SPECIALTY STORES

Autozone
http://www.autozone.com

Body Shop (UK)
http://www.the-body-shop.com

Borders Books and Music
http://www.borders.com

Burlington Coat Factory
http://www.coat.com

Casual Male/Big & Tall
http://www.thinkbig.com

Container Store
http://containerstore.com

Disney Store
http://store.disney.com

Express
http://www.express.style.com

Eddie Bauer
http://www.ebauer.com

FAO Schwarz
http://www.faoschwarz.com

Foot Locker
http://www.footlocker.com

The Gap
http://www.gapinc.com

The Nature Company
http://www.natureco.com

Pep Boys
http://www.pepboys.com

Pier 1 Imports
http://www.pier1.com

Radio Shack
http://www.radioshack.com

Roots
http://www.roots.com

Warner Brothers Store
http://www.studio.warnerbrothers.com

Western Auto
http://www.westernauto.com

CATEGORY SPECIALISTS

Best Buy
http://www.bestbuy.com

Blockbuster
http://www.blockbuster.com

Circuit City
http://www.circuitcity.com/

CompUSA
http://www.compusa.com

Media Play
http://www.mediaplay.com

Office Max
http://www.officemax.com

PETsMART
http://www.petsmart.com

Sports Authority
http://www.pwr.com/SportsAuthority

Staples
http://www.staples.com

Toys "R" Us
http://www.tru.com

OFF-PRICE RETAILERS

Ross Stores
http://www.rossstores.com

Tuesday Morning
http://www.tuesdaymorning.com

WAREHOUSE CLUBS

Meijers
http://www.meijers.com

Price/Costco
http://www.pricecostco.com

Sam's Club
http://www.samsclub.com

HOME IMPROVEMENT CENTERS

Home Depot
http://www.homedepot.com

Lowe's
http://www.lowes.com

Payless Cashway
http://www.cashways.com

Wickes Lumber
http://www.wickes.com

CATALOG RETAILERS

Lands' End
http://www.landsend.com

L.L. Bean
http://www.llbean.com

Patagonia
http://www.patagonia.com

INTERNET RETAILERS

Amazon Books
http://www.amazon.com

CDNow
http://www.cdnow.com

Hot Sauces
http://www.hothothot.com

PC Flowers and Gifts
http://www.pcflowers.com

Peapod
http://www.peapod.com

INTERNET MALLS

Cybershop
http://www.cybershop.com

Cybertown
http://www.cybertown.com

Dreamshop
http://www.pathfinder.com

Internet Shopping Network
http://www.internet.net

World Avenue
http://worldavenue.com

THIRD EDITION

Retailing Management

Lehmann & Winer
Product Management, *2/E*

Levy & Weitz
Retailing Management, *3/E*

Levy & Weitz
Essentials of Retailing

Loudon & Della Bitta
Consumer Behavior: Concepts &
Applications, *4/E*

Lovelock & Weinberg
Marketing Challenges: Cases and
Exercises, *3/E*

Mason, Mayer & Ezell
Retailing, *5/E*

Mason & Perreault
The Marketing Game!

McDonald
Modern Direct Marketing

Meloan & Graham
International and Global Marketing Concepts
and Cases, *2/E*

Monroe
Pricing, *2/E*

Moore & Pessemier
Product Planning and Management: Designing
and Delivering Value

Oliver
Satisfaction: A Behavioral Perspective on the
Consumer

Patton
Sales Force: A Sales Management Simulation
Game

Pelton, Strutton & Lumpkin
Marketing Channels: A Relationship
Management Approach

Perreault & McCarthy
Basic Marketing: A Global Managerial
Approach, *12/E*

Perreault & McCarthy
Essentials of Marketing: A Global Managerial
Approach, *7/E*

Peter & Donnelly
A Preface to Marketing Management, *7/E*

Peter & Donnelly
Marketing Management: Knowledge and
Skills, *5/E*

Peter & Olson
Consumer Behavior and Marketing
Strategy, *4/E*

Peter & Olson
Understanding Consumer Behavior

Quelch
Cases in Product Management

Quelch, Dolan & Kosnik
Marketing Management: Text and Cases

Quelch & Farris
Cases in Advertising and Promotion
Management, 4/E

Quelch, Kashani & Vandermerwe
European Cases in Marketing Management

Rangan
Business Marketing Strategy: Cases, Concepts
& Applications

Rangan, Shapiro & Moriarty
Business Marketing Strategy: Concepts &
Applications

Rossiter & Percy
Advertising and Promotion Management, *2/E*

Stanton, Spiro, & Buskirk
Management of a Sales Force, *10/E*

Sudman & Blair
Marketing Research: A Problem-solving
Approach

Thompson & Stappenbeck
The Marketing Strategy Game

Ulrich & Eppinger
Product Design and Development

Walker, Boyd & Larreche
Marketing Strategy: Planning and
Implementation, *2/E*

Weitz, Castleberry & Tanner
Selling: Building Partnerships, *3/E*

Zeithaml & Bitner
Services Marketing

THIRD EDITION

Retailing Management

MICHAEL LEVY, Ph.D.
University of Miami

BARTON A. WEITZ, Ph.D.
University of Florida

Boston, Massachusetts   Burr Ridge, Illinois   Dubuque, Iowa
Madison, Wisconsin   New York, New York   San Francisco, California   St. Louis, Missouri

Irwin/McGraw-Hill

A Division of The McGraw-Hill Companies

This book is printed on acid-free paper.

4 5 6 7 8 9 0 VNH/VNH 9 0 9   (U.S. edition)

4 5 6 7 8 9 0 VNH/VNH 9 0 9   (International edition)

ISBN 0-256-22346-7

Editorial director and vice president: *Michael W. Junior*
Executive editor: *Stephen M. Patterson*
Developmental editor: *Libby Rubenstein*
Marketing manager: *Colleen J. Suljic*
Project manager: *Lynne Basler/Carrie Sestak*
Production supervisor: *Melonie Salvati*
Senior photo research coordinator: *Keri Johnson*
Designer: *Michael Warrell*
Cover image: *courtesy of Photofest, NY. Copyright 1961 by Paramount Pictures Corporation and Jurow-Shepard Productions*
Compositor: *PC&F, Inc.*
Typeface: *10/12 Janson Text*
Printer: *Von Hoffmann, Press, Inc.*

Library of Congress Cataloging-in-Publication Data

Levy, Michael.
    Retailing management/Michael Levy, Barton A. Weitz.—3rd ed.
      p.   cm.—(The Irwin/McGraw-Hill series in marketing)
    Includes index.
    ISBN 0-256-22346-7.—ISBN 0-07-115387-X
    1. Retail trade—Management. I. Title. II. Series.
HF5429.L4828 1998   97-25683
658.8'7—dc21

http://www.mhhe.com

To my wife, Marcia, and my daughter, Eva
Michael Levy

To my wife, Shirley
Barton Weitz

ABOUT THE AUTHORS

Michael Levy, Ph.D.
University of Miami

Michael Levy received his Ph.D. from The Ohio State University. He taught at Southern Methodist University before joining the faculty as Professor and Chair of the Marketing Department at the University of Miami. He has taught retailing management for 19 years.

Professor Levy has developed a strong stream of research in retailing, business logistics, financial retailing strategy, pricing, and sales management that has been published in over 30 articles in leading marketing and logistics journals including the *Journal of Retailing, Journal of Marketing,* and *Journal of Marketing Research.* He currently serves on the editorial review board of *Journal of Retailing, Journal of the Academy of Marketing Science, International Journal of Logistics Management,* and *International Journal of Logistics and Materials Management.*

Professor Levy has worked in retailing and related disciplines throughout his professional life. Prior to his academic career, he worked for several retailers and a housewares distributor in Colorado. He has performed research projects with many retailers, including Andersen Consulting, Burdines Department Stores, Mervyn's, Neiman Marcus, and Zale Corporation.

Barton A. Weitz, Ph.D.
University of Florida

Barton A. Weitz received an undergraduate degree in electrical engineering from MIT and an MBA and Ph.D. in business administration from Stanford University. He has been a member of the faculty at the UCLA Graduate School of Business and the Wharton School at the University of Pennsylvania. He is presently the JCPenney Eminent Scholar Chair in Retail Management in the College of Business Administration at the University of Florida and Chair of the Marketing Department.

Professor Weitz is the Executive Director of the Center for Retailing Education and Research at the University of Florida. The activities of the center are supported by contributions by 20 national and regional retailers, including JCPenney, Sears, Burdines, Wal-Mart, Home Depot, Richs, Office Depot, Bealls, and Electronic Boutique. Each year the center places over 150 undergraduates in paid summer internships with retail firms and funds research on retailing issues and problems.

Professor Weitz has won awards for teaching excellence and has made numerous presentations to industry and academic groups. He has published over 40 articles in leading academic journals on salesperson effectiveness, sales force and human resource management, and channel relationships and is on the editorial review boards of the *Journal of Retailing, Journal of Marketing, Journal of Interactive Marketing, International Journal of Research in Marketing,* and *Journal of Marketing Research.* He is a former editor of the *Journal of Marketing Research* and is presently co-editor of *Marketing Letters.*

Professor Weitz is a member of the Board of Directors of the National Retail Federation, the National Retail Institute, and the American Marketing Association. He is a former board member of the Direct Selling Association and Direct Selling Educational Foundation and a former academic trustee of the Marketing Science Institute.

PREFACE

RETAILING, ONE OF THE LARGEST SECTORS in the global economy, is going through a period of dramatic change. Innovative retail entrepreneurs are using new technologies and changing customer needs to build the next generation of industry giants. Traditional retailers are adapting or going out of business. Our objective in writing this textbook is to capture this excitement and challenge in the retail industry as we inform students about the state-of-the-art management practices of these important institutions in our society.

NEW FEATURES IN THE THIRD EDITION

In preparing this third edition, we have made the following changes to reflect the evolving nature of retailing:

- **Emergence of electronic retailing**—While electronic retail sales are relatively small today, this new format's potential is dramatic. Every major retailer has a home page on the Internet, many of which sell merchandise and services. Entrepreneurs like Amazon.com, a bookstore, take advantage of the opportunities offered by electronic retailing to tailor information to the specific needs of individual customers. The third edition of this book addresses these new formats as follows:

  - Chapter 3, a new chapter on nonstore retailing, focuses on the present and potential impact of this retailing format.
  - Examples involving electronic retailers are used to illustrate the concept in other chapters.
  - Internet sites with information about retailing are spread throughout this edition.

- **Utilization of information and communication technology**—Retailing has become a high-tech business. Data collected for each transaction is used to automatically place orders with vendors and trigger warehouse deliveries. An alphabet soup of retail systems—POS, ECR, EDI, QR—to exploit these data are now commonplace in the industry. POS data are used by retailers to develop frequent-shopper promotion programs targeted at specific customers. Several new features in this new edition that address this industry trend are:

  - Strategic and implementation issues involving information, communication, and distribution systems appear in Chapters 6 and 11.
  - The widely used Arthur© by Comshare Retail merchandise planning system is used to illustrate the merchandise planning process. A version of the system is included with this book on a computer disk. Also included with the book on disk are tutorials and interactive computer exercises.
  - Use of customer information to target promotions and the development of frequent shopper programs are discussed in Chapter 16.

- **Globalization of retailing**—Retailing is rapidly becoming a global industry. Wal-Mart has stores in China; Ahold, a Dutch retailer, owns major supermarket chains on the U.S. East Coast; and McDonald's operates in over 60 countries. To emphasize the international aspects of retailing, the third edition includes:
  - Global sourcing of merchandise (Chapter 14).
  - Consumer behavior (Chapter 5), employee management (Chapter 17), and customer service (Chapter 19) in international markets.

- **Growth of services retailing**—Services retailing is becoming increasingly important in our economy. The treatment of services retailing is expanded as follows:
  - Review similarities and differences between merchandise and services retailing (Chapter 2).
  - Greater use of service retail examples through the text ranging from new concepts like America On-Line and Starbucks to more traditional service retailers like Marriott, Domino's, and Disneyland.
  - Boxed inserts on special issues for service retailers in selected chapters.

- **Entrepreneurship**—While the activities of large retail corporations dominate the business press, retailing continues to provide opportunities for people to start their own businesses. To support this entrepreneurial spirit, this edition includes:
  - More discussion of how small retailers compete effectively against the giants by focusing their efforts and developing effective retail mixes for their businesses.
  - More illustrations of successful retail entrepreneurs operating both store-based and nonstore businesses.

- **Reader-friendly textbook**—In the third edition, we have continued to interest and involve students in the material by making the textbook a "good read" via:
  - More interesting facts about retailing, called "Refacts," in the margin of each chapter. Did you know that a Montgomery Ward buyer created Rudolph the Red-Nosed Reindeer as a Christmas promotion in 1939?
  - Greater use of vignettes, called "Retailing Views," in each chapter to relate concepts to activities and decisions made by retailers. These vignettes involve both small start-ups and major retailers like Sears, Wal-Mart, JCPenney, and Home Depot that interview students on campus for management training positions.
  - Student computer disks with both interactive tutorials and exercises to help students learn experientially.

BASIC PHILOSOPHY

The third edition of *Retailing Management* maintains the basic philosophy of the previous two editions. We continue to focus on the key issues facing the retail industry as the new millennium approaches.

Preparing for the New Millennium

Strategic Perspective   To be successful in a highly competitive, rapidly changing environment, retailers must develop a strategic approach. The entire textbook is organized around a model of strategic decision making outlined in Exhibit 1–5 in Chapter 1. Each section and chapter is related back to this overarching strategic framework. In addition, the second section of the book focuses exclusively on critical strategic decisions such as selecting target markets, developing a sustainable competitive advantage, and building an organizational structure and information and distribution systems to support the strategic direction.

Financial Analysis   The business side of retailing is becoming increasingly important. The financial problems experienced by some of the largest retail firms like Kmart and Macy's highlight the need for a thorough understanding of the financial implications of retail decisions. Financial analysis is emphasized in selected chapters such as Chapter 7 on the overall strategy of the firm and Chapter 13 on retail buying systems. Financial issues are also raised in the sections on negotiating leases, bargaining with suppliers, pricing merchandise, developing a communications budget, and compensating salespeople.

Store Management   Traditionally, retailers have exalted the merchant prince—the buyer who knew what the hot trends were going to be. This text, by devoting an entire section to store management, reflects the changes that have occurred over the past 10 years—the shift in emphasis from merchandise management to store management. Retailers now recognize that a key source of competitive advantage is providing high-quality customer service in an attractive environment. Due to this shift toward store management, most students embarking on retail careers go into store management rather than merchandise buying.

Balanced Approach   The third edition offers a balanced approach for teaching an introductory retailing course by including descriptive, how-to, and conceptual information in a highly readable format.

Descriptive Information   Students can learn about the vocabulary and practice of retailing from the descriptive information throughout the text. Examples of some of this material are:

- Management decisions made by retailers (Chapter 1).
- Types of store-based and nonstore retailers (Chapters 2 and 3).
- Changing demographics and values of retail customers (Chapter 4).
- Retail locations (Chapter 8).
- Organization structure of typical retailers (Chapter 10).
- Flow of information and merchandise (Chapter 11).
- Branding strategies (Chapter 14).
- Store layout options and merchandise display equipment (Chapter 18).
- Career opportunities (Appendix A).

How-to Information   *Retailing Management* goes beyond this descriptive information to illustrate how and why retailers, large and small, make decisions. Step-by-step procedures with examples are provided for making the following decisions:

- Comparison shopping (Appendix A to Chapter 2).
- Scanning the environment and developing a retail strategy (Chapter 6).
- Analyzing the financial implications of retail strategy (Chapter 7).
- Evaluating location decisions (Chapter 9).
- Developing a merchandise assortment and budget plan (Chapters 12 and 13).

- Negotiating with vendors (Chapters 14).
- Pricing merchandise (Chapter 15).
- Recruiting, selecting, training, evaluating, and compensating sales associates (Chapter 17).
- Selling a customer (Chapter 20).
- Starting a retail business (Appendixes B and C).

Conceptual Information   *Retailing Management* also includes conceptual information that enables students to understand why decisions are made as outlined in the text. As Mark Twain said, "There is nothing as practical as a good theory." Students need to know these basic concepts so they can make effective decisions in new situations. Examples of this conceptual information in the third edition are:

- Retail evolution theories (Appendix B to Chapter 2).
- Customers' decision-making process (Chapter 5).
- The strategic profit model (Chapter 7).
- Price theory and marginal analysis (Chapters 15 and 16).
- The Gaps model for service quality management (Chapter 19).

Supplemental Material

To improve the student learning experience, the third edition includes new cases and videos illustrating state-of-the-art retail practices, a computer exercise package for students, and a comprehensive instructor's manual with additional cases and teaching suggestions.

Cases   The text includes new cases, including "Sears Rebounds from the Brink of Bankruptcy," "Michaels Decreases Its Merchandise Assortment," "The Home Shopping Network: Dealing with a Sales Slowdown," "Bloomingdale's: Customer Service Reaches Abroad," "Virtual Vineyards: Wine On-Line," "Levi Stores: Mass Customization of Jeans," "Marriott's Success Comes from Its Human Resources," "Delta Airlines Finds Customer Service at a High Price," "The Gap Opens Old Navy," "NikeTown," and "Nieman Marcus's Preferred Customer Program."

Videos   The video package includes, "Sears' Transformation," "Electronic Article Surveillance at Walgreens," "The Rainforest Cafe," "Holiday Inn Customer Service," "Steinmart, Upscale Off-Price Retailer," "Burdines' Implementing the Florida Store Concept," "Direct Selling in a Global Economy," and the "JCPenney Catalog Design and Fulfillment System."

ACKNOWLEDGMENTS

Throughout the development of this text, several outstanding individuals were integrally involved and made substantial contributions. We wish to express our sincere appreciation to Evan Koenig and Marcia Levy for their assistance in developing a superior *Instructor's Manual,* and to Thomas K. Pritchett and Betty M. Pritchett of Kennesaw College for their comprehensive *Manual of Tests.* The disks included with each copy of *Retailing Management* include an exciting array of tutorials and exercises—including the popular Arthur© inventory planning system—was prepared by Hal Koenig of Oregon State University and Ann Delusia of Comshare Retail. Kathy Brown and Margaret Jones (Center for Retailing Education and Research, University of Florida) provided invaluable assistance in preparing the manuscript.

The support, expertise, and occasional coercion from our editors and marketing manager at Irwin/McGraw-Hill, Steve Patterson, Libby Rubenstein, and Colleen Suljic, are greatly appreciated. The book would also never have come together without the production staff at Irwin/McGraw-Hill: Carrie Sestak, Lynne Basler, Michael Warrell, Melonie Salvati, Jon Christopher, Bruce Sylvester, and Harriett Stokanes.

Retailing Management has also benefited significantly from contributions by several leading executives and scholars in retailing and related fields. We would

William Alcorn
JCPenney

Mason Allen
Steinmart

Edward Beiner
Mr. I's Optical

Cynthia Cohen
MARKETPLACE 2000

Evan Cole
Claritas/UDS Data Services

Terry Donafrio
Retail Systems and Services

Tom Drake
University of Miami

Barry Dunne
Information Resources, Inc.

Joan Fox
Host Marriott

Deanne Gipson
Holiday Inn

Erik Gordon
University of Florida

Steven Kirn
Sears

John F. Konarski III
National Council of Shopping Centers

Douglas Lambert
The Ohio State University

Kathleen McManus
Rich's/Lazarus/Goldsmith's

Edward Nolan
Eckerd

Coleman Peterson
Wal-Mart

Cynthia Ray
Federated Department Stores, Inc.

Tom Redd
Comshare Retail

Ann Rupert
Burdines

Carol Sanger
Federated Department Stores

Arun Sharma
University of Miami

Kathleen Seiders
Babson College

Don Singletary
Home Depot

Ken Smith
May Department Stores

Daniel Sweeney
IBM Retail Group

Kathleen Seiders
Babson College

Douglas Tigert
Babson College

Herbert Tobin
The Ben Tobin Companies

Petey Wasserman
Bloomingdales

Robert Wery
Sears

Walter Zinn
University of Miami

The third edition of *Retailing Management* has benefited from the reviews of several leading scholars and teachers of retailing and related disciplines. Together, these reviewers spent hundreds of hours reading and critiquing the manuscript. We gratefully acknowledge:

Jeff Blodgett
University of Mississippi

Robert Miller
Central Michigan University

Lon Camomile
Colorado State University

Mary Anne Milward
University of Arizona

Kevin Fertig
University of Illinois

Laura Scroggins
California State University—Chico

Tom Gross
University of Wisconsin

Janet Wagner
University of Maryland

Tony Henthorne
University of Southern Mississippi

Ron Zallocco
University of Toledo

Harold McCoy
Virginia Commonwealth University

We also thank the following reviewers for their diligence and insight in helping us prepare previous editions:

Mary Barry
Auburn University

Peter Gordon
Southeast Missouri State University

George W. Boulware
Lipscomb University

Larry Gresham
Texas A&M University

Leroy M. Buckner
Florida Atlantic University

Tony L. Henthorne
University of Southern Mississippi

David J. Burns
Purdue University

Eugene J. Kangas
Winona State University

J. Joseph Cronin, Jr.
Florida State University

Herbert Katzenstein
St. John's University

Ann DuPont
The University of Texas

Terrence Kroeten
North Dakota State University

Chloe I. Elmgren
Mankato State University

Elizabeth Mariotz
Philadelphia College of Textiles & Science

Richard L. Entrikin
George Mason University

John J. Porter
West Virginia University

Kenneth R. Evans
University of Missouri—Columbia

Shirley M. Stretch
California State University—LA

Richard Feinberg
Purdue University

William R. Swinyard
Brigham Young University

We received cases from professors all over the world. Although we would like to have used more cases in the text and the *Instructor's Manual,* space was limited. We would like to thank all who contributed but are especially appreciative of the following authors whose cases were used in *Retailing Management* or in the *Instructor's Manual.*

Ronald Adams
University of North Florida

Laura Bliss
Stephens College

James Camerius
Northern Michigan University

David Ehrlich
Marymount University

Ann Fairhurst
Indiana University

Linda F. Felicetti
Clarion University

Joseph P. Grunewald
Clarion University

K. Douglas Hoffman
University of North Carolina—Wilmington

Laura Hooks
University of Florida

Dilip Karer
University of North Florida

Robert Kenny
Saint Michael's College

Alison T. Knott
University of Florida

Evan Koenig
University of Miami

Robert Letovsky
Saint Michael's College

Debra Murphy
Saint Michael's College

Jan Owens
University of Wisconsin

Catherine Porter
University of Massachusetts

Richard Rausch
Hofstra University

William R. Swinyard
Brigham Young University

Irvin Zaenglein
Northern Michigan University

Heather Zuilkoski
University of Florida

Michael Levy
Barton A. Weitz

BRIEF CONTENTS

SECTION ONE

The World of Retailing

1. Introduction to the World of Retailing, 2
2. Store-Based Retailing, 28
3. Nonstore Retailing—Electronic Retailing and Catalogs, 66
4. The Retail Customer, 96
5. Customer Buying Behavior, 120

SECTION TWO

Retailing Strategy

6. Retail Market Strategy, 160
7. Financial Strategy, 196
8. Retail Locations, 230
9. Site Selection, 256
10. Organization Structure and Human Resource Management, 284
11. Integrated Retail Logistics and Information Systems, 314

SECTION THREE

Merchandise Management

12. Planning Merchandise Assortments, 338
13. Buying Systems, 370
14. Buying Merchandise, 402
15. Pricing, 440
16. Retail Promotion Mix, 472

SECTION FOUR

Store Management

17. Managing the Store, 506
18. Store Layout, Design, and Visual Merchandising, 540
19. Customer Service, 570
20. Retail Selling, 600

SECTION FIVE

Cases

1–37, C–1 through C–53

SECTION SIX

Appendixes

Appendix A: Careers in Retailing, A
Appendix B: Starting Your Own Retail Business, A–15
Appendix C: Starting a Franchise Business, A–28

GLOSSARY, G
CREDITS, CR
INDEXES, I

CONTENTS

SECTION ONE   The World of Retailing   2

1 **Introduction to the World of Retailing 4**

What Is a Retailer? 7
   Retailing's Role in Distribution
   Channels, 7
   Functions Performed by Retailers, 8
   Organization of the Distribution
   Channel, 9
Economic Significance of Retailing, 11
   Retail Sales, 11
   Employment, 11
   The Top 25 Retailers, 12
Opportunities in Retailing, 14
   Management Opportunities, 14
   Entrepreneurial Opportunities, 15

Retail Management Decision-Making
Process, 17
   Understanding the World of
   Retailing, 17
   Developing a Retail Strategy, 20
   Implementing the Retail Strategy, 22
Summary, 24
Key Terms, 25
Suggested Readings, 25
Appendix: Trade Publications for
Retailers, 25
Notes, 27

2 **Store-Based Retailing 28**

Types of Retailers, 29
   Nature of Retail Mix, 29
Food Retailers, 33
   Conventional Supermarkets, 33
   Big Box Food Retailers, 34
   Convenience Stores, 35
   Competition in Food Retailing, 35
Traditional General Merchandise
Retailers, 36
   Specialty Stores, 36
   Department Stores, 38
   General Merchandise Discount
   Stores, 41
New Retail Store Formats, 42
   Category Specialists, 42
   Home-Improvement Centers, 42
   Warehouse Clubs, 43
   Off-Price Retailers, 43
   Catalog Showrooms, 46
   Hypermarkets and Supercenters, 46

Services Retailing, 47
   Types of Services Retailers, 47
   Differences between Services and
   Merchandise Retailers, 49
Types of Ownership, 52
   Independent, Single-Store
   Establishments, 52
   Corporate Retail Chains, 53
   Franchising, 55
   Other Forms of Ownership, 56
Summary, 56
Key Terms, 58
Discussion Questions & Problems, 58
Suggested Readings, 58
Appendix 2A: Comparison
Shopping, 59
Appendix 2B: Theories of the
Evolution of Retailing, 61
Notes, 64

3   **Nonstore Retailing—Electronic Retailing and Catalogs 66**

Nonstore versus Store-Based
Retailers, 67

Catalog and Direct-Mail Retailing, 69

    Types of Catalog and Direct-Mail
Retailers, 70

    Complement to In-Store Retail
Format, 70

    Keys to Success, 71

Vending Machine Retailing, 73

Television Home Shopping, 74

Direct Selling, 75

Interactive Home Shopping, 77

    Growth Potential for Interactive Home
Shopping, 79

What Type of Merchandise Will Be
Sold Effectively through the IHS
Format? 84

Impact of IHS on the Retail Industry—
What Might Happen in the Future? 86

    A Nutshell View of IHS, 90

Summary, 90

Key Terms, 91

Discussion Questions & Problems, 91

Suggested Readings, 91

Appendix: Retail Internet Sites, 92

Notes, 94

4   **The Retail Customer 96**

Generational Cohorts, 97

    Generation Y, 98

    Generation X, 100

    The Baby Boomers, 101

    Silver Streakers: The Older
Population, 103

Ethnic Diversity, 104

    African-Americans, 105

    Hispanic-Americans, 105

    Asian-Americans, 106

Income, 107

    The Upscale Customer, 107

    The Mass Middle and Lower-Income
Markets, 108

Decline of Household Managers, 110

    The Changing Women's Market, 110

    The Time-Poor Society, 111

Changes in Consumer Values, 113

    Social Consciousness, 113

    Green Marketing, 114

    The Value-Oriented Customer, 114

    Cocooning, 115

    Dress-Down Fashion, 115

Summary, 116

Key Terms, 116

Discussion Questions & Problems, 117

Suggested Readings, 117

Notes, 118

5 Customer Buying Behavior 120

Types of Buying Decisions, 120
   Extended Problem Solving, 121
   Limited Problem Solving, 122
   Habitual Decision Making, 123
The Buying Process, 124
   Need Recognition, 125
   Information Search, 129
   Evaluation of Alternatives: The Multiattribute Model, 130
   Choice of Alternatives, 133
   Implications for Retailers, 134
   Purchasing the Merchandise, 136
   Postpurchase Evaluation, 137
Factors Affecting the Decision Process, 137
   Family, 137
   Reference Groups, 139
   Culture and Subculture, 140

Market Segmentation, 141
   Criteria for Segmenting Markets, 142
   Approaches to Segmenting Markets, 144
   Composite Segmentation Approaches, 147
Summary, 147
Key Terms, 149
Discussion Questions & Problems, 149
Suggested Readings, 150
Appendix: Customer Behavior toward Fashion, 150
Notes, 154

SECTION TWO   ## Retailing Strategy   158

6 Retail Market Strategy 160

What Is Retail Strategy? 160
   Definition of Retail Market Strategy, 161
Target Market and Retail Format, 162
Building a Sustainable Competitive Advantage, 164
   Customer Loyalty, 165
   Location, 167
   Vendor Relations, 168
   Management Information and Distribution Systems, 168
   Low-Cost Operations, 169
   Multiple Sources of Advantage, 169
Growth Strategies, 170
   Market Penetration, 170
   Market Expansion, 171
   Retail Format Development, 171
   Diversification, 172
   Strategic Opportunities and Competitive Advantage, 173
International Growth Opportunities, 173
The Strategic Retail Planning Process, 179

Step 1: Define the Business's Mission, 180
Step 2: Conduct a Situation Audit, 181
Step 3: Identify Strategic Opportunities, 185
Step 4: Evaluate Strategic Opportunities, 186
Step:5 Establish Specific Objectives and Allocate Resources, 187
Step: 6 Develop a Retail Mix to Implement Strategy, 187
Step: 7: Evaluate Performance and Make Adjustments, 187
Strategic Planning in the Real World, 188
Summary, 188
Key Terms, 188
Discussion Questions & Problems, 189
Suggested Readings, 189
Appendix: Using the Market Attractiveness/Competitive Position Matrix, 190
Notes, 192

7 Financial Strategy 196

The Strategic Profit Model:
An Overview, 197
The Income Statement (Path 1), 200
   Net Sales, 201
   Gross Margin, 201
   Expenses, 201
   Net Profit, 202
The Balance Sheet (Path 2), 203
   Current Assets, 204
   Accounts Receivable, 204
   Merchandise Inventory, 205
   Cash and Other Current Assets, 207
   Current Assets Cycle, 207
   Fixed Assets, 208
   Asset Turnover, 209
   Liabilities and Owners' Equity, 210
The Strategic Profit Model, 211
   Return on Assets, 212

Integrating Marketing and Financial
Strategies for Joanne Phillips's Gift
Stores, 214
   Profit Path, 214
   Turnover Path, 215
   Return on Assets, 217
Recap of the Strategic Profit
Model, 217
Setting Performance Objectives, 218
   Top-Down versus Bottom-Up
   Process, 219
   Accountability, 220
   Performance Measures, 220
   Types of Measures, 220
Summary, 222
Key Terms, 222
Discussion Questions & Problems, 222
Suggested Readings, 223
Appendix: Activity-Based Costing, 224
Notes, 228

8 Retail Locations 230

Types of Retail Locations, 231
   Central Business Districts (CBDs), 231
   Shopping Centers, 232
   Strip Shopping Centers, 234
   Shopping Malls, 237
   Other Retail Location
   Opportunities, 242
Location and Retail Strategy, 243
   Department Stores, 243
   Specialty Apparel Stores, 244
   Category Specialists, 245
   Grocery Stores, 246
   Example: Optical Boutique, 246

Site Evaluation, 247
   Accessibility, 247
   Locational Advantages within a
   Center, 248
   Terms of Occupancy, 249
   Legal Considerations, 251
Summary, 252
Key Terms, 253
Discussion Questions & Problems, 253
Suggested Readings, 254
Notes, 254

9 Site Selection 256

Location Decisions, 256
   Region/Market Area, 258
   Trade Area, 258
Factors Affecting the Attractiveness of
Region/Market and Trade Areas, 260
   Demographics, 260
   Business Climate, 260
   Competition, 261
Measuring Demand, 261
   Decennial Census of the United States, 261
   Buying Power Index, 264
   Demographic Data Vendors, 264

Measuring Competition, 267
Measuring Trade Area Potential, 268
   Analog Approach, 268
   Multiple Regression Analysis, 271
   Gravity Models, 274
Summary, 279
Key Terms, 280
Discussion Questions & Problems, 280
Suggested Readings, 281
Notes, 282

10 Organization Structure and Human Resource Management 284

Challenging Issues, 286
Objectives of Human Resource
Management, 286
Designing the Organization Structure
for a Retail Firm, 286
   Organization Design
   Considerations, 287
Retail Organization Structures, 289
   Organization of Small Stores, 289
   Organization of a Regional Department
   Store Chain, 290
   Corporate Organization of Regional
   Department Store Chains, 293
   Organization Structure of Other Types
   of Retailers, 295
Organization Design Issues, 296
   Centralized versus Decentralized
   Decision Making, 296
   Coordinating Buying and Store
   Management Activities, 297
   New Developments in the Organization
   of Retail Activities, 300

Motivating and Coordinating
Employees, 302
   Policies and Supervision, 302
   Incentives, 302
   Organization Culture, 303
Building Employee Commitment and
Reducing Turnover, 304
   Promotion from Within, 305
   Balancing Careers and Families, 306
Managing Diversity, 307
   Programs for Managing Diversity, 309
Summary, 310
Key Terms, 311
Discussion Questions & Problems, 311
Suggested Readings, 311
Notes, 312

11 Integrated Retail Logistics and Information Systems 314

Strategic Advantages Gained through Logistics and Information Systems, 315
Improved Product Availability, 315
Improved Assortment, 315
Improved Return on Investment, 316
The Physical Flow of Merchandise—Logistics, 317
The Distribution Center, 319
Outsourcing, 323
Store versus Distribution Center Delivery, 325
Pull versus Push Logistics Strategies, 327
The Flow of Information, 328
Database Retailing, 329
Build and Manage Dialogues with Customers, 329

Integrate Marketing Campaigns, 329
Improve Inventory Management, 330
Improve Marketing Productivity, 330
Calculate the Value of a Customer or Prospect, 330
Difficulties, 330
Quick Response (QR) Delivery Systems, 331
Benefits of a QR System, 331
Costs of a QR System, 331
Value Added Networks (VANs), 333
Summary, 333
Key Terms, 334
Discussion Questions & Problems, 334
Suggested Readings, 334
Notes, 335

SECTION THREE   Merchandise Management   336

12 Planning Merchandise Assortments 338

Organizing the Buying Process by Categories, 339
Category Management, 340
The Buying Organization, 341
Setting Merchandise Financial Objectives, 344
Putting Profits, Sales, and Turnover Together: GMROI, 345
Measuring Inventory Turnover, 348
Sales Forecasting, 351
The Assortment Planning Process, 360
The Trade-offs between Variety, Assortment, and Product Availability: A Strategic Decision, 362

Determining Variety and Assortment, 362
Determining Product Availability, 364
The Assortment Plan, 365
Summary, 367
Key Terms, 368
Discussion Questions & Problems, 368
Suggested Readings, 368
Notes, 369

13 Buying Systems 370

Merchandise Budget Plan, 371
 Monthly Sales Percent Distribution to Season (Line 1), 373
 Monthly Sales (Line 2), 375
 Monthly Reductions Percent Distribution to Season (Line 3), 375
 Monthly Reductions (Line 4), 376
 BOM (Beginning-of-Month) Stock-to-Sales Ratio (Line 5), 376
 BOM (Beginning-of-Month) Stock (Line 6), 378
 EOM (End-of-Month) Stock (Line 7), 378
 Monthly Additions to Stock (Line 8), 378
 Evaluating the Merchandise Budget Plan, 379
Open-to-Buy, 379
 Calculating Open-to-Buy for Past Periods, 380
 Calculating Open-to-Buy for Current Period, 380
 Calculating Open-to-Buy for Future Periods, 381

Evaluating Open-to-Buy, 381
Staple Merchandise Buying Systems, 383
 What the System Does, 384
 The Inventory Management Report, 384
Allocating Merchandise to Stores, 387
Analyzing Merchandise Performance, 389
 ABC Analysis, 390
 Sell-through Analysis, 392
 Multiple-Attribute Method, 392
Summary, 394
Key Terms, 395
Discussion Questions & Problems, 395
Suggested Readings, 396
Appendix 13A: Retail Inventory Method (RIM), 396
Appendix 13B: Alternatives to the Stock-to-Sales Ratio, 399
Notes, 401

14 Buying Merchandise 402

Branding Strategies, 403
 Manufacturer Brands, 403
 Private-Label Brands, 406
International Sourcing Decisions, 409
 Costs Associated with Global Sourcing Decisions, 410
 Managerial Issues Associated with Global Sourcing Decisions, 413
 Source Closer to Home or Buy "Made in America," 413
Meeting Vendors, 414
 Wholesale Market Centers, 415
 Trade Shows, 415
 Buying on Their Own Turf, 415
 Resident Buying Offices, 415
Establishing and Maintaining Strategic Partnerships with Vendors, 416
 Establishing Strategic Partnerships, 416
 Maintaining Strategic Partnerships, 418

Ethical and Legal Issues in Purchasing Merchandise, 419
 Slotting Allowances, 420
 Commercial Bribery, 420
 Counterfeit Merchandise, 421
 Gray-Market and Diverted Merchandise, 421
 Exclusive Territories, 423
 Exclusive Dealing Agreements, 424
 Tying Contracts, 424
 Refusals to Deal, 424
 Dual Distribution, 424
Summary, 425
Key Terms, 426
Discussion Questions & Problems, 426
Suggested Readings, 427
Appendix 14A: Negotiating with Vendors, 427
Appendix 14B: Terms of Purchase, 432
Notes, 438

15 Pricing 440

Pricing Strategies and Practices, 441
   Everyday Low Pricing (EDLP), 441
   High/Low Pricing, 441
   Deciding Which Strategy Is Best, 442
   The Future of EDLP and High/Low Pricing Strategies, 444
   Coupons, 445
   Rebates, 446
   Leader Pricing, 446
   Price Bundling, 446
   Multiple-Unit Pricing, 447
   Price Lining, 448
   Odd Pricing, 448
Contrasting Cost-Oriented and Demand-Oriented Methods of Setting Retail Prices, 449
The Cost-Oriented Method of Setting the Retail Price, 450
   Determining the Initial Markup from Maintained Markup and Gross Margin, 450
   Determining the Initial Retail Price under Cost-Oriented Pricing, 452
Adjustments to the Initial Retail Price, 453

Markdowns, 453
Markdown Cancellations, 457
Additional Markups, 458
Additional Markup Cancellations, 458
Profit Impact of Adjustments to the Retail Price: The Use of Break-Even Analysis, 458
The Demand-Oriented Method of Setting the Retail Price, 460
   Factors That Affect Customers' Sensitivity to Price, 460
   Determining the Initial Retail Price under Demand-Oriented Pricing, 461
Legal Issues in Retail Pricing, 463
   Price Discrimination, 463
   Vertical Price-Fixing, 464
   Horizontal Price-Fixing, 464
   Predatory Pricing, 465
   Comparative Price Advertising, 465
   Bait-and-Switch Tactics, 466
Summary, 467
Key Terms, 468
Discussion Questions & Problems, 469
Suggested Readings, 469
Notes, 470

16 Retail Promotion Mix 472

Role of the Retail Promotion Program, 473
   Tasks Performed by the Promotion Program, 473
   Methods for Communicating with Customers, 474
   Strengths and Weaknesses of Communication Methods, 475
   Integrated Marketing Communications, 476
Planning the Retail Communication Program, 477
   Setting Objectives, 477
   Setting the Promotion Budget, 481
   Evaluating a Specific Promotion Opportunity, 484
Allocating the Promotion Budget, 485
   Implementing and Evaluating, 486
Implementing Advertising Programs, 487
   Developing the Advertising Message, 487

Assistance in Developing Advertising, 487
Choosing the Most Effective Advertising Medium, 490
Factors in Selecting Media, 493
Determining Ad Frequency and Timing, 495
Implementing Sales Promotion Programs, 495
   Types of Sales Promotions, 495
Implementing Publicity Programs, 497
   Publicity Tools, 498
   Publicity's Effect on Employees and Stockholders, 499
   An Illustration: A Store Opening, 499
Summary, 500
Key Terms, 501
Discussion Questions & Problems, 501
Suggested Readings, 502
Notes, 502

SECTION FOUR   Store Management   504

17   Managing the Store 506

Store Management
Responsibilities, 507
Recruiting and Selecting Store
Employees, 508
  Job Analysis, 508
  Job Description, 509
  Locating Prospective Employees, 510
  Screening Applicants to Interview, 511
  Selecting Applicants, 512
Socializing and Training New Store
Employees, 512
  Orientation Program, 512
  Training Store Employees, 514
Motivating and Managing Store
Employees, 517
  Leadership, 517
  Motivating Employees, 518
  Maintaining Morale, 519
Evaluating Store Employees and
Providing Feedback, 520
  Who Should Do the Evaluation? 520
  How Often Should Evaluations Be
  Made? 520
  Format for Evaluation, 521
  Evaluation Errors, 522
Compensating and Rewarding
Employees, 523

  Extrinsic Rewards, 523
  Intrinsic Rewards, 524
  Compensation Programs, 525
Legal and Ethical Issues in Managing
Store Employees, 528
  Hiring and Promotion, 528
  Selection, 529
  Compensation, 529
  Health and Safety, 529
  Sexual Harassment, 529
  Labor Relations, 530
Controlling Costs, 530
  Labor Scheduling, 530
  Store Maintenance, 531
  Energy Management, 531
Reducing Inventory Losses, 531
  Calculating Shrinkage, 532
  Detecting and Preventing
  Shoplifting, 532
  Reducing Employee Theft, 534
Summary, 535
Key Terms, 536
Discussion Questions & Problems, 536
Suggested Readings, 537
Notes, 537

18 Store Layout, Design, and Visual Merchandising 540

Store Layout, 543
Types of Design, 544
Types of Display Area, 547
Flexibility of Store Design, 550
Recognizing the Needs of the Disabled, 550

Space Planning, 551
Location of Departments, 552
Location of Merchandise within Departments: The Use of Planograms, 555
Evaluating Space Productivity, 556

Merchandise Presentation Techniques, 558
Idea-Oriented Presentation, 559
Style-Item Presentation, 559
Color Presentation, 559

Price Lining, 559
Vertical Merchandising, 559
Tonnage Merchandising, 560
Frontal Presentation, 560
Fixtures, 560

Atmospherics, 562
Visual Communications, 562
Lighting, 564
Color, 564
Music, 565
Scent, 566

Summary, 566
Key Terms, 567
Discussion Questions & Problems, 567
Suggested Readings, 568
Notes, 568

19 Customer Service 570

Strategy Advantage through Customer Service, 571
Nature of Customer Service, 572
Customer Service Strategies, 572
Cost of Customer Service, 575

Customer Evaluation of Service Quality, 576
Role of Expectations, 576
Perceived Service, 578
Situations That Stimulate Satisfactory and Unsatisfactory Experiences, 579

Gaps Model for Improving Retail Service Quality, 580

Knowing What Customers Want: The Knowledge Gap, 581
Researching Customer Expectations and Perceptions, 581
Using Customer Research, 584

Setting Service Standards: The Standards Gap, 584
Commitment to Service Quality, 585
Exploring Solutions to Service Problems, 585
Defining the Role of Service Providers, 587

Setting Service Goals, 587
Measuring Service Performance, 589

Meeting and Exceeding Service Standards: The Delivery Gap, 589
Giving Information and Training, 589
Providing Instrumental and Emotional Support, 590
Improving Internal Communications and Reducing Conflict, 590
Empowering Store Employees, 591
Providing Incentives, 592

Communicating the Service Promise: The Communications Gap, 592
Realistic Commitments, 592
Managing Customer Expectations, 593

Service Recovery, 593
Listening to the Customer, 593
Providing a Fair Solution, 594
Resolving Problems Quickly, 595

Summary, 596
Key Terms, 596
Discussion Questions & Problems, 596
Suggested Readings, 597
Notes, 597

20 Retailing Selling 600

Roles of Salespeople, 601

The Retail Selling Process, 602

   Approaching Customers, 603

   Collecting Information, 605

   Presenting the Merchandise, 606

   Demonstrating the Merchandise, 607

   Handling Reservations, 608

   Making the Sale, 611

   Selling Multiple Items, 614

   Building Relationships and Future Sales, 614

Knowledge and Skills for Effective Selling, 618

   Knowledge, 618

   The Art of Listening, 619

   The Art of Asking Questions, 621

   Interpreting and Using Nonverbal Communication, 622

   Flexibility and Adaptive Selling, 622

Summary, 625

Key Terms, 625

Discussion Questions & Problems, 625

Suggested Readings, 626

Notes, 626

SECTION FIVE

C Cases

Case 1   Cleveland Clinic, C–1

Case 2   Rainforest Cafe: A Wild Place to Shop and Eat, C–1

Case 3   NikeTown, C–2

Case 4   Virtual Vineyards: Wine On-Line, C–3

Case 5   The Home Shopping Network: Dealing with a Sales Slowdown, C–5

Case 6   Peapod: Electronic Grocery Shopping, C–6

Case 7   The Lab: AKA the Antimall, C–7

Case 8   The McGees Buy Three Bicycles, C–9

Case 9   Bloomingdale's: Customer Service Reaches Abroad, C–10

Case 10   Toys "R" Us: A New Beginning, C–11

Case 11   The Gap Opens Old Navy, C–12

Case 12   Sears Rebounds from the Brink of Bankruptcy, C–13

Case 13   Lindy's Bridal Shoppe, C–14

Case 14   Retailing in China, C–16

Case 15   Winn-Dixie Stores, Inc., and Dillard Department Stores, Inc.: Comparing Strategic Profit Models, C–22

Case 16   Stephanie's Boutique, C–25

Case 17   Hutch: Locating a New Store, C–24

Case 18   Fuller's: Whom to Let Go? C–30

Case 19   Marriott's Success Comes from Its Human Resources, C–31

Case 20   Lawson Sportswear, C–32

Case 21   Michaels Decreases Its Merchandise Assortment, C–35

Case 22   Merchandise Planning Problems, C–36

Case 23   McFaddens Department Store: Preparation of a Merchandise Budget Plan, C–37

Case 24   Star Hardware, C–39

Case 25   Urban Outfitters and the Coffee Crowd, C–42

Case 26   Stan's Shirts, C–43

Case 27   Pricing Problems, C–43

Case 28   An Advertising Plan, C–44

Case 29   Nieman Marcus's Preferred Customer Program, C–45

Case 30   Dexter Brown, Star Salesperson, C–46

Case 31   The Tardy Trainee, C–47

Case 32   Borders Book Store, C–48

Case 33   The Best Display? C–48

Case 34   Olathe Lanes East Bowling Center: Retail Space to Mirror Customers' Lifestyles, C–49

Case 35   Levi Stores: Mass Customization of Jeans, C–51

Case 36   Delta Airlines Finds Customer Service at a High Price, C–52

Case 37   Best Buy Uses Kiosks to Improve Customer Service, C–53

SECTION SIX   Appendixes

Appendix A
Careers in Retailing

Career Opportunities, A

Store Management, A–1

Merchandise/Buying, A–1

Careers in Corporate (Support Areas), A–2

Is Retailing for Me? A–5

Compensation and Benefits, A–5

Working Conditions, A–7

Responsibility, A–7

Employment Security, A–7

Decentralized Job Opportunities, A–8

Career Advancement, A–8

Women in Retailing, A–8

Characteristics Necessary to Be a Successful Retailer, A–8

Commonly Asked Questions, A–10

Getting Ready for a Retail Interview, A–11

Summary, A–12

Notes, A–12

Appendix B
Starting Your Own Retail Business

Do You Have What It Takes to Run Your Own Business? A–16

Demands in Owning a Business, A–16

Opportunities and Potential Problems of Owning a Business, A–17

What Should the Business Plan Include? A–18

Marketing Plan, A–18

Financial Plan, A–19

Legal Requirements, A–22

Business Plan Assistance, A–23

Value of the Business Plan, A–24

Where Can You Get the Financing to Start Your Business? A–24

Equity Financing, A–24

Debt Financing, A–25

What Should You Do If You're Considering the Purchase of an Existing Small Business? A–26

Summary, A–26

Suggested Readings, A–27

Notes, A–27

Appendix C
Starting a Franchise Business

Why Buy a Franchise? A–28

Advantages of Buying a Franchise, A–29

Disadvantages of Buying a Franchise, A–29

Are You Ready? A–29

Evaluating and Choosing a Franchise, A–30

Step 1: Initial Investigation, A–30

Step 2: Visiting Other Franchisees, A–31

Step 3: Visiting the Franchisor's Headquarters, A–31

Step 4: Financial Analysis, A–31

Step 5: Professional Assistance, A–33

Step 6: Contract and Franchise Agreement, A–33

Step 7: Final Decision, A–34

Suggested Readings, A–41

GLOSSARY, G

CREDITS, CR

INDEXES, I

Retailing Management

The World of Ret

CHAPTER 1 DESCRIBES THE FUNCTIONS RETAILERS pe
variety of decisions they make to satisfy customers' nee
changing, highly competitive environment. The remain
this section give you background information to under.

CHAPTER ONE
Introduction to the
World of Retailing

CHAPTER TWO
Store-Based Retailing

CHAPTER THREE
Nonstore Retailing—
Electronic Retailing
and Catalogs

CHAPTER FOUR
The Retail Customer

CHAPTER FIVE
Customer Buying
Behavior

environment. • Chapters 2 a
ferent types of retailers, both in-
store retailers. • Chapter
impact of changing consumer
lifestyles, and values on retailing
5 discusses factors consumers
choosing stores and buying
These chapters provide the bac.
mation about retail customers a
to develop and effectively imp.
strategy. • Section II outline
decisions retailers make. Secti
explore tactical decisions concer
dise and store management.

James E. Oesterreicher, Chairman and CEO, JCPenney Company, Inc.

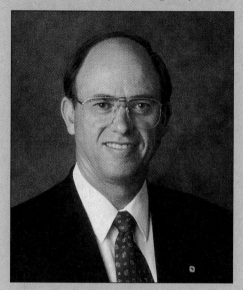

THE EXTENT AND SPEED OF CHANGE among consumers and in the retail industry is accelerating. We have one foot in the predictable world of the past and one foot in the unknown future • I believe retailers are operating on at least four important frontiers today. Each raises questions all retailers must address. • The frontier of consumer expectations. One factor that fuels the pace of change is the intense scarcity of time most American consumers experience. They struggle to find time for shopping. They also demand higher quality, more fashion, greater selection, and ease of shopping—all at a better price. How do retailers meet these expectations while still growing their businesses with acceptable profit margin? • The frontier of human resources. Systems, processes, bricks and mortar can all be duplicated, but people can't—what they know and how they work together. How can retailers build well-trained, motivated, and focused teams? • The frontier of technology. The big challenge here is to use information technologies to make faster and better decisions. We must also explore how these technologies will affect our customers' demands for shopping convenience and value. How can retailers marry their human talent with technology to best serve the customer and the shareholder? • The frontier of the global marketplace. Whether or not to go global is no longer a question for major retailers. The question is: When? Taking businesses global creates huge opportunites and risks for retailers, as JCPenney has learned by opening stores in Mexico and Chile. Related to this is another issue: How can retailers best serve customers and employees holding diverse interests, needs, and backgrounds? • There are no safe harbors in the years ahead. Companies must keep finding new strategies for staying ahead. • Here we can learn from Wayne Gretzky. He says his secret in leading the NHL in goals year after year has been to skate to where the puck is *going to be*, not where it *was*. That's exactly the skill retailers today must develop. Our challenge is to develop a vision of where consumers are going and then get there before they do or, more importantly, before the competition does.

Introduction to the World of Retailing

THE WORLD OF RETAILING

1. Introduction to the World of Retailing

2. Store-Based Retailing

3. Nonstore Retailing—Electronic Retailing and Catalogs

4. The Retail Customer

5. Customer Buying Behavior

↓

RETAILING STRATEGY

↓

MERCHANDISE MANAGEMENT

STORE MANAGEMENT

QUESTIONS

- What is retailing?

- What do retailers do?

- Why is retailing important in our society?

- What career and entrepreneurial opportunities does retailing offer?

- What types of decisions do retail managers make?

RETAILING, ONE OF THE LARGEST SECTORS in the global economy, is going through a period of exciting, dramatic change. The corner grocery store has evolved into an international business. McDonald's has over 8,000 outlets in 87 countries—over 1,500 in Japan alone. Wal-Mart is operating stores from Brazil to China. Some of the largest food retailers in the United States, such as A&P, Food Lion, Stop & Shop, Shaw's, and 7-Eleven, are owned by retail companies with headquarters in Europe and Japan.

Consumer demographics and needs are changing, and retailers are responding to these changes. With the increasing number of two-income families, people just don't have as much time to shop. So retailers are developing ways to help customers find what they want as quickly as possible. If you are interested in a big-screen TV, you can go to one store, a Circuit City or Best Buy, and know that you will see all the brands available, have someone there to answer questions, and pay a reasonable price. Electronic retailing enables consumers to shop the world from their house. Some experts forecast that electronic retailing and catalogs will account for 55 percent of all retail sales (compared to the present 15 percent).[1]

Consumers are more knowledgeable, demanding better value and customer service, and retailers are addressing these needs. At a General Nutrition Alive store, you can design your own personalized beauty care products and regimen of food supplements and vitamins developed for your specific needs. The products are developed in the store at the time of sale with each bottle marked with a customized label specifying the ingredients and your name.[2] Levi stores offer custom-fitted jeans for men and women. Department stores have personal shoppers to provide special showings of merchandise selected for the needs of their best customers.

Innovative retail concepts are providing more value to the consumer. Eatzi's (left) is a convenience store that offers to take meals home, and the General Nutrition Alive store (right) sells custom-designed nutrition supplements.

INTERNET EXERCISE   To experience electronic retailing, go to http://bf2.cstar.ac.com/bf/ where an agent will provide the prices for CD music albums from electronic retailers or http://bf2.cstar.ac.com/lifestyle/ where Waldo will suggest Internet sites based on your lifestyle. At http://www.ffly.com/ an agent will suggest movies and records you might like.

REFACT Wal-Mart is the largest retailer and the largest employer in the world.[3]

Stores are becoming more than just a place to buy products. They are offering exciting, visual experiences to attract customers. Niketown on Michigan Avenue is the most popular tourist attraction in Chicago. In 1995, 4.5 million tourists visited the Potomac Mills outlet mall in Dade City, Virginia, making it the number one tourist attraction in the state—ahead of Williamsburg, Arlington National Cemetery, and Mount Vernon.[4] Children around the world are entertained in Disney and Warner stores.

REFACT The Mall of America in Minnesota drew 40 million visitors, including 12 million tourists—more than Disney World, the Grand Canyon, and Graceland combined.[5]

Retailing is becoming a high-tech business. When you buy something at a supermarket, you trigger a sequence of electronic communications and decisions that determines what products will be delivered from the company's warehouse to the store tomorrow. Every day 500 gigabytes of data are transmitted via satellite from the point-of-sale (POS) terminals in JCPenney's 1,200 U.S. stores to its corporate headquarters in Dallas. Computer programs analyze this data and then automatically transmit orders to Penney's vendors, designating what merchandise should be shipped to each of its stores. Lands' End maintains a data warehouse with information about what each customer has bought and returned. With this information, mailings can be tailored to specific customers, and salespeople can make helpful suggestions when customers call in.[6]

In this dynamic environment, some entrepreneurs have launched new companies and concepts and become industry leaders, while traditional firms have had to rethink their business or go bankrupt. Thirty years ago, some of the largest retailers

Retail stores like Niketown (left) and the Warner Brothers store (right) are so exciting and entertaining that they have become tourist destinations.

1.1

New Ways to Buy a Car

MANY CONSUMERS VIEW GOING to a dealer to buy a car as being about as pleasurable as going to the dentist. But now new technology, modern retail merchandising, and old-fashioned entrepreneurship are providing alternatives to the traditional car dealers. Already 10 percent of car buyers bypass dealers and get their cars through superstores and third parties such as warehouse clubs and affinity groups.

CarMax, a division of Circuit City, applies the category-killer concept to develop a used-car superstore. It offers huge assortments, over 2,000 cars, in a comfortable atmosphere with everyday low pricing and no-hassle shopping. Customers identify cars they are interested in using an interactive computer kiosk that provides information on all cars at that location and other CarMax locations. For example, customers can enter the down payment and monthly payments they can make and the model and options they are considering. Cars meeting these criteria are then displayed on the terminal with their prices.

The salesperson's job is to help customers use the kiosk and find the car on the lot. There is no haggling over price. All cars are sold at the listed price and carry a 30-day warranty. If you want to trade in your car, the company buys the car at its appraised value in a separate transaction.

A car on display illustrates the 110-point performance and safety checkup that all used cars go through. Customers can return a car within five days of purchase and get a full refund, no questions asked.

Consumers are buying new cars using the Internet. First buyers determine the car they want by looking through extensive information provided by Edmund's (http://www.edmunds.com) or AutoNet New Cars (http://autosite.com). Then they place an order with a broker like Auto-By-Tel (http://autobytel.com). The broker arranges for a local dealer with the selected car to call the customer and sell the car at the wholesale price.

Source: "Revolution in the Showroom," *Business Week,* February 19, 1996, pp. 70–75; Alex Taylor, "How to Buy a Car on the Internet," *Fortune,* March 4, 1996, pp. 164–68; and Michael Hartnet, "Superstores Reshape Used Car Business," *Stores,* June 1996, pp. 30–32.

in the world—Wal-Mart, The Limited, The Gap, Home Depot, and Toys "R" Us—were either small start-ups or did not even exist. Over the last 10 years, a number of retailers with over $1 billion in annual sales—Revco, Macy's, Allied, Carter Hawley Hale, Ames, Best Products, Zale, and Grand Union—have filed for bankruptcy. Some of these companies, like Federated Department Stores, have reorganized to emerge as strong retailers, while other have disappeared. Retailing View 1.1 illustrates the dramatic changes in the retailing of automobiles.

Retailing is such a part of our everyday life that it's often taken for granted. Customers aren't aware of the sophisticated business decisions managers make and the technologies they use to provide goods and services. Retail managers must make complex decisions in selecting target markets, locating stores, determining what merchandise and services to offer, negotiating with suppliers, and deciding how to price, promote, and display merchandise. Making these decisions in a highly competitive, rapidly changing environment is challenging and exciting, with big opportunities for financial rewards.

This book describes the retail environment and gives principles for effectively managing businesses in this dynamic environment. Knowledge of retailing principles and practices will help you develop management skills for many business contexts. For example, a high-technology company like Dell Computer (America's fourth-largest computer designer and manufacturer) views direct-mail retailing skills as the key to its success. "We're more like Mary Kay Cosmetics than we are

Dell Computer views itself primarily as a retailer, even though it is a major computer designer and manufacturer.

like General Motors."[7] Financial and health care institutions are using retail principles to develop assortments of services, improve customer service, and make their offers available at convenient locations. Many firms ultimately sell their products and services to retailers. Thus students interested in professional selling, advertising, and many other retail-related careers will find this book useful.

WHAT IS A RETAILER?

Retailing's Role in Distribution Channels

A **retailer** is a business that sells products and services to consumers for their personal or family use. A retailer is the final business in a distribution channel that links manufacturers with consumers.[8] Exhibit 1–1 shows retailers' position within the distribution channel. Manufacturers make products and sell them to retailers or wholesalers. Wholesalers buy products from manufacturers and resell these products to retailers, while retailers resell products to consumers. Wholesalers and retailers may perform many of the same functions described in

EXHIBIT 1–1
Distribution Channel

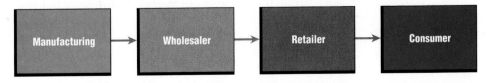

1.2

$20 for a Bottle of Aspirin

THE JAPANESE DISTRIBUTION SYSTEM is so complex and inefficient that consumers pay $20 for a bottle of 96 aspirins. A top priority of the Japanese economic policy is to protect small neighborhood retailers. A set of second- and third-level wholesalers have developed to make daily deliveries to these small retailers. Thus, merchandise might pass through three distributors between the manufacturer and retailer. Over one-fifth of the Japanese labor force is employed in distribution.

With Japanese consumers demanding lower prices, retailers are bypassing the distribution system to deal directly with manufacturers. For example, Daiei, a department store chain, opened a warehouse club, Kou, that attracted 146,000 members during its first year. The club offers discounts up to 80 percent on merchandise ranging from refrigerators to salad oil. By buying directly from U.S. manufacturers, Kou sells 12 Spaulding Magna Plus golf balls at $26.80, compared to the $72 price for the same balls going through the Japanese distribution system.

Source: Emily Thorton, "Revolution in Japanese Retailing," *Fortune,* February 1, 1994, pp. 143–46.

---

the next section. But wholesalers satisfy retailers' needs, while retailers direct their efforts to satisfying needs of ultimate consumers. Some retail chains (like Home Depot and Sam's) are both retailers and wholesalers. They're retailers when they sell to consumers; they're wholesalers when they sell to other businesses like building contractors or restaurant owners.

U.S. consumers are able to buy merchandise at low prices from convenient locations because the U.S. distribution system is very efficient. Retailing View 1.2 illustrates how the Japanese distribution system affects the prices its consumers pay.

Functions Performed by Retailers

Retailers undertake business activities and perform functions that increase the value of the products and services they sell to consumers. These functions are

1. Providing an assortment of products and services.
2. Breaking bulk.
3. Holding inventory.
4. Providing services.

Providing Assortments Supermarkets typically carry 15,000 different items made by over 500 companies. Offering an assortment enables customers to choose from a wide selection of brands, designs, sizes, colors, and prices in one location.

Manufacturers specialize in producing specific types of products. For example, Campbell's makes soup, Kraft makes dairy products, Kellogg makes breakfast cereals, and McCormick makes spices. If each of these manufacturers had its own stores that only sold its own products, consumers would have to go to many different stores to buy groceries to prepare a single meal.

All retailers offer assortments of products, but they specialize in the assortments they offer. Supermarkets provide assortments of food, health and beauty aids (HBA), and household products, while The Gap provides assortments of clothing and accessories. Most consumers are well aware of the product assortments retailers offer. Even small children know where to buy different types of products. But new types of retailers offering unique assortments appear each year, such as Play It Again Sports (used sporting goods), Michaels (craft supplies), and Mini Maid (home cleaning services).

REFACT The word *retail* is derived from the French word *retaillier,* meaning to cut a piece off or to break bulk.

Breaking Bulk   To reduce transportation costs, manufacturers and wholesalers typically ship cases of frozen dinners or cartons of blouses to retailers. Retailers then offer the products in smaller quantities tailored to individual consumers' and households' consumption patterns. This is called **breaking bulk.**

Holding Inventory   A major function of retailers is to keep inventory so that products will be available when consumers want them. Thus, consumers can keep a much smaller inventory of products at home because they know the retailers will have the products available when they need more.

By maintaining an inventory, retailers provide a benefit to consumers—they reduce the consumer's cost of storing products.[9] The investment to store products ties up consumers' money that could go into an interest-earning bank account or some other use.

Providing Services   Retailers provide services that make it easier for customers to buy and use products. They offer credit so consumers can have a product now and pay for it later. They display products so that consumers can see and test them before buying. Retailers may have salespeople on hand to answer questions and provide additional information about products.

Increasing the Value of Products and Services   By providing assortments, breaking bulk, holding inventory, and providing services, retailers increase the value consumers receive from their products and services. To illustrate, consider a door in a shipping crate in an Iowa manufacturer's warehouse. The door won't satisfy the needs of a do-it-yourselfer (DIYer) who wants to replace a closet door today. For the DIYer, a home improvement center like Home Depot or Lowe's sells one door at a conveniently located store that is available when the DIYer wants it. The home improvement center helps the customer select the door by displaying them so they can be examined before they're purchased. An employee is available to explain which door is best for closets and how the door should be hung. The center provides an assortment of hardware, paint, and tools that the DIYer will need for the job. Thus, retailers increase the value of products and services bought by their customers. Retailing View 1.3 illustrates how retailers provide value to their communities as well as their customers.

Retailing is the set of business activities that adds value to the products and services sold to consumers for their personal or family use. Often people think of retailing only as the sale of products in stores. But retailing also involves the sale of services: overnight lodging in a motel, a doctor's exam, a haircut, a videotape rental, or a home-delivered pizza. Not all retailing is done in stores. Examples of nonstore retailing are the direct sales of cosmetics by Avon, catalog sales by L.L. Bean and Patagonia, and the Home Shopping Network on cable TV.

Organization of the Distribution Channel

In some distribution channels, the manufacturing, wholesaling, and retailing activities are performed by independent firms. But most distribution channels have some vertical integration.

Vertical integration means that a firm performs more than one level of activity in the channel. For example, most large retailers—such as Kmart, Safeway, Wal-Mart, and Macy's—do both wholesaling and retailing. They buy

1.3

Community Pride Food Store Brings Pride Back to the Community

Jonathon Johnson, founder of Community Pride Stores and community leader in Richmond, Virginia.

WHEN JONATHAN JOHNSON WAS growing up in Richmond, Virginia, his neighbors took great pride in their homes and community. Now the neighborhood bears the scars of economic hardship, crime, and drugs. Johnson started Community Pride Food Stores in 1992 with the objective of developing a new spirit of community in Richmond's inner city.

Community Pride has seven clean, well-managed stores in urban Richmond that offer affordable, quality products. Eighty percent of its employees live within three miles of the store where they work. Each store has two delivery vans providing rides to customers who aren't mobile. Customers can also cash checks, pay utility bills, and buy bus tickets, postage stamps, and money orders at the stores.

Johnson stresses the importance of education. Employees are encouraged to enroll in many structured training programs. Also, $5,000 scholarships are awarded to employees who pursue college education. Families of high school students who earn all As and Bs and don't miss more than one day of classes get a 10 percent discount on food.

Source: "Retail Entrepreneur of the Year," *Chain Store Age Executive,* December 1995, pp. 74, 78.

REFACT The tea bag was developed by a Macy's buyer. A JCPenney buyer developed panty hose.

directly from manufacturers, have merchandise shipped to their warehouses for storage, and then distribute the merchandise to their stores. Other retailers, such as The Gap and The Limited, are even more vertically integrated. They design the merchandise they sell and then contract with manufacturers to produce it exclusively for them.

Thus, retailers undertake a wide variety of activities to add value to the merchandise and services they sell to ultimate users. Besides traditional retailing activities, many retailers are vertically integrated and perform manufacturing and wholesaling functions.

EXHIBIT 1–2

Employment by
Industry, 1995
(millions of
employees)

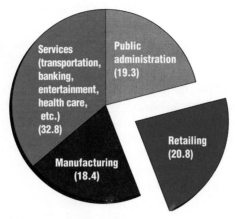

Source: U.S. Department of Commerce.

ECONOMIC SIGNIFICANCE OF RETAILING

Because activities performed by retailers are important to consumers, retailing is a significant economic institution and a big business in our society.

Retail Sales

REFACT In 1995, total expenditures on goods sold by retailers were greater than expenditures on medical care, housing, and recreation combined.[11]

Retailing affects every facet of life. Just think of how many contacts you have with retailers when you eat meals, furnish your apartment, have your car fixed, and buy clothing for a party or job interview. U.S. retail sales in 1995 were $2,340 trillion.[10] These official statistics include only store and catalog sales; they don't include other types of nonstore retail sales, such as direct sales to consumers, TV home shopping, and sales of services to consumers such as movie theaters, hotel rooms, and legal assistance.

Contrary to popular belief, most retail firms are not large businesses. In 1992, there were 1.4 million retail firms, but only 4.9 percent of them had more than one store. Of the retail firms in the United States only 7.9 percent of them have annual sales over $2.5 million dollars.[12]

Employment

Retailing is one of the nation's largest industries in terms of employment. As Exhibit 1–2 shows, 20 million people are employed in retailing—approximately 18 percent of the U.S. workforce. Exhibit 1–3 illustrates the growth in employment in the major sectors of the U.S. economy. Over the next 10 years, it is estimated that employment in retail trades will grow by 1.2 million jobs, while there will be a loss of 0.6 million jobs in manufacturing.[13] Note that these figures understate the impact of retailing as an employer because many of the 4.8 million service jobs involve firms retailing services to consumers.

EXHIBIT 1–3

Change in Jobs,
1990–95

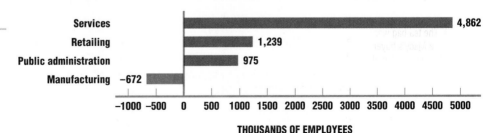

Source: U.S. Department of Commerce.

1.4

Sam Walton Builds the World's Largest Retailer

THE WALTON FAMILY IS ranked by *Forbes* magazine as one of the wealthiest in the world. But Sam Walton disliked the tag of America's richest person, saying, "It's just paper. All I own is a pick-up truck and a little Wal-Mart stock."

Walton majored in economics at the University of Missouri, graduating in 1940. He considered selling insurance, but an interview with JCPenney attracted him to retailing. He began working as a management trainee in the Des Moines store for $85 a month. In 1942, he left to join the military.

At the end of World War II, Walton sought a retail business to buy with money he had saved in the army. He bought a Ben Franklin variety store franchise in Newport, Arkansas. When his landlord declined to renew his lease in 1950, Walton relocated to Bentonville, Arkansas (which remains Wal-Mart's corporate headquarters), and opened a Walton five-and-dime. By 1962, his business had grown to 15 stores (most Ben Franklin franchises).

In the 1960s, the pioneers of modern discounting were building their businesses, primarily in the Northeast. Walton visited these stores, observed their merchandising techniques, and became convinced that discounting would revolutionize retailing. After failing to get people at Ben Franklin's headquarters to join him in opening discount stores, he opened his first Wal-Mart discount store in Rogers, Arkansas, in 1962. "Old Number 1" has now been joined by over 2,000 stores in the United States, 250 Wal-Mart Discount City stores, and over 300 stores outside the United States.

Wal-Mart's initial strategy was to offer name-brand merchandise at discount prices to small communities. Walton felt that the key to

Sam Walton's understanding of his customers and employees was instrumental in building Wal-Mart into one of the largest retailers in the world.

his success is people: his customers and his employees (called "associates," a term adopted from his initial job at Penney). He said, "Our goal has always been in our business to be the very best. We believe completely that in order to be the very best you've got to make a good situation and put the interests of your associates first. If we really do that consistently, they will in turn cause our business to be successful." Sam Walton died in 1992, but his spirit and ideas remain a driving force at Wal-Mart.

Source: Patrica Sellers, "Can Wal-Mart Get Back the Magic?" *Fortune,* April 1996, pp. 130–35; David Hatch, "Sam Walton: Master Change Agent," *Executive Excellence,* June 1992, p. 19; and Bill Saporito, "What Sam Walton Taught America," *Fortune,* May 4, 1992, pp. 104–5.

The Top 25 Retailers

Exhibit 1–4's list of the 25 largest U.S. retailers reveals the diverse and dynamic nature of retailing as well as the economic importance of retailing. The list includes companies that sell a few categories of merchandise (Toys "R" Us and McDonald's) as well as companies that sell a wide variety of merchandise through different retail formats, such as JCPenney (department stores and catalog)

EXHIBIT **1–4**

The 25 Largest U.S.
Retail Corporations

RANK (RETAILERS)	COMPANY (HEADQUARTERS)	1995 SALES (MILLIONS)	1995 PROFITS (MILLIONS)	RANK (ALL U.S. FIRMS)
1	Wal-Mart (Bentonville, AR)	$93,607	$2,740	4
2	Sears Roebuck (Hoffman Estates, IL)	35,181	1,801	15
3	Kmart (Troy, MI)	34,654	(571)	16
4	JCPenney (Plano, TX)	26,416*	931	34/268
5	Kroger (Cincinnati, OH)	23,939	303	27
6	Dayton Hudson (Minneapolis, MN)	23,516	311	28
7	American Stores (Salt Lake City, UT)	18,309	316	45
8	Price/Costco (Issaquah, WA)	18,247	134	46
9	Safeway (Oakland, CA)	16,398	326	54
10	Home Depot (Atlanta, GA)	15,470	731	66
11	Federated Depart. Stores (Cincinnati, OH)	15,049	75	69
12	Albertson's (Boise, ID)	12,585	465	96
13	May Dept Stores (St. Louis, MO)	12,187	752	99
14	Winn-Dixie (Jacksonville, FL)	11,788	232	103
15	Melville (Rye, NY)	11,516	(657)	110
16	Walgreen (Deerfield, IL)	10,395	320	123
17	McDonald's (Oak Brook, IL)	9,975	1,427	132
18	Publix Super Markets (Lakeland, FL)	9,470	242	136
19	Toys "R" Us (Paramus, NJ)	9,427	148	137
20	Staples/Office Depot (Framingham, MA)	8,381†	206	404/239
21	Woolworth (New York, NY)	8,224	(164)	161
22	Limited (Columbus, OH)	7,881	961	167
23	Lowe's (North Wilksboro, NC)	7,075	226	184
24	USAA (San Antonio, TX)	6,611	730	200
25	Dillard Dept Stores (Little Rock, AR)	6,097	470	214

Source: "Fortune 500 Largest U.S. Corporations," *Fortune*, April 29, 1996, pp. F1–F19.
*Based on acquisition of Eckerd by JCPenney completed in 1997.
†Based on the potential acquisition of Office Depot by Staples completed in 1997.

Note: Great American & Pacific Tea Company (A&P), Food Lion, and Southland (7-Eleven) are not on the list because they are owned by larger, foreign companies. Other large retailers who also have substantial sales to businesses as well as directly to consumers are Prudential Insurance of America (1995 sales $41,330), State Farm ($40,810), PepsiCo ($30,421), Metropolitan Life Insurance ($27,977), Allstate ($22,793), Cigna ($18,955), AMR (American Airlines) ($16,910), New York Life ($16,202), UAL (United Airlines) ($14,943), Aetna Life & Casualty ($12,978), Delta ($12,194), Walt Disney ($12,114), Viacom ($11,780), Nationwide Life ($11,702), TIAA ($11,646), Northwest Mutual Life ($11,483), Northwest Airlines ($9,085), Marriott ($8,961), Time Warner ($8,067), and USAir ($7,474) (all figures in millions).

REFACT One out of every five workers in the United States is employed in retailing.[14]

REFACT Wal-Mart's, Kmart's, and Sears' annual sales are much greater than the annual sales of Procter & Gamble, PepsiCo, and RJR Nabisco—the three largest consumer product companies.[16]

and Dayton Hudson (department and discount stores). USAA sells insurance and financial services exclusively through direct mail and telemarketing. Six firms on the list (The Limited, Price, Toys "R" Us, Costco Warehouse, Food Lion, and Wal-Mart) have developed into major retailers during the past 30 years. Retailing View 1.4 describes how Wal-Mart grew into the world's largest retailer.

Some of the top 25 retailers have completely changed their retailing approach over this period. For example, Kmart (Kresge) and Woolworth began as variety stores but became leading discount and specialty store operators.[15] Sears began as a catalog retailer, expanded to a national chain of retail stores, diversified into financial services and insurance, and is now refocusing on in-store retailing.

1.5

Managing a Business in a Retail Corporation

AFTER GRADUATING FROM SANTA CLARA University with a B.S. in marketing, Del Hernandez went to work for Macy's. Hernandez's initial assignment was department manager for children's and infants' apparel in the Oakridge Mall store. A month after college, he was responsible for managing a department with $3 million in annual sales. In this position, he worked with buyers to make sure his department had the merchandise customers wanted, he developed and implemented plans for presenting merchandise, and he supervised 20 salespeople.

After 10 months, Hernandez was promoted to assistant buyer for junior separates at the division headquarters in San Francisco. In 18 months, he was promoted again to group sales manager in the Oakridge Mall store. The three departments he managed employed over 100 salespeople; their annual sales totaled $15 million.

A little over three years after he had graduated, Hernandez was promoted again. He became buyer for the $12 million of advanced consumer electronics and video games sold annually in all 25 Macy–California stores. He was responsible for selecting merchandise, negotiating with vendors, pricing merchandise, and providing guidelines for its presentation in stores.

Macy's consumer electronics department has an unusual assortment of merchandise that appeals to an upscale market. To locate unique items, Hernandez went to toy fairs, sporting goods shows, and gift shows. Three years later, he saw some dancing flowers in an East Coast store and decided to make a major commitment to this novelty item. He placed a large order with the manufacturer and designed a 100-square-foot "flower garden" with 50 to 60 dancing flowers in each Macy's store.

Hernandez's investment in inventory, selling space, and promotion of the dancing flowers was risky, but it paid off. Macy's was the first West Coast store to sell dancing flowers. Early commitment and significant investment resulted in sales of 50,000 pieces during 1989.

Ten years after graduation, Hernandez was promoted again to manage the Bullock's (a division of Macy's) store in Palm Desert. Annual sales for his store total $30 million; it employs 200 people.

Due to Hernandez's performance as a department manager, assistant buyer, group sales manager, buyer, and store manager, his salary was more than five times his starting salary when he graduated from college 10 years ago.

Source: Personal communication.

OPPORTUNITIES IN RETAILING

Management Opportunities

To cope with a highly competitive and challenging environment, retailers are hiring and promoting people with a wide range of skills and interests. Students often view retailing as a part of marketing because management of distribution channels is part of a manufacturer's marketing function.[17] But retailers undertake most of the traditional business activities. Retailers raise capital from financial institutions; purchase goods and services; develop accounting and management information systems to control operations; manage warehouses and distribution systems; and design and develop new products as well as undertake marketing activities such as advertising, promotions, sales force management, and market research. Thus, retailers employ people with expertise and interest in finance, accounting, human resource management, logistics, and computer systems as well as marketing. Retail managers are often given considerable responsibility early in their careers. Retailing View 1.5 describes one college graduate's career path and responsibilities.

Retail management is also financially rewarding. After completing a management trainee program in retailing, managers can double their starting salary in three to five years if they perform well. The typical buyer in a department store earns $50,000 to $60,000 per year. Store managers working for department or discount store chains often make over $100,000. At the end of this book, Appendix A describes retail career opportunities in detail.

Entrepreneurial Opportunities

Retailing also provides opportunities for people wishing to start their own business. Many retail entrepreneurs are among the Forbes 400 wealthiest people in the United States. Highly successful retail entrepreneurs include Leslie Wexner (The Limited), David Thomas (Wendy's), Donald Fisher (The Gap), Gary Comer (Lands' End), and Thomas Monaghan (Domino's Pizza).

REFACT Ninety-three percent of U.S. retailers have only one store, while only 0.1 percent of U.S. retailers have more than 100 stores.[18]

Leslie Wexner's parents owned a retail clothing store, working 70 hours a week, but never earned more than $10,000 in a year. Wexner dropped out of law school and went to work in the family store. When he disagreed with its buying and marketing techniques, he borrowed $5,000 from an aunt and opened his first sportswear store for young women in 1963, naming it Leslie's. Leslie's was changed to The Limited. Over the past 30 years, it has grown to 5,100 stores with over $7.8 billion in annual sales. The firm acquired Henri Bendel, Victoria's Secret, Abercrombie & Fitch, Lane Bryant, and Lerner Shops and started Limited Express, Structure, Limited Two, Bath & Body Works, Victoria's Secret Bath, and Cacique.[19]

REFACT Wendy's International was named after one of Dave Thomas's daughters, Melinda Lou, whose nickname is Wendy. She is a graduate of the University of Florida.[21]

After appearing in over 300 TV commercials, Dave Thomas has become the most well known living restaurateur. His unassuming persona conveys an image that the chain is owned by a caring grandfather rather than a faceless corporation, a lesson he learned from Colonel Sanders, founder of KFC. Thomas never knew his parents. His adoptive mother died when he was five. His involvement in the restaurant business began at the age of 12. After dropping out of high school and completing service in the army, he bought a run-down KFC franchise. At the age of 35, he became a millionaire when he sold his KFC franchises. He decided to open some fast-food restaurants to pay for his children's college educations. Wendy's success is attributed to his focusing on young adults and offering them sandwiches made to order with the condiments selected by the customer.[20]

Donald Fisher was a finance major and a star swimmer at the University of California at Berkeley. After graduating in 1950, he entered his family's real estate development business. He cofounded The Gap with his wife in 1969 out of his frustration at not being able to find blue jeans that would fit his normally proportioned six-foot–one, 34-inch waist frame. The Gap stores were unique in offering every size and style of Levi's, arranged by size for convenience. When the teen-jean craze slowed in the mid-1970s, stores were repositioned for a more mature customer. Now The Gap sells only private-label merchandise under its own brand name.

REFACT After working with consultants to develop a name for his new retail concept, Mickey Drexler settled on Old Navy after seeing it on a building during a walk around Paris.[23]

Reminiscent of the founding of The Gap, GapKids was started when chief operating officer Mickey Drexler couldn't find comfortable clothing for his children. Drexler also developed Old Navy to cater to the new lifestyle when being hip is not to spend money on clothing.[22]

Gary Comer was an award-winning copywriter for the Young & Rubicam advertising agency. Then he went to work as a salesperson for a sail-making company and competed in the sailing trials for the 1968 Olympics. Comer started the Lands' End mail-order catalog for sailing supplies and accessories, with a small

1.6

Patagonia Reflects the Personality of Its Founder and Owner

Merchandise offered in the Patagonia catalog reflects the founder, Tvon Chouinard, a rugged outdoorsman, shown surfing above.

TVON CHOUINARD, FOUNDER AND OWNER of Patagonia, started his business career selling handmade mountain-climbing tools from his car. In 1974, he founded Patagonia, the California-based retailer and manufacturer of high-quality outdoor clothing. As an expert climber, surfer, skier, kayaker, and fisherman, Chouinard travels the world, personally testing the products his company manufacturers and sells in its 17 stores and internationally distributed catalog. The catalog is known for its breath-taking images of high-risk sports activities in exotic locations. The clothes and equipment in the catalog are designed to withstand the most rugged environments.

Chouisand is a legendary extreme adventurer and dedicated environmentalist. He donates 1 percent of Patagonia's sales to environmental causes. In 1991, the company undertook an environmental audit to examine the impact of its clothing on the environment. On the basis of the audit, the company eliminated 30 percent of its product because the items used too many natural resources.

Chouinard's personality is reflected throughout the company. Patagonia was one of the first companies to offer on-site day care. The work atmosphere is friendly and casual. Employees can work up to one month a year for a nonprofit organization with full pay from Patagonia.

Source: "Patagonia Comes of Age," *Industry Week,* April 3, 1995, pp. 42–44; and "Retail Entrepreneurs of the Year," *Chain Store Age Executive,* December 1994, pp. 46–47.

clothing section. More apparel items were added to the catalog, and by 1977, the sailing items were eliminated. Lands' End features entertaining catalogs and polite telephone operators. As Comer says, "I treat customers the way I want to be treated. What is best for our customers is best for all of us at Lands' End."[24]

Thomas Monaghan was fatherless at four and raised in orphanages. After being thrown out of a seminary for misconduct, he joined the Marines. In 1960, he bought his first pizza parlor in Ypsilanti, Michigan, with a $500 loan from his brother. One year later he swapped his Volkswagen for his brother's interest in the business.

His strategy was to focus on home delivery when other pizza restaurants thought delivery was a nuisance. Tailoring the operations to the delivery business included the design of everything from the ovens to the pizza boxes. Monaghan met his wife when he delivered a pizza to her dormitory. Domino's now has over 5,500 stores worldwide and annual sales over $3 billion.[25]

Retailing View 1.6 provides the background on the founder of Patagonia. Appendices B and C at the end of the book describe steps for starting a retail business and buying a franchise business.

RETAIL MANAGEMENT DECISION-MAKING PROCESS

The success of a small retailer or a major retail corporation depends largely on how much it embraces the retailing concept. The **retailing concept** is a management orientation that focuses a retailer on determining its target market's needs and satisfying those needs more effectively and efficiently than its competitors.[26]

The retailing concept emphasizes that high-performance retailers must be strong competitors. They can't achieve high performance by simply satisfying customers' needs. They must also keep a close watch to ensure that competitors don't attract their customers.

Retailers attempt to minimize competition by offering unique merchandise and services that can't be copied easily. But gaining long-term competitive advantage is particularly difficult in retailing. Since retailers typically purchase the products they sell, competitors can often purchase and sell the same products. Retailers can't patent a unique store design, merchandise assortment, or service. For example, if one supermarket develops a successful takeout deli, its competitors can install and operate a similar deli counter within weeks.

This book is organized around the management decisions retailers make to provide value to their customers and develop an advantage over their competitors. Exhibit 1–5 identifies chapters in this book associated with each type of decision.

Understanding the World of Retailing

The first step in the retail management decision process, as Exhibit 1–5 shows, is getting an understanding of the world of retailing. Retail managers need a good understanding of their environment, especially their customers and competition, before they can develop and implement effective strategies. The first section of this book provides a general overview of the retailing industry and its customers. Then Chapter 6 describes how an individual retailer performs a situation analysis as part of a strategic planning process.

Three critical environmental factors in the world of retailing are (1) competition; (2) consumer demographics and lifestyle trends and their impact on retail institutions, and (3) the needs, wants, and decision-making processes of retail consumers.

Competition   At first glance, identifying competitors appears easy. A retailer's primary competitors are those with the same format. Thus, department stores compete against other department stores and supermarkets compete with other supermarkets. This competition between retailers with the same format is called **intratype competition.**

To appeal to a broader group of consumers and provide one-stop shopping, many retailers are increasing their variety of merchandise. For example, clothing and food are now available in grocery, department, discount, and drugstores. The offering of merchandise not typically associated with the store type, such as clothing in a drugstore, is called **scrambled merchandise.**

EXHIBIT 1–5

Retail Management
Decision Process

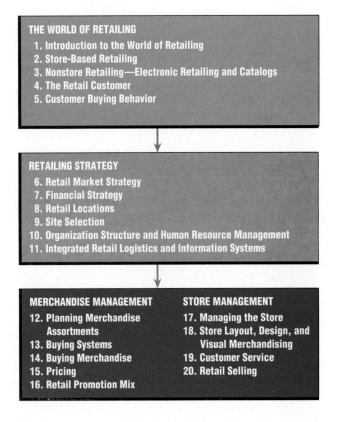

THE WORLD OF RETAILING

1. Introduction to the World of Retailing
2. Store-Based Retailing
3. Nonstore Retailing—Electronic Retailing and Catalogs
4. The Retail Customer
5. Customer Buying Behavior

RETAILING STRATEGY

6. Retail Market Strategy
7. Financial Strategy
8. Retail Locations
9. Site Selection
10. Organization Structure and Human Resource Management
11. Integrated Retail Logistics and Information Systems

MERCHANDISE MANAGEMENT

12. Planning Merchandise Assortments
13. Buying Systems
14. Buying Merchandise
15. Pricing
16. Retail Promotion Mix

STORE MANAGEMENT

17. Managing the Store
18. Store Layout, Design, and Visual Merchandising
19. Customer Service
20. Retail Selling

REFACT When Wal-Mart converts one of its general merchandise discount stores into a supercenter by adding groceries, sales of nongrocery items rise 30 to 50 percent.[27]

Competition between retailers that sell similar merchandise using different formats, such as discount and department stores, is called **intertype competition.** Increasing intertype competition has made it harder for retailers to identify and monitor their competition. Most retailers now have scrambled merchandise to tailor their merchandise to a target segment's needs. In one sense, all retailers compete against each other for the dollars consumers spend buying goods and services. But the intensity of competition among firms is greatest when customers view the retail mixes as very similar.

Since convenience of location is important in store choice, a store's proximity to competitors is a critical factor in identifying competition. Consider two videotape rental stores, Blockbuster and Harry's Video, in two suburbs 10 miles apart. The stores are the only specialty videotape rental retailers within 50 miles, but a grocery store also rents videotapes in the same strip center as Blockbuster. Due to the distance between Blockbuster and Harry's Video, they probably don't compete against each other intensely. Customers who live near Harry's Video will rent tapes there, while customers close to Blockbuster will rent tapes at Blockbuster or the grocery store. In this case, Harry's major competitor may be movie theaters and cable TV because it's too inconvenient for customers close to Harry's to rent videotapes elsewhere. On the other hand, Blockbuster competes most intensely with the grocery store.

Management's view of competition also can differ, depending on the manager's position within the retail firm. For example, the manager of the Neiman Marcus women's sportswear department in the Bal Harbor Shops near Miami Beach, Florida, views the women's sportswear specialty stores in the same mall as her major competitors. But the Neiman Marcus store manager views the Saks store in

Blockbuster competes against independent video rental stores (on the right) and a wide variety of other retailers that rent videos.

the nearby Aventura Mall as her strongest competitor. These differences in perspectives arise because the department sales manager is primarily concerned with customers for a specific category of merchandise, while the store manager is concerned with customers seeking the selection of all merchandise and services offered by a department store.

On the other hand, the CEO of a retail chain views competition from a much broader geographic perspective. For example, Nordstrom identifies The Bon Marche as its strongest competitor in the Northwest, Macy's West in northern California, and Bloomingdale's in New York City. At a national level, Kmart considers Wal-Mart to be its strongest competitor.

The CEO may also take a strategic perspective and recognize that other activities compete for consumers' disposable income. For example, Blockbuster Video's CEO takes the consumer's perspective and recognizes that videotape rental stores are competing in the entertainment industry with other videotape rental stores, other retailers who rent videotapes (such as grocery and convenience stores), movie theaters, regular and cable TV, theater, opera, ballet, nightclubs, and restaurants.[28]

Retailing is intensely competitive. Understanding the different types of retailers and how they compete with each other is critical to developing and implementing a retail strategy. Chapters 2 and 3 discuss various types of retailers and retail strategies.

Consumer Trends   The second background factor is consumer trends. Today's retailers confront a particularly challenging business environment. Customer needs are continually changing at an increasing rate.[29] Retailers need to respond to broad demographic and lifestyle trends in our society, such as the growth in the elderly and minority segments of the U.S. population and the importance of shopping convenience to the rising number of two-income families. Chapter 4 tells of important changes in retail customers.

REFACT Fred Lazarus Jr., founder of the Lazurus department stores, promoted the idea of fixing Thanksgiving on the fourth weekend in November to expand the Christmas shopping season. Congress adopted his proposal in 1941.[30]

Customer Buying Behavior   Customers are the third factor in the situation analysis. To develop and implement an effective strategy, retailers need to know the information in Chapter 5 about why customers shop, how they select a store, and how they select among that store's merchandise.

Ethical and Legal Issues   Ethical standards and legal and public policy considerations guide management decisions. Strategy development and implementation must be consistent with corporate values, legal opinions, and public policies. Federal, state, and local laws are enacted to ensure that business activities are consistent with society's interests. Some laws define unfair competitive practices related to suppliers and customers. They regulate advertising, promotion, and pricing practices and restrict store locations.

Retailers often use ethical standards to guide decision making when confronting questionable situations not covered by laws. For example, retail salespeople may wonder if they should use high-pressure, manipulative sales techniques to sell merchandise that seems inappropriate for a customer. Buyers may have to decide whether to accept a supplier's offer of free tickets to a football game. Some retailers have policies that outline correct behavior of employees in these situations, but in many situations people must rely on their own code of ethics.

Due to the importance of these issues, we discuss ethical and legal considerations throughout this book and relate them to each retail management decision area.

REFACT Sit-ins to protest racial discrimination began in 1960 when four black college students were denied service at a lunch counter in a Woolworth store in Glassboro, North Carolina. [31]

Developing a Retail Strategy

Using the situation analysis, the next stages in the retail management decision-making process are formulating and implementing a retail strategy. Section 2 focuses on decisions related to developing a retail strategy. Sections 3 and 4 concern implementation decisions.

The **retail strategy** indicates how the firm plans to focus its resources to accomplish its objectives. It identifies (1) the target market toward which the retailer will direct its efforts, (2) the nature of the merchandise and services the retailer will offer to satisfy needs of the target market, and (3) how the retailer will build a long-term advantage over competitors.

The nature of a retail strategy can be illustrated by comparing strategies of Wal-Mart and Toys "R" Us.[32] Initially Wal-Mart identified its target market as small towns (under 35,000 in population) in Arkansas, Texas, and Oklahoma. It offered name-brand merchandise at low prices in a broad array of categories, ranging from laundry detergent to girls' dresses. While Wal-Mart stores have many different categories of merchandise, selection in each category is limited. A store might have only three brands of detergents in two sizes, while a supermarket carries eight brands in five sizes.

In contrast to Wal-Mart, Toys "R" Us identified its target as consumers living in suburban areas of large cities. Rather than carrying a broad array of merchandise categories, Toy "R" Us stores specialize in toys, games, bicycles, and furniture primarily for children. While Toys "R" Us has few categories of merchandise, it has almost all the different types of toys and games currently available in the market.

Both Wal-Mart and Toys "R" Us emphasize self-service. Customers select their merchandise, bring it to the checkout line, and then carry it to their cars. Frequently customers must assemble the merchandise at home. Since Wal-Mart and Toys "R" Us emphasize low price, they've made strategic decisions to develop a cost advantage over competitors. Both firms have sophisticated distribution and management information systems to manage inventory. Their strong relationships with suppliers enable them to buy merchandise at low prices.

Strategic Decision Areas   The key strategic decisions areas are determining a market strategy, financial strategy, location strategy, organizational structure and human resource strategy, and information systems strategy.[33] Chapter 6 discusses how selection of a retail market strategy is based on analyzing the environment and the firm's strengths and weaknesses. When major environmental changes occur, the current strategy and the reasoning behind it are reexamined. The retailer then decides what, if any, strategy changes are needed to take advantage of new opportunities or avoid new threats in the environment.

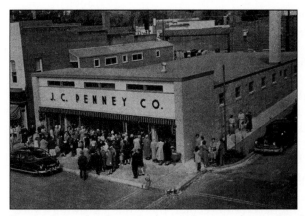

Penney's has made a dramatic strategic change in its move from Main Street in small towns to become the second largest U.S. department chain in regional malls.

The retailer's market strategy must be consistent with the firm's financial objectives. Chapter 7 reviews how financial variables such as sales, costs, expenses, profits, assets, liabilities, and owner's equity are used to evaluate the market strategy and its implementation.

Decisions concerning location strategy (reviewed in Chapters 8 and 9) are important for both consumer and competitive reasons. First, location is typically consumers' top consideration when selecting a store. Generally consumers buy gas at the closest service station and patronize the shopping mall that's most convenient to their home or office. Second, location offers an opportunity to gain long-term advantage over competition. When a retailer has the best location, a competing retailer has to settle for the second-best location.

A retailer's organization design and human resource management strategy are intimately related to its market strategy. For example, retailers that attempt to serve national or regional markets must make trade-offs between the efficiency of centralized buying and the need to tailor merchandise and services to local needs. Retailers that focus on customer segments seeking high-quality customer service must motivate and enable sales associates to provide the expected levels of service. The organization structure and human resources policies discussed in Chapter 10 coordinate the implementation of the retailing strategy by buyers, store managers, and sales associates.

Retail information and control systems will be a significant opportunity for retailers to gain strategic advantage in the coming decade. Chapter 11 reviews how some retailers are developing sophisticated computer and distribution systems to monitor flows of information and merchandise from vendors to retail distribution centers to retail stores. Point-of-sale (POS) terminals read price and product information that's coded into Universal Product Codes (UPCs) affixed to the merchandise. This information is then transmitted to distribution centers or directly to vendors electronically, computer-to-computer. These technologies are part of an overall inventory management system that enables retailers to (1) give customers a more complete selection of merchandise and (2) decrease their inventory investment.

JCPenney Moves from Main Street to the Mall   The interrelationships among these retail strategy decisions—market strategy, financial strategy, organization structure and human resource strategy, and location strategy—are illustrated by a major strategic change JCPenney made in the early 1960s.[34]

In the late 1950s, Penney was one of the most profitable national retailers. Its target market was small towns. In its Main Street locations, Penney sold staple soft goods—underwear, socks, basic clothing, sheets, tablecloths, and so forth—at low prices with minimal service. All sales were cash; the company didn't offer credit to its customers. Penney had considerable expertise in the design and purchase of soft goods with private labels—brands developed by the retailer and sold exclusively at its stores.

Organization structure was decentralized. Each store manager controlled the type of merchandise sold, the pricing of merchandise, and the management of store employees. Promotional efforts were limited and also controlled by store managers. Penney store managers were active participants in their community's social and political activities.

Although Penney was a highly successful retailer, there was a growing awareness among company executives that environmental trends would have a negative impact on the firm. First, as the nation's levels of education and disposable income rose, consumers grew more interested in fashionable rather than staple merchandise. Second, with the development of a national highway system, the growth of suburbs, and the rise of regional malls, small-town residents were attracted to conveniently located, large, regional shopping malls. Third, Sears (the nation's largest retailer) was beginning to locate stores and auto centers in regional malls. These trends suggested a decline in small-town markets for staple soft goods.

In the early 1960s, Penney undertook a new strategic direction that was consistent with changes it saw in the environment. All new Penney stores were located in regional malls across the United States. Penney opened several mall locations in each metropolitan area to create significant presence in each market. The firm began to offer credit to its customers and added new merchandise lines: appliances, auto supplies, paint, hardware, sporting goods, consumer electronics, and moderately priced fashionable clothing.

Besides altering its merchandise and locations, Penney made its organization structure more centralized. Store managers continued to have considerable responsibility for selecting merchandise and managing store operations, but advertising was done centrally, using national print and TV media. Penney emphasized a consistent presentation and similar merchandise in all locations. Buyers at corporate headquarters had more responsibility for providing the general merchandise direction the firm would pursue.

To effectively control its 1,500 stores, Penney installed a sophisticated communication network. Each store manager can monitor daily sales of each type of merchandise in her store and every other store in the chain. Buyers at corporate headquarters in Dallas communicate daily with merchandise managers in each store over a satellite TV link.

This illustrates how retailers must respond to a changing environment. These changes often result in new strategic directions that must be supported by new locations, new organization design, and new information and communication systems.

Implementing the Retail Strategy

To implement a retail strategy, management develops a retail mix that satisfies the needs of its target market better than its competitors. The retail mix is the combination of factors retailers use to satisfy customer needs and influence their purchase decisions. Elements in the **retail mix** (Exhibit 1–6) include the types of merchandise and services offered,

The interior of a Burdines stores illustrates how the firm implements the Florida store strategy through its merchandise and visual design. The tropical colors and palm tree identify the store, with its Florida target market.

merchandise pricing, advertising and promotional programs, store design, merchandise display, assistance to customers provided by salespeople, and convenience of the store's location.

To determine the retail mix, managers in the buying organization must decide how much and what types of merchandise to buy (Chapters 12 and 13), the vendors to use and the purchase terms (Chapter 14), the retail prices to set (Chapter 15), and how to advertise and promote merchandise (Chapter 16).

Store managers must determine how to recruit, select, and motivate sales associates (Chapter 17), where and how merchandise will be displayed (Chapter 18), the nature of services to provide customers (Chapter 19), and the selling skills needed by sales associates (Chapter 20).

Burdines: The Florida Store   Implementation decisions must be consistent with and reinforce the retailer's strategic direction—the core of Exhibit 1–6 from which elements of the retail mix emerge. Burdines illustrates this interrelationship between retail strategy and mix.

In 1898, two years after the East Coast Railroad was completed, William M. Burdine opened the first Burdines store in Miami. It sold work clothes, notions, and piece goods. The first branch store opened in 1912, followed by additional

EXHIBIT 1–6

Elements in the Retail Mix

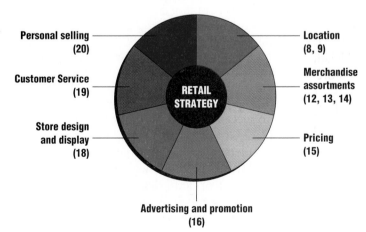

Personal selling (20)

Customer Service (19)

Store design and display (18)

Advertising and promotion (16)

RETAIL STRATEGY

Location (8, 9)

Merchandise assortments (12, 13, 14)

Pricing (15)

outlets in south Florida. In 1973, Burdines began to expand to central Florida and the west coast of Florida. By 1993, Burdines' 30 stores had annual sales over $1 billion. The chain is now part of Federated Department Stores, Inc., a corporation composed of regional department store chains.

Burdines' long-term strategy considered the possibilities of expanding beyond Florida to other southeastern states either through acquisitions or by opening new stores. In 1988, department store competition in south Florida increased dramatically as two Macy's and two Bloomingdale's stores opened. These northern retailers' invasion of Burdines' Florida market led to a reevaluation of Burdines' long-term strategy. Burdines decided to focus exclusively on the Florida market, identify itself as The Florida Store, and forsake expansion plans through the Southeast. It would defend its position in its Florida target market by creating unique merchandise tailored to Florida's climate and displaying this merchandise in a unique Florida style. This focused strategy would be difficult for out-of-state retailers to copy cost-effectively because those competitors lacked enough Florida stores to justify developing unique buying plans and visual presentations.

To implement this strategy, Burdines' visual merchandise department redesigned stores to be tropical, colorful, and whimsical. One clearly identifiable Florida symbol used throughout the stores is the palm tree. In the newest stores, palms are used as column enclosures and as symbols to denote entrances and significant areas in the store. In addition, the palm frond often is used for a table to display merchandise.

Lighting is another key element reinforcing the Florida theme. Daylight from atrium skylights, filtered by a unique shutter system, is introduced into the store to reinforce the tropical atmosphere and establish a focal point for customers. Burdines uses pastel colors extensively. White in the cosmetics and electronics departments is an exciting innovation. Traditionally electronics departments use dark colors, which results in a cavernlike atmosphere, while cosmetics are usually displayed with an odd assortment of colors selected by the manufacturer.

Burdines' unique visual merchandising isn't the only aspect of creating The Florida Store. Buyers have adapted their buying seasons to Florida's climate. For example, Florida customers continue to buy summer merchandise through autumn, so Burdines' buyers ask vendors to make extra cuttings of summer merchandise in new colors rather than buying merchandise made for autumn that's sold to northern department stores.

SUMMARY

An important institution in our society, retailing provides considerable value to consumers while giving people opportunities for rewarding and challenging careers. Due to significant shifts in consumers' needs and technology, the retail industry too is changing. Retail formats and companies that were unknown 30 years ago are now major factors in the industry.

The key to successful retailing is offering the right product, at the right price, in the right place, at the right time and making a profit. To accomplish all this, retailers must understand what customers want and what competitors are offering now and in the future. Retailers' wide range of decisions extends from setting a brown wool sweater's price to determining whether a new multimillion-dollar store should be built in a mall. This book is written to provide insights and directions for making such decisions.

KEY TERMS

breaking bulk, *9*	**providing assortments,** *8*	**retailer,** *7*	**scrambled merchandise,** *17*
intertype competition, *18*	**retail mix,** *22*	**retailing,** *9*	**vertical integration,** *9*
intratype competition, *17*	**retail strategy,** *20*	**retailing concept,** *17*	

SUGGESTED READINGS

Ailawadi, Karim, Norm Borin, and Paul Farris. "Market Power and Performance: A Cross-Industry Analysis of Manufacuters and Retailers," *Journal of Retailing* 71(Fall 1995), pp. 211–48.

Barmmash, Isadore. *Macy's for Sale.* New York: Weidenfeld & Nicolson, 1989.

"Global Powers of Retailing," *Chain Store Age,* December 1995, pp. 1–37.

Harris, L. *Merchant Princes.* New York: Berkeley Books, 1980.

Hollander, Stanley. *Discount Retailing.* New York: Garland, 1986.

Hollander, Stanley, and Glenn Omura. "Chain Store Development and Their Political, Strategic, and Social Interdependence." *Journal of Retailing* 65 (Fall 1989), pp. 299–326.

Katz, D. R. *The Big Store: Inside the Crisis and Revolution at Sears.* New York: Viking, 1987.

Peppers, Don, and Martha Rogers. "The End of Mass Marketing." *Marketing Tools,* March/April 1995, pp. 42–50.

"Retailing: Change at the Checkout." *The Economist,* March 4, 1995, pp. 1–18.

"State of the Industry: Seven Pillars of Future Success." *Chain Store Age,* August 5, 1996, pp. 9A–15A.

Tedlow, Richard. *New and Improved: The Story of Mass Marketing in America.* Boston: Harvard Business School Press, 1996.

Tordjman, Andre, "European Retailing: Convergences, Differences, and Perspectives." *International Journal of Retail & Distribution Management* 22, no. 5 (1994), pp. 3–19.

Trade Publications for Retailers

American Bookseller. Monthly magazine for book retailers covers buying, advertising and promotion, inventory control, display techniques, and publisher–bookseller relations.
http://www.bookweb.org/

Apparel Merchandising. Monthly magazine for retail buyers forecasts and interprets apparel merchandising trends and strategies in women's, men's, and children's wear.
http://www.lf.com/pubs/amseg.htm/

Chain Store Age Executive. Monthly magazine for retail headquarters executives and shopping center developers. Deals with management, operations, construction, modernization, store equipment, maintenance, real estate, financing, materials handling, and advertising. More oriented to operations than stores.
http://www.chainstoreage.com/

Convenience Store News. Monthly magazine for convenience store and oil retailing executives, managers, and franchisees. Covers industry trends, news, and merchandising techniques.
http://www.csnews.com

Daily News Record. Daily newspaper on retail fashion, product, merchandising, and marketing for men's and boys' wear. Geared to retailers, wholesalers, and manufacturers.
http://www.dailynewsrecord.com/

Discount Store News. Biweekly national newspaper describing marketing developments and productivity reports from executives in full-line discount stores, catalog showrooms, warehouse clubs, and specialty discount chains.
http://www.discountstorenews.com/

Furniture/Today. Weekly newspaper for retail executives in furniture and department stores and for executives in manufacturing firms.
http://www.brcb.com/mainmag/ft.htm/

HFD. Weekly newspaper for retailers and manufacturers in the home products industry including furniture, bedding, decorative accessories, lamps, home electronics, major appliances, tabletop, domestics, bath shop, and giftware.
http://www.homefurnishingsnews.com

Home Improvement Centers. Monthly magazine for full-line and specialty retailers and wholesale distributors of home-improvement products. Covers systems and products to sell to customers ranging from do-it-yourselfers to professional remodelers.

Hotel and Motel Management. Bimonthly magazine reports news and trends affecting the lodging industry.

Mass Market Retailers. Biweekly newspaper for executives in supermarket, chain drug, and chain discount headquarters. Reports news and interprets its effects on mass merchandisers.

Modern Grocer. Weekly newspaper covers regional and national food retailing.

Modern Jeweler. Monthly magazine for jewelry retailers looks at trends in jewelry, gems, and watches.

Private Label Product. Bimonthly magazine for buyers, merchandisers, and executives involved in purchasing private, controlled packer, and generic-labeled products for chain supermarkets and drug, discount, convenience, and department stores.

Progressive Grocer. Monthly magazine reporting on the supermarket industry. Original research and analysis includes industry data, special product category reports, tracking studies of trade and consumer trends, and retailer and wholesaler case histories.
http://www.pgshowdaily.com

Retail Info Systems News. Monthly magazine addressing system solutions for corporate/financial, operations, MIS, and merchandising management at retail.

Retailing/Technology and Operations. Monthly magazine reporting on and interpreting technologies available for all levels of the fashion distribution chain from manufacturers to retailers. Includes computers, retail point-of-sales systems, computer-aided design and manufacturing, software, electronic retailing, credit systems, visual merchandising, and factory automation.

Shopping Center World. Monthly magazine providing news, statistical analyses, and feature articles on new-center developments and leasing, redevelopments and releasing, management, operations, marketing, design, construction, and financing of shopping centers.
http://www.internetreview.com/pubs/scw.htm

Stores. Monthly magazine published by the National Retail Federation (NRF), formerly the National Retail Merchants Association. Aimed at retail executives in department and specialty stores, it emphasizes broad trends in customer behavior, management practices, and technology.
http://www.stores.org/

Upscale Discounting. A monthly merchandising magazine for catalog showrooms, discount department stores, hypermarkets, specialty discounters, home shopping/TV/mail order, and warehouse clubs in the upscale discount market.

VM/SD. (Visual Merchandising/Store Design). Monthly magazine for people involved in merchandise display, store interior design and planning, and manufacturers of equipment used by display and store designers.
http://www.visualstore.com

Women's Wear Daily. Daily newspaper reports fashion and industry news on women's and children's ready-to-wear, sportswear, innerwear, accessories, and cosmetics. http://www.wwd.com/

NOTES

1. *Vision for the New Millennium . . . Evolving to Consumer Response*, Atlanta: Kurt Salmon Associates, 1995.

2. "GNC Targets Health and Wellness with Alive," *Chain Store Age*, April 1996, pp. 35–36.

3. "Fortune 500 Largest US Corporations," *Fortune*, April 29, 1996, F1.

4. Edwin McDowell, "America's Hot Tourist Spot: The Outlet Mall," *The New York Times*, May 26, 1996, pp. 1, 17.

5. Ibid, p.17.

6. Janet Novack, "The Data Miners," *Forbes*, February 12, 1996, pp. 96–97.

7. Kyle Pope, "For Compaq and Dell Accent Is on Personal in the Computer Wars," *The Wall Street Journal*, July 2, 1993, p. A2.

8. For a more detailed discussion of distribution channels, see Louis Stern, Adel El-Ansary, and James Brown, *Management in Marketing Channels*, 3d ed. (Englewood Cliffs, NJ: Prentice Hall, 1996).

9. For a discussion of the trade-off between retailer and consumer inventory holding costs, see Robert Blattberg, Gary Epen, and Joshua Lieberman, "A Theoretical and Empirical Evaluation in Price Deals for Consumer Nondurables," *Journal of Marketing* (Winter 1981), pp. 116–29; and Robert Meyer and Joao Assuncao, "The Optimality of Consumer Stockpiling Strategies," *Marketing Science* 35 (Winter 1990), pp. 18–41.

10. U.S. Department of Commerce, Bureau of the Census.

11. "Retailing: Mirror on America" (New York: National Retail Federation, 1996, p. 5).

12. U.S. Department of Commerce, Bureau of the Census.

13. *Retail Industry Indicators.* Washington, DC: National Retail Federation, May 1996, p. 13.

14. U.S. Department of Commerce.

15. A. Raucher, "Dime Store Chains: The Making of Organization Men 1880–1940," *Business History Review* 65 (Spring 1991), pp. 130–63.

16. "Fortune 500 Largest U.S. Corporations," *Fortune*, April 29, 1996, p. F1.

17. William Swinyard, Fred Langrehr, and Scott Smith, "The Appeal of Retailing as a Career: A Decade Later," *Journal of Retailing* 67 (Winter 1991), pp. 451–65.

18. 1992 U.S. Census of Retail Trade.

19. Thomas Jaffee, "One Last Throw," *Forbes*, December 18, 1955, p. 45; Penny Gill, "Les Wexner: Unlimited Success Story," *Stores*, January 1993, pp. 81–122; and Laura Zinn, "Maybe the Limited Has Limits After All," *Business Week*, Febrary 3, 1992, p. 30.

20. Carolyn Walkup, "R. David Thomas: Founder of Wendy's International," *Nation's Restaurant News*, February 1996, p. 162; and Louise Kramer, "Pioneer of the Year: Dave Thomas," *Nation's Restaurant News*, October 9, 1995, p. 152.

21. Kramer, Pioneer, p. 152.

22. Susan Caminiti, "Will Old Navy Fill the Gap?" *Fortune*, March 18, 1996, pp. 59–64; Laura Zinn, "The New Stars of Retailing," *Business Week*, December 16, 1991, pp. 120–22; and Bertrand Frank, "Merchandising Private Label Apparel," *Retail Business Review*, April 1992, pp. 24–26.

23. Caminiti, "Old Navy," p. 60.

24. Susan Chandler, "Lands' End Looks for Terra Firma," *Business Week*, July 8, 1996, p. 128; and Jeff Haggin and Bjorn Kartomkin, "Show Your Customer Respect," *Catalog Age*, October 1992, pp. 91–92.

25. Louise Kramer, "Thomas S. Monaghan," *Nation's Restaurant News*, 1996, p. 114; and John Cortez, "Monaghan's Goal to Reheat Domino's Pizza," *Advertising Age*, December 16, 1991, p. 13.

26. George Day and Robin Wensley, "Marketing Theory with a Strategic Orientation," *Journal of Marketing* 47 (Fall 1983), pp. 79–89; Alfred Oxenfeldt and William Moore, "Customer or Competitor: Which Guideline for Marketing?" *Management Review*, August 1978, pp. 43–48.

27. Joanne Frederick, "Supercenters: The Threat du Jour," *Grocery Marketing*, March 1995, pp. 14–17.

28. Patricia Sellers, "Wal-Mart's Big Mac Puts Blockbuster on Fast Forward," *Fortune*, November 25, 1996, pp. 111–15.

29. T. Mullen, "Preparing for Change," *Stores*, December 1992, pp. 18–20; Joseph Antonni, "Trends in Retailing in the Nineties," *Retail Control*, December 1991, pp. 3–7; and Michael Gade and Jacquelyn Bivens, "Fundamental Changes," *Discount Merchandiser*, May 1992, pp. 66, 69.

30. "Rating the Stores," *Consumer Reports*, November 1994, p. 714.

31. "Cold War, Hot Development," *Chain Store Age Executive*, June 1994, p. 67.

32. Jennifer Reese, "America's Most Admired Companies," *Fortune*, February 8, 1993, pp. 44–47ff; Mark Maremont, "Brawls in Toyland," *Business Week*, December 21, 1992, pp. 36–37; and Debra Chanil, "The Toy Game: Increasing Market Share," *Discount Merchandiser*, February 1992, pp. 60–67ff.

33. C. Caroll, "Developing Competitive Strategies in Retailing," *Long Range Planning* 25 (April 1992), pp. 81–88; and Michael Porter, *Competitive Strategy* (New York: Free Press, 1980).

34. Based in part on "The JC Penney Company (A): Marketing and Financial Strategy," in William Davidson, Daniel Sweeney, and Ronald Stampfl, *Retailing Management*, 6th ed. (New York: Wiley, 1988), pp. 261–64.

Store-Based Retailing

THE WORLD OF RETAILING

1. Introduction to the World of Retailing
2. **Store-Based Retailing**
3. Nonstore Retailing—Electronic Retailing and Catalogs
4. The Retail Customer
5. Customer Buying Behavior

RETAILING STRATEGY

MERCHANDISE MANAGEMENT

STORE MANAGEMENT

QUESTIONS

- What are the different types of in-store retailers?

- How do retailers differ in terms of their retail mixes?

- How do services retailers differ from merchandise retailers?

- What are the types of ownership for retail firms?

YOU WANT TO HAVE REAL COFFEE in the morning, not instant, but you don't want to bother with boiling water, pouring it through ground coffee in a filter, and waiting. You decide to buy an automatic coffee maker with a timer so your coffee will be ready when you wake up. Think of all of the different retailers you could buy the coffee maker from. You could buy the coffee maker at a discount store like Wal-Mart or Kmart, a department store like Macy's, a drug store, a category specialist like Electric Avenue, or a catalog showroom like Service Merchandise; you could also order a coffee maker from the JCPenney catalog. All of these retailers are competing against each other to sell you a coffee maker. Many of them are selling the same brands, but they offer different atmospheres, services, prices, and location convenience.

To develop and implement a retail strategy, you need to understand the nature of competition in the retail marketplace. The next two chapters describe different types of retailers. Retailers differ in terms of the types of merchandise and services they offer to customers, the nature of the retail mixes used to satisfy customer needs, the degree to which their offerings emphasize services versus merchandise, and the ownership of the firm. This chapter focuses on retailers offering merchandise and services in a store environment. Chapter 3 examines nonstore retailing—retailers that sell goods and services to consumers by catalogs and electronic media.

TYPES OF RETAILERS

The 1.4 million retailers in the United States range from street vendors selling hot dogs to large corporations such as Sears that have become an integral part of American culture. Each retailer survives and prospers by satisfying a group of consumers' needs more effectively than its competitors. Over time, different types of retailers have emerged and prospered because they have attracted and maintained a significant customer base. A retail institution is a group of retailers that provide a similar retail mix designed to satisfy the needs of a specific segment of customers.

Nature of Retail Mix

The most basic characteristic of a retailer is its retail mix—the elements used by retailers to satisfy their customers' needs. (See Exhibit 1–6.) Four elements of the retail mix are particularly useful for classifying retailers: the type of merchandise sold, the variety and assortment of merchandise sold, the level of customer service, and the price of the merchandise. Appendix 2A at the end of this chapter provides guidelines for comparing retailers based on their retail mixes.

As you read about the different types of retailers, notice how patterns among retail mix elements arise. For example, department stores appeal to consumers looking for fashionable apparel and home furnishings. Typically department stores have higher prices because they have higher costs due to stocking a lot of fashionable merchandise, providing high levels of service with considerable personal selling, and having more convenient and expensive mall locations. On the other hand, discount stores appeal to customers who are looking for lower prices and are less interested in services and a wide range of merchandise sizes and colors.

Type of Merchandise The U.S. Bureau of the Census developed and uses a classification scheme to collect data on retail activity in the United States. It classifies all retail firms into a hierarchical set of four-digit Standard Industrial Classification (SIC) codes (Exhibit 2–1). Each of the exhibit's eight two-digit categories is broken down further into three-digit categories. For example, food retailers (SIC 54) are divided into grocery stores (SIC 541), meat and fish markets (SIC 542), fruit and vegetable markets (SIC 543), and so forth. Exhibit 2–2 shows the annual sales of the larger categories as reported in the Census of Retail Trade.

While a retailer's principal competitors may be other retailers in the same SIC classification, there are many exceptions. For example, convenience stores (such as 7-Eleven and Circle K), traditional supermarkets, and warehouse grocery stores are all classified as SIC 541. These food stores all sell the same type of merchandise, but they satisfy different consumer needs and thus appeal to different market segments. The convenience store caters to customers who value convenience but don't seek low prices or a broad selection. The warehouse grocery store, on the other hand, caters to customers who want low prices and don't place much importance on service or store atmosphere.

REFACT Over one-third of all U.S. retail sales are for automobiles, gas, and food. Department and discount stores only account for 10 percent of U.S. retail sales.[1]

INTERNET EXERCISE Some data on U.S. retail sales are available at The U.S. Bureau of the Census Internet site at http://www.census.gov/econ/www.monret.html. Look at the unadjusted monthly sales by SIC. Which categories of retailers have the largest percentage of sales in the fourth quarter (the Christmas season)?

EXHIBIT 2–1

Standard Industrial
Classification System
for Retailers

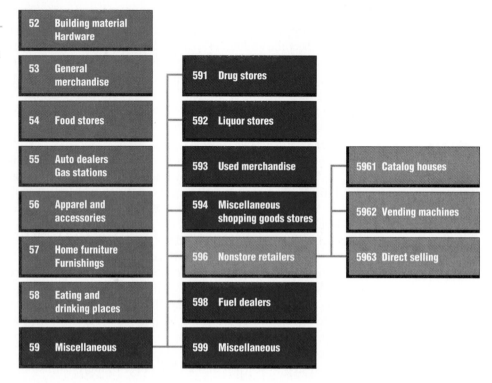

The degree to which retailers compete against each other isn't simply based on the similarity of their merchandise. The variety and assortment of the merchandise they offer and the services they provide must also be considered.

Variety and Assortment   **Variety** is the number of different merchandise categories a retailer offers. **Assortment** is the number of different items in a merchandise category. Each different item of merchandise is called an **SKU (stock keeping unit).** For example, a 32-ounce box of Tide laundry detergent or a white, long-sleeved, button-down–collar Tommy Hilfinger shirt, size 16-33, is an SKU.

Department stores, discount stores, and toy stores all sell toys. However, department stores sell many other categories of merchandise in addition to toys. Stores specializing in toys stock more types of toys (more SKUs). For each type of toy, such as dolls, the toy specialist will offer more models, sizes, and brands than general merchants such as department or discount stores.

Variety is often referred to as the **breadth of merchandise** carried by a retailer; assortment is referred to as the **depth of merchandise.** Exhibit 2–3 shows the breadth and depth of bicycles carried in a local bicycle shop (a specialty store), in Toys "R" Us (a category specialist), and in Wal-Mart (a general merchandise discount store). Toys "R" Us carries three types and has a narrower variety than the bicycle shop (four types). Toys "R" Us has the greatest depth of assortment in children's bicycles. Wal-Mart has the lowest number of SKUs (62) compared to 119 at Toys "R" Us and 66 at the bicycle shop. Note, however, that Wal-Mart and Toys "R" Us have many of the same brands, but the bicycle shop offers a completely different set of brands.

EXHIBIT 2–2   Retail Sales by SIC Category, 1995

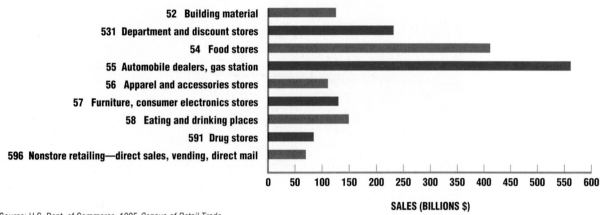

Source: U.S. Dept. of Commerce, 1995 *Census of Retail Trade.*

Customer Services   Retailers also differ in the services they offer customers. For example, the bicycle shop offers assistance in selecting the appropriate bicycle, adjusting bicycles to fit the individual, and repairing bicycles. Toys "R" Us and Wal-Mart don't provide any of these services.

Customers expect retailers to provide some services: accepting personal checks, providing parking, and displaying merchandise. Some retailers charge customers for other services, such as home delivery and gift wrapping. Retailers that cater to service-oriented consumers offer customers most of these services at no charge.

Cost of Offering Breadth and Depth of Merchandise and Services   Stocking a broad variety and deep assortment like the Toys "R" Us offering in bicycles is appealing to customers but costly for retailers. When a retailer offers customers many SKUs, inventory investment increases because the retailer must have backup stock for each SKU.

Similarly, services attract customers to the retailer, but they're also costly. More salespeople are needed to provide information and assist customers, to alter merchandise to meet customers' needs, and to demonstrate merchandise. Child care facilities, rest rooms, dressing rooms, and check rooms take up valuable store

The local bike shop on the left offers a deeper assortment of performance bicycles and different brands than Toys "R" Us on the right.

EXHIBIT 2–3

Variety and
Assortment of
Bicycles in
Different Retail
Outlets

TYPES OF BICYCLES	RETAILERS		
	BICYCLE SHOP	TOYS "R" US	WAL-MART
Adult Road	Diamond Back Klein Trek		Murray
	# of SKUs = 12 $89–539		# of SKUs = 3 $108.96
Adult Hybrid	Diamond Back Klein Trek	Huffy Magna Pacific Cycle Paragon Royce Union	Murray Huffy Roadmaster
	# of SKUs = 28 $219–1359	# of SKUs = 31 $74.90–199.99	# of SKUs = 11 $119.96–199.96
Mountain	Diamond Back Klein Trek	Pacific Cycle	
	# of SKUs = 14 $489–3,500	# of SKUs = 1 $299.95	
Child	Diamond Back Klein Trek	Asoma Kent Magna Murray Pacific Cycle Paragon Pinnacle Rand Rallye Roadmaster Royce Union Viken	Huffy Kawasaki Murray Roadmaster RideHard
	# of SKU's = 12 $89–539	# of SKUs = 87 $19.99–179.95	# of SKUs = 47 $49.96–149.96

space that could be used to stock and display merchandise. Offering delayed billing, credit, and installment payments requires a financial investment that could be used to buy more merchandise.

A critical retail decision involves the trade-off between costs and benefits of maintaining additional inventory or providing additional services. Chapters 7 and 12 address the considerations in making this trade-off.

While there are over 1 million retailers in the United States, there are a limited number of retail institutions. The following sections discuss some common store-based retail institutions: traditional food and general merchandise retailers, newer retail institutions (such as category specialists), and services retailers. Appendix 2B at the end of the chapter outlines some theories about the evolution of retail institutions.

By adding a drive-through service, this convenience store attracts more customers.

FOOD RETAILERS

Exhibit 2–4 shows the number of stores, sales revenues, and retail mixes for different types of food retailers.

Conventional Supermarkets

Prior to 1930, most food was purchased in small neighborhood markets referred to as mom-and-pop stores because they were family-owned and -operated. These have been replaced by larger self-service supermarkets, which offer considerably lower prices. Societal changes stimulating the development of supermarkets include the widespread use of cars, improved road systems, development of national mass media, rise of national brands, consumers' growing sophistication, and improved packaging and refrigeration. These changes made it easier for consumers to go to a store beyond the walking distance from their home. Also as a result of these changes, consumers have information that lessens their need for their store employees' assistance when they make purchase decisions.[2]

A **conventional supermarket** is a self-service food store offering groceries, meat, and produce with annual sales of over $2 million and size of under 20,000 square feet. In conventional supermarkets, the sale of nonfood items, such as health and beauty aids and general merchandise, is limited.

Half of the conventional supermarkets are very promotional. One day each week, they advertise that week's sale items in local papers. These promotion-oriented supermarkets also offer their own coupons or may agree to reimburse customers double or triple the face value of manufacturer coupons. This is called a hi-lo pricing strategy.

The other half of conventional supermarkets use very few promotions and sell almost all merchandise at the same price every day. This is called an everyday low pricing (EDLP) policy. Typically, everyday prices in these supermarkets are lower

REFACT The first self-service grocery store was opened in 1930 by King Kullen in Jamaica, New York.[3]

EXHIBIT 2–4   Types of Food Retailers

	CONVENIENCE STORES	CONVENTIONAL SUPERMARKETS	SUPERSTORES, COMBINATION STORES, SUPERCENTERS, HYPERMARKETS	WAREHOUSE SUPERMARKETS, WHOLESALE CLUBS
Sales ($ millions)*	$27.3	$141.6	$130.1	$40.0
Number of stores	56,000	18,425	7,800	3,575
Sales per store ($ millions)	$0.5	$7.7	$16.7	$11.2
Number of checkout lines	1–2	6–10	10–20	5–10
SKUs*	2,000–3,000	20,000	30,000	20,000
Variety	Narrow	Average	Broad	Broad
Assortment	Shallow	Average	Deep	Average
Services	Average	Average	Low	Low
Prices	High	Average	Low	Low
Size (sq. ft.)	2,000–4,000	8,000–20,000	20,000–100,000	50,000–150,000
Largest U.S. chains	7-Eleven	A&P	Wal-Mart	Price/Costco
	Circle K	Winn-Dixie	Kmart	Sam's
		Kroger		
		Safeway		
		American Stores		

Source: Data on sales and number of stores from "1995 Grocery Sales" in "63rd Annual Report of the Grocery Industry," *Progressive Grocer,* April 1996, p. 13.

*Supermarket items.

than regular prices in promotional supermarkets. For example, Food Lion (a Salisbury, North Carolina–based chain that uses an everyday–low-price strategy) grew 25 percent annually during the 1980s, with net profits double the typical supermarket's. Food Lion keeps its costs low by offering a "no-frills" shopping experience. The store environment is Spartan—displays consist of recycled banana crates. By adopting everyday low pricing, Food Lion reduces advertising costs to 25 percent of typical advertising expenses for a supermarket. Cereal and pet food are sold at cost to draw people into the store. The company philosophy is to do "1,000 things 1 percent better" than competitors.[4] Hi-lo and EDLP strategies are discussed in detail in Chapter 15.

Big Box Food Retailers

Over the past 20 years, supermarkets have increased in size and have begun to sell a broader variety of merchandise. In 1979, conventional supermarkets accounted for 85 percent of supermarket sales. By 1995, only 45 percent of supermarket sales were in conventional supermarkets due to the growth of "big box" food retailing formats—superstores, combination stores, and warehouse-type stores. [6]

Superstores are large supermarkets (20,000 to 50,000 square feet). **Combination stores** are food-based retailers of 30,000 to 100,000 square feet that have over 25 percent of their sales from nonfood merchandise such as flowers, health and beauty aids, kitchen utensils, film developing, prescription drugs, and videotape rentals.

REFACT A full 8.2 percent of disposable income is spent on food consumed at home while 4.0 percent goes to food consumed away from home.[5]

Warehouse Stores   **Warehouse stores** are discount food retailers that offer merchandise in a no-frills environment. There are different types of warehouse stores. **Limited-line warehouse stores** (also called **box stores**) typically carry 1,500 items (one size and brand per item), with no refrigerated or perishable merchandise. Merchandise is often displayed in cut boxes on shipping pallets and service is limited.

Food retailers range from convenience stores (left) carrying 2,000 SKUs to supermarkets (right) carrying over 20,000 SKUs.

Much of the merchandise in warehouse stores is bought when a supplier offers a special deal. Thus customers may not be able to buy the same brands and sizes each time they visit the stores.

The largest and fastest-growing type of warehouse store is the super-warehouse. These stores range from 50,000 to 70,000 square feet and generate $30 to $50 million in sales per store. Super-warehouse stores typically sell nationally branded packaged goods at low prices and make low profits as a percentage of sales.

Convenience Stores

Convenience stores provide a limited variety and assortment of merchandise at a convenient location in a 3,000-to-8,000–square-foot store with speedy checkout. They are the modern version of the neighborhood mom-and-pop grocery store.

Convenience stores enable consumers to make purchases quickly, without having to search through a large store and wait in long checkout lines. Over half the items bought are consumed within 30 minutes of purchase. Due to their small size and high turnover, convenience stores typically receive deliveries every day.

Convenience stores only offer a limited assortment and variety and charge higher prices than supermarkets. Milk, eggs, and bread once represented the majority of their sales. Now groceries, dairy, and baked goods represent less than 20 percent of sales. The major merchandise categories are tobacco products, beer and wine, soft drinks, and prepared foods.[7]

Competition in Food Retailing

Over the past 10 years, food retailers have been facing increased competition from discount chains. In addition to selling grocery store items at low prices in their general merchandise discount stores, Wal-Mart and Kmart are aggressively opening supercenters offering broad assortments of grocery and general merchandise under one roof. The super-centers offer customers one-stop shopping. Customers will typically drive farther to shop at these stores than to visit conventional supermarkets (which offer a smaller selection). General merchandise items (nonfood items) are often purchased on impulse when customers' primary reason for coming to the store is to buy groceries. The general merchandise has higher margins, enabling the super-centers to price food items more aggressively. However, since supercenters are very large, it takes customers more time to find the items they want.

Supermarkets continue to sell over 75 percent of the produce, meat, dry/canned goods, frozen food, dairy, bakery, and seafood. However, the other food retail formats now account for over 50 percent of the sales of pet food, paper products, beer, and personal care products.[8] Exhibit 2–5 illustrates that supermarkets remain the preferred place to shop for food merchandise.

EXHIBIT 2–5

Shopping Patterns by
Type of Retail Outlet

OUTLET	% SHOPPING	NUMBER OF WEEKLY TRIPS	WEEKLY SPENDING
Supermarkets	100%	2.4	$72.82
General merchandise discount stores	68	1.3	32.53
Fast-food restaurants	65	1.9	16.32
Drug stores	39	1.2	18.70
Convenience stores	37	2.4	19.72
Wholesale clubs	27	1.7	75.12
Specialty food stores	9	1.0	23.70

Source: "Consumers Are Skeptical Again," "63rd Annual Report of the Grocery Industry," *Progressive Grocer,* April 1996, p. 42.

Sales in convenience stores have not grown over the past five years primarily because of the lack of interest in the major merchandise categories in convenience stores; beer, tobacco, and salty snacks. In addition, convenience stores have an image of "truck stops" where men go to buy beer and magazines at midnight. To stimulate growth, convenience stores and entrepreneurs are experimenting with new concepts emphasizing prepared meals. For example, EatZi's in Dallas combines a convenience store and takeout restaurant in an 8,000-square-foot location. Customers can park, walk in, pick up tonight's dinner and tomorrow's breakfast, and be back in their cars in 10 minutes.[9]

Supermarket sales might suffer with these changes in convenience stores. As convenience stores upgrade their merchandise assortments and presentations, consumers are more willing to pay higher prices and save time by going to them.

In response to the inroads being made by supercenters and convenience stores, supermarkets are placing more emphasis on perishables and meal solutions (prepared meals and side dishes). In addition, they are offering the larger pack sizes that attracted family shoppers to the warehouse clubs. They are also reducing their costs by using more efficient distribution systems. (See Chapter 11.) Retailing View 2.1 describes how a supermarket chain holds its own against increased competition.

TRADITIONAL GENERAL MERCHANDISE RETAILERS

The traditional general merchandise retail stores are specialty stores, department stores, and discount stores. During the past 30 years, however, a number of new types of general merchandise retailers have emerged and are becoming increasingly important to consumers. These include category specialists, home improvement centers, off-price retailers, catalog showrooms, warehouse clubs, and hypermarkets. Exhibit 2–6 summarizes characteristics of general merchandise retailers that sell through stores. Nonstore retailers are discussed in the next chapter.

Specialty Stores

A traditional **specialty store** concentrates on a limited number of complementary merchandise categories and provides a high level of service in an area typically under 8,000 square feet. Exhibit 2–7 lists some of the largest U.S. specialty store chains.

In contrast to department and discount stores, specialty stores focus on a narrow market segment or niche. By carrying a narrow variety but deep assortment, they offer customers a better selection and sales expertise in that category than department or discount stores provide. Consumers are attracted to specialty stores by deep assortments, personal attention, and more intimate store atmosphere. A unique retail chain concentrating on chocolate is discussed in Retailing View 2.2.

2.1

Wegman's Lures Customers with Quality and Style

WHILE SHOPPING IN WAREHOUSE and discount stores is growing in other parts of the country, Wegman's Food Market's 50-store chain is winning the battle in Rochester, New York. Wegman's has transformed grocery shopping into entertainment. Chefs in white hats toss fresh pasta. Dining areas in the stores offer Sunday brunch and chilled wine.

Its produce section is five times larger than the average supermarket's section. Produce is replenished 12 times a day. Many suppliers deliver produce directly to the store, which reduces cost and bruising when it is handled in and out a warehouse. All produce is inspected rigorously. The Wegman's produce manager emphasizes that "Once you turn down a few loads of pears, or strawberries, whether they are from Chile, California, or Mexico, people don't waste their time, money, or effort to send products we'll reject."

Wegman's is also a leader in the trend for supermarkets to provide precooked food for their customers. Wegman's offers an extensive variety of prepared meals ranging from Caesar salads to Chinese food made by chefs in full view of its customers. A satisfied customer says, "They have the drama. I ask for a fresh salmon sautéed with a little lemon, browse 10 minutes in the store, and take it home to my wife for dinner."

Source: Rosanne Harper, "Prepared Food Revolution," *Supermarket News,* September 9, 1996, p. 37; and Wendy Bounds, "As Big as Kodak Is in Rochester, N.Y., It Still Isn't Wegman's," *The Wall Street Journal,* December 27, 1994, pp. A1, A6.

Apparel specialty store retailing grew rapidly in the 1970s and 1980s, but by the mid-90s, their sales growth has slowed to below the growth rate for total U.S. retail sales. One exciting new concept is called lifestyle retailing. **Lifestyle retailing** tailors merchandise to the lifestyle of a specific group of customers. For example, Los Angeles–based Rampage targets teenagers by offering a stream of new fashions in stores with an urban atmosphere. Stores have tin-stamped ceilings, wood-planked floors, and brick walls complete with graffiti. In addition to T-shirts and jeans, 30 percent of the merchandise is nonapparel items like makeup, jewelry, candles, and picture frames.

EXHIBIT 2–6   Characteristics of Different General Merchandise Retailers

TYPE	VARIETY	ASSORTMENT	SERVICE	PRICES	SIZE (SQ. FT.)	SKUS	LOCATION
Department stores	Broad	Deep to average	Average to high	Average to high	100,000–200,000	100,000	Regional malls
Traditional discount stores	Broad	Average to shallow	Low	Low	60,000–80,000	25,000–30,000	Stand-alone, power strip centers
Traditional specialty stores	Narrow	Deep	High	High	4,000–12,000	5,000	Regional malls
Category specialists	Narrow	Very deep	Low	Low	50,000–120,000	25,000–40,000	Stand-alone, power strip centers
Warehouse clubs	Average	Shallow	Low	Very low	80,000–100,000	4,000–5,000	Stand-alone
Hypermarkets	Broad	Average	Low	Low	200,000	50,000	Stand-alone
Off-price stores	Average	Deep, but varying	Low	Low	25,000–40,000	100,000	Stand-alone, power strip centers Outlet malls

2.2 Rocky Mountain Chocolate Factory

FRANK CRAIL WAS A SUCCESSFUL OWNER of a software firm specializing in the development of billing and reporting systems for cable companies. But at 41, he realized he was not having fun. The idea of setting up a retail store and interacting with people rather than computers was appealing. He decided to settle in Durango, Colorado, and establish a chocolate store to appeal to tourists. Tourists would buy in the summer; residents would buy during the holidays like Valentine's Day, Easter, and Christmas. He is now doing a lot better in retailing than he had in his computer business, and he's having more fun. He says, "There are a lot of hours in retailing but it's a real people business and that's what I enjoy."

Crail built the The Rocky Mountain Chocolate Factory into a 175-store chain, mostly franchised. His key to success is making and selling the best chocolate products and making the store interesting for customers. *Money* magazine taste testers compared Rocky Mountain Chocolates favorably with Godiva. In the stores, chocolates are merchandised from traditional copper kettles in an atmosphere of country Victorian charm. Customers are lured back by the visual appeal and aromas.

Source: Bruce Goldberg, "Candy Is Dandy Colorado Business," *Colorado Business,* September 1996, pp. 6–8; and "Retail Entrepreneur of the Year," *Chain Store Age Executive,* December 1995, p. 90.

Drug stores are specialty stores that concentrate on health and personal grooming merchandise. The preparation and sale of pharmaceuticals often represents over 50 percent of drug store sales and profits. Drug stores are facing considerable competition from discount stores and supermarkets adding pharmacies as well as from mail order retailers filling prescriptions. In response drug stores are providing new services such as drive-through windows for picking up prescriptions and personal attention from the pharmacist. Firms are also increasing the size of their stores and stocking more merchandise traditionally sold at convenience stores.[10]

Department Stores

Department stores are retailers that carry a broad variety and deep assortment, offer considerable customer services, and are organized into separate departments for displaying merchandise.[11] Each department within the store has a specific selling space allocated to it, a POS terminal to transact and

EXHIBIT 2-7

Largest Specialty
Stores Chains
(sales in $ millions)

APPAREL

The Limited	**$7,881**
The Gap	**4,395**
Intimate Brands	**2,517**
Charming Shop	**1,102**
Ann Taylor	**731**

SHOES

Payless Shoes	**$2,330**
Famous Footwear	**741**

DRUG STORES

Walgreen	**$10,395**
Rite Aid	**5,446**
Eckerds	**4,997**
American Drug	**4,995**
CVS	**4,885**
Thrifty	**4,569**
Revco	**4,432**

FURNITURE

Heileg-Meyers	**$1,359**
Levitz	**983**
Pier 1	**811**
IKEA	**510**
W.S. Badcock	**410**
Haverty Furniture	**395**
Bombay Co.	**345**

AUTO PARTS

Western Auto	**$1,958**
AutoZone	**1,800**
Pep Boys	**1,594**

JEWELRY

Zales	**$1,046**
Sterling Jewelers	**855**
Tiffany's	**803**
Helzberg Diamonds	**320**

MUSIC

Musicland	**$1,723**
Tower Records	**950**

OPTICAL

Lenscrafter	**$858**
Pearle Vision	**600**
Sunglass Hut	**418**

Source: "The Top 100 Specialty Stores," *Stores*, August 1996, pp. S3–S23; and "State of the Industry: Seven Pillars to Future Sucess," *Chain Store Age Executive,* August 1996, section 2.

record sales, and salespeople to assist customers. The department store often resembles a collection of specialty shops. The largest department store chains in the United States are Sears (1995 sales of $22 billion), JCPenney ($17 billion), Federated Department Stores ($15 billion), May Department Stores ($10.5 billion), and Dayton Hudson ($7.7 billion).[12]

The major departments are women's, men's, and children's clothing and accessories; home furnishings and furniture; toys and games; consumer electronics such as TVs, VCRs, and stereos; and kitchenware and small appliances. Since women's wear typically accounts for over half the sales volume, women's merchandise is divided into departments based on size (petite, full-figure), usage occasion (sportswear, business attire, evening wear), lifestyle (conservative, traditional, update), or age (juniors, misses).

In some situations, departments in a department store or discount store are leased and operated by a firm specializing in retailing a specific type of merchandise or service. A **leased department** is an area in a retail store that is leased or rented to an independent firm. The lease holder is typically responsible for all retail mix decisions involved in operating the department and pays the store a percentage of its sales as rent.

Retailers lease departments when they feel they lack expertise to efficiently operate the department. Commonly leased departments are in-store beauty salons, pharmacies, shoes, jewelry, photography studios, and repair services. To ensure that operation of the leased department is consistent with the retailer's image, operating requirements are included as part of the lease agreement. But problems can arise when the lease holder's operations differ from the store's.

This specialty department store offers moderately priced, national and private brands of women's apparel.

Department stores are unique in terms of their services to customers. Their labor costs are higher than other types of general merchandise retailers because they employ more sales associates to offer information and assistance to customers. Most department stores offer the full range of customer services. Chapter 7 gives financial implications of the retail mixes offered by a department store and a low-service, low-assortment warehouse club.

To make the shopping experience exciting, department stores also emphasize promotions such as elaborate displays during the Christmas season. Some department stores hold special promotions throughout the year such as back-to-school and white sales.

Twenty years ago, two forms of department stores emerged: specialty and promotional. **Specialty department stores** use a department store format but focus primarily on apparel and soft home furnishings. Neiman Marcus and Parisian are examples. A **promotional department store** is a specialty department store that sells a substantial portion of its merchandise on weekly promotion. In a promotional department store, a group of regular merchandise items are selected to be promoted in weekly multipage inserts in local newspapers.

The nature of traditional department stores has changed considerably over the years, so the distinction between traditional, specialty, and promotional department stores has blurred. With few exceptions, traditional department stores have eliminated many of the departments they originally had. No longer can a customer buy a new outfit and then walk to the next aisle for a record album, refrigerator, best-selling book, or toy. Traditional department stores are concentrating more on apparel and soft home furnishings (sheets, bedspreads, pillows) and cutting back or eliminating toys and games, furniture, and consumer electronics. Thus, traditional and specialty department stores are offering similar merchandise mixes.

REFACT Sixty to 80 percent of all merchandise sold by department stores is on sale.[13]

The number of special promotions undertaken by traditional department stores has increased dramatically, and promotional department stores such as Mervyn's and Uptons have reduced the amount of merchandise bought for special promotions. Mervyn's, the largest promotional department store chain and a division of Dayton Hudson, now operates similarly to many traditional department stores offering moderately priced national and private brands. Like those stores, Mervyn's has weekly promotions on merchandise it normally sells. These promotions are advertised in high-quality, multipage, preprinted inserts in local papers.

Circuit City is a category specialist offering a deep assortment of consumer electronics.

Department stores' overall sales have stagnated in recent years due to increased competition from discount stores and specialty stores. Discount stores offer lower prices and are beginning to sell some of the same brand-name clothing as department stores. On the other hand, many customers now feel that specialty stores provide better service and merchandise assortments than department stores.

In response to this increased competition, department stores are improving their customer service and altering their merchandise mix and presentation of merchandise. Besides focusing more on apparel, department stores are developing unique, private-label merchandise that consumers can buy only at their stores. For example, strong private-label jeans have been developed by JCPenney (Arizona) and Sears (Canyon River Blues). Private-label merchandise accounts for 25 percent of Nordstrom's sales.[15]

REFACT Consumers go to discount stores an average of 4.7 times per month and visit department stores 2.7 times per month.[14]

General Merchandise Discount Stores

A **general merchandise discount store** is a retailer that offers a broad variety of merchandise, limited service, and low prices. They offer national brands, but these brands are typically less fashion-oriented than brands in department stores. The "big three" general merchandise discount store chains, Wal-Mart (with 1995 annual sales of $54.3 billion), Kmart ($26.8 billion), and Target, a division of Dayton Hudson ($15.8 billion), account for over 80 percent of the U.S. sales made by general merchandise discount stores.[16]

Discount stores can charge lower prices than department stores because they provide less service at low-cost locations in a more Spartan atmosphere. Discount stores emphasize self-service. Customers pick out their merchandise, put it in their cart, and take it to the checkout counter at the front of the store. Salespeople are available only in departments where they're absolutely needed, such as photography, consumer electronics, and jewelry.

REFACT Hudson's Bay Company, the oldest retailer in North America, conquered the Canadian wilderness by trading furs over 300 years ago. Today one of it divisions, Zellers, is the largest general merchandise discount chain in Canada.[17]

Discount and department stores offer similar numbers of SKUs. But discount stores tend to offer more variety and less depth of merchandise. They typically carry fewer brands and sizes in each category than department stores. Merchandise categories that are typically available in discount stores but not department stores include hardware, auto supplies, athletic equipment, and gardening supplies.

Just as department stores face intense competition from specialty stores that focus on a single category of merchandise, the category specialists compete intensely with traditional discount stores. (Category specialists are described in a subsequent section.) To respond to category specialists' domination of hard goods (appliances, consumer electronics, automotive, sporting goods, etc.), many general merchandise discount retailers are making it easier to shop in the stores, increasing the level of customer service, upgrading their apparel offerings, and offering more grocery products.[18]

NEW RETAIL STORE FORMATS

A group of new general merchandise retailers has emerged on the retailing scene during the past 20 years. These new retailers include category specialists, home-improvement centers, warehouse clubs, off-price retailers, and hypermarkets.

Some of these new formats including office supply category specialists, home improvement centers, and warehouse clubs are patronized by both consumers and small businesses. For example, many small restaurants buy supplies, food ingredients, and desserts from a warehouse club rather than from food distributors. Similarly, small businesses buy office supplies from category specialists, while building contractors buy materials and tools in home-improvement centers. Thus some of these new retail formats function as wholesalers for businesses as well as retailers for consumers.

REFACT When Wal-Mart converts a general merchandise discount store into a supercenter by adding groceries, sales of nongrocery items go up 30 to 50 percent.[19]

Category Specialists

A **category specialist** is a discount store that offers a narrow variety but deep assortment of merchandise. These retailers are basically discount specialty stores. Their stores are about the same size as traditional discount stores and located in stand-alone sites or power strip shopping centers. But their merchandise assortment is the exact opposite of a traditional discount store where you find broad variety but narrow assortment.

Most category specialists use a self-service approach, but some specialists in consumer durables offer assistance to customers. For example, Office Depot stores have a warehouse atmosphere, with cartons of copying paper stacked on pallets and equipment in boxes on shelves. However, some models are displayed in the middle of the store, and salespeople in the display area are available to answer questions and make suggestions.[20]

By offering a complete assortment in a category at low prices, category specialists can "kill" a category of merchandise for other retailers and thus are frequently called "category killers." For example, Toys "R" Us accounts for over 40 percent of all toys and games sold in the United States. Because category specialists dominate a category of merchandise, they can use their buying power to negotiate lower prices, excellent terms, and assured supply when items are scarce. Department stores and traditional discount stores located near a Toys "R" Us store typically have to reduce their offerings of toys and games because local consumers are drawn to the deep assortment and low prices at Toys "R" Us. Exhibit 2–8 lists the largest category specialists in the United States.

Home-Improvement Centers

A **home-improvement center** is a category specialist that combines the traditional hardware store and lumber yard. It focuses on providing material and information that enable do-it-yourselfers to maintain and improve their homes. Merchandise includes an extensive assortment of building materials, paints and painting equipment, plumbing materials, electrical supplies, hardware, power tools, and garden and yard equipment. The largest U.S. home-improvement

This warehouse club sells an inconsistent assortment of brand merchandise to consumers and small businesses.

chains are Home Depot ($15.5 billion in annual sales), Lowe's Companies ($7.1 billion), Payless Cashways ($2.7 billion), Builders Square ($2.7 billion), and Hechinger ($2.3 billion).[21]

While merchandise in home-improvement centers is displayed in a warehouse atmosphere, salespeople are available to assist customers

EXHIBIT 2–8

Largest Category Specialists

COMPANY	($ MILLIONS)	NUMBER OF STORES	AVERAGE STORE SIZE (000 SQ.FT.)
HOME FURNISHINGS			
Bed, Bath & Beyond	$ 601	80	38
Linens 'N Things	554	145	33
IKEA US	511	13	200
CRAFTS			
Michaels	1,295	442	16
Fabri-Centers of America	835	936	12
TOYS			
Toys "R" Us	6,060	653	46
BOOKS			
Barnes & Noble	1,349	358	16
Borders	684	116	17
BABY			
Baby Superstores	291	46	40
SPORTING GOODS			
Sports Authority	1,046	136	43
Sports and Recreation	526	80	47
PET SUPPLY			
PETsMART	1,030	262	26
OFFICE SUPPLY			
Office Depot	5,300	504	35
Staples	3,068	443	20
Office Max	2,543	468	24
COMPUTERS			
CompUSA	2,813	96	26
Computer City	1,800	99	22
CONSUMER ELECTRONICS			
Best Buy	7,200	251	45
Circuit City	7,030	419	30

Source: "DSN Top 200," *Discount Store News*, July 1, 1996; and "State of the Industry: Seven Pillars to Future Success," *Chain Store Age Executive*, August 1996, section 2.

Home Depot (left) sells home improvement merchandise at low prices but still offers personalized customer service. Warehouse clubs (right) offer low prices and appeal to customers with large families and to small business owners.

in selecting merchandise and to tell them how to use it. For example, most Home Depot stores have a licensed electrician. Experts in specific areas lead workshops to show customers how to do things themselves. All Home Depot salespeople are required to attend "product knowledge" classes and are paid for the time they spend learning about water heaters and power tools.[22]

Warehouse Clubs

A **warehouse club** is a general merchandise retailer that offers a limited merchandise assortment with little service at low prices to ultimate consumers and small businesses. Stores are large (about 100,000 square feet) and located in low-rent districts. They have simple interiors and concrete floors. Aisles are wide so forklifts can pick up pallets of merchandise and arrange them on the selling floor. Little service is offered. Customers pick merchandise off shipping pallets, take it to checkout lines in the front of the store, and pay with cash. The largest warehouse club chains are Sam's Warehouse, a division of Wal-Mart (annual sales of $19.0 billion) and Price/Costco Club ($17.9 billion).[23]

Along with low-cost locations and store designs, warehouse clubs reduce inventory holding costs by carrying a limited assortment of fast-selling items. Merchandise usually is sold before the clubs need to pay for it.

Merchandise in warehouse clubs is about half food and half general merchandise. Specific brands and items may differ from time to time because the stores buy merchandise available on special promotions from manufacturers.

Most warehouse clubs have two types of members. Wholesale members are small-business people and individual members who purchase for their own use. Some clubs require individual members to have an affiliation with a government agency, utility, or credit union. Typically members must pay an annual fee of $25 to $35. In some stores, individual members pay no fee, but pay 5 percent over items' ticketed price. Wholesale members typically represent less than 20 percent of the customer base, but account for over 50 percent of sales.

Off-Price Retailers

Off-price retailers offer an inconsistent assortment of brand-name, fashion-oriented soft goods at low prices. America's largest off-price retail chains are T. J. Maxx (1995 annual sales of $6.2 billion including annual sales of Marshalls), Burlington Coat Factory ($1.6 billion), and Ross Stores ($1.4 billion).[24]

Off-price retailers can sell brand-name and even designer-label merchandise at low prices due to their unique buying and merchandising practices. Most merchandise is bought opportunistically from manufacturers or other retailers with excess inventory at the end of the season. This merchandise might be in odd sizes or unpopular colors and styles, or there may be minor mistakes in garments' construction (irregulars). Typically, merchandise is purchased at one-fifth to one-fourth of the original wholesale price. Off-price retailers can buy at low prices because they don't ask suppliers for advertising allowances, return privileges, markdown adjustments, or delayed payments. (Terms and conditions associated with buying merchandise are detailed in Chapter 14.)

Due to this pattern of opportunistic buying, customers can't be confident that the same type of merchandise will be in stock each time they visit the store. Different bargains will be available on each visit. To improve their offerings' consistency, some off-price retailers complement opportunistically bought merchandise with merchandise bought at regular wholesale prices. Three special types of off-price retailers are outlet, closeout, and single-price stores.

Outlet Stores   **Outlet stores** are off-price retailers owned by manufacturers or by department or specialty store chains. Outlet stores owned by manufacturers are frequently referred to as **factory outlets.**

Many manufacturers have one or two outlet stores. Manufacturers with a significant number of outlets include Warnaco (manufacturer of Hathaway shirts and Warner's lingerie), Reebok (athletic shoes), Van Heusen (men's shirts), Palm Beach (manufacturer of Evan Picone women's wear), and Ralph Lauren (men's and women's clothing).

Manufacturers view outlet stores as an opportunity to improve their revenues from irregulars, production overruns, and merchandise returned by retailers. Outlet stores also allow manufacturers some control over where their branded merchandise is sold at discount prices.

Retailers with strong brand names such as Saks and Brooks Brothers operate outlet stores too. By selling excess merchandise in outlet stores rather selling it at markdown prices in their primary stores, department and specialty store chains can maintain an image of offering desirable merchandise at full price.

Closeout Retailers   **Closeout retailers** are off-price retailers that sell a broad but inconsistent assortment of general merchandise as well as apparel and soft home goods. Some closeout stores, like Bud's Warehouse Outlets, sell both merchandise purchased opportunistically and excess merchandise from other retail chains owned by the parent corporation. The largest closeout chains are Odd Lots/Big Lots ($1.3 million in annual sales), MacFrugal's ($705 million), and Bud's Warehouse Outlets, a division of Wal-Mart ($570 million).[25]

Single-Price Retailers   **Single-price retailers** are closeout stores that sell all their merchandise at a single price, typically $1. The largest single-price retailer is Dollar Tree ($300 million in annual sales).[26]

Over the past several years, the sales growth of off-price retailers has slowed. With the increase in sales and promotions in department stores, consumers often are able to get fashionable, brand name merchandise in department stores at the same discounted prices offered by off-price retailers. In addition, more sophisticated inventory management systems has reduced the amount of excess production that can be bought by off-price retailers. In response to these conditions, off-price retailers are buying more current merchandise to complement the excess merchandise bought at the end of a fashion season.[27]

Some outlet stores, like the Liz Claiborne store (right) are owned by manufacturers, and others are owned by retailers like Nordstrom.

Catalog Showrooms

A **catalog showroom** is a retailer whose showroom is adjacent to its warehouse. The largest catalog showroom chains in the United States are Service Merchandise (annual sales of $4.0 billion) and Best Products ($1.5 billion).[28]

These retailers typically specialize in hard goods such as housewares, jewelry, sporting equipment, garden equipment, and consumer electronics. Jewelry frequently accounts for 25 percent of showroom sales. Catalog showrooms can offer low prices because they minimize the cost of displaying merchandise, focus on a narrow range of merchandise, provide minimal service, and are located in lower-cost areas than regional malls.

In most showrooms, the customer writes up an order for merchandise using the number on the display item or in a catalog. Then the order is handed to a clerk, who gets the merchandise from a warehouse.

The attractiveness of this retailing format has been declining. Category specialists can offer the same low prices and let customers browse through their "warehouse," selecting merchandise they want to buy. In addition, some customers find it inconvenient to wait for merchandise to be retrieved from the warehouse.

Hypermarkets and Supercenters

Hypermarkets   A **hypermarket** is a very large retail store offering low prices. It combines a discount store and superstore food retailer in one warehouselike building. Hypermarkets can be up to 300,000 square feet—larger than six football fields—and stock over 50,000 different items. Hypermarkets are unique in the size of the general merchandise assortment, store size, and low operating margins and prices. Annual revenues are typically over $100 million per store.

Hypermarkets were created in France after World War II. By building large stores on the outskirts of metropolitan areas, French retailers could attract customers and not violate strict land use laws. In 1987, the first hypermarket (Hypermart*USA) was opened in the United States in Dallas by Wal-Mart and Cullum. Wal-Mart was responsible for the discount store merchandise, and Cullum operated the grocery business.

Hypermarkets haven't been very successful in the United States. Land use laws are much less restrictive in the United States than in Europe so American consumers can conveniently shop elsewhere for merchandise sold in hypermarkets. Discount stores often are located at three-mile intervals in metropolitan areas, and supermarkets appear at even closer intervals. While shopping for groceries and general merchandise in the same store appeals to some consumers, many U.S. consumers find that shopping in stores of over 200,000 square feet is too time-consuming. It's hard to find merchandise, and checkout lines can be very long.

Supercenters   In reaction to weak consumer response to hypermarkets, Wal-Mart and Kmart are concentrating on smaller supercenters. **Supercenters** are 150,000-to-200,000–square-foot stores that combine a superstore (a large supermarket) and a general merchandise discount store. Wal-Mart's sales in supercenters have grown from $4.6 billion from 143 stores in 1994 to $17.6 billion from 350 stores in 1996. The largest supercenter chains in the United States are Wal-Mart Supercenters (1995 annual sales of $11.5 billion), Meijer ($5.6 billion), Super Kmart Centers ($3.7 billion), and Fred Meyers ($3.4 billion).[29]

INTERNET EXERCISE   Two large associations of retailers are
National Retail Federation http://www.nrf.com
Food Marketing Institute http://www.fmi.org
Visit these sites and report the latest retail developments and issues confronting the industry.

SERVICES RETAILING

The retail firms discussed in the previous sections sell products to consumers. However, **services retailers** are a large and growing part of the retail industry. Consider a typical Saturday. After a bagel and cup of coffee at a nearby Noah's Bagels, you go to the laundromat to wash and dry your clothes, drop a suit off at a dry cleaners, leave film to be developed at a Walgreen drug store, and make your way to the Jiffy Lube to have your car's oil changed. Since you are in a hurry, you drive through a Taco Bell so you can eat lunch quickly and not be late for your haircut at 1 P.M. By mid-afternoon, you're ready for a swim at your health club. After stopping at home for a change of clothes, you're off to dinner, a movie, and dancing with a friend. Finally, you end your day with a caffe latte at Starbucks, having interacted with 10 different services retailers during the day.

In Chapter 4, we discuss trends that suggest considerable future growth in services retailing. For example, the aging of the population will increase demand for health services. Younger people too are spending more time and money on health and fitness. Parents in two-income families are willing pay to have their homes cleaned, lawns maintained, clothes washed and pressed, and meals prepared so they can spend more time with their families.

REFACT Services account for 55 percent of the U.S. gross domestic product (the value of goods and services produced) and 79 percent of nonfarm employment in the United States.[30]

Types of Services Retailers

Exhibit 2–9 shows the wide variety of services retailers along with the national companies that provide these services. These companies are retailers because they sell goods and services to consumers. However, some of these companies are not just retailers. For example, airlines, banks, hotels, and insurance and express mail companies sell their services to businesses as well as consumers. Also, a large number of services retailers such as lawyers, doctors, and dry cleaners are not in the exhibit because they focus on local markets and do not have a national presence.

EXHIBIT 2–9

Examples of
Services Retailers

TYPE OF SERVICE	SERVICE RETAIL FIRMS
Airlines	American, Delta, British Airways, Singapore Airways
Automobile maintenance and repair	Jiffy Lube, Midas, AAMCO
Automobile rental	Hertz, Avis, Budget, Alamo
Banks	Citibank, NCNB, Bank of America
Child care centers	Kindercare, Gymboree
Credit cards	American Express, VISA, MasterCard
Education	University of Florida, UCLA
Entertainment parks	Disney, Universal Studios, Six Flags
Express package delivery	Federal Express, UPS, U.S. Postal Service
Financial services	Merrill Lynch, Dean Witter
Fitness	Jazzercise, Bally's, Gold's Gym
Health care	Humana, HCA
Home maintenance	Chemlawn, Mini Maid, Roto-Rooter
Hotels and motels	Hyatt, Sheraton, Marriott, Days Inn
Income tax preparation	H&R Block
Insurance	Allstate, State Farm
Internet access/Electronic information	America On-Line, CompuServ
Long-distance telephone	AT&T, MCI, Sprint
Movie theaters	AMC, Loews/Sony, Universal
Real estate	Century 21, Coldwell Banker
Restaurants	TGI Friday's, Wendy's, Pizza Hut
Truck rentals	U-Haul, Ryder
Weight loss	Weight Watchers, Jenny Craig
Video rental	Blockbuster
Vision centers	Lenscrafter, Pearle

Many organizations that offer services to consumers—such as banks, hospitals, health spas, legal clinics, entertainment firms, and universities—traditionally haven't considered themselves as retailers. Due to increased competition, these organizations are adopting retailing principles to attract customers and satisfy their needs. For example, banks are following the practices of retailers by emphasizing the need to deliver products and services conveniently, quickly, and knowledgeably to consumers. They are placing branches in convenient locations, switching from "banker hours" to "retail hours," and adapting services offered and branch design to the needs of the local communities.[31]

All retailers provide goods and services for their customers. However, the emphasis placed on the merchandise versus the services differs across retail formats, as Exhibit 2–10 shows. On the left side of the exhibit are supermarkets and warehouse clubs. These retail formats consist of self-service stores that offer very little services. However, these formats do offer a few services such as check cashing and some assistance from store employees. Moving along the continuum from left to right, we find category specialists, which also emphasize self-service, but have employees who can answer questions, demonstrate merchandise, and make recommendations. Next, department and specialty stores provide even higher levels of service. In addition to assistance from sales associates, these stores offer services such as gift wrapping, bridal registers, and alterations.

Optical centers and restaurants lie somewhere in the middle of the merchandise/service continuum. In addition to selling frames, eyeglasses, and contact lenses, optical centers also provide important services like eye examinations and fitting

EXHIBIT **2-10**   Merchandise/Service Continuum

Wholesale club	Supermarket	Category specialist	Speciality/ department store	Optical center	Restaurant	Airline	Banks/ University

ALL GOODS/NO SERVICES   ALL SERVICES/NO GOODS

eyeglasses. Similarly, restaurants offer food plus a place to eat, music in the background, a pleasant ambiance, and table service. As we move to the right end of the continuum, we encounter retailers whose offering is primarily services. However, even these retailers have some products associated with the services offered, such as a meal on the airplane or a check book. **Services retailers** are defined as retailers for which the major aspect of their offerings is services versus merchandise. Blockbuster, described in Retailing View 2.3, is an international services retailer that is changing its strategy to sell more merchandise.

Differences between Services and Merchandise Retailers

As a retailer falls more to the right on the merchandise/service continuum, services become a more important aspect of the retailer's offering. Four important differences in the nature of the offering provided by services and merchandise retailers are (1) intangibility, (2) simultaneous production and delivery, (3) perishability, and (4) inconsistency of the offering to customers.[32]

Intangibility   Services are generally intangible—customers cannot see, touch, or feel them. On the other hand, services are performances or actions rather than objects. For example, health care services cannot been seen or touched by a patient. Even after diagnosis and treatment, the patient may not realize the full extent of the service that has been performed.

Intangibility introduces a number of challenges for services retailers. First, since customers can't touch and feel services, it's difficult for customers to evaluate services before they buy them or even after they buy and consume them. Due to the intangibility of their offering, services retailers often use tangible symbols to inform customers about the quality of their services. For example, lawyers frequently have elegant, carpeted offices with expensive antique furniture. The design of service retailing outlets is discussed in Chapter 18.

Services retailers also have difficulty in evaluating the quality of services they are providing. For example, it's hard for a law firm to evaluate how well its lawyers are performing their jobs. To evaluate the quality of their offering, services retailers emphasize soliciting customer evaluations and complaints.

Simultaneous Production and Consumption   Products are typically made in a factory, stored and sold by a retailer, and then used by consumers in their homes. Service providers, on the other hand, create and deliver the service as the customer is consuming it. For example, when you eat at a restaurant, the meal is prepared and consumed almost virtually the same time.

The simultaneity of production and consumption creates some special problems for services retailers. First, the customers are present when the service is produced, may even have an opportunity to see it produced, and in some cases may be

2.3

Blockbuster Video Shifts from Services to Merchandise

BLOCKBUSTER REVOLUTIONIZED THE video rental business. In eight years it grew from 32 to 3,400 outlets with 25 percent of sales made outside the United States. Blockbuster dominated by offering a broader, deeper assortment of video rentals than the small independent retailers. The typical video rental store has 1,500 square feet and 2,500 tapes. In comparison, Blockbuster stores are more than four times larger (6,500 square feet) with four times more tapes (10,000). Each Blockbuster usually has 50 copies of new releases, while the typical video store only has five.

Blockbuster doesn't just offer selection; it also provides better service than the typical video rental store. Most Blockbusters are open until midnight. They all have outside return boxes so customers can return tapes when the store's closed. Salespeople are trained to know the selection of tapes and to be polite in responding to customers.

A company-wide computer and communication system enables Blockbuster to monitor inventory and sales transactions at each store. By combining demographic data about the store's trade area and buying patterns, Blockbuster can refine its selection of tapes and tailor the selection to local markets. For example, research indicated that the typical Blockbuster customer rents two tapes at a time. To accommodate such customers, Blockbuster adopted a unique rental fee of $3 for three nights and two days.

Blockbuster emphasizes that it's a family-oriented store by refusing to stock soft-core pornographic videos and X-rated films. Stores are careful to rent R-rated videos only to people over 17.

In 1995, Blockbuster founder and CEO Wayne Huizenga sold the firm to Viacom, an entertainment conglomerate. William Fields, former executive vice president of Wal-Mart and CEO of Blockbuster, charted a new course for Blockbuster. With the potential for the delivery of videos on demand through satellite and cable systems, Fields decided to convert Blockbuster stores into entertainment centers selling videos, music CDs, books, and computer games. In addition, he expanded. Facing declines in sales and profits, Fields left Blockbuster in 1996. Viacom is now developing a new strategy for coping with its changing environment.

Source: Patrica Sellers, "Wal-Mart's Big Man Puts Blockbuster on Fast Forward," *Fortune,* November 25, 1996, pp. 111–115; and Duncan Anderson, Michael Warshaw, and Nari-Aylssa Mulvihill, "#1 Entrepreneur in America: Wayne Huizenga," *Success,* March 1995, pp. 12–15.

part of the production process, as in making their own salad at a salad bar. Second, other customers consuming the service at the same time can affect the quality of the service provided. For example, an obnoxious passenger next to you on an airline can make the flight very unpleasant. Finally, the services retailer often does not get a second chance to satisfy the needs of its customers. While customers can return damaged merchandise to a store, customers that are dissatisfied with services have limited recourse. Thus it is critical for services retailers to get it right the first time.

Because services are produced and consumed at the same time, it is difficult to reduce costs through mass production. For this reason, most services retailers are small, local firms. Large national retailers are able to reduce costs by "industrializing" the services they offer. They make substantial investments in equipment and training to provide a uniform service. For example, McDonald's has a detailed procedure for cooking french fries and hamburgers to make sure they come out the same whether cooked in Paris, France, or Paris, Illinois.

Since it is difficult to judge service quality, service retailers like the Ritz-Carlton, London (left) and a bank (right) provide tangible clues of service quality in the design of the hotel lobby and offices.

Perishability   Because the creation and consumption of services are inseparable, services are perishable. They can't be saved, stored, or resold. Once the airline takes off with an empty seat, the sale is lost forever. This is in contrast to merchandise that can be held in inventory until a customer is ready to buy it.

Due to the perishability of services, an important aspect of services retailing is matching supply and demand. Most services retailers have a capacity constraint, and the capacity cannot be changed easily. There are a fixed number of tables in a restaurant, seats in a classroom, beds in a hospital, and electricity that can be generated by a power plant. To increase capacity, services retailers need to make major investment such as buying more airplanes and building an addition to increase the size of the hospital or restaurant.

In addition, demand for service varies considerably over time. Consumers are most likely to fly on airplanes during holidays and the summer, eat in restaurants at lunch and dinner time, and use electricity in the evening rather than earlier in the day. Thus services retailers often have times when their services are underutilized and other times when they have to turn customers away because they can't accommodate them.

Services retailers use a variety of programs to match demand and supply. For example, airline and hotels set lower prices on weekends when they have excessive capacity because businesspeople aren't traveling. To achieve more capacity flexibility, health clinics stay open longer in the flu season, while tax preparation services are open on weekends during March and April. Restaurants increase staffing on weekends, may not open until dinner time, and use a reservation system to guarantee service delivery at a specific time. Finally, services retailers attempt to make customers' waiting time more enjoyable. For example, videos and park employees entertain customers while they wait in line in Disney theme parks.

Inconsistency   Merchandise is often produced by machines with very tight quality control so customers are reasonably assured that each box of Cheerios will be identical. Because services are performances produced by people, employees and customers, no two services will be identical. For example, tax accountants can have different knowledge and skills for preparing tax returns. The waiter at the Olive Garden can be in a bad mood and make your dining experience a disaster.

Thus an important challenge for services retailers is providing consistently high-quality services. Many factors determining service quality are beyond the control of the retailers; however, services retailers expend considerable time and effort selecting, training, managing, and motivating their service providers.

Due to the differences in merchandise and services retailing, some sections of this text will be of greatest interest to merchandise retailers while others will be more important to services retailers. For example, all retailers need to understand consumer trends and behaviors (Chapters 4 and 5), develop a retail strategy (Chapter 6), locate sites (Chapters 8 and 9), manage human resources (Chapter 10), and develop information systems (Chapter 11). However, because services can't be inventoried, services retailers aren't involved in the inventory control issues raised in Chapters 6 and 11 and the merchandise planning, controlling, and buying systems in Section III. On the other hand, since employees are intimately involved in the production and delivery of the service offering, the decisions on store operations and employee management, the provision of customer service, and retail selling in Section IV are particularly important to services retailers.

TYPES OF OWNERSHIP

The first three sections of this chapter discussed how retailers can be classified in terms of the merchandise they sell (food, general merchandise, and specific categories of merchandise), their retail mix (the variety and depth of merchandise and services offered to customers), and the relative importance of merchandising and services in their offering. Another way to classify retailers is by their ownership. The major classifications of retail ownership are (1) independent, single-store establishments, (2) corporate chains, and (3) franchises.

Independent, Single-Store Establishments

Retailing is one of the few sectors in our economy where entrepreneurial activity is extensive. In 1995, over 60,000 new retail businesses were started in the United States.[34] Many such stores are owner-managed. Thus, management has direct contact with customers and can respond quickly to their needs. Small retailers are also very flexible. They aren't bound by bureaucratic rules that restrict store location or types of merchandise sold.

While single-store retailers can tailor their offering to their customers' needs, corporate chains can more effectively negotiate lower prices for merchandise and advertising due to their larger size. In addition, corporate chains have a broader management base, with people who specialize in specific retail activities. Single-store retailers typically have to rely on owner-managers' capabilities to make the broad range of necessary retail decisions.

To better compete against corporate chains, some independent retailers join a retail-sponsored cooperative group or wholesale-sponsored voluntary chain. A **retailer-sponsored cooperative** is an organization owned and operated by small, independent retailers to improve operating efficiency and buying power. Typically, the retail-sponsored cooperative operates a wholesale buying and distribution system and requires its members to concentrate their purchases from the cooperative's wholesale operation.

REFACT Over 95 percent of all U.S. retailers own and operate a single store. Yet single-store retailers account for less than 50 percent of all retail store sales.[33]

A **wholesale-sponsored voluntary cooperative group** is an organization operated by a wholesaler offering a merchandising program to small, independent retailers on a voluntary basis. Independent Groceries Alliance (IGA) and Ace Hardware are wholesale-sponsored voluntary cooperative groups. In addition to buying, warehousing, and distribution, these groups offer members services such as store design and layout, site selection, bookkeeping and inventory management systems, and employee training programs.

Corporate Retail Chains

A **retail chain** is a company operating multiple retail units under common ownership and usually having some centralization of decision making in defining and implementing its strategy. Retail chains can range in size from a drug store with two stores to retailers with over 1,000 stores such as Safeway, Wal-Mart, Kmart, and JCPenney. Some retail chains are divisions of larger corporations or holding companies. For example, The Limited owns Abercrombie & Fitch, Henri Bendel, Lerner Shops, Structures, and Lane Bryant; Intimate Brands owns Victoria's Secret, Cacique, and Body & Bath Works; and Dayton Hudson Corporation owns Dayton's, Hudson's, Marshall Fields, Mervyn's, and Target.

REFACT Fewer than 500 retail chains have over 100 stores, but these chains account for more than 30 percent of all retail store sales in the United States.[35]

There has been considerable concern that corporate retail chains will eventually drive independent retailers out of business. For example, Wal-Mart and other discount store chains have pursued a strategy of opening stores on the outskirts of small rural towns with populations between 25,000 and 50,000. These stores offer a broader selection of merchandise at much lower prices than previously available from local retailers. Due to scale economies and an efficient distribution system, corporate chains can sell at lower prices. This forces some competing local retailers out of business and alters the community fabric. On the positive side, the stores do employ 200 to 300 people from the local community.

But local retailers offering merchandise and services that aren't available at corporate chains can still prosper. When large discount stores open, more consumers are attracted to the community from surrounding areas. While chain stores may have cost advantages over local retailers, large retail chains can be very bureaucratic, stifling managers' creativity with excessive rules and procedures. Often, all stores in the chain have the same merchandise and services, while local retailers can provide merchandise compatible with local market needs.

Trends in Corporate Retail Chains   Over the past 10 years there has been—and will continue to be—considerable restructuring of corporate retail chains. For example, Federated Department Stores has acquired Macy's; Penney has acquired Eckerd Drug; Staples and Office Depot, the two largest office supply category specialists, have attempted to merge; PETsMART acquired two smaller pet supply category specialists (Pet Food Giant and Petstuff); Melville sold a number of divisions including Kay-Bee Toys, Wilson's, This End Up, and Marshalls to focus on its drug store chain, CVS; and Kmart divested Sports Authority, Borders, Builders Square, and Office Max to focus on its general merchandise discount store chain.

These restructuring activities illustrate two important trends in corporate retail chains: consolidation and focus. Fewer large chains are dominating discount and department store retailing formats. For example, Wal-Mart, Kmart, and Target account for a growing percentage of sales in the general merchandise discount format with some regional discount store chains experiencing decreased sales and profits and several going bankrupt. Similarly, regional department store chains have been acquired by more nationally oriented chains. Ten years ago there were 20 large office supply category specialists. Now there are only three.

2.4

The New Federated Department Store Chain

FEDERATED DEPARTMENT STORES was founded as a holding company by several family-owned, regional department store chains including Abraham & Strauss (New York), F&R Lazarus (Columbus, Ohio), Filene's (Boston), and Shillito's (Cincinnati, Ohio). Over the next 30 years, Bloomingdale's (New York), Rike's (Dayton, Ohio), Goldsmith's (Memphis), Burdines (Miami), and Rich's (Atlanta) joined Federated. In addition, the company started Filene's Basement (an off-price retailer) and Gold Circle (a general merchandise discounter) and acquired Ralphs (a West-Coast supermarket chain). Each of these chains was operated as an independent division with its own buying office, distribution center, corporate offices, and human resource policies. While the divisions were profitable, the stock price was low.

In 1986, Robert Campeau, a successful Canadian real estate developer, felt that the stock for retail holding companies like Federated was low and he bought Allied, a similar holding company, for $3.5 billion. In April 1988, he bought Federated for $6.6 billion. To finance these acquisitions, he sold off over 25 chains owned by the two holding companies (including Brooks Brothers, Ann Taylor, Ralphs, Filene's, Joske's, Miller's, Bonwit Teller, and Gold Circle) and attempted to cut operating costs. However, most of the acquisition was financed by issuing bonds and taking out loans. On January 15, 1990, the Campeau Corporation could not pay the interest on its debt and filed for bankruptcy, the largest bankruptcy in U.S. history.

Under the protection of the bankruptcy court, Federated's new management team closed unprofitable stores, sold divisions unrelated to its core department store activities, and reduced operating costs dramatically by developing information, distribution, and buying systems used by most of the department store divisions. In 1992, Federated emerged from bankruptcy as one of the largest and best managed retail chains. The company has since acquired Macy's, Horne's (Pittsburgh), and The Broadway (Los Angeles) but maintained its focus on developing synergies between its department store divisions. Federated appears to have a long-term strategy of operating three national retail chains—Bloomingdale's, Macy's, and Stern's—positioned at three points on the price/quality continuum. The Bullock's and Broadway stores in Southern California and the Jordan Marsh stores in New England were converted to the Macy's nameplate in 1995 and 1996. Chapter 10 details the organization and management of Federated.

Source: Linda Grant, "Miracle or Mirage on 34th Street," *Fortune,* February 1996, pp. 84–91; Barbara Solomon, "The Federated–Macy's Merger," *Management Review,* March 1995, pp. 34–39; and Jeffrey Trachtenberg, "Federated Rises from the Ashes, Still Faces Hurdles," *The Wall Street Journal,* June 22, 1992, pp. A1, A6.

The primary force behind this consolidation is the development of sophisticated communications, information, and distribution systems that enable large chains to reduce their costs. As chains grow in size, they can increase their sales without increasing the expense of hiring more buying and corporate staffs. With modern communications systems, the headquarters staff can be fully informed about what is going on in the individual stores across the world.

In addition to the consolidation in the industry, the retail chains are focusing their expertise on managing a specific retail format rather than operating as a holding company for a diverse set of retail formats. For example, TJX is focusing on off-price retailing, Melville on drug store retailing, May Company on department stores, and Kmart on general merchandise discount stores. By focusing their efforts, they are in a better position to develop a strategic advantage and increase their profitability, as Chapters 6 and 7 relate. These trends toward consolidation and focus are illustrated in the changing structure of Federated Department Stores. (See Retailing View 2.4.)

Franchising   **Franchising** is a contractual agreement between a franchisor and a franchisee that allows the franchisee to operate a retail outlet using a name and format developed and supported by the franchisor. Approximately one-third of all U.S. retail sales are made by franchisees.[36] Exhibit 2–11 lists some retailers governed by franchise agreements.

In a franchise contract, the franchisee pays a lump sum plus a royalty on all sales for the right to operate a store in a specific location. The franchisee also agrees to operate the outlet in accordance with procedures prescribed by the franchisor. The franchisor provides assistance in locating and building the store, developing the products and/or services sold, management training, and advertising. To maintain the franchisee's reputation, the franchisor also makes sure that all outlets provide the same quality of services and products.

The franchising ownership format attempts to combine advantages of owner-managed businesses with efficiencies of centralized decision making in chain store operations. Franchisees are motivated to make their store successful because they receive the profits (after the royalty is paid). The franchisor is motivated to develop new products and systems and to promote the franchise because

EXHIBIT 2–11

Franchise Retailers

NAME	TYPE	NUMBER OF OUTLETS*	START-UP COST ($000)	ROYALTY (% OF SALES)
FAST FOOD/RESTAURANTS				
McDonald's	Hamburgers	17,407	$363–601	12.5% and up
Subway	Sub sandwiches	12,233	54–140	8.0
KFC	Chicken, fast food	9,181	950–1,400	4.0
Pizza Hut	Pizza	8,400	281–1,300	6.5
Burger King	Hamburgers	8,022	320–1,320	3.5–6.0
Dairy Queen	Ice cream	5,692	181–572	4.0
Taco Bell	Mexican food	4,947	191–470	5.5
Dunkin' Donuts	Donuts	4,382	70–482	4.9
Denny's	Restaurant	1,595	Varies	4.0
Long John Silver's	Seafood, fast food	1,480	Varies	4.0
MERCHANDISE RETAILERS				
7-Eleven	Convenience stores	15,385	12+	Varies
GNC	Health food	2,704	75–135	6.0
Medicine Shoppe	Pharmacy	1,172	47–89	5.5
SERVICES RETAILERS				
Century 21	Real estate services	6,176	Up to 25	6.0
Mail Boxes Etc	Postal services	3,133	69–122	5.0
Coldwell Banker	Real estate services	2,511	8–37	Up to 6.0
Holiday Inn	Hotels/motels	2,208	Varies	5.0
Carlson Wagonlit	Travel services	1,164	3–8	None
Merry Maids	House cleaning	1,062	6–16	5.7
Midas Intern'l.	Mufflers, brakes	2,675	234–337	10.0
Budget	Auto rental	3,027	Varies	7.5
Jazzercise	Fitness	4,458	1–17	Up to 20

Source: "18th Annual Franchise 500," *Entrepreneur,* January 1997, pp. 206–305.
*Company-owned and -franchised.

2.5

A New Approach to Retailing Used Merchandise

STORES SELLING USED MERCHANDISE are referred to as **thrift stores**. Two nonprofit organizations, the Salvation Army and Goodwill, are the largest operators of thrift stores in the United States.

When you think about a thrift, you probably think of a store in a low-income area, a store with a musty smell and used merchandise strewn haphazardly. Grow Biz founders are changing this image by opening stores in middle-class suburban strip malls. Grow Biz sells used merchandise, only its stores look like any other retail stores—well signed, well fixtured, well lit, and well managed.

Grow Biz develops and franchises value-oriented retail concepts. The stores buy, sell, trade, and consign used and new merchandise. One of their chains is Play It Again Sports with over 7,000 outlets in the United States, Europe, and Australia. Its target market is parents seeking value in sporting goods because their kids are cycling through new sports equipment and are ready to get rid of equipment for sports that no longer interest them. Adults also patronize Play It

Again Sports, selling the Nordic Track they bought and only used for a few months and picking up a set of golf clubs. Prices are 50 to 70 percent less than prices of new sports equipment.

A big problem is finding enough used merchandise to sell. Franchisees get most of their merchandise by advertising in the papers and going to garage sales. Some merchandise (such as in-line skates) is so popular that it's impossible to get an extensive selection so the company complements the used merchandise with some new merchandise.

In addition to Play It Again Sports, Grow Biz operates several other franchise formats including Once upon a Child (used children's apparel, furniture, and accessories), Computer Renaissance (used computer equipment), Disc Go Round (used compact discs), and Music Go Round (used musical instruments.)

Source: "Grow Biz: A Recycling Retailer," *Discount Merchandiser,* May 1996, pp. 92–96, and "Grow Biz International: Building on a Used Foundation," *Stores,* May 1996, p. 81.

it receives a royalty on all sales. Advertising, product development, and system development are efficiently done by the franchisor, with costs shared by all franchisees. Retailing View 2.5 describes an interesting franchisor of used merchandise outlets. Appendix C at the end of this book relates considerations in starting a franchise.

Other Forms of Ownership

Some retail outlets are owned by their customers; others are owned by government agencies. In **consumer cooperatives,** customers own and operate the retail establishment. Customers have ownership shares, hire full-time managers, and share in the store's profits through price reductions or dividends. The most well-known consumer cooperatives are credit unions that provide financial services. Retailing View 2.6 describes a unique cooperative selling outdoors equipment.

Local, state, and federal government agencies sometimes own retail establishments. For example, the Army and Air Force Exchange Service, with sales over $7 billion, provides retail services for military personnel at 24,000 retail outlets on military bases in 24 countries.

SUMMARY

This chapter explained different types of retailers and how they compete with different retail mixes to sell merchandise and services to customers. To collect statistics about retailing, the federal government

2.6

REI Is Owned by Its Customers

RECREATIONAL EQUIPMENT INC. (REI) is one of the largest outdoor specialty retail chains and also the nation's largest consumer cooperative. By paying a $15 one-time fee, customers become members and owners of the company. Their share in the company profits is based on the amount of their purchases. REI's goal is to refund 10 percent of purchases to members in form of dividends that can be used to make future purchases at REI or redeemed for cash.

REI's 48 stores in two states, generate over $475 million annually. The company is noted for its commitment to high-performance outdoor gear. Julie Writing, REI merchandise manager for footware and apparel, asserts, "People know they can walk into REI and see the best hiking boot wall in the U.S." an assertion most people in the industry support. REI works closely with its vendors to improve the performance of the products it sells. For example, REI consulted with a vendor to reengineer a hiking boot for women. The hiking boot buyer says, "We don't jump on trends. We have been selling hiking boots for 58 years. That's the core of our business and that will never

change." And employees are encouraged to try out REI merchandise on their outdoor adventures supported by the company's REI Brand Employee Challenge Grant program.

Source: Mark Tedeschi, "2 Ways Out: Managing the Outdoor Market," *Footwear News,* April 1994, p. 12; and company documents.

classifies retailers by type of merchandise and services sold. But this classification method may not be useful in determining a retailer's major competitors.

A more useful approach for understanding the retail marketplace is classifying retailers based on their retail mix—the merchandise variety and assortment, services, location, pricing, and promotion decisions made to attract customers.

Over the past 30 years, U.S. retail markets have been characterized by the emergence of many new retail institutions. Traditional institutions (supermarkets and department, discount, and specialty stores) have been joined by category specialists, superstores, convenience stores, home-improvement centers, warehouse clubs, off-price retailers, catalog showrooms, and hypermarkets.

In addition, there has been substantial growth in services retailing. The inherent differences between services and merchandise result in services retailers emphasizing store management while merchandise retailers emphasize inventory control issues.

Traditional retail institutions have changed in response to these new retailers. For example, department stores have increased their emphasis on fashion-oriented apparel and improved the services they offer. Supermarkets are focusing more attention on meal solutions and perishables.

Appendix A describes theories of retail change and Appendix B provides guidelines for comparing competing retailers' retail mixes.

KEY TERMS

assortment, *30*

box store, *34*

breadth of merchandise, *30*

catalog showroom, *46*

category specialist, *42*

closeout retailer, *45*

combination store, *34*

consumer cooperative, *56*

convenience store, *35*

conventional super-market, *33*

department store, *38*

depth of merchandise, *30*

drug store, *38*

factory outlet, *45*

franchising, *55*

general merchandise discount store, *41*

home-improvement center, *42*

hypermarket, *46*

leased department, *39*

lifestyle retailing, *37*

limited-line warehouse story, *34*

off-price retailer, *43*

outlet store, *45*

promotional department store, *40*

retail chain, *53*

retail institution, *29*

retail-sponsored cooperative, *52*

services retailer, *47*

single-price retailer, *45*

SKU (stock keeping unit), *30*

specialty department store, *40*

specialty store, *36*

supercenter, *47*

superstore, *34*

super-warehouse store, *35*

thrift store, *56*

variety, *30*

warehouse club, *43*

warehouse store, *34*

wholesale-sponsored voluntary cooperative group, *53*

DISCUSSION QUESTIONS & PROBLEMS

1. Distinguish between variety and assortment. Why are these important elements of retail market structure?

2. How can an independent retailer compete against a corporate chain?

3. Compared to merchandise retailers, why are services retailers more concerned with employee management issues and less concerned with inventory control issues?

4. Some department and specialty store retailers argue that factory outlet stores, such as Ralph Lauren/ Polo, compete with their businesses to the point that sales are lost. Others argue that factory outlets don't affect their store sales. Discuss reasons for each position.

5. Distinguish between retail mixes in traditional discount stores and off-price retailers.

6. Give examples of retailers involved in intratype and intertype competition.

7. Many experts believe that customer service is one of retailing's most important issues in the 1990s. How can retailers that emphasize low price (such as discount stores, category specialists, and off-price retailers) improve customer service without increasing costs and, thus, prices?

8. Compare and contrast the retail mixes of convenience stores, traditional supermarkets, superstores, and warehouse stores. Can all of these food retail institutions survive over the long run? Why?

9. A chef wants to open an Italian restaurant and plans to do an analysis of the competition. Besides other Italian restaurants in town, what types of retailers might be considered competition for her restaurant?

10. The same brand and model personal computer is sold in specialty computer stores, discount stores, category specialists, and warehouse stores. Each type of retailer offers a different retailing mix for selling it. Why?

11. Since the 1970s, U.S. department store sales haven't kept pace with overall retail sales growth. Specialty stores, category specialists, and mail-order firms have captured American consumers' interest, reducing traditional department stores' market shares and profits. Will this trend continue and eventually cause the department store as we now know it to become extinct? Why? How might department stores reverse this trend?

SUGGESTED READINGS

Berry, Leonard, and Kathleen Seiders. "Growing through Portfolio Retailing." *Marketing Management* 2 (Fall 1993), pp. 9–20.

Brown, Stephen, and Mary Jo Bittner. "Services Marketing." In *AMA Management Handbook*, 3d Ed. New York: AMA-CON Books, 1994, pp. 15:5–15:15.

"The DSN Top 200." *Discount Store News*, July 1, 1996, pp. 37–85.

Larke, Roy. "Japanese Retailing: Fascinating, but Little Understood." *International Journal of Retail & Distribution Management*, January-February 1992, pp. 3–15.

Michman, Ronald, and Alan Greco. *Retailing Triumphs and Blunders*. Westport, CT: Quorum, 1995.

Nowatakhtar, Susan, and Richard Widdows. "The Structure of the General Merchandise Industry, 1959–1983: An Empirical Analysis." *Journal of Retailing* 63 (Winter 1987), pp. 426–35.

"Reinventing the Discount Store," *Discount Store News*, May 15, 1995, pp. 37–71.

Schultz, David. "Nation's Biggest Retail Companies," *Stores*, August 1996, pp. S1–S52.

"63rd Annual Report of the Grocery Industry." *Progressive Grocer*, April 1996, pp. 6–78.

"The State of the Industry: Seven Pillars to Future Success." *Chain Store Age Executive*, August 1996, section 2.

Zeithaml, Valarie, and Mary Jo Bitner. *Services Marketing*. New York: McGraw-Hill, 1996.

APPENDIX 2A

Comparison Shopping

All retailers learn about their competitors through comparison shopping. Comparison shopping might be as informal as walking through a competitor's store and looking around. But a structured analysis is more helpful in developing a retail offering that will attract consumers from a competitor's store.

EXHIBIT **2–12**

Examples of
Issues to Address
in Comparison
Shopping

MERCHANDISE PRESENTATION

1. How is the selling floor laid out? What selling areas are devoted to specific types of merchandise? How many square feet are devoted to each area?
2. Where are the different selling areas located? Are they in heavy traffic areas? By restrooms? On the main aisle? On a secondary aisle? How does this location affect sales volume for merchandise in the area?
3. What kind of fixtures are used in each selling area (faceouts, rounders, cubes, bunkers, tables, gondolas)?
4. Are aisles, walls, and columns used to display merchandise?
5. What is the lighting for sales areas (focus, overhead, bright, toned down)?
6. How is the merchandise organized in the selling areas (by type, price point, vendor, style, color)?
7. Evaluate the housekeeping of the selling areas. Are they cluttered or messy? Are they well maintained and organized?
8. What's the overall atmosphere or image of the selling areas? What effect does the lighting, fixturing, spacing, and visual merchandising have on customers?
9. What type of customer (age, income, fashion orientation) would be attracted to the store and each selling area within it?

SALES SUPPORT/CUSTOMER SERVICES

1. How many salespeople are in each department? Is the department adequately staffed?
2. How are salespeople dressed? Do they have a professional appearance?
3. Do salespeople approach customers promptly? How soon after entering a selling area is a customer greeted? How do customers respond to the level of service?
4. Evaluate salespeople's product knowledge.
5. Do salespeople suggest add-on merchandise?
6. Where, if applicable, are fitting rooms in relation to the selling floor? In what condition are they? Are they supervised? Are there enough fitting rooms to meet demand?
7. How many registers are on the selling floor? Are they well staffed and well stocked with supplies?
8. What services (credit charges acceptance, gift wrapping, delivery, special ordering, bridal registry, alterations, other) does the store offer?
9. What level of customer service is provided in the selling area?

MERCHANDISE (EACH CATEGORY)

1. Who are the key vendors?
2. How deep are the assortments for each vendor?
3. What are the private labels and how important are they?
4. What are the low, average, and top prices for merchandise in the category?

SUMMARY AND CONCLUSIONS

1. Who is the store's target customer?
2. What are the competitor's strengths and weaknesses?
3. How can we capture more business from the competitor?

The first step in the process is to define the scope of the comparison. For example, the comparison might be between two retail chains, two specific stores, two departments, or two categories of merchandise. The appropriate scope depends on the responsibilities of the person undertaking the comparison. For example, CEOs of retail chains would be interested in comparing their chain with a competitor's. Comparisons might focus on chains' financial resources, inventory levels, number of stores and employees, store locations, merchandise sold, employee compensation programs, and return policies. Thus, CEOs would examine factors for which the corporate office is responsible.

On the other hand, store managers would be interested in comparing their store with a competing store. For example, department store managers would want to know more about other department stores anchoring the mall where they're located. Buyers and department managers would focus on specific areas of merchandise for which they're responsible. Exhibit 2–12 lists questions to consider when comparison shopping. Exhibit 2–13 suggests a format for comparing merchandise, in this case lug-sole shoes in JCPenney and a men's shoe store.

EXHIBIT 2–13   Format for Merchandise Comparisons

Retailer	Factors	Lug sole casual shoes			Comments
J.C. Penney	Style	3 eyelet oxford			
	Brands	St. Johns Bay (private)			
	Price	$35			
	% mix	5%			
	Depth	36 pair			
	Breadth	4 colors			
Father/Son Shoes	Style	3 eyelet oxford	Tie suede	Chukka suede	
	Brands	British Knights Private	Private	Private	
	Price	$38.99–39.99	$29.99	$37.95	
	% mix	10%	5%	5%	
	Depth	24 pairs	36 pairs	12 pairs	
	Breadth	3 colors	3 colors	2 colors	
Harwyns	Style	2 eyelet oxford	Tie suede		
	Brands	British Knights	Private		
	Price	$39.99	$29.95		
	% mix	5%	5%		
	Depth	36 pairs	36 pairs		
	Breadth	3 colors	3 colors		

Style For clothing, style might be the fabric or cut. For example, sweater styles might be split into wool, cotton, or polyblend and V-neck, crewneck, or cardigan.

Brands The identifying label. Indicate whether or not the brand is a national brand or store brand.

Price The price marked on the merchandise. If the item has been marked down, indicate the original price and the marked down price.

Percent mix The percentage of the total assortment devoted to this style of merchandise.

Depth The amount of inventory for this style. The amount on display is one indicator of inventory depth. Another indicator is the amount of space devoted to the style.

Breadth The number of SKUs in this style.

EXHIBIT 2–14
Theories of Retail
Institution Change

CYCLICAL THEORIES
Wheel of retailing (price/service)
Accordion theory (assortment)

EVOLUTIONARY THEORIES
Dialectic process (retailer)
Natural selection (customer)

APPENDIX 2B

**Theories of the Evolution
of Retailing**

A number of theories have been developed to explain the present structure of the retail industry and predict how the structure will change. No individual theory explains all of the changes in the retailing environment. Yet as a whole, the theories provide insight for understanding the evolution of retail institutions.

Exhibit 2–14 details four theories of change in retail institutions. The first two theories, the wheel of retailing and accordion theory, are cyclical theories. These theories suggest that retail institutions go through cycles, beginning with one state and then returning to that state at some time in the future. The last two theories, dialectic process and natural selection, are evolutionary theories suggesting that changes in retail institutions are similar to patterns observed in biological evolution.

The Wheel of Retailing   One of the first and most famous frameworks for explaining changes in retailing institutions is the wheel of retailing (Exhibit 2–15).[37] The wheel represents phases through which some types of retailers pass. The cycle begins with retailers attracting customers by offering low price and low service. Over time, these retailers want to expand their market and they begin to stock more expensive merchandise, provide more services, and open more convenient locations. This trading-up process increases the retailers' costs and the prices of their merchandise, creating opportunity for new low-price retailers to enter the market.

The evolution of the department store illustrates the wheel of retailing theory. The first department store is attributed to Bon Marche, founded in Paris in 1852 by Aristide Boucicaut as an innovative response to small specialty stores.[38] In this entry phase, as Exhibit 2–15 shows, the department store was a low-cost, low-service venture. After World War II, department stores moved into the trading-up phase. They upgraded their facilities, stock selection, advertising, and service. Today, department stores are in the vulnerability phase. They're vulnerable to various types of low-cost, low-service formats such as general merchandise discount stores and category specialists.

The first phase of general merchandise discount stores was the national mass merchandise chains such as Sears and JCPenney. But over the years, these retailers have also succumbed to the turning of the wheel of retailing. Both of these retailers have made a concerted effort to upgrade their stores and merchandise. For instance, it is now hard to distinguish between a new Penney store and a department store at the same mall, so Sears and Penney became vulnerable to new forms of low-price, low-service retailers just like other department store chains.

Now these low-cost, low-service general merchandise discount stores such as Target, Kmart, and Wal-Mart stores offer credit, name-brand merchandise, some carpeted departments, and some limited service. One could view these discount stores as beginning to enter the trading-up phase of the wheel of retailing.

EXHIBIT 2–15

The Wheel of
Retailing

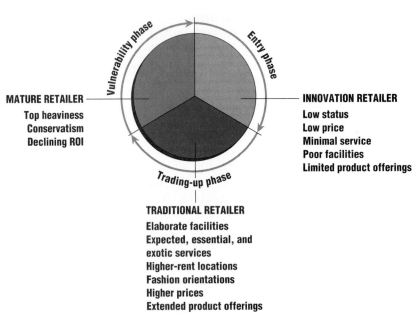

Another example on the wheel of retailing is off-price retailers. This type of retailer generally purchases branded end-of-season or closeout merchandise at significant discounts and passes the savings on to customers. Yet off-price retailers may also be facing maturity. The first generation of off-price retailers, such as Loehmann's, primarily sold manufacturer leftovers. Now off-price retailers aren't too different in appearance from regular-price specialty stores.

The new entry in the low-status/low-price arena is the warehouse club. These stores, such as Sam's Wholesale Club and Price/Costco, require customers to become members and are a cross between wholesale warehouses and discount stores. The question remaining for warehouse clubs is whether they'll proceed to the trading-up phase on the wheel of retailing. This question raises a general criticism of the wheel—some types of retailers never trade up. A corollary criticism is that some institutions don't begin as low-price/low-service entrants. Upscale fashion specialty stores, for instance, have never fit the wheel of retailing pattern.

The Accordion Theory   The second cyclical theory, the accordion theory, proposes that the retail institutions fluctuate from the strategy of offering many merchandise categories with a narrow assortment to the strategy of offering a wide assortment with a limited number of categories. This expansion and contraction calls to mind an accordion. During this nation's early development, relatively small general stores succeeded by offering rural Americans many categories of merchandise under one roof. As towns grew, they were able to support retail specialists like shoe, clothing, drug, and food stores. Department stores developed during the next expansion of the accordion. Department stores, somewhat like giant general stores, again offered customers multiple merchandise categories under one roof. This time, however, the depth of selection improved as well. The next contraction of the retail accordion results from specialty stores' tendency to have become even more specialized in the past two decades. These retail formats—known as category killers or category specialists (such as Toys "R" Us, Foot Locker, and Sports Authority)—offer consumers deep selections in a limited number of merchandise categories.[39]

Dialectic Process   The first of the two evolutionary theories of change in retail institutions is the dialectic process of thesis, antithesis, and synthesis (Exhibit 2–16). This theory implies that new retail institutions result from stores borrowing characteristics from other very different competitors, much like children are a combination of the genes of their parents. The established retail institution, known for relatively high margins, low turnover, and plush facilities, is the department store—the thesis. Discount stores in their early form were the antithesis of department stores. That is, they were characteristically low-margin, high-turnover, Spartan operations. Over time, characteristics from both department stores and discount stores were synthesized to form discount department stores like Kmart and Wal-Mart.[40]

Natural Selection   A final theory, with the strongest intuitive appeal for explaining change in retailing institutions, is natural selection. It follows Charles Darwin's early view that organisms evolve and change on the basis of survival of the fittest. In retailing, those institutions best able to adapt to changes in customers, technology, competition, and legal environments have the greatest chance of success. For instance, the increased number of women in the work force and America's physical fitness craze have made salad bars successful in some grocery stores. Video stores appeared in virtually every neighborhood in America only a few years after videocassette recorder technology was developed. Department stores have tried to battle specialty stores' competitive inroads by creating small specialty stores or boutiques within their stores.[41]

EXHIBIT **2–16**

The Dialectic
Process

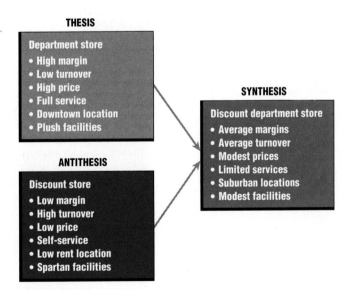

Source: Reprinted with the permission of Macmillan College Publishing Company, from *Retailing*, 4th edition, by Dale M. Lewison. Copyright © 1991 by Macmillan College Publishing Company, Inc.

NOTES

1. U.S. Department of Commerce, Bureau of Census, *Census of Retail Trade*, 1994.

2. David Appel, "The Supermarket: Early Development of an Institutional Innovation," *Journal of Retailing* 48 (Spring 1972), pp. 39–53; and Arieh Goldman, "Stages in the Development of the Supermarket," *Journal of Retailing* 51 (Winter 1975–76), pp. 49–64.

3. "Roaring 20's Ends in Depression," *Chain Store Age Executive*, June 1994, p. 49.

4. Michael Garry, "How to Fight Food Lion and Win— or at Least Break Even," *Progressive Grocer*, April 1992, pp. 72–76.

5. "Spending Slide Continues," in "63rd Annual Report of the Grocery Industry," *Progressive Grocer*, April 1996, p. 15.

6. "The Challenge Mounts," in "63rd Annual Report of the Grocery Industry," *Progressive Grocer*, April 1996, p. 13.

7 "Grabbing Share with Vice Grip," *Supermarket Business*, September 1996, pp. 17–25.

8. "The Battle Royal," in "63rd Annual Report of the Grocery Industry," *Progressive Grocer*, April 1996, p. 30.

9. "Convenience Stores Get Fresh," *Chain Store Age*, August 1996, section II, p. 18A; and "A New Recipe for Success," *Supermarket Business*, September 1996, p. S13.

10. Matt Murray, "Merger Mania among Drug Stores Is Likely to Continue," *The Wall Street Journal*, January 15, 1997, p. 12.

11. The *Census of Retail Trade* published by the U.S. Bureau of the Census adopts a much broader definition of department stores—a definition that is not consistent with practice in the retail industry. To be classified as a department store for the census, a store must employ more than 25 people; sell dry goods, household items, family apparel, home furnishings, furniture, appliances, and TV sets; and have no more than 80 percent of its sales from one category of merchandise or have sales over $1 million in the smallest two categories. Using this definition, the *Census of Retail Trade* considers traditional department stores such as Macy's, Burdines, and Marshall Field's to be in the same category as discount stores such as Wal-Mart and Kmart.

12. "Department Stores: The Big Squeeze," *Chain Store Age*, August 1996, section II, p. 25A.

13. *Women's Wear Daily*, April 16, 1995, section 2, p. 2.

14. "How to Lure Diverse Groups without Alienating Either," *Discount Store News*, June 3, 1996, p. 28.

15. "Retail Perspectives," *Women's Wear Daily*, September 26, 1996, p. 21.

16. "The DSN Top 200," *Discount Store News*, July 1, 1996, p. 59.

17. Larry Greenberg, "Hudson's Bay Faces Challenge from Southern Rival," *The Wall Street Journal*, May 24, 1996, p. B4.

18. "Reinventing the Discount Store," *Discount Store News*, May 15, 1995, pp. 37–71; and Sandra Sjkrova and Tereska Buzek, "Discount Department Stores: Growing Fashion and Food," *Chain Store Age*, August 1995, section 2, pp. 27A–28A.

19. Joanne Frederick, "Supercenters: The Threat du Jour," *Grocery Marketing*, March 1995, pp. 14–17.

20. Michael Gelfand, "Consumer Electronics Superstores," *Discount Merchandiser*, January 1993, pp. 60–66ff; and Dean Foust, "Circuit City's Wires Are Sizzling," *Business Week*, April 27, 1992, p. 76.

21. "State of Industry: Seven Pillars to Future Success," *Chain Store Age*, August 1996, section 2, p. 21A.

22. Cyndee Miller, "Big Chains Battle for Market Share in Home Improvement," *Marketing News*, September 28, 1992, pp. 1, 10–11; and Roger Thompson, "There's No Place Like Home Depot," *Nation's Business*, February 1992, pp. 30–33.

23. "The DSN Top 200," *Discount Store News*, July 1, 1996, p. 79.

24. Ibid., p. 63.

25. Ibid., p. 67.

26. Ibid., p. 74.

27. Sharon Edelson, "Once a Poor Relation, Outlets Go Legit—and Trouble Looms," *Women's Wear Daily*, April 4, 1995, pp. 1, 8.

28. Ibid., p. 67.

29. Ibid., p. 62.

30. Statistical Abstract of the United States, 115th ed. (Washington, DC: U.S. Government Printing Office, 1996).

31. Jennifer Porter, "Supermarket Banker Personifies the New Way in Bank Sales," *Bank Marketing*, October 1996, pp. 8–10; Jeffrey Westegren, "The 'New' Bank Marketing," *Bank Marketing*, July 1996, pp. 7–8; and Beverly Wayne and Curtis Wayne, "Tailoring Retailing to Fit Banking," *Bank Marketing*, February 1996, pp. 43–47.

32. Valarie Zeithaml, A. Parasuraman, and Leonard Berry, "Problems and Strategies in Services Marketing," *Journal of Marketing* 49 (Spring 1985), pp. 33–46.

33. *Retailing: A Mirror on America* (Washington, DC: National Retail Federation, 1996), p. 6.

34. *Dun and Bradstreet Corporate Starts* (New York: Dun and Bradstreet, 1996), p. 74.

35. *Census of Retail Trade* (U.S. Department of Commerce, Bureau of the Census, 1996), p. 15.

36. Louis Stern, Adel El-Ansary, and Ann Coughlin, *Marketing Channels*, 6th ed. (Englewood Cliffs, NJ: Prentice Hall, 1996), p. 32.

37. Stephen Brown, "The Wheel of Retailing: Past and Future," *Journal of Retailing*, Summer 1990, p. 147; Stephen Brown, "Postmodernism, the Wheel of Retailing, and Will to Power," *The International Review of Retail, Distribution, and Consumer Research*, July 1995, pp. 387–412; and Arieh Goldman, "Institutional Change in Retailing: An Updated Wheel of Retailing," in *Foundations of Marketing Channels*, ed. A. Woodside, J. Sims, D. Lewison, and I. Wilkenson (Austin, TX: Lone Star, 1978), pp. 193–201.

38. Tom Mahoney and Leonard Sloane, *The Great Merchants* (New York: Harper & Row, 1974), p. 2.

39. Stanley C. Hollander, "Notes on the Retail Accordion," *Journal of Retailing* 42 (Summer 1966), pp. 20–40, 54.

40. Thomas J. Maronick and Bruce J. Walker, "The Dialectic Evolution of Retailing," in *Proceedings: Southern Marketing Association*, ed. Barnett Greenberg (Atlanta: Georgia State University, 1974), p. 147.

41. A. C. R. Dreesmann, "Patterns of Evolution in Retailing," *Journal of Retailing*, Spring 1968; and Murray Forester, "Darwinian Theory of Retailing," *Chain Store Age*, August 1995, p. 8.

Nonstore Retailing— Electronic Retailing and Catalogs

THE WORLD OF RETAILING

1. Introduction to the World of Retailing
2. Store-Based Retailing
3. **Nonstore Retailing**—Electronic Retailing and Catalogs
4. The Retail Customer
5. Customer Buying Behavior

RETAILING STRATEGY

MERCHANDISE MANAGEMENT

STORE MANAGEMENT

QUESTIONS

- What are the different types of nonstore retailers?

- Which types of nonstore retailing formats have the most growth potential?

- Will electronic home shopping be a significant retail format in the future?

- What types of merchandise are most easily sold through a nonstore format?

WHILE ONLY 10 PERCENT OF RETAIL SALES are made through nonstore channels, sales in nonstore formats are growing faster than store sales. The most exciting and potentially most significant form of nonstore retailing is interactive home shopping, also referred to as electronic retailing. Electronic retail sales were very low in 1996, but most experts feel this format has the greatest potential of all the nonstore formats. New computer and communication technologies make it possible for consumers to shop the world from their home. For example, many people are buying gifts over the Internet.[1] From your home computer, you can buy a rare movie poster from the Chisholm Larsson Gallery (http://www.chisholm-poster.com) for a friend in Los Angeles, a cashmere blanket from Royal Cashmere (http://www. royalcashmere.com) for grandmother, and a pair of warm gloves from L.L. Bean (http://www.llbean.com) for Dad in Vermont. You look over the gifts before you buy them, transmit your order and credit card information electronically to the retailers, and have the gifts shipped directly to your friends and relatives.

Many major retailers sell merchandise through an electronic retail format using the Internet. A few of the many retail Internet sites are listed in the Appendix to this chapter. Although only in its infancy, interactive home shopping has the potential to fundamentally change the way people shop as well as the structure of the consumer goods and retail industries.

The Hudson Bay Company, one of the oldest retailers in North America, is selling merchandise over the newest retail format.

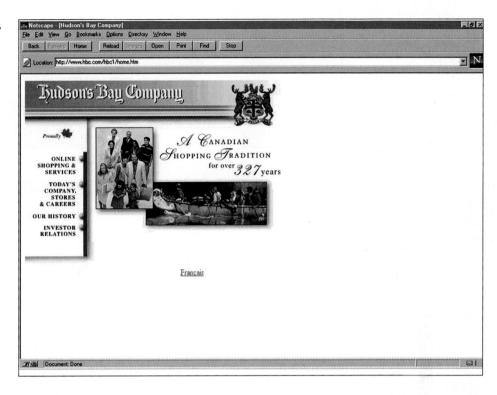

In this chapter, we review the various nonstore retailing formats—catalog and direct mail retailing, TV home shopping, vending machines, direct selling, and electronic retailing. The last section focuses on electronic retailing—the present electronic retail offerings, what the future holds for this format, and how electronic retailing may change the nature of the retail industry.

NONSTORE VERSUS STORE-BASED RETAILERS

Nonstore retailing is a form of retailing in which sales are made to consumers without using stores. The various types of nonstore retailers are defined in terms of the medium they use to communicate with their customers. As Exhibit 3–1 shows, direct selling retailers communicate with customers through a personal, face-to-face contact by a salesperson, vending machine retailers have limited communications through the display of the merchandise in the machine, catalog and direct-mail retailers communicate using printed material, TV home shopping retailers use television, and electronic retailers use an interactive computer or computerlike interface.[2]

The nature of the communications between the retailer and its customers differs for the various nonstore retailing formats. Communications in direct selling are highly interactive. The salesperson responds immediately to customer comments and questions; responses are tailored to the needs of each customer. As we discuss later in the chapter, electronic retailing has the potential for providing this same high level of interactivity. On the other hand, the communications in TV home shopping, vending machines, and catalog retailing are not very interactive.

EXHIBIT 3–1

Types of Nonstore
Retailers

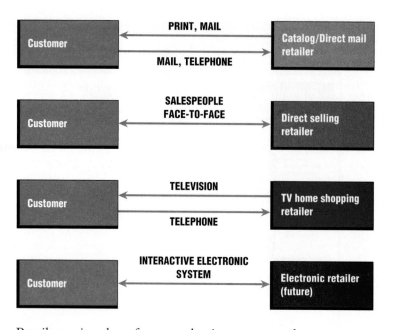

Retailers using these formats take time to respond to customers, and the responses are relatively standardized. All customers get the same information from the catalogs and vending machines.

REFACT Wal-Mart's sales in 1996 were greater than all nonstore retail sales.

The annual sales made by the nonstore format are shown in Exhibit 3–2. More than 90 percent of all retail sales are made in stores. However, nonstore sales now are growing at a rate of 7 percent a year, while sales in retail stores are increasing at only 4 percent per year. The high growth rate for nonstore retailing is primarily due to the growth of catalog and direct-mail retailing—the most significant nonstore retailing formats. However, the growth of catalog retail sales is slowing and sales in other nonstore retailing formats such as TV home shopping, direct selling, and vending machines are stagnant. As we discuss later in the chapter, the prospects for electronic retailing are promising, but very uncertain.

Most nonstore retailers offer consumers the convenience of selecting and purchasing merchandise at a time and location of their choosing. Usually, after the choice is made and the order placed, the merchandise is delivered a few days later to the customer's home. But nonstore retailing transactions also take place at work or at a neighbor's house.[3] These benefits of nonstore retailing are very appealing to time-conscious consumers and consumers who can't easily go to stores, such as the handicapped, the elderly, mothers with young children, and rural residents.[4]

EXHIBIT 3–2

Sales by Nonstore
Retail Format, 1996

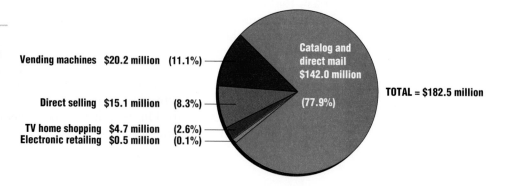

Vending machines $20.2 million   (11.1%)

Direct selling $15.1 million   (8.3%)

TV home shopping $4.7 million   (2.6%)
Electronic retailing $0.5 million   (0.1%)

Catalog and direct mail
$142.0 million

(77.9%)

TOTAL = $182.5 million

3.1

U.S. Catalog Retailers Prove Popular in Japan

L.L. BEAN, PATAGONIA, LANDS' END, and Eddie Bauer catalog sales have been so high in Japan that the retailers are opening stores. While other U.S. businesses are struggling in Japan, these retailers are succeeding because they are satisfying unfulfilled consumer needs. The Japanese find it difficult to get quality fashionable apparel at reasonable prices. Apparel offered in Japanese department stores is very expensive. While direct-mail retailing in Japan is extensive, much like it is in the United States, the merchandise offered in catalogs is a mix of cheap dresses, necklaces, diapers, and dog food.

Upper- and middle-income consumers—especially the younger generation and urban residents—find the merchandise offered by U.S. catalogers attractive. Two other appealing aspects of U.S. catalog retailers are the lifetime no-questions-asked guarantee and the use of top models wearing the merchandise in the catalogs. Even with the import duty and transportation costs, the catalog merchandise prices are still reasonable for Japanese consumers.

While U.S. catalog retailers are a popular new alternative in Japan now, once U.S. catalogs become commonplace, it may be harder to be successful in Japan. Although the Japanese clamor for authentic U.S. goods, U.S. marketers may want to tailor offerings to fit Japanese tastes and needs. For example, Patagonia has found that its Japanese customers prefer brighter colors for apparel.

Source: Mari Yamaguchi, "Japanese Consumers Shun Local Catalogs to Buy American," *Marketing News*, December 2, 1996, p. 12; and Melissa Dowling, "Catching the Wave to Japan," *Catalog Age*, February 1996, pp. 55–59.

Nonstore retailing can involve highly personalized services (such as those provided by Mary Kay beauty consultants) or the very impersonal interactions associated with a vending machine. The merchandise offered by a nonstore retailer range from the broad assortment found in the 1,000-page JCPenney catalog to the narrow product line of Belgian chocolates offered by Internet retailer Geldof Chocolatier (http://www.he.net/~geldof).

While nonstore retailing provides unique convenience benefits over in-store retailing, frequently consumers can't get some important services provided by store-based retailers. For example, customers ordering through a catalog or over the Internet can't touch and feel the merchandise, try it on, attend sessions on how to use it, or have it altered prior to purchase. If customers are dissatisfied with the merchandise, they can't simply go to a store and return it. When returning merchandise to a nonstore retailer, customers have to repackage the merchandise and send it to the retailer, often at their own expense.

The following sections discuss each of the major nonstore forms of retailing.

CATALOG AND DIRECT-MAIL RETAILING

Catalog retailing is a nonstore retail format in which the retail offering is communicated to a customer through a catalog, while **direct-mail retailers** communicate with their customers using letters and brochures. Historically, catalog and direct-mail retailing were most successful with rural consumers, who lacked ready access to retail stores. With the rise of dual-income families and other people with limited time for shopping in stores, catalog retailing has grown in popularity and now appeals to a broad cross section of consumers. Retailing View 3.1 describes the success of U.S. catalog retailers in Japan.

The typical U.S. household receives more than one catalog a week. However, the growth in catalog retailing sales is declining.

REFACT In 1489, Aldus Manutius of Venice, Italy, offered the first catalog listing 15 books written in Latin and Greek. The first American catalog, produced in 1744 by Benjamin Franklin, sold scientific instruments and academic books.[5]

In 1995, $142 billion of merchandise and services were sold to consumers through catalogs and direct mail. Approximately 60 percent of the sales were for merchandise with the remaining 40 percent for services such as insurance. Direct mail accounted for 10 percent of the U.S. sales of general merchandise but only 3.7 percent of all U.S. retail sales.

Catalog and direct-mail retail sales grew by 7.5 percent in 1995. Merchandise categories experiencing higher than average growth included apparel, hosiery, computer hardware and software, gifts, pharmaceuticals, and vitamins. On the other hand, cosmetics, books, food, gardening supplies, photographic products, and hardware and tools had lower than average growth.[6]

Over two-thirds of all U.S. adults (113 million people) made a purchase in response to catalogs and direct mail with 42 percent spending more than $100 on catalog purchases in 1995. The average U.S. household receives 1.7 catalogs and a similar number of direct-mail solicitations per week. However, households that patronize catalog retailers receive three times as many catalogs as the average household.[7]

Types of Catalog and Direct-Mail Retailers

Two types of firms selling products through the mail are (1) general merchandise and specialty catalog retailers and (2) direct-mail retailers. General merchandise catalog retailers offer a broad variety of merchandise in catalogs that are periodically mailed to their customers. For example, JCPenney distributes a 1,000-page catalog with over 50,000 SKUs to its customers twice a year. Besides its general merchandise catalog, Penney distributes 70 specialty catalogs each year. Specialty catalog retailers focus on specific categories of merchandise, such as fruit (Harry and David), gardening tools (Smith & Hawken), and seeds and plants (Burpee).

REFACT Orvis, the oldest catalog still being published in the United States, began in 1856 selling fishing gear.[8]

Direct-mail retailers typically mail brochures and pamphlets to sell a specific product or service to customers at one point in time. For example, USAA sells automobile insurance and a division of JCPenney sells life insurance through the mail. In addition to the focus on a specific product or service, most direct-mail retailers are primarily interested in making a single sale from a specific mailing, while catalog retailers typically maintain relationships with customers over time.

Exhibit 3–3 lists the nation's largest catalog and direct-mail retailers and illustrates the variety of products and services sold directly to customers through impersonal methods. About two-thirds of the sales are for merchandise; one-third are for services. The fastest-growing areas are apparel, drugs and vitamins, and sporting goods. Sales of low-cost jewelry and gifts, insurance, food, books, and photo processing are growing more slowly.

Complement to In-Store Retail Format

Many in-store retailers use direct mail to complement their in-store retailing efforts. More than half of the top 50 department stores also sell through catalogs. For example, PETsMART, a pet supplies category specialist, acquired Sporting Dog Specialty, the largest catalog retailer of dog supplies. With this combination of in-store and catalog retailing, PETsMART could expand its reach to markets that are too small to support a

EXHIBIT 3–3

Leading U.S. Catalog and Direct-Mail Retailers

COMPANY	DIRECT MAIL/CATALOG SALES 1995 ($ MILLIONS)	MERCHANDISE AND SERVICES OFFERED
United Services Automobile Association	$5,784	Insurance
Tele-Communications	4,464	Cable TV
Dell Computer	4,042	Computers
AARP/Prudential	3,584	Insurance
Gateway 2000	3,500	Computers
JCPenney	3,424	Insurance, general merchandise
Time Warner Cable	3,371	Cable TV
GEICO	2,700	Insurance
AT&T	2,000	Communication services
Fingerhut	1,743	General merchandise
Comp-U-Card	1,555	General merchandise
MCI	1,470	Communication services
Micro Warehouse	1,308	Consumer electronics
Comcast Cable	1,131	Cable TV
Federated Department Stores	1,100	General merchandise
Spiegel	1,084	General merchandise
Cox Communications	1,074	Cable TV
Reader's Digest	1,053	Books, publications
Continental Cablevision	1,052	Cable TV
Lands' End	959	General merchandise

Source: "Highlights of the 1995 Mail Order Market Place," *Direct Marketing*, August 1996, pp. 54–55.

REFACT The largest catalog retailer in the world is Otto Versand, a German company with 1995 sales of $1.8 billion. Spiegel, a general merchandise catalog retailer in the United States, is owned by Otto Versand.[9]

store. Thus it could build up a reputation in markets where stores will be opened in the future. In addition, the catalog enables PETsMART to offer a broader assortment to its customers. PETsMART stores have 12,000 SKUs while the five Sporting Dog Specialty catalogs offer 60,000 SKUs.[10] On the other hand, more than half of all catalog retailers have no stores and a third have only one store.

To make a clear and consistent statement, retailers prefer to offer the same merchandise in their catalogs as in their stores. But some retailers selling more fashionable apparel (such as Bloomingdales) deviate from this policy because their direct-mail customers, compared to in-store customers, tend to be younger, have lower income, and buy merchandise at lower price points.[11]

Keys to Success   Direct-mail and catalog retailing are attractive business opportunities, because the start-up costs are relatively low. An entrepreneur can launch a direct mail business with minimal inventory and can use her garage as a warehouse and office. There is no need to rent a store in a high-rent location, use expensive fixtures, create an attractive shopping environment, or hire salespeople. Mailing lists tailored for a target market can be purchased inexpensively. Retailing View 3.2 describes two neighbors who started a successful catalog retail business.

On the other hand, catalog and direct-mail retailing can be very challenging. Mailing and printing costs are high since catalog retailers mail out 10 to 20 catalogs for each order they receive. It is increasingly hard to capture consumers' attention as they receive more catalogs in their mail each year. Second, costs of paper and third-class mail have been increasing 20 to 25 percent per year. Third, some direct-mail retailers' misleading and deceptive practices have led to government regulations

3.2

Starting a Catalog Retail Business

JOANN MARTIN MET VICKIE HUTCHINS when she moved in next door in Delaware, Ohio. Sharing a love of decorating and antiques, they spent weekends together shopping at flea markets and auctions. Then they decided to go into the catalog retail business, putting up $5,000 apiece and naming the business Gooseberry Patch. Their first catalog featured craft items they would like to have: a $195 Redware punch bowl, a $75 handmade mohair teddy bear, and a $400 handcrafted chair. Sales from their glossy, full-color, 12-page catalog were disappointing. They got only $27,000 in orders and lost $20,000. However, they discovered that the best-selling items were inexpensive country style crafts with a touch of nostalgia.

They got rid of the slick catalog and expensive items, shifting from country expensive to country whimsical. Their next catalog had a folksier flavor. It was printed on heavy brown paper stock with illustrations by a local artist rather than photos. The second catalog did much better, generating sales of $85,000.

Gooseberry Patch now mails out 2 million catalogs a year, generating $5 million in sales. Price points are $5 to $100. The catalogs feature decorating and party ideas, recipes, as well as updates on the private lives of the owners. The all-time best-seller is a $13 "heart-in-hand" cookie cutter, which creates a heart-shaped cookie with a heart-shaped hole in the middle. Cinnamon is the top-selling fragrance with nutmeg a close second. New opportunities the owners are considering include selling their Gooseberry Patch Books in traditional bookstores and wholesaling Gooseberry private-label potpourris, cookie cutters, home fragrances, and cards.

Source: Marla Matzer, "Selling Smells," Forbes, January 16, 1995, pp. 89–90; and "Retail Entrepreneur of the Year," Chain Store Age Executive, December 1995, pp. 56–57.

---

concerning return policies and notification of delays in delivery. Finally, the length of time required to design, develop, and distribute catalogs makes it difficult for catalog and direct-mail retailers to respond quickly to new trends and fashions.[12]

Successful direct-mail and catalog retailers have sophisticated information, communication, and distribution systems. For example, Lands' End maintains a mailing list of 9 million people, 45 percent of whom have purchased merchandise from the firm in the previous 36 months. In 1996, it mailed out 150 million catalogs, which generated sales of $925 million. When customers call the toll-free number to place orders, Lands' End operators can access information about their past purchases and address, making it easier for customers to order. Operators can also access information about merchandise and provide detailed information about measurements for a garment and its fabrication. Ninety percent of all orders are mailed to the customer in 24 hours. If customers don't like their merchandise, they can return it for a cash refund, and Lands' End will pay the return mail costs.[13] Retailing View 3.3 illustrates how Sears—the largest catalog retailer in the United States—went out of the catalog business because it did not keep up with technological changes.

While some catalog retailers have very sophisticated operations, many catalogers do not utilize much customer information in developing and mailing their catalogs. Less than 75 percent of them keep track of the items and dollar amounts purchased by their customers. Fewer than 10 percent of the catalog retailers relate their sales to demographic information about individual customers or the ZIP codes in which they live.[15] While the use of customer information helps catalog retailers improve their efficiency, many consumers are concerned about companies collecting and using this private information.[16]

REFACT Consumers rate the L.L. Bean catalog as the best in terms of consumer satisfaction. Patagonia was rated second; Lands' End was third.[14]

3.3

The Fall of the Sears Catalog

THE SEARS CATALOG, AN AMERICAN tradition, closed in 1993 because the company's distribution and communication systems were outmoded. Sears started as a catalog retailer when Richard Sears, a railroad agent, bought a shipment of returned watches and resold them to other agents on the rail line. In 1893, Sears moved to Chicago and formed Sears, Roebuck and Company with Alvah Roebuck, a watchmaker. They built their company by sending farmers their 500-page catalog featuring clothing, musical instruments, buggies, housewares, and even houses (assembly required).

Richard Sears had a grand vision, but was not a detail person. At the turn of the century, a customer wrote, "For heaven sakes, quit sending me sewing machines. Every time I go to the station I find another one there. You have sent me five already." This sewing machine incident was prophetic of problems the Sears catalog would experience in the future.

In 1992, the Sears catalog generated $3.3 billion in sales, but lost $175 million because the company's ordering system was not automated or computerized. In addition, the company didn't analyze its customer database and target small catalogs to customers with specific interests. All customers were sent the same 1,000-page catalog whether they ordered $1,000 of merchandise or only an item or two.

However, Sears has reentered catalog retailing by setting up joint ventures with other firms. Sears contributes the information in its database of 24 million credit customers; its partners produce and mail specialty catalogs and take and fill orders. The new catalog operation now employs 20 people compared to 19,000 employees in the old division.

Source: Jason Hudson, "Nonstore Retailing: Paper Remains King," *Chain Store Age,* August 1995, p. 27; Cyndee Miller, "Catalogs Alive and Thriving," *Marketing News,* February 28, 1994, pp. 1, 9; and "The Sears Catalog," *Consumer Reports,* October 1994, p. 625.

CD ROM Catalogs   Several catalog retailers are now offering their catalog on CD ROM disks that can be read by a personal computer. Other companies are selling collections of 25 to 40 different catalogs on a disk. Using a mouse, you can browse through the "pages" of the catalog, even hear parts of a record from a music catalog, and use keywords to locate specific items.

While the disks are interactive, the amount of merchandise presented and the ability to perform complex searches (such as displaying all white cotton sweaters under $50) is limited. Some companies link the CD ROM catalog to their Internet site so prices and merchandise can be updated and orders can be placed electronically. However, this electronic catalog technology will probably be replaced by interactive home shopping retailers using the Internet directly rather than in conjunction with a CD ROM.

VENDING MACHINE RETAILING

Vending machine retailing is a nonstore format in which merchandise or services are stored in a machine and dispensed to customers when they deposit cash or use a credit card. The vending machines are placed at convenient, high-traffic locations such as in airports for selling travel insurance, in factory and office work areas for snacks, and near university classrooms for soft drinks. Since the transaction can be completed without personal interaction, customers can acquire merchandise or services at any time during the day.

While $20.2 billion in goods is sold annually through vending machines in the United States, almost all products sold are hot and cold beverages, food, and candy. Vending machine sales have experienced little growth over the past five

Around the world, vending machines are primarily used to sell cold beverages, food, and candy.

years largely due to changes in the workplace. Employment growth has been limited, and the largest growth in the work force is white and "pink" collar employees rather than the blue collar workers that buy most heavily from vending machines.[17] Presently, merchandise priced over $1 has not sold well from vending machines because of the number of coins required to complete the transaction. Only 57 percent of the vending machines take dollar bills and very few accept credit cards. In addition, consumers are reluctant to buy more expensive merchandise based on the limited information provided by the vending machine.

Technological developments in vending machine design may result in long-term sales growth. New video kiosk vending machines enable consumers to see the merchandise in use, have more information about the merchandise, and use their credit cards to make a purchase. The new vending machine designs also enable the retailers to increase the productivity of the machines. Electronic systems in the machine keep track of sales and inventory and signal the operator when stockouts and malfunctions occur.

TELEVISION HOME SHOPPING

Television home shopping retailing is a retail format in which customers watch a TV program demonstrating merchandise and then place orders for the merchandise by telephone. The three forms of electronic retailing are (1) cable channels dedicated to television shopping, (2) infomercials, and (3) direct-response advertising shown on broadcast and cable TV. **Infomercials** are TV programs, typically 30 minutes long, that mix entertainment with product demonstrations and then solicit orders placed by telephone. **Direct-response advertising** includes advertisements on TV and radio that describe products and provide an opportunity for consumers to order them.

More than 60 million American consumers now have access to a television shopping channel network; however, only 20 percent of the potential viewing audience even watches. To increase the audience, the shopping channels have increased the level of entertainment included in the programs. For example, QVC has 4 million customers, but 50 percent of the purchases are made by its top 300,000 customers.[18] TV home shopping sales in 1995 were $4.7 billion, including the $2.6 billion sales made by the two largest networks with dedicated channels: The Home Shopping Network and QVC.

REFACT The typical person watches 36 hours of programming on QVC before making a purchase.[19]

The major advantage of TV home shopping compared to catalog retailing is that customers can see the merchandise demonstrated on the TV screen. However, customers can't look at a particular type of merchandise or a specific item when they want to, as they can with catalogs. They have to wait for the time when the merchandise will be shown. To address this limitation, home shopping networks schedule categories of merchandise for specific times so customers looking for specific merchandise can plan their viewing time.

The two major shopping networks, QVC and HSN, have sophisticated telemarketing and distribution systems to support the orders stimulated by television programs.

TV home shopping retailers appeal primarily to lower-income consumers. Forty percent of TV home shopping sales are inexpensive jewelry. Other major categories are apparel, cosmetics, and exercise equipment. To broaden its target market, TV home shopping channels have attempted to upgrade the quality of merchandise sold and sell more fashion-oriented apparel. Calvin Klein and Donna Karan were considering offering their designer apparel and Saks has experimented with selling merchandise on QVC. But these efforts to sell more upscale merchandise have been unsuccessful.[20]

DIRECT SELLING

Direct selling is a retail format in which a salesperson, frequently an independent distributor, contacts a customer directly in a convenient location, either at the customer's home or at work, and demonstrates merchandise benefits, takes an order, and delivers the merchandise to the customer. Direct selling is a highly interactive form of retailing in which considerable information is conveyed to customers through face-to-face discussions with a salesperson. However, providing this high level of information, including extensive demonstrations, is costly. Retailing View 3.4 describes an entrepreneur who started a direct selling retail business and now focuses on helping others.

Annual U.S. sales for direct selling total $15.1 billion. The largest categories of merchandise sold through direct selling are cosmetics, fragrances, decorative accessories, vacuum cleaners, home appliances, cooking and kitchenware, jewelry, food and nutritional products, and encyclopedias and educational materials. For these products, the benefits of the information provided by direct selling outweigh the cost of providing the information. About three-quarters of all direct sales are made in the home, with 12 percent in the workplace, and 8 percent over the phone.[21]

Almost all of the 5.5 million salespeople who work in direct sales are independent agents. They aren't employed by the direct sales firm but act as independent distributors, buying merchandise from the firms and then reselling it to consumers. Eighty percent of the salespeople work part-time (less than 30 hours per week). In most cases, direct salespeople may sell their merchandise to anyone. But some companies (such as Avon) assign territories to salespeople who regularly contact each household in their territory.

REFACT Annual sales by direct selling in Japan are almost twice as high as in the United States. About one-half of new automobile sales are made by door-to-door salespeople in Japan.[22]

3.4

Success Means Helping Others to Succeed

JOE DUDLEY, SR., one of 11 children, grew up in a three-room farmhouse in a small North Carolina town. Labeled mentally retarded, he was held back in first grade. Today he is the owner and founder of a multimillion-dollar hair care and cosmetics company based in Greensboro, North Carolina.

Dudley Products is one of the largest minority-owned businesses in the Southeast. Dudley got his start in retailing by selling Fuller Brush products door-to-door while he was a student at North Carolina A&T. Since 1967, when he and his wife began making their own line of hair products, Dudley Products uses direct selling to distribute its products to consumers and beauty salons throughout the United States.

Dudley realized his personal goal of making $1 million by his 40th birthday. Since that time, he has devoted much of his effort to helping others reach their goals. Dudley Products instituted a high school mentor program. Students in the program meet bimonthly with Dudley executives and get a firsthand view of what it takes to succeed. Dudley and his company were honored with the North Carolina Governor's Business Award in Education and a designation as one of the 1,000 points of light by former President Bush.

Source: Company documents.

Two special types of direct selling are party plan and multilevel selling. About 20 percent of all direct sales are made using a party plan system. In a **party plan system,** salespeople encourage customers to act as hosts and invite friends or coworkers to a "party" at which the merchandise is demonstrated in a partylike atmosphere. Sales made at the party are influenced by the social relationship of the people attending with the host. The host or hostess receives a gift or commission for arranging the meeting.[23]

Almost two-thirds of all direct sales are made through multilevel sales networks. In a **multilevel network,** people serve as master distributors, recruiting other people to become distributors in their network. The master distributors either buy merchandise from the firm and resell it to their distributors or receive a commission on all merchandise purchased by the distributors in their network. In addition to selling merchandise themselves, the master distributors are involved in recruiting and training other distributors.

The Mary Kay beauty consultant provides information and services for customers that are typically not available from store-based retailers.

Some multilevel direct selling firms are illegal pyramid schemes. A pyramid scheme develops when the firm and its program are designed to sell merchandise and services to other distributors rather than to end users. The founders and initial distributors in pryamid schemes profit from the inventory bought by later participants but little merchandise is sold to consumers who use it.[24]

INTERACTIVE HOME SHOPPING

Interactive home shopping (IHS), also known as **electronic retailing,** is a retail format in which the retailer and customer communicate with each other through an interactive electronic system. In response to the customer's inquiries, the retailer transmits information and graphics to the customer's TV or computer. After an electronic dialog between the retailer and customer, the customer can order merchandise directly through the interactive system and the merchandise is typically delivered to the customer's home. Exhibit 3–4 illustrates a somewhat futuristic form of IHS.[25]

The scenario portrayed in Exhibit 3–4 is highly interactive. Judy specifies the type of merchandise sought and then FRED communicates with retailers around the world, locating a large group of alternatives. Using information about Judy's tastes, FRED reduces the large number of alternatives down to a small set that are

EXHIBIT 3–4

A Futuristic IHS Scenario

[Judy Jamison sits in front of her home electronic center reviewing her engagement calendar displayed on her TV screen. She sees that she has accepted an invitation to a formal cocktail party on Friday night and she decides to buy a new dress for the occasion. She switches to her personal electronic shopper, FRED, and initiates the following exchange:]

FRED: Do you wish to browse, go to a specific store, or buy a
       specific item?

Judy: Specific item

FRED: Type of item?

Judy: Black dress

FRED: Occasion? [menu appears on screen]

Judy: Formal cocktail party

FRED: Price range? [menu appears]

Judy: $200-$400

FRED: 497 items have been identified. How many do you want to review?

Judy: Just 5

[Five pictures of Judy in each dress appear on the screen with the price, brand name, and the IHS retailer selling it listed beneath each one. Judy clicks on one of the dresses and it is enlarged on the screen. Another click and Judy views the dress from different angles. Another click and specifications such as fabric and laundering instructions appear. Judy repeats this routine with each dress. She selects the one she finds most appealing. FRED knows her measurements and picks the size that fits her best.]

FRED: How would you like to pay for this? [menu appears]

Judy: American Express

FRED: Nieman Marcus [the firm selling the dress Judy selected] suggests a Xie scarf
       and Koslow belt to complement this dress.

[Judy clicks on the items and they appear on the screen. Judy inspects these items as she inspected the dresses. She decides to purchase both accessories. FRED then asks Judy about delivery. Judy selects two-day delivery at a cost of $5.00.]

FRED: Just a reminder. You have not purchased hosiery in 30 days. Do
       you wish to reorder at this time?

Judy: Yes

FRED: Same shades?

Judy: Yes

of most interest to Judy and personalizes the display of the merchandise for Judy. After Judy selects the merchandise she wants to buy, the retailer suggests accessories. Again the presentation of these accessories is personalized for Judy.

INTERNET EXERCISE   Go to the following retail sites and shop for a pair of pants. How do you compare your experience shopping for pants on the Internet to shopping in a local store? What are the advantages and disadvantages of the Internet shopping experience? How does your shopping experience differ from the scenario in Exhibit 3–4?

JCPenney http://www.penney.com/
Wal-Mart http://www.walmart.com/
L.L. Bean http://www.llbean.com/
Lands' End http://www.landsend.com/

Current Internet retailing sites are not like the IHS example in Exhibit 3–4. Shopping at the current retail sites is like looking through a lot of catalogs. The present Internet retail sites do not offer a broad selection of merchandise, the opportunity to easily search through a wide range of options, or the individualized presentation of merchandise illustrated in Exhibit 3–4.[26] However, it is predicted that the Internet shopping experience in Exhibit 3–4—along with the design and production of customized clothing[27]—will be available to consumers sometime soon, perhaps in less than five years.[28]

Sales forecasts for IHS range from $5 to 300 billion by the year 2000. In contrast to such projections, current sales are barely noticeable—less than $500 million in 1996.[29] While retail sales through the IHS format are small now, demographic and cultural changes suggest that an "electronic culture" is developing that will support IHS retailing. Many young people are very familiar with computers and computers themselves are taking on the status of household appliances. Penetration of home computers is currently about 30 percent and is projected to reach 60 percent by the beginning of the new millennium.[30] Integrated computer/television sets and low-cost "information appliances" designed specifically to "surf the Net" are available. In addition, technological barriers to secure, interactive communications to homes are rapidly disappearing. Retailing View 3.5 describes Cybersmith, a cyber cafe offering consumers access to the Internet and a social experience.

While U.S. consumers appear to be on the verge of accepting IHS, European consumers are more reluctant to venture on the information highway. Even technically sophisticated Europeans are reluctant to have electronic networks in their homes. For example, a 30-year-old German who owns a software design company says, "Are we going to be a society of everybody just staying at home, doing home working, home banking, and home shopping?" Europeans are also much less likely to engage in shopping patterns compatible with IHS such as renting videos and having food delivered to the home.[32]

In the remaining portion of this section, we consider three questions: (1) Will IHS become a major retail format? (2) What kind of merchandise can be sold by IHS retailers? and (3) How might this new format affect the retail industry?

REFACT Five million children under the age of 18 are regular users of the Internet. On average, children between the age of 5 and 18 who have access to computers use them 5.3 hours per week.[31]

3.5

Cybersmith—A Public Beach for Surfing the Web

CYBERSMITH IN CAMBRIDGE, MASSACHUSETTS, offers its customers high-speed access to the Internet from its 55 workstations. It also offers caffe lattes and biscottis. The access is not cheap—$10 per hour—but even people who have access from their home drop in to soak up the atmosphere, hear good music, and hang around with other cyberhipsters.

Most weekend business is families, but during the week college students and profes-sionals are Cybersmith's best customers. "They come here instead of going to the movies," says Eric McNulty, director of marketing. The Cambridge store was voted "best first date" in Boston in 1995.

Source: Cyndee Miller, "New Services for Consumers without Home Page at Home," *Marketing News*, April 23, 1996, pp. 1–2.

Growth Potential for Interactive Home Shopping

Although the IHS experience described in Exhibit 3–4 is exciting and attractive, current retail formats effectively satisfy most cus-tomer needs. A wide variety of stores are convenient to most con-sumers in the United States. Just think of the number of stores you could go to in 15 minutes to buy a VCR, a shirt, or milk. And consumers who can't get to a store easily have a wide selection of catalogs they can order from. IHS sales will grow only if the format offers consumer advantages over other existing retail formats.

Exhibit 3–5 compares the benefits and costs to consumers of six retail formats: three store-based formats (described in Chapter 2) and three nonstore formats (the traditional catalog, the present Internet offering, and the IHS format described in Exhibit 3–5).

REFACT Two-thirds of the Internet users are male. Internet users also have higher incomes and better education than the avarage U.S. citizen.[33]

Entertainment and Social Experience   Retail formats provide a variety of ben-efits to consumers other than helping them buy merchandise. For example, in-store shopping can be a stimulating experience for some people, providing a break in their daily routine and enabling consumers to interact with friends. Mall devel-opers and in-store retailers place considerable emphasis on attracting customers by satisfying these needs.

All nonstore retail formats are limited in the degree to which they can satisfy these entertainment and social needs. Even the most attractive and inventive web pages and video clips will not be as exciting as the displays and activities in a store such as Niketown. Note that Exhibit 3–5 suggests that grocery stores have less opportunity to satisfy these entertainment and social needs than other store-based retail for-mats because most people view grocery shopping as a chore to be accomplished as quickly as possible.

In-store retailers provide entertainment and oppor-tunities for social experiences that are difficult for IHS retailers to provide.

Safety   Security in malls and shopping areas is becoming an important con-cern for many shoppers. Nonstore retail formats have an advantage over store-based retailers by enabling cus-tomers to review merchandise and place orders from a safe environment—their homes.[34]

EXHIBIT 3–5   Dimensions Affecting Relative Attractiveness to Consumers of Alternative Retail Formats

DIMENSIONS	STORE-BASED RETAIL FORMATS			NON-STORE RETAIL FORMATS		
	SUPERMARKET	DEPARTMENT STORE	CATEGORY SPECIALIST	CATALOG	CURRENT INTERNET RETAILER	IHS FORMAT
Entertainment	Low	High	Medium	Low	Low	Medium
Social interaction	Medium	High	Medium	Low	Low	Low
Personal security	Low	Low	Low	High	High	High
ORDERING AND GETTING MERCHANDISE						
Locations for placing orders	Few	Few	Few	Everywhere	Many	Many
Delivery time	Immediate	Immediate	Immediate	Days	Days	Days
NUMBER OF ALTERNATIVES						
Number	Medium	Medium	Low	Low	Low	High
ASSISTANCE IN SCREENING ALTERNATIVES						
Assistance	Medium	High	Medium	Low	Low	High
MERCHANDISE INFORMATION						
Quantity of information	Medium	Medium	Medium	Medium	Medium	High
Comparison information	Medium	Medium	High	Low	Low	High
COST OF MERCHANDISE						
Retail cost for operating stores	High	High	High	Low	Low	Low
Customer time costs	High	High	High	Low	Low	Low
Customer shipping costs	Low	Low	Low	High	High	High

Ordering and Getting Merchandise   The IHS format, like most nonstore retail formats, enables consumers to order merchandise from many locations at any time of the day. However, consumers usually have to wait several days to get the merchandise. Thus, all nonstore retailers suffer in comparison to stores on this dimension.

The importance of getting merchandise to customers immediately depends on the type of buying situation and merchandise. For example, Hispanics typically buy wedding gifts just before they attend the ceremony and reception. Thus, they would be unlikely to buy wedding presents from nonstore retailers. Many items bought in a supermarket are perishable and must be taken home and stored in a refrigerator or consumed shortly after they are purchased. Thus an IHS supermarket retailer must be able to deliver orders to customers shortly after they are picked from a store or warehouse.

Number of Alternatives   As Exhibit 3–5 shows, a potential benefit of IHS compared to other retail formats is the vast number of alternatives that become available to consumers. Through IHS, a person living in Columbus, Ohio, can shop at Harrod's in London in less time than it takes to visit the local supermarket.

Having a lot more alternatives to consider might not be that much of a benefit. Consumers rarely visit more than two outlets even when buying expensive consumer durables.[35] While it is easy to go from one web site to another, finding what you want is not so easy because each web site has a different format that customers have to learn to get the information they want.

Consider Judy Jamison's search with FRED. Does Judy really care if FRED found 50 or 497 dresses initially? Having identified 497 Internet retail sites selling a product you might like, how many sites would you take the time to visit? The advantages of having a lot of alternatives is only meaningful if you have a FRED to search through them and find a few you might like to look at in detail.

Assistance in Screening Alternatives   Another potential, and more significant, benefit of IHS is the ability to have an electronic shopper like FRED search through a wide range of alternatives and select a small group for the customer to look at in detail. As indicated in Exhibit 3–5, service-oriented retailers like department stores also have this capability. Some department and specialty store sales associates know what their customers want, select a few outfits, and arrange to show these outfits to a preferred customer before the store opens or even in the customer's office. FRED provides the same service as these super sales associates; however, FRED never is in a bad mood, is not paid anything to do its job, and is always available.

FRED is called a search engine. A **search engine** or **intelligent agent** is a computer program that locates and selects alternatives based on some predetermined characteristics.[36] In the future, search engines may be computer software programs bought by consumers. The program could learn about a consumer's tastes by asking questions when it's installed on the consumer's computer. For example, when Judy adds the FRED software to her home electronic systems, the software asks her questions to learn about her tastes and preferences.

Search engines could also be used by IHS retailers, like a super sales associate in a department store, to locate merchandise the customer might like. Finally, search engines might be operated by independent companies like *Consumer Reports* to help consumers locate merchandise.

INTERNET EXERCISE   To see an example of a search engine that makes suggestions on movies and music, go to http://www.agents.com. The agent will ask you questions about the movies and music you like and then suggest other movies or albums you might enjoy. How good are the agent's predictions about what you might like?

Another agent that searches all of the companies selling CD albums on the Internet is Bargain Finder (http://bf.cstar.ac.com/). Go to this site and use the agent to find the retailer selling an album you want at the lowest cost. Did all of the retailers allow the agent into their retail sites? Why?

The Amazing Waldo (http://bf.cstar.ac.com/lifestyle) is an example of a search engine that looks for web sites compatible with your lifestyle. Was Waldo able to suggest sites of interest to you?

Providing Information to Evaluate Merchandise   One primary service benefit offered by retailers is providing information that helps customers make better purchase decisions. The retail formats shown in Exhibit 3–5 differ in terms of how much information they provide and whether customers can easily make side-by-side comparisons of different brands.

Quantity of Information   Retailers vary in the sheer amount of information provided about the merchandise they offer. For instance, some catalogs provide only a few specifications per item, such as price, weight, and brand/model. Other catalogs provide much more detail about each item carried. For many clothing items, Lands' End not only provides color pictures but often gives extensive detail about the construction process, stitching, and materials.

Electronic agents are critical for sifting through the vast amount of information available and present only information useful to the customer. The Bargainfinder agent searching for CD album prices is "blocked" by retailers who do not want customers shopping on price alone.

BargainFinder Agent

BargainFinder is now searching nine stores for their prices of your album. Clicking on the name of a store will take you directly to your album in that store.

Bear in mind that BargainFinder is an experimental prototype agent, built to support research. It may not be able to handle all of the conditions and variations that a commercial agent would. Andersen Consulting does not guarantee BargainFinder's results.

While three stores are blocking out our agents, seven others have approached us to be included in the BargainFinder experiment. Some stores may not like the agent, but most see it as an opportunity. What do you think? After BargainFinder finishes searching, <u>tell us what you think!</u>

● NEW: When BargainFinder is finished, check out <u>LifestyleFinder, featuring Waldo the Web Wizard</u>, our latest intelligent agent that recommends Web pages to you based on your lifestyle.

● Going to <u>Comdex Fall '96</u>? Come to the <u>Panel on Intelligent Agents</u>, featuring a presentation on our <u>research projects.</u>

Four by Blues Traveler :

$14.97 <u>Emusic</u> (Shipping starts at $1.99 first item, $0.49 each additional item.)
$ 14.98 <u>CD Universe</u> (Shipping starts at $2.49. World-wide shipping. 30 day returns.)
$8.00 (new) <u>GEMM</u> (Broker service for independent sellers; many used CDs, imports, etc.)
$ 14.97 <u>CDworld</u> (Variety of shipping options, starting at $2.74 for first item.)
$ 13.98 <u>Music Connection </u>(Shipping from $3.25, free for 9 or more. 20 day returns.)
<u>CDnow</u> is blocking out our agents. You may want to try browsing there yourself.
<u>NetMarket</u> is blocking out our agents. You may want to try browsing there yourself.
<u>CDLand</u> was blocking out our agents, but decided not to. You'll see their prices here soon.
<u>IMM</u> did not respond. You may want to try browsing there yourself.

Store-based retailers also differ in the information they make available to consumers. Specialty and department stores typically have trained, knowledgeable sales associates, while most discount stores do not. Customers for durable goods such as appliances report that salespeople are the most useful information source, more useful than *Consumer Reports*, advertising, and friends.[37]

Knowledgeable sales associates are able to dramatically increase the usefulness of the information they provide through their face-to-face interaction with customers. They ask questions about a customer's needs and provide specific information the customer seeks. On the other hand, many discount retailers, catalog retailers, and present Internet retailers are limited in the amount of information that they can provide on signs in the stores or through pictures and specifications on printed pages on a CRT screen.

As Exhibit 3–4 shows, IHS retailers have more opportunity to provide information to their customers than specialty and department stores. Using an interactive electronic communication channel, retailers can respond to customers' inquires just like a sales associate would. However, the information provided by the electronic database can be frequently updated and will always be available, while store-based retailers may have a difficult time retaining knowledgeable sales associates, and in many cases it is not cost-effective for them to do so. The cost of adding information to an IHS database is likely to be far less than the cost of continually training thousands of sales associates.

Comparison of Alternatives   Some retail formats allow customers to easily compare alternatives they might consider; others do not. For example, most in-store retailers stock alternative colors, styles, and brands in each merchandise product category. An appealing characteristic of category specialists such as Circuit City and Office Depot is the number of different brands and models they sell and the opportunity to make side-by-side comparisons. Similarly, consumers shopping for apparel can try on different slacks to compare their fit. Current Internet, TV home shopping, and catalog retailers do not offer this opportunity.

Consider the difficulty in comparing alternative laptop computers using the Internet sites for Toshiba (http://www.toshiba.com) and Texas Instruments (http://www.ti.com). One can directly compare alternatives only by printing the on-screen information and using the printout as a catalog or by going through a slow process of downloading images to obtain information about a single model. One cannot search for all laptops that have hard drives greater than a gigabyte, Pentium Pro processors, active matrix color screens, and 16 megabytes of RAM, and then make side-by-side comparisons of the alternatives that meet these criteria. In addition, current IHS retailers selectively present information, whereas consumers going to in-store retailers can get information they want to compare alternatives by looking over the merchandise and asking questions.

Now consider the scenario describing IHS in the future as described in Exhibit 3–4. Through FRED, Judy can compare the five dresses she was considering, side-by-side. In addition, this comparison information is tailored to Judy—she can see how the dresses look on her, not on a model in a picture. Similarly, future IHS systems will have the capability to provide side-by-side comparison information that's important to the specific customer. For example, an unsophisticated customer interested in buying audio speakers might want size and price data, while an audiophile might want details about speakers' performance.

Cost of Merchandise   Some experts suggest that IHS retailers will have much lower costs, as much as 25 percent lower than in-store retailers, because IHS retailers do not have to spend money building and operating stores at convenient locations.[38] However, IHS retailers, or their customers, will have to pay for the considerable costs of delivering merchandise in small quantities to customers' homes. Customers presently incur these costs when they spend their time and money going to stores to pick out and take merchandise home and then going back to the stores to return merchandise they don't want.

A potential cost savings for IHS retailers compared to catalog retailers is eliminating the cost of printing and distributing catalogs. However, maintaining and updating electronic presentations of merchandise information might be quite expensive.

Even though sales by Internet retailing are small now, IHS has the potential for being a major retail format and realizing optimistic sales estimates in the future, because the format can offer consumers superior benefits to those offered by present in-store and nonstore formats. Due to the interactive nature of the IHS retail format, customers can have a selection of merchandise and information about the merchandise tailored to their needs. In effect, the IHS format has the potential for preparing an individually tailored catalog for the customer each time the customer goes shopping. Using this individually tailored catalog, customers will be able to make more satisfying selections of merchandise using the IHS format compared to other formats. The key to providing these individually tailored catalogs is the availability of search engines like FRED described in Exhibit 3–4.

What Type of Merchandise Will Be Sold Effectively through the IHS Format?

In addition to the amount and presentation of information, retail formats also differ in the type of information they can present effectively. For instance, when you purchase apparel, some critical information might be "look-and-see" attributes like color and style, as well as "touch-and-feel" attributes like how the apparel fits. Customers can get both the look-and-see and touch-and-feel information when they buy merchandise in a store. When buying merchandise through nonstore outlets, touch-and-feel information isn't available. Customers' ability even to assess color depends on how good the photographic reproduction is and whether there are variations in dyeing garments from piece to piece. Fit cannot be predicted well, unless the nonstore retailer has consistent sizing and the consumer has learned over time what size to buy for a particular brand. It is impossible to feel the fabric in a dress, taste a sample of an ice cream flavor, or smell a perfume before buying the product from a nonstore retailer.

Based on the difficulty of providing touch-and-feel information through nonstore channels, one might conclude that nonstore retailers will not be able to successfully sell merchandise such as clothing, perfume, flowers, and food with important touch-and-feel attributes. However, this type of merchandise is presently sold by nonstore retailers.

The critical issue determining what types of merchandise can be sold successfully by IHS retailers is whether the IHS retailer can provide enough information prior to the purchase to make sure the customer will be satisfied with the merchandise once he gets it. Consider branded merchandise like Nautica perfume or Levi's 501 jeans. Even though you can't smell a sample of the perfume before buying it, you know that it will smell like your last bottle when you get it from the IHS retailer because the manufacturer of Nautica makes sure each bottle smells the same. Similarly, if you wear a size 30" waist, 32" inseam Levi 501 jean, you know it will fit when you buy it from an IHS or catalog retailer.

In some situations, the IHS retailer might even be able to provide superior information, compared to store retailers. For example, a parent might want to see a new toy before buying one for her child. So the parent goes to toy store to look at the toy. But there the toys are not typically displayed, so the parent can only see a picture on the side of the box containing the toy. This same picture could be displayed by an IHS retailer. In addition, the IHS retailer could provide superior information to the parent through a full-motion video clip of a child playing with the toy.

In other situations, touch-and-feel information might be important, but the information in a store is not much better than the information provided by an IHS retailer. For example, suppose you're buying a bottle of perfume for your mother. Even if you go to the store and smell the samples of all the new scents, you might not get much information to determine which one your mother would like.

The Travelocity site by the Sabre Group is very successful because it delivers all of the information customers need to make travel arrangements.

Travel Reservations

Destinations & Interests

Points of View

Travel Merchandise

Win A Pair Of Volkls! You, too, can be bad on the slopes with a new pair of Volkl skis. The price? About 30 seconds of your time. Enter our **Winter Sports contest** today.

Mo' Better Miles. Earn more miles and points each time you travel. Get the latest information on award programs and how to earn miles without even flying in **@Frequent Flyer**. Travel Merchandise's newest service store.

Tales From The Middle Seat. We've all been there. Wedged in the middle seat for a long flight. Stuck in a resort that wasn't *anything* like the brochure promised. Share your tales or be square in **Rants**.

Thursday, March 20, 1997

Spring Fare Specials.
America West and **American** are offering special advance-purchase fares in the United States and Canada until 3/25, travel good thru 9/30...**Lufthansa** is offering European blitzes until 6/17 from major U.S. cities to Paris, Brussels, Zurich and Milan...**US Airways** is offering r/t fares from $228 to $588 in major U.S. markets until 3/25 for travel until 9/30 (advance-purchase and minimum-stay requirements). Check **Flights** for details.

 Flight Paging Arrives. If you own an alphanumeric pager with national access, you can subscribe to **Flight Paging**, our *new, free* event-notification service that tells you via pager of flight delays, arrival, departure and gate information for many airlines.

Don't Wait For Spring. Go to *it*. **Travelocity Cruises** by Cruises Inc. offers you the sweetest deals on **vacations that'll float your boat.**

Saving You Money. Radisson Hotels is the latest member of our growing cadre of **Last Minute Deals**.

Go All Out. Travelocity and *ComputerLife* magazine is the winning combination for a free trip for two to Miami and a stay at a Miami Hilton. Enter the **"All-Out Adventure Sweepstakes"** by 3/31 and you could win this or other adventuresome prizes.

ABOUT - FEEDBACK - HELP

In this situation, in-store retailers have no benefit over IHS and other nonstore retailers in terms of information about the merchandise. Nonstore retailers might even have a benefit over in-store retailers because they will save you the time and effort in packaging and sending the gift to your mother. For this reason, gifts represent a substantial portion of sales made by present IHS and catalog retailers.

Some services retailers have been very successful over the Internet, because their look-and-see offering can be delivered over the system. For example, Travelocity (http://www.travelocity.com) is an Internet travel planning service offered by the Sabre Group. After you go to the Internet site and fill in an on-line form indicating your

Electronic and in-store retailers have advantages and disadvantages from the consumer's perspective. Why would some consumer choose to buy jewelry from Wal-Mart's electronic offering while others would prefer to shop for jewelry in a store?

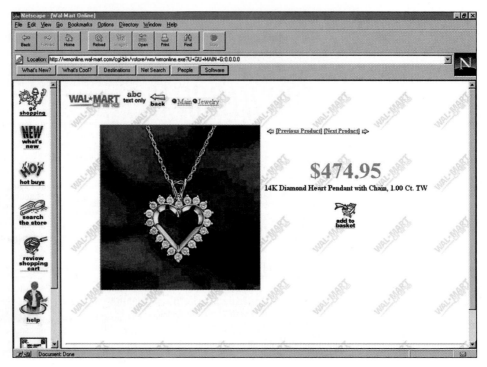

destination and preferred departure time, the electronic agent locates the lowest-cost fare for the flight. To purchase a ticket, you simply click on the purchase ticket icon, enter your credit card information, and get an E-ticket confirmation number. Travel service providers like Travelocity and Expedia (http://expedia.msn.com) provide detailed information about destinations like the location of hotels on a map.[39] Due to the appeal of the Internet for providing services, NCNB, the 20th largest bank in the United States, is making major investments to provide banking services over the Internet.[40]

Impact of IHS on the Retail Industry—What Might Happen in the Future?

The IHS channel provides an attractive opportunity for retailers and manufacturers to expand their customer base with relatively low cost and risk. Local and regional retailers can become national and international retailers overnight without making significant investments in store locations, visual merchandising, and leases.[41]

This opportunity is particularly attractive to firms with strong brand names but limited locations and distribution. For example, retailers such as Harrod's, Bloomingdale's, and Nieman Marcus are widely known for offering unique, high-quality merchandise but require customers to travel to England or major U.S. cities to buy many of the items they carry. Similarly, manufacturers such as Godiva Chocolates with strong brand names but limited distribution due to a small market base can reach customers across the world through the Internet.[42]

On the other hand, retailers with extensive distribution are concerned about the IHS channel because it might cannibalize their in-store sales. Most in-store retailers view IHS as a college football coach would view an inquiry by the NCAA Infractions Committee. It is something they prefer to avoid but find too dangerous to ignore. Thus most large in-store retailers are just "putting their toe in the water" and establishing Internet sites with a limited number of offerings; such

Customers stopping at Boston's Cybersmith café can drink exotic coffees while doing their shopping on-line.

sites don't have the features and merchandise assortments to attract a large number of customers. Many of the sites are used to support their in-store business rather than develop substantial sales. For example, JCPenney has a nationwide bridal registry that can be accessed from its stores and also through the Internet.

Large in-store retail firms have two primary concerns about IHS retailing: intensified price competition and disintermediation. Let's look at these concerns.

Greater Price Competition Many retailers offer similar assortments of branded merchandise and thus have difficulty differentiating themselves on the basis of their merchandise offering. However, price competition is reduced by geography. Consumers typically shop at the stores and malls closest to where they live and work. However, with IHS retailing, consumers can search for merchandise across the globe at low cost. The number of stores that a consumer can visit to compare prices is not limited by physical distance.

To limit price comparisons, present IHS retailers make it hard for customers to go from one Internet site to another. IHS retailers do not use a standard interface so customers need to learn how to search through the offerings at each new site they visit. In addition, Internet retailers electronically prevent search agents like FRED from accessing their sites and collecting information about the products sold at the site.

As mentioned previously, one key benefit of the IHS format is the ability to shop the world and easily compare alternatives from different retailers. Thus by making these comparisons difficult, IHS retailers are limiting the attractiveness and growth of the format. However, consumers eventually will insist on making these comparisons and will reward IHS retailers that offer this service by going to their sites. If FRED is not allowed in at a site, FRED's owner will buy from competing sites that let FRED in.

3.6

Amazon.com: Selling Books on the Internet

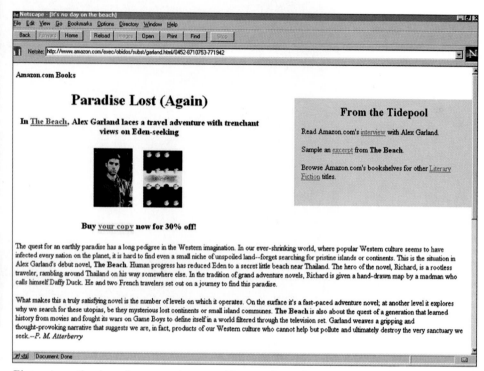

Electronic retailers have the opportunity to provide up-to-date information tailored to customer needs. For example, Amazon.com offers book reviews, sample excerpts, and interviews with authors.

ONE OF THE MOST SUCCESSFUL Internet retailers, Amazon.com was started by Jeffrey Bezos, a former programmer on Wall Street. Amazon.com (http://www. amazon.com/) has used the technology of the Internet to provide services for book lovers and buyers that they can't get from traditional in-store retailers or catalogers. Customers can search through a database of 1.1 million books on-line (five times more titles than Barnes & Noble offers in its superstores) and access reviews or short synopses for titles they find interesting. After you select a book, the system is programmed to suggest other books by the same author or of the same genre. An electronic chat room is provided for customers to share their own opinions about different books; authors frequently drop in electronically to post their comments. Recently a book entitled *Sponging: A Guide to Living Off Those You Love* got rave reviews, catapulting it to Amazon's best-seller list. Finally, customers can tell Amazon about their favorite authors and subjects and then receive E-mail on new books that might be of interest.

Traditional bookstores still have some advantages over Amazon. While books from Amazon are discounted 10 to 30 percent, a $3 service charge plus $.95 per book is added to each order. It takes Amazon about a week to deliver books that aren't best-sellers—even longer for some obscure titles.

Amazon's retail operation demonstrates the potential economies for IHS retailers. The company generates about $20 million in annual sales, is open 24 hours a day, and has customers in 66 countries. To support this retail activity, Amazon has only 33 employees and a 17,000–square-foot warehouse.

Source: G. Bruce Knecht, "How Wall Street Whiz Found a Niche Selling Books on the Internet," *The Wall Street Journal,* May 16, 1996, pp. A1, A6; and "A Literary Hangout—without the Latte," *Business Week,* September 23, 1996, p. 108.

Rather than using location to reduce price competition, IHS retailers might resort to selling more unique private-label merchandise or partnering with national brand manufacturers to develop unique cobranded merchandise such as Levi's for Sears.

Another approach for reducing the emphasis on price is providing better services and information. Because of these services, customers might be willing to pay high prices for the merchandise. Retailing View 3.6 describes an innovative IHS book retailer offering unique services for its customers.

An interesting parallel can be drawn between the introduction of IHS into the present retail environment and the development of discount stores 40 years ago.[43] Discount stores offered consumers a chance to give up personalized service in return for lower prices. In response, department and specialty stores attempted to avoid such competition by having state and federal governments pass fair trade laws—laws that forced all retailers to sell merchandise at the same price. Proponents of fair trade laws argued that without some protection, discount stores would drive department and specialty stores out of business. Meanwhile, consumers would become more price sensitive, and retailers would adjust over time to focus on offering low price and no services. Ultimately some consumers would suffer because no retailer would be motivated to provide the services that those consumers find valuable. While discount stores did increase price competition in some merchandise categories, many consumers continue to shop at retailers such as Nordstrom that provide superior information and services even though they charge a higher price.

Although consumers shopping through an IHS channel will be able to collect price information with little effort, they will also be able to get a lot of other information about the quality and performance of products at a low cost. For instance, an electronic merchant of custom oriental rugs can clearly show real differences in patterns and materials used for construction. An electronic grocery service such as Peapod can allow the customer to sort cereals by nutritional content, thus making it easier to use that attribute in decision making.

Disintermediation   Both in-store and nonstore retailers are concerned about disintermediation. **Disintermediation** is when a manufacturer sells directly to consumers bypassing retailers. This concern arises because manufacturers can get direct access to consumers by establishing a retail site on the Internet without making the heavy investment that retailers have made in store locations. But retailers are more efficient in dealing with customers directly than manufacturers are. They have considerably more experience than manufacturers in (1) distributing merchandise directly to customers, (2) providing assortments, and (3) collecting and using information about customers.

Distribution Efficiency   As mentioned previously, when customers shop at retail stores, they bear the cost of transporting merchandise from stores to their homes and bringing unsatisfactory merchandise back to the store. When buying from an IHS retailer, the cost of home delivery is included in the purchase price and this cost can be substantial.

Manufacturers have distribution systems designed to receive large orders from retail firms and deliver truckloads of goods to retailers' stores or warehouses. However, many retailers, particularly catalog retailers, have very efficient systems for taking orders from individual customers, packaging the merchandise ordered for shipping, and delivering it to homes.

Assortments of Complementary Merchandise   The opportunity for an IHS retailer to make multiple-item sales is important for two reasons. First, by making multiple-item purchases from an IHS supplier, customers reduce the shipping costs, thereby reducing the price. Second, the IHS retailer is in an ideal position to tailor a second offering to a customer based on the customer's primary purchase. Remember how the retailer in Exhibit 3–4 suggested the belt and scarf to go with the dress Judy ordered. Present retailers are skillful at putting assortments of merchandise together, a skill that most manufacturers lack. For example, if consumers want to buy a dress shirt and tie directly from the manufacturers, they must visit two different Internet sites and still can't be sure that the shirt and tie will go together.

Collection and Utilization of Customer Information   As mentioned previously, an important benefit that can be provided by IHS retailers is tailoring information to the needs of a specific customer. Present retailers have considerable information about their customers that they use to perform this service. However, manufacturers have limited information about specific customers who buy their products.

A Nutshell View of IHS   Sales by IHS retailers are very small now but have substantial growth potential. However, IHS retailers will be successful when they design their format to provide superior benefits over existing retail formats. The critical benefit that IHS retailers can provide is the opportunity for consumers to search across a broad range of alternatives, develop a smaller set of alternatives based on their needs, and get the specific information about alternatives they want. Current Internet retailers do not provide these benefits; however IHS retailers in the future will provide these benefits in response to consumer demand.

The type of merchandise sold by IHS retailers depends on delivery costs, the consumer's need for immediacy, and the degree to which electronic retailers can provide prepurchase information that helps a customer determine whether he will be satisfied with the merchandise. Successful IHS retailers will overcome the limitations of collecting touch-and-feel data by offering testimonials from other buyers, providing video information about the experience with the merchandise, or using information about brand–size combinations that fit specific members of the household. For experienced consumers, brand name alone may be enough information to predict satisfaction with the purchase decision.

Disintermediation by manufacturers will be rare because most manufacturers do not have the capability of efficiently distributing merchandise to individual consumers, providing assortments, and using information about specific consumers to develop individual catalogs for specific customers.

SUMMARY   Nonstore retailing is a small, but growing sector in the retail industry. The major nonstore retailing formats are direct selling, vending machines, catalog and direct-mail retailing, TV home shopping, and interactive home shopping (electronic retailing). Each of these formats communicates with customers using different media and offers different levels of interactivity.

Electronic retailing (interactive home shopping) has substantial growth opportunities. Present offerings on the Internet are very attractive, but in the future Internet retailers will give customers the chance to shop the world and use electronic agents to help them sift through the information quickly and locate what they want.

KEY TERMS

catalog retailing, *69*

direct-mail retailing, *69*

direct-response
  advertising, *74*

direct selling, *75*

disintermediation, *89*

electronic retailing, *77*

infomercial, *74*

intelligent agent, *81*

interactive home shopping
  (IHS), *77*

multilevel network, *76*

nonstore retailing, *67*

party plan system, *76*

search engine, *81*

TV home shopping
  retailing, *74*

vending machine
  retailing, *73*

DISCUSSION QUESTIONS & PROBLEMS

1. What are the five different nonstore retail formats? Which format has the greatest annual sales? Which format has the greatest annual growth rate?

2. Why do vending machine retailers primarily sell merchandise priced below $1?

3. Why do consumers like to buy gifts from nonstore retailers?

4. Which of the following categories of merchandise do you think could be sold effectively by nonstore retailers: jewelry, TV sets, computer software, high-fashion apparel, pharmaceuticals, and health care products such as toothpaste, shampoo, and cold remedies? Why?

5. If interactive home shopping retail sales increase dramatically, which retailers will experience declines? Why? Which of the following retail formats are most vulnerable to lose sales to IHS retailers: catalog and direct-mail retailers, supermarkets, category specialists, home improvement centers, and drug stores?

6. At this point in time, the typical person who surfs the Internet is male and has a relatively high income. If you were going to develop a retail site on the Internet, what typical lines of merchandise and services would you offer to attract this typical user?

SUGGESTED READINGS

Bartlett, Richard. *The Direct Option.* College Station, TX: Texas A&M University, 1994.

Deighton, John. "The Future of Interactive Marketing." *Harvard Business Review,* November-December 1996, pp. 151–65.

Gehrt, Kenneth, Laura Yale, and Diana Lawson. "The Convenience of Catalog Shopping: Is There More to It than Time?" *Journal of Direct Marketing* 10 (Autumn 1996), pp. 19–28.

"Mail-Order Shopping: Which Is Best?" *Consumer Reports,* October 1994, pp. 620–27.

Milne, George, and Mary Ellen Gordon. "A Segmentation Study of Consumers' Attitudes toward Direct Mail." *Journal of Direct Marketing* 8 (Spring 1994), pp. 45–52.

Peterson, Robert, and Gerald Albaum. "What Is Direct Selling? Definition, Perspectives, and Research." *Journal of Personal Selling and Sales Management* 16 (Fall 1996), pp. 1–16.

Rayport, Jeffrey, and John Sviokla. "Managing in the Marketspace." *Harvard Business Review,* November-December 1994, pp. 141–49.

"Retailing on the Internet: Seeking the Truth beyond the Hype." *Chain Store Age,* September 1995, pp. 33–72.

Shields, Grainne. "Direct Marketing in the UK: Rhetoric and Reality." *Journal of Direct Marketing* 10 (Winter 1996), pp. 59–70.

Topol, Martin, and Elaine Sherman. "Trends and Challenges of Expanding Internationally via Direct Marketing." *Journal of Direct Marketing* 8 (Winter 1994), pp. 12–19.

"Wired Kingdom." *Chain Store Age,* January 1997, pp. 1A–14A.

Retail Internet Sites

RETAIL TRADE ASSOCIATIONS

Food Marketing Institute	http://www.fmi.org
Grocery Manufacturers Association	http://www.gmabrands.org
National-America Wholesale Grocers Association	http://www.nawga-ifda.org
National Association of Convenience Stores	http://www.cstorecentral.com
National Grocer Association	http://www.onetoone.com/nga
National Retail Federation	http://www.nrf.com
National Retail Hardware Association	http://www.nhra.org

FOOD RETAILERS

A&P	http://www.aptea.com
AUCHAN (France)	http://one.auchen.com
Food Lion	http://www.foodlion.com
Fred Meyer	http://www.fredmeyer.com
Hannaford	http://www.hannaford.com
H.E. Butt	http://www.heb.com
IGA (Independent Grocers Alliance)	http://www.igainc.com
Ralphs	http://www.ralphs.com
J. Sainsbury (UK)	http://www.j-sainsbury.co.uk
Tesco (UK)	http://www.tesco.co.uk
Trader Joe's	http://www.traderjoes.com
Wegmans	http://www.wegmans.com
Whole Foods Market	http://www.wholefoods.com

CONVENIENCE STORES

RaceTrac	http://www.racetrac.com
7-Eleven	http://www.7elevenusa.com

DEPARTMENT STORES

Bloomingdale's	http://www.bloomingdales.com
Bon-Ton Stores	http://www.bonton.com
Boscov's Department Stores	http://www.boscovs.com
Carson Pirie Scott	http://www.carsons.com
Dillards	http://www.azstarnet.com/dillards
Eaton's (Canada)	http://www.eatons.com
Federated Department Stores	http://www.fedrated-fds.com
Gottschalks	http://www.gotts.com
JCPenney	http://www.jcpenney.com
Macy's	http://www.macys.com
Marks & Spencer (UK)	http://www.marks-and-spencer.com
Marshall Fields	http://www.shop-at.com/marshallfields
May Company	http://www.maycompany.com
Mercantile Stores	http://www.mercstores.com
Neiman Marcus	http://www.neimanmarcus.com
Nordstrom	http://www.nordstrom-pta.com
Sears, Roebuck	http://www.sears.com

GENERAL MERCHANDISE DISCOUNT STORES

Carrefour (France)	http://www.carrefour.fr.
Kmart	http://www.kmart.com
Target	http://www.targetstores.com
Wal-Mart	http://www.wal-mart.com

APPENDIX

Retail Internet Sites
(continued)

SPECIALTY STORES	
Autozone	http://www.autozone.com.
Body Shop (UK)	http://www.the-body-shop.com
Borders Books and Music	http://www.borders.com
Burlington Coat Factory	http://www.coat.com
Casual Man/Big & Tall	http://www.thinkbig.com
Container Store	http://www.containerstore.com
Disney Store	http://store.disney.com
Express	http://www.express.style.com
Eddie Bauer	http://www.ebauer.com
FAO Schwarz	http://www.faoschwarz.com
Foot Locker	http://www.footlocker.com
The Gap	http://www.gapinc.com
The Nature Company	http://www.natureco.com
Pep Boys	http://www.pepboys.com
Pier 1 Imports	http://www.pier1.com
Radio Shack	http://www.radioshack.com
Roots	http://www.roots.com.
Warner Brothers Store	http://www.studio.warnerbrothers.com
Western Auto	http://www.westernauto.com

DRUG STORES	
Arbor Drugs	http://www.arbordrugs.com
CVS	http://www.cvs.com
Drug Emporium	http://www.drugemporium.com
Eckerds	http://www.eckerd.com
Osco	http://www.americandrugstores.com
Revco	http://www.revco.com
Rite-Aid	http://www.riteaid.com
Save-on Drugs	http://www.americandrugstores.com
Walgreens	http://www.walgreens.com

CATEGORY SPECIALISTS	
Best Buy	http://www.bestbuy.com
Blockbuster	http://www.blockbuster.com
Circuit City	http://www.circuitcity.com/
CompUSA	http://www.compusa.com
Media Play	http://www.mediaplay.com
Office Max	http://www.officemax.com
PETsMART	http://www.petsmart.com
Sports Authority	http://www.pwr.com/SportsAuthority
Staples	http://www.staples.com
Toys "R" Us	http://www.tru.com

OFF-PRICE RETAILERS	
Ross Stores	http://www.rossstores.com
Tuesday Morning	http://www.tuesdaymorning.com

APPENDIX

Retail Internet Sites
(concluded)

WAREHOUSE CLUBS	
Meijers	http://www.meijers.com
Price/Costco	http://www.pricecostco.com
Sam's Club	http://www.samsclub.com
HOME IMPROVEMENT CENTERS	
Home Depot	http://www.homedepot.com
Lowe's	http://www.lowes.com
Payless Cashway	http://www.cashways.com
Wickes Lumber	http://www.wickes.com
CATALOG RETAILERS	
Lands' End	http://www.landsend.com
L.L. Bean	http://www.llbean.com
Patagonia	http://www.patagonia.com

NOTES

1. "A Mouse-Potato's Guide to Holiday Shopping," *Websight*, November-December 1996, pp. 24–28.

2. See also Connie Bauer and John Miglautsch, "A Conceptual Definition of Direct Marketing," *Journal of Direct Marketing* 6 (Spring 1992), pp. 7–17.

3. Caryne Brown, "Door-to-Door Selling Grows Up," *Black Enterprise*, December 1992, pp. 76–90; and Kate Ballen, "Get Ready for Shopping at Work," *Fortune*, February 15, 1988, pp. 96–97.

4. Cynthia Crossen and Ellen Graham, "Pressed for Time or Pressed for Money?" *The Wall Street Journal*, March 8, 1996, p. B4; George Milne and Mary Ellen Gordon, "A Segmentation Study of Consumers' Attitudes toward Direct Mail," *Journal of Direct Marketing* 8 (Spring 1994), pp. 45–52; Robert Mamis, "Toward Hassle-Free Mail Order," *Inc.*, January 1993, p. 42; Soyean Shim and Marianne Mahoney, "The Elderly Mail-Order Catalog User of Fashion Products," *Journal of Direct Marketing* 6 (Winter 1992), pp. 49–58; and James Pelter and John Schribowsky, "The Use of Need-Based Segmentation for Developing Segment-Specific Direct Marketing Strategies," *Journal of Direct Marketing* 6 (Summer 1992), pp. 44–53.

5. "Mail-Order Shopping: Which Catalogs Are Best?" *Consumer Reports*, October 1994, p. 622.

6. "Highlights of the Mail Order Marketplace," *Direct Marketing*, August 1996, p. 49.

7. *1996 Statistical Fact Book* (New York: Direct Marketing Association, 1996).

8. "Mail-Order Shopping: Which Catalogs Are Best?" pp. 622–23.

9. "25 Leading Mail-Order Companies Worldwide," *Direct Marketing*, August 1996, p. 56.

10. Kelly Shermach, "Retail Catalogs Designed to Boost In-Store Sales," *Marketing News*, July 3, 1995, pp. 1–3.

11. John Simone, "The Mailing of America," *VM&SD*, November 1992, pp. 24–32.

12. "Critical Issues," *Catalog Age*, December 1996, pp. 54–61.

13. Personal communication.

14. "Mail-Order Shopping: Which Catalogs Are Best?" p. 627.

15. *1996 Statistical Fact Book*, p. 113.

16. Glen Nowak and Joseph Phillips, "Understanding Privacy Concerns," *Journal of Direct Marketing* 6, no. 2 (1992), pp. 28–39.

17. "1996 State of the Vending Industry Report," *Automatic Merchandiser*, August 1996, pp. 19–44.

18. "Home Shopping: Home Alone?" *Economist*, October 12, 1996, pp. 67–68.

19. Jason Hudson, "Paper Remains the King," *Chain Store Age*, April 1, 1995, p. 56.

20. "Amid Turmoil, QVC Eyes the Future," *Chain Store Age Executive*, August 1994, pp. 23–24; Sharon Edelson, "Home Shopping Club Tones Down the Glitz and Puts on the Ritz," *Women's Wear Daily*, October 11, 1994, pp. 1, 13; Sharon Edelson, "Fashion Reevaluates Flickering Fortunes of TV Home Shopping," *Women's Wear Daily*, November 8, 1995.

21. *Worldwide Direct Sales Data* (Washington, DC: World Federation of Direct Selling Associations, July 1995); and Gerald Albaum and Robert Peterson, *Consumer Preferences for Buying from Direct Selling Companies*, (Washington, DC: Direct Selling Educational Foundation, 1987).

22. *Worldwide Direct Sales Data*; and Valarie Retiman, "In Japan's Car Market, Big Three Face Rivals Who Go Door to Door," *The Wall Street Journal*, September 28, 1994, pp. a1, a6.

23. John Anderson, "Hitting the Party Circuit," *Selling*, September 1994, pp. 28–31.

24. Mario Brossi and Joseph Marino. *Multilevel Marketing: A Legal Primer* (Washington, DC: Direct Selling Association, 1990).

25. This section is based on Joseph Alba, John Lynch, Barton Weitz, Chris Janiszewski, Richard Lutz, and Stacy Wood, "Interactive Home Shopping and the Retail Industry," working paper (Cambridge, MA: Marketing Science Institute, 1997).

26. Joan Rigdon, "Caught in the Web," *The Wall Street Journal*, June 17, 1996, p. R14; and Michael Martin, "Why the Web Is Still a No Shop Zone," *Fortune*, February 5, 1996, pp. 127–28.

27. Louise Lee, "Garment Scanner Could Be Perfect Fit," *The Wall Street Journal*, September 20, 1994, pp. B1, B8.

28. "The Future of Clothing," *Wired*, November 1996, p. 76; Donna Hoffman, Thomas Novak, and Patrali Chatterjee, "Commercial Scenarios for the Web: Opportunities and Challenges," *Journal of Computer Mediated Communications*, Special Issue on Electronic Commerce 1 (December 1995), pp. 12–25.

29. Bruce Fox, "Retailing on the Internet: Seeking Truth beyond the Hype," *Chain Store Age Executive*, September 1995, pp. 33–35; and Jennifer Pellet, "The Future of Electronic Retail," *Discount Merchandiser*, January 1996, pp. 36–46.

30. "U.S. Computer Sales Said to Slow," *The New York Times*, March 20, 1996, p. D7.

31. Leslie Miller, "Surfing Kids Share Their Cyberspace View," *The Wall Street Journal*, October 24, 1996, p. 4D.

32. Tara Parker-Pope, "Interactive Services Have Less Appeal in Europe than in U.S., Survey Says," *The Wall Street Journal*, June 20, 1995, p. B10.

33. Thomas Weber, "Who Uses the Internet?" *Chain Store Age*, December 9, 1996, p. R6.

34. Reid Claxton, "Customer Safety: Direct Marketing's Undermarketed Advantage," *Journal of Direct Marketing* 9 (Winter 1995), pp. 67–78.

35. William Wilkie and Peter R. Dickson, "Consumer Information Search and Shopping Behavior," working paper (Cambridge, MA: Management Science Institute, 1985).

36. "'Intelligent Agent' Test Probes Consumers' On-Line Shopping Needs," *Stores*, November 1996, pp. 47–88; and Patricia Maes, "Agents That Reduce Work and Information Overload," *Communications of the ACM* 37 (July 1994), pp. 31–40.

37. Wilkie and Dickson, "Consumer Information Search and Shopping Behavior."

38. John Verity and Robert Hof, "The Internet: How Will It Change the Way You Do Business?" *Business Week*, November 14, 1994, pp. 80–88.

39. Stan Gibson, "10 Who Dared to Be Different," *PC Week*, January 6, 1997, pp. 21–24; and Mary Behr, "Travel: Book Now for the Best," *PC Magazine*, January 1997, p. 103.

40. Nikhil Deogun, "A Tough Bank Boss Takes On Computers, with Real Trepidation," *The Wall Street Journal*, July 25, 1996, pp. A1, A4.

41. W. R. Rennie, "Global Competitiveness: Born Global," *McKinsey Quarterly*, September 22, 1993, pp. 42–52.

42. John Quelch and Lisa Klein, "The Internet and International Marketing," *Sloan Management Review*, Spring 1996, pp. 60–75.

43. Mary Jane Sheffet and Debra L. Scammon, "Resale Price Maintenance: Is It Safe to Suggest Retail Prices?" *Journal of Marketing* 49 (Fall 1985), pp. 82–91.

4

The Retail Customer

THE WORLD OF RETAILING

1. Introduction to the World of Retailing
2. Store-Based Retailing
3. Nonstore Retailing—Electronic Retailing and Catalogs
4. **The Retail Customer**
5. Customer Buying Behavior

RETAILING STRATEGY

MERCHANDISE MANAGEMENT

STORE MANAGEMENT

QUESTIONS

- How are retailers responding to demographic trends such as the maturing baby boomers and emerging Generation Xers?

- What are the fastest-growing ethnic groups in the United States?

- Should retailers target upper-, middle-, or lower-income groups?

- How are retailers meeting the needs of time-starved consumers?

- Do most people still have to get dressed up to go to work?

CONSIDER THE NEAR FUTURE in the year 2001. The place: Dimlit Drug Store in downtown Hartigan, a modest town in the southwestern United States. The poorly lit store is filled with a random assortment of somewhat dusty merchandise. It's 5 P.M., and business is slow as usual. One teenage clerk behind a cash register ponders why he took such a boring job, while the 60-year-old owner/pharmacist is wondering why business is so bad. He'll worry about it tomorrow; the store closes at 5:30, just as always.

Out in the suburbs at the new Walgreens drugstore in the shopping center next to Blockbuster Video and the Safeway supermarket, the scene is quite different. The parking lot is jammed with men and women coming home from work. Since they're in a hurry to do some errands before they get dinner on the table for their families, they do one-stop shopping to save time. They can go to either the supermarket or drugstore to pick up milk and a prescription. Although Blockbuster has a broader selection, they could also rent a film at Safeway. Both stores are open late, seven days a week.

Walgreens' part-time pharmacist is a man in his 70s who retired from his own drugstore a few years ago. It's not unusual for retailers to seek out older part-time workers since they're experienced and reliable, and there's a shortage of young workers. He's filling a prescription for a tourist from New Jersey. The pharmacist can get the tourist's prescription information from a Walgreens in the tourist's hometown via satellite. The pharmacist gives the prescription to a young woman who works after school as part of a vocational training program. She scans the bar code on the prescription label at the point-of-sale terminal. This information is used to update the inventory management system that automatically reorders merchandise and produces a sales receipt.

Customers don't just wander aimlessly through aisles of cluttered merchandise as they might at Dimlit. Walgreens has a computer terminal for customers to place special orders plus databases that they can use to get information on products and health-related matters. Some products as well as the music are geared to the store's primarily Hispanic-American clientele. Most employees are bilingual; announcements are made in both English and Spanish. The store is readily accessible to the handicapped. Signs use large, easy-to-read lettering. Employees are trained to cater to special needs of the elderly.

Walgreens employees are encouraged to participate in civic events and charities. The store manager is a Girl Scout leader; one pharmacist coordinates a food drive for the homeless with other area retailers and restaurants. Recycling bins are found in the parking lot. The store also attempts to purchase products that are ecologically safe.

The difference between these two stores is that one anticipated and accommodated the profound demographic trends of today's population, while the other tried to resist them and ended up losing.

This chapter is the first of two that focuses on the customer. In this chapter, we examine several consumer trends and how retailers are reacting to them. Next, Chapter 5 concentrates on customer needs, buying behavior, and how retailers segment their markets. This chapter begins with three sections that describe important shifts in consumer **demographics** (vital statistics about populations): generational cohorts, ethnic diversity, and income. The fourth section discusses the decline of traditional household managers. Specifically it examines how the women's market has changed and how our time-poor society has created opportunities for many retailers. The last section looks at changes in consumer values. Social consciousness, environmental sensitivity, the value-oriented customer, cocooning, and dress-down fashions are discussed.

INTERNET EXERCISE   *American Demographics* is an interesting magazine with articles on changing U.S. lifestyles. Go to their site on the Internet (http://www.demographics.com), select an article in an issue of the magazine, and discuss how the information in the article can help retailers better understand and appreciate the needs of their changing customer base. What should retailers do based on the information in this article to improve their performance?

GENERATIONAL COHORTS

Retailers and their vendors find it useful to group people into generations and then market to them differently. In general, a **generational cohort**—people within the same generation—have similar purchase behaviors because they have shared experiences and are in the same stage of life. For instance, although baby boomers (people born after World War II, 1946 through 1964) and Generation Xers (people born between 1965 and 1976) gravitate toward products and services that foster a casual lifestyle, they do so for different reasons. Baby boomers are desperately trying to maintain their youth. This group, who grew up in jeans and khakis, continue this

4.1

Generational Retailing: Targeting the Generations

THE MARKETERS AT LEVI STRAUSS are masters in selling to different generations. They first introduced the firm's wildly successful Dockers line of loose-fitting casual pants in 1986, aiming their promotions directly at baby boomers. The ads featured middle-aged men fishing on a dock. More recent promotions are aimed straight at Xers. Why the shift in promotional strategy? The company had successfully penetrated the older market, but it wasn't appealing to the Xers. The youth-seeking boomer customer could identify with the imagery of younger men, but that didn't work the other way around. That's why you don't see overweight, balding men in Dockers commercials anymore.

Domain, a chain of high-fashion furniture, has learned through research that its core baby boomer clientele, who have always valued personal growth, is as concerned about self-improvement issues as it is about decorating. So it launched a series of in-store seminars—one on women's issues such as how to start a business, the other on design issues. Repeat business among this segment has nearly doubled since the new programs began.

Domain has also launched a new furniture series for older clients. The sofas are narrower, with more back support, and aren't as deep as boomer sofas—that makes getting out of them easier.

Source: Faye Rice, "Making Generational Marketing Come of Age," *Fortune*, June 26, 1995, pp. 110–14.

practice and have brought casual dressing into their businesses. Xers wear jeans and khakis because they are less impressed with symbols of conspicuous consumption than their parents. Besides, jeans are comfortable and relatively inexpensive— and at this stage of their lives, many Xers don't have much money. Retailing View 4.1 examines how Levi Strauss and Domain target multiple generations.

Although there are many ways to cut the generational pie, we will discuss four major groups. Also, the exact definitions for these groups shift as time goes by. For instance, older baby boomers have become young silver streakers. Meanwhile, the youngest group—Generation Y—gets bigger with each new birth. For our purposes, however, the four generational cohorts are

GENERATIONAL COHORT	DATES OF BIRTH	AGE IN 1998
Generation Y	1977–1998	0–21
Generation X	1965–1976	22–33
Baby boomers	1946–1964	34–52
Silver streakers	Before 1946	53 and older

Generation Y Americans aged 21 and younger will form a generation as big as the original baby boom (discussed later in this section.)[1] **Generation Y**—no fewer than 72 million Americans—represents 28 percent of the population, compared to 30 percent for the baby boomers. They are also growing up in a very different world than their parents did. Exhibit 4–1 compares 10 cultural attributes of the original baby boom with today's youth.

If you could sum up Generation Y in a single word, the word would be *diverse*. First, the original baby boomers are 75 percent non-Hispanic white, compared to only 67 percent in this group. As a result, retailers and their vendors develop

EXHIBIT **4–1**

Ten Cultural Attributes of the Original Baby Boom and Generation Y

ORIGINAL BABY BOOM

1. cold war
2. nuclear threat
3. mother's care
4. "Father Knows Best"
5. TV dinners
6. network TV
7. 45s and "American Bandstand"
8. Ma Bell
9. VW buses
10. free love

GENERATION Y

1. regional wars
2. terrorist threats
3. day care
4. father isn't home
5. low-fat fast food
6. cable TV
7. CDs and MTV
8. Internet
9. minivans
10. condoms

Source: Susan Mitchell, "The Next Baby Boom," *American Demographics,* October 1995, pp. 22–31.

REFACT Teenagers spend almost $100 billion a year.[2]

products and promotions with much broader appeal than in the past. For instance, Fisher-Price (a subsidiary of toymaker Mattel) has Dream Doll House families that are African-American, Hispanic, Asian, and Caucasian. Some firms shoot different versions of the same ad using rap, alternative rock, and even country music to reach different groups of teens and children. Second, Generation Y is more likely to live with single mothers, never-married mothers, or grandparents than children in previous generations. If they do live with both parents, it's likely that both parents are working outside the home. Finally, there is likely to be more gender-bending—acceptance of products and advertising that appeal to both sexes. For instance, Calvin Klein is marketing a unisex fragrance called "cK one." Tomorrow's young men are more likely to try hair color and jewelry, while women will be more likely to visit the hardware store.

Generation Y's market shows similar attitudes and shopping patterns throughout the world.[3] They watch MTV and "90210," drink Coke, eat Big Macs, watch the same movies, surf the Internet, and wear baggy Levi's

Teenagers throughout the world have similar attitudes and shopping patterns because they have been influenced by a worldwide media web; for example, many eat Big Macs.

Toys "R" Us is one of the most successful retailers to target Generation Y and their Baby Boomer parents.

or Diesel jeans, T-shirts, and Nikes. Most experts believe that the reason for the similarities is that this is the first generation tied together by a worldwide media web. The influence has a strong American flavor. Although the emergence of the European Union (EU) has brought teens from those countries closer together, these teens tend to embrace products and fashions made in Europe.

The opportunity for marketing to these children and teens is threefold. First, they have their own money to spend. Second, children influence household purchases through their requests to parents or by shopping themselves. Finally, and possibly most important, children are a future market for all goods and services.

Retailers have realized the gigantic opportunity to sell goods to children and their baby boomer parents. Probably the most successful retailer to target this group is Toys "R" Us, the supermarket for toys. Strategies retailers use to meet children's special needs include

- Present merchandise in manageable groupings to eliminate the feeling of having "too many choices."
- Create "touchy-feely" departments. Lechmere, for example, has a children's learning section with working computers and video games that children can play with.
- Kids seem comfortable visiting the same stores over and over, so some retailers are developing "frequent shopper" programs.
- Retailers are developing partnerships with schools. For instance, Pizza Hut offers grade school children free food if they read at least 20 minutes a day.[4]
- Stores are getting involved in community service. McDonald's hopes to make a sick child's stay in the hospital less frightening, while creating brand loyalty, by placing its mascot's image on pediatric hospital gowns.[5]
- Retailers attempt to get kids involved. Genuardi's Family Markets in Pennsylvania has created a vegetable club for kids. Since children love to collect things, they're given cards of the vegetables they buy and try each time they visit the store.[6] Some stores arrange MTV-inspired fashion shows or other promotional ideas to get children and their parents through their doors.
- Children tend to be environmentally conscious. Thus products and programs related to the environment should do well with them. (See "Green Marketing" later in this chapter.)

Generation X

The next oldest group is **Generation X** (Xers). Born between 1965 and 1976, Xers represent some 41 million Americans. There are only three generalizations we can make about this group: They are Americans, they are in their 20s and 30s, and they don't like the labels that have been bestowed on

Retailers can appeal to children by getting them involved in the shopping decision.

them by the media—which isn't surprising since their other choices are baby busters and the lost generation.

This group is very different from their baby boomer parents. For instance, they're the first generation of **latchkey children** (those who grew up in homes where both parents worked) and, as with the youth population, over 50 percent of their parents' marriages ended in divorce. Whereas their parents were an optimistic group unified on many issues such as Vietnam and Civil Rights, the Xers are often pessimistic about their future and not as unified as their parents. Generation Xers are more likely to be unemployed, to live at home longer, and to stay single longer than their parents. No longer does a college education guarantee a job for the recent graduate, which leads to frustration among many Xers. Furthermore, Xers have different values, shopping habits, and income levels than their parents. On the average, members of Generation X have about one less year of college education than baby boomers. Even those with the same education earn much lower salaries than boomers did at the same age.

REFACT Xers like to exercise their eyeballs with art, TV, and movies, but they are less fond of exercise for the rest of their bodies.[7]

Although the Xers are a group in disarray, they possess considerable spending power. From a retailer's perspective, they're much less interested in shopping than their parents, especially for home furnishings and home purchases. Instead, Xers are more likely to spend their disposable income on items such as CDs, computers, fax machines, microwaves, sneakers, clothing, beer, and cosmetics. Xers are also considered to be astute consumers, more cynical than their boomer parents. They're more likely to disbelieve advertising claims and what salespeople tell them. Xers developed shopping savvy at an early age because many grew up in dual-career households where the parents didn't have much time for shopping. As a result, as teenagers many Xers learned how to make shopping decisions, so they grew more knowledgeable about products and more risk-averse than other shoppers. Finally, Xers are much less interested in status products than older generations. It is not that they can't afford luxury brands—they just don't see the point. They ask, Why buy Calvin Klein jeans when Levi's look just as good?

To effectively target the valuable Generation X market, many companies have revised their ad campaigns to adapt to the more knowledgeable, cynical group. Gone are the days of ads portraying luxury items. Today's retailers of athletic shoes, cosmetics, fashion, and fast food (who flourish because of Xers) are making their ads more candid, while not pushing the actual product too hard on the customer. Many retailers have found success by focusing on green marketing (discussed later in the chapter) to lure environmentally conscious Xers.

The Baby Boomers

After World War II, the birth rate rose sharply, giving rise to a group known as the **baby boomers**—the 78 million Americans born between 1946 and 1964. This huge generation spans 18 years, so it's almost impossible to fit them into one group. The older baby boomers were 17 to 23 years

Natural products appeal to Generation Xers.

old during a time of economic prosperity and political tumult (the Vietnam War and the Civil Rights movement). Younger boomers were still growing up during Watergate, the oil embargo, and a contracting economy. These vastly different experiences during their coming-of-age years has affected their outlook toward life in general and consumption behavior in particular. Further, many older baby boomers are quickly reaching a stage in their family life cycle called *empty nest* where their families have grown up and left home. Younger boomers, on the other hand, are in the throes of childrearing. As a result, many older boomers have more disposable income and time than the younger boomers.

Despite the differences between older and younger boomers, experts agree that they share several traits that set them apart from people born before World War II.[8] First, they are individualistic. Second, leisure time is a high priority for them. Third, they believe that they can always take care of themselves. They have a feeling of economic security, even though they are a little careless about the way they spend their money. Fourth, as we noted in Retailing View 4.1, they have an obsession with maintaining their youth. Finally, they will always love rock and roll.

No matter what shape their tummies are in, Baby Boomers will never give up their jeans.

Although significant in size and wealth, aging baby boomers pose significant challenges to retailers. First, unlike busters, they don't need to make those first-time purchases of furniture, appliances, or business attire. Further, as people reach middle age, they're thought to become less materialistic. For instance, The Sharper Image based its success in the 1980s on providing expensive toys to yuppies (Young Urban Professionals). In the 1990s, it had to redefine its merchandising strategy to provide more practical products and lower price points.

How will retailers reach this large group?

Sell Natural They believe "natural" is better.[10] While the term *natural* means different things to different people, retailers and their vendors will continue to design and sell products that are perceived to be natural to their baby boomer customers. Boomers also respond well to firms with a social consciousness. Personal products chain The Body Shop (which donates a share of its profits to save the Amazonian rain forest) has been particularly successful in appealing to boomers.

Sell Youth and Fitness Another boomer characteristic that's consistent with their desire to maintain their youth is their obsession with exercise and diet. Experts believe that this is more than a fitness fad. As boomers watch their parents grow old, they're seeing that they have to keep themselves fit to stay out of the nursing home. Retailers of exercise equipment, sports apparel, and sports-related foods such as Gatorade will continue to benefit from boomers' passion for fitness. Service providers such as exercise clubs, personal trainers, diet clinics, and plastic surgeons will also benefit.

Sell Technology Boomers are more likely than older or younger adults to own a computer and use a computer at home on a daily basis. Many boomers grew up with and feel comfortable with computers. Also, many boomer households have computers partly because they have children at home. As Xers earn more money, however, they may surpass boomers in their fondness for computers.

Silver Streakers: The Older Population

This is America's fastest-growing group. Between 1996 and 2010, the number of people age 55 to 64 will grow 65.2 percent, mostly as a result of aging baby boomers. But those 65 and older in 1996 will increase 16.3 percent and those 85 and older will increase 51.3 percent.[12]

Are they an important market segment for retailers to pursue? The American Association of Retired Persons (AARP) reports that they're more likely to complain, need special attention, and take time browsing before making a purchase, and that they don't like changes, compared to other age groups.[13] On the other hand, they have time to shop and money to spend. Although their household income is lower than other groups', the income is likely to be from one individual.

In the past, **silver streakers** were very conservative with their savings. They wanted something to pass on to their children. But that attitude is changing. Older people seem to be buying goods and services at the same pace as younger generations. What do they spend this money on? Travel, second homes, luxury cars, electronic equipment, investments, home furnishings, clothing, and gifts are frequent purchases.

Silver streakers like "made in the USA" items, natural fibers, recognizable brand names (but generally not designer labels), value, quality, and classic styles. They're loyal and willing to spend, but are extremely quality-conscious and demand hassle-free shopping. Since most mature customers don't need basics, they would prefer to buy a few high-quality items rather than a larger number of low-quality items. Convenient locations are a major consideration for them. They also don't like long checkout lines—but who does?

Some retailers have created special programs for the mature segment of their customer base. Many Kmart stores, for example, offer an annual "seniors-only shopping spree" one day each December. On that day, the store opens for special shopping hours just for senior citizens and provides gift selection counseling, free gift wrapping, mailing services, and other specials.

REFACT In 1997, for the first time since the last baby boomer was born in 1964, the number of people in this huge generation may decline. But the smaller X generation will not be larger than the boomers until around 2040. But by that time, the youngest Generation Xer will be 64 years old![9]

REFACT Nearly 40 percent of baby boomers regularly take a walk of one mile or more.[11]

REFACT Mick Jagger of the Rolling Stones qualifies as a silver streaker. He was born in 1943.

REFACT Households headed by people age 55 and older account for one in four dollars spent by all U.S. households. That share will grow steadily over the next two decades.[14]

EXHIBIT 4–2

Retailing to the
Silver Streakers[15]

BETTER SERVICE

Retailers are making shopping easier for older people.

1. Have someone available who knows where things are to help older shoppers find things in the store.

2. Train all people to understand older citizens' needs, including simple, clear explanations and reassurance.

3. Employ older people. They can help other older people. They can reduce shoplifting losses because it is harder to steal from nice older people than from huge impersonal corporations. Wal-Mart hires older people as greeters to make customers of all ages feel welcome.

4. Encourage older people to order things by telephone or mail when they wish.

5. Provide places for them to sit down in different parts of the store.

6. Put up plenty of signs with big print and contrasting colors.

7. Don't move products to new locations all the time.

8. Have good lighting. Make sure lighting changes gradually, especially from the outside.

9. Locate restrooms in the front of the store for convenience and security.

10. Post directories throughout the store as convenient points of reference.

11. Don't put products that older shoppers tend to buy on the very top or bottom shelves.

12. Make store, mall, and parking lot security prevalent and visible.

13. Provide product information, such as information cards and brochures.

BETTER VALUE

Older people are often retired and on fixed (sometimes limited) incomes so retailers targeting these customers provide them with good value for their money.

1. Offer senior citizen discount days.

2. Have special "savings for seniors" sales that go beyond senior citizen discount days and feature products for older people.

The May Department Stores Company is a corporate sponsor of the non-profit Older Adult Service and Information System (OASIS) program. OASIS members are provided with meeting rooms in May Company stores where they can socialize, relax, or participate in cultural and educational programs. Members also get a 10 percent discount on store merchandise on specified days and can shop during special members-only hours during holiday shopping periods. Exhibit 4–2 describes how some retailers are providing better service and value to older consumers.

ETHNIC DIVERSITY

America has become ethnically diverse due to immigration and increasing birth rates for various ethnic and racial groups.[16] Approximately 80 percent of all population growth for the next 20 years is expected to come from the African, Hispanic, and Asian communities. Minorities now represent about a quarter of the population; by 2010 they will represent about a third. Most of the foreign-born population and recent immigrants are concentrated in a handful of states and metropolitan areas, primarily on the East and West coasts and along the U.S.–Mexican border. In other areas such as Detroit and Atlanta, they are barely noticeable. Some retailers are correctly focusing on the large and growing middle and affluent classes of these minorities. Minorities also make up a bigger share of the retail work force than in the past. Immigrant entrepreneurs have revitalized neighborhoods and small towns. Food stores, restaurants, and service retailers such as dry cleaners and gasoline stations are particularly attractive to these entrepreneurs.

African-Americans

African-Americans represent about 12 percent of the U.S. population.[17] The African-American population tends to be younger than the rest of the population, and half are single heads of households, compared to a third of white households.

Their annual spending power is about $220 billion. The average African-American household income is $21,100 compared to $32,300 for all U.S. households. But they spend about 5 percent more than whites on an average trip to a mall. Unlike many other consumer groups, the majority of black African-Americans believe it's "fun and exciting" to shop for clothes.

Although African-American households are less affluent than other groups, they're some retailers' best customers. For instance, African-Americans spend 75 percent more per capita than other groups on boys' clothing, but 1 percent less than whites on girls' clothing. They also spend almost twice as much for TV, appliance, and furniture rentals than other groups. Retailers providing products and services that enhance personal appearance should take special note of this market. The average annual household expenditure for hair styling, massages, and manicures is $530 in African-American households, 34 percent higher than the U.S. average. They also spend more than average on hosiery, women's accessories, and jewelry.

Retailers have seized the opportunity of targeting directly to African-Americans. For instance, JCPenney has opened boutiques that sell authentic African clothing, housewares, and art. Spiegel Inc. (the giant mail-order company) and *Ebony* magazine have successfully targeted blacks with *E Style*, a quarterly fashion, accessories, and home-decor catalog for black women. Kmart and Toys "R" Us have used minority advertising agencies to develop campaigns designed specifically for African-American customers. In Atlanta, the South DeKalb Mall has repositioned itself as an "Afrocentric retail center." Several retailers in the mall have tried to orient their goods to blacks. Camelot Music more than doubled its selection of gospel, jazz, and rhythm and blues. Foot Locker stocks styles that do well in black markets, such as suede and black athletic shoes and baseball shirts from the Negro League of the 1930s.

Hispanic-Americans

Many retailers see the Hispanic market's worth. JCPenney, for instance, spends about $6 million on Hispanic marketing per year. Why is there all this interest? About 350,000 Hispanic immigrants come to the United States every year. They and their U.S.-born children should increase the number of Hispanic-Americans from just under 28 million in 1996 to over 32 million in 2001.[18] Hispanic households tend to be larger than other groups. Hispanics represent a $171 billion annual market. Forty-one percent of Hispanic households have annual incomes of at least $25,000, with Cubans having a much higher income than either Mexican or Puerto Rican consumers. Importantly, there's little difference in education, employment, and income between whites and Hispanics who were born in the United States or have lived here at least five years. The Hispanic market is particularly large in certain states and cities, such as California, Arizona, New Mexico, Texas, Miami, New York City, and Chicago.

Many retailers see the Hispanic market's worth. JCPenney, for instance, spends about $6 million annually on Hispanic marketing.

Like many ethnic markets, the Hispanic market isn't homogeneous. Spanish-speaking people include Cubans, Mexicans, Puerto Ricans, and Central and South Americans—each with their own traditions and cultural backgrounds. As a result, retailers and their vendors must adapt their strategies to fit these groups. For instance, Goya Foods targets its black beans to Cubans in Miami and targets red beans to Puerto Ricans in New York. Burdines in Miami purchases merchandise and has bilingual sales associates and ads to satisfy its large Latin clientele.

Retailers and their vendors must also be careful, however, when advertising to their Hispanic customers. The California Milk Processors ran an ad campaign in English with the theme "Got Milk?" When looking to expand the campaign to target California's Hispanics, they discovered that the literal translation was "Are you lactating?" Fortunately, they caught the error before they caused any damage.[20] Retailing View 4.2 describes how the Publix supermarket chain caters to its Hispanic clientele.

Asian-Americans

Although Asian-Americans comprise only about 3 percent of the U.S. population, they're the fastest-growing minority population. They also earn more, have more schooling, and are more likely to be professionally employed or own a business than whites. But as with Hispanics, retailers shouldn't assume that they can target all Asians with one strategy. The

4.2

A Taste of Home: A Supermarket with Salsa

THERE'S NO MAGIC TRICK for reaching the Hispanic market. But marketers need to recognize cultural differences and Spanish-language nuances. They must understand what Hispanic customers want and like, who they are, and how they use products. Publix Supermarkets, with over 400 stores in Florida, Georgia, and South Carolina, tries hard to cater to its Hispanic customers in South Florida.

The best-sellers in a store in a heavily Latin section of Dade County (Miami) are tortillas, baby cologne from Spain, olives and olive oil, beans (nine feet of aisle space), and white cheese, plus *bolas* (beef rounds), ox tails, half pigs, and *tasajo* (dried beef) at the meat counter.

This store has been a specially designated bilingual store since it opened in 1991. Publix carefully tracks census data and the number of Hispanic items it sells. When they hit certain percentages, the supermarket is designated a bilingual, bicultural store.

Once a store is so designated, signs in the aisles and on banners and other promotional materials are bilingual. The merchandise assortment also attains a Latin flavor. *Picadillo* begins appearing along with ground beef on labels; *empanadas* and *croquetas* become staples in the deli cases; and the tubers yucca, malanga, and boniato appear in the produce section. The store also stocks beverages with the taste of home. There's Inca Kola from Peru, Milca red soda from Nicaragua, several types of malta, and fruit nectars in tamarind, mamey, papaya, and passion fruit flavors. The store even attempts to stock imported cleaning products and toiletries that shoppers were familiar with in their homelands.

"Hay para todos" (There's something for everyone), Publix tells its Hispanic customers.

Source: Mimi Whitefield, "How Companies Do It," *The Miami Herald,* October 30, 1995, pp. 25–26.

Chinese, Japanese, Indian, Korean, and southeast Asian subgroups such as Vietnamese and Cambodian all speak different languages as well as come from different cultures.

REFACT One out of seven Californians speaks a language other than English at home.[21]

The Aberdeen Centre near Vancouver, British Columbia, Canada, has targeted the large Asian market in its area. Nearly 80 percent of the merchants and customers are Chinese-Canadians. The mall has shops with Hong Kong–made clothing and traditional Chinese medicines. Chinese movies, Kung fu martial arts demonstrations, and Chinese folk dances help make this mall an important destination for its customers.

INCOME Income distribution in the United States is becoming more polarized—the highest-income groups are growing, while some middle- and lower-income groups' real purchasing power is declining. Polarization of income has helped to polarize retail institutions. Many retailers have increasingly targeted upscale customers, while others have found success with middle- and lower-income groups.

The Upscale Customer In 1993, the richest 20 percent of the households in the country accounted for nearly half of the nation's income. The top five percent had 21 percent of the income. The bottom 20 percent of the households, on the other hand, accounted for just 3.6 percent of the income.[22] There are more wealthy families than in the past because the general population is maturing, there is an increase in dual-income households, and the overall level of education is higher.

The Asian-American population is so dominant in certain parts of the United States, particularly on the West Coast, that retailers can market directly to them.

REFACT Sales of luxury goods—from Gucci handbags to Montblanc pens—experienced approximately 20 percent increases over the previous year in both 1995 and 1996.[24]

Retailers have adapted to meet the needs of the better-educated, high-income customer by adjusting their market strategies. Some middle-market retailers—particularly specialty stores—have upgraded their stores and merchandise. The Williams Sonoma chain of cooking utensil stores, for instance, caters specifically to upscale customers. It continually sells out of its $250 two-slice toasters. In 1996, Neiman Marcus sold all 50 of the $75,000 Jaguars advertised in its Christmas catalog. Hermes "Kelly" $4,000 bags, $400 Prada pajamas, and $40,000 Patek Phillipe watches are also in short supply.[23] Retailing View 4.3 describes one of the most upscale retailers in the world, Sulka.

The Mass Middle and Lower-Income Markets

The mass middle and lower-income markets are more appealing markets today than ever before. The lower-income market represents consumers with household incomes below $25,000, whereas the mass middle market includes households between $25,000 and $50,000.

Why are customers searching for value more today than in recent decades? For the first three decades after World War II, most American families experienced real income growth. But in the late 1970s and 1980s, that growth began to stagnate. Some economists believe that all wage increases accruing in the United States in the past 20 years have gone to the top 20 percent of the population.[25] Family incomes have stayed slightly ahead of inflation, while health care costs, property taxes, and tuition bills have risen much faster than inflation. To compound the problem of income stagnation, the recession and resulting increased unemployment of the late 1980s and 1990s profoundly affect both consumers and

4.3

Sulka: Luxury and Tradition

APART FROM BEING FAMOUS SCREEN ACTORS, what do Jeremy Irons, Warren Beatty, Al Pacino, and Hugh Grant have in common? The answer is that they have all worn clothes from Sulka, a store that enjoys a level of celebrity in the world of sumptuous dressing gowns, pajamas, and shirts on a par with the celebrity these people enjoy on the silver screen. Irons sported silk jacquard pajamas in *Reversal of Fortune,* Beatty graced *Vanity Fair* in a blue paisley silk robe and pink silk pajamas, and Pacino wore a navy silk robe in *Casino.*

As a retailer, Sulka may not be a regular on international catwalks, but it is synonymous with a kind of timeless luxury that manages to transcend the seasonal vicissitudes of fashion. Sulka is a totally vertical operation that integrates design, sourcing, product development, finishing of goods, and finally retail stores. The firm was founded by two immigrants in New York a century ago, and opened in Paris in 1911 and London in 1924. It first made uniforms for professional workers, but they were so admired by the employers themselves that they too started to patronize the firm. Sulka swiftly made the transition from downstairs to upstairs. Today, there are eight Sulka stores worldwide.

Unsurprisingly, its merchandise bears the lavish price tags that deny that recessions ever happen, proving that regardless of economic conditions, there are always people with money somewhere in the world. Indeed, this global attitude is central to Sulka's strategy. It was one of the first international brands. "Our customer is international, affluent, accustomed to the best. . . . And if he isn't he wants to be. He also does not wish to wear his labels on the outside, but still enjoys a thoroughly designer experience," explains Neil J. Fox, CEO and president of Sulka. To this end, he has created a kind of glossy international continuity. "All the stores look the same and carry similar merchandise. Our customer can pick up a jacket in London and find a shirt to go with it in New York." To this he has added a level of service that many other expensive shops have forgotten. They even offer in-house laundering "because we don't want our shirts decimated by the standard commercial laundry," says Fox.

Source: John Morgan, "Luxe et Tradition," *Hommes International Mode Vogue,* Spring-Summer 1996, p. 22.

---

retailers. But retailers appealing to the lower-income group may see their fortunes change as blue-collar employment increases.[26]

The 1980s were the heyday for upscale retailers. Many department stores including JCPenney upgraded their stores and merchandise. But the 1990s are different. Notably, Penney has scaled back its fashion image by searching for products offering customers better value—more quality for less money. In 1994, The Gap opened a chain called the Old Navy Clothing Company that competes directly with discount stores on price, but offers more distinctive clothes made with higher-quality fabrics and attention to detail.

Another venue for lower-income customers involves used, distressed, or odd-lot merchandise at rock-bottom prices. Companies such as Dollar General, Grow Biz International, and Consolidated Stores have done well by dispensing with many of the shopping amenities found even at traditional discounters. (See Chapter 2.)

Traditional choices for the lower-income groups are Mervyn's, Wal-Mart, Kmart, and Target. These stores have three key success factors in common. First, their atmosphere communicates value. They're nice, but not too nice. If fixtures and lighting are too plush, it implies expensive merchandise. Second, the merchandise assortment is credible. These stores carry a mix of moderately priced national brands that people recognize as well as quality, lower-priced private-label merchandise. Finally, the stores relentlessly promote both sale merchandise and everyday low prices.[27]

DECLINE OF HOUSEHOLD MANAGERS

When baby boomers were growing up in the 1950s and 60s, it wasn't unusual for women to be at home raising a family. That scenario has changed! More women are working and more households are headed by single women. Teenagers and men have taken on more household responsibilities, including purchasing groceries. Unfortunately, women's changing role in the family coupled with the career pressures on all adults have resulted in a society that's short on time. These shifts have created significant opportunities for retailers, however. Let's look at the changing women's market and implications for the time-poor society.

The Changing Women's Market

From cars to copiers, from sweaters to sweeteners, women make the majority of purchasing decisions and influence most of the rest.[29] For instance, they purchase about 80 percent of men's merchandise in department stores and over 50 percent of merchandise bought at Home Depot. Further, women now head almost 30 percent of American households. Clearly, the working women's segment is a large, complex, lucrative market for retailers. Women's roles in the workplace have even changed in traditional Russia, as Retailing View 4.4 relates.

One of the most challenging issues in retailing today is how women's apparel retailers are dealing with their changing customers.[30] Women of every generation appear to have less need and interest in apparel. Baby boomers with children have more pressing uses for their disposable income. **Empty-nesters**—households whose children are grown and have left home—are saving for retirement. In general, older women are less swayed by fashion trends. They buy less, they buy classics, and they look for value. Generation X women purchase casual clothing because that's what they can afford and what they like.

Gone are the days when Mom is the only one who does the family's grocery shopping.

Cultural trends are reinforcing a disinterest in fashion. Business dress is becoming more casual (a phenomenon explored later in this chapter). Increasingly women find that one relaxed, stylish wardrobe can fit almost all situations. Also, an environment of everyday low pricing (discounters and off-price outlets) and continuous sales (department and specialty stores) encourages women to never pay "full retail."

Retailers are fighting back with a vengeance. Retailers competing at the lower price points (e.g., discounters) continue to provide their customers with value—better merchandise at lower prices. They have also increased

4.4

For Mary Kay Sales Reps in Russia, Hottest Shade Is the Color of Money

IN RUSSIA, THE COLOR OF money is pink. Mary Kay Cosmetics Inc., with its trademark pink everything, raked in $9 million in sales in 1994 and has positioned itself as a major player in Russia's booming retail cosmetics trade.

The company, a unit of Mary Kay Corp., of Dallas, has tapped a market where women are hungry for makeup, after years of finding only baby-blue eye shadow in stores. Moreover, Mary Kay's can-do style has struck a chord with Russian women, many of whom feel disenfranchised in the new market economy.

Mary Kay began here with 30 or so sales representatives. By the end of 1995, it expects to have 17,000. Mary Kay sales staff buy the products from the company at 40 percent of retail and sell at full price. Unlike Avon ladies (who go door-to-door), Mary Kay reps gather women in small groups to pitch their products.

On any given day, out-of-town saleswomen cram around a distribution counter in Mary Kay's cotton-candy–pink Moscow headquarters, stuffing boxes and duffel bags full of moisturizers and makeup to take back home.

Ms. Ageyeva travels two days each week to Moscow to pick up products for a dozen other saleswomen, or "consultants," in Pyatigorsk. They are among 80 in the town of 180,000. While she grumbles slightly about the haul (a problem Mary Kay is trying to resolve), the fact that she makes $1,500 a month in a country where the average salary is $112 a month keeps her coming back. The average Mary Kay salesperson earns $300 to $400 a month.

Most saleswomen are drawn to the job because selling cosmetics seems genteel in this prefeminist society. Moreover, because the women determine their own schedules, they can spend time with their families. About 60 percent of Mary Kay's Russian sales staff is full-time, with the remainder working second jobs.

Source: Neela Banerjee, "For Mary Kay Sales Reps in Russia, Hottest Shade Is the Color of Money," *The Wall Street Journal*, August 30, 1995, p. A5.

their assortment of women's apparel. Department stores have expanded their private-label lines to keep their prices down (see Chapter 14), are mixing apparel categories to help women put together new ways of dressing for work and play, and offer the high-end market an array of designer boutiques. Specialty stores are expanding their product lines into footwear and personal care, and expanding their traditional merchandising focus. For example, Banana Republic has added more careerwear, while Talbots and Ann Taylor are bringing in more leisurewear.

The Time-Poor Society

When both husband and wife work while still raising a family, leisure time is in short supply. In the past, shopping provided an opportunity for social interaction and entertainment. Today, shopping takes time away from other activities that many customers either must do or would prefer to be doing. To succeed in this environment, retailers are adopting some of the following strategies.[31]

REFACT In 1989, the average customer spent 142 hours a year shopping. By 1993, the average was 40 hours. "Shopping is over. Just looking is over."[32]

Be Available When the Customer Needs You   Selling to a family that includes a working woman calls for adaptive strategies that weren't necessary in previous generations. To accommodate time-sensitive consumers, retailers should be there when the customer wants to shop. OfficeMax, for instance, opens at 7 A.M. because many of their customers want to shop before they start their own business day.

Improve Customer Service   Many retailers recognize the opportunity to serve the short-on-time customer by providing strong customer service. For instance, numerous department stores are again attempting to provide the benefits that originally attracted customers to the stores. To economize in previous decades, they eliminated services such as gift wrapping and alterations, and cut their sales staffs. In response, customers who sought the service traditionally offered in department stores began to shop more at specialty stores providing such service.

Many department stores, such as Nordstrom and Neiman Marcus, have lately refocused their attention on customer service by using more full-time salespeople and offering higher compensation to attract better people. Some discount and off-price retailers now provide services formerly reserved for their more upscale competition. Most now accept discount cards, have salespeople in some departments such as consumer electronics and jewelry, and offer **layaway**—a method of deferred payment in which a store holds merchandise for a customer until it's completely paid for. As we said earlier in this chapter, Wal-Mart employs a **greeter**—a person who greets customers when they enter the store and provides information and/or assistance.

Another strategy for improving customer service is to empower salespeople to make decisions. Customers don't like to wait for authorization for check approval, merchandise returns, or other interactions with store staff. Retailers from Montgomery Ward to Neiman Marcus authorize sales associates to make these decisions without managerial approval.

Give Information   Providing customers with important information can reduce their shopping time. Many specialty stores keep track of their good customers' sizes and preferences so that they can call them up when appropriate merchandise arrives. Informative signage and coordinated merchandise can also speed shopping. For instance, Crate & Barrel places small, tasteful, informative signs beside merchandise to act as a "silent salesperson." Some fashion stores, like Saks Fifth Avenue, offer personalized salespeople who can help speed the decision process. These fashion consultants may even meet with customers in their home or office.

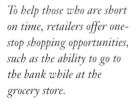

To help those who are short on time, retailers offer one-stop shopping opportunities, such as the ability to go to the bank while at the grocery store.

Automate Processes   Automated selling or service processes can help save customers time. For instance, A&P, Shop Rite, and Publix are experimenting with automated grocery checkout systems that reduce waiting time in checkout lines. Another supermarket chain, Wegman's, has computerized its deli department. The customer simply enters the order and picks up the items on the way out of the store. Electronic kiosks for information and special-order purposes, inventory control, and customer-directed ad programs are available at some retailers.

Offer Opportunities for One-Stop Shopping   Finally, retailers should offer customers opportunities to make multiple purchases in one location. For instance, some grocery stores have videotape rentals and branches of traditional banks within their stores. Retailers and shopping center developers can create partnerships in which several retailers are strategically clustered together to facilitate time-saving shopping. A shopping center specializing in services—such as a packaging and mail service, dry cleaner, shoe repair store, and printer—would boast significant customer convenience.

Provide Alternatives to Store Visits   Nonstore retailing has expanded in many directions, as Chapter 3 said. Specialty catalogs such as L.L. Bean are very successful. Major retailers such as JCPenney and Neiman Marcus have expanded their use of catalogs. Although some are struggling, TV home shopping stations provide time-saving alternatives to shopping in stores. Wal-Mart, Kmart, OfficeMax, and Borders, among others, are frantically experimenting with Interactive Home Shopping.

Feed the Customer   One of the best opportunities to capitalize on time-poor customers is to provide them with high-quality, healthy food that's ready-to-eat. If you're in Dallas, you can go to Eatzi's, where you can choose from 450 ready-to-eat entrees along with fresh produce, from-scratch baked goods, wines, cheeses, snacks, beverages, and other consumables. Eatzi's average core customer visits two to five times per week. If you're in St. Louis, try Gourmet to Go![33]

CHANGES IN CONSUMER VALUES

The previous section examined retail customers' changing demographic makeup. As a result of these changes and other environmental factors, consumer values are also changing. For instance, certain demographic groups (notably baby boomers and their children, Generation X) respond well to retailers with a strong social consciousness and commitment to the environment. Dual-income families and older Americans appear to be searching for convenience and value. This section examines changing consumer values and retailers' reactions to them.

Social Consciousness

Retailers and their employees play an important role in their communities. A retail manager's influence extends beyond the business world and into the society in which she lives. In other words, a manager's business actions often may have serious repercussions—for good or bad—on society at large. Because companies often directly or indirectly affect our society's mores, they must look beyond the bottom line and factor in societal needs. For example, Target contributes 5 percent of sales back to the community. Also, because nutrition is so vital in everyone's life, many fast-food retailers have added healthier items to their menus and make nutritional information readily

REFACT Patagonia, the purveyor of upscale sporting apparel and equipment, gives 10 percent of pretax profits to saving places that its customers like to climb to and survive in.

available. Retailers that are perceived to actively improve citizens' lives are, in turn, esteemed by society.

Green Marketing

Green marketing is a strategic focus by retailers and their vendors to supply customers with environmentally friendly merchandise.[34] The movement was rekindled in the early 1990s after a relatively dormant period. Baby boomers and Generation Xers are sympathetic to environmental concerns. Although by 1993 the majority of Americans were environmentally active to some degree, the rest remain apathetic. Part of the problem is that consumers have been confused about what is a "good" or "bad" environmental practice. Many correctly believe that retailers and their vendors tout environmental benefits to gain a short-term sales advantage. Few people believe, for instance, that because a liquid detergent is clear, it is more environmentally friendly than one with color. Also, the average American is more concerned with price, quality, and his personal experience with a product than he is with a brand or a store's environmental record.

Retailers should not ignore environmental issues altogether. They should simply be selective in their appeals. Consumers are likely to pay more attention to environmental issues when buying things that have an obvious direct impact on the environment, such as lawn-and-garden products and household cleaners. Environmental considerations are less critical when purchasing things like fast food and cars. These products may have a significant impact on the environment, but the impact is obscured.

The most effective methods of appealing to the environmentally sensitive consumer are

- Address consumer skepticism head on. Tell people about the environmentally correct things being done. Advertising messages with "new" or "improved" just don't cut it.
- Communications with the customer should show a concern for consumer well-being. For instance, an ad should discuss health and safety benefits.
- Convey a companywide commitment to the environment by communicating what's being done throughout the organization.

REFACT The Body Shop sells natural cosmetics. One reason for its success is that the owner has taken a public stand against such practices as testing products on animals and burning the rain forests.

The Value-Oriented Customer

Stagnation in real household income growth, baby boomers with families, and Generation Xers with little disposable income have forced retailers to take a hard look at offering their customers a better value than they did in the past.[35] For example, during the 1980s, JCPenney became more fashion-forward and higher-priced as it pushed more national brands like Oshkosh B'Gosh and Levi's. But in the 1990s, it returned to its moderately priced roots. Now Penney sells an $84 suit that is similar to a $600 St. John Knit at Saks Fifth Avenue. Although Penney's model is made of a synthetic fabric instead of wool, other details make it look remarkably like the original.

Fashionable clothing at budget prices has become a priority for other retailers as well. At Wal-Mart, the Kathie Lee Gifford line of women's apparel is displayed in an in-store boutique similar to what you would find in a department store. Wal-Mart salespeople are trained to help women put together outfits.

Manufacturers cut corners in ways that are imperceptible to most customers. For instance, a men's dress shirt manufacturer can make a shirt that will retail for $9.99 instead of $25 for a department store shirt simply by making the shirt a little shorter, using fewer stitches per inch, and putting just one button on the cuff. Retailers like JCPenney and Target subject garments to tough quality control tests. It's often hard for consumers to tell the difference. *Consumer Reports* ranked a $26 women's sweater from Sears on par with a $340 sweater from Barney's New York.

In their search for bargains, value-oriented customers often sacrifice the perceived safety of purchasing national brands for merchandise offered on sale, through coupons, or by manufacturers' rebates. (See Chapters 14 and 15.) In fact, many retailers have increased their budgets for such promotions, often at the expense of more traditional advertising. Special promotions (such as frequent shopper plans, Discover Card cumulative discounts, magazine subscriptions, gifts, and sweepstakes) are expected to become even more popular in the future.

Cocooning

Cocooning is a behavioral pattern of consumers who increasingly turn to the nice, safe, familiar environment of their homes to spend their precious leisure time. Increasingly, people are working at home. The cocooning phenomenon is due to (1) a return to traditional values, (2) families having children later in life, and (3) individuals' time-consciousness. Cocooning means strong markets for VCRs, home computers, stereo systems, security systems, answering machines, and other products used in the home. As we noted earlier, restaurants and supermarkets are offering home delivery and gourmet prepared foods, while many supermarkets have hired professional chefs to oversee preparation of carry-out items.

Some predict a countercocooning trend, however. With so many single-person households and so few traditional families, cocooning may become less prevalent in the future.[36]

Dress-Down Fashion

Gone are the men in their gray flannel suits of the 1950s and 60s.[37] As baby boomers enter the boardrooms and Generation Xers enter the workplace, their khakis and sneakers are coming with them. This important fashion trend creates significant opportunities for retailers and their vendors. Many workers are purchasing a third wardrobe, somewhere between business suits and jeans and a T-shirt. Retailers at both ends of the fashion/price spectrum stand to gain. Lower-priced stores benefit because people can go to work in casual pants and a shirt rather than a $500 suit. Other customers are devoting their suit budget to upscale designer fashions.

Some workers, particularly men, have had trouble learning what's appropriate casual business attire. So, smart retailers and their vendors are attempting to educate them. Target and Men's Warehouse have run TV commercials based on a casual dress-for-success theme. Saks Fifth Avenue's corporate casual campaign includes videos, seminars, and consultations between Saks fashion directors and corporate senior executives. Macy's has built a catalog around a campaign called "Casual That Works."

REFACT Ninety percent of U.S. workers are dressing down at least some of the time. IBM and Ford Motor Company have converted to five-days-a-week casual.[38]

Most believe that a casual workplace is here to stay. Once people get used to the comfort and functionality of casual clothing, they will not go back.

INTERNET EXERCISE   Levi Strauss and Co. provides fashion assistance for people who are dressing more casually in their jobs. Go to: http://www.dockers.com on the Internet and indicate how an apparel retailer might use this information in developing its assortment.

SUMMARY

Not many years ago, customers had relatively few choices. They could choose among department and specialty stores for clothing, appliances, and home furnishings; discount stores for housewares, tools, and bargain clothing; grocery stores for food; and convenience stores for a candy bar or pack of cigarettes. Successful retailers have adapted to changes in their customer base to improve their previous offerings. Others have opened new retail formats.

Some retailers target the affluent youth market; others concentrate on older groups. Yet one of the hardest groups to reach is Generation X—those born between 1965 and 1976. Since the United States is becoming more ethnically diverse, and assorted ethnic groups are growing larger and more economically viable, several retailers have specific marketing programs to meet their needs. The number of women in the work force and the fact that they make the majority of purchasing decisions provide interesting challenges to retailers. To meet upscale, dual-income, well-educated, time-poor customers' needs, department and specialty stores have rediscovered how to provide excellent service. Retailers that offer mail-order catalogs and those that specialize in products that can be used at home, like videocassettes and gourmet food, are prospering as these customers spend their limited leisure time at home (cocooning).

Retailers are also responding to changes in consumer values. Many have found that a strong social consciousness is good not only for society, but also for business. Many consumers have had to adjust to lower real incomes than previous generations enjoyed. Retailers who've developed strategies to attract and maintain more price-sensitive, value-oriented customers have thrived. Others have become more environmentally conscious. Fashion retailers are providing customers in all categories with functional clothing that can be used for both work and play.

KEY TERMS

baby boomers, *101*	empty nesters, *110*	generational cohort, *97*	latchkey children, *101*
Cocooning, *115*	Generation X, *100*	green marketing, *114*	layaway, *112*
demographics, *97*	Generation Y, *98*	greeter, *112*	silver streakers, *103*

DISCUSSION QUESTIONS & PROBLEMS

1. Explain the dramatic changes in the women's market over the past 25 years. Discuss various business strategies that could be useful for targeting this group.

2. In many ways, Generation X has changed the face of retailing. How does Generation X differ from baby boomers? How can retailers that once catered to boomers alter their marketing strategy to appeal to Xers?

3. What is your favorite retailer of luxury products? What makes people willing to pay extra dollars to acquire their merchandise?

4. Cocooning is a direct result of America's time-poor society. Explain cocooning. What strategies can retailers use to cater to time-poor customers?

5. Some service retailers such as Chem Lawn that provide lawn care services (e.g., planting, feeding, and general lawn care) have been very successful in recent years. How do such companies benefit consumers? For what markets are they positioning themselves?

6. Assume that Kmart is opening three new locations in the New York City area. Location A's area is 75 percent African-American. Location B's trade area is 80 percent Hispanic; of those, half are Cuban and half are Mexican. Location C is in Chinatown. How can Kmart target each ethnic group in each area? Discuss potential marketing problems.

7. To remain competitive, retailers and their employees must play an important part in their communities at both local and national levels. Give examples of how various companies can give back to the community and respond to America's environmental concerns.

8. What tips could you give Walgreens to help it cater to its large and growing group of elderly customers?

9. How does your favorite clothing store address the trend of wearing casual clothing to the office?

SUGGESTED READINGS

Braus, Patricia. "The Baby Boom at Mid-Decade." *American Demographics*, April 1995, pp. 40–45.

Dortch, Shannon. "Rise and Fall of Generations." *American Demographics*, July 1996, pp. 6–7, 43.

Emondson, Brad. "Hispanic Americans in 2001." *American Demographics*, January 1997, p. 17.

Fisher, Christy. "Black, Hip, and Primed (to Shop)." *American Demographics*, September 1996, pp. 52–58.

Hoeffel, John. "The Next Baby Boom." *American Demographics*, October 1995, pp. 22–31.

Macarenhus, Oswald A. J., and Mary A. Higby. "Peer, Parent, and Media Influences in Teen Apparel Shopping." *Journal of the Academy of Marketing Science* 21, no. 1 (Winter 1993), pp. 53–58.

Mitchell, Susan. *The Official Guide to the Generations.* New Strategist, 1995.

Morris, Eugene. "The Difference Is Black and White." *American Demographics*, January 1993, pp. 44–49.

Moschis, George P. "Life Stages of the Mature Market." *American Demographics*, September 1996, pp. 44–47.

Peracchio, Laura A. "How Do Young Children Learn to Be Consumers? A Script-Processing Approach." *Journal of Consumer Research* 18, no. 4 (March 1992), pp. 425–40.

Peterson, Robert A. *The Future of U.S. Retailing: An Agenda for the 21st Century.* New York: Quorum Books, 1992.

Russell, Cheryl. *The Master Trend—How the Baby Boom Generation Is Remaking America.* New York: Plenum, 1993.

Stisser, Peter. "A Deeper Shade of Green." *American Demographics*, March 1994, pp. 25–29.

Underhill, Paco. "Seniors in Stores." *American Demographics*, April 1996, pp. 44–48.

Zill, Nicholas and John Robinson. "The Generation X Difference." *American Demographics*, April 1995, pp. 24–33.

NOTES

1. John Hoeffel, "The Next Baby Boom," *American Demographics*, October 1995, pp. 22–31.

2. J. Paul Peter and Jerry C. Olson, *Consumer Behavior and Marketing Strategy* (Burr Ridge, IL: Irwin, 1996), p. 420.

3. Cyndee Miller, "Teens Seen as the First Truly Global Consumers," *Marketing News*, March 27, 1995, p. 9.

4. "Retailers at Play," *Design Forum Ideations* 3, no. 1 (January-February 1996).

5. Ibid.

6. Ibid.

7. Nicholas Zill and John Robinson, "The Generation X Difference," *American Demographics*, April 1995, pp. 24–33.

8. Cheryl Russell, *The Master Trend—How the Baby Boom Generation Is Remaking America* (New York: Plenum, 1993), cited in Patricia Braus, "The Baby Boom at Mid-Decade," *American Demographics*, April 1995, pp. 40–45.

9. Shannon Dortch, "Rise and Fall of Generations," *American Demographics*, July 1996, pp. 6–7, 43.

10. Braus, "The Baby Boom at Mid-Decade."

11. Ibid.

12. Dortch, "Rise and Fall of Generations," pp. 6–7.

13. Mary Ellen Kelly, "Discounters Grow Wiser to Seniors' Spending Potential," *Discount Store News*, May 18, 1992, pp. 113–14; atttributed to Professor George Moschis of Georgia State University.

14. Paco Underhill, "Seniors in Stores," *American Demographics*, April 1996, pp. 44–48.

15. Ibid; "Marketing to Older Shoppers Makes Good Sense," *Discount Store News*, June 20, 1994, pp. 23, 28; "Retailers Slow to Target Older Consumers" *Chain Store Age Executive*, August 1988; and Marianne Wilson, "Sixty Something," *Chain Store Age Executive*, July 1991. Copyright Lebhar-Friedman, Inc., 425 Park Avenue, New York, NY 10022.

16. "Immigration's Impact on Real Estate and Retailing," *Chain Store Age*, October 1996, pp. 68–74; and "Minority Customers to Become a Major Marketing Target," *Discount Store News*, May 18, 1992, p. 100.

17. Christy Fisher, "Black, Hip, and Primed (to Shop)," *American Demographics*, September 1996, pp. 52–58; "J.C. Penney Finds Profit in America," *American Demographics*, November 1992, p. 12; Laurie M. Grossman, "After Demographic Shift, Atlanta Mall Restyles Itself as Black Shopping Center," *The Wall Street Journal*, February 2, 1992, pp. B1, B7; and Eugene Morris, "The Difference Is Black and White," *American Demographics*, January 1993, pp. 44–49.

18. Brad Emondson, "Hispanic Americans in 2001," *American Demographics*, January 1997, p. 17.

19. Ibid.; attributed to Yankelovich Hispanic MONITOR in Norwalk, Connecticut.

20. Deborah Shaw, "Habla Espanol? That's Spanish for 'Want to Survive?'," *Discount Store News*, September 2, 1996, p. 12.

21. Martha Farnsworth Riche, "Vital Trends in Consumer Demographics (1)," *Retail Control*, March 1987, pp. 20–36.

22. Susan Reda, "Beyond Discounting," *Stores*, May 1996, pp. 24–28; statistics taken from Bureau of the Census and Kurt Salmon Associates.

23. "Qualty, Not Flash, Marks New Gains in Luxury Sales," *New York Times*, December 12, 1996, pp. A1ff (national edition).

24. Ibid.

25. Reda, "Beyond Discounting"; statistics attributed to MIT economist Lester Thurow.

26. Michael P. Niemira, "Are the Fortunes of Retailers That Appeal to Lower-Income Groups about to Change?" *Chain Store Age*, April 1996, p. 24.

27. Joseph Ellis, "The Mass Middle Market for Apparel," (New York: Goldman Sachs Investment Research, April 20, 1993); Jack Kasulis, "The Frugal Family of the Nineties," *Retailing Issues Letter* 3, no. 5 (September 1991); and Wendy Zellner, "Penney's Rediscovers Its Calling," *Business Week*, April 5, 1993, pp. 51–52.

28. Carl Steidmann, "5 Down and 5 to Go," Management Horizons, A Consulting Division of Price Waterhouse LLP, 1995.

29. Roger Selbert, "Retailing's Five Most Important Trends," *Retailing Issues Letter* 3, no. 2 (March 1991); and "Women in Charge," *American Demographics*, September 1989, pp. 27–29.

30. This section draws heavily from Stephanie S. Shern, "Women's Apparel: Changing Market Trends Demand New Strategies," *Ernst & Young's Retail News*, Fall 1995, pp. 2–3.

31. Adapted from Laura Liebeck, "Shoppers Need Ways to Beat the Clock," *Discount Store News*, May 6, 1996, pp. 88–94; and Eugene Fram, "The Time Compressed Shopper," *Marketing Insights*, Summer 1991, pp. 34–39.

32. Scott Martin, "Death of a Bike Shop," *Bicycling*, November 1994, pp. 71–76; statistics and quotation attributed to retail consultant Geter Glen.

33. "Gourmet to Go Creates Healthy Meals That Can Be Pre-Ordered and Picked Up on the Way Home," *Chain Store Age*, December 1995, pp. 31–32; "Eatzi's Serves Up Fine Food Fast," *Discount Store News*, April 15, 1996, pp. 6, 15; and Debra Sykes, "Eatzi's Finds Market Niche on Fine Line between Restaurant and Supermarket," *Stores*, May 1996, pp. 48–49.

34. Peter Stisser, "A Deeper Shade of Green," *American Demographics*, March 1994, pp. 25–29.

35. Teri Agins, "Why Cheap Clothes Are Getting More Respect," *The Wall Street Journal*, October 16, 1995, pp. B1, B3.

36. Carl Steidmann, "5 Down and 5 to Go."

37. Mark Manoff, "Smart Companies Capitalize on Corporate Dress-Down Policies," *Ernst & Young's Retail News*, Fall 1995, pp. 4–6.

38. Ibid.

Customer Buying Behavior

THE WORLD OF RETAILING

1. Introduction to the World of Retailing
2. Store-Based Retailing
3. Nonstore Retailing—Electronic Retailing and Catalogs
4. The Retail Customer
5. **Customer Buying Behavior**

RETAILING STRATEGY

MERCHANDISE MANAGEMENT

STORE MANAGEMENT

QUESTIONS

- What stages do customers go through when selecting a retailer and purchasing merchandise?

- What do customers consider when they decide to visit a store, scan a catalog, or surf the Internet?

- How do culture, family, and opinion leaders affect the customer's buying process?

- How can retailers get customers to visit their stores more frequently and buy more merchandise during each visit?

- Why and how do retailers group customers into market segments?

THE RETAILING CONCEPT (discussed in Chapter 1) emphasizes that an effective retail strategy satisfies customer needs better than competitors' strategies. Thus, understanding customer needs and buying behavior is critical for effective retail decision making. Chapter 4 reviewed retail implications of some broad consumer trends, such as the aging population and the growth in two-income families. This chapter focuses on the needs and buying behavior of individual customers and market segments. It describes the stages customers go through to purchase merchandise and the factors that influence the buying process. We then use the information about the buying process to discuss how consumers can be grouped into market segments.[1] The appendix to this chapter examines special aspects of consumer behavior that concern retailers selling fashion merchandise.

TYPES OF BUYING DECISIONS

Retailing View 5.1 describes how Maria Sanchez, a student, bought a new suit for job interviews. Such purchases typically involve several stages. The buying process begins when customers recognize an unsatisfied need. Then they seek information about how to satisfy the need: what products might be useful and how they can be bought. Customers evaluate the various alternative sources of merchandise such as stores, catalogs, and electronic retailers and choose

5.1

Maria Sanchez Buys a New Suit

MARIA SANCHEZ, at Cal State–Long Beach in southern California, is beginning to interview for jobs. For the first interviews on campus, Maria had planned to wear the blue suit her parents bought her three years ago. But looking at her suit, she realizes that it's not very stylish and that the jacket is beginning to show signs of wear. Wanting to make a good first impression during her interview, she decides to buy a new suit.

Maria looks through a few catalogs sent to her apartment to see the styles being offered. But she decides to buy the suit in a store so she can try it on and have it for her first interview next week. She likes to shop at the Express and The Gap, but neither sells business suits. She remembers an ad in the *Los Angeles Times* for women's suits at Macy's. She decides to go to Macy's in the mall close to her apartment and asks her friend Brenda to come along. Maria values Brenda's opinion, because Brenda is a clothes horse and has good taste.

Walking through the store, they see some Liz Claiborne suits. Maria looks at them briefly and decides they're too expensive for her budget and too stylish. She wants to interview with banks and thinks she needs a more conservative suit.

Maria and Brenda are approached by a salesperson in the career women's department. After asking Maria what type of suit she wants and her size, the salesperson shows her three suits. Maria asks Brenda what she thinks about the suits and then selects one to try on. When Maria comes out of the dressing room, she feels that the shoulder pads in the suit make her look too heavy, but Brenda and the salesperson think the suit is attractive. Maria decides to buy the suit after another customer in the store tells her she looks very professional in the suit.

Maria doesn't have a Macy's charge card, so she asks if she can pay with a personal check. The salesperson says yes, but the store also takes Visa and MasterCard. Maria decides to pay with her Visa card.

As the salesperson walks with Maria and Brenda to the cash register, they pass a display of scarves. The salesperson stops, picks up a scarf, and shows Maria how well the scarf complements the suit. Maria decides to buy the scarf also.

---

a store or Internet site to visit or a catalog to review. This encounter with a retailer provides more information and may alert customers to additional needs. After evaluating the retailer's merchandise offering, customers may make a purchase or go to another retailer to collect more information. Eventually, customers make a purchase, use the product, and then decide whether the product satisfies their needs.

REFACT Women spend $50 billion on work apparel. Sixty percent of purchases are made in department and specialty stores, 17 percent in off-price outlets, 12 percent in discount stores, and 7 percent through mail order.[2]

In some situations, customers like Maria spend considerable time and effort selecting a retailer and/or evaluating the merchandise. In other situations, buying decisions are made automatically with little thought. Three types of customer decision-making processes are extended problem solving, limited problem solving, and habitual decision making.

Extended Problem Solving

Extended problem solving is a purchase decision process in which customers devote considerable time and effort to analyzing alternatives. Customers typically engage in extended problem solving when the purchase decision involves a lot of risk and uncertainty. There are many types of risks.[3] Financial risks arise when customers purchase an expensive product. Physical risks are important when customers feel a product may affect their health or safety. Social risks arise when customers believe a product will affect how others view them.

Consumers engage in extended problem solving when they are making a buying decision to satisfy an important need or when they have little knowledge about the product or service. Due to high risk and uncertainty in these situations, customers go beyond their personal knowledge to consult with friends, family

Customers typically engage in extended problem solving when buying an automobile because the purchase decision involves considerable expense and risk.

members, or experts. They may visit several retailers before making a purchase decision.

Retailers can influence such decisions by providing the necessary information in a manner that customers can understand and easily use and by offering money-back guarantees. For example, retailers that sell merchandise involving extended problem solving might provide brochures describing the merchandise and its specifications; have informational displays in the store (such as a sofa cut in half to show its construction); and use salespeople to make presentations and answer questions. Retailing View 5.2 shows how manufacturers and retailers provide information to help consumers minimize the social risks in dressing inappropriately for casual days at work.

Limited Problem Solving

Limited problem solving is a purchase decision process involving a moderate amount of effort and time. Customers engage in this type of buying process when they have had some prior experience with the product or service and their risk is moderate. In these situations, customers tend to rely more on personal knowledge than on external information. They usually choose a retailer they have shopped at before and select merchandise they have bought in the past. The majority of customer decision making involves limited problem solving.

Retailers attempt to reinforce this buying pattern when customers are buying merchandise from them. If customers are shopping elsewhere, however, retailers need to break this buying pattern by introducing new information or offering different merchandise or services.

Maria Sanchez's buying process illustrates both limited and extended problem solving. Her store choice decision was based on her prior knowledge of the merchandise in various stores she had shopped in and an ad in the *Los Angeles Times*. Considering this information, she felt the store choice decision was not very risky and engaged in limited problem solving when deciding to visit Macy's. But her buying process for the suit was extended. This decision was important to her, and she spent time acquiring information from a friend and the salesperson to evaluate and select a suit.

One common type of limited problem solving is impulse buying. **Impulse buying** is a buying decision made by customers on the spot after seeing the merchandise.[5] Maria's decision to buy the scarf was an impulse purchase.

Retailers encourage impulse buying behavior by using prominent displays to attract customer attention and stimulate a purchase decision based on little analysis. For example, sales of a grocery item are greatly increased when the item is featured in an end-aisle display, when a BEST BUY sign is placed on the shelf with the item, when the item is placed at eye level (typically on the third shelf from

5.2

What to Wear on Casual Days at Work

WHILE CLOTHING DESIGNERS are promoting a return to glamour by outfitting models in stiletto heels and vinyl miniskirts, consumers are dressing more casually, and not just on the weekends, but also at work. Even IBM abandoned its blue suit, white shirt, and red tie tradition, encouraging employees to dress more casually. Sales of tailored clothing, including dresses and suits, are declining, while demand for no-iron slacks and sweaters increases.

However, most consumers are still concerned about wearing the wrong clothing when "dressing down" at work. Retailers and manufacturers are addressing these concerns by offering special styles for casual days. Haggar has a "relaxed but tailored" line of clothing using the brand name City Casual. Special point-of-purchase material is developed to help retailers sell this merchandise line. Haggar's "How to Dress Down" brochure, available in these displays, has tips like "Suede suspenders, belts, and shoes add a warmer, more casual touch. But save the little suede shorts for Oktoberfest."

Marshall Field's, a Chicago-based department store chain, features an article on casual work wear in its monthly customer newsletter and holds one-hour seminars on the subject complete with a free box lunch.

Source: Cyndee Miller, "A Casual Affair," *Marketing News,* March 13, 1995, p. 12.

---

the bottom), or when items are placed at the checkout counter so customers can see them as they wait in line. Supermarkets use these displays and prime locations for the profitable items that customers tend to buy on impulse, such as gourmet food, rather than commodities such as flour and sugar, which are usually planned purchases.

Habitual Decision Making

Habitual decision making is a purchase decision process involving little or no conscious effort. As Chapter 4 said, today's customers have many demands on their time. One way they cope with these time pressures is by simplifying their decision-making process. When a need arises, customers may automatically respond with, "I'll buy the same thing I bought last time from the same store." Typically, this habitual decision-making process is used when decisions aren't very important to customers and involve familiar merchandise they have bought in the past.

Brand loyalty and store loyalty are examples of habitual decision making. **Brand loyalty** occurs when customers like and consistently buy a specific brand in a product category. They are reluctant to switch to other brands if their favorite brand isn't available. Thus, retailers can only satisfy these customers' needs if they offer the specific brands desired.

Brand loyalty creates both opportunities and problems for retailers. Customers are attracted to stores carrying popular brands. But, since retailers must carry the high-loyalty brands, they may not be able to negotiate favorable terms with the supplier—the brand manufacturer. Chapters 12 and 14 cover buying and stocking branded merchandise.

Store loyalty means that customers like and habitually visit the same store to purchase a type of merchandise. All retailers would like to increase their customers' store loyalty. Some approaches for increasing store loyalty are selecting a convenient location (see Chapter 11), offering complete assortments and reducing

REFACT The typical supermarket customer spends 15 seconds and looks at only one brand when buying laundry detergent.[8]

REFACT The grocery product categories with the highest brand loyalty are cigarettes, mayonnaise, and hot cereal. Milk, cookies, and cold cereal have the lowest brand loyalty.[9]

Supermarkets use a variety of approaches to increase impulse buying, including in-store coupons, end-aisle displays, and point-of-sale advertising.

the number of stockouts (Chapter 13), rewarding customers for frequent purchases (Chapter 16), and providing good customer service (Chapter 19).

THE BUYING PROCESS

Exhibit 5–1 outlines the **buying process**—the stages in selecting a retailer and buying merchandise. Understanding the steps of the buying process is helpful in developing and implementing a retailing strategy. Each stage in the buying process is addressed in the following sections.

As the stages in the buying process are discussed, you should recognize that customers may not go through the stages in the same order shown in Exhibit 5–1. For example, a person might see an ad for Jiffy Lube, go to the nearest Jiffy Lube for an oil change, encounter a long line, leave the Jiffy Lube, and drop his car off at a gas station near work. Here the customer decides what service he wants and selects the specific retailer at the same time.

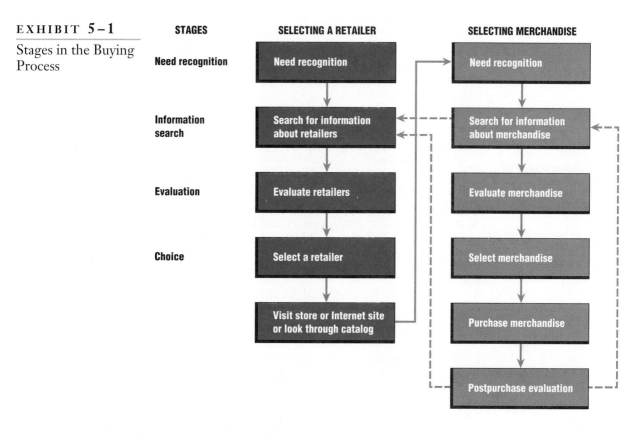

EXHIBIT 5–1

Stages in the Buying Process

Need Recognition   The buying process is triggered when people recognize they have an unsatisfied need. Unsatisfied needs arise when a customer's desired level of satisfaction differs from his or her present level of satisfaction. For example, Maria Sanchez recognized that she had a problem when she considered interviewing for jobs in her blue suit. She needed a suit that would make a good impression and realized her worn, outdated blue suit wouldn't satisfy this need.

Need recognition can be as straightforward as discovering there's no milk in the refrigerator or it can be as ambiguous as feeling the need for an uplifting experience after a final exam. Visiting stores, looking through catalogs, and purchasing products are approaches to satisfying different types of needs.

Types of Needs   The needs motivating customers to go shopping and purchase merchandise can be classified as functional or psychological.[10] **Functional needs** are directly related to the performance of the product. For example, people who need to style their hair might be motivated to purchase a hair dryer. This purchase is based on the expectation that the hair dryer will assist the customer in styling hair.

Psychological needs are associated with the personal gratification customers get from shopping or from purchasing and owning a product. For example, a Tommy Hilfinger shirt may not serve the function of clothing any better than a knit shirt from Kmart, but the Hilfinger shirt may also satisfy the customer's need to be perceived as a fashionable dresser. When products are purchased to satisfy psychological needs, the product's functional characteristics are typically less important.

Many products satisfy both functional and psychological needs. The principal reason for purchasing a Tommy Hilfinger shirt may be to enhance one's self-image, but the shirt also satisfies the functional need for clothing. Most Americans have more income than they require to satisfy their functional needs for food, liquid, clothing, and shelter. As disposable income rises, psychological needs become increasingly important.[11] Thus, store ambiance, service, and fashionable merchandise are more important to American retail customers than to customers in countries with less-developed economies.

Functional needs are often referred to as rational, while psychological needs are called emotional. These labels suggest that visiting stores or buying products to satisfy psychological needs is irrational. But is it really irrational for people to buy designer clothing because it makes them feel more successful? Anything customers do to improve their satisfaction should be considered rational, whether the action satisfies a functional or a psychological need. Successful retailers attempt to satisfy both the functional and psychological needs of their customers. Psychological needs that can be satisfied through shopping and purchasing merchandise include[13]

REFACT Ralph Lauren has established the world's most successful designer brands generating over $5 billion in annual sales for his firm, including $1 billion in royalties from 26 licensees.[12]

- **Stimulation.** Retailers and developers use background music, visual displays, scents, and demonstrations in stores and malls to create a carnival-like, stimulating experience for their customers.[14] These environments encourage consumers to take a break in their daily environment and visit these sites. Catalog and electronic retailers also attempt to stimulate customers with exciting graphics and photography.

L.L. Bean stimulates customer interest in its Internet sites with colorful graphics and information about national parks.

- **Social experience.** Marketplaces have traditionally been centers of social activity—places where people could meet friends and develop new relationships.[15] Regional shopping malls in many communities have replaced open markets as social meeting places, especially for teenagers. Mall developers satisfy the need of social experiences by providing places for people to sit and talk in food courts. Borders and Barnes and Noble bookstores have cafes where customers can discuss novels while sipping a latte. Electronic retailers provide similar social experiences through chat rooms for people visiting their sites. For example, visitors to the Amazon.com electronic bookstore (http://www.amazon.com) share information and opinions about books with other visitors.

- **Learning new trends.** By visiting stores, people learn about new trends and ideas. These visits satisfy customers' needs to be informed about their environment. For example, record stores use displays to show shoppers what new trends and artists are emerging.

- **Status and power.** Some customers have a need for status and power that's satisfied through shopping. When shopping, a person can be waited on without having to pay for the service. For some people, a store is one of the few places where they get attention and respect they need. Ralph Lauren's store on Madison Avenue satisfies this need by creating an atmosphere of aristocratic gentility and the good life in a refurbished mansion in New York City. The store is furnished with expensive antiques. Cocktails and canapés are served to customers in the evening.[16]

- **Self-reward.** Customers frequently purchase merchandise to reward themselves when they have accomplished something or want to dispel depression. Perfume and cosmetics are common self-gifts. Retailers satisfy these needs by "treating" customers to personalized makeovers while they are in the store.[17]

REFACT The most frequently cited reasons for disliking shopping are long checkout lines, crowds, and poorly trained salespeople.[18]

Conflicting Needs   Most customers have multiple needs. Moreover, these needs often conflict. For example, Maria Sanchez would like to wear a Liz Claiborne suit. Such a suit would enhance her self-image and earn her the respect and admiration of her college friends. But this need conflicts with her budget and her need to get a job. Employers might feel that she's not responsible if she wears an expensive suit to an interview for an entry-level position. Typically customers make trade-offs between their conflicting needs. Later in this chapter we will discuss a model of how customers make these trade-offs.

Often a consumer's needs cannot be satisfied in one store or by one product. Retailing View 5.3 describes how consumers are engaging in more cross-shopping to satisfy their needs for value and self-esteem.

Stimulating Need Recognition   As we have said, customers must recognize unsatisfied needs before they are motivated to visit a store and buy merchandise.[19] Sometimes these needs are stimulated by an event in a person's life. For example, Maria's department store visit to buy a suit was stimulated by her impending interview and her examination of her blue suit. An ad motivated her to look for the suit at Macy's.

Retailers use a variety of approaches to stimulate problem recognition and motivate customers to visit their stores and buy merchandise. Advertising, direct mail, publicity, and special events communicate the availability of merchandise or special prices. Within the store, visual merchandising and salespeople can

5.3

Cross-Shopping Patterns Are Hard to Predict

MANY CONSUMERS APPEAR to be inconsistent in their shopping behavior. For example, an executive might own an expensive Mercedes-Benz auto and buy gas from a discount service station. A grocery shopper might buy an inexpensive store brand of paper towels and a premium national brand of orange juice. The pattern of buying both premium and low-priced merchandise or patronizing expensive, status-oriented retailers and price-oriented retailers is called **cross-shopping.**

Cross-shopping is of particular concern to department stores because 70 percent of department store customers shop in discount stores but only 47 percent of discount store shoppers shop in department stores. Thus, the growth in cross-shopping is drawing more consumers to discount stores. The middle-class cross-shopper has the profile of a department store customer but is seeking more value through cross-shopping.

While cross-shoppers are seeking value, their perception of value varies across product classes. Thus, a cross-shopper might feel it is worth the money to buy an expensive sweater in a boutique, but feel there is little quality difference between jeans at Kmart and designer brands at the boutique. Similarly, consumers may cut back on dining at an expensive restaurant but still want to treat themselves to expensive, high-quality jams, mustards, and olive oils in the supermarket. While retailers might think the buying patterns for cross-shopping do not make sense to them, it makes sense to their customers.

Source: Jerry Olson and J. Paul Peter, *Consumer Behavior and Marketing Strategy,* 4th ed. (Burr Ridge, IL: Richard D. Irwin, 1996), p. 204; and "Cross-Shopping," *Women's Wear Daily,* April 26, 1995, section II.

---

stimulate need recognition. For example, a salesperson showed Maria a scarf to stimulate her need for an accessory to complement her new suit.

One of the oldest methods for stimulating needs and attracting customers is still one of the most effective. The Saks Fifth Avenue store in Manhattan has 310 feet of store frontage along 49th and 50th Streets and the famed Fifth Avenue. Each day at lunchtime, about 3,000 people walk by the 31 window displays. Saks has 1,200 different window displays each year, with the Fifth Avenue windows changing each week. These displays can dramatically impact sales. For example, when Donna Karan clothes were featured in window displays, they sold over five times better than comparable designer lines.[20]

Window displays can stimulate need recognition. These bypassers are looking for a touch of retailing class in a Cartier window.

Information Search   Once customers identify a need, they may seek information about retailers and/or products that might help them satisfy the need. Maria's search was limited to the three suits shown her by the salesperson at Macy's. She was satisfied with this level of **information search** because she and her friend Brenda had confidence in Macy's merchandise and pricing, and she was pleased with the selection of suits presented to her. More extended buying processes may involve collecting a lot of information, visiting several retailers, and deliberating a long time before making a purchase.[21]

Amount of Information Searched   In general, the amount of information search depends on the value customers feel they'll gain from searching versus the cost of searching. The value of the search is in how it improves the customer's purchase decision. Will the search help the customer find a lower-price product or one that will give superior performance? The cost of search includes both time and money. Traveling from store to store can cost money for gas and parking, but the major cost incurred is the customer's time. Electronic retailing can dramatically reduce the cost of information. Consumers can collect information about merchandise sold across the world by "surfing the Net" from their home computer. However, electronic agents, like FRED described in Exhibit 3–4, are needed to make it easier to search electronically across the globe.

Factors influencing the amount of information searched include (1) the nature and use of the product being purchased, (2) characteristics of the individual customer, and (3) aspects of the market and buying situation in which the purchase is made.[22] Some people search more than others. For example, customers who enjoy shopping search more than those who don't like to shop. Also, customers who are self-confident or have prior experience purchasing and using the product tend to search less.

Marketplace and situational factors affecting information search include (1) the number of competing brands and retail outlets and (2) the time pressure under which the purchase must be made. When competition is greater and there are more alternatives to consider, the amount of information searched may increase. The amount decreases as time pressure increases.

Sources of Information   Customers have two sources of information: internal and external. **Internal sources** are information in a customer's memory such as names, images, and past experiences with different stores. For example, Maria relied on an internal source (her memory of an ad) when choosing to visit Macy's. **External sources** are information provided by ads and other people. Customers see hundreds of ads in print and the electronic media and notice signs for many retail outlets each day. In addition, customers get information about products and retailers from friends and family members. External sources of information are particularly important in the selection of fashion merchandise.

A major source of information is the customer's past shopping experience. Even if they remember only a small fraction of the information they are exposed to, customers have an extensive internal information bank to draw upon when deciding where to shop and what to buy.

If customers feel that their internal information is inadequate, they may turn to external information sources. Say a person wants to go to a movie. In selecting the film, he might rely on his past experiences—his satisfaction with movies with the same actors or director. He might also collect additional information by talking to friends or reading movie reviews. Remember how Maria Sanchez asked a respected

Video rental retailers assist customers in the information search phase by providing descriptions of the films and kiosks to find films of interest.

friend to help her make the purchase decision.[23] External sources of information play a major role in the acceptance of fashions, as discussed in the appendix to this chapter.

Reducing the Information Search
The retailer's objective at this stage of the buying process is to limit the customer's information search to its store. Each element of the retailing mix can be used to achieve this objective.

First, retailers must provide a good selection of merchandise so customers can find something to satisfy their needs within the store. Providing a wide variety of products and a broad assortment of brands, colors, and sizes increases the chances that customers will do so. For example, Blockbuster has a wide selection of video and uses in-store terminals to help customers locate alternative videos if their first choice is unavailable.[24]

Services provided by retailers can also limit search. The availability of credit and delivery may be important for consumers who want to purchase large durable goods such as furniture and appliances. And salespeople can provide enough information to customers so they won't feel the need to collect additional information by visiting other stores. For example, mail-order retailer of sportswear and sports equipment L.L. Bean gives employees 40 hours of training before they interact with their first customer. Due to this extensive training, people across the United States call L.L. Bean for advice on such subjects as what to wear for cross-country skiing and what to take on a trip to Alaska. If the employee answering the phone can't provide the information, the customer is switched to an expert within the company.[25] Thanks to L.L. Bean's reputation for expertise in sportswear and sporting goods, customers feel they can collect all the information they need to make a purchase decision from this one retailer.

Everyday low pricing is another way retailers increase the chance that customers will buy in their store and not search for a better price elsewhere. Since Wal-Mart and Circuit City have everyday-low-pricing policies, customers can feel confident that they won't offer that merchandise at a lower price in the future. Many stores with everyday low pricing offer money-back guarantees if a competitor offers the same merchandise at a lower price. Chapter 15 talks about benefits and limitations of various pricing strategies.

Evaluation of Alternatives: The Multiattribute Model

Customers collect and review information about alternative products or stores, evaluate the alternatives, and select one that best satisfies their needs. A multiattribute attitude model provides a useful way to look at the customer's evaluation process. We will discuss it in detail since it offers a framework for developing a retailing strategy.[26]

A **multiattribute attitude model** is based on the notion that customers see a retailer or a product as a collection of attributes or characteristics. The model is designed to predict a customer's evaluation of a product or retailer based on (1) its performance on several attributes and (2) those attributes' importance to the

EXHIBIT 5–2

Information Used to
Evaluate Stores

A. INFORMATION ABOUT STORES SELLING GROCERIES			
STORE CHARACTERISTICS	**CONVENIENCE STORE**	**SUPERMARKET**	**WAREHOUSE STORE**
Grocery prices	30% over average	average	20% below average
Double coupons	no	yes	no
Travel time (minutes)	5	15	25
Typical checkout time (minutes)	2	5	10
Number of products, brands, and sizes	2,000	15,000	5,000
Fresh produce	no	yes	yes
Fresh fish	no	yes	no
Atmosphere	unexciting	exciting	unexciting
Check cashing	no	yes	yes

B. BELIEFS ABOUT STORES' PERFORMANCE BENEFITS*			
PERFORMANCE BENEFITS	**CONVENIENCE STORE**	**SUPERMARKET**	**WAREHOUSE STORE**
Economy	3	6	10
Convenience	10	5	4
Assortment	2	10	6
Shopping Environment	4	8	2

*10 = Excellent; 1 = Poor

customer. Retail buyers can also use the multiattribute model to evaluate merchandise and vendors. (See Chapter 14.)

Beliefs about Performance   To illustrate this model, consider the store choice decision confronting a young single person who needs groceries. He considers three stores: the neighborhood convenience store, supermarket, and wholesale club compared in Exhibit 5–2.

The customer mentally processes Exhibit 5–2A's "objective" information about each store and forms an impression of the benefits the stores provide. Exhibit 5–2B shows his beliefs about these benefits. Notice that some benefits combine several objective characteristics. For example, the convenience benefit combines travel time, checkout time, and check-cashing privileges. Grocery prices and double-coupon offers affect the customer's beliefs about the economy of shopping at the stores.

The degree to which each store provides the benefit is represented on a 10-point scale: 10 means the store performs well in providing the benefit; 1 means it performs poorly. Here no store has superior performance on all benefits. The convenience store is high on convenience but low on assortment. The supermarket performs well on assortment and environment, but its performances on convenience and economy are modest. Finally, the wholesale club offers good economy but unappealing atmosphere.

Importance Weights   The young person in the preceding example forms an overall evaluation of each store based on the importance he places on each benefit the stores provide. The importance he places on a benefit can also be represented using a 10-point rating scale, with 10 indicating the benefit is very important and 1 indicating it's very unimportant.[27] Using this rating scale, the importance of the store benefits for the young single person and a parent with four children are shown in Exhibit 5–3, along with the performance beliefs previously discussed.

5.4

Gender Differences in Supermarket Shopping

ELAINE MORALES GIVES HER HUSBAND Jake Bramhall a C− grade for grocery shopping. He might be a great management consultant and know a lot about cars, but "He comes back [from the supermarket] with candies, just like a kid."

While 19 percent of households indicate that a male is the primary grocery shopper for the family, the supermarket is still a woman's world. Men show little ability or interest in honing their shopping skills, while women view the supermarket as a place where they can demonstrate their expertise in getting the most value for their money. Rather than looking for items on sale or making price comparisons, men tend to select well-known brands. They also tend to not pay attention at the checkout register, while women watch the cashier to be sure they're charged the right price.

Men and women even buy different merchandise. Women buy more health-oriented foods (such as cottage cheese and refrigerated yogurt) and household essentials (such as cleaning and personal health products). Men's shopping baskets contain more beer, cupcakes, ice cream, and hot dogs.

Men also do less planning and make numerous last-minute grocery trips. Single men visit supermarkets 99 times a year, while single women make 80 trips a year. These 11th-hour trips make men more susceptible to impulse purchases such as potato chips and cookies.

Over time these differences between male and female shopping patterns may fade. Even now, busy career women shop more like men than their mothers.

Source: Suein Hwang, "From Choices to Checkout, the Genders Behave Very Differently in Supermarkets," *The Wall Street Journal*, March 22, 1994, pp. A1, A4; and Rosemary Polegato and Judith Zaichkowsky, "Family Food Shopping; Strategies Used by Husbands and Wives," *Journal of Consumer Affairs* 28 (Winter 1994), pp. 278–99.

Notice that the single man values convenience much more than economy, assortment, and store environment. But the parent places a lot of importance on economy, assortment is moderately important, and convenience and store environment aren't very important.

Every customer has a unique set of needs when she is about to go shopping. The importance of a store's benefits differs for each customer and may also differ for each shopping trip. For example, the parent with four children may stress economy because food expenditures are high. Since the parent has a baby-sitter for the children during the weekly shopping trip, convenience isn't so important. Retailing View 5.4 describes some basic differences in how men and women shop for groceries.

EXHIBIT 5–3 Information Used in Evaluating Stores

| CHARACTERISTIC | IMPORTANCE WEIGHTS | | PERFORMANCE BELIEFS | | |
	YOUNG SINGLE MAN	PARENT WITH FOUR CHILDREN	CONVENIENCE STORE	SUPERMARKET	WAREHOUSE STORE
Economy	3	10	3	6	10
Convenience	10	2	10	5	4
Assortment	1	6	2	7	5
Shopping environment	3	3	4	8	2
OVERALL EVALUATION OF EACH STORE					
Parent			74	136	144
Young single man			123	99	81

Men often show little interest or ability in shopping.

In Exhibit 5–3, the single man and parent have the same beliefs about each store's performance, but they differ in the importance they place on benefits the stores offer. In general, customers can differ on their beliefs about the stores' performance as well as on their importance weights.

Evaluating Stores   Research has shown that a customer's overall evaluation of an alternative (in this situation, a store) is closely related to the sum of the performance beliefs multiplied by the importance weights.[28] Thus, we calculate the young single man's overall evaluation or score for the convenience store as follows:

$$
\begin{array}{rcr}
3 \times 3 &=& 9 \\
10 \times 10 &=& 100 \\
1 \times 2 &=& 2 \\
3 \times 4 &=& 12 \\
\hline
&& 123
\end{array}
$$

Choice of Alternatives   Exhibit 5–3 shows the overall evaluations for the three stores using the importance weights of the single man and the parent. For the single man, the convenience store has the highest score, 123, and thus the most favorable evaluation. He would probably select this store to buy coffee, milk, a frozen dinner, and ice cream. On the other hand, the wholesale club has the highest score, 144, for the parent, who'd probably buy the family's weekly groceries there.

When customers are about to select a store, they don't actually go through the process of listing store characteristics, evaluating stores' performance on these characteristics, determining each characteristic's importance, calculating each store's overall score, and then visiting a store with the highest score! The multiattribute attitude model doesn't reflect customers' actual decision process, but it does predict their evaluation of alternatives and their choice.[29] In addition, the model provides useful information for designing a retail offering. For example, if the supermarket here could increase its performance rating on assortment from 8 to 10 (perhaps by adding a bakery), customers like the parent might shop at the supermarket more often than at the wholesale club. Later in this chapter we'll discuss how retailers can use the multiattribute attitude model to increase their store's evaluation.

EXHIBIT 5-4

Information Maria
Sanchez Used in
Buying a Suit

BENEFITS PROVIDED BY SUITS	IMPORTANCE WEIGHTS	BELIEFS ABOUT PERFORMANCE		
		SUIT A	SUIT B	SUIT C
Economy	6	6	5	5
Quality	6	10	7	8
Conservative look	8	6	6	10
Complement to wardrobe	8	7	6	9
Fashion	4	7	10	5
Fit	10	?	?	8
Overall evaluation				330

The application of the multiattribute attitude model in Exhibit 5–3 deals with a customer who's evaluating and selecting a retail store. The same model can also be used to describe how a customer evaluates and selects merchandise in a store. For example, Exhibit 5–4 shows Maria Sanchez's beliefs and importance weights about the three suits shown to her by the salesperson in Retailing View 5.1. Maria didn't evaluate suits A and B on fit because she didn't try them on. She bought suit C because it was good enough. Its overall evaluation passed some minimum threshold (which in terms of this multiattribute attitude model might be a score of 320).

Customers often make choices as Maria did. They don't thoroughly evaluate each alternative as suggested in the multiattribute attitude model. They simply buy merchandise that's good enough or very good on one particular attribute. In general, customers don't spend the time necessary to find the very best product. Once they've found a product that satisfies their need, they stop searching.[30]

INTERNET EXERCISE   McGraw-Hill (the publisher of this textbook and *Business Week*) maintains an Internet site with information about personal computers. Go to the site, http://www.maven.businessweek/, and look for information to purchase a laptop computer for yourself. How does this experience compare to shopping for a computer in a store?

Implications for Retailers   How can a retailer use the multiattribute attitude model to encourage customers to shop at its store more frequently? First, the model indicates what information customers use to decide which store to visit. Thus, to develop a program for attracting customers, the retailer must do market research to collect the following information:

1. Alternative stores that customers consider.
2. Characteristics or benefits that customers consider when making their store evaluation and choice.
3. Customers' ratings of each store's performance on the characteristics.
4. The importance weights that customers attach to the characteristics.

Armed with this information, the retailer can use several approaches to influence customers to select its store.

Hermanos uses billboard advertising to build top-of-the-mind awareness and ensure that the store will be in the customer's consideration set when buying boots.

Getting into the Consideration Set   The retailer must make sure that its store is included in the customer's consideration set. The **consideration set** is the set of alternatives the customer evaluates when making a selection.[31] To be included in the consideration set, the retailer must develop programs to increase the likelihood that customers will remember its store when they're about to go shopping. The retailer can influence this top-of-the-mind awareness through advertising and location strategies. Heavy advertising expenditures that stress the store's name increase top-of-the-mind awareness. When a retailer locates several stores in a geographic area, customers are exposed more frequently to the store name as they drive through the area.[32]

After ensuring that its store is in the consideration set, the retailer can use four methods to increase the chances that its store will be selected for a visit:

1.   Increase the belief about its store's performance.
2.   Decrease the performance belief for competing stores in the consideration set.
3.   Increase customers' importance weights.
4.   Add a new benefit.

Changing Performance Beliefs   The first approach involves altering customers' beliefs about the retailer's performance—increasing the retailer's performance rating on a characteristic. For example, the supermarket in Exhibit 5–3 would want to increase its overall rating by improving its rating on all four benefits. The supermarket could improve its rating on economy by lowering prices and could improve its rating on assortment by stocking more gourmet and ethnic foods.

It's costly for a retailer to improve its performance on all benefits. Thus, a retailer should focus efforts on improving performance on benefits that are important to customers in its target market. For example, 7-Eleven's market research found that women avoid convenience stores because they view them as dingy and unsafe. To attract more women, 7-Eleven has improved the shopping environment in a number of its stores. To create a sense of space, brighter lighting was installed and aisles were widened. Cigarette racks and other clutter were cleared off checkout counters, and colorful signage was used to designate merchandise areas.[33]

A change in the performance belief concerning an important benefit results in a large change in customers' overall evaluation. In Exhibit 5–3's situation, the supermarket should attempt to improve its convenience ratings if it wants to attract more young single men who presently shop at convenience stores. If its convenience rating rose from 5 to 8, its overall evaluation for young single men would be slightly greater (129 versus 123) than the overall evaluation of the convenience store. Note that a larger increase in rating— from 6 to 10 on both less-important benefits such as economy and shopping environment—would have no great effect on the store's overall evaluation. The supermarket might try to improve its rating on convenience by increasing the number of checkout stations, using scanners to reduce checkout time, or providing more in-store information so customers could locate merchandise more easily.

Another approach is to try to decrease customers' performance ratings of a competing store. This approach may be illegal and usually isn't very effective, because customers typically don't believe a firm's negative comments about its competitors.

Changing Importance Weights   Altering customers' importance weights is another approach to influencing store choice. A retailer would want to increase the importance customers place on benefits for which its performance is superior and decrease the importance of benefits for which it has inferior performance.

For example, if the supermarket in Exhibit 5–4 tried to attract families who shop at wholesale clubs, it should increase the importance of assortment. Typically changing importance weights is harder than changing performance beliefs because importance weights reflect customers' values.[34]

Adding a New Benefit   Finally, retailers might try to add a new benefit to the set of benefits customers consider when selecting a store. Since JCPenney is America's only national department store, a customer can purchase a gift at a local Penney store and send it to a person in another part of the country knowing that, if necessary, the recipient can exchange it at her local Penney store. Normally, customers wouldn't consider this when selecting a retail store. This approach of adding a new benefit is often effective because it's easier to change customer evaluation of new benefits than old benefits.

Purchasing the Merchandise

Customers don't always purchase a brand or item of merchandise with the highest overall evaluation. The item with the highest evaluation may not be in the specific store they visit or the store might not have the size and color the customer wants. Even if the customer locates the item he wants, the store might not be open when he wants to buy it or the store might not accept his credit card. Retailers must take steps to ensure that customers can easily convert their merchandise evaluation and choice decisions into purchases at the cash register.

JCPenney, as a national department chain, offers an unusual benefit. Customers from around the world can use the bridal registry on the Internet to order gifts. The recipient can then return merchandise to any store location.

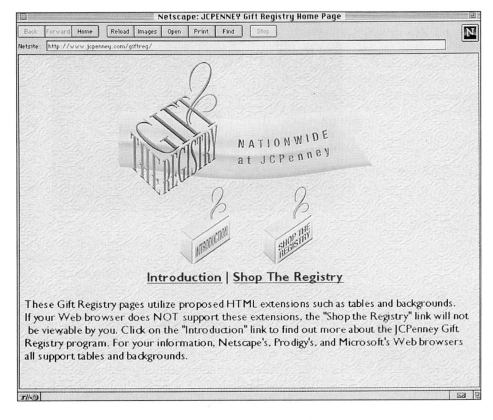

Postpurchase Evaluation   The buying process doesn't end when a customer purchases a product. After making a purchase, the customer consumes or uses the product and then evaluates the experience to determine whether it was satisfactory or unsatisfactory. **Satisfaction** is a postconsumption evaluation of how well a store or product meets or exceeds customer expectations.[36]

This **postpurchase evaluation** becomes part of the customer's internal information that affects future store and product decisions. Unsatisfactory experiences can motivate customers to complain to the retailer and to patronize other stores.[37] Chapter 17 discusses means to increase customer satisfaction such as offering quality merchandise, providing accurate information about merchandise, and contacting customers after a sale.

REFACT About two-thirds of women and three-fourths of men go into a store wanting to purchase a specific item only to find it's not there.[35]

FACTORS AFFECTING THE DECISION PROCESS

Factors that influence customers' decision-making process include family, reference groups, and cultural environment.

Family

To develop effective retail programs, retailers must understand how families make purchase decisions, how various family members influence these decisions, and how decision making changes over the family life cycle.

Family Decision Making   In the discussion of the consumer decision-making process, we focused on how one person makes a decision—how Maria purchases a suit for herself. When families make purchase decisions, they often consider the

Children can play an important role in family purchase decisions. This boy may influence the family to buy the telephone being demonstrated by the salesperson.

needs of all family members.[38] In a situation such as choosing a vacation site, all family members may participate in the decision-making process. In other situations, one member of the family may assume the role of making the purchase decision. Women typically have the authority to make decisions on goods and services needed to sustain day-to-day operation of the household, while men are more involved in purchasing financial services like household loans and investments.[39]

Retailers need to consider these different roles when selling to families. For example, the husband might buy the groceries, while the wife uses them to prepare their child's lunch, and the child consumes the lunch in school. In this situation, the store choice decision might be made by the husband, while the brand choice decision might be made by the mother but greatly influenced by the child.

Children play an important role in family buying decisions. It's estimated that children between ages 4 and 12 themselves spend or influence their parents' purchases of $135 million in merchandise. Shopping ranks among the top seven interests and activities of American youth.[40]

Satisfying the needs of children is particularly important for many baby boomers deciding to have children late in life. They often have high disposable income and want to stay in luxury resorts, but they still want to take their children on vacations. Resort hotels now realize they must satisfy children's needs as well as adults'. For example, Hyatt hotels greet families by offering books and games tailored to the children's ages. Parents checking in with infants receive a first-day supply of baby food or formula and diapers at no charge. Baby-sitting and escort services to attractions for children are offered.[41]

Retailers can attract consumers who shop with other family members by satisfying the needs of all family members. For example, IKEA, a Swedish furniture store chain, has a "ball pit" in which children can play while their parents shop. Nordstrom has sitting areas in its store and pubs where men can have a beer and watch a football game while their wives shop. By accommodating the needs of men and children who might not be interested in shopping, the family stays in the stores longer and buys more merchandise.[42]

Family Life Cycle   The **family life cycle** describes how a family's needs and expenditures change over time.[43] The traditional stages in the family life cycle are

- Bachelor—young, single people typically living away from their parents.
- Newly married couples with no children.

REFACT Eighty-five percent of the men's clothing sold in department stores is bought by women, and over 50 percent of Home Depot's sales are made to women.

- Young married couples with youngest child under six.
- Young married couples with youngest child over six.
- Older married couples with dependent children.
- Older married couples, still working, with independent children.
- Retired married couples.
- Solitary survivors.

Of course, as mentioned in Chapter 4, there are a substantial number of non-traditional families in the United States, and many traditional families do not pass through all the stages in the life cycle. However, the life cycle is useful for understanding the needs of families and how they change over time. For example, with two incomes and no expenses for children, young married people typically are less concerned about the price of merchandise and more interested in luxury goods. Young married couples with young children are more interested in health care services and the nutritional value of food.

Reference Groups

A **reference group** is one or more people whom a person uses as a basis of comparison for beliefs, feelings, and behaviors. A consumer might have a number of different reference groups, although the most important reference group is the family, as discussed in the previous section. These reference groups affect the buying decision process by (1) providing information, (2) administering rewards for specific purchasing behaviors, and (3) enhancing a consumer's self-image.

Reference groups provide information to consumers directly through conversation or indirectly through observation. For example, Maria received valuable information from her friend about the suits she was considering. On the other hand, Maria might look to women tennis players like Monica Seles and Martina Hingis to guide her selection of tennis apparel. The role of reference groups in creating fashion is discussed in the appendix to this chapter.

Some reference groups influence purchase behaviors by rewarding behavior that meets with their approval. For example, the reference group of employees in a company might define the appropriate dress style and criticize fellow workers who violate this standard. When retailers provide information about "dress-down" days, as discussed in Retailing View 5.2, they are helping customers avoid sanctions from their reference group.

By identifying and affiliating with reference groups, consumers create, enhance, and maintain their self-image. Customers who want to be seen as members of an elite social class may shop at prestige retailers, while others who want to create an image of an outdoors person might buy merchandise from the L.L. Bean catalog.

Department stores use their teen boards to provide a reference group influence on teenaged shoppers. The teen board members are selected because they are a group of students that other students would like to emulate. By buying apparel worn by teen board members, other students can identify with these student leaders.

Affinity marketing provides an opportunity for consumers to express their identification with an organization. It's an example of the use of reference groups to influence purchase behavior. The common example of affinity marketing is banks offering consumers affinity credit cards tied to reference groups like their university, an NFL team, or a town such as South Orange, New Jersey.

REFACT Over 26 million people have at least one of the 3,600 affinity credit cards available.[44]

Culture and Subculture

Culture is the meaning and values shared by most members of a society. For example, core values shared by most Americans include individualism, freedom, mastery and control, self-improvement, achievement and success, material comfort, and health and fitness.[45]

As retailers expand beyond their domestic markets, they need to be sensitive to how cultural values affect customer needs and buying behavior. For example, gift giving plays a much more important role in Japanese than American culture. Most Japanese feel a need to bring gifts for family and friends when they return from a trip. In one study, about half of the Japanese tourists returning home from Los Angeles bought gifts for over 15 family members and friends. They spent as much on gifts for others as on merchandise for their own use. Gift packaging and wrapping offered by retailers is particularly important to these Japanese tourists because gifts aren't opened in front of the gift giver. Thus, the gift's appearance is particularly important to the giver.[46]

Even the meaning of colors differs across cultures. In China, white is the color of mourning and brides wear red dresses. When Domino's Pizza opened its first outlet in Japan, it needed to educate Japanese consumers about the toppings on American pizzas. In this educational process, Domino's learned that it needed to develop new toppings like apple, rice, burdock root, and squid to please the Japanese palate.[47]

Subcultures are distinctive groups of people within a culture. Members of a subculture share some customs and norms with the overall society but also have some unique perspectives. Subcultures can be based on geography (Southerners), age (baby boomers), ethnicity (Asian Americans), or lifestyle (punks).

The two largest ethnic subcultures in the United States are African American and Hispanic. The African American subculture is the largest, accounting for 13 percent of the population. While the 17 million relatively poor African Americans living in the inner city are very visible, 8 million African Americans are more affluent, living in the suburbs.

The overall spending patterns of African Americans and whites are similar, and differences are largely due to social class and income rather than ethnic differences. However, African Americans do spend more than whites on some product categories like encyclopedias and reference books, cooking ingredients, baby products, and cosmetics. Retailing View 5.5 outlines some differences between white and African American shopping behaviors.

REFACT In 1994, furniture retailer IKEA aired the first mainstream TV ad targeted toward the gay subculture by featuring a gay relationship.[48]

REFACT If African Americans were a separate nation, their buying power would rank 12th among Western nations.[49]

Many retailers are selling merchandise and providing services to satisfy the needs of specific subcultures.

5.5

Still Shopping Till They Drop

AS DISCUSSED IN CHAPTER 4, the time-pressured consumer is less inclined to do recreational shopping. However, African Americans are still hitting the malls. Sixty percent of African American consumers say shopping is "fun and exciting," while only 35 percent of white consumers hold this view.

African Americans are more prone to shop in department and specialty stores than whites. Department stores such JCPenney, Sears, and Nordstrom are committed to serving the needs of this subculture. Stores with numerous African American patrons carry merchandise tailored to this segment's needs. For example, African American women buy more and higher-quality hosiery than other women. They prefer to be more dressed up and are less likely to wear casual clothes to work. African American women also spend three times more annually on cosmetics than white women.

In addition to tailoring their assortments toward African Americans, many retailers are committed to increasing the representation of minorities and women in their senior management ranks. These managing-diversity programs are discussed in more detail in Chapter 10.

Source: Christy Fisher, "Black, Hip, and Primed to Shop," *American Demographics,* September 1996, pp. 52–58.

Some retailers assume that African American consumers will develop the values of the white community as they move up the social ladder. However, middle-class African Americans have a strong sense of their ethnicity and respond to products and retailers that appeal to their racial pride.

The Hispanic subculture represents 8 percent of the U.S. population and is the fastest-growing ethnic group. However, the subculture is very diverse, including people from a number of different Spanish-speaking countries such as Cuba, Puerto Rico, Mexico, and the Dominican Republic. Two important demographic characteristics of the Hispanic market are its youth and family size. The average age of Hispanics is 23, while the U.S. average is 32. Hispanic households have 3.5 people compared to the U.S. average of 2.7.[50]

Family plays a central role in Hispanic subculture. Hispanics take considerable pride in their children's clothing. They're also attracted to labor-saving products, but Hispanic homemakers are willing to spend the extra time if their families will benefit. Long distance services that offer lower rates for calls to family members would offend Hispanics, who view needing a price discount to call family insulting.[51] Retailing View 5.6 describes Carnival supermarkets, which are designed to meet the needs of Hispanic shoppers.

REFACT Brand loyalty among Asian Americans is very low. In a study of Chinese families in San Francisco, one-third of the households couldn't name the brand of laundry detergent they used.[52]

MARKET SEGMENTATION

The preceding discussion focused on (1) how individual customers evaluate and select stores and merchandise and (2) factors affecting their decision-making processes. To lower their costs, retailers identify groups of customers (market segments) and target their offerings to meet the needs of typical customers in that segment rather than the needs of a specific customer. A **retail market segment** is a group of customers whose needs are satisfied by the same retail mix because they have similar needs and go through similar buying processes. For example, families traveling on a vacation have different needs than an executive on a business trip. Thus, Marriott offers hotels with different retail mixes for each of these segments.

5.6

Retailing to the Hispanic Market

WHEN MINYARD REALIZED that more than 50 percent of the people within three of its supermarkets were Hispanics, it decided to reconfigure those outlets to meet its customers' needs. The stores were renamed Carnival, and decor was changed to bright Sunbelt colors: yellows, greens, and oranges. Signage in Spanish was added. The music was changed from country-and-western and easy listening to Mexican tunes.

Based on an analysis of the spending patterns in the stores, the meat and produce departments were expanded. Whole chickens and fish were displayed on ice rather than as prepackaged parts and fillets.

A carnival atmosphere was emphasized by using food products sold as decorations such as large tin tubs full of pinto beans and hanging piñatas sold at bargain prices. Many of the strands of chili peppers and garlic decorating the produce department were bought as gifts.

Source: Bob Ingram, "At Minyard, Big 'D' Stands for Diversity," *Supermarket Business Magazine,* May 1994, pp. 41–45; and Richard Turcsik, "A Latino Accent," *Supermarket News,* January 25, 1993, pp. 15–16.

Criteria for Segmenting Markets

Customers are grouped into segments in many different ways. For example, customers can be grouped based on the fact that they live in the same city, have similar incomes and education, or barbecue at their homes twice a week or more. Exhibit 5–5 shows different methods for segmenting retail markets. There's no simple way to determine which method is best. Five criteria for evaluating whether a retail segment is a viable target market are actionability, identifiability, accessibility, stability, and size.

Actionability The fundamental criteria for evaluating a retail market segment are (1) customers in the segment must have similar needs, seek similar benefits, and be satisfied by a similar retail offering and (2) those customers' needs are different from the needs of customers in other segments. Actionability means that the definition of a segment must clearly indicate what the retailer should do to satisfy its needs. Based on this criterion, it makes sense for Lane Bryant (a division of The Limited catering to full-figure women) to segment the apparel market based on a demographic characteristic—physical size. Customers who wear large sizes have different needs than customers in small sizes, so they are attracted to a store offering a unique merchandise mix. In the context of the multiattribute attitude model discussed previously, women who wear large sizes place more importance on fit and fashion because it's harder for them to satisfy these needs. They should also feel that Lane Bryant performs better on these characteristics than retailers such as JCPenney, Kmart, or Limited Express that don't carry as wide an assortment of large sizes.

It wouldn't make sense for a supermarket to segment its market based on customer size. Large and small men and women probably have the same needs, seek the same benefits, and go through the same buying process for groceries. They have similar importance weights for store attributes. This segmentation approach wouldn't be actionable for a supermarket retailer because the retailer couldn't develop unique mixes for large and small customers. Thus, supermarkets usually segment markets using demographics such as income or ethnic origin to develop their retail mix.

Identifiability Retailers must be able to identify the customers in a target segment. Identifiability is important because it permits the retailer to determine (1) the segment's size and (2) with whom the retailer should communicate when promoting its retail offering.

Accessibility   Once a segment is identified, retailers must be able to deliver the appropriate retail mix to the customers in it. Customers for Marriott convention hotels and resort hotels are accessed in different ways because they use different sources to collect information about products and services. Convention hotel customers are best reached through newspapers such as *USA Today* and *The Wall Street Journal*, while resort hotel customers are best reached by ads on TV and travel and leisure magazines.

EXHIBIT 5–5   Methods for Segmenting Retail Markets

SEGMENTATION BASES/DESCRIPTORS	ILLUSTRATIVE CATEGORIES
GEOGRAPHIC	
Region	Pacific, Mountain, West North Central, West South Central, East North Central, East South Central, South Atlantic, Middle Atlantic, New England
Size of city, country, or standard metropolitan statistical area (SMSA)	Under 5,000, 5,000–19,999, 20,000–49,999, 50,000–99,999, 100,000–249,999, 250,000–499,999, 500,000–999,999, 1,000,000–3,999,999, 4,000,000 or over
Population density	Urban, surburban, rural
Climate	Warm, cold
DEMOGRAPHIC	
Age	Under 6, 6–12, 13–19, 20–29, 30–39, 40–49, 50–59, 60–70, 70+
Gender	Male, female
Family size	1–2, 3–4, 5+ persons
Family life cycle	Young, single; young, married, no children; young married, youngest child under 6; young, married, youngest child 6 or over; older, married, with children; older, married, no children under 18; older, single, other
Income	Under 10,000, 10,000–14,999, 15,000–24,999, 25,000–34,999, 35,000–49,999, 50,000–74,999, over 75,000
Occupation	Professional and technical; manager, official, and proprietor; clerical, sales; craftsperson, foreperson; operative; farmer; retired; student; housewife or househusband; unemployed
Education	Grade school or less; some high school; graduated from high school; some college; graduated from college; some graduate work; graduate degree
Religion	Catholic, Protestant, Jewish, other
Race	White, Asian, African American, Hispanic American
NATIONALITY	
	U.S., British, French, German, Italian, Japanese
PSYCHOSOCIAL	
Social class	Upper class, middle class, working class, lower class
Lifestyle	Traditionalist, sophisticate, swinger
Personality	Compliant, aggressive, detached
FEELINGS AND BEHAVIORS	
Attitudes	Positive, neutral, negative
Benefits sought	Convenience, economy, prestige
Readiness stage	Unaware, aware, informed, interested, desirous, intention to purchase
Perceived risk	High, moderate, low
Innovativeness	Innovator, early adopter, early majority, late majority, laggard, nonadopter
Involvement	Low, high
Loyalty status	None, some, total
Usage rate	None, light, medium, heavy
User status	Nonuser, exuser, potential user, current user
Usage situation	Home, work, commuting, vacation

Source: J. Paul Peter and Jerry C. Olson, *Consumer Behavior and Marketing Strategy,* 3d ed. (Burr Ridge, IL: Richard D. Irwin, 1996), pp. 488–89.

Stability   Attractive segments (segments that provide opportunities for long-term profits) are stable over time. Banana Republic, for example, targeted its retail stores toward a group of people with a unique lifestyle. Customers in this segment led casual, active lives and perceived themselves to be cosmopolitan and adventuresome. This segment provided a basis for growth and profits for Banana Republic for a while. But as the values of society—in particular, of customers in this segment—changed, Banana Republic's fortunes declined.

Size   A target segment must be large enough to support a unique retailing mix. For example, in the past, health food and vitamins were found primarily in small, owner-operated stores that catered to a relatively small market. In the wake of a higher consciousness about exercise and nutrition, health food stores like General Nutrition have flourished. Supermarkets have also expanded their offering of health foods and vitamins to meet this substantial market segment's needs.

Approaches to Segmenting Markets

Exhibit 5–5 illustrates the wide variety of approaches for segmenting retail markets. No one approach is best for all retailers. They must explore various factors that affect customer buying behavior and determine which factors are most important. Now we'll discuss methods for segmenting retail markets.

Geographic Segmentation   **Geographic segmentation** groups customers by where they live. A retail market can be segmented by countries (United States, Mexico), states, counties, cities, and neighborhoods. Since customers typically shop at stores convenient to where they live and work, individual retail outlets usually focus on the customer segment reasonably close to the outlet.

Many department store chains concentrate on regions of the country. For example, Lazarus concentrates on Ohio and surrounding states, while Bergstroms concentrates on Milwaukee. Even though national retailers such as The Gap and JCPenney have no geographic focus, they do tailor their merchandise selections to different regions of the country. Snow sleds don't sell well in Florida and surfboards don't sell well in Colorado. Even within a metropolitan area, stores in a chain must adjust to unique needs of customers in different neighborhoods. For example, supermarkets in affluent neighborhoods typically have more gourmet foods than stores in less affluent neighborhoods.

Segments based on geography are identifiable, accessible, durable, and substantial. It's easy to determine who lives in a geographic segment such as the Chicago area and to target communications and locate retail outlets for customers in Chicago.

Because customers in different geographic segments may have similar needs, it could be inappropriate to develop unique retail offerings by geographic markets. For example, a fast-food customer in Detroit probably seeks the same benefits as a fast-food customer in Los Angeles. Thus, it wouldn't be useful to segment the fast-food market geographically. Even though Target and The Gap vary some merchandise assortments geographically, the majority of their merchandise is identical in all of their stores because customers who buy basic clothing (underwear, slacks, shirts, and blouses) have the same needs in all regions of the United States.

Demographic Segmentation   **Demographic** variables are the most common means to define segments because such customer segments can be easily identified and accessed. The media used by retailers to communicate with customers are

REFACT Across the United States, vanilla is the number one flavor and chocolate is number two of Häagen-Dazs ice cream; however, coffee is most popular in New York, butter pecan elsewhere in the East, and chocolate chip in California.[53]

defined in terms of demographic profiles. Chapter 4 discussed special demographic segments retailers focus on such as African Americans, Hispanic Americans, the elderly, and baby boomers.

While segments based on demographics are easily identified and accessed, demographics aren't always related to customer needs and buying behavior. Thus, demographics may not be useful for defining segments for some retailers. For example, demographics are poor predictors of users of active wear such as jogging suits and running shoes. At one time, retailers assumed that active wear would be purchased exclusively by young people, but the health and fitness trend has led people of all ages to buy this merchandise. Initially, retailers felt that VCRs would be a luxury product purchased mainly by wealthy customers. But retailers found that low-income customers and families with young children were strongly attracted to VCRs because they offered low-cost, convenient entertainment.

REFACT Consumers over 50 are only 25 percent of the population but control over 77 percent of all of the financial assets in the United States.[54]

Lifestyle Segmentation   Lifestyle refers to how people live, how they spend their time and money, what activities they pursue, and their attitudes and opinions about the world they live in. Retailers today are placing more emphasis on lifestyles or psychographics than on demographics to define a target segment.

VALS2 is one of several commercially available segmentation approaches based on consumer values and lifestyles.[55] Segments are based on two national surveys of 2,500 consumers conducted by SRI International. The surveys ask consumers to indicate whether they agreed or disagreed with statements such as "My idea of fun in a national park would be to stay in an expensive lodge and dress up for dinner" and "I could not stand to skin a dead animal." Based on an analysis of responses to the survey, eight lifestyle segments (Exhibit 5–6) were identified. Note how consumers in each segment are described in terms of different attitudes, ambitions, and buying behaviors rather than their age or where they live.

The eight lifestyle segments are arranged in two dimensions. The vertical dimension indicates the amount of resources (money, education, health, self-confidence, and energy level) people in the segment have. Actualizers have a lot of resources; strugglers have limited resources.

The horizontal dimension describes the self-orientation of consumers in the segment. The behavior of people in principle-oriented segments (fulfilled and believers) is based on their beliefs about how the world is or should be. People in status-oriented segments are guided by the actions and opinions of others. Those in action-oriented segments are guided by their need for social and physical activity, variety, and risk taking.

INTERNET EXERCISE   Want to know what VALS2 segment you are in? Go to http://future.sri.com:80/vals/survey.html and take a survey to find out your profile. Search associated sites and compare Web users with the general population. How do they differ? What does this mean for a retailer targeting Web users?

Many businesses use the VALS2 segments to better understand their customers and target markets. For example, a survey of air travelers found that 37 percent were actualizers compared to 8 percent of the general population. Since actualizers buy merchandise that reflects their high income and status, the research suggests that stores like The Nature Company and Sharper Image would succeed in airport locations.[56]

EXHIBIT 5–6

VALS2 Lifestyle Segments

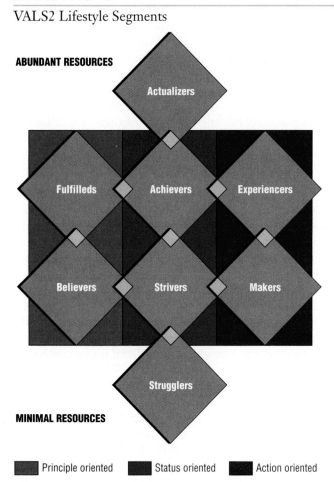

ABUNDANT RESOURCES

MINIMAL RESOURCES

▓ Principle oriented   ▓ Status oriented   ▓ Action oriented

ACTUALIZERS
Highest income. High self-esteem. Indulge in self-oriented activities. Image is important. Wide range of interests. Open to change. Want the finer things in life.

FULFILLEDS
Mature, responsible, well-educated professionals. Leisure activities center on the home. Well informed about what is going on in the world. Open to new ideas and social change. High income but practical, value-oriented consumers.

ACHIEVERS
Successful. Work-oriented. Life centers around jobs and family. Politically conservative. Respect authority. Favor established products that demonstrate their status to their peers.

EXPERIENCERS
Youngest of all segments. Want to affect the environment in meaningful way. Have a lot of energy. Spend time on physical and social activities. Avid consumers. Spend heavily on clothing, fast food, music, and anything new.

BELIEVERS
Modest income. Conservative and predictable consumers. Favor American products and established brands. Life centers around family, church, and community.

STRIVERS
Similar values as Achievers but have fewer resources. Style is very important. Attempt to emulate people who they wish they were.

MAKERS
Practical. Value self-sufficiency. Focus activities on family, work, and physical recreation. Have little interest in events outside their immediate surroundings. Not impressed by material possessions.

STRUGGLERS
Lowest income. Oldest segment. Tend to be brand loyal.

Source: Martha Farnsworth Riche, "Psychographics for the 1990s," *American Demographics*, July 1989, p. 26. Reprinted with permission. © *American Demographics*, July 1989, Ithaca, New York.

The Merrill Lynch advertising campaign "Bullish on America" was altered based on a VALS2 analysis. The original campaign showed a thundering herd of buffalos. The analysis revealed that this ad appealed primarily to "belongers" rather than "achievers," the customer profile Merrill Lynch was seeking. The ad was changed to depicting a lone bull using the theme "A Breed Apart."

SRI International provides information about the number of people in each segment living in different zip-code areas and buying different products. While it's harder to identify and access consumers in a **lifestyle segment** than in a demographic segment, lifestyles are typically more closely related to consumer needs and buying behavior. Thus, it's easier to develop an effective retail mix for a lifestyle segment than for a demographic segment.

Buying Situation Segmentation   Buying behavior of customers with the same demographics or lifestyle can differ depending on their buying situation. For example, the parent with four children evaluated the wholesale club higher than the convenience store or supermarket for weekly grocery purchases in Exhibit 5–3.

But if the parent ran out of milk during the week, he'd probably go to the convenience store rather than the wholesale club for this fill-in shopping. In terms of Exhibit 5–3's multiattribute attitude model, convenience would be more important than assortment in the fill-in shopping situation. Similarly, the same executive will stay at a convention hotel on a business trip and a resort on a family vacation.

Benefit Segmentation Another approach for defining a target segment is to group customers seeking similar benefits. In the multiattribute attitude model, customers in the same benefit segment would have a similar set of importance weights on the attributes of a store or a product. For example, customers who place high importance on fashion and style and low importance on price would form a fashion segment, while customers who place more importance on price would form a price segment.

Benefit segments are very actionable. Benefits sought by customers in the target segment clearly indicate how retailers should design their offerings to appeal to the segment. But customers in benefit segments aren't easily identified or accessed. It's hard to look at a person and determine what benefits she's seeking. Typically, the audience for media used by retailers is described by demographics rather than by the benefits sought.

Composite Segmentation Approaches

As we've seen, no one approach meets all the criteria for useful customer segmentation. For example, demographic and geographic segmenting are ideal for identifying and accessing customers, but these characteristics are often unrelated to customers' needs. Thus, these approaches don't indicate the actions necessary to attract customers in these segments. On the other hand, knowing what benefits customers are seeking is useful for designing an effective retail offering, but presents a problem in identifying which customers are seeking these benefits. For these reasons, **composite segmentation** plans use multiple variables to identify customers in the target segment. They define target customers by benefits sought, lifestyles, and demographics.

JCPenney's Segmentation of the Women's Apparel Market The market for women's apparel is typically segmented into five categories: conservative, traditional, update, bridge, and designer or fashion-forward. The conservative segment is the most price-conscious and least fashion-oriented. The designer segment seeks just the opposite—fashion and style with little regard for price.

Penney customers are in the first three segments, but the firm is targeting its offering to customers in the traditional and updated segments. Exhibit 5–7A shows characteristics of each apparel segment. Note how these descriptions include segment size, customers' values, benefits they seek, and demographic information. Penney has different departments within each store and different private labels tailored to meet each segment's needs. Exhibit 5-7B lists Penney's retail offerings directed toward these segments.

SUMMARY

To satisfy customer needs, retailers must thoroughly understand how customers make store choice and purchase decisions and the factors they consider when deciding. This chapter describes the buying process's six stages (need recognition, information search, evaluation of alternatives, choice of alternatives, purchase, and postpurchase evaluations) and how retailers can influence each stage. A stage's importance depends on the nature of the customer's

EXHIBIT 5–7   JCPenney Segments for Women's Apparel

A. SEGMENT DESCRIPTION		
	CONSERVATIVE	**TRADITIONAL**	**UPDATE**
Size	23% of population	38% of population	16% of population
	16% of total sales	40% of total sales	24% of total sales
	35–55 years old	25–49 years old	25–49 years old
Age	Conservative values	Traditonal values	Contemporary values
Values	Satisfied with present status	Active, busy, independent, self-confident	Active, busy, independent, very self-confident
Employment	Has job, not career	Family- and job/career-oriented	Family- and job/career-oriented
Income	Limited disposable income	Considerable income	Considerable income
Benefits sought	Price-drive, reacts to sales	Quality-driven, will pay a little more	Fashion-driven, expresses self through apparel
	Wants easy care and comfort	Wants traditional styling, seeks clothes that last	Wants newness in color and style
	Not interested in fashion	Interested in newness	Shops often
	Defines value as	Defines value as	Defines value as
	price	quality	fashion
	quality	fashion	quality
	fashion	price	price

B. RETAIL OFFERING		
RETAIL MIX	**CONSERVATIVE**	**TRADITIONAL**	**UPDATE**
Pricing	Budget	Moderate	Moderate to better
Merchandise	Basic styles, easy-care fabrics, comfortable fit	Traditional styling, good quality, tailored look	Fashion-forward, more selection, newer colors
Brands	Alica	Joneswear	Claude
	Cobble Lane	Worthington	Mary McFadden
	Motion	Halston	Counterparts
	Cabin Creek	Wyndham	Jacqueline Ferrar
		Russ Togs	
		Hunt Club	
		Dockers	
Merchandising approach	Price signing, "save stories," stack-out tables	Well-coordinated merchandise, collections, uncluttered displays, knowledgeable salespeople	Color statements, mannequins, theme areas

decision. When decisions are important and risky, the buying process is longer; customers spend more time and effort on information search and evaluating alternatives. When buying decisions are less important to customers, they spend little time in the buying process and their buying behavior may become habitual.

The buying process of individual consumers is influenced by their families, reference groups, culture, and subcultures. The largest ethnic subcultures in the United States, African American and Hispanic, have their own values and needs.

To develop cost-effective retail programs, retailers group customers into segments. Some approaches for segmenting markets are based on geography, demographics, lifestyles, usage situations, and benefits sought. Since each approach has its advantages and disadvantages, retailers typically define their target segment by several characteristics.

KEY TERMS

affinity marketing, *139*

benefit segmentation, *146*

brand loyalty, *123*

buying process, *124*

buying situation segmentation, *146*

composite segmentation, *146*

consideration set, *135*

cross-shopping, *128*

culture, *140*

demographic segmentation, *144*

extended problem solving, *121*

external sources of information, *129*

family life cycle, *138*

fashion, *150*

functional needs, *125*

geographic segmentation, *144*

habitual decision making, *123*

impulse buying, *122*

information search, *129*

internal sources of information, *129*

lifestyle, *145*

lifestyle segmentation, *145*

limited problem solving, *122*

multiattribute attitude model, *130*

postpurchase evaluation, *137*

psychological needs, *125*

reference groups, *139*

retail market segment, *141*

satisfaction, *137*

store loyalty, *123*

subculture, *140*

DISCUSSION QUESTIONS & PROBLEMS

1. What are the stages in selecting a retailer to patronize?

2. Does the customer buying process end when a customer buys some merchandise? Explain your answer.

3. What would get a consumer to switch from making a habitual choice decision to eat at Wendy's to making a limited or extended choice decision?

4. Reflect on your decision process in selecting a college. (State universities are nonprofit service retailers.) Was your decision-making process extensive, limited, or habitual? Did you go through all of Figure 5–1's stages?

5. What actions can a retailer take to ensure that customers have a satisfactory experience with a catalog retailer?

6. When would a retailer want to increase the amount of information searched for by consumers? When would it want to decrease the amount?

7. Using the VALS2 categories, suggest a retail strategy for a chain of movie theaters to attract each category of consumer.

8. What advantages and disadvantages do consumers receive by purchasing from an Internet retailer rather than from a store? What type of merchandise do consumers prefer to purchase in a store? From the electronic retailer? Why?

9. What might be some differences in the various stages of Hispanic Americans' and Anglos' decision-making processes when selecting a grocery store?

10. A family-owned bookstore across the street from a major university campus wants to identify the various segments in its market. What approaches might the store owner use to segment its market? List the potential target market segments based on this segmentation approach. Then contrast the retail mix that would be most appropriate for two potential target segments.

11. What factors do consumers use to determine what bank to use? How does the importance of these factors differ between businesspeople and consumers? Between people looking for a loan and a checking account?

12. Any retailer's goal is to get a customer in his store to stop searching and buy a product there. How can a record retailer ensure that the customer buys a CD there?

13. Using the multiattribute attitude model and the information on the top of page 150, identify the probable choice of an auto repair outlet for a young single businesswoman and for a retired couple with limited income.

CHARACTERISTICS	IMPORTANCE WEIGHT		PERFORMANCE BELIEFS		
	YOUNG SINGLE	RETIRED COUPLE	LOCAL GAS STATION	NATIONAL SERVICE CHAIN	LOCAL CAR DEALER
Price	2	10	9	10	3
Time to complete repair	5	8	5	9	7
Reliability	9	2	2	7	10
Convenience	6	2	3	6	8

SUGGESTED READINGS

Burt, Steve, and Mark Gabbott. "The Elderly Consumer and Non-Food Purchase Behavior." *European Journal of Marketing* 29, no. 2 (1995), pp. 43–57.

Carsky, Mary, Roger Dickenson, and Mary Smith. "Toward Consumer Efficiency: A Model for Improving Buymanship." *Journal of Consumer Affairs* 29, no. 2 (1995), pp. 442–58.

Gladwell, Malcolm. "The Science of Shopping." *New Yorker*, October 5, 1996, pp. 32–55.

Kranzin, Kent, and Erhard Valentin. "Using Consumer Logistics to Segment Retail Markets." *Stores*, April 1995, pp. RR1–RR3.

McNeal, James, and Chyon-Hwa Yeh. "Born to Shop." *American Demographics*, June 1993, pp. 34–39.

Moschic, George, and Julie Sneath. *Existing Retail Strategies and the Older Consumer.* New York: International Council of Shopping Centers, 1995.

Mueller, Rene, and Amanda Broderick. "East European Retailing: A Consumer Perspective." *International Journal of Retail & Distribution Management* 23, no. 1 (1995), pp. 32–40.

Peter, J. Paul, and Jerry Olson. *Consumer Behavior and Marketing Strategy*, 4th ed. Burr Ridge, IL: Richard D. Irwin, 1996.

Rose, Herman. "Are You Ready for the Future? Trends in Consumer Behavior." *Grocery Marketing*, May 1995, pp. 26–30.

Solomon, Michael. *Consumer Behavior: Buying, Having, and Being*, 3d ed. Englewood Cliffs, NJ: Prentice-Hall, 1996.

Walker, Chip. "The Age of Self-Navigation," *American Demographics*, September 1996, pp. 36–43.

APPENDIX

Customer Behavior toward Fashion

Fashion is a type of product or a way of behaving that is temporarily adopted by a large number of consumers because the product or behavior is considered to be socially appropriate for the time and place. For example, in some social groups, it is—or was—fashionable to have brightly colored hair, play golf, wear a coat made from animal fur, have a beard, or go to an expensive health spa for a vacation. In many retail environments, however, the term *fashion* is associated with clothing.

Customer Needs Satisfied by Fashion   Fashion gives people an opportunity to satisfy many emotional and practical needs. Through fashions, people develop their own identity. They can use fashions to manage their appearance, express their self-image and feelings, enhance their egos, and make an impression on others. Through the years, fashions have become associated with specific lifestyles or roles people play. You wear different clothing styles when you are attending class, going out on a date, or interviewing for a job.

Fashion also can be used to communicate with others. For example, you might wear a classic business suit when interviewing for a job at Neiman Marcus but more informal attire when interviewing for a job with The Gap. These different dress styles would indicate your appreciation and understanding of the differences in the cultures of these firms.

People use fashions both to develop their own identity and to gain acceptance from others. These two benefits of fashion can be opposing forces. If you choose to wear something radically different, you will achieve recognition for your individuality but might not be accepted by your peers. To satisfy these conflicting needs, manufacturers and retailers offer a variety of designs and combinations of designs that are fashionable and still enable consumers to express their individuality.

What Creates Fashion?   Fashion is affected by economic, sociological, and psychological factors.

Economic Factors   Fashion merchandise is a luxury. It includes design details that go beyond satisfying basic functional needs. Thus, demand for fashion merchandise is greatest in countries with a high level of economic development and in market segments with the greatest disposable income.

Sociological Factors   Fashion changes reflect changes in our social environment—our feelings about class structure, the roles of women and men, and the structure of the family. For example, time pressures arising from the increased number of women in the work force have led to the acceptance of low-maintenance, drip-dry, wrinkle-resistant fabrics. Rising concern for the environment has resulted in natural fibers becoming fashionable and fur coats going out of fashion. Interest in health and fitness has made it fashionable to exercise and wear jogging clothes, leotards, and running shoes.

Psychological Factors   Consumers adopt fashions to overcome boredom. People get tired of wearing the same clothing and seeing the same furniture in their living room. They seek changes in their lifestyles by buying new clothes or redecorating their houses.

How Do Fashions Develop and Spread?   Fashions are not universal. A fashion can be accepted in one geographic region, country, or age group and not in another. In the 1970s, the fashion among young women was ankle-length skirts, argyle socks, and platform shoes, while older women were wearing pantsuits, double-breasted blazers, and midheeled shoes. During the 1970s, natural hairstyles were fashionable among African Americans, while corn-row hairstyles became fashionable in the early 1980s.

The stages in the fashion life cycle are shown in Exhibit 5–8. The cycle begins with the creation of a new design or style. Then some consumers recognized as fashion leaders adopt the fashion and start a trend in their social group. The fashion spreads from the leaders to others and is accepted widely as a fashion. Eventually the fashion is accepted by most people in the social group and can become overused. Saturation and overuse set the stage for the decline in popularity and the creation of new fashions.

EXHIBIT 5–8

Stages in the Fashion Life Cycle

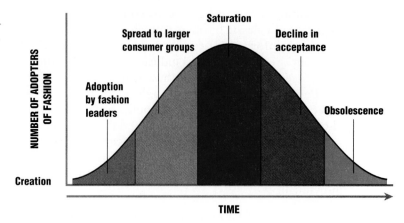

Creation   New fashions arise from a number of sources. Couture fashion design-ers are only one source of the creative inspirations. Fashions are also developed by creative consumers, celebrities, and even retailers. Andre Agassi has influenced fashion worn by tennis players. *Miami Vice* popularized such men's fashions as T-shirts worn under jackets and the stubble beard.

Adoption by Fashion Leaders   The fashion life cycle really starts when the fash-ion is adopted by leading consumers. These initial adopters of a new fashion are called fashion leaders or innovators. They are the first people to display the new fashion in their social group. If the fashion is too innovative or very different from currently accepted fashion, the style might not be accepted by the social group, thus prematurely ending the life cycle.

Three theories have been proposed to explain how fashion spreads within a society. The trickle-down theory suggests that the fashion leaders are consumers with the highest social status—wealthy, well-educated consumers. After they adopt a fashion, the fashion trickles down to consumers in lower social classes. When the fashion is accepted in the lowest social class, it is no longer acceptable to the fashion leaders in the highest social class.

The mass-market theory proposes that fashions spread across social classes. Each social class has its own fashion leaders who play a key role in their own social networks. Fashion information "trickles across" social classes rather than down from the upper classes to the lower classes.

The subculture theory is based on the development of recent fashions. Subcultures of mostly young and less affluent consumers, such as motorcycle rid-ers and urban rappers, started fashions for such things as colorful fabrics, T-shirts, sneakers, jeans, black leather jackets, and surplus military clothing. These fashions started with people in small, less moneyed consumer groups and "trickled up" to mainstream consumer classes.

These theories of fashion development indicate that fashion leaders can come from many different places and social groups. In our diverse society, many types of consumers have the opportunity to be the leaders in setting fashion trends. Retailing View 5A.1 describes how a buyer predicts fashion for homewear.

5A.1

Barbara Turf Predicts Consumer Tastes for Crate & Barrel

CRATE & BARREL is a Chicago-based chain of 54 housewares and furnishings stores catering to fashion-conscious customers who want something different, something that is not available in department and discount stores. The stores have a homey atmosphere with merchandise displayed in colorful arrangements. Sales clerks wearing aprons are readily available to answer questions about the latest merchandise.

Barbara Turf, executive vice president of merchandising, is Crate's secret weapon in the battle to anticipate fashion trends and have the right merchandise available. In 1995, she bet that customers would want housewares, from tablecloths to bedspreads, in blues and greens with yellow tones, and she placed orders so the merchandise would be in the stores in 1997.

To make her predictions, she travels widely, reads a lot of magazines, and simply observes everything around her. She always has an eye on Europe, where she says trends often develop 18 months before they do in the United States. But she also looks out for trends in the United States. For example, when people started to drive Jeep Cherokees rather than Cadillacs, she began buying more casual dinnerwear.

But predicting fashions is a tricky business, and even Ms. Turf makes mistakes. The pinkish plaid place mats she bought in 1995 were losers and had to be deeply discounted before they would sell.

Source: Christina Duff, "How Barbara Turf Chooses the Hot Place Mats of 1997," *The Wall Street Journal*, March 16, 1995, pp. B1–B2; and Suzanne Slesin, "Is New York Ready for Nice?" *New York Times*, March 2, 1995, p. C1.

Spread to Large Consumer Groups   During this stage, the fashion is accepted by a wider group of consumers referred to as early adopters. The fashion becomes more visible, receives greater publicity and media attention, and is readily available in retail stores.

The relative advantage, compatibility, complexity, trialability, and observability of a fashion affect the time it takes the fashion to spread though a social group. New fashions that provide more benefits have a higher relative advantage compared to existing fashions, and these new fashions spread faster. Fashions are often adopted by consumers because they make people feel special. Thus more exclusive fashions like expensive clothing are adopted more quickly in an affluent target market. On a more utilitarian level, clothing that is easy to maintain, such as wrinkle-free pants, will diffuse quickly in the general population.

Compatibility is the degree to which the fashion is consistent with existing norms, values, and behaviors. When new fashions aren't consistent with existing norms, the number of adopters and the speed of adoption are lower. Since the mid-1960s, the fashion industry has repeatedly attempted to revive the miniskirt. It has had only moderate success because the group of women with the most disposable income to spend on fashion are baby boomers—many of whom no longer find the miniskirt a relevant fashion for their family-oriented lifestyles.

Complexity refers to how easy it is to understand and use the new fashion. Consumers have to learn how to incorporate a new fashion into their lifestyle. *Trialability* refers to the costs and commitment required to initially adopt the fashion. For example, when consumers need to spend a lot of money buying a new type of expensive jewelry to be in fashion, the rate of adoption is slower than if the fashion simply requires wearing jewelry that the consumer already owns on a different part of the body.

Observability is the degree to which the new fashion is visible and easily communicated to others in the social group. Clothing fashions are very observable compared to fashions for the home, such as sheets and towels. It is therefore likely that a fashion in clothing will spread more quickly than a new color scheme or style for the bathroom.

Fashion retailers engage in many activities to increase the adoption and spread of a new fashion through their target market. Compatibility is increased and complexity is decreased by showing consumers how to coordinate a new article of fashion clothing with other items the consumer already owns. Trialability is increased by providing dressing rooms so customers can try on clothing and see how it looks on them. Providing opportunities for customers to return merchandise also increases trialability. Retailers increase observability by displaying fashion merchandise in their stores and advertising it in newspapers.

Saturation   In this stage, the fashion achieves its highest level of social acceptance. Almost all consumers in the target market are aware of the fashion and have decided to either accept or reject it. At this point, the fashion has become old and boring to many people.

Decline in Acceptance and Obsolescence   When fashions reach saturation, they have become less appealing to consumers. Because most people have already adopted the fashion, it no longer provides an opportunity for people to express their individuality. Fashion creators and leaders are beginning to experiment with new fashions. The introduction of a new fashion speeds the decline of the preceding fashion.

NOTES

1. For a detailed discussion of customer behavior, see J. Paul Peter and Jerry C. Olson, *Consumer Behavior and Marketing Strategy*, 4th ed. (Burr Ridge, IL: Richard D. Irwin, 1997). See also Jagdish Sheth, "An Integrative Theory of Patronage Preference and Choice," in William Darden and Robert Lusch, eds., *Patronage Theory and Retail Management* (New York: North-Holland, 1989), pp. 9–28.

2. "Working Women: $50 Billion in Sales," *Women's Wear Daily*, May 8, 1996, Section II, p. 14.

3. Joel Urbany, Peter Dickson, and William Wilkie, "Buyer Uncertainty and Information Search," *Journal of Consumer Research* 16 (September 1989), pp. 208–15; James Lumpkin, "Perceived Risk and Selection of Patronage Mode," *Journal of the Academy of Marketing Science* 14

(Winter 1986), pp. 38–42; and Patrick Murphy and Gerald Skelly, "The Influence of Perceived Risk on Brand Preference for Supermarket Products," *Journal of Retailing* 62 (Summer 1986), pp. 204–16.

4. Ignacio Galceran and Jon Berry, "A New World of Consumers," *American Demographics*, March 1995, p. 30.

5. Francis Piton, "Defining Impulse Purchasing," in R. Hillman and M. Houston, eds., *Advances in Consumer Research* vol. 19 (Provo, UT: Association for Consumer Research, 1990), pp. 509–14; and Dennis Rock, "The Buying Impulse," *Journal of Consumer Research*, September 1987, pp. 189–99.

6. Bruce Whalen, "Retail Customer Service: Marketing's Last Frontier," *Marketing News*, March 15, 1995, pp. 16, 18.

7. Michael Wahl, "Eye POPing Persuasion," *Marketing Insights*, June 1989, p. 130.

8. Joel Urbany, Peter Dickson, and Rosemary Kalapurakai, "Price Search in the Retail Grocery Market," *Journal of Marketing* 60 (April 1996), pp. 91–111; and Peter Dickson and Alan Sawyer, "The Price Knowledge and Search of Supermarket Shoppers," *Journal of Marketing*, July 1991, pp. 49–59.

9. "Consumer Buying Patterns: Beyond Demographics," *Progressive Grocer*, May 1995, p. 136.

10. Barry Babin, William Darden, and Mitch Griffin, "Work and/or Fun: Measuring Hedonic and Utilitarian Shopping Value," *Journal of Consumer Research* 20 (March 1994), pp. 644–56.

11. This hierarchical structure needs is based on Abraham Maslow, *Motivation and Personality* (New York: Harper & Row, 1954).

12. Susan Caminiti, "Ralph Lauren: The Emperor Has Clothes," *Fortune*, November 11, 1996, p. 82.

13. "Shop, Shop, Shop," *Advertising Age*, August 22, 1994, p. 3; Betsy Morris, "As a Favored Pastime, Shopping Ranks High with Most Americans," *The Wall Street Journal*, July 30, 1987, pp. 1, 113; Robert A. Westbrook and William C. Black, "A Motivational-Based Shopper Typology," *Journal of Retailing* 61 (Spring 1985), pp. 78–103; Edward Tauber, "Why Do People Shop?" *Journal of Marketing* 36 (October 1972), pp. 42–49; and Scott Dawson, Peter Dawson, and Nancy Ridgeway, "Shopping Motives, Emotional States, and Retail Outcomes," *Journal of Retailing* 66 (Winter 1990), pp. 408–27.

14. Jacquelyn Bivens, "Fun and Mall Games," *Stores*, August 1989, p. 35; Peter Block, Nancy Ridgeway, and Scott Dawson, "The Shopping Mall as Consumer Habitat," *Journal of Retailing* 70 (Winter 1994), pp. 23–42.

15. Kenneth Evans, Tim Christiansen, and James Gill, "The Impact of Social Influence and Role Expectations on Shopping Center Patronage Intentions," *Journal of the Academy of Marketing Science* 24 (Summer 1996), pp. 208–18; and Yong-Soon Kang and Nancy Ridgeway, "The Importance of Consumer Market Interactions as a Form of Social Support for Elderly Consumers," *Journal of Public Policy & Marketing* 15 (Spring 1996), pp. 108–17.

16. Caminiti, p. 84.

17. David Mick, Michelle DeMoss, and Ronald Faber, "A Projective Study of Motivations and Meanings of Self-Gift," *Journal of Retailing*, Summer 1992, pp. 112–44.

18. "How to Lure Diverse Groups without Alienating Either," *Discount Store News*, June 3, 1996, p. 28.

19. Gordon Bruner and Richard Pomazal, "Problem: Recognition: The Crucial First State of the Consumer Decision Process," *Journal of Consumer Marketing*, Summer 1987, pp. 59–66.

20. Lisa Gubernick, "Through a Glass, Brightly," *Forbes*, August 11, 1986, p. 34.

21. Philip Titus and Peter Everett, "The Consumer Retail Search Process: A Conceptual Model and Research Agenda," *Journal of the Academy of Marketing Science* 23 (Spring 1995), pp. 106–19.

22. John Hauser, Glen Urban and Bruce Weinberg, "How Consumers Allocate Their Time When Searching for Information," *Journal of Marketing Research* 30 (November 1993), pp. 452–66; Sharon E. Beatty and Scott M. Smith, "External Search Effort: An Investigation across Several Product Categories," *Journal of Consumer Research* 8 (June 1986), pp. 119–26; Joel Urbany, Peter Dickson, and William Wilkie, "Buyer Uncertainty and Information Search," *Journal of Consumer Research* 16 (Septembser 1989), pp. 10–25; and Girish Punj, "Presearch Decision Making in Consumer Durable Purchases," *Journal of Consumer Marketing* 4 (Winter 1987), pp. 71–82.

23. Lawrence Feick, Linda Prie, and Robie Higie, "People Who Use People: The Other Side of Opinion Leadership," in R. Lutz, ed., *Advances in Consumer Research* (Provo, UT: Association of Consumer Research, 1986), pp. 10–12.

24. Eugene Fram, "The Time Compressed Shopper," *Marketing Insghts*, Summer 1991, pp. 12–23.

25. George Russell, "Where the Customer Is Still King," *Time*, February 2, 1987, pp. 56–57.

26. Adam Finn and Jordan Louviere, "Shopping Center Image, Considerations, and Choice: Anchor Store Contribution," *Journal of Business Research* 35 (1996), pp. 241–51; and Don James, Richard Durand, and Robert Dreves, "The Use of a Multi-Attribute Attitude Model in a Store Image Study," *Journal of Retailing* 52 (Summer 1976), pp. 23–32.

27. Robert Hansen and Terry Deutscher, "An Empirical Investigation of Attribute Importance in Retail Store Selection," *Journal of Retailing* 53 (Winter 1978), pp. 59–72.

28. William L. Wilkie and Edgar D. Pessimier, "Issues in Marketing's Use of Multi-Attribute Attitude Models," *Journal of Marketing Research*, November 1973, pp. 428–41; and Richard J. Lutz and James R. Bettman, "Multi-Attribute Models in Marketing: A Bicentennial Review," in A. G. Woodside, J. N. Sheth, and P. D. Bennett, eds., *Consumer and Industrial Buying Behavior* (New York: Elsevier-North Holland, 1977), pp. 13–50.

29. Eric Johnson and Robert Meyer, "Compensatory Models of Non-Compensatory Choices Processes: The Effect of Varying Context," *Journal of Consumer Research* 5 (June 1984), pp. 52–58.

30. For a discussion of the different decision rules customers use, see James R. Bettman, *An Information Processing Theory of Consumer Choice* (Reading, MA: Addison-Wesley, 1979).

31. Ronald LeBlanc and L. W. Turley, "Retail Influence on Evoked Set Formation and Final Choice of Shopping Goods," *International Journal of Retail & Distribution Management* 22 (1994), pp. 10–17; John Hauser and Birger Wernerfeldt, "An Evaluation Cost Model of a Consideration Set," *Journal of Consumer Research*, March 1990, pp. 393–408; Susan Spiggle and Murphy Sewall, "A Choice Set Model of Retail Selection," *Journal of Marketing* 51 (April 1987), pp. 97–111.

32. Wayne Hoyer and Steven Brown, "Effects of Brand Awareness of Choice for a Common, Repeat-Purchase Product," *Journal of Consumer Research*, September 1990, pp. 141–49.

33. Masaaki Kiotabe, "The Return of 7-Eleven . . . from Japan: The Vanguard Program," *Columbia Journal of World Business* 30 (Winter 1995), pp. 70–81; and Kevin Helliker, "Some 7-Elevens Try Selling a New Image," *The Wall Street Journal*, October 25, 1991, pp. B1–B2.

34. Richard J. Lutz, "Changing Brand Attitudes through Modification of Cognitive Structure," *Journal of Consumer Research* 1 (March 1975), pp. 49–59.

35. "Survey Says Shoppers Aren't Satisfied," *WWD Infotracs*, May 1996, p. 14.

36. Jagdip Singh, "A Typology of Consumer Dissatisfaction Response Styles," *Journal of Retailing*, Spring 1990, pp. 57–98; and Richard Oliver and Wayne DeSarbo, "Response Determinants in Satisfaction Judgments," *Journal of Consumer Research* 15 (March 1988), pp. 495–507.

37. Richard L. Oliver, "A Cognitive Model of the Antecedents and Consequences of Satisfaction Decisions," *Journal of Marketing Research* 17 (November 1980), pp. 460–69; and Richard L. Oliver, "Measurement and Evaluation of Satisfaction Processes in a Retail Setting," *Journal of Retailing* 57 (Fall 1981), pp. 26–31.

38. Conway Lachman and John Lanasa, "Family Decision-Making Theory, An Overview and Assessment," *Psychology & Marketing* 10 (March–April 1993), pp. 81–94; Robert Boutlier, "Pulling the Family Strings," *American Demographics*, August 1993, pp. 44–48; Irene Foster and Richard Olshavsky, "An Exploratory Study of Family Decision Making Using a New Taxonomy of Family Role Structure," in T. Srull, ed., *Advances in Consumer Research* (Provo, UT: Association for Consumer Research, 1989), pp. 665–700.

39. Marilyn Lavin, "Husband-Dominant, Wife-Dominate, Joint: A Shopping Typology for Baby Boom Couples," *Journal of Consumer Marketing* 10, no. 3 (1993), pp. 33–42.

40. Sharen Kindal, "They May Be Small, but They Shop Big," *Adweek*, February 10, 1992, p. 38.

41. Christy Fisher, "Kidding Around Makes Sense," *Advertising Age*, June 27, 1994, pp. 34, 37; and Ken Wells, "Hotels and Resorts Are Catering to Kids: Day Care and Activities Programs Help Welcome the Traveling Family," *The Wall Street Journal*, August 11, 1988, p. 25.

42. Dianne Pogoda, "It's a Matter of Time: Stores Keep Traffic Moving, Cash Flowing," *Women's Wear Daily*, April 9, 1996, pp. 1, 8.

43. "The Future of Households," *American Demographics*, December 1993, pp. 48–52; Robin Douthitt and Jaoanne Fedyk, "Family Consumption, Parental Time, and Market Goods: Life-Cycle Tradeoffs," *Journal of Consumer Affairs*, Summer 1990, pp. 110–33.

44. G. Bruce Knecht, "The Residents of South Orange, N.J. Won't Leave Home without It," *The Wall Street Journal*, April 12, 1994, p. B1.

45. Pogoda, "It's a Matter of Time."

46. Terrence Witkowski and Yoshito Yamamoto, "Omiyage Gift Purchasing by Japanese Traveler to the US," in *Advances in Consumer Research*, vol. 18 (Provo, UT: Association of Consumer Research, 1991), pp. 123–28.

47. Yumiko Ono, "Pizza in Japan Is Adapted to Local Tastes," *The Wall Street Journal*, June 4, 1993, p. B1.

48. Cyndee Miller, "Top Marketers Take a Bolder Approach in Targeting Gays," *Marketing News*, July 4, 1994, pp. 1, 2.

49. Monroe Anderson, "Advertising's Black Magic Helping Corporate America Tap a Lucrative Market," *Newsweek*, February 19, 1986, p. 60.

50. Joe Schwartz, "Hispanic Opportunities," *American Demographics*, May 1987, pp. 56–59.

51. Stacy Vollmers and Ronald Goldsmith, "Hispanic American Consumers and Ethnic Marketing," *Proceedings of the Atlantic Marketing Association*, 1993, pp. 46–50.

52. Betsy Wiesendanger, "Asian-Americans: The Three Biggest Myths," *Sales & Marketing Management*, September 1993, p. 86.

53. Florence Fabricant, "The Geography of Taste," *New York Times Magazine*, March 10, 1996, pp. 40–41.

54. "Marketing to Older Shoppers Makes Sense," *Discount Store News*, June 20, 1994, p. 23.

55. Martha Farnsworth Riche, "Psychographics for the 1990s," *American Demographics*, July 1989, pp. 25–31, 53–54. See also Lynne Kahle, Sharon Beatty, and Pamela Homer, "Alternative Measurement Approaches to Consumer Values: The List of Values (LOV) and Values and Lifestyles (VALS)," *Journal of Consumer Research* 13 (December 1986), pp. 40–50.

56. Rebecca Pirto, "VALS the Second Time," *American Demographics*, July 1991, p. 6.

Retailing Strategy

SECTION I DESCRIBED RETAIL management decisions; the different types of retailers; the changing nature of retailing in terms of consumer needs and technology; and factors that affect consumers' choice of retailers and merchandise. This broad overview of retailing provides the background information needed to develop and implement an effective retail strategy. • Section II discusses strategic decisions made by retailers, including development of a retail market strategy (Chapter 6), the financial strategy associated with the market strategy (Chapter 7), the location strategy for retail outlets (Chapters 8 and 9), the firm's organization and human resource strategy (Chapter 10), and systems used to control the flow of information and merchandise (Chapter 11). As outlined in Chapter 1, these decisions are strategic rather than tactical because they involve committing considerable resources to developing long-term advantages over competition in a target market segment. • Sections III and IV review tactical decisions concerning merchandise and store management to implement and evaluate the retail strategy. These implementation or tactical decisions impact a retailer's efficiency, but their impact is shorter term than the strategic decisions reviewed in Section II.

CHAPTER SIX
Retail Market Strategy

CHAPTER SEVEN
Financial Strategy

CHAPTER EIGHT
Retail Locations

CHAPTER NINE
Site Selection

CHAPTER TEN
Organization Structure and Human Resource Management

CHAPTER ELEVEN
Integrated Retail Logistics and Information Systems

Arthur C. Martinez, Chairman and CEO, Sears, Roebuck and Co.

WHEN I ARRIVED AT SEARS IN 1992, I found that, beyond deteriorating financial performance and market share, Sears had become totally self-centered, neglecting the person who mattered most to us: the customer.   •   We also suffered from a massive identity crisis, not knowing who *we* were anymore—a department store, discounter, mass merchandiser, or a collection of specialty stores. But, by evaluating our existing strengths and designing a plan to hone them while also transforming the organization, we were able to, once again, define Sears.   •   Our three key strengths were: the equity and trust we enjoyed with American families; our unrivaled brands—Kenmore, Craftsman, and Diehard—and our superior real estate position in regional shopping centers across the country.   •   These strengths were the cornerstone upon which we began to build our future. We established five strategic initiatives that would guide our ongoing transformation and adopted a goal that would serve as our universal theme—to make Sears a compelling place to shop, work, and invest. Those five strategies are to focus on our core businesses; make Sears a more compelling place to shop; establish greater local market focus; improve cost structure and productivity; develop a winning culture.   •   We began our transformation by defining our target customer. It is the woman who acts as the chief purchasing agent for her family. She makes 70 percent of the appliance purchasing decisions and half of the home improvement and automotive-related sales, for example. For her, we renovated stores, updated merchandise, and diversified product assortments. While she was used to shopping at Sears for her kids, her husband, and her home, she wasn't shopping for herself. Our "Softer Side of Sears" marketing efforts were aimed to lure her back to see our increased emphasis on fashionable apparel and new cosmetics.   •   We also started practicing our shared belief that people add value. Our associates began to participate in the strategic direction of the company, identifying necessary changes and proposing solutions in their day-to-day activities. We created associate education and development opportunities, initiating financial incentive opportunities and employee stock options to reward performance and promote a sense of associate ownership. The result? Our employees are more motivated and involved, and their attitudes about working at Sears have improved. This, in turn, has produced better customer service, enhanced customer satisfaction, and, ultimately, increased sales.   •   We're not done. We'll never be "done." Instead, we'll continue to foster and embrace healthy change in search of continuous improvement.

Retail Market Strategy

THE WORLD OF RETAILING

RETAILING STRATEGY
6. Retail Market Strategy
7. Financial Strategy
8. Retail Locations
9. Site Selection
10. Organization Structure
    and Human Resource
    Management
11. Integrated Retail Logistics
    and Information Systems

MERCHANDISE MANAGEMENT

STORE MANAGEMENT

QUESTIONS

- What is a retail strategy?

- How can a retailer build a sustainable competitive advantage?

- What steps do retailers go through to develop a strategy?

- What different strategic opportunities can retailers pursue?

THE GROWING INTENSITY OF RETAIL COMPETITION due to the emergence of new formats and technology plus shifts in customer needs (outlined in Chapter 4) is forcing retailers to devote more attention to long-term strategic thinking.[1]

As the retail management decision-making process indicates, retailing strategy (Section II) is the bridge between understanding the world of retailing—the analysis of the retail environment (Section I)—and the more tactical merchandise management and store operations activities (Sections III and IV) to implement the retail strategy. The retail strategy provides the direction retailers need to deal effectively with their environment, customers, and competitors.

The first part of this chapter defines the term *retail strategy* and discusses three important elements of retail strategy: the target market segment, retail format, and sustainable competitive advantage. Next, it outlines approaches for building a sustainable competitive advantage. The chapter concludes with a discussion of the strategic retail planning process.

WHAT IS A RETAIL STRATEGY?

The term *strategy* is frequently used in retailing. For example, retailers talk about their merchandise strategy, promotion strategy, location strategy, and private-brand strategy. In fact, the term is used so commonly it appears that all retailing decisions are now strategic decisions. But retail strategy isn't just another expression for retail management.

Definition of Retail Market Strategy

A **retail strategy** is a statement identifying (1) the retailer's target market, (2) the format the retailer plans to use to satisfy the target market's needs, and (3) the bases upon which the retailer plans to build a sustainable competitive advantage.[2] The **target market** is the market segment(s) toward which the retailer plans to focus its resources and retail mix. A **retail format** is the retailer's type of retail mix (nature of merchandise and services offered, pricing policy, advertising and promotion program, approach to store design and visual merchandising, and typical location). Here are examples of retail strategies.

REFACT The word *strategy* comes from the Greek word meaning the "art of the general."[3]

- **Autozone.** Autozone, a Memphis-based auto parts retailer with annual sales exceeding $2 billion, is the largest auto supply retailer in the United States. Its target market is lower-income people who repair their cars themselves out of economic necessity—they can't afford to have their cars repaired by others. Autozone builds loyalty in this segment by providing exceptional convenience and service. Stores are located in neighborhoods near their customers and stay open until midnight. Almost all employees (called Autozoners) have prior automotive repair experience. They're encouraged to go out to the store parking lot with a customer to check on the exact part needed and even help the customer install simple items like headlights and hoses.[4]

- **Talbots.** Talbots is a national catalog and specialty store and retailer. Its target market is 35-to-55-year-old women. Sixty percent of its customers are college educated with an average family income $70,000. Talbots offers private brand, moderate- to better-priced women's classic apparel, shoes, and accessories. Its stores are located in village locations and upscale regional malls. Synergies between the store and catalog operations provide a competitive advantage over other retailers.[5]

- **Starbucks.** Starbucks, a national chain of gourmet coffee cafes, generates annual sales over $500 million. Friendly, knowledgeable counter servers called *baristas* (Italian for bartenders), educate customers about Starbucks' products. The company has entered into some creative partnerships to put its cafes in Nordstrom and Barnes & Nobles stores and serve its coffee on United Airlines.[6]

- **Gymboree.** Gymboree is a specialty store retailing children's apparel and accessories. It targets families with children under age seven. Annual sales are about $100 million. Its retail format offers high-quality, traditional, private-label apparel in bright colors and bold "fun" prints. Salespeople use a "MATCHmatics formula" to help parents create multiple outfits using the same set of garments. Gymboree creates a unique shopping environment for families in its colorful, brightly lit 1,000- to 1,300-square-foot stores in regional malls. Coordinated outfits are displayed on store walls to make it easy for customers to select wardrobes and still have floor space to maneuver strollers. While parents are shopping, children are encouraged to play with small toys and watch Gymboree videos.[7]

Each of these retail strategies involves (1) selecting a target market segment and retail format and (2) developing sustainable competitive advantage that enables the retailer to reduce the level of competition it faces. Now let's examine these central concepts in a retail strategy.

Gymboree's retail strategy is to offer high quality, private-label boys' and girls' apparel in colorful, brightly lit 1,000 to 1,300 square foot mall locations.

INTERNET EXERCISE   Visit the Autozone homepage (http://www.autozone.com/) and the Talbots catalog page (http://www./catalogsite.com/Gen/Talbots Pl.html). Do these Internet sites reflect the retail strategies for the companies as discussed above?

TARGET MARKET AND RETAIL FORMAT

The retailing concept (discussed in Chapter 1) emphasizes that retailers must consider both their customers and their competitors when developing a retail strategy. Successful retailers satisfy the needs of customers in their target market segment better than the competition does. The selection of a target market focuses the retailer on a group of consumers whose needs it will attempt to satisfy. The selection of a retail format outlines the retail mix to be used to satisfy needs of customers in the target market.

The retail strategy determines the markets in which a retailer will compete. Traditional markets, like a farmers' market, are places where buyers and sellers meet and make transactions—a consumer buys six ears of corn from a farmer. But in modern markets, potential buyers and sellers aren't located in one place—transactions can occur without face-to-face interactions. For example, many customers contact retailers and place orders over the Internet using a computer.

We define a **retail market,** not as a specific place where buyers and sellers meet, but as a group of consumers with similar needs (a market segment) and a group of retailers using a similar retail format to satisfy those consumer needs.[8]

Exhibit 6–1 illustrates a set of retail markets for women's clothing. A number of retail formats are listed down the left-hand column. As Chapter 2 said, each format offers a different retail mix to its customers. Customer segments are listed in the exhibit's top row. As mentioned in Chapter 5, these segments can be defined

In traditional retail markets like this farmer's market, face-to-face transactions are made between buyers and sellers.

in terms of the customer's demographics, lifestyle, buying situation, or benefits sought. In this illustration we use the JCPenney fashion segments described in Chapter 5. Each square of the matrix shown in Exhibit 6–1 describes a potential retail market where two or more retailers compete with each other. For example, The Limited and The Gap stores in the same geographic area compete with each other in two squares: the specialty store format catering to the needs of traditional and updated customers. Wal-Mart and Kmart compete with each other by providing a discount retail format directed toward a conservative fashion segment.

The women's clothing market in Exhibit 6–1 is just one of several representations that could have been used. Retail formats could be expanded to include outlet stores and electronic retailing. Rather than being segmented by fashion orientation, the market could have been segmented using the other approaches described in Chapter 5. While Exhibit 6–1 isn't the only way to describe the women's retail clothing market, it does illustrate how retail markets are defined in terms of retail format and customer market segment.

EXHIBIT 6–1

Retail Markets for Women's Apparel

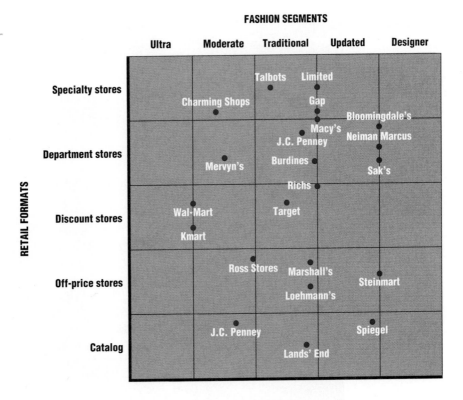

Basically, Exhibit 6–1's matrix describes the battlefield where women's clothing retailers compete. The position in this battlefield indicates the first two elements of a retailer's strategy: its target market segment and retail format. Consider the situation confronting The Gap as it develops a retail strategy for the women's clothing market. Should The Gap compete in all 25 retail markets shown in Exhibit 6–1, or should it focus on a limited set of retail markets? If The Gap decides to focus on a limited set of markets, which should it pursue? The Gap's retail strategy indicates how it plans to focus its resources.

BUILDING A SUSTAINABLE COMPETITIVE ADVANTAGE

The final element in a retail strategy is the retailer's approach to building a sustainable competitive advantage. A **sustainable competitive advantage** is an advantage over competition that can be maintained over a long time. Exhibit 6–2 shows some approaches a retailer can use to gain an advantage over its competitors. The list isn't exhaustive. Any business activity that a retailer engages in can be a basis for a competitive advantage.

But some advantages are sustainable over a long period of time, while others can be duplicated by competitors almost immediately.[10] For example, it would be hard for Jiffy Lube to get a long-term advantage over Pep Boys Automotive Center by simply offering an oil change at a lower price. Pep Boys would realize quickly—within hours—that Jiffy Lube had lowered its prices and match Jiffy Lube the next day if it found the lower prices were attracting customers. Similarly, it's hard for retailers to develop a long-term advantage by offering broader or deeper assortments. If broader and deeper assortments attracted a lot of customers, competitors could simply go out and buy the same merchandise for their stores.

EXHIBIT 6–2

Methods for Developing Competitive Advantage

A. ADVANTAGES BASED ON EXTERNAL RELATIONSHIPS		
		SUSTAINABLE ADVANTAGES
Customer relations (Chapters 6, 19)		More loyal customers
		Extensive customer information
Legal		Zoning laws to prohibit competitive entry
		Tax advantages
Location (Chapters 9–10)		Convenient locations
Vendors		Strong relationships (Chapter 14)
B. ADVANTAGES BASED ON INTERNAL OPERATIONS		
		SUSTAINABLE ADVANTAGES
Merchandise management (Chapters 12–16)	More merchandise	Exclusive merchandise
	Better assortments	Lower costs for merchandise— scale economies
	Better terms	
	Lower prices	
	Better buyers	
	Better advertising	
	More sales	
Store operations (Chapters 17–20)	Better visual presentation	Better service
	Better security, less theft	
	Better sales associates	Better store managers
		Better management information systems
		More efficient distribution
		Better inventory control

Establishing a competitive advantage means that a retailer builds a wall around its position in the retail market. This wall makes it hard for competitors outside the wall to contact customers in the retailer's market. If the retailer has built a wall around an attractive market, competitors will attempt to break down the wall. Over time, all advantages will be eroded due to these competitive forces; but by building high walls, retailers can sustain their advantage, minimize competitive pressure, and boost profits for a longer time. Thus, establishing a sustainable competitive advantage is the key to long-term financial performance.

Five important opportunities for retailers to develop sustainable competitive advantages are (1) customer loyalty, (2) location, (3) vendor relations, (4) management information and distribution systems, and (5) low-cost operations. Let's look at each of these approaches.

Customer Loyalty

Customer loyalty means that customers are committed to shopping at a store. Loyalty is more than simply liking one store over another. Loyalty means that customers are committed. For example, loyal customers will continue to shop at Home Depot home-improvement centers even if Builders Square opens a store nearby and provides a slightly superior assortment or slightly lower prices. Some ways that retailers build customer loyalty are (1) positioning, (2) service, (3) database retailing, and (4) merchandise.[11]

REFACT Over one-third of supermarkets have programs to build customer loyalty.[12]

Positioning A retailer builds customer loyalty by developing a clear, distinctive image of its retail offering and consistently reinforcing that image through its merchandise and service. **Positioning** is the design and implementation of a retail mix to create an image of the retailer in the customer's mind relative to its competitors.[13] Positioning emphasizes that the image in the customer's mind (not the retail manager's mind) is critical. Thus, the retailer needs to research what its image is and make sure that its image is consistent with what customers in its target market want. A perceptual map is frequently used to represent the customer's image and preference for retailers.

Exhibit 6–3 is a hypothetical perceptual map of retailers selling women's clothing in the Washington, D.C., area. The two dimensions in this map—fashion style and service—represent the two primary characteristics that consumers in this example might use in forming their impression of retail stores. Perceptual maps are developed so that the distance between two retailers' positions on the map indicates how similar the stores appear to consumers.[14] For example, Neiman Marcus and Bloomingdale's are very close to each other on the map because consumers in this illustration see them as offering similar service and fashion. On the other hand, Nordstrom and Kmart are far apart, indicating consumers' belief that they're quite different. Note that stores close to each other compete vigorously with each other because consumers feel they provide similar benefits.

Based on this example, The Limited has an image of offering moderately fashionable women's clothing with good service. T.J. Maxx offers more fashionable clothing with less service. Sears is viewed as a retailer offering women's clothing that's not fashionable with poor service.

The ideal points (marked by blue dots on the map) indicate characteristics of an ideal retailer for consumers in different market segments. For example, consumers in segment 3 prefer a retailer that offers high-fashion merchandise with low service, while consumers in segment 1 want more traditional merchandise and aren't concerned about service. The ideal points are located so that the distance between the retailer's position and the ideal point indicates how consumers in the segment evaluate the retailer. Retailers that are closer to an ideal point are

EXHIBIT 6–3

Hypothetical Perceptual Map of Women's Apparel Retailers in Washington, D.C.

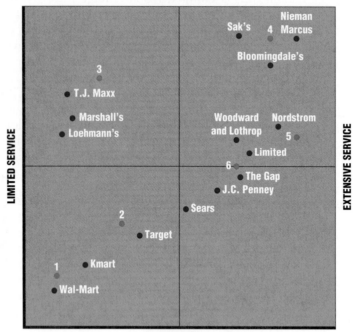

evaluated more favorably by the consumers in the segment than retailers located further away. Thus, consumers in segment 6 prefer The Gap to Penney because The Gap is closer to their image of their ideal retailer. Retailing View 6.1 describes Sears' efforts to reposition itself from a mass merchandise store appealing to segment 1 to a national department store targeting segment 6. Chapter 16 outlines how retailers develop positions in the minds of their customers using marketing communications.

Service Retailers can build customer loyalty by offering excellent customer service. But offering good service consistently is difficult, because customer service is provided by retail employees—and humans are less consistent than machines. Retailers that offer good customer service instill its importance in their employees over a long period of time. For example, Neiman Marcus's service tradition began on opening day in 1907, when Al Neiman met and greeted every customer who visited the store.[15]

It takes considerable time and effort to build a tradition and reputation for customer service, but good service is a valuable strategic asset. Once a retailer has earned a service reputation, it can sustain this advantage for a long time because it's hard for a competitor to develop a comparable reputation. Chapter 19 discusses how retailers develop a service advantage.

Databased Retailing **Databased retailing** is the development and implementation of retailing programs utilizing a computerized file **(data warehouse)** of customer profiles and purchase patterns.[16] Retailing View 6.2 describes how a small menswear chain uses customer information to improve services and target its promotional activities. Databased retailing is discussed in more detail in Chapters 11 and 16.

6.1

Sears Repositions to the Softer Side

IN THE BEGINNING OF THE 1990s, Sears was a textbook example of a once mighty retailer falling on hard times because it had failed to adapt to changing customer tastes. Sales and profits from regional mall stores stagnated. Mall shoppers were mostly in segments 4, 5, and 6 in Exhibit 6–3. They sought fashionable clothing from retailers in regional malls and went to category specialists such as Home Depot, Circuit City, Best Buy, and Pep Boys in strip shopping centers for car batteries, hardware, and refrigerators. But Sears was continuing to sell basic apparel alongside its Craftsman tools and Kenmore appliances in its mall stores.

In 1993, Sears' new CEO Arthur Martinez decided to rekindle growth in its mall locations by emphasizing fashion apparel at value prices.

More floor space was devoted to apparel, jewelry, and shoes; cosmetic departments were added; and $4 billion was spent on renovating stores to make them more appealing to female customers. The "Softer Side of Sears" advertising campaign communicated this new positioning to Sears' customers. These changes in Sears' retail mix were designed to move Sears' image closer to the ideal point of segment 6.

Source: Susan Reda, "Goodbye Bloomingdale's . . . Hello Sears," *Discount Store News,* September 16, 1996. p. A64–65; Cyndee Miller, "Redux Deluxe: Sears Comeback, an Event Most Marketers Would Kill For," *Marketing News,* July 15, 1996, p.1; and Scott McMurray, "Sears Fashions a New Future for Itself," *US News and World Report,* June 15, 1996, p. 61.

INTERNET EXERCISE   Rackes Direct is an Internet retailer selling better women's apparel. Go to the site (http://www.rackes.com), complete the questionnaire as if you were a customer, and think about how Rackes Direct would use the information you provided.

Merchandise   It's difficult for retailers to develop customer loyalty through merchandise because competitors typically can purchase and sell the same items. But a retailer may achieve a sustainable competitive advantage based on its merchandise offering by having the merchandise made exclusively for it (as a private label).[17]

Consistency   To develop loyal customers, retailers must offer a consistent retail mix. For example, Neiman Marcus needs to be consistent in offering service, merchandise, and prices compatible with its image. Its customers expect to find excellent service and the latest in fashions. If customers didn't consistently find the most fashionable clothing, perfumes, and cosmetics and a staff of well-trained, service-oriented sales associates to assist them, they might shift to another store.

Location   The classic response to the question "What are the three most important things in retailing?" is "Location, location, and location." Besides being a critical factor in consumers' selection of a store, location lets a retailer gain a sustainable advantage over its competition. For example, when a Holiday Inn motel occupies the best location on a highway, competing motels are at a disadvantage. Days Inn and LaQuinta can overcome this disadvantage only if Holiday Inn abandons its location. Chapters 8 and 9 discuss this approach to developing a sustainable competitive advantage.

6.2

Harry Rosen Knows a Lot about Its Customers

HARRY ROSEN, A 24-STORE MENSWEAR retailer based in Toronto, Canada, uses information to provide better customer service and build long-term relationships. Each Harry Rosen salesperson can access the firm's data warehouse with customer information from any POS terminal in any store. The database tells what the customer has bought in the past and also provides personal information. All sales associates are urged to contribute to the database. If a wife buys a birthday gift for her husband, salespeople are encouraged to find out his birthday and how old he is and include this information in the system rather than their personal notebook.

The information system improves customer service and targeting of retail promotions. For example, when garments are left in the store for alterations, the system tracks their progress and electronically notifies the salesperson of any delay so the salesperson can relay this information to the customer. Heavy spenders are easily identified and invited to special promotional events. The system is also used to sell slow-moving merchandise. For example, a store may have too many size-44-short suits. A salesperson can go to a terminal, generate a list of all customers who have bought 44-short suits in the past month, and offer them a discount if they make a purchase now. When new merchandise arrives, the salesperson can identify customers who have bought that type of merchandise in the past and inform them of the new merchandise.

Source: "RITA '96," *Chain Store Age Executive*, September 1996, pp. 50–52.

Vendor Relations

By developing strong relations with vendors, retailers may gain exclusive rights (1) to sell merchandise in a region, (2) to buy merchandise at lower prices or with better terms than competitors who lack such relations, or (3) to receive merchandise in short supply. Relationships with vendors, like relationships with customers, are developed over a long time and may not be easily offset by a competitor.[18]

Kmart has electronic links with 2,600 of its 3,000 vendors and provides 250 vendors with point-of-sale data. By developing computer links with its vendors, Kmart increases its opportunity to have the right merchandise at the right store when the customer wants it. Chapter 14 discusses vendor relationships in detail.

Management Information and Distribution Systems

A key to Wal-Mart's success is its distribution system.[19] It was very costly and took a long time for Wal-Mart to develop enough sales volume in different areas to justify an efficient distribution system. But now that Wal-Mart has developed this advantage, it may be even more costly and difficult for Kmart (which competes in the same retail market) to establish the same level of sales and same low-cost distribution system. In other words, Wal-Mart can maintain its low-cost–distribution advantage for a long time. Similarly, its management information systems enable Wal-Mart to respond quickly to customer needs.

Family Dollar is a discount retailer that has gained a competitive advantage through its efficient distribution system. The firm has over 2,500 stores generating $1.5 billion in annual sales targeting families with incomes between $15,000 and $25,000. Family Dollar keeps prices low for families with limited disposable income by operating a no-frills discount retail format. The format is a cross between a discount store and a convenience store. Stores are small (6,000 to 8,000 square feet); have limited service, few employees, and cash-and-carry sales; and are conveniently located in neighborhood centers. Family Dollar has developed a cost advantage over its competition through its distribution system. Merchandise is shipped to stores weekly from a fully automated distribution center based on inventory reports reviewed by buyers and on orders placed directly by store managers using electronic handheld calculators. Cases are routed across 6.2 miles of mechanized conveyer belts past laser scanners that divert them to one of 14 shipping lanes. Each lane has a telescoping extension that enables merchandise to be directly loaded into a tractor trailer.[20]

Chapter 11 discusses various types of operating systems and shows how some retailers have developed sustainable competitive advantages through them.

Low-Cost Operations

All retailers are concerned about the costs of providing their retail offering. Costs are important even to retailers such as Nordstrom that offer excellent service and sell high-priced merchandise to customers who aren't very price-sensitive. If Nordstrom can offer the same merchandise quality and service as its competitor at a lower cost, then Nordstrom will either make a higher profit margin than its competitors or use the potential profits to attract more customers and increase sales. If Nordstrom feels that its customers aren't very price-sensitive, it may decide to attract more customers from its competitors by offering even better service, merchandise assortments, and visual presentation rather than lower prices.

Multiple Sources of Advantage

To build a sustainable advantage, retailers typically don't rely on a single approach such as low cost or excellent service.[21] They need multiple approaches to build as high a wall around their position as possible. For example, McDonald's success is based on developing loyal customers, maintaining good vendor relations, having excellent information and distribution systems, and controlling costs.

The McDonald's target market segment doesn't expect a lot of customer service. Customers know they will not get a meal prepared to their specific tastes. But customers do expect that the food will be hot, available with a minimal wait, and reasonably priced. McDonald's has developed a loyal group of customers by meeting these expectations every time a customer visits a store.

To consistently meet customer expectations, McDonald's has developed capabilities in a number of areas. Its relationships with vendors ensure that it will always have quality ingredients. Its distribution and inventory control systems enable it to make sure that the ingredients are available at each location. By developing a system for producing its food and using extensive training for store managers, McDonald's reduces customers' wait in line. This training also means that customers will be handled quickly and courteously. By developing unique capabilities in a number of areas, McDonald's has built a high wall around its position as a service retailer, using a fast-food format directed toward families with young children.

REFACT McDonald's has 11,400 outlets in the United States and 7,000 additional restaurants in 89 other countries. Each day 7 percent of the U.S. population eats at McDonald's.[22]

Starbucks has developed several bases of competitive advantage, one of which is the service provided by this barista.

6.3

Calyx & Corolla Builds Competitive Advantage through Distribution

IN 1987, RUTH OSWADES formed a direct-mail firm, Calyx & Corolla, retailing fresh-cut flowers based on an innovative distribution concept giving a sustainable competitive advantage by directly linking customer and supplier.

Annual flower and plant retail sales are over $9 billion in the United States. Most sales are made through retail florists (60 percent) and supermarkets (20 percent). Florists are very service-oriented, making special arrangements and providing home delivery. FTD, a worldwide cooperative owned by 25,000 retail florists, enables florists to make deliveries beyond their trading area.

Describing her retail concept, Oswades says, "I envision a table with three legs, and Calyx & Corolla is only one of them. The second is the best flower growers available, and the third is Federal Express." Each month Calyx & Corolla mails out over 100,000 catalogs describing a variety of floral offerings. Orders are transmitted directly to growers, who ship directly to customers using Federal Express.

Since most growers are very small businesses, Calyx & Corolla educates them as to how to perform their retail activities. Growers are provided with shipping boxes, labels, vases, and sales forecasts. Growers tell Calyx & Corolla when their stock of certain flowers is low so substitutes can be discussed with the customer. Federal Express delivery people are trained not to leave packages to freeze when no one is home to receive a delivery.

Customers can enjoy their flowers one to two weeks longer if they order from Calyx & Corolla than if they buy flowers from a local florist. Due to its unique distribution system, customers receive flowers two days after they're cut, while flowers ordered through FTD or bought in a retail florist are typically cut one to two weeks earlier.

Source: David Wylie, "Calyx and Corolla," Harvard Business School (Boston), Case 9-592-035, revised October 28, 1992; Patti Hagan, "Hearts and Flowers: The Nose Gay Express," *The Wall Street Journal,* February 14, 1991, p. 36; and "Ruth Oswades," *Working Woman,* February 1991, pp. 10–12.

Each of the retail strategies outlined at the beginning of the chapter involves multiple sources of advantage. For example, Starbucks has developed a strong competitive position through its unique locations, strong brand name, and high-quality service provided by committed employees.

Retailing View 6.3 describes an entrepreneur who developed a successful mail-order retail flower business and maintains its performance by developing a unique distribution system and building strong vendor and customer relationships.

GROWTH STRATEGIES

Four types of growth opportunities that retailers may pursue (market penetration, market expansion, retail format development, and diversification) are shown in Exhibit 6–4.[23] The vertical axis indicates whether the growth opportunities involve market segments that the retailer is presently pursuing or new market segments. The horizontal axis indicates whether the growth opportunities involve using the retailer's present format or a new format.

Market Penetration

A **market penetration opportunity** involves directing investments toward existing customers using the present retailing format. An example is attempting to increase sales by inducing current customers to visit the store more often or by attracting consumers in the retailer's target market who don't shop at its stores.

EXHIBIT 6-4

Growth
Opportunities

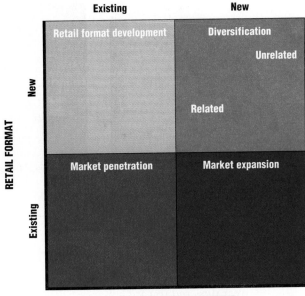

One approach for accomplishing this objective would be to open more stores in the target market in locations convenient to more of the firm's customers. Another approach would be training salespeople to cross-sell. **Cross-selling** means that sales associates in one department attempt to sell complementary merchandise from other departments to their customers. For example, a sales associate who has just sold a dress to a customer will take the customer to the accessories department to sell her a handbag or scarf that will go with the dress. More cross-selling will increase sales from existing customers.

Market Expansion A **market expansion opportunity** employs the existing retail format in new market segments. For example, The Gap's strategy is using a specialty store retail format to sell updated sportswear to upscale men and women between ages 20 and 45. GapKids was a market expansion opportunity in which the same specialty store format was directed toward a different segment—families with children aged 2 to 12. Another example is the opening of Toys "R" Us stores in Japan and Germany. This opportunity involved entering a new geographic segment with the same retail format.

Retail Format Development A **retail format development opportunity** involves offering customers a new retail format. For example, Talbots, a catalog retailer, exploited a format development opportunity when it opened specialty stores to sell its present line of merchandise to the same target segment through a new retail format. Another example of a retail format development opportunity would be a retailer's adding additional merchandise categories or altering the breadth and depth of assortments in its stores. Adjusting the type of merchandise or services offered typically involves a small investment, while providing an entirely different format—such as a department store going into catalog retailing—would be a much larger investment.

Diversification

A **diversification opportunity** involves an entirely new retail format directed toward a market segment that's not presently served. Sears' entry into retail financial services (Dean Witter) and real estate services (Coldwell Banker) was a diversification investment.

Vertical Integration   **Vertical integration** is an example of diversification involving investments by retailers' wholesaling and/or manufacturing merchandise.[24] Examples of vertical integration are The Limited's acquisition of Mast Industries (a trading company that contracts for private-label manufacturing) and Zale's manufacturing of jewelry. Backward integration into manufacturing represents diversification because manufacturing merchandise is a very different "format" from retailing merchandise—different operating skills are required. In addition, the immediate customers for a manufacturer's merchandise are retailers, while the retailer's customers are consumers. Thus, a manufacturer's marketing activities are very different from a retailer's. Note that some manufacturers and designers like Nike, Levi, and Ralph Lauren forward-integrate into retailing. In these situations, the manufacturer is also diversifying, undertaking a new set of business activities and customers.

Related versus Unrelated Diversification   Diversification opportunities are either related or unrelated. In a **related diversification opportunity,** the present retail strategy shares something in common with the opportunity that the retailer is entering. This commonality might be purchasing from the same vendors, using the same distribution and/or management information system, or advertising in the same newspapers to similar target markets. In contrast, an **unrelated diversification** lacks any commonality between the present business and the new business.

Two of JCPenney's past investments in electronic shopping (TeleAction and JCPenney Television Shopping Channel) illustrate the differences between related and unrelated diversification opportunities. TeleAction was an interactive electronic home shopping system selling a variety of merchandise, from food to ticket reservations. Since little of the merchandise was sold through the Penney stores or catalog, the system was an unrelated diversification because it didn't involve Penney's catalog ordering and distribution system. Basically, managing TeleAction was like managing an electronic mall.

On the other hand, the Television Shopping Channel was a related diversification because it offers predominantly Penney merchandise shipped through its mail-order catalog distribution system. Thus, it's an electronic catalog TV show rather than an electronic mall.

Strategic Opportunities and Competitive Advantage

Typically, retailers have the greatest competitive advantage in opportunities that are very similar to their present retail strategy. Thus, retailers would be most successful engaging in market penetration opportunities that don't involve entering new, unfamiliar markets or operating new, unfamiliar retail formats.

When retailers pursue market expansion opportunities, they build on their strengths in operating a retail format and applying this competitive advantage in a new market. In a retail format extension opportunity, retailers build on their reputation and success with present customers. Even if a retailer doesn't have an advantage in operating the new format, it hopes to attract its loyal customers to it. For example, Talbots, mentioned at the beginning of this chapter, started as a catalog retailer and then opened retail stores. It used its information about its customers to locate its stores and exploit the synergies between its catalog and store operations. New merchandise lines are tested in the catalog and then rolled out to the stores. The catalog serves as an advertising vehicle for the stores and also accommodates customers when the store is out of stock of an item.

Retailers have less competitive advantage when dealing with opportunities that involve new markets or new retail formats. But retailers must often consider market expansion or retail format extension opportunities. For example, Kmart felt it had saturated its U.S. target market using a general merchandise discount format and decided to pursue (1) a market expansion strategy by opening discount stores in Eastern Europe and Mexico and (2) a retail format expansion strategy by opening category specialist stores (Sports Authority, Pace Warehouse, and Builders Square) in the United States. Both of these growth strategies diverted Kmart's attention from its core discount business. To refocus its strategy on the U.S. discount store market, Kmart divested the category specialist businesses and the international expansion plans.

Retailers have the least competitive advantage when they pursue diversification opportunities. Thus, these opportunities are very risky. In part, Sears' financial problems resulted from its diversification into insurance, real estate, and consumer financial services.

INTERNATIONAL GROWTH OPPORTUNITIES

International expansion is one form of a market expansion strategy.[25] Many U.S. companies are expanding beyond the United States. The most commonly targeted regions are Mexico, Europe, China, and Japan. Like foreign companies entering the United States, American companies entering these countries face specific government regulations and different cultural traditions and languages. U.S. retailers have strong incentives to expand globally, because U.S. markets are saturated in terms of the number of stores, available locations, and competition.[26]

Experts believe that some American retailers, particularly category killers, have a natural advantage when competing globally.[27] American retailers are leaders in the use of technology to manage inventories, control global logistical systems, and tailor merchandise assortments to local needs. In addition, the American culture is emulated in many countries.

U.S. restaurant franchises have been very successful in the international market.

More affluent consumers in most developed countries share the same important characteristics that the best American specialty retailers already understand. Specifically, they enjoy a relatively high level of disposable income—due, in part, to having fewer children per household than in the past, dual-income families, generous benefits from employers and governments, and a strong work ethic—and they appreciate the selection, convenience, and prices available in the United States.

Category killers may be particularly suited to succeed internationally because of the expertise they've already developed at home. For instance, firms such as Toys "R" Us provide consumers with an assortment of brand-name merchandise procured from sources around the world. This advantage is particularly valuable if brand-name merchandise is important to consumers. Second, retailers like Wal-Mart have become the low-price provider in every market they enter because of their buying economies of scale and efficient distribution systems. Third, despite idiosyncrasies in the international environment, category killers have developed unique systems and standardized formats that facilitate control over multiple stores—and these should work well regardless of the country of operation. Fourth, because of the category killer's narrow assortment and focused strategy, communications across national boundaries and cultures are specifically focused, which improves management coordination. Finally, at one time people felt that consumers outside the United States were used to high levels of personalized service and would not accept the self-service concept employed by U.S. discounters. However, a substantial number of international consumers are willing to forgo the service for lower prices.[28]

Next we'll look at specific issues and opportunities for retailers in Latin America, Europe, and Asia.

Latin America   Latin America provides an attractive opportunity for retailers. The market is growing rapidly. Many young consumers will have increasing disposable income as a result of economic and political reforms. There is considerable pent-up demand for basic as well as high-priced consumer goods. Consumers are demanding higher-quality products, greater selection, lower prices, and better service.[29]

Latin America has the world's greatest income differential between the upper and lower classes. Each of the sectors is served by different retail structures. A formal retail industry, with formats similar to those in developed countries, caters to needs of the upper-class sector. The lower-income sector in urban slums and rural areas deals primarily with retailers who sell from kiosks on wheels, in open markets, or directly to homes.

While Latin America is a large and growing market, investments in Latin America are risky. Economic and political instability persist; high inflation rates could return. Exhibit 6–5 summarizes the trade-off between potential sales and risk for major Latin American countries.

EXHIBIT **6–5**

Risk and Rewards in Latin America: Country Risk Assessment

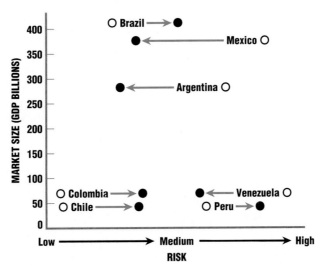

Source: Coopers & Lybrand Analysis, "Global Retailing: Assignment Latin America," *Chain Store Age Executive,* April 1996, section 2, p. 4.

6.4

Wealthy Latin Americans Shop at the Galleria Mall in Houston

HOUSTON'S GALLERIA MALL and its retailers have targeted the Latin American market for 15 years. Travel agencies throughout Latin America offer tour packages including round-trip air fares and two nights' accommodations in one of the two Westin hotels connected to the mall. During the Christmas season, over 9,000 Latin American shoppers will stay at the hotels.

On the Saturday after Thanksgiving, Neiman Marcus closed its store early to hold an invitation-only party for its Latin American charge cardholders, many of whom flew up for the event. The store manager promotes visits to the store by holding fashion shows several times a year in Monterrey and Mexico City.

Retailers have found that Latin American shoppers differ from U.S. consumers. They are more conscious of brands and reluctant to buy private labels. They buy what's in stock and will not wait for special orders, alterations, or promotions. Finally, they're reluctant to buy computers or complex consumer electronics that can't be easily serviced in their country.

Source: Bob Ortega, "Wealthy Mexicans Head Stateside to Shop," *The Wall Street Journal*, December 22, 1994, pp. B1–B2.

Mexico has become particularly attractive to U.S. retailers for several reasons.[30] The North American Free Trade Agreement (NAFTA) provides complete access for U.S. retailers to invest in Mexico and Canada. Mexico has the 14th largest economy in the world, and it's projected to be in the top 10 in the first decade of the 21st century. Its demographics are also changing. It's a relatively young nation in that over one-third of its population is under 14 years of age, and 50 percent is between ages 15 and 44, indicating a growing consumer base. However, the peso devaluation in 1995 made the market less attractive and resulted in many U.S. retailers such as JCPenney, Kmart, and Wal-Mart scaling back their expansion plans.[31]

Many upper-income Latin Americans come to the United States to buy merchandise that is not as readily available in their countries. Retailing View 6.4 describes how the Galleria Mall and its retailers in Houston cater to Latin Americans.

Europe   Western Europe has been part of many U.S. retailers' expansion strategies for some time. Toys "R" Us has been particularly successful. Entering Europe through England in 1985, the category-killer toy store has spread to France, Germany, Spain, and Austria. Food retailers such as McDonald's, TGI Friday's, Pizza Hut, and Häagen-Dazs have also done well in Western Europe. With its purchase of Cityvision PLC, Blockbuster Entertainment has over an 850-store presence in Great Britain in addition to stores in Germany and Spain.

Exhibit 6–6 divides the countries on degree of restriction in the marketplace on the vertical axis and by growth rate on the horizontal axis. Based on these criteria, Spain, Italy, France, and Germany have the most potential. While Portugal and Belgium have had, and are expected to continue to have, somewhat higher than average growth rates, their markets aren't as easily accessible. The U.K. and the Netherlands have had slower growth even though they're relatively open markets. Luxembourg, Ireland, and Greece have had lower than average growth and relatively heavy restrictions. Denmark is dominated by the "co-op" and is the most restricted retail market in the European Community.

The development of the European Community (EC) in general and of retailing in particular has the potential for removing many physical, fiscal, and technical trade barriers.[32] However, there are still considerable differences in habits,

EXHIBIT 6–6

EXHIBIT 6–6

Evaluation of
Retail Market
Opportunities
in European
Community

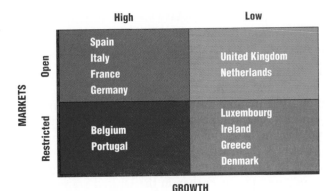

High **Low**

MARKETS

Open
Spain
Italy
France
Germany

United Kingdom
Netherlands

Restricted
Belgium
Portugal

Luxembourg
Ireland
Greece
Denmark

GROWTH

Source: Thomas J. Schiro and Amy M. Skolnik, "Europe 1992—Impact on Retail Sector,"
Retail Control, May-June 1990, p. 9

tastes, customs, and laws across Europe. For instance, national planning restrictions have prevented hypermarkets from expanding in many countries. Some European governments have restricted advertising and sales to specific times—mainly end-of-summer and post-Christmas clearances. Unions, sometimes backed by religious organizations, force retailers to close during the evening and on Sunday.

A number of EC proposals, directives, and cultural trends influence the retail industry. Consumer protection and environmental concerns have become hot issues. For instance, rules on labeling refillable containers and the civil liability of producers of batteries and other waste products impact retailing within the EC. Retailers in Germany must recycle packaging materials sold in their stores.

Some Western European and a few U.S. retailers are carefully moving into Eastern Europe. Many obstacles face retailing in Eastern Europe. Bureaucracies still prevail, and privatization of business has been slow. Laws about land and business

REFACT The average U.S. consumer purchases about 1.5 pairs of athletic footwear per year, compared to about one pair every five years for the average European.[33]

Gift stores in the Houston Galleria Mall focus on brand-name china to build sales from Latin American visitors.

ownership are still unclear. Workers are unfamiliar with market economies and many aren't used to working hard. Production distribution, technology, and in some cases electrical power are insufficient. Finally, unemployment is high.[34]

Asia   Retailing is a different business in Asia.[35] In the United States, merchandise mix, positioning, and vendor merchandise are critical success factors. Tenant management and manufacturer partnerships play a more important role in Asian retailing. In Asia, retailers develop competitive advantage through partnerships with real estate firms, manufacturers, and designers.

Most U.S. retail activities occur in the suburbs, while Asian retailing is an urban activity with higher rents and greater need for high sales per square foot. Labor costs and taxes are lower than in the United States; however, managers with skills comparable to American retail executives' are scarce. The distribution system is typically under government control and inefficient, requiring stores to carry higher inventory levels than they would in the United States.

Japan   Like Europeans, the Japanese thrive on American culture and fashion. Not too many years ago, many people wore traditional dress like the kimono. Today, streetwear is strictly Western. Brides typically wear the traditional bridal kimono only for pictures. Then they change into a white bridal gown that could be found at any American wedding.

Japanese department stores are three to four times the size of their U.S. counterparts. It's not uncommon for 1 million people to walk into a department store on a Saturday. Most departments in the store are leased and operated as independent firms. Thus, managing a Japanese department store is more similar to managing a U.S. mall than a U.S. department store. The Japanese have two gift-giving seasons. Each season represents 20 to 25 percent of their annual business.

The distribution system is different from that in the United States. Wholesalers are very strong in Japan, and merchandise sold on consignment is prevalent. For example, a wholesaler may own the merchandise and negotiate with the retailer to obtain space and operate the department. In effect, the retailer has less risk, but also has a lower profit margin than a similar American retailer.[36]

The repeal of the Large-Scale Retail Stores Law provides significant opportunities for foreign retailers in Japan. The law prohibited the opening of large stores (over 500 square meters) without the agreement of a majority of small independent stores in the market area and thus protected both small retailers and larger concerns that were already entrenched in the market.[37]

China   With 25 percent of the world's population, China will become a major retail market. At present, the market is undeveloped in terms of retail outlets and consumer spending power. Operating retail outlets is extremely complex and costly due to government restrictions and a poor distribution infrastructure.

Retailers from around the world are attracted to the United States. IKEA, Swedish furniture retailers, and Gucci, an Italian designer and retailer of hand leather goods, increase the level of competition in retail markets.

6.5

Retailing Invasion from Abroad

MANY FOREIGN RETAILERS FIND the United States to be a prime expansion opportunity because it's the world's largest consumer market and has relatively few legislative, cultural, or other barriers to entry. However, some international retailers have floundered in the United States.

Carrefour, a Paris-based global hypermarket giant, was unsuccessful in launching its hypermarket concept in the United States. Galeries Lafayette, the largest department store chain in France, lost $20 million before it closed its store on Fifth Avenue in New York. Makro (a Dutch-based, global retailer) couldn't establish a foothold in the United States for its cash-and-carry grocery warehouse concept.

However, a number of European food retailers have entered the U.S. market through acquisitions. Delhaize of Belgium has the controlling interest in Food Lion. A&P was acquired by the German firm Tengelmann. Ahold, a Dutch food retailer, owns six supermarket chains in the United States, including Bi-Lo, Tops, Edwards, and Stop & Shop. Sainsbury, one of the largest food retailers in Great Britian, acquired Giant Food and Shaw's. The acquiring companies have taken steps to improve distribution systems, consolidate buying, and introduce private labels in the U.S. outlets.

Source: Helen Arnold, "Looking for a New Oasis: Foreign Expansion of UK Retailers," *Super Marketing*, August 23, 1996, p. 18; Carla Rappoport and Justin Martin, "Retailers Go Global," *Fortune*, February 20, 1995, pp. 102–8; E. S. Browning, "Ahold's Supermarkets 'Go Native' to Succeed in U.S.," *The Wall Street Journal*, October 4, 1994, p. B4.

Many of the world's leading retailers, including Wal-Mart, McDonald's, and Makro (a Dutch warehouse retail chain), are moving quickly to establish a presence in China.[38] Even with all of the problems making it difficult to run a profitable business, these retailers are eager to learn how to operate in this new environment.

Retailing View 6.5 describes how many foreign retailers are finding it attractive to enter the U.S. market. The rest of this chapter outlines steps in developing a retail strategy.

REFACT The 10 major Asian countries have over one-half of the world's population.[39]

THE STRATEGIC RETAIL PLANNING PROCESS

The **strategic retail planning process** is the set of steps a retailer goes through to develop a strategic retail plan.[40] (See Exhibit 6–7.) It describes how retailers select target market segments, determine the appropriate retail format, and build sustainable competitive advantages. The planning process can be used to formulate strategic plans at different levels within a corporation. For example, American Express's corporate strategic plan indicates how resources are to be allocated across the corporation's various businesses such as credit cards and travel services. Each business within American Express has its own strategic plan, and then strategies are developed for products in a business such the American Express Gold card.

As we discuss the steps in the retail planning process, we will apply each of these steps to the planning process Joanne Phillips is undertaking. Joanne owns Gifts To Go, a small, two-store chain in the Chicago area. One of her 1,000-square-foot stores is in the downtown area; the other is in an upscale suburban mall. The target market for Gifts To Go is upper-income men and women looking for gifts in the $50 to $500 price range. The stores have an eclectic selection of merchandise, including handmade jewelry and crafts, fine china and glassware,

EXHIBIT 6–7

Steps in the Strategic
Retail Planning
Process

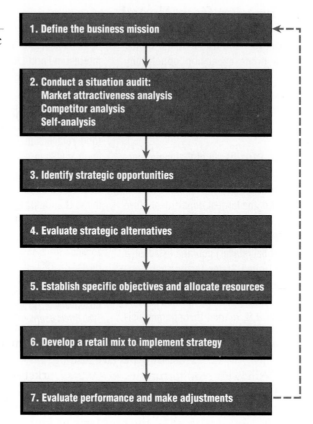

perfume, watches, writing instruments, and a variety of one-of-a-kind items. The stores have developed a number of loyal customers who are contacted by sales associates when anniversaries and birthdays come up. In many cases, customers know a sales associate and have enough confidence in his or her judgment that they tell the associate to pick out the gift. The turnover of Gifts To Go sales associates is low for the industry, because Ms. Phillips treats associates as part of the family. The company pays for medical and dental insurance for all associates. Sales associates share in the profits of the firm.

Step 1: Define the Business's Mission   The first step in the strategic retail planning process is to define the business's mission. The **mission statement** is a broad description of a retailer's objectives and the scope of activities it plans to undertake.[41]

The objective of a publicly held firm is to maximize its stockholders' wealth by increasing the value of its stock and paying dividends.[42] Owners of small, privately held firms frequently have other objectives such as providing a specific level of income and avoiding risks rather than maximizing income.

The mission statement should define the general nature of the target segments and retail formats that the firm will consider. For example, OfficeMax's mission statement, "Serve the customer, build value for shareholders, and create opportunities for associates,"[43] is too broad. It does not provide a sense of strategic direction.

In developing the mission statement managers must answer: (1) What business are we in? (2) What should be our business in the future? (3) Who are our customers? (4) What are our capabilities? (5) What do we want to accomplish? Gifts To Go's mission statement might read, "The mission of Gifts To Go is to be the leading retailer of higher-priced gifts in Chicago and provide a stable income of $100,000 per year for the owner."

Since the mission statement defines the retailer's objectives and the scope of activities it plans to undertake, Gifts To Go's mission statement indicates its management won't consider retail opportunities outside the Chicago area, won't consider opportunities for selling low-priced gifts, and won't consider opportunities that would jeopardize its ability to generate $100,000 in annual income.

Step 2: Conduct a Situation Audit

After developing a mission statement and setting objectives, the next step in the strategic planning process is to do a situation audit. A **situation audit** is an analysis of the opportunities and threats in the retail environment and the strengths and weaknesses of the retail business relative to its competitors. The elements in the situation analysis are shown in Exhibit 6–8.[44]

Market Factors   Market size and growth as well as sales cyclicity and seasonality are related to the nature of consumers and their buying patterns. Market size, typically measured in retail sales dollars, is important because it indicates a firm's opportunity for generating revenues to cover its investment. Large markets are attractive to large retail firms. But they are also attractive to small entrepreneurs because they offer more opportunities to focus a market segment.

Growing markets are more attractive than mature or declining markets. For example, retail markets for specialty stores are growing faster than those for department stores. Typically, margins and prices are higher in growing markets because competition is less intense than in mature markets. Since new customers are just beginning to patronize stores in growing markets, they may not have developed strong store loyalties and thus might be easier to attract to a new store.

Firms are often interested in minimizing the business cycle's impact on their sales. Thus, retail markets for merchandise affected by economic conditions (such as cars and major appliances) are less attractive than retail markets unaffected by economic conditions (such as food).

EXHIBIT 6–8

Elements in a Market Analysis

MARKET FACTORS
Size
Growth
Seasonality
Business cycles

COMPETITIVE FACTORS
Barriers to entry
Bargaining power of vendors
Competitive rivalry
Threat of superior new formats

ENVIRONMENTAL FACTORS
Technology
Economic
Regulatory
Social

ANALYSIS OF STRENGTHS AND WEAKNESSES
Management capabilities
Financial resources
Locations
Operations
Merchandise
Store management
Customer loyalty

In general, markets with highly seasonal sales are unattractive because a lot of resources are needed to accommodate the peak season, but then resources are underutilized the rest of the year. For example, to minimize these problems due to seasonality, ski resorts have been promoting the opportunities for vacations during all four seasons.

To do an analysis of the market factors for Gifts To Go, Joanne Phillips went to the library to get information about the size, growth, cyclicity, and seasonality of the gift market in general and, more specifically, in Chicago. Based on her analysis, she concluded that the market factors were attractive. The market for more expensive gifts was large, growing, and not vulnerable to business cycles. The only negative aspect was the seasonality with peaks at Valentine's Day, Easter, June (due to weddings), and Christmas.

REFACT Seventy percent of all toy sales are made during the Christmas season.

Competitive Factors   The nature of the competition in retail markets is affected by barriers to entry, bargaining power of vendors, competitive rivalry, and threat of superior new formats.[45]

Retail markets are more attractive when new competitors have little opportunity to enter. **Barriers to entry** are conditions in a retail market that make it difficult for firms to enter the market. These conditions include scale economies, customer loyalty, and availability of locations.

Scale economies are cost advantages due to a retailer's size. Retailers are reluctant to enter a market when a competitor has a cost advantage due to its size. For example, a small entrepreneur would avoid becoming an office supply category specialist because the market is dominated by two large firms: Staples/The Office Depot and OfficeMax. These firms would have a considerable cost advantage over the entrepreneur because they can buy merchandise cheaper and operate more efficiently by investing in the latest technology and spreading their overhead across more stores. Similarly, firms are cautious about entering retail markets dominated by a well-established retailer that has developed a loyal group of customers. For example, Home Depot's high loyalty among its customers in Atlanta makes it hard for a competing home-improvement center to enter the Atlanta market.

Retailing View 6.6 discusses how some small retailers develop sustainable advantages over national chains with larger-scale economies.

Finally, the availability of locations may impede competitive entry. JCPenney department stores aren't very strong in the Northeast. Lack of available mall locations makes it difficult for Penney to enter and build a strong position there.

Entry barriers are a two-edged sword. A retail market with high entry barriers is very attractive for retailers presently competing in that market, because those barriers limit competition. However, markets with high entry barriers are unattractive for retailers not already in the market. For example, the lack of good new mall locations in the Northeast makes this market attractive for Macy's and Filene's (department stores already in the region), but unattractive for department stores such as Penney that desire to enter the market.

Another competitive factor is the **bargaining power of vendors.** Markets are unattractive when a few vendors control the merchandise sold in it. In these situations, vendors have an opportunity to dictate prices and other terms (like delivery dates), reducing retailer's profits. For example, the market for retailing fashionable cosmetics is less attractive because two suppliers, Elizabeth Arden and Estée Lauder, provide the most desired brands. Since department stores need these brands to support a fashionable image, these suppliers have the power to sell their products to retailers at high prices.[46]

6.6

Competing against the Giants

SMALL RETAILERS CAN EFFECTIVELY compete head-to-head against industry giants like Wal-Mart and Home Depot. These large retailers with buying power can sell merchandise at lower prices than small retailers. However, small retailers can compete effectively by (1) offering unique merchandise tailored to the local community, (2) giving customers a personal touch, and (3) developing ties with the local community. For example, Toys "R" Us and Wal-Mart are primarily interested in selling well-known toys and games at low prices and letting their manufacturers advertise how the toys work. But many toys are too complicated to explain in a 30-second commercial. Playmobil construction toys are only sold through independent toy stores, because these stores are interested in setting up Playmobil playpens on their floors so parents and children can have "an out-of-box experience."

At Classic Creations, a Venice, Florida, jewelry store, owners of the store rather than a commissioned salesperson wait on customers. By offering personal attention they build customer loyalty. For example, a man recently bought a $4,000 engagement ring based on a recommendation he received from his parents, who had their wedding bands redesigned there several years ago.

Independent fishing tackle shops compete against discount giants like Wal-Mart and Toys "R" Us and sporting goods category specialists by offering special services. In Sarasota, Florida, Mr. CB's Bait & Tackle teams up with local charter boat captains to offer seminars and discounted trips. The captains get the fishing trips and Mr. CB's sells the fishing gear. K & K True Value Hardware in Bettendorf, Iowa, focuses on fishing experts who want to make their own lures. The store stocks the raw materials: spinner blades in 14 sizes, tinsel in 40 colors, chicken feathers, deer fur, weights, and hooks.

Bookseller's in Fridley, Minnesota, competes against Barnes & Noble by specializing in books on Christianity. Customers include pastors, Sunday school teachers, and people who need spiritual guidance. For example, the owner suggested some books for a mother concerned about her son's drug problems. The son is now an honors student in college. A pet store builds its reputation among children by inviting classes from the local school to visit the store and learn about pets.

Source: Alina Matus, "Taking on the Retail Giants," *Miami Herald*, May 22, 1995, pp. 12–13; Kenneth Stone, *Competing against the Giants* (New York: Wiley, 1995); and Michael Sele, "Small Retailers Fare Well Despite Chains' Onslaught," *The Wall Street Journal*, September 12, 1994, p. B2.

The final industry factor is the level of competitive rivalry in the retail market. **Competitive rivalry** is the frequency and intensity of reactions to actions undertaken by competitors. When rivalry is high, price wars erupt, employee raids occur, advertising and promotion expenses increase, and profit potential falls.

Conditions that may lead to intense rivalry include (1) a large number of competitors that are all about the same size, (2) slow growth, (3) high fixed costs, and (4) the lack of perceived differences between competing retailers.

When Joanne Phillips started to analyze the competitive factors for Gifts To Go, she realized that identifying her competitors wasn't easy. While there were no gift stores carrying similar merchandise and price points in the Chicago area, there were a number of other retailers where a customer could buy these types of gifts. She felt her primary competitors were department stores, craft galleries, and catalogs. Joanne felt there might be some scale economies in developing customer databases to support gift retailing. The lack of large suppliers meant that vendors' bargaining power wasn't a problem and competitive rivalry was minimal because the gift business was not a critical part of the department store's overall business. In addition, merchandise carried by the various retailers offered considerable opportunity to differentiate the retailers.

Environmental Factors   Environmental factors that affect market attractiveness span technological, economic, regulatory, and social changes.[47] When a retail market is going through significant changes in technology, present competitors are vulnerable to new entrants that are skilled at using the new technology. For example, JCPenney, a late entrant into the catalog retail market, adopted new data-processing and communication technology faster than Sears, which had 50 years' more experience in catalog retailing.

Some retailers may be more affected by economic conditions than others. For example, Neiman Marcus and Nordstrom employ many well-paid salespeople to provide high-quality customer service. When unemployment is low, their costs may increase significantly, as salespeople's wages rise due to the difficulty in hiring qualified people. But retailers like Wal-Mart that provide little service and have much lower labor costs as a percentage of sales may be less affected by low unemployment.

Government regulations can reduce the attractiveness of a retail market. For example, regulations make it costly for American retailers to build stores (zoning laws) and hire employees (limitations on terminating employees). These regulations may serve as barriers to entry—they may make a market more attractive to retailers already in the market and less attractive to potential new entrants.

Finally, trends in demographics, lifestyles, attitudes, and personal values affect retail markets' attractiveness. Chapter 3 covered many of these changes and their implications.

Retailers need to answer three questions about each environmental factor:

1. What new developments or changes might occur, such as new technologies and regulations or different social factors and economic conditions?
2. What is the likelihood that these environmental changes will occur? What key factors affect whether these changes will occur?
3. How will these changes impact each retail market, the firm, and its competitors?

Joanne Phillips' primary concern when she did an environmental analysis was the potential growth of traditional catalog and electronic retailers in the gift business. Gifts seem to be ideal for nonstore retailing. Typically, customers would not get much benefit out of visiting the store, because they were not buying the merchandise for themselves. Even when they saw and touched the merchandise, they wouldn't know how the recipient would feel about it. In addition, many Gift To Go customers had the store ship the present rather than taking the present with them. Finally, Joanne felt that catalog and potential electronic retailers could effectively collect information about customers and then target promotions and suggestions to them when gift-giving occasions arose.

Strengths and Weaknesses Analysis   The most critical aspect of the situation audit is for a retailer to determine its unique capabilities—its **strengths and weaknesses** relative to the competition.[49] These strengths and weaknesses indicate how well the business can seize opportunities and avoid harm from threats in the environment. Exhibit 6–9 outlines issues to consider in performing a self-analysis.

EXHIBIT 6–9

Strengths and
Weaknesses Analysis

In performing self-analysis, the retailer considers the potential areas for developing a competitive advantage listed below and answers the following questions:

- At what is our company good?
- In which of these areas is our company better than our competitors?
- In which of these areas does our company's unique capabilities provide a sustainable competitive advantage or a basis for developing one?

MANAGEMENT CAPABILITY
Capabilities and experience of top management
Depth of management—capabilities of middle management
Management's commitment to firm

MERCHANDISING CAPABILITIES
Knowledge and skills of buyers
Relationships with vendors
Capabilities in developing private brands
Advertising and promotion capabilities

FINANCIAL RESOURCES
Cash flow from existing business
Ability to raise debt or equity financing

STORE MANAGEMENT CAPABILITIES
Management capabilities
Quality of sales associates
Commitment of sales associates to firm

OPERATIONS
Overhead cost structure
Quality of operating systems
Distribution capabilities
Management information systems
Loss prevention systems
Inventory control system

LOCATIONS

CUSTOMERS
Loyalty of customers

Here is Joanne Phillips' analysis of Gifts To Go's strengths and weaknesses:

Management capability	Limited—Two excellent store managers and a relatively inexperienced person who helped Joanne with buying merchandise. An accounting firm kept the financial records for the business.
Financial resources	Good—Gifts To Go had no debt and a good relationship with a bank. — Joanne had saved $255,000 that she had in liquid securities.
Operations	Poor—While Joanne felt Gifts to Go had relatively low overhead, the company did not have a computer-based inventory control system or management and customer information systems. Her competitors (local department stores and catalog retailers) certainly had superior systems.
Merchandise capabilities	Good—Joanne had a flair for selecting unique gifts and she had excellent relationships with vendors providing one-of-a-kind merchandise.
Store management capabilities	Excellent—The store managers and sales associates were excellent. They were very attentive to customers and loyal to the firm. Employee and customer theft were kept to a minimum.
Locations	Excellent—Both of Gifts To Go's locations were excellent. The downtown location was convenient for office workers. The suburban mall location was at a heavily trafficked juncture.
Customers	Good—While Gifts To Go did not do the sales volume in gifts done in department stores, the company had a loyal base of customers.

Step 3: Identify Strategic Opportunities After completing the situation audit, the next step is to identify opportunities for increasing retail sales. These strategic alternatives are defined in terms of the squares in the retail market matrix shown in Exhibit 6–1 and the growth strategies in Exhibit 6–4.

Joanne Phillips competes in gift retailing using a specialty store format. Growth options that she's considering for Gifts To Go include:

Market penetration	1. Increase size of present stores and amount of merchandise in stores.
	2. Open additional gift stores in Chicago area.
Market expansion	1. Open gift stores outside the Chicago area (new geographic segment).
	2. Sell lower-priced gifts in present stores or open new stores selling low-priced gifts (new benefit segment).
Retail format development	1. Sell apparel and other nongift merchandise to same customers in same or new stores.
	2. Sell similar gift merchandise to same market segment using a catalog or electronic retailing.
Diversification	1. Manufacture craft gifts.
	2. Open apparel stores targeted at teenagers.
	3. Open a category specialist selling low-price gifts.

Note that some of these growth opportunities involve a redefinition of her mission.

Step 4: Evaluate Strategic Opportunities

The fourth step in the strategic planning process is to evaluate opportunities that have been identified in the situation audit. The evaluation determines the retailer's potential to establish a sustainable competitive advantage and reap long-term profits from the opportunities under evaluation. Thus, a retailer must focus on opportunities that utilize its strengths—its area of competitive advantage. For example, expertise in developing private-label apparel is one of The Limited's sources of competitive advantage. Thus, The Limited would positively evaluate opportunities that involve development of private-label merchandise. Some areas retailers need to examine when evaluating new strengths and weaknesses are are shown in Exhibit 6–9.

Market Attractiveness/Competitive Position Matrix   The **market attractiveness/competitive position matrix** (Exhibit 6–10) provides a method for analyzing opportunities that explicitly considers both the retailer's capabilities and the retail market's attractiveness.[50] The matrix's underlying premise is that a market's attractiveness determines its long-term profit potential, and the retailer's competitive position indicates how much the retailer's profits can surpass competitors'. The matrix indicates that the greatest investments should be made in market opportunities where the retailer has a strong competitive position.

Joanne evaluated the growth opportunities as follows:

OPPORTUNITY	MARKET ATTRACTIVENESS	COMPETITIVE POSITION
Increase size of present stores and amount of merchandise in stores.	Low	High
Open additional gift stores in Chicago area.	Medium	Medium
Open gift stores outside the Chicago area (new geographic segment).	Medium	Low
Sell lower-priced gifts in present stores or open new stores selling low-priced gifts (new benefit segment).	Medium	Low
Sell apparel and other nongift merchandise to same customers in same or new stores.	High	Low
Sell similar gift merchandise to same market segment using a catalog or electronic retailing.	High	Medium
Manufacture craft gifts.	High	Low
Open apparel stores targeted at teenagers.	High	Low
Open a category specialist selling low-price gifts.	High	Low

EXHIBIT 6–10

Market
Attractiveness/
Competitive Position
Martrix

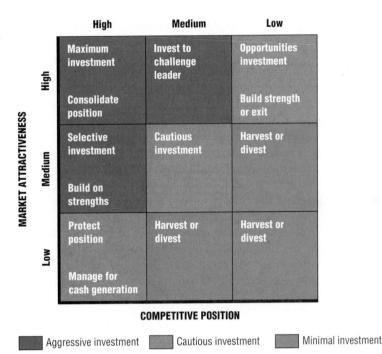

COMPETITIVE POSITION

Aggressive investment   Cautious investment   Minimal investment

Step 5: Establish Specific Objectives and Allocate Resources

After evaluating the strategic investment opportunities, the next step in the strategic planning process is to establish a specific objective for each opportunity. The retailer's overall objective is included in the mission statement. The specific objectives are goals against which progress toward the overall objective can be measured. Thus, these specific objectives have three components: (1) the performance sought, including a numerical index against which progress may be measured, (2) a time frame within which the goal is to be achieved, and (3) the level of investment needed to achieve the objective. Typically, the performance levels are financial criteria such as return on investment, sales, or profits. Another commonly used objective, market share, is becoming more popular because it's easier to measure and often more objectively assessed than financial measures based on accounting information (which can be dramatically affected by accounting rules). Research indicates that market share is a good surrogate for long-term profitability in many businesses.[51]

Step 6: Develop a Retail Mix to Implement Strategy

The sixth step in the planning process is to develop a retail mix for each opportunity in which investment will be made and to control and evaluate performance. Decisions related to the elements in the retail mix are discussed in Sections III and IV.

Step 7: Evaluate Performance and Make Adjustments

The final step in the planning process is evaluating the results of the strategy and implementation program. If the retailer is meeting or exceeding its objectives, changes aren't needed. But if the retailer fails to meet its objectives, reanalysis is needed. Typically, this reanalysis starts with reviewing the implementation programs; but it may indicate that the strategy (or even the mission statement) needs to be reconsidered. This conclusion would result in starting a new planning process, including a new situation audit.

Strategic Planning in the Real World

The planning process in Exhibit 6–7 indicates that strategic decisions are made in a sequential manner. After the business mission is defined, the situation audit is performed, strategic opportunities are identified, alternatives are evaluated, objectives are set, resources are allocated, the implementation plan is developed, and, finally, performance is evaluated and adjustments are made. But actual planning processes have interactions among the steps. For example, the situation audit may uncover a logical alternative for the firm to consider, even though this alternative isn't included in the mission statement. Thus, the mission statement may need to be reformulated. Development of the implementation plan might reveal that resource allocation to the opportunity is insufficient to achieve the objective. In that case, the objective would need to be changed or the resources would need to be increased, or the retailer might consider not investing in the opportunity at all.

Strategic planning is an ongoing process. Every day, retailers audit their situations, examine lifestyle trends, study new technologies, and monitor competitive activities.[52] But the retail strategy statement isn't changed every year or every six months. The strategy statement is reviewed and altered only when major changes in the retailer's environment or capabilities occur.

When a retailer undertakes a major reexamination of its strategy, the process for developing a new strategy statement may take a year or two. Potential strategic directions are generated by people at all levels of the organization. These ideas are evaluated by senior executives and operating people to ensure that the eventual strategic direction is profitable in the long run and can be implemented.

SUMMARY

A retailer's long-term performance is largely determined by its strategy. The strategy coordinates employees' activities and communicates the direction the retailer plans to take. Retail market strategy describes both the strategic direction and the process by which the strategy is to be developed.

The strategic planning process consists of a sequence of steps including a detailed analysis of (1) the environment in which the retailer operates and (2) the retailer's unique capabilities. Based on this analysis, the retailer can evaluate alternatives using financial theory and a market attractiveness/competitive position matrix.

The retail strategy statement includes identification of a target market and the retail offering to be directed toward the target market. The statement also needs to indicate the retailer's methods to build a sustainable competitive advantage.

KEY TERMS

bargaining power of vendors, *182*

barriers to entry, *182*

competitive rivalry, *183*

cross-selling, *171*

customer loyalty, *165*

data warehouse, *166*

databased retailing, *166*

diversification opportunity, *172*

market attractiveness/ competitive position matrix, *186*

market expansion opportunity, *171*

market penetration opportunity, *170*

mission statement, *180*

positioning, *165*

related diversification, *172*

retail format, *161*

retail format development opportunity, *171*

retail market, *162*

retail strategy, *161*

scale economies, *182*

situation audit, *181*

strategic retail planning process, *179*

strengths and weaknesses analysis, *184*

sustainable competitive advantage, *164*

target market, *161*

unrelated diversification, *172*

vertical integration, *172*

DISCUSSION QUESTIONS & PROBLEMS

1. What approaches can a retailer use to develop a competitive advantage?

2. Give an example of a market penetration opportunity, a retail format extension, and a market extension opportunity for Kentucky Fried Chicken (KFC).

3. For each of the four retailers discussed at the beginning of the chapter, describe their strategy and basis of competitive advantage.

4. Do a situation analysis for McDonald's. What is its mission? What are its strengths and weaknesses? What environmental threats might it face over the next 10 years? How could it prepare for these threats?

5. Give an example of a retailer using the retail format development growth strategy.

6. Disney decided to expand its retail operations by opening specialty stores in malls. What are the advantages and disadvantages of Disney's pursuing this opportunity?

7. Many retailing experts have suggested that improving customer service is the basis for capturing a sustainable competitive advantage in the 1990s. What practical changes can a food/grocery retailer make to improve customer service?

8. Evaluate the strategic alternatives being considered by Gifts To Go as outlined in the chapter. Which do you think the company should pursue and why?

9. The Limited expanded its operations through the purchase of Lane Bryant, Lerner Shops, Victoria's Secret, Henri Bendel, and Limited Express. One might argue that it was good for The Limited to enter new markets and formats and thus improve its market share as well as its profit level. On the other hand, one could argue that The Limited has lost its focus and now is susceptible to being involved in too many businesses. How can The Limited continue to expand and grow and at the same time maintain a clear mission for its businesses?

SUGGESTED READINGS

Aaker, David. *Strategic Market Management*, 4th ed. New York: Wiley, 1995.

Collins, David and Cynthia Montgomery. "Competing on Resources: Strategy for the 1990s." *Harvard Business Review* 73(July-August 1995), pp. 118–28.

"Going Global: Best Practice Strategy Development and Brand Development." *Chain Store Age*, November 1995, pp. 76–84.

Hunt, Shelby, and Robert Morgan. "The Comparative Advantage Theory of Competition." *Journal of Marketing* 59 (April 1995), pp. 1–15.

Lehmann, Donald, and Russell Winer. *Analysis for Marketing Planning*, 3d ed. Burr Ridge, IL: Irwin, 1994.

Morris, Tim, and R. Nicholas Gerlich. "Effects of Wal-Mart Supercenters on Local Market Food Retailers: Survival Strategies for the Small Grocer." *Journal of Business and Entrepreneur* 7 (March 1995), pp. 31–44.

Peppers, Don, and Martha Rogers. *The One to One Future: Building Relationships One Customer at a Time*. New York: Doubleday, 1993.

Porter, Michael. *Competitive Advantage*. New York: Free Press, 1985.

"Retailers with a Future: The New Value Equation." *Chain Store Age*, October 1996, pp. 4D–7D.

Samiee, Saeed. "Strategic Considerations in European Retailing." *Journal of International Marketing*, 1995, pp. 49–76.

Smart, Denise, and Robert Solano-Mendez. "Generic Retailing Types, Distinctive Marketing Competencies, and Competitive Advantage." *Journal of Retailing* 69 (Fall 1993), pp. 254–79.

Wines, Leslie. "Know Thy Customer: Lessons in Value." *Journal of Business Strategy* 16 (November-December 1995), pp. 13–15.

Woods, Robert. "Strategic Planning : A Look at Ruby Tuesday." *Cornell Hotel & Restaurant Administration Quarterly* 35 (June 1994), pp. 41–49.

APPENDIX

Using the Market Attractiveness/Competitive Position Matrix

The following example illustrates an application of the market attractiveness/competitive position matrix shown in Exhibit 6–10. There are six steps in using the matrix to evaluate opportunities for strategic investments:

1. Define the strategic opportunities to be evaluated. For example, a store manager could use the matrix to evaluate departments in a store; a vice president of stores for a specialty store chain could use it to evaluate stores or potential store sites; a merchandise vice president could use it to evaluate merchandise categories sold by the retailer; or a retail holding company's CEO could use it to evaluate the retail chains it owns.

2. Identify key factors determining market attractiveness and the retailer's competitive position. Factors that might be selected are discussed in the market attractiveness, competitor analysis, and self-analysis sections of the situation audit.

3. Assign weights to each factor used to determine market attractiveness and competitive position. The weights assigned to each factor indicate that factor's importance in determining the market attractiveness and competitive position. Typically, weights are selected so that they add up to 100.

4. Rate each strategic investment opportunity on (1) the attractiveness of its market and (2) the retailer's competitive position in that market. Typically, opportunities are rated on a 1-to-10 scale, with 10 indicating a very attractive market or very strong competitive position and 1 indicating a very unattractive market or very weak competitive position.

5. Calculate each opportunity's score for market attractiveness and competitive position. Scores are calculated by (1) multiplying the weights by each factor's rating and (2) adding across the factors.

6. Plot each opportunity on the matrix in Exhibit 6–11.

In this example, a department store chain is evaluating seven merchandise categories it sells:

1. Women's clothing (target age group 30 to 60).
2. Juniors' clothing (ages 13 to 30).
3. Men's and boys' clothing (ages 13 to 60).
4. Children's clothing, toys, and games (ages 0 to 12).
5. Furniture.
6. Consumer electronics.
7. Soft home (bedding, draperies) and kitchen items.

EXHIBIT 6–11   Opportunities' Market Attractiveness Ratings

	WEIGHT	WOMEN'S (1)	JUNIORS' (2)	MEN'S (3)	CHILDREN'S (4)	FURNITURE (5)	CONS. ELEC. (6)	SOFT HOME (7)
				FACTORS				
Market size	20	9	7	5	4	5	6	7
Growth	20	4	3	6	5	4	8	6
Vendor power	15	5	4	10	9	2	1	8
Competitive intensity	20	4	3	10	2	5	2	10
Social trends	25	5	5	6	6	7	4	9
Score	100	540	445	720	505	485	435	805

To evaluate each merchandise category's market attractiveness, management identified five market factors, assigned a weight to each factor, rated the merchandise category markets on each factor, and calculated a market attractiveness score for each alternative (Exhibit 6–11). Here management assigned the highest weight to social trends (25) and lowest to vendor power (15).

Ratings for market size and market growth are based on industry data and projections. Vendors' bargaining power is rated low for consumer electronics (1) and furniture (2) due to the limited number of suppliers for these merchandise categories. (A high rating [i.e., 10] on vendor power means that vendors aren't very powerful. A high rating on competitive intensity means that competition isn't very intense.) Soft home items (8), men's clothing (10), and children's clothing (9) are viewed as fragmented industries with many small suppliers. The retailer evaluates competition as very strong in consumer electronics (2) and children's clothing (2) due to the region's growth of category specialists such as GapKids, Kids "R" Us, and Circuit City. Finally, the trend toward spending more time at home makes home merchandise and furniture more attractive because consumers will increase spending in these categories and be less price-sensitive.

Exhibit 6–12 shows the factors, weights, and ratings used to evaluate the retailer's competitive position in each merchandise category versus the competition. In evaluating competitive position, management assigned more weight to vendor relationships (25) and the store's image for the merchandise category (25) because it views these factors as critical for maintaining an assortment of high-fashion brands from which customer loyalty develops. Buyers' skills (10) are less critical because management felt that poor buyers could be easily replaced by better ones.

The store location in a leading regional mall is appropriate for clothing but less so for consumer electronics. Thus, management indicates a strong competitive position on location for women's and juniors' clothing (9), but a weak position for consumer electronics (2). Management felt that relationships with consumer electronics vendors are poor (3) and that the skills of buyers responsible for this category are below average (4). Finally, the store's image with customers is particularly good in women's and juniors' clothing and soft home items (8).

Evaluations for each merchandise category are plotted on Exhibit 6–13's business attractiveness/competitive position matrix. Based on the recommended investment level and objectives associated with each cell in the exhibit, the department store should invest substantially in home merchandise and men's clothing categories; consider reducing investments in or discontinue the furniture,

EXHIBIT **6–12**   Opportunities' Competitive Position Ratings

	WEIGHT	WOMEN'S (1)	JUNIORS' (2)	MEN'S (3)	CHILDREN'S (4)	FURNITURE (5)	CONS. ELEC. (6)	SOFT HOME (7)
				FACTORS				
Location	20	9	9	8	6	4	2	4
Vendor relationship	25	8	7	5	7	4	3	7
Costs	20	8	8	5	6	3	1	7
Skills of buyers	10	6	7	5	9	5	4	8
Image with customer	25	8	8	5	6	5	2	8
Score	100	800	785	560	655	415	225	675

EXHIBIT 6–13

Evaluation of
Department Store
Opportunities

children's clothing, and consumer electronics lines; make selective investments in
juniors' clothing; and invest to achieve a leadership position in men's clothing.
While this example is hypothetical, similar analyses have led many department
store chains to reach the same conclusions and reduce or discontinue consumer
electronics and furniture.[53]

NOTES

1. Nancy Karch, "The New Strategic Era in Retailing, Part I,"
Retail Control 53 (October 1985), pp. 36–49; Nancy Karch,
"The New Strategic Era in Retailing, Part 2," *Retail Control*
53 (November 1985), pp. 10–19; and Bert Rosenbloom,
"Strategic Planning in Retailing: Prospects and Problems,"
Journal of Retailing 56 (Spring 1980), pp. 98–106.

2. Roger Evered, "So What Is Strategy?" *Long Range
Planning* 16 (Fall 1983), pp. 120–25; and Barton Weitz
and Robin Wensley, "What Is Marketing Strategy?"
working paper, College of Business Administration,
University of Florida, Gainesville.

3. Evered, "So What Is Strategy?" p. 120.

4. Howard Rudnitsky, "Keeping the Family Buggy on the
Road," *Forbes*, March 11, 1996, pp. 52–53; and John
Wirebach, "Autozone Strikes the Heartland," *Automotive
Marketing*, October 1996, pp. 19–21.

5. Susan Reda, "Talbots Thrives with Innovative Synergies,
Consumer Research," *Stores*, July 1995, pp. 34–37; and
Richard Baum, *The Talbots, Inc.* (New York: Goldman,
Sachs, December 31, 1993).

6. Adrian Slywatsky and Kevin Mundt, "Hold the Sugar,"
Across the Board, September 1996, pp. 39–41; and
"Starbucks Rides the Caffeine Wave," *Chain Store Age*,
April 1996, pp. 80–81.

7. "Retail Entrepreneur of the Year," *Chain Store Age Executive*,
December 1994, p. 35; and Richard Baum, *Gymboree
Corporation* (New York: Goldman, Sachs, May 5, 1993).

8. Anthony Boardman and Aidan Vining, "Defining Your
Business Using Product–Customer Matrices," *Long Range
Planning* 29 (February 1996), pp. 38–48; and R. L.
Rothschild, *How to Gain and Maintain Competitive
Advantage in Business* (New York: McGraw-Hill, 1984).
Chapter 2 gives other examples of this approach to map-
ping competitive markets.

9. "The Best Stores," *Women's Wear Daily*, Special Report, October 1994.

10. Denise Smart and Robert Solano-Mendez, "Generic Retailing Types, Distinctive Marketing Competencies, and Competitive Advantage," *Journal of Retailing* 69 (Fall 1993), pp. 254–79; Gary Hamel and C. K. Prahalad, "Thinking Differently," *Business Quarterly* 59 (Summer 1995), pp. 22–25ff; David Collins and Cynthia Montgomery, "Competing on Resources: Strategy for the 1990s," *Harvard Business Review* 73 (July-August 1995), pp. 118–28; William Werther and Jeffery Kerr, "The Shifting Sands of Competitive Advantage," *Business Horizons* 38 (May-June 1995), pp. 11–17; and David Aaker, "Managing Assets and Skills: The Key to Sustainable Competitive Advantage," *California Management Review* 32 (Winter 1989), pp. 91–106.

11. Leonard Berry, "Relationship Marketing of Services— Growing Interest, Emerging Perspectives," *Journal of the Academy of Marketing Sciences* 23 (Fall 1995), pp. 236–45; and Mary Jo Bitner, "Building Service Relationships: It's All About Promises," *Journal of the Academy of Marketing Sciences* 23 (Fall 1995), pp. 246–51.

12. Jane Laker, "Supermarkets Still Ahead in Battle to Keep Customers Loyal," *Marketing Week*, September 13, 1996, p. 34.

13. Bernd Schmitt, Alex Simonson, and Joshua Marcus, "Managing Corporate Image and Identity," *Long Range Planning* 28 (October 1995), pp. 82–92; David Aaker, "Positioning Your Product," *Business Horizon*, May-June 1982, pp. 56–62; and George Lucas and Larry Gresham, "How to Position for Retailing Success," *Business*, April-June 1989, pp. 31–32.

14. For examples of this type of research, see James Mammarella, "Value Rules Apparel Decisions as Battle for Share Sharpens," *Discount Store News*, October 7, 1996, pp. 21–25; and Mary R. Zimmer and Linda L. Golden, "Impressions of Retail Stores: A Content Analysis of Consumer Images," *Journal of Retailing* 64 (Fall 1988), pp. 266–93.

15. Stanley Marcus, *Minding the Store* (Boston: Little, Brown, 1974), p. 81.

16. Susan Greco, "The Road to One to One Marketing, *Inc.*, October 1995, pp. 56–58; Leslie Wines, "Know Thy Customer: Lessons in Value," *Journal of Business Strategy* 16 (November-December 1995), pp. 13–15; and Rashi Glazer, "Marketing in an Information Intensive Environment: Strategic Implications of Knowledge as an Asset," *Journal of Marketing* 55 (October 1991), pp. 1–19.

17. Diane Halstead and Cheryl Ward, "Assessing the Vulnerability of Private Label Brands," *Journal of Product & Brand Management*, July 1995, pp. 38–48; and Walter J. Salmon and Karen A. Carr, "Private Labels Are Back in Fashion," *Harvard Business Review* 65 (May-June 1987), pp. 99–106.

18. Gerald Smith, Meera Venkatraman, and Lawrence Wortzel, "Strategic Marketing Fit in Manufacturer–Retailer Relationships: Price Leaders versus Merchandise Differentiators," *Journal of Retailing* 71 (Fall 1995), pp. 297–316; Margaret Gilliam, "The Impact of Partnerships on Retailers and Manufacturers," *Retail Control*, March 1992, pp. 11–18; Wendy Zellner, "Clout! More and More, Retail Giants Rule the Marketplace," *Business Week*, December 21, 1992, pp. 66–73; and Erin Anderson and Barton Weitz, "Forging a Strategic Distribution Alliance," *Chief Executive*, November-December 1991, pp. 70–73.

19. John Cooke, "The Retail Revolution Is Coming!" *Logistics Management*, April 1996, pp. 48–51.

20. Debra Chanil, "A Year of Change," *Discount Merchandiser*, January 1996, pp. 10–12ff; and Family Dollar 1995, *Annual Report.*

21. William Werther and Jeffrey Kerr, "The Shifting Sands of Competitive Advantage," *Business Horizons*, 38 (May-June 1995), pp. 11–17.

22. Stephen Drucker, "Who's the Best Restaurateur in America? McDonald's," *New York Times Magazine*, March 10, 1995, pp. 45–47.

23. H. Igor Ansoff, *Corporate Strategy* (New York: McGraw-Hill, 1965); and Roger Kerin, Vijay Mahajan, and P. Rajan Varadarajan, *Contemporary Perspectives on Strategic Market Planning* (Boston: Allyn & Bacon, 1990), chapter 6. See also Susan Mudambi, "A Topology of Strategic Choice in Retailing," *International Journal of Retail & Distribution Management*, 1994, pp. 22–25.

24. Erin Anderson and Barton Weitz, "Make-or-Buy Decisions: Vertical Integration and Marketing Productivity," *Sloan Management Review* 28 (Spring 1986), p. 319.

25. Eithel Simpson and Dayle Thorpe, "A Conceptual Model of Strategic Considerations for International Retail Expansion," *Service Industries Journal*, October 1995, pp. 16–24; Mel Redman, "Preparation and Study Central to International Expansion," *Chain Store Age*, October 1995, pp. 92–93; Susan Reda, "Global Expansion: Will Retailers Get Burned?" *Stores*, November 1994, pp. 19–24; and Michael Bier and David Mish, "Best Practices in Retailing: Going Global: Best Practice Strategy and Brand Development," *Chain Store Age*, November 1995, pp. 76–84.

26. Jay Johnson, "Why American Retailers Are Going Global," *Discount Merchandiser*, September 1995, pp. 37–38; and "Building around the World," *Chain Store Age Executive*, February 1995, pp. 88–92.

27. Robert Verdisco, "The Future of Mass Retailing Is Global," *Discount Store News*, October 5, 1992, p. 11; and Joseph R. Baczko, former president, Blockbuster Entertainment and Toys "R" Us International Division, at the Executive Education Symposium, Center for Retail Education and Research, University of Florida, May 13, 1993.

28. Jay Johnson, "The Globe Trotters: Retail's Multinationals," *Discount Merchandiser*, September 1995, pp. 40–41.

29. "Global Retailing: Assignment Latin America," *Chain Store Age*, April 1996, section 2, pp. 1–16.

30. Keith Kohler, "Retailing in Latin America: Fewer Surprises, Greater Opportunities," *Chain Store Age*, April 1996, section 2, p. 5; Mary Ellen Kelly, "U.S. Retailers Begin Mexican Invasion," *Discount Store News*, May 18, 1992, pp. 43–48; "Retailers Must Avoid Pitfalls of New Market," *Discount Store News*, May 18, 1992, pp. 43–48; Mary Ellen Kelly, "JCPenney to Enter Mexico," *Discount Store News*, February 15, 1993, p. 3; Tracy Mullin, "NAFTA: A Win/Win for Retailers," *Stores*, October 1992, p. 20; and Arthur Markowitz, "Costco Thinks International: Club Eyes France and Spain," *Discount Store News*, August 5, 1991, p. 7.

31. "Mexico: Peso Devaluation Forces Global Retailers to Stall Plans," *Chain Store Age*, December 1995, Coopers & Lybrand Global Powers of Retailing Supplement, pp. 32–34.

32. Saeed Samiee, "Strategic Considerations in European Retailing," *Journal of International Marketing*, 1995, pp. 49–76.

33. Joseph H. Ellis, Richard N. Baum, and Mary Ann Casati, "International Retailing: Opportunities and Pitfalls," Goldman Sachs Investment Research, May 14, 1993, p. 6.

34. Paul Dooley, "Euro-Retailing," *Stores*, July 1992, pp. 76–78; Timothy Harper, *Cracking the New European Markets* (New York: Wiley, 1994); Thomas J. Schiro and Amy M. Skolnik, "Europe 1992—Impact on Retail Sector," *Retail Control*, May-June 1990, pp. 3–9; Laura Liebeck, "Kmart Czechs into Europe," *Discount Store News*, June 15, 1992, pp. 3, 20; Arthur Markowitz, "Status Quo in Western Europe," *Discount Store News*, May 6, 1991, pp. 99ff; Laura Liebeck, "Eastern Europe a Risky Business," *Discount Store News*, May 6, 1991, pp. 103ff; and Carrie Dolan, "Levi Tries to Round Up Counterfeiters," *The Wall Street Journal*, February 19, 1992, pp. B1, B10.

35. Janet Zhang, "Asia: Opportunities Large and Small," *Chain Store Executive*, January 1995, section 2, pp. 7–8.

36. Yung-Fang Chen and Brenda Sternquist, "Differences between International and Domestic Japanese Retailers," *Service Industries Journal*, October 1995, pp. 118–33.

37. Stanley Marcus and Lawrence R. Katzen, "Japan's Best Practices: Lessons and Opportunities," *Retail Business Review*, January 1993, pp. 6–9; "Japanese vs. American Retailing," *Stores*, June 1992, p. 29; and Tony Lisanti, "Japanese Retailing's Tug-of-War," *Discount Store News*, May 6, 1991, pp. 77ff.

38. Joan Bergmann, "China Reassessed," *Discount Merchandiser*, May 1995, pp. 94–97ff; and Alan Treadgold, "The Asian Opportunity," *Discount Merchandiser*, December 1995, pp. 33, 70.

39. "Global Retailing: Asian Assignment," *Chain Store Age Executive*, January 1995, section 2, p. 5.

40. See Steve Weinstein, "How Retailers Set Goals and Reach Them," *Progressive Grocer*, April 1990, pp. 155–60; William Rothschild, *Putting It All Together: A Guide to Strategic Thinking* (New York: AMACON, 1976); Donald Lehman and Russell Winer, *Analysis for Marketing Planning*, 3d ed. (Burr Ridge, IL: Irwin, 1995); and Myron Gable and Martin Topol, "Planning Practices of Small-Scale Retailers," *American Journal of Small Business*, Fall 1987, pp. 19–32.

41. Fred R. Davis, "How Companies Define Their Mission," *Long Range Planning*, February 1990, pp. 90–94.

42. Alfred Rappaport, *Creating Shareholder Value: The New Standard for Business Performance* (New York: Wiley, 1988).

43. Jay Johnson, "OfficeMax: Maximizing the Office Product Superstore," *Discount Merchandiser*, November 1995, p. 37.

44. Adam Finn, "Characterizing the Attractiveness of Retail Markets," *Journal of Retailing* 63 (Summer 1987), pp. 129–62.

45. Michael Porter, *Competitive Strategy* (New York: Free Press, 1980).

46. See "Reaching for Prestige," *Women's Wear Daily*, June 1, 1990, pp. 12–13.

47. Masoud Yasai-Ardekani and Paul Nystrom, "Designs for Environmental Scanning Systems: Tests of a Contingency Theory," *Management Science*, 42 (February 1996), pp. 187–204; Xian-zhong Xu and G. Roland Kaye, "Building Market Intelligence Systems for Environment Scanning," *Logistics Information Management* 8 (1995), pp. 22–29; and P. Rajan Varadarajan, Terry Clark, and William Pride, "Controlling the Uncontrollable: Managing Your Market Environment," *Sloan Management Review* 33 (Winter 1992), pp. 39–47.

48. "Mail-Order Shopping: Which Catalogs Are Best?" *Consumer Reports*, October 1994, pp. 622-23.

49. George Day and Robin Wensley, "Assessing Advantage: A Framework for Diagnosing Competitive Superiority," *Journal of Marketing* 52 (April 1988), pp. 1–20; C. K. Prahalad and Gary Hamel, "The Core Competencies of the Corporation," *Harvard Business Review* 68 (May-June 1970), pp. 79–97; G. Stalk, "Competing on Capabilities: The New Rules of Corporate Strategy," *Harvard Business Review*, March-April 1992, pp. 51–69; and Donna Cartwright, Paul Boughton, and Stephen Miller, "Competitive Intelligence Systems: Relationships to Strategic Orientation and Perceived Usefulness," *Journal of Managerial Issues* 7 (Winter 1995), pp. 420–34.

50. See Kerin, Mahajan and Varadarajan, *Contemporary Perspectives*, chapter 3. Another matrix that is often used in strategic planning is the Boston Consulting Group (BCG) market growth/market share matrix. Rather than considering all of the factors that determine market attractiveness and competitive position, the BCG matrix focuses on just two factors: market growth and market share. Research indicates that concentrating on these two

factors may result in poor strategic decisions. See Robin Wensley, "Strategic Marketing: Betas, Boxes, and Basics," *Journal of Marketing* 45 (Summer 1981), pp. 173–82.

51. Robert Buzzell, Bradley Gale, and Ralph Sultan, "Market Share—Key to Profitability," *Harvard Business Review* 55 (January-February 1975), pp. 97–106; and Robert Jacobson and David Aaker, "Is Market Share All That It's Cracked Up to Be?" *Journal of Marketing* 49 (Fall 1985), pp. 11–22.

52. Henry Mintzberg, "Crafting Strategy," *Harvard Business Review* 65 (July-August 1987), pp. 66–79; Henry Mintzberg, "What Is Planning Anyway?" *Strategic Management Journal* 2 (1981), pp. 319–24; and James Brian Quinn, "Strategic Goals: Process and Politics," *Sloan Management Review*, Fall 1977, pp. 21–35.

53. David Schultz, "Porteous: Repositioning through Remerchandising," *Stores*, April 1992, pp. 52–53.

7

Financial Strategy

THE WORLD OF RETAILING

↓

RETAILING STRATEGY
6. Retail Market Strategy
7. Financial Strategy
8. Retail Locations
9. Site Selection
10. Organization Structure
    and Human Resource
    Management
11. Integrated Retail Logistics
    and Information Systems

↓

MERCHANDISE MANAGEMENT

STORE MANAGEMENT

QUESTIONS

- How are the income statement and balance sheet used as "report cards" for retail organizations?

- What is the strategic profit model, and how is it used?

- Why must retailers evaluate their performance?

- What different measures do retailers use to assess their performance?

AS THE RETAIL MANAGEMENT decision-making process shows, financial decisions are an integral component in every aspect of a retailer's strategy. In Chapter 6, we examined how retailers develop their strategy for sustaining a competititve advantage. In this chapter, we look at financial tools retailers use to measure and evaluate their performance.

Retailers continually receive information about their performance. Joanne Phillips, owner of the Gifts To Go store we described in Chapter 6, sees how many customers enter her store and counts up the receipts at the end of the day to find out how well she's doing. Large national retailers can get instantaneous sales information for each item at every store using sophisticated data communications networks linked to point-of-purchase terminals.

Retailers use this information to evaluate their performance relative to their objectives. If the retailer is achieving its objectives, changes in strategy or implementation programs aren't needed. But if the performance information indicates that objectives aren't being met, the retailer needs to reanalyze its plans and programs. For example, after reviewing her accountant's financial report, Joanne might conclude that she's not earning a fair return on the time and money she's invested in the store. Based on this evaluation, she might consider changing her strategy by appealing to a different target market and lowering the average price point of the gifts that she carries.

We'll first show how financial information taken from standard accounting documents can be used to plan and evaluate strategies. Specifically, retailers have two paths available to achieve a high level of performance: the *profit path* and the *turnover path*. Different retailers, however, pursue different strategies, resulting in different types of financial performance. The two paths are combined into the strategic profit model to illustrate that retailers using very different strategies and financial performance characteristics can be financially successful. As a vehicle for discussion, we'll compare the financial performance of two very different retailers: Nordstrom, Inc. (a national department store chain) and Price/Costco (a national chain of warehouse clubs).

REFACT The first ware-house club was opened by Sol Price in 1976.

Then we will discuss how retailers set performance objectives and how different performance measures are used throughout the organization. The chapter concludes with an appendix that describes activity-based costing and its use throughout retail organizations.

We begin our examination of corporate-level performance measures by looking at the strategic profit model.

THE STRATEGIC PROFIT MODEL: AN OVERVIEW

Every retailer wants to be financially successful. One way to define financial success is to provide the owners of the firm a good return on their investment. Although retailers pursue a similar financial goal, they employ different strategies. For instance, Nordstrom department stores, described in Retailing View 7.1, has broad assortments of merchandise, exceptionally high levels of service, and opulent surroundings. Price/Costco warehouse clubs, described in Retailing View 7.2, take the opposite approach. They have narrow assortments, little service, and functional decor. Based on this description, why would anyone shop at Price/Costco? The answer is that Price/Costco strives for low prices. The strategic profit model is used to evaluate the performance of different retailers that, like Nordstrom and Price/Costco, may employ very different strategies.

The strategic profit model is based on three very common financial ratios: net profit margin, asset turnover, and return on assets. (Don't worry if you aren't currently familiar with these ratios. They're explained in this chapter.)

To illustrate how the strategic profit model works, consider the two very different hypothetical retailers in Exhibit 7–1. La Madeline Bakery has a net profit margin of 1 percent and asset turnover of 10 times, resulting in a return on assets of 10 percent. The profit margin is low due to the competitive nature of this commodity-type business. Asset turnover is relatively high, because the firm doesn't have its own credit card system (no accounts receivable). Also, it rents its store, so fixed assets are relatively low, and it has a very fast inventory turnover—in fact, its inventory turns every day!

EXHIBIT 7–1

Return on Assets Model for a Bakery and Jewelry Store

	NET PROFIT MARGIN	×	ASSET TURNOVER	=	RETURN ON ASSETS
La Madeline Bakery	1%	×	10 times	=	10%
Kalame Jewelry	10%	×	1 time	=	10%

7.1

Nordstrom—Retailing's Service Leader

NORDSTROM DEPARTMENT STORES are full of tales of loyal sales associates outdoing each other for their customers. Consider Nicole Honzik, a men's sportswear manager. She once drove two hours in Los Angeles traffic to personally replace a distraught shopper's $110 velour jumpsuit four hours after it was stolen. Then there is Anita Dziedzic, who sells women's sportswear. She spent a lunch hour tracking down a Liz Claiborne sweater to match a customer's suit. Nordstrom didn't have any in stock, so she bought one from a competitor and had it sent.

Nordstrom has become the envy of America's best service-oriented retailers. Several have even studied how this specialty department store does business. The Nordstrom philosophy is simple: "Offer the customer the best service, selection, quality, and value." How does it implement this strategy? It employs a highly trained sales staff who are interested in making sure that customers' needs are met. They provide gift suggestions and wardrobe planning, and even travel from department to department with customers to help them find exactly what they want. The Personal Touch department will provide complimentary wardrobe consulting. Nordstrom will send a consultant to the customer's home free of charge to look over the customer's wardrobe.

Stores are designed with customer service in mind. Customers may check coats and packages at the store's concierge desk. Large dressing rooms with three-way viewing mirrors facilitate purchasing. Customers are encouraged to take coffee and soft drinks, sit in comfortable chairs while waiting, and enjoy live in-store piano music. These services positively impact sales, but load up the operating expenses.

Nordstrom has 35 departments merchandised by lifestyle, including 5 for shoes and 10 for women's apparel. Some stores carry as many as 150,000 pairs of men's, women's, and children's shoes. Women's clothes and shoes represent about 80 percent of Nordstrom's business. Although this deep assortment provides customers with an unsurpassed assortment, it can take its toll on inventory turnover.

Main aisles are a minimum of 8 to 10 feet wide and free of product displays and perfume-spritzing fragrance models, so shoppers move through the store with ease. Stores are adorned with rich brass fixtures and Italian-marble flooring. Each level offers seating areas with family-room–style furniture, so customers can rest. Additionally, all stores have a full-service cafe and espresso bar. Nordstrom's commitment to an elegant environment is not cheap. Its heavy investment in fixed assets can adversely affect its asset turnover ratio.

Source: George Hunter, "How to Keep Customers Coming Back: Retailers Stress Service to Survive," *The Detroit News,* August 12, 1996, p. 6; Bill Lubinger, "At Your Service; Going Above and Beyond the Call of Duty Is the Norm for Nordstrom's Sales Staff," *The Plain Dealer,* November 3, 1996, p. 1H; and "Why Nordstrom Got There," *Stores,* January 1990, pp. 75–76.

On the other hand, Kalame Jewelry Store has a net profit margin of 10 percent and asset turnover of one time, again resulting in a return on assets of 10 percent. The difference is that even though the jewelry store has higher operating expenses than the bakery, its gross margin is much more—it may double the cost of jewelry to arrive at a retail price. Kalame's asset turnover is so low compared to the bakery's because Kalame has very expensive fixtures and precision jewelry-manufacturing

7.2

Price/Costco: A Lean, Mean Warehouse Club

IN 1993, PRICE CO. and Costco Wholesale Corporation (then the nation's second-largest and third-largest warehouse club chains) merged into a 200-store giant called Price/Costco. The merger provides tremendous synergy. The company's huge buying clout enables it to secure merchandise at rock-bottom prices.

These low prices are generally passed on to the customer, causing a slim gross margin. Recently, however, Price/Costco has opened ancillary businesses within existing stores, such as pharmacies, optical shops, food courts, one-hour photo labs, and an expanded fresh-food program that will boost gross margin.

Clubs like Price/Costco have established their ability to deliver attractive-branded products at the lowest possible price by sacrificing selection and service. Attempts to become more like other retailers (e.g., by expanding assortments or by spending more money on marketing, merchandising, and presentation) have been resisted because they increase a warehouse club's expenses and, hence, prices, thereby jeopardizing the loyalty of the key, price-sensitive wholesale customer.

Price/Costco and other clubs carry relatively few SKUs; most merchandise is nonfashion staples. As a result, inventory turnover is relatively rapid—compared to that of department and specialty stores.

The economies of scale achieved through the merger have also enabled it to further streamline operations and cut operating expenses. Price/Costco is typically located in stand-alone locations, which are much less expensive than malls. Since it's buying fewer SKUs than department and specialty stores, its buying staff (an administrative expense) can be quite lean. Merchandise is delivered directly to stores, eliminating the necessity for distribution centers (a fixed asset) and their staffs (an operating expense).

Source: Debra Chanil, "Fine-tuning the Wholesale Club Industry," *Discount Merchandiser,* November 1995, pp. 56–59; George C. Strachan and Daniel M. Dauber, "Warehouse Clubs: Still a Growth Industry?" *Investment Research Report* (New York: Goldman Sachs, April 22, 1993); and Pauline Yoshihashi, "Price Co. Plans a Combination with Costco," *The Wall Street Journal,* June 17, 1993, pp. A3–A4.

---

equipment (fixed assets), offers liberal credit to customers (accounts receivable), and has very slow inventory turnover—possibly only one-half to one turn per year. In sum, these two very different types of retailers could have exactly the same return on assets.

Thus, La Madeline is achieving its 10 percent return on assets by having a relatively high asset turnover—the *turnover path*. Kalame Jewelry, on the other hand, achieves its return on assets with a relatively high net profit margin—the *profit path*.

Jewelry stores typically have a higher net profit margin than bakeries, but their asset turnover is much lower. How can return on assets of a jewelry store and a bakery be the same?

In the next three sections we will take a close look at these three financial ratios. Specifically, we will examine the relationship between these ratios and retailing strategy, and describe where the information can be found in traditional accounting records.

EXHIBIT 7–2

Income Statements for Price/Costco Wholesale Corporation and Nordstrom, Inc., 1995 (in 000s)

	PRICE/COSTCO	NORDSTOM
Net sales	$16,480,643	$3,894,478
Less: Cost of goods sold	$14,662,891	$2,599,553
Gross margin	$1,817,752	$1,294,925
Less: Operating expense	$1,563,725	$928,703
Less: Interest expense	$50,472	$30,664
Total expense	$1,614,197	$959,367
Net profit, pretax	$203,555	$335,558
Less: Taxes*	$92,657	$132,600
Tax rate	45.52%	39.52%
Net profit after tax	$110,898	$202,958

*Effective tax rates often differ among corporations due to different tax breaks and advantages.

Source: *Fairchild's Financial Manual of Retail Stores, 1996,* 68th ed. (New York. Fairchild Books, Division of Fairchild Fashion and Merchandising Group).

THE INCOME STATEMENT (PATH 1)

The income statement summarizes a firm's financial performance over a period of time. Exhibit 7–2 shows income statements adapted from corporate reports of Price/Costco Wholesale Corporation stores and Nordstrom, Inc., department stores. The *profit path* portion of the strategic profit model that utilizes these income statement data appears in Exhibit 7–3. Let's look at each item in the income statement.

EXHIBIT 7–3   Profit Margin Models for Price/Costco Wholesale Corporation and Nordstrom, Inc., 1995 (in 000s)

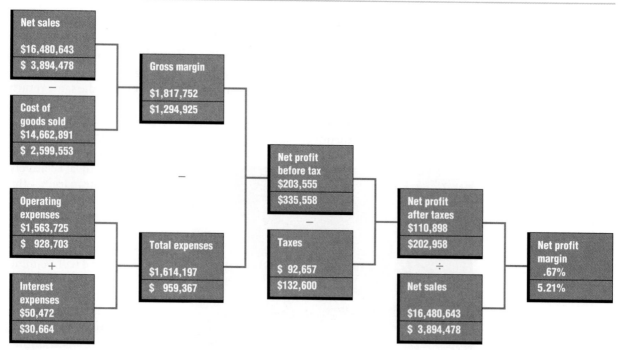

Top number = Price/Costco
Bottom number = Nordstrom

Net Sales   The term **net sales** refers to the total number of dollars received by a retailer after all refunds have been paid to customers for returned merchandise:

Net sales = Gross amount of sales – Customer returns – Customer allowances

REFACT Ninety percent of the purchases of Avon products in Patrocino, Brazil, are made with gold dust.[1]

Customer returns represents the value of merchandise that customers return because it's damaged, doesn't fit, and so forth. Customer allowances represents any additional price reduction given to the customer. For instance, if an item at Gifts To Go regularly retails for $5 but is sold for $4.50 because it's scratched, the 50-cent difference is the customer allowance.

Sales are an important measure of performance because they indicate the activity level of the merchandising function. Retailers are particularly interested in sales growth due to its direct link to the firm's overall profitability. Chapters 12 and 13 cover sales forecasting techniques.

Gross Margin   Gross margin = Net sales – Cost of goods sold

Gross margin, also called **gross profit**, is an important measure in retailing. It gives the retailer a measure of how much profit it's making on merchandise sales without considering the expenses associated with operating the store.

Gross margin, like other performance measures, is also expressed as a percentage of net sales so retailers can compare (1) performances of various types of merchandise and (2) their own performance with other retailers.

$$\text{Gross margin \%} = \frac{\text{Gross margin}}{\text{Net sales}}$$

$$\text{Price/Costco:} \quad \frac{\$1,817,752}{\$16,480,643} = 11.03\%$$

$$\text{Nordstrom:} \quad \frac{\$1,294,925}{\$3,894,478} = 33.25\%$$

(Throughout this chapter, dollar figures are expressed in thousands.)

Superficially, Nordstrom appears to outperform Price/Costco on gross margin. However, further analysis will show that other factors interact with gross margin to determine overall performance. But first, let's consider the factors that contribute to differences in gross margin performance.

REFACT Talk about markup! Tiffany & Co. has a 52 percent gross margin, compared to an average of only 37.9 percent for other specialty stores.[2]

Warehouse clubs like Price/Costco generally have lower gross margins than department stores because the clubs pursue a deliberate strategy of offering merchandise at low prices with minimal service to several cost-oriented market segments. Warehouse clubs have tried to increase their average gross margin by adding specialty products and departments like gourmet foods and jewelry. But the warehouse club store's overall average gross margin lags behind the department store's. Chapters 12, 13, and 15 explore the use of gross margin in merchandise and pricing decisions.

Expenses   Expenses are costs incurred in the normal course of doing business to generate revenues. One expense category in Exhibit 7–3, operating expenses, is further defined in Exhibit 7–4.

Another major expense category, interest, is the cost of financing everything from inventory to the purchase of a new store location. For instance, if a bank charges Nordstrom 10 percent interest, Nordstrom pays $49 million in interest to borrow $490 million.

EXHIBIT 7–4

Types of Retail
Operating Expenses

Selling expenses	**= Sales staff salaries + Commissions + Benefits**
General expenses	**= Rent + Utilities + Miscellaneous expenses**
Administrative expenses	**= Salaries of all employees other than salespeople + Operations of buying offices + Other administrative expenses**

Nordstrom has significantly higher total expenses as a percentage of net sales than Price/Costco. Like gross margin, total expenses are also expressed as a percentage of net sales to facilitate comparisons across items and departments within firms.

$$\text{Total expenses/Net sales ratio} = \frac{\text{Total expenses}}{\text{Net sales}}$$

Price/Costco: $\dfrac{\$1,614,197}{\$16,480,643} = 9.79\%$

Nordstrom: $\dfrac{\$959,367}{\$3,894,478} = 24.63\%$

The total expenses/net sales ratio is only approximately 10 percent for Price/Costco; at Nordstrom, it's almost 25 percent. This difference is to be expected. Warehouse clubs have relatively low selling expenses. They're also typically located on less expensive real estate so rent is lower. Finally, warehouse clubs operate with a smaller administrative staff. For instance, buying expenses are much lower for warehouse clubs. Their buyers don't have to travel as far, and much of the purchasing consists of rebuying staple merchandise that's already in the stores. On the other hand, a department store's total expenses are much higher because its large, experienced sales staff requires a modest salary plus commission and benefits. Unlike a warehouse club, the department store is located in select areas, commanding high rent and other expenses.

REFACT Total expenses as a percentage of net sales is a whopping 36.3 percent at catalog retailer Lands' End, compared to an average specialty store's 9.5 percent ratio.[3]

Net Profit **Net profit** is a measure of the firm's overall performance:

Net profit = Gross margin – Expenses

Net profit can be expressed either before or after taxes. Generally, it's more useful to express net profit after taxes, since this is the amount of money left over to reinvest in the business, disburse as dividends to stockholders or owners, or repay debt.

Net profit margin, like gross margin, is often expressed as a percentage of net sales:

$$\text{Net profit margin} = \frac{\text{Net profit}}{\text{Net sales}}$$

However, net profit measures the profitability of the entire firm, while gross margin measures the profitability of merchandising activities. In Exhibit 7–3, the after-tax net profit margin is .67 percent for Price/Costco and 5.21 percent for Nordstrom. From a profit perspective alone, Nordstrom is outperforming Price/Costco. Even though Nordstrom has a higher total expenses/net sales ratio, its gross margin percentage is so large compared to Price/Costco's that it still surpasses the warehouse club store's profit performance.

THE BALANCE SHEET (PATH 2)

The income statement summarizes the financial performance over a period of time, while the balance sheet summarizes a retailer's financial position at a given point in time, such as the last day of the year. The balance sheet shows the following relationship:

Assets = Liabilities + Owner's equity

Assets are economic resources (such as inventory or store fixtures) owned or controlled by an enterprise as a result of past transactions or events. **Liabilities** are an enterprise's obligations (such as accounts or notes payable) to pay cash or other economic resources in return for past, current, or future benefits. **Owners' equity** (owners' investment in the business) is the difference between assets and liabilities. It represents the amount of assets belonging to the owners of the retail firm after all obligations (liabilities) have been met.

Exhibit 7–5's balance sheet for Nordstrom and Price/Costco continues the comparison between them. The turnover path portion of the strategic profit model is shown in Exhibit 7–6's asset turnover model. The remainder of this section covers elements of the balance sheet.

EXHIBIT 7–5

Balance Sheets for Price/Costco Wholesale Corporation and Nordstrom, Inc. ($ in 000s)

	PRICE/COSTCO (AS OF 8/28/94)	NORDSTROM (AS OF 1/31/95)
ASSETS		
Current assets		
Accounts receivable	$ 130,278	$ 675,891
Merchandise inventory	1,260,476	627,930
Cash	53,638	32,497
Other current assets	89,906	61,395
Total current assets	1,534,298	1,397,713
Fixed assets		
Building, equipment, and other fixed assets, less depreciation	$2,701,361	$ 999,070
Total assets	$4,235,659	$2,396,783
LIABILITIES		
Current liabilities		
Accounts payable	$1,073,326	$ 273,084
Notes payable	149,340	87,388
Other current liabilities	424,641	329,982
Total current liabilities	$1,647,307	$ 690,454
Long-term liabilities	$ 868,613	$ 362,529
Total liabilities	$2,515,920	$1,052,983
OWNERS' EQUITY		
Common stock	$ 576,525	$ 163,334
Retained earnings	1,143,214	1,180,466
Total owners' equity	$1,719,739	$1,343,800
Total liabilities and owners' equity	$4,235,659	$2,396,783

Source: *Fairchild's Financial Manual of Retail Stores, 1996*, 68th ed. (New York: Fairchild Books, Division of Fairchild Fashion and Merchandising Group).

EXHIBIT 7–6

Asset Turnover
Model for
Price/Costco
Wholesale
Corporation and
Nordstrom, Inc.
($ in 000s)

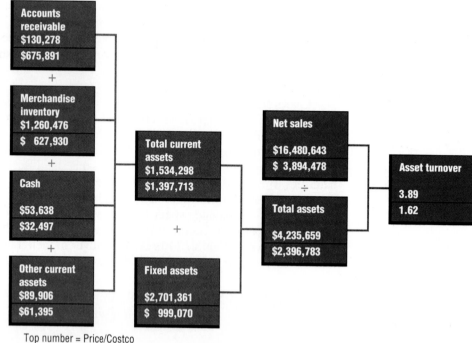

Accounts receivable	
$130,278	
$675,891	

+

Merchandise inventory	
$1,260,476	
$ 627,930	

+

Cash	
$53,638	
$32,497	

+

Other current assets	
$89,906	
$61,395	

Total current assets	
$1,534,298	
$1,397,713	

+

Fixed assets	
$2,701,361	
$ 999,070	

Net sales	
$16,480,643	
$ 3,894,478	

÷

Total assets	
$4,235,659	
$2,396,783	

Asset turnover	
3.89	
1.62	

Top number = Price/Costco
Bottom number = Nordstrom

Current Assets

By accounting definition, **current assets** are those that can normally be converted to cash within one year. In retailing

Current assets = Accounts receivable + Merchandise inventory + Cash
+ Other current assets

Accounts Receivable

Accounts receivable are monies due to the retailer from selling merchandise on credit. This current asset is substantial for some retailers. For example, Price/Costco's investment in accounts receivable is much smaller than Nordstrom's due to Price/Costco customers' high propensity to pay cash.

To ease the burden of carrying accounts receivable, retailers use third-party credit cards such as Visa or MasterCard.

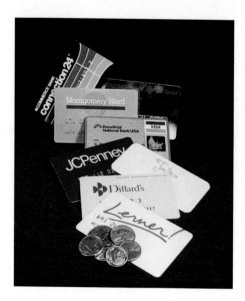

Accounts receivable:

Price/Costco: $130,278, or .8 percent of sales

Nordstrom: $675,891, or 17 percent of sales

From a marketing perspective, the accounts receivable generated from credit sales may be the result of an important service provided to customers. The retailer's ability to provide credit, particularly at low interest rates, could make the difference between making or losing a sale. Paying cash for a sizable purchase like a bedroom suite or car may be difficult for many people!

Unfortunately, having a large amount of accounts receivable is expensive for retailers, who of course would like to sell a product for cash and immediately reinvest the cash in new merchandise. When merchandise is sold on credit, proceeds of the sale are tied up as accounts receivable until collection is made. The money invested in accounts receivable costs the retailer interest expense and keeps the retailer from investing proceeds of the sale elsewhere. To ease the financial burden of carrying accounts receivable, retailers can use third-party credit cards such as Visa or MasterCard, give discounts to customers who pay with cash, discourage credit sales, and control delinquent accounts.

Merchandise Inventory

Merchandise inventory is a retailer's lifeblood. It represents approximately 30 percent of total assets for Price/Costco and 26 percent of total assets for Nordstrom. An exception to this generalization is service retailers such as ChemLawn, Marriott Hotels, and your local barber shop/beauty salon, which carry little or no merchandise inventory.

$$\frac{\text{Inventory}}{\text{Total assets}}$$

$$\text{Price/Costco:} \quad \frac{\$1,260,476}{\$4,235,659} = 29.76\%$$

$$\text{Nordstrom:} \quad \frac{\$627,930}{\$2,396,783} = 26.20\%$$

Inventory turnover is used to evaluate how effectively managers utilize their investment in inventory. Inventory turnover is defined as follows:

$$\text{Inventory turnover} = \frac{\text{Net sales}}{\text{Average inventory}}$$

Note that average inventory is expressed at retail rather than at cost.

Think of inventory as a measure of the productivity of inventory—how many sales dollars can be generated from $1 invested in inventory. Generally, the larger the inventory turnover, the better. Exhibit 7–7 illustrates the concept of inventory

Think of inventory as "merchandise in motion." The faster it moves through the store, the greater the inventory turnover.

turnover. Inventory is delivered to the store, spends some time in the store, and then is sold. We can think of inventory turnover as how many times, on average, the inventory cycles through the store during a specific period of time (usually a year).

Price/Costco's inventory turnover is almost three times Nordstrom's—11.64 compared to 4.16.[4]

REFACT The inventory turnover for Home Shopping Network is approximately 6.1.[5]

$$\text{Inventory turnover} = \frac{\text{Net sales}}{\text{Average inventory}}$$

Price/Costco: $\dfrac{\$16,480,643}{\$1,416,265}$ = 11.64

Nordstrom: $\dfrac{\$3,894,478}{\$937,209}$ = 4.16

Nordstrom's slower inventory turnover is expected due to the nature of department stores. First, many items in warehouse clubs are grocery products

Nordstroms, like most department stores, has slower inventory turnover than warehouse clubs. They carry specialty products, have extensive assortments, and often have to purchase merchandise months in advance.

such as baked goods, frozen meat, and produce. And, unlike department stores, warehouse clubs carry commodities that are available at every other club or grocery store. Thus, warehouse clubs are very price-competitive, which results in rapid turnover. Third, warehouse clubs carry a simpler stock selection than department stores do. In a warehouse club, for example, there may be only two brands of ketchup, each in two sizes, which represents four inventory items. Department stores, on the other hand, may stock three brands of men's short-sleeve knit shirts, but each knit shirt comes in four sizes and 10 colors, representing 120 inventory items.

Cash is a current asset on the balance sheet. Retailers should keep no more cash in their stores than is necessary to make change for their customers.

Fourth, due to the nature of fashion apparel, department store buyers often must order merchandise three to six months in advance of delivery. Finally, since department store merchandise is often made to order in another country for a specific season, stores may have only one chance per season to order some merchandise. Warehouse clubs, on the other hand, order items daily or weekly. These factors, when taken together, explain why Price/Costco has a faster inventory turnover than Nordstrom.

Management of this aspect of retailing permeates most retailing decisions. Chapters 12 and 13 address the crucial subject of merchandise inventory management.

Cash and Other Current Assets

Cash = Monies on hand
+ Demand and savings accounts in banks to which a retailer has immediate access
+ Marketable securities such as Treasury bills

Other current assets = Prepaid expenses + Supplies

REFACT Twenty-four percent of all retailers don't accept checks. Of the retailers accepting checks, 56 percent won't accept checks over $250.[6]

Price/Costco reports cash of about .33 percent of sales, whereas Nordstrom's cash percentage is only .83 percent.

Current Assets Cycle

Exhibit 7–8 shows the relationship between the current assets. Cash is used to purchase inventory. Inventory is sold for cash—or on credit, in which case it becomes an account receivable. When a receivable is collected for cash, it can then be recycled directly into inventory.

EXHIBIT 7–8
Current Assets Cycle

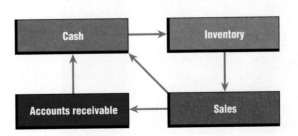

Retailers must know the productivity of their current assets. Inventory is their most important asset—without inventory, there are no sales. Accounts receivable is a necessary cost of doing business for some retailers, yet unless a retailer operates its own credit card system for profit, accounts receivable isn't directly a productive asset. Finally, cash is useful primarily for making change for customers. Retailers therefore keep a minimum amount of cash on hand.

Fixed Assets

Fixed assets are assets that require more than a year to convert to cash. In retailing,

Fixed assets = Buildings (if store property is owned rather than leased)
+ Fixtures (such as display racks)
+ Equipment (such as forklift or delivery trucks)
+ Long-term investments such as real estate or stock in other firms

Fixed assets represent 63.78 percent and 41.68 percent of total assets for Price/Costco and Nordstrom, respectively.

Fixed assets = Asset cost – Depreciation

Since most fixed assets have a limited useful life, those assets' value should be less over time—in other words, they're depreciated. For instance, styles of mannequins in department stores change almost as often as the merchandise they're designed to display. One year, fashion may dictate realistic mannequins; the next year, the style may be more abstract. Thus, mannequins are depreciated in 3 to 5 years, whereas a building may be depreciated over 25 years.

Mannequins are a fixed asset that are depreciated over three to five years.

*Nordstrom and Price/
Costco stock is part of the
owner's equity section of
their balance sheet.*

Asset Turnover

Asset turnover is an overall performance measure from the asset side of the balance sheet.

$$\text{Asset turnover} = \frac{\text{Net sales}}{\text{Total assets}}$$

Although fixed assets don't turn over as quickly as inventory, asset turnover can be used to evaluate and compare how effectively managers use their assets. When a retailer redecorates a store, for example, old fixtures, carpeting, and lights are removed and replaced with new ones. Thus, like inventory, these assets cycle through the store. The difference is that the process is a lot slower. The life of a fixture in a store may be five years (instead of five months, as it might be for a diamond ring in the store's inventory), yet the concept of turnover is the same. When a retailer decides to invest in a fixed asset, she should determine how many sales dollars can be generated from that asset.

Suppose that Joanne Phillips, owner of Gifts To Go, considers purchasing a new fixture. She has the choice of buying an expensive antique display cabinet for $5,000 or having a simple plywood display constructed for $500. Using the expensive antique, she forecasts sales of $50,000 in the first year, whereas the plywood display is expected to generate only $40,000. Ignoring all other assets for a moment,

$$\text{Asset turnover} = \frac{\text{Net sales}}{\text{Assets}}$$

$$\text{Antique cabinet} \quad \frac{\$50,000}{\$5,000} = 10$$

$$\text{Plywood cabinet} \quad \frac{\$40,000}{\$500} = 80$$

The antique cabinet will certainly help create an atmosphere conducive to selling expensive designer shoes. Exclusively from a marketing perspective, the antique would thus appear appropriate. But it costs much more than the plywood shelves. From a strict financial perspective, Joanne should examine how much additional sales can be expected to be generated from the added expenditure in assets. Clearly, by considering only asset turnover, the plywood shelves are the way to go. In the end, a combination of marketing and financial factors should be considered when making the asset purchase decision.[7]

Price/Costco outperforms Nordstrom on asset turnover. The asset turnover for Price/Costco and Nordstrom are 3.89 and 1.62, respectively. This finding is consistent with the different strategies each firm is implementing. We saw earlier that Price/Costco has a higher inventory turnover. Its other assets are relatively lower than Nordstrom's as well. For instance, the fixed assets involved in outfitting a store (such as fixtures, lighting, and mannequins) would be relatively lower for a warehouse store than a department store.

Liabilities and Owners' Equity

The other side of the balance sheet equation from assets involves liabilities and owners' equity. Now let's look at the major liabilities and components of owners' equity.

Current Liabilities   Like current assets, **current liabilities** are debts that are expected to be paid in less than one year. The most important current liabilities are accounts payable, notes payable, and accrued liabilities.

Accounts Payable   **Accounts payable** refers to the amount of money owed to vendors, primarily for merchandise inventory. Accounts payable are an important source of short-term financing. Retailers buy merchandise on credit from vendors. The longer the period of time they have to pay for that merchandise, the larger their accounts payable—and the less they need to borrow from financial institutions (notes payable), issue bonds or stock, or finance internally through retained earnings. Since retailers normally don't have to pay interest to vendors on their accounts payable, they have strong incentive to negotiate for a long time period before payment for merchandise is due. (See Chapter 14.) Note that accounts payable as a percentage of net sales are almost identical for the two firms: 6.51 percent for Price/Costco and 7.01 percent for Nordstrom.

Notes Payable   **Notes payable** under the current liabilities section of the balance sheet are the principal and interest the retailer owes to financial institutions (banks) that are due and payable in less than a year. Retailers borrow money from financial institutions to pay for current assets, such as inventory. Although Price/Costco generates more in sales than Nordstrom, its notes payable as a percentage of sales is much smaller.

Accrued Liabilities   **Accrued liabilities** include taxes, salaries, rent, utilities, and other incurred obligations that haven't yet been paid. These are called accrued liabilities because they usually accumulate daily but are only paid at the end of a time period, such as a month.

Long-Term Liabilities   **Long-term liabilities** are debts that will be paid after one year. The notes payable entry in the long-term liability section of the balance sheet is similar to the one in the current liability section except that it's due to be paid in more than one year. Other long-term liabilities include bonds and mortgages on real estate.

Although Price/Costco's sales are over 4.23 times Nordstrom's, Price/Costco's total other long-term liabilities are only 2.4 times as large—$868.613 million compared to $362.529 million. Thus, Nordstrom utilizes relatively more long-term debt to finance its operations than Price/Costco does.

Owners' Equity   Owners' equity, also known as **stockholders' equity,** represents the amount of assets belonging to the owners of the retail firm after all obligations (liabilities) have been met. In accounting terms, the relationship can be expressed as

Owners' equity = Total assets – Total liabilities

Although there are several entries in the owners' equity category, two of the most common are common stock and retained earnings.

Common stock is the type of stock most frequently issued by corporations.[8] Owners of common stock usually have voting rights in the retail corporation. They also have the right to share in distributed corporate earnings. If the firm is liquidated, common stock owners have the right to share in the sale of its assets. Finally, they have the right to purchase additional shares to maintain the same percentage ownership if new shares are issued.

Retained earnings refers to the portion of owners' equity that has accumulated over time through profits but hasn't been paid out in dividends to owners. The decision of how much of the retailer's earnings should be retained in the firm and how much should be returned to the owners in the form of dividends is related to the firm's growth potential. Specifically, retailers with a propensity toward and opportunities for growth will retain and reinvest their profits to fund growth opportunities. For example, a high-growth retailer such as Wal-Mart retains most of its earnings to pay for the new stores, inventory, and expenses associated with its growth.

Total owners' equity is over $1,719 million for Price/Costco and over $1,343 million for Nordstrom.

THE STRATEGIC PROFIT MODEL

The previous sections defined the most important balance sheet and income statement entries as well as the most useful performance ratios. Yet many of these items are interrelated, and when examined alone they can be confusing. More importantly, it's hard to compare the performance of retailers with different operating characteristics, such as Nordstrom and Price/Costco. The strategic profit model (Exhibit 7–9) combines the two performance ratios from the income statement and balance sheets: net profit margin and asset turnover. By multiplying these ratios together, you get return on assets.

INTERNET EXERCISE   Go to the Price/Costco site on the Internet (http://www.pricecostco.com:80/about/finance/financi.html) and use the financial information from the most recent annual report to update the numbers in the strategic profit model in Exhibit 7–9.

EXHIBIT 7–9   The Strategic Profit Model

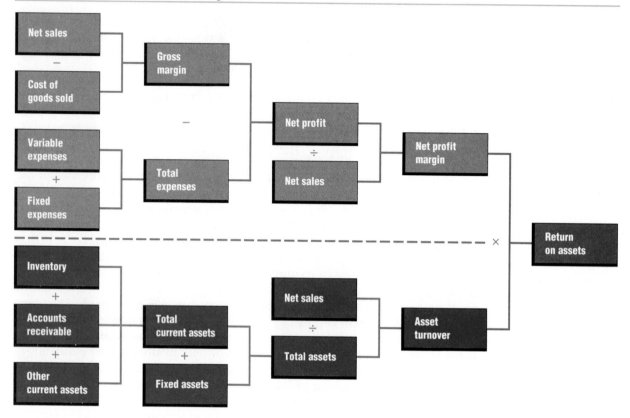

Return on Assets   Return on assets = Net profit margin × Asset turnover

$$= \frac{\text{Net profit}}{\text{Net sales}} \times \frac{\text{Net sales}}{\text{Total assets}}$$

$$= \frac{\text{Net profit}}{\text{Total assets}}$$

Return on assets determines how much profit can be generated from the retailer's investment in assets. (Note that when we multiply net profit margin by asset turnover, net sales drops out of the equation.)

The most important issue associated with return on assets is that the money that would be invested in retailing could also be invested in any other asset, such as a CD or Treasury bill. For instance, if a retailer can achieve 9 percent return on assets by opening a new store, and 10 percent by investing in a nearly risk-free Treasury bill, the retailer should take the higher-yield, lower-risk investment. In fact, should the return on assets of another investment with similar risk be greater, it would be the manager's fiduciary duty to invest in the other asset. In general, return on assets is effective in evaluating the profitability of individual investments in assets because it can easily be compared with yields of other investments with similar risk. It has also been shown to be an effective predictor of business failures.[9]

$$\text{Return on assets} = \frac{\text{Net profit}}{\text{Total assets}}$$

7.3

The Strategic Profit Model of a Service Retailer: HealthSouth

HEALTHSOUTH IS THE SECOND LARGEST health care company in the United States and the largest in terms of geographic coverage. Now in 45 states, HealthSouth boasts over 850 locations.

HealthSouth isn't just any health care provider, however. It has become the leader in outpatient rehabilitation and sports medicine centers. It provides sports medicine coverage for hundreds of high school and college teams, 40 professional teams, the NCAA's Southeastern Conference, the Ladies' Professional Golf Association, and USA Hockey. The HealthSouth Sports Medicine Center at the Colorado Springs Olympic Complex provides advanced training and sports medicine care to Olympic athletes.

Although very successful, the firm's strategic profit model looks quite different from those of the merchandise retailers we've looked at in this chapter. Let's first look at HealthSouth's profit path. It has no gross margin per se because it has no cost of *goods* sold. It sells only service! Operating expenses as a percentage of sales is 73 percent, compared to almost 10 and 25 percent for Price/Costco and Nordstrom, respectively. HealthSouth's net profit in 1995 was about 5 percent.

The turnover path is just as different. Its accounts receivable represent almost 14 percent of total assets, compared to 3 and 28 percent for Price/Costco and Nordstrom, respectively. But inventory as a percentage of total assets is only 1.36 percent, compared to 29.76 for Price/Costco and 26.20 percent for Nordstrom. Clearly, a service provider like HealthSouth has little need for inventory.

HealthSouth's asset turnover is only .63, compared to 3.89 and 1.62 for Price/Costco and Nordstrom, respectively. So, although a service provider like HealthSouth doesn't have to maintain a heavy inventory position, it does maintain a heavy investment in the long-term assets necessary to run these facilities, that is, the real estate investment and medical equipment. For instance, the cost of a Gamma Knife used to remove brain tumors without invasive surgery is about $3 million—HealthSouth currently owns two!

HealthSouth achieved a 3.2 percent return on assets in 1995, compared to 2.62 for Price/Costco and 8.47 for Nordstrom. Relatively low asset turnover adversely affected its return on assets. In summary, although many of the component ratios for a service provider like HealthSouth are different than merchandise retailers like Price/Costco and Nordstrom, HealthSouth earned a return on assets that was between the two.

Source: *HealthSouth 1995 Annual Report.*

Price/Costco: $$\frac{\$110,898}{\$4,235,659} = 2.62\%$$

Nordstrom: $$\frac{\$202,958}{\$2,396,783} = 8.47\%$$

Nordstrom outperformed Price/Costco on return on assets—8.47 percent versus 2.62 percent, respectively. Nordstrom can generate a larger profit with its investment in assets. Even though Price/Costco generated a higher asset turnover than Nordstrom — 3.89 compared to 1.62 (Exhibit 7–6)—Nordstrom generated a much higher net profit margin of 5.21 percent versus 0.67 percent for Price/Costco (Exhibit 7–3). So, when we multiply asset turnover by net profit margin to generate return on assets, Nordstrom comes out the clear winner!

Exhibit 7–10 shows strategic profit model (SPM) ratios for a variety of retailers. In the next section, we continue the strategic plan developed for Joanne Phillips in Chapter 6. Retailing View 7.3 looks at the very different strategic profit model of a service retailer.

EXHIBIT **7-10**   Strategic Profit Models for Selected Retailers

	(1) NET PROFIT MARGIN (NET PROFIT ÷ NET SALES) (%)	(2) ASSET TURNOVER (NET SALES ÷ TOTAL ASSETS)	(3) RETURN ON ASSETS (NET PROFIT MARGIN × ASSET TURNOVER) (%)
DISCOUNT STORES			
Wal-Mart Stores, Inc.	3.25%	2.51	8.16%
Kmart Corporation	0.86	2.02	1.74
Best Buy Co., Inc.	1.14	3.39	3.84
GROCERY STORES			
Food Lion, Inc.	3.19	3.23	10.30
Vons Companies, Inc.	1.55	2.97	4.60
The Kroger Co.	1.06	4.88	5.17
Safeway, Inc.	1.53	3.11	4.76
DEPARTMENT STORES			
May Department Stores	4.85	1.22	5.92
Dillard Department Stores	4.93	1.20	5.92
Federated Department Stores, Inc.	2.26	0.67	1.51
SPECIALTY STORES			
Circuit City Stores, Inc.	2.80	2.79	7.81
The Limited, Inc.	6.56	1.80	11.81
The Gap, Inc.	8.60	1.86	16.00
Tiffany & Co.	4.30	1.24	5.33
Service Merchandise Company, Inc.	2.17	1.98	4.30
CATALOGS			
Spiegel, Inc.	0.93	1.06	0.99
Lands' End	3.64	3.33	12.12

Source: *Fairchild's Financial Manual of Retail Stores, 1996*, 68th ed. (New York: Fairchild Books, Division of Fairchild Fashion and Merchandising Group).
Note: Some variations may occur due to rounding.

INTEGRATING MARKETING AND FINANCIAL STRATEGIES FOR JOANNE PHILLIPS'S GIFT STORES

Recall from Chapter 6 that Joanne Phillips owns Gifts To Go, a two-store chain in the Chicago area. She's considering several growth options, one of which is to open a new store selling lower-priced gifts than her other store. She determined that the market for such a store is high but very competitive. Now she needs to do a financial analysis for the proposed store, called Thrifty Gifts, and compare the projections with Gifts To Go.

We'll first look at the profit path, followed by the turnover path. Then we'll combine the two and examine the stores' return on assets. Exhibit 7–11 shows income statements for one of her Gifts To Go stores and her projections for Thrifty Gifts.

Profit Path   **Gross Margins**   We expect Thrifty Gifts to have a lower gross margin than Gifts To Go because it will compete on the basis of low prices. To be able to offer these low prices, it will seek out less expensive merchandise and be willing to accept a lower gross margin than at Gifts To Go.

EXHIBIT 7–11

Income Statements
for Gifts To Go and
Thrifty Gifts

	GIFTS TO GO	THRIFTY GIFTS (PROJECTED)
Net sales	$200,000	$200,000
Less: Cost of goods sold	110,000	140,000
Gross margin	90,000	60,000
Less: Total expenses	30,000	20,000
Net profit, pretax	60,000	40,000
Less: Taxes	27,000	18,000
Tax rate	45%	45%
Net profit after tax	$33,000	$22,000

$$\text{Gross margin \%} = \frac{\text{Gross margin}}{\text{Net sales}}$$

Gifts To Go:
$$\frac{\$90,000}{\$200,000} = 45\%$$

Thrifty Gifts:
$$\frac{\$60,000}{\$200,000} = 30\%$$

Total Expenses/Net Sales Ratio   The total expenses/net sales ratio is projected to be lower for Thrifty Gifts because it will have a smaller sales staff (selling expenses) and be in a less expensive location (rent).

$$\text{Total expenses/Net sales ratio} = \frac{\text{Total expenses}}{\text{Net sales}}$$

Gifts To Go:
$$\frac{\$30,000}{\$200,000} = 15\%$$

Thrifty Gifts:
$$\frac{\$20,000}{\$200,000} = 10\%$$

Net Profit Margins   Although Gifts To Go has higher expenses than Thrifty Gifts is projected to have, Gifts To Go's gross margin is also higher, so in the end, it maintains a higher net profit margin.

$$\text{Net profit margin} = \frac{\text{Net profit}}{\text{Net sales}}$$

Gifts To Go:
$$\frac{\$33,000}{\$200,000} = 16.5\%$$

Thrifty Gifts:
$$\frac{\$22,000}{\$200,000} = 11\%$$

Turnover Path   Now let's compare the two stores using the turnover path. Exhibit 7–12 shows balance sheets for Gifts To Go and Thrifty Gifts.

Accounts Receivable and Inventory Turnover   Like Gifts To Go, Thrifty Gifts would have no accounts receivable due to taking credit cards like Visa, MasterCard, and American Express.

	GIFTS TO GO	THRIFTY GIFTS
ASSETS		
Current assets		
Merchandise inventory	$44,000	$35,000
Cash	2,000	1,500
Other current assets	3,000	2,500
Total current assets	49,000	39,000
Fixed assets	$125,000	$70,000
Total assets	$174,000	$109,000
LIABILITIES		
Current liabilities		
Accounts payable	$35,000	$30,000
Notes payable	7,500	5,000
Total current liabilities	$42,000	$35,000
Long-term liabilities	$10,000	$12,000
Total liabilities	$52,000	$47,000
OWNERS' EQUITY		
	$122,000	$62,000
Total liabilities and owners' equity	$174,000	$109,000

Thrifty Gifts should have a faster projected inventory turnover than Gifts To Go for the same reasons that Price/Costco's turnover is greater than Nordstrom's. Specifically, Thrifty Gifts would carry less expensive, less exclusive merchandise priced competitively to encourage quick turnover. Its stock selection wouldn't be as deep as Gifts To Go's. Finally, it could receive replenishment merchandise more quickly.

$$\text{Inventory turnover}[10] = \frac{\text{Net sales}}{\text{Average inventory}}$$

$$\text{Gifts To Go} = \frac{\$200,000}{\$80,000} = 2.5$$

$$\text{Thrifty Gifts} = \frac{\$200,000}{\$50,000} = 4$$

Fixed Assets   Gifts To Go and Thrifty Gifts rent their store space. Thus, their fixed assets consist of the fixtures, lighting, and other leasehold improvements in their store as well as equipment such as point-of-sale terminals and computers.

Asset Turnover   As we would expect, Thrifty Gifts' projected asset turnover (1.83) is significantly higher than Gifts To Go's (1.15). Thrifty is projected to have a higher inventory turnover. Its other current assets should be lower as well. Importantly, Thrifty's fixed assets are projected to be much smaller, since the store's interior design will be less opulent and more utilitarian.

$$\text{Asset turnover} = \frac{\text{Net sales}}{\text{Total assets}}$$

$$\text{Gifts To Go} = \frac{\$200,000}{\$174,000} = 2.5$$

$$\text{Thrifty Gifts} = \frac{\$200,000}{\$109,000} = 4$$

Return on Assets $$\text{Return on assets} = \frac{\text{Net profit}}{\text{Total assets}}$$

$$\text{Gifts To Go:} \qquad \frac{\$33,000}{\$174,000} = 19\%$$

$$\text{Thrifty Gifts:} \qquad \frac{\$22,000}{\$109,000} = 20\%$$

Although Gifts To Go's net profit margin is much higher than that projected for Thrifty Gifts (16.5 percent versus 11 percent), Thrifty's asset turnover should be greater than Gifts To Go's (1.83 versus 1.15). Yet, when we multiply the asset turnovers by the net profit margins, the resulting return on assets ratios are almost identical: 19 percent for Gifts To Go and 20 percent projected for Thrifty Gifts. Thus, stores with very different retailing strategies can achieve similar financial performance. If Joanne believes she's receiving an acceptable return on her investment with Gifts To Go, then based on this financial analysis alone, Thrifty Gifts becomes a very viable alternative. She must, however, combine this financial analysis with her findings from the strategic audit described in Chapter 6 before determining whether to proceed.

RECAP OF THE STRATEGIC PROFIT MODEL

The strategic profit model is useful to retailers because it combines two decision-making areas—margin management and asset management—so managers can examine interrelationships among them. The strategic profit model uses return on assets as the primary criterion for planning and evaluating a firm's financial performance.

The strategic profit model can also be used to evaluate financial implications of new strategies before they're implemented. For instance, suppose Joanne Phillips wishes to increase sales by 10 percent at Gifts To Go. Using the strategic profit model, she can estimate this action's impact on other parts of the strategic profit model. For instance, to increase sales, she may choose to have a sale. Lowering prices will reduce gross margin. She would have to advertise the sale and hire additional sales help, thus increasing operating expenses. So, although she may be able to achieve the 10 percent sales increase, net profit margin would go down. Looking at the turnover path, increasing sales without an appreciable change in inventory will increase inventory turnover. Assuming other assets aren't affected, asset turnover will also increase. When she multiplies the lower net profit margin by the higher asset turnover, the resulting return on assets may remain unchanged.

We'll look at another method of evaluating strategic options in this chapter's appendix on activity-based costing. First, however, let's see how financial performance objectives are set in retailing organizations.

7.4

Why Pay So Much Attention to the Numbers? The Case of Merry-Go-Round

"HOW IMPORTANT IS THIS financial stuff to me? After all, I'm not a finance major." This comment is heard all too often in schools of business and human sciences. The answer is that it's very important—if you don't understand the basics, you can lose everything.

Consider Leonard "Boogie" Weinglass, founder of the now defunct Merry-Go-Round apparel chain. It all began in the 1950s in Baltimore, where Weinglass was a not so serious student who spent most of his spare time hanging out in diners with Harold Goldsmith (who became his partner and the financial brains behind Merry-Go-Round) and Barry Levinson (the Academy Award–winning movie director who based a main character in his classic movie *Diner* on Weinglass).

After working as a traveling clothing salesperson in the 1960s, Weinglass opened his first Merry-Go-Round in 1968. By all accounts, Weinglass had a flair for picking fashions that would become popular across the country. For instance, in the 1980s, he brought in the *Flashdance* look of off-the-shoulder sweatshirts and *Top Gun* jackets.

In 1983, Merry-Go-Round went public. About the same time, Weinglass and Levinson pulled out of the day-to-day operations of the business but remained on the board, staying active in deciding the direction of the company. The stock price tripled from 1985 to 1990 and *Forbes* magazine named it one of the 25 best companies for the period.

Disaster struck in 1991 when Harold Goldsmith, the firm's financial guru, died in a plane crash. About the same time, Merry-Go-Round started to lose touch with its core customer, the 15- to 24-year-olds. Though antisyle fashion was sweeping the nation, Merry-Go-Round maintained its strategy of picking a hot fashion item and running with it. While other firms, such as The Gap, carefully utilized marketing research, Merry-Go-Round continued to "wing it." This approach may work for a chain with only a few stores, but by this time Merry-Go-Round had over 800 stores across the United States.

Merry-Go-Round's next major mistake was to purchase Chess King—an ailing competitor. Though Goldsmith vetoed the acquisition twice prior to his death, Merry-Go-Round was able to pick up someone else's problem at what it thought was a very low price.

By 1993, the chain was in real trouble. It took a $46 million loss for the fiscal year and a $35 million write-down on unsold inventory. About the same time, Weinglass returned to active duty, albeit for a short time. In early 1994, Merry-Go-Round filed for protection under Chapter 11 of the bankruptcy code. In the next 18 months, Merry-Go-Round went through four CEOs and several unsuccessful turnaround strategies—but to no avail. Early in 1996, the firm announced it was going out of business. And now nothing is left.

The moral of the story: There's no substitute for paying attention to the numbers!

Source: Jennifer Steinhauer, "Bankrupt Merry-Go-Round Decides to Go Out of Business," *New York Times,* February 3, 1996, p. 37; Justin Martin, "The Man Who Boogied Away a Billion," *Fortune,* December 23, 1996, pp. 89–97; and David Harrison, "MGR Still Means Business," *Baltimore Business Journal,* April 12, 1996, p. 1.

Retailing View 7.4 preaches the Holy Grail—why it is so important to pay attention to the numbers.

SETTING PERFORMANCE OBJECTIVES

Setting performance objectives is a necessary component of any firm's strategic planning process. How would a retailer know how it has performed if it doesn't have specific objectives in mind to compare actual performance against? Performance objectives should include (1) the performance sought, including a numerical index against which progress may be measured, (2) a time frame within which the goal is to be achieved, and (3) the resources needed to achieve the objective. For example, "earning reasonable profits" isn't a good objective. It doesn't provide specific goals that can be used to evaluate performance. What's reasonable? When do you want to realize the profits? A better objective would be "earning $100,000 in profit during calendar year 1999 on $500,000 investment in inventory and building."

Top-Down versus Bottom-Up Process

Setting objectives in large retail organizations entails a combination of the top-down and bottom-up approaches to planning. **Top-down planning** means that goals are set at the top of the organization and filter down through the operating levels.

In a retailing organization, top-down planning involves corporate officers developing an overall retail strategy and assessing broad economic, competitive, and consumer trends. Armed with this information, they develop performance objectives for the corporation. This overall objective is then broken down into specific objectives for each merchandise category and each region or store.

The overall strategy determines the merchandise variety, assortment, and product availability plus store size, location, and level of customer service. Then the merchandise vice presidents decide which types of merchandise are expected to grow, stay the same, or shrink. Next performance goals are established for each category manager or buyer. A category manager, discussed in Chapter 12, is like a "super buyer" in many retail organizations.

The director of stores works on the performance objectives with each regional store manager. Next these regional managers develop objectives with their store managers. The process then trickles down to department managers in the stores.

This top-down planning is complemented by a **bottom-up planning** approach. Category managers and store managers are also estimating what they

Top-down planning means that goals are set at the top of the organization and filter down through the operating levels.

can achieve. Their estimates are transmitted up the organization to the corporate planners. Frequently there are disagreements between the goals that have trickled down from the top and those set by lower-level employees of the organization. For example, a store manager may not be able to achieve the 10 percent sales growth set for the region because a major employer in the area has announced plans to lay off 2,000 employees.

These differences between bottom-up and top-down plans must be resolved through a negotiation process involving corporate planners and operating managers. If the operating managers aren't involved in the objective-setting process, they won't accept the objectives and thus will be less motivated to achieve them.

Accountability

At each level of the retail organization, the business unit and its manager should be held accountable only for revenues and expenses it directly controls. Thus, expenses that benefit several levels of the organization (such as the labor and capital expenses incurred in operating a corporate headquarters) shouldn't be arbitrarily assigned to lower levels. In the case of a store, for example, it may be appropriate to set performance objectives based on sales and employee productivity. If the buyer lowers prices to get rid of merchandise and therefore profits suffer, then it's not fair to assess a store manager's performance based on the store's profit. (Activity-Based Costing, discussed in this chapter's appendix, provides a vehicle for allocating costs.)

Performance measures should only be used to pinpoint problem areas. Reasons why performance is above or below planned levels must be examined. Perhaps the people involved in setting the objectives aren't very good at making predictions. If so, they may need to be trained in forecasting. Also, a manager may misrepresent a business unit's ability to contribute to the firm's financial goals in order to get a larger inventory budget than is warranted. In either case, funds could be misallocated.

Actual performance may be different than the plan due to circumstances beyond the manager's control. For example, there may have been a recession. Assuming the recession wasn't predicted, or was more severe or lasted longer than anticipated, there are several relevant questions: How quickly were plans adjusted? How rapidly and appropriately were pricing and promotional policies modified? In short, did the manager react to salvage an adverse situation or did those reactions worsen the situation?

Performance Measures

Many factors contribute to a retailer's overall performance. Thus, it's hard to find one single measure to evaluate performance. For instance, sales is a global measure of how much activity is going on in the store. However, a store manager could easily increase sales by lowering prices, but the profit realized on the merchandise (gross margin) would suffer as a result. Clearly, an attempt to maximize one measure may lower another. Managers must therefore understand how their actions affect multiple performance measures. It's usually unwise to use only one measure since it rarely tells the whole story.

The measures used to evaluate retail operations vary depending on (1) the level of the organization where the decision is made and (2) the resources the manager controls. For example, the principle resources controlled by store managers are space and money for operating expenses (such as wages for sales associates and utility payments to light and heat the store). Store managers focus on performance measures like sales per square foot and employee costs.

Types of Measures

Exhibit 7–13 breaks down a variety of retailers' performance measures into three types: output measures, input measures, and productivity measures. **Input measures** assess the amount of resources or money used by the retailer to achieve outputs. These inputs are used by the retailer to generate sales and profits. **Output measures** assess the results of retailers' investment decisions. For example, sales revenue results from decisions on how many stores to build, how much inventory to have in the stores, and how much to spend

EXHIBIT 7-13   Examples of Performance Measures Used by Retailers

LEVEL OF ORGANIZATION	OUTPUT	INPUT	PRODUCTIVITY (OUTPUT/INPUT)
Corporate (measures of entire corporation)	Net sales Net profits Growth in sales, profits	Square feet of store space Number of employees Inventory Advertising expenditures	Return on assets Asset turnover Sales per employee Sales per square foot
Merchandise management (measures for a merchandise category)	Net sales Gross margin Growth in sales	Inventory level Markdowns Advertising expenses Cost of merchandise	Gross Margin Return on Investment (GMROI) Inventory turnover Advertising as a percentage of sales* Markdown as a percentage of sales*
Store operations (measures for a store or department within a store)	Net sales Gross margin Growth in sales	Square feet of selling areas Expenses for utilities Number of sales associates	Net sales per square foot Net sales per sales associate or per selling hour Utility expenses as a percentage of sales*

*These productivity measures are commonly expressed as an input/output.

on advertising. A **productivity measure** (the ratio of an output to an input) determines how effectively a retailer uses a resource.

Exhibit 7–14 shows productivity measures used at different levels of a retailing organization. This chapter has concentrated on productivity measures used at the corporate level since they are most closely tied to a retailer's overall strategy. Productivity measures used to evaluate merchandise are discussed in Chapters 12 and 13, whereas we look at productivity measures for evaluating the space in stores in Chapter 18.

In general, since productivity measures are a ratio of outputs to inputs, they can be used to compare different business units. Suppose Joanne Phillips's two stores are different sizes: One has 5,000 square feet and the other has 10,000 square feet. It's hard to compare stores' performances using just output or input measures. The larger store will probably generate more sales and have higher expenses. But if the larger store generates $210 net sales per square foot and the smaller store generates $350 per square foot, Joanne knows that the smaller store is operating more efficiently even though it's generating lower sales.

EXHIBIT 7-14   Illustrative Productivity Measures Used by Retailing Organizations

LEVEL OF ORGANIZATION	OUTPUT	INPUT	PRODUCTIVITY (OUTPUT/INPUT)
Corporate (chief executive officer)	Net Profit	Owners' equity	Net profit / Owners' equity = Return on owners' equity
Merchandising (merchandise manager and buyer)	Gross margin	Inventory*	Gross margin / inventory* = GMROI
Store operations (director of stores, store manager)	Net sales	Square foot	Net sales/square foot

*Inventory = Average inventory at cost.

SUMMARY   This chapter explains some basic elements of retailing financial strategy and examines how retailing strategy affects the financial performance of a firm. We used the strategic profit model as a vehicle for understanding the complex interrelations between financial ratios and retailing strategy. We found that different types of retailers have different financial operating characteristics. Specifically, department store chains like Nordstrom generally have higher profit margins and lower turnover than warehouse clubs like Price/Costco. Yet, when margin and turnover are combined into return on assets, we showed that it's possible to achieve similar financial performance.

We also described some financial performance measures used to evaluate different aspects of a retailing organization. Although the return on assets ratio in the strategic profit model is appropriate for evaluating the performance of retail operating managers, other measures are more appropriate for more specific activities. For instance, gross margin return on investment (GMROI) is appropriate for buyers, whereas store managers should be concerned with sales or gross margin per square foot.

The chapter concludes with an appendix describing the use and benefits of activity-based costing. Based on contribution analysis, activity-based costing is a method of allocating the cost of all major activities a retailer performs to products, product lines, SKUs, and the like. Using activity-based costing, retailers can make more informed and profitable decisions, since they have a clear understanding of the costs associated with the different activities involved in making those decisions. There are several reasons for using activity-based costing, not the least of which is that it can be adapted for use throughout the retail organization.

KEY TERMS

accounts payable, *210*	current assets, *204*	liabilities, *203*	output measure, *220*
accounts receivable, *204*	current liabilities, *210*	long-term liabilities, *210*	owners' equity, *203*
accrued liabilities, *210*	fixed assets, *208*	net profit, *202*	productivity measure, *221*
activity-based costing, *224*	gross margin, *201*	net sales, *201*	retained earnings, *211*
assets, *203*	gross profit, *201*	notes payable, *210*	stockholders' equity, *211*
bottom-up planning, *219*	input measure, *220*	opportunity cost of capital, *225*	top-down planning, *219*

DISCUSSION QUESTIONS & PROBLEMS

1. Why must a retailer use multiple performance measures to evaluate its performance?

2. Describe how a multiple-store retailer would set its annual performance objectives.

3. Buyers' performance is often measured by their gross margin. Why is this figure more appropriate than net profit or loss?

4. How does the Strategic Profit Model (SPM) assist retailers in planning and evaluating marketing and financial strategies?

5. Mayor's Jewelry (a regional high-end jewelry store) and Target Stores (a national discount retailer) target different groups of customers. Which should have the higher asset turnover, net profit margin, and return on assets? Why?

6. Given the following information on page 223, construct an income statement for the Neiman Marcus Group, Inc., and determine if there was a profit or loss in 1994.

THE NEIMAN MARCUS GROUP, INC., 1994 ($000)	
Sales	$ 2, 092,906
Cost of goods sold	1, 465,656
Operating expenses	567,914
Interest expense	31,878
Taxes	11,532

7. Using the following information taken from the balance sheet of the 1994 income statement for The Sharper Image Corporation, determine the asset turnover.

SHARPER IMAGE CORPORATION, 1995 ($000)	
Net sales	$ 188,535
Total assets	64,036
Total liabilities	31,244

8. Using the following information taken from the 1995 balance sheet and 1995 income statement for Lands' End, Inc., develop a strategic profit model.

LANDS' END, INC. 1995 ($000)	
Sales	$ 992,106
Cost of goods sold	568,634
Operating expenses	358,540
Interest expense	1,769
Inventory	168,652
Accounts receivable	4,459
Other current assets	25,057
Accounts payable	52,762
Notes payable	0
Other current liabilities	49,948
Fixed assets	96,991
Long-term liabilities	5,379

9. Assume that Sports Authority evaluates its store managers based on return on assets. You've been hired by the CEO to examine this practice and you're considering using activity-based costing as an alternative. Write a position statement defending the use of either ROA or activity-based costing.

SUGGESTED READINGS

Activity-Based Costing for Food Wholesalers and Retailers. Ernst & Young LLP and the Joint Industry Project on Efficient Consumer Response, 1994.

Ailawadi, Kusum L., Norm Borin, and Paul W. Farris. "Market Power and Performance: A Cross-Industry Analysis of Manufacturers and Retailers." *Journal of Retailing* 71, no. 3 (Fall 1995), pp. 211–49.

Borin, Norm, and Paul Farris. "An Empirical Comparison of Direct Product Profit and Existing Measures of SKU Productivity." *Journal of Retailing* 66, no. 3 (Fall 1990), pp. 297–314.

Chow, James, and Anthony Koh. "An Empirical Study of Retailers' Perceptions of Direct Product Profitability." In Robert King, ed., *Retailing: Theories and Practices for Today and Tomorrow.* Proceedings of the Fourth Triennial National Retailing Conference, Richmond, VA, 1994, pp. 51–55.

Compton, Ted R. "Implementing Activity-Based Costing." *The CPA Journal,* March 1996, pp. 20–27.

Cooper, Robin, and Robert S. Kaplan. "Profit Priorities from Activity-Based Costing." *Harvard Business Review,* May–June 1991, pp. 130–35.

Direct Product Profit Manual. Washington, DC: Food Marketing Institute, 1986.

Fairchild's Financial Manual of Retail Stores, 1996, 68th ed. New York: Fairchild Books, Division of Fairchild Fashion and Merchandising Group.

Gardiner, Stanley C. "Measures of Product Attractiveness and the Theory of Constraints." *International Journal of Retail & Distribution Management* 21, no. 7 (November 1993), pp. 37–46.

Lambert, Douglas M., and James R. Stock. *Strategic Logistics Management,* 3d ed. Burr Ridge, IL: Irwin, 1993.

Mecimore, Charles D., and Alice T. Bell. "Are We Ready for Fourth-Generation Activity-Based Costing?" *Management Accounting,* January 1995, pp. 22–26.

Moran, Alexandra, ed. *MOR 1996 Edition: Merchandising and Operating Results of Retail Stores in 1995,* 71st ed. New York: John Wiley & Sons, 1996, pp. 4–7.

Rappaport, Alfred. *Creating Shareholder Value: The New Standard for Business Performance.* New York: Macmillan, 1986.

Solomons, David. *Divisional Performance: Measurement and Control.* Burr Ridge, IL: Richard D. Irwin, 1965.

APPENDIX

Activity-Based Costing

A financial management tool that has been quite popular as a method of improving retailing performance is activity-based costing. **Activity-based costing** is an accounting method that enables a retailer to better understand how and where it makes a profit than more traditional methods allow. In activity-based costing, all major activities within a cost center are identified and costs of performing each are calculated. The resulting costs are then charged to the product, product line, customer, or vendor that caused the activity to be performed.[11]

Activity-based costing isn't a new idea. Various forms of activity-based costing have been used under different names since the 1960s. Although each variation of activity-based costing has its own nuances, all are based on contribution margin analysis.[12] Residual income has been used in several applications.[13] Many consulting and retailing firms (e.g., Deloitte & Touche,[14] Andersen Consulting,[15] Neiman Marcus, and Kmart[16]) have used direct product profitability (DPP). DPP was particularly popular in supermarket retailing but appears to have been supplanted by activity-based costing.[17]

Consider the following hypothetical example illustrated in Exhibit 7–15. Suppose Safeway pays $75 per case for Smuckers strawberry jelly and sells it for $100. The gross margin is $25; the gross margin percentage is also 25. Safeway pays $70 per case for its private-label jelly and sells it for $93.30—again resulting in a 25 percent gross margin.

By using the traditional gross margin measure of profitability, the "real" profit is obscured. There are additional costs that can be applied directly to these products to determine the "real" profit using activity-based costing. The cost of handling the private-label jelly is actually much greater than meets the eye. The private label is shipped to a Safeway distribution center, stored, and then shipped to individual stores. The private-label vendor demands payment in 10 days, rather than 30, and is not responsive to damaged goods claims. Smuckers, on the other hand, delivers directly to each store, allows 30 days before payment is due, and gives immediate credit for any damaged merchandise. Using activity-based costing, the additional cost assigned to the case of private-label jelly is $42, compared to $10 for Smuckers. Activity-based costing analysis indicates that Safeway makes $1.50 per case on Smuckers, while losing $18.70 per case for the private–label jelly.

A major shortcoming of activity-based costing is that the cost allocation may be arbitrary. To solve the problem of which costs should be included, use the following decision rule: Don't include costs that will remain unchanged as a result of a particular decision.[18] For instance, if a retailer won't be able to reduce its administrative staff if it decides to bypass a distribution center and deliver merchandise directly to stores, then the administrative staff expense shouldn't be included in the decision.[19]

EXHIBIT 7–15

Activity-Based Costing Profitability Statement for Smuckers and Private-Label Jelly at Safeway

	SMUCKERS	PRIVATE-LABEL JELLY
Retail price per case	$100.00	$93.30
Cost per case	75.00	70.00
Gross margin	25.00	23.30
Other "relevant" costs	10.00	42.00
Contribution margin	1.50	−18.70

In the next few pages, we discuss why activity-based costing is so useful. First, it helps retailers make more profitable decisions. Also, it's more flexible than other evaluation tools because (1) it rewards managers for their ability to increase sales and (2) it considers the risk inherent in making any financial decision. Finally, unlike the specialized evaluation measures we've examined throughout *Retailing Management*, activity-based costing can be used throughout a retailing organization.

Benefit 1: Making More Profitable Decisions There's a problem with using some of the productivity ratios discussed earlier in this chapter. For instance, conflicting results may ensue when traditional gross margin and inventory turnover measures instead of activity-based costing are used to plan and evaluate merchandising performance. Management tends to try to maximize these measures or to set target goals too high.

Using activity-based costing analysis, the buyer would frame the problem as follows:

Contribution Margin (CM) = Gross margin – Relevant costs

An important cost that impacts a merchandising decision is the cost of carrying the inventory:[20]

Cost of carrying inventory = Average inventory value (at cost)
× Opportunity cost of capital

The **opportunity cost of capital** is the rate available on the next best use of the capital invested in the project at hand. It should be no lower than the rate at which a firm borrows funds, since one alternative is to pay back borrowed money. But it can be higher, depending on the range of other opportunities available. Typically, this rate rises with the investment's risk. So, if average inventory is $100,000 and the cost of borrowing money is 10 percent per year, the inventory carrying cost is $10,000.

Consider a buyer facing the decision of putting a category of slow-moving merchandise on sale (Exhibit 7–16). After he cuts prices, gross margin percentage falls from 50 to 33.3 percent, but inventory turnover increases from .5 to .6 times.

EXHIBIT 7–16

Gross Margin, Turnover, and Contribution Margin for an SKU, Three-Month Period without and with a Sale

	WITHOUT A SALE	WITH A SALE
Net sales	$100,000	$150,000
Cost of goods sold	50,000	100,000
Gross margin	$ 50,000	$ 50,000
Gross margin percentage	50%[a]	33.3%
Average inventory at cost	$100,000	$166,666
Three-month inventory turnover	.5[b]	.6
Opportunity cost of capital (three-month)[c]	2.5%	2.5%
Contribution margin	$ 47,500[d]	$ 45,833

[a] Gross margin % = $\dfrac{\text{Gross margin}}{\text{Net sales}}$

$50\% = \dfrac{\$50,000}{\$100,000}$

[b] Inventory turnover = $\dfrac{\text{Cost of goods sold}}{\text{Average inventory at cost}}$

$.5 \text{ times} = \dfrac{\$50,000}{\$100,000}$

[c] A 2.5 percent opportunity cost of capital for a three-month period is equivalent to an annual rate of 10 percent.
[d] Contribution margin = Gross margin – [(Opportunity of cost of capital) × (Average inventory at cost)]
$47,500 = $50,000 – [(0.025) x ($100,000)]

It's hard to determine whether the buyer should take the markdown because of the countervailing goals of maximizing both margin and turnover. By using the activity-based costing model, the correct profit impact of such a decision is easily determined. Based on Exhibit 7–16's parameters, the buyer should maintain the higher price because the contribution margin is higher.

Benefit 2: Rewarding Sales Growth   Sales growth, an important corporate goal, is an integral part of the activity-based costing model. Examine Exhibit 7–16 for the SKU without a sale. Suppose sales are expected to be twice the original estimate—$200,000 versus $100,000. The buyer must buy twice as many units, so total assets and net profit also double. Most important, contribution margin doubles from $47,500 to $95,000 [or $100,000 – ($200,000 × .025)]! Yet gross margin percentage and inventory turnover remain unchanged. A buyer being evaluated on these two ratios alone wouldn't get credit for the increases in sales and profits.

Benefit 3: Using Activity-Based Costing throughout Retailing Organizations
As we saw in the previous section, different—often conflicting—performance evaluation tools are used in retail organizations. Different tools are also used to make different types of decisions at various levels of the organization. For example, upper management may be evaluated on an ROI measure such as return on assets; buyers may strive to achieve gross margin and inventory turnover goals; whereas sales growth and the ability to control operating expenses may be used to evaluate store managers. By using an activity-based costing paradigm throughout the organization, employees can plan their activities and be evaluated using one basic measure.

Exhibit 7–16 is for a category of merchandise. Contribution margins (CMs) for individual SKUs are aggregated across vendors:

$$CM_{vendor} = CM_{SKU1} + CM_{SKU2} + CM_{SKU3} + \ldots CM_{SKU\,n}$$

In the same way, contribution margins for each vendor are aggregated to obtain the contribution margin for each category:

$$CM_{category} = CM_{vendor1} + CM_{vendor2} + CM_{vendor3} + \ldots CM_{vendor\,n}$$

How would decisions change as activity-based costing data are aggregated further up the retail organization? At the buyer and merchandise manager levels, additional relevant administrative expenses should be included such as costs associated with clerical help and assistant buyers. Managers can analyze whether the benefit derived from adding additional labor would more than offset the costs.

This decision-making process is similar in store operations. The appropriate measure for planning and evaluating salespeople's performance is the contribution margin of the SKUs they sell. Although salespeople have no direct control over cost of goods sold or any other costs associated with the product, they do have some control over the mix of merchandise they sell. Some retailers would rather not share the details of these costs with salespeople, but they could use different commission percentages based on the different margins. This would give salespeople the correct incentive to sell the desired mix of goods. For instance, suppose the contribution margin as a percentage of sales is higher for women's accessories than for dresses. If management wishes to emphasize the higher–contribution-margin accessories, they would give the salespeople a higher commission for selling them.

The appropriate measure for sales managers is the sum of the contribution margins generated by each salesperson less the costs relevant to the manager:

$$CM_{\text{sales manager}} = CM_{\text{salesperson1}} + CM_{\text{salesperson2}} + CM_{\text{salesperson3}}$$
$$+ \ldots CM_{\text{salesperson } n} - \text{Other relevant expenses}$$

Some relevant costs are in-store promotions, point-of-sale displays, and overtime salaries—so long as the decisions to make these expenditures are done by the sales manager. If the sales manager has hiring responsibility, salaries and benefits of the sales staff would also reduce contribution margin. In this way, the sales manager can determine whether it's profitable to hire additional salespeople and decide the mix of part-time help.

The store manager is responsible for all revenues and costs under the control of sales managers, plus more. For instance, store managers can impact the costs of security and utilities. As such, using activity-based costing they can make rational decisions regarding the costs/benefits of improving antitheft devices or installing and maintaining energy-efficient lighting or air conditioning. In some retail firms (e.g., JCPenney), the store manager controls the level of inventory and should thus be charged for the cost of these assets.

$$CM_{\text{store manager}} = CM_{\text{sales manager1}} + CM_{\text{sales manager2}} + CM_{\text{sales manager3}}$$
$$+ \ldots CM_{\text{sales manager } n} - \text{Other relevant expenses} -$$
$$\text{Cost of carrying assets}$$

Retail space allocation is an important decision both store and merchandise managers face. A commonly used performance measure for allocating space for merchandise and evaluating that space's productivity is sales per square foot. (See Chapter 18.) But retailers can't survive on sales without profits. Contribution margin per square foot of selling space is a more useful space performance measure for stores that display merchandise primarily on one level because it captures the true profit-generating ability of the merchandise. Grocery and discount stores that use long gondolas of multishelved displays should use contribution margin per linear foot, whereas warehouse stores that stack merchandise on pallets 20 or more feet in the air should use contribution margin per cubic foot. Like other decisions previously discussed, retailers would aggregate the contribution margins of SKUs to vendors, merchandise classifications, departments, and so on.

Some of the most important decisions facing retailers are those capital expenditures that affect multiple time periods (e.g., equipment purchases and store renovation). The appropriate way to evaluate these investments is through value-based planning. Value-based planning is a managerial tool for measuring the desired increase in wealth to a firm's owners.[21] The corporate goal of creating value for the firm's owners is accomplished by using the financial concepts of discounted cash flow to measure the value of a particular investment or strategy. Yet, the results of value-based planning aren't consistent with retailers' control models based on accrual accounting.[22] Fortunately, activity-based costing can be used in a capital budgeting problem to yield results that are identical to a discounted cash flow analysis. Similar to the single-period example in Exhibit 7–15 and 7–16, the projected income statements are explicitly charged with the opportunity cost of capital in each period within the planning horizon. The sum of the contribution margins across each period equals the net present value of the cash streams.

Broadening the application base for activity-based costing beyond merchandising decisions benefits retailers along several dimensions. First, as activity-based costing becomes integrated into multiple decision-making arenas, employees throughout the organization will all be working toward the same common goal—maximizing contribution margin! Second, one consistent decision-making and evaluation tool simplifies training and facilitates the transfer of managerial skills throughout the organization. Finally, the use of activity-based costing analysis is consistent with value-based planning, discounted cash flow capital budgeting procedures, and operating budgets.

NOTES

1. "Harper's Index," *Harpers*, February 1994, p. 13.

2. *Fairchild's Financial Manual of Retail Stores, 1996*, 68th ed. (New York: Fairchild Books, Division of Fairchild Fashion and Merchandising Group); and Alexandra Moran, ed., *MOR 1996 Edition: Merchandising and Operating Results of Retail Stores in 1995*, 71st ed. (New York: John Wiley & Sons, 1996), pp. 4–7.

3. Ibid.

4. Average retail inventory is estimated from the balance sheet inventory. Assume the end-of-year inventory on the balance sheet is average cost inventory. Average retail inventory = average cost inventory/1 – gross margin percent (expressed as a decimal).

5. *Fairchild's Financial Manual of Retail Stores, 1996*, p. 134.

6. *Chain Store Age Executive*, January 1996, section II, p. 23A.

7. Although the use of asset turnover presented here is helpful for gaining appreciation of the performance ratio, capital budgeting or present value analyses are more appropriate for determining long-term return of a fixed asset.

8. All categories of stock (including preferred, paid-in capital, and treasury stock) are included with common stock for simplicity.

9. B. S. Chakravarthy, "Measuring Strategic Performance," *Strategic Management Journal* 7 (1986), pp. 437–58; R. A. D'Aveni, "The Aftermath of Organizational Decline: A Longitudinal Study of the Strategic and Managerial Characteristics of Declining Firms," *Academy of Management Journal* 32, no. 3 (1989), pp. 577–605; D. C. Hambrick and R. A. D'Aveni, "Large Corporate Failures as Downward Spirals," *Administrative Science Quarterly* 33 (1988), pp. 1–23; R. Rust, and D. C. Schmittlein, "A Bayesian Cross-Validated Likelihood Method for Comparing Alternative Specifications of Quantitative Models," *Marketing Science* 4, no. 1 (1985), pp. 20–28; and S. Sharma, and V. Mahajan, "Early Warning Indicators of Business Failure," *Journal of Marketing*, Fall 1980, pp. 80–89.

10. Average retail inventory is estimated from the balance sheet inventory. Assume the end-of-year inventory on the balance sheet is average cost inventory. Average retail inventory = average cost inventory/1 – gross margin percent (expressed as a decimal).

11. *Activity Based Costing for Food Wholesalers and Retailers* (Ernst & Young LLP and the Joint Industry Project on Efficient Consumer Response, 1994), p. 53. See also Robin Cooper and Robert S. Kaplan, "Profit Priorities from Activity-Based Costing," *Harvard Business Review*, May–June 1991, pp. 130–35; Ted R. Compton, "Implementing Activity-Based Costing," *The CPA Journal*, March 1996, pp. 20–27; Robin Cooper and Robert S. Kaplan, "Activity-Based Systems: Measuring the Costs of Resource Usage," *Accounting Horizons*, September 1992, pp. 1–13; Charles D. Mecimore and Alice T. Bell, "Are We Ready for Fourth-Generation Activity Based Costing?" *Management Accounting*, January 1995, pp. 22–26; Michael D. Woods, "Economic Choices with Activity Based Costing," *Management Accounting*, December 1992, pp. 53–57; Harper A. Roehm, Melissa A. Critchfield, and Joseph F. Castellano, "Yes, Activity Based Costing Works with Purchasing Too," *Journal of Accountancy*, November 1992, pp. 59–62; and Kenneth H. Manning, "Distribution Channel Profitability," *Management Accounting*, January 1995, pp. 44–48.

12. Frank H. Mossman, Paul M. Fischer, and W. J. E. Crissy, "New Approaches to Analyzing Marketing Profitability," *Journal of Marketing* 38, no. 2 (April 1974), pp. 43–48.

13. David Solomons, *Divisional Performance: Measurement and Control* (Burr Ridge, IL: Richard D. Irwin, 1965); Michael Levy and Charles A. Ingene, "Residual Income Analysis: A Method of Inventory Investment Allocation and Evaluation," *Journal of Marketing* 48 (Summer 1984), pp. 93–104; Michael Levy and Michael van Breda, "A Financial Perspective on the Shift of Marketing Functions," *Journal of Retailing* 60, no. 4 (Winter 1984), pp. 23–42; Michael Levy and Michael F. van Breda, "The Decomposition of Firm Value in a Hierarchical Retailing Organization," *Journal of Retailing* 64, no. 2 (Summer 1988), pp. 215–25; and Michael Levy and Daniel J. Howard, "An Experimental Approach to Planning the Duration and Size of Markdowns," *International Journal of Retailing* 3, no. 2 (1988), pp. 48–58.

14. *"Supermarket/Wholesale Advanced Merchandising Technology Survey."* (San Francisco: Deloitte & Touche, 1992).

15. "Attacking the Parts," *Stores*, June 1988, pp. 79–84.

16. "Not Only for Groceries," *Stores*, July 1988, pp. 48–52.

17. *Direct Product Profit Manual* (Washington, DC: Food Marketing Institute, 1986).

18. Herein lies the fundamental difference between activity-based costing and DPP. DPP captures all direct costs, such as the cost of shipping and storage, and allocates them to products, and so on. Activity-based costing allocates both direct and indirect costs. An example of an indirect cost of a product is the salary of the people working in a distribution center. Using activity-based costing, an analysis would be made of the activities that a warehouseperson performed. That person's compensation would then be allocated to a product based on the time spent handling the product. We propose that some indirect costs should not be allocated based on our decision rule.

19. See Douglas M. Lambert and James R. Stock, *Strategic Logistics Management* 3d ed. (Burr Ridge, IL: Irwin, 1993), pp. 608–10; and Woods, "Economic Choices with Activity-Based Costing."

20. Barnard J. LaLonde and Douglas M. Lambert, "A Methodology for Calculating Inventory Carrying Costs," *International Journal of Physical Distribution* 7, no. 4 (1977), pp. 195–231.

21. Alfred Rappaport, *Creating Shareholder Value: The New Standard for Business Performance* (New York: Macmillan, 1986); A. Hax and N. Majluf, *Strategic Management: An Integrated Perspective* (Englewood Cliffs, NJ: Prentice Hall, 1984); William Alberts and James McTaggart, "Value Based Strategic Investment Planning," *Interfaces* (January-February 1984), pp. 138–51; William Fruhan, *Financial Strategy: Studies in the Creation, Transfer, and Destruction of Shareholder Value* (Burr Ridge, IL: Richard D. Irwin, 1979); Levy and van Breda, "The Decomposition of Firm Value in a Hierarchical Retailing Organization"; Roger Kerin, and Nikhil Varaiya, "Value-Based Planning in Retailing," *Journal of Retailing* 61 (Winter 1985), pp. 5–10; and Nikhil Varaiya, Roger A. Kerin, and David Weeks, "The Relationship between Growth, Profitability, and Firm Value," *Strategic Management Journal* 8 (1987), pp. 487–97.

22. G. E. Pinches, "Myopia, Capital Budgeting and Decision Making," *Financial Management* (Autumn 1982), pp. 6–19; and Michael F. van Breda, "Integrating Capital and Operating Budgets," *Sloan Management Review* (Winter 1984), pp. 49–58.

Retail Locations

THE WORLD OF RETAILING

↓

RETAILING STRATEGY
  6. Retail Market Strategy
  7. Financial Strategy
  8. Retail Locations
  9. Site Selection
  10. Organization Structure
     and Human Resource
     Management
  11. Integrated Retail Logistics
     and Information Systems

↓

MERCHANDISE MANAGEMENT

STORE MANAGEMENT

QUESTIONS

- What types of locations are available to retailers?

- What are the relative advantages of these types of locations?

- What factors should retailers consider when deciding on a particular site?

FOR SEVERAL REASONS, STORE LOCATION is often the most important decision made by a retailer. First, location is typically the prime consideration in a customer's store choice. For instance, when choosing where you're going to have your car washed, you usually pick the location closest to your home or work.

Second, location decisions have strategic importance because they can be used to develop a sustainable competitive advantage. As Chapter 6 said, retailers can change their pricing, service, and merchandise assortments in a relatively short time. However, location decisions are harder to change because retailers frequently have to either make substantial investments to buy and develop real estate or commit to long-term leases with developers. It's not unusual, for instance, for a national chain store to sign a lease from 7 to 10 years. Thus, retailers with excellent locations have a strategic advantage competitors can't easily copy.

Location decisions have become even more important in recent years. First, there are more retailers (particularly national chains like The Gap and Toys "R" Us) opening new locations, making the better locations harder to obtain. This problem is made more complex by a slowdown in both population growth and new shopping center construction. A retailer may find a suitable location, but high rent, complicated leases, and expensive fixturing and remodeling can make it very costly.

This chapter describes the types of locations available to retailers and the relative advantages of each. We then examine factors that retailers should consider when choosing a particular site within a shopping center. In the next chapter, the topic of location continues. Chapter 9 examines issues in selecting appropriate regions of the country and trade areas for locating retail stores. (A **trade area** is a geographic sector that contains potential customers for a particular retailer or shopping center.) Specifically, we examine the qualitative and quantitative issues that define the sales potential for a retail location. As such, Chapters 8 and 9 are designed to be studied together.

Special Issues for Services Retailers

HAVING A GOOD LOCATION may be even more important for a service retailer than it is for a merchandise retailer. After all, services are a perishable commodity. If it isn't available when the customer wants it, there is no second chance. A sustainable competitive advantage will accrue to those service retailers who maintain convenient locations.

Consider, for instance, automatic teller machines (ATMs). Not too many years ago, the only way a bank customer could get cash or make a withdrawal was via a face-to-face interaction with a teller during the bank's limited hours. Interestingly, many banks are still closed during the hours that people have time to go to the bank such as early morning, evenings, and weekends. Not only have ATMs partially solved the "bankers' hours" problem by being open 24 hours a day, but they are conveniently located virtually everywhere in the Western world.

TYPES OF RETAIL LOCATIONS

Many types of locations are available for retail stores—each with its own strengths and weaknesses. Choosing a particular site involves evaluating a series of trade-offs. These trade-offs generally concern the cost versus the value of the site for a particular type of retailer. For instance, the best location for a 7-Eleven convenience store isn't necessarily—or usually—the best location for a Saks Fifth Avenue specialty store.

Retailers have three basic types of sites to choose from: a central business district (CBD), a shopping center, or a freestanding location. They can also choose carts, kiosks, retail merchandising units (RMUs), or tall wall units, which are selling spaces within a shopping center. Finally, retailers can locate in a mixed-use development. The following sections describe each type of location and present criteria for choosing a particular site.

Central Business Districts (CBDs)

The **central business district** is the traditional downtown business area in a city or town. Due to its business activity, it draws many people into the area. Also, people must go to the area for work. The CBD is also the hub for public transportation, and there is a high level of pedestrian traffic. Finally, the most successful CBDs for retail trade are those with a large number of residents living in the area.[2]

But central business district locations in the United States have their drawbacks. Retailers are less attracted to CBDs because higher security is required, shoplifting can be more common, and parking is often a problem. High crime rates, urban decay, and no control over the weather can discourage shoppers from the suburbs. Shopping in the evening and on weekends can be particularly slow in many CBDs. Also, unlike modern shopping centers, CBDs tend to suffer from a lack of planning. One block may contain upscale boutiques while the next may be populated with low-income housing, so consumers may not have enough interesting retailers that they can visit on a shopping trip.

Some central business districts have undergone a process of **gentrification** in which old buildings are torn down or restored with new offices, housing developments, and retailers.[3] Why is it happening?

- Gentrification is part of a natural evolution in retailing. Starting in the 1950s, retailers followed their customers to the suburbs by locating in suburban shopping centers. As cities restored their urban areas, people began to move back. Retailers simply continue to follow their customers to where they live and work.

- Developers aren't building as many malls as before, and it's often hard to find a good location in a successful mall.

REFACT A convenient location means close. But close to what? Either close to other stores or close to home. For apparel shopping, over 40 percent of consumers feel convenience means proximity to other stores where they like to shop. But for food, two-thirds of consumers measure in terms of closeness to home.[1]

- Successful national chain stores still need to expand.
- Chains are finding that occupancy costs in malls are too high.
- Cities often provide significant incentives to locate in urban centers. Shopper's World in Detroit, for instance, is a discount department store that successfully targets the urban poor. A significant property tax incentive was provided to the landlord as an inducement to enter a neighborhood in the urban core. Not only is the store very successful, but it has generated employment for 200 people—most from the immediate vicinity.

Many cities use entertainment to draw people to the gentrified CBD. Craft and cooking fairs, horse-drawn carriages, sidewalk cafes, and historical points of interest draw people to downtown shopping areas in cities like San Francisco, New Orleans, San Antonio, Denver, Cincinnati, and Orlando.

Central business district gentrification in larger cities isn't always successful. It's hard to get people to drive in from the suburbs just to find merchandise similar to what they can find at a shopping center close to home. Also, today's value-oriented, back-to-basics customer isn't likely to be attracted to these redeveloped areas since many are populated by high-end retailers.

The gentrification process in neighborhood central business districts appears to be more successful, however. A **neighborhood CBD** is the traditional shopping area located in smaller towns, or a secondary business district in a suburb or within a larger city. Neighborhood CBDs share most of the characteristics of the primary CBD. But their occupancy costs are generally lower than a primary CBD's. They do not draw as many people as the primary CBD because fewer people work in the area, and fewer stores generally means a smaller overall selection. Finally, neighborhood CBDs typically don't offer the entertainment and recreational activities available in the more successful primary CBDs.

Some drawbacks of CBDs and neighborhood CBDs in the United States are not found in cities and towns in other industrialized countries, particularly in Europe. Retailing View 8.1 examines how main-street locations in Europe are fighting to maintain their traditional advantage over the encroachment of large retailers.

Shopping Centers

From the 1950s through the 1980s, retailing declined in many central business districts, while suburban shopping centers grew as populations shifted to the suburbs. Life in the suburbs has created a need for stores a short drive from home. Large shopping centers provide an assortment of merchandise that often exceeds the CBD's. Combining many stores under one roof creates a synergy that attracts more customers than if the stores had separate locations. It's not uncommon, for instance, for one department store's sales to increase after a competing store enters a shopping center.

The term *shopping center* has been evolving since the early 1950s.[4] A **shopping center** is a group of retail and other commercial establishments that is planned, developed, owned, and managed as a single property. The two main configurations of shopping centers are strip centers and malls. **Strip centers** usually have parking in front of the stores. Open canopies may connect the store fronts, but a strip center does not have enclosed walkways linking the stores. **Malls,** on the other hand, have a pedestrian focus. Customers park in outlying areas and walk to the stores. Traditional malls are enclosed, with a climate-controlled walkway between two facing strips of stores.

8.1

Mainstreet Europe: The Fate of Mom-and-Pop Stores

DURING THE 1990s EUROPEAN retailing has been changing at the expense of the traditional mom-and-pop retail stores. In the past, mom-and-pop stores were the town or village meeting place. The locals would shop at these stores for convenience and service and because the owner was their neighbor.

Yet in most of Europe, the number of small and medium-size stores has fallen drastically over the past several years. Downtown and corner stores are threatened with extinction as suburban superstores selling everything under one roof—from food and cosmetics to clothing and electronics—become more popular. For example, in Italy, the number of superstores doubled between 1988 and 1993. The two countries experiencing the largest expansion of superstores are Germany (in particular, what was East Germany) and the Commonwealth of Independent States (formerly the USSR).

In countries where this change has been occurring steadily over the past few years, local governments have tried to restrain superstores' growth by limiting their size, thus helping local entrepreneurs compete. For instance, in metropolitan Norwich, England, a horse trots down a dirt lane. It may sound sleepy and pastoral, but this is all happening only three miles from the center of this county capital of 250,000. The nearby downtown has more than 500 shops and 200 restaurants, an open-air market, and a new mall that lures a quarter of a million shoppers into the city center each week.

Were this an American city of similar size, the dirt lane no doubt would be replaced by a highway, the plowed field by a Wal-Mart, and the meadows by a multiplex cinema. European cities such as Norwich like to do things differently, partly because they have less space and partly because they take great pride in their heritage. Strict planning and greenbelt laws force a sharp division between town and country. Suburbs are few. There is no place for the urban area to sprawl.

The efforts help Main Streets thrive and protect the underdeveloped countryside. The London-based Association of Town Center Management says 80 percent of United Kingdom retail sales are still conducted in towns, despite a crusade by food superstores, mall developers, and other big retailers who want to locate outside downtown. In the United States, only 4 percent of the retail market is still downtown, according to the International Downtown Association in Washington.

But preservation comes at a cost for Europe. The limits on out-of-town retailing reduce competition and retailing efficiency, causing higher prices. Looking for a Trivial Pursuit game? It will cost about $55 in downtown Norwich. A short-sleeve Polo shirt from Ralph Lauren? $90.

What's more, the protection of town centers may also be a culprit behind Europe's chronic unemployment woes. A McKinsey & Co. study said policies such as strict zoning laws "represent the most obvious and easily correctable barriers to increased employment" in retail.

Toys "R" Us, which has located 41 of its 49 U.K. stores out of town, has tried repeatedly to build a store in the Norwich area that would bring 150 new jobs. But it has been consistently rejected by Norwich and its neighbors. Phillip Kerrigan, after buying a toy for his daughter at Langleys (a pricey shop in town), says he isn't sorry the Toys "R" Us application was rejected. "I'd come into the city anyway. I want it to be a going concern, not a row of empty shops."

The rewards of Norwich's efforts: It has kept 95 percent of nonfood sales in the town center. The retail store occupancy rate is 95 percent as well.

Source: Cacilie Rohwedder, "Europe's Smaller Food Shops Face Finis," *The Wall Street Journal,* May 12, 1993, pp. B1, B7; and Dana Milbank, "Guarded by Greenbelts, Europe's Town Centers Thrive," *The Wall Street Journal,* May 3, 1995, pp. B1, B9.

The International Council of Shopping Centers has defined eight principal shopping center types, as shown in Exhibit 8–1.[5] Retailing View 8.2 gives a historical perspective on shopping centers.

EXHIBIT 8-1   Shopping Center Definitions

TYPE	CONCEPT	SQ. FT. INCLUDING ANCHORS	NUMBER OF ANCHORS	TYPE OF ANCHORS	TRADE AREA*
Neighborhood	Convenience	30,000–150,000	1 or more	Supermarket	3 miles
Community	General merchandise; convenience	100,000–350,000	2 or more	Discount dept. store; supermarket; drug; home improvement; large specialty/discount apparel	3–7 miles
Power	Category-dominant anchors; few small tenants	250,000–600,000	3 or more	Category killer; home improvement; discount department store; warehouse club; off-price	5–10 miles
Regional	General merchandise; fashion (mall, typically enclosed)	400,000–800,000	2 or more	Full-line department store; junior department store; mass merchant; discount department store; fashion apparel	5–15 miles
Superregional	Similar to regional but has more variety and assortment	800,000+	3 or more	Full-line department store; junior department store; mass merchant; fashion apparel	5–25 miles
Fashion/specialty	Higher-end, fashion-oriented	80,000–250,000	N/A	Fashion	5–15 miles
Outlet	Manufacturers' outlet stores	50,000–400,000	N/A	Manufacturers' outlet stores	25–75 miles
Theme/festival	Leisure; tourist-oriented	80,000–250,000	N/A	Restaurants; entertainment	N/A

* The area from which 60 to 80 percent of the center's sales originate.
Source: International Council of Shopping Centers.

INTERNET EXERCISE   The International Council of Shopping Centers, the premier trade organization for the shopping center industry, publishes a newsletter called *Shopping Centers Today*. Go to its site on the Internet (http://www.icsc.org) and click on SCT/VRN Magazine. Find an article that discusses a new trend or innovation in shopping centers.

Strip Shopping Centers   There are three types of strip shopping centers: the neighborhood center, the community center, and the power center. Strip centers have been successful in the United States because they offer customers convenient locations, easy parking, and relatively low rents for retailers. The neighborhood centers of today have fewer mom-and-pop stores than in the past. Instead, there are more national tenants like Blockbuster Video, Little Caesar's, and Walgreens. National specialty store chains like Payless Shoe Source are able to compete effectively in strip centers against their rival stores in malls. They can offer lower prices, partly because of the lower rents incurred by being in a community center, plus their customers can drive right up to the door.

8.2

Shopping Centers: A Historical Perspective

Strip centers offer customers convenient locations, easy parking, and relatively lower rents for retailers. Planned shopping malls offer customers variety, a planned tenant mix, and a controlled environment.

REGIONAL SHOPPING CENTERS are a post–World War II phenomenon. Their growth was sparked by such explosive elements as a booming population, marked rise in incomes, widespread population shift from city to suburbs, and (last but far from least) tremendous growth in the use of cars and the development of the interstate highway system.

Historically, shopping centers trace their beginnings to centuries ago. The public plaza stalls of 13th-century Venice, Italy, were a forerunner of today's malls. Of more recent vintage is Milan's glass-roofed Galeria Vittorio Emanuele erected around 125 years ago.

The first neighborhood shopping center with off-street parking was Roland Park Shopping Center about five miles north of downtown Baltimore. Dating from 1907, it grew from one drugstore to a half dozen convenience stores.

Market Square, in Lake Forest, Illinois, opened in 1916. The National Register of Historic Places calls it the first suburban retail center. Country Club Plaza, on 40 acres five miles south of Kansas City, Missouri, was erected in 1922 by J. C. Nichols Co., a real estate organization. Nichols also developed a 5,000-acre housing area nearby, providing a built-in, walk-in shopping population of 40,000 persons. The center's retailers were local merchants. There were then no anchors. However, Country Club Plaza pointed the way to today's regional malls.

Seven miles north of downtown Seattle, Allied Stores' Northgate was the prototype in 1950 of the centrally controlled shopping center. At the outset, it boasted a 200,000–square-foot Bon Marche, a smaller department store, at least two variety stores, supermarkets, and other types of merchants. Other innovations were a 5,000-space parking lot, a truck tunnel, a children's nursery, and a kiddieland for older children. Expanding over the years to 1.2 million square feet, Northgate has always had a merchant's association strongly supported by both tenants and the landlord.

In 1956, Southdale (the first enclosed, climate-controlled regional mall) was opened in Edina, a Minneapolis suburb, by the Dayton Co. There were then more than 2,000 shopping centers in the United States, the great majority being strip centers.

In the 1950s, a large center ran from 200,000 to 300,000 square feet. Even then there were realtors and retailers who insisted that the United States had all the shopping centers it needed, and that any new malls would encounter market saturation difficulties.

Source: Samuel Feinberg, "The Godfather of Malls Born in Venice, Italy," *Women's Wear Daily*, July 5, 1989, p. 13.

Neighborhood Centers A neighborhood center is designed to provide convenience shopping for the day-to-day needs of consumers in the immediate neighborhood. Roughly half of these centers are anchored by a supermarket, while about a third have a drugstore anchor. These anchors are supported by stores offering sundries, food, and a variety of personal services.

The first shopping center, a marketplace with retail stores, was the Agora at the foot of the Parthenon in Athens in 600 BC. It was the center of all commerce, politics, and entertainment in ancient Greece.[6]

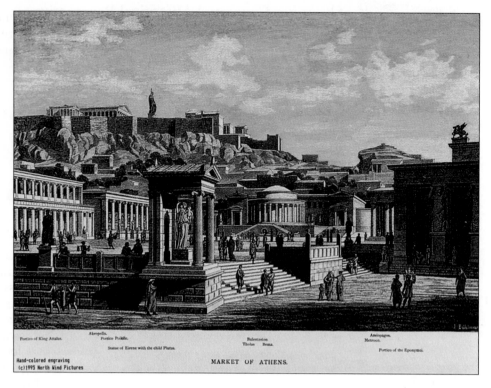

Portico of King Attalos.   Akropolis.   Portico Poikîle.   Bulenterion   Areiopagos.
     Statue of Eirene with the child Plutus.   Tholas   Bema.   Metroon.
                                                       Portico of the Eponymoi.

Hand-colored engraving
(c)1995 North Wind Pictures   MARKET OF ATHENS.

REFACT In 1995, according to the National Research Bureau, there were a total of 41,235 shopping centers in the United States, representing a total leasable retail area of 4.97 billion square feet.[7]

Community Centers   A community center typically offers a wider range of apparel and other soft goods than the neighborhood center does. Among the more common anchors are supermarkets, super drugstores, and discount department stores. Community center tenants sometimes contain off-price or category-dominant retailers selling such items as apparel, home improvement/furnishings, toys, shoes, pet supplies, and electronics and sporting goods.

Of the eight center types, community centers encompass the widest range of formats. For example, certain centers that are anchored by a large discount department store refer to themselves as discount centers. Others with a high percentage of square footage allocated to off-price retailers can be termed off-price centers.

Power Centers   This type of center is dominated by several large anchors, including discount department stores (Target), off-price stores (Marshalls), warehouse clubs (Price/Costco), or category killers (also known as "big-box" stores) such as Home Depot, Office Depot, Circuit City, Sports Authority, PETsMART, and Toys "R" Us. Unlike the centers previously discussed, a power center often includes several freestanding (unconnected) anchors and only a minimum number of small specialty tenants. They are typically unenclosed in a strip center configuration, or they can be arranged in a "village" cluster.

Power centers were virtually unknown a decade ago, but have become the mainstay of shopping center development activity. The typical new power center has increased in size throughout the 1990s. Many are now larger than some regional malls. Why have they become so popular? First and foremost, their tenants have experienced tremendous growth and prosperity, and there are new entries into the category killer arena all the time. A power center is a natural location for these large tenants. They don't want to pay the high rents of regional shopping malls and they benefit from the synergy of being with other big-box stores. Also, shoppers are seeking "value" alternatives to the stores found in shopping malls.[8]

Shopping Malls   Shopping malls have several advantages over alternative locations. First, because of the many different types of stores, the merchandise assortments available within those stores, and the opportunity to combine shopping with entertainment, shopping malls have become the Main Street for current shoppers. Teenagers hang out and meet friends, older citizens in Nikes get their exercise by walking the malls, and families make trips to the mall an inexpensive form of entertainment (as long as they don't buy anything). To enhance the total shopping experience, many malls incorporate food and entertainment.

The second major advantage of locating in a shopping mall is that the tenant mix can be planned. Shopping mall owners control the number of different types of retailers so that customers can have a one-stop–shopping experience with a well-balanced assortment of merchandise. For instance, it's important to have several women's clothing stores in a major mall to draw in customers. Yet, too many such stores could jeopardize any one store's success. Mall managers also attempt to create a complementary tenant mix. They like to have all stores that appeal to certain target markets (such as all upscale specialty clothing stores) located together. Using this approach, customers know what types of merchandise they can expect to find in a particular mall or location within a mall. Managers also strive for a good mix between shopping and specialty goods stores. A strong core of shopping goods stores, like shoe stores, brings people to the mall. Specialty stores, like computer software stores, also bring shoppers to the mall. While specialty store customers are in the mall, they'll likely be attracted to other stores.

The third advantage of planned shopping malls is that individual retailers don't have to worry about their external environment. The mall's management takes care of maintenance of common areas. Mall tenants can look forward to a strong level of homogeneity with the other stores. For instance, most major malls enforce uniform hours of operation. Many malls even control the external signage used for window displays and sales.

Although planned shopping centers are an excellent site option for many retailers, they have some disadvantages. First, mall rents are higher than those of some freestanding sites and many central business districts. As a result, retailers that require large stores, such as home-improvement centers, typically seek other options. Second, some tenants may not like mall managers' control of their operations. Finally, competition within shopping centers can be intense. It may be hard for small specialty stores to compete directly with large department stores. In the past few years, some shopping centers have had a particularly hard time keeping their space rented. Retailing View 8.3 shows how they've addressed this problem.

Regional Centers   This center type provides general merchandise (a large percentage of which is apparel) and services in full depth and variety. Its main attractions are its anchors: traditional, mass merchant, or discount department stores or fashion specialty stores. A typical regional center is usually enclosed with an inward orientation of the stores connected by a common walkway, while parking surrounds the outside perimeter.

8.3

Shopping Malls Combat Vacant Space Problem with Entertainment, a Town Square Environment, and Demalling

SHOPPING MALLS ARE FACING competition from power centers, outlet centers, catalogs, the Internet, and other retail locations. Many of today's shoppers are looking for "value" alternatives to stores found in shopping malls. Also, the apparel business, which makes up a large percentage of mall tenants, has continued to be weak, causing some specialty store chains to close. The result is lots of empty space in America's shopping malls.

What are they doing about their problem? Mall owners are turning their centers into traditional town squares with lots of entertainment opportunities. They believe if they can encourage people to spend more time in the mall, people will spend more money there. The owners are renting to nontraditional mall tenants like dry cleaners, doctors' offices, and even chapels—everything that you would have found in a Town Square in the 1950s. Others are forging links to their communities by opening wellness centers, libraries, city halls, and children's play areas. Some malls view their new role as a family entertainment center.

Consider the following strategies some malls have pursued.

The new Circle Center mall in Indianapolis has no shops on the fourth floor. Instead, you can play virtual reality games like throwing "virtual" grenades at your friends wearing Space-Age wraparound goggles. If you don't want to play games, you can go to a movie, a theme restaurant, or bar.

The Town West Square Mall in Wichita, Kansas, has a services center with an auditorium where classes and workshops are held daily. The center also does a range of screenings for cholesterol and the like.

The St. Gtherese Chapel at the Bergen Mall in Paramus, New Jersey, conducts services that draw 400 people.

A more extreme approach to revitalizing a mall is known as demalling. **Demalling** usually involves demolishing a mall's small shops, scrapping its common space and food courts, enlarging the sites once occupied by department stores, and adding more entrances onto the parking lot. For example, Anaheim Plaza was one of the first enclosed malls in Orange County, California, near Disneyland. During the 1980s, it had lost most of its original glamour. Its owner bulldozed most of the mall and built in its place a string of stores, opening onto a parking lot. The new tenants include a Wal-Mart, CompUSA, The Gap's budget store Old Navy, Radio Shack, Petco, and Payless Shoes.

Source: Mitchell Pacelle, "The Aging Shopping Mall Must Either Adapt or Die," *The Wall Street Journal*, April 16, 1996, pp. B1, B16; Sharon Edelson, "Regional Malls Borrow Town Square Concept as Apparel Sales Fall," *Women's Wear Daily*, May 8, 1996, pp. 1, 8–9; and Mitchell Pacelle, "Malls Add Fun and Games to Attract Shoppers," *The Wall Street Journal*, January 23, 1996, pp. B1–B9.

Super-regional Centers   Similar to a regional center, but because of its larger size, a super-regional center has more anchors and a deeper selection of merchandise, while it draws from a larger population base. As with regional centers, the typical configuration is an enclosed mall, frequently with multilevels. Mall of America near Minneapolis, Minnesota—the largest shopping center in the United States—offers customers just about anything they could want. (See Retailing View 8.4.)

INTERNET EXERCISE   The largest mall in the world is the Mall of America in Minnesota. Go to http://www.primenet.com/~trix/mall.htm. and take a tour. Do you think retailers in the mall complement each other? Why?

Mall of America Has It All

Mall of America in Minneapolis is America's largest shopping mall—4.2 million square feet, including a seven-acre Knott's Camp Snoopy Theme Park.

THE PHILOSOPHY OF THE MALL of America in Minneapolis is appeal to all of the people all of the time. Hence the name, Mall of America. Inside the largest shopping center in the United States (surpassed in size only by the Edmonton Mall in Canada) are 4.2 million square feet, 2.5 million of which are devoted to retail space! This is equivalent to four regional shopping centers connected together. This immense real estate project sits on 78 acres of land in Bloomington, Minnesota. It houses four department stores, over 400 other shops, 45 restaurants, nine nightclubs, 14 cinema screens, 12,750 on-site parking spaces, a roller coaster, a seven-acre

Knott's Camp Snoopy theme park, Lego city, and a synthetic rain forest. What makes this mall unique besides its size is that it has four themed "streets" to connect the anchor stores: Sears, Nordstrom, Macy's, and Bloomingdale's. What may be most interesting is the combination of upscale and off-price retailers in the tenant mix, which is designed to provide one-stop shopping for consumers with various sizes of pocketbooks.

Source: "Consolidate or Bust," *The Economist,* March 4, 1995, p. 11; Debra Hazel, "At Long Last, The Megamall," *Chain Store Age Executive,* September 1992, pp. 53–55; and Paul Doocey, "Mall of America Fallout," *Stores,* May 1993, pp. 44–47.

Fashion/Specialty Centers   A fashion/specialty center is composed mainly of upscale apparel shops, boutiques, and gift shops carrying selected fashion or unique merchandise of high quality and price. These centers need not be anchored, although sometimes gourmet restaurants, drinking establishments, and theaters can function as anchors. The physical design of these centers is very sophisticated, emphasizing a rich decor and high-quality landscaping.

Anaheim Plaza in Orange County, California, has gone through a demalling process. Its owner bulldozed most of the mall and built in its place a string of stores opening onto a parking lot.

Fashion/specialty centers usually are found in trade areas having high income levels, in tourist areas, or in some central business districts. These centers' large trade area may be large because of the specialty nature of the tenants and their products. Customers are more likely to travel greater distances to shop for specialty products sold at nationally known shops such as Neiman Marcus and Ralph Lauren/Polo than for other types of shopping centers.

A great example of a fashion/specialty center is the newly renovated Sommerset Collection in the wealthy Detroit, Michigan, suburb of Troy. Although the mall is over 25 years old, it has recently become the fashion focus of Michigan and Western Ontario. The owners believed that their upscale customers were traveling to trendy shops in New York and Chicago, so they expanded the mall and brought in anchor stores like Neiman Marcus, Hudson's, Nordstrom, and Saks Fifth Avenue as well as specialty shops like F.A.O. Schwarz, Crate & Barrel, and Rand McNally. Mall management offers customers a variety of services, including free valet parking and car washes, as well as complimentary beverages from a cafe in the mall.[9]

Outlet Centers Outlet centers consist mostly of manufacturers' outlet stores selling their own brands supposedly at a discount. These centers also sometimes include off-price retailers such as T.J. Maxx and Burlington Coat Factory. Similar to power centers, a strip configuration is most common, although some are enclosed malls, and others can be arranged in a "village" cluster.

Outlet centers have progressed rather quickly from no-frills warehouses to well-designed buildings with landscaping, gardens, and food courts that make them hard to distinguish from more traditional shopping centers. Outlet center tenants have also upgraded their offerings by adding credit, dressing rooms, and higher-quality fixtures and lighting. There are now more than 10,000 outlet stores in the United

States. Manufacturers have opened so many such stores that they can no longer fill them with irregulars and overruns. So outlet tenants now offer first-quality, full-line merchandise. Although outlet-mall developers typically require their tenants to cut at least 20 percent off the suggested retail price, many shoppers are finding that they can do just as well or better at the regional mall closer to home.[10]

Outlet centers are often located some distance from regional shopping centers so outlet tenants don't compete directly with department and specialty store customers. They're also located in strong tourist areas. For instance, since shopping is a favorite vacation pastime, and Niagara Falls attracts 15 million tourists per year, the 1.2 million–square-foot Factory Outlet Mega Mall in Niagara Falls, New York, is a natural location for an outlet center. Some center developers actually organize bus tours to bring people hundreds of miles to their malls. As a result, the primary trade area for some outlet centers is 50 miles or more. Finally, outlet centers are located in metropolitan markets that have no traditional regional mall competition nearby. For instance, Franklin Mills in Philadelphia is several (inconvenient) miles away from traditional regional malls.

Theme/Festival Centers These centers typically employ a unifying theme that is carried out by the individual shops in their architectural design and, to an extent, in their merchandise. The biggest appeal of these centers is to tourists. These centers typically contain tenants similar to those in the specialty centers, except that there are usually no large specialty stores or department stores. They can be anchored by restaurants and entertainment facilities. Because they lack traditional anchor stores and are often perceived as being trendy, these centers are viewed by some industry experts as being risky, unstable investments.

REFACT In 1994 there were 294 outlet centers in the United States, accounting for sales of $11.4 billion, compared to just 183 centers in 1990 and sales of $6.3 billion.[11]

Laura Ashley is one of the many well-known designer/manufacturers who sell irregulars, overruns, and first-quality merchandise through their own outlet stores.

8.5

The New Shopping Experience: Entertainment or Reality?

HOW FAR CAN SHOPPING CENTER developers reach into the entertainment arena? At what point will the two meet? Welcome to CityWalk. This new entertainment and shopping promenade developed by MCA is 20 miles east of Los Angeles in the San Fernando Valley.

The developers designed a promenade that has the feel of a problem-free Los Angeles. Besides the faux Venice Beach, it has the billboards and neon of Sunset Boulevard, the neo-Mexican facades of Olivera Street, and the chic shops of Melrose Avenue—all without the hassles of interfacing with crime, homelessness, and traffic. This is the classic G-rated shopping promenade.

MCA expects locals to make up the largest group of visitors, but it's also counting on tourists to support this $100 million project. MCA specifically located it next to one of the country's highest-grossing cinemas and conveniently close to Universal Studios. Besides the retailing environment, CityWalk sports a ShowMotion Theatre in which Showscan Corp. features a "motion-simulated ride-film" similar to Disneyland's Star Tours. Simulated visual entertainment isn't the only art here. The Museum of Neon Art has relocated its headquarters to CityWalk from downtown Los Angeles. UCLA has also set up an extension center where adults can take night classes. There's also what MCA calls a "futuristic electronics pavilion" created by Steven Spielberg.

This new venture into the realm of a total shopping/entertainment experience will be closely studied by many developers. Will this be the sanitized shopping experience of the future or will it be labeled "only in L.A."?

Source: Thomas R. King, "Mall Replicates a Sanitized Los Angeles," *The Wall Street Journal*, May 10, 1993, pp. B1, B6.

A theme/festival center can be located in a place of historical interest such as Faneuil Hall in Boston or Ghirardelli Square in San Francisco. Alternatively, they can attempt to replicate a historical place (such as the Old Mill Center in Mountain View, California) or create a unique shopping environment (like MCA's CityWalk in Los Angeles, described in Retailing View 8.5).

Other Retail Location Opportunities

Although most retailers locate in strip centers or planned shopping malls, a frequent option for large retailers is a freestanding site. Carts, kiosks, RMUs (retail merchandising units), and tall wall units are location alternatives within malls that have become popular. Mixed-use developments are also examined in this section.

Freestanding Sites   A **freestanding site** is a retail location that's not connected to other retailers, although many are located adjacent to malls. Retailers with large space requirements, such as warehouse clubs and hypermarkets, are often freestanding. Category killers such as Toys "R" Us also utilize freestanding sites. Advantages of freestanding locations are lower rents, ample parking, no direct competition, as well as fewer restrictions on signs, hours, or merchandise (which might be imposed in a shopping center). The most serious disadvantage is the lack of synergy with other stores. A retailer in a freestanding location must be a primary destination point for customers. It must offer customers something special in merchandise, price, promotion, or services to get them into the store.

Carts, Kiosks, RMUs, and Tall Wall Units   Carts, kiosks, retail merchandising units, and tall wall units are selling spaces typically found in mall common areas.[13] A **cart** offers the simplest presentation, is mobile, and is often on wheels. A **kiosk** is larger than a cart, is stationary, and has many conveniences of a store such as

REFACT The Wal-Mart Store in the U.S.-Mexican border town of Laredo, Texas, is one of the chain's largest conventional discount stores. At 151,915 square feet, it's almost the size of three football fields. It employs 350 associates who staff 36 departments including a photo-finishing lab, auto oil-and-lube center, pharmacy, and currency exchange.[12]

movable shelves, telephone, and electricity. **Retail merchandising units (RMUs)** are a relatively new and sophisticated location alternative offering the compactness and mobility of a cart, but the more sophisticated features of a kiosk. For instance, they can be locked or enclosed, so they can serve as a display when closed for business. Finally, the newest innovation, **tall wall units,** are six-to-seven–foot selling spaces placed against a wall instead of in the middle of an aisle.

These selling spaces are typically between 40 and 500 square feet, and can be in prime mall locations. They're relatively inexpensive compared to a regular store. For instance, a cart called The Sportsman's Wife at Mall of America was started with $15,000 ($10,000 of which was for inventory). They usually have short-term leases, shielding tenants from the liability of having to pay long-term rent in case the business fails. Of course, vendors also can be evicted on little notice. These alternatives to regular stores are often a great way for small retailers to begin or expand.

Mall operators see these alternative selling spaces as an opportunity to generate rental income in otherwise vacant space. They also can generate excitement leading to additional sales for the entire mall. For instance, Woodbridge Center in Woodbridge, New Jersey, typically has several carts selling ethnic merchandise such as clothing and art made by Africans and Native Americans. Mall operators must be sensitive to their regular mall tenants' needs, however. These selling units can block a store, be incompatible with its image, or actually compete with similar merchandise.

Mixed-Use Developments (MXDs)   Mixed-use developments (MXDs) combine several different uses in one complex, including shopping centers, office towers, hotels, residential complexes, civic centers, and convention centers. MXDs are popular with retailers because they bring additional shoppers to their stores. Developers like MXDs because they use space productively. For instance, land costs the same whether a developer builds a shopping mall by itself or builds an office tower over the mall or parking structure.

A good example of an MXD is found in Seattle's central business district. Metropolitan Plaza is an eight-acre pocket of luxury stores and restaurants. The developers have created a special human feeling by concentrating on small things like wide sidewalks, generous display windows, plush carpeting in interior hallways, and an open arcade that welcomes people the way an Italian courtyard offers a visual invitation to leave the intensity of the street. The retail offering focuses on owner-operated stores rather than on franchised chains.

LOCATION AND RETAIL STRATEGY

Now that we've examined the types of locations available to retailers, let's see why some retailers choose the locations they do. Exhibit 8–2 reviews relative advantages of the major retail locations. In this section, we'll examine the location strategies of department stores, specialty apparel stores, category specialists, grocery stores, and an independent optical boutique.

Department Stores

Department stores, like those owned by May Department Stores Company (Foley's) or Federated Department Stores (Bloomingdale's) are usually located in central business districts and regional or super-regional shopping centers. Department stores have historically been the backbone of CBDs. Since the 1950s, they have become the anchors for most regional and super-regional shopping centers.

EXHIBIT 8–2

Relative Advantages
of Major Retail
Locations

LOCATION ISSUES	CBD	NEIGHBORHOOD CBD	STRIP CENTER	SHOPPING MALL	FREESTANDING
Large size draws people to area	+	–	–	+	–
People working/living in area provided source of customers	+	+	+	–	–
Source of entertainment/recreation	?	–	–	+	
Protection against weather	–	–	–	+	–
Security	–	–	–	+	–
Long, uniform hours of operation	–	–	+	+	+
Planned shopping area/balanced tenant mix	–	–	–	+	–
Parking	–	–	+	?	+
Occupancy costs (e.g., rent)	?	+	+	–	+
Pedestrian traffic	+	+	–	+	–
Landlord control	+	+	+		+
Strong competition	+	+	+	–	+
Tax incentives	?	?	?	?	?

CBDs and shopping centers are a natural location for department stores. These locations draw a large number of people due to their large size and merchandise selection. Of course, the department stores create their own traffic for the CBD or mall. CBDs have the advantage of having potential customers working in the area. Most malls and some CBDs are a source of entertainment and recreation. Some cities in the United States and around the world have CBDs where residents can enjoy a leisurely stroll. In Italy, for instance, it is customary to take a walk through the shopping district every night before dinner between 6 and 8 P.M. As we noted earlier, malls have become America's Main Street where people gather, walk, and simply hang out.

It is not difficult to understand why the regional and super-regional shopping centers are the location of choice for department stores. Since they're enclosed, they protect shoppers against the weather. Most people would rather stroll around the climate-controlled malls during Minnesota's winters than venture out to the CBDs. Malls also afford customers the feeling of a secure environment. Department stores appreciate malls' uniform and long hours of operation. Also, better malls design their tenant mix so that stores appealing to certain target markets are located together. For instance, upscale specialty stores will tend to be clustered near Neiman Marcus or Nordstrom, while more moderately priced stores will be near Sears.

Specialty Apparel Stores   Specialty apparel stores like The Limited or The Gap thrive in central business districts, neighborhood CBDs, and most types of malls including regional and super-regional shopping centers, fashion/specialty centers, and theme/festival centers. These locational venues appeal to these specialty stores

Specialty stores like The Limited thrive in central business districts and other locations with similar merchandise because their customers often go from store to store comparing merchandise.

for the same reasons that they are popular with department stores. These locations are all capable of drawing large numbers of people, and provide entertainment and recreational opportunities for their customers. Shopping centers also provide protection against weather, security, uniform and long hours of operation, and a balanced tenant mix that is consistent with their target market.

Specialty apparel stores carry **shopping goods**—products for which consumers spend time comparing alternatives. It's not uncommon, for instance, for a woman to go from The Limited to The Gap and on to other apparel stores during one shopping trip. Malls and to some extent CBDs facilitate this type of shopping behavior by having several stores with the same types of merchandise so that customers can compare across stores.

Category Specialists   Category specialists like Home Depot, Sports Authority, and Toys "R" Us are likely to be found in power centers or in freestanding locations. Category specialists have different locational needs than department stores or specialty apparel stores. Category specialists choose power centers or freestanding locations for several reasons. First, these stores typically compete on price, and these locations cost less than CBDs or malls. Second, easy access to parking is important to customers of category specialists since purchases are often

Retailers like Toys "R" Us use freestanding sites because rents are lower, there is ample parking, and there is no direct competition. Also, there are fewer restrictions on signs, hours, or merchandise.

large and difficult to carry. Finally, category specialists are destination stores. A **destination store** is one in which the merchandise, selection, presentation, pricing, or other unique features act as a magnet for customers. As such, it is not as important for these stores to be located adjacent to stores selling similar merchandise or in areas that have a natural customer draw. People in the market for a kitchen faucet or a child's birthday present will seek out Home Depot or Toys "R" Us, irrespective of the store's location.

Grocery Stores

Grocery stores are typically located in neighborhood strip centers. Like category specialists, grocery stores are price competitive, and neighborhood strip centers have relatively inexpensive rent. These centers' readily accessible parking is also important to grocery store customers. People generally aren't willing to travel long distances to shop for groceries. Grocery stores carry **convenience goods**—products consumers aren't willing to spend effort to evaluate prior to purchase, such as milk and bread. The location success factor that's critical to stores carrying convenience goods is being readily accessible to customers. Neighborhood strip centers meet these criteria.

Wholesale clubs, like Sam's Wholesale Club and Price/Costco, are stores that carry food, but aren't located in neighborhood strip centers. Like other category specialists, these stores are very price competitive. Their customers are willing to give up some of the convenience of shopping at their neighborhood grocery store for lower prices.

Optical Boutique

Let's examine the location options for Mr. I's Optical Boutique, a South Miami, Florida , store specializing in upper-end high-fashion eyewear. Mr. I's has chosen a neighborhood CBD (NCBD). Although this NCBD does not draw from a trade area as large as a CBD or a shopping center, it serves the people working and living in the area.

 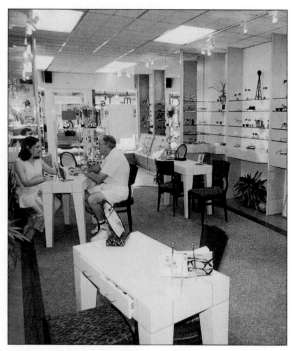

Mr. I's Optical Boutique, a store in a South Miami, Florida neighborhood, specializes in upper-end, high-fashion eyewear.

The retailers in this NCBD recognize that their location lacks the entertainment and recreation found in shopping centers, so they sponsor art and music festivals to bring people to the area. On Halloween, each store provides candy to its future customers and their parents.

Mr. I's recognizes other issues that make the South Miami CBD less than perfect. There's no protection against the heavy rains that characterize this subtropical climate. Security also could be an issue, but most stores are closed at night (when most of their customers have the time to shop). Although most of the stores cater to upscale customers living in surrounding neighborhoods, the tenant mix isn't always balanced. For instance, Mr. I's shares its block with a secondhand clothing store and an inexpensive diner. Finally, parking is often a problem.

In general, though, Mr. I's finds this neighborhood CBD attractive. The rent is much less expensive than it would be in a shopping mall. There is usually good pedestrian traffic. Since the properties in the NCBD are owned by several individuals, the landlords have less control over the tenants than they would in a shopping mall. Finally, although there are other optical stores in the area, the competition is not intense due to the exclusive lines Mr. I's carries.

SITE EVALUATION

We've seen that certain types of stores will be more successful in specific types of locations—Mr. I's Optical Boutique in a neighborhood central business district, for example. Now let's look at the issues that make a particular site attractive. Specifically, we'll examine the site's accessibility, locational advantages within the center, terms of occupancy, and legal considerations.

Accessibility

The accessibility of a site is the ease with which a customer may get into and out of it. The accessibility analysis has two stages: a macro analysis and then a micro analysis.

The macro analysis considers the primary trade area, such as the area two to three miles around the site in the case of a supermarket or drugstore. To assess a site's accessibility on a macro level, the retailer simultaneously evaluates several factors, such as road patterns, road conditions, and barriers.

In the macro analysis, the analyst should consider the road pattern. The primary trade area needs major arteries or freeways so customers can travel easily to the site. A related factor is the road condition (including the age, number of lanes, number of stoplights, congestion, and general state of repair of roads in the primary trade area). For instance, a location on an old, narrow, congested secondary road in disrepair with too many stoplights wouldn't be a particularly good site for a retail store.

Natural barriers (such as rivers or mountains) and artificial barriers (such as railroad tracks, major highways, or parks) may also impact accessibility. These barriers' impact on a particular site primarily depends on whether the merchandise or services are available on both sides of the barrier. If, for instance, only one supermarket serves both sides of a highway, people on the opposite side must cross to shop.

The micro analysis concentrates on issues in the immediate vicinity of the site such as visibility, traffic flow, parking, congestion, and ingress/egress.

Visibility refers to customers' ability to see the store and enter the parking lot safely. Good visibility is less important for stores with established and loyal customers and for stores with limited market areas because customers know where the store is. Nonetheless, large national retailers like Kmart insist that there be no impediments to a direct, undisturbed view of their store. In an area with a highly transient population (such as a tourist center or large city), good visibility from the road is particularly important.

The success of a site with a good traffic flow is a question of balance. The site should have a substantial number of cars per day but not so many that congestion impedes access to the store. To assess the level of vehicular traffic, you can usually obtain data from the regional planning commission, county engineer, or state highway department. But you may have to adjust these data for special situations. As a result, it's sometimes easier and more accurate to do the analysis in-house. For instance, the analyst must consider that the presence of large places of employment, schools, or large trucks may lessen a site's desirability. Also, areas congested during rush hours may have a good traffic flow during the rest of the day when most shopping takes place. Finally, some retailers might wish to adjust the raw traffic counts by excluding out-of-state license plates or counting only homeward-bound traffic.

The amount and quality of parking facilities are critical to a shopping center's overall accessibility. If there aren't enough spaces or if they're too far from the stores, customers will be discouraged from entering the area. On the other hand, if there are too many open spaces, the shopping center may be seen as a failure or as having unpopular stores. It's hard to assess how many parking spaces are enough, although location analysts use parking ratios as a starting point. A standard rule of thumb is 5:1, (five spaces per thousand square feet of gross leasable area).[14] Nevertheless, there's no good substitute for observing the shopping center at various times of the day, week, and season. You must also assess the availability of employee parking, the proportion of shoppers using cars, parking by nonshoppers, and the typical length of a shopping trip. One retailer examines outlying parking spaces for engine grease. If there's a lot of grease, he assumes that the parking lot is often filled and therefore the site is successful.

An issue that's closely related to the amount of available parking facilities, but extends into the shopping center itself is the relative congestion of the area. Congestion can refer to the amount of crowding of either cars or people. There's some optimal range of comfortable congestion for customers. Too much congestion can make shopping slow, irritate customers, and generally discourage sales. On the other hand, a relatively high level of activity in a shopping center creates excitement and can stimulate sales.[15]

The last factor to consider in the accessibility analysis is ingress/egress—the ease of entering and exiting the site's parking lot. Often, medians or one-way streets make entering or exiting difficult from one or more directions, limiting accessibility.

Locational Advantages within a Center

Once the center's accessibility is evaluated, you must evaluate the locations within it. Since the better locations cost more, retailers must consider their importance. For instance, in a neighborhood shopping center, the more expensive locations are closest to the supermarket. A liquor store or a flower shop that may attract impulse buyers should thus be close to the supermarket. But a destination store, such as a shoe repair store (which shouldn't expect impulse customers) could be in an inferior location because customers in need of this service will seek out the store.

The same arguments hold for regional multilevel shopping centers. It's advantageous for shopping goods stores like The Limited or Ann Taylor to be clustered in the more expensive locations near a department store in a mall. Women shopping for clothing may start at the department store and naturally gravitate to stores near it. Yet stores such as Foot Locker—another destination store—needn't be in the most expensive location, since many of its customers know they're in the market for this type of product before they even get to the center.

Another consideration is to locate stores that appeal to similar target markets close together. In essence, customers want to shop where they'll find a good assortment of merchandise. This is based on the principle of **cumulative attraction** in which a cluster of similar and complementary retailing activities will generally have greater drawing power than isolated stores that engage in the same retailing activities. This is why antique shops, car dealers, and shoe and clothing stores all seem to do better if they're close to one another. Of course, an area can become overstored when it has too many competing stores to profitably satisfy demand.

The principle of cumulative attraction applies to both stores that sell complementary merchandise and those that compete directly with one another. Consider Exhibit 8–3's map of Dallas's North Park Center. The more fashion-forward, higher-income customers will find stores like Alfred Dunhill of London and other exclusive boutiques between Neiman Marcus and Lord & Taylor. Some stores sell exactly the same merchandise categories, while others sell complementary products, such as perfumes in one store and lingerie in another. A similarly healthy tenant mix is found in the more moderately priced wing between Dillard's and JCPenney. Customers can buy shoes at Penney or a Kinney Shoe store. At the same time they can find a gift at Dillard's and a card at Bolen's Hallmark Shop. Thus a good location is one whose tenant mix provides (1) a good selection of merchandise that competes with itself and (2) complementary merchandise.

Terms of Occupancy

Once a particular site is chosen, retailers still face a multitude of decisions, including types of leases and terms of the lease.

Types of Leases   Most retailers lease store sites. Although there are advantages to owning a store site (such as stable mortgage payments and freedom from lease covenants), most retailers don't wish to tie up their capital by owning real estate. Also, most of the best locations—such as in shopping malls—are only available by leasing.

There are two basic types of leases: a percentage and a fixed-rate lease. Although there are many combinations within each type, the most common form is a **percentage lease,** in which rent is based on a percentage of sales. Most malls use some form of percentage lease. Since retail leases typically run from 5 to 10 years, it appears to be equitable to both parties if rents go up (or down) with sales and inflation.

A **percentage lease with specified maximum** is a lease that pays the lessor, or landlord, a percentage of sales up to a maximum amount. This type of lease rewards good retailer performance by allowing the retailer to minimize rent above a certain level of sales. A similar variation, the **percentage lease with specified minimum,** specifies that the retailer must pay a minimum rent no matter how low sales are.

Another type of percentage lease uses a **sliding scale** in which the percentage of sales paid as rent decreases as sales go up. For instance, a retailer may pay 4 percent on the first $200,000 in sales, and 3 percent on sales greater than $200,000.

EXHIBIT 8–3

Map of Dallas's
North Park Center

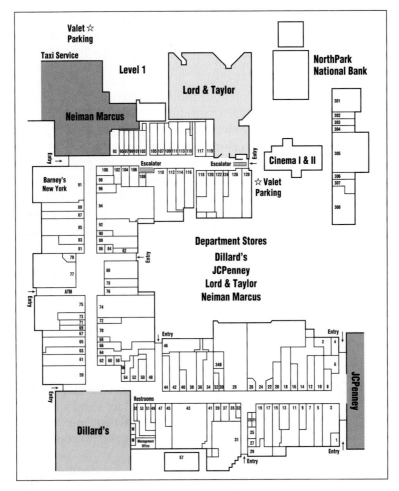

Like the percentage lease with specified maximum, the sliding scale rewards high-performing retailers.

The second basic type of lease is a **fixed-rate lease.** These leases are more commonly used by community and neighborhood centers. Here a retailer pays a fixed amount per month over the life of the lease. With a fixed-rate lease the retailer and landlord know exactly how much will be paid in rent, but, as noted earlier, this type doesn't appear to be as popular as the various forms of percentage leases.

A variation of the fixed-rate lease is the **graduated lease.** Here rent increases by a fixed amount over a specified period of time. For instance, rent may be $1,000 per month for the first three years and $1,250 for the next five years.

A **maintenance-increase-recoupment lease** can be used with either a percentage or fixed-rate lease. This type of lease allows the landlord to increase the rent if insurance, property taxes, or utility bills increase beyond a certain point.

Finally, a **net lease** is a popular form of leasing arrangement. In a net lease, the retailer is responsible for all maintenance and utilities. Thus the landlord is freed from these responsibilities. A net lease can also be used with either a fixed-rate or percentage lease.

REFACT The Port Authority of New York and New Jersey, developer of New York City's World Trade Center office/hotel/retail complex, requires all of its 70 stores to open at 7:30 A.M. on weekday mornings to serve office workers and commuters on their way to work.[16]

Terms of the Lease   Although leases are formal contracts, they can be changed to reflect the relative power and specific needs of the retailer.[17] Recognize that since most leases' basic format is developed by the **lessor** (the property's owner), the lease's terms may be slanted in favor of the lessor. It's up to the **lessee** (the party signing the lease, in this case the retailer) to be certain that the lease reflects the lessee's needs. Let's look at some clauses retailers may wish to include in a lease.

A **prohibited use clause** limits the landlord from leasing to certain kinds of tenants. Many retailers don't want the landlord to lease space to establishments that take up parking spaces and don't bring in shoppers—for example, a bowling alley, skating rink, theater, meeting hall, dentist, or real estate office. Retailers may also wish to restrict the use of space to those establishments that could harm the shopping center's wholesome image. Prohibited use clauses often specify that bars, pool halls, game parlors, off-track betting establishments, massage parlors, and pornography retailers are unacceptable.

An **exclusive use clause** prohibits the landlord from leasing to retailers selling competing products. For example, a discount store's lease may specify that the landlord can't lease to other discount stores, variety stores, dollar stores, or discount clothing outlet stores.

Some retailers are particular about how the storefront appears. For instance, a women's specialty store may specify that the storefront must have floor-to-ceiling glass to maximize window displays to improve customers' ability to see into the store. Other retailers believe it's important that nothing block the view of the store from the street, so they specify that the landlord can't place any outparcels in the parking lot. An **outparcel** is a building (like a bank or McDonald's) or kiosk (like an automatic teller machine) in the parking lot of a shopping center, but not physically attached to the shopping center.

It's crucial to some retailers that they be in shopping centers with specific types of tenants. For instance, a chain of moderately priced women's apparel shops benefits from the traffic flow of Kmart and Wal-Mart stores. It therefore specifies in its leases that if the major retailer leaves the shopping center, it has the option of canceling its lease or paying a reduced rent.

An interesting feature that any retailer would want to have in a lease, if it could get away with it, is an **escape clause.** An escape clause allows the retailer to terminate its lease if sales don't reach a certain level after a specified number of years, or if a specific co-tenant in the center terminates its lease.

Finally, retailers must attempt to protect themselves from legal actions by citizens or government agencies that result from a landlord's action or inaction. Clauses may be inserted into leases that protect retailers from these legal problems. The next section looks at some of these legal issues.

Legal Considerations

Laws regarding how land is used have become so important that they should be a retailer's first consideration in a site search. Legal issues that affect the site decision include environmental issues, zoning, building codes, signs, and licensing requirements.

Environmental Issues   The Environmental Protection Agency plus state and local agencies have become increasingly involved with issues that could affect retail stores.[18] Two environmental issues have received particular attention in recent years. First is "above-ground risks" such as asbestos-containing materials or lead pipes used in construction. These materials can be removed relatively easily.

The second issue is hazardous materials that have been stored in the ground. This can be particularly important for a dry cleaner because of the chemicals used, or an auto repair shop because of disposal of used motor oil and battery fluid. The costs of cleaning up hazardous materials can range from $10,000 to over $6 million.

Real estate transactions almost always require an environmental impact statement on the property. But relying on past public filings of buried tanks and other potential hazards can be unreliable and not a protection in court. Retailers have two remedies to protect themselves from these environmental hazards. The best option is to stipulate in the lease that the lessor is responsible for removal and disposal of this material if it's found. Alternatively, the retailer can buy insurance that specifically protects it from these risks.

Zoning and Building Codes   Zoning determines how a particular site can be used. For instance, some parts of a city are zoned for residential use only; others are zoned for light industrial and retail use. Building codes are similar legal restrictions determining the type of building, signs, size and type of parking lot, and so forth that can be used at a particular location. Some building codes require a certain size parking lot or architectural design. In Santa Fe, New Mexico, for instance, building codes require buildings to keep the traditional mud stucco (adobe) style.

Signs   Restrictions on the use of signs can also impact a particular site's desirability. Size and style may be restricted by building codes, zoning ordinances, or even the shopping center management. At the Bal Harbour Shops in North Miami Beach, for example, all signs (even sale signs) must be approved by the shopping center management.

Licensing Requirements   Licensing requirements may vary in different parts of a region. For instance, some Dallas neighborhoods are dry, meaning no alcoholic beverages can be sold; in other areas, only wine and beer can be sold. Such restrictions can affect retailers other than restaurants and bars. For instance, a theme/festival shopping center that restricts the use of alcoholic beverages may have limited clientele at night.

Legal issues such as those mentioned here can discourage a retailer from pursuing a particular site. These restrictions aren't always permanent, however. Although difficult, time-consuming, and possibly expensive, lobbying efforts and court battles can change these legal restrictions.

SUMMARY

Decisions about where to locate a store are critical to any retailer's success. A clear, coherent strategy should specify location goals. A location decision is particularly important because of its high cost and long-term commitment. A location mistake is clearly more devastating to a retailer than a buying mistake, for instance.

Retailers have a plethora of types of sites to choose from. Many central business districts have become a more viable option than in the past due to gentrification of the area and lack of suburban mall opportunities. Retailers also have many types of shopping centers from which to choose. They can locate in a neighborhood, community, or power strip center, or they can go into a mall. We examined the relative advantages of several types of malls including regional and superregional centers, fashion/specialty centers, theme/festival centers, and outlet centers. We also examined the viability of freestanding sites, carts, kiosks, RMUs, tall wall units, and mixed-use developments.

Retailers have a hard time finding a perfect site. Each site has its own set of advantages and disadvantages. In assessing the viability of a particular site, a retailer must make sure the store's target markets will patronize that location. They must also consider the location's accessibility as well as locational advantages within the center. The location analyst's job isn't finished until terms of occupancy and other legal issues are considered.

Chapter 9 continues the discussion of how to locate a retail store by examining the issues used to determine which region and trade areas are best and how to obtain and analyze data for making these decisions.

KEY TERMS

cart, *242*

central business district (CBD), *231*

convenience goods, *246*

cumulative attraction, *249*

demalling, *238*

destination store, *246*

escape clause, *251*

exclusive use clause, *251*

fixed-rate lease, *250*

freestanding site, *242*

gentrification, *231*

graduated lease, *250*

kiosk, *242*

lessee, *251*

lessor, *251*

maintenance-increase-recoupment lease, *250*

mall, *232*

mixed-use development (MXD), *243*

neighborhood CBD, *232*

net lease, *250*

outparcel, *251*

percentage lease, *249*

percentage lease with specified maximum, *249*

percentage lease with specified minimum, *249*

prohibited use clause, *251*

retail merchandising unit (RMU), *243*

shopping center, *232*

shopping goods, *245*

sliding scale, *249*

strip center, *232*

tall wall unit, *243*

trade area, *230*

DISCUSSION QUESTIONS & PROBLEMS

1. Why have location decisions become more important in recent years?

2. There are many types of selling spaces besides a standard enclosed "store design." What are the advantages and disadvantages of each? What types of merchandise would benefit from each of these alternative types of selling spaces?

3. Home Depot, a rapidly growing chain of large home-improvement centers, typically locates in either a power center or a freestanding site. What are the strengths of each location for a store like Home Depot?

4. What are the advantages and disadvantages of a retailer's leasing space in a shopping center in an area with extensive zoning restrictions?

5. Retailers have a tradition of developing shopping centers and freestanding locations. These stores are often located in neighborhoods or central business districts that have suffered decay. Some people have questioned the ethical and social ramifications of this process, which is known as gentrification. What are the benefits and problems associated with gentrification?

6. What is the best location option for a Tommy Hilfiger outlet store? Justify your answer.

7. In many malls, fast-food retailers are frequently located together in an area known as a food court. What are this arrangement's advantages and disadvantages to the fast-food retailer?

8. Some specialty stores prefer to locate next to or close to an anchor store. But Little Caesar's, a take-out pizza retailer typically found in strip centers, wants to be at the end of the center away from the supermarket anchor. Why?

9. Retailers have a choice of locating on a mall's main floor or second or third level. Typically, the main floor offers the best, but most expensive locations. Why would specialty stores such as Radio Shack and Foot Locker choose the second or third floor?

10. Why would a Payless ShoeSource store locate in a neighborhood shopping center instead of a regional shopping mall?

SUGGESTED READINGS

Burns, David J. "Image Transference and Retail Site Selection." *International Journal of Retail & Distribution Management* 20, no. 5 (September 1992), pp. 38–47.

Cohen, Eric. "Miles, Minutes, & Custom Markets." *Marketing Tools*, July-August 1995, pp. 16–21.

Davies, R. L., and D. S. Rogers, eds. *Store Location and Store Assessment Research.* New York: John Wiley & Sons, 1984.

Drezner, Tammy. "Optimal Continuous Location of a Retail Facility, Facility Attractiveness, and Market Share: An Interactive Model." *Journal of Retailing* 70 (Spring 1994), pp. 49–64.

Finn, Adam, and Jordan Louviere. "Shopping-Center Patronage Models: Fashioning a Consideration Set Segmentation Solution." *Journal of Business Research*, November 1990, pp. 259–75.

Ghosh, Avijit, and Sara L. McLafferty. *Location Strategies for Retail and Service Firms.* Lexington, MA: D.C. Heath, 1987.

Ghosh, Avijit, and Sara McLafferty. "The Shopping Center: A Restructuring of Post-War Retailing." *Journal of Retailing* 67 (Fall 1991), pp. 253–67.

ICSC Research Quarterly. New York: International Council of Shopping Centers.

Tayman, Jeff, and Louis Pol. "Retail Site Selection and Geographic Information Systems." *Journal of Applied Business Research* 11, no. 2 (Spring 1995), pp. 46–54.

Thompson, John S. *Site Selection.* New York: Lebhar-Friedman, 1982.

NOTES

1. Mark Kingdom, "Consumer Enhancement & Development," *Chain Store Age*, January 1996, section 3, p. 5.

2. Personal communication, John Konarski III, Ph.D., director of research, International Council of Shopping Centers, September 1996.

3. Debra Hazel, "Cityscape Retail: The Last Frontier?" *Chain Store Age Executive*, September 1994, pp. 21–28.

4. This section draws from *The ICSC Research Quarterly* no. 1 (1994).

5. The definitions and exhibit are meant to be guidelines for understanding major differences between the basic types of shopping centers. They are not meant to encompass the operating characteristics of every center.

6. John Fleischman, "In Classic Athens, a Market Trading in Currency of Ideas," *Smithsonian* 24 (July 1993), pp. 38–47.

7. "The Scope of the Shopping Center Industry in the United States, 1996," International Council of Shopping Centers, p. 2.

8. John McCloud, "Power Center Development Explodes across U.S.," *Shopping Center World*, August 1994, pp. 34–41.

9. Heidi Gralla, "Turning a Mall into an Intimate 'Collection,'" *Shopping Centers Today*, December 1992, pp. 7, 10.

10. Christina Duff, "Brighter Lights, Fewer Bargains: Outlets Go Upscale," *The Wall Street Journal*, April 11, 1994, p. B1.

11. Ira Apfel, "What Is an Outlet Center," *American Demographics*, July 1996, pp. 14–15.

12. Richard Gibson, "Location, Luck, Service Can Make a Store Top Star," *The Wall Street Journal*, February 1, 1993, p. B1.

13. This section uses information in Joseph Weishar, "Temporary Tenants: Cars, Kiosks, RMUs and In-Lines," *Visual Merchandising and Store Design*, December 1992, pp. 34–35; Barbara Marsh, "Kiosks and Carts Can Often Serve as Wall Magnets," *The Wall Street Journal*, November 23, 1992, pp. B1–B2; and "Specialty Carts Mix It Up Ethnically," *Chain Store Age Executive*, November 1992, pp. 56–57.

14. Personal communication, Kenard E. Smith, Ph.D, vice president—Area Research, The May Department Stores Company, July 1996.

15. Sevgin Eroglu and Gilbert D. Harrell, "Retail Crowding: Theoretical and Strategic Implications," *Journal of Retailing* 62 (Winter 1986), pp. 346–63.

16. "Early Bird Special in NYC," *Chain Store Age Executive*, June 1991, pp. 31–32.

17. Corporate sources, The Ben Tobin Companies.

18. Lisa Holton, "Policies Protect Tenants, Developers from Unseen Environmental Risks," *Stores*, February 1996, p. 64.

Site Selection

THE WORLD OF RETAILING

RETAILING STRATEGY
6. Retail Market Strategy
7. Financial Strategy
8. Retail Locations
9. Site Selection
10. Organization Structure and Human Resource Management
11. Integrated Retail Logistics and Information Systems

MERCHANDISE MANAGEMENT

STORE MANAGEMENT

QUESTIONS

- What issues should be considered when determining in which region or market area to locate a store?

- What is a trade area, and why should a retailer choose one over another?

- How should retailers define their current trade areas and the trade areas for new stores?

- How can retailers forecast sales for new store locations?

CHAPTER 8 EXAMINED DIFFERENT TYPES of locations available to retailers and factors retailers should consider when deciding on a particular site. In this chapter, we look at the issues retailers use to select a region, market area, and trade area for their stores. Then we explore retailers' methods for predicting sales for a particular location. To assess a location's sales potential, retailers must answer two questions. First, what is or will be the demand for a store's merchandise based on the potential customer base? Retailers seek locations that maximize demand for their products. However, if the area is overstored because too many stores are selling competing products, then the value of any particular location is small. Thus, the second question is, how strong is the supply of competitive stores in the area? Exhibit 9–1 outlines the decisions to be made when choosing a region and market area and evaluating a trade area.

LOCATION DECISIONS

Exhibit 9–2 breaks the location decision into three levels: region, trade area, and specific site. The decisions affecting the specific site, such as type of location and the attractiveness of a specific location, were discussed in Chapter 8. The **region** refers to the part of the country, a particular city, or Metropolitan Statistical Area (MSA). An **MSA** is a city with 50,000 or more inhabitants or an urbanized area of at least 50,000 inhabitants and a total MSA population of at least 100,000 (75,000 in

EXHIBIT 9–1

Retail Location
Decision-Making
Process

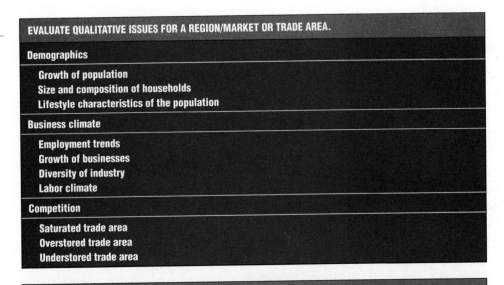

EVALUATE QUALITATIVE ISSUES FOR A REGION/MARKET OR TRADE AREA.

Demographics

Growth of population
Size and composition of households
Lifestyle characteristics of the population

Business climate

Employment trends
Growth of businesses
Diversity of industry
Labor climate

Competition

Saturated trade area
Overstored trade area
Understored trade area

ESTIMATE SALES FOR A SPECIFIC LOCATION.

Estimate demand for merchandise sold in store.
Estimate level of competition in trade area.

New England). A **trade area** is a contiguous geographic area that accounts for the majority of a store's sales and customers. A trade area may be part of a city, or it can extend beyond the city's boundaries, depending on the type of store and the density of potential customers surrounding it. For instance, a video rental store's trade area may be only a few city blocks within a major metropolitan area. On the other hand, a Wal-Mart store's trade area in the rural South may encompass 50 square miles.

In making store location decisions, retailers must examine all three levels simultaneously. For instance, suppose Taco Bell is expanding operations in the Pacific Northwest. Its research indicates that competition in the Tacoma, Washington, market is relatively weak. But maybe it can't find a suitable site in Tacoma, so it must temporarily postpone locating there.

This section examines factors that are important to retailers when choosing a region/market area and trade area.

EXHIBIT 9–2   Three Levels of Spatial Analysis

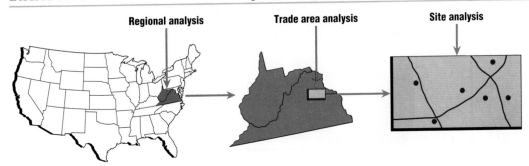

Regional analysis   Trade area analysis   Site analysis

Region/Market Area   Regardless of the general economy's state, certain regions or markets may be more attractive to some retailers than to others. It would be misleading to think that simply because a market is large or growing economically, it's attractive to all retailers. For example, a swimming pool supply store would have less potential in rural Maine than in San Diego, California. Heavily populated regions aren't always better either. Although the emphasis has shifted in recent years, Wal-Mart's early growth came from regions with small cities, not from large metropolitan markets. Although potential sales were limited in these small cities, competition was also limited.

Some retailers focus on certain geographic regions. For instance, Davenport, Iowa-based Von Maur is a regional department store chain that currently has 12 stores.[1] Although it can compete with larger, national chains on several dimensions, one of its advantages stems from its regional orientation. It can maintain a loyal customer base by remaining a regional chain. It has excellent visibility and is well known throughout the area. Second, its merchandising, pricing, and promotional strategies specifically target the needs of a regional market rather than a national market. For instance, Von Maur knows that merchandise that's popular in Davenport will also sell in Des Moines. Finally, the management team can have greater locus of control over a regional market. Managers can easily visit the stores and assess competitive situations.

Trade Area   A **trade area** is a contiguous geographic area that accounts for the majority of a store's sales and customers. Trade areas can be divided into two or three zones, as depicted by Exhibit 9–3's concentric polygons. Such trade areas are called **polygons** because their boundaries conform to streets and other map features. The zones' exact definitions should be flexible to account for particular areas' nuances. The following rules of thumb are often used.

The **primary zone** is the geographic area from which the store or shopping center derives 60 to 65 percent of its customers. This zone is usually three to five miles radius from the store, or less than a 10-minute drive from the site.

EXHIBIT 9–3

Narrowing Effect on Trade Area Caused by Major Highways and Natural Boundaries

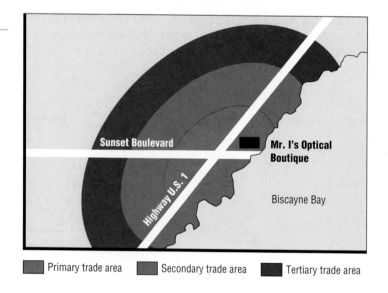

Sunset Boulevard

Highway U.S. 1

Mr. I's Optical Boutique

Biscayne Bay

☐ Primary trade area   ☐ Secondary trade area   ■ Tertiary trade area

The **secondary zone** is the geographic area of secondary importance in terms of customer sales, generating about 20 percent of a store's sales. It usually extends three to seven miles radius from the store, or is no more than a 15-to-20–minute drive from the site.

The **tertiary zone** (the outermost ring) includes customers who occasionally shop at the store or shopping center. There are several reasons for the tertiary zone. First, these customers may lack adequate retail facilities closer to home. Second, there are excellent highway systems to the store or center so customers can get there easily. Third, customers may drive near the store or center on the way to or from work. Finally, customers are drawn to the store or center because it is in or near a tourist area. The tertiary zone typically extends 15 miles in major metropolitan markets and as far as 50 miles in smaller markets.

The actual boundaries of a trade area are determined by the store's accessibility, natural and physical barriers, type of shopping area, type of store, and competition. Exhibit 9–3 illustrates the trade area for Mr. I's Optical Boutique, a store in South Miami, Florida, specializing in upper-end high-fashion eyewear. A major highway (US 1) is often difficult to cross due to heavy traffic, thus limiting the primary trade area on the west. Biscayne Bay limits the primary trade area on the east, causing the trade area to be oblong. Other barriers (such as a river, mountain range, or high-crime area) may also influence the shape and size of a trade area.

Trade area size is also influenced by the type of store or shopping area. A 7-Eleven convenience store's trade area, for example, may extend less than one mile, whereas a category specialist like Toys "R" Us may draw customers from 20 miles away. The difference is due to the nature of the merchandise sold and the total size of the assortment offered. Convenience stores succeed because customers can buy products like milk and bread quickly and easily. If customers must drive great distances, the store's no longer convenient. Category specialists offer a large choice of shopping and specialty products that customers are willing to put forth additional effort to shop for. Thus customers will generally drive some distance to shop at a category specialist. Mr. I's Optical Boutique is located in a neighborhood central business district rather than a major shopping center. Thus, its trade area is smaller than it would be if it were located in a regional shopping center.

Another way of looking at how the type of store influences the size of a trade area is whether it's a destination or a parasite store. A **destination store** is one in which the merchandise, selection, presentation, pricing, or other unique features

This flower store is a parasite store, but not because it has bugs. It is a parasite store because it does not create its own traffic. People tend to stop here on the way to and from other stores.

act as a magnet for customers. In general, destination stores have larger trade areas than parasite stores. Mr. I's Optical Boutique would qualify as a destination store due to the exclusive nature of its merchandise. A **parasite store** is one that does not create its own traffic and whose trade area is determined by the dominant retailer in the shopping center or retail area. A dry cleaner would qualify as a parasite store to a grocery store. People tend to stop at this cleaner on the way to or from the grocery and other stores. Its business is thus derived from other businesses in the area.

The level of competition also affects the size and shape of a trade area for a particular store. If two convenience food stores are too close together, their respective trade areas will shrink since they offer the same merchandise. On the other hand, Mr. I's Optical Boutique is one of several optical shops in this business district. Having similar shopping goods stores in the same vicinity generally expands the trade area boundaries; more people are drawn to the area to shop because of its expanded selection. Additionally, Mr. I's Optical Boutique's trade area is limited on the south by a large regional shopping center that has several stores carrying similar merchandise.

FACTORS AFFECTING THE ATTRACTIVENESS OF REGION/MARKET AND TRADE AREAS

The best regions and trade areas are those that generate the highest demand or sales for a retailer. Although the region or market analysis is distinct from the trade area analysis, the factors that make them attractive are the same. To assess overall demand in a particular region/market or trade area, the retail analyst considers the population's demographics and business climate as well as competition from other retailers in the area.

Demographics

In most cases, areas where the general population is growing are preferable to those with declining populations. Yet population growth alone doesn't tell the whole story. Mr. I's Optical Boutique, for example, is in a mature neighborhood with a stable population. A reason for the success of this store and similar independently owned retailers in the area is that household income in the trade area is relatively high.

Size and composition of households in an area can also be important success determinants. For instance, Ann Taylor (a chain specializing in traditional and business apparel for women) generally locates in areas with high-income households and in tourist areas; household size, however, isn't a particularly critical issue. Toys "R" Us, on the other hand, is interested in locations with heavy concentrations of families with young children.

Finally, other demographic and lifestyle characteristics of the population may be relevant, depending on the target market(s) a particular retailer is pursuing. We'll describe how retailers use these population statistics later in this chapter.

Business Climate

It's important to examine a market's employment trends because a high level of employment usually means high purchasing power. Also, it's useful to determine which areas are growing quickly and why. For instance, the east side of Seattle, Washington, has become a desirable retail location because of its proximity to Microsoft's corporate headquarters. Retail location analysts must determine how long such growth will continue and how it will affect demand for their merchandise. For instance, the economies of some rustbelt cities like Flint, Michigan, experience greater peaks and valleys due to their dependence on specific industries such as automobiles.

Employment growth in and of itself isn't enough to ensure a strong retail environment in the future. If growth isn't diversified in a number of industries, the area may suffer from adverse cyclical trends. For instance, many towns with military bases are expected to decline in population into the next millennium as the military downsizes and bases close in towns like Plattsburgh, New York, and Moreno Valley, California.

Competition   The level of competition in an area also affects demand for a retailer's merchandise. The level of competition can be defined as saturated, understored, or overstored. A **saturated trade area** offers customers a good selection of goods and services, while allowing competing retailers to make good profits. Since customers are drawn to these areas because of the great selections, retailers who believe they can offer customers a superior retail format in terms of merchandise, pricing, or service may find these areas attractive. Some restaurants such as Burger King seek locations where their major competition—McDonald's—has a strong presence. They believe that it's important to go head-to-head with their strongest competitors so that they can develop methods and systems that will allow them to successfully compete with them. They contend that locating in areas with weak competition allows them to become complacent. The strongest competitor will eventually enter the trade area. By then, however, it will have lost its competitive edge.[2]

Another strategy is to locate in an **understored trade area**—an area that has too few stores selling a specific good or service to satisfy the needs of the population. Wal-Mart's early success was based on a location strategy of opening stores in small towns that were relatively understored. Now these stores experience high market share in their towns and draw from surrounding communities.

In effect, these areas have gone from being understored before Wal-Mart arrived to being **overstored**—an area that has so many stores selling a specific good or service that some stores will fail. Unable to compete head-to-head with Wal-Mart on price or breadth of selection, many family-owned retailers in those towns have either had to reposition their merchandising and/or service strategies or else go out of business.

MEASURING DEMAND

Retailers have many sources of information available for estimating demand for new store locations so that they can understand the demographic and lifestyle characteristics of their customers. The most widely used sources of information about such characteristics are the *Decennial Census of the United States* published by the U.S. Department of Commerce, *Sales & Marketing Management's* "Buying Power Index," and materials from demographic data vendors like Urban Decision Systems. Each of these inexpensive sources is readily available to small and large retailers alike.

Decennial Census of the United States   The *Decennial Census of the United States* is the most complete source of information for making location decisions. But as the name implies, it's taken only once every 10 years so it's often out of date and requires supplementary reports and updates by government agencies and private firms. In the census, each household in the country is counted to determine the number of persons per household, household relationships, sex, race, age, and marital status. Additionally, a report on each building identifies the number of housing units at the address, the status of plumbing facilities, the number of rooms, whether the dwelling is owned or rented, whether the dwelling is owner-occupied, the housing value, the rent, and the vacancy status. Additional information is obtained for approximately one-sixth of U.S. households. A summary of census items is found in Exhibit 9–4.

EXHIBIT 9–4

Sample Information Contained in the Decennial Census of the United States

COMPLETE COUNT DATA ITEMS	
(SHOWN FOR ALL CENSUS AREAS INCLUDING CITY BLOCKS)	
POPULATION ITEMS	**HOUSING ITEMS**
Relationship to head of household	Number of units at this address
Color or race	Telephone
Age	Private entrance to living quarters
Sex	Complete kitchen facilities
Marital status	Rooms
	Water supply
	Flush toilet
	Bathtub or shower
	Basement
	Tenure (owner/renter)
	Commercial establishment on property
	Value
	Contract rent
	Vacancy status
	Months vacant
SAMPLE DATA ITEMS	
(NOT SHOWN IN SOME REPORTS)	
POPULATION ITEMS	**HOUSING ITEMS**
State or country of birth	Components of gross rent
Years of school completed	Heating equipment
Number of children ever born	Year structure built
Employment status	Number of units in structure and whether a trailer
Hours worked last week	Farm residence
Weeks worked in 1969	Source of water
Last year in which worked	Sewage disposal
Occupation, industry, and class of worker	Bathrooms
Activity five years ago	Air conditioning
Income in 1969 by type	Automobiles
Country of birth of parents	
Mother tongue	
Year moved into this house	
Place of residence five years ago	
School or college enrollment (public or private)	
Veteran status	
Place of work	
Means of transportation to work	

Source: *The Census and You*, U.S. Department of Commerce, Bureau of the Census.

The Decennial Census
of the United States *has
information on every city
block in the United States.
You can find, for instance,
the number of people per
household, household
relationships, sex, race,
age, and marital status.*

The decennial census data are available in many formats. Data can be obtained for areas as small as a city block or as large as the entire country. One of the most useful designations for regional evaluations is the Metropolitan Statistical Area (MSA). Census tracts are subdivisions of an MSA with an average population of 4,000. Because of their smaller size, they are more useful than MSAs for doing trade area or site analyses.

Census data reports and maps are available through on-line services, computer tapes, CD-ROMs, and TIGER (Topologically Integrated Geographic Encoding and Reference system). TIGER is a minutely detailed computerized map of the entire United States. When combined with a database, such as the results of the 1990 census or a company's own customer files, TIGER gives desktop computer users for the first time the cartographic equivalent of a computerized spreadsheet known as Geographic Information Systems (GIS). Software companies have written TIGER-based programs that allow small companies to create maps with demographic information on their own computers. Users can ask various "what if" questions and print out the answers in map form. Information using the TIGER system is also available from private research firms.[3]

Not only is the census taken only once a decade, but also the information is not totally published for up to three years after the census has been conducted. Fortunately, the Census Bureau does release preliminary reports in the interim. It also publishes a variety of supplementary reports that the analyst can use as an update even after the census is published. The census, supplementary reports, and maps are usually available in public libraries, from state data centers that operate in conjunction with the Census Bureau, or directly from the U.S. Government Printing Office in Washington, D.C.

Some information from the census is also available through vendors, regional planning commissions, and state, local, and county agencies.[4] Caution should be exercised when using some vendors and local sources, however, since an optimistic bias may be built into the data.

Buying Power Index Retailers often use the Buying Power Index (BPI) published annually by *Sales & Marketing Management* to forecast demand for new
stores and to evaluate the performance of existing stores. BPI measures the overall retail demand in an area expressed as a percentage of total demand in the
United States. BPI is calculated as follows:

$$BPI = .5 \times (\text{Percentage of U.S. effective buying income})$$
$$+ .3 \times (\text{Percentage of U.S. retail sales})$$
$$+ .2 \times (\text{Percentage of U.S. population})$$

For instance, the BPI for New England is calculated as follows[5]:

$$BPI = .5 \times (260,740,921 \div 4,436,178,724)$$
$$+ .3 \times (121,795,586 \div 2,241,319,080)$$
$$+ .2 \times (13,285,600 \div 282,213,300)$$
$$= 2.939 + 1.630 + .942$$
$$= 5.51$$

This BPI for New England means that 5.51 percent of the buying power of the
United States is concentrated in the New England states. By comparison, the
highest BPI of any census region is in the South Atlantic states, which represent
17.83 percent of national buying power.

The rationale for this weighted average is that an area's income level has the
largest impact on retail sales and thus should receive the highest weight (.5). The
preceding year's retail sales total receives the second highest weight (.3), followed
by population size (.2).

BPIs for regions and states will not be broken down enough for specific location decisions. Fortunately, though, BPIs are available for counties, metropolitan
areas, cities, and TV viewing areas. Also, the BPI reports provide indices for different types of products such as food, eating and drinking places, general merchandise, furniture/home furnishings and appliances, automotive, and drugs.

The BPI is one piece of information, used in conjunction with others, to help
make location decisions. In general, retailers want to have stores in locations with
high buying power. Thus, a region with a high BPI is preferable to a low-BPI
area, all other factors held constant.

Demographic Data Vendors Demographic data vendors, such as Urban Decision Systems, Inc.,
have become quite popular by repackaging and updating census-
type data in a format that's easy to understand, easy and quick to obtain, and relatively inexpensive.[6] A retailer can contract from such firms for specific services on
a long-term basis, or order several reports to meet its requirements. Reports are
often delivered within 24 hours at a cost of $75 to $150 each. For instance, an
analyst can choose from an unlimited array of area sizes and shapes, such as concentric rings (or bands), neighborhood sectors, polygons, **travel-time contours**
(rings around a particular site based on travel time instead of distances), and
reports by state, county, city, and zip-code area.

To illustrate the depth and breadth of information available through demographic data vendors, Exhibits 9–5, 9–6, and 9–7 describe the primary trade area
(three-mile ring) for Mr. I's Optical Boutique in South Miami, Florida.[7] Urban
Decision Systems' Distibution Report (Exhibit 9–5) contains detailed household
income figures as well as growth projections. With the estimated year 2000
average household income at $99,080, and 18.5 percent of the households with

EXHIBIT 9-5

Income Distribution
of Three-Mile Ring
Surrounding Mr. I's
Optical Boutique

	1990 CENSUS		1995 ESTIMATE		2000 PROJECTION	
Population	90,951		88,365		85,621	
In group quarters	4,213		3,327		2,612	
Per capita income	$26,479		$32,051		$38,456	
Aggregate income ($ mil)	2,398.7		2,832.1		3,292.7	
Households	34,675	%	34,078	%	33,120	%
By income						
Less than $ 5,000	1,809	5.2	1,998	5.9	1,673	5.1
$ 5,000–$ 9,999	1,977	5.7	2,102	6.2	2,470	7.5
.						
.						
$ 40,000–$49,999	3,105	9.0	3,263	9.6	2,881	8.7
$ 50,000–$ 59,999	2,436	7.0	2,440	7.2	2,266	6.8
$ 60,000–$ 74,999	2,804	8.1	2,543	7.5	2,747	8.3
$ 75,000–$149,000	5,935	17.1	6,011	17.6	6,148	18.5
$150,000+	3,271	9.4	3,371	9.9	4,011	12.1
Median household income	$40,476		$41,814		$45,202	
Average household income	$69,178		$82,757		$99,080	

EXHIBIT 9-6

Demographic Trends
for Three-Mile Ring
Surrounding Mr. I's
Optical Boutique

	1990 CENSUS	%	1995 ESTIMATE	%	2000 PROJECTED	%
Population	90,591	%	88,365	%	85,621	%
Households	34,675		34,073		33,110	
1 person	9,619	27.7	9,653	28.3	9,529	28.8
2 persons	11,747	33.9	11,550	33.9	11,229	33.9
3–4 persons	9,955	28.7	9,771	28.7	9,502	28.7
5+ persons	3,353	9.7	3,099	9.1	2,849	8.6
Average hhld. size	2.49		2.50		2.51	
Race						
White	78,010	86.1	74,779	84.6	70,774	82.7
Black	8,617	9.5	8,892	10.1	9,598	11.2
Asian/Pacific Islander	1,901	2.1	2,548	2.9	2,992	3.5
American Indian	121	0.1	133	0.2	141	0.2
Other	1,941	2.1	2,011	2.3	2,115	2.5
Hispanic origin	31,617	34.9	37,354	42.3	42,893	50.1
Median age	36.0		36.8		37.9	
Males	43,670		42,676		41,481	
0–20	11,839	27.1	11,764	27.6	11,899	28.7
21–44	17,195	39.4	16,255	38.1	14,624	35.3
45–64	9,378	21.5	9,427	22.1	10,018	24.2
65–84	4,907	11.2	4,810	11.3	4,420	10.7
85+	350	0.8	419	1.0	520	1.3
Females	46,921		45,689		44,140	
0–20	10,951	23.3	10,936	23.9	11,079	25.1
21–44	17,982	38.3	17,147	37.5	15,574	35.3
45–64	10,276	21.9	10,179	22.3	10,688	24.2
65–84	6,927	14.8	6,538	14.3	5,761	13.1
85+	785	1.7	889	1.9	1,037	2.4
Owner-occupied hhlds.	22,627		22,257		21,695	
Renter-occupied hhlds.	12,047		11,815		11,415	

Source for both exhibits: 1990 Census, March 15, 1995, UDS estimates.

Which PRIZM cluster do you think these people best represent: "Pools and Patios" or "Young Influentials"?

incomes between $75,000 and $149,000 and 18.5 percent with incomes over $150,000, the three-mile ring surrounding Mr. I's Optical is very affluent.

Urban Decision Systems' demographic trends report (Exhibit 9–6) includes data on population, households by number of persons, race, ethnic origin, age by sex, and ownership of housing units. An interesting characteristic of the area surrounding Mr. I's Optical is that an estimated 50 percent of the population will be of Hispanic descent by 2000.

Developed by the Claritas Corporation, the Potential Rating Index for Zip Markets (PRIZM) is one of several commercially available services that combines census data, nationwide consumer surveys, and other statistics as well as information from 1,600 municipal and regional agencies. This information is analyzed by social rank, mobility, ethnicity, family life cycle, and housing. Clients can order reports by zip codes, census tracts, and zip-plus-four. The PRIZM system categorizes the nation's neighborhoods into 62 types. PRIZM is based on the premise that people like to live in neighborhoods with their peers and that people in a neighborhood tend to have similar consumer behavior patterns.[8]

Exhibit 9–7 summarizes the most prominent PRIZM lifestyle report for the three-mile ring surrounding Mr. I's Optical. These segments are described in Exhibit 9–8. Like the income and demographic trends reports, the PRIZM reports indicate that the surrounding area would be ideal for selling exclusive and expensive eyewear.

INTERNET EXERCISE   Claritas' PRIZM clusters is only one type of geo-demographic data that are commercially available. Go to www.scanus.com and describe how this firm's products could help you make retail site selection decisions.

EXHIBIT 9–7

PRIZM Neighborhood Lifestyle Clusters for Three-Mile Ring Surrounding Mr. I's Optical

CLUSTER	POPULATION	PERCENTAGE
Blue Blood Estates	15,956	18.1
Pools & Patios	8,639	9.8
Young Influentials	9,416	10.7
Upstarts & Seniors	11,020	12.5

EXHIBIT 9–8

Descriptions
of Largest
PRIZM Clusters
Surrounding
Mr. I's Optical

BLUE BLOOD ESTATES	UPSTARTS & SENIORS
Blue Blood Estates are America's wealthiest socioeconomic neighborhoods, populated by upper-class, established managers, professionals, and heirs to "old money." They are accustomed to privilege and living in luxurious surroundings. One in 10 millionaires can be found in Blue-Blood Estates, and there is a considerable drop from these heights to the next highest level of affluence.	Upstarts & Seniors includes both youths and seniors. It shows that, if employable, single, and childless, they have much in common. They share average educations and incomes in several fields, such as business, finance, retail, health, and public service. This group lives in condos and apartments, and prefers the nation's retirement areas in the Sunbelt and West. This group is middle income, predominantly white, and either under 24 or 65 and older.
POOLS & PATIOS	YOUNG INFLUENTIALS
Pools & Patios are found in upscale green-belt suburbs. Most of their children have grown and departed, leaving aging couples and aging nests too costly for young homemakers. Good education, high white-collar employment levels, and double incomes ensure "the good life" in these neighborhoods.	Young Influentials are young metropolitan sophisticates with exceptional high-tech, white-collar employment levels. Double incomes afford high spending. Lifestyles are open, with singles, childless couples, and unrelated adults predominating in expensive one- and two-person homes, apartments, and condos.

MEASURING COMPETITION

Estimating the demand for a retailer's products is a critical success factor, but it only tells half the story. It's equally important to determine the level of competition in the trade area. Earlier in this chapter, we concluded that either a saturated or an understored trade area offers a potentially good location opportunity, but that retailers should avoid trade areas that are overstored. How can a retailer like Mr. I's Optical determine the level of saturation of the trade area for a potential new location? In other words, what's the level of trade area competition?

Information on competition can be found in the Census of Retail Trade, trade association publications, shopping center and retail tenant directories, and even the Yellow Pages. For instance, a relatively easy way to determine level of competition is to calculate total square footage of retail space devoted to a type of store per household.[9] From published sources, Mr. I's can determine the total square feet devoted to optical retailers in their trade area and divide it by the number of households. The higher the ratio, the higher the level of competition. Of course, there's no substitute for personal visits to stores to assess competition.

To illustrate the process of measuring competition, consider the situation in which Mr. I's Optical is assessing the relative level of competition for four potential new sites using Exhibit 9–9's information.

Based on the information in Exhibit 9–9, Mr. I's Optical should locate its new store at Site B. The trade area potential is high and competition is relatively low. Of course, relative competition is only one issue to consider. Later in this chapter we'll consider competition along with other issues to determine which is the best new location for Mr. I's Optical. (See Exhibit 9–11.)

Other types of retailers could perform a similar analysis. Competititve analyses are easiest for large chains selling commodity-type merchandise, like grocery stores. First, they have information on sales and competition for all of the trade areas in which they have stores. The data are readily available and can be used to estimate what sales would be for a new store. Second, it is relatively easy to determine how much people spend on food or other commodities in a trade area and how much of the demand is being adequately satisfied by stores in the area. On the other hand,

EXHBIT 9–9   Competitive Analysis for Mr. I's Optical Boutique

TRADE AREA (1)	EYEGLASSES/ YEAR/ PERSON (2)	TRADE AREA POPULATION (3)	TOTAL EYEGLASSES POTENTIAL (4)	ESTIMATED EYEGLASSES SOLD (5)	TRADE AREA POTENTIAL UNITS (6)	TRADE AREA POTENTIAL PERCENTAGE (7)	RELATIVE LEVEL OF COMPETITION (8)
South Miami	0.2	85,621	17,124	7,550	9,574	55.91%	Low
Site A	0.2	91,683	18,337	15,800	2,537	13.83	Medium
Site B	0.2	101,972	20,394	12,580	7,814	38.32	Low
Site C	0.2	60,200	12,040	11,300	740	6.15	High
Site D	0.2	81,390	16,278	13,300	2,978	18.29	Medium

*Column 2: To perform the analysis, estimate the number of eyeglasses sold per year per person. This information could be obtained from industry sources.[a]

*Column 3: Trade area population is taken from information provided by Urban Decision Systems (Exhibit 9–3).

*Column 4: The total trade area potential for eyeglasses is column 2 times column 3.

*Column 5: Estimates of the number of eyeglasses sold in the trade areas are taken from industry sources, from customer surveys, and/or from visits to competitive stores.

*Column 6: The unit sales potential for eyeglasses in the trade areas is column 4 minus column 5.

*Column 7: The trade area potential percentage is column 6 divided by column 4. For instance, since the total eyeglasses potential for the South Miami store trade area is 17,124 pairs and we estimate that an additional 9,574 pairs could be sold in that trade area, 55.91 percent of the eyeglasses market in this area is left untapped. We could also say that 44.09 percent of the market is saturated (100 – 55.91 percent.)

*Column 8: The relative level of competition is subjectively estimated based on column 7. Remember, unlike other optical stores in the trade area, Mr. I's Optical carries a very exclusive merchandise selection. In general, however, the higher the trade area potential, the lower the relative competition will be.

[a]The appropriate ratio will vary depending upon the situation. For instance, a retailer may use average sales per square foot of selling space, average sales per household, or number of persons in the target market per store.

these analyses are more difficult for retailers with few outlets that carry exclusive merchandise. As we have seen from our analysis of Mr. I's Optical, they do not have data from multiple trade areas from which they can derive their analysis. Also, since they carry exclusive merchandise, it is more difficult to define their competition.

MEASURING TRADE AREA POTENTIAL

A number of complementary analytical methods are used to measure the sales potential of trade areas. One of the most widely used techniques—the analog approach—was first developed by William Applebaum for the Kroger Company in the 1930s. A more formalized statistical version of the analog approach uses multiple regression analysis. A third approach uses gravity models, based on Newton's law of gravity. Finally, a natural extension to the gravity approach attempts to locate multiple stores simultaneously. We discuss these location analysis methods below.

Analog Approach

The analog approach could just as easily be called the *similar store approach*. Suppose Mr. I's Optical Boutique wants to open a new location. Since its present location in South Miami has been very successful, it would like to find a location whose trade area has similar characteristics. We would estimate the size and customer demographic characteristics of its current trade area and then attempt to match those characteristics to new potential locations. Thus, knowledge of customer demographics, the competition, and sales of currently operating stores can be used to predict the size and sales potential of a new location.

The analog approach is divided into three steps.[10] First, the current trade area is determined by using a technique known as customer spotting in which customers are identified and their locations are plotted on a map. Second, based on the density of customers from the store, the primary, secondary, and tertiary trade area zones are defined. Finally, we match the characteristics of our current store with the potential new stores' locations to determine the best site.

EXHIBIT 9-10   Example of a Questionnaire Used in Customer Spotting Survey for Mr. I's Optical Boutique

---

1. What is your address? _____
   Street   City/Town   State   Zip code

2. What is the closest street to your house which crosses the street you live on?

   _____

3. How often do you shop at this store?

   _____ every other month or less   _____ once a month   _____ 2–3 times a month

   _____ once a week   _____ twice a week or more often

4. How much did you spend today? _____

5. What other store do you shop at for that type of merchandise?
   (Accept up to 3 responses—list in order mentioned.)

   _____

   _____

   _____

6. What newspapers do you normally read? *(Accept up to 3 responses—list in order mentioned.)*

   Daily?   *Sunday?*   *Other?*

   _____   _____   _____

   _____   _____   _____

   _____   _____   _____

7. How many persons live in your household? _____

8. What are the occupations of each full-time worker living in your household?

   _____

   _____

   _____

9. Do you own or rent your home? _____ Own _____ Rent

10. To what age category do you belong? *(Show respondent Card A)*
    Response code _____

11. What is the total income of all full-time workers in your household?
    (Show respondent Card B)
    Response code _____

12. *(Do not ask)*   Sex   M   F
                     Race   W   B   Other

Card A	
Code	Age
Z	18–24
G	25–34
B	35–44
Q	45–54
A	55–64
X	64+

Card B	
Code	Total household income ($)
N	under 20,000
W	20,000–39,999
K	40,000–59,999
D	60,000–79,999
I	80,000–99,999
F	100,000–119,000
R	120,000 and over

Source: Adapted from G. L. Drummey, "Traditional Methods of Sales Forecasting," in *Store Location and Store Assessment Research,* R. L. Davies and D. S. Rogers, eds. Copyright © 1984 by John Wiley & Sons, Ltd. Reprinted by permission of John Wiley & Sons, Ltd.

Customer Spotting   The purpose of the customer spotting technique is to spot, or locate, the residences of customers for a store or shopping center. This can be accomplished in a number of ways. Automobile license plates can be recorded in the parking lot and traced to the owner by purchasing the information from state governments or private research companies. Experts believe that at least 500 plates are necessary to provide a good sample. The Motor Statistical Division of R.L. Polk and Co. in Detroit can match the plates against its national vehicle registration database and summarize where the vehicles originate. Another method is to take addresses from customer checks or credit cards.

These unobtrusive methods are easy, but an in-store interview of customers, although more expensive, can provide richer information, such as the demographic composition, shopping behavior, and media habits of the customers. Exhibit 9–10 shows an example of an in-store questionnaire that Mr. I's Optical might use. Besides the address information that's essential for locating customers, other important data are collected. Customer demographic and socioeconomic information is useful to determine the retailer's typical customer. If, for example, the survey indicates that customers are relatively old and live in high-income areas, then—all other factors held equal—we should attempt to find new locations in such areas.

Competitive information is the final important component of the customer spotting survey. If customers believe that there's significant store competition, then additional information on those stores is required. We need to determine relative distance and size of the competing stores, general store appearance, and merchandising expertise.

Processing the Data   We can process the data in two ways: by manually plotting the location of each customer on a map or by using a computer.

Once the customers are spotted, we delineate the trade area. (See Exhibit 9–3.) Since this process involves a lot of subjectivity, follow the guidelines presented earlier in this chapter.

Choosing a New Location Using the Analog System   Once Mr. I's Optical has defined the trade area for its existing store, it can use the information to choose a new store location. The trick is to find a location whose market area is similar or analogous to its existing store.

Based on the information we examined earlier in the chapter, we conclude that the five factors that contribute most to the success of Mr. I's current location are high income, predominantly white-collar occupations, relatively larger percentage of older residents, upscale PRIZM profile, and relatively low competition for expensive, high-fashion eyewear. Exhibit 9–11 compares Mr. I's current location with four potential locations on these five factors.

The best location for Mr. I's Optical Boutique should contain many older professionals with high incomes.

Although the potential customers of site A typically have white-collar occupations, they have relatively low incomes and are comparatively young. Young Suburbans also tend to have young families, so expensive eyewear may not be a priority purchase. Finally, there's a medium level of competition in the area.

The Gray Power residents surrounding site B have moderate incomes and are mostly retired. Even though competition would be low and most residents need glasses, these customers are more interested in value than in fashion.

Site C has strong potential since the Young Literati

EXHIBIT 9–11   Descriptions of Mr. I's Optical Boutique and Four Potential Locations'
Trade Areas

STORE LOCATION	AVERAGE HOUSEHOLD INCOME	WHITE-COLLAR OCCUPATIONS	PERCENTAGE OF RESIDENTS AGE 45 AND OVER	PREDOMINANT PRIZM PROFILE	LEVEL OF COMPETITION
Mr. I's Optical	$99,000	High	38%	Blue Blood Estates	Low
Site A	$60,000	High	25	Young Suburbia	Medium
Site B	$70,000	Low	80	Gray Power	Low
Site C	$100,000	High	30	Young Literati	High
Site D	$120,000	High	50	Money and Brains	Medium

Average household income is taken from Exhibit 9–5, year 2000 projections. Level of white-collar occupations is estimated from PRIZM data in Exhibit 9–7. Percentage of residents 45 years old and over is estimated from Exhibit 9–6. Level of competition was subjectively determined.

residents in the area have high incomes and are a mix of executives, professionals, and students living near an urban university. They would appreciate Mr. I's fashionable assortment. Unfortunately, other high-end optical stores are entrenched in the area.

Site D is the best location for Mr. I's. The residents are older professionals with high incomes. Money and Brains are sophisticated consumers of adult luxuries like high-fashion eyewear. Importantly, this PRIZM cluster is similar to Blue Blood Estates but not as wealthy.

Unfortunately, finding analogous situations isn't always as easy as in this example. The weaker the analogy, the more difficult the location decision will be. When a retailer has a relatively small number of outlets (say, 20 or fewer), the analog approach is often best. Even retailers with just one outlet like Mr. I's Optical can use the analog approach. As the number of stores increases, it becomes more difficult for the analyst to organize the data in a meaningful way. More analytical approaches such as multiple regression analysis are necessary.

Multiple Regression Analysis

Multiple regression analysis is a common method of defining retail trade area potential for retail chains with greater than 20 stores. Although multiple regression analysis uses logic similar to that of the analog approach, it uses statistics rather than judgment to predict sales for a new store.

The initial steps in multiple regression analysis are the same as those in the analog approach. First, the current trade areas are determined by using the customer spotting technique. Second, the primary, secondary, and tertiary zones are determined by plotting customers on a map. But then the multiple regression procedure begins to differ from the analog approach. Instead of matching characteristics of trade areas for existing stores with a potential new store by using the location analyst's subjective experience, a mathematical equation is derived.

Using "canned" statistical packages, three steps are followed to develop the multiple regression equation:

1. Select appropriate measures of performance, such as per capita sales or market share.
2. Select a set of variables that may be useful in predicting performance.
3. Solve the regression equation and use it to project performance for future sites.[11]

Family income is a good predictor (independent) variable to use in a regression analysis to predict sales for a new jewelry store.

Determine Store Performance Measure and Variables Used to Predict Performance   Sales or per capita sales is the store performance measure most often used in location regression analyses.

Potential variables used to predict performance include demographic composition of the individual store trading areas; specific information on the location; image; strength of each potential competitor; and site-related real estate variables such as visibility, access, or other types of tenants at the site.[12] The predictor variables should differ, depending on the type of store being analyzed. For instance, household income may be an important variable when predicting sales of a new Peoples Jewelry store, whereas the number of school-age children per household would be appropriate for predicting sales of a McDonald's restaurant.

Estimate Regression Equation   Data for each store's performance measure and predictor variables are input to a computerized regression program. The end result of the regression analysis is an equation that can be used to predict sales of a new store, given data on the predictor variables for that store. A simple example illustrates how the multiple regression procedure works.[13] Exhibit 9–12 provides data for 10 hypothetical home-improvement centers. (The example has been

EXHIBIT 9–12

Yearly Sales, Population, and Income for 10 Home-Improvement Centers

STORE	YEARLY SALES ($000)	0-TO 3–MILE RADIUS POPULATION
1	$402	54,000
2	367	29,500
3	429	49,000
4	252	22,400
5	185	18,600
6	505	61,100
7	510	49,000
8	330	33,200
9	210	26,400
10	655	83,200

Source: John S. Thompson, *Site Selection* (New York: Lebar-Friedman, 1982), p. 130.

simplified considerably; simple regression should not be performed without at least 30 stores. Also, only one predictor variable is used: population within a three-mile radius of the store.)

Exhibit 9–13 plots yearly sales and population. A regression line has been drawn on the plot that best describes the relationship between sales and population. Specifically, the regression line is statistically defined as that which minimizes the squared distances from the points to the line. (The exact form of this line can be determined by any statistical package designed for personal or mainframe computers as well as some handheld calculators.) The closer the points are to the line, the better the fit and, therefore, the better the sales forecast. As indicated by the line, as population increases, so do sales. Assume a proposed site had a zero-to-three-mile radius population of 40,000. To estimate sales, extend a vertical line from the 40 mark on the horizontal axis of the graph to the regression line, then extend it horizontally to the vertical axis. (See the dotted line in Exhibit 9–13.) Sales would be approximately $366,000.

The regression line is derived from the equation

$$\text{Sales} = a + b_1 x_1$$

where

 $a =$ A constant derived by the regression program; a also defines where the regression line in Exhibit 9–13 intercepts the y-axis and is therefore also known as the y-intercept.

EXHIBIT 9–13

Regression of
Population on Sales

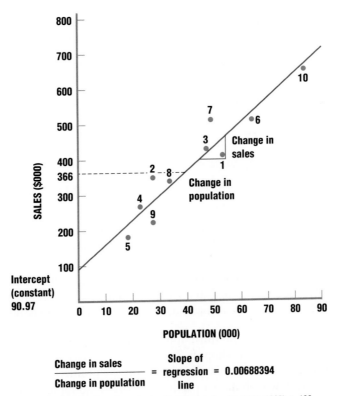

Change in sales / Change in population = Slope of regression line = 0.00688394

Source: John S. Thompson, *Site Selection* (New York: Lebar-Friedman, 1982), p. 133.
Note: Each number on the graph corresponds to the store number on Exhibit 9–12.

b_1 = A number derived by the regression program that defines the relationship between sales and the predictor variable(s); it is also the slope of the regression line.

x_1 = The predictor variable (zero-to-three–mile population).

Continuing with the example,

$$Sales = \$91,000 + (\$6.88 \times 40,000)$$
$$= \$366,200$$

In this case, the regression-derived b indicates that sales will increase positively at a rate of $6.88 for every person in the zero-to-three–mile population. Since the zero-to-three–mile population is 40,000 people, and a is derived as $91,000, the sales total is forecast as $366,200. Note that the mathematical and graphic approaches give the same answer (within one's ability to read the graph).

This simplified illustration used only one predictor variable. Assume that other predictor variables were tested and that average family income was also shown to have a strong and statistically significant relationship to sales. (The number of predictor variables is limited to two in this example for simplification purposes.) The new regression equation is

$$Sales = a + b_1 x_1 + b_2 x_2$$

where

a, b_1, and x_1 are as previously defined.

b_2 = A number derived by the regression program that defines the relationship between sales and average family income.

x_2 = The predictor variable (average family income).

Assume the new store has a zero-to-three–mile radius population of 55,000, and average family income is $28,000. After solving the regression equation,

a = –144,146
b_1 = 6.937
b_2 = 10.132

Substituting these values into the equation, the new sales forecast is derived:

$$Sales = -144,146 + (6.937 \times 55,000) + (10.132 \times 28,000)$$
$$= \$521,085$$

Using the multiple regression method, then, a retailer can predict sales of a new store if variables that have been successfully used to predict sales in other stores are known. Regression analysis does have limitations, however. First, to be reliable, a large database is required. Second, the analyst must be properly trained and must adhere to strict statistical procedures. Finally, since regression is an averaging technique, it seldom identifies extremely good or extremely poor potential locations.

Gravity Models

The third approach for forecasting retail sales potential of a store or shopping center uses gravity models. These models, following Newton's law of gravity, are based on the premise that the probability that a given customer will shop in a particular store or shopping center becomes larger as the size of the store or center grows and the distance or travel time from customers to the store or center shrinks.

Reilly's Law of Retail Gravitation: A Numerical Example

THE FORMULA FOR REILLY'S LAW of retail gravitation is

$$\frac{B_a}{B_b} = \left(\frac{P_a}{P_b}\right)\left(\frac{D_a}{D_b}\right)^2$$

where

B_a = The business that city A draws from the intermediate place.

B_b = The business that city B draws from the intermediate place.

P_a = Population of city A.

P_b = Population of city B.

D_a = Distance from city A to intermediate place.

D_b = Distance from city B to intermediate place.

Arlington, Texas, is approximately 12 miles from Dallas (city A) and 8 miles from Fort Worth (city B). Dallas has a population of about 1 million people, whereas Fort Worth has only about 430,000. Using Reilly's formula

$$\frac{B_{Dallas}}{B_{Fort\ Worth}} = \left(\frac{1,000,000}{430,000}\right) \times \left(\frac{8}{12}\right)^2 = 1.03$$

Reilly's model predicts that customers living in Arlington spend about the same amount of money in Dallas as in Fort Worth, that is, $1.03 in Dallas and $1 in Fort Worth.

Gravity models have had a prominent place in the retail location literature since the early 1930s. For a historical perspective and an understanding of the basic principles underlying gravity models, we briefly examine the works of Reilly, Converse, and Christaller. Their research spawned a more practical approach by Huff and others for defining trade areas and forecasting sales.

Reilly's Law of Retail Gravitation   Reilly's law defines two cities' relative abilities to attract customers from the area between them.[14] The larger the town, the greater its ability to attract customers. Likewise, the greater the distance from town, the less likely a customer is to shop there. A numerical illustration of Reilly's law is found in the accompanying information insert.

Gravity models for measuring trade areas would predict that the trade area for the Baskin Robbins ice cream store in the regional shopping mall is much larger than the similar store in the strip mall. People are attracted to larger shopping centers because they have better and larger assortments.

Converse's Breaking-Point Model: A Numerical Illustration

THE FORMULA for Converse's model is

$$D_{ab} = \frac{d}{1 + \sqrt{\dfrac{P_b}{P_a}}}$$

where

D_a = breaking point from city A, measured in miles to city B.

d = Distance between city A and city B.

P_a = Population of city A.

P_b = Population of city B.

Continuing with the previous example, the distance (d) between Dallas and Fort Worth, Texas, is about 20 miles. Dallas has about 1 million people (P_a), compared to about 430,000 for Fort Worth (P_b).

$$D_{ab} = \frac{20}{1 + \sqrt{\dfrac{430,000}{1,000,000}}} = 12.08$$

Thus, the breaking point from Dallas is 12.08 miles along the road to Fort Worth. People living within 12.08 miles will most likely shop in Dallas, while those living more than 12.08 miles from Dallas will shop in Fort Worth.

Reilly's principal contribution was to define the relationship between shopping area size and the distance to customers. Its usefulness is limited in practice, however. If the towns aren't isolated in rural areas, competition for business from other areas will distort the results from Reilly's formula. Also, the model assumes that population size of a town is a perfect substitute for availability of shopping facilities and that distance is the same as travel time. Finally, this law implicitly assumes that people shop in one town or the other, but not both.

Converse's Breaking-Point Model   Converse extended Reilly's law by defining the breaking point—the location between two towns where customers on one side of the location patronize one town, while those on the other side patronize the other town.[15] The accompanying box provides an example of this model. Although the breaking-point model gives a different view of trade area definition, it suffers from the same limitation as Reilly's law.

Christaller's Central Place Theory   Christaller developed his central place theory in Germany about the same time that Reilly was publishing his law of retail gravitation in the United States.[16] A **central place** is a center of retailing activity such as a town or city. The theory argues that there's a hierarchy of central places according to the assortment of goods available. Thus, a village would be at the bottom of the hierarchy, since it provides a relatively small assortment of goods. A large city is at the top of the hierarchy, since its assortment is large. Small towns can usually support a relatively limited group of retailers such as grocery stores, gas stations, and convenience stores. People will drive longer distances to shop in cities with a large assortment of merchandise. Like the law of retail gravitation, the central place theory uses size of retail business activity and distance from consumers as the two critical parameters for analyzing retail locations.

The central place theory is useful for identifying appropriate markets for new stores for three reasons:[17]

- The theory supports the notion that not all locations are appropriate for all retailers. While convenience stores are as successful in small towns as in large cities, people expect to drive to large cities to find specialty goods like Ferrari sports cars. Also, retailers that specialize in convenience

Both the Grand Avenue mall in downtown Milwaukee, Wisconsin, and the downtown shopping area of Flossmoor, Illinois, are known as central places—centers of retailing activity. Yet more people would be willing to drive farther to the Grand Avenue mall because it has a more comprehensive assortment.

and necessity items can be successful in small shopping centers. But purveyors of specialty goods, which must draw from a larger trade area to ensure a sufficient customer base, should locate in larger regional malls or shopping areas.

- Growing communities and shopping areas will be able to support larger numbers of shopping and specialty goods retailers.
- Since larger communities and shopping areas contain both convenience and necessity items as well as shopping and specialty goods, people will travel farther to these areas to satisfy all their shopping needs in one location. Thus, the larger cities and shopping areas will do a disproportionately larger amount of business. The hypermarkets in Europe are successful, in part, because they provide customers with one-stop shopping that isn't available in the central shopping areas of small villages.

Huff's Model   The objective of Huff's approach is to determine the probability that a customer residing in a particular area will shop at a particular store or shopping center.[18] To forecast sales, the location analyst multiplies the probability that the customer will shop at a particular place by an estimate of the customer's expenditures. Then, all the estimated expenditures in an area are aggregated to estimate sales from the area. To begin the process of estimating sales using the Huff method, the general model is defined as follows:

$$P_{ij} = \frac{S_j \div T_{ij}^{\ b}}{\sum_{j=1}^{n} S_j \div T_{ij}^{\ b}}$$

where

P_{ij} = Probability of a customer at a given point of origin i traveling to a particular shopping center j

S_j = Size of shopping center j

T_{ij} = Travel time or distance from customer's starting point to shopping center

b = An exponent to T_{ij} that reflects the effect of travel time on different kinds of shopping trips

Huff's Gravity Model: A Numerical Illustration

TO ILLUSTRATE THE USE of Huff's model, examine Exhibit A. Assume a local shoe store is thinking of opening a new store at University Park Center shopping center. Two major shopping centers provide competition for women's shoes: The Falls and Old Town. Exhibit B summarizes the information on these shopping centers.

The following four steps are repeated for each area surrounding the shopping center. Since University Park Center will draw heavily from a nearby university, the process for determining a sales forecast from the university students is described.

1. Determine the probability that a student at this university will shop at University Park Center. Using the formula for Huff's model and data in Exhibit B:

$$P_{ij} = \frac{1{,}000 \div 3^2}{(1{,}000 \div 3^2) + (500 \div 5^2) + (100 \div 1^2)}$$

Probability = .48

2. Determine the number of students who will buy their shoes at University Park Center. The probability is multiplied by the number of students:

.48 × 12,000 students = 5,760 customers

3. Determine the sale forecast. Assuming each customer will spend an average of $150 on shoes, the forecasted sales will be

5,760 customers × $150 = $864,000

4. Estimate sales for the entire trade area. The university population represents only part of the trade area for University Park Center. To estimate sales for the entire trade area, repeat steps 1 to 3 for the remaining areas and then sum them.

EXHIBIT A   University and Shopping Centers: Gravity Model Illustration

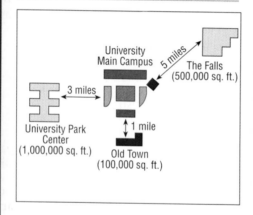

EXHIBIT B   Summary Information for Three Shopping Centers

SHOPPING CENTER	SIZE (000 SQ. FT.)	DISTANCE FROM UNIVERSITY (MI.)
University Park Center	1,000	3
The Falls	500	5
Old Town	100	1

(The exponent, b, is assumed to be 2.)

The model indicates that the larger the size (S_j) of the shopping center compared to competing shopping centers' sizes, the larger the probability that a customer will shop at the center. A larger size is generally better in the customer's eye because it means more assortment and variety. Travel time or distance (T_{ij}) has the opposite effect on the probability that a customer will shop at a given shopping center. The greater the travel time or distance from the customer compared to competing shopping centers, the smaller the probability that the customer will shop at the center. Generally, customers would rather shop at a close center than a distant one.

The exponent T_{ij}^{b} reflects travel time's effect on different kinds of shopping trips. The larger the value of b, the larger the effect of travel time or distance (T_{ij}) on the probablity that a customer will shop at a given center. Travel time or distance is generally more important with convenience goods that with shopping goods—people are less willing to travel a great distance for a quart of milk than for a new pair of shoes. Thus a larger value for b is assigned if the store or shopping center being studied specializes in convenience goods rather than shopping goods. b is usually determined through surveys of shopping patterns or from previous experience.

The Huff model is currently being used by retailers to define their trade areas and forecast sales. The accompanying box explains how the Huff model works.

Location Allocation Models   The preceding methods of analyzing trade areas are useful for a retailer trying to determine the best location for one store. The problem is much more difficult if the retailer plans to open a number of new locations all at the same time. For instance, the single best location for a new ice cream store may be inferior if five stores are all opening at once. To some extent, the stores will compete with each other, and sales from one store will cannibalize sales from another.

Although their description is beyond the scope of this book, a number of location allocation models have been developed that simultaneously select multiple location sites in order to optimize specific criteria such as sales, market share, or a profitability measure like gross margin or contribution margin.[19]

Choosing the Best Method(s)   In any decision, the more information that's available, the better the outcome is likely to be. This is true for research in general and location analysis in particular. Therefore, if a combination of the techniques is applied and the same conclusion is reached, the retailer should have more confidence in the decision.

Some methods used for analyzing trade areas are better in certain situations, however. The analog and gravity approaches are best when the number of stores with obtainable data is small, usually fewer than 30. These approaches can also be used by smaller retailers. The regression approach, on the other hand, is best when there are multiple variables expected to explain sales, since it's hard to keep track of multiple predictor variables when using a manual system like the analog approach. Also, the gravity models explicitly consider the attractiveness of competition and customers' distance or travel time to the store or shopping center in question. Location allocation models are most appropriate when trying to locate several stores at the same time. Finally, since neither gravity nor location allocation models usually utilize demographic variables, it's particularly important to use these methods in conjunction with the analog or regression methods.

SUMMARY   In this chapter, we looked at the qualitative issues that location analysts use to choose a region/market and a trade area. Retailers choose a particular region or market area for two reasons. First, some types of merchandise sell better in certain areas than in others. Second, some stores choose to maintain a regional focus so that they can maintain a strong image with their customers and be able to manage their stores and distribution more efficiently.

Trade areas are typically divided into primary, secondary, and tertiary zones. The boundaries of a trade area are determined by how accessible it is to customers, the natural and physical barriers that exist in the area, the type of shopping area in which the store is located, the type of store, and the level of competition.

Retailers consider several issues when assessing the attractiveness of a particular region, market, or trade area. They want to know about the people living in the area. What are their lifestyles? How wealthy and large are the households? Is the area growing or declining? Does it have a favorable business climate? Importantly, what is the level of competition? Retailers should only locate in areas with heavy competition if they believe their retailing format is superior to their competition's. A safer strategy is to locate in an area with little competition. Of course, in today's overbuilt retail environment, such areas are nearly impossible to find.

We then examined the sources of data and the quantitative tools necessary for evaluating a trade area's sales potential. First, data sources and some conventional tools for estimating demand for a store's merchandise at a particular location were discussed. The *Decennial Census of the United States* is a complete source of information for virtually any size area—from the entire country to a city block. The Buying Power Index (BPI) provides information about overall retail demand in an area. Finally, several demographic data vendors offer census-type data in easy-to-understand, inexpensive formats.

To provide a complete picture of the sales level that could be expected in an area, we described how a retailer would assess the level of competition in an area.

The chapter concluded by evaluating various methods and models for delineating trade areas and estimating their sales. The analog approach—one of the easiest to use—can be particularly useful for smaller retailers. Using this approach, the retailer makes predictions about the sales of a new store based on sales in stores in similar areas. Multiple regression analysis uses the same logic as the analog approach but is statistically based and requires more objective data. Finally, several gravity models are described. All are based on the premise that customers are more likely to shop at a given store or shopping center if it's conveniently located and offers a large selection. Although Reilly's law, Converse's model, and Christaller's theory provide a good historical perspective, Huff's model has more possibilities for application.

KEY TERMS

central place, *276*	overstored, *261*	region, *256*	trade area, *257*
destination store, *259*	parasite store, *260*	saturated trade area, *261*	travel-time contours, *264*
MSA (Metropolitan Statistical Area), *256*	polygons, *258*	secondary zone, *259*	understored trade area, *261*
	primary zone, *258*	tertiary zone, *259*	

DISCUSSION QUESTIONS & PROBLEMS

1. What are the shape and size of the trade area zones of a shopping center near your school?

2. When measuring trade areas, why is the analog approach not a good choice for a retailer with several hundred outlets?

3. True Value Hardware Stores plans to open a new store. Two sites are available, both in middle-income neighborhood centers. One neighborhood is 20 years old and has been well maintained. The other was recently built in a newly planned community. Which site is preferable for True Value? Why?

4. Large companies that specialize in measuring demand are extensively used by larger retailers but are often out of the financial reach of smaller retail firms. Sometimes, the smaller retailer must rely on data from sources such as the local chamber of commerce. What are the advantages and disadvantages of using data from such sources?

5. What are the limitations of Reilly's law and Converse's breaking-point model?

6. How is the Buying Power Index used in location analysis?

7. Levytown has approximately 800,000 people. The population of Weitzville is 100,000. The cities are 15 miles apart. What is the breaking point?

8. An automobile retailer has decided to locate in either Levytown or Weitzville. The retailer has discovered that the locations have about the same sales potential. In between the two cities is Gant City. Gant City is about 10 miles from Levytown and 14 miles from Weitzville. Using the following additional information and the formula for Converse's breaking-point model, determine which location the auto retailer should select.

	WEITZVILLE	LEVYTOWN
Population	539,421	656,937

9. A drug store is considering opening a new location at shopping center A, with hopes of capturing sales from a new neighborhood under construction. Two nearby shopping centers, C and E, will provide competition. Using the following information and Huff's probability model, determine the probability that residents of the new neighborhood will shop at shopping center A.

SHOPPING CENTER	SIZE (000 SQ. FT.)	DISTANCE FROM NEW NEIGHBORHOOD (MILES)
A	2,500	3
C	1,250	3
E	250	2

(Assume that $b = 2$)

10. Suppose you work for Safeway and have been assigned to assess the level of market saturation in a trade area that already has a Kroger, a Skaggs Alpha Beta, and Evan's Supermarket. Explain how you would perform the analysis.

SUGGESTED READINGS

Brown, Stephen. "Christaller Knew My Father: Recycling Central Place Theory." *Journal of Macromarketing* 15, no. 1 (Spring 1995) pp. 60–73.

Curry, Bruce, and Luiz Moutinho. "Computer Models for Site Location Decisions." *International Journal of Retail & Distribution Management* 20, no. 4 (July 1992), pp. 12–20.

Davies, R. L., and D. S. Rogers, eds. *Store Location and Store Assessment Research.* New York: John Wiley & Sons, 1984.

Drezner, Tammy. "Locating a Single New Facility among Existing, Unequally Attractive Facilities." *Journal of Regional Science* 34 (1994), pp. 237–52.

Drezner, Tammy. "Optimal Continuous Location of a Retail Facility, Facility Attractiveness, and Market Share: An Interactive Model." *Journal of Retailing* 70, no. 1 (March 22, 1994), pp. 49–64.

Durvasula, Srinivas, Subhash Sharma, and J. Craig Andrews. "STORELOC: A Retail Store Location Model Based on Managerial Judgments." *Journal of Retailing* 68, no. 4 (Winter 1992), pp. 420–45.

Eiselt, H. A., G. Laporte, and J. F. Thisse. "Competitive Location Models: A Framework and Bibliography." *Transportation Science* 27 (1993), pp. 44–54.

Ghosh, Avijit, and C. Samuel Craig. "FRANSYS: A Franchise Distribution System Location Model." *Journal of Retailing* 67, no. 4 (Winter 1991), pp. 446–96.

Ghosh, Avijit, and Sara L. McLafferty. *Location Strategies for Retail and Service Firms.* Lexington, MA: D.C. Heath, 1987.

Ghosh, Avijit, and Sara McLafferty. "The Shopping Center: A Restructuring of Post-War Retailing." *Journal of Retailing* 67 (Fall 1991), pp. 253–67.

Hodges, James S., Kirthi Kalyanam, and Daniel S. Putler. "A Bayesian Approach for Estimating Target Market Potential with Limited Geodemographic Information." *Journal of Marketing Research* 33 (Spring 1996), pp. 134–50.

Jones, Ken, and Jim Simmons. *Location Location Location: Analyzing the Retail Environment.* Toronto: Methuen, 1987.

Jones, Ken, and Jim Simmons. *The Retail Environment.* New York: Rutledge, Chapman and Hall, 1990.

Kohsaka, Hiroyuki. "Three-Dimensional Representation and Estimation of Retail Store Demand by Bicubic Splines." *Journal of Retailing* 68, no. 2 (Summer 1992), pp. 221–41.

Mitchell, Susan. "Birds of a Feather." *American Demographics,* February 1995, pp. 40–48.

Okoruwa, Ason A., Hugh O. Nourse, and Joseph V. Terza. "Estimating Sales for Retail Centers: An Application of the Poisson Gravity Model." *Journal of Real Estate Research* 9, no. 1 (Winter 1994), pp. 85–97.

O'Malley, Lisa, Maurice Patterson, and Martin Evans. "Retailing Applications of Geodemographics: A Preliminary Investigation." *Marketing Intelligence & Planning* 13, no. 2 (1995), pp. 29–35.

Roca, Ruben A., ed. *Market Research for Shopping Centers.* New York: International Council of Shopping Centers, 1985.

Rust, Roland T., and Naveen Donthu. "Capturing Geographically Localized Misspecification Error in Retail Store Choice Models." *Journal of Marketing Research* 32, no. 1 (February 1995), pp. 103–10.

Tayman, Jeff, and Louis Pol. "Retail Site Selection and Geographic Information Systems." *Journal of Applied Business Research* 11, no. 2 (Spring 1995), pp. 46–54.

Thompson, John S. *Site Selection.* New York: Lebhar-Friedman, 1982.

Weiss, Michael J. *The Clustering of America.* New York: Harper & Row, 1988.

NOTES

1. Debra Hazel, "The Resurgence of the Regionals," *Chain Store Age,* January 1996, pp. 65–70.

2. See Michael E. Porter, *The Competitive Advantage of Nations* (New York: Free Press, 1990).

3. Private firms using TIGER technology include Equifax, Urban Decision Systems, C.A.C.I., Donneley, and ScanUS. Eugene Carlson, "Business Map Plans for Use of TIGER Geographical Files: Census Bureau Data, Now on Disk, Offer Opportunities and Headaches," *The Wall Street Journal,* June 8, 1990, p. B2; *Tiger: The Coast-to-Coast Digital Map Data Base* (Washington, DC: U.S. Bureau of the Census, November 1990); and *TIGER Resource List* (Washington, DC: U.S. Bureau of the Census, October 1993).

4. A list of regional planning commissions is available through the National Association of Regional Councils, 1700 K Street NW, Washington, DC 20006.

5. "1995 Regional and State Summaries of Population," *1995 Survey of Buying Power, Sales & Marketing Management,* pp. B2–B4.

6. Urban Decision Systems, 4676 Admiralty Way, Marina del Rey, CA 90292, telephone 1-800-633-9568; and 3975 Fair Ridge Drive, Fairfax, VA 22033, telephone 1-800-364-4837.

7. We described Mr. I's trade area in Exhibit 9–3. To simplify the analysis, we've defined its primary trade area with a circle rather than the polygons described earlier. For ease of explication, Exhibits 9–5, 9–6 and 9–7 have been simplified.

8. Susan Mitchell, "Birds of a Feather," *American Demographics,* February 1995, pp. 40–48. PRIZM is available from Claritas, 201 North Union Street, Alexandria, VA 22314, telephone 1-800-284-4868. Other major cluster systems are ACORN from CACI Marketing Systems,

1100 North Glebe Road, Arlington, VA 22201, telephone 1-800-292-2224; ClusterPLUS 2000 from Strategic Mapping, Inc., 70 Seaview Avenue, Stamford, CT 06192-0058, telephone (203) 353-7500; and MicroVision from Equifax National Decision Systems, 5375 Mira Sorrento Place, Suite 400, San Diego, CA 92121, telephone 1-800-866-6510.

9. Personal communication, Kenard E. Smith, Ph.D., vice president—area research, The May Department Stores Company, July 1996.

10. G. L. Drummey, "Traditional Methods of Sales Forecasting," in R. L. Davies and D. S. Rogers, eds., *Store Location and Store Assessment Research* (New York: John Wiley & Sons, 1984), pp. 279–99.

11. J. Dennis Lord and Charles D. Lynds, "The Use of Regression Models in Store Location Research: A Review and Case Study," *Akron Business and Economic Review,* Summer 1981, pp. 13–19.

12. B. L. Wilson, "Modern Methods of Sales Forecasting; Regression Models," in *Store Location,* Davies and Rogers, eds., p. 303.

13. John S. Thompson, *Site Selection* (New York: Lebhar-Friedman, 1982), pp. 13–40.

14. W. J. Reilly, *The Laws of Retail Gravitation* (New York: Knickerbocker Press, 1931).

15. P. D. Converse, "New Laws of Retail Gravitation," *Journal of Marketing* 14 (1949), pp. 379–84.

16. Walter Christaller, *Central Places in Southern Germany,* 1935, trans. Carlisle W. Baskin (Englewood Cliffs, NJ: Prentice-Hall, 1966).

17. Robert F. Lusch, Patrick Dunne, and Randall Gebhardt, *Retail Management,* 2d ed. (Cincinnati: South-Western, 1993), p. 350.

18. David L. Huff, "Defining and Estimating a Trade Area," *Journal of Marketing* 28 (1964), pp. 34–38; D. S. Rogers, "Modern Methods of Sales Forecasting," in *Store Location*, Davies and Rogers, eds., pp. 319–31; C. Samuel Craig, Avijit Ghosh, and Sara McLafferty, "Models of the Retail Location Process: A Review," *Journal of Retailing* 60, no. 1 (Spring 1981), p. 536; M. Nakanishi and L. G. Cooper, "Parameter Estimate for Multiplicative Interaction Choice Model: Least Squares Approach," *Journal of Marketing Research* 11 (1974), pp. 303–11; A. K. Jain and V. Mahajan, "Evaluating the Competitive Environment in Retailing Using Multiplicative Competitive Interactive Models," in J. Sheth, ed., *Research in Marketing* (Greenwich, CT: JAI), 1 (1979), pp. 217–35.

19. Craig, Ghosh, and McLafferty, "Models of the Retail Location Process"; Tammy Drezner, "Optimal Continuous Location of a Retail Facility, Facility Attractiveness, and Market Share: An Interactive Model," *Journal of Retailing* 70, no. 1 (1994), pp. 49–64; Dale Achabal, W. L. Gorr, and Vijay Mahajan, "MULTILOC: A Multiple Store Location Model," *Journal of Retailing* 58, no. 2, pp. 5–25; Avijit Ghosh and C. Samuel Craig, "FRANSYS: A Franchise Distribution System Location Model," *Journal of Retailing* 67, no. 4 (Winter 1991), pp. 446–96; J. R. Beaumont, "Location Allocation Models and Central Place Theory," *Spatial Analysis and Location-Allocation Models*, A. Ghosh and G. Rushton, eds. (New York: Van Nostrand Reinhold, 1987), pp. 21–54; T. Drezner, "Locating a Single New Facility among Existing, Unequally Attractive Facilities," *Journal of Regional Science* 34 (1994), pp. 237–52; S. Durvasula, S. Sharma, and J. C. Andrews, "STORELOC: A Retail Store Location Model Based on Managerial Judgments," *Journal of Retailing* 68 (1992), pp. 420–44; and H. A. Eiselt, G. Laporte, and J. F. Thisse, "Competitive Location Models: A Framework and Bibliography," *Transportation Science* 27 (1993), pp. 44–54.

Organization Structure and Human Resource Management

THE WORLD OF RETAILING

↓

RETAILING STRATEGY
6. Retail Market Strategy
7. Financial Strategy
8. Retail Locations
9. Site Selection
10. Organization Structure and Human Resource Management
11. Integrated Retail Logistics and Information Systems

↓

MERCHANDISE MANAGEMENT

STORE MANAGEMENT

QUESTIONS

● Why does the management of human resources play a vital role in a retailer's performance?

● What activities do retail employees undertake and how are they typically organized?

● How do retailers coordinate employees' activities and motivate them to work toward organization goals?

● What are the new human resource management programs for managing diversity, empowering employees, and building employee commitment?

RETAILERS ACHIEVE THEIR FINANCIAL objectives by effectively managing their four critical assets: their locations, merchandise inventory, stores, and employees. This chapter focuses on the organization and management of employees—the retailer's human resources.

Human resource management is particularly important in retailing because employees play a major role in performing retail functions. In many manufacturing firms, capital equipment (machinery, computer systems, robotics) is now used to perform jobs employees once did. But retailing and other service businesses remain labor-intensive. Retailers still rely on people to perform the basic retailing activities such as buying, displaying merchandise, and providing service to customers.

Bernard Marcus and Arthur Blank, cofounders of Home Depot, attribute their firm's phenomenal success to its 103,000 employees. Retailing View 10.1 describes Home Depot's innovative approaches to human resource management.

Two chapters in this text are devoted to human resource management because it's such an important issue in the management and performance of retail firms. This chapter focuses on the broad strategic issues involving organization structure, the general approaches used to coordinate and motivate employee activities, and new approaches for building a committed work force and reducing

10.1

Human Resource Management at Home Depot

THE FOLLOWING QUOTATIONS from Home Depot's annual reports illustrate its human resource philosophy:

- *Candid two-way communications*—We make sure our employees know what is expected of them and what they should expect—even demand from their managers. We value free expression, individuality, and self-reliance within the context of team work, experimentation, and risk-taking. . . . We will lose our entrepreneurial focus if we evolve into a company of many thousands of people marching in lockstep, all with the same mentality, same behaviors, and same politically correct attitudes.

- *Training*—Our company does not manage by memo or edict. . . . Our officers and senior managers don their orange aprons and spend significant amount[s] of time in the stores, working alongside, teaching and learning from our store employees.

- *Compensation*—We believe that the best way to create wealth is to share it. Our philosophy is to pay people what they are worth. We have no set pay scales and no one makes minimum wage. Through our stock purchase plans, all of our employees are able to become owners of the Company.

- *Diversity*—We believe in the strength that comes from diversity and continue to make progress in the hiring and promotion of women and minorities. In an industry [home-improvement centers] that has traditionally been male-dominated, we have managed to develop an employee base that is a reasonable representation of the communities where we do business.

Source: Company documents.

Due to Home Depot's stock ownership plan, company employees are dedicated to achieving the company's objective of providing outstanding customer service.

REFACT Labor costs typically are over 25 percent of sales and 50 percent of operating costs in fashion-oriented department and specialty stores.[1]

turnover. Specific activities undertaken to implement the retailer's human resource strategy—including recruiting, selecting, training, supervising, evaluating, and compensating sales associates—are typically undertaken by store management. We discuss these operational issues in more detail in Chapter 17 on store management.

CHALLENGING ISSUES

Human resource management in retailing is very challenging. Most retailers are open long hours and weekends to respond to the needs of family shoppers and working people. In addition, peak shopping periods occur during lunch hours, at night, and during sales. To accommodate these peak periods and long hours, retailers must complement their one or two shifts of full-time (40-hours-per-week) employees with part-time workers. Part-time workers can be more difficult to manage than full-time employees. They often are less committed to the company and the job and are more likely to quit than full-time employees.

REFACT Thirty-five percent of all retail employees work part-time; 3.3 million of these part-time workers are enrolled in high school or college.[2]

Retailers must also control expenses and thus are cautious about paying high wages to hourly employees who perform low-skill jobs. Often retailers hire people with little or no experience to work as sales associates, bank tellers, waiters and waitresses, and stock clerks. High turnover, absenteeism, and poor performance often result from use of inexperienced, low-wage employees.

The lack of experience and motivation among retail employees is particularly troublesome because these employees are often in direct contact with customers. Unlike manufacturing employees on an assembly line, retail employees work in areas that are highly visible to the firm's customers. Poor appearance, manners, and attitudes can hinder sales.

REFACT Wal-Mart is the largest private employer in the world with over 500,000 employees.[3]

Finally, the changing demographic patterns outlined in Chapter 4 will result in a chronic shortage of qualified sales associates and other hourly retail employees. To satisfy their human resource needs, retailers are increasing the diversity of their work force, employing more minorities, handicapped people, and older people. Managing the growing diversity in retail work forces creates opportunities and problems for human resource managers.[4]

OBJECTIVES OF HUMAN RESOURCE MANAGEMENT

The strategic objective of human resource management is to increase **employee productivity**—the retailer's sales or profit divided by its employee costs. Employee productivity can be increased by increasing the sales generated by each employee and/or reducing labor costs. This chapter examines two important human resource strategies that affect employee productivity: the design of the organization structure and the programs used to develop a committed, motivated work force.

The first part of this chapter describes how retail firms are typically organized. Then we discuss the retailers' approaches to improve coordination between departments and employees. The last sections review human resource programs using incentives and organization culture to motivate employees to work toward achieving company goals and build their commitment to the firm.

DESIGNING THE ORGANIZATION STRUCTURE FOR A RETAIL FIRM

The **organization structure** identifies the activities to be performed by specific employees and determines the lines of authority and responsibility in the firm. The first step in developing an organization structure is to determine the tasks that must be performed. Exhibit 10–1 shows tasks typically performed in a retail firm.

These tasks are divided into four major categories: strategic management, administrative management (operations), merchandise management, and store management. The organization of this textbook is based on these tasks, which are performed by different types of managers.

The strategic decisions discussed in Chapters 7 and 8 are undertaken primarily by senior management in the retail firm.

Section II of the text focuses on the strategic and administrative tasks. The strategic market and finance decisions (discussed in Chapters 6 and 7) are undertaken primarily by senior management: the CEO, president, vice presidents, and the board of directors representing shareholders in publicly held firms. Administrative tasks (discussed in Chapters 8 through 11) are performed by corporate staff employees who have specialized skills in human resource management, finance, accounting, management information systems, site location, and distribution. These administrative activities provide plans, procedures, and information to assist operating managers in implementing the firm's strategic plans.

In a retail firm, the primary operating managers are involved in merchandise management (Section III) and store management (Section IV). These operating managers implement the strategic plans with the assistance of administrative personnel. They make the day-to-day decisions that directly affect the firm's performance.

To illustrate the connection between the tasks performed and the organization structure, the tasks are color coded. Red is used to represent the strategic tasks, blue for the administrative tasks, brown for the merchandising tasks, and green for the store management tasks.

Organization Design Considerations

Once the tasks have been identified, the retailer groups them into jobs to be assigned to specific individuals and determines the reporting relationships.[5] Rather than performing all the tasks shown in Exhibit 10–1, individual employees are typically responsible for only one or two tasks.

Specialization Specialization enables employees to develop expertise and increase productivity. For example, a real estate manager can concentrate on becoming expert at selecting retail sites, while a benefit manager can focus on becoming expert in developing creative and cost-effective employee benefits. Through specialization, employees work only on tasks for which they were trained and have unique skills.

EXHIBIT 10-1   Tasks Performed in a Retail Firm

STRATEGIC MANAGEMENT
- Develop a retail strategy
- Identify the target market
- Determine the retail format
- Design organizational structure
- Select locations

MERCHANDISE MANAGEMENT
- Buy merchandise
  Locate vendors
  Evaluate vendors
  Negotiate with vendors
  Place orders
- Control merchandise inventory
  Develop merchandise budget plans
  Allocate merchandise to stores
  Review open-to-buy and stock position
- Price merchandise
  Set initial prices
  Adjust prices

STORE MANAGEMENT
- Recruit, hire, train store personnel
- Plan work schedules
- Evaluate performance of store personnel
- Maintain store facilities
- Locate and display merchandise
- Sell merchandise to customers
- Repair and alter merchandise
- Provide services such as gift wrapping and delivery
- Handle customer complaints
- Take physical inventory
- Prevent inventory shrinkage

ADMINISTRATIVE MANAGEMENT (OPERATIONS)
- Promote the firm, its merchandise, and services
  Plan communication programs
  Develop communication budget
  Select media
  Plan special promotions
  Design special displays
  Manage public relations
- Manage human resources
  Develop policies for managing store personnel
  Recruit, hire, train managers
  Plan career paths
  Keep employee records
- Distribute merchandise
  Locate warehouses
  Receive merchandise
  Mark and label merchandise
  Store merchandise
  Ship merchandise to stores
  Return merchandise to vendors
- Establish financial control
  Provide timely information on financial performance
  Forecast sales, cash flow, profits
  Raise capital from investors
  Bill customers
  Provide credit

But employees may become bored when they're assigned a narrow set of tasks such as putting price tags on merchandise all day long, every day. Also, extreme specialization may increase labor costs. For example, salespeople often don't have many customers when the store first opens, mid-afternoon, or at closing. Rather than hiring a specialist in stocking shelves and arranging merchandise, many retailers have salespeople perform these tasks during slow selling periods.

Responsibility and Authority   Productivity is increased when employees have the proper amount of authority to effectively undertake the responsibilities assigned to them. For example, buyers who are responsible for the profitability of merchandise in a category should also have the authority to make decisions that will enable them to fulfill this responsibility. They should have the authority to select and price merchandise for their category and determine how the merchandise is displayed and sold.

Sometimes benefits of matching responsibility and authority conflict with benefits of specialization. For example, buyers rarely have authority over how their merchandise is sold. Other employees, such as store managers who specialize in management of salespeople, have this authority.

Reporting Relationships   After assigning tasks to employees, the final step in designing the organization structure is determining the reporting relationships. Productivity can decrease when too many or too few employees report to a supervisor. A specific manager can effectively supervise a limited number of people. On the other hand, if managers are supervising very few employees, the number of managers increases and costs go up.

The appropriate number of subordinates ranges from 4 to 12, depending on the nature of their tasks, their skills, and their location. The number of subordinates is greater when they perform simple standardized tasks, when they're well trained and competent, and when they perform tasks at the same location as the supervisor. Under these conditions, supervision isn't very difficult, and the supervisor can effectively manage more people.

Matching Organization Structure to Retail Strategy   The design of the organization structure needs to match the firm's retail strategy. For example, category specialists and warehouse clubs such as Circuit City and Price/Costco target price-sensitive customers and thus are very concerned about building a competitive advantage based on low cost. They minimize the number of employees by having decisions made by a few people at corporate headquarters. These centralized organization structures are very effective when there are limited regional or local differences in customer needs.

On the other hand, high-fashion clothing customers often aren't very price-sensitive, and tastes vary across the country. Retailers targeting these segments tend to have more managers and decision making at the local store level. By having more decisions made at the local store level, human resource costs are higher, but sales also increase since merchandise and services are tailored to meet the needs of local markets.

RETAIL ORGANIZATION STRUCTURES

Retail organization structures differ according to the type of retailer and the size of the firm. For example, a retailer with a single store will have an organization structure quite different from a national chain.

Organization of Small Stores

Owner-managers of small stores may be the entire organization. When they go to lunch or go home, the store closes. As sales grow, the owner-manager hires employees. Coordinating and controlling employee activities is easier in a small store than in a large firm. The owner-manager simply assigns tasks to each employee and watches to see that these tasks are performed properly. Since the number of employees is limited, small retailers have little specialization. Each employee must perform a wide range of activities, and the owner-manager is responsible for all management tasks.

When sales increase, specialization in management may occur when the owner-manager hires management employees. Exhibit 10–2 illustrates the common division of management responsibilities into merchandise and store management. The owner-manager continues to perform strategic and store management tasks. The store manager also may be responsible for administrative tasks associated with receiving and shipping merchandising and managing the employees.

EXHIBIT 10-2
EXHIBIT 10-2

Organization of a
Small Retailer

The merchandise manager or buyer may handle the advertising and promotion tasks as well as the merchandise tasks. Often the owner-manager contracts with an accounting firm to perform financial control tasks for a fee.

Organization of a Regional Department Store Chain

In contrast to the management of small retailers, retail chain management is complex. Managers must supervise units that are geographically distant from each other. In this section, we use Rich's/Lazarus/Goldsmith's (a regional department store chain headquartered in Atlanta, Georgia, and owned by Federated Department Stores) to illustrate the organization of a large, multi-unit retailer.

The Rich's/Lazarus/Goldsmith's division was formed in 1995 when Federated Department Stores merged three regional department store chains. The division employs 17,700 people in 75 stores located in nine Midwest and Southeast states with annual sales of $2.1 billion.[6] While the stores in each region continue to carry the name of the regional chains, there's only one headquarters office. Rather than using the full name of the division, we'll refer to it as Rich's in the following discussion.

Traditionally, department stores were family-owned and -managed. Organization of these firms was governed by family circumstances—executive positions were designed to accommodate family members involved in the business. Then, in 1927, Paul Mazur proposed a functional organization plan that has been adopted by most retailers.[7] The organization structures of retail chains, including Rich's, continue to reflect principles of the Mazur plan such as separating merchandising and store management tasks into separate divisions.

Exhibit 10–3 shows Rich's organization. Most retail chains such as The Gap, Home Depot, and T.J. Maxx have similar organization structures. Vice presidents responsible for specific merchandise, store, and administrative tasks report to the chairperson and president.

In most retail firms, the chairperson and president work closely together in managing the firm. They are frequently referred to as principals or partners. One member of the partnership is primarily responsible for the merchandising activities of the firm—the merchandise, stores, and marketing divisions. The other partner is primarily responsible for the human resource, distribution, information systems, and finance divisions. For example, James Zimmerman and Terry Lundgren are CEO and president, respectively, of Federated Department Stores.

EXHIBIT 10–3   Organization of a Regional Department Store: Rich's

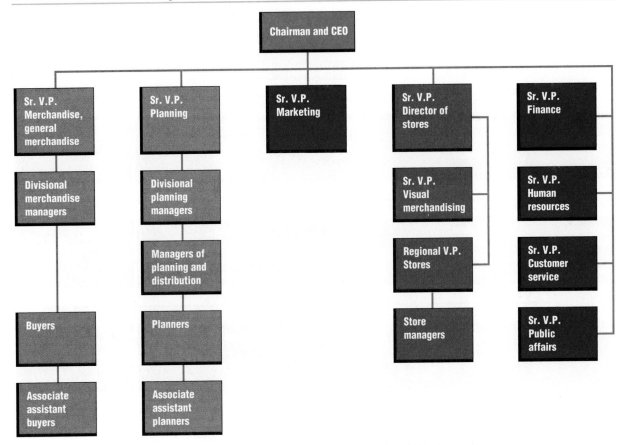

While they share a lot of responsibilities for developing and implementing Federated's strategy, Lundgren is primarily concerned with merchandising while Zimmerman is more involved in operations.

Most managers and employees in the stores division work in stores located throughout the geographic region. Distribution center employees and managers work in one or two distribution centers in the region. Senior executives and merchandise, marketing, and human resource division employees work at corporate headquarters.

Merchandise Division   The merchandise division is responsible for procuring the merchandise sold in the stores and ensuring that the quality, fashionability, assortment, and pricing of merchandise is consistent with the firm's strategy. Chapters 12 through 15 discuss major activities performed in the merchandise division.

Exhibit 10–4 shows a detailed organization structure of Rich's merchandise division. Each general merchandise manager (GMM) is responsible for specific categories of merchandise. GMMs report directly to the chairperson, the partner in charge of the merchandising activities.

The organization structure of the merchandising division in retail chains has changed significantly over the past five years. Previously, the buyer was the key operating manager in the merchandising division. Each buyer was responsible for

EXHIBIT 10–4   Merchandise Division Organization: Rich's

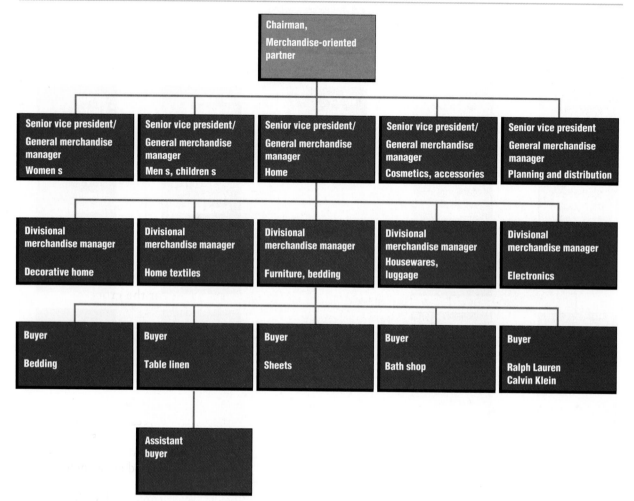

a specific category of merchandise, such as bed sheets and comforters and managed that category as if it were a separate business. Buyers actually selected merchandise and priced it. They determined what merchandise was stocked and sold in each store and managed their business with profit-and-loss responsibility.

Giving this much responsibility and authority to buyers can cause problems. First, the merchandise strategy across categories might not be consistent. For example, the buyer for preteens' accessories might select merchandise that wasn't compatible with the merchandise bought by the preteen's apparel buyer. Second, the allocation of merchandise to specific stores wasn't coordinated. For example, some buyers might allocate more expensive merchandise to stores in high-income areas, while others wouldn't make this adjustment.

To address these problems, most retail chains created a merchandise planning group, with a SR VP of Planning & Distribution which is often as important as the merchandise managers in the buying organization. Each merchandising planner is responsible for tailoring the assortment in several categories for specific stores in a geographic area. For example, the planner at The Gap would alter the basic assortment of sweaters for the different climatic conditions in South Florida and the Pacific Northwest.

EXHIBIT 10–5

Department Store
Organization at
Rich's/Lazarus/
Goldsmith's

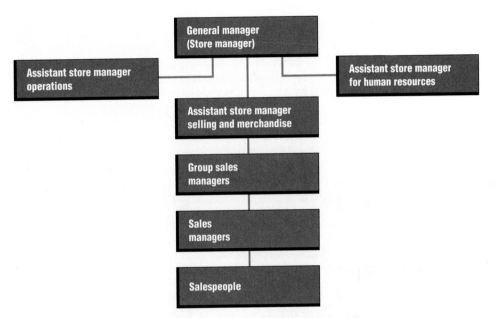

Stores Division   The stores division is responsible for the group of activities undertaken in stores where merchandise is sold and services are provided for customers. Each vice president is in charge of a set of stores. A general manager or store manager is responsible for activities performed in each store.

Exhibit 10–5 shows the organization chart of a Rich's store. The general manager has three assistant store managers reporting to him. The assistant store manager for sales and merchandising manages the sales associates and presentation of the merchandise in the store. The assistant manager for human resources is responsible for selecting, training, and evaluating employees. The assistant store manager for operations is responsible for store maintenance; store security; some customer service activities (such as returns, complaints, and gift wrapping); the receiving, shipping, and storage areas of the store; and leased areas including the restaurant and hair styling salon.

Group sales managers, sales managers, and the salespeople work with customers in a specific area of the store. For example, a sales manager might be responsible for the entire area in which kitchen appliances, gifts, china, silver, and tableware are sold, while a group sales manager might be responsible for an entire floor of the store.

Only the largest Rich's stores have different people in all of the positions in Exhibit 10–5. In smaller stores, for example, the general manager may perform the tasks done by an assistant store manager for merchandise.

Administrative Divisions   Exhibit 10–6 summarizes responsibilities for the departments in Rich's administrative divisions: marketing, human resources, customer service, community affairs, and finance.

Corporate Organization
of Regional Department
Store Chains

As mentioned in Chapter 2, many regional chains, such as Rich's, are owned by retail corporations. Exhibit 10–7 shows the organization chart of Federated's corporate headquarters in Cincinnati, Ohio. The decisions made at the corporate office involve activities that reduce costs by coordinating the regional chains' activities. For example, having one corporate management information system and one private-label merchandise program is much more efficient and effective than having separate systems and programs in each regional chain.

EXHIBIT 10-6

Responsibilities of
the Administrative
Divisions at Rich's

MARKETING DIVISION
Development of marketing strategy and management of advertising and special events.

ADVERTISING DEPARTMENT
Design and placement of newspaper, radio, and TV ads; the design and distribution of
catalogs sent through the mail; and customer research.

SPECIAL EVENTS DEPARTMENT
Planning and implementation of special events such as Elizabeth Taylor's store visits
to promote Passion perfume.

VISUAL MERCHANDISING AND STORE PLANNING DEPARTMENT
Design and development of window and interior displays. Displays are sent to the stores
and then are installed by store personnel.

HUMAN RESOURCES DIVISION
Personnel planning and policies. Recruits, selects, and trains hourly management trainees
and executives. Establishes and administers personnel policies and procedures. Determines
employee benefit packages and negotiates with vendors that provide these benefits. Develops
and administers employee compensation programs. Administers employee evaluation and
career planning activities. Hiring, training, evaluating, and supervising hourly employees is
done in the stores. Chapter 17 details these activities.

OPERATIONS DIVISION
Loss prevention programs, the physical distribution of merchandise from vendors to the stores,
and special services provided in some stores (such as restaurants and hair styling salons).

LOSS PREVENTION
Minimizes inventory shrinkage by designing stores appropriately, installing procedures and
systems to monitor and locate the cause of losses, and communicating the importance of
loss prevention to employees.

DISTRIBUTION CENTER
Moves merchandise from vendors to the stores.

FINANCE DIVISION
Long-range financial planning, budgeting, and financial control activities. Maintains accounting
records, prepares financial records. Assists other divisions in preparing budgets and monitors
performance of these budgets. Manages the firm's credit program. Receives and disburses cash.

MIS DEPARTMENT
Collects data and provides reports that assist buyers in managing the inventory for which
they're responsible.

Corporate Functions   Merchandising and administrative activities performed by
the Federated corporate office, rather than by the regional chain level, include

- Corporate (Cincinnati, Ohio): Support services cover tax, audit, accounting,
  cash management and finance, planning, insurance, forecasting, law, corporate communications and marketing, purchasing, store design/construction,
  and real estate.

- Merchandising and Product Development (New York): Development of merchandising strategies, coordinating relationships with vendors, designing and
  sourcing private-label merchandise, and managing marketing programs for
  private-label merchandise. Among Federated's private labels are The Cellar,
  Charter Club, Arnold Palmer, Club Room, and Affini.

- Financial Credit Services Group (Mason, Ohio): This group provides proprietary credit services for each regional department store chain. Federated
  has over 40 million credit card holders. The group also is responsible for
  payroll, benefits processing, and accounts payable.

- Systems Group (Norcross, Georgia): Sabre, a wholly owned subsidiary, designs, installs, and manages the information system used by all divisions.
- Logistics (Secaucus, New Jersey): Logistics coordinates and manages the logistics functions and also manages the Quick Response and EDI activities.

Organization Structure of Others Types of Retailers

Most retail chains have an organization structure very similar to Rich's structure in Exhibit 10–3 with people in charge of the merchandising, store management, and administrative tasks reporting to the CEO and president. Only corporations that operate several different chains such as Dayton Hudson, The Limited, and The Gap have the overarching corporate structure shown in Exhibit 10–7. Large supermarket chains such as Publix and Kroger's are often organized geographically, like Federated Department Stores, with each region operating as a semi-independent unit having its own merchandise and store management staff.

The primary difference between the organization structure of a department store and other retail formats is the numbers of people and management levels in the merchandising and store management areas. Many national retailers such as The Gap, Sears, and Circuit City centralize merchandise management activities at corporate headquarters and have fewer buyers and management levels in the merchandise group. On the other hand, these national retailers have many more

EXHIBIT 10–7

Corporate Organization: Federated Department Stores

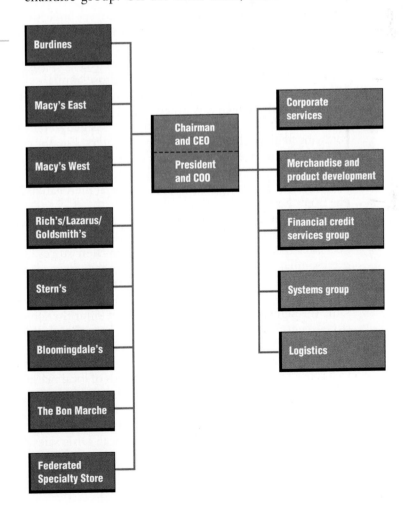

stores than a regional department store chain like Rich's; thus they have more people and management levels in the stores division. For example, one person is responsible for stores and operations at The Gap, in contrast to the regional chain executives for stores and operations in the decentralized Federated Stores organization. But The Gap, with over 900 stores, needs more levels of store management (14 zone vice presidents, 18 regional managers, 195 district managers) than Rich's, which only has 75 stores.

ORGANIZATION DESIGN ISSUES

Centralized versus Decentralized Decision Making

Federated Department Stores, Inc., is an example of a retail corporation with a geographically decentralized organization structure. Many retailing decisions are made by the regional department store chains, not by corporate managers. **Centralization** is the degree to which authority for retailing decisions is delegated to corporate managers rather than to geographically dispersed regional, district, and store managers.

Advantages and Disadvantages of Centralization   Retailers can reduce costs when decision making is centralized in corporate management. First, overhead falls because fewer managers are required to make the merchandise, human resource, marketing, and financial decisions. For example, Federated has both regional women's blouse buyers and corporate buyers coordinating the regional chains and buying private-label blouses. The Gap has one buyer for women's blouses at the corporate headquarters.

With annual sales of about $2.1 billion, Rich's has over 90 people in its buying organization. The Gap has about twice those annual sales and only half as many buyers. Centralized retail organizations can similarly reduce personnel in administrative functions such as marketing and human resources.

Second, by coordinating its efforts across geographically dispersed stores, the company achieves lower prices from suppliers. Finally, centralization provides an opportunity to have the best people make decisions for the entire corporation. For example, in a centralized organization, people with the greatest expertise in areas such as MIS, buying, store design, and visual merchandise can have all stores benefit from their skills.[8]

Most centralized retail organizations emphasize efficiency. Standard operating policies are used for store and personnel management; these policies limit the decisions made by store managers. Often their stores are similar physically and carry similar merchandise. Corporate merchandisers do considerable research to determine the best method for presenting merchandise. They provide detailed guides for displaying merchandise to each store manager so that all stores look the same throughout the country. Because they offer the same core merchandise in all stores, centralized retailers can achieve economies of scale by advertising through national media rather than more costly local media.

While centralization has advantages in reducing costs, it's harder for the centralized retailer to tailor its offering to the needs of local markets. However, retailers are relying more on their information systems to react to local market conditions. For example, American Drug Stores use data collected by point-of-sale terminals to understand local conditions. Most drug stores chains are cutting back on the space devoted to automotive supplies. But American Drug sales data indicated that people in the inner city are more likely to change their own oil so it maintained its automotive supply offering in these stores.[9] Retailing View 10.2 discusses how another large drug store chain uses decentralized management to cater to local market needs.

10.2

Longs Drug Store Managers Are Entrepreneurs

TYPICALLY, EACH OF THE LINKS in a chain store look alike. The stores stock the same merchandise, have the same prices, and use the company handbook. Longs Drug, Inc., with 1995 sales of $2.6 billion from 350 stores in six western states, has one of the highest sales per square foot of any drug store chain by using a different approach.

Longs has a tradition of treating its store managers as independent entrepreneurs. The store manager determines what merchandise to carry and how it will be organized in the store. To illustrate the effects of decentralization, consider the two Longs stores in Walnut Creek, California, a suburb northeast of San Francisco. One store, near a retirement community, promotes aspirin, laxatives, and other products used by the elderly. Small sizes rather than fam-

ily sizes are carried. The store across town, in an area of upper-income professionals with young families, emphasizes disposable diapers, feminine hygiene products, cameras, and VCRs.

While Longs' decentralized approach generates high sales, it's also very costly. After the chain installed POS terminals in 1994, corporate category managers started work with store managers to develop a common core of merchandise so the chain could buy merchandise in quantity at lower prices. Longs also incorporates unique features in its stores such as soda fountains and in-store demonstrations.

Source: Allene Symons, "Annual Report: Longs Drug Store," *Drug Store News,* April 29, 1996, pp. 114–16; and Allene Symons, "Category Management Sparks Longs' Turnaround," *Drug Store News,* March 24, 1996, pp. 61–62.

In addition to problems with catering to local needs, the centralized retailer may have difficulty responding to local competition and labor markets. Since merchandise mix and pricing are established centrally, individual stores may not be able to respond quickly to competition in their market. Finally, centralized personnel policies can make it hard for local managers to pay competitive wages in their area or to hire appropriate types of salespeople.

Coordinating Buying and Store Management Activities

Small independent retailers can effectively coordinate their stores' buying and selling activities. Owner-managers typically buy the merchandise and work with their salespeople to sell it. Being in close contact with customers, they know what their customers want.

On the other hand, large retail firms organize the buying and selling functions into separate divisions. Buyers specialize in buying merchandise and have limited contact with the store management responsible for selling it. While this specialization increases buyers' skills and expertise, it makes it harder for them to understand customers' needs. Four approaches large retailers use to coordinate buying and selling are (1) improving communications between buyers and sellers, (2) making store visits, (3) assigning employees to coordinating roles, and (4) decentralizing the buying decisions.

Improving Communications Fashion-oriented retailers use several methods to increase buyers' contact with customers and to improve informal communication between buyers and store personnel who sell the merchandise they buy. Management trainees, who eventually become buyers, are required by most retailers to work in the stores before they enter the buying office. During this 6-to-10–month training period, prospective buyers gain appreciation for the activities performed in the stores, the problems salespeople and department managers encounter, and the needs of customers.

297

Making Store Visits   Another approach to increasing customer contact and communication is to have buyers visit the stores and work with the departments they buy for. At Wal-Mart, all managers (not just the buyers) are required to visit stores frequently and practice the company philosophy of MBWA (Management by Wandering Around). Managers leave corporate headquarters in Bentonville, Arkansas, Sunday night and return to share their experiences at the traditional Saturday morning meetings.[10]

This face-to-face communication provides managers with a richer view of store and customer needs than they can get from impersonal sales reports from the company's management information system. Spending time in the stores improves buyers' understanding of customer needs, but this system is costly because it reduces the time the buyer has to review sales patterns, plan promotions, manage inventory, and locate new sources of merchandise.

Assigning Employees to Coordinating Roles   Some retailers, like Rich's, have people in the merchandise division (the planner/distributors who work for buyers) and the stores (the managers of operations who work for the store managers) who are responsible for coordinating buying and selling activities. Most national retail chains have regional and even district staff personnel to coordinate buying and selling activities. For example, Target's regional merchandise managers in Chicago work with stores in the North Central region to translate plans developed by corporate buyers into programs that meet the regional needs of consumers.

Involving Store Management in Buying Decisions   Another way to improve coordination between buying and selling activities is to increase store employees' involvement in the buying process. Rather than centralizing the buying decisions at corporate headquarters in Seattle, Nordstrom has buyers who live in each geographic region and buy merchandise for that region. For example, merchandise for the four Nordstrom stores in northern California is bought by buyers in San Francisco. Because these buyers work with a limited number of stores in close proximity to their offices, they're in the stores frequently.

JCPenney has a tradition of decentralized store management. **Decentralization** is when authority for retail decisions is made at lower levels in the organization. Management in each JCPenney

This store owner does not have a problem coordinating employee activities because she has daily, face-to-face contact with her employees and her customers.

JCPenney achieves the efficiencies of centralized buying and the tailoring of assortments for local markets by using satellite communication systems and CD ROMs to involve local store managers in merchandise assortment decisions.

store determines what merchandise that store will sell. Each season, buyers at corporate headquarters in Dallas select merchandise and present it over closed-circuit TV to managers in all Penney stores. Prior to the transmission, store managers are given an order planning form with retail prices, margins, and suggested quantities and assortments for their store size. During the broadcast, store managers can call corporate buyers in Dallas, ask questions, and suggest different types of merchandise that might be popular in their local markets. One week after the broadcast, store merchandise managers place their orders for the merchandise presented through computer terminals linked to the Penney management information system. Buyers then accumulate all of the store orders and place an order for the company with the vendor.

Using regional buyers and involving store managers in buying decisions enables Nordstrom and JCPenney to better tailor their merchandise to local markets. But the firms lose some buying efficiency. At Nordstrom, regional buyers only place orders for four stores. They can't use the chain's entire buying power to get prices as low and delivery as quick as comparably sized competing chains can get. By pooling orders from all its stores, Penney can place large orders and get favorable prices from its vendors. But corporate buyers may be reluctant to make and get firm commitments from vendors until they receive orders from individual stores.

While the buying decisions are made by Penney merchandise managers who interact daily with their customers, these managers have limited buying expertise. Frequently, they've just completed a management training program after graduating from college. Corporate buyers with significant experience and expertise are often frustrated because the store merchandise managers aren't quick to adapt to fashion trends that buyers see coming. Finally, merchandise managers in the stores only see the merchandise on TV or from CD ROMs. They can't feel the merchandise or see its true colors.

In conclusion, each approach for coordinating buying and selling has limitations. Retail firms constantly make trade-offs between the efficiency gained through centralized buying and the greater sales potential obtained through decentralized buying decisions that tailor merchandise to local markets.

10.3

Taco Bell Unleashes the Power of Its People

IN THE EARLY 1980s, TACO BELL was losing money. It had such a weak reputation that people in the Eastern United States thought it was a Mexican telephone company. Prices were rising and a typical family of four was reluctant to spend $25 for a fast-food dinner.

A new management team, headed by John Martin, was brought in to reengineer the business, reduce costs, and improve customer service. Consolidated sites were set up to perform a lot of slicing, dicing, and cooking formerly done at the back of each restaurant. This centralization of food preparation reduced cost, improved food quality and safety, and increased restaurants' space for servicing customers.

The team concept was introduced to extend the notion of ownership and responsibility to the people who interact with the 50 million customers Taco Bell serves weekly. Restaurants were organized as team managed units (TMUs). Instead of having a full-time manager, the crews work together as a TMU to run the restaurant. To reduce the 16 hours a week being spent on administrative tasks, Taco Bell developed a computerized system for employee scheduling and food ordering. Front-line crew members are given responsibility for hiring and training other crew members, handling customer requests and complaints, and even reviewing the financial statements to see how well the restaurant is doing. They decide among themselves about what can be done to improve performance.

Taco Bell's reengineering efforts have built the chain from 1,500 restaurants with less than $600 million in sales in 1982 to over 20,000 locations with $5 billion annual sales. Taco Bell feels that benefits of the TMU concept go beyond improving restaurant performance. For many people, Taco Bell is their first real job. The TMU experience introduces them to the notion of accepting responsibility and developing a work ethic that can serve them throughout their lifetime.

Source: Roger Hallowell, Leonard Schlesinger, and Jeffery Zornitsky, "Internal Service Quality, Customer and Job Satisfaction; Linkages and Implications for Management," *Human Resource Planning* 19, no. 2 (1996), pp. 20–31; and John Martin, "Unleashing the Power of Your People," *Andersen Retail Issues Letter*, College Station, TX: Center for Retailing Studies, Texas A&M University, 1994.

New Developments in the Organization of Retail Activities

To improve financial performance in the face of increased competition, retailers are changing their organizations. These changes reduce cost by flattening the organization structure, outsourcing, and improving employee productivity through empowerment. Retailing View 10.3 illustrates how Taco Bell reengineered its organization to reduce cost and increase customer value.

Flattening the Organization   **Flattening the organization** means reducing the number of management levels. For example, the Rich's merchandise department in Exhibit 10–4 has five levels: partner, general merchandise manager, divisional merchandise manager, buyer, and associate buyer. A flatter organization structure might have three levels: partner, divisional manager, and buyer. Using this structure, there might be more buyers and divisional merchandise managers, but the general merchandise manager and associate buyer levels would be eliminated.

Cutting management levels reduces the total number of managers and increases the organization's responsiveness to customers and competitors. Higher-level managers then become closer to the customer. Fewer levels of approval are needed to make changes and implement new programs.

On the other hand, in a flatter organization, managers have more subordinates reporting to them so they can't supervise them closely. They must trust their subordinates to do their jobs well.[11]

Outsourcing   Retailers, like other businesses, are reviewing the activities performed by company employees and deciding if these activities can be performed more efficiently by other companies. **Outsourcing** is purchasing from suppliers services that previously had been performed by company employees. For example, many retailers outsource logistical services, store maintenance, and management of their information systems. These retailers find that companies specializing in providing these business services perform them at a lower cost due to their scale economies and use of up-to-date technologies. Another example of outsourcing is having vendors rather than retail employees put labels and price tags on merchandise. This example of outsourcing is discussed in more detail in Chapter 11.

While outsourcing these services can reduce costs, some retailers are concerned that outsourcing may result in loss of a strategic advantage. As Chapter 6 said, retailers can develop competitive advantages based on their distribution and information systems. If these activities are outsourced, competitors can achieve similar performance levels by using the vendors. Even a mundane activity like cleaning the store can be a source of strategic advantage that retailers are reluctant to outsource. The Bloomingdale's flagship store on 59th Street in New York City is known for its exciting store atmosphere. When asked about outsourcing the maintenance of the store, the store's operations manager responded, "There is so much that is unique about this store . . . I don't believe any outsider would bring the same sense of passion to the job we do in house."[12]

Empowerment   **Empowerment** is the process of managers sharing power and decision making authority with employees. When employees have authority to make decisions, they become more confident in their abilities, have greater opportunity to provide service to customers, and feel they're more important contributors to their firm's success.

The first step in empowering employees is to review any employee activity requiring a manager's approval. In many cases, the approval is just a formality because the manager relies completely on the employee's advice. Approvals are usually required to minimize mistakes, but errors are often reduced and service increased when employees are empowered to make these decisions without getting approval.[13]

For example, Parisian, a regional specialty department store chain, changed its check authorization policy, empowering sales associates to accept personal checks of up to $1,000 without a manager's approval. Under the old policy, customers frequently had to wait 10 minutes for a sales associate to locate a manager for approval. Then the busy manager simply signed the check without reviewing the customer's identification. When sales associates were empowered to make approvals, service improved and the number of bad checks decreased because the sales associates felt personally responsible and checked the identification carefully.

Empowerment of retail employees transfers authority and responsibility for making decisions to the organization's lower levels.

Many retailers are empowering their sales associates. This sales associate can do what is necessary to satisfy the complaining customer without getting approval from a supervisor.

These employees are closer to customers and in a better position to satisfy customers' needs. For these empowerment efforts to work, managers must change their attitudes from distrust and control to trust and respect.[14]

MOTIVATING AND COORDINATING EMPLOYEES

A fundamental task of human resource management is to motivate and coordinate employees to work toward achieving the firm's goals and implementing its strategy. The task is often difficult because employees' goals may differ from the firm's. For example, a sales associate might find it more personally rewarding to finish arranging a display than to help a customer.

Retailers generally use three methods to motivate and coordinate their employees' activities: (1) written policies and supervision, (2) incentives, and (3) organization culture.[15]

Policies and Supervision

Perhaps the most fundamental method of coordination is to (1) prepare written policies that indicate what employees should do and (2) have supervisors enforce these policies. For example, retailers may set policies on when and how merchandise can be returned by customers. If employees use the written policies to make these decisions, their actions will be consistent with the retailer's strategy.

But strict reliance on written policies can reduce employee motivation. Employees might have little opportunity to use their own initiative to improve performance of their areas of responsibility. As a result, they eventually might find their jobs uninteresting.

Relying on rules as a method of coordination leads to a lot of red tape. Situations will arise that aren't covered by a rule. Employees will need to talk to a supervisor or wait for a new policy before they can deal with a new situation.

Incentives

The second method of motivating and coordinating employees uses incentives to direct their actions. Incentives can be used to motivate employees to perform activities consistent with the retailer's objectives. For example, buyers will be motivated to focus on the firm's profits if they receive a bonus based on the profitability of the merchandise they buy.

Types of Incentives Two types of incentives are commissions and bonuses. A **commission** is compensation based on a fixed formula such as 2 percent of sales. For example, many retail salespeople's compensation is based on a fixed percentage of the merchandise they sell. A **bonus** is additional compensation awarded periodically based on an evaluation of the employee's performance. For example, store managers often receive bonuses at the end of the year based on their store's performance relative to its budgeted sales and profits.[16] Chapter 17 details advantages and disadvantages of compensation plans.

Besides incentives based on individual performance, retail managers often receive additional income based on their firm's performance. These profit-sharing arrangements can be offered as a cash bonus based on the firm's profits or as a grant of stock options that link additional income to performance of the firm's stock. Retailing View 10.4 describes a JCPenney program to give managers a stake in the ownership of the company.

A number of retailers such as Wal-Mart, Home Depot, and Toys "R" Us use stock incentives to motivate and reward all employees including sales associates. Employees are encouraged to buy shares in their companies at discounted prices through payroll deduction plans. Stores compete to have the highest percentage

10.4

Partners in JCPenney

IN 1902, THOMAS CALLAHAN and William Guy Johnson opened a new store in Kemmerer, Wyoming. When they invited James Cash Penney to manage the store and become a one-third partner, a retailing tradition was launched. Mr. Penney has said that this simple act was the key to his success. Becoming a partner fired his ambition to succeed, and he made it a cornerstone in the company he built.

Presently, all JCPenney managers who've been with the firm for five years are inducted into the partnership program and participate in the company's profit-sharing program. Entering the partnership program is a milestone in a Penney manager's career. In October 1996, over 1,000 new partners were inducted. Mr. Penney made the following comment about the significance of being a partner at the 1942 induction meeting:

When the JCPenney Company is faced with the opportunity of choosing partners . . . I say partners because we believe that all our associates work together as partners . . . we make our selection of partners according to the character qualities that best fit into our business, that build rapidly into the principles of our business: Honor, Confidence, Service, and Cooperation (HCSC).

At the first induction meeting in 1913 in Salt Lake City, the following HCSC company motto was outlined:

- Honor is the fundamental ingredient of character. It confers respect and esteem, because it is a constant guide to what is right and true. Our sense of honor will continue to ensure our customers' respect for us. May your every thought and your every act be prompted by that which is honorable.

- Confidence is important. We must have confidence in ourselves and confidence in others in order to inspire confidence. May your conduct and your influence be such that you inspire confidence—at all times—in yourself and in this Company.

- Service is the keynote of success; it attracts customers. Service is the art of making ourselves useful—to our jobs, to our associates, and to our communities.

- Cooperation is the fourth essential of the Penney partnership. The goals toward which we all strive can be reached only through cooperation with each other and with all those with whom we deal.

Source: Company documents.

---

of employee stockholders. These stock incentives align employees' interests with the company's and can be very rewarding when the company does well. However, if growth in the company's stock prices declines, employee morale declines too, corporate culture is threatened, and demands for higher wages and more benefits develop.[17]

Drawbacks of Incentives   Incentives are very effective in motivating employees to perform the activities on which the incentives are based. But incentives may cause employees to ignore other activities. For example, salespeople whose compensation is based entirely on their sales may be reluctant to spend time arranging merchandise. Excessive use of incentives to motivate employees also can reduce employee commitment. Company loyalty falls because employees feel that the firm hasn't made a commitment to them (since it's unwilling to guarantee their compensation). Thus if a competitor offers to pay a higher commission rate, they'll feel free to leave.[18]

REFACT A sales associate who paid $1,650 for 100 shares of Wal-Mart when it went public in 1970 would now have stock worth over $4 million.

Organization Culture

The final method for motivating and coordinating employees is to develop a strong organization culture. An **organization culture** is the set of values, traditions, and customs in a firm that guides employee behavior. These guidelines aren't written in a set of policies and procedures, but are traditions passed along by experienced employees to new employees.[19]

303

Many retail firms have strong organization cultures that give employees a sense of what they ought to do on their jobs and how they should behave to be consistent with the firm's strategy. For example, Nordstrom's strong organization culture emphasizes customer service, while Wal-Mart's organization culture focuses on reducing costs so the firm can provide low prices to its customers.

An organization culture often has a much stronger effect on employees' actions than rewards offered in compensation plans, directions provided by supervisors, or written company policies. Nordstrom emphasizes the strength of organization culture in the policy manual given to new employees. The manual has one rule: Use your best judgment to do anything you can to provide service to our customers.

Lack of written rules doesn't mean that Nordstrom employees have no guidelines or restrictions on their behavior. Its organization culture guides employees' behavior. New salespeople learn from other employees that they should always wear clothes sold at Nordstrom, that they should park their cars at the outskirts of the parking lot so customers can park in more convenient locations, that they should approach customers who enter their department, that they should accept any merchandise returned by a customer even if the merchandise wasn't purchased at a Nordstrom store, and that they should offer to carry packages to the customer's car.

Developing and Maintaining a Culture   Organization cultures are developed and maintained through stories and symbols.[20] Values in an organization culture are often explained to new employees and reinforced to present employees through stories. For example, Nordstrom's service culture is emphasized by stories describing the "heroic" service undertaken by its salespeople. Salespeople will relate how a fellow salesperson went across the mall and bought a green extra-large Ralph Lauren/Polo shirt for a customer who was upset because Nordstrom didn't have the shirt in his size. Department sales managers encourage story telling by holding contests in which the salesperson with the best hero story for the day wins a prize.

Using symbols is another technique for managing organization culture and conveying its underlying values. Symbols are an effective means of communicating with employees because the values they represent can be remembered easily.

Wal-Mart makes extensive use of symbols and symbolic behavior to reinforce its emphasis on controlling costs and keeping in contact with its customers. Photocopy machines at corporate headquarters have cups on them for employees to use to pay for any personal copying. At a traditional Saturday morning executive meeting, employees present information on cost-control measures they've recently undertaken. Managers who've been traveling in the field report on what they've seen, unique programs undertaken in the stores, and promising merchandise. Headquarters are Spartan. Founder Sam Walton (one of the world's wealthiest people before he died) lived in a modest house and drove a pickup truck to work.

Finally, the CEO's philosophies and actions play a major role in establishing corporate culture.[21] Retailing View 10.5 illustrates the two principles used by Herbert Kelleher to establish the distinctive organization culture at Southwest Airlines.

BUILDING EMPLOYEE COMMITMENT AND REDUCING TURNOVER

As mentioned in the beginning of this chapter, turnover in retail firms is very high. **Turnover** is the percentage of employees at the beginning of a time period (usually a year) who aren't employed by the firm at the end of the time period. High turnover reduces sales and increases costs. Sales are lost because inexperienced employees lack the skills and knowledge about company policies and merchandise to effectively interact with customers. Costs increase due to the need to continually recruit and train new employees.

10.5

Humor and Altruism: The Cornerstones of Southwest Airlines' Corporate Culture

THE AIRLINE INDUSTRY HAS gone through dramatic changes since deregulation. While established carriers like Pan Am and Eastern have gone bankrupt, Southwest Airlines has emerged as a leading financial performer by developing a distinctive culture that knits together people working toward the company's goals. Herbert Kelleher built Southwest's corporate culture on two principles: (1) work should be fun and (2) people are important—each person makes a difference. Servicing 49 cities, Southwest Airlines has grown to $3 billion in annual sales, but Kelleher never wants the business to be so big that he can't have a personal relationship with its people. Kelleher goes out of his way to meet Southwest's employees. In 1996, during his visit to the field, he met with 5,000 of Southwest's 22,000 employees.

Humor plays an important role at Southwest because it encourages the frank expression of ideas and feelings without making people uncomfortable. Kelleher hires people with a sense of humor—people who don't take themselves too seriously and don't use humor to make others uncomfortable.

The importance of people is expressed through altruism. Southwest emphasizes that its employees must be motivated to help others. Southwest employees treat each other as family. When a Midland, Texas, agent's son was dying of leukemia, 3,000 Southwest employees (60 percent of its employees at the time) sent cards to him on their own.

Source: Dan Reed, "Flying like a Madman," *Sales & Marketing Management,* October 1996, pp. 92–97; and James Quick Campbell, "Crafting an Organization Culture: Herb's Hand at Southwest Airlines," *Organizational Dynamics,* December 1992, pp. 45–56.

Consider what happens when Bob Roberts, meat department manager in a supermarket chain, leaves the company. His employer promotes a meat manager from a small store to take Bob's position, then promotes an assistant department manager to the position in the small store, promotes a meat department trainee to assistant manager's position, and hires a new trainee. Now the supermarket chain needs to train two meat department managers and one assistant manager, and hire and train one trainee. The estimated cost for replacing Bob Roberts is almost $10,000.[22]

REFACT: Specialty retail chains often have 100 percent annual turnover among salespeople and 50 percent among managers.

To reduce turnover, retailers need to build an atmosphere of mutual commitment in their firms. When a firm invests in developing its employees and demonstrates its commitment, employees respond by developing loyalty to the company. Employees improve their skills and work hard for the company when they feel the company is committed to them over the long run, through thick and thin. For example, when retailers communicate their commitment to their buyers, buyers have the confidence to explore new opportunities and merchandising approaches. They invest time in learning how to do their job better because they know they'll be around when this investment begins to pay off. Some approaches that retailers take to build mutual commitment are (1) adopting promotion-from-within policies, (2) developing employee skills through training, and (3) instituting programs so employees can balance their careers and families.

Promotion from Within

Promotion from within is a staffing policy that involves hiring new employees only for positions at the lowest level in the job hierarchy and then promoting employees for openings at higher levels in the hierarchy. Home Depot, JCPenney, and Wal-Mart have promotion-from-within policies, while others frequently hire people from competitors when management positions open up.

Many retailers have day care facilities so that employees can balance career and family responsibilities.

Promotion-from-within policies establish a sense of fairness. When employees do an outstanding job and then outsiders are brought in over them, employees feel that the company doesn't care about them. Promotion-from-within policies also commit the retailer to develop its employees.[23]

Training   The empowerment trend means that retailers need to provide these empowered employees with the skills to make decisions. Investing in developing employee skills tells employees that the firm considers its employees to be important.

In response to the difficulty in finding qualified service workers, Marriott has made a considerable investment in recruiting and training entry-level workers. The training goes beyond the basics of doing the job to include improving grooming habits and teaching basic business etiquette like calling when you can't come to work.

Employees involved in this program have a strong commitment to Marriott. For example, Sara Redwell started working at Marriott as a housekeeper after emigrating from Mexico. She's now a housekeeping manager supervising 20 employees and mentoring other Mexican immigrants. "What Marriott gave to me, I want to give to others," she says. Tom Lee (a bartender at the Seattle Marriott) proudly proclaims, "Every day I put on this uniform just like an NBA player."[24]

Balancing Careers and Families   The increasing number of two-income and single-parent families makes it difficult for employees to effectively do their jobs and manage their households. Retailers build employee commitment by offering services like job sharing, child care, and employee assistance programs to help their employees manage these problems.

Flextime is a job scheduling system that enables employees to choose the times they work. With **job sharing,** two employees voluntarily are responsible for a job that was previously held by one person. Both programs let employees accommodate their work schedules to other demands in their life such as being home when children return from school.

Many retailers offer child care assistance. Sears' corporate headquarters near Chicago has a 20,000–square-foot day care center. At Eddie Bauer (a catalog retailer in Seattle), the corporate headquarters cafeteria stays open late and prepares take-out

In the early 1900s, people from diverse cultures came to America to assimilate into the mainstream culture. Now the "salad bowl" has replaced the "melting pot" analogy as people from diverse cultures want to maintain their cultural identity.

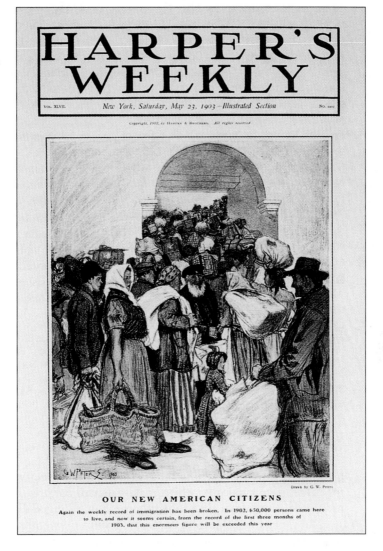

OUR NEW AMERICAN CITIZENS

Again the weekly record of immigration has been broken. In 1902, 650,000 persons came here to live, and now it seems certain, from the record of the first three months of 1903, that this enormous figure will be exceeded this year

meals for time-pressed employees. Some companies will even arrange for a person to be at an employee's home waiting for the cable guy to come or to pick up and drop off dry cleaning.[25]

By investing in employees, companies are able to hire better employees and reduce turnover. Retailing View 10.6 illustrates how Starbucks created strong commitment in its employees. In the next section, we discuss another critical issue facing retailers—building a diverse work force to sell merchandise and services to increasingly diverse consumers.

MANAGING DIVERSITY

Managing diversity is a human resource management activity designed to realize the benefits of a diverse work force. Today diversity means more than differences in skin color, nationality, and gender. Diversity also includes differences in religion, age, disability status, and sexual orientation.

Managing a diverse work force isn't a new issue for retailers. In the late 1800s and early 1900s, waves of immigrants entering America went to work in retail stores. The traditional approach for dealing with these diverse groups was to

10.6

Starbucks Captures the Romance of Italy

THE INSPIRATION FOR STARBUCKS came to Howard Schultz (founder and CEO) as he wandered through the ancient piazzas of Milan. Passing the cheerful espresso bars, he realized that Americans lacked the opportunity to savor a good cup of coffee in a pleasant atmosphere. "I saw what Italy had captured was the romance of the beverage." He opened his first Starbucks in Seattle in 1988 and built a chain of 1,000 coffee bars across the United States with over $500 million in annual sales.

Starbucks develops a passion for coffee in its customers by providing the perfect cup in an entertaining atmosphere. Recognizing that its front-line employees are critical to providing the perfect cup, the company has built an organization culture based on two principles: (1) strict standards for how coffee should be prepared and delivered to customers and (2) a laid-back, supportive, empowering attitude toward employees.

All new hires go through a 24-hour training program that instills a sense of purpose, commitment, and enthusiasm. The new staff are treated with dignity and respect that go along with their title as *baristas* (Italian for bartender). To emphasize their responsibility in pleasing customers, they're presented with a scenario in which a customer complains that a pound of beans was ground incorrectly. The preferred response is to replace the beans on the spot without checking with the manager or someone with greater authority.

So the firm can hold on to these motivated, well-trained employees, all are eligible for health benefits and a stock option plan called "Bean Stock." *Baristas* know about and are encouraged to apply for promotion to store management positions. Due to the training, empowerment, benefits and opportunities, Starbucks' turnover is only 60 percent of its store employees, considerably less than similar food service firms.

Source: Seanna Browder, "Starbucks Does Not Live on Coffee Alone," *Business Week,* August 5, 1996, p. 78; Adrian Slywatsky and Kevin Mundt, "Hold the Sugar," *Across the Board,* September 1996, pp. 39–41; and Bob Filipczak, "Trained by Starbucks," *Training,* June 1995, pp. 73–80.

blend them into the "melting pot." Minority employees were encouraged to adopt the values of the majority, white, male-oriented culture. To keep their jobs and get promoted, employees abandoned their ethnic or racial distinctiveness.

But times have changed. Minority groups now embrace their differences and want employers to accept them for what they are. The appropriate metaphor now is a salad bowl, not a melting pot. Each ingredient in the salad is distinctive, preserving its own identity, but the mixture of ingredients improves the combined taste of the individual elements.[26]

Some legal restrictions promote diversity in the workplace by preventing retailers from practicing discrimination based on non–performance-related employee characteristics. But retailers now recognize that promoting employee diversity can improve financial performance.

As Chapter 4 said, retail customers' racial and ethnic backgrounds are increasingly diverse. To compete in this changing marketplace, retailers need management staffs that match the diversity of their target markets. For example, 85 percent of the men's clothing sold in department stores is bought by women, while over 50 percent of Home Depot's sales are made to women. To better understand customer needs, department store and home-improvement retailers feel that they must have women in senior management positions—people who really understand their female customers' needs.

Retailers recognize that the diversity among the firm's employees and managers needs to match the diversity of their customers.

Besides gaining greater insight into customer needs, retailers must deal with the reality that their employees will become more diverse in the future. By the year 2000, women will make up 47 percent of the U.S. work force, and minorities and immigrants will hold 26 percent of all jobs.[27] Many retailers have found that these emerging groups are more productive than their traditional employees.

After renovating its national reservation center to accommodate workers with disabilities, Days Inn found that turnover among disabled workers was only 1 percent annually compared with 30 percent for its entire staff. Lowes, a home-improvement center chain, changed floor employees' responsibilities so they wouldn't have to lift heavy merchandise. By assigning these tasks to the night crew, the firm was able to shift its floor personnel from teenagers to older employees who provided better customer service and had personal experience with do-it-yourself projects.[29] Effectively managing a diverse work force isn't just morally correct—it's necessary for business success.[30]

REFACT Eighty-five percent of the new entrants into the labor market between 1995 and 2005 will be women and minorities.[28]

Programs for Managing Diversity

The fundamental principle of managing diversity is the recognition that employees have different needs and require different approaches for accommodating those needs. Managing diversity goes beyond meeting equal employment opportunity laws. It means accepting and valuing differences. Some programs that retailers use to manage diversity involve offering diversity training, providing support groups and mentoring, and managing career development and promotions.[31]

Diversity Training   Toys "R" Us has all employees attend a diversity training program so they can identify and reduce their biases and develop skills to manage a diverse work force. The program begins by creating an awareness of employees' different needs and expectations; it includes developing skills to effectively deal with other employees and customers who aren't like them.

Support Groups and Mentoring   Many retailers help form minority networks to exchange information and provide emotional and career support for members who traditionally haven't been included in the majority's networks. In addition, mentors are often assigned to minority managers. **Mentoring programs** assign higher-level managers to help lower-level managers learn the firm's values and meet other senior executives. At Giant Foods, a Maryland-based supermarket chain, the mentoring program has reduced turnover of minorities by making them more aware of the resources available to them and giving them practical advice for solving problems that arise on their jobs.

Career Development and Promotions   While laws provide entry-level opportunities for women and minority groups, these employees often encounter a glass ceiling as they move through the corporation. A **glass ceiling** is an invisible barrier that makes it difficult for minorities and women to be promoted beyond a certain level. To break through this glass ceiling, JCPenney monitors high-potential minorities and women employees and makes sure they have opportunities for store and merchandise management positions that are critical for eventual promotion to senior management.

Similarly, women in the supermarket business have traditionally been assigned to peripheral departments like bakery and deli, while men were assigned to the critical departments in the store: meat and grocery. Even in the supermarket chain corporate office, women traditionally have been in staff-support areas like human resource management, finance, and accounting, while men are more involved in store operations and buying. To make sure that more women have an opportunity to break through the glass ceiling in the supermarket industry, firms are placing them in positions critical to the firm's success.

SUMMARY

Human resource management plays a vital role in supporting a retailing strategy. The organization structure defines supervisory relationships and employees' responsibilities. Principles to be considered in developing an organization structure are specialization, responsibility and authority, unity of command, and the number of subordinates reporting to managers.

In developing an organization structure, retailers must make trade-offs between the scale economies gained through centralized decision making and the benefits of tailoring the merchandise offering to local markets—benefits that arise when decisions are made in a decentralized manner.

Besides developing an organization structure, human resource management undertakes a number of activities to improve employee performance. Retailers motivate employees and direct their efforts in a manner consistent with the retailer's strategy through supervision, policies and procedures, compensation programs, and organization culture. Effective human resource management uses all of these approaches to ensure that the firm's retail strategy is effectively implemented.

Two critical human resource management issues are the development of a committed work force and the effective management of a diverse work force. Building a committed work force is critical in retailing because high turnover has a major impact on profitability. A key factor in reducing turnover is developing an atmosphere of mutual commitment. Managing diversity is important in retailing because customers are becoming more diverse and new entrants into the retail work force will come largely from the ranks of women and minorities. Programs for managing diversity include diversity training, support groups and mentors, and promotion management.

KEY TERMS

bonus, *302*

centralization, *296*

commission, *302*

decentralization, *298*

employee productivity, *286*

empowerment, *301*

flattening the
organization, *300*

flextime, *306*

glass ceiling, *310*

job sharing, *306*

managing diversity, *307*

mentoring program, *310*

organization culture, *303*

organization structure, *286*

outsourcing, *301*

promotion from within, *305*

specialization, *287*

turnover, *304*

DISCUSSION QUESTIONS & PROBLEMS

1. Why is human resource management more important in retailing than in manufacturing firms?

2. What three methods do retailers use to motivate and coordinate employee activities? What are the advantages and disadvantages of each?

3. What are the different types of decisions that should be made by operating managers, administrative managers, and senior managers? What position titles are these types of managers given?

4. What key government regulations affect human resource management?

5. How can national retailers like Sears and The Gap, which both use a centralized buying system, make sure that their buyers are aware of the local differences in consumer needs?

6. To motivate employees, several major department stores are experimenting with incentive compensation plans. Frequently compensation plans with a lot of incentives don't promote good customer service. How can retailers motivate employees to aggressively sell merchandise and at the same time not jeopardize customer service?

7. You've been promoted to manage a general merchandise discount store. Your assistant managers are a black male, an Hispanic, a white female, and a 65-year-old veteran of the Vietnam War. What are the strengths of your management group, and what problems do you see arising?

8. Describe the similarities and differences between the organization of small and large retail companies. Why do these similarities and differences exist?

9. Assume that you're starting a new restaurant catering to college students and plan to use college students as waiters and waitresses. What human resource management problems would you expect to have? How could you build a strong organization culture in your restaurant to provide outstanding customer service?

SUGGESTED READINGS

Cappelli, Peter, and Anne Crocker-Hefler. "Distinctive Human Resources Are Firms' Core Competency." *Organizational Dynamics* 24 (January 1996), pp. 6–17.

Dolan, Kerry. "When Money Isn't Enough." *Forbes*, November 18, 1996, pp. 164–70.

Gable, Myron, Susan Fiorito, and Martin Topol. "The Current State of Women in Retailing." *Journal of Retailing* 70 (Spring 1994), pp. 65–74.

Galbraith, J. R. *Designing Complex Organizations: An Executive Briefing on Strategy, Structure, and Process.* San Francisco: Jossey-Bass, 1995.

Hammonds, Keith. "Balancing Work and Family." *Business Week*, September 16, 1996, pp. 74–80.

Henkoff, Susan. "Finding, Training and Keeping the Best Service Workers." *Fortune*, October 1994, pp. 118–25.

Pfeffer, Jeffrey. *Competitive Advantage through People: Unleashing the Power of the Workforce.* Boston: Harvard Business School Press, 1994.

Quinn, James Brian, Phillip Anderson, and Sydney Finkelstein. "Leveraging Intellect." *Academy of Management Executive* 10 (1996), pp. 7–27.

Smith, Gerald. "Organization Structure and Management for the Small and Mid-Size Retailer." *Retail Control*, November 1990, pp. 25–28.

Spector, Robert, and Patrick McCarthy. *The Nordstrom Way: The Inside Story of America's #1 Service Company.* New York: Wiley, 1995.

Yang, Katherine. "Low Wage Lessons." *Business Week*, November 11, 1996, pp. 108–16.

NOTES

1. *Merchandising and Operations Costs Report* (New York: Fairchild Publications, 1996).

2. *Retailing: Mirror on America* (Washington, DC: National Retail Institute, 1996).

3. Company documents.

4. W. Johnson and A. Packer, *Workforce 2000: Work and Workers for the 21st Century* (Indianapolis: Hudson Institute, 1987).

5. John Burdett and Lawson Mardon, "A Template for Organization Design," *Business Quarterly*, Summer 1992, p. 40.

6. *1996 Corporate Fact Book* (Cincinnati, OH: Federated Department Stores, 1996).

7. Paul M. Mazur, *Principles of Organization Applied to Modern Retailing* (New York: Harper & Brothers, 1927).

8. Walter Loeb, "Unbundling or Centralize: What Is the Answer?" *Retailing Issues Letter*, Center for Retailing Studies, Texas A&M University, May 1992.

9. Susan Reda, "American Drug Stores Custom Fits Each Market," *Stores*, September 1994, pp. 22–24.

10. Bill Saporito, "A Week aboard the Wal-Mart Express," *Fortune*, August 24, 1992, pp. 77–84.

11. John McClenahen, "Managing More People in the 90s," *Industry Week*, March 1989, pp. 30–38.

12. "Outsourcing," *Chain Store Age*, September 1996, pp. 22B–24B; and Susan Reda, "Bringing 'A Sense of Passion' to Vital Housekeeping Needs," *Stores*, August 1996, pp. 79–80.

13. Lawrence Sternberg, "Empowerment: Trust vs. Control," *The Cornell H.R.A. Quarterly*, February 1992, pp. 69–72.

14. Manuel Werner, "The Great Paradox: Responsibility without Empowerment," *Business Horizons*, September-October 1992, pp. 55–58; D. Quinn Mills, "The Truth about Empowerment," *Training & Development*, August 1992, pp. 31–32; and J. Conder and R. Kanungo, "The Empowerment Process: Integrating Theory and Practice," *Academy of Management Review* 13 (1988) pp. 471–82.

15. William Ouchi, "A Conceptual Framework for the Design of Organizational Control Mechanisms," *Management Science* 25 (September 1979), pp. 833–49; and Bernard Jaworski, "Toward a Theory of Marketing Control: Environmental Context, Control Types, and Consequences," *Journal of Marketing* 52 (July 1988), pp. 23–39.

16. Jules Abend, "A Bonus Does Pay Off," *Stores*, July 1987, pp. 69–73.

17. Patrica Sellers, "Can Home Depot Fix Its Stagging Stock?" *Fortune*, March 4, 1996, pp. 139–45; and Bob Ortega, "What Does Wal-Mart Do If Stock Drop Cuts into Workers' Morale?" *The Wall Street Journal*, January 4, 1995, pp. A1, A5.

18. Linda Good, Grovalynn Sisler, and James Gentry, "Antecedents of Turnover Intentions among Retail Management Personnel," *Journal of Retailing* 64 (Fall 1988), pp. 295–314; and William Darden, Ronald Hampton, and Roy D. Howell, "Career versus Organizational Commitment: Antecedents and Consequences of Retail Salespeople's Commitment," *Journal of Retailing* 65 (Spring 1989), pp. 80–89.

19. John Case, "Corporate Culture," *Inc.*, November 1996, pp. 42–50; Scott Kelley, Tomothy Longfellow, and Jack Malehorn, "Organizational Determinants of Service Employees' Exercise of Routine, Creative, and Deviant Discretions," *Journal of Retailing* 72 (June 1996), pp. 135–45; Don Soderquist, "Wal-Mart: Competing with Culture," *Inside Retailing*, Fall 1994, pp. 3–5; and Cynthia Webster, "Toward the Measurement of Marketing Culture in a Service Firm," *Journal of Business Research* 21 (December 1990), pp. 345–62.

20. David Boje, "Stories of the Story Telling Organization: A Post Modern Analysis of Disney as 'Tamara-Land'," *Academy of Management Journal*, August 1995, pp. 997–1015; and Charles O'Reilly, "Corporations, Culture, and Commitment: Motivation and Social Control in Organization," *California Management Review* 31 (Summer 1989), pp. 9–25.

21. John Slocum and Sara McQuaid, "Cultural Values and the CEO: Alluring Companions?" *Academy of Management Executives* 2, no. 1 (1988), pp. 39–49.

22. Frank Hammel, "Tackling Turnover," *Supermarket Business*, October 1995, pp. 103–08.

23. Shankar Ganesan and Barton Weitz, "The Impact of Staffing Policies on Retail Buyer Job Attitudes and Behaviors," *Journal of Retailing*, Spring 1996, pp. 231–45.

24. Catherine Yang, "Low Wage Lessons," *Business Week*, November 11, 1996, pp. 108–16.

25. Kerry Dolan, "When Money Isn't Enough," *Forbes*, November 18, 1996, pp. 164–70; and Keith Hammonds, "Balancing Work and Family," *Business Week*, September 16, 1996, pp. 74–79.

26. R. Roosevelt Thomas, "From Affirmative Action to Diversity," *Harvard Business Review*, March-April 1990, pp. 107–17; and "Race in the Workplace: Is Affirmative Action Working?" *Business Week*, July 8, 1991, pp. 50–61.

27. William Johnson and Arnold Packer, *Workforce 2000: Work and Worker for the 21st Century* (New York: Hudson Institute, 1987).

28. Ibid.

29. T. Cox and S. Blake, "Managing Cultural Diversity: Implications for Organizational Competitiveness," *Academy of Management Executive* 5 (August 1991), pp. 45–56.

30. A. Ramirez, "Making Better Use of Older Workers," *Fortune*, June 30, 1989, pp. 179–87; C. Fyock, *America's Work Force Is Coming of Age* (Lexington, MA: Lexington Books, 1990); N. Perry, "The Workers of the Future," *Fortune*, May 15, 1991, pp. 68–72; and Gary Robbins, "Employment of the Disabled," *Stores*, November 1991, pp. 71–75.

31. Marianne Wilson, "JCPenney Embraces Diversity," *Chain Store Age Executive*, June 1995, pp. 19–25; and Steve Weinstein, "Managing Diversity," *Progressive Grocer*, April 1996, pp. 28–30.

11

Integrated Retail Logistics and Information Systems

THE WORLD OF RETAILING

RETAILING STRATEGY
6. Retail Market Strategy
7. Financial Strategy
8. Retail Locations
9. Site Selection
10. Organization Structure and Human Resource Management
11. Integrated Retail Logistics and Information Systems

MERCHANDISE MANAGEMENT
STORE MANAGEMENT

QUESTIONS

● How do merchandise and information flow from vendor to retailer to consumer and back?

● How can logistics systems help retailers achieve a sustainable competitive advantage?

● What are Quick Response Delivery Systems?

● How are some retailers using databases to develop a one-on-one relationship with their customers?

Until recently, most retailers knew only what merchandise was going into their stores. Until employees counted the merchandise, they had no clear idea about what was selling (or not selling). And by that time, it was often too late to implement corrective action such as taking early markdowns or buying additional merchandise.

Today, many retailers work closely with their vendors to predict customer demand, shorten lead times for receiving merchandise, and reduce inventory investment. They've established on-line systems that link their point-of-sale (POS) cash registers to computer terminals on their desks. They can determine exactly what's selling by item, classification, store, or vendor on a minute-by-minute basis. As a result, inventory investment can be reduced and customer service levels improved.

In this final chapter of the "Retailing Strategy" section, we describe how retailers can gain a strategic advantage through logistics and computer information systems. We then examine how merchandise and information flows from the point of sale at the store, to distribution centers, and on to vendors. The chapter concludes with discussions of two major strategic thrusts that many retailers are adopting. The first, on database retailing, examines how many retailers employ huge databases of information to create individual relationships with their customers by providing them with unique promotions and product offerings. The second, on Quick Response Inventory Systems, examines how retailers are

The flow of merchandise and information starts at the point of sale. The sale is recorded at a POS terminal.

developing strategic alliances with vendors to get merchandise to the stores quickly, with less inventory investment, and with a higher level of service than was ever possible in the past.

INTERNET EXERCISE Retail Systems Alert publishes articles dealing with the latest in retail technology and information systems. Go to their website and click on Top of the Net (http://www.retail-info.com/news/TONentry.html). Find an article that supplements material that is found in the text.

STRATEGIC ADVANTAGES GAINED THROUGH LOGISTICS AND INFORMATION SYSTEMS

Logistics decisions have become an increasingly important component of a retailer's overall corporate strategy. Retailers have realized that profit growth can't be obtained solely through sales growth. Many retailers have stores in mature, stagnant markets. Competition is more intense than in the past. Retailers have realized there's incredible profit potential in having more efficient logistics systems. Retailing View 11.1 describes how Wal-Mart developed a competitive advantage through its logistics and information systems.

Improved Product Availability

An efficient logistics system can improve the retailer's ability to offer customers the exact merchandise they want when they want it. Leda Perez recently went to her local department store on a Saturday afternoon when she saw an ad for silk blouses. Unfortunately the store was out of her size in all the colors she liked. The store gave her a rain check so she could come back and still pay the sale price when it received a new shipment. Perez wasn't impressed. She had fought the traffic, waited in line, and generally wasted her afternoon. In the end, Perez never returned to the store and she told all of her friends about her problems there. The problem could have been avoided since the merchandise was available in the distribution center, but it hadn't been delivered to the store on time.

REFACT Total distribution cost as a percentage of retail sales averages over 17 percent![1]

Improved Assortment

Consumer wants and tastes are changing more rapidly today than ever before. Retailers are attempting to meet these demands by carrying more stock keeping units (SKUs). For instance, only a few years ago a bath department consisted of three sizes of towels in five colors. Now there are

11.1

Wal-Mart Builds a Competitive Advantage through Distribution and Information Systems

WAL-MART'S INITIAL RETAIL STRATEGY was to target customers in small towns with a discount store format. Because the stores were in rural areas while manufacturers and independent wholesalers were used to servicing urban areas, Wal-Mart's distribution costs were quite high. High distribution costs were inconsistent with its strategy of providing everyday low prices in all its markets. To lower its distribution costs, Wal-Mart decided to perform the distribution function itself by using its own distribution centers. Only after building a distribution center does Wal-Mart open stores to be serviced by that center. Each distribution center is designed to service 175 stores within a 150-to-300–mile radius.

As Wal-Mart developed its distribution centers in the 1970s, it utilized two innovative logistics techniques: cross-docking and electronic data interchange. Vendors ship merchandise to a Wal-Mart cross docking distribution center; merchandise is prepackaged in quantities required for each store. Wal-Mart price labels with UPC bar-coding have already been affixed to the merchandise, and apparel is already on hangers. The merchandise is delivered to one side of the distribution center, and then transferred to the other side for delivery to an individual store. That is,

the merchandise goes from delivery dock to shipping dock, thus the expression *cross-docking*. The distribution centers are equipped with miles of laser-guided conveyor belts that read the bar codes on incoming cases and direct them to the right truck for their onward journey. Wal-Mart saves millions of dollars annually by not having to process and store merchandise in its distribution centers.

By the early 1980s Wal-Mart not only had set up computer links between each store and the distribution centers through a system called EDI (electronic data interchange), it also hooked up with the computers of the firm's main suppliers. The final step was to buy a satellite to transmit the firm's enormous data load.

As a result of cross-docking and EDI, Wal-Mart's distribution costs in 1992 were under 3 percent of sales, compared with 4.5 to 5 percent for the firm's competitors—a saving of close to $750 million in that year alone.

Sources: "Stores of Value," *The Economist*, March 4, 1995, pp. 5–6; "Sam Walton: CEO of the Decade," *Financial World*, April 4, 1989, pp. 60–62; and Pankaj Ghemawat, "Wal-Mart Stores' Discount Operations," Harvard Business School, case no. 11-387-018, Rev. 7–87.

---

twice as many SKUs in towels plus rugs, shower curtains, wastebaskets, toothbrush holders, and other accessories—all in matching colors and patterns. This SKU explosion means that additional inventory must be carefully managed and distributed, or the associated costs will far outweigh the profits generated by the additional sales.

Improved Return on Investment   One measure of retailing performance is the ability to generate a target return on investment (ROI). (See Chapter 7.) Consider the commonly used return on investment measure, return on assets:

$$\text{Return on assets} = \frac{\text{Net profit}}{\text{Total assets}}$$

Better logistics and information systems can increase net profit, while at the same time reducing total assets. Net profit can increase by either raising gross margin or lowering expenses. Consider the silk blouse that Perez was trying to purchase. Another retailer with a strong consumer database would have information about the group of customers who like silk blouses including their color and

EXHIBIT 11–1

Information and
Merchandise Flows

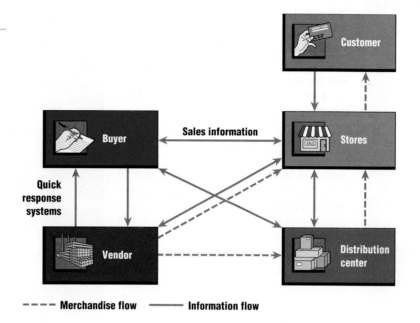

- - - - **Merchandise flow** ———— **Information flow**

style preferences. They would not only try to stay in stock on these items, but they would entice this group into the store with promotions designed and sent directly to them. Their information system between buying staffs and vendors could take advantage of special buying opportunities and obtain the silk blouses at a lower cost—thus improving the gross margin. This same retailer can lower operating expenses by coordinating deliveries, thus cutting transportation expenses. The retailer's distribution center is so efficient that merchandise can be received, prepared for sale, and shipped to stores with minimum handling. Its inventory management system, which is directly linked to the vendor's computer, is so sophisticated that the retailer needs to carry relatively little back-up inventory to stay in stock. Thus, since inventory investment is low, the cost of carrying that inventory is also low. In sum, although it may be increasingly difficult for retailers to achieve higher returns through new store openings and the resulting sales growth, there's still untapped opportunity for many retailers to improve their performance through better distribution and information systems.

Exhibit 11–1 shows the complexities of the merchandise and information flows in a typical multistore chain. In the next two sections we describe how information on customer demand is captured at the store and then triggers a series of responses from the buyer, distribution center, and vendor that are designed to ensure that merchandise is available at the store when the customer wants it.

THE PHYSICAL FLOW OF MERCHANDISE— LOGISTICS

Logistics is the organized process of managing the flow of merchandise from the source of supply—the vendor, wholesaler, or distributor—through the internal processing functions—warehousing and transportation—until the merchandise is sold and delivered to the customer. This section examines how logistics has increased in importance as the complexities of retail management have increased. Retailing View 11.2 discusses how Sears has saved about $45 million by improving its logistics system.

11.2 There Is More to the New Sears than the "Softer Side"

IN THE EARLY 1990s, Sears, Roebuck & Co. was dismissed as a retail dinosaur with its earnings and customer base dwindling. Chief executive officer Arthur Martinez has been credited with the turnaround. The most visible initiative is the successful implementation of "the Softer Side of Sears." Sears had been known for its quality hardlines—Diehard batteries, Kenmore appliances, and Craftsman tools—but not for fashion. Today, Sears is successfully competing against JCPenney and others for the lucrative moderately priced apparel business.

But there is more to the "new" Sears than the "Softer Side." Martinez hired the three-star Army general who was chief of logistics for the entire U.S. military during the Gulf War: William G. Pagonis.

Prior to Martinez's and Pagonis's arrivals, Sears had multiple channels of distribution operating separately under different lines of authority, with no effort to cooperate to get savings or delivery speed. The size of the logistics operation is intimidating, even for a general. Sears has 600,000 truckload shipments a year from 160 warehouses and distribution centers to 800 stores, plus home deliveries of about 4 million items a year.

From total logistics spending of about $1.3 billion in 1995, Pagonis has cut about $45 million, contributing to a companywide 1.2 percent reduction in sales, general, and administrative expense as a percentage of domestic sales. Let's see how Pagonis did it:

- **Simplified and sped-up Sears' distribution system.** Store managers who had to order products through as many as 12 different channels soon dealt with only four. That helped increase the average load of delivery trucks from 60 to 90 percent.

- **Dictated how and when suppliers make deliveries.** Financial penalties are now

General Gus Pagonis, a three-star army general who was chief of logistics for the entire U.S. military during the Gulf War, is now in charge of logistics for Sears. In one year, he saved them $45 million.

imposed on suppliers that fail to meet delivery deadlines or pack and label boxes according to Sears' standards. In 1995, these penalties amounted to $2 million.

- **Reduced delivery times.** Apparel now takes 7 instead of 14 days to get to stores. Home appliances can now be delivered in 24 hours in 70 percent of its markets; a year ago, the company took 48 hours.

- **Reduced inventories.** Faster deliveries from suppliers enabled Sears to reduce its inventory by $10 million in 1995, while 1995 domestic sales increased 7.2 percent.

Source: Robert Berner, "Retired General Speeds Deliveries, Cuts Costs, Helps Sears Rebound," *The Wall Street Journal*, July 16, 1996, p. A1, A7.

Examine Exhibit 11–1. Merchandise flows from vendor to distribution center to stores, or directly from the vendor to stores. Sometimes merchandise is temporarily stored at the distribution center; other times it's immediately prepared to be shipped to individual stores. This preparation may include breaking shipping

cartons into smaller quantities that can be more readily utilized by the individual stores, as well as tagging merchandise with price stickers, UPC codes, and the store's label. A **UPC code** (the black-and-white bar code printed on the package of most products) is illustrated in the cartoon. UPC stands for Universal Product Code. Later in this chapter we'll discuss why some retailers use distribution centers, while others have vendors ship directly to stores.

The Distribution Center   To fully understand the logistics function within a retailing organization, consider a shipment of Hanes hosiery and underwear arriving at a Sears distribution center. The distribution center performs several functions for Sears: coordinating inbound transportation, receiving, checking, storing and cross-docking, ticketing, marking, filling orders, and coordinating outbound transportation.

EXHIBIT 11–A

Merchandise Flows

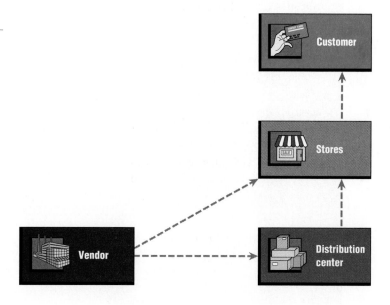

Management of Inbound Transportation   Buyers have traditionally worked with vendors to determine merchandise assortments, pricing, promotions, and the terms of purchase such as discounts to take for early payment. Now, however, buyers and their staffs get much more involved in coordinating the physical flow of merchandise to the stores. The Hanes buyer has arranged for a truckload of hosiery and underwear to be delivered to the Detroit distribution center on Monday between 1 and 3 P.M. The truck must arrive within the specified time because the distribution center has all of the receiving docks allocated throughout the day, and much of the merchandise on this particular truck is going to be shipped to stores that afternoon. Unfortunately the truck was delayed in a snow storm. The **dispatcher**—the person who coordinates deliveries to the distribution center—reassigns the Hanes truck to a Wednesday morning delivery slot and fines the firm several hundred dollars for missing its delivery time. Although many manufacturers pay transportation expenses, some retailers negotiate with their vendors to absorb this expense. The retailers believe they can lower net merchandise cost and better control merchandise flow if they negotiate directly with truck companies and consolidate shipments from many vendors.[2]

Receiving and Checking   **Receiving** refers to the process of recording the receipt of merchandise as it arrives at a distribution center. **Checking** is the process of going through the goods upon receipt to make sure they arrived undamaged and that the merchandise ordered was the merchandise received.

Voice recognition technology is also being applied to the distribution center receiving function. Receiving clerks can process key data by talking into a headset. The system, designed to recognize about 50 words and numbers typically used to designate store and purchase order information, converts spoken commands into printed bar code labels. The operator places the label onto the carton and the merchandise continues along a conveyor belt for sorting and subsequent outbound shipping.[4]

In this cross-docking distribution center, merchandise is unloaded from a vendor's truck onto this conveyor system. Merchandise is then sorted and loaded onto the store's truck.

An order is sent from a store to the distribution center, where it is filled using sophisticated material handling equipment.

REFACT Federated Department Stores Inc. expects all merchandise coming into its distribution centers to be marked with UPC bar code labels and suggested retail price tags. It also requires vendors to provide garments on hangers, when appropriate, and pay penalties for noncompliance of $.15 per hanger.[5]

Storing and Cross-Docking   Since the Hanes shipment is two days late, it has to be temporarily stored rather than shipped immediately to stores. The merchandise is loaded onto forklift trucks that carry it to prespecified locations in the distribution center.

In the past, distribution centers' primary function was to store merchandise received by vendors until it was needed in the stores. Although the Hanes shipment was stored, many retailers are using distribution centers and designing logistics systems around cross-docking. As we said in Retailing View 11.1, *cross-docking* is a system in which vendors ship merchandise to a distribution center prepackaged in the quantity required for each store. The floor-ready merchandise is then transferred to the other side of the distribution center for delivery to a store. Cross-docking distribution centers are less costly than traditional centers because there is little or no storage required, processing at the distribution center is minimal, and the centers can be much smaller than traditional centers.[6]

Had the Hanes shipment been delivered on time, it could have been immediately moved to the shipping area, combined with merchandise from other vendors, and immediately shipped to stores. Retailers want to move merchandise through the inventory pipeline as quickly as possible. After all, retailers can't sell merchandise in a distribution center.

Ticketing and Marking   In a traditional distribution center, **ticketing and marking** refers to making price and identification labels and placing them on the merchandise. In the past, retailers like Sears have ticketed and marked merchandise on the store's selling floor. Unfortunately the selling process is disrupted if new merchandise is scattered throughout the store and retail salespeople spend their time ticketing and marking price labels. Thus it's more efficient to ticket and mark price labels at a distribution center. Identification labels using universal product codes (UPCs) or other identifiers also facilitate the smooth flow of merchandise to the stores. These labels can be affixed to shipping cartons and then scanned at the store to quickly check them in.

Of course, the best approach from the retailer's perspective is to get vendors like Hanes to ship the merchandise floor-ready by ticketing and marking their merchandise and shipping cartons at the factory, thus totally eliminating this expensive, time-consuming process for Sears. Floor-ready merchandise is discussed later in the chapter.

Filling orders   Point-of-sale terminals in a Sears store in East Lansing, Michigan, record each purchase. These data are transmitted to buyers and their staffs so they may formulate replenishment orders for Hanes underwear and hosiery as well as for all other items in the store. (Chapters 12 through 14 detail how merchandise is purchased.) The order for the East Lansing store is transmitted computer-to-computer to the distribution center. The computer at the distribution center creates a **pick ticket** (a document that tells the order filler how much of each item to get from the storage area). The pick ticket is printed in warehouse location sequence so the order fillers don't waste time crisscrossing the distribution center looking for merchandise. The computer knows which items are out of stock so it doesn't even print them on the pick ticket. Order fillers take the merchandise to a staging area where it's consolidated with other merchandise and loaded onto trucks.

In two ways, retailers and their vendors have improved the efficiency of the order-filling function over what we just described. First, using a Quick Response inventory system that we describe later in the chapter, retailers may turn over the inventory management function to their vendors. The POS sales data are transmitted directly to the vendor, who ships an appropriate amount of floor-ready merchandise directly to the stores, thus bypassing the distribution center entirely. Second, if the retailer chooses to use a cross-docking distribution center, the floor-ready merchandise can be moved from the vendor's to the retailer's truck without going through all the steps involved in filling orders.

Management of Outbound Transportation   Due to increased use of distribution centers by retailers, the management of outbound transportation from distribution center to stores has become increasingly complex. The Sears distribution center runs almost 100 routes in one day. To handle its complex transportation problem, the center uses a sophisticated routing and scheduling computer system. This system considers customer service levels, road conditions, and transportation operating constraints to develop the most efficient routes possible. It utilizes an accurate road network to provide stores with an accurate time of arrival and to maximize vehicle utilization.

Another challenge to multistore chains is the transportation problems associated with interstore transfers. For instance, Leda Perez may not have been disappointed if the silk blouse she wanted was properly transferred to the store. Buyers and their staffs can balance stocks by shifting sizes or colors to stores where they're needed. In an era of ever more demanding customers, special orders are on the rise. Buying staffs must handle these important but time-consuming orders through interstore transfers or special orders from vendors. Finally, buying staffs at some retail firms consolidate all sale merchandise into one location, like the "Last Call Sale" at Neiman Marcus, resulting in a giant interstore transfer. Buyers may incur additional outbound transportation expenses when merchandise is returned to a vendor because it's damaged or defective merchandise, unsold consigned merchandise, or unsold merchandise that has been authorized by the vendor to be returned.

Now we will look at some additional logistics issues facing retailers today. First, retailers are outsourcing many functions. Outsourcing is obtaining a service from outside the company that had previously been done by the firm itself. Second, the relative advantages of delivering merchandise directly to stores or using a distribution center are examined. Finally, we will look at the conditions under which it's best to use a pull versus a push logistics strategy.

Outsourcing   To streamline their operations and make more productive use of their assets and personnel, retailers are constantly looking to outsource logistical functions if those functions can be performed better or less expensively by someone else. Sometimes these functions are passed back to the vendor, as is the case with floor-ready merchandise. Other times retailers contract with third-party logistics companies.

Floor-ready merchandise   **Floor-ready merchandise** is merchandise that's ready to be placed on the selling floor. Prior to the advent of a floor-ready merchandise system, each carton had to be unpacked and its contents checked to make sure the merchandise received was the merchandise ordered. Price labels and security devices used to prevent shoplifting were generated and attached to each item. Bar codes were attached to shipping labels. Garments were placed on appropriate hangers. Shipments were checked before they were sent to stores.

The following example illustrates how Hanes provides Sears with floor-ready merchandise. The Hanes shipment is received and checked in using scanners. Hanes marks the boxes with unique identifying bar codes. The person on the receiving dock simply scans the bar-coded boxes, and the merchandise is automatically checked in. Unless the merchandise appears to be damaged, there's no need to break open cartons and count merchandise, since the contents have been electronically recorded.

All merchandise inside the boxes is marked with Sears' retail price, other identifying information, and UPC bar codes so it can be read by the point-of-sale scanners in the stores. Also, apparel is on hangers, if appropriate. Finally, every item has a source tag. A **source tag** is a very small electronic device that is

Retailers are demanding and receiving "floor-ready" merchandise from their vendors.

unobtrusively affixed to merchandise to prevent shoplifting and provide retailers with merchandise movement information. (Source tagging is explored in the next section.)

Having floor-ready merchandise provides the retailer with several benefits. The cost of making the merchandise floor-ready is passed onto vendors. Large vendors, like Hanes, have developed their own systems to meet their customers' demands. Some smaller vendors, however, have decided it's too costly to provide floor-ready merchandise and have decided to concentrate on smaller specialty stores.

Source Tagging   Although source tagging is only part of a vendor's program to provide retailers with floor-ready merchandise, it has the potential to transform the way merchandise information is collected and used.[7] Source tags are quickly replacing the traditional hard tags used for loss prevention. They are currently less than two inches long and are wafer thin so they can be permanently attached to merchandise. Cloth source tags can be sewn directly into apparel items.

There are two primary reasons why source tagging is an important innovation for retailers. First, source tags are more efficient than traditional loss-prevention systems. Since the source tags are so small, they can be used on higher-priced, theft-prone items such as fashion jewelry, fragrances, and CDs. Once tagged, these items can be brought out of locked cases and made accessible to customers. Source tags are also perfect for apparel. Traditional loss-prevention hard tags make trying on clothing uncomfortable and interfere with the fit.

The second reason for using source tags is that it streamlines the distribution system and provides the retailer with useful information. The retailer is relieved of many time-consuming, expensive loss-prevention activities. The vendor affixes the label onto the merchandise, and it remains permanently on the merchandise. The retailer doesn't have to put it on or take it off.

In the future, source tags will include microchips containing a wealth of information, such as a product's date and point of manufacture, time of departure from the distribution center, date of arrival in the store, warranty parameters, and owner identification. This will enable the retailer to track merchandise even after it is sold, thus reducing counterfeiting, eliminating fraudulent returns, and increasing the potential for recovery of stolen merchandise.

Third-Party Logistics Companies   Many retailers are outsourcing logistics functions to **third-party logistics companies.** These firms facilitate the movement of merchandise from manufacturer to retailer, but are independently owned. Specifically, they provide transportation, warehousing, consolidation of orders, and documentation, or a combination of several of these services. Increasingly, third-party logistics companies provide information services called value added networks (VANs) that facilitate the electronic data interchange that is such an integral part of quick response inventory systems. VANs are discussed later in the chapter.

Transportation   Retailers must choose their shippers carefully and demand reliable, customized services. After all, to a large extent, the retailer's lead time and the variation in lead time are determined by the chosen transportation company. Also, many retailers are finding that airfreight is worth the added costs. Some retailers mix modes of transportation to reduce overall cost and time delays. For example, many Japanese shippers send Europe-bound cargo by ship to the U.S.

REFACT Saks Fifth Avenue outsources its transportation to American Airlines, making Saks its second-largest freight customer.[8]

West Coast. From there, the cargo is flown to its final destination in Europe. By combining the two modes of transport, sea–air, the entire trip takes about two weeks, as opposed to four or five weeks with an all-water route, and the cost is about half of an all-air route.[9]

Warehousing To meet the increasingly stringent demands retailers are placing on their vendors to meet specific delivery times for floor-ready merchandise, many vendors must store merchandise close to their retail customers. Rather than owning these warehouses themselves, vendors typically use **public warehouses** which are owned and operated by a third party. By using public warehouses, vendors can provide their retailers with the level of service demanded without having to invest in warehousing facilities.

Freight Forwarders *Freight forwarders* are companies that purchase transport services. They then consolidate small shipments from a number of shippers into large shipments that move at a lower freight rate. These companies offer shippers lower rates than the shippers could obtain directly from transportation companies because small shipments generally cost more per pound to transport than large shipments.[10]

One of the most daunting tasks for a retailer involved in importing merchandise to the United States is government bureaucracy. International freight forwarders not only purchase transport services, but also prepare and expedite all documentation, such as government-required export declarations and consular and shipping documents.[11]

Integrated Third-Party Logistics Services Traditional definitions distinguishing between transportation, warehousing, and freight forwarding have become blurred in recent years. Some of the best transportation firms, for example, now provide public warehousing, freight forwarding, and VANs. The same diversification strategy is being used by the other types of third-party logistics providers. Retailers are finding this "one-stop shopping" quite useful.

Retailing View 11.3 tells how fresh lobsters get from Canada to locations around the world using third-party logistics services.

Store versus Distribution Center Delivery

Today, more merchandise is distributed directly by retailers rather than by wholesalers or manufacturers to retailers.[12] More and more national and regional chains like The Limited and Toys "R" Us are doing their own distribution. Many of these chains have developed sophisticated logistics systems for bringing merchandise into central distribution centers and then reshipping it to stores. Yet others prefer to have merchandise delivered directly to stores.

To determine which distribution system—distribution centers or direct store delivery—is better, the retailer must consider the total cost associated with each alternative versus the customer service criterion of having the right merchandise at the store when the customer wants to buy it. What are the advantages of using a distribution center? First, more accurate sales forecasts are possible when the retailer does a combined forecast for all stores that draw from a distribution center rather than doing a forecast for each store. Consider, for instance, a chain with 10 stores, each carrying a Black & Decker toaster oven. Each store normally stocks five units—a total of 50 units in the system. By

11.3

Lobsters—Get Them While They're Fresh!

LOBSTER, PERHAPS ONE of the most sensitive and highly perishable of products, provides logistics challenges for retailers and their suppliers. Lobster must arrive alive and in good health at the final destination, which for Ferguson's Lobster Pound, Ltd., based in Halifax, Nova Scotia, Canada, includes countries all over the world. The average length of time a lobster survives out of water is 30 to 40 hours. Shipping costs are too high to ship lobster in water containers. Managing the lobster shipping logistics is a 24-hour-a-day, seven-day-a-week business.

In response to the shipping challenges, Ferguson's has implemented several innovative programs. First, it formed an arrangement that would ensure regular delivery to European destinations. Before the arrangement, low-volume cargo—lobster included—moved on a space-available basis. As a result, last-minute changes in airline scheduling were fairly common. These changes could literally kill a marketplace. European buyers want 8 A.M. delivery so they can get the goods to restaurants in time for lunch and dinner. If a flight doesn't get there until 4 P.M., you have lost a day's business.

Ferguson's solved the problem by working closely with Air Canada to quicken turnaround times at London's Heathrow airport, to establish state-of-the-art in-flight cooler facilities, and to ease the customs process. For lobster shipments to Japan, Air Canada flies the lobster to Los Angeles or San Francisco, where it's turned over to Japan Airlines for transport to Tokyo. Particularly for these trips from Halifax to Japan, which last about 30 hours, temperature control is critical. Rather than being wrapped in wet newspaper and packed in waxed corrugated boxes (as done

These lobsters travel in style from Halifax, Nova Scotia, to Canada to Japan in 30 hours. Temperature control is critical. The lobsters are packed in an insulated container that has a separate compartment for dry ice and an attachment to a machine that periodically pumps in cool oxygen.

for European delivery), Japanese-bound lobsters travel in style: in an insulated container with a separate compartment for dry ice and an attachment to a machine that periodically pumps in cool oxygen.

Source: Jay Gordon, "The Logistics of Lobster," *Distribution*, October 1991, pp. 38–40. Taken from Michael R. Czinkota and Ilkka A. Ronkainen, *Global Marketing* (New York: Harcourt Brace, 1996), p. 474.

carrying the item at each store, the retailer must develop 10 individual forecasts, each with the possibility of error resulting in either too much or too little merchandise. Alternatively, by carrying most inventory in a distribution center and feeding the stores toaster ovens as they need them, only one forecast is required, reducing the forecast error. Second, distribution centers enable the retailer to carry less merchandise in the individual stores, resulting in a lower inventory investment systemwide. If the stores get frequent deliveries from the distribution center, they need to carry relatively little extra merchandise as back-up stock. Third, it's easier to avoid running out of stock or having too much stock in any particular store since merchandise is ordered from the distribution center as needed. Finally, retail space is typically much more expensive than space at a distribution center, and distribution centers are better equipped than stores to prepare merchandise for sale. As a result, many retailers find it cost-effective to store merchandise and get it ready for sale at a distribution center rather in individual stores.

But distribution centers aren't viable for all retailers. If a retailer has only a few outlets, then the expense of a distribution center is probably unwarranted. Also, if many outlets are concentrated in metropolitan areas, then merchandise can be consolidated and delivered by the vendor to all the stores in one area. In some cases, it's quicker to get merchandise to stores by avoiding the extra step of shipping to a distribution center. Finally, if the vendor pays freight charges, then direct store delivery will probably result in a lower total merchandise cost.

What type of retailer should use a distribution center?

- Retailers with wildly fluctuating demand for specific items at the store level, like CDs, since more accurate sales forecasts are possible when demand from many stores is aggregated at distribution centers.

- Stores that require frequent replenishment (like grocery stores) because a direct store delivery system would require stores to spend too much time receiving and processing orders from many vendors. There wouldn't be enough hours in the day to process that many trucks.

- Stores that carry a relatively large number of items or order in less than full-case quantities.

- Retailers with a large number of outlets that aren't geographically concentrated within a metropolitan area, but are within 150 to 200 miles of a distribution center.

Pull versus Push Logistics Strategies

As retail operations become more complex and the information systems described in the next section become more prevalent, more retailers will utilize a pull logistics strategy instead of a push one. With a **pull logistics strategy,** orders for merchandise are generated at the store level on the basis of demand data captured by point-of-sale terminals. With a **push logistics strategy,** merchandise is allocated to stores based on historical demand, the inventory position at the distribution center, as well as the stores' need.

A pull strategy is the embodiment of the marketing concept in that stores can order merchandise based on their customers' needs. Further, since inventory at the store is based on consumer demand, there's less likelihood of being overstocked or out of stock. There's also less need for store-to-store transshipments to balance inventories.

Pull logistics strategies can't be used by all retailers, however. It's harder to forecast sales for each store than for a distribution center. Therefore, retailers with less sophisticated forecasting and information systems should probably use a push strategy. Also, a push logistics strategy works well for retailers whose merchandise isn't too desirable but still must be sold. An example of a push strategy that's still used by one of the world's largest firms is General Motors. As sophisticated as General Motors is, it still allocates cars and trucks to its retail dealers based on its production instead of consumer demand.

REFACT More than half of the retailers in a recent survey report using a pull method of inventory or a combination of pull and push. Grocery/supermaket companies rely on the pull method almost exclusively.[13]

INTERNET EXERCISE   The Council of Logistics Management is the premiere industry organization in the logistics area. Go to their site on the Internet (http://www.clml.org/) and find out about new trends in logistics.

THE FLOW OF INFORMATION

The flow of information is complex in a retail environment. Although Leda Perez was disappointed that the store was out of the silk blouse that she wanted, she was successful in purchasing a new pair of Guess? jeans. This purchase triggers a series of information messages throughout the system.

The sales associate scans the UPC tag on the jeans. A sales receipt is created for Perez, and the purchase information is recorded in the POS terminal.

The sales data are also often communicated directly to vendors using a system called **electronic data interchange (EDI)**—the computer-to-computer exchange of business documents from retailer to vendor, and back. In addition to sales data, purchase orders, invoices, and data about returned merchandise are transmitted from retailer to vendor. Information about when orders will be shipped (known as **advanced shipping notice, ASN**), on-hand inventory status, and price changes can be transmitted from vendor to retailer. It's also possible to exchange information about purchase order changes, order status, and transportation routings by EDI. EDI is part of a comprehensive merchandise replenishment system known as quick response that is discussed in the last section of this chapter.

Besides sharing sales data with vendors for replenishment purposes, many retailers have created huge databases, also known as data warehouses, that are used throughout their organization to develop marketing strategies to target specific customer groups. We explore specific uses of these databases in the next section.

REFACT Service Merchandise sends approximately 85 percent of purchase orders and receives nearly 85 percent of invoices via EDI.[14]

EXHIBIT 11–B

Information Flows

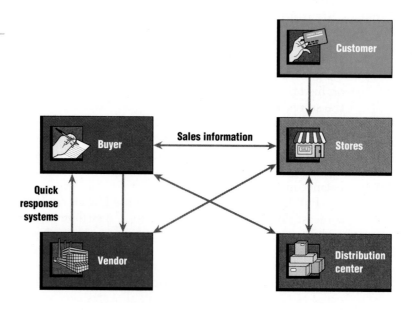

DATABASE RETAILING

In marketing's infancy, at the beginning of the century, all customers were treated the same. Henry Ford said that people could have any color of car they wanted as long as it was black. By the 1960s, marketers concentrated on selling to segments of customers that shared common wants and needs. Today, computer databases allow them to treat customers as individuals. **Database retailing** is a retail management and marketing approach based on an organizationwide database system that gathers and stores data to identify and understand customers and prospective customers as individuals and/or groups.[15]

Database retailing has several advantages over traditional approaches to reaching customers.[16] First, it can be used to build and manage dialogues with customers. Second, all aspects of a marketing campaign can be coordinated using database retailing. Third, these systems can be used to improve inventory management and overall marketing productivity. Finally, the databases can be used to calculate the value of a customer or prospective customer. Now let's explore each of these advantages.

Build and Manage Dialogues with Customers

In a traditional retailing environment, retailers attempt to purchase what they think their customers will buy. They place the merchandise in the store, and wait and see if their customer responds. Retailers utilizing sophisticated databases can develop a dialogue with their customers that can help nurture a long-term relationship.

Not only does the retailer know what was purchased and who purchased it, it also knows a lot about that customer and the household in which he or she lives. The retailer uses the information to seek out and communicate with precisely defined target audiences. The incentives, coupons, and promotions that these customers receive are designed specifically for them. For instance, a grocery chain in Southern California generates coupons printed on the supermarket shopper's receipt, offering discounts on future purchases. The coupons are based on the purchases the consumer has just made. For instance, the system can offer a customer who buys a product's trial size an incentive to try the large size. It can encourage a user of one variant to sample the rest of the line. Each coupon is not haphazard, but a precisely targeted promotional tool.

The database can also identify and target customers who have stopped shopping at a store and encourage customers to come in for special events such as birthdays and anniversaries. For instance, mail-order catalog Fingerhut produces a monthly series of birthday flyers, tailored to a specific age group and sex, which include selections of merchandise. Parents of children with upcoming birthdays receive an appropriately targeted flyer with a personalized message, such as, "Here's wishing Jimmy a happy birthday in May. With your order, you'll get special birthday gifts for him, PLUS three other free gifts."[17]

Integrate Marketing Campaigns

A database program can coordinate different marketing tools to maximize their potency. For instance, a department store introducing a new fragrance would coordinate TV advertising with a sampling program of customers who have previously purchased fragrances. In an attempt to create a loyal customer, after some time it would send these customers a promotional offer to induce them to make a second purchase.

Improve Inventory Management

By maintaining a database on what specific customers purchase, retailers can more efficiently forecast their inventory needs. For instance, Talbots, the women's clothing retailer and mail-order catalog, maintains a database of 7 million customers that includes information about customers' sizes. This leads to more accurate forecasts of which sizes will sell in particular stores.[18]

A men's specialty retailer uses its database to sell overstocked merchandise. After finding it has too many suits in size 40-regular, it can contact customers who wear that size and offer them a special promotional price.[19]

Improve Marketing Productivity

In the past, retailers had only rudimentary knowledge of their marketing efforts' effectiveness. Effective use of retailing databases can improve by linking expenditures with results. They will know whether a specific individual received a communication and whether she responded. Also, retailers can identify and reach market niches too small to be served by mass marketing methods. For instance, suppose a retailer like Bed, Bath, and Beyond recognizes that a small fraction of its customers require hypoallergenic pillows and other white goods. Using a database, it could profitably reach this small niche—a niche that wouldn't have been worth the effort using traditional marketing methods.

Calculate the Value of a Customer or Prospect

Earlier, we discussed how retailers evaluate their return on their investment in assets. These assets were in the form of things we can touch and see, such as inventory and fixtures. Yet a retailer's customers may be its most valuable asset. By maintaining a customer database, retailers can compute the discounted lifetime value of each customer. Knowing the value of a customer enables retailers to evaluate their customers' response to their marketing actions.

Difficulties

If retailing databases are so wonderful, why aren't all retailers using them?[20] First, databases are expensive to collect and analyze. Consider, for instance, the grocery industry. Each store may maintain several hundred thousand different items or stock keeping units. Around 10,000 new items are introduced each year. And this is only half of the problem. Each store must also maintain records on thousands of customers.

The second problem with successfully implementing these databases is that customers may expect big discounts or rebates in return for their loyalty. For instance, The Great Atlantic & Pacific Tea Company (A&P) has developed a frequent-shopper program similar to those used by airlines and hotels. Customers can sign up for free Bonus Saver cards, which entitle them to check-cashing privileges. In addition, hundreds of items are marked with special discounts for cardholders.

Finally, these databases are viewed by some as an invasion of privacy. Government, the press, and the public are all questioning the way personal information is gathered, stored and used. The National Retail Federation urges retailers to disclose how they're using the data in an effort to head off restrictions imposed from outside. Outside of the United States, the European Community has called for full disclosure to consumers of all potential uses of database information.[21]

Clearly, some of the benefits described in this section will only be realized by the most sophisticated retailers. Now let's look at how some of the best retailers combine aspects of logistics and information systems into quick response delivery systems.

QUICK RESPONSE (QR) DELIVERY SYSTEMS

There are only two groups of retail businesses today—the quick and the dead.[22]

Quick response (QR) delivery systems are inventory management systems designed to reduce the retailer's lead time for receiving merchandise, thereby lowering inventory investment, improving customer service levels, and reducing logistics expenses. Quick response systems are known as efficient consumer response (ECR) in the grocery industry.[23]

To illustrate a QR system, consider how the system works at Wal-Mart using its Retail Link system: On Monday afternoon, a customer buys a denim shirt manufactured under a private label for the chain by Americo Group Inc. Every day, Retail Link downloads information from Wal-Mart's computers to Americo's computer. Information includes point-of-sale data by stock keeping unit and by store, warehouse movement, forecast analysis, electronic mail, and remittance advice. A decision support system gives the vendor 100 weeks of product sales history and tracks products' performance globally and by market. Specific sales information on a product is available only to that vendor.

America picks the order, affixes Wal-Mart's price label, UPC code, and source tag for shrinkage protection to the merchandise, places it on hangers, and ships it to Wal-Mart's distribution center on Tuesday. Using a cross-docking system described earlier in the chapter, the merchandise is unloaded and sent immediately to a Wal-Mart truck on the other side of the distribution center. By Wednesday, the shipment is in the store, ready for purchase by another customer. Three days to get the merchandise ready for sale may not seem that amazing, except for the fact that in the mid-1980s the process would have taken a month.

Wal-Mart and its customers aren't the only ones to benefit from this QR system. With sales information on an individual store and SKU level, Americo can customize assortments according to region and climate, and plan more accurately. For example, tracking denim shirt sales (which were high in early summer) will allow Americo to beef up stock for back to school. Analysis of sales data leads to more frequent changes in color palettes and concentration in specific sizes in certain stores.[25]

Quick Response Delivery Systems were originally designed for use with basic merchandise. Retailing View 11.4 shows how retailers now recognize QR's benefits in the fashion apparel arena.

REFACT Quick response yields the general retail community annual savings of almost $10 billion after an initial investment of $3.6 billion.[24]

Benefits of a QR System

Reduces Lead Time By eliminating the need for paper transactions using the mail, overnight deliveries, or even fax, EDI in the QR system reduces lead time. (**Lead time** is the amount of time between the recognition that an order needs to be placed and its arrival in the store, ready for sale.) Since the vendor's computer acquires the data electronically, no manual data entry is required on the recipient's end. As a result, lead time is reduced even more, and vendor recording errors are eliminated. Thus use of EDI in the QR system can cut lead time by a week or more. Shorter lead times further reduce the

11.4

Quick Response: Not Just for Basics

ORIGINALLY, QUICK RESPONSE delivery systems seemed better suited to basic items, such as underwear, paper towels, or toothpaste, than to high fashion. By its nature, fashion dictates being able to quickly adjust to seasons as well as to new colors and styles. Yet Quick Response is as important in managing fashion inventories as in managing basic item inventories. Fashion retailers need to determine what's selling (so it can be reordered quickly) and what isn't selling (so it can be marked down).

Saks Fifth Avenue has been using quick response for basics like Coach handbags since the early 1990s. In the mid-1990s, Saks began to work with vendors of fashion merchandise like Donna Karan. Saks' POS system records each day's sales. If stock falls below preset minimum levels, the system will automatically generate a replenishment order. The order is transmitted electronically to Karan and processed within 48 hours.

Donna Karan and Saks Fifth Avenue have had a Quick Response Replenishment System since the mid-1990s.

Another chain of fashion retailers, Dayton Hudson, has about 25 percent of its apparel vendors participating in quick response programs. Its goal is to get fashion merchandise selling in the stores in six days from the time it is ordered.

Source: Faye Brookman, "Fashioning Quick Response," *Stores*, December 1994, pp. 54–56.

---

need for inventory because the shorter the lead time, the easier it is to forecast demand; therefore the retailer needs less inventory.

Increases Product Availability and Lowers Inventory Investment   In general, as a retailer's ability to satisfy customer demand by being in stock increases, so does its inventory investment. (This concept is explored in Chapter 12.) Yet with QR, the ability to satisfy demand can actually increase while inventory decreases! Since the retailer can make purchase commitments closer to the time of sale, its inventory investment is reduced. Stores need less inventory because they're getting less merchandise on each order, but they receive shipments more often. Inventory is further reduced because the retailer isn't forecasting sales so far into the future. For instance, in the past, retailers may have made purchase commitments six months in advance and received merchandise far in advance of actual sales. QR systems align deliveries more closely with sales.

The ability to satisfy customer demand by being in stock also increases in QR systems as a result of the more frequent shipments. For instance, if a Wal-Mart store is running low on a medium kelly-green sweater, its QR system will ensure a shorter lead time than that of more traditional retailers. As a result, it's less likely that the Wal-Mart store will be out of stock before the next sweater shipment arrives.

Reduces Logistics Expenses   QR systems also have the potential to significantly reduce logistics expenses. Many retailers receive merchandise in their distribution centers, consolidate shipments from multiple vendors, attach price labels, and then reship the merchandise to stores. Until retailers started using QR systems, the use of a distribution center lowered inventory in the store and raised customer service levels. With QR systems, retailers can negotiate a direct store delivery system in which the vendors deliver floor-ready merchandise to each store rather than to the distribution center. The costs of a distribution center (DC) and transportation from the DC to stores are eliminated. Since the merchandise is floor-ready, there's no need to devote expensive retail space for receiving and processing merchandise in the store—space that can be more productively used to sell merchandise.

Costs of a QR System

Although retailers achieve great benefits from a QR system, it's not without its costs.[26] The logistics function has become much more complicated with more frequent deliveries. With greater order frequency come smaller orders, which are more expensive to transport. The greater order frequency also makes deliveries and transportation more difficult to coordinate. Computer hardware and software must be purchased by both parties. Retailers attempt to get their vendors to absorb many of these expensive logistics costs.

Value Added Networks (VANs)

Value added networks are third-party logistics companies that facilitate the electronic data interchange (EDI) part of QR systems by making computer systems between vendors and retailers compatible. Suppose Wal-Mart has contracted with a manufacturer in Mexico to supply toys. Since Wal-Mart insists that its vendors utilize an EDI system, and their computer systems may be incompatible, it might contract with a VAN like General Electric Information Services to provide the communications link. Computer files would be sent to the VAN via EDI, translated to Wal-Mart's format, and sent on to Wal-Mart's computer.

SUMMARY

The changing complexities of the retail environment have forced many retailers to adopt a systems approach to merchandise and information flows. This chapter has discussed why and how they should be linked together.

Logistics has become much more important to the success of a retail enterprise in recent years. Customers are demanding better product availability and broader assortments than in the past. There are simply more retail outlets for chains to service. Many retailers can no longer count on double-digit annual sales increases to sustain growth in profits. Developing more efficient methods of distributing merchandise creates an opportunity to reduce expenses and improve customer service levels in an era of slow growth—or even no growth—in sales.

Retailers are reacting to today's environmental opportunities and threats by changing the way they distribute merchandise. Some are using distribution centers for cross-docking instead of for storing merchandise. Others are forcing their vendors to supply them with floor-ready merchandise and adhere to strict delivery schedules as part of a quick response delivery system. Other retailers are having vendors deliver merchandise directly to their stores and are using pull logistics strategies which base inventory policy on consumer demand. Retailers are outsourcing these logistics functions to third-party logistics companies.

The systems used to control the flow of information to buyers and onto vendors have become quite sophisticated. Retailers have developed databases that provide them with intimate knowledge of who their customers are and what they like to buy. These databases are being used to strengthen the relationship with their customers and improve the productivity of their marketing and inventory management efforts.

Finally, quick response delivery systems represent the culmination of many of the trends described in this chapter. QR systems reduce lead time, increase product availability, lower inventory investment, and reduce overall logistics expenses.

KEY TERMS

advanced shipping notice (ASN), *328*

checking, *320*

cross-docking, *316*

database retailing, *329*

dispatcher, *320*

electronic data interchange (EDI), *328*

floor-ready merchandise, *323*

lead time, *331*

logistics, *317*

outsourcing, *323*

pick ticket, *322*

public warehouse, *325*

pull logistics strategy, *327*

push logistics strategy, *327*

quick response (QR) delivery system, *331*

receiving, *320*

source tag, *323*

third-party logistics company, *324*

ticketing and marking, *321*

UPC code, *319*

value added networks (VANs), *333*

DISCUSSION QUESTIONS & PROBLEMS

1. Retail system acronyms include QR, EDI, POS, and UPC. How are these terms related to each other?

2. It's often hard to introduce new technology such as EDI in retail operations. What practical steps can a manager take to ensure that the introduction of EDI will be successful?

3. Explain how QR systems can increase a retailer's level of product availability and decrease its inventory investment.

4. Draw a picture of what you think a cross-docking distribution center looks like.

5. This chapter has presented trends in logistics and information systems that benefit retailers. How do vendors benefit from these trends?

6. Some retail experts might argue that many expensive and complex computerized checkout stations, particularly in small stores, are nothing more than glorified cash registers. Under what circumstances is this true?

7. What would you include in the ideal retailing database? Why would you include it?

8. The vice president of logistics and information systems for Pearle Vision Centers has been assigned to improve the time it takes to get "hard-to-fit" eyeglasses and contact lenses. What would you advise him to do?

9. Explain the differences between pull and push logistics strategies.

10. Why is global logistics much more complicated than domestic logistics?

SUGGESTED READINGS

Bessen, Jim. "Riding the Marketing Information Wave." *Harvard Business Review*, September–October 1993, pp. 150–63.

Bienstock, Carol C., John T. Mentzer, and Monroe Murphy Bird. "Measuring Physical Distribution Service Quality." *Journal of the Academy of Marketing Science* 25, no. 1 (1995), pp. 31–44.

Blattberg, Robert C., and John Deighton. "Interactive Marketing: Exploiting the Age of Addressability." *Sloan Management Review* 33, no. 5 (September 1991), pp. 5–17.

Buzzell, Robert D., and Gwen Ortmeyer. "Channel Partnerships Streamline Distribution." *Sloan Management Review* 36, no. 3 (March 22, 1995), pp. 85–97.

Christ, Paul F., and Jack Gault. "The Benefits, Costs and Strategic Implications of Quick Response Systems." *1995 AMA Summer Educators' Conference Proceedings.* Chicago: American Marketing Association, pp. 485–91.

Fiorito, Susan S., Eleanor G. May, and Katherine Straughn. "Quick Response in Retailing: Components and Implementation." *International Journal of Retail & Distribution Management* 23, no. 5 (May 1995), pp. 12–17.

Germain, Richard, Cornelia Droge, and Patricia J. Daugherty, "The Effect of Just-in-Time Selling on Organizational Structure: An Empirical Investigation." *Journal of Marketing Research* 31, no. 3 (November 1994), pp. 471–83.

Haley, George T., and R. Krishnan. "It's Time for CALM: Computer-Aided Logistics Management." *International Journal of Physical Distribution & Logistics Management* 25, no. 4 (1995), pp. 46–60.

Lambert, Douglas M. "Developing a Customer-Focused Logistics Strategy." *International Journal of Physical Distribution & Logistics Management* 22, no. 6 (1992), pp. 12–19.

Phillips, Lisa, and Cornelia Droge. "Quick Response: A Theoretical Framework." *1995 AMA Winter Educators'*

Conference Proceedings. Chicago: American Marketing Association, pp. 295–302.

Rogers, Dale S., Patricia J. Daugherty, and Theodore P. Stank. "Enhancing Service Responsiveness: The Strategic Potential of EDI." *International Journal of Physical Distribution & Logistics Management* 22, no. 8 (1992), pp. 15–20.

Kurt Salmon Associates, Inc. *Efficient Consumer Response: Enhancing Consumer Value in the Grocery Industry.* Washington, DC: Food Marketing Institute, January 1993.

Wu, Haw-Jan, and Steven C. Dunn. "Environmentally Responsible Logistics Systems." *International Journal of Physical Distribution & Logistics Management* 25, no. 2 (1995), pp. 20–38.

NOTES

1. Bernard J. LaLonde, Martha Cooper, and Thomas Norrdewier, *1987 Customer Service: A Managerial Perspective* (Chicago: Council of Logistics Management, 1988).

2. "Delivery Systems: The Key to Controlling Inventory," *Chain Store Age*, August 1996, pp. 3T–5T.

3. Paul Olson, "Megashifts and Future Trends in EDI," *EDI Forum*, 1992.

4. Susan Reda, "Voice Recognition System Takes Giant Step toward More Efficient Distribution," *Stores*, September 1996, pp. 38–39.

5. Kathleen DesMarteau, "Floor Ready Is Here to Stay," *Bobbin* 36, no. 7 (March 1995), pp. 56–67.

6. Gary Robins, "Less Work, More Speed," *Stores*, March 1994, pp. 24–26.

7. "Source Tagging: Beyond Loss Prevention," Advertising Supplement to *Stores*, sponsored by Sensormatic, January 1997.

8. "Change at the Check-Out," *The Economist*, March 4, 1995, pp. 31–32.

9. "Sea-Air: Cheap and Fast," *Global Trade*, February 1992, pp. 16–18, taken from Michael R. Czinkota and Ilkka A. Ronkainen, *Global Marketing* (Orlando, FL: Harcourt Brace, 1996), p. 486.

10. Douglas M. Lambert and James R. Stock, *Strategic Logistics Management*, 3d ed. (Burr Ridge, IL: Irwin, 1993), p. 181.

11. Ibid.

12. The authors appreciate the assistance of Professor John T. Mentzer at the University of Tennessee in the development of this section.

13. "Managing the Supply Chain," *Chain Store Age*, October 1996, section 2, p. 12.

14. "Service Merchandise: EDI—A Jewel in the Crown of America's Leading Jeweler," in *Competing with Key*

Technologies, Fifth Annual Retail Technology Study, CSC/RIS News Supplement, June 1995, p. 35.

15. Harrison Donnelly, "Jumping into Database Marketing," *Stores*, December 1994, pp. 36–38; definition by the Direct Marketing Association.

16. Robert C. Blattberg and John Deighton, "Interactive Marketing: Exploiting the Age of Addressability," *Sloan Management Review*, 33, no. 5 (September 1991), pp. 5–17.

17. Jim Bessen, "Riding the Marketing Information Wave," *Harvard Business Review*, September-October 1993, pp. 150–63.

18. "Computer-Dating the Customer," *The Economist*, March 4, 1995, p. 7.

19. Donnelly, "Jumping into Database Marketing."

20. Bessen, "Riding the Marketing Information Wave."

21. Susan Reda, "Retailers Respond to Growing Privacy Debate," *Stores*, December 1996, pp. 20–25.

22. "Flow-Through DC Yields Savings for Fred Meyer," *Chain Store Age*, October 1995, pp. 64–66; quote by Mary Sammons, senior vice president, Fred Meyer.

23. Kurt Salmon Associates, Inc., *Efficient Consumer Response: Enhancing Consumer Value in the Grocery Industry* (Washington, DC: Food Marketing Institute, January 1993); and Gary Robins, "Sailing into ECR's Unchartered Waters," *Stores*, 1994, pp. 43–44.

24. John Ross, "EDI/QR: Dispelling the Myths, Reaping the Benefits," *Retail Systems Reseller* 4, no. 5 (June 1995), p. 2.

25. Georgia Lee, "Wal-Mart's Tool: Data for Vendors," *Women's Wear Daily*, December 5, 1995, p. 10.

26. Paul F. Christ and Jack Gault, "The Benefits, Costs and Strategic Implications of Quick Response Systems," *1995 AMA Summer Educators' Conference Proceedings* (Chicago: American Marketing Association), pp. 485–91.

SECTION III

Merchandise Management

CHAPTERS 6 AND 7 (Retail Market Strategy and Financial Strategy), provided an overall framework for making the tactical decisions that will

CHAPTER TWELVE
Planning Merchandise
Assortments

CHAPTER THIRTEEN
Buying Systems

CHAPTER FOURTEEN
Buying Merchandise

CHAPTER FIFTEEN
Pricing

CHAPTER SIXTEEN
Retail Promotion Mix

be examined more closely in Section III. • In Sections III and IV, we offer tactical solutions to the strategic problems posed in Section II. Section III provides an in-depth discussion of the activities involved in the basic functions of retailing. Chapter 12 discusses how retailers develop profitable assortments and forecast sales. The buying systems used to make these decisions are examined in Chapter 13. • No treatise on merchandise management is complete without an examination of processes involved in buying merchandise. Chapter 14 explores branding options, sourcing internationally, and establishing and maintaining a competitive advantage by developing long-term relationships with vendors. The important question of how to set and adjust retail prices is the subject of Chapter 15. • Chapter 16 looks at the relative advantages of various promotional vehicles available to retailers and at how promotion affects the consumer decision-making process. The chapter also describes how to develop a promotion program and how to set a budget.

Laura Farris, Buyer, Wal-Mart

THROUGH THE CENTER FOR RETAILING EDUCATION AND RESEARCH at the University of Florida, I was able to participate in the internship program and had my first summer internship after my sophomore year at a Wal-Mart store in Johnson City, Tennessee. The following summer, after gaining store operations experience, I interned at the corporate headquarters in Bentonville, Arkansas, in the merchandising division. After I graduated in 1995, I accepted a position in merchandising in the general office. • Today, I am one of seven buyers for the toy department. The categories that I am responsible for are large dolls, plush stuffed animals, junior electronics, and miscellaneous rack toys. These categories will produce over $450 million in sales for Wal-Mart this year. In managing these categories, I am responsible for sourcing exciting new products that will drive sales, promoting the product, getting it to the right stores at the right times, and managing the assets like a portfolio. Buying merchandise is like making a series of investments; I have to make the same risk-return trade-offs that a portfolio manager makes, and I have to watch the performance of my portfolio. At all times, I attempt to maximize my assets by buying more of what's hot, and by marking down and getting rid of items that have not met my expectations. • Another important factor in buying is being a visionary by reacting to current trends and translating them into merchandise that will bring people into your store. For example, a toy with new technology was introduced at this year's toy show in New York. It allows a child to "raise" a virtual pet. After working with senior management and deciding that we wanted to strongly support this item, as the buyer for this category, I put together a plan to ensure that Wal-Mart would be among the first to have this product in significant quantities. I worked with the manufacturer to secure large quantities for an early promotion, then worked with marketing to develop a signing concept, information packet, and flyers to hand out at the stores so that we could create excitement at store level about this new item. Since this is a completely new concept and item, we were taking a large risk, but so far the investment has paid off! Although buyers must always take risks, the returns must always outweigh the risk. However, as with any risk taking, large rewards can only be reaped when large calculated risks are taken.

12 Planning Merchandise Assortments

THE WORLD OF RETAILING

↓

RETAILING STRATEGY

↓

MERCHANDISE MANAGEMENT

12. Planning Merchandise Assortments

13. Buying Systems
14. Buying Merchandise
15. Pricing
16. Retail Promotion Mix

STORE MANAGEMENT

17. Managing the Store
18. Store Layout, Design, and Visual Merchandising
19. Customer Service
20. Retail Selling

QUESTIONS

● How is the buying process organized?

● How do retailers determine the profitability of their merchandising decisions?

● How do retailers forecast sales for merchandise classifications?

● What trade-offs must retailers make to ensure that stores carry the appropriate type and amount of merchandise?

● How do retailers plan their assortments?

MOST RETAILERS' PRIMARY GOAL IS to sell merchandise. Nothing is more central to the strategic thrust of the retailing firm. Deciding what to buy and how much is a vital task for any retailer.

This is the first of five chapters that deal with merchandise management. **Merchandise management** is the process by which a retailer attempts to offer the *right* quantity of the *right* merchandise in the *right* place at the *right* time while meeting the company's financial goals. This chapter examines strategic and planning issues that lay the foundation for the merchandise management process shown in the top portion of Exhibit 12–1. The issues examined in this chapter are used as input into the buying systems described in Chapter 13, as shown in the bottom portion of Exhibit 12–1. As such, Chapters 12 and 13 are integrally related and are designed to be studied together.

Small and large retailers are required to make decisions about thousands of individual items from hundreds of vendors. If the buying process is not organized in a systematic, orderly way, chaos will result. Thus, in the first section we describe how and why merchandise is organized by categories for buying purposes.

As in any business, a retailer's ultimate objective is to achieve an adequate return on the investment to the owners. In Chapter 7 we looked at how retailers set and evaluate their financial objectives. In this chapter, we show how these financial objectives trickle down the merchandising organization, and how these objectives are used to make buying decisions. Specifically, we look at how gross margin and inventory turnover merge together into a merchandise-specific return on investment measure called Gross Margin Return on Investment (GMROI). We also describe how retailers forecast sales.

EXHIBIT **12–1**

Merchandise
Management Issues

PLANNING MERCHANDISE ASSORTMENTS (CHAPTER 12)

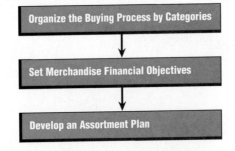

BUYING SYSTEMS (CHAPTER 13)

Once the financial objectives are set, the retailer starts the task of determining what to buy. Superficially, one would think this would be easy. If the store is a women's clothing store, then the retailer would purchase women's clothing. Unfortunately, it isn't that simple. The retailer is limited by the amount of money available for merchandise and the space in the store. He must decide whether to carry a large variety of different types of clothing (categories)—for example, dresses, blouses, and jeans—or carry fewer categories but a larger assortment of more styles and colors within each category. To complicate the situation, he needs to decide how much backup stock to carry for each item. The more backup stock, the less likely he is to run out of a particular item. On the other hand, if he decides to carry a lot of backup stock, he will have less money available to invest in a deeper assortment or in more categories. The process of trading off variety, assortment, and backup stock is called assortment planning.

The culmination of planning the financial and merchandising objectives for a particular merchandise category is the assortment plan. An **assortment plan** is a list of merchandise that indicates in very general terms what should be carried in a particular merchandise category. For instance, an assortment plan for girls' jeans would include the average number and percentage of each style/fabric/color/size combination that the retailer would have in inventory.

From the assortment plan, we move to the more formal buying systems described in Chapter 13.

ORGANIZING THE BUYING PROCESS BY CATEGORIES

The category is the basic unit of analysis for making merchandising decisions. In this section we examine the process of category management and describe where the category fits into the buying organization.

Girls' jeans are a merchandise category because they are purchased from a similar set of vendors. Also, the merchandise is priced and promoted to appeal to a similar target market.

Category Management

It would be virtually impossible to keep the buying process straight without grouping items into categories. In general, a **category** is an assortment of items that the customer sees as reasonable substitutes for each other. Girls' apparel, boys' apparel, and infants' apparel are categories. Each of these categories has similar characteristics. For instance, girls' jeans are purchased from a similar set of vendors. Also, the merchandise is priced and promoted to appeal to a similar target market. The price promotions are timed to occur at the same times of the year, such as back-to-school in August.

As we discussed in Chapter 10, many retail organizations divide responsibility for buying merchandise between a buyer or category manager and a merchandise planner. Although a category manager is more than a buyer in the traditional sense, we will interchange the terms. Since the merchandise planning function is a relatively new concept, it's handled in various ways by different retailers. In some organizations, the category manager or buyer supervises the planners, while in others they're equal partners.

In general, the buyer oversees every aspect of the merchandising function.[1] For instance, she's responsible for working with vendors, selecting merchandise, pricing merchandise, and coordinating promotions with the advertising department and stores. The planner's role is more analytical. She's responsible for buying the correct quantities of each item, allocating those items to stores, monitoring sales, and suggesting markdowns. Together, the buyer and planner are the merchandising team.

The merchandising process can be very inefficient for retailers who don't embrace category management. Without a buyer who serves as a category manager, no one individual is totally responsible for the success or failure of a category. It's also harder to identify the source of a problem and solve it without category management. Suppose, for instance, an ad is placed in the newspaper for a Memorial Day Sale, but the store doesn't receive the merchandise. Who caused the problem? Was it because the buyer didn't order the merchandise in time? Did the

The responsibility for buying merchandise at many retail organizations is divided between a buyer or category manager and a merchandise planner.

advertising manager fail to inform the buyer or the logistics manager that the ad was going to run? Did the distribution center fail to get the merchandise to the stores? Importantly, without the emphasis on category management, the buyer doesn't have the power to solve the problem. By using category management, all of the activities and responsibilities mentioned above come under the control of the buyer and her staff.

The importance of establishing strategic partnerships with vendors has been stressed throughout *Retailing Management*. (See Chapters 6 and 14.) Since retailers and their vendors share the same goals—to sell merchandise and make profits—it's only natural for them to share the information that will help them achieve those goals. Since vendors can develop systems for collecting information for all of the areas that they service, they can provide buyers with valuable information.

Some retailers turn to one favored vendor to help them manage a particular category. Known as the **category captain,** this supplier forms an alliance with a retailer to help gain consumer insight, satisfy consumer needs, and improve the performance and profit potential across the entire category.[3]

Levi Strauss, for example, works with key retailers by balancing stock selections. Levi's account executives work with buyers and sales associates in the stores. They provide merchandising advice and fixtures as well as an electronic ordering system.[4]

A potential problem with establishing a category captain, however, is that vendors could take advantage of their position. It's somewhat like letting the fox into the henhouse. Suppose, for example, that a large candy manufacturer like Mars has become the category captain for a grocery store chain like Safeway. Part of its responsibility is to provide Safeway with planograms. A **planogram** is a diagram that illustrates exactly where every SKU should be placed. Will the planogram provide an assortment that maximizes the profitability for Safeway, or will there be a tendency for the plan to be biased in favor of Mars?[5]

The Buying Organization

All retailers—even those with only one buyer, who may also be the owner-operator of the store—should organize their buying activities around categories to maintain an orderly buying process. Although each retailer has its own system of categorizing merchandise, we have chosen the standard merchandise classification scheme used by the National Retail Federation

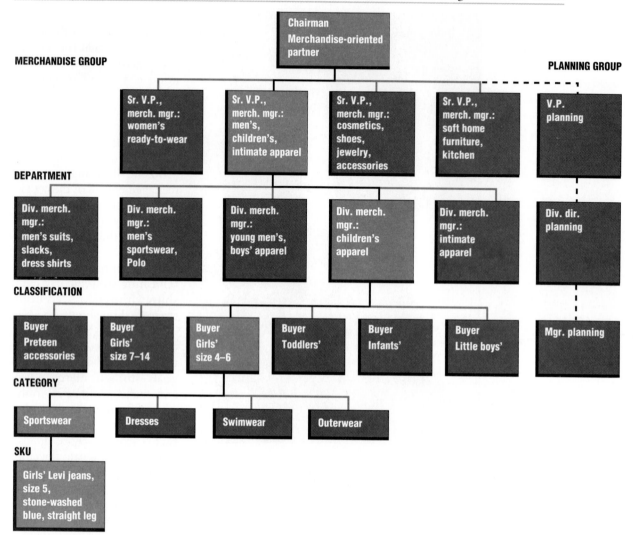

(NRF) for illustrative purposes. Exhibit 12–2 shows how the NRF scheme is used at major department store chains like Federated Stores, Inc. (Bloomingdale's, Lazarus, and others). In Exhibit 12–2, we have concentrated on the buyer. Recall from Chapter 10, there is a merchandise planning group that works with the buying organization. See Exhibits 10–3 and 10–4. Similar schemes are used by other types of stores such as specialty chain stores (The Gap), power retailers (Toys "R" Us), and discount stores (Wal-Mart). These stores typically carry fewer items and have fewer buyers than department stores.

Recall from Chapter 10 that the largest classification level is the **merchandise group.** The merchandise group is managed by the vice presidents of merchandise, also called general merchandise managers or GMMs (Exhibit 12–2). These merchandise managers are responsible for several departments. For instance, the second vice president on the chart in the exhibit is responsible for men's, children's, and intimate apparel.

The second division in the classification scheme in the exhibit is the **department.** These departments are managed by divisional merchandise managers who report to the vice presidents. For example, the vice president of merchandising for

How many SKUs are there in this picture?

men's, children's, and intimate apparel has responsibility for five divisional merchandise managers. Each divisional merchandise manager is responsible for a department. For example, the divisional merchandise manager highlighted in red in Exhibit 12–2 is responsible for children's apparel.

The classification is the third level in the exhibit's classification scheme. Each divisional merchandise manager is responsible for a number of buyers. The children's apparel divisional merchandise manager here is responsible for six buyers. Each buyer purchases a **classification**—a group of items or SKUs for the same type of merchandise (such as pants as opposed to jackets or suits) supplied by different vendors. The exhibit highlights the one buyer responsible for girls' apparel sizes 4 to 6. In some cases, a buyer is responsible for several classifications.

Categories are the next level in the classification scheme. Each buyer purchases a number of categories. The girls' size 4 to 6 buyer in Exhibit 12–2 purchases several categories, such as sportswear, dresses, swimwear, and outerwear. A category like swimwear may be made up of merchandise from one or several manufacturers.

Defining categories isn't always as straightforward as in Exhibit 12–2. Without marketing research, it isn't always clear how the customer perceives the products. For example, a manufacturer might view shampoos and conditioners as separate categories. Yet shoppers choose between purchasing a shampoo combined with a conditioner or buying the shampoo and conditioner separately. Although shampoo and conditioner are not substitutable products, the customer uses them in similar ways.

12.1

Category Management Benefits Vendors Too

MANCO WAS ONCE ONE AMONG many vendors of specialty tape. Now it's credited with being a pioneer in the development of category management.

In the 1970s it was having a hard time merchandising its tape products. The products were found in departments all over the store and were purchased by several buyers. Manco came up with the idea of a tape center, merchandising all kinds of tape in one place.

The idea was so successful that in the 1980s, Manco applied the same concept to a mailing center, a weatherproofing center, and a crafts department—each an extension of a single product (mailing tape, weatherproofing tape, and glue).

The mailing center was the most successful. Several other vendors had attempted to get mailing products like bubble wrap and mailing envelopes into discount stores, but most failed. Manco started with a 19-SKU assortment of mailing supplies. Now it has up to 32 feet in many office superstores.

Manco's tape center was one of the first category management concepts to be used in the United States.

Source: Pete Hisey, "Category Management: Retail's New Changemaker," *Discount Store News*, May 1, 1995, pp. 22, 43.

Therefore, they should probably be grouped as one category.[6] Sometimes it makes sense to make vendors their own category. For instance, since department stores are often organized into vendor boutiques, they sometimes define categories by vendors such as Polo/Ralph Lauren, Liz Claiborne, Estée Lauder, or Clinique.

A **stock keeping unit (SKU)** is the smallest unit available for keeping inventory control. In soft goods merchandise, for instance, a SKU usually means size, color, and style. For example, a pair of girls' size 5, stone-washed blue, straight-legged Levis is one SKU.

Category management can be beneficial to vendors as well, as Retailing View 12.1 shows.

Now that we've examined how and why retailers manage their merchandise by categories, let's consider the financial implications of their actions.

SETTING MERCHANDISE FINANCIAL OBJECTIVES

Retailers cannot hope to be financially successful unless they preplan the financial implications of their merchandising activities. Financial plans start at the top of the retail organization and are broken down into categories, while buyers and merchandise planners develop their own plans and negotiate up the organization. Top management looks at the big merchandising picture. They set the merchandising direction for the company by making (1) projections about how the company will do overall and (2) decisions about which areas deserve more or less emphasis. Buyers and merchandise planners, on the other hand, take a more micro approach. They study their categories' past performance, look at trends in the market, and try to project their merchandise needs for the coming seasons. The financial planning process is similar for smaller retailers. Although there aren't as many layers of management involved in planning and negotiations, they still start with the firm's overall financial goals and break them down into categories.

The resulting merchandise plan is a financial buying blueprint for each category. It considers the firm's financial objectives along with sales projections and merchandise flows. The merchandise plan tells the buyer and planner how much money to spend on a particular category of merchandise in each month so that the sales forecast and other financial objectives are met. Once the merchandise plan is set, the buyers and planners develop the assortment plan. The buyers work with vendors choosing merchandise, negotiating prices, and developing promotions. The merchandise planners break down the overall financial plan into how many of each item to purchase and how they should be allocated to stores. In Chapter 13 we'll describe specific systems used for merchandise and assortment planning.

As you can imagine, there's a great deal of negotiating at each step. Merchandise managers and buyers compete for large sales forecasts because the forecast determines how much money they'll have available to spend on merchandise. Buyers and merchandise managers have to plan elaborate presentations to convince their superiors to increase their sales forecast. Of course, they must be honest with themselves. If they succeed in having a larger sales forecast approved, and the merchandise doesn't sell, their profitability—and their performance evaluation—will suffer.

The next section examines the important merchandise performance measure GMROI and its component ratios: inventory turnover and gross margin percentage. The section concludes with a discussion of how retailers forecast sales.

Putting Profits, Sales, and Turnover Together: GMROI

At the corporate level, return on assets is used to plan and evaluate performance of overall retail operations. (See Chapter 7.)

$$\text{Return on assets} = \text{Net profit margin} \times \text{Asset turnover}$$

$$= \frac{\text{Net profit}}{\text{Net sales}} \times \frac{\text{Net sales}}{\text{Total assets}}$$

$$= \frac{\text{Net profit}}{\text{Total assets}}$$

Using the Strategic Profit Model, we found that we could use return on assets to plan and compare the performance of store managers and other operating executives since they have some control over how assets are employed to produce profits in their store.

But at the merchandise management level, not all components of return on assets are important. Buyers generally have control over gross margin, but not operating expenses. Likewise, they have control over their inventory investment, but not other assets. As a result, the financial ratio that is important to plan and measure *merchandising* performance is a return on investment measure called gross margin return on inventory investment (GMROI).[7] It measures how many gross margin dollars are earned on every dollar of inventory investment.

GMROI is a similar concept to return on assets, only its components are under the control of the buyer rather than higher-level executives. Instead of combining net profit margin and asset turnover, GMROI uses gross margin percentage and the sales-to-stock ratio (which is similar to inventory turnover).

$$\text{GMROI} = \text{Gross margin percentage} \times \text{Sales-to-stock ratio}$$

$$= \frac{\text{Gross margin}}{\text{Net sales}} \times \frac{\text{Net sales}}{\text{Average inventory}}$$

$$= \frac{\text{Gross margin}}{\text{Average inventory}}$$

Average inventory in GMROI can be expressed at retail or at cost. Some retailers use retail inventory since it closely reflects the market price of their goods. The spreferred method of calculating GMROI is to express average inventory at cost, however, because inventory in the denominator of a return on investment is measured at cost. A retailer's investment in inventory is the cost of the inventory, not its retail value. This measure is called the sales-to-stock ratio.

$$\text{Sales-to-stock ratio} = \frac{\text{Net sales}}{\text{Average cost inventory}}$$

So if sales $= \quad \$100,000$

and average cost inventory $= \quad \$33,333$

then sales-to-stock ratio $= \quad \dfrac{\$100,000}{\$33,333} = 3$

Thus,

Inventory turnover = Sales-to-stock ratio $\times$ (100% – Gross margin %)

Continuing the example, if gross margin = 40 percent, then

Inventory turnover = 3 $\times$ (100% – 40%) = 1.8 (expressed as a decimal)

Like return on assets, GMROI combines the effects of profits and turnover. It's important to use a combined measure so that departments with different margin/turnover profiles can be compared and evaluated. For instance, within a supermarket, some departments (such as wine) are high margin/low turnover, whereas other departments (such as dairy products) are low margin/high turnover. If the wine department's performance was compared to that of dairy products using inventory turnover alone, wine wouldn't fare well. On the other hand, if only gross margin was used, wine would be the winner.

Consider the situation in Exhibit 12–3. Here a supermarket manager wants to evaluate performance of two classifications: milk and wine. If evaluated on gross margin percentage or sales alone, wine is certainly the winner with a 50 percent gross margin and sales of $300,000 compared to milk's gross margin of 1.333 percent and sales of $150,000. Yet wine turns (sales-to-stock ratio) only four times a year, whereas milk turns 150 times a year. Using GMROI, both classifications achieve a GMROI of 200 percent and so are equal performers from a return on investment perspective.

GMROI is used as a return on investment profitability measure to evaluate departments, merchandise classifications, vendor lines, and items. It's also useful for management in evaluating buyers' performance since it contains both the gross margin ratio and the inventory turnover ratio. As we showed above, merchandise

EXHIBIT 12–3

Illustration of GMROI

				MILK	WINE
			Gross margin	$2,000	$150,000
			Sales	$150,000	$300,000
			Average inventory	$1,000	$75,000

			$\dfrac{\text{Gross margin}}{\text{Net sales}}$	$\times$	$\dfrac{\text{Net Sales}}{\text{Average inventory}}$	$=$	$\dfrac{\text{Gross margin}}{\text{Average inventory}}$
	GMROI	=					
Milk	GMROI	=	$\dfrac{\$2,000}{\$150,000}$	$\times$	$\dfrac{\$150,000}{\$1,000}$	$=$	$\dfrac{\$2,000}{\$1,000}$
		=	1.333%	$\times$	150 times	$=$	200%
Wine	GMROI	=	$\dfrac{\$150,000}{\$300,000}$	$\times$	$\dfrac{\$300,000}{\$75,000}$	$=$	$\dfrac{\$150,000}{\$75,000}$
		=	50%	$\times$	4	$=$	200%

with different margin/turnover characteristics can be compared. Exhibit 12–4 shows GMROI percentages for selected departments from department and specialty stores. The range is from 110 percent (for footwear in department stores) to 350 percent (for female apparel in specialty stores). It's no wonder that both department and specialty stores devote so much space to female apparel.

Although GMROI is a composite of gross margin and inventory turnover, gross margin plays a more important role in pricing decisions. (See Chapter 15.) But inventory turnover is more important when making decisions about merchandise. The following section explains how we measure inventory turnover and the advantages and disadvantages of a rapid rate of inventory turnover.

The GMROI for low margin/high turnover products like milk can be the same as high margin/low turnover products like wine.

EXHIBIT 12–4

GMROI and
Inventory Turnover
for Selected
Departments in
Department and
Specialty Stores

	GMROI		INVENTORY TURNOVER	
	DEPARTMENT STORES	SPECIALTY STORES	DEPARTMENT STORES	SPECIALTY STORES
Female apparel	230	350	2.6	3.2
Adult female accessories	180	280	1.9	2.5
Men's/boys' apparel and accessories	160	220	2.0	2.4
Infants'/children's clothing and accessories	210	160	2.6	2.4
Footwear	110	140	1.4	1.7
Home furnishings	120	220	1.7	1.8

Source: Alexandra Moran, ed., *MOR 1996 Edition: Merchandising and Operating Results of Retail Stores in 1995,* 71st ed. (New York: John Wiley & Sons), pp. 4–7.

Measuring Inventory Turnover

The notion of inventory turnover was introduced in Chapter 7 as "merchandise in motion." Jeans are delivered to the store through the loading dock in the back, spend some time in the store on the racks, and then are sold and go out the front door. The faster this process takes place, the higher the inventory turnover will be. We thus can think of inventory turnover as how many times, on average, the jeans cycle through the store during a specific period of time, usually one year. It's a measure of the productivity of inventory—that is, how many sales dollars can be generated from a dollar invested in jeans.

Inventory turnover is defined as follows:

$$\text{Inventory turnover} = \frac{\text{Net sales}}{\text{Average inventory at retail}}$$

or

$$\text{Inventory turnover} = \frac{\text{Cost of goods sold}}{\text{Average inventory at cost}}$$

Since most retailers tend to think of their inventory at retail, the first definition is preferable. Arithmetically there's no difference between these two definitions, and they yield the same result.[8] Be careful, however, since both the numerator and denominator must be at retail or at cost.

Retailers normally express inventory turnover rates on an annual basis rather than for parts of a year. Suppose the net sales used in an inventory turnover calculation is for a three-month season. If turnover for that season is calculated as 2.3 turns, then annual turnover will be four times that number (9.2). Thus, to convert an inventory turnover calculation based on part of a year to an annual figure, multiply it by the number of such time periods in the year.

Exhibit 12–4 shows inventory turnover ratios for selected departments from department and specialty stores. The range is from 3.2 (for female apparel in specialty stores) to 1.4 (for footwear in department stores).

Calculating Average Inventory   Average inventory is calculated by dividing the sum of the inventory for each of several months by the number of months:

$$\text{Average inventory} = \frac{\text{Month}_1 + \text{Month}_2 + \text{Month}_3 + \ldots}{\text{Number of months}}$$

But how many months should be used? How could we determine the inventory for the month? One approach is to take the end-of-month (EOM) inventories for several months and divide by the number of months available. For example,

MONTH	RETAIL VALUE OF INVENTORY
EOM January	$22,000
EOM February	$33,000
EOM March	$38,000
Total inventory	$93,000
Average inventory = $93,000 ÷ 3 = $31,000	

This approach is adequate only if the end-of-month figure doesn't differ in any appreciable or systematic way from any other day. For instance, January's end-of-month inventory is significantly lower than the other two since it represents the inventory position at the end of the winter clearance sale and before the spring buildup.

Most retailers no longer need to use physical "counts" to determine average inventory. Point-of-sale (POS) terminals capture daily sales and automatically subtract them from on-hand inventory. Retailers with POS systems can get accurate average inventory estimates by averaging the inventory on hand for each day in the year.

Advantages of Rapid Turnover   Retailers want rapid inventory turnover—but not too rapid, as we'll soon see. Advantages of rapid inventory turnover include increased sales volume, improved salesperson morale, more money for market opportunities, decreased operating expenses, and increased asset turnover.[9]

Increased Sales Volume   A rapid inventory turnover increases sales volume since fresh merchandise is available to customers, and fresh merchandise sells better and faster than old, shopworn merchandise. Notice the produce next time you're in a less-than-successful supermarket. Brown bananas! Since turnover is slow, the produce is old, which makes it even harder to sell.

Recall from Chapter 11 that quick response (QR) delivery systems are inventory management systems designed to reduce retailers' lead time for receiving merchandise. Retailers order less merchandise, more often, so merchandise supply is more closely aligned with demand. As a result, inventory turnover rises since inventory investment falls, and sales climb since the retailer is out of stock less often.

Less Risk of Obsolescence and Markdowns   The value of fashion and other perishable merchandise is said to start declining as soon as it's placed on display. When inventory is selling quickly, merchandise isn't in the store long enough to become obsolete. As a result, markdowns are reduced and gross margins increase.

Improved Salesperson Morale   With rapid inventory turnover and the fresh merchandise that results, salesperson morale stays high. No one likes to sell yesterday's merchandise. Salespeople are excited over new merchandise, the assortment of sizes is still complete, and the merchandise isn't shopworn. When salespeople's morale is high, they try harder so sales increase—increasing inventory turnover even further.

A rapid rate of inventory turnover ensures fresh merchandise. Since fresh merchandise is easier to sell, sales increase and so does employee morale.

More Money for Market Opportunities   When inventory turnover is high, money previously tied up in inventory is freed to buy more merchandise. Having money available to buy merchandise late in a fashion season can open tremendous profit opportunities. Suppose Levi Strauss overestimates demand for its seasonal products. It has two choices: (1) holding the inventory until next season and (2) selling it to retailers at a lower-than-normal price. If retailers have money available because of rapid turnover, they can take advantage of this special price. Retailers can pocket the additional markup or choose to maintain their high-turnover strategy by offering the special merchandise at a reduced cost to the consumer. In either case, sales and gross margin increase.

Decreased Operating Expenses   An increase in turnover may mean that a lower level of inventory is supporting the same level of sales. And lower inventory means lower inventory carrying costs. In this case there are lower interest costs on money borrowed for inventory. Inventory insurance and taxes are also lower.

Increased Asset Turnover   Finally, since inventory is a current asset, and if assets decrease and sales stay the same or increase, then asset turnover increases. This directly affects return on assets, the key performance measure for top management.

Disadvantages of Overly Rapid Turnover   Retailers should strike a balance in their rate of inventory turnover. An excessively rapid inventory turnover can hurt the firm due to a lower sales volume, an increase in the cost of goods sold, and an increase in buying and order-processing time.

Lowered Sales Volume   One way to increase turnover is to limit the number of merchandise categories or the number of SKUs within a category. But if customers can't find the size or color they seek—or even worse, if they can't find the product line at all—a sale is lost. Customers who are disappointed on a regular basis will shop elsewhere and will possibly urge their friends to do the same. In this case, not only is a sale lost, but so are the customers and their friends.

Increased Cost of Goods Sold   To achieve rapid turnover, merchandise must be bought more often and in smaller quantities, which reduces average inventory without reducing sales. But by buying smaller quantities, the buyer can't take advantage of quantity discounts and transportation economies of scale. It may be possible, for instance, to buy a year's supply of Levis at a quantity discount that offsets the high costs of carrying a large inventory.

Retailers who pay transportation costs must consider that the more merchandise shipped and the slower the mode of transportation, the smaller the per-unit transportation expense. For instance, to ship a 10-pound package of jeans from Dallas to Denver, overnight delivery, would cost about $50 ($5 per pound). If the retailer could order 50 pounds of jeans at the same time and could wait 5 to 10 days for delivery, the cost would be only about $30 (60 cents per pound). In this example, it costs over eight times more to ship small packages quickly.

Increased Operating Expenses   Economies of scale can also be gained when a retailer purchases large quantities. A buyer spends about the same amount of time meeting with vendors and writing orders whether the order is large or small. It also takes about the same amount of time, for both large and small orders, to print invoices, receive merchandise, and pay invoices—all factors that increase merchandise's cost.

In summary, rapid inventory turnover is generally preferred to slow turnover. But the turnover rate can be pushed to the point of diminishing returns—a key concern for merchandise managers in all retail sectors.

Sales Forecasting

An integral component of any merchandising plan is the sales forecast. Without knowing how much is forecast to be sold, you can't determine how much to buy. We begin the sales forecasting section by (1) discussing category life cycles and (2) then developing a forecast based on historical sales data and other sources.

Category Life Cycles   When developing a sales forecast, you must be able to predict how well product categories will sell over time. Product categories typically follow a predictable sales pattern—sales start off low, increase, plateau, and then ultimately decline. Yet the shape of that pattern varies considerably from category to category. This information enables buyers to understand what customer groups will be buying the products, the variety of products that customers will expect, the nature of competition, and the appropriate type of promotion and level of prices. Knowing whether merchandise is a fashion, a fad, a staple, or seasonal merchandise is equally important for developing a sales forecast and other aspects of a category's merchandise strategy.

This section describes the most fundamental form of sales pattern, the category life cycle. Using the category life cycle as a basis, we'll examine some commonly found variations on it: fad, fashion, staple, and seasonal.

The *category life cycle* describes a merchandise category's sales pattern over time. The category life cycle (Exhibit 12–5) is divided into four stages: introduction, growth, maturity, and decline. Knowing where a category (or specific item within a category) is in its life cycle is important in developing a sales forecast and merchandising strategy. Specifically, the stage a particular category is in impacts target market, variety, distribution intensity, price, and promotion.

EXHIBIT 12–5
The Category
Product Life Cycle

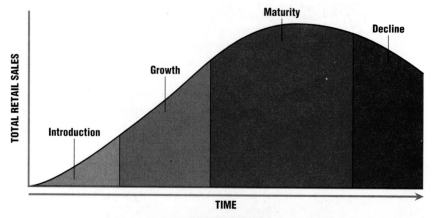

Strategy variable	INTRODUCTION	GROWTH	MATURITY	DECLINE
Target market	High-income innovators	Middle-income adopters	Mass market	Low-income and laggards
Variety	One basic offering	Some variety	Greater variety	Less variety
Distribution intensity	Limited or extensive	More retailers	More retailers	Fewer retailers
Price	Penetration or skimming	Wide range	Lower prices	Lower prices
Promotion	Informative	Persuasive	Competitive	Limited

REFACT Fashion experts believe that "fashion cycles" run from 18 months to several years. Predicting where a category is in the cycle is essential for accurately forecasting sales.[10]

The target market for newly introduced categories is often high-income innovators. For instance, when Motorola's StarTAC™ telephone was first introduced, its target market was high-use customers like doctors and business executives who were willing to pay for the convenience of having a very small phone. It was very expensive compared to older, larger models, and not available at all stores that normally sell cellular phones. As categories reach the growth and maturity stages, they usually appeal to more middle-income, mass market customers—discount store and category killer customers in the case of cellular phones. Finally, as categories eventually go into decline, they're made available to low-income customers who follow rather than lead fashions. Some new merchandise categories gain popularity in unlikely places, however. Pagers were first marketed to doctors and salespeople. Parents now find them useful for keeping track of their children.

The variety available for newly introduced categories is typically fairly small, but grows through maturity and then is cut back as the category goes into decline. For example, pagers were initially available in black, but as the category grew and approached maturity, they became available in a multitude of colors—even Day-Glo. As demand for a category declines, retailers will again reduce the variety to better control inventory costs.

Distribution intensity refers to the number of retailers carrying a particular category. In the introductory stage, categories can be distributed more or less intensely, depending on the type of category and its availability. A high-tech category

Sales Forecasting for Services Retailers

DUE TO THE PERISHABLE nature of services, service retailers can't stockpile as merchandise retailers can. Instead they must have extra equipment (e.g., ski lifts) or additional service providers (telephone repair people) to meet surges in demand. Of course, having idle equipment and service providers is a waste of resources. So service retailers have devised strategies for handling surges in demand.

Many service retailers attempt to match customers with service providers by taking reservations or making appointments. Physicians are notorious for making their patients wait, but patients are fighting back—they walk out and don't come back.[11] Other service retailers use different strategies for lessening the impact of having to wait for service. Sticking a television in front of customers is a simple, inexpensive method used by service providers from airlines to barbershops. Distracting customers by allowing them to watch the service being performed is a strategy used by car washes, photo finishers, and restaurants. The most innovative service retailers, however, actually devise methods to perform the service better. United Parcel Services of America, Inc. (UPS) now guarantees overnight delivery of packages and letters by 8:30 A.M. The next best alternative is Federal Express and other major carriers that promise overnight delivery by 10:30 A.M. The UPS service isn't inexpensive, however. Delivery of a letter, for instance, costs $40, almost four times the price of a letter delivered at 10:30.[12] Finally, some retailers have devised innovative pricing strategies that entice customers to utilize service during off-peak times. (See Chapter 15.)

---

like cellular phones would initially be available only through a few retailers. A manufacturer of a new hand tool, on the other hand, would want its category distributed intensively—through as many retailers as possible. As a category gains popularity in the growth and maturity stages, distribution intensity usually increases. Thus, cellular phones have become available at many retailers. But when a category goes into decline, fewer retailers will be interested in stocking it because of decreased demand.

The pricing strategy for newly introduced categories can be either high **(skimming)** or low **(penetration),** depending on the type of category and the level of distribution intensity. A skimming policy is typically used with categories that are in short supply and available through a limited number of retailers. Cellular phones were originally very expensive when they were available only through a small set of retailers. A new grocery store item, on the other hand,

Pagers were first marketed to doctors and salespeople. You could only get them in black. Now that pagers are in the maturity stage of the category product life cycle, they come in a multitude of colors. Parents now find them useful for keeping track of their children.

would initially use a low price to achieve high market penetration as soon as possible. As a category moves through growth into maturity and decline, the price generally decreases since the category becomes readily available and demand slows. You can now get a cellular phone for a dollar!

Promotion in a new category's introductory stage is designed to inform the customer about the category. With a high-tech item like cellular phones, ads showed pictures of the category, where it was available, and its cost. But as a category goes into growth and maturity stages, promotions become much more competitive and are designed to persuade customers to shop at a particular store. Retailers limit their promotion for categories in the decline stage and divert those funds to categories that can generate more sales.

Knowing where a category is in its life cycle is useful for predicting sales. For instance, the choice of a penetration or skimming pricing strategy in the introductory stage will influence whether the product will have high or modest sales. Care must be taken, however, that use of the category life cycle as a predictive tool does not adversely affect sales. If a product is classified as being in decline, it's likely that retailers will stock less variety and limit promotions. Naturally, sales will go down. Thus, the "decline" classification may actually become a self-fulfilling prophesy. Many products have been successfully maintained at the maturity stage because their buyers have maintained innovative strategies that are consistent with a mature product. For instance, Kellogg's Frosted Flakes continues to be successful over many decades because it has innovative advertising and is priced competitively.

Variations on the Category Life Cycle   Most categories follow the basic form of the category life cycle: sales increase, peak, and then decline. Variations on the category life cycle—fad, fashion, staple, and seasonal—are shown in Exhibit 12–6. The distinguishing characteristics between them are whether the category lasts for many seasons, whether a specific style sells for many seasons, and whether sales vary dramatically from one season to the next.

A **fad** is a merchandise category that generates a lot of sales for a relatively short time—often less than a season. Examples are Rubik's Cubes, Troll Dolls, and some licensed characters like Disney's Hunchback of Notre Dame. More mainstream examples are certain computer games, new electronic equipment, and some apparel. Fads are often illogical and unpredictable. The art of managing a fad comes in recognizing the fad in its earliest stages and immediately locking up distribution rights for merchandise to stores nationwide before the competition does. Marketing fads is one of the riskiest ventures in retailing because even if the company properly identifies a fad, it must still have the sixth sense to recognize the peak so it can bail out before it's stuck with a warehouse full of merchandise.

EXHIBIT 12–6

Variations on the Category Life Cycle

	FAD	FASHION	STAPLE	SEASONAL
Sales over many seasons	No	Yes	Yes	Yes
Sales of a specific style over many seasons	No	No	Yes	Yes
Sales vary dramatically from one season to the next	No	Yes	No	Yes
Illustration (Sales against Time)				

Unlike a fad, a **fashion** is a category of merchandise that typically lasts several seasons, and sales can vary dramatically from one season to the next. A fashion is similar to a fad in that a specific style or SKU sells for one season or less. A fashion's life span depends on the type of category and the target market. For instance, double-breasted suits for men or certain colors in domestic goods (sheets and towels) are fashions whose life may last several years. On the other hand, fashions like see-through track shoes may last only a season or two.

Items within the **staple merchandise** (also called **basic merchandise**) category are in continuous demand over an extended period of time. Even certain brands of basic merchandise, however, ultimately go into decline. Most merchandise in grocery stores, as well as housewares, hosiery, blue jeans, and women's intimate apparel, are considered to be staple merchandise.

Seasonal merchandise is inventory whose sales fluctuate dramatically according to the time of the year. Both fashion and staple merchandise usually have seasonal influences. For instance, fashionable wool sweaters sell better in fall and winter, while staples like lawn mowers and garden tools are more popular in spring and summer. Retailers carefully plan their purchases and deliveries to coincide with seasonal demand.

Fad, Fashion, or Staple?   When pagers were first introduced, no one knew if they would be a fad, a fashion, or a staple. Buyers in electronics stores purchased the category carefully at first. They bought small quantities to see how they would sell. As they began to sell, they reordered throughout the season and into the next. Had the merchandise sold briskly for a few months and then died, it would have been considered a fad. Now pagers are increasingly popular. Considered a staple, they've become available in a large variety of colors through many retail outlets at competitive prices. Ultimately, however, with today's technological breakthroughs, the pager will go the way of other staples like rotary phones and vinyl disc record players—they'll be readily available only at your local secondhand store.

The inventory management systems used for fads and fashion merchandise are very different than those used for staples. Managing fashion merchandise can be tricky. Since there is little or no history for specific SKUs, buyers forecast sales by category rather than by item. Then skill, experience, and creativity enable the buyer to select quantities for specific SKUs.

On the other hand, managing staple merchandise is fairly straightforward. Since there's a rich sales history for each SKU, SKU-based inventory management systems are readily available that forecast future sales using information from the past. Chapter 13 examines these systems.

Armed with information about where an item or a category is in its life cycle, retailers develop their sales forecast.

Developing a Sales Forecast   We develop a sales forecast by adjusting a category's past sales to make projections into the future. Buyers utilize a variety of sources in making these decisions. We divide the discussion into examining previous sales volume, published sources, and customer information, by shopping at the competition, as well as by utilizing vendors and buying offices.

Previous Sales Volume   Exhibit 12–7 shows Levi sales by season over a 10-year period. Sales have been increasing by about 25 percent per season for several years. The exhibit illustrates a strong seasonality pattern. Typically 40 percent of

Which of these products is a fad? Which is a fashion?

the annual sales occur in fall, 30 percent in winter, and 15 percent each in spring and summer. In the eighth year, the fall season was unusually strong due to early cold weather, whereas spring sales were particularly weak because of a temporary turndown in the local economy. For fashion merchandise, where styles change from year to year, sales figures older than three years probably aren't very useful. When forecasting sales, we must identify real trends (either up or down), and try to isolate a real change in demand from random occurrences. Thus, the unusually high and low sales in the eighth year should be ignored when trying to forecast sales for the current season. The "More Information" box on page 357 shows a simple method of forecasting sales, using Exhibit 12–7's data. Chapter 13 covers more sophisticated methods to forecast sales of staples at the SKU level. Retailing View 12.2 describes how retailers should take weather into consideration when forecasting sales.

EXHIBIT 12–7

Sales for Levi Jeans at Trendsetters Department Store

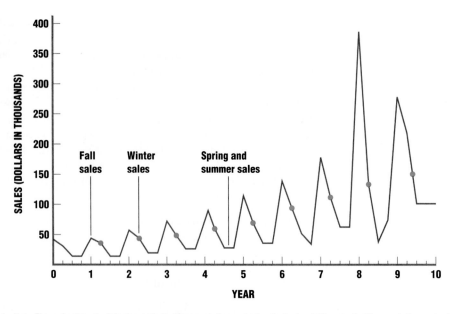

Note: The peaks show the fall sales, typically 40 percent of annual sales; the horizontal lines typify 15 percent of annual sales each in spring and summer; and the dots (the winter sales) are typically 30 percent of annual sales. These data are for illustrative purposes only. They do, however, represent typical growth patterns for a category like jeans.

Forecasting Sales for Levi Jeans

THE PROCEDURE FOR FORECASTING sales by season is accomplished in two steps. First, we determine a sales forecast for the entire year. Then we consider seasonal sales patterns for each season.

The accompanying exhibit summarizes sales by season for Levi jeans for years 6 through 9 from Exhibit 12–7. For instance, during the fall season of year 6, the store sold $152,587 in jeans, which represents 41.9 percent of the total sales for year 6 ($152,587 ÷ $364,247 = 41.9 percent). The last column indicates the percentages of the increases for the previous three years: 30.1, 48.5, and 5 percent. The 30.1 percent increase from year 6 to year 7 was calculated as follows: ($364,247 − $476,835) ÷ $364,247. Unfortunately these data don't show a consistent pattern due to unusually high sales in year 8. The buyer should probably discount the impact of year 8 sales on the forecast and examine sales increases from earlier years as well as more qualitative factors. The average sales increase over the previous nine years has been 25 percent, general economic indicators in the area are strong, and top management sees an opportunity to "grow" this classification, so the buyer estimates the sales increase for year 10 to be 30 percent. Thus, the sales forecast for year 10 is [($745,056 x .3) + $745,056] or $968,573.

The second step is to apply the seasonal sales pattern to the annual sales forecast to determine sales for each season. The percentage of annual sales occurring in each season has been fairly stable except in year 8. Thus, the buyer decides to apply the same percentages as those in years 7 and 9. To forecast sales for each season, the buyer multiplies the annual sales by each of the seasonal sales percentages. For instance, fall sales for year 10 should equal ($968,573 x .4) or $387,429.

YEAR	SEASON				TOTAL	PERCENTAGE INCREASE
	FALL	WINTER	SPRING	SUMMER		
6	$152,587	$114,440	$57,220	$40,000	$364,247	
	41.9%	31.4%	15.7%	11.0%	100%	
7	190,734	143,051	71,525	71,525	476,835	30.1%
	40.0%	30.0%	15.0%	15.0%	100%	
8	400,000	178,813	40,000	89,406	708,219	48.5%
	56.5%	25.3%	5.6%	12.6%	100%	
9	298,023	223,517	111,758	111,758	745,056	5.0%
	40.5%	30.0%	15.0%	15.0%	100%	
6–9 (total)	1,041,344	659,821	280,503	312,689	2,294,357	
	45.4%	28.2%	12.2%	13.6%	100%	
10 (forecast)	387,429	290,572	145,286	145,286	968,573	

Published Sources Adjustments to sales trends are based on economic trends in the geographic area for which the forecast is developed. For example, a buyer for The Gap would consider national economic indicators such as gross national product (GNP), interest rates, and employment rates, whereas an independent local clothing store would primarily consider local conditions. Even if national unemployment rates are low, they may be significantly higher where a particular retailer has a store. If so, people may spend less money on fashion in this region than in other areas.

12.2

Whether or Not to Use Weather to Forecast Sales

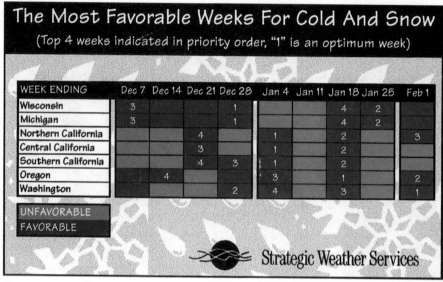

The Most Favorable Weeks For Cold And Snow
(Top 4 weeks indicated in priority order, "1" is an optimum week)

WEEK ENDING	Dec 7	Dec 14	Dec 21	Dec 28	Jan 4	Jan 11	Jan 18	Jan 25	Feb 1
Wisconsin	3			1			4	2	
Michigan	3			1			4	2	
Northern California			4		1		2		3
Central California			3		1		2		
Southern California			4	3	1		2		
Oregon		4			3		1		2
Washington				2	4		3		1

UNFAVORABLE
FAVORABLE

Strategic Weather Services

Do you want to sell some snow shovels in Wisconsin? Make sure you are in stock during the weeks of December 28, January 25, December 7, and January 18.

OF ALL THE FACTORS that drive sales in retailing, probably none is more significant than the weather. For instance, when early warm weather drives sales of spring and summer apparel, or when a mid-September heat wave dampens sales of fall fashions, it's weather that gets the blame or credit in the monthly sales reports of chain retailers.

For all this talk about the weather, as the old saying goes, "Nobody does anything about it." Certainly in the world of retailing, the traditional tendency has been to regard weather, when it's regarded at all, as a great unknown factor. Merchandise allocation plans tend to be based on the previous year's sales, which means they assume that the previous year's weather conditions will be repeated.

But according to Richard J. Fox (chairman of Strategic Weather Services in Wayne, Pennsylvania), weather only repeats itself from year to year about 35 percent of the time. Thus, retailers who assume a repeat of the previous year's weather will be wrong two seasons out of three.

The result can be devastating. For example, consumers coming into a department store in the Northeast looking for wool socks and thermal underwear during a brutally cold late February may find none to be had, as the store is all decked out with spring merchandise.

Fox's company is a long-range and short-range weather forecasting and consulting firm that has an extensive track record working with such industries as agriculture, manufacturing and feature film production.

Several years ago it began advising the retail industry, with an array of proprietary methods that apply future weather to decisions in receipt timing, merchandise allocation and distribution, advertising, promotions, and markdowns. Today, some 50 retail chains routinely factor weather into their plans in order to increase sales and profits.

Source: Rachel J. Dickinson, "Retailers Weather the Odds," *American Demographics,* April 1996, pp. 20–21; "Better Forecasts-System Ties Weather To Merchandise." *Chain Store Age Executive,* July 1994, p. 40; Amanda Meadus and Wendy Hessen, "Falling Temperatures Trigger Sharp Rise in Accessories Sales," *Women's Wear Daily,* December 19, 1994, pp. 1, 8–10; Gary Robins, "Weather Watch," *Stores,* December, 1994, pp. 46–47; For more information, contact Strategic Weather Services, 1325 Morris Drive, Wayne, PA 19087, telephone (610) 640-9485.

Sales & Marketing Management's Survey of Buying Power gives demographic and annual sales data by major line of merchandise broken down into geographic units as small as cities of more than 25,000 people. (See Chapter 11 for more details.) Similar data on a monthly basis are obtainable from the *Monthly Retail Trade Report* published by the U.S. Department of Commerce. These two sources of information cover general trends, but may not be particularly helpful for a buyer forecasting sales for a particular merchandise category.

Retailers and their vendors can also buy data from private firms like InfoScan.[13] InfoScan buys information from individual supermarkets on price and promotion activity that has been scanned through their POS terminals, and aggregates the data by region, chain, or market area. Information on customer demographics and psychographics as well as competitive information is available from firms like Urban Decision Systems.[14] (See Chapter 11.) Finally, general retail trade publications such as *Stores, Women's Wear Daily, Chain Store Age,* and *Discount Store News* analyze general retail trends.

INTERNET EXERCISE   InfoScan's website is located at: http://www.infores.com/external/prodserv/HI/samplecf.htm on the Internet. Go to their site and describe the services they offer retailers.

Customer Information   Customer information can be obtained either by measuring customer reactions to merchandise through sales, by asking customers about the merchandise, or by observing customers and trendsetters. Knowing what customers want today is very helpful in predicting what should be purchased in the future.

Obtaining market information about the merchandise directly from the customer is probably the easiest yet most underused method. For example, a cashier at a restaurant may ask how a customer liked a meal, but not record the answer in any systematic way. Another excellent source of customer information is retail salespeople. They have the direct contact with the customer necessary to determine customer attitudes in depth. Unless the store is owner-operated, however, this information doesn't filter in to the buyer automatically. Salespeople require both training and incentives to pass customer information on to buyers. Some retailers maintain a **want book** in which salespeople record out-of-stock or requested merchandise. This information is collected by buyers for making purchasing decisions.

Customer information can be collected through traditional forms of marketing research like depth interviews and focus groups. The **depth interview** is an unstructured personal interview in which the interviewer uses extensive probing to get individual respondents to talk in detail about a subject. For example, one grocery store chain goes through the personal checks they've received each day and selects all customers with large purchases of groceries and several with small purchases. They call these customers and interview them to find out what they like and don't like about the store.

A more informal method of interviewing customers is to require buyers to spend some time on the selling floor waiting on customers. In most national retail chains, buyers are physically isolated from their customers. For example, buying offices for Mervyn's and The Gap are both in northern California, yet their stores are throughout America. It has become increasingly hard for buyers in large chains to keep a pulse on local customer demand. Frequent store visits help the situation. Some retailers require their buyers to spend a specified period of time, like a day a week, in a store.

A **focus group** is a small group of respondents interviewed by a moderator using a loosely structured format. Participants are encouraged to express their views and to comment on the views of others in the group. To keep abreast on the teen market, for instance, some stores have teen boards comprised of opinion leaders that meet to discuss merchandising and other store issues.[15]

One of the most useful methods of spotting new fashion trends is to observe trendsetters. Where in the past, designers dictated fashions, today's fashions are often discovered by observing cool city kids. By definition, fashion is fickle. Yet, retailers and their vendors need time, usually several months, to bring new fashions to market. Unless they can spot these trends in advance of the typical mall shopper, their opportunity will have passed. So they hire research firms that specialize in spotting fashion trends. Some go to rock concerts, underground dance clubs, and extreme sports competitions to observe and take pictures of the participants. One firm finds people whom they deem especially hip and pay them several hundred dollars to interview dozens of their peers on videotape.[16]

Shop Competition   Buyers need to observe their competition. They need to remain humble and keep in mind that, no matter how good they are, their competition and similar stores in other markets may be even better. Shopping at local competition helps buyers gauge the immediate competitive situation. For instance, a Macy's buyer shopping at a Nordstrom store may determine that Macy's prices on a particular line of handbags are too high. Shopping markets in buying centers such as New York, Milan, London, and Paris provides information on trends. Retailing View 12.3 tells how Crate & Barrel spots trends for tableware.

Vendors and Resident Buying Office   Buyers musk seek information from vendors and resident buying offices. **Resident buying offices** either are independent organizations or are directly associated with particular retailers that offer a number of services associated with the procurement of merchandise. (Chapter 14 gives details.) Vendors and resident buying offices are excellent sources of market information. They know what's selling in markets around the world. Buyers, vendors, and buying offices must share such information if all are to succeed.

Now that we have set the financial and sales goals for a merchandise category, we can begin to look at what type of merchandise to buy.

THE ASSORTMENT PLANNING PROCESS

All retailers face the fundamental strategic question of what type of retail format to maintain to achieve a sustainable competitive advantage. (See Chapters 6 and 7.) A critical component of this decision is determining what merchandise assortment will be carried. Merchandise decisions are constrained by the amount of space available in the store and the amount of money available to spend on inventory. Based on the financial objectives that have been set at the top and have trickled through the retail organization, decisions regarding variety, assortment, and product availability must be made.

In this section we first define variety, assortment, and product availability. Then we examine the strategic trade-offs between them. In the next section, we zero in on the assortment plan itself.

12.3

Picking Fashions for the Table

NEVER MIND WHAT'S ON your table now. In two years, you'll be hankering for place mats in blue or green with thick black borders. And you'll be thinking what great taste you have, not knowing that the decision about what adorns your table was made months—if not years—before by a former math teacher who's one of the leading buyers in the housewares industry.

Barbara Turf, merchandising chief for Crate & Barrel stores, is a betting woman. Blues and greens with a yellow tone are all the rage in Europe right now. In 18 months, she figures, that color scheme will spread to households across the United States—and she wants to be ready. By traveling, reading magazines, and astutely observing everything around her, Ms. Turf is Crate's secret weapon in the battle to anticipate and provide for consumers' changing tastes.

Ms. Turf considers what we eat, drive, and wear before deciding what we'll want to buy for our homes. She always has an eye on Europe, where she says trends often begin about 18 months before they reach our shores. But she's watching what's happening here as well. When people started driving Jeep Cherokees instead of Cadillacs, she moved to more casual dinnerware. Changes in eating habits led her to stock pasta and fajita makers and ease up on waffle irons. A resurgence of linen in clothes, she says, will translate to linen in the home.

Whether copying a successful European competitor or following a hunch, this is a tricky, unscientific business. If Ms. Turf guesses wrong, Crate is stuck with excess merchandise that will have to be sharply discounted. But when she gets it very, very right, Crate doesn't necessarily buy more of the hit item. The company updates its products and colors at least three times a year to stay ahead of imitators—an industry rule of thumb, but one some of their competitors have a tough time following.

Source: Christina Duff, "How Barbara Turf Chooses the Hot Place Mats of 1997," *The Wall Street Journal*, March 16, 1995, pp. B1–B2.

Variety **Variety** is the number of different merchandising categories within a store or department. Stores with a large variety are said to have good breadth— the terms *variety* and *breadth* are often used interchangeably. Some stores, like Banana Republic, carry a large variety of categories of sportswear to meet all the needs of their target customers. Banana Republic carries traditional slacks, sweaters, shirts, outerwear, and other categories for both men and women. County Seat, on the other hand, carries a much more limited number of categories (variety): jeans and related apparel.

REFACT The JCPenney catalog has over 100,000 SKUs in 400 categories. Now that's real depth of assortment.[17]

Assortment **Assortment** is the number of SKUs within a category. Stores with large assortments are said to have good depth—the terms *assortment* and *depth* are also used interchangeably. County Seat, for instance, carries a large assortment of jeans and accessories, such as shirts and belts, that complement jeans. Banana Republic, on the other hand, has a narrow assortment of jeans because it appeals to a more narrowly defined target market and doesn't have the space to devote to jeans due to its emphasis on variety.

Product Availability **Product availability** defines the percentage of demand for a particular SKU that is satisfied. For instance, if 100 people go into a County Seat store to purchase a pair of tan jeans in size 33–34, and it sells only 90 pairs before it runs out of stock, its product availability is 90 percent. Product availability is also referred to as the **level of support** or **service level.**

Assortment Planning for Service Retailers   Consider health clubs. Some offer a large variety of activities and equipment from exercise machines to swimming, wellness programs, and New Age lectures. Others, like Gold's Gym, don't offer much variety, but have an excellent assortment of body building equipment and programs. Some hospitals, such as big municipal hospitals found in most urban areas, offer a large variety of medical services. Smaller private hospitals often specialize in physical rehabilitation or psychiatry. For service retailers, the level of product availability is a sales forecasting issue. (See the "More Information" box on page 353.)

The Trade-offs between Variety, Assortment, and Product Availability: A Strategic Decision

How do retailers make the trade-off between variety, assortment, and product availability? It depends on their particular marketing strategy. Recall from Chapter 6 that a retail strategy identifies (1) the target market toward which a retailer plans to commit its resources, (2) the nature of the retail offering that the retailer plans to use to satisfy the target market's needs, and (3) the bases upon which the retailer will attempt to build a sustainable competitive advantage.

As a specialty store, Banana Republic tries to be the one-stop shopping alternative for its target markets. It carries a large variety of merchandise categories for both men and women. As a result, it can't physically or financially carry either gigantic assortments within each category or sufficiently high backup stock so as never to be out of stock. Alternatively, County Seat has developed its marketing strategy around a target market of people who are particularly interested in buying jeans. As a result, it provides a large assortment of a limited number of categories. Its product availability is high; it doesn't want to miss a sale because it doesn't have the right size. If any of these three elements—variety, assortment, or product availability—aren't what the customer expects or needs, a retailer will likely lose the sale and possibly the customer.

The trade-offs between variety, assortment, and product availability are strategic issues. Of the three issues, variety is the most strategic. Variety is most important in defining the retailer in the customer's eyes. For instance, is the retailer perceived to be a category specialist like Toys "R" Us or a generalist like a department store? Variety also defines the retailer's vendor structure. Does it purchase from many different types of manufacturers or just a few? Finally, decisions regarding variety are typically made less often and at higher levels in the organization than decisions regarding assortment or product availability. Top managers, for instance, make decisions about whether to delete categories or even departments from the store. Since these decisions have important ramifications, they're made only after serious consideration.

Determining Variety and Assortment

In attempting to determine the variety and assortment for a category like jeans, the buyer would consider the following factors: profitability of the merchandise mix, the corporate philosophy toward the assortment, physical characteristics of the store, and the degree to which categories of merchandise complement each other.

Profitability of Merchandise Mix   Since retailers are constrained by the amount of money they have to invest in merchandise and space to put the merchandise in, they're always trying to find the most profitable mix of products. Thus, for a chain like County Seat to add a category like Levi's Dockers to the assortment, a reduction must be made elsewhere. It would attempt to take the inventory investment

REFACT Lack of inventory and high prices are why customers don't buy. In every category, out of stock, wrong size, or wrong brand items or insufficient advertised items in stock account for 33 percent of failed food shopping trips and 40 percent of apparel and home goods shopping trips not resulting in a purchase.[18]

that it's been making in a less profitable merchandise category (a private label in which it's invested $1 million to generate $2 million in sales) and shift it to Dockers, which it hopes will generate $2.5 million.

Corporate Philosophy toward the Assortment   The corporate philosophy toward the assortment helps the buyer determine the number of styles and colors to purchase. To illustrate, let's again consider the hypothetically different philosophies of County Seat and Banana Republic. Both stores have a merchandise budget of $150,000 to spend on jeans that retail for $50. Thus, both stores can purchase 3,000 pairs. County Seat purchases 30 different style/color combinations (100 units per combination); Banana Republic purchases 10 (300 per combination). Similar to a portfolio of stocks, County Seat, with 30 styles and colors, is more diversified than Banana Republic.

As with stocks, the more diversified the portfolio, the less risk of large losses. With County Seat, since there are so many style/color combinations, on average the category will perform adequately even if a few don't sell. But by spreading the 3,000 pairs across so many style/color combinations, the buyer runs the additional risk of **breaking sizes,** which means running out of stock on particular sizes. Typically, retailers take markdowns on assortments with broken sizes since they become harder to sell. Additionally, a large assortment of styles and colors won't enable the buyer to maximize profits by investing a large portion of the budget on the big winners.

Another issue is whether top management wants to grow or shrink a particular merchandise category. Some department stores, for instance, have dropped furniture and major appliances altogether because of low turnover, low profit margins, or lack of space. Many stores, however, have taken a fairly aggressive stance on men's sportswear in recent years. So even if a category is shrinking, if the retailer's overall strategy is to enlarge the department, the category could be expanded.

Physical Characteristics of the Store   Retailers must consider how much space to devote to the category. If many styles and colors are in the assortment, more space will be required to properly display and store the merchandise. The display area's physical characteristics are also important. A rack, for instance, may hold 300 pairs of jeans. It wouldn't be aesthetically pleasing to display only 100 units on the rack or to mix the jeans with another merchandise category.

Retailers typically divide their chain into A, B, and C stores on the basis of their ability to generate sales. Not only will A stores get the largest total inventory allocation, but they can also handle the largest assortment. C stores, for instance, may not receive the extreme sizes or the more avant-garde styles or colors. It's important, however, to assign merchandise that's expected to be best-sellers to the C stores and to judiciously add assortment to the larger A and B stores. Chapter 13 discusses how retailers assign merchandise to stores. Chapters 18 examines how retailers assign space to merchandise.

Complementary Merchandise   When retailers plan to add to their assortment, they must consider whether the merchandise under consideration complements other merchandise in the department. For instance, Dockers may stimulate the sale of plaid shirts and belts, and vice versa. Further, retailers may decide to carry other merchandise, such as men's underwear and socks, as a service because their customers expect it.

EXHIBIT 12–8

EXHIBIT 12–8

Relationship between Inventory Investment and Product Availability

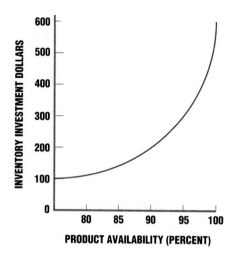

Determining Product Availability

The third dimension of the assortment planning process is product availability. Recall that product availability defines the percentage of demand for a particular SKU that is satisfied. The higher the product availability, the higher the amount of backup stock necessary to ensure that the retailer won't be out of stock on a particular SKU when the customer demands it. Choosing an appropriate amount of backup stock is critical to successful assortment planning because if the backup stock is too low, the retailer will lose sales—and possibly customers too—due to stockouts. If the level is too high, scarce financial resources will be wasted in needless inventory that could be more profitably invested in more variety or assortment.

Exhibit 12–8 shows the trade-off between inventory investment and product availability. Although the actual inventory investment varies in different situations, the general relationship is that a very high level of service results in a prohibitively high inventory investment. This relationship can be explained by the relationship between cycle stock and backup stock.

Cycle stock, also known as **base stock,** is inventory that results from the replenishment process and is required to meet demand when the retailer can predict demand and replenishment times (lead times) perfectly, as depicted in green in Exhibit 12–9.[19] In this case, 96 units of an SKU are ordered. During the next two weeks, much of the inventory is sold. But before the store is out of stock, the next order arrives. The cycle then repeats in this typical zigzag fashion.

Unfortunately, most retailers are unable to predict demand and replenishment times without error. As a result, retailers carry **backup stock,** also known as **safety stock** or **buffer stock,** as a safety cushion for the cycle stock so they won't run out before the next order arrives. Backup stock is depicted in orange in the exhibit.

Several issues determine the level of required backup stock. First, backup stock and, therefore, overall inventory investment depend on the product availability the retailer wishes to provide. If, for instance, County Seat wants to satisfy almost all its customers who wish to purchase a pair of Levi's 501 jeans in size 31–32, it must carry a great deal of backup stock compared to what it needs if it decides to satisfy only 75 percent of the demand for the SKU.

Second, the higher the fluctuations in demand, the greater the need for backup stock. Suppose County Seat sells an average of 100 pairs of Levi's 501 jeans in size 31–32 in two weeks. Yet in some weeks, sales are greater or less than

EXHIBIT 12–9

Cycle and Backup
Stock

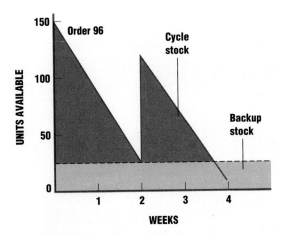

the average. When sales are less than average, the retailer ends up carrying a little more merchandise than it needs. But if sales are more than average, there must be some backup stock to ensure that the retailer doesn't go out of stock. Note in Exhibit 12–9 that during week 4, sales were greater than average so the retailer had to dip into backup stock to avoid a stockout.

The amount of backup stock also depends on lead time from the vendor. **Lead time** is the amount of time between recognition that an order needs to be placed and the point at which the merchandise arrives in the store and is ready for sale. If it takes two months to receive a shipment of Levi's Dockers, the possibility of running out of stock is greater than if lead time were only two weeks because County Seat would have to forecast for a longer period. The shorter lead times inherent in quick response inventory systems (described in Chapter 11) result in a lower level of backup stock required to maintain the same level of product availability.

Fluctuations in lead time also affect the amount of backup stock. If County Seat knows that lead time for Dockers is always two weeks, plus or minus one day, it can more accurately plan its inventory levels. But if lead time is plus or minus one day on one shipment and then plus or minus five days on the next shipment, County Seat must carry additional backup stock to cover the uncertainty in lead time. Many retailers using quick response inventory systems are forcing their vendors to deliver merchandise within a very narrow window—sometimes two or three hours—to reduce the fluctuations in lead time and thus the amount of required backup stock.

Finally, the vendor's product availability also affects the retailer's backup stock requirements. For example, County Seat can more easily plan its inventory requirements if Levi normally ships every item that County Seat orders. If, on the other hand, Levi only ships 75 percent of the ordered items, County Seat must maintain a higher backup stock to be certain that the jeans' availability to its customers isn't adversely affected.

THE ASSORTMENT PLAN

After setting financial goals and determining the relative importance of variety, assortment, and product availability, the retailer is ready to determine what merchandise to stock using an assortment plan. An assortment plan describes in very general terms what should be carried in a particular merchandise category. The assortment plan for fashion merchandise doesn't identify specific SKUs since fashions change from

EXHIBIT 12-10   Assortment Plan for Girls' Jeans

STYLES	TRADITIONAL	TRADITIONAL	TRADITIONAL	TRADITIONAL	TRADITIONAL	TRADITIONAL
Price levels	$20	$20	$35	$35	$45	$45
Fabric composition	Regular demim	Stone-washed	Regular denim	Stone-washed	Regular denim	Stone-washed
Colors	Light blue	Light blue	Light blue	Light blue	Light blue	Light blue
	Indigo	Indigo	Indigo	Indigo	Indigo	Indigo
	Black	Black	Black	Black	Black	Black
STYLES	BOOT-CUT	BOOT-CUT	BOOT-CUT	BOOT-CUT		
Price levels	$25	$25	$40	$40		
Fabric composition	Regular demim	Stone-washed	Regular denim	Stone-washed		
Colors	Light blue	Light blue	Light blue	Light blue		
	Indigo	Indigo	Indigo	Indigo		
	Black	Black	Black	Black		

year to year. The more fashion-oriented the category, the less detail will be found in the assortment plan because the merchandise planner requires more flexibility to adjust to fashion changes.

Historical precedence is the starting point for developing the assortment plan for the current season. The merchandise planner uses the sales, GMROI, and turnover forecast along with the assortment plan from the previous season to develop the plan for the current season. Adjustments are then made based on the merchandise planner's expectations for what items or fashions will be important in the coming season. For instance, if a particular style, such as boot-cut jeans, is expected to be especially popular in the coming season, the merchandise planner will use more of the merchandise budget for that style and cut back on traditional jeans.

Exhibit 12–10 shows an abbreviated assortment plan for girls' jeans. This assortment plan identifies general styles (traditional five-pocket straight-leg jeans and boot-cut jeans), general price levels ($20, $35, and $45 for traditional jeans; $25 and $40 for boot-cut jeans), composition of fabric (regular denim and stone-washed), and colors (light blue, indigo, and black).

Assortment plans for apparel and shoes also typically include a size distribution. To illustrate, Exhibit 12–11 breaks down size and length for the 429 units for girls' traditional $20 denim jeans in light blue. Thus, the store wants to have nine units of size 1-short, which represent 2 percent of the 429 total. The process of applying the size distribution is then repeated for each style/color combination for each store.

The development of an assortment plan can be complicated. In an actual multistore chain, the process is even more complex than in our example. A good assortment plan requires a good forecast for sales, GMROI, and inventory turnover along with a mix of subjective and experienced judgment. A good inventory management system that combines these elements is also critical to successful merchandise management. These systems are described in the next chapter.

EXHIBIT **12–11**

Size Disbribution
for Traditional $20
Denim Jeans in
Light Blue for a
Large Store

					SIZE					
LENGTH	1	2	4	5	6	8	10	12	14	
Short	2	4	7	6	8	5	7	4	2	%
	9	17	30	26	34	21	30	17	9	units
Medium	2	4	7	6	8	5	7	4	2	%
	9	17	30	26	34	21	30	17	9	units
Long	0	2	2	2	3	2	2	1	0	%
	0	9	9	9	12	9	9	4	0	units
									Total	**100%**
										429 units

SUMMARY This chapter was the first of five on merchandise management. As such, it examined basic strategic issues and planning tools for managing merchandise. First, merchandise must be broken down into categories for planning purposes. Buyers and their partners, merchandise planners, control these categories, often with the help of their major vendors. Without a method of categorizing merchandise like the one described here, retailers could never purchase merchandise in any rational way.

Tools to develop a merchandising plan include GMROI, inventory turnover, and sales forecasting. GMROI is used to plan and evaluate merchandise performance. The GMROI planned for a particular merchandise category is derived from the firm's overall financial goals broken down to the category level. Gross margin percentage and inventory turnover work together to form this useful merchandise management tool.

Calculating inventory turnover and determining inventory turnover goals are important. Retailers strive for a balanced inventory turnover. Rapid inventory turnover is imperative for the firm's financial success. But if the retailer attempts to push inventory turnover to its limit, severe stockouts and increased costs may result.

When developing a sales forecast, retailers must know what stage of the life cycle a particular category is in and whether the product is a fad, fashion, or staple so they can plan their merchandising activities accordingly. Creating a sales forecast involves such sources of information as previous sales volume, published sources, customer information, and shopping at the competition as well as utilizing vendors and buying offices.

The trade-off between variety, assortment, and product availability is a crucial issue in determining merchandising strategy. Examining this trade-off helps retailers answer the important question of what type of store to be: a specialist or generalist.

The culmination of planning the GMROI, inventory turnover, sales forecast, and assortment planning process is the assortment plan. The assortment plan supplies the merchandise planner with a general outline of what should be carried in a particular merchandise category. Yet the merchandise planner's repertoire of tools is still incomplete. In the next chapter, we show how GMROI, inventory turnover, and the sales forecast are integral components to (1) the merchandise budget plan used for fashion merchandise and (2) inventory management systems used for staple products.

KEY TERMS

assortment, *361*	cycle stock (base stock), *364*	level of support (service level), *361*	seasonal merchandise, *355*
assortment plan, *339*	department, *342*	merchandise group, *342*	skimming, *353*
backup stock (safety stock, buffer stock), *364*	depth interview, *359*	merchandise management, *338*	staple merchandise (basic merchandise), *355*
breaking sizes, *363*	distribution intensity, *352*	penetration, *353*	stock keeping unit (SKU), *344*
category, *340*	fad, *354*	planogram, *341*	variety, *361*
category captain, *341*	fashion, *355*	product availability, *361*	want book, *359*
classification, *343*	focus group, *360*	resident buying office, *360*	
	lead time, *365*		

DISCUSSION QUESTIONS & PROBLEMS

1. What are the differences between a fashion, fad, and staple? How should a merchandise planner manage these types of merchandise differently?

2. How can depth (assortment) and breadth (variety) of merchandise affect a consumer's search for merchandise?

3. Simply speaking, increasing inventory turnover is an important goal for a retail manager. What are the consequences of turnover that's too slow?

4. What does an 85 percent product availability mean from a practical point of view?

5. An assortment plan indicates that a buyer can purchase 1,000 units of fashion wristwatches. The buyer must choose between buying 20 styles of 50 units each or 5 styles of 200 units each. In terms of the store's philosophy toward risk and space utilization, how does the buyer make this decision?

6. A buyer has had a number of customer complaints that he has been out of stock on a certain category of merchandise. The buyer subsequently decides to increase this category's product availability from 80 percent to 90 percent. What will be the impact on backup stock and inventory turnover?

7. How would you go about forecasting sales for a new fashion item?

8. The fine jewelry department in a department store has the same GMROI as the small appliances department even though characteristics of the merchandise are quite different. Explain this situation.

9. Calculate GMROI and inventory turnover given

Annual sales	$10,000
Average inventory (at cost)	$5,000
Gross margin	40%

10. Calculate GMROI and inventory turnover given

Average inventory (at cost)	$25,000
Annual sales	$25,000
Average inventory (at cost)	$10,000
Gross margin	32%

SUGGESTED READINGS

Blattberg, Robert C., and Edward J. Fox. *Category Management.* Washington, DC: Food Marketing Institute and the Center for Retail Management, Northwestern University, 1995.

Category Management: Positioning Your Organization to Win. Chicago: NTC Business Books, Nielsen Marketing Research, and the American Marketing Association, 1992.

Emmelhainz, Margaret A., James R. Stock, and Larry W. Emmelhainz. "Consumer Responses to Stock-Outs." *Journal of Retailing* 67, no. 2 (Summer 1991), pp. 138–47.

Kelly, J. Patrick, Hugh M. Cannon, and H. Keith Hunt. "Customer Responses to Rainchecks." *Journal of Retailing* 67, no. 2 (Summer 1991), pp. 122–37.

Kline, Barbara, and Janet Wagner. "Information Sources and Retail Buyer Decision-Making: The Effects of Product-Specific Buying Experience." *Journal of Retailing* 70 (Spring 1994), pp. 75–88.

McIntyre, Shelby H., Dale D. Achabal, and Christopher M. Miller. "Applying Case-Based Reasoning to Forecasting Retail Sales." *Journal of Retailing* 69, no. 4 (December 22, 1993), pp. 372–83.

Morwitz, Vicki G., and David Schmittlein. "Using Segmentation to Improve Sales Forecasts Based on Purchase Intent: Which 'Intenders' Actually Buy?" *Journal of Marketing Research* 29, no. 4 (November 1992), pp. 391–405.

Nanadan, Shiva, and Roger Dickinson. "Private Brands in the United States: An Historical Perspective." In Robert King, ed., *Retailing: Theories and Practices for Today and Tomorrow, Proceedings of the Fourth Triennial National Retailing Conference.* Richmond, VA: The Academy of Marketing Science, pp. 89–94.

Smith, Stephen A., Shelby H. McIntyre, and Dale D. Achabal. "A Two-Stage Sales Forecasting Procedure Using Discounted Least Squares." *Journal of Marketing Research* 31 (Winter 1994), pp. 44–53.

NOTES

1. Faye Brookman, "Category Management: A New Way of Life," *Women's Wear Daily*, June 1995, pp. 36–37. The concept of category management is particularly popular in the grocery industry where many experts believe it is needed the most. In fact, the Food Marketing Institute (FMI), the primary trade organization in the grocery industry, has published a series of five books on the subject. See Robert C. Blattberg and Edward J. Fox, *Category Management* (Washington, DC: Food Marketing Institute and the Center for Retail Management, Northwestern University, 1995).

2. Faye Brookman, "Category management: A New Way of Life," *Women's Wear Daily*, June 1995.

3. Arthur Friedman, "KSA's Guide to Managing a Category," *Women's Wear Daily*, March 6, 1996, p. 12.

4. "Denim Brands Are Controlling Their Own Destinies," *Women's Wear Daily*, March 6, 1996, p. 12.

5. "Avoid Pitfalls of Category Management," *Discount Store News*, May 1, 1995, p. 25.

6. *Category Management: Positioning Your Organization to Win* (Chicago: NTC Business Books, Nielsen Marketing Research, and the American Marketing Association, 1992), pp. 32–35.

7. Daniel J. Sweeney, "Improving the Profitability of Retail Merchandising Decisions," *Journal of Marketing*, January 1973, pp. 60–68.

8. To illustrate, suppose net sales = $50,000 and average inventory at retail = $10,000; inventory turnover = $50,000 ÷ $10,000 = 5. To convert inventory turnover expressed at retail to turnover at cost, we multiply by the cost complement, which is the percentage of net sales represented by the cost of goods sold. If the gross margin is 40 percent, the cost complement is 60 percent (100% − 40%). By multiplying the numerator and denominator by 60 percent, the result is cost of goods sold ÷ the average inventory at cost.

$$\$50,000 \times .6 = \$30,000 = 5$$
$$\$10,000 \times .6 = \$6,000 = 5$$

Thus, inventory turnover is 5 whether it is calculated using retail or cost figures.

9. This section is adapted from William R. Davidson, Daniel J. Sweeney, and Ronald W. Stampfl, *Retailing Management*, 5th ed. (New York: John Wiley & Sons, 1984).

10. Robert Frank, "UPS Plans Deliveries before Workday Starts, but, as Always, Time Is Money," *The Wall Street Journal*, September 29, 1994, p. A4.

11. Marilyn Chase, "Whose Time Is Worth More: Yours or the Doctor's?" *The Wall Street Journal*, October 24, 1994, p. B1.

12. David Moin, Sharon Edelson, and Mark Tosh, "Charting the Cycles: Predictable Patterns Meet Chaos Theory," *Women's Wear Daily*, March 25, 1996, pp. 1, 14–15.

13. InfoScan is available through Information Resources Inc., 150 N. Clinton St., Chicago, IL 60661, telephone (312) 726-1221.

14. Urban Decision Systems, 4676 Admiralty Way, Marina del Rey, CA 90292, telephone 1-800-633-9568; and 3975 Fair Ridge Drive, Fairfax, VA 22033, telephone 1-800-364-4837.

15. *Focus Groups: Issues and Approaches* (New York: Advertising Research Foundation, 1985); David Steward and Prem Shamdasani, *Focus Groups: Theory and Practice* (Newbury Park, CA: Sage, 1990); and Richard Krueger, *Focus Groups: A Practical Guide for Applied Research* (Newbury Park, CA: Sage, 1989).

16. Roger Riclefs, "Marketers Seek Out Today's Coolest Kids to Plug into Tomorrow's Mall Trends," *The Wall Street Journal*, July 11, 1996, pp. B1–B2. Specialized marketing research firms include Sputnik Inc. in New York; Cheskin + Masten/ImageNet in Redwood Shores, CA; the Zandl Group in New York; Lambesis Inc. in San Diego; and Teenage Research Unlimited in Northbrook, IL.

17. Bruce Fox, "Penney Wins Top RITA," *Chain Store Age Executive*, September 1991, pp. 62–64.

18. Mark Kingdom, "Consumer Enhancement & Development," *Chain Store Age*, January 1996, section 3, p. 5.

19. James R. Stock and Douglas M. Lambert, *Strategic Logistics Management*, 3d ed. (Burr Ridge, IL: Richard D. Irwin, 1993), p. 400.

13

Buying Systems

THE WORLD OF RETAILING

↓

RETAILING STRATEGY

↓

MERCHANDISE MANAGEMENT
12. Planning Merchandise
    Assortments
13. Buying Systems
14. Buying Merchandise
15. Pricing
16. Retail Promotion Mix

STORE MANAGEMENT
17. Managing the Store
18. Store Layout, Design, and
    Visual Merchandising
19. Customer Service
20. Retail Selling

QUESTIONS

- What are a merchandise budget plan and open-to-buy, and how are they prepared?

- How does a staple merchandise buying system operate?

- How do multistore retailers allocate merchandise to stores?

- How do retailers evaluate their merchandising performance?

IN CHAPTER 12, WE EXAMINED the assortment plan, which indicates in very general terms what should be carried in a particular merchandise category. As Exhibit 13–1 shows, this chapter continues the merchandise management process by showing how retailers utilize many principles and tools introduced in Chapter 12 into formal buying systems. Specifically, these systems help buyers and merchandise planners determine how much to buy. Retailers use two distinct types of buying systems: (1) a merchandise budget for fashion merchandise and (2) a staple merchandise buying system for basics.

While the assortment plan provides a general outline of what types of merchandise should be carried, the merchandise budget plan is used to determine how much money to spend in each month on a particular category of fashion merchandise, given the sales forecast, inventory turnover, and GMROI goals. It's not a complete buying guide because it doesn't indicate how much of a particular SKU should be purchased. To forecast sales for a particular SKU, buyers must know how much was sold in the past. Yet there's little or no sales history for fashions at the SKU level. For instance, even though dresses are purchased year after year, their styles and fabrics change. Buyers must determine the quantity of specific SKUs to purchase based on many of the issues described in Chapter 12.

Forecasting sales is much more straightforward for staples than for fashion merchandise. Since there's an established sales history for each staple SKU, standard statistical techniques are used to forecast sales.

EXHIBIT 13–1

Merchandise
Management Issues

PLANNING MERCHANDISE ASSORTMENTS (CHAPTER 12)

Organize the Buying Process by Categories

Set Merchandise Financial Objectives

Develop an Assortment Plan

BUYING SYSTEMS (CHAPTER 13)

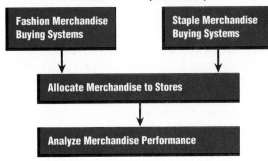

Fashion Merchandise
Buying Systems

Staple Merchandise
Buying Systems

Allocate Merchandise to Stores

Analyze Merchandise Performance

The chapter begins with buying systems for fashion merchandise: the merchandise budget plan and an ancillary system known as open-to-buy. Buying systems for staple merchandise are then examined. The chapter then discusses how multistore retailers allocate merchandise among stores. At the end of this chapter, Appendix 13A describes the retail inventory method (RIM), while Appendix 13B provides alternatives to the stock-to-sales ratio (an integral part of the merchandise budget plan). Retailing View 13.1 provides a glimpse of how not to order merchandise.

MERCHANDISE BUDGET PLAN

The merchandise budget plan's aims are to set up specific merchandise objectives (in dollars) and to plan the financial aspects of the merchandise side of the business. The merchandise budget plan isn't a complete buying plan since it doesn't indicate what kind of merchandise to buy or in what quantities. The plan just specifies how much money should be spent each month to support sales and achieve turnover and GMROI objectives.

Exhibit 13–2 shows a six-month merchandise budget plan for men's tailored suits at a national specialty store chain. This chain uses Arthur, a merchandise management system available through Comshare Retail of Wilmington, Delaware. Available in 29 countries, Arthur is currently used by over 300 retailers including The Gap, Kay-Bee Toy Stores, Carson Pirie Scott, Sherwin-Williams, Pier 1 Imports, Victoria's Secret, Best Buy, Neiman Marcus, and Zales.[1] Even relatively small stores now use advanced computer technologies like Arthur to plan

13.1

How Not to Order

- The salesperson shows the merchandise to the buyer in a cramped, noisy stockroom.
- The buyer assumes that there's enough money in the budget to make the purchase, without really checking. The buyer doesn't stipulate when the merchandise should be delivered.
- The salesperson submits the order to the vendor without checking its accuracy.
- The vendor receives the order, but can't read it clearly. The vendor doesn't bother to confirm the order with the retailer.
- The order is delayed while a credit check on the retailer is performed. The buyer receives a "request for information" from the vendor's credit department. The buyer turns the request over to the accounting department. They put it into a "to do" file.
- Time passes.
- Business at the store has been great and this order is really needed.
- The buyer calls the salesperson to ask where the order is.
- The salesperson calls the vendor to ask where the order is.
- The vendor checks with their credit department to ask where the approval is.

- The credit department calls the retailer to ask where the credit information is.
- The credit information is faxed to the credit department, which immediately releases the order.
- The vendor finds that 40 percent of the order isn't available so it substitutes six styles for the unreadable and unavailable merchandise.
- The retailer receives the shipment, checks in goods, but can't find the original purchase order, so it has no idea which items have been substituted.
- The buyer inspects the shipment and finds partial shipment and substitutions, so she holds the merchandise off the selling floor.
- More time passes.

This nightmarish scenario is unfortunately more common than you would expect. However, at least some of the situations outlined above can be avoided, or their negative effects can be mitigated with proper planning and recordkeeping.

Source: Bill Pearson, "Playing Hard-Ball with Your Orders . . . It's the Follow Through That Counts," *Stores*, November 1993, pp. 73–74.

---

merchandise budgets. Retailing View 13.2 shows how Arthur rescued a tough year at sportswear retailer REI.

INTERNET EXERCISE Comshare Retail's Arthur has its own website on the Internet (http://www.comshare.com/retail/retail.htm). To see all that Arthur can do and see how retailers around the world have embraced Arthur's power, go to their site.

Before we get into the detail of the plan, look at the last line of Exhibit 13–2, monthly additions to stock—or how much we want to purchase in each month. All of the previous entries are used to derive the monthly additions to stock. As we'll see, based on the sales forecast, monthly fluctuations in sales, GMROI, and inventory turnover goals, we should purchase $4,260 in January. Now, let's start at the beginning.

13.2

Arthur Rescues REI

IN LATE **1994,** merchandise planners at Recreational Equipment Inc. (REI) were full of optimism for the year ahead. And who could blame them? Sales from 1992 through 1994 had hit record levels, climbing an average of 16 percent each year. With 44 stores and a large mail-order business, REI was suddenly in the heady position of being the nation's sixth largest sports apparel retailer, behind the likes of Foot Locker, L.L. Bean, and Eddie Bauer.

Like many apparel retailers, REI hit a tough year in 1995. Its sales rose only 2.8 percent. Compared to its competitors, it was lucky to do that well.

Amazingly, however, the huge shortfall from the original plan was no catastrophe. REI came out of the year healthy and profitable, with inventories well in line with actual sales.

REI credits the Arthur planning system from Comshare Retail with saving its year. With its old merchandise planning system, REI would have spent the whole year trying to stay close to its original plan. With Arthur, it quickly recognized the need to reforecast, replan, and reallocate its inventories.

At first, Arthur was designated for use only by the merchandising department, but REI is integrating the system with planning strategies of other departments. Arthur enables the vision of senior management to balance with the vision of merchandise planners so there's a common ground for consensus building.

Source: "Single Version of the Truth Rescues a Tough Year for REI," *Chain Store Age*, September 1996, p. 77.

Monthly Sales Percent Distribution to Season (Line 1)

Line 1 of the plan projects what percentage of the total sales is expected to be sold in each month. Thus, in Exhibit 13–2, 21 percent of the six-month sales is expected to occur in January. The

EXHIBIT 13–2

Six-Month Merchandise Budget Plan

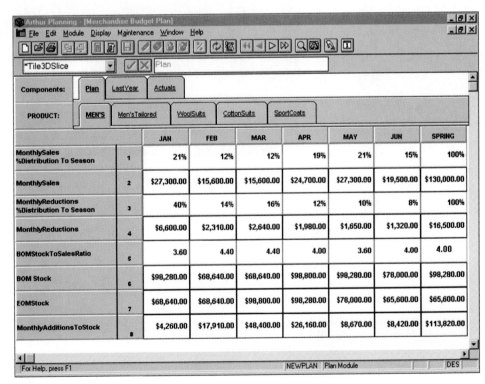

		JAN	FEB	MAR	APR	MAY	JUN	SPRING
MonthlySales %Distribution To Season	1	21%	12%	12%	19%	21%	15%	100%
MonthlySales	2	$27,300.00	$15,600.00	$15,600.00	$24,700.00	$27,300.00	$19,500.00	$130,000.00
MonthlyReductions %Distribution To Season	3	40%	14%	16%	12%	10%	8%	100%
MonthlyReductions	4	$6,600.00	$2,310.00	$2,640.00	$1,980.00	$1,650.00	$1,320.00	$16,500.00
BOMStockToSalesRatio	5	3.60	4.40	4.40	4.00	3.60	4.00	4.00
BOM Stock	6	$98,280.00	$68,640.00	$68,640.00	$98,800.00	$98,280.00	$78,000.00	$98,280.00
EOMStock	7	$68,640.00	$68,640.00	$98,800.00	$98,280.00	$78,000.00	$65,600.00	$65,600.00
MonthlyAdditionsToStock	8	$4,260.00	$17,910.00	$48,400.00	$26,160.00	$8,670.00	$8,420.00	$113,820.00

13.3

One Week for 40 Percent

RETAILING HAS VIOLENT sales peaks throughout the year. These peaks must be accounted for when calculating the sales percentage per month in a merchandise budget plan. At JCPenney, sales increase dramatically, especially during the seven days prior to Christmas.

Over the past few years, consumers have been shopping closer and closer to Christmas, culminating in the week before the holiday. In fact, the seven days before Christmas represent 40 percent of December's sales, and the month overall accounts for 50 percent of Penney's fourth-quarter business. Even more astounding is the fact that 25 percent of its December sales come during four days—December 21 through 24. In most departments weekly sales average between 1 and 2 percent of annual sales, yet after Thanksgiving, sales rise steeply, peaking at around 9 percent in the week before Christmas.

Retailers can make a fortune during this period but only if they properly plan for a leap in sales. Stores must offer consumers a competitive selection of the right merchandise in key sizes and colors, and can't have stockouts in the most popular SKUs that customers wish to buy. By using past sales figures combined with the merchandise budget plan, stores like Penney can better prepare themselves for the hectic but profitable holiday season.

Source: JCPenney report, "7 days, 40 percent."

At JCPenney, the seven days before Christmas represent 40 percent of December's sales, and the month overall accounts for 50 percent of Penney's fourth-quarter business.

sum of these monthly percentages must equal 100 percent of sales. Retailing View 13.3 discusses the holiday season's impact on sales at JCPenney.

MonthlySales %Distribution To Season	1	21%	12%	12%	19%	21%	15%	100%

The starting point for determining the percent distribution of sales by month is historical records. The percentage of total sales that occurs in a particular month doesn't vary appreciably from year to year. Even so, it's helpful to examine each month's percentage over a few years to check for any significant changes. For instance, the merchandise planner realizes that the autumn selling season for men's tailored suits continues to be pushed further back into summer. Over time, this general shift toward earlier purchasing will affect the percent distribution of sales by month. The distribution may also vary due to changes in the planner or her competitors' marketing strategies. She must include special sales that didn't occur in the past, for instance, in the percent distribution of sales by month in the same way that they're built into the overall sales forecast.

Monthly Sales (Line 2) Monthly sales equal the forecast total sales for the six-month period (last column = $130,000) multiplied by each sales percentage by month (line 1). In Exhibit 13–2, monthly sales for January = $130,000 × 21% = $27,300.

MonthlySales	2	$27,300.00	$15,600.00	$15,600.00	$24,700.00	$27,300.00	$19,500.00	$130,000.00

Monthly Reductions Percent Distribution to Season (Line 3) Reductions include markdowns, discounts, and shrinkage. To have enough merchandise every month to support the monthly sales forecast, the planner must consider factors that reduce the inventory level. Although sales are the primary reduction, the value of the inventory is also reduced by markdowns, shrinkage, and discounts to employees. Note that in Exhibit 13–2, 40 percent of the season's total reductions occur in January.

MonthlyReductions %Distribution To Season	3	40%	14%	16%	12%	10%	8%	100%

REFACT In 1994, markdowns (including employee discounts) had a median of 23.9 percent of sales for department stores and 18.7 percent for specialty stores.[2]

Markdowns can be forecast fairly accurately from historical records. Of course, changes in markdown strategies—or changes in the environment, such as competition or general economic activity—must be taken into consideration when forecasting markdowns. (Chapter 15 discusses markdowns.)

Discounts to employees are like markdowns, except that they're given to employees rather than to customers. Cost of the employee discount is tied fairly closely to the sales level and number of employees. Thus, its percentage of sales and dollar amount can be forecast fairly accurately from historical records.

Shrinkage is caused by shoplifting by employees and/or customers, by merchandise being misplaced or damaged, or by poor bookkeeping. The planner measures shrinkage by taking the difference between (1) the inventory's recorded value based on merchandise bought and received and (2) the physical inventory in stores and distribution centers. (Physical inventories are typically taken semiannually.) Shrinkage varies by department and season. Typically shrinkage also varies directly with sales. So if sales of men's tailored suits rise 10 percent, then the planner can expect a 10 percent increase in shrinkage.

To reduce losses from internal theft, this sophisticated security device enables security personnel to monitor checkout lanes and sales transactions simultaneously.

Monthly Reductions (Line 4)

The planner calculates the monthly reductions like she calculates monthly sales. She multiplies the total reductions by each percentage in line 3. In Exhibit 13–2,

January reductions = $16,500 × 40% = $6,600

MonthlyReductions	4	$6,600.00	$2,310.00	$2,640.00	$1,980.00	$1,650.00	$1,320.00	$16,500.00

BOM (Beginning-of-Month) Stock-to-Sales Ratio (Line 5)

The stock-to-sales ratios are calculated in four steps:

Step 1: Calculate Sales-to-Stock Ratio Begin with the planned GMROI, gross margin, and sales-to-stock ratio that was assigned to the category based on overall corporate financial objectives. (See Chapter 12.)

GMROI = Gross margin % × Sales-to-stock ratio
122.72% = 45% × 2.727

Note that the sales-to-stock ratio is based on six-month rather than annual sales.

Step 2: Convert the Sales-to-Stock Ratio to Inventory Turnover As Chapter 12 said,

Inventory turnover = Sales-to-stock ratio × (100% – Gross margin %, expressed as a decimal)

1.5 = 2.727 × .55

This adjustment is necessary since the sales-to-stock ratio defines sales at retail and inventory at cost, whereas inventory turnover defines both sales and inventory either at retail or at cost. This inventory turnover is based on a six-month period.

Step 3: Calculate Average Stock-to-Sales Ratio

$$\text{Average stock-to-sales ratio} = 6 \text{ months} \div \text{Inventory turnover}$$
$$4 = 6 \div 1.5$$

(If preparing a 12-month plan, the planner must divide 12 into the annual inventory turnover!) This ratio specifies the amount of inventory that should be on hand at the beginning of the month to support the sales forecast and maintain the inventory turnover objective. As with inventory turnover, both the numerator and denominator can be either at cost or at retail. Since Exhibit 13–2's merchandise budget plan is based on retail, it's easiest to think of the numerator as BOM (beginning-of-month) retail inventory and the denominator as sales for that month. Thus, to achieve a six-month inventory turnover of 1.5, on average, the planner must plan to have a BOM inventory that's four times the amount of sales for a given month.

Even a planner must be careful when thinking about the average stock-to-sales ratio. It can be easily confused with the sales-to-stock ratio. One isn't the inverse of the other, however. Sales are the same in both ratios. But stock in the sales-to-stock ratio is the average inventory at cost over all days in the period, whereas stock in the average stock-to-sales ratio is the average BOM inventory at retail. Also, the BOM stock-to-sales ratio is an average for all months. Adjustments are made to this average in line 5 to account for seasonal variation in sales.

Step 4: Calculate Monthly Stock-to-Sales Ratios

The monthly stock-to-sales ratios in line 5 must average the BOM stock-to-sales ratio calculated above to achieve the planned inventory turnover. Generally, monthly stock-to-sales ratios vary in the opposite direction of sales. That is, in months when sales are larger, stock-to-sales ratios are smaller, and vice versa.

The merchandise planner must consider the seasonal pattern for men's tailored suits in determining her monthly stock-to-sales ratios. In the ideal situation, men's tailored suits arrive in the store the same day and in the same quantity that customers demand them. Unfortunately the real-life retailing world isn't this simple. Note in Exhibit 13–2 (line 8) that men's tailored suits for the spring season start arriving slowly in January, yet demand lags behind these arrivals until the weather starts getting warmer. Monthly sales then jump from 12 percent of annual sales in March to 19 percent in April (line 1). But the stock-to-sales ratio (line 5) decreased from 4.4 in March to 4.0 in April. Thus, in months when sales increase (e.g., April), beginning-of-month inventory also increases (line 6) but at a slower rate. This causes stock-to-sales ratios to decrease. Likewise, in months when sales decrease dramatically, like in June (line 1), inventory also decreases (line 6), again at a slower rate, causing stock-to-sales ratios to increase (line 5).

BOMStockToSalesRatio	5	3.60	4.40	4.40	4.00	3.60	4.00	4.00

How, then, should specific monthly stock-to-sales ratios be determined? When doing a merchandise budget plan for a classification that has accumulated history (like men's tailored suits), the planner examines previous stock-to-sales ratios. To judge how adequate these past ratios were, the planner determines if inventory levels were exceedingly high or low in any months. Then she makes minor corrections to adjust for a previous imbalance in inventory levels.

We must also make adjustments for changes in the current environment. For instance, assume the planner is planning a promotion for Groundhog Day. Since this promotion has never been done before, the stock-to-sales ratio for that February should be adjusted downward to allow for the expected increase in sales. Caution: Monthly stock-to-sales ratios don't change by the same percentage as the percent distribution of sales by month is changing. In months when sales increase, stock-to-sales ratios decrease, but at a slower rate. Since there's no exact method of making these adjustments, the buyer must make some subjective judgments.

BOM (Beginning-of-Month) Stock (Line 6)

The amount of inventory planned for the beginning of the month (BOM) equals

Monthly sales (line 2) × BOM stock-to-sales ratio (line 5)

When doing this multiplication, sales drops out of the equation, leaving BOM stock. In Exhibit 13–2,

BOM stock for January = $27,300 × 3.6 = $98,280

BOM Stock	6	$98,280.00	$68,640.00	$68,640.00	$98,800.00	$98,280.00	$78,000.00	$98,280.00

EOM (End-of-Month) Stock (Line 7)

The BOM stock from the current month is the same as the EOM (end-of-month) stock in the previous month. So, to derive line 7, the planner simply moves the BOM stock in line 6 down one box and to the left.

In Exhibit 13–2, the EOM stock for January is the same as the BOM stock for February—$68,640. We must forecast ending inventory for the last month in the plan.

EOMStock	7	$68,640.00	$68,640.00	$98,800.00	$98,280.00	$78,000.00	$65,600.00	$65,600.00

Monthly Additions to Stock (Line 8)

The monthly additions to stock is the amount to be ordered for delivery in each month, given turnover and sales objectives.

Additions to stock = Sales (line 2) + Reductions (line 4)
+ EOM inventory (line 7) − BOM inventory (line 6)

In Exhibit 13–2,

Additions to stock for January = $27,300 + 6,600 + 68,640 − 98,280 = $4,260

MonthlyAdditionsToStock	8	$4,260.00	$17,910.00	$48,400.00	$26,160.00	$8,670.00	$8,420.00	$113,820.00

This formula isn't particularly enlightening, so consider the following explanation. At the beginning of the month, the inventory level equals BOM stock. During the month, merchandise is sold and various reductions, such as markdowns, occur. So BOM stock minus monthly sales minus reductions equals EOM stock if nothing is purchased. But something must be purchased to get back up to the forecast EOM stock. The difference between EOM stock if nothing is purchased (BOM stock – sales – reductions) and the forecast EOM stock is the additions to stock.

Evaluating the Merchandise Budget Plan

GMROI, inventory turnover, and the sales forecast are used for both planning and control. The previous sections have described how they all fit together in planning the merchandise budget. A merchandise planner negotiates a GMROI, inventory turnover, and sales forecast goal based on the top-down/bottom-up planning process described in Chapter 12. This plan is used to purchase men's tailored suits for the upcoming season. Well in advance of the season, the planner purchases the amount of merchandise found in the last line of the merchandise budget plan to be delivered in those specific months—the monthly additions to stock.

After the selling season, the planner must determine how well she actually performed compared to the plan for control purposes. If the actual GMROI, turnover, and forecast are greater than those in the plan, then performance is better than expected. No performance evaluation should be based on any one of these measures, however. Several additional questions must be answered to evaluate her performance: Why did her performance exceed or fall short of the plan? Was the deviation from the plan due to something under her control? (For instance, was too much merchandise purchased? Did she react quickly to changes in demand by either purchasing more or having a sale? Was the deviation due to some external factor, such as a change in competitive level or economic activity?) Every attempt should be made to discover answers to these questions. Later in this chapter, we'll examine several additional tools used to evaluate merchandise performance.

OPEN-TO-BUY*

The open-to-buy starts where the merchandise budget plan ends. That is, the merchandise budget provides the merchandise planner with a plan for purchasing merchandise to be delivered in a particular month. The **open-to-buy** system keeps track of merchandise flows while they're occurring. Specifically, open-to-buy records how much is spent each month (and therefore how much is left to spend). For the merchandise budget plan to be successful (i.e., meet the sales, inventory turnover, and GMROI goals for a category), the merchandise planner attempts to buy merchandise in quantities and with delivery dates such that the actual EOM (end-of-month) stock for a month will be the same as the projected EOM stock. For example, at the end of June, which is the end of the spring season, the planner would like to be completely out of men's tailored suits in this category so there will be room for the summer collection. Thus, the planner would want the projected EOM stock and the actual EOM stock to both equal zero.

Using the Arthur planning system, Exhibit 13–3 presents the six-month open-to-buy for the same category of men's suits discussed in the merchandise planning section earlier in the chapter. The first row of numbers for each entry represents the *plan*, whereas the second row represents what has *actually* occurred. So, for instance, in January our BOM (beginning-of-month) stock was planned to be

*We thank Ann Delusia of Comshare Retail for her assistance in the preparation of this section.

EXHIBIT 13–3

Six-Month Open-
to-Buy

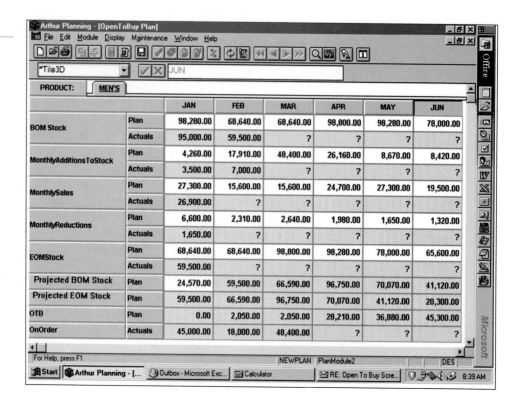

$98,280, but it was actually $95,000. Note also that the first five row entries also appear in the merchandise budget plan: BOM stock, monthly additions to stock, monthly sales, monthly reductions, and EOM stock.

Calculating Open-to-Buy for Past Periods

The way we view open-to-buy and how it is calculated vary depending on whether we're looking at a past period, the current period, or a future period. Let's start with a past period. We're now in the middle of February—January is over. Notice that there's an entry for actual January EOM stock ($59,500), but not one for February. The calculation of open-to-buy at the end of a period is easy. Since the month is over, we know that the projected EOM stock is equal to the actual EOM stock. Open-to-buy is zeroed out because there's no point in buying merchandise for a month that's already over. Thus,

$$\text{Projected EOM stock} = \text{Actual EOM stock}$$
$$\$59,500 = \$59,500$$
$$\text{Open-to-buy} = 0$$

Calculating Open-to-Buy for Current Period

Now let's look at February, the current month. Notice that there is a BOM stock of $59,500, but not an EOM (end-of-month) stock because the month has started but it hasn't finished. When calculating the open-to-buy for the current month, the projected EOM stock comes into play. Think of the projected EOM stock as a new and improved estimate of the planned EOM stock from the merchandise budget plan. This new and improved version takes information into account that wasn't available when the merchandise budget plan was made. The formula for projected EOM stock is

Projected EOM stock =	$66,590 =
Actual BOM stock	59,500
+ Actual monthly additions to stock (what was actually received)	+ 7,000
+ Actual on order (what is on order for the month)	+ 18,000
– Plan monthly sales	– 15,600
– Plan reductions for the month	– 2,310

Although this formula may seem complicated, think of it this way: The projected EOM stock is equal to the inventory we have at the beginning of the month plus what we buy minus what we get rid of through sales or other inventory reductions.

The open-to-buy formula used during the current month is simply the difference between what you originally planned to end with from the merchandise budget plan (planned EOM stock) and what you think you will end with based on information collected during the month (projected EOM stock):

$$\text{Open-to-buy} = \text{Planned EOM stock} - \text{Projected EOM stock}$$
$$\$2,050 \quad = \quad \$68,640 \quad - \quad \$66,590$$

This means that we have $2,050 left to spend in February if we want to reach our planned EOM stock of $68,640.

Calculating Open-to-Buy for Future Periods

Now we'll calculate open-to-buy for March. Since we are still in February, we have no actual data for March except for what is actually on order. The formula for projected EOM (end-of-month) stock is

Projected EOM stock =	$96,750 =
Projected BOM stock	66,590
+ Actual on order (what is on order for the month)	+ 48,400
– Plan monthly sales	–15,600
– Plan reductions for the month	–2,640

This is the same formula that we used to calculate open-to-buy for a current period except there are no actual monthly additions to stock. We assume that what is on order is the same as the planned additions to stock for that month.

We also use the same open-to-buy formula as we did before:

$$\text{Open-to-buy} = \text{Planned EOM stock} - \text{Projected EOM stock}$$
$$\$2,050 \quad = \quad \$98,800 \quad - \quad \$96,750$$

This means that we have $2,050 left to spend if we want to reach our planned EOM stock of $98,800. (It's just a coincidence that the open-to-buys for February and March are the same.)

Evaluating Open-to-Buy

Even if everything in the planner's merchandise budget for men's tailored suits goes according to plan, without careful attention to the record keeping performed in the open-to-buy, she'll fail. In the same way that you must keep track of the checks you write, the planner must keep careful records of the merchandise she purchases and when it's to be delivered. Otherwise she would buy too much or too little. Merchandise would be delivered in months when it wasn't needed, and would be unavailable when it was needed. Sales and

13.4

If She Wants Lime Green, You Had Better Not Have Orange

SPECIALTY RETAILER Mothers Work Inc. figured out early in the season that lime green fashions sell five times faster than orange. This allowed the firm to start cranking out more lime-green clothes for its 450-plus maternity shops.

The Mothers Work information system provides a picture of the entire inventory pipeline, down to single garments. Every day, the company knows what is selling, what isn't, what is in transit, and how long it will take before it can make or order more merchandise.

Using the system, the company test markets fashion ideas in stores before committing itself to large production runs, and replenishes inventory at stores daily. It can produce more of a hot-selling style in less than two weeks and rush a new idea from a design stage to the store in less than a month. While most specialty retailers live and die with styles selected six months in advance, Mothers Work doesn't have to place its bets so far ahead. It's really planned procrastination. By waiting until the last possible minute, the company minimizes its exposure to markdowns.

Source: Laura Bird, "High-Tech Inventory System Coordinates Retailer's Clothes with Customers' Taste," *The Wall Street Journal*, June 12, 1996, pp. B1, B7.

Mothers Work test markets fashion ideas in stores before committing itself to large production runs, and replenishes inventory at stores daily from distribution centers like this one.

inventory turnover would suffer, and the merchandise budget plan would be useless. Thus, the open-to-buy system presented here is a critical component of the merchandise management process.

Retailing View 13.4 illustrates the importance of having an open-to-buy system that can adjust quickly to fashion trends.

As this section's example shows, the assortment planning process for fashion merchandise can be complicated. In an actual multistore chain, the process is even more complex than in our example. A good assortment plan requires a fine mix of subjective and experienced judgments, a good information system, and a systematic method of keeping historical records. Now let's look at buying systems for staple items.

STAPLE MERCHANDISE BUYING SYSTEMS

A very different, more mechanical system of inventory management is used for staple merchandise as opposed to the system for fashion merchandise. Staple merchandise buying systems are used for merchandise that follows a predictable order–receipt–order cycle. Most merchandise fits this criterion. These systems don't work well with fashion merchandise, however, because they use past history to predict sales for the future—and fashion merchandise has no history from previous seasons on specific SKUs. But most items found in food and discount stores are good candidates for these systems. So are categories in specialty and department stores like underwear, socks, and housewares.

Numerous inventory management systems for staple merchandise are currently available for both micro- and mainframe computers for retailers of all sizes. Let's explore the basics of these systems using IBM's INFOREM (Inventory Forecasting and Replenishment Modules) as an example.[4]

INTERNET EXERCISE   Go to IBM's INFOREM on the Internet. Go to: http://204.146.47.38/disi3.htm. How is INFOREM being used by retailers today? Which retailers are using INFOREM?

Retailers like Target would use a SKU-based inventory management system to control staple merchandise like these plates.

$4.99 gets you dinner for four.
(Food not included.)

TARGET

What the System Does   Staple merchandise buying systems contain a number of program modules that show how much to order and when. These systems assist merchandise planners by performing three functions:

- Monitoring and measuring average current demand for items at the SKU level.
- Forecasting future SKU demand with allowances made for seasonal variations and changes in trend.
- Developing ordering decision rules for optimum restocking.

The Inventory Management Report   The inventory management report provides information on sales velocity, inventory availability, the amount on order, inventory turnover, sales forecast, and, most important, the quantity to order for each SKU. The inventory management report is given to the planner on a prespecified schedule, depending on how often he wishes to review the vendor's inventory and make purchases. For instance, he may review some vendors' lines every week, while he reviews others' every three weeks. Exhibit 13–4 shows an actual inventory management report for Rubbermaid, a large manufacturer of household plastic products.

Basic Stock List   The first four columns of Exhibit 13–4 represent what many retailers call the basic stock list. The **basic stock list** describes each SKU and summarizes the inventory position. Specifically, it contains the stock number and description of the item, how many items are on hand and on order, and sales for the past 12 and 4 weeks. The basic stock list differs from the assortment plan used in the fashion-based systems in that it defines each SKU in precise rather than general terms.

Examine the first item: stock number 4050, a Rubbermaid bath mat in avocado green. There are 6 on hand and 120 on order. Thus, the quantity available is 126. (Quantity on hand + quantity on order = quantity available.) Sales for the past 12 and 4 weeks were 215 and 72 units, respectively.

The basic stock list is a necessary component of any inventory management system, yet many retailers go beyond the basic record-keeping function. The last four columns of Exhibit 13–4 are needed too. Using this information, the inven-

EXHIBIT 13–4   Sample Inventory Management Report for Rubbermaid

STOCK NUMBER	DESCRIPTION	QUANTITY ON HAND (ON ORDER)	SALES LAST 12 WKS. (LAST 4 WKS.)	TURNOVER ACTUAL (PLAN)	PRODUCT AVAILABILITY (BACK-UP STOCK)	FORECAST CURRENT 4 WKS. (NEXT 8 WKS.)	ORDER POINT (ORDER QTY.)
4050	RM bath mat avocado	6 (120)	215 (72)	9 (12)	96 (20)	94 (117)	167 (42)
4051	RM bath mat blue	0 (96)	139 (56)	5 (9)	100 (17)	58 (113)	110 (96)
4052	RM bath mat gold	1 (60)	234 (117)	9 (12)	95 (27)	42 (196)	200 (144)
4053	RM bath mat pink	2	41 (31)	5 (9)	95 (10)	41 (131)	58 (60)

Source: Banner Distributing Company, Denver, Colorado; used with permission.

tory management part of the system manipulates the numbers in the basic stock list to arrive at sales forecasts and suggested order quantities. Now let's talk about the remaining entries in Exhibit 13–4 and how they fit into the system.

Inventory Turnover   Like the merchandise budget plan, a planned inventory turnover, based on overall financial goals, drives the inventory management system. The planner achieves an actual inventory turnover of 9 for the avocado bath mat, but the planned turnover was 12.

Product Availability   In Exhibit 13–4's avocado bath mat example, on average, out of every 100 customers wanting the item, 96 found it in stock. Determining the appropriate planned level of product availability for staple merchandise can be difficult and requires considerable managerial judgment.

Backup Stock   **Backup stock,** also known **as safety stock** or **buffer stock,** is inventory used to guard against going out of stock when demand exceeds forecasts or when merchandise is delayed. (See Chapter 12.) Backup stock for the avocado bath mat is 20 units.

Forecast   Sales forecasts for staple items are fairly straightforward and mechanical compared to those for fashion merchandise. With fashion merchandise, past trends and other issues that help determine the future are examined. Forecasting sales of staple items entails extending sales trends from the past into the future.

Exponential smoothing is a forecasting technique in which sales in previous time periods are weighted to forecast future periods. To understand exponential smoothing, again consider the Rubbermaid avocado bath mat whose average sales forecast over the past few four-week periods is 100 units (not shown in Exhibit 13–4). But the sales total for the past four-week period was 72 units. To forecast the next four-week period, the planner wants to be responsive to the decrease in

Forecasting (as mentioned above) for high-fashion merchandise involves examining past trends and other issues that help determine the future.

sales from 100 to 72, but doesn't want to overreact by ignoring the historical average since the decrease could be a random occurrence. The following formula takes into account the two sales forecasting objectives of being responsive and ignoring random occurrences:

New forecast = Old forecast + α (Actual demand – Old forecast)

The Greek letter alpha (α) is a constant between 0 and 1 that determines the influence of actual demand on the new forecast. When demand is increasing or decreasing sharply, high values of alpha, such as .5, cause the forecast to react quickly. Low values of alpha, such as .1, are appropriate when demand is changing very slowly. Let's continue the forecast for the bath mat using high and low alphas:

New forecast = Old forecast + α (Actual demand – Old forecast)
96 + .1 (72 – 96) = 94
96 + .5 (72 – 96) = 84

Alpha in Exhibit 13–4 is .1, indicating a forecast for the next four-week period of 94. Determining what alpha to use requires experimentation. If the planner believes the last period's decrease in demand represents a real shift rather than a random occurrence, the .5 alpha is more appropriate since it yields the much lower forecast of 84 bath mats. In general, if alpha is too high, an unstable forecasting process results because the forecasts overreact to random changes in demand. If alpha is too low, the forecast will always lag behind or ahead of the trend. Once the system is forecasting properly, the software will automatically adjust alpha when necessary.

Even staple items like bath mats have some seasonality—typically demand rises slightly around spring-cleaning time. The new forecast, which the planner calculated using exponential smoothing, is called the deseasonalized demand. **Deseasonalized demand** is forecast demand without the influence of seasonality. The season's influence is removed before making the calculations. To obtain the actual forecast of demand including the influence of seasonality, the inventory management system multiplies deseasonalized demand times a seasonality index in the same way that it was done in the first two lines in the merchandise budget plan in Exhibit 13–2. In the bath mat case, there was no seasonality for the example month.

Order Point   There are two types of reordering systems: perpetual and periodic. Using the **perpetual ordering system,** the stock level is monitored perpetually and a fixed quantity, known as EOQ (economic order quantity), is purchased when the inventory available reaches a prescribed level known as the order point. The **order point** is the amount of inventory below which the quantity available shouldn't go or the item will be out of stock before the next order arrives. Using the perpetual system, the review time (the period of time between reviews of the vendor) is variable. That is, the review time could be one day, while the next review time could be 20 days. The perpetual reordering system isn't usually used in retailing because it requires buyers to review their lines on a daily basis to determine whether an order should be placed. This isn't usually feasible since buyers are responsible for purchasing from multiple vendors with potentially hundreds of SKUs from each vendor. An exception would be meat or produce in a grocery store.

Most retailers use a **periodic reordering system** for staple merchandise. The periodic reordering system is an inventory management system in which the review time is a fixed period (e.g., two weeks), but the order quantity can vary. Using the periodic system, buyers don't need to review every line daily. The order point in the periodic system is defined as

Order point = [(Demand/Day) (Lead time + Review time)] + (Back-up stock)

The **lead time** is the amount of time between recognition that an order needs to be placed and when it arrives in the store and is ready for sale. Assume demand/day is 1 and lead time is zero days. (This may be the case in a pharmacy receiving shipments from its wholesaler more than once a day.) Here the order point would be zero. The buyer would wait until stock ran out, and then order and replenish the merchandise almost instantaneously.

With lead time of two weeks, there's some point below which the buyer shouldn't deplete the inventory without ordering, or the retailer would start selling the back-up stock before the next order arrived. Further, the buyer only reviews the line once a week, and 20 units of back-up stock are necessary to maintain a high service level. In this case, if demand is 7 units per day, then

Order point = [(7 units) × (14 + 7 days)] + (20 units) = 167 units

Here the buyer orders if quantity available falls to 167 units or fewer.

Order Quantity   The question remains, how much should the planner order when the quantity available is less than the order point? He should order enough so the cycle stock isn't depleted and sales dip into back-up stock before the next order arrives—this is the difference between the quantity available and the order point. Using the avocado bath mats in Exhibit 13–4, since quantity available is 126, the planner orders 41 units, because the order point is 167 (i.e., 167 – 126 = 41). The actual suggested order quantity is 42 since the bath mats are packed 6 to a carton, and the computer rounds up to the next whole carton.

ALLOCATING MERCHANDISE TO STORES

Once the merchandise is purchased for either fashion or staple merchandise, it must be allocated to stores. Exhibit 13–5 illustrates how a planner allocates additions to stock of $150,000 among 15 stores to girls' traditional $35 denim jeans in light blue.

Chain stores typically classify their stores into A, B, and C stores based on their potential sales volume (column 1). This chain has four A stores, each of which is expected to sell 10 percent of the total, equaling $15,000

EXHIBIT 13–5

Breakdown by Store of Traditional $35 Denim Jeans in Light Blue

(1) TYPE OF STORE	(2) NUMBER OF STORES	(3) PERCENTAGE OF TOTAL SALES, EACH STORE	(4) SALES PER STORE (TOTAL SALES X COL. 3)	(5) SALES PER STORE TYPE (COL. 2 X COL. 4)	(6) UNIT SALES PER STORE (COL. 4/$35)
A	4	10.0%	$15,000	60,000	429
B	3	6.7	10,000	30,000	286
C	8	5.0	7,500	60,000	214
Total sales $150,000					

per store; three B stores, each expected to sell 6.7 percent, equaling $10,000 per store; and eight C stores, each expected to sell 5 percent, equaling $7,500 per store (columns 2 and 3). The percentage breakdown (column 3) is based on historical records for similar merchandise for that chain.

Every chain's allocation of merchandise to stores is different, but it should be based on the total number of stores in the chain and the distribution of sales among stores. Each store in the chain, regardless of size, must carry a large proportion of the assortment offered by the largest store in the chain. Otherwise, customers would perceive the smaller stores as having an inferior assortment. Hence, smaller stores require a higher-than-average stock-to-sales ratio. The opposite is true for stores with larger-than-average sales. For instance, one major department store chain allocates merchandise to stores as follows:[5]

	FEWER SALES, MORE INVENTORY						MORE SALES, LESS INVENTORY	
Percentage of total sales	1	1.5	2.5	3.5	4	6	8	12
Percentage of total inventory	1.5	2	3	4	4	4	6	10

This means that if a store generates 4 percent of the sales of a classification for the chain, it should also receive 4 percent of the inventory. Note that stores with sales below 4 percent require proportionately more inventory. For instance, the smallest store, which generates only 1 percent of sales, requires 1.5 percent of the total inventory—inventory equals $1\frac{1}{2}$ times the level of sales. Even though this store has low sales, it still needs to stock an adequate assortment and back-up stock. Customers must not feel that just because the store is small or has relatively low sales that it isn't well stocked.

At the other extreme, stores with sales greater than 4 percent require proportionately less inventory. The largest store, with sales of 12 percent, requires only 10 percent of the inventory allocation for the classification—here inventory equals 83 percent of sales. This store can boost inventory turnover by receiving more frequent shipments. Also, thanks to high sales, the largest store can present an aesthetically pleasing, well-stocked look with less inventory.

Sales per store (column 4 of Exhibit 13–5) is total sales multiplied by the percentage of total sales for each store. Thus, the four A stores are each expected to generate sales of $15,000.

Sales per store type (column 5) is the number of stores (column 2) times sales per store (column 4). Thus, combined sales for the four A stores is $60,000.

The jeans are expected to sell for $35. Therefore, unit sales per store is dollar sales per store (column 4) divided by $35. Thus, each A store is expected to sell 429 units.

The buyer must also adjust the breakdown by store according to individual store differences. See Retailing View 13.5.

The process of allocating merchandise to stores that we just described is useful for fashion merchandise and new staple items. As merchandise sells, it must be replenished, either by the vendor or through distribution centers. As Chapter 11 said, retailers use either a pull or a push distribution strategy to replenish merchandise. With a pull distribution strategy, orders for merchandise are generated at the store level on the basis of demand data captured by point-of-sale terminals.

13.5

Assortment Plan Adjustments by Store

ALL STORES ARE NOT created equal. To adjust to the different needs of local markets, retailers develop their assortment plan by market and sometimes by store. Retailers consider the following:

- More petite sizes in areas where there is a high Hispanic or Asian population.
- Brighter colors and fancier children's apparel in Hispanic areas.
- Western-theme merchandise in stores located in the West.
- More women's accessories in areas with a concentration of African Americans.
- Ski clothing near ski resorts.
- Wider assortment of apparel in smaller towns because there are usually fewer apparel outlets for customers than larger towns offer.

How do some retailers fine-tune their assortments? First, they give store managers some buying authority to meet the needs of their local customers. Second, they develop a scheme to define the micromarkets of their stores. For instance, Kmart divides its 2,200 stores into retirement-area stores, beach-area stores, and western locations. Target's micromarketing efforts are based on age, climate, small-town community, and African American, Hispanic, or Asian heritage.

Source: Barbara Solomon, "Mass Chains Tuning Stocks Store by Store," *Women's Wear Daily,* June 8, 1994, pp. 1, 17.

All stores are not created equal. Assortments should be varied on a store-by-store basis. For instance, retailers should stock brighter colors and fancier children's apparel in Hispanic areas.

With a push distribution strategy, merchandise is allocated to the stores based on historical demand, the inventory position at the distribution center, as well as the needs of the stores. As Chapter 11 noted, a pull strategy is used by more sophisticated retailers because it's more responsive to customer demand.

ANALYZING MERCHANDISE PERFORMANCE

Retailers should continually ask when to add or delete SKUs, vendors, classifications, or departments. Here we examine three procedures for analyzing merchandise performance. The first, known as ABC analysis, is a method of rank-ordering merchandise to make inventory stocking decisions. The second procedure, a sell-through analysis, compares actual and planned sales to determine whether early markdowns are required or whether more merchandise is needed to satisfy demand. The third approach is a method for evaluating vendors using the multiple-attribute (or multiattribute) model.

ABC Analysis   ABC analysis rank-orders merchandise by some performance measure to determine which items should never be out of stock, which items should be allowed to be out of stock occasionally, and which items should be deleted from the stock selection.[6] An ABC analysis can be done at any level of merchandise classification, from the SKU to the department. The SKU is the level of analysis discussed in this section.

ABC analysis utilizes the general 80-20 principle that implies that approximately 80 percent of a retailer's sales or profits come from 20 percent of the products. This means that retailers should concentrate on products that provide the biggest bang for their buck.

The first step in the ABC analysis is to rank-order SKUs using one or more criteria. The most important performance measure for this type of analysis is contribution margin:

Contribution margin = Net sales – Cost of goods sold – Other variable expenses

An example of an "other variable expense" in retailing is sales commissions. It's important to do ABC analyses using multiple performance measures since different measures give the buyer different information. Other measures commonly used in ABC analysis are sales dollars, sales in units, gross margin, and GMROI (gross margin return on investment).

Some less profitable items, like portable appliances, may be high in sales dollars or units. Such items are often important because they draw people into the store. It may also be important to carry some low-profit/high-volume merchandise because such merchandise complements other items in the store. For instance, batteries may sell at a low price, but they're necessary to sell cameras, radios, and flashlights.

Sales or gross margin per square foot measures are also useful in ABC analyses. For instance, a line of sunglasses may not appear particularly profitable in comparison to other items on the basis of contribution margin, sales, or units. But the display also takes relatively little space. Thus, performance of the merchandise on a square-foot basis may be very high.

The next step is to determine how items with different levels of profit or volume should be treated differently. Consider the dress shirts for a chain of men's stores in Exhibit 13–6. Even though the exact distribution varies across products, the general shape of the curve is the same for most types of products due to the 80-20 principle. Here the buyer has defined the A, B, C, and D SKUs by rank-ordering each SKU by sales volume and examining the distribution of those sales.

The buyer defines A items as those that account for 5 percent of items and represent 70 percent of sales. These items should never be out of stock. A items can be expensive to carry because they generally require high levels of back-up stock to buffer against variations in demand and lead times. They include most sizes of long- and short-sleeve white and blue dress shirts.

B items represent 10 percent of the SKUs and an additional 20 percent of sales. The store should pay close attention to the B items, which include some of the other better-selling colors and patterned shirts. Occasionally, however, it will run out of some SKUs in the B category because it's not carrying the same amount of back-up stock.

EXHIBIT **13–6**

ABC Analysis for
Dress Shirts

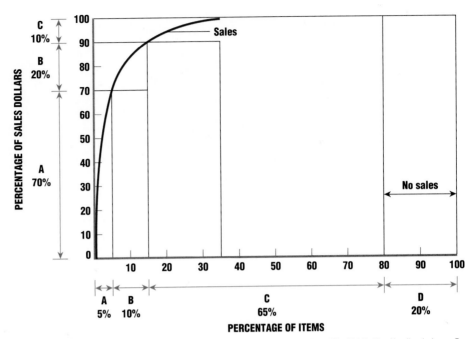

Source: Reprinted with permission of The Free Press, a Division of Macmillan, Inc., from *The Distribution Handbook,* James F. Robeson and Robert G. House, eds. Copyright © 1985 by The Free Press.

C items account for 65 percent of SKUs but contribute only 10 percent of sales. The buyer may plan to carry C items only in certain odd sizes, with special orders used to solve out-of-stock conditions.

Although the analysis is called ABC, there are also D items. D items, the remaining 20 percent of SKUs, had no sales whatsoever during the past season, having become out-of-date or shopworn. Not only is excess merchandise an unproductive investment, but it also distracts from the rest of the inventory and clutters the store. Most retailers with excess merchandise should have a simple decision strategy: Mark it down or give it away, but get rid of it.

Retailers should never be out of A items like these white and blue dress shirts. The shirt on the right, however is a D item. It had no sales during the past season. What should the retailer do with this shirt? Get rid of it!

EXHIBIT 13-7

Sell-through Analysis
for Blouses

STOCK NUMBER	DESCRIPTION		WEEK 1			WEEK 2		
			PLAN	ACTUAL	ACTUAL-TO-PLAN PERCENTAGE	PLAN	ACTUAL	ACTUAL-TO-PLAN PERCENTAGE
1011	Small	White Silk V-neck	20	15	-25%	20	10	-50%
1011	Medium	White Silk V-neck	30	25	-16.6	30	20	-33
1011	Large	White Silk V-neck	20	16	-20	20	16	-20
1012	Small	Blue Silk V-neck	25	26	4	25	27	8
1012	Medium	Blue Silk V-neck	35	45	29	35	40	14
1012	Large	Blue Silk V-neck	25	25	0	25	30	20

Sell-through Analysis

A sell-through analysis is a comparison between actual and planned sales to determine whether early markdowns are required or whether more merchandise is needed to satisfy demand. Exhibit 13–7 shows a sell-through analysis for blouses for the first two weeks of the season. Because the blouses are a very high-fashion item, the buyer believes that, if necessary, corrective action should be made to the buying plan after only two weeks.

Examine the week 1 column for the first SKU, the small white blouse. Planned sales were 20 units. The actual sales were 15 units. Therefore, the actual-to-plan percentage was –25 percent [(15 – 20)/20 = –25 percent]. This means that actual sales were 25 percent less than the planned sales. In fact, the actual-to-plan percentage is negative for all of the white blouses and positive for all of the blue blouses.

What should the buyer do? There's no exact rule for determining when a markdown is necessary or when more merchandise should be ordered. The decision depends on experience with the merchandise in the past, whether the merchandise is scheduled to be featured in advertising, whether the vendor can reduce the buyer's risk by providing markdown money (funds a vendor gives a retailer to cover lost gross margin dollars that result from markdowns), and other merchandising issues. In this case, however, it appears that the white blouses are selling significantly less than planned. Therefore, early markdowns are probably justified to ensure that the merchandise isn't left unsold at the end of the season.

The decision regarding the blue blouses isn't so clear, though. The small blue blouses are selling slightly ahead of the plan. The medium blue blouses are selling briskly. The large blue blouses are selling ahead of plan only in the second week. In this case, the buyer may need to wait another week or two before a distinct sales pattern emerges. If actual sales stay significantly ahead of planned sales, a reorder should be made.

Multiple-Attribute Method

The multiple-attribute (or multiattribute) method for evaluating vendors uses a weighted average score for each vendor. This score is based on the importance of various issues and the vendor's performance on those issues.[7] This method is very similar to the multiattribute approach that can be used to understand how customers evaluate stores and merchandise (discussed in Chapter 5) and the market attractiveness/competitive position matrix (examined in Chapter 6).

To illustrate the multiattribute method for evaluating vendors, either current or proposed, consider the example in Exhibit 13–8 for a vendor of men's tailored suits. A buyer can evaluate vendors by using the following five steps:

EXHIBIT 13–8

Evaluating a Vendor:
A Weighted Average
Approach

ISSUES (1)	IMPORTANCE EVALUATION OF ISSUES (I) (2)	PERFORMANCE EVALUATIONS OF INDIVIDUAL BRANDS ACROSS ISSUES			
		BRAND A (P_a) (3)	BRAND B (P_b) (4)	BRAND C (P_c) (5)	BRAND D (P_d) (6)
Vendor reputation	9	5	9	4	8
Service	8	6	6	4	6
Meets delivery dates	6	5	7	4	4
Merchandise quality	5	5	4	6	5
Markup opportunity	5	5	4	4	5
Country of origin	6	5	3	3	8
Product fasionability	7	6	6	3	8
Selling history	3	5	5	5	5
Promotional assistance	4	5	3	4	7
Overall evaluation = $\sum_{i=1}^{n} I_i * P_{ij}$		290	298	212	341

$\sum_{i=1}^{n}$ = Sum of the expression

I_i = Importance weight assigned to the ith dimension
P_{ij} = Performance evaluation for jth brand alternative on the ith issue
1 = Not important
10 = Very important

1. Develop a list of issues to consider in the decision (column 1).[8] A balance should be made between having too short or too comprehensive a list of issues. Too short a list will ignore some relevant issues. Too long a list will be hard to use. Also, the list should be balanced so that one dimension of vendor performance doesn't receive too much attention. For instance, if there are three issues dealing with different aspects of a vendor's promotional package and only one with product characteristics, promotional considerations will receive too much attention in the overall evaluation.

2. Importance weights for each issue in column 1 should be determined by the buyer in conjunction with the merchandise manager (column 2). Here we used a scale of 1 to 10, where 1 equals not important and 10 equals very important. In developing these importance scores, be sure that all issues don't receive high (or low) ratings. For instance, the buyer and her merchandise manager might believe that vendor reputation should receive a 9 since it's very important. Merchandise quality could receive a 5 since it's moderately important. Finally, a vendor's selling history is less important, so it could be rated 3.

3. Make judgments about each individual brand's performance on each issue (the remaining columns). This procedure should also be a joint decision between the category and merchandise managers. Note that some brands have high ratings on some issues, but not on others.

4. We can't evaluate the overall performance of the vendors without combining the importance and performance scores. We do this by multiplying the importance for each issue by the performance for each brand or its vendor. For instance, vendor reputation importance (9) multiplied by the performance rating (5) for brand A is 45. Vendor promotional assistance importance (4) multiplied by the performance rating (7) for vendor D is 28. This type of analysis illustrates an important point: It doesn't pay to perform well on issues that customers don't

believe are very important. Although vendor D performed well on promotional assistance, the buyer didn't rate this issue highly on importance so the resulting score was still low.

5.   To determine a vendor's overall rating, sum the product for each brand for all issues. In Exhibit 13–8, brand D has the highest overall rating (341) so D's is the preferred vendor.

SUMMARY

This chapter (the second to deal with merchandise management) built on basic concepts and tools of assortment planning described in Chapter 12. The sales forecast and inventory turnover described in Chapter 12 work together to drive the merchandise budget plan for fashion merchandise. The sales forecast is broken down by month, based on historical seasonality patterns. It's necessary to purchase more in months when sales are forecast to be higher than average. Planned inventory turnover is converted to stock-to-sales ratios and used in the merchandise budget plan to determine the inventory level necessary to support sales. Monthly stock-to-sales ratios are then adjusted to reflect seasonal sales patterns. The end product of the merchandise budget planning process is the dollar amount of merchandise a planner should purchase each month for a category if the sales forecast and inventory turnover goals are to be met.

The open-to-buy system begins where the merchandise budget plan leaves off. It starts with the additions to stock from the merchandise budget plan and keeps track of how much merchandise is purchased for delivery in each month. Using an open-to-buy system, merchandise planners know exactly how much money they've spent compared to how much they plan to spend.

While the merchandise budget plan provides a spending plan in dollars, it doesn't specify the exact SKUs to purchase. The assortment plan described in Chapter 12 supplies the merchandising team with a general outline of what should be carried in a particular merchandise category for fashion merchandise. The selection of specific fashion items and the quantities to be purchased requires a blend of skill, style, and experience. Buyers collect information on trends from vendors, customers, and competition.

Buying systems for staple merchandise are very different. They provide specific information on how much of a particular SKU to purchase.

Once the merchandise is purchased, merchandise planners in multistore chains must allocate the merchandise to stores. Not only must the planners look at the differences in sales potential among stores, they also must consider the differences in the characteristics of the customer base.

In the end, the performance of buyers, vendors, and individual SKUs must be determined. We examined three different approaches to evaluating merchandise performance. In ABC analysis, merchandise is rank-ordered from highest to lowest. The merchandising team uses this information to set inventory management policy. For example, the most productive SKUs should carry sufficient back-up stock so as to never be out-of-stock. The second evaluation technique, sell-through analysis, is more useful for examining the performance of individual SKUs. The planner compares actual-to-planned sales to determine whether more merchandise needs to be ordered or whether the merchandise should be put on sale. Finally, the multiple-attribute method is most useful for evaluating vendors' performance.

The chapter concludes with two appendixes. In Appendix A, we examine the retail inventory method. Appendix B provides several alternatives to using the stock-to-sales ratio in the merchandise budget plan. Specifically, we discuss the week's supply method, the basic stock method, and the percentage variation method.

KEY TERMS

back-up stock (buffer stock, safety stock), *385*

basic stock list, *384*

deseasonalized demand, *386*

lead time, *387*

open-to-buy, *379*

order point, *386*

periodic reordering system, *387*

perpetual ordering system, *386*

DISCUSSION QUESTIONS & PROBLEMS

1. One of the most popular reasons for working in retailing is that employees usually receive a substantial discount when buying merchandise from their employer. In fact, employee purchases can make up a relatively large percentage of sales. Given that employee discounts must be counted as a reduction, how do reductions affect additions to stock in the merchandise budget plan, and what can a retailer do to account for them?

2. Using the following information, calculate additions to stock:

Sales	$24,000
EOM stock	$90,000
BOM stock	$80,000

3. Using the following information, calculate the average beginning-of-month stock-to-sales ratio for a six-month merchandise budget plan:

GMROI	150%
Gross margin	40%

4. Today is July 19. The merchandise planner is attempting to assess his current open-to-buy given the following information:

BOM stock for July	$50,000
Merchandise already received in July	25,000
Merchandise on order to be delivered in July	10,000
Planned monthly sales for July	30,000
Planned reductions	5,000
Planned EOM stock	65,000

What is the open-to-buy on July 19? What does this number mean to you?

5. Now it is July 31 and we need to calculate the open-to-buy for August given the following information:

Planned monthly sales	$20,000
Merchandise on order	40,000
Planned markdowns	5,000
Projected BOM stock	50,000
Planned EOM stock	30,000

Calculate open-to-buy and explain what the number means to you.

6. Typically, August school supplies sales are relatively low. In September, sales increase tremendously. How does the September stock-to-sales ratio differ from the August ratio?

7. Using the 80–20 principle, how can a retailer make certain that there's enough inventory of fast-selling merchandise and a minimal amount of slow-selling merchandise?

8. What's the order point, and how many units should be reordered if a food retailer has an item with a 7-day lead time, 10-day review time, and daily demand of 8 units? Say 65 units are on hand and the retailer must maintain a back-up stock of 20 units to maintain a 95 percent service level.

9. A buyer at a sporting goods store in Denver receives a shipment of 400 ski parkas on October 1 and expects to sell out by January 31. On November 1, she still has 375 parkas left. What issues should she consider in evaluating the selling season's progress?

10. A buyer is trying to decide from which vendor to buy a certain item. The item can be purchased as either a manufacturer brand or private-label brand. Using the following information, determine which vendor the buyer should use.

PERFORMANCE EVALUATIONS OF BRANDS			
ISSUES	IMPORTANCE WEIGHT	MANUFACTURER BRAND	PRIVATE-LABEL BRAND
Vendor reputation	8	5	5
Service	7	6	7
Meets delivery dates	9	7	5
Perceived merchandise quality	7	8	4
Markup opportunity	6	4	8
Demand-generating ability	5	7	5
Promotional assistance	3	6	8

SUGGESTED READINGS

Cash, R. Patrick. *The Buyer's Manual.* New York: National Retail Federation (NRF), 1979.

Department and Specialty Stores: Merchandising and Operating Results Fiscal 1995, 71st ed. New York: John Wiley, 1996.

Goodwin, David R. "The Open-to-Buy System and Accurate Performance Measurement." *International Journal of Retail and Distribution Management* 20, no. 2 (March 1992), pp. 16–27.

INFOREM: Principles of Inventory Management. White Plains, NY: IBM Corp., 1978.

Powers, James T. *The Retail Inventory Method Made Practical.* New York: National Retail Federation, 1971.

Robeson, James F., and Robert G. House. *The Distribution Handbook.* New York: Free Press, 1985.

Stock, James R., and Douglas M. Lambert. *Strategic Logistics Management*, 3d ed. Burr Ridge, IL: Richard D. Irwin, 1993.

Switzer, Gerald J. "A Modern Approach to Retail Accounting." *Management Accounting* 75, no. 8 (February 1994), pp. 55–64.

Taylor, Charles G. *Merchandise Assortment Planning.* New York: National Retail Federation, 1970.

APPENDIX 13A

Retail Inventory Method (RIM)

Like firms in most industries, retailers can value their inventory at cost—and in fact, some retailers do so. Yet many retailers find significant advantages to the retail inventory method (RIM).[9] RIM has two objectives:

1. To maintain a perpetual or book inventory in terms of retail dollar amounts.

2. To maintain records that make it possible to determine the cost value of the inventory at any time without taking a physical inventory.

The Problem   Retailers generally think of their inventory at retail price levels rather than at cost. They take their initial markups, additional markups, markdowns, and so forth as percentages of retail. (These terms are thoroughly defined in Chapter 15 and the Glossary.) When retailers compare their prices to competitors', they compare their retail prices. The problem is that when retailers design their financial plans, evaluate performance, and prepare financial statements, they need to know the cost value of their inventory. One way to keep abreast of their inventory cost is to take physical inventories. Anyone who has worked in retailing knows that this process is time-consuming, costly, and not much fun. So retailers usually only take physical inventories once or twice a year. By the time management receives the results of these physical inventories, it's often too late to make any changes.

Many retailers use POS terminals that easily keep track of every item sold, its original cost, and its final selling price. The rest of the retail world faces the problem of not knowing the cost value of its inventory at any one time. RIM can be used by retailers with either computerized or manual systems.

Advantages of RIM   RIM has five advantages over a system of evaluating inventory at cost.

- The retailer doesn't have to "cost" each time. For retailers with many SKUs, keeping track of each item at cost is expensive and time-consuming, and it increases the cost of errors. It's easier to determine the value of inventory with the retail prices marked on the merchandise than with unmarked or coded cost prices.

- RIM follows the accepted accounting practice of valuing assets at cost or market, whichever is lower. The system lowers the value of inventory when markdowns are taken but doesn't allow inventory's value to increase with additional markups.

- As a by-product of RIM, the amounts and percentages of initial markups, additional markups, markdowns, and shrinkage can be identified. This information can then be compared with historical records or industry norms.

- RIM is useful for determining shrinkage. The difference between the book inventory and the physical inventory can be attributed to shrinkage.

- The book inventory determined by RIM can be used in an insurance claim in case of a loss (e.g., due to fire).

Disadvantages of RIM   RIM is a system that uses average markup. When markup percentages change substantially during a period, or when the inventory on hand at a particular time isn't representative of the total goods handled in terms of markup, the resulting cost figure may be distorted. As with inventory turnover, merchandise budget planning, and open-to-buy, RIM should be applied on a category basis to avoid this problem.

The record-keeping process involved in RIM is burdensome. Buyers must take care so that changes made to the cost and retail inventories are properly recorded.

Steps in RIM   Exhibit 13–9 is an example of RIM in action. The following discussion, which outlines the steps in RIM, is based on this exhibit.

Calculate total goods handled at cost and retail   To determine the total goods handled at cost and retail:

1. *Record beginning inventory at cost* ($60,000) *and at retail* ($84,000). The initial markup is reflected in the retail inventory.
2. *Calculate net purchases* ($39,000 at cost and $54,600 at retail) by recording gross purchases ($50,000 at cost and $70,000 at retail) and adjusting for merchandise returned to vendor ($11,000 at cost and $15,400 at retail).
3. *Calculate net additional markups* ($2,000) by adjusting gross additional markups ($4,000) by any additional markup cancellations ($2,000). Note: These are recorded only at retail because markups affect only the retail value of inventory.

EXHIBIT 13–9

Retail Inventory
Method Example

TOTAL GOODS HANDLED	COST		RETAIL	
Beginning inventory		$60,000		$84,000
Purchases	$50,000		$70,000	
– Return to vendor	(11,000)		(15,400)	
Net purchases		39,000		54,600
Additional markups			4,000	
– Markup cancellations			(2,000)	
Net markups				2,000
Additional transportation		1,000		
Transfers in	1,428		2,000	
– Transfers out	(714)		(1,000)	
Net transfers		714		1,000
Total goods handled		$100,714		$141,600

REDUCTIONS	RETAIL	
Gross sales	$82,000	
– Customer returns and allowances	(4,000)	
Net sales		$78,000
Markdowns	6,000	
– Markdown cancellations	(3,000)	
Net markdowns		3,000
Employee discounts		3,000
Discounts to customers		500
Estimated shrinkage		1,500
Total reductions		$86,000

4. *Record transportation expenses* ($1,000). Here transportation is recorded at cost because it affects only the cost of the inventory.

5. *Calculate net transfers* ($714 at cost and $1,000 at retail) by recording the amount of transfers in and out. A transfer can be from one department to another or from store to store. Transfers are generally made to help adjust inventory to fit demand. For instance, a sweater may be selling well at one store but not at another. A transfer is, in effect, just like a purchase (transfer in) or a return (transfer out). Thus, it's recorded at both cost and retail.

6. *The sum is the total goods handled* ($100,714 at cost and $141,600 at retail).

Calculate retail reductions   Reductions are the transactions that reduce the value of inventory at retail (except additional markup cancellations, which were included as part of the total goods handled). Reductions are calculated as follows:

1. *Record net sales.* The largest reduction in inventory is sales. Gross sales ($82,000) are reduced to net sales ($78,000) by deducting customer returns and allowances ($4,000).

2. *Calculate markdowns.* Net markdowns ($3,000) are derived by subtracting any markdown cancellations ($3,000) from gross markdowns ($6,000).

3. *Record discounts to employees* ($3,000) and customers ($500).

4. *Record estimated shrinkage* ($1,500). Estimated shrinkage is used to determine the ending book inventory if the buyer is preparing an interim financial statement. The estimate is based on historical records and is presented as a percentage of sales. Estimated shrinkage wouldn't be included, however, if a physical inventory was taken at the time the statement was being prepared. In this case, the difference between physical inventory and book inventory would be the amount of shrinkage due to loss, shoplifting, and so forth.

5. *The sum is the total reductions* ($86,000).

Calculate the cumulative markup and cost multiplier The cumulative markup is the average percentage markup for the period. It's calculated the same way the markup for an item is calculated:

$$\text{Cumulative markup} = \frac{\text{Total retail} - \text{Total cost}}{\text{Total retail}}$$

$$28.87\% = \frac{\$141,600 - \$100,714}{\$141,600}$$

The cumulative markup can be used as a comparison against the planned initial markup. If the cumulative markup is higher than the planned initial markup, then the category is doing better than planned.

The cost multiplier is similar to the cost complement.

$$\text{Cost multiplier} = (\$100\% - \text{Cumulative markup }\%)$$
$$71.13\% = 100\% - 28.87\%$$

or

$$\frac{\text{Total cost}}{\text{Total retail}} = \frac{\$100,714}{\$141,600} = 71.13\%$$

The cost multiplier is used in the next step to determine the ending book inventory at retail.

Determine ending book inventory at cost and retail

$$\text{Ending book inventory at retail} = \text{Total goods handled at retail} - \text{Total reductions}$$
$$\$55,600 = \$141,600 - \$86,000$$

The ending book inventory at cost is determined in the same way that retail has been changed to cost in other situations—multiply the retail times (100% – gross margin percentage). In this case,

$$\text{Ending book inventory at cost} = \text{Ending book inventory at retail} \times \text{Cost multiplier}$$
$$\$39,548 = \$55,600 \times 71.13\%$$

APPENDIX 13B

Alternatives to the Stock-to-Sales Ratio

The average BOM (beginning-of-month) stock-to-sales ratio was derived directly from the planned inventory turnover to determine monthly additions to stock in the merchandise budget plan in Chapter 13. This appendix looks at some retailers' similar methods of defining the relationship between inventory and sales.

Week's Supply Method   The week's supply method is the inventory management method most similar to the stock-to-sales method. The difference is that everything is expressed in weeks rather than months. The average BOM stock-to-sales ratio equals the number of months in the period divided by the planned inventory turnover for the period. For instance, if the plan is for 12 months and planned turnover is 6, the average BOM stock-to-sales ratio = 12 ÷ 6 = 2.

Using the week's supply method, 52 weeks are substituted for 12 months. Thus, 52 weeks ÷ 6 turns = 8.66 weeks of supply. This means the buyer is planning to have 8.66 weeks of supply at the beginning of the month. (Of course, 8.66 weeks is equivalent to two months.)

Basic Stock Method   The basic stock method is the inventory management method used to determine the BOM inventory by considering both the sales forecast for the month and the back-up stock.

BOM inventory = Forecast monthly sales + Basic stock

So basic stock and back-up stock are really the same thing. Like the stock-to-sales ratio and the week's supply methods, the basic stock method uses inventory turnover to calculate BOM inventory. Exhibit 13–10 illustrates the basic stock method.

1. Given the monthly sales, the average sales for the period is $16,666 (total period sales ÷ number of months).
2. Assuming inventory turnover for the three-month period is 2 (eight annual turns), average inventory for the period is $25,000.

$$\text{Average inventory} = \text{Total period sales} \div \text{Inventory turnover}$$
$$\$25,000 = \$50,000 \div 2$$

3. Basic stock = Average inventory − Average sales
   $8,334 = $25,000   − $16,666

4. BOM inventory for October = Basic stock + Planned sales for October
   $23,334 = $8,334   + $15,000

The basic stock method has some shortcomings. First, it won't work if inventory turnover is greater than 12 times a year. In this case, average inventory would be less than average monthly sales, causing basic stock to be negative. Further, the basic stock is the same for every month, no matter what the sales. By comparison, in the stock-to-sales method, monthly stock-to-sales ratios fluctuate with the forecast level of sales. This makes more sense for months with higher sales, where there's greater need for back-up stock.

Percentage Variation Method   The percentage variation method considers the same factors as the basic stock method. The formula used to calculate BOM inventory can be expressed as

$$\text{BOM inventory} = \text{Average inventory} \times \frac{1}{2}\left(1 + \frac{\text{Planned sales for the month}}{\text{Average monthly sales}}\right)$$

Using Exhibit 13–10's data, the BOM inventory for October is

$$\$25,000 \times \frac{1}{2}\left(1 + \frac{\$15,000}{\$16,666}\right) = \$23,750.45$$

EXHIBIT 13–10

Basic Stock and
Percentage Variation
Methods for One
Category

MONTH	SALES	BOM INENTORY: BASIC STOCK METHOD	BOM INVENTORY: PERCENTAGE VARIATION METHOD
October	$15,000	$23,334	$23,750
November	$15,000	$23,334	$23,750
December	$20,000	$28,335	$27,500
Total	$50,000		
Average sales	$16,666		
Average inventory	$25,000		
Basic stock	$ 8,334		

November and December BOM inventories are calculated the same way.

Note the similarities between the BOM inventories in the basic stock and the percentage variation methods. In fact, the percentage variation gives the same results as the basic stock method when an annual inventory turnover of 6 is planned. When higher inventory turnovers are planned, however, the percentage variation method gives BOM inventories less than the basic stock method.[10]

The percentage variation method has the same shortcomings as the basic stock method. In addition, the "1/2" in the formula is arbitrarily set.

NOTES

1. "Why a Single Version of the Truth Matters," *Chain Store Age*, June 1996, p. C3.

2. *Department and Specialty Stores: Merchandising and Operating Results Fiscal 1994*, 70th ed. (New York: National Retail Federation, 1995), pp. 1–2.

3. Ibid.

4. *INFOREM: Principles of Inventory Management* (White Plains, NY: IBM Corp., 1978).

5. The department store chain wishes to remain anonymous. The allocation of inventory to stores is based on each store's standard deviation of sales. Larger stores will have a proportionally smaller standard deviation, causing the back-up stock to be proportionally smaller.

6. See James R. Stock and Douglas M. Lambert, *Strategic Logistics Management*, 3d ed. (Burr Ridge, IL: Richard D. Irwin, 1993), pp. 419–21; and Lynn E. Gill, "Inventory and Physical Distribution Management," in *The Distribution Handbook*, ed. James F. Robeson and Robert G. House (New York: Free Press, 1988), pp. 664–67.

7. For a review of multiattribute decision models, see Kenneth R. MacCrimmon, "An Overview of Multiple Objective Decision Making," in *Multiple Criteria Decision Making*, ed. J. L. Cochrane and M. Zeleny (Columbia: University of South Carolina Press, 1973), pp. 18–44. For other attitudinal approaches to vendor evaluation, see John S. Berens, "A Decision Matrix Approach to Supplier Selection," *Journal of Retailing* 47, no. 4 (1971–72), pp. 47–53; Elizabeth C. Hirschman, "An Exploratory Comparison of Decision Criteria Used by Retail Buyers," in *Retailing Patronage Theory*, ed. Robert F. Lusch and William R. Darden (Norman: Center for Economic and Management Research, University of Oklahoma, 1981), p. 15; Elizabeth C. Hirschman and David Mazursky, "A Trans-Organizational Investigation of Retail Buyers' Criteria and Information Sources," New York University Institute of Retail Management Working Paper, 1982, pp. 82–88; Rom J. Markin, *Retail Management: A Systems Approach* (New York: Macmillan, 1971); William F. Massey and Jim D. Savvas, "Logical Flow Models for Marketing Analysis," *Journal of Marketing* 28 (January 1964), pp. 30–37; and Janet Wagner, Richard Ettenson, and Jean Parrish, "Vendor Selection among Retail Buyers: An Analysis by Merchandise Division," *Journal of Retailing* 65, no. 1 (Spring 1989), pp. 58–79.

8. These issues were taken from Wagner, Ettenson, and Parrish, "Vendor Selection."

9. For a thorough treatment of the retail inventory method, see James T. Powers, *The Retail Inventory Method Made Practical* (New York: National Retail Merchants Association, 1971).

10. Robert F. Lusch and Patrick Dunne, *Retail Management* (Cincinnati: South-Western, 1990), p. 356.

14

Buying Merchandise

THE WORLD OF RETAILING

↓

RETAILING STRATEGY

↓

MERCHANDISE MANAGEMENT

12. Planning Merchandise
    Assortments
13. Buying Systems
14. Buying Merchandise
15. Pricing
16. Retail Promotion Mix

STORE MANAGEMENT

17. Managing the Store
18. Store Layout, Design, and
    Visual Merchandising
19. Customer Service
20. Retail Selling

QUESTIONS

- What branding options are available to retailers?

- What issues should retailers consider when sourcing internationally?

- How and where do retailers meet with their vendors?

- How can retailers establish and maintain a competitive advantage by developing long-term relationships with vendors?

- What ethical and legal issues are associated with purchasing merchandise?

IN THE PRECEDING TWO CHAPTERS, we discussed the process that buyers go through to determine what and how much merchandise to buy. This chapter focuses on the process of buying merchandise: making branding and international sourcing decisions, meeting with vendors, establishing and maintaining strong vendor relationships, and ethical and legal issues.

Branding is one of the most important strategic merchandising decisions facing retailers. The types of brands a retailer chooses to carry are essential cues that customers use to evaluate a store. Brands influence consumers' loyalty to a store and image of it. The choice of brands also dictates margins and the degree of flexibility retailers have with their vendors.

The issue of branding goes hand in hand with international sourcing decisions, particularly for those retailers purchasing private-label merchandise. Not only does a product's country of origin denote its quality, it will also influence the merchandise cost and how long it takes to get. Recently, international sourcing decisions have been complicated with charges of human rights and child labor violations.

Whether the retailer decides to buy merchandise domestically or from an international source, it must "go to market" to view the merchandise and negotiate with vendors. It can meet vendors in a market center where there's a concentration of hundreds—or possibly thousands—of vendors. Or it can buy in its own office. A third alternative is to have a third party, called a resident buying office, prearrange meetings with potential vendors.

Is Banana Republic a brand or the name of a store?

As merchandise is purchased from the same vendors over and over, relationships develop. Developing strong relationships with vendors is a good way to achieve a sustainable competitive advantage. Simply buying from the same vendor, however, doesn't necessarily end in a competitive advantage. Both parties must agree to a strategic partnership based on trust, shared goals, and a strong financial commitment.

Given the number of transactions between a retailer and each of its vendors, there are lots of opportunities for unethical and even illegal behavior. The ethical issues involved in purchasing merchandise are often subtle, yet they define the principles of conduct that govern the behavior of category managers and their employees. The law formalizes society's ethical concerns and dictates what, when, why, and how things are sold, and who may sell them. Failure to be aware of the impact of these issues can result in crippling, if not ruinous, consequences for a retailer. On the other hand, retailers that take a positive, proactive role can benefit financially and psychologically from the knowledge that they're doing the right thing.

We conclude this chapter with two appendixes. In the first, we provide tips for retailers negotiating with their vendors. Negotiations—a basic form of human interaction—are particularly important when making buying decisions. A good negotiator can easily make her yearly salary in one good negotiating session.

The second appendix examines the terms under which merchandise is purchased from vendors. Unfortunately, buying from vendors isn't as simple as when you buy from a store. Retailers must choose between several types of discount and payment date combinations. Although these discounts are relatively small compared to the total cost of an order, over a year they can become sizable. In fact, the discounts could make the difference between realizing a profit or a loss for small gross-margin retailers like grocery stores.

BRANDING STRATEGIES

Think about the products that you've bought recently. Have you bought manufacturer brands like Levi's, Kellogg's, or Black & Decker; private labels like Gap jeans, America's Choice cookies from A&P, or Craftsman tools from Sears? As they develop their merchandise and assortment plans, buyers must also decide the mix of manufacturer versus private-label brands to buy. In this section, we examine the relative advantages of these branding decisions, which are summarized in Exhibit 14-1.

Manufacturer Brands

Manufacturer brands, also known as **national brands,** are products designed, produced, and marketed by a vendor. The manufacturer is responsible for developing the merchandise and establishing an image for the brand. In some cases, the manufacturer will use its name as part of the brand name for a specific product such as Kellogg's corn flakes. However, some manufacturers like Procter & Gamble (manufacturer of Tide, Cheer, and Ivory) don't associate their name with the brand. Exhibit 14–2 shows some of the most recognized names in women's fashion.

EXHIBIT 14–1

Relative Advantages of Manufacturer versus Private Brands

IMPACT ON STORE	TYPE OF VENDOR	
	MANUFACTURER BRANDS	PRIVATE-LABEL BRANDS
Store loyalty	?	+
Store image	+	+
Traffic flow	+	+
Selling and promotional expenses	+	–
Restrictions	–	+
Differential advantages	–	+
Margins	?	?

+ advantage to the retailer
– disadvantage to the retailer
? depends on circumstances

EXHIBIT 14–2

The Most Recognized Brands in Women's Fashion

BRAND	PRODUCT
1. L'eggs	Legwear
2. Timex	Watches
3. Lee	Jeans and sportswear
4. Hanes	Hosiery, activewear
5. Levi Strauss	Jeans and sportswear
6. Hanes Her Way	Underwear, daywear, bras, casual wear, socks, casual shoes
7. Fruit of the Loom	Underwear, daywear, activewear
8. Reebok	Athletic shoes, activewear
9. Calvin Klein	Designer apparel, jeans, fragrance, licensing, retail
10. No Nonsense	Hosiery
11. Nike	Athletic shoes, activewear
12. Dockers	Sportswear
13. Seiko	Watches
14. Playtex	Bras, shapewear
15. Wrangler	Jeans, denim sportswear
16. Jordache	Jeans, sportswear
17. London Fog	Rainwear, outerwear
18. Guess?	Jeans and sportswear, licensing
19. L.A. Gear	Athletic shoes, activewear
20. Bugle Boy	Jeans, sportswear
21. Liz Claiborne	Sportswear
22. Rolex	Watches
23. Adidas	Athletic shoes, activewear
24. The Gap	Jeans, casual sportswear
25. Gitano	Jeans, denim sportswear

Source: "The Fairchild 100," *Women's Wear Daily,* November 1995, pp. 7–14.

Some retailers organize some of their categories around their most important national brands. For instance, buyers in department stores are responsible for brands, such as Clinique or Estée Lauder, rather than for products, such as lipstick and fragrances. Clothing is also often organized by manufacturer brand (e.g., Polo/Ralph Lauren, Levi's, Liz Claiborne, or DKNY). These brands often have their own boutique within stores. Managing a category by national brand, rather than a more traditional classification scheme, is useful so that merchandise can be purchased in a coordinated manner around a central theme.

Buying from vendors of manufacturer brands can help store image, traffic flow, and selling/promotional expenses. (See Exhibit 14–1.) Retailers buy from vendors of manufacturer brands because they have a customer following—people go into the store and ask for them by name. Loyal customers of manufacturer brands generally know what to expect from the products and feel comfortable with them.

Manufacturers devote considerable resources to creating demand for their products. As a result, relatively less money is required by the retailer for selling and promotional expenses for manufacturer brands. For instance, Guess? Inc., manufacturer of jeans and other casual clothing, attempts to communicate a constant and focused message to the consumer by coordinating advertising with in-store promotions and displays. But manufacturer brands typically have lower realized gross margins than private-label brands. These lower gross margins are due to the manufacturer assuming the cost of promoting the brand and increased competition among retailers selling these brands. Typically many retailers offer the same manufacturer brands in a market so customers compare prices for these brands across stores. Retailers often offer significant discounts on some manufacturer brands to attract customers to their stores.

Stocking national brands may increase or decrease store loyalty. If the manufacturer brand is available through a limited number of retail outlets (e.g., Lancôme cosmetics or DKNY sportswear), customers loyal to the manufacturer brand will also become loyal to the store. If, on the other hand, manufacturer brands are readily available from many retailers in a market, customer loyalty may decrease because the retailer can't differentiate itself from competition. Another problem with manufacturer brands is that they can limit a retailer's flexibility. Vendors of strong brands can dictate how their products are displayed, advertised, and priced. Jockey underwear, for instance, tells retailers exactly when and how their products should be advertised.

Licensed Brands   A special type of manufacturer brand is a **licensed brand,** in which the owner of a well-known brand name (licensor) enters a contract with a licensee to develop, produce, and sell the branded merchandise. The licensee may be either (1) the retailer that contracts with a manufacturer to produce the licensed product or (2) a third party that contracts to have the merchandise produced and then sells it to the retailer.

Licensed brands' market share has grown increasingly large in recent years. Owners of trade names not typically associated with manufacturing have also gotten into the licensing business. For instance, the manufacturer of the sweatshirt or baseball cap emblazoned with your university's logo pays your school a licensing fee. If it didn't, it would be infringing on the university's logo (a trademark) and therefore be involved in counterfeiting. (Counterfeiting is discussed later in this chapter.) Retailing View 14.1 describes the growth of Looney Tunes licensed brands.

14.1

The Licensing of Bugs Bunny

BUGS BUNNY, DAFFY DUCK, Porky Pig, and the rest of Warner Brothers Consumer Products' (WBCP) Looney Tunes characters are everywhere! Worldwide retail sales of these licensed brands are estimated to be over $3.5 billion.

To ensure that the Looney Tunes brand continues to generate tremendous retail sales and consumer excitement, WBCP decided to use the familiar logo featuring Bugs Bunny inside red rings because it exemplifies the heritage, nostalgia, and classic attributes of the brand. It also developed a unifying theme for packaging and display so the products will look like they belong together.

Looney Tunes characters are found in several merchandise categories. Bugs and his buddies are found on all sorts of apparel. For instance, Hanes has created "tween" underwear and related knit separates for girls. Looney Tunes Lovables, a successful line of baby products, has baby versions of the popular Looney Tunes characters. Warner Bros. Interactive Entertainment and Virgin Sound and Vision are producing a line of Looney Tunes CD-ROM titles targeting children under 12. In conjunction with Spalding Sports Worldwide, WBCP is marketing a line of equipment and accessories for tennis, basketball, football, and other sports. Even housewares and soft home departments are getting into the act. The characters are found on coordinated bedding, pillows, rugs, wallpaper, juvenile furniture, dinnerware, and clocks.

Source: Advertising Insert, *Discount Store News,* August 19, 1996.

Private-Label Brands

Private-label brands (also called **store brands**) are products developed and marketed by a retailer. Exhibit 14–3 gives examples. Typically, retail buyers or category managers develop specifications for the merchandise and then contract with a vendor to manufacture it. But the retailer, not the manufacturer, is responsible for promoting the brand.

Retailers' use of private labels has been relatively small in the past for several reasons. First, national brands have been heavily advertised on TV and other media for decades, creating a strong consumer franchise. Second, it has been hard for retailers to gain the economies of scale in design and production necessary to compete against manufacturer brands. Third, many retailers haven't been sophisticated enough to aggressively compete against manufacturer brands. Finally, private labels have had a reputation of being inferior to manufacturer brands. Although consumers are looking for value, they still want quality.

Many predict a much greater presence of private-label brands in the future. As we discussed in Chapter 4, customers are becoming more value-conscious. Although value has traditionally been defined as the relationship between quality and price, today's consumers are not willing to give up quality. Thus, retailers who can provide products perceived to be equal to or better than national brands' quality at a less expensive or parity price will be successful.

Of course, only larger retailers are in a position to create private labels and compete with manufacturer brands. In the past two decades, retailers have become larger and more powerful in relation to their suppliers. Retail leaders like Wal-Mart, The Limited, Federated Department Stores, and Kroger all have the economic power and level of sophistication necessary to create private labels that can compete against manufacturer brands.

To meet the growing taste for gourmet and specialty foods, some grocery store chains are producing "premium" private labels, like A&P's Master Choice. A Gallup survey found that 90 percent of the consumers who say they buy "premium" private-label merchandise rate the products equal to or better than national brands.[2]

REFACT Private labels are becoming the category leaders for milk, cheese, paper napkins, and dozens of other products found in supermarkets, drugstores, and retail outlets.[3] They account for $48 billion in revenues in grocery stores.[4]

EXHIBIT **14–3**

Examples of Private-Label Brands

INDUSTRY	STORE	BRAND
Grocery stores	Safeway	Shurfine, Empress
	King Soopers	Topco
	A&P	America's Choice, Master Choice (premium private label)
	Winn-Dixie	Maid
Chain stores	Sears	Kenmore, Diehard, Craftsman, Canyon River Blues, Toughskins
	Wal-Mart	Sam's Choice Cola, Great Value, Decadent Cookie, Better Homes and Gardens
	Kmart	Ora-Pure, Kgro, Jaclyn Smith
	JCPenney	Arizona, Fox, Stafford, Hunt Club
Department stores	Macy's	I.N.C. International Concepts
	Saks Fifth Avenue	SFA Collections, Real Clothes
	Bloomingdale's	East Island, Metropolitan View
	Nordstrom Inc.	Classiques Entier
Specialty stores	Neiman Marcus	One-Up
	The Limited, Limited Express	Forenza, Hunters Run, Outback Red, EXP
	Kids "R" Us	Legends

Fashion retailers have stepped up their private-label offerings as well. Flooded with competition from factory-outlet and off-price stores that carry manufacturer brands, department stores are using private-label brands to present an exclusive image. These stores are better able to appeal to regional tastes by using private labels than they could with manufacturer brands. For example, stores in the South can design and carry bright colors and lighter fabrics in the winter. This strategy is much harder for retailers who depend on manufacturer brands.[5] The strategy appears to be paying off for some. For instance, in a *Women's Wear Daily* survey of the most recognized brands in women's sportswear, Kmart's Jaclyn Smith Collection came in fourth ahead of Calvin Klein and Ralph Lauren.[6] JCPenney's phenomenal Arizona brand of jeans hit $900 million in retail sales in 1995 and is expected to hit $1 billion by 2000.[7] Retailing View 14.2 gives details.

Offering private labels provides a number of benefits to retailers, as Exhibit 14–1 shows. First, the exclusivity of strong private labels boosts store loyalty. For instance, Hunters Run, a brand of traditional women's sportswear owned by The Limited, won't be found at Macy's. A second advantage of buying from private-label vendors is that they can enhance store image if the brands are high quality and fashionable. Third, like manufacturer brands, successful private-label brands can draw customers to the store. Fourth, retailers that purchase private-label brands don't have the same restrictions on display, promotion, or price that often encumber their strategy with manufacturer brands. Retailers purchasing private brands also have more control over manufacturing, quality control, and distribution of the merchandise. Talbots, for instance, can contract with any vendor to manufacture its private-label sweaters. Finally, gross margin opportunities may be greater. Due to these advantages, many people think that private-label merchandise

REFACT Sears plans to increase its share of private-label goods in apparel and home fashion to 50 percent. Private-label sales in 1996 constituted 26 percent of total apparel volume, up from less than 15 percent in 1994.[8]

14.2

Private Label Jeans Mount Aggressive Attack on Market

The success of Sears' Canyon River Blues line of jeans for men, juniors, and children has far exceeded Sears' expectations.

WITH DYED-IN-BLUE JEANS LOYALISTS becoming a thing of the past, a growing number of retailers have moved aggressively to make this huge market their "private" preserve. Propelled by consumers who place a higher priority on value and quality than on designer names, updated finishes, or trendy silhouettes, private-label jeans have become the fastest-growing segment of the $8 billion jeans business.

Led by JCPenney's Original Arizona Jeans Co. and The Gap, this rapidly growing segment has captured an estimated 26 percent of the denim market, up from 15 percent in 1991. The launch of Canyon River Blues (Sears' line of jeans for men, juniors, and children) moreover has bumped the private-label share even higher. So far, the success of Canyon River Blues has far exceeded Sears' expectations.

The success of Penney's Arizona brand has also far surpassed what company executives envisioned when they launched the label in late 1989. Today, the Arizona brand can be found in men's, women's, children's, infants', and toddlers' departments and ranks among the top 10 best-selling jeans brands across all JCPenney stores nationwide. When the Arizona brand was introduced, it dovetailed with shoppers' desire for fashion at a value price. And as tastes have changed over the years, the Plano, Texas-based retailer has successfully adapted the brand to stay in tune with shifts in the market.

Other major retailers are also bidding for a new share of the denim business. Saks Fifth Avenue has introduced a line of women's jeans under its SFA private label. Kids "R" Us has successfully marketed its Legends brand for several years, while mass market operators such as Kmart, Wal-Mart, and Target are paying increased attention to private-label jeans. Aggressive brand management and marketing is what sets today's private-brand denim labels apart from those of the past. Retailers are investing heavily in product development, quality control, store presentation, and advertising just as a traditional manufacturer builds its brand.

The cumulative effect of these private-brand jeans is taking its toll on such national labels as Guess?, Calvin Klein, Lee, Wrangler, and even the kingpin, Levi Strauss. Although none will admit to market share erosion, each is reshaping its merchandising and marketing efforts in an attempt to woo shoppers lured by the heavily advertised, competitively priced private brands.

What remains to be seen, however, is whether this added push on the part of national brands will be enough to slow the advance of private brands, particularly Arizona and Canyon River Blues. Most experts predict that the growing strength of these labels will ultimately result in a shakeout among jeans makers.

Source: Susan Reda, "Private Label Jeans Mount Aggressive Attack on Market," *Stores,* February 1996, pp. 68–69.

will become as popular in the United States as it is in Europe. For instance, in a French hypermarche—a huge supermarket—everything from TV sets to champagne is private-label.[9]

But there are drawbacks to using private-label brands. Although gross margins may be higher for private-label brands than for manufacturer brands, there are other expenses that aren't readily apparent. Retailers must make significant investments to design merchandise, create customer awareness, and develop a favorable image for their private-label brands. When private-label vendors are located outside the United States, the complications become even more significant, as we'll see in the next section.

Sales associates may need additional training to help them sell private-label brands against better-known brands. If the private-label merchandise doesn't sell, the retailer can't return the merchandise to the vendor. These problems are most severe for high-fashion merchandise.

Generic Products   A special category of private-label merchandise is known as generics. **Generic products** are unbranded, unadvertised merchandise found mainly in drug, grocery, and discount stores. Generics are popular in a few product categories. Some industry experts think generic pharmaceuticals capture 25 to 50 percent of the market in their first year on the market. The reasons for their success are simple: lower price (around 70 percent less than the name-brand equivalent); flat-rate Medicare reimbursements; demands made by health maintenance organizations (HMOs) to use generic products; and pharmacists who endorse the lower-priced products. Generic cigarettes' popularity is also growing as the tax causes prices to skyrocket.

Sometimes it's hard to distinguish a brand from a store and vice versa. See Retailing View 14.3.

INTERNATIONAL SOURCING DECISIONS

Take a look at what you are wearing to see if anything is made in the United States. Chances are your shirt or blouse was made in Hong Kong, your jeans were made in Italy, those beautiful new shoes are Brazilian, while those old sweat socks are from China. Your undergarments may be from Honduras. To top it off, your watch is probably from Japan or Switzerland.

A decision that's closely associated with branding decisions, which we discussed in the previous section, is to determine where the merchandise is made. Retailers involved in private branding are faced with all of the issues that we'll examine in this section. Although retailers buying manufacturer brands usually aren't responsible for determining where the merchandise is made, a product's country of origin is often used as a signal of quality. Certain items are strongly associated with specific countries, and products from those countries, such as gold jewelry from Italy or cars from Japan, often benefit from those linkages.[11]

In this section we'll first examine the cost implications of international sourcing decisions. Superficially, it often looks like retailers can get merchandise from foreign suppliers cheaper than from domestic sources. Unfortunately, there are a lot of "hidden" costs, including managerial issues, associated with sourcing globally that make this decision more complicated. We then examine the trend toward sourcing closer to home or actually reversing the trend toward international sourcing by buying "Made in America." This section concludes by exploring ethical issues associated with retailers who buy from vendors engaged in human rights and child labor violations.

REFACT Over the past 20 years, importing has gone from a small segment of the production strategy for apparel to a dominant force, now accounting for about 67 percent of all goods sold at retail.[10]

14.3

A Brand or a Store?

THE DISTINCTION BETWEEN A STORE and a brand has become blurred in recent years. Some large retailers have developed strong private-label merchandise. Other retailers, like The Gap and its sister store, Banana Republic, have such a strong "brand name" that the average consumer cannot make a distinction between store or brand. The Gap has capitalized on its strong name recognition by widening the variety of merchandise offered at its stores. It now sells personal care products like perfume, lotion, and lip gloss. Brooks Brothers (the traditional clothing retailer) and Crate & Barrel (the upscale soft home store chain) only carry merchandise with their names on it. The Limited takes a slightly different tactic, selling multiple private-label brands to reach different target markets. Hunters Run is traditional, whereas EXP is targeted for the juniors market. (See Exhibit 14–3.)

A natural extension of the retailer's brand strategy is to exploit a strong retail name recognition by selling its products through channels other than its own stores. For instance, Tiffany's, the upscale jewelry store with its flagship store in Manhattan and other outlets around the country, now sells it products to other jewelry stores. Starbucks staged one of the most aggressive moves by a retailer to broaden its customer base. The coffee shop retailer that brought Middle America the "short, skinny, decaf latte" has teamed up with PepsiCo to market the Frappuccino—a coffee-and-milk blend sold through traditional grocery channels. Starbucks also is engaged in a joint venture with Dreyer's Grand Ice Cream to distribute Starbucks coffee-flavored ice cream.

On the other side of the distribution spectrum, several firms that have traditionally been exclusively manufacturers have become retailers. Examples are Guess?, Calvin Klein, Ralph Lauren, Georgio Armani, Levi's, Harley-Davidson, Sony, and Nike. Why have these manufacturers chosen to become retailers? First, by becoming retailers they have total control over the way their merchandise is presented to the public. They can price, promote, and merchandise their line with a unified strategy. They don't have to worry about retailers cherry-picking certain items or discounting the price, for instance. Second, they can use these stores to test new merchandise and merchandising concepts. Based on these tests' results, they can better advise other retailers what to buy and how to merchandise their stores. Third, these manufacturers/retailers use their stores to showcase their merchandise to the public as well. The Sony and Nike stores in Chicago and Ralph Lauren's flagship store in Manhattan have an atmosphere that enhances the manufacturer's image as well as helps to sell merchandise. Finally, although these stores often compete with stores that carry the same merchandise, some would argue that having a stronger retail presence creates a name recognition and synergy between the manufacturer and retailer that benefit both parties.

Costs Associated with Global Sourcing Decisions

A demonstrable reason for sourcing globally rather than domestically is to save money. Retailers must examine several cost issues when making these decisions. The cost issues discussed in this chapter are country-of-origin effects, foreign currency fluctuations, tariffs, free trade zones, inventory carrying costs, and transportation costs.

Country-of-Origin Effects The next time you're buying a shirt made in Western Europe (e.g., Italy, France, or Germany), notice that it's probably more expensive than a comparable shirt made in a developing country like Hungary, Ecuador, or Taiwan. These Western European countries have a reputation for high fashion and quality. Unfortunately for the U.S. consumer, however, the amount of goods and services that can be purchased in those countries with U.S. dollars is significantly less than in the developing countries. When making international sourcing decisions, therefore, retailers must weigh the savings associated with buying from developing countries with the panache associated with buying merchandise from a country that has a reputation for fashion and quality.

Other countries might have a technological advantage in the production of certain types of merchandise and can therefore provide their products to the world market at a relatively lower price than other countries. For example, Japan has always been a leader in the development of consumer electronics. Although these products often enter the market at a high (penetration) price, the price soon drops as manufacturers learn to produce the merchandise more efficiently.

REFACT JCPenney buys its goods from suppliers spread across 50 countries.[12]

Foreign Currency Fluctuations   An important consideration when making global sourcing decisions is fluctuations in the currency of the exporting firm. Unless currencies are closely linked, for example, between the United States and Canada, changes in the exchange rate will increase or reduce the cost of the merchandise.

Suppose, for instance, that Service Merchandise is purchasing watches from Swatch in Switzerland for $100,000, which is equivalent to 120,000 Swiss Francs (SFr) since the exchange rate is 1.2 Sfr for each U.S. dollar. If the dollar falls to, say, 1.1 SFr, before the firm has to pay for the watches, it would end up paying $109,090 (or 120,000 SFr ÷ 1.1).

Tariffs   A **tariff,** also known as a **duty,** is a list of taxes placed by a government upon imports.[13] Import tariffs have been used to shield domestic manufacturers from foreign competition and to raise money for the government. In general, since tariffs raise the cost of imported merchandise, retailers have always had a strong incentive to reduce them. The General Agreement on Tariffs and Trade, the North American Free Trade Agreement, and foreign trade zones all help reduce tariffs.

The General Agreement on Tariffs and Trade (GATT) and the World Trade Organization (WTO)   In 1946, the average U.S. tariff rate was 26 percent, compared to approximately 5 percent in 1987.[14] The General Agreement on Tariffs and Trade is partially responsible for this reduction. Started in 1947, GATT has evolved into a group of 125 member countries that sponsors international trade negotiations. In January 1995, the World Trade Organization was formed to supervise and arbitrate GATT agreements and encourage future negotiations.

Maquiladores are manufacturing plants in Mexico that make goods and parts or process food for export to the United States. They are very popular because their costs are lower than those of their U.S. counterparts.

North American Free Trade Agreement (NAFTA)   The ratification of NAFTA on January 1, 1994, created a tariff-free market with 364 million consumers and a total output of $6 trillion.[15] NAFTA members are currently the United States, Canada, and Mexico. Other Latin American countries are expected to join in the next few years.

REFACT In 1995, the volume of imports from Mexico, propelled by NAFTA, grew 61 percent, and the country was the third-largest foreign apparel supplier to the United States. Right behind Mexico was the Dominican Republic. Nevertheless, China remains the number one apparel supplier, followed by Hong Kong.[16]

U.S. retailers stand to gain from NAFTA for two reasons. First, Mexican labor is relatively low-cost and abundant. Thus, retailers can either search for lower-cost suppliers in Mexico or begin manufacturing merchandise there themselves. **Maquiladoras** (plants in Mexico that make goods and parts or process food for export to the United States) are plentiful, have lower costs than their U.S. counterparts, and are located throughout Mexico, particularly in border towns such as Nogales and Tijuana. Second, with the growing importance of quick response inventory systems, the time it takes to get merchandise into stores has become even more critical than in the past. Transit times are shorter and managerial control problems are reduced when sourcing from Mexico, compared to the Far East or Europe.

Foreign Trade Zones   Retailers involved in foreign sourcing of merchandise can lower import tariffs by using foreign trade zones. A **foreign trade zone** is a special area within a country that can be used for warehousing, packaging, inspection, labeling, exhibition, assembly, fabrication, or transshipment of imports without being subject to that country's tariffs.

To illustrate how a foreign trade zone can benefit retailers, consider how German cars are imported to a foreign trade zone in Guatemala for distribution throughout Central America. The duty for passenger vehicles is 100 percent of the landed cost of the vehicle. The duty for commercial vehicles, however, is only 10 percent. The German manufacturer imported commercial vans with no seats or carpeting, and with panels instead of windows. After paying the 10 percent import duty, they converted the vans to passenger station wagons in the foreign trade zone in Guatemala and sold them throughout Latin America.

Cost of Carrying Inventory   The cost of carrying inventory is likely to be higher when purchasing from suppliers outside the United States than from domestic suppliers. Recall from Chapter 7 that

$$\text{Cost of carrying inventory} = \text{Average inventory value (at cost)} \times \text{Opportunity cost of capital}$$

The **opportunity cost of capital** is the rate available on the next best use of the capital invested in the project at hand.

There are several reasons for the higher inventory carrying costs. Consider The Spoke bicycle store in Aspen, Colorado, which is buying Moots bicycles manufactured in Steamboat Springs, Colorado. They know that the **lead time**—the amount of time between recognition that an order needs to be placed and the point at which the merchandise arrives in the store and is ready for sale—is usually two weeks, plus or minus three days. But if The Spoke is ordering bikes from Italy, the lead time might be three months, plus or minus three weeks. Since lead times are longer, retailers must maintain larger inventories to ensure that merchandise is available when the customer wants it. Larger inventories mean larger inventory carrying costs.

It's also more difficult to predict exactly how long the lead time will be when sourcing globally. When the bicycle goes from Steamboat Springs to Aspen, the worst that could happen is that it gets caught in a snowstorm for a day or two. On the other hand, the bicycle from Italy might be significantly delayed because of multiple handlings at sea or airports, customs, strikes of carriers, poor weather, or bureaucratic problems. Similar to longer lead times, inconsistent lead times require the retailer to maintain higher levels of safety stock.

Transportation Costs   In general, the further merchandise has to travel, the higher the transportation cost will be for any particular mode of transportation. For instance, the cost of shipping a container of merchandise by ship from China to New York is significantly higher than from Panama to New York.

Managerial Issues Associated with Global Sourcing Decisions   In the previous section we examined the specific costs associated with global sourcing decisions. In most cases, retailers can obtain hard cost information that will help them make their global sourcing decisions. The managerial issues discussed in this section—quality control and developing strategic alliances—are not as easily evaluated.

Quality Control   When sourcing globally, it's harder to maintain and measure quality standards than when sourcing domestically. Typically these problems are more pronounced in countries that are further away and that are less developed. For instance, it's easier to address a quality problem if it occurs on a shipment of dresses from Costa Rica to the United States than if the dresses were shipped from Singapore.

There are both direct and indirect ramifications for retailers if merchandise is delayed because it has to be remade due to poor quality. Suppose Banana Republic is having pants made in Haiti. Before the pants leave the factory, Banana Republic representatives find that the workmanship is so poor that the pants need to be remade. This delay reverberates throughout the system. Banana Republic could carry extra safety stock to carry it through until the pants can be remade. More likely, however, they won't have advance warning of the problem, so the stores will be out of stock.

A more serious problem occurs if the pants are delivered to the stores without the problem having been detected. This could happen if the defect is subtle, such as inaccurate sizing. Customers can become irritated and question merchandise quality. Also, markdowns ensue because inventories become unbalanced and shopworn.

Building Strategic Alliances   The importance of building strategic alliances is examined later in this chapter. It is typically harder to build these alliances when sourcing globally, particularly when the suppliers are further away and are from less developed countries. Communications are more difficult. There is often a language barrier, and there are almost always cultural differences. Business practices—everything from terms of payment to the mores of trade practices such as commercial bribery—are different in a global setting. The most important element in building a strategic alliance—maintaining the supplier's trust—is more arduous in an international environment.

Source Closer to Home or Buy "Made in America"   Some U.S. retailers are shifting suppliers from Asia and Europe to nearby Central American and Caribbean countries, or they're seeking products made in America. There are four reasons for this shift. First, it may be more profitable for all of the reasons that we detailed above.

Second, Quick Response Delivery Systems described in Chapter 11 and sourcing globally are inherently incompatible. Yet both are important and growing trends in retailing. Quick Response Systems are based on short and consistent lead times. Vendors provide frequent deliveries with smaller quantities. There's no room for defective merchandise. For a Quick Response System to work properly, there needs to be a strong alliance between vendor and retailer that is based on trust and a sharing of information through electronic data interchange (EDI). In the preceding section we argued that each of these activities is more difficult to perform globally than domestically. Further, the level of difficulty increases with distance and the vendor's sophistication.[17]

Retailers are searching for merchandise closer to home so that they can police potential violations of human rights and child labor.

REFACT In a national survey, 84 percent indicated a preference for buying American-made products; 64 percent said they would spend 10 percent more for domestically produced goods over foreign-made items.[19]

The third reason why retailers are taking a closer look at domestic sources of supply is that some of their customers prefer products that are "made in America." A national survey of consumers indicates that Americans purchase goods based first on quality, then features, followed by price, warranty, and country of origin. Importantly, American-made products are perceived as being superior in quality to foreign-made goods, especially tools, clothing, candy and confections, and toys.[18] Retailers are simply reacting to their customers' quality perceptions.

The fourth reason for sourcing closer to home is that it's easier to police potential violations of human rights and child labor. Wal-Mart, The Gap, JCPenney, Dayton Hudson, Liz Claiborne, and Eddie Bauer, among many others, have had to publicly deflect allegations about human rights, child labor, or other abuses involving factories and countries where their goods are made.[20]

Some firms respond by promising an inquiry. They require their contractors to sign strict codes of conduct that threaten withdrawal of business if labor abuses occur. Many companies are asking their quality control people to look out for worker abuses while also watching that zippers are sewn on straight.

INTERNET EXERCISE   Buyers can use the Internet to find merchandise and buying services such as freight forwarders from around the world. Go to WOMEX (World Merchandise Exchange Inc.) at www.womex.com and find out what other services are available to buyers.

MEETING VENDORS

Now that we've examined the different branding decisions available to retailers and the issues surrounding global sourcing, we concentrate on how and where retailers meet with their vendors. Retailers "go to market" to see the variety of available merchandise and to buy. A **market,** from the retail buyer's perspective, is a concentration of vendors within a specific geographic location, perhaps even under one roof. These markets may be permanent wholesale market centers or temporary trade fairs. Retailers may also buy on their own turf, either in stores or at corporate headquarters. Finally, resident buying offices prearrange opportunities for buyers to visit vendors in major market centers in this country and abroad.

Wholesale Market Centers

For many types of merchandise, retailers can do much of their buying in established market centers. Wholesale market centers have permanent vendor sales offices retailers can visit throughout the year. Probably the world's most significant wholesale market center for many merchandise categories is in New York City. The Fashion Center, also known as the Garment District, is located from Fifth to Ninth avenues and from 35th to 41st streets. An estimated 22,000 apparel buyers visit every year for five market weeks and 65 annual related trade shows. The Garment District has 5,100 showrooms and 4,500 factories.[21]

The United States also has a number of regional wholesale market centers. The Dallas Market Center, the world's largest, is a 6.9-million–square-foot complex of six buildings. Over 26,000 manufacturers and importers display their international products in its 2,400 permanent showrooms and more than 2,000 temporary spaces. Some regional centers have developed into national markets for specific merchandise categories (for example, the Miami Merchandise Mart for swimwear).

Trade Shows

Many wholesale market centers host **trade shows** (also known as **merchandise shows** or **market weeks**). Permanent tenants of the wholesale market centers as well as vendors leasing temporary space participate. Here retailers place orders and get a concentrated view of what's available in the marketplace. The Dallas Market Center hosts over 40 shows annually for products ranging from floor coverings to toys, apparel, jewelry, and gifts. Trade shows are also staged by convention centers not associated with wholesale market centers. McCormick Place in Chicago (the nation's largest convention complex with almost 2 million square feet) hosts over 65 meetings and trade shows per year, including the National Hardware Show, National Housewares Manufacturers Association International Exposition, and National Sporting Goods Association Market.

Buying on Their Own Turf

Although buyers go to wholesale market centers and trade shows to search for new merchandise, place orders, and meet with vendors, vendors also work with buyers in their offices. Most buying activity in buyers' offices is for basic merchandise or rebuys on fashion merchandise.

Resident Buying Offices

Resident buying offices are organizations located in major buying centers that provide services to help retailers buy merchandise. To illustrate how buying offices operate, consider how David Smith of Pockets Men's Store in Dallas utilizes his resident buying offices when he goes to market in Milan. Smith meets with market representative Alain Bordat of the Doneger Group. Bordat, an English-speaking Italian, knows Smith's store and his upscale customers, so in advance of Smith's visit he sets up appointments with Italian vendors he believes would fit Pockets' image.

When Smith is in Italy, Bordat accompanies him to the appointments and acts as translator, negotiator, and accountant. Bordat informs Smith of the cost of importing the merchandise into the United States, taking into account duty, freight, insurance, processing costs, and so forth.

The Fashion Center in New York City, also known as the Garment District, is located from Fifth to Ninth Avenues and from 35th to 41st Streets. The Garment District has 5,100 show-rooms and 4,500 factories.

Once the orders are placed, Bordat writes the contracts and follows up on delivery and quality control. The Doneger Group also acts as a home base for buyers like Smith, providing office space and services, travel advisors, and emergency aid. Bordat and his association continue to keep Smith abreast of what's happening on the Italian fashion scene through reports and constant communication. Without the help of a resident buying office, it would be difficult, if not impossible, for Smith to penetrate the Italian wholesale market.

There are four general types of buying offices. The first, a **syndicated office,** is a division of a corporation that operates a group of retail companies. Examples are Federated Merchandising (a division of Federated Department Stores) and May Merchandising (a division of May Department Stores Company). The second type of buying office, a **salaried** or **fee office,** is an independent office where noncompeting retailers purchase professional services. Price Breakers is an off-price women's wear specialist, while Martin Bayer Associates is a men's wear and women's wear office. The Doneger Group in our example is the largest buying office of this type. The third type, a **cooperative** or **associated office,** is owned by its member retailers. Examples are Associated Merchandising Corporation (AMC) and Frederick Atkins, Inc. Cooperative offices have become less important in recent years due to the continued consolidation of department store chains. The last type of buying office, called a **private office,** is owned by and serves one company. Neiman Marcus and Stein Mart operate in this environment.

ESTABLISHING AND MAINTAINING STRATEGIC PARTNERSHIPS WITH VENDORS

As we discussed in Chapter 6, maintaining strong vendor relationships is an important method of developing a sustainable competitive advantage. Meeting with vendors is only the first step in this process. In this section we examine how retailers can develop relationships with their vendors that can evolve into a strategic partnership. Like a good marriage, strategic partnerships require a lot of work. We therefore conclude this section with a discussion of several characteristics of a successful long-term relationship that, if present, should result in a strategic partnership.

Establishing Strategic Partnerships

Relationships between retailers and vendors are often based on "splitting up a profit pie."[22] Both parties may be interested exclusively in their own profits and are unconcerned about the other party's welfare. These relationships are common when the products are commodities

Retailers from all over the world come to trade shows like this one to place orders and get a concentrated view of what is available in the marketplace.

and have no major impact on the retailers' performance. This type of relationship is basically a "win–lose" relationship because when one party gets a larger portion of the pie, the other party gets a smaller portion. This type of arrangement does not have any of the qualities necessary to achieve a competitive advantage.

To develop a strategic partnership that will lead to a competitive advantage, the retailer and vendor must commit to a long-term business relationship in which partners make significant investments to improve both parties' profitability. In these relationships, it's important for the partners to "put their money where their mouth is." They've taken risks to "expand the pie"—to give the partnership a strategic advantage over other companies.

Thus a strategic partnership is a win–win relationship. Both parties benefit because the size of the pie has increased. Strategic partnerships are created explicitly to uncover and exploit joint opportunities.[23] Members in strategic partnerships depend on and trust each other heavily; they share goals and agree on how to accomplish those goals; and they're willing to take risks, share confidential information, and make significant investments for the sake of the relationship.

Wal-Mart has made great strides in developing strategic partnering relationships with its vendors. Wal-Mart and many of its suppliers have created cross-functional teams composed of individuals from various areas of the firm such as marketing, finance, operations, distribution, and management information systems. Wal-Mart's teams work closely with similar teams from Procter & Gamble, Kraft General Foods, James River, Black & Decker, and other companies to develop unique information systems and promotional programs tailored to markets served by Wal-Mart and its vendors.

REFACT Wal-Mart is Procter & Gamble's largest customer, buying as much as the household-products giant sells to the entire country of Japan.[24]

Similarly, Levi Strauss teams worked with JCPenney to create a specially designed area for stores to display Docker merchandise. Then the teams developed sophisticated inventory control systems to make sure the stores were always stocked with strong-selling styles and sizes. As a result, JCPenney is now Levi's largest customer. Penney also increased its profits by offering customers a unique display and in-stock merchandise competing department stores lacked.

Levi Strauss has developed a strategic partnership with JCPenney to create a specially designed area for stores to display Docker merchandise.

A strategic partnership is like a marriage. When businesses enter strategic partnerships, they're wedded to their partner for better or worse. For example, if the Levi Docker merchandise hadn't sold well, Penney and Levi would have lost money. Strategic partnerships are risky and reduce flexibility. Once Penney formed a true strategic partnership with Levi, it couldn't "date around" with Levi's competitors.

Now let's look at characteristics that are necessary to maintain strategic partnerships.

Maintaining Strategic Partnerships

Maintaining a strategic partnership accomplishes both parties' goals. Successful buyer–vendor relationships involve increasing the mutual benefits as the partners learn to trust and depend on each other more and more. Additionally, the buyer and vendor can resolve conflicts as they arise, settle differences, and compromise when necessary. The four foundations of successful strategic partnerships are mutual trust, open communication, common goals, and credible commitments.

Mutual Trust The key to developing a strategic partnership is trust. Lou Pritchett, former senior vice president of sales for Procter & Gamble, once said, "Cost reduction throughout the total system can be accomplished when trust replaces skepticism. Trusting suppliers, customers and employees is one of the most effective, yet most underutilized techniques available to management."[25]

Trust is a belief by one party that the other party will fulfill its obligations in a relationship.[26] When vendors and buyers trust each other, they're more willing to share relevant ideas, clarify goals and problems, and communicate efficiently. Information shared between the parties becomes increasingly comprehensive, accurate, and timely. There's less need for the vendor and buyer to constantly monitor and check up on each other's actions because each believes the other wouldn't take advantage of him, given the opportunity.[27]

For example, an apparel manufacturer might want to develop Quick Response relationships with a retailer. (See Chapter 11.) To do so, it must get cooperation from the retailer. The manufacturer has a better chance of realizing its goal by approaching a retailer that (1) can visualize the benefits from working together with the manufacturer and (2) is willing to take the risks associated with altering its normal routines. If the manufacturer and retailer trust each other, they'll be more willing to try new and different ways of doing business because they know their partner is similarly committed to the relationship. Further, they believe that any gains and losses resulting from their partnership will even out over the long run so they aren't afraid to sustain a short-term loss for the sake of gaining a greater long-term advantage.

Vendors develop trust in buyers when the salespeople consistently take the buyers' needs and interests into account. A vendor who has a track record of consistent deliveries and reliable performance and cultivates a positive, interpersonal relationship with the customer earns valuable trust.

Open Communication   Open, honest communication is a key to developing successful relationships. Buyers and vendors in a relationship need to understand what's driving each other's business, their roles in the relationship, each firm's strategies, and any problems that arise over the course of the relationship.

Common Goals   Vendors and buyers must have common goals for a successful relationship to develop. Shared goals give both members of the relationship incentive to pool their strengths and abilities, and to exploit potential opportunities between them. There's also greater assurance that the other partner won't do anything to hinder goal achievement within the relationship.

For example, if Johnson & Johnson (J&J) and Kmart commit to reducing out-of-stock occurrences at the store level, then they both must work toward this goal. J&J can't fall behind on its shipments and Kmart can't be lackadaisical about getting the product on the shelf in a timely manner. With a common goal, both firms have incentive to cooperate because they know that by doing so, each can boost sales.

Shared goals also help to sustain the partnership when expected benefit flows aren't realized. If one J&J shipment fails to reach a Kmart store on time due to an uncontrollable event like misrouting by a trucking firm, Kmart won't suddenly call off the whole arrangement. Instead, Kmart is likely to view the incident as a simple mistake and will remain in the relationship. This is because Kmart knows it and J&J are committed to the same goal in the long run.

Credible Commitments   Successful relationships develop because both parties make credible commitments to the relationship. Credible commitments are tangible investments in the relationship. They go beyond just making the hollow statement "I want to be a partner." Credible commitments involve spending money to improve the supplier's products or services provided to the customer.[28]

For example, a vendor may train sales associates, invest in special displays, and develop a special system to interface with the retailer's computer. These investments signal a partner's long-run commitment to the relationship.

ETHICAL AND LEGAL ISSUES IN PURCHASING MERCHANDISE

As you can imagine, given the thousands of relationships and millions of transactions between retailers and their vendors, unethical or illegal situations may arise. In this section we'll view ethical and legal issues from both retailers' and vendors' perspectives. Retailers should not take advantage of their position of power in the marketing channel. In this regard, we'll examine slotting allowances and commercial bribery. To protect their customers' interests and their own reputation, retailers must be cognizant of whether the merchandise is counterfeit or from the gray market. From the vendor's perspective, they aren't likely to become legally entangled with their retailers so long as they sell to whoever wants to buy, whatever they want, all at the same price. In this regard, we'll look at exclusive territories, exclusive dealing agreements, tying contracts, refusals to deal, and dual distribution.

Slotting Allowances

Slotting allowances (also called **slotting fees**) are fees paid by a vendor for space in a retail store. Slotting allowances currently aren't illegal.[29] You may decide, however, that in certain circumstances they're unethical. Here's an example. When General Foods or any other consumer package goods manufacturer wants to introduce a new product, it often pays a slotting allowance to grocery and discount store chains for the space (slot) on the shelf. The fee varies depending on the nature of the product and the relative power of the retailer. Products whose brand names command relatively low customer loyalty pay the highest slotting allowances. Likewise, large grocery chains can demand higher slotting allowances than small mom-and-pop stores can. Fees can be significant—as high as $10,000 per store! It may cost close to $1 million to get national distribution of a new product.

Slotting fees are present not only in the food industry. For instance, in the music industry, retailers regularly charge vendors for the right to display and sell their merchandise. Coconuts leases out its windows to the highest bidder. In a busy midtown Manhattan store, companies like Time Warner Inc. and Sony pay $200,000 per window per year! The top six companies in the music industry each pay at least $10 million a year to secure desirable locations in major cities.[30]

Some retailers argue that slotting allowances are a reasonable method for ensuring that their valuable space is used efficiently. Of course, manufacturers view slotting allowances as extortion.

Some retailers may use slotting allowances as a short-term profit-generating device, which may harm long-term customer relationships. For example, a retailer may stock an inferior new product for six to eight weeks, discontinue the product due to inferior performance, and use the slotting allowance as its profit. If the retailer stocks too many inferior products, customers may switch to a competitor with more attractive merchandise.

As part of a program to develop strategic partnerships, some manufacturers avoid slotting allowances by working closely with retail stores and sharing the financial risk of new products. For instance, to avoid slotting allowances, Campbell Soup has launched a "failure fee" program that guarantees each new Campbell item will achieve certain sales after six months or Campbell will pay the retailer a specified fee.

Commercial Bribery

Commercial bribery occurs in retailing when a vendor or its agent offers to give or pay a retail buyer "something of value" to influence purchasing decisions. Say a sweater manufacturer offers to take a department store buyer to lunch at a fancy private club and then proposes a ski weekend at Vail. The buyer enjoys the lunch but graciously turns down the ski trip. These gifts could be construed as bribes or kickbacks, which are illegal. In fact, the Internal Revenue Service doesn't allow money paid for bribes to be deducted as a business expense. From an ethical perspective, there's a fine line between the social courtesy of a free lunch and an elaborate free vacation.

To avoid these problems, many companies forbid employees to accept any gifts from vendors. Kmart specifically forbids the taking of "bribes, commissions, kickbacks, payments, loans, gratuities or other solicitations, including any item of value from suppliers to the company."[31] But many companies have no policy against receiving gifts, and some unethical employees accept and even solicit gifts, even if their company has a policy against it. A good rule of thumb is to accept only limited entertainment or token gifts, such as flowers or a bottle of wine, for Christmas, birthdays, or other occasions. When the gift or favor is perceived to be large enough to influence a buyer's purchasing behavior, it's considered to be commercial bribery and therefore illegal.

Counterfeit Merchandise

Counterfeit merchandise includes goods made and sold without the permission of the owner of a trademark, a copyright, or a patented invention that is legally protected in the country where it is marketed.[32] The nature of counterfeiting has changed over the last decade. Although manufacturers of high-visibility, strong–brand-name consumer goods are still tortured by counterfeiters, there's now a thriving business in counterfeit high-tech products such as software, CDs, and CD-ROMs. For instance, it is estimated that the software publishing and distribution industries lose over $12 billion a year.[33] Why is this type of merchandise so attractive to counterfeiters? It has a high unit value, is relatively easy to duplicate and transport, and has high consumer demand. For instance, suppose *Retailing Management* were available on a CD-ROM. It could be easily duplicated as a CD or reprinted as a book for a few dollars in a foreign country. Neither the publishers nor the authors would receive any money. In fact, it's likely that they wouldn't even know about the copyright infringement.

Retailers and their vendors have four avenues to pursue to protect themselves against the ravages of counterfeiting and intellectual property rights violations: product registration, legislative action, bilateral and multilateral negotiations, and measures taken by companies.[34]

First, the product must be trademarked, copyrighted, and/or patented in the countries in which it's sold. Unfortunately, registration in the United States provides no protection in another country although treaties and other international agreements provide some protection outside the United States.[36]

The second method of protection is through legislative action. Several laws protect businesses against counterfeiting. For instance, the Trademark Counterfeiting Act of 1984 made counterfeiting a criminal rather than a civil offense, and established stiff penalties for the practice.

Third, the U.S. government is engaged in bilateral and multilateral negotiations and education to limit counterfeiting. For instance, the GATT agreement described earlier in this chapter includes rules on intellectual property protection.[37]

Finally, companies are aggressively taking steps to protect themselves. The International Anti-Counterfeiting Coalition is a group of 375 firms that lobby for stronger legal sanctions worldwide. Individual companies are also taking a more aggressive stance against counterfeiting. Retailing View 14.4 describes Levi Strauss and Co.'s war against counterfeiting.

REFACT Counterfeit merchandise causes a significant drain in the world economy. The International Trade Commission estimates that U.S. companies lose a total of $60 billion every year because of product counterfeiting and other fringement of intellectual property.[35]

Gray-Market and Diverted Merchandise

A **gray-market good** possesses a valid U.S. registered trademark and is made by a foreign manufacturer but is imported into the United States without permission of the U.S. trademark owner. Gray-market merchandise is not counterfeit. This merchandise is the same quality and may actually be identical to merchandise brought into the country legally.

14.4

Levi's War against Counterfeiting

ROLEX, CHANEL, POLO, CARTIER, and many other famous manufacturers must deal with the rising problems involving counterfeit merchandise. The Levi Strauss Company is no exception. Millions of pairs of fake Levi jeans have been seized around the world during the 1990s, meaning millions more have been sold.

Denim detectives and security officials for companies like Levi search the world for manufacturers and distributors of counterfeit products. In 1993, an eight-month investigation uncovered an operation distributing tens of thousands of fake jeans around the world. Jeans were allegedly manufactured somewhere in China and bought by a Fort Lauderdale business, which shipped them to a warehouse in Guadalajara, Mexico. From there, they were distributed to middlemen throughout the world, including Milan, Paris, and Reykjavik, Iceland. During this operation, 7,200 fake jeans were seized in retail stores in Iceland, and another 28,000 in other European countries. For these illegal sales, Levi is seeking multimillion dollars in damages against the defendants who allegedly ran this operation.

Source: Anthony Faiola, "Tracking Fake Levi's," *The Miami Herald*, September 8, 1993, p. C1.

REFACT Up to $10 billion of gray-market merchandise enters the United States annually.[40]

Without realizing it, we see gray-market goods in the marketplace all the time. Manufacturers of cars, jewelry, perfume, liquor, watches, cameras, crystal ware, ski equipment, tractors, baby powder, and batteries are all involved in gray marketing in the United States.[38] Gray markets are not restricted to the United States. Due to the high value of the yen and the subsidization of cheaper exports through high taxes, some Japanese retailers find it cheaper to reimport versions of Japanese-made products from the United States.[39]

Diverted merchandise is similar to gray-market merchandise except there need not be distribution across international boundaries. Suppose, for instance, fragrance manufacturer Givenchy grants an exclusive territory to all May Department Stores, including a Lord & Taylor store in Denver. A discount store in Denver purchases Givenchy products from a wholesale distributor in Las Vegas and sells it for 20 percent below the suggested retail price. The merchandise is *diverted* from its legitimate channel of distribution, and the wholesaler in this case would be referred to as a *diverter*.

Here's an example of how the gray market for watches might work in the United States. To help create a prestigious image, to offset an unfavorable exchange rate, and to pad profit margins, Swiss watch manufacturers often charge a higher wholesale price in the United States than in Europe and other countries. A Swiss watchmaker such as Patek Philippe may sell 1,000 watches to a distributor in Egypt. But instead of shipping the watches to Egypt, the watchmaker sends the shipment to the free-trade zone in Panama. Gray Goods, Inc., in New York buys the entire shipment in Panama from the Egyptian distributor. It's then imported into the United States, where it's sold to a chain of discounters called Mel's Jewelry Stores. Mel can sell these watches at a significantly lower price than a traditional jewelry store can and still make an adequate profit margin.

Some discount store operators argue that customers benefit from the lack of restriction on gray-market and diverted goods because it lowers prices. Competition with retailers selling gray-market and diverted merchandise forces authorized dealers to cut their price.

Traditional retailers, on the other hand, claim gray-market and diverted merchandise has a negative impact on the public. They believe that important service after the sale will be unavailable through retailers of gray-market or diverted goods. They also think that a less expensive gray-market or diverted product may hurt the trademark's image. Importantly, the gray-market product may be an out-of-date model or not work properly in a different country. For example, in 1993, the U.S. Court of Appeals ruled that U.S. discounters could no longer sell Lever Brothers' Sunlight brand of dishwashing detergent produced for the British market. Since tap water is generally harder in Britain, it requires a different formulation to work properly.[41]

Under a 1988 Supreme Court decision, U.S. retailers may import gray-market goods without the consent of the U.S. trademark owner under certain circumstances. However, in 1991, the U.S. Customs Service enacted a rule whereby trademarked goods that have been authorized for manufacture and sale abroad by U.S. trademark holders will no longer be allowed into the United States.[42] Clearly, the legality of gray-market merchandise is still "gray." Diverting merchandise does not appear to be illegal. However, this hasn't stopped fragrance manufacturers such as Givenchy and Boucheron from bringing suit against unauthorized retailers of their products.[43]

Vendors wishing to avoid the gray-market problem have several remedies. First, they can require all of their retail and wholesale customers to sign a contract stipulating that they will not engage in gray marketing. If a retailer is found in violation of the agreement, the vendor will refuse to deal with it in the future. Another strategy is to produce different versions of products for different markets. For instance, a camera manufacturer could sell the same camera in the United States and the European Union but with different names and warranties.

Exclusive Territories

Vendors often grant **exclusive geographic territories** to retailers so no other retailer in the territory can sell a particular brand. These territorial arrangements can benefit vendors by assuring them that "quality" retailers represent their products. In cases of limited supply, providing an exclusive territory to one retailer helps ensure that enough inventory can be carried to make a good presentation and offer the customer an adequate selection. If, for instance, the luxury Ferrari Automobile Company allowed its products to be distributed through all dealers that want to carry them, there wouldn't be enough Ferraris to go around, leading to customer confusion. Being granted exclusive territories helps retailers as well because it gives them a monopoly for the product—a strong incentive to push that vendor's products. They know there will be no competing retailers to cut prices so their profit margins are protected. The retailer with an exclusive territory has the incentive to carry more inventory; use extra advertising, personal selling, and sales promotions; provide special displays and display areas; and develop special services for customers.

The courts have tended to hold exclusive territories illegal when they restrict competition. Competition is restricted when other retailers have no access to similar products. For example, having exclusive Ferrari dealers wouldn't be a restraint of trade since other luxury cars are readily available to the public. On the other hand, if De Beers, the South African diamond cartel, granted exclusive territories to certain jewelry retailers, this would probably be seen as a restraint of trade because diamonds wouldn't be readily available through other sources.

Exclusive Dealing Agreements

Exclusive dealing agreements occur when a manufacturer or wholesaler restricts a retailer into carrying only its products and nothing from competing vendors. The effect on competition determines these contracts' legality. For instance, suppose a retailer signs an agreement with Lee's to sell only its jeans. There's no real harm done to competition because other manufacturers have many alternative retail outlets, and Lee's market share isn't large enough to approach monopolistic levels.

On the other hand, in 1987, Hartz Mountain (which has a majority market share in the pet products market) was fined $1 million by a St. Louis federal court for attempting to monopolize the pet supplies market. The court ruled that Hartz had attempted to draw retailers away from a wholesaler selling competing pet products.[44] The difference in the legal interpretation of these two cases is based on the relative impact on competition. Because Hartz Mountain has such a large market share, smaller competitors could be severely injured.

Tying Contracts

When a vendor and a retailer enter into an agreement that requires the retailer to take a product it doesn't necessarily desire (the "tied product") to ensure that it can buy a product it does desire (the "tying product"), a tying contract exists. Tying contracts are illegal if they may substantially lessen competition or tend to create a monopoly.

A vendor is entitled to create tying contracts to protect its goodwill and quality reputation. For instance, the Italian knitwear manufacturer Benetton may legally require its retail stores to purchase all their sweaters from Benetton since the legitimate purpose is to maintain the brand name's image. Alternatively, an auto manufacturer probably wouldn't be allowed to force its dealers to purchase only the automaker's radios with its cars. Dealers could legitimately argue that the manufacturer's image or the functioning of the cars wouldn't be impaired by purchasing radios from another vendor.

Refusals to Deal

The practice of refusing to deal can be viewed from both suppliers' and retailers' perspectives. Generally, both suppliers and retailers have the right to deal or refuse to deal with anyone they choose. But there are exceptions to this general rule when there's evidence of anticompetitive conduct.

A manufacturer may refuse to sell to a particular retailer, but it can't do so for the sole purpose of benefiting a competing retailer. Levi Strauss & Co. refuses to deal with any retailer ordering less than $10,000 worth of goods a year. The company says that it's part of an effort to eliminate processes that aren't cost-effective.[45] The courts would probably allow the situation in which Bob's Western Wear Store is cut from Levi's list of outlets because it can't make the minimum annual purchases. It would, however, be unlawful for a competitor of Bob's to pressure Levi into not selling to Bob, but from a practical perspective it's hard to prove such coercive influence.

Dual Distribution

Dual distribution occurs when a manufacturer or wholesaler competes directly with its retailers. Dual distribution systems usually arise when a vendor decides to vertically integrate by starting retailing activities. Dual distribution isn't always illegal. But there may be a restraint on competition and trade if vendors sell to independent retailers at higher prices than they sell to the retailers they own, and thus cause a severe and continuous decline among competing retailers.

The retail gas market is a good example of a dual distribution system. Oil companies like Mobil and Texaco own some of their stations, while others are independently owned. In this scenario, the oil company is in competition with itself if its company-owned service stations are located near the independent stations. If the company charges a higher price for its products to the independent stations than to nearby company stations, this may be viewed as an illegal restraint on competition and free trade.

In summary, anytime two parties interact, there's a potential for ethical and legal problems. Buyers face issues such as how much to charge a vendor for shelf space in their stores or whether they should accept a gift or favor from a vendor with "no strings attached." An eye toward fairness and the desire to maintain a strong relationship should dictate behavior in these areas. Retailers must also be concerned with the origin of their merchandise. Specifically, is it counterfeit or gray-market? Vendors encounter a different set of issues. In general, vendors need not worry about legal problems when selling to retailers so long as they sell whatever the retailers want, to whoever wants to buy, all at the same price. But when vendors start making restrictions and exceptions, there may be legal violations.

SUMMARY

This chapter examined issues surrounding vendor relations and purchasing merchandise. Simply put, retailers can't succeed without their vendors. To survive, they must be able to count on a predictable supply of merchandise at competitive prices and with sufficient promotional support.

Retailers can purchase either manufacturer's brands or private-label brands. Each type has its own relative advantages. Choosing brands and a branding strategy is an integral component of a firm's merchandise and assortment planning process.

A large percentage of the merchandise we buy is manufactured outside of the United States. The decision to buy from domestic manufacturers or source internationally is a complicated one. We examined the cost, managerial, and ethical issues surrounding global sourcing decisions.

Buyers and their merchandise managers have several opportunities to meet with vendors, view new merchandise, and place orders. They can visit their vendors at wholesale market centers such as New York, Paris, or Milan. Virtually every merchandise category has at least one annual trade show where retailers and vendors meet. Buyers often meet with vendors on their own turf—in the retail store or corporate offices. Finally, meetings with vendors are facilitated by resident buying offices. Market representatives of these resident buying offices facilitate merchandising purchases in foreign markets.

Retailers who can successfully team up with their vendors can achieve a sustainable competitive advantage. There needs to be more than just a promise to buy and sell on a regular basis. Strategic partnerships require trust, shared goals, strong communications, and a financial commitment.

With thousands of annual transactions taking place between retailers and their vendors, there's plenty of room for ethical and legal problems. The issues of charging vendors for shelf space or taking bribes were discussed. We also examined problems associated with counterfeit and gray-market merchandise. We then looked at the issues (such as exclusive territories and tying contracts) that vendors face when selling to retailers. We concluded that care should be taken when making restrictions on which retailers they will sell to, what merchandise, how much, and at what price.

The chapter concludes with two appendixes. In Appendix A, we look at how a retailer should prepare for and conduct a negotiation with a vendor. Successful vendor relationships depend on planning for and being adept at negotiations. Appendix B reviews the purchase and payment terms given to retailers. Retailers face a plethora of discount/payment-date combinations. A working knowledge of these terms of purchase is essential for any person involved in merchandising. More importantly, the most advantageous application of the terms can make a significant impact on corporate profits.

KEY TERMS

cooperative office (associated office), *416*

counterfeit merchandise, *421*

diverted merchandise, *422*

exclusive geographic territory, *423*

foreign trade zone, *412*

generic product, *409*

gray-market good, *421*

lead time, *412*

licensed brand, *405*

manufacturer brand (national brand), *403*

Maquiladoras, *412*

market, *414*

opportunity cost of capital, *412*

private-label brand (store brand), *406*

private office, *416*

resident buying office, *415*

salaried office (fee office), *416*

slotting allowance (slotting fee), *420*

syndicated office, *416*

tariff (duty), *411*

trade show (merchandise show, market week), *415*

trust, *418*

DISCUSSION QUESTIONS & PROBLEMS

1. What name is given to the private-brand sport shirts sold in the department store near your college? What's the name of the manufacturer brand in competition with the private-label sport shirts? How does the department store promote its private label?

2. Assume you have been hired to consult with The Gap on sourcing decisions for sportswear. What issues would you consider when deciding whether you should buy from Mexico or China, or find a source in the United States?

3. How would a category manager in a women's specialty store in Des Moines, Iowa, use a New York resident buying office with satellite operations in Milan, Paris, and Tokyo?

4. How can having a strategic partnership with a vendor help create a sustainable competitive advantage?

5. What kinds of social courtesies or gifts (lunches, theater tickets, etc.) are appropriate and acceptable for buyers to accept from vendors?

6. What are the advantages and disadvantages to retailers carrying licensed brands?

7. When setting goals for a negotiation session with a vendor, what issues should a buyer consider?

8. A $500 invoice is dated October 1, the merchandise arrives October 15, and the terms are 3/30, n/60 ROG.

   a. How many days does the retailer have to take advantage of the discount?

   b. What is the percentage of discount?

   c. How much is due November 10?

   d. What's the final date the retailer can pay the invoice without being considered late?

9. Price/Costco is contemplating the purchase of some gray-market TV sets. What are the ramifications, both positive and negative, of such a purchase?

10. What factors should a buyer consider when deciding which vendors to develop a close relationship with?

SUGGESTED READINGS

Ailawadi, Kusum L., Norm Borin, and Paul W. Farris. "Market Power and Performance: A Cross-Industry Analysis of Manufacturers and Retailers." *Journal of Retailing* 71, no. 3 (September 22, 1995), pp. 211–19.

Buzzell, Robert D., and Gwen Ortmeyer. "Channel Partnerships Streamline Distribution." *Sloan Management Review* 36, no. 3 (March 22, 1995), pp. 85–97.

Fisher, Roger, and William Ury. *Getting to Yes.* New York: Penguin, 1981.

Ganesan, Shankar. "Negotiation Strategies and the Nature of Channel Relationships." *Journal of Marketing Research* 30 (May 1993), pp. 183–203.

Gundlach, Gregory T., and Patrick E. Murphy. "Ethical and Legal Foundations of Relational Marketing Exchanges." *Journal of Marketing* 57, no. 4 (October 1993), pp. 35–46.

Hoch, Stephen, and Shumet Bamerji. "When Do Private Labels Succeed?" *Sloan Management Review* 34, no. 4 (Summer 1993), pp. 57–70.

Krapel, Robert, Deborah Salmond, and Robert Spekman. "A Strategic Approach to Managing Buyer–Seller Relationships." *European Journal of Marketing* 25 (1991), pp. 22–37.

Mohr, Jakki, and Robert Spekman. "Characteristics of Successful Partnerships: Attributes, Communication Behavior, and Conflict Resolution Techniques." *Strategic Management Journal*, February 1993, pp. 23–45.

Morgan, Robert, and Shelby Hunt. "The Commitment-Trust Theory of Relationship Marketing." *Journal of Marketing* 38 (July 1994), pp. 20–38.

Olsen, Janeen E., and Kent L. Grazin. "Gaining Retailers' Assistance in Fighting Counterfeiting: Conceptualization and Empirical Test of a Helping Model." *Journal of Retailing* 68, no. 1 (Spring 1992), pp. 90–109.

Nevin, John R., and Mark T. Spriggs. "The Legal Status of Trade and Functional Price Discounts." *Journal of Public Policy & Marketing* 13, no. 1 (Spring 1994), pp. 61–71.

Quelch, John, and David Husling. "Brands vs. Private Labels: Fighting to Win." *Harvard Business Review* 74 (1996), pp. 99–111.

Richardson, Paul S., Alan S. Dick, and Arun K. Jain. "Extrinsic and Intrinsic Cue Effects on Perceptions of Store Brand Quality." *Journal of Marketing* 58, no. 4 (October 1994), pp. 28–36.

Richardson, Paul S., Arun K. Jain, and Alan S. Dick. "Household Store Brand Proneness: A Framework." *Journal of Retailing* 72, no. 2 (Summer 1996), pp. 159–86.

Swamidass, Paul M. "Import Sourcing Dynamics: An Integrative Perspective." *Journal of International Business Studies* 24, no. 4 (December 22, 1993), pp. 671–82.

APPENDIX 14A

Negotiating with Vendors

Negotiations are as basic to human nature as eating or sleeping.[46] A negotiation takes place any time two parties confer with each other to settle some matter. Negotiations take place between parents and their children about issues like allowances. People negotiate with their friends about what to do on the weekend.

Business negotiations occur almost daily. People negotiate for higher salaries, better offices, and bigger budgets. Negotiations are crucial in buyers' discussions with vendors.

No one should go into a negotiation without intensive planning. We first provide guidelines for planning negotiations with vendors. Then we discuss some tips for conducting the negotiation face-to-face.

GUIDELINES FOR PLANNING NEGOTIATIONS WITH VENDORS

As a vehicle for describing how a buyer should prepare for and conduct a negotiation with a vendor, consider the hypothetical situation in which Carolyn Swigler, men's designer shirt buyer at Lord & Taylor, is preparing to meet with Dario Carnevale, the salesman from Tommy Hilfiger, in her office in New York. Swigler is ready to buy Tommy Hilfiger's spring line, but she has some merchandising problems that have yet to be resolved from last season. Let's go over seven general guidelines for planning a negotiation session and seven for conducting a face-to-face negotiation session, all described in terms of Swigler's hypothetical situation.

KNOWLEDGE IS POWER! The more the buyer knows about the vendor, the better his negotiating strategy will be.

Consider History

Buyers need a sense of what has occurred between the retailer and the vendor in the past. Though Swigler and Carnevale have only met a few times in the past, their companies have had a long, profitable relationship. A sense of trust and mutual respect has been established, which may work to Swigler's advantage in the upcoming meeting. An established vendor may be more likely to take care of old problems and accept new demands if a long-term, profitable relationship already exists.

Assess Where Things Are Today

Although Tommy Hilfiger shirts have been profitable for Lord & Taylor in the past, three patterns sold poorly last season. Some vendors believe that once they've sold merchandise to the retailer, their responsibility ends. This is a short-term perspective, however. If the merchandise doesn't sell, a good vendor, like Tommy Hilfiger, will arrange to share the risk of loss. Swigler will ask Carnevale to let her return some merchandise. Or Carnevale may provide markdown money—funds a vendor gives a retailer to cover lost gross margin dollars due to markdowns and other merchandising issues—usually in the form of a credit to the Lord & Taylor account.

Set Goals

Besides taking care of last season's leftover merchandise, the buyer Swigler has set goals in six areas for the upcoming meeting: additional markup opportunities, terms of purchase, transportation, delivery and exclusivity, communications, and advertising allowances.

Additional Markup Opportunities   Vendors may have excess stock (manufacturers' overruns) due to order cancellations, returned merchandise from retailers, or simply an overly optimistic sales forecast. To move this merchandise, vendors offer it to retailers at lower than normal prices. Retailers can then make a higher than normal gross margin and/or pass the savings on to the customer. Since Lord & Taylor is noted as a fashion leader, it probably isn't interested in any excess inventory that Tommy Hilfiger has to offer. Off-price retailers, such as T. J. Maxx, Marshalls, Loehmann's, and Burlington Coat Factory, specialize in purchasing manufacturers' overruns. Another opportunity for additional markups is with private-label merchandise, which we discussed earlier in this chapter.

Terms of Purchase   It's advantageous for buyers to negotiate for a longer time period in which to pay for merchandise. Longer terms of payment improve the firm's cash flow position, lower its liabilities (accounts payable), and can cut its interest expense if it's borrowing money from financial institutions to pay for its inventory. According to the Robinson-Patman Act, however, a vendor can't offer different terms of purchase or prices to different retailers unless the difference can be cost-justified. But buyers would be remiss if they didn't ask for the best terms of purchase available. (Terms of purchase are detailed in Appendix B to this chapter.)

Transportation   Transportation costs can be substantial, though this doesn't pose a big problem with the Tommy Hilfiger shirts due to their high unit cost and small size. Nonetheless, the question of who pays for shipping merchandise from vendor to retailer can be a significant negotiating point. (Transportation issues are part of the terms of purchase discussed in this chapter's Appendix B.)

Delivery and Exclusivity   In retailing in general (and in fashion in particular), timely delivery is essential. Being the only retailer in a market to carry certain products helps a retailer hold a fashion lead and achieve a differential advantage. Swigler wants to be certain that her shipment of the new spring line arrives as early in the season as possible, and that some shirt patterns won't be sold to competing retailers.

Communications   Vendors and their representatives are excellent sources of market information. They generally know what is and isn't selling. Providing good, timely information about the market is an indispensable and inexpensive marketing research tool, so Swigler plans to spend at least part of the meeting talking to Carnevale about market trends.

Advertising Allowances   Retailers have the choice of advertising any product in the store. They can sometimes share the cost of advertising through a cooperative arrangement with vendors known as co-op advertising—a program undertaken by a vendor in which the vendor agrees to pay all or part of a pricing promotion. By giving retailers advertising money based on a percentage of purchases, vendors can better represent their product to consumers. (Chapter 16 describes cooperative advertising.) Under the Robinson-Patman Act, vendors are allowed to give advertising allowances on a proportionately equal basis—the same percentage to everyone—usually based on a percentage of the invoice cost. As a fashion leader, Lord & Taylor advertises heavily. Swigler would like Tommy Hilfiger to support a number of catalogs with a generous ad allowance.

Know the Vendor's Goals and Constraints   Negotiation can't succeed in the long run unless both parties believe they've won. By understanding what's important to Carnevale and Tommy Hilfiger, Swigler can plan for a successful negotiating session. Generally, vendors are interested in the following issues.

A Continuous Relationship   Vendors want to make a long-term investment in their retailers. For seasonal merchandise like men's designer shirts, they have to plan their production in advance so it's important to Tommy Hilfiger that certain key retailers like Lord & Taylor will continue their support. Swigler plans to spend some time at the beginning of the meeting reviewing their mutually profitable past and assuring Carnevale that Lord & Taylor hopes to continue their relationship.

Testing New Items   There's no better way to test how well a new product will sell than to put it in a store. Retailers are often cautious with new items due to the risk of markdowns and the opportunity cost of not purchasing other, more successful merchandise. Yet vendors need their retailers to provide sales feedback for new items. Lord & Taylor has always been receptive to some of Tommy Hilfiger's more avant-garde styles. If these styles do well in certain Lord & Taylor stores, they'll likely succeed in similar stores around the country.

Communications   Just as Carnevale can provide market information to Swigler, she can provide sales information to him. Also, Swigler travels the world market. On one buying trip to England, she found an attractive scarf. She bought the scarf and gave it to Carnevale, who had it copied for a shirt. It was a big success!

Showcase   In certain urban centers—notably New York, Los Angeles, Dallas, London, Milan, and Paris—vendors use large stores to showcase their merchandise. For instance, many U.S. buyers go to market in New York. Most stop at Lord & Taylor to see what's new, what's selling, and how it's displayed. Thus Carnevale wants to make sure that Tommy Hilfiger is well represented at Lord & Taylor.

A good understanding of the legal, managerial, and financial issues that constrain a vendor will facilitate a productive negotiating session. For instance, Swigler should recognize from past experience that Tommy Hilfiger normally doesn't allow merchandise to be returned, but does provide markdown money. If Carnevale initially says that giving markdown money is against company policy, Swigler will have strong objective ammunition for her position.

Plan to Have at Least as Many Negotiators as the Vendor

There's power in numbers. Even if the vendor is more powerful, aggressive, or important in the marketplace, the retailer will have a psychological advantage at the negotiating table if the vendor is outnumbered. At the very least, the negotiating teams should be of equal number. Swigler plans to invite her merchandise manager into the discussion if Carnevale comes with his sales manager.

Plan to Negotiate on Your Own Turf

Swigler has a natural advantage in the upcoming meeting since it will be in her office. She'll have everything at her fingertips, such as information plus secretarial and supervisory assistance. From a psychological perspective, people generally feel more comfortable and confident in familiar surroundings. Unfortunately, negotiations often take place at the vendor's showroom, which can be in such unfamiliar locations as Hong Kong or Milan.

Be Aware of Real Deadlines

To illustrate the importance of deadlines, consider when labor strikes are settled. An agreement is often reached one minute before everyone walks out. There's always pressure to settle a negotiation at the last minute. Swigler recognizes that Carnevale must go back to his office with an order in hand since he has a quota to meet by the end of the month. She also knows that she must get markdown money or permission to return the unsold shirts by the end of the week or she won't have sufficient open-to-buy to cover the orders she wishes to place. Recognizing these deadlines will help Swigler come to a decisive closure in the upcoming negotiation.

GUIDELINES FOR FACE-TO-FACE NEGOTIATIONS

The most thoughtful plans can go astray if the negotiators fail to follow some important guidelines in the meeting. Here are seven tips for successful negotiations, including separating people from the problem, insisting on objective criteria, and inventing options for mutual gain.[47]

Separate People from the Problem

Suppose Swigler starts the meeting with "Carnevale, you know we've been friends for a long time. I have a personal favor to ask. Would you mind taking back $10,000 in shirts?" This personal plea puts Carnevale in an uncomfortable situation. Swigler's personal relationship with Carnevale isn't the issue here and shouldn't become part of the negotiation.

An equally detrimental scenario would be for Swigler to say, "Carnevale, your line is terrible. I can hardly give the stuff away. I want you to take back $10,000 in shirts. After all, you're dealing with Lord & Taylor. If you don't take this junk back, you can forget about ever doing business with us again." This approach serves as a personal attack on Carnevale. Even if he had nothing to do with the shirts' design, Swigler is attacking his company. Reminding Carnevale that he's dealing with a large concern like Lord & Taylor is threatening and would probably further alienate him. Finally, threats usually don't work in negotiations; they put the other party on the defensive. Threats may actually cause negotiations to break down, in which case no one wins.

Conversely, if Carnevale takes a personal, aggressive, or threatening stance in the negotiations, what should Swigler do? Let him talk. If Swigler allows Carnevale to work through his aggression or anger, it will probably dissipate like a tropical storm going out to sea. Listen. Swigler may find that Carnevale's problem can be easily resolved. Finally, apologize if necessary. Even if Swigler doesn't believe she or Lord & Taylor did anything to cause Carnevale's anger, an apology that doesn't admit to any personal or corporate responsibility will probably calm him down.

Insist on Objective Criteria

The best way to separate people from the problem is to insist on objective criteria. Swigler must know exactly how many shirts need to be returned to Tommy Hilfiger or how much markdown money is necessary to maintain her gross margin.

If Carnevale argues from an emotional perspective, Swigler should stick to the numbers. For instance, suppose that after Swigler presents her position, Carnevale says that he'll get into trouble if he takes back the merchandise or provides markdown money. With the knowledge that Tommy Hilfiger has provided relief in similar situations in the past, Swigler should ask what Tommy Hilfiger's policy is regarding customer overstock problems. She should also show Carnevale a summary of Lord & Taylor's buying activity with Tommy Hilfiger over the past few seasons. Using this approach, Carnevale is forced to acknowledge that providing assistance on this overstock situation—especially if it has been done in the past—is a small price to pay for a long-term profitable relationship.

Invent Options for Mutual Gain

Inventing multiple options is part of the planning process, but knowing when and how much to give (or give up) requires quick thinking at the bargaining table.

Consider Swigler's overstock problem. Her objective is to get the merchandise out of her inventory without significantly hurting her gross margin. Carnevale's objective is to maintain a healthy yet profitable relationship with Lord & Taylor. Thus Swigler must invent options that could satisfy both parties. Her options are

- Sell the shirts to an off-price retailer at 10 cents on the retail dollar.
- Have Carnevale take back the shirts.
- Get Tommy Hilfiger to provide markdown money and put the shirts on sale.
- Return some of the shirts and get markdown money for the rest.

Clearly, selling the shirts to an off-price retailer would cause Swigler to take a loss. But from Carnevale's perspective, taking back the merchandise may be unacceptable because the styles are from last season and some shirts may be shopworn. Swigler could, however, present this option first with the knowledge that it will probably be rejected. Then she could ask for markdown money. Carnevale would believe he got off easy, and Swigler would have her problem solved.

In developing her plan for the meeting, Swigler followed some important rules of negotiation. She identified viable options for both parties. Then she determined which options would satisfy both parties' objectives. When presenting the options, she held back the one she believed would be most acceptable to Carnevale so he would think he was a winner.

Let Them Do the Talking   There's a natural tendency for one person to continue to talk if the other person involved in the conversation doesn't respond. If used properly, this phenomenon can work to the negotiator's advantage. Suppose Swigler asks Carnevale for special financial support on Lord & Taylor's Christmas catalog. Carnevale begins with a qualified no and cites all the reasons why he can't cooperate. But Swigler doesn't say a word. Although Carnevale appears nervous, he continues to talk. Eventually, he comes around to a yes. In negotiations, those who break the silence first, lose!

Know How Far to Go   There's a fine line between negotiating too hard and walking away from the table with less than necessary. If Swigler overnegotiates by getting the markdown money, better terms of purchase, and a strong advertising allowance, the management of Tommy Hilfiger may decide that other retailers are more worthy of early deliveries and the best styles. Carnevale may not be afraid to say no if Swigler is pushing him beyond a legal, moral, profitable relationship.

Don't Burn Bridges   Even if Swigler gets few additional concessions from Carnevale, she shouldn't be abusive or resort to threats. Professionally, Lord & Taylor may not wish to stop doing business with Tommy Hilfiger on the basis of this one encounter. From a personal perspective, the world of retailing is relatively small. Swigler and Carnevale may meet at the negotiating table again—both working for different companies. Neither can afford to be known in the trade as being unfair, rude, or worse.

Don't Assume   Many issues are raised and resolved in any negotiating session. To be certain there are no misunderstandings, participants should orally review the outcomes at the end of the session. Swigler and Carnevale should both summarize the session in writing as soon as possible after the meeting.

APPENDIX 14B

Terms of Purchase

Now that we have chosen our merchandise, developed relationships with our suppliers, and considered the legal ramifications of our actions, we must negotiate the terms of purchase. There are two sides to the pricing equation. In Chapter 15 (pricing), we'll examine the price at which merchandise is sold. In this section, we look at the price at which merchandise is *purchased*. When determining price, vendors must examine the different types of discounts they may offer. These discounts—referred to as the terms of purchase—include trade or functional discounts, chain discounts, quantity discounts, seasonal discounts, cash discounts, anticipation discounts, and shipping terms and conditions.

Trade Discounts (Functional Discounts)

Trade or functional discounts are reductions in a manufacturer's suggested retail price granted to wholesalers or retailers. For instance, suppose a TV's suggested retail price is $100. If the manufacturer sells to a wholesaler, the price is 50 percent off the suggested retail price, or $50. Alternatively, if the set is bought by the retailer, the cost is 33.3 percent off the suggested retail price, or $66.67.

Many issues come to mind when thinking about this rather quaint tradition in pricing. First, why is it called a trade or functional discount? It's because different prices are offered to different lines of trade (i.e., wholesalers versus retailers). It's also known as a functional discount since retailers and wholesalers often perform different functions in the channel of distribution.

Under the cost justification defense of the Robinson-Patman Act, vendors can offer different prices to wholesalers and retailers for the same merchandise and quantity if they can show that costs of manufacture, sale, or delivery are different. The costs of manufacture wouldn't often be different, but selling and delivery could be more expensive to retailers than to wholesalers. Because there are multiple retail outlets within a chain, a manufacturer's sales staff may expend more effort when selling to retailers than to wholesalers. The manufacturer may also incur larger transportation expenses due to multiple delivery points and smaller shipments to retailers.

In recent years, however, some large retailers (notably Kmart and Wal-Mart) have convinced some vendors to give them the lowest prices offered. These retailers argue that they perform all the functions that would otherwise be performed by an independent wholesaler, such as transportation from distribution centers to stores, price marking, and inventory management. Thus, they say, they should receive the lowest price.

Another question is, why would the manufacturer discount a suggested retail price rather than simply quoting a net cost? It's because retailers generally think of their merchandise in terms of retail rather than cost. By quoting prices as discounted suggested retail prices, the manufacturer's practice remains consistent with retailing thought. Further, by providing suggested retail prices, the manufacturer has some subtle influence on the retail price. Note, however, that manufacturers can influence retailers to maintain suggested retail prices only under certain circumstances. (See "Vertical Price Fixing" in Chapter 15.)

Chain Discounts   In some lines of trade—such as housewares and hardware—chain discounts are used. A chain discount is a number of different discounts taken sequentially from the suggested retail price. An example is 50-10-5 (spoken fifty, ten, and five). Using the previous example, if the TV set has a suggested retail price of $100, then the price is calculated as follows:

1. A 50 percent reduction is taken: $100 \times .5 = $50.
2. An additional 10 percent reduction from the remaining $50 is taken: $50 - ($50 \times .1) = $50 - $5 = $45.
3. A 5 percent discount from the remaining $45 is taken: $45 - ($45 \times .05) = $45 - $2.25 = $42.75.

So, with a 50-10-5 chain discount on a $100 suggested retail item, the retailer pays $42.75. But note that the discounts can't be added! A 50-10-5 discount isn't the same as a 65 percent discount: $100 - (100 \times .65) = $35.

Why do vendors and retailers use such an awkward pricing scheme? Simply because it's traditional. In the precalculator era, it was easier for people to calculate chain discount prices in their heads without having to resort to tedious computations.

Quantity Discounts   Quantity discounts are of two types: cumulative and noncumulative. Retailers earn cumulative quantity discounts by purchasing certain quantities over a specified period of time. For instance, a vendor may grant an additional discount to a retailer that purchases $100,000 worth of merchandise in one year. These discounts have the same effect as a year-end rebate. Vendors grant cumulative quantity discounts as an incentive to buy more merchandise and to encourage retailer loyalty. Under the Robinson-Patman Act, however, it's hard for a vendor to justify lower costs for higher quantities on a cumulative basis.[48] To justify

EXHIBIT 14-4

A Sample Price List

QUANTITY PER ORDER	PRICE TO WHOLESALER		PRICE TO RETAILER	
	DISCOUNT	PRICE	DISCOUNT	PRICE
1–10	40–5%	$57*	30%	$70
11–25	50–10	45	40	60
26+	50–10–5	42.75	40–10	54

* Based on a $100 suggested retail price.

cumulative quantity discounts, a vendor could show that having retailers commit to certain levels of purchases in advance allows the vendor to plan production more efficiently and thus cut costs. Cumulative quantity discounts could be easily justified in the garment industry, for instance, since garment manufacturers must commit to their cloth suppliers months in advance.

Noncumulative quantity discounts are offered to retailers as an incentive to purchase more merchandise on a single order. Larger, less frequent orders may save vendors order processing, sales, and transportation expenses. These expenses are often found in retailing and are more easily cost-justified than cumulative quantity discounts.[49]

Exhibit 14–4 presents a sample price list that combines trade/functional, chain, and noncumulative quantity discounts for an appliance manufacturer. The headings "Price to Wholesaler" and "Price to Retailer" illustrate trade/functional discounts. The "40–5%," "50–10," and "50–10–5" under "Price to Wholesaler, Discount" represent different chain discounts. Finally, the first column, "Quantity per Order," illustrates noncumulative quantity discounts.

Examine the columns under "Price to Retailer." At which price should the retailer buy? At first glance, the lowest price appears to be $54. But the lowest price isn't always the most profitable. If the dealer purchases 26 or more TV sets all at once, it may have more than a year's supply. Inventory turnover and the cost of carrying the inventory would be unsatisfactory. The merchandise may become shopworn, and the large quantity might even require more space than is available.[50]

Seasonal Discounts

A seasonal discount is an additional discount offered as an incentive to retailers to order merchandise in advance of the normal buying season. For instance, Black & Decker garden tools may be offered to retailers at a special price in January. Black & Decker can more easily plan its production schedules and lower its finished goods inventory if it can ship early in the season. Retailers, on the other hand, must consider the benefits of a larger gross margin from the discount versus the additional cost of carrying the inventory for a longer period of time.[51]

Cash Discounts

A cash discount is a reduction in the invoice cost for paying the invoice prior to the end of the discount period. It's applied after the functional/trade, chain, quantity, and seasonal discounts. An example is 1/30, n/60 (spoken as one, thirty, net sixty). This means the retailer can take a 1 percent discount if it pays on or before the 30th day after the date of invoice. Or the full invoice amount is due 60 days after the date of invoice. Thus there are three components of a cash discount: the percentage of the discount, the number of days in which the discount can be taken, and the net credit period (when the full amount of the invoice is due). For example, a typical cash discount is 1/30, n/60. This

```
               1/30, N/60

      |          |           |
    Nov. 1     Dec. 1      Jan. 1
    Date of    30 days     60 days
    invoice      1%        Full
               discount    amount
                            due
```

means that if the invoice is dated on November 1, the retailer has 30 days (until December 1) to take the 1 percent discount. The full amount is due 60 days after the invoice date, on January 1. (If retailers really counted days, the full amount would be due on December 31 since there are 31 days in December. But retailers usually don't pay that much attention to number of days in a month for the purpose of taking cash discounts.)

There are a number of variations on the basic cash discount format known as dating. The term *dating* refers to the dates on which discounts can be taken and full amounts are due in a cash discount pricing policy. Here are four examples of common forms of dating.

Receipt of Goods (ROG) Dating   Using ROG dating, the cash discount period starts on the day the merchandise is received. If the merchandise is shipped and invoiced on November 1, but doesn't arrive until November 15, using dating of 1/30, n/60, ROG, the cash discount can be taken until December 15, and the full amount is due January 15.

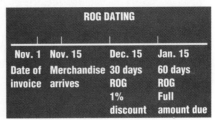

```
                  ROG DATING

     |        |         |          |
   Nov. 1   Nov. 15   Dec. 15    Jan. 15
   Date of  Merchandise 30 days   60 days
   invoice  arrives     ROG       ROG
                        1%        Full
                        discount  amount due
```

End-of-Month (EOM) Dating   In EOM dating, the discount period starts at the end of the month in which the invoice is dated (except when the invoice is dated the 25th or later—as we'll discuss shortly). As in the previous example, if merchandise is invoiced on November 1, using dating of 1/30, n/60, EOM, the cash discount can be taken until January 1, and the full amount is due February 1. The retailer can pay 30 days later than the same terms without the EOM designation.

```
                  EOM DATING

     |         |          |         |
   Nov. 1    Dec. 1     Jan. 1     Feb. 1
   Date of   30-days    30 days    60 days
   invoice   discount   EOM        EOM
             period     1%         Full
             begins     discount   amount
                                   due
```

EOM Dating, Grace Period   A grace period is often given when an invoice with EOM dating is dated after the 25th of the month. The vendor starts counting on the first of the next month. If the merchandise is invoiced on October 25, using the same dating of 1/30, n/60, EOM, the cash discount can still be taken until January 1, and the full amount is due February 1. This time the retailer gets 36 days longer to pay than without the EOM designation! So if the retailer wanted to maximize the length of time to pay for the merchandise and still take the cash discount, the merchandise would be ordered so that it would be invoiced as close to the 25th of the month as possible.

EOM DATING, GRACE PERIOD				
Oct. 25	Nov. 1	Dec. 1	Jan. 1	Feb. 1
Date of invoice		30-days discount period begins	30 days EOM 1% discount	60 days EOM Full amount due

Extra Dating   With extra dating, the retailer receives an extra amount of time to pay the invoice and still take the cash discount. Assume again that the merchandise is invoiced on November 1. Using dating of 1/30, n/60, EOM, 60 days extra (also written 60X or 60 ex.), the cash discount could be taken until March 1, with the net amount due April 1. That is, the discount period starts December 1, due to the EOM designation. The buyer gets 30 days for the regular discount period, plus an additional 60 days.

EXTRA DATING						
Nov. 1	Dec. 1	Jan. 1	Feb. 1	Mar. 1		Aug. 1
Date of invoice	30-day discount period begins	60-day Extra discount period begins		60-day Extra 1% discount		Full amount due

The rationale for offering extra dating is similar to that for the seasonal discount. The vendor may need to give the retailer an additional incentive to purchase risky or seasonal merchandise. Instead of giving the retailer a lower price (as is the case with the seasonal discount), the vendor grants the retailer a longer time in which to pay.

Anticipation Discounts   Under the previously discussed dating policies, a retailer has no incentive to pay earlier than the last day of the discount period. An anticipation discount provides this incentive. It's a discount offered in addition to the cash discount or dating if an invoice is paid before the end of the cash discount period. Let's say the dating is 1/30, n/60, EOM, with anticipation of 18 percent per year, and the invoice is dated November 1, the 30-day discount period ends at the end of December, but the retailer pays on December 1, 30 days earlier. Let's calculate the net cost on a $100 item.

Cash discount = $100 × .01 = $1
Invoice less discount = $100 − $1 = $99

Since the anticipation is 18 percent a year, but the retailer is paying 30 days early, we calculate the anticipation as

Anticipation = $99 × .18 × (30 days early ÷ 360 days per year) = $1.49
Net amount = $99.00 − $1.49 = $97.51

The retailer can earn an extra $2.49 (or $100 − $97.51) by paying early, taking the cash discount, and taking the anticipation.

Shipping Terms and Conditions

The last question in any terms of purchase policy is who (the retailer or the vendor) has responsibility for the different aspects of shipping the merchandise. Two basic issues must be agreed upon when designating the shipping terms and conditions: Who pays the freight charges, and who owns the merchandise while it's in transit?

Transportation costs for shipping merchandise from vendor to retailer can be substantial. If the retailer incurs this expense, it increases the cost of the merchandise.

The party owning the merchandise in transit is responsible for filing a claim with the transportation company in case of lost or damaged merchandise. This is a time-consuming, potentially expensive process. The party filing the claim may have to wait months before it's reimbursed for the loss or damage. Also, the party owning the merchandise while in transit may be responsible for paying insurance that might be needed above the liability of the transportation company to cover merchandise lost or damaged in transit.

Many forms of shipping terms and conditions are used. Exhibit 14–5 outlines the most common ones. The designation *freight prepaid* means freight is paid by the vendor; *freight collect* means the retailer pays the freight. The term *FOB (free on board) origin* means ownership of the merchandise changes hands at the location where the shipment originates. When the ownership changes hands, so does responsibility for filing claims and insurance in case of lost or damaged merchandise. Thus FOB origin is beneficial to the vendor. The term *origin* is often substituted for plant or factory. *FOB destination* means ownership of the merchandise changes hands at the store. So the term *destination* is often substituted for *store* or *retailer*.

EXHIBIT 14–5

Alternative Shipping Terms and Conditions

	PAYS FREIGHT CHARGES	OWNS MERCHANDISE IN TRANSIT AND FILES CLAIMS (IF ANY)
FOB origin, freight collect	Retailer	Retailer
FOB origin, freight prepaid	Supplier	Retailer
FOB destination, freight collect	Retailer	Supplier
FOB destination, freight prepaid	Supplier	Supplier

NOTES

1. Robin Lewis, "What's a Brand Worth?" *Women's Wear Daily*, November 8, 1995, pp. 10–11, taken from the 1995 brand survey issue of *Financial World.*

2. "Private Label on the Rise," *Chain Store Age*, May 1996, p. 31.

3. Marcia Mogelonsky, "When Stores Become Brands," *American Demographics*, February 1995, pp. 32–38.

4. Raj Sethuraman, "National Brand and Store Brand Price Competition: Who Hurts Whom?" Marketing Science Institute Technical Working Paper, report no. 95-105, 1995.

5. Teri Agins, "Big Stores Put Own Labels on Best Clothes," *The Wall Street Journal*, September 26, 1994, pp. B1, B10.

6. Susan Reda, "Private Label Transformation," *Stores,* January 1995, pp. 28–32.

7. "Brands Devise to Conquer," *Women's Wear Daily*, May 2, 1996, pp. 1, 8–9.

8. Mark Tosh, "Sears' New Private Label Weapon," *Women's Wear Daily*, April 17, 1996, p. 14.

9. E. S. Browning, "Europeans Witness Proliferation of Private Labels," *The Wall Street Journal*, October 20, 1992, pp. B1, B5.

10. Arthur Friedman, "Sourcing Now: The Proximity Factor, Imports: A Change of Venue," *Women's Wear Daily*, May 26, 1996, p. 6, citing the U.S. Department of Commerce.

11. See Gary M. Erickson, Johny K. Johansson, and Paul Chao, "Image Variables in Multi-Attribute Information on Product Evaluation: An Information Processing Perspective," *Journal of Consumer Research* 16 (September 1989), pp. 175–87; Sung-Tai Hong and Robert S. Wyer, Jr., "Effects of Country-of-Origin and Product-Attribute Information on Product Evaluation: An Information Processing Perspective," *Journal of Consumer Research* 16 (September 1989), pp. 175–87; and Michael R. Solomon, *Consumer Behavior* (Boston: Allyn & Bacon, 1992), p. 262.

12. "Change at the Checkout," *The Economist*, March 4, 1995.

13. Export tariffs are used in some less developed countries to generate additional revenue. For instance, the Argentine government may impose an export tariff on wool that is exported. An export tariff actually lowers the competitive ability of domestic manufacturers, rather than protecting them, as is the case with import tariffs.

14. Thomas R. Graham, "Global Trade: War and Peace," *Foreign Policy*, Spring 1983, pp. 124–37, taken from Michael R. Czinkota and Ilkka A. Ronkainen, *Global Marketing* (Fort Worth: Harcourt Brace, 1996), p. 85.

15. *The Likely Impact on the United States of a Free Trade Agreement with Mexico* (Washington, DC: U.S. International Trade Commission, 1991).

16. "Asia's Fertile Fields," *Women's Wear Daily*, May 1, 1996, pp. 8–9.

17. Stanley E. Fawcett and Laura M. Birou, "Exploring the Logistics between Global and JIT Sourcing," *International Journal of Physical Distribution & Logistics Management* 22 no. 1 (1992), pp. 3–14.

18. "Asia's Fertile Fields."

19. "'Buy American' Emotional Appeal No Match for Bargains," *Discount Store News*, June 20, 1994, p. 23.

20. This section is adapted from Joanna Ramey, "Apparel's Ethics Dilemma," *Women's Wear Daily*, March 18, 1996, pp. 10–12; and Susan Chandler, "Look Who's Sweating Now," *Business Week*, October 16, 1995, pp. 96–97.

21. "The Fashion Center," *Women's Wear Daily*, Advertising Supplement, September 1995, p. 4.

22. Sandy Jap and Barton Weitz, "A Taxonomy of Long-Term Relationships," Working Paper, College of Business Administration, University of Florida, Gainesville, 1994; F. Robert Dwyer, Paul Schurr, and Sejo Oh, "Developing Buyer–Seller Relationships," *Journal of Marketing* 51 (April 1987), pp. 11–27.

23. Robert Krapel, Deborah Salmond, and Robert Spekman, "A Strategic Approach to Managing Buyer–Seller Relationships," *European Journal of Marketing* 25 (1991), pp. 22–37; B. G. Yovovich, "Dos and Don'ts of Partnering," *Business Marketing*, March 1992, pp. 38–39; and "Smart Selling: How Companies Are Winning Over Today's Tough Customers," *Business Week*, August 3, 1992, pp. 46–52.

24. "Change at the Checkout."

25. "Pritchett on Quick Response," *Discount Merchandiser*, April 1992, p. 64.

26. John Swan and Johannah Nolan, "Gaining Customer Trust: A Conceptual Guide for the Salesperson," *Journal of Personal Selling and Sales Management*, November 1985, pp. 39–48; and John Swan, I. Fred Trawick, David Rink, and Jenney Roberts, "Measuring Dimensions of Purchaser Trust of Industrial Salespeople," *Journal of Personal Selling and Sales Management*, May 1988, pp. 1–9.

27. Erin Anderson and Barton Weitz, "The Use of Pledges to Build and Sustain Commitment in Distribution Channels," *Journal of Marketing Research* 29 (February 1992), pp. 18–34.

28. Ibid.

29. Gene R. Laczniak and Patrick E. Murphy, *Marketing Ethics* (Needham Heights, MA: Allyn & Bacon, 1992).

30. Jeffrey A. Trachtenberg, "Record Stores Lease Out Windows, Walls, Whatever," *The Wall Street Journal*, April 19, 1995, p. B1.

31. Read Hayes, "Retailers Toughen Ethics Codes to Curb Employee Abuses," *Stores*, July 1996, pp. 83–84.

32. Trademarks, copyrights, and patents are all under the general umbrella of intellectual property. *Intellectual property* is intangible and is created by intellectual (mental) effort as opposed to physical effort. A *trademark* is any mark, word, picture, or design associated with certain merchandise (for instance, the crown on a Rolex watch and the GE on General Electric products). A *copyright* protects original work of authors, painters, sculptors, musicians, and others who produce works of artistic or intellectual merit. The copyright protects only the physical expression of the effort,

not the idea. This book is copyrighted, so these sentences cannot be used by anyone without the consent of the copyright owner. However, anyone can take the ideas in this book and express them in different words. The owner of a **patent** controls the right to make, sell, and use a product for a period of 17 years or a design for 14 years. Edward J. Conry, Gerald R. Ferrera, and Karla H. Fox, *The Legal Environment of Business* (Boston: Allyn & Bacon, 1993), pp. 185–91.

33. "Software Piracy Continues to Plague Industry," *Business Software Alliance*, April 27, 1994.

34. This section draws from Czinkota and Ronkainen, *Global Marketing*, pp. 401–4.

35. Faye Rice, "How Copycats Steal Billions," *Fortune*, April 22, 1991, pp. 157–64.

36. "An Introductory Guide for US Businesses on Protecting Intellectual Property Abroad," *Business America*, July, 1, 1991, pp. 2–7.

37. "Intellectual Property . . . Is Theft," *The Economist*, January 22, 1993, pp. 72–73.

38. Louis P. Bucklin, "The Gray Market Threat to International Marketing Strategies," Marketing Science Institute, Working Paper no. 90-116, September 1990.

39. This section draws from Czinkota and Ronkainen, *Global Marketing*, pp. 466–69.

40. Bucklin, "The Gray Market Threat."

41. "Brand Battles," *International Business*, April 1993, p. 83.

42. Ellen Klein and J. D. Howard, "Strings Attached," *North American International Business* 6 (May 1991), pp. 54–55.

43. Faye Brookman, "Stores Seeking New Options as the Gray Market Darkens," *Women's Wear Daily*, March 1996, pp. 6, 8.

44. "Hartz Mountain Gets Knocked," *Sales & Marketing Management*, April 1987, p. 4.

45. Janet Ozzard, "Levi's Cutoff Bugs Small Stores," *Women's Wear Daily*, July 27, 1994, p. 16.

46. This section was developed with the assistance of Howard Kreitzman, vice president, Duty Free Stores.

47. These guidelines are based on Roger Fisher and William Ury, *Getting to Yes* (New York: Penguin, 1981).

48. Itzhak Sharav, "Cost Justification under the Robinson-Patman Act," *Management Accounting*, July 1978, pp. 15–22.

49. For different perspectives on determining a quantity discount pricing policy see Abel P. Jeuland and Steven M. Shugan, "Managing Channel Profits," *Marketing Science* 2 (Summer 1983), pp. 239–72; Rajiv Lal and Richard Staelin, "An Approach for Developing an Optimal Discount Pricing Policy," *Management Science* 30 (December 1984), pp. 1524–39; Michael Levy, William Cron, and Robert Novack, "A Decision Support System for Determining a Quantity Discount Pricing Policy," *Journal of Business Logistics* 6, no. 2 (1985), pp. 110–41; James Monahan, "A Quantity Discount Pricing Model to Increase Vendor Profits," *Management Science* 30 (June 1984), pp. 720–27; Kent B. Monroe and Albert J. Della Bitta, "Models for Pricing Decisions," *Journal of Marketing Research* 15 (August 1990), pp. 413–28; James B. Wilcox, Roy D. Howell, Paul Kuzdrall, and Robert Britney, "Price Quantity Discounts: Some Implications for Buyers and Sellers," *Journal of Marketing* 51, no. 3 (July 1987), pp. 60–71; and Pinhas Zusman and Michael Etgar, "The Marketing Channel as an Equilibrium Set of Contracts," *Management Science* 27 (March 1981), pp. 284–302.

50. Michael Levy and Michael van Breda, "A Financial Perspective on the Shift of Marketing Functions," *Journal of Retailing* 60, no. 4 (Winter 1984), pp. 23–42.

51. Ibid.

15

Pricing

THE WORLD OF RETAILING

↓

RETAILING STRATEGY

↓

MERCHANDISE MANAGEMENT
12. Planning Merchandise
    Assortments
13. Buying Systems
14. Buying Merchandise
15. **Pricing**
16. Retail Promotion Mix

STORE MANAGEMENT
17. Managing the Store
18. Store Layout, Design, and
    Visual Merchandising
19. Customer Service
20. Retail Selling

QUESTIONS

- Why do some retailers have frequent sales while others attempt to maintain an everyday low price strategy?

- How do retailers set retail prices?

- Why are markdowns taken, and what are some guidelines for taking them?

- Under what circumstances can retailers' pricing practices get them into legal difficulties?

TODAY'S CUSTOMERS ARE LOOKING for a good value in what they purchase. To some people, a good value means a low price. Many different types of consumers have become much more price-sensitive. Others are willing to pay more as long as they believe they're getting their money's worth in terms of product quality or service.

Retailers have responded to their customers' needs with retail formats that emphasize low prices as a means of creating a differential advantage. National discount store chains that offer everyday low prices (EDLP)—such as Wal-Mart, Target, and Kmart—dominate many markets in many product categories. A close competitor in the price-oriented market is the membership-only warehouse club, such as Sam's Warehouse Club and Price/Costco. Another retail format is the off-price retailer (e.g., Loehmann's, T. J. Maxx, and Marshalls), which purchases closeout and end-of-season merchandise at lower-than-normal prices and passes the savings on to the customer. (Chapters 2 and 4 describe these stores and trends.)

Some of the more mature retailing institutions have come to grips with these new forms of price competition in various ways. Dayton Hudson, for example, has expanded beyond its traditional department store boundaries to offer discounting (Target) and heavy price promotion (Mervyn's). Other retailers, from department stores to supermarkets, have taken on more of a price promotion orientation. Finally, many retailers—notably Dillard's and Nordstrom—have successfully maintained their market appeal by offering customers high-quality merchandise and service without attempting to offer the lowest prices on a particular product category.

Wal-Mart's Everyday Low Pricing (EDLP) strategy has helped make them the market leader in every market they enter, and the largest retailer in the world.

In the middle of this price competition among national giants are the smaller retailers. Typically unable to purchase in large quantities to receive lower prices like their larger competitors, "ma-and-pa" retailers have either learned to use other strategies to compete or gone out of business. For instance, to compete with Wal-Mart's low prices, small retailers have developed niche strategies by providing a broader assortment of merchandise within a given product category *and* better service. Wal-Mart may have the lowest average price on the few guns and rifles that it carries. A good sporting goods specialty store, however, might have a larger assortment than Wal-Mart and would be willing to special-order merchandise so that its customers could get exactly the guns they're looking for. It could also give advice on the product itself as well as local hunting information.

This chapter begins by comparing everyday low pricing with high/low pricing. In addition, we describe several additional pricing practices that retailers use to get a competitive edge. Then we describe two complementary methods of setting retail prices: cost-oriented and demand-oriented approaches. We conclude this chapter with a discussion of important legal issues involved in making price decisions.

PRICING STRATEGIES AND PRACTICES

Retailers have made the pricing problem interesting by adding various nuances to the basic process of adding a markup to the cost of merchandise. In today's retail market, two opposing pricing strategies prevail: everyday low pricing and high/low pricing.[1]

Everyday Low Pricing (EDLP)

Many retailers have adopted an **everyday low pricing (EDLP)** strategy. This strategy stresses continuity of retail prices at a level somewhere between the regular nonsale price and the deep discount sale price of the retailer's competitors. The term *everyday low pricing* is therefore somewhat of a misnomer. *Low* doesn't necessarily mean lowest. Although retailers using EDLP strive for low prices, they aren't always the lowest price in the market. At any given time, a sale price at a competing store or a special purchase at a wholesale club store may be the lowest price. A more accurate description of this strategy is therefore everyday *stable* prices because the prices don't have significant fluctuations. Four of the most successful U.S. retailers—Home Depot, Wal-Mart, Office Depot, and Toys "R" Us—have adopted EDLP.

High/Low Pricing

In a **high/low pricing strategy,** retailers offer prices that are sometimes above their competition's EDLP, but they use advertising to promote frequent sales. Like EDLP, the use of high/low strategies has become more intense in recent years. In the past, fashion retailers would mark down merchandise at the end of a season; grocery and drug stores would only have sales when their vendors offered them special prices or when they were overstocked. Today, many fashion retailers respond to increased competition and a more value-conscious customer by promoting more frequent sales. Vendors to grocery and drug stores are taking advantage of increasingly frequent deal periods—a limited time period allowed by manufacturers to purchase merchandise at a special price. Some of these retailers buy almost all of their merchandise "on deal."

Deciding Which Strategy Is Best

An EDLP has five relative benefits in relation to high/low.

- *Reduced price wars.* Many customers—particularly Generation X customers—are increasingly skeptical about shelf prices. They have become conditioned to buying only on sale—the main characteristic of a high/low pricing strategy. A successful EDLP strategy enables retailers to withdraw from highly competitive price wars with competitors. Once customers realize that prices are fair, they'll buy more each time and buy more frequently.
- *Reduced advertising.* The stable prices caused by EDLP limit the need for weekly sale advertising used in the high/low strategy. Instead, retailers can focus on more image-oriented messages. Also, catalogs don't become obsolete as quickly since prices don't change as often.
- *Improved customer service.* Without sale-stimulated throngs of people, salespeople can spend more time with customers. Retailers that participate in high/low pricing can offer high levels of customer service during sales, but only if they hire additional salespeople during the sales.
- *Reduced stockouts and improved inventory management.* An EDLP reduces the large variations in demand caused by frequent sales with large markdowns. As a result, retailers can manage their inventory with more certainty. Fewer stockouts mean more satisfied customers, higher sales, and fewer rain checks. (**Rain checks** are given to customers when merchandise is out of stock; they're written promises to sell customers merchandise at the sale price when the merchandise arrives.) In addition, a more predictable customer demand pattern enables the retailer to improve inventory turnover by reducing the average inventory needed for special promotions and backup stock. (**Backup stock** is inventory used to guard against going out of stock when demand exceeds forecasts or when merchandise is delayed; see Chapter 12.)
- *Increased profit margins.* Even though prices are generally lower with EDLP, overall profit margins can increase since merchandise is no longer sold at large reductions as it is using a high/low strategy. Prices change much less often with EDLP. This lowers costs of (1) making price changes and (2) mistakenly charging customers sale prices on merchandise that's no longer on sale.

But EDLP policy isn't for every retailer. A high/low strategy has five relative strengths too.

- *The same merchandise appeals to multiple markets.* When fashion merchandise first hits the store, it's offered at its highest price. Fashion leaders, those who are less sensitive to price, and hard-to-fit customers often buy as soon as the merchandise is available. As the season progresses and markdowns are taken, more people enter the market. Finally, hard-core bargain hunters enter the market for the end-of-season deep-discount sales like the Neiman Marcus Last Call Sale at the end of each season—25 percent off merchandise that has already been marked

A high/low pricing strategy enables retailers to appeal to multiple markets with the same merchandise. One group buys at the beginning of the season at "full retail price," while another group waits until the merchandise is marked down.

down 33 to 50 percent. Grocery and drug store customers react to high/low prices in a similar manner. Some customers pay little attention to the prices they pay, while others will wait for merchandise to go on sale and stockpile for future use.

• *It creates excitement.* A "get them while they last" atmosphere often occurs during a sale. Sales draw crowds, and crowds create excitement. Some retailers augment low prices and advertising with special in-store activities like product demonstrations, giveaways, celebrity appearances, and very-short-term special prices that last only a few minutes.

• *It moves merchandise.* All merchandise will eventually sell—the question is, at what price? Frequent sales enable retailers to move the merchandise, even though profits erode.

• *Emphasis is on quality or service.* A high initial price sends a signal to customers that the merchandise is high-quality and/or excellent service is provided. When merchandise goes on sale, customers still use the original price to gauge quality. An EDLP policy may send the wrong signal to customers. They may assume that since prices are low, quality or services may suffer.

• *It's hard to maintain EDLP.* EDLP is difficult for most retailers. Those who promote an EDLP policy must, in fact, have low prices on merchandise that customers can compare with that of the competition, such as national brands at a department store or commodity products, such as milk or sugar in a supermarket. Merchandise must be purchased frequently since customers are aware of these products' prices. Given these constraints, it's generally hard for certain types of retailers such as fashion or small retailers to implement an EDLP strategy.

Retailers using EDLP are eventually doomed if their prices are higher than competitors' but they still advertise EDLP. Home Depot, Wal-Mart, and others have succeeded in the long run by consistently offering everyday low prices.

15.1

Stable Prices—the Key to Success at Dillard's

DILLARD'S HAS EMERGED as the nation's fourth-largest traditional department store chain—fifth if JCPenney is included in the list. One reason for its meteoric growth is that it was the first major department store company to adopt an everyday stable price strategy that reverses the trend of ever-increasing "special sales" that dominates the department store industry. These special sales tend to cause higher, artificial initial markups that produce higher "regular prices" against which ever-increasing quantities of "sale" merchandise can be priced.

Dillard's success with this strategy far exceeds several other department stores'. One reason is that it has replaced its sale catalogs with handsome catalogs of regular-priced goods. Catalogs often focus on major categories of merchandise such as menswear, women's dresses, and home. You can only appreciate the selling power of these quality, full-page selling presentations by comparing them with the price-oriented newspaper ads and inserts that characterize promotions for much of the department store industry.

Of course, everyday stable prices and quality promotional vehicles are only two elements of a successful strategy. Experts believe that Dillard's success is a result of coordinating pricing and promotion efforts with improvements in the actual merchandise offerings and store environment as well as sophisticated merchandise information and Quick Response inventory management systems.

Source: *The Wall Street Journal,* May 11, 1994, pp. A1, A6; and Joseph H. Ellis, "Dillard's Department Stores," Goldman Sachs Investment Research, February 5, 1991.

The Future of EDLP and High/Low Pricing Strategies

Retailing is always in a state of flux. Retailers who've pioneered an everyday low pricing strategy (like Wal-Mart and Kmart) are using more frequent promotions, while retailers engaged primarily in a high/low strategy are attempting to stabilize their wild price fluctuations with more everyday low prices. Retailing View 15.1 tells how Dillard Department Stores has adopted its own form of everyday stable prices.

INTERNET EXCERCISE   Go to the websites for Bloomingdale's (http://www.bloomingdales.com/) and Dillard's Department Stores (http://www.azstarnet.com/dillards) on the Internet. Which department store chain is using an everyday low pricing strategy and which is using a high/low strategy? How can you tell?

We offer guidelines for how to deal with this basic pricing strategy.[2] First, EDLP should not be used for all product categories. Brands that enjoy high consumer loyalty and have a high market share in a category with relatively few players are likely to benefit from EDLP. Generally, it's hard for a brand that already has a relatively high market share to increase its share through promotions. For example, the profitability in the diaper category—where Procter & Gamble's Pampers and Luvs, along with Kimberly-Clark's Huggies, account for about 75 percent of total sales—should benefit from EDLP. People are more likely to respond to high levels of promotion in a product category like shampoos with lots of highly competitive products. Thus, retailers can adopt EDLP for some product categories and use price to promote others.

Second, some retailers have developed strategies to wean customers off high/low strategies.[3] Dayton Hudson Corp., for instance, has reduced the number

of sales "events" at its department stores. Kmart has reduced the number of items featured in its newspaper sales circulars. Ann Taylor and others are trying to encourage customers to buy at full price by displaying fewer clothes. They assume that if customers believe the item is scarce, they are more likely to buy now (at full price) rather than take the chance of waiting for it to go on sale.

Third, those retailers who have embraced an EDLP strategy must convince their customers that they do, in fact, have low prices, even if they don't have the lowest price on every item. For instance, you may be able to find items that are lower-priced than at Wal-Mart, but the chain's loyal customers probably won't believe you. Promotions can play an important role in creating a perception of EDLP. For instance, Daffy's is an off-price clothing retailer that thrives on no advertised discount or sale, only an increasing perception that it's a great place to shop every day.[4] (See the ad above.)

Finally, retailers must recognize that they generally can't avoid sales altogether. Sure, if they don't buy enough merchandise or buy a narrow assortment, they can avoid sales. Unfortunately, they'll also pass up the chance to satisfy more customers by doing so. It's a tough trade-off.

Although retailers' basic pricing strategies lie along a continuum from everyday low pricing to high/low strategies, they use other practices too—coupons, rebates, leader pricing, price bundling, multiple-unit pricing, price lining, and odd pricing—in conjunction with their basic strategy.

Coupons   **Coupons** are documents that entitle the holder to a reduced price or x cents off the actual purchase price of a product or service.[6] Coupons are issued by manufacturers and retailers in newspapers, on products, on the shelf, at the cash register, and through the mail. Retailers' use of coupons is staggering. It's estimated that 292 billion coupons were issued in 1995. But only about 2 percent were redeemed, compared to about 4 percent in 1980. The decline is partly because manufacturers have cut the average time before expiration by more than half to limit their exposure.[7]

Coupons are thought to be an important sales promotional tool because they induce customers to try products for the first time, convert those first-time users to regular users, encourage larger purchases, increase usage, and protect market share against competition.[8]

Coupons induce customers to try products for the first time, convert those first-time users to regular users, encourage larger purchases, increase usage, and protect market share against competition.

The evidence on couponing's overall profitability is mixed. Since coupons have the seemingly positive effect of encouraging larger purchases, the coupon promotion may be stealing sales from a future period without any net increase in sales. For instance, if a supermarket runs a coupon promotion on sugar, households tend to buy a large quantity of sugar and stockpile it for future use. Thus, unless the coupon is used mostly by new buyers, the net impact on sales will be negligible, and there will be a negative impact on profits by the amount of the redeemed coupons and cost of the coupon redemption procedures. Unfortunately, it's very hard to isolate a market for new users without allowing current users to take advantage of the coupon promotion.[9]

Competition among retailers for coupon-prone customers has become so intense that retailers often offer double- and even triple-coupon promotions, which allow the customer double or triple the face value of the coupon. But compelling evidence indicates that customers who redeem these coupons are the stores' present customers, not customers from competing stores.[10] As a result, retailers are paying for coupon redemption without increasing sales or market share. Finally, besides the additional cost of a coupon price war, coupons are expensive to handle.

Rebates

A **rebate** is money returned to the buyer based on a portion of the purchase price. Generally, the customer sends a proof of purchase to the manufacturer, and the manufacturer sends the customer the rebate. Rebates are most useful when the dollar amount is relatively large. Otherwise, it's not worth the customer's time and postage to redeem the rebate. For instance, rebates are often offered on cars, major and portable appliances, and electronic products. From the retailer's perspective, rebates are more advantageous than coupons since they increase demand in the same way coupons may, but the retailer has no handling costs.

Leader Pricing

In **leader pricing,** certain items are priced lower than normal to increase customers' traffic flow and/or to boost sales of complementary products. Reasons for using leader pricing are similar to those for coupons. The difference is that with leader pricing, merchandise has a low price to begin with so customers, retailers, and vendors don't have to handle the coupons. Some retailers call these products loss leaders. In a strict sense, loss leaders are sold below cost. But a product doesn't have to be sold below cost for the retailer to be using a leader pricing strategy. The best items for leader pricing are products purchased frequently, primarily by price-sensitive shoppers.[11] For instance, supermarkets typically use white bread, eggs, and milk as loss leaders. Price-sensitive customers take note of ads for these products because they're purchased weekly. The retailer hopes consumers will also purchase their weekly groceries while buying loss leaders. Toys "R" Us has successfully used a leader pricing strategy for disposable diapers. New parents get in the habit of shopping at Toys when their children are infants and become loyal customers throughout their parenting period.

Price Bundling

Price bundling is the practice of offering two or more different products or services for sale at one price.[12] For instance, a travel agency may sell a tour that includes airfare, a cruise, and meals, all for $1,500. If purchased separately, the items might total $2,600. Price bundling is used to increase both unit and dollar sales by bringing traffic into the store. The strategy can also be used to move less desirable merchandise by including it in a package with merchandise in high demand.

INTERNET EXCERCISE Price bundling is very common in the travel and vacation industry. Go to the webpage for Sandals and see what you can get—all for one price (http://www.sandals.com/general/about.html).

Multiple-Unit Pricing **Multiple-unit pricing** is similar to price bundling, except the products or services are similar rather than different. For example, a convenience store may sell three liters of soda for $2.39 when the price per unit is 99 cents—a savings of 58 cents. Like price bundling, this strategy is used to increase sales volume. Depending on the type of product, however, customers may stockpile for use at a later time. For example, although you typically purchase and consume one liter of soda a week, you may purchase several if you perceive a substantial cost savings. If customers stockpile, demand is shifted back in time with no long-term effect on sales.

Some retailers abuse price bundling and multiple-unit prices by implying a savings when there really isn't one (say, 49 cents each or two for 98 cents; or even worse, 49 cents each or three for $1.59). This type of deceptive practice has received considerable attention from consumer groups.

Which ad is using price bundling and which is using multiple-unit pricing?

Price Lining   In **price lining,** retailers offer a limited number of predetermined price points within a classification. For instance, a tire store may offer tires only at $29.99, $49.99, and $79.99. Both customers and retailers can benefit from such a strategy for several reasons:

- Confusion that often arises from multiple price choices is essentially eliminated. The customer can choose the tire with either the low, medium, or high price. (There need not be three price lines; the strategy can use more or fewer than three.)
- From the retailer's perspective, the merchandising task is simplified. That is, all products within a certain price line are merchandised together. Further, when going to market, the firm's buyers can select their purchases with the predetermined price lines in mind.
- Price lining can also give buyers greater flexibility. If a strict initial markup is required, there could be numerous price points. But with a price lining strategy, some merchandise may be bought a little below or above the expected cost for a price line. Of course, price lining can also limit retail buyers' flexibility. They may be forced to pass up potentially profitable merchandise because it doesn't fit into a price line.
- Although many manufacturers and retailers are simplifying their product offerings to save distribution and inventory costs and to make the choice simpler for consumers, price lining can be used to get customers to "trade up" to a more expensive model. Research indicates a tendency for people to choose the product in the middle of a price line. So, for example, if a camera store starts carrying a "superdeluxe" model, customers will be more likely to purchase the model that was previously the most expensive. Retailers must decide whether it's more profitable to sell more expensive merchandise or save money by paring down their stock selection.[13]

Odd Pricing   **Odd price** refers to a price that ends in an odd number (such as 57 cents or 63 cents) or to a price just under a round number (such as $98 instead of $100). Odd pricing has a long history in retailing. In the 19th and early 20th centuries, odd prices were used to reduce losses due to employee theft. Because merchandise had an odd price, salespeople typically had to go to the cash register to give the customer change and record the sale. This reduced salespeople's chances to take money for an item from a customer, keep the money, and never record the sale. Odd pricing was also used to keep track of how many times an item had been marked down. After an initial price of $20, the first markdown would be $17.99, the second markdown $15.98, and so on.

While odd pricing originally had loss prevention and accounting functions, some retailers believe that odd pricing can increase sales. Most empirical studies, however, don't support this proposition.[14]

Toys "R" Us has successfully used a leader pricing strategy for disposable diapers. New parents get in the habit of shopping at "Toys" when their children are infants and become loyal customers throughout the parenting process.

Does odd pricing—a price that ends in an odd number—really work?

Nonetheless, many retailers use some rules of thumb regarding odd prices. Odd pricing may be less successful for products that require some thought. For instance, when purchasing a car, most customers wouldn't have to think long to realize that $17,995 is almost $18,000. Also, odd pricing seems to imply a low price. So retailers interested in maintaining an upscale image probably shouldn't use odd pricing. For instance, Tiffany's doesn't advertise diamond rings for $6,999. But if it put a ring on sale, it might use an odd price to signal a price reduction. Odd pricing, then, may be most successful for impulse purchases at lower-end retailers or on sale merchandise.

CONTRASTING COST-ORIENTED AND DEMAND-ORIENTED METHODS OF SETTING RETAIL PRICES

The previous section examined general strategies for setting retail prices. The following sections examine two distinct methods of setting retail prices: cost-oriented and demand-oriented. Under the **cost-oriented method,** the retail price is determined by adding a fixed percentage to the cost of the merchandise. For instance, Primrose Fashions, a family-owned women's specialty store in Dallas, uses the **keystone method** of setting prices in which it simply doubles the cost of the merchandise to obtain the original retail selling price. If a dress costs Primrose $50, the original selling price is $100. In the **demand-oriented method,** prices are based on what customers expect or are willing to pay. In this case, Primrose may have found a particularly good value at $50, but believe that the profit-maximizing price is $115.

Which method is best? The answer is both! The cost-oriented method's strength is that it's designed to achieve target levels of profits. Also, it's quick, mechanical, and relatively simple to use. The demand-oriented method's strength is its consistency with the marketing concept. That is, it considers customers' wants and needs. Further, the demand-oriented method can determine profit-maximizing prices. But demand-oriented pricing is hard to implement, especially in a retailing environment with thousands of SKUs that require individual pricing decisions.

A combined demand- and cost-oriented method is useful. The cost-oriented method would be the basis of the pricing strategy. The demand-oriented method, on the other hand, would be used for fine-tuning the strategy. Retailers would start with a price based on their profit goals and perform tests to determine if it's the most profitable price. The initial retail price could then be changed according to the findings.

THE COST-ORIENTED METHOD OF SETTING THE RETAIL PRICE

This section shows how retail prices are set based on cost of the merchandise. Unfortunately, the process isn't always as simple as doubling the cost, which we described earlier. For instance, the retail price at which the product is originally sold may not be the same as the final retail selling price due to markdowns. So retailers have devised methods of keeping track of changes in the retail price so they can achieve their overall financial goals, as we discussed in Chapter 7.

Recall that the retailer's financial goals are set by top management in terms of a target return on investment—either return on assets or return on owners' equity. In the strategic profit model, return on assets is calculated as net profit margin multiplied by asset turnover. Pricing goals are determined primarily from net profit margin.

For pricing decisions, the key component of net profit margin is gross profit margin percentage (gross margin ÷ net sales). Retailers set initial prices high enough so that after markdowns and other adjustments (known as reductions) are made, they'll end up with a gross margin consistent with their overall profit goals.

First, we describe how retailers determine their initial selling price based on their gross margin goal. Then we examine various adjustments to the retail price such as markdowns and additional markups.

Determining the Initial Markup from Maintained Markup and Gross Margin

The performance measure usually used to evaluate pricing decisions is gross margin. Exhibit 15–1 summarizes its components. But retailers use an additional term called *maintained markup* that's similar to gross margin. The relationship can be expressed as

$$\text{Maintained markup percentage} = \frac{\text{Net sales} - \text{Cost of goods sold}}{\text{Net sales}}$$

$$\frac{\text{Gross margin}}{\text{percentage}} = \frac{\text{Maintained markup} - \text{Workroom costs} + \text{Cash discounts}}{\text{Net sales}}$$

Thus, the only difference between the two terms is the workroom costs and cash discounts. Why do retailers make this distinction between maintained markup and gross margin? In many retail organizations, wookroom (or alteration) costs aren't controlled by the person who makes the pricing decision. For instance, the furniture buyer doesn't have control over costs associated with assembling a dining room table. In the same way, a buyer typically has no control over whether the accounting department takes the cash discounts offered. But remember that conceptually, maintained markup and gross margin are very similar.

The term **maintained markup** is very descriptive. It's the amount of profit (markup) a retailer plans to maintain on a particular category of merchandise. For example, in Exhibit 15–1, planned maintained markup is $62,000 on sales of

EXHIBIT 15–1

Sample Income Statement Showing Gross Margin

Net sales	$120,000
– Cost of goods sold	58,000
= Maintained markup	62,000
– Alteration costs + Cash discounts	3,000
= Gross margin	$ 59,000

$120,000, or 51.67 percent ($62,000/$120,000). In other words, to meet its profit goals, this retailer must obtain a 51.67 percent maintained markup.

A retailer's life would be relatively simple if the amount of markup it wanted to maintain (maintained markup) were the same as the initial markup.

Initial markup = Retail selling price *initially* placed on the merchandise
– Cost of goods sold

However, the maintained markup is the *actual* sales that you get for the merchandise minus cost of goods sold. Why is there a difference? A number of reductions to the value of retail inventory occur between the time the merchandise is originally priced (initial markup) and the time it's sold (maintained markup). **Reductions** include markdowns, discounts to employees and customers, and inventory shrinkage (due to shoplifting, breakage, or loss). Initial markup must be high enough so that after reductions are taken out, the maintained markup is left.

A few retail customers might feel slightly guilty when buying a product that has been drastically marked down. They shouldn't, however. Retailers that successfully plan their sales and markdowns also build the markdown into the initial price. Even though a customer may receive a very good price on a particular purchase, other people paid the premarkdown price. So, on average, the markup was maintained.

Retailers expect shrinkage and include this loss in the price customers pay. To illustrate, consider a TV campaign that ran a few years ago showing someone shoplifting. The message was "When you shoplift, you are ripping off your neighbor." If two retailers plan to achieve the same maintained markup, but one has a high percentage of shrinkage due to shoplifting, that store needs a higher initial markup if all other factors are held constant.

The relationship between initial markup and maintained markup is

$$\text{Initial markup percentage} = \frac{\begin{array}{c}\text{Planned operating expenses + Planned profit}\\ \text{+ Workroom costs – Cash discounts}\\ \text{+ Planned reductions}\end{array}}{\text{Planned net sales + Planned reductions}}$$

Returning to the example in Exhibit 15–1, suppose the retailer expects reductions to be $14,400. To reach its maintained markup goal, its initial markup will have to be

$$\text{Initial markup} = \frac{\$17,000 + \$42,000 + \$3,000 + \$14,400}{\$120,000 + \$14,400} = 56.85\%$$

This formula can be simplified since

Gross margin = Operating expenses + Net profit

Likewise,

Maintained markup = Gross margin + Workroom costs – Cash discounts

$$\text{Initial markup} = \frac{\text{Maintained markup + Reductions}}{\text{Net sales + Reductions}}$$

or

$$\text{Initial markup} = \frac{\begin{array}{c}\text{Maintained markup (as a \% of net sales)}\\ \text{+ Reductions (as a \% of net sales)}\end{array}}{100\% + \text{Reductions (as a \% of net sales)}}$$

Using the information in Exhibit 15–1 and knowing that reductions of $14,400 here equal 12 percent of net sales,

$$\text{Initial markup} = \frac{\$62,000 + 14,400}{\$120,000 + 14,400} = 56.85\%$$

or

$$\text{Initial markup} = \frac{51.67\% + 12\%}{100\% + 12\%} = 56.85\%$$

Note that the same answer is obtained using all three formulas. Also, initial markup is always greater than maintained markup so long as there are any reductions. Finally, initial markup is expressed either in dollars or as a percentage of retail price. This is because retailers using the retail inventory method (RIM) of inventory accounting (described in Appendix 13A) think of their inventory in "retail" rather than "cost" terms. Also, expressing initial markup as a percentage of retail price closely resembles the other accounting conventions of expressing net profit, gross margin, and maintained markup as percentages of net sales, which are, of course, at retail.

Determining the Initial Retail Price under Cost-Oriented Pricing

Continuing the preceding example, with the initial markup of 56.85 percent, assume that the suggested retail price of a certain item is $100. What are the dollar markup and the merchandise cost?

Retail = Cost   + Markup
$100 = Cost   + (56.85% × Retail)
$100 = Cost   + $56.85
$100 = $43.15 + $56.85

The dollar markup is $56.85, and the merchandise cost is $43.15.

Here's another example. A salesperson comes into a buyer's office with a great new product that will cost $100. What will be the retail price if the initial markup is still 56.85 percent?

There are two ways to solve this problem. First, the buyer can convert the initial markup as a percentage of retail to initial markup as a percentage of cost using the formula[15]

$$\text{Initial markup as a \% of cost} = \frac{\text{Initial markup as a \% of retail}}{100\% - \text{Initial markup as a \% of retail}}$$

$$131.75\% = \frac{56.85\%}{100\% - 56.85\%}$$

Then the problem can be set up as before:

Retail   = Cost + Markup
Retail   = $100 + (131.75% × Cost)
$231.75 = $100 + $131.75

The second way to solve this problem uses algebra:

Retail = Cost + Markup
Retail = $100 + (56.85% × Retail)
R   = $100 + .5685   × R

15.2

Final Final Sale! Stores Unload Buyers' Errors

APPROACHING THE CASHIER, Susanne Lemberger can hardly carry all the designer dresses, jackets, and shoes she has picked out. But the price is light—about $200. "It almost seems like a mistake," she says.

It is, and Dillard Department Stores, Inc., is paying for it. Ms. Lemberger is shopping in what some department store executives call a repository of mistakes: the Dillard clearance center in Kansas City, Kansas. One of the oldest kinds of discount stores, it's the ignoble home of merchandise that failed to sell—even at 50 percent off—in Dillard Department Stores. At its half-dozen clearance centers, Dillard unloads some merchandise for less than wholesale. The full retail price of Ms. Lemberger's booty exceeded $1,000.

The existence of these centers shows that department store retailing remains an art—despite predictions that technology would make it a science. Dillard's computer system tracks every purchase and informs company officials which items aren't selling and need promotion and which are selling out and need replenishing. But as yet, computers can't predict consumer tastes.

Not long ago, Dillard bet on an American Film Classics necktie featuring illustrations from *Gone With the Wind;* on a polka-dot sweatshirt for teenage girls; and on a dark-brown all-cotton Liz Claiborne lady's jacket. Today, dozens—even hundreds—of these items fill the Dillard clearance centers.

At Neiman Marcus, whose clearance centers are named Last Call, buyers are required to "visit their mistakes" twice a year. Any buyer whose goods consistently land there won't survive. But buyers whose choices never enter a clearance center may be buying too little or not taking the risks necessary to purchase unique and interesting merchandise.

Source: Kevin Helliker, "Final Final Sale! Stores Unload Buyers' Errors," *The Wall Street Journal,* November 4, 1994, pp. B1, B4.

By subtracting $.5685 \times R$ from both sides of the equation, the resulting initial retail price can be figured as follows:

$$.4315 \times R = \$100$$
$$R = \$231.75$$

ADJUSTMENTS TO THE INITIAL RETAIL PRICE

The initial retail price isn't always the price at which the merchandise is ultimately sold. The four adjustments to the initial retail price are markdowns, markdown cancellations, additional markups, and additional markup cancellations.

Markdowns

Markdowns are reductions in the initial retail price. Let's examine why retailers take markdowns, how to reduce the amount of markdowns, how large a markdown should be, the duration of the markdown period, how to liquidate markdown merchandise, and the mechanics of taking markdowns.

Reasons for Taking Markdowns   Retailers' many reasons to take markdowns can be classified as either clearance (to get rid of merchandise) or promotional (to generate sales).

Many retailers think of markdowns as mistakes. (See Retailing View 15.2.) When merchandise is slow-moving, obsolete, at the end of its selling season, or priced higher than competitors' goods, it generally gets marked down for clearance purposes. This merchandise can become an eyesore and impair a store's image. Further, even if the merchandise can be sold in the following season, it

Retailers use markdowns to get rid of merchandise or to generate sales.

may become shopworn or out of style. Also, cost of carrying inventory is significant.[16] If a buyer has to carry $10,000 of unwanted inventory at cost for a year with an annual inventory carrying cost of 35 percent, the cost would be $3,500 (or $10,000 × .35)—not a trivial amount! Markdowns are part of the cost of doing business. As we've said, retailers plan their markdowns. They set an initial markup high enough so that after markdowns and other reductions are taken, the planned maintained markup is achieved. Thus, a retailer's objective shouldn't necessarily be to minimize markdowns. If markdowns are too low, the retailer is probably pricing the merchandise too low, not purchasing enough merchandise, or not taking enough risks with the merchandise being purchased.

Using a high/low pricing strategy described earlier in this chapter, retailers employ markdowns to promote merchandise to increase sales. A buyer may decide to mark down some merchandise to make room for something new. An additional benefit is that the markdown sale generates cash flow to pay for new merchandise. Markdowns are also taken to increase customers' traffic flow. Retailers plan promotions in which they take markdowns for holidays, for special events, and as part of their overall promotional program. (Chapter 16 gives details.) In fact, small portable appliances (such as toasters) are called traffic appliances because they're often sold at reduced prices to generate in-store traffic. Retailers hope that customers will purchase other products at regular prices while they're in the store. Another opportunity created by markdowns is to increase the sale of complementary products. For example, a supermarket's markdown on hot dog buns may be offset by increased demand for hot dogs, mustard, and relish—all sold at regular prices.

Reducing the Amount of Markdowns   Although retailers should expect and plan for a certain amount of markdowns, it's crucial not to have more than an optimal amount. The most important means to reduce potential markdowns is to have a good merchandise budget plan (detailed in Chapter 13). A good plan will ensure that the *right* amount of merchandise is on hand when the customer wants it. A number of other issues also affect the amount of markdowns.

Retailers should make sure that merchandise selections are coordinated. For example, a buyer for a traditional men's clothier wouldn't purchase avant-garde Italian neckwear to go with traditional button-down shirts.

Another means to reduce markdowns is to obtain timely deliveries. Although not often possible, the best plan is to purchase a small amount of a new product as a test. If it gets a favorable response, the retailer buys again. At the very least, retailers should try to avoid deliveries too early in the season. The fashion "season" seems to be pushed back further every year. It's not uncommon now to see newly arrived heavy winter coats for sale in July. By the time customers are ready to purchase, the merchandise may look shopworn. On the other hand, when merchandise arrives too late, retailers may have trouble selling the entire stock without taking markdowns. Quick response (QR) inventory systems (Chapter 11) are becoming increasingly popular with retailers. By reducing lead time for receiving merchandise, retailers can more closely monitor changes in trends and customer demand, thus reducing markdowns.

Retailers must work with their vendors. Vendors have a vested interest in retailers' success. Vendors who are knowledgeable of the market and competition can help with stock selections. Of course, a retailer must also trust its own taste and intuition; otherwise, its store will have the same merchandise as all other stores. Retail buyers can often obtain **markdown money**—funds a vendor gives the retailer to cover lost gross margin dollars that result from markdowns and other merchandising issues. For instance, assume a retailer has $1,000 worth of ties at retail that are given a 25 percent markdown. Thus, when the ties are sold, the retailer receives only $750. But if the vendor provides $250 in markdown money, the maintained markup remains. In this way, the vendor helps share the risk. Wal-Mart has informed some of its vendors that any markdown will be paid for by the vendors.[17] According to the Robinson-Patman Act, markdown money should be provided to all retailers on a proportionally equal basis—typically as a percentage of purchases. (Markdown money falls under the umbrella of price discrimination discussed later in this chapter.)

When to Take Markdowns Retailers must keep good records. This means keeping track of (1) types of merchandise that required markdowns in the past and (2) what's not selling in the current season. If, for example, certain sizes required significant markdowns in the past, the retailer would cut purchases in those sizes for the current season. Part of keeping good records is doing sell-through analyses. Recall from Chapter 13 that **sell-through analysis** is a comparison between actual and planned sales to determine whether early markdowns are required or whether more merchandise is needed to satisfy demand.

Size of the Markdown and Duration of the Markdown Period Many retailers take some markdowns early in the season, when demand is still fairly active. By taking markdowns early, price reductions don't have to be as deep as those for markdowns taken late in the selling season. As noted above, early markdowns free up selling space for new merchandise and improve the retailer's cash flow position. And customer traffic rises due to marked-down merchandise.

Storewide clearance sales (late-markdown policy) are usually conducted twice a year, after the peak selling seasons of Christmas and the Fourth of July, although recently these sales have started earlier in the season. A late-markdown policy is commonly used by upscale department and specialty stores, though most retailers with seasonal merchandise also find this policy useful. One advantage is that a longer period is available to sell merchandise at regular prices. But it's likely that retailers using a late-markdown policy will need to offer larger markdowns, 40 to 50 percent, to make sure the merchandise is sold. Also, as we discussed earlier in this chapter, frequent markdowns that are inherent in a high/low pricing strategy can destroy customer confidence in a store's regular pricing policy. Finally, clearance sales limit bargain hunting to twice a year.

A combination of early and late markdown strategies has become popular in recent years. In fact, many large fashion retailers follow a strict markdown policy, such as 20 percent off after six weeks, followed by an additional 30 percent three weeks later, and so on until the merchandise is gone. Research shows that this approach is relatively more profitable than having fewer but more severe markdowns.[18] This may be because customers believe they must rush to buy before the sale ends and before the retailer runs out of merchandise. When coupled with promotion, the relatively short markdown periods, each with consecutively higher markdowns, help keep customers interested and stimulate repeat visits to the store. Also, customers who weren't induced to buy during the first wave of markdowns may subsequently buy. The increasing price reductions help alleviate the negative attitude toward leftover merchandise. The combination strategy's disadvantage is that a retailer may be selling merchandise at a loss after the first or second markdown.

The size of the markdown required to sell the merchandise is hard to determine. Highly perishable merchandise, like fresh meat and produce as well as fashion, typically requires more substantial markdowns than staple merchandise. A markdown's absolute dollar amount may be different for different products.[19] For instance, a 10 percent reduction on a $10,000 car would probably be viewed as a greater incentive than a 10 percent reduction on a $1 ice cream cone.

Liquidating Markdown Merchandise   No matter what markdown strategy a retailer uses, some merchandise may still remain unsold. Retailers can use one of three strategies to liquidate this merchandise:

1. They can "job-out" the remaining merchandise to another retailer.
2. They can consolidate the marked-down merchandise.
3. They can carry the merchandise over to the next season.

Selling the remaining marked-down merchandise to another retailer has been very popular among retailers. For instance, Boston-based department store Filene's, T. J. Maxx, and Marshalls have traditionally purchased end-of-season merchandise from other retailers and sold it at deep discounts. (See Chapter 2 for details.) This strategy enables the retailer to have a relatively short markdown period, provides space for new merchandise, and at the same time eliminates the often unappealing sale atmosphere. The problem with this strategy is that the retailer can only recoup a small percentage of the merchandise's cost—often a mere 10 percent.

Marked-down merchandise can be consolidated in a number of ways. First, the consolidation can be made into one or a few of the retailer's regular locations. Second, marked-down merchandise can be consolidated into another retail chain or an outlet store under the same ownership. Saks Fifth Avenue and Neiman Marcus use this strategy. Finally, marked-down merchandise can be shipped to a distribution center for final sale. Retailers that use these strategies condition customers to anticipate out-of-stock situations at locations that don't participate in the consolidation sales, since the merchandise is only at those locations for a relatively short time. This practice encourages a successful yet relatively short markdown period. Further, customers who shop during the consolidation sale enjoy a better selection than they'd find in the individual stores. But consolidation sales can be complex and expensive due to the extra transportation and record-keeping involved.

The final liquidation strategy—to carry merchandise over to the next season—is used with relatively high-priced nonfashion merchandise, such as traditional men's clothing and furniture. Generally, however, it's not worth carrying over merchandise due to excessive inventory carrying costs.

EXHIBIT 15–2

Retail Adjustments to
Merchandise Cost

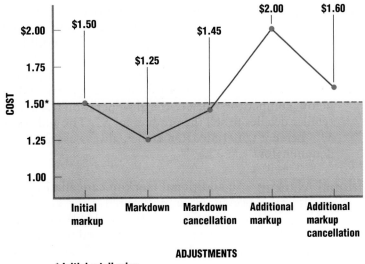

ADJUSTMENTS

* Initial retail price

Mechanics of Taking Markdowns   Using Exhibit 15–2 as a point of reference,
assume that a product costs $1, initial markup is 33.3 percent of retail price, and
initial retail price *(R)* is $1.50.

Retail = Cost + Markup
Retail = $1 + (33.3% × Retail)
$R = \$1.00 + .333 \times R$

Subtracting $.333 \times R$ from both sides of the equation, we get

$.667 \times R = \$1.00$
$R = \$1.50$

For a three-day weekend sale, the retailer decides to mark down the product
from $1.50 to $1.25. The markdown of 25 cents represents 16.7 percent (.25 ÷ 1.50).
Note: To determine the markdown percentage, always use the previous selling
price as the denominator.

Markdown Cancellations   A **markdown cancellation** is the amount by which the retail price
is raised after a markdown is taken. A markdown cancellation is
used only for promotional markdowns, since there's no reason to raise the price of
merchandise that the retailer is trying to liquidate. On Monday, the retailer
records a markdown cancellation by raising the price of the previously marked-
down product from $1.25 to $1.45. The markdown cancellation is 20 cents, or
16 percent (.20 ÷ 1.25).

We must keep markdown cancellations and markups separate, since many
retailers use the retail inventory method described in Chapter 13's Appendix A.
Using this method, retailers must track all price changes carefully. Conservative
accounting practices dictate that the value of inventory should be either at cost or
the market value, whichever is lower. By keeping track of changes in initial retail
price in this way, the inventory's value is allowed to fall in the case of a markdown
but can't rise with a markup. Finally, note that in Exhibit 15–2, a markdown cancellation is in effect only up to the initial retail price of $1.50. Raising the price
above the initial retail price is called an additional markup.

Additional Markups

An **additional markup** is an increase in the retail price after the initial markup percentage has been applied but before the merchandise is placed on the selling floor. Using Exhibit 15–2's example, a certain product's initial retail price is $1.50. But suppose the retailer got a particularly good buy, and the competition is selling the same product for $2. The retailer decides that the product is price-inelastic. That is, if the retailer lowers the price below competitors' price, the product won't sell appreciably more. So the retailer decides to sell the product for $2. The additional markup is 50 cents, or 33.3 percent (.50/1.50). Remember, always use the previous selling price as the denominator.

Additional Markup Cancellations

An **additional markup cancellation** is the amount by which the retail price is lowered after an additional markup is taken. Continuing with Exhibit 15–2's example, suppose the competition lowers its price on the product to $1.60, and the retailer decides to match it. The additional markup cancellation is 40 cents ($2.00 – $1.60) or 20 percent (.40/2.00). The rationale for an additional markup cancellation is the same as for a markdown cancellation. Any decrease in retail price beyond the initial retail price of $1.50 is considered to be a markdown.

Profit Impact of Adjustments to the Retail Price: The Use of Break-Even Analysis

Now that we've examined the mechanics of setting an initial retail price and making adjustments to that price, we must understand the profit impact of our actions. A useful analytical tool here is **break-even analysis,** which analyzes the relationship between total revenue and total cost to determine profitability at various sales levels. Break-even analysis has many applications in retailing. Let's look at two that directly relate to pricing: the break-even volume of a new private-label product and the break-even sales change needed to cover a price change.

Calculating Break-Even for a New Product   Assume that a large retailer like The Gap is interested in developing a new private-label product—a ribbed sleeveless T-shirt for women. Cost of developing this shirt is about $300,000, including executives' and designers' salaries, rent on the design team's buildings, and warehousing. Since these costs are stable and don't change with the quantity of product that's produced and sold, they're known as **fixed costs.** Management plans to sell the T-shirt for $12—the unit price. Cost of the shirt is $5. In economic terms, this is known as the **variable cost**—the sum of the firm's expenses that vary directly with the quantity of product produced and sold. Variable costs often include direct labor and materials used in producing the product. But in this case, The Gap is purchasing the shirt from a third party. Thus, the only variable cost is the shirt's cost. The break-even point (BEP) is the quantity at which total revenue equals total cost, and beyond which profit occurs.

$$\text{BEP}_{quantity} = \frac{\text{Fixed cost}}{\text{Unit price} - \text{Unit variable cost}}$$

In this example,

$$\text{BEP}_{quantity} = \frac{\$300,000}{\$12 - \$5} = 42,857 \text{ units}$$

This means The Gap must sell 42,857 T-shirts to break even. To make things interesting, let's assume The Gap wishes to make a $100,000 profit. The break-even quantity now becomes

$$BEP_{quantity} = \frac{\$300,000 + \$100,000}{\$12 - \$5} = 57,142 \text{ units}$$

If it decides to reduce the selling price to $10, the break-even quantity is

$$BEP_{quantity} = \frac{\$300,000 + \$100,000}{\$10 - \$5} = 80,000 \text{ units}$$

To convert the break-even quantity to break-even sales dollars, simply multiply the $BEP_{quantity}$ by the selling price: 80,000 units × $10 = $800,000.

Calculating Break-Even Sales   A closely related issue to the calculation of a break-even point is determining how much sales would have to increase to profit from a price cut, or how much sales would have to decline to make a price increase unprofitable.[21] Continuing with The Gap example, assume our break-even quantity is 57,142 units (based on the $300,000 fixed cost, the $100,000 profit, a selling price of $12, and a cost of $5). We want to know how many units we must sell to break even if we lower our selling price by 16.6 percent to $10. Using the formula

$$\% \text{ break-even sales change} = \frac{-\% \text{ price change}}{\%CM + \% \text{ price change}} \times 100$$

%CM stands for percent contribution margin. **Contribution margin** is gross margin less any expense that can be directly assigned to the merchandise. In this example, since there are no variable costs besides the cost of the shirt, the contribution margin is the same as the gross margin. Also, don't forget the minus sign in the formula's numerator.

CM   = Selling price – Variable costs
CM   = $12 – $5 = $7
%CM = (CM ÷ Selling price) × 100
%CM = ($7 ÷ $12) × 100 = 58.33%

Substituting the %CM into the formula, we can calculate the break-even sales change:

$$\% \text{ break-even sales change} = \frac{-(-16.6)}{58.33 + (-16.6)} \times 100 = 39.78\%$$

Unit break-even sales change = 39.78% × 57,142 units = 22,731 units

Thus, if The Gap reduces its price to $10, it must sell an additional 22,731 units to break even. It should come as no surprise that when we add the break-even quantity at $12 to the break-even sales change to $10, we get 79,873 units (57,142 + 22,731)—almost the same break-even of 80,000 units that we obtained using the first formula. (The difference is due to rounding.) The same formula can be used to determine the sales change necessary to break even with a price increase.

As you'll see in the next section, the concepts of costs and revenues you've become familiar with in studying break-even analysis are useful when determining the initial retail price under demand-oriented pricing.

THE DEMAND-ORIENTED METHOD OF SETTING THE RETAIL PRICE

Demand-oriented pricing should be used in conjunction with the cost-oriented method to determine retail prices. Using this method, retailers not only consider their profit structure but also pay close attention to price changes' impact on sales. For instance, if customers are extremely sensitive to price, then a price cut increases demand so much that profits actually increase. Alternatively, if customers are insensitive to price, raising the price also boosts profits, since sales don't decrease. Demand-oriented pricing seeks to determine the price that maximizes profits.

This section examines (1) factors that affect customers' sensitivity to price and (2) how to establish the initial retail price using the demand-oriented method.

Factors That Affect Customers' Sensitivity to Price

When retailers determine how to set initial retail prices, they must consider how sensitive customers are to price.[22] In general, retailers set relatively higher prices on products for which customers are less price-sensitive. Let's look at the factors that determine customers' price-sensitivity.

Substitute Awareness Effect   The substitute awareness effect occurs when customers become more sensitive to price because there are a lot of substitutes for a product or for a retailer. Some markets are overstored—an area that has so many stores selling a specific good or service that some stores will fail. For instance, within a three-mile radius in Dallas, there are three regional shopping centers sporting Foley's, Sears, JCPenney, Neiman Marcus, Lord & Taylor, Saks Fifth Avenue, Macy's, Marshall Field's, and others. In other words, there are many alternatives for fashion. In these overstored markets, price competition is keen, since the retailers are vying for the same fashion customers.

Total Expenditure Effect   Customers are more price-sensitive when the expenditure is large, both in dollars and as a percentage of income. Home-improvement centers like Home Depot thus attempt to be very price-competitive on expensive products like major appliances. But for small purchases such as bulk nuts and bolts, customers will tolerate higher prices.

Difficult Comparison Effect   Customers are more sensitive to price when it's easy to compare competing offerings. A problem facing many retailers—notably fashion retailers, particularly department stores—is finding unique product offerings. Some manufacturer brands, like Levi's, are so strong that customers demand that they be stocked. As a result, customers can purchase Levis almost anywhere. Customers can easily compare similar products, making it hard for any one retailer to command higher prices.

To combat this problem and make product comparison more difficult, some retailers have developed their own private-label merchandise. **Private label** means that the brand name or logo identifying the product is owned by the retailer rather than the manufacturer. Chapter 14 discusses private labels.

Benefits/Price Effect   The benefits/price effect defines the relationship between people's perception of the benefits they receive from a product and its price.[23] For some "image" or "exclusive" products, customers are less sensitive to price—they feel they receive higher benefits from the product because it's more expensive. For example, a Chanel original evening gown may be priced 10 times higher than a department store's gown of equal quality. The customer who purchases the Chanel gown values the recognition or ego gratification that comes from buying an original—and isn't sensitive to price.

Most research indicates people use price as a cue for determining value only when little other information is available. For instance, people generally have a difficult time evaluating the quality of diamonds. Due to their relatively high price and people's lack of information and knowledge about them, customers perceive diamonds to be a risky purchase. They therefore equate high price with high quality. Zale jewelry stores found this human characteristic to be so strong that it developed an entire ad campaign around the concept. The campaign's theme was that customers should go to a jeweler they can trust because it's so hard to evaluate diamonds' quality. Of course, the trustworthy jewelry store is Zale!

Products can also be priced so low that consumers perceive a lack of quality. For instance, Pathmark's Premium All-Purpose Cleaner was packed like Fantastik, a top-seller in the category. Its chemical composition was the same as well. Best of all, Premium cost shoppers only 89 cents, compared with $1.79 for Fantastik. Unfortunately the product failed, probably because customers believed its low price meant it couldn't be high quality.[24]

Situation Effect   Driving down a country road, we spot an old store all by itself. Approaching the store, we see a sign—FINE ANTIQUES FOR SALE. Driving past the store, on the other side we see another sign—WE BUY JUNK. This story illustrates the situation effect—consumers' sensitivity to price can be different depending on the situation. Why are movie patrons willing to pay $2.50 for popcorn that would cost about five cents if they made it themselves at home? Eating popcorn is part of the overall movie-going experience. Also, people expect to pay a premium for merchandise purchased under certain situations.[25] Many restaurants also take advantage of the situation effect. Their lunches cost less than their dinners because people expect to pay less for lunch. Upscale fashion retailers also take advantage of the situation effect. Customers expect to pay more in a plush atmosphere with attentive service. Alternatively, many off-price and warehouse stores maintain a sparse, utilitarian environment to create the "low-price" atmosphere customers expect when looking for bargains. Thus, understanding how to manipulate situations to impact customers' perception of price can influence overall corporate strategy and profitability.

Determining the Initial Retail Price under Demand-Oriented Pricing

To illustrate how an initial retail price is set using the demand-oriented method, we continue the hypothetical situation of The Gap's new ribbed sleeveless T-shirt for women. Recall that fixed cost of developing the product was $300,000 and variable cost was $5 each. One benefit of private-label merchandise is the flexibility of being able to set any retail price. The Gap decides to test the T-shirt in four markets at different prices. Exhibit 15–3 shows the pricing test's results. It's clear (from column 5) that a unit price of $10 is by far the most profitable ($450,000). Unfortunately, determining the most profitable retail price isn't as simple as this

EXHIBIT 15-3

Results of
Pricing Test

MARKET	(1) UNIT PRICE	(2) MARKET DEMAND AT PRICE (IN UNITS)	(3) TOTAL REVENUE (COL. I X COL. 2)	(4) TOTAL COST OF UNITS SOLD ($300,000 FIXED COST + $5 VARIABLE COST)	(5) TOTAL PROFITS (COL. 3 – COL. 4)
1	$8	200,000	$1,600,000	$1,300,000	$300,000
2	10	150,000	1,500,000	1,050,000	450,000
3	12	100,000	1,200,000	800,000	400,000
4	14	50,000	700,000	550,000	150,000

example suggests. The primary difficulty is that most retailers carry so many products that these tests become a very expensive proposition. Also, a retailer must have multiple outlets to be able to manipulate prices in this manner. Obtaining data for demand-oriented pricing can be done through experiments and consumer panel data.[26]

Experiments   In a pricing experiment, a retailer actually changes the price in a systematic manner to observe changes in purchases or purchase intentions. Of all the methods of discovering customers' sensitivities to price, experiments are generally the most accurate and useful, but in the past, they've also been the most costly and time-consuming.

Exhibit 15–4 shows an example of a simple experiment—a classic before/after experiment with control group design. Two stores are similar in size and customer characteristics. Their weekly sales for a compact microwave oven are almost identical (10 and 12 units per week), and the ovens are selling at the same price, $100. Price at the first store is changed to $80, but the second store's price is left at $100. Thus, the second store is used as a control to make sure that any change in sales is due to the price change rather than to some outside force such as competition or weather. Now sales at the first store jump to 21 units per week, while sales at the control store hit 13 units. Barring any circumstances unknown to the retailer, the change in sales is due to the price cut. And, by the way, the $100 price is more profitable than the $80 price in the second store! Since product cost is $50, the $100 retail price provides a $650 gross margin [($100 – $50) × 13 units], whereas the $80 price provides a $630 gross margin [($80 – $50) × 21 units].

In the past, these pricing experiments weren't regularly applied due to the time and expense of administering them. But now any retailer with point-of-sale (POS) terminals can run large-scale experiments. These combination cash registers/computers capture sales and price information instantaneously so data for experiments are readily at hand. Retailers and their vendors can also buy from private firms like InfoScan.[27] InfoScan purchases information from individual supermarkets on price and promotion activity that has been scanned through their POS terminals; it then aggregates data by region, chain, or market area.

EXHIBIT 15-4

A Pricing
Experiment

	BEFORE	AFTER
Store 1	10 units @ $100 Gross margin = $500	21 units @ $80 Gross margin = $630
Store 2 (control)	12 units @ $100 Gross margin = $600	13 units @ $100 Gross margin = $650

Consumer Panel Data   A more traditional approach for collecting data on customers' sensitivities to price changes is through consumer panel data. Here a number of marketing research companies collect individual purchase data from panels of a few thousand households. The data can then be purchased by retailers and their vendors. These records cover what customers have purchased, prices paid, and conditions of sale (such as coupon usage and price specials). Various demographic information on the customer makes it possible to correlate price sensitivity with customer profiles.

Retail POS technology has eliminated the requirement that panel members record their purchases on a questionnaire and return them weekly. Instead, purchases are recorded automatically by in-store scanners whenever panel members identify themselves at the checkout counter. This technology has made panel membership easier so a more representative sample of households is possible.

Now that we have looked at methods of setting retail prices, let's examine the legal ramifications of our decisions.

LEGAL ISSUES IN RETAIL PRICING

The legal environment surrounding retail pricing is complex. Let's examine legal issues surrounding the buying of merchandise (price discrimination and vertical price-fixing) and legal issues affecting the customer (horizontal price fixing, predatory pricing, comparative price advertising, and bait and switch tactics).

Price Discrimination

Price discrimination occurs when a vendor sells the same product to two or more retailers at different prices. Although price discrimination is generally illegal, there are three situations where it's acceptable.

First, different retailers can be charged different prices as a result of differences in the cost of manufacture, sale, or delivery resulting from the differing methods or quantities in which such commodities are sold or delivered. Under what conditions may these differences exist?

It's often less expensive per unit to manufacture, sell, or deliver large quantities than small quantities. Manufacturers can achieve economies of scale through the longer production runs achieved with large quantities. Cost of selling to a customer also decreases as the quantity of goods ordered increases because it costs almost the same for a salesperson to write a small order as a large order. Finally, delivery or transportation expenses decrease on a per unit basis as quantities of goods ordered increase. These exceptions give rise to **quantity discounts,** the practice of granting lower prices to retailers who buy in higher quantities. (See Chapter 14.)

The differences in methods of sale that allow for differing prices refer specifically to the practice of granting **functional discounts** (also known as **trade discounts**). Functional discounts are different prices, or percentages off suggested retail prices, granted to customers in different lines of trade (e.g., wholesalers and retailers). Wholesalers often receive a lower price than retailers for the same quantity purchased. This is legal, for wholesalers perform more functions in the distribution process than do retailers. For instance, wholesalers store and transport merchandise, and they use salespeople for writing orders and taking care of problems in the stores. Essentially, manufacturers "pay" wholesalers for servicing retailers by giving the wholesalers a lower price.

With the growth of large chain retailers like The May Department Stores Company and Wal-Mart, functional discounts become more difficult to justify. Wal-Mart performs virtually all the functions an independent wholesaler provides.

Therefore, Wal-Mart demands and should receive the same low prices as wholesalers. These lower prices make it hard for smaller retailers to compete.

The second exception to the no–price-discrimination rule is when the price differential is in response to changing conditions affecting the market for or the marketability of the goods concerned. The third exception is when the differing price is made in good faith to meet a competitor's equally low price. Suppose, for example, that Borden ice cream is experiencing severe price competition with a locally produced ice cream in Wisconsin. Borden is allowed to lower its price in this market below its price in other markets to meet the low price of local competition. In this case, market conditions have changed and Borden has reacted by meeting the competition's price.

Large retailers often benefit from subtle forms of price discrimination. For instance, book publishers have been accused of charging independent booksellers more than chain operators even though their individual orders are the same size. Many manufacturers take back merchandise that isn't selling at large retailers without penalty or give the retailers markdown money to help them defray the markdown cost—a perk not available to smaller stores.

Unless a particular situation comes within one of the exceptions just discussed, retailers should never ask a vendor for or accept a net price (after all discounts, allowances, returns, and promotional allowances) that they know—or experience tells them—won't be offered to their competitors on a proportional basis for similar merchandise to be purchased at about the same time.

Vertical Price-Fixing

In a letter to retailers, Specialized, a bicycle manufacturer, stated that it "will discontinue sales of all its goods to any dealer whom it learns has engaged in the sale of Specialized products below suggested retail prices."[28] This practice, known as **vertical price-fixing,** involves agreements to fix prices between parties at different levels of the same marketing channel (e.g., retailers and vendors). **Resale price maintenance laws (fair trade laws)** were enacted in the early 1900s to curb vertical price-fixing, and have had a mixed history ever since.

Initially, resale price maintenance laws were primarily designed to help protect small retailers. Congress believed that these small, often family-owned, stores couldn't compete with large chain stores like Sears or Woolworth, which could buy in larger quantities and sell at discount prices. By requiring retailers to maintain manufacturers' suggested retail prices, however, prices to the consumer may have been higher than they would have been in a freely competitive environment. Due to strong consumer activism, the **Consumer Goods Pricing Act (1975)** repealed all resale price maintenance laws and enabled retailers to sell products below suggested retail prices. Congress's attitude was to protect customers' right to buy at the lowest possible free market price—even though some small retailers wouldn't be able to compete. For instance, in a 1996 decision, the Federal Trade Commission (FTC) ordered New Balance Athletic Shoe Co. to stop "fixing, controlling or maintaining prices at which retailers advertise" the company's products and refrain from "coercing any retailer to maintain or adopt any resale price."[29]

Horizontal Price-Fixing

Horizontal price-fixing involves agreements between retailers that are in direct competition with each other to have the same prices. Consider the hypothetical case of two large discount stores, Mel's and KD's, that conspire to fix retail paint prices at an extremely low level. Big G, a small chain of three paint stores, can't compete with their low prices. Mel's and KD's can sell the paint as a loss leader. But Big G sells only paint. If the price fixing continues, Big G may have to close. With Big G out of the market, Mel's and KD's could raise their paint prices. Clearly, such behavior by Mel's and KD's is anticompetitive. Horizontal price fixing is always illegal since it suppresses competition while often raising the cost to the consumer.

As a general rule of thumb, retailers should refrain from discussing prices or terms or conditions of sale with competitors. **Terms** or **conditions of sale** may include charges for alterations, delivery, or gift wrapping, or the store's exchange policies. If a buyer or store manager needs to know a competitor's price on a particular item, it's permissible to "shop" at the competitor's store by going personally or sending an assistant to the store to examine the product. But the buyer or manager shouldn't call the competitor to get the information. Further, retailers shouldn't respond to any competitor's request to verify those prices. The only exception to the general rule is when a geographically oriented merchants association, such as a downtown area or a shopping center, is planning a special coordinated event. In this situation, the retailer may announce that merchandise will be specially priced during the event, but the specific merchandise and prices shouldn't be identified.

Predatory Pricing

Establishing merchandise prices to drive competition from the marketplace is called **predatory pricing.** It's illegal. A retailer can, however, sell the same merchandise at different geographic locations for different prices if its costs of sale or delivery are different. For instance, a national specialty store chain like The Limited may charge more for a dress in California than in Ohio, since the cost of shipping the dress from its distribution center in Columbus, Ohio, to California is higher than the cost of shipping it to a store in Ohio. A competing retailer in Ohio may not be able to meet The Limited's lower price on this dress. But because the lower price is due to The Limited's lower distribution cost rather than an attempt to drive the competitor out of business, the tactic is allowable.

It's also illegal to sell merchandise at unreasonably low prices. However, a retailer generally may sell merchandise at any price so long as the motive isn't to destroy competition. Retailing View 15.3 examines Wal-Mart's everyday low pricing strategy.

Comparative Price Advertising

A department store in Denver was selling two cutlery sets on "sale"—reduced from "original" or "regular" prices of $40 and $50. The true regular prices were $19.99 and $29.99. They sold few at the "original" price for two years. This common retailing practice, known as **comparative price advertising,** compares the price of merchandise offered for sale with a higher "regular" price or a manufacturer's list price. Consumers use the higher price, known as the **reference price,** as a benchmark for what they believe the "real" price of the merchandise should be.

This practice may be a good strategy, since it gives customers a price comparison point and makes the merchandise appear to be a good deal. Retailers, like the one in Denver, may use comparative price advertising to deceive the consumer, however. To avoid problems with the Federal Trade Commission and state governments that have been actively prosecuting violators, retailers should follow these guidelines:

REFACT In 1911, John Wanamaker's initial department store in Philadelphia was the first big store to offer a one-price, no-haggle policy with a money-back guarantee.[30]

15.3

Wal-Mart's Predatory Pricing Practices under Attack

INDEPENDENT RETAILERS in small towns across the country have long accused Wal-Mart of selling goods below cost to drive them out of business, and then boosting prices after seizing control of the local market. The sheer size of the company—the world's largest retailer—gives it leverage to demand goods at the lowest possible cost from suppliers. Facing increased competition from other large retailers as it moves into urban areas, Wal-Mart acted aggressively to be the leader in using an everyday low price strategy.

Some smaller retailers, however, have accused Wal-Mart of predatory pricing by selling items—including Crest and over-the-counter drugs—below cost. Wal-Mart maintains that it hasn't violated the law because it didn't intend to hurt competitors. But it admits it has sold some products below cost, as do other retailers. The chain claims its intent was only to provide the best everyday low price to customers. Wal-Mart's everyday low price strategy bases prices on local competition—more competition leads to lower prices; less competition leads to higher prices.

Wal-Mart's so-called predatory pricing strategy has been tested in the courts. After an earlier conviction in a lower court, the Arkansas Supreme Court ruled that the chain had no intent to destroy competition through its practice of selling a revolving selection of prescription and nonprescription drugs at less than cost.

Source: Bob Ortega, "Suit over Wal-Mart's Pricing Practices Goes to Trial Today in Arkansas Court," *The Wall Street Journal*, August 23, 1993, p. A3; and Pete Hisey, "Ark. Supreme Court Rules Wal-Mart's No Predator: Lack of Proof Overturns Price Conviction," *Discount Store News*, February 6, 1995, pp. 3, 89.

- Have the reference price in effect at least one-third of the time the merchandise is on sale.
- Disclose how "sale" prices are set and how long they will be offered.
- Offer a "satisfaction guaranteed policy" in which customers can return the merchandise for any reason for a full refund, including those who feel they were deceived. This strategy doesn't stop deception, but acts as a "good faith" effort if the retailer gets caught.
- Be careful when using a manufacturer's suggested list price. Don't use it as the reference price unless it is the "regular" price.
- Use objective terms. "Special," "valued at," and "worth" are too subjective.
- If a retailer advertises that it has the lowest prices in town, or that it will meet or beat any competitor's price, it should have proof that its prices are, in fact, the lowest in town before the ad is placed.
- If a retailer advertises that it will meet or beat any competitor's prices, the retailer must have a company policy that enables it to adjust prices to preserve the accuracy of its advertising claims.[31]

Bait-and-Switch Tactics Bait-and-switch is an unlawful deceptive practice that lures customers into a store by advertising a product at a lower than usual price (the bait) and then induces the customer to switch to a higher-priced model (the switch). Bait-and-switch can occur in two ways. Suppose customer Smith is in the market for a new refrigerator. Smith shops the ads in the newspaper and finds a particularly attractively priced unit. At the store, however, Smith finds that the retailer has significantly underestimated demand for the advertised product and no longer has any available for sale. The person begins pushing a higher-priced model that's heavily stocked.

In the second bait-and-switch method, the retailer has the advertised model in stock but disparages its quality while highlighting the advantages of a higher-priced model. In both cases, the retailer has intentionally misled the customer.

To avoid disappointed customers and problems with the Federal Trade Commission, retailers should have sufficient quantities of advertised items. If they run out of stock on these items, they should offer customers a rain check. Finally, they should caution salespeople not to disparage the lower-priced advertised items with the intent of trading customers up to a higher-priced model.

In summary, retailers, wholesalers, and manufacturers should be aware that whenever they decide to sell the same merchandise for different prices at different locations, or to sell merchandise at extraordinarily low prices to attract customers, they may be susceptible to federal and state prosecution and to lawsuits from competitors. But as a practical matter, the length of time and the expense of acquiring sufficient data and legal assistance to prove injury by a competitor may be so great that the injured party may still lose its business. Retailing View 15.4 examines the common practice of charging a higher price to women than to men.

SUMMARY

There's more to setting retail prices than just taking the manufacturer's suggestions. Everyday low pricing (EDLP), coupons, and rebates are popular alternatives to the frequent use of sales. Leader pricing, price bundling, price lining, and odd pricing are also commonly used strategies for pricing product lines.

After examining the relative merits of the demand- and cost-oriented methods of setting retail prices, we've concluded that a mix of the two methods is best. Since the initial retail price isn't necessarily the price at which the merchandise is finally sold, you must understand how to use the cost-oriented method to adjust the initial retail price and how these adjustments affect profits. Specifically, we examined several issues regarding markdowns (such as reasons for taking markdowns, when to take markdowns, and markdown cancellations), additional markups, additional markup cancellations, and break-even analysis.

As for demand-oriented methods of setting retail prices, several qualitative factors affect customers' sensitivity to prices. Specifically, customers are more sensitive to price when there are many alternative stores from which to choose, when the total expenditure is large, when comparisons between existing brands are easy, and when it's hard to perceive special benefits from the products or retailers. Experiments, consumer panel data, and surveys can help retailers determine initial retail prices using demand-oriented methods. Although all these approaches are useful, they're harder to use than the cost-oriented method, especially for small retailers.

Legal issues that impact pricing decisions come from two sides. Those that affect the buying of merchandise include price discrimination and vertical price fixing. The legal pricing issues that affect the consumer are horizontal price-fixing, predatory pricing, comparative price advertising, and bait-and-switch.

15.4

Why Do Women Pay More?

IT'S WELL KNOWN THAT WOMEN often earn less than men in similar jobs, even when they have similar education and experience. It's also true that they pay more for products and services ranging from haircuts to cars. For the most part, trying to explain gender-differentiated prices is like trying to justify racial discrimination—it just doesn't cut it.

Why do women's haircuts cost more than men's? The "traditional" response is that it takes longer to cut more hair. But two in three haircutters surveyed by the New York City Department of Consumer Affairs charge women 25 percent more than men for a basic shampoo, cut, and blow dry, averaging $20 versus $16 for men. Does it really take 25 percent longer to cut women's hair, regardless of its length, texture, and amount of styling?

For years, dry cleaners have cited the same reasons for pricing women's services higher. It's harder to press a woman's shirt with equipment designed for men's shirts. Clothing merchants usually have different staff altering men's and women's clothing, so it's harder to make true comparisons based on job difficulty. However, the fact remains that many stores still offer most alterations free to men, but not to women.

Unlike alterations, dry cleaning, and haircuts, where the actual service provided to men and women may vary slightly, there is no comparable explanation why women pay more for cars. In some cases, salespeople simply don't offer women the same deals they offer men because they think they can get away with it. But women are less likely than men to bargain on car prices, partly because they're less knowl-

edgeable about the process. Salespeople perceive that women are not comfortable about dickering on prices, and they take advantage of the situation.

There's little reason to believe that salespeople will automatically knock their own prices down just because a customer is unwilling to ask for a deal. There is another solution, however—one-price stickers, used by Saturn and others.

Some states are advocating legislation to alleviate gender-bias pricing. California, Massachusetts, and New York have already passed such laws. But even when laws are in place, they are hard to enforce. The Massachusetts attorney general's office sent surveys to dry cleaners to ascertain prices for men's and women's shirts. The results indicated that women were charged up to $2.50 more per item. Cleaners claimed that they had to do women's shirts by hand or dry-clean them because they didn't fit the presses. The attorney general's office found this not to be the case and sent letters explaining that gender-bias pricing is against the law. A year and a half later, a follow-up survey found that many dry cleaners were conforming.

In many businesses, however, the price women pay is not seriously challenged or addressed. Until women get fed up with paying more, they will continue to be taken to the cleaners.

Source: Gerry Myers, "Why Women Pay More," *American Demographics,* April 1996, pp. 40–41. For more details about gender and pricing, see Frances Cerra Whittelsey, *Why Women Pay More* (Washington, DC: Center for Study of Responsive Law).

KEY TERMS

break-even analysis, *458*

comparative price advertising, *465*

Consumer Goods Pricing Act (1975), *464*

contribution margin, *459*

cost-oriented method, *449*

coupon, *445*

demand-oriented method, *449*

everyday low pricing (EDLP), *441*

fixed cost, *458*

functional discount (trade discount), *463*

high/low pricing strategy, *441*

initial markup, *451*

keystone method, *449*

leader pricing, *446*

maintained markup, *450*

markdown, *453*

markdown cancellation, *457*

markdown money, *455*

multiple-unit pricing, *447*

odd price, *448*

predatory pricing, *465*

price bundling, *446*

price lining, *448*

private label, *460*

quantity discount, *463*

rain check, *442*

rebate, *446*

reduction, *451*

reference price, *465*

resale price maintenance laws (fair trade laws), *464*

backup stock, *442*

sell-through analysis, *455*

terms of sale (conditions of sale), *465*

variable cost, *458*

verticle price-fixing, *464*

DISCUSSION QUESTIONS & PROBLEMS

1. What's the difference between initial markup and maintained markup? Can initial markup and maintained markup ever be the same?

2. Simple examination of markdowns could lead us to believe that they should be taken only when a retailer wants to get rid of merchandise that's not selling. What other reasons could a retailer have to take markdowns?

3. Do you know any retailers who have violated any of the legal issues discussed in this chapter? Explain your answer.

4. Which of the pricing strategies discussed in this chapter are used by your favorite retailer? Do you think they're used effectively? Can you suggest a more effective strategy?

5. A department's maintained markup is 38 percent, reductions are $560, and net sales are $28,000. What's the initial markup percentage?

6. Maintained markup is 39 percent, net sales are $52,000, alterations are $1,700, shrinkage is $500, markdowns are $5,000, employee discounts are $2,000, and cash discounts are 2 percent. What are gross margin in dollars and initial markup as a percentage? Explain why initial markup is greater than maintained markup.

7. Cost of a product is $150, markup is 50 percent, markdown is 30 percent, and markdown cancellation is 10 percent. What's the final selling price?

8. Manny Perez bought a tie for $9 and priced it to sell for $15. What was his markup on the tie?

9. Alex Fox says he gets a markup of 33⅓ percent. What markup on cost does he get?

10. Mary White has one blouse in inventory marked to sell for $50. She wants to take a 25 percent markdown on the blouse. What price should she put on the blouse?

SUGGESTED READINGS

Berry, Leonard L., and Manjit S. Yadav. "Capture and Communicate Value in the Pricing of Services." *Sloan Management Review* 37, no. 4 (June 22, 1996), pp. 41–48.

Compeau, Larry D., Dhruv Grewal, and Diana S. Grewal. "Adjudicating Claims of Deceptive Advertised Reference Prices: The Use of Empirical Evidence." *Journal of Public Policy & Marketing* 14 (Fall 1994), pp. 52–62.

Dickson, Peter R., and Joel E. Urbany. "Retailer Reactions to Competitive Price Changes." Journal of Retailing 70, no. 1 (Spring 1994), pp. 1–22.

Hoch, Stephen J., Xavier Dreze, and Mary E. Purk. "EDLP, Hi–Lo, and Margin Arithmetic." *Journal of Marketing* 58, no. 4 (Fall 1994), pp. 16–28.

Karande, Kiran W., and V. Kumar. "The Effect of Brand Characteristics and Retailer Policies on Response to Retail Price Promotions: Implications for Retailers." *Journal of Retailing* 71, no. 3 (September 22, 1995), pp. 249–63.

Kaufmann, Patrick J., N. Craig Smith, and Gwendolyn K. Ortmeyer. "Deception in Retailer High–Low Pricing: A 'Rule of Reason' Approach." *Journal of Retailing* 70, no. 2 (June 22, 1994), pp. 115–29.

Krishnan, Trichy V., and Ram C. Rao. "Double Couponing and Retail Pricing in a Couponed Product Category." *Journal of Marketing Research* 32 (November 1995), pp. 419–32.

Mazumdar, Tridib, and Sung Youl Jun. "Consumer Evaluations of Multiple versus Single Price Change." *Journal of Consumer Research* 20, no. 3 (December 1993), pp. 441–53.

Monroe, Kent B. *Pricing: Making Profitable Decisions*, 2d ed. New York: McGraw-Hill, 1990.

Mulhern, Francis J., and Daniel T. Padgett. "The Relationship between Retail Price Promotions and Regular Price Purchases." *Journal of Marketing* 59, no. 4 (Fall 1995), pp. 83–91.

Nagle, Thomas T. *The Strategy and Tactics of Pricing*. Englewood Cliffs, NJ: Prentice-Hall, 1987.

Rajendram, K. N., and Gerard J. Tellis. "Contextual and Temporal Components of Reference Price." *Journal of Marketing* 58, no. 2 (Winter 1994), pp. 22–31.

Smith, Gerald, and Thomas Nagle. "Frames of References and Buyers' Perceptions of Price and Value." *California Management Review* 38, no. 1 (1995), pp. 98–117.

Venkatesh, R., and Vijay Mahajan. "A Probabilistic Approach to Pricing a Bundle of Products or Services." *Journal of Marketing Research* 30 (Fall 1993), pp. 494–505.

Yadav, Manjit S., and Kent B. Monroe. "How Buyers Perceive Savings in a Bundle Price: An Examination of a Bundle's Transaction Value." *Journal of Marketing Research* 30 (Summer 1993), pp. 350–58.

NOTES

1. Alan Sawyer and Peter Dickson, "Everyday Low Prices vs. Sale Price," *Retailing Review* 1, no. 2 (1993), pp. 1–2, 8; and Gwen Ortmeyer, John A. Quelch, and Walter Salmon, "Restoring Credibility to Retail Pricing," *Sloan Management Review* 33, no. 1 (Fall 1991), pp. 55–56.

2. Andrew Shore, Gary Giblen, and Margaret Lenahan, "Household Products and Cosmetics: Everyday Low (or 'Value') Pricing: An Idea Whose Time Has Come," *PaineWebber*, October 13, 1992.

3. Laura Bird, "Apparel Stores Seek to Cure Shoppers Addicted to Discounts," *The Wall Street Journal*, May 29, 1996, pp. A1, A10.

4. Ellis Verdi, "The Great Retailer Advertising Wars," *Chain Store Age*, September 1995, pp. 30–31.

5. Zachary Schiller, "First Green Stamps. Now, Coupons?" *Business Week*, April 22, 1996.

6. This section draws from Kent B. Monroe, *Pricing: Making Profitable Decisions*, 2d ed. (New York: McGraw-Hill, 1990).

7. Schiller, "First Green Stamps. Now, Coupons?" Information provided by coupon processor, NCH Promotional Services in Lincolnshire, IL.

8. William O. Bearden, Donald R. Lichtenstein, and Jesse E. Teel, "Comparison Price, Coupon, and Brand Effects on Consumer Reactions to Retail Newspaper Advertisements," *Journal of Retailing* 60, no. 2 (Summer 1984), pp. 11–34.

9. Kapil Bawa and Robert W. Shoemaker, "The Coupon-Prone Consumer: Some Findings Based on Purchase Behavior across Product Classes," *Journal of Marketing* 51 (October 1987), pp. 99–110; and Jesse E. Teel, Robert H. Williams, and William O. Bearden, "Correlates of Consumer Susceptibility to Coupons in New Grocery Product Introductions," *Journal of Advertising* 9, no. 3 (1980), pp. 31–35.

10. Rockney G. Walters and Heikki J. Rinne, "An Empirical Investigation into the Impact of Price Promotions on Retail Store Performance," *Journal of Retailing* 62, no. 3 (Fall 1986), pp. 237–66.

11. Thomas T. Nagle, *The Strategy and Tactics of Pricing* (Englewood Cliffs, NJ: Prentice-Hall, 1987), p. 185.

12. See Joseph P. Guiltinan, "The Price Bundling of Services: A Normative Framework," *Journal of Marketing* 51 (April 1987), pp. 74–85; Rockney G. Walters, "Assessing the Impact of Retail Price Promotions on Product Substitution, Complementary Purchase, and Interstore Sales Displacement," *Journal of Marketing* 55, no. 2 (1991), pp. 17–28; and Francis J. Mulhern and Robert Leone, "Implicit Price Bundling of Retail Products: A Multiproduct Approach to Maximizing Store Profitability," *Journal of Marketing* 55, no. 4 (October 1991), pp. 63–76.

13. Itamar Simonson, "Shoppers Easily Influenced Choices," *New York Times*, November 6, 1994, based on research by Itamar Simonson and Amos Tversky.

14. Robert Blattberg and Kenneth Wisniewski, "How Retail Price Promotions Work: Empirical Results," Marketing Working Paper no. 42 (Chicago: University of Chicago, December 1987). This study indicated that odd pricing increases sales. The following studies don't support this proposition, however: Robert M. Schindler, and Thomas Kibarian, "Testing Perceptual Underestimation of 9-ending Prices," *Advances in Consumer Research* 11 (Association for Consumer Research, 1993), pp. 580–85; Zarrel V. Lambert, "Perceived Prices as Related to Odd and Even Price Endings," *Journal of Retailing* 51 (Fall 1975), pp. 13–22; Robert M. Schindler and Alan R. Wiman, "Consumer Recall of Odd and Even Prices," Working Paper (Boston: Northeastern University, 1983); Robert Schindler, "Consumer Recognition of Increases in Odd and Even Prices," *Advances in Consumer Research* 11 (Association for Consumer Research, 1983), pp. 459–62; and Eli Ginzberg, "Customary Prices," *American Economic Review* 26 (1936), p. 296.

15. In some rare situations, retail price and initial markup as a percentage of cost are known, and the retailer is seeking to determine the cost. In this case the following formula applies:

$$\frac{\text{Initial markup}}{\text{as \% of retail}} = \frac{\text{Initial markup as a \% of cost}}{100\% + \text{Initial markup as a \% of cost}}$$

16. See James R. Stock and Douglas M. Lambert, *Strategic Logistics Management*, 2d ed. (Burr Ridge, IL: Richard D. Irwin, 1987), chapter 9, for a method of calculating inventory carrying costs.

17. "Wal-Mart's New Policy Makes Suppliers Pay," *Discount Store News*, May 20, 1996, p. 1.

18. Michael Levy and Daniel J. Howard, "An Experimental Approach to Planning the Duration and Size of Markdowns," *International Journal of Retailing* 3, no. 2 (1988), pp. 48–58.

19. Peter Cooper, "Subjective Economics: Factors in Psychology of Spending," and "The Begrudging Index and the Subjective Value of Money," in *Pricing Strategy*, Bernard Taylor and Gordon Wills, eds. (Princeton, NJ: Brandon/Systems, 1970), pp. 112–31; and Steward Henderson Britt, "How Weber's Law Can Be Applied to Marketing," *Business Horizons*, February 1975, pp. 21–29.

20. "The Great 'Sale'-ing Season," *Chain Store Age Executive*, February 1992, p. 17.

21. This section is based on Nagle, *The Strategy and Tactics of Pricing*, pp. 30–31.

22. This section draws from Nagle, *The Strategy and Tactics of Pricing*.

23. Kent B. Monroe, *Pricing: Making Profitable Decisions*, 2d ed. (New York: McGraw-Hill, 1990); Kent B. Monroe and William B. Dodds, "A Research Program for Establishing the Validity of the Price–Quality Relationship," *Journal of the Academy of Marketing Science* 16 (Spring 1990), pp. 151–68; Akshay R. Rao and Kent B. Monroe, "The Effect of Price, Brand Name, and Store Name on Buyers' Perceptions of Product Quality: An Integrative Review," *Journal of Marketing Research* 26 (August 1990), pp. 351–57; Valarie A. Zeithaml, "Consumer Perceptions of Price, Quality, and Value: A Means–End Model and Synthesis of Evidence," *Journal of Marketing* 52 (July 1988), pp. 2–22; and Gerald J. Tellis, "Consumer Purchasing Strategies and the Information in Retail Prices," *Journal of Retailing* 63, no. 3 (Fall 1987), pp. 279–97.

24. Alix M. Freedman, "A Price That's Too Good May Be Bad," *The Wall Street Journal*, November 15, 1988, p. 1B.

25. Richard Thaler, "Mental Accounting and Consumer Choice," *Marketing Science* 4 (Summer 1985), pp. 199–214.

26. This section draws from Nagle, *The Strategy and Tactics of Pricing*, chapter 11.

27. InfoScan is available through Information Resources Inc., 150 N. Clinton St., Chicago, IL 60661, telephone (312) 726-1221.

28. Paul M. Barrett, "Anti-Discount Policies of Manufacturers Are Penalizing Certain Cut-Price Stores," *The Wall Street Journal*, February 27, 1991.

29. Ken Rankin, "Let's Hear Some Balance in Price-Fixing Cases," *Discount Store News*, October 7, 1996, p. 14.

30. "Rating the Stores," *Consumer Reports*, November 1994, p. 714.

31. Larry D. Compeau, Dhruv Grewal, and Diana S. Grewal, "Adjudicating Claims of Deceptive Advertised Reference Prices: The Use of Empirical Evidence," *Journal of Public Policy & Marketing* 14 (Fall, 1994); Dhruv Grewal, Diana S. Grewal, and Larry D. Compeau, "States' Crackdown on Deceptive Price Advertising: Retail and Public Policy Implications," *Pricing Strategy & Practice: An International Journal* 1, no. 2 (1993), pp. 33–40; Dhruv Grewal and Larry D. Compeau, "Comparative Price Advertising: Informative or Deceptive?" *Journal of Public Policy and Marketing* 11 (Spring 1992), pp. 52–62; Robert N. Corley and O. Lee Reed, *The Legal Environment*, 7th ed. (New York: McGraw-Hill, 1987); Teri Agins, "Low Prices or Low Practice? Regulators Cast Wary Eye on Retailers' Many Sales," *The Wall Street Journal*, February 13, 1990, pp. B1, B7; and *Do's and Don'ts in Advertising Copy* (Council of Better Business Bureaus, 1987).

16

Retail
Promotion Mix

THE WORLD OF RETAILING

↓

RETAILING STRATEGY

↓

MERCHANDISE MANAGEMENT
12. Planning Merchandise
    Assortments
13. Buying Systems
14. Buying Merchandise
15. Pricing
16. Retail Promotion Mix

STORE MANAGEMENT
17. Managing the Store
18. Store Layout, Design, and
    Visual Merchandising
19. Customer Service
20. Retail Selling

QUESTIONS

- What are the strengths and weaknesses of the different methods for communicating with customers?

- Why do retailers need to have an integrated marketing communication program?

- What steps are involved in developing a promotion program?

- How do retailers establish a promotion budget?

- How can you use the different elements in a promotion mix to alter customers' decision-making processes?

- What factors should retailers consider when designing advertising, sales promotion, and publicity programs?

THE PRECEDING CHAPTERS DESCRIBED how retailers develop a merchandise budget plan and then buy and price an assortment of merchandise. The next step in the retail management decision-making process is developing and implementing a promotion program to attract customers to stores and encourage them to buy merchandise. The promotion program informs customers about the store as well as the merchandise and services it offers.

In addition, retailers are using promotion programs to build repeat business and store loyalty. For example, Gary Mead, a 34-year-old entrepreneur, uses databased marketing to take on the giants: Domino's, Little Caesar's, and Pizza Hut. With a $10,000 computer system, he keeps track of the purchase history of customers patronizing his restaurant, Mi Amore Pizza & Pasta in Lompac, California. If a customer doesn't order for 60 days, the system spits out a postcard with a discount to lure her back. Other promotions encourage customers to try all of the dishes offered by suggesting pasta dishes to pizza lovers. The database has 8,500 customers in a town of 11,000; business has been increasing 25 to 30 percent each year.[1]

Retailers communicate with customers through five vehicles: advertising, sales promotion, publicity, store atmosphere and visual merchandising, and personal selling. This chapter focuses on the first three of these vehicles—the **promotion mix.** In large retail firms, the promotion mix is managed by the firm's marketing or advertising department and the buying organization. Store atmosphere and personal selling are managed by store personnel and are thus discussed in more detail in Section IV.

EXHIBIT **16–1**
The Retail Promotion Mix

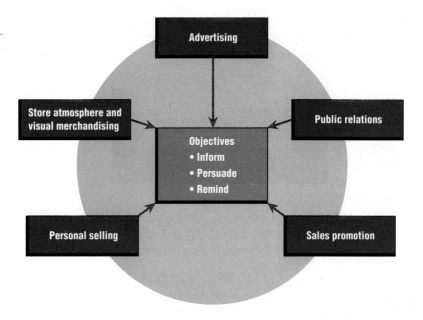

EXHIBIT **16–1**

The Retail Promotion Mix

ROLE OF THE RETAIL PROMOTION PROGRAM

The ultimate goal of the retail promotion program is to generate sales for customers in the retailer's target market. To accomplish this goal, retailers use a variety of methods to inform, persuade, and remind customers about the retailer. (See Exhibit 16–1.)

Tasks Performed by the Promotion Program

In Chapter 5, we discussed how customers go through a number of stages as they decide which store to visit and what to purchase there. The retailer's promotion program moves customers through the stages in the buying process outlined in Exhibit 5–1.

Informing The first task performed by the promotion program is informing customers about the retailer and the merchandise and services it offers. For example, a carpet cleaning company places ads in the Yellow Pages to make customers aware of its services and its phone number. Supermarkets advertise special prices on groceries in the daily newspaper and place signs on the shelves next to products on sale. Home-improvement centers make announcements on radio for classes they're holding to show customers how to install a new kitchen sink.

Persuading The second task is motivating customers to visit the retailer and buy merchandise and services. For example, the department store salesperson described in Chapter 5 encouraged the college student to buy a suit for her upcoming interviews. Mi Amore Pizza & Pasta, the restaurant described at the beginning of the chapter, sends out coupons offering discounts to motivate customers to order pizzas.

Reminding As we discussed in Chapter 5, simply making a sale isn't enough. Although a customer may like a retailer, the retailer is vulnerable to appeals made by competitors. Retailers need to build repeat sales and loyalty by reminding customers about their offering and its benefits.

More and more retailers are using frequent shopper programs to perform this reminding task. **Frequent shopper programs** are reward and communication programs to encourage continued sales from the retailer's best customers. For example, many department chains identify their best customers, send them periodic

REFACT Zellers discount store chain's frequent shopper program, Club Zed, has 8 million members out of Canada's population of 30 million.[2]

EXHIBIT 16–2

Communication
Methods

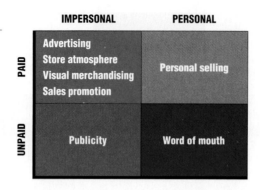

newsletters announcing programs, invite the customers to special showings, assign personal shoppers to them, and offer special discounts.³ These programs are discussed in detail later in the chapter.

Methods for Communicating with Customers

Exhibit 16–2 classifies retailers' communication methods to inform, persuade, and remind customers. The classification is based on whether the methods are impersonal or personal and paid or unpaid.

Paid Impersonal Communications   Advertising, sales promotions, and store atmosphere are examples of paid impersonal communications. **Advertising** is a form of paid communication to customers using impersonal mass media such as newspapers, TV, radio, and direct mail.

Sales promotions are paid impersonal communication activities that offer extra value and incentives to customers to visit a store and/or purchase merchandise during a specific period of time. The most common sales promotion is a sale. Other sales promotions involve special events, in-store demonstrations, coupons, and contests.

Sales promotion activities typically are used to influence customer behavior during a short period of time. For example, Kmart's "blue-light specials" are a dramatic way to increase sales of specific items. They're announced over the store's public address system and a flashing blue light is placed near the item on sale. The sales last only 5 to 15 minutes. Since the stock of sale items is limited, customers rush to the merchandise to make sure they get it before it runs out or the sale ends. Besides increasing sales of specific items, blue-light specials reinforce Kmart's image of providing good value to its customers.

While sales promotions are effective at generating short-term interest among customers, they aren't very useful for building long-term loyalty. Customers attracted by sales promotions are interested in the promoted merchandise, not the store. But customers who participate in the promotion might learn more about a store and return to it. Unfortunately, when a specific promotion is effective for a retailer, competing retailers learn about it quickly and offer the same promotion, which prevents the innovating retailer from gaining any long-term advantage.

Finally, the retail store itself provides paid impersonal communications to its customers. **Store atmosphere** is the combination of the store's physical characteristics, such as architecture, layout, signs and displays, colors, lighting, temperature, sounds, and smells, which together create an image in the customer's mind. The atmosphere communicates information about the store's service, pricing, and fashionability of its merchandise.⁶ Chapter 18 discusses elements of store atmosphere.

REFACT Department and specialty store chains typically spend 8 percent of their sales revenue on personal selling and 3 percent on advertising and direct mail.⁴

REFACT The Christmas story about Rudolph the Red-Nosed Reindeer was developed by a Montgomery Ward copywriter in 1939 for a store promotion.⁵

This Alberton store in Wichita, Kansas, staged a karaoke contest to generate publicity for the store opening.

Paid Personal Communications   Retail salespeople are the primary vehicle for providing paid personal communications to customers. **Personal selling** is a communication process in which salespeople assist customers in satisfying their needs through face-to-face exchange of information.

Unpaid Impersonal Communications   The primary method for generating unpaid impersonal communication is publicity. **Publicity** is communications through significant unpaid presentations about the retailer (usually a news story) in impersonal media. Examples of publicity are the newspaper and TV coverage of Macy's Thanksgiving Day parade in New York and the Sears trophy for the national collegiate football championship.[7]

REFACT People who have an unsatisfactory experience with retail service tell nine other people on average about their experience.[9]

Unpaid Personal Communications   Finally, retailers communicate with their customers at no cost through **word of mouth** (communication between people about a retailer).[8] For example, retailers attempt to encourage favorable word-of-mouth communication by establishing teen boards composed of high school student leaders. Board members are encouraged to tell their friends about the retailer and its merchandise. On the other hand, unfavorable word-of-mouth communication can seriously affect store performance.

Strengths and Weaknesses of Communication Methods

Exhibit 16–3 compares communication methods in terms of control, flexibility, credibility, and cost.

EXHIBIT 16–3

Comparison of Communication Methods

	Control	Flexibility	Credibility	Cost
Paid impersonal				
• Advertising	●	○	○	◑
• Sales promotions	●	◕	—	◕
• Sales atmosphere	●	◕	—	◑
Paid personal				
• Personal selling	◐	●	○	◐
Unpaid impersonal				
• Publicity	○	○	●	◕
Unpaid personal				
• Word of mouth	○	○	●	○

● High   ◕ High to moderate   ◐ Moderate   ◔ Moderate to low   ○ Low

Control   Retailers have more control when using paid versus unpaid methods. When using advertising, sales promotions, and store atmosphere, retailers determine the message's content and the time of its delivery. But because each salesperson can deliver different messages, retailers have less control over personal selling than other paid communication methods. Retailers have very little control over the content or timing of publicity and word-of-mouth communications. Since unpaid communications are designed and delivered by people not employed by the retailer, they can communicate unfavorable as well as favorable information. For example, extensive news coverage of food poisoning at Jack-in-the-Box restaurants and discrimination at Denney's resulted in significant declines in sales.[10]

Flexibility   Personal selling is the most flexible communication method, because salespeople can talk with each customer, discover her specific needs, and develop unique presentations for her. Other communication methods are less flexible. For example, ads deliver the same message to all customers.

Credibility   Because publicity and word of mouth are communicated by independent sources, their information is usually more credible than the information in paid communication sources. For example, customers see their friends and family as highly credible sources of information. Customers tend to doubt claims made by salespeople and in ads since they know retailers are trying to promote their merchandise.

Cost   Publicity and word of mouth are classified as unpaid communication methods, but retailers do incur costs to stimulate them. Creating an event that merits significant news coverage can be costly for a retailer. For example, Penney's incurs cost sponsoring Lynn St. James and her Spirit of the American Woman race car in the Indianapolis 500 and the JCPenney/LPGA skins game.

REFACT Sears is the third largest advertiser in the United States. McDonald's is seventh largest.[11]

Paid impersonal communications often are economical. For example, a full-page ad in *The Los Angeles Times* costs about two cents per person to deliver the message in the ad. In contrast, personal selling is more effective than advertising, but more costly. A 10-minute presentation by a retail salesperson paid $6 per hour costs the retailer $1—almost 100 times more than exposing a customer to a newspaper, radio, or TV ad.

Due to the differences just described, communication methods differ in their effectiveness in performing communication tasks. Typically, advertising and publicity are most cost-effective at informing customers about the retailer and its offering. Personal selling, sales promotion, store atmosphere, and visual merchandise are used to persuade customers to purchase merchandise. Remembering and repeat purchase are developed through image advertising and service offered by sales associates.

Integrated Marketing Communications

The elements in the retail communication program must work together and reinforce each other so the retailer can achieve its objectives. As described above, the communication methods vary in their effectiveness in performing tasks in the promotion program. Rather than creating unique programs for sales associates, advertising, sales promotion, and direct mail, retailers need to coordinate these activities into an integrated marketing communication program. Without this coordination, the communication methods might work at cross-purposes. For example, the retailer's TV advertising campaign might attempt to build an image of exceptional customer service, but the firm's sales promotions might all emphasize low prices. If communication methods aren't used consistently, customers may become confused about the retailer's image and therefore may not patronize the store.

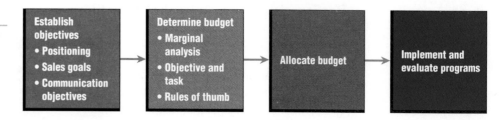

EXHIBIT 16-4

Steps in Developing a Retail Promotion Program

Integrated marketing communications is the strategic integration of multiple communication methods to form a comprehensive, consistent message. For example, Lane Bryant used an integrated approach to target African American markets. The focus of the program was a a five-city mall tour coordinated by *Essence* magazine. Radio and TV ads were used to inform customers about the tour and the special mall event. Prior to the arrival of the tour, direct mail announcements were sent to consumers in the city announcing the mall event and presenting Lane Bryant's offering for African American customers. Ads with discount coupons placed in the *Essence* issues distributed during the tour offered additional encouragement to visit Lane.[12]

INTERNET EXERCISE   Trader Joe's is an interesting retail concept—an off-price retailer selling food and wine. Go to http://www.traderjoes.com and see how the firm uses its Internet site to promote its retail offering. How effective do you think the site is in promoting the store?

Retailing View 16.1 describes how the Body Shop has an integrated communication program to build the loyalty of socially conscious cosmetics customers. The next section of this chapter is devoted to planning the promotion program.

PLANNING THE RETAIL COMMUNICATION PROGRAM

Exhibit 16–4 illustrates the four steps in developing and implementing a retail promotion program: setting objectives, determining a budget, allocating the budget, and implementing and evaluating the mix. The following sections detail each of these steps.

Setting Objectives

Retailers establish objectives for promoting a program to provide (1) direction for people implementing the program and (2) a basis for evaluating its effectiveness. Some promotion programs have a long-term orientation, such as creating or altering customers' image of the retailer. Other promotion programs focus on improving short-term performance, such as increasing store traffic on weekends.

Positioning: A Long-Term Objective   **Positioning** is the design and implementation of a retail communication program to create an image in the customer's mind of the retailer relative to its competitors. As Chapter 6 said, a long-term competitive advantage can be developed through positioning.

A positioning objective typically links the retailer to a specific category of merchandise or benefit in the customer's mind. Specific positioning objectives retailers pursue include[13]

16.1

Profits with Principle at the Body Shop

THE BODY SHOP IS AN 800-STORE chain selling natural-ingredient hair and skin care products in 40 countries. Anita Roddick, the founder and CEO, strongly believes that her business should contribute to the community and the environment beyond selling cosmetics. The company has developed an integrated marketing communications program to link its brand name with the "profits with principle" theme.

The company and its founder "walk the walk" by publicizing its position against testing cosmetics on animals, and for preserving the rain forest, protecting endangered species, and using recycled materials. A special line of children's bath products comes with informative story books about endangered species.

Sales associates not only wear Body Shop T-shirts with social messages, they believe in the company's causes. The company pays its store employees to spend 10 hours each week on community and charitable activities.

To better communicate with its customers, The Body Shop created a club for them. Customers pay a $25 annual fee and receive the latest information on Body Shop products, a T-shirt, a quarterly newsletter with updates about causes The Body Shop supports (such as Amnesty International and banning animal testing of

The Body Shop has an integrated marketing communication program involving personal selling, store design, and advertising to reinforce its image of quality, natural cosmetics, and personal hygiene.

cosmetics), and a three-ring binder (made from recycled soda bottles) to keep the newsletter and product information.

Members also complete a personal profile questionnaire. Information from the questionnaire is used to tailor direct-mail programs to customers' needs and lifestyles.

Source: Erich Joachimsthaler and David Aaker, "Building Brands without Mass Media," *Harvard Business Review*, January–February 1997, pp. 39–48; Julian Lee and Patrick Barrett, "Body in Need of Reshaping," *Marketing*, April 4, 1996, p. 10; and "The Body Shop Club: Frequency Marketing Politically Correct Cosmetics," *Colloquy* 3, no. 1 (1993), pp. 1–2.

1. *Merchandise category.* The most common method for positioning is to make the retailer distinctive in a category of merchandise offered. For example, Circuit City is closely related in consumers' minds with consumer electronics. Consumers view Circuit City as having any electronic item they might want in stock at all times.

2. *Price/quality.* Some retailers (such as Neiman Marcus) position themselves as offering high prices and high fashion. Other retailers (such as Wal-Mart) are positioned as offering low prices, adequate merchandise and service, and good value.[14]

3. *Specific attribute or benefit.* A retailer can link its stores to attributes such as convenience (7-Eleven) or service (Nordstrom).

4. *Lifestyle or activity.* Some retailers associate themselves with a specific lifestyle or activity. For example, The Nature Company, a retailer offering books and equipment to study nature, is linked to a lifestyle of interacting with the environment. Electronic Boutique is associated with home use of computer software.

Retail advertising can be used to achieve long-term positioning goals and short-term sales goals. The Fashion Bug ad is used to position the retailer for its fashion-oriented target market. The Payless ad builds sales of children's shoes during a sale.

Sales Goals: Short-Term Objectives   A common short-term objective for a promotion program is to increase sales during a specified time period. For example, retailers often have sales during which some or all merchandise is priced at a discount for a short time. Grocery stores usually place weekly ads with coupons that can be used to save money on purchases made during the week.

Communication Objectives   While retailers' overall objective is to generate long- and short-term sales and profits, they often use objectives related to the communication tasks discussed previously rather than sales objectives to plan and evaluate their promotion programs.[15] **Communication objectives** are specific goals related to the retail promotion mix's effect on the customer's decision-making process.

Exhibit 16–5 shows hypothetical information about customers in the target market for a Safeway supermarket. This information illustrates goals related to stages in the consumer decision-making process. Note that 95 percent of the customers are aware of the store (the first stage in the decision-making process) and 85 percent know the type of merchandise it sells. But only 45 percent of the customers in the target market have a favorable attitude toward the store. Thirty-two percent intend to visit the store during the next few weeks; 25 percent actually visit the store during the next two weeks; and 18 percent regularly shop at the store.

In this hypothetical example, most people know about the store and its offering. The major problem confronting the Safeway supermarket is the big drop between knowledge and favorable attitude. The store should develop a communication program with the objective of increasing the percentage of customers with a favorable attitude toward it.

To effectively implement and evaluate a communication program, objectives must be clearly stated in quantitative terms. The target audience for the promotion mix needs to be defined along with the degree of change expected and the time period over which the change will be realized.

EXHIBIT 16–5

Communication
Objectives and Stages
in Consumers'
Decision-Making
Process

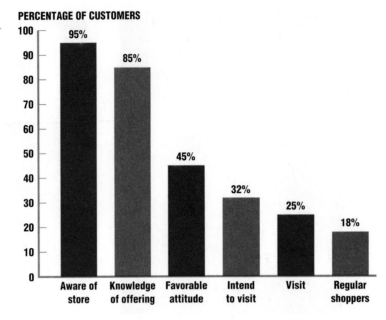

PERCENTAGE OF CUSTOMERS

Aware of store	Knowledge of offering	Favorable attitude	Intend to visit	Visit	Regular shoppers
95%	85%	45%	32%	25%	18%

For example, the communication objective for the Safeway program might be to increase from 45 percent to 55 percent within three months the percentage of customers within a five-mile radius of the store who have a favorable attitude toward the store. This objective is clear and measurable. It indicates the task the program should address. The people who implement the program know what they're supposed to accomplish.

Exhibit 16–6 describes how the communication objectives and approaches used by vendors and retailers differ and how these differences can lead to conflicts.

EXHIBIT 16–6

Differences between
Retailer and Vendor
Communication
Programs

LONG-TERM VERSUS SHORT-TERM GOALS

Most communications done by vendors (manufacturers) are directed toward building a long-term image of their products. On the other hand, most retailer communications are typically used to announce promotions and special sales that generate short-term revenues.

PRODUCT VERSUS LOCATION

When vendors advertise their branded products, they don't care where the customer buys them. On the other hand, retailers don't care what brands customers buy as long as they buy them in their store. Vendors want to sell their specific brands, while retailers want to sell the most profitable brands.

GEOGRAPHIC COVERAGE

Since people tend to shop at stores near their homes or workplaces, most retailers use local newspapers, TV, and radio to target their communications. On the other hand, most vendors sell their brands nationally and thus tend to use national TV and magazines.

BREADTH OF MERCHANDISE OFFERED

Typically, vendors have a relatively small number of products to advertise. They can devote a lot of attention to developing consistent communication programs for each brand they make. Since retailers offer a much broader set of products and often focus on building short-term sales, retail communications can easily confuse customers if they focus on different products and don't develop a consistent overall store image.

EXHIBIT 16–7   Marginal Analysis for Setting Diane West's Promotion Budget

	PROMOTION EXPENSES (1)	SALES (2)	GROSS MARGIN REALIZED (3)	RENTAL EXPENSE (4)	PERSONNEL EXPENSE (5)	CONTRIBUTION BEFORE PROMOTION EXPENSES (6) = (3) − (4) − (5)	PROFIT (7) = (6) − (1)
	$ 0	$240,000	$ 96,000	$44,000	$52,200	($200)	($200)
	5,000	280,000	112,000	48,000	53,400	10,600	5,600
	10,000	330,000	132,000	53,000	54,900	24,100	14,100
	15,000	380,000	152,000	58,000	56,400	37,600	22,600
	20,000	420,000	168,000	62,000	57,600	48,400	28,400
	25,000	460,000	184,000	66,000	58,800	59,200	34,200
Last year	30,000	500,000	200,000	70,000	60,000	70,000	40,000
	35,000	540,000	216,000	74,000	61,200	80,800	45,800
	40,000	570,000	228,000	77,000	62,100	88,900	48,900
	45,000	600,000	240,000	80,000	63,000	97,000	52,000
	50,000	625,000	250,000	82,500	63,750	103,750	53,750
	55,000	650,000	260,000	85,000	64,500	110,500	55,500
	60,000	670,000	268,000	87,000	65,100	115,900	55,900
Best profit	65,000	690,000	276,000	89,000	65,700	121,300	56,300
	70,000	705,000	282,000	90,500	66,150	125,350	55,350
	75,000	715,000	286,000	91,500	66,450	128,050	53,050
	80,000	725,000	290,000	92,500	66,750	130,750	50,750
	85,000	735,000	294,000	93,500	67,050	133,450	48,450
	90,000	745,000	298,000	94,500	67,350	136,150	46,150
	95,000	750,000	300,000	95,000	67,500	137,500	42,500
	100,000	750,000	300,000	95,000	67,500	137,500	37,500

Setting the Promotion Budget

The second step in developing a retail promotion program is determining a budget (as Exhibit 16–4 shows). The economically correct method for setting the promotion budget is marginal analysis. Even though retailers usually don't have enough information to perform a complete marginal analysis, the method shows how managers should approach budget-setting programs.

Marginal Analysis Method   **Marginal analysis** is based on the economic principle that firms should increase promotion expenditures so long as each additional dollar spent generates more than a dollar of additional contribution. To illustrate marginal analysis, consider Diane West, owner-manager of a specialty store selling women's business clothing. Exhibit 16–7 shows her analysis to determine how much she should spend next year on her promotion mix.[16]

For 21 different promotion expense levels (column 1), she estimated store sales (column 2), gross margin (column 3), and other expenses (columns 4 and 5). Then she calculated the contribution excluding expenses on promotions (column 6) and the profit when the promotion expenses are considered (column 7). To estimate the sales generated by different levels of promotions, West could have simply relied on her judgment and experience, or she might have analyzed past data to determine the relationship between promotion expenses and sales. Historical data also provide information about the gross margin and other expenses as a percentage of sales.

Notice that at low levels of promotion expenses, an additional $5,000 in promotion expenses generates more than a $5,000 incremental contribution. For example, increasing the promotion expense from $15,000 to $20,000 increases contribution by $10,800 (or $48,400 – $37,600). When the promotion expense reaches $65,000, further increases of $5,000 generate less than $5,000 in additional contributions. For example, increasing the budget from $65,000 to $70,000 generates only an additional $4,050 in contribution ($125,350 – $121,300).

In this example, West determined that the maximum profit would be generated with a promotion expense budget of $65,000. But she noticed that expense levels between $55,000 and $70,000 all result in about the same level of profit. Thus, West might make a conservative decision and establish a $55,000 budget for promotion expenses.

In most cases, it's very hard to do a marginal analysis because managers don't know the relationship between promotion expenses and sales. Note that the numbers in Exhibit 16–7 are simply West's estimates—they may not be accurate.

Sometimes retailers do experiments to get a better idea of the relationship between promotion expenses and sales.[17] Say, for example, a catalog retailer selects several geographic areas in the United States with the same sales potential. The retailer then distributes 100,000 catalogs in the first area, 200,000 in the second area, and 300,000 in the third area. Using the sales and costs for each distribution level, he could go through an analysis like the one in Exhibit 16–7 to determine the most profitable distribution level. (Chapter 15 described the use of experiments to determine the relationship between price and sales.)

Some other methods that retailers use to set budgets are the objective-and-task method and rules of thumb, such as the affordable, percentage-of-sales, and competitive parity methods. These methods are less sophisticated than marginal analysis, but easier to use.

Objective-and-Task Method   The **objective-and-task method** determines the budget required to undertake specific tasks for accomplishing communication objectives. To use this method, the retailer first establishes a set of communication objectives. Then the necessary tasks and their costs are determined. The sum total of all costs incurred to undertake the tasks is the promotion budget.

Exhibit 16–8 illustrates how Diane West used the objective-and-task method to complement her marginal analysis. West established three objectives: to increase the awareness of her store, to create a greater preference for her store among customers in her target market, and to promote the sale of merchandise remaining at the end of each season. The total promotion budget she requires to achieve these objectives is $55,300.

EXHIBIT 16–8

Illustration of Objective-and-Task Method for Setting a Promotion Budget

Objective: Increase the percentage of target market (working women living and/or working within 10 miles of our store) who know of our store's location and that it sells women's business attire from 25 percent to 50 percent over the next 12 months.	
Task: 480, 30-second radio spots during peak commuting hours (7:00 to 8:00 A.M. and 5:00 to 6:00 P.M.).	$12,300
Task: Sign with store name near entrance to mall.	4,500
Task: Display ad in the Yellow Pages.	500
Objective: Increase the percentage of target market who indicate that our store is their preferred store for buying their business wardrobe from 5 percent to 15 percent in 12 months.	
Task: Develop TV campaign to improve image and run 50, 30-second commercials.	$24,000
Task: Hold four "Dress for Success" seminars followed by a wine-and-cheese social.	8,000
Objective: Attract new customers to store.	
Task: Special event.	6,000
Total budget	**$55,300**

EXHIBIT 16–9

Financial Implications
of Increasing the
Promotion Budget

	LAST YEAR	NEXT YEAR
Sales	$500,000	$650,000
Gross margin (realized)	200,000	260,000
Rental, maintenance, etc.	70,000	85,000
Personnel	60,000	64,500
Communications	30,000	55,300
Profit	$ 40,000	$ 55,200

Besides defining the objectives and tasks, West also rechecked the financial implications of the promotion mix by projecting the income statement for next year using the promotion budget. (See Exhibit 16–9.) This income statement includes an increase of $25,300 in promotion expenses over last year. But West feels that this increase in the promotion budget will boost annual sales from $500,000 to $650,000. Based on West's projections, the increase in promotion expenses will raise store profits. The results of the marginal analysis and the objective-and-task methods suggest a promotion budget between $55,000 and $65,000.

Rule-of-Thumb Methods   In the previous two methods, the promotion budget is set by estimating promotion activities' effects on the firm's future sales or communication objectives. The **rule-of-thumb methods** discussed in this section use the opposite logic. These methods use past sales and promotional activity to determine the present promotion budget.[18]

Affordable Method   When using the affordable budgeting method, retailers first forecast their sales and expenses excluding promotion expenses during the budgeting period. The difference between the forecast sales and expenses plus desired profit is then budgeted for the promotion mix. In other words, the **affordable method** sets the promotion budget by determining what money is available after operating costs and profits are budgeted.

The major problem with the affordable method is that it assumes that the promotion expenses don't stimulate sales and profit. Promotion expenses are just a cost of business, like the cost of merchandise. When retailers use the affordable method, they typically cut "unnecessary" promotion expenses if sales fall below the forecast rather than increase promotion expenses to increase sales.

Percentage-of-Sales Method   The **percentage-of-sales method** sets the promotion budget as a fixed percentage of forecast sales. Retailers use this method to determine the promotion budget by forecasting sales during the budget period and using a predetermined percentage to set the budget. The percentage may be the retailer's historical percentage or the average percentage used by similar retailers.

The problem with the percentage-of-sales method is that it assumes the same percentage used in the past, or by competitors, is still appropriate for your firm. Consider a retailer that hasn't opened new stores in the past but plans to open many new stores in the current year. It must create customer awareness for these new stores so the promotion budget should be much larger in the current year than in the past.

Using the same percentage as competitors also may be inappropriate. For example, a retailer might have better locations than its competitors. Due to these locations, customers may already have a much higher awareness of the retailer's stores. Thus, the retailer may not need to spend as much on promotions as competitors with poorer locations spend.

REFACT Furniture stores spend 7.2 percent of sales on advertising, while grocery stores only spend 1.4 percent of sales on advertising.[19]

One advantage of both the percentage-of-sales method and the affordable method for determining a promotion budget is that the retailer won't spend beyond its means. Since the level of spending is determined by sales, the budget will only go up when sales go up and the retailer generates more sales to pay for the additional promotion expenses. When times are good, these methods work well because they allow the retailer to communicate more aggressively with customers. But when sales fall, promotion expenses are cut, which may accelerate the sales decline.

Competitive Parity Method   Under the **competitive parity method,** the promotion budget is set so that the retailer's share of promotion expenses equals its share of market. For example, consider a sporting goods store in a small town. To use the competitive parity method, the owner-manager would first estimate the total amount spent on promotions by all of the sporting goods retailers in town. Then the owner-manager would estimate the store's market share for sporting goods and multiply the market share by sporting goods stores' total advertising expenses to set its budget. Assume that the owner-manager's estimate of advertising for sporting goods was $5,000 and the estimate of the store's market share was 45 percent. Based on these estimates, the owner-manager would set the store's promotion budget at $2,250 to maintain competitive parity.

Like the other rule-of-thumb methods, the competitive parity method doesn't allow retailers to exploit the unique opportunities or problems they confront in a market. If all competitors used this method to set promotion budgets, their market shares would stay about the same over time (assuming that the retailers develop equally effective campaigns).

Evaluating a Specific Promotion Opportunity   Many promotion opportunities undertaken by retailers are initiated by vendors. For example, Procter & Gamble might offer the following special promotion to Kroger: During a one-week period, Kroger can order Tide laundry detergent in the 48-ounce size at 15 cents below the standard wholesale price. However, if Kroger elects to buy Tide at the discounted price, the grocery chain must feature the 48-ounce container of Tide in its Thursday newspaper ad at $1.59 (20 cents off the typical retail price). In addition, Kroger must have an end-aisle display of Tide.

Before Kroger or any other retailer decides whether to accept such a trade promotion and then promote Tide to its customers, it needs to assess the promotion's impact on its profitability. Such a promotion may be effective for the vendor but not for the retailer.

To evaluate a trade promotion, the retailer considers

- The realized margin from the promotion.
- The cost of the additional inventory carried due to buying more than the normal amount.
- The potential increase in sales from the promoted merchandise.
- The potential loss suffered when customers switch to the promoted merchandise from more profitable unpromoted brands.
- The additional sales made to customers attracted to the store by the promotion.[20]

When Tide's price is reduced to $1.59, Kroger will sell more Tide than it normally would. But Kroger's margin on the Tide will be less because the required retail discount of 20 cents isn't offset by the wholesale discount of 15 cents. In addition, Kroger might suffer losses because the promotion encourages customers to buy

16.2

Marshalls Advertising to Build Sales and Profits

WHEN TJX, THE CORPORATION that owns T. J. Maxx, bought Marshalls, another off-price retail chain, the firm reduced Marshalls' ad budget by $28 million and eliminated Marshalls' "buy one, get one free" promotion program—and sales actually increased. Bernard Cammaratus, TJX's CEO, attributes the sales increase to a new communication strategy that "reestablished the true off-price mentality in the Marshalls organization and got the Marshalls shopper all excited again."

Prior to the acquisition by TJX, Marshalls' advertising frequently featured new shipments of clothing and products. An ad would say, "We just got in a boatload of Armani suits, please come down and see us," or it would highlight prices of specific items, emphasizing the size of the discount off list price. Shoppers were attracted to the stores by these ads, but they just cherry picked the advertised items. (**Cherry-picking** is customers visiting a store and buying only merchandise sold at big discounts.)

Cammaratus believes that advertising is different for off-price retailers than for other retailers. Visiting an off-price retailer is like going on a treasure hunt. Shoppers can find apparel, glassware, and jewelry at 30 to 60 percent below department store prices. The chance of finding a real bargain keeps customers going through the merchandise until they find something to buy. But Marshalls' advertising told customers what was new and what were the good buys and thus eliminated the adventure in the off-price shopping experience.

Marshalls' new advertising campaign stresses everyday low prices. One ad features a shopper named Marsha thinking out loud about what she might find at Marshalls. The tagline is "Brand Names for Less Everyday."

Source: Joseph Pereira, "TJX Slashes Ad Budget to Revitalize Unit," *The Wall Street Journal,* October 8, 1996, p. B4.

Tide, which has a lower margin than Kroger's private-label detergent the customer might have bought. In fact, customers may stockpile Tide, buying several boxes, which will reduce sales of Kroger's private-label detergent for some time after the special promotion ends. On the other hand, the promotion may attract customers to the store—customers who don't normally shop at Kroger but who will visit to buy Tide at the discounted price. These customers might buy additional merchandise, providing a gain to the store that it wouldn't have realized if it hadn't promoted Tide.

Allocating the Promotion Budget

After determining the size of the promotion budget, the third step in the promotion planning process is allocating the budget. (See Exhibit 16–4.) In this step, the retailer decides how much of its budget to allocate to specific communication elements, merchandise categories, geographic regions, or long- and short-term objectives. For example, Dillard's must decide how much of its promotion budget to spend in each area where it has stores: Arkansas, Texas, Florida, North Carolina, Arizona, and Ohio. Sears decides how much to allocate to appliances, hardware, and apparel. The sporting goods store owner-manager must decide how much of the store's $900 promotion budget to spend on promoting the store's image versus generating sales during the year and how much to spend on advertising and special promotions.

Research indicates that allocation decisions are more important than the decision on the size of the promotion.[21] In other words, retailers often can realize the same objectives by reducing the size of the promotion budget, but allocating the budget more effectively. Retailing View 16.2 illustrates how Marshalls cut its advertising budget and increased sales.

An easy way to make such allocation decisions is just to spend about the same in each geographic region or for each merchandise category. But this allocation rule probably won't maximize profits because it ignores the possibility that promotion programs might be more effective for some merchandise categories or for some regions than for others. Another approach is to use rules of thumb such as basing allocations on the sales level or contribution for the merchandise category.

Allocation decisions, like budget-setting decisions, should use the principles of marginal analysis. The retailer should allocate the budget to areas that will yield the greatest return. This approach for allocating a budget is sometimes referred to as the high assay principle. Consider a miner who can spend his time digging on two claims. The value of the gold on one claim is assayed at $10,000 per ton, while the assay value on the other claim is $5,000 per ton. Should the miner spend 2/3 of his time at the first mine and 1/3 third of his time at the other mine? Of course not! The miner should spend all of his time mining the first claim until the assay value of the ore mined drops to $5,000 a ton, at which time he can divide his time equally between the claims.

Similarly, a retailer may find that its customers have a high awareness and very favorable attitude toward its women's clothing but may not know much about the store's men's clothing. In this situation, a dollar spent on advertising men's clothing might generate more sales than a dollar spent on women's clothing.

Implementing and Evaluating

The final two stages in developing a retail promotion program are implementation and evaluation. (See Exhibit 16–4.) Due to differences in implementing advertising, sales promotion, and publicity programs, we'll discuss each element of the promotion mix separately at the end of the chapter and focus on the evaluation stage in this section.

When evaluating promotion programs, a retailer needs to compare the results of the program to the objectives developed during the first part of the planning process. Here's an example of the use of market research to evaluate a promotion program.

South Gate West is one of several specialty import furniture stores competing for upscale shoppers in Charleston, South Carolina. The store has the appearance of both a fine antique store and a traditional furniture shop, but most of its merchandise is new Asian imports.

The owner realized his promotion budget was considerably less than the budget of the local Pier 1 store. (Pier 1 is a large national import furniture chain.) He decided to concentrate his limited budget on a specific segment and use highly distinctive copy and art in his advertising. His target market was experienced, sophisticated consumers of household furniture. His experience indicated the importance of personal selling for more seasoned shoppers because they (1) make large purchases and (2) seek considerable information before making a decision. Thus the owner spent part of his promotion budget on training his sales associates.

The advertising program he developed stressed his store's distinctive image. The owner used the newspaper as his major vehicle. Competitive ads contained line drawings of furniture with prices. His ads emphasized the imagery associated with Asian furniture by featuring off-the-beaten-path scenes of Asian countries with unusual art objects. This theme was also reflected in the store's atmosphere.

To measure his campaign's effectiveness, the manager conducted an inexpensive tracking study. Telephone interviews were conducted periodically with a representative sample of furniture customers in his store's trading area. Communication objectives were assessed using the following questions:

COMMUNICATION OBJECTIVE	QUESTION
Awareness	What stores sell East Asian furniture?
Knowledge	Which stores would you rate outstanding on the following characteristics?
Attitude	On your next shopping trip for East Asian furniture, which store would you visit first?
Visit	Which of the following stores have you been to?

The survey results over one year were:

COMMUNICATION OBJECTIVE	BEFORE CAMPAIGN	SIX MONTHS AFTER	ONE YEAR AFTER
Awareness (% mentioning store)	38%	46%	52%
Knowledge (% giving outstanding rating for sales assistance)	9	17	24
Attitude (% first choice)	13	15	19
Visit (% visited store)	8	15	19

The results show a steady increase in awareness, knowledge of the store, and choice of the store as a primary source of East Asian furniture. This research provides evidence that the advertising is conveying the intended message to the target audience.[22]

In the rest of this chapter we discuss specific issues in implementing advertising, sales promotion, and publicity programs.

IMPLEMENTING ADVERTISING PROGRAMS

Retail advertising is used to develop and reinforce a firm's image, inform customers about merchandise and prices, and announce a sale. While some national retailers invest in image advertising (see Retailing View 16.3), most retail advertising focuses on short-term objectives. Implementing an ad program involves developing the message, choosing the specific media to convey the message, and determining the frequency and timing of the message. Next we'll look at each of these decisions.

Developing the Advertising Message

Most retail advertising messages have a short life and are designed to have an immediate impact. This immediacy calls for a copy writing style that grabs the reader's attention. Exhibit 16–10 outlines specific suggestions for developing advertising aimed at local markets.[24]

Assistance in Developing Advertising

Cooperative Advertising Cooperative (co-op) advertising is a program undertaken by a vendor. The vendor pays for part of the retailer's advertising. But the vendor dictates some conditions for the advertising. For example, Procter & Gamble may have a co-op program that pays for half of a retailer's ads for Tide detergent.

Co-op advertising enables a retailer to increase its advertising budget. In the previous paragraph's example, the retailer only pays for half of its expenses (for ads including Tide). In addition to lowering costs, co-op advertising enables the retailer to associate its name with well-known national brands using attractive art work.

REFACT The average consumer sees over 2,000 advertising messages per week. [23]

16.3

Penney's Advertises to Attract the Value-Conscious Consumer

THE OBJECTIVE OF JCPENNEY'S communication program is to bridge the gap between the new JCPenney and the 1990s consumer. In the 80s, Penney's made a number of changes in its merchandise offering and visual presentation to target traditional and updated customer segments. National brands such as Bugle Boy, Henry Grethel, Maidenform, and Guess? now complement Penney's private-label merchandise. Consumer electronics, appliances, and sporting goods were deleted so that Penney's could focus on apparel lines. Over $50 million was spent to renovate stores and provide superior visual displays.

Research by Penney's and its advertising agency, N.W. Ayer, found that 90s consumers exhibit four characteristics:

- They're optimistic but have concerns about their ability to provide economically for their families.
- They're interested in getting good values, beating the system, and getting more for less.
- They spend more time at home with their family and are less self-indulgent.
- They're attracted to authentic natural clothing, not trendy high-fashion apparel.

To communicate how the new JCPenney meets the needs of 90s consumers, N.W. Ayer developed a communication program built on the theme "fashion comes to life." Within this overall theme, the following slogans are stressed:

- "A great new fashion feeling at JCPenney."
- "A new spirit of style."
- "Fashions that cater to every lifestyle."
- "Hundreds of brands."
- "Dozens of newly designed departments."
- "Reminder of JCPenney value."

The tone of the TV commercials was uplifting, warm, emotional, and realistic. The stores and merchandise were shown as being part of real people's everyday lives. Models represented the wide range of ages and ethnic groups in Penney's target market.

Print ads were placed in leading men's and women's fashion magazines. They emphasized Penney's private labels using a lifestyle approach. The focus was on the brand name, with JCPenney placed in the lower left-hand corner of the ad. The merchandise was shown as a quality national brand available at JCPenney, not as a Penney's brand.

N.W. Ayer pretested the campaign by comparing consumers' attitudes about Penney's before and after seeing the ads. After seeing the ads, more consumers agreed with the following statements about JCPenney:

- "Offers well-known brand-name apparel."
- "Has clothing that will help me project the image I want to project."
- "Is changing to fit my needs."
- "Has quality merchandise."
- "Has up-to-date fashions."
- "Has up-to-date men's and women's apparel."
- "Is a contemporary store."
- "Makes me feel confident about its merchandise."

When the ad campaign was launched, Penney's discovered consumers also felt its merchandise was high priced and didn't offer good value. Thus, the campaign achieved the fashion image desired, but had a negative effect on Penney's value image.

Source: Company documents.

REFACT Co-op advertising accounts for approximately 50 percent of all department store and 75 percent of all grocery store advertising.[25]

Co-op advertising has some drawbacks. First, vendors want the ad to feature their products, while retailers are more interested in featuring their store's name, location, and assortment of merchandise and services offered. This conflict in goals can reduce co-op advertising's effectiveness from the retailer's perspective. In addition, ads developed by the vendor often are used by several competing retailers and

EXHIBIT **16–10**

Suggestions for
Developing Local
Ads

Retail Owner-Managers	
Have a dominant headline	The first question a consumer asks is, What's in if for me? Thus, retailers need to feature the principal benefit being offered in the headline along with a reason why the consumer should act immediately. The benefit can be expanded on in a subhead.
Use a dominant element	Ads should include a large picture or headline. Typically, photographs of real people attract more attention than drawings. Action photographs are very effective in getting readers' attention.
Stick to a simple layout	The ad's layout should lead the reader's eye through the message from the headline to the illustration and then to the explanatory copy, price, and retailer's name and location. Complex elements, decorative borders, and many different typefaces distract the reader's attention from the retailer's message.
Provide a specific, complete presentation	Ad readers are looking for information that will help them decide whether to visit the store. The ad must contain all of the information pertinent to this decision, including the type of merchandise, brands, prices, sizes, and colors. Consumers are unlikely to make a special trip to the store on the basis of vague information. Broadcast ads, particularly radio ads, tend to be very creative but often leave the consumer thinking, Gee that was a clever ad, but what was it advertising?
Use easily recognizable, distinct visuals	Consumers see countless ads each day. Thus, to get the consumers' attention, retailers must make their ads distinct from the competition's. Ads with distinctive art, layout, design elements, or typeface generate higher readership.
Give the store's name and address	The store's name and location are the two most important aspects of a retail ad. If consumers don't know where to go to buy the advertised merchandise, the retailer won't make a sale. The retailer's name and location must be prominently displayed in print ads and repeated several times in broadcast ads.

may list the names and locations of all retailers offering their brands. Thus, co-op ads tend to blur any distinctions between retailers. Finally, restrictions the vendor places on the ad may further reduce its effectiveness for the retailer. For example, the vendor may restrict advertising to a period of time when the vendor's sales are depressed—a time when the retailer might not normally be advertising.

Advertising Agencies   Most large retailers have a department that creates advertising for sales and special events. Advertising agencies are often used by large retailers to develop ads for store image campaigns. Many small retailers use local agencies to plan and create their advertising. These local agencies are often more skilled in planning and executing advertising than the retailer's employees are. Agencies also work on other aspects of the promotion programs, such as contests, direct mail, and special promotions.

Local Media   Besides selling newspaper space and broadcast time, the advertising media offer services to local retailers ranging from planning an ad program to actually designing the ads. Media companies also do market research on their audiences and can provide information about shopping patterns in the local area.

This Kmart free-standing insert supports a co-op advertising program that Kmart developed with Rubbermaid.

Choosing the Most Effective Advertising Medium

After developing the message, the next step is deciding what medium to use to communicate the message to customers.

Types of Media   The media used for retail advertising are newspapers, magazines, direct mail, radio, TV, outdoor, shopping guides, and the Yellow Pages. Exhibit 16–11 summarizes their characteristics.

Newspapers   Retailing and newspaper advertising grew up together over the past century. But the growth in retail newspaper advertising has slowed recently as retailers have begun using other media. Still, 16 of the nation's 25 largest newspaper advertisers are retailers.[26]

EXHIBIT 16–11

Media Capability

MEDIA	TARGETING	TIMELINESS	INFORMATION PRESENTATION CAPABILITIES	LIFE	COST
Newspapers	Good	Good	Modest	Short	Modest
Magazines	Poor	Poor	Modest	Modest	High
Direct mail	Excellent	Modest	High	Modest	Modest
Radio	Modest	Good	Low	Short	Low
Television	Modest	Modest	Low	Short	Modest
Outdoor	Modest	Poor	Very low	Long	Modest
Shopping guides	Modest	Modest	Low	Modest	Low
Yellow Pages	Modest	Poor	Low	Long	Low

In addition to printing ads with their editorial content, newspapers distribute free-standing inserts. A **free-standing insert (FSI),** also called a **preprint,** is an ad printed at the retailer's expense and distributed as an insert in the newspaper.

Since newspapers are distributed in a well-defined local market area, they're effective at targeting retail advertising. For large retailers with multiple stores, the local market covered by a newspaper is similar to the market served by the retailer. Newspapers are beginning to offer opportunities for small retailers to target their advertising by developing editions for different areas of a city. For example, *The Los Angeles Times* has 11 special editions for regions of southern California, including editions for Ventura County, the desert cities, and San Diego County.

Newspapers also offer quick response. There's only a short time between the deadline for receiving the ad and the time that the ad will appear. Thus, newspapers are very useful for delivering messages on a short notice.

Newspapers, like all print media, effectively convey a lot of detailed information. Readers can go through an ad at their own pace and refer back to part of the ad when they want to. In addition, consumers can save the ad and take it to the store with them. This makes newspaper ads very effective at conveying information about the prices of sale items. But newspaper ads aren't effective for showing merchandise (particularly when it's important to illustrate colors) because of the poor reproduction quality.

While newspapers are improving their printing facilities to provide better reproductions and color in ads, retailers continue to rely on preprints to get good reproduction quality. JCPenney uses FSIs extensively, distributing them to over 50 million newspaper readers weekly. However, FSIs are so popular that the insert from one retailer is lost among the large number of inserts in the newspaper. Walgreen has reduced its FSIs from two to one a week because of the clutter and because it has found that younger people don't read newspapers as much as their parents. However, Walgreen is trying to increase the effectiveness of its FSIs by streamlining the message and using a better grade of paper.[28]

The life of a newspaper ad is short because the newspaper is usually discarded after it's read. In contrast, magazine advertising has a longer life since consumers tend to save magazines and read them several times during a week or month.

Finally, the cost of developing newspaper ads is very low, but the cost of delivering the message may be high if the newspaper's circulation is broader than the retailer's target market, thus requiring the retailer to pay for exposures that won't generate sales. Newspaper ads can be developed by less experienced people and don't require expensive color photography or typesetting.

Magazines   Retail magazine advertising is mostly done by national retailers such as Lord & Taylor and The Gap. But magazine advertising is increasing with the growth of local magazines and regional editions of national magazines. Retailers tend to use this medium for image advertising because the reproduction quality is high. Due to the lead time (time between submitting the ad and publication), a major disadvantage is that the timing of a magazine ad is difficult to coordinate with special events and sales.

Direct Mail   Retailers frequently use data collected at POS terminals to target their advertising and sales promotions to specific customers using direct mail. (See Chapter 11.) For example, Neiman Marcus keeps a database of all purchases made by its credit card customers. With information on each customer's purchases, Neiman Marcus can target direct mail on a new perfume to customers with a history of purchasing such merchandise.

16.4

Service Merchandise Collects Phone Numbers

WHEN A CUSTOMER PURCHASES an item at Service Merchandise, the sales associate asks for the customer's phone number. Ninety percent of the customers comply with the request and then the phone number is used as a unique identifier for maintaining a record of the customer's purchase history. When the sales associate enters the phone number in the POS terminal, it's transmitted to a central file in Nashville. Then the customer's name and address is sent back to the store for verification by the sales associate.

A full 250 million transactions from 24 million customers over the past eight years are in the database. The database includes information about the transactions (selling price, regular and sale prices, payment method, date, store, clerk number) and details about the merchandise.

Service Merchandise regularly mails flyers and an annual 600-page catalog to its top customers. The top 2 percent of its customers contribute 25 percent of sales and profits, the top 30 percent contribute 80 percent of the retailer's sales and profits. By analyzing the database, Service Merchandise identified 1 million customers who just shop during Christmas season no matter how many mailings are sent. These customers now only get mailings during the Christmas season. Another example of targeting direct mail is sending a flyer promoting the store's gift registry to customers who have just purchased an engagement ring.

Source: Gary Witkin, "Effective Use of Retail Data Base," *Direct Marketing,* December 1995, pp. 32–35.

Many purchases are made with cash or use third-party credit cards like Visa and MasterCard. Thus, retailers lack information about many purchases if they rely on store credit card transactions to create a mailing list. Retailing View 16.4 discusses how Service Merchandise overcomes this problem and then uses the database of customer purchases to build sales and customer loyalty.

Retailers without their own mailing list can purchase a wide variety of lists for targeting consumers with specific demographics, interests, and lifestyles. For example, a store could buy a list of subscribers to *Architectural Digest* magazine in its trading area and then mail information about home furnishings to those upscale consumers. Finally, many retailers encourage their salespeople to maintain a preferred customer list and use it to mail personalized invitations and notes.

While direct mail can be very effective due to the ability to personalize the message, it's also costly. Many consumers ignore direct-mail advertising and treat it as junk mail.

Radio   Many retailers use radio advertising because messages can be targeted to a specific segment of the market.[29] Some radio stations' audiences are highly loyal to their announcers. When these announcers promote a retailer, listeners are impressed. The cost of developing and broadcasting radio commercials is quite low.

One disadvantage of radio advertising is that listeners generally treat the radio broadcast as background, which limits the attention they give the message. As with all broadcast media, consumers must get the information from a radio commercial when it's broadcast—they can't refer back to the ad for information they didn't hear or remember.

INTERNET EXERCISE   You can find more information about the use of radio as an advertising media at the Radio Advertising Bureau site http://www.rab.com. Based on this information, what types of retail messages can be delivered most effectively by radio compared to other media?

Television   TV commercials can be placed on a national network or a local station. A local commercial is called a spot. Retailers typically use TV for image advertising. They take advantage of the high reproduction quality and the opportunity to communicate through both visual images and sound. TV ads can also demonstrate product usage. For example, Eckerd Drug's TV ad program is built around the theme "It's Right at Eckerds." The ads summarize the advantages of shopping at Eckerd on many levels—convenient location, available parking, broad assortment, easy and fast checkout. Lifestyle ads connect Eckerd as a vital link to an active, healthy, reduced-stress lifestyle. On the other hand, Walgreen's advertising campaign stresses its position as the leading national drugstore using the theme "The Pharmacy America Trusts."[30]

REFACT Americans spend 1,645 hours annually watching TV and only 175 hours a year reading newspapers.[31]

Besides high production costs, broadcast time for national TV advertising is expensive. **Spots,** ads on local and cable TV, have relatively small audiences and may be economical for local retailers. To offset the high production costs, many suppliers provide modular commercials, in which the retailer can insert its name or a "tag" after information about the vendor's merchandise.

Outdoor   Billboards and other forms of outdoor advertising can effectively create awareness for a limited amount of information to a narrow audience. Thus, outdoor advertising has limited usefulness in providing information about sales. Outdoor advertising is typically used to remind customers about the retailer or to inform people in cars of nearby retail outlets.[32]

Shopping Guides   **Shopping guides** are free papers delivered to all residents in a specific area. This medium is particularly useful for retailers that want to saturate a specific trading area. Shopping guides are very cost-effective and assure the local retailer of 100 percent coverage in a specific area. In contrast, subscription newspapers typically offer only 30 to 50 percent coverage.[33]

An extension of the shopping guide concept is the coupon book or magazine. These media contain coupons offered by retailers for discounts. Shopping guides and coupon books make no pretense about providing news to consumers. They're simply delivery vehicles for ads and coupons.

Yellow Pages   The Yellow Pages are useful for retailers because they have a long life. The Yellow Pages are used as a reference by consumers who are definitely interested in making a purchase and seeking information.

Factors in Selecting Media

To convey their message with the most impact to the most consumers in the target market at the lowest cost, retailers need to evaluate media in terms of coverage, reach, cost, and impact of the advertising messages delivered through the medium.

Coverage   **Coverage** refers to the number of potential customers in the retailer's target market that could be exposed to an ad in a given medium. For example, assume that the size of the target market is 100,000 customers. The local newspaper is distributed to 60 percent of the customers in the target market, 90 percent of the potential customers have a TV set that picks up the local station's signal, and 5 percent of the potential customers drive past a billboard. Thus, the coverage for newspaper advertising would be 60,000; for TV advertising, 90,000; and for the specific billboard, 5,000.

REFACT Cable TV has a broad reach with teens. A full 72 percent of male teens and 75 percent of female teens watch MTV weekly. Also, 67 percent of male teens watch ESPN weekly.

Reach   In contrast to coverage, **reach** is the actual number of customers in the target market exposed to an advertising medium. If on any given day, 60 percent of the potential customers who receive the newspaper actually read it, then the newspaper's reach would be 36,000 (or 60 percent × 60,000). Retailers often run an ad several times, in which case they calculate the **cumulative reach** for the sequence of ads. For example, if 60 percent of the potential customers receiving a newspaper read it each day, 93.6 percent (or 1 – .40 × .40 × .40) of the potential customers will read the newspaper at least one day over the three-day period in which the ad appears in the paper. Thus, the cumulative reach for running a newspaper ad for three days is 56,160 (or 93.6 percent × 60,000)—which almost equals the newspaper's coverage.

Cost.   The **cost per thousand (CPM)** measure is often used to compare media. Typically, CPM is calculated by dividing an ad's cost by its reach. Another approach for determining CPM would be to divide the cost of several ads in a campaign by their cumulative reach. If, for instance, in the previous example, one newspaper ad costs $500 and three ads cost $1,300, the CPM using simple reach is $13.89 (or $500/36). Using cumulative reach, the CPM is $23.15 (or $1,300/56.16). Note that the CPM might be higher using cumulative reach rather than simple reach, but the overall reach is also higher, and many potential customers will see the ad two or three times.

CPM is a good method for comparing similar-size ads in similar media, such as full-page ads in *The Los Angeles Times* and *The Orange County Register.* But CPM can be misleading when comparing the cost-effectiveness of ads in different types of media, such as newspaper and TV. A TV ad may have a lower CPM than a newspaper ad, but the newspaper ad may be much more effective at achieving the ad's communication objectives, such as giving information about a sale.

Impact   Impact is an ad's effect on the audience. Due to their unique characteristics, different media are particularly effective at accomplishing different promotion tasks. Exhibit 16–12 shows various media's effectiveness for different communication tasks. TV is particularly effective at getting audience attention, demonstrating merchandise, changing attitudes, and announcing events. Magazines are particularly appropriate for emphasizing the quality and prestige of a store and its offering, and for providing detailed information to support quality claims. Newspapers are useful

EXHIBIT **16–12**

Effectiveness of Six Media on Communication Objectives

Communication tasks	TV	Magazines	Newspaper	Radio	Outdoor	Direct mail
Getting attention	●	◗	○	◑	◕	◕
Demonstrating merchandise	●	◕	◗	○	◑	●
Emphasizing quality	◗	●	◑	○	◕	●
Providing information	◔	●	◕	◗	◔	●
Changing attitudes	●	◗	◕	○	◑	●
Identifying name	◗	◕	○	◔	●	○
Stimulating imagination	◕	◗	◑	●	○	◕
Announcing events	●	○	◕	◗	◑	●

● Most effective   ◕ More effective   ◗ Moderately effective   ◔ Less effective   ○ Least effective

Source: Adapted from Michael Rothschild, *Advertising: From Fundamentals to Strategies* (Lexington, MA: D. C. Heath, 1987), pp. 449, 452.

for providing price information and announcing events. Radio's principal strength, other than its low cost, is stimulating listeners' imagination. Outdoor advertising is most effective at promoting a retailer's name and location. Finally, direct mail is one of the most effective media since it can be targeted to specific families and can convey considerable information

Determining Ad Frequency and Timing

Ads' frequency and timing determines how often and when customers will see the retailer's message.

Frequency   **Frequency** is how many times the potential customer is exposed to an ad. The appropriate frequency depends on the ad's objective. Typically, several exposures to an ad are required to influence a customer's buying behavior. Thus, campaigns directed toward changing purchase behavior rather than creating awareness emphasize frequency over reach. Ads announcing a sale are often seen and remembered after one exposure. Thus, sale ad campaigns emphasize reach over frequency.

Timing   Typically, an ad should appear on, or slightly preceding, the days consumers are most likely to purchase merchandise. For example, if most consumers buy groceries Thursday through Sunday, then supermarkets should advertise on Thursday and Friday. Similarly, consumers often go shopping after they receive their paychecks at the middle and the end of the month. Thus, advertising should be concentrated at these times.

Retailers should avoid advertising during periods of limited demand. Seasonal merchandise should only be advertised during periods when it's bought—lawn mowers at the beginning of summer and skimobiles at the beginning of winter. Advertising isn't very effective during bad weather because customers are reluctant to leave their homes to visit a store. But these might be good times for direct-mail retailers to advertise.

IMPLEMENTING SALES PROMOTION PROGRAMS

The most commonly used sales promotions by retailers are special sales supported by advertising. Other forms of retail sales promotion are merchandise demonstrations, premiums, and coupons as well as games, sweepstakes, and contests. Many retailers are initiating frequent shopper programs to target sales promotion to building loyalty among the store's best customers.

Types of Sales Promotions

Special Sales   Retailers often have special sales to promote store traffic and reduce their inventory of older merchandise. These sales promotions can be advertised or just announced through signs in the store. Special sales can be used to sell merchandise that's still in inventory at the end of the season.

Merchandise Demonstrations and Sampling   Some retailers use in-store demonstrations and offer free samples of merchandise to build excitement in the store and stimulate purchases. In department stores, fashion shows and cooking demonstrations draw customers to the store and encourage impulse purchases.

Sampling in supermarkets is very effective because most consumers often do not know what they want to buy before entering the stores. For example, when 10-year-old Alex Rolfson likes a free sample of a new frozen pizza, his father Chuck tosses a couple of them in his shopping cart. Chuck Rolfson says, "That's why I bring my kids along. If I buy it without a sample, they won't eat it." Bigg's (a supermarket chain in Cincinnati) finds that over 60 percent of its customers sample products and 37 percent buy the sampled product.[34]

Premiums   A **premium** is merchandise offered at a reduced price, or even for free, to encourage customers to make a purchase. Premiums are often used to promote cosmetics and fragrances. Manufacturers such as Estée Lauder will offer a gift box of bath powder with every purchase of a new cologne to stimulate trial of the new fragrance.

Games, Sweepstakes, and Contests   Promotional games of chance differ from premiums and price-off deals in that (1) only a few customers receive rewards and (2) winners are determined by luck. For example, fast-food restaurants frequently have contests associated with major films (such as *The Lion King*) or sports events (such as the Super Bowl).

Coupons   **Coupons** offer a discount on the price of specific items when they're purchased at a store. Coupons are the most common promotional tool used by supermarkets. Retailers distribute them in their newspaper ads and in direct-mail programs. For example, Publix, a Florida-based supermarket chain, targeted a promotion at affluent customers using a direct-mail piece that included recipes for a gourmet meal with coupons to purchase the products needed to prepare it.

INTERNET EXERCISE   Some manufacturers now deliver coupons through the Internet rather than by mail or in FSIs. Go to H.O.T.! Coupon site at http://hotcoupons.com for coupons offered over the Internet. How does this distribution system compare to more traditional distribution systems?

Manufacturers also distribute coupons for their products that can be used at retailers that stock the products. To attract customers, some supermarkets accept coupons distributed by competing retailers. Another technique is for a retailer to offer double or triple the value of coupons distributed by manufacturers. Coupons are often tied into frequent shopper programs discussed in the next section. Retailing View 16.5 describes a system for targeting coupons at the point of sale to specific customers.

Frequent Shopper Programs   Fresh Farm, a Norfolk, Virginia–based supermarket chain, has a frequent shopper program, called the Gold Card program, for its best customers. When Gold Card member Tina Williams enters the store, she "swipes" her card at a kiosk, and a high-speed printer provides a personalized shopping list with up to 25 deals. The deals offered are based on Tina's purchase history.

Coupons offering special prices for merchandise are distributed in newspapers, free-standing inserts, and in-store coupon dispensers.

16.5

Targeting Coupons

CATALINA MARKETING HAS DEVELOPED a system for targeting coupons to grocery shoppers. The company has installed coupon printers at 80,000 checkout aisles in 8,400 supermarkets. Manufacturers and supermarkets contract with Catalina to print specific coupons for customers based on their purchases. For example, Coca-Cola might offer a coupon to each customer who purchased a six-pack of Pepsi-Cola or the supermarket might offer a coupon for a store-brand detergent to customers buying Tide. The redemption rate for Catalina's coupons is 9 percent, four times greater than the redemption rate for coupons printed on free-standing inserts. In addition, these coupons are targeted to specific groups that the manufacturer and supermarkets want to reach. Catalina also automatically enrolls customers in a sweepstakes based on the merchandise they purchase or prints out telephone debit cards for long-distance calling with a personal identification number.

Catalina has recently launched a new program called Supermarkets Online, which uses the internet to bring retailers and manufacturers together on special promotions. On the Internet site (http://www.hotcoupons.com), the manufac-

This Bold coupon was automatically printed out for a customer when the POS terminal recognized that the customer had purchased a competing detergent brand on this shopping trip.

turers section from Bumble Bee Tuna, Listerine, and General Foods International Coffees offers coupons, information, and vouchers for samples. The supermarket section has listings of weekly specials, checkout rebate offers, and coupons for local retailers.

Source: Matt Walsh, "Point-of-Sale Persuaders," *Forbes,* October 24, 1994, p. 232; and Richard De Santa, "In-store Marketing Continues to Surge," *Supermarket Business*, February 1996, p. 26.

For example, Tina's history shows she frequently purchases corn chips but does not buy dip. She'll get a deal on bean dip printed on her shopping list to encourage her to try a new product. If she passes up the deal this time in the market, the next time the value of the bean dip coupon will be automatically increased.[37]

Frequent shopper programs are based on two principles: (1) all customers are not equal and (2) behavior follows rewards. Most retailers have found that 20 percent of their customers account for an overwhelming share of their sales and profits. Frequent shopper programs reward those important customers to motivate them to develop loyalty. Due to these programs' success, many retailers are shifting their expenditure on newspaper advertising and newspaper coupons to frequent shopper programs. Exhibit 16–13 provides suggestions for developing frequent shopper programs.

REFACT At the end of 1996, 44 percent of consumers belonged to a supermarket frequent shopper club, nearly double the number belonging in 1992.[38]

IMPLEMENTING PUBLICITY PROGRAMS

The objectives of publicity typically are to generate awareness, improve the retailer's image, help the community, and develop community members' goodwill toward the retailer. Publicity can be generated by events held within the store (such as a visit by Elizabeth Taylor to promote her line of perfume) or by the sponsorship of entertainment,

EXHIBIT 16–13

Brian Woolf's 10 P's
for Frequent
Shopper Programs

Brian Woolf, the guru of frequent shopper programs, offers the following points for developing an effective program:

1. *Price*—Members of the program should receive lower prices than nonmembers.
2. *Purchases*—The more you spend, the more rewards you should receive. For example, offer a free turkey at Thanksgiving if the customer spends X dollars during the previous six weeks.
3. *Points*—Award points based on customer purchases. Then allow customers to use the points to buy what they like.
4. *Partners*—Bring noncompetitive retailers into the program. For example, airline frequent flyer programs have partnerships with rental car companies, hotels, and restaurants. General merchandise retailers can team up with local restaurants, gas stations, banks, and movie theaters.
5. *Prizes*—Big Y in New England ran a $1 million sweepstakes plus weekly prizes of $1,000 in cash for members of its frequent shopper club.
6. *Privileges*—If you stay in a Disney hotel, you have the privilege of entering the park an hour early. Marks & Spencer in England has a special shopping evening before Christmas only for its best customers. As American Express says in its ads, "Membership has its privileges."
7. *Pro bono*—Tie in with local charities. Have your best customers select a charity and donate 1 percent of their money from purchases to the charity.
8. *Personalization*—When the frequent shopper card is scanned by the POS terminal, have the screen give the sales associate the opportunity to say "Good morning, Ms. Ramirez." A bakery in Ireland can tell the salesperson that the card holder's birthday is within a week and then the sales associate gets a free birthday cake for the customer.
9. *Participation*—Involve your best customers in decisions. Ask them to participate in focus groups.
10. *Presto*—Treat special customers special. Empower sales associates to make favorable decisions for these customers.

Source: Murray Raphael, "Customer Specific Marketing," *Direct Marketing,* June 1996, pp. 22–27; Brian Woolf, "Differentiate or Die," *Progressive Grocer,* May 1996, pp. 71–73; and "Select Few," *Marketing Week,* March 29, 1996, pp. 53–56.

educational, or community-service activities. Retailers frequently sponsor fund-raising benefit concerts or fashion shows for charitable organizations. Finally, some merchandising programs are so unusual, such as the his-and-hers gifts in the Neiman Marcus Christmas catalog (see Retailing View 16.6), that they become newsworthy.

Publicity Tools

Press releases, press conferences, bylined articles, and speeches are among retailers' methods to get favorable coverage of events involving their firm.

Press Releases   A **press release** is a statement of facts or opinions that the retailer would like to see published by the news media. Press releases are used to announce special events, new store openings, quarterly and annual sales and profits, and changes in strategy.

The press release needs to contain the information that news reporters are trained to seek: who, what, when, where, why, and how. Typically, press releases are one or two pages long, double-spaced so the editor can easily change the copy before authorizing its publication, and printed on company letterhead with the name and phone number of someone to contact for additional information. In some cases, a photograph and caption might be sent with the news release. Major retail firms' public relations departments maintain press lists used for distributing releases to relevant news media.

Press Conferences   A **press conference** is a meeting with representatives of the news media that is called by a retailer. This publicity tool is used for major news events such as the merger of two large retail chains. The press conference gives the media an opportunity to get more information than would be provided by a press release. Major players in the news story are often present at the conference to answer reporters' questions.

16.6

The Ultimate His-and-Hers Gift

THE NEIMAN MARCUS CHRISTMAS catalog is perhaps the nation's best-known retail catalog. Its reputation is largely due to its annual tradition of ultraextravagant his-and hers gifts.

The Christmas catalog was first distributed in 1915 as a Christmas card inviting Neiman Marcus customers to visit the store during the holiday season. In the late 50s, customers were asking Neiman Marcus about unique gifts—merchandise not available in the store or from other catalogs. The first unique gift was a pair of vicuna coats offered in 1951. In 1959, the gift of a black angus steer, delivered on the hoof or in steaks, generated a lot of publicity and elevated the catalog gifts to national prominence.

The next year, Neiman Marcus offered the first his-and-hers gift—a pair of Beechcraft airplanes—and a tradition was born. His-and-hers gifts have included ermine bathrobes, hot-air balloons, Chinese junks, and a pair of camels. The most expensive gift was a set of his-and-hers diamonds priced at $2 million. Most of these gifts are actually sold. A highly publicized chocolate Monopoly set was purchased by Christie Hefner, president of Playboy Enterprises, for her father, Hugh Hefner, founder of *Playboy* magazine.

The 1996 gift was an Airstream motor couch designed and owned by noted husband-and-wife team Victoria and Richard MacKenzie-Child. The couch, selling for $195,000, sleeps four and is decorated with rich fabrics, oil-paint murals, and antique rugs.

Source: Preston Gratiot, "Christmas Catalog Couch," *Trailer Life,* December 1996, p. 54; and Anne Dingus, "The Neiman Marcus Catalog," *Texas Monthly,* December 1996, p. 184.

Bylined Articles   Many publications, particularly trade magazines, accept and publish articles about a particular issue written by an expert working for the retailer. These articles offer retailers an opportunity to express their viewpoint on an issue and demonstrate the firm's expertise.

Speeches   Speeches also enable the retailer to express its views in a public forum. Retail managers have many chances to speak in front of industry groups, business luncheons, conferences, civic groups, and college students. Most speeches can be covered with a press release and photos to generate additional publicity.

Publicity's Effect on Employees and Stockholders

Most advertising is directed toward potential customers. Publicity, however, is often used to communicate with additional audiences. Favorable news stories generated by publicity can build employee morale and help improve employee performance. Much of this publicity is provided by internal newsletters, magazines, bulletin board notices, handbooks, and inserts into pay envelopes. However, news about the retailer published in newspapers or broadcast over TV and radio can have a greater impact on employees than internally distributed information. Just like customers, employees place more credibility on information provided by news media than on information generated by the retailer. Similarly, stockholders, the financial community, vendors, and government agencies are influenced by publicity generated by retailers.

An Illustration: A Store Opening

Let's look at how publicity can be used to generate awareness and interest for a store opening in a target customer group. Consider a local entrepreneur's opening of a new store that sells expensive gifts. One approach for attracting people to the opening would be to offer free T-shirts or posters that commemorate the opening. A T-shirt or poster might

This entrepreneur opening his new restaurant has a person who enjoys good food participate in the store-opening ceremony.

attract some customers but probably won't attract the more affluent customers in the store's target market. Simply offering free posters and T-shirts will certainly not get press coverage.

To get press coverage, the store needs to do something unusual. A ribbon-cutting ceremony isn't unique but might get coverage if a newsworthy person, such as the mayor, cuts the ribbon. If the person is well known and respected by people in the retailer's target market, then the opening will attract the right types of customers.

Another approach for generating publicity would be to link the store opening to a theme. For example, the opening could be tied to a set of new services or merchandise categories offered. If this approach is taken, press kits and press conferences might be needed so that the local media can get enough information to write a detailed story about the opening and the event it's linked to.

Finally, the opening could be tied to a community issue and used to demonstrate the retailer's interest and involvement in the community. For example, a store opening in a downtown location might be linked with redeveloping the downtown area.[39]

SUMMARY

Retailers communicate with customers through advertising, sales promotions, store atmosphere, publicity, personal selling, and word of mouth. These elements in the promotion mix must be coordinated so customers will have a clear, distinct image of the retailer and won't be confused by conflicting information.

The promotion mix can be designed to achieve a variety of objectives for the retailer. Objectives include positioning the retailer in the customer's mind, increasing sales and store traffic, providing information about the retailer's location and offering, and announcing special activities.

Many retailers use rules of thumb to determine the size of the promotion budget. Marginal analysis (the most appropriate method for determining how much must be spent to accomplish the retailer's objectives) should be used to determine whether the level of spending maximizes the profits that could be generated by the promotion mix.

The largest portion of a retailer's promotion budget is typically spent on advertising and sales promotions. A wide array of media can be used for advertising—each medium has its pros and cons. Newspaper advertising is effective for announcing sales, while TV ads are useful for developing an image. Sales promotions are typically used to achieve short-term objectives, such as increasing store traffic over a weekend. Most sales promotions are supported in part by promotions offered to the retailer by its vendors. Publicity and word of mouth generate the most credible information, but both are hard to control.

KEY TERMS

advertising, *474*

affordable method, *483*

cherry-picking, *485*

communication objectives, *479*

competitive parity method, *484*

cooperative (co-op) advertising, *487*

cost per thousand (CPM), *494*

coupon, *496*

coverage, *493*

cumulative reach , *494*

free-standing insert (FSI), *491*

frequency, *495*

frequent shopper program, *473*

impact, *494*

integrated marketing communications, *477*

marginal analysis, *481*

objective-and-task method, *482*

percentage-of-sales method, *483*

personal selling, *475*

positioning, *477*

premium, *496*

preprint, *491*

press conference, *498*

press release, *498*

promotion mix, *472*

publicity, *475*

reach, *494*

rule-of-thumb methods, *483*

sales promotion, *474*

shopping guide, *493*

spot, *493*

store atmosphere, *474*

word of mouth, *475*

DISCUSSION QUESTIONS & PROBLEMS

1. As a means of communicating with customers, how does advertising differ from publicity?

2. How can advertising, personal selling, and promotion complement each other in an integrated marketing communications program?

3. Why is the newspaper the favorite medium used by retailers for advertising? What are the advantages and disadvantages of newspaper advertising? Why is the use of newspaper decreasing and use of direct mail increasing?

4. What factors should be considered in dividing up the budget among a store's different merchandise areas? Which of the following should receive the highest advertising budget: fashionable women's clothing, men's underwear, women's hosiery, or kitchen appliances? Why?

5. Outline some elements in a promotion program to achieve the following objectives:

   a. Increase store loyalty by 20 percent.

   b. Build awareness of the store by 10 percent.

   c. Develop an image as a low-price retailer.

   How would you determine whether the program met the objective?

6. A potential market's size is 357,000, the local newspaper is distributed to 52 percent of the population, 34 percent of those who receive the newspaper actually read it, and a retailer runs an ad for two days. What's the cumulative reach?

7. TV is a popular advertising medium for retailers. TV advertisers have identified many types of markets based on the day, time, and type of show during which their ads may appear. During which days, times, and types of shows would retailers advertise fresh produce and meat, power drills, beer, and health club memberships? Why?

8. Some retailers direct their advertising efforts toward reaching as wide an audience as possible. Others try to expose the audience to an advertisement as many times as possible. When should a retailer concentrate on reach? When should a retailer concentrate on frequency?

9. The U.S. auto industry is extremely competitive. New car lines are quite often a big risk for manufacturers and retailers alike. Suppose an auto retailer decides it needs extensive sales promotion to achieve high sales for a new line of cars. Make some suggestions for using the five types of sales promotions.

10. A retailer plans to open a new store near a university. It will specialize in collegiate merchandise such as T-shirts, fraternity/sorority accessories, and sweat shirts. What specific advertising media should the new store use to capture the university market?

11. Cooperative (co-op) advertising is a good way for a retailer to extend an ad budget. Why isn't it always in a retailer's best interests to rely extensively on co-op advertising?

SUGGESTED READINGS

Achabal, Dale, Shelby McIntyre, and Stephen Smith. "Maximizing Profits from Periodic Department Store Promotions." *Journal of Retailing*, Winter 1990, pp. 383–407.

Belch, George, and Michael Belch. *Introduction to Advertising and Promotion Management*, 2d ed. Burr Ridge, IL: Richard D. Irwin, 1996.

Cuneo, Alice, "Savvy Frequent-Buyer Plans Build on a Loyal Base." *Advertising Age*, March 20, 1995, pp. S10–S11.

Falk, Edgar. *1,001 Ideas to Create Retail Entertainment.* Englewood Cliffs, NJ: Prentice-Hall, 1995.

Hathcote, Jan. "Institutional and Promotional Newspaper Advertising in the US Apparel Retailing Industry from 1971 to 1991." *International Journal of Advertising*, March 22, 1995, pp. 165–73.

Karande, Kiram, and V. Kumar. "The Effects of Brand Characteristics and Retailer Policies on Response to Retail Price Promotion: Implications for Retailers." *Journal of Retailing* 71 (Fall 1995), pp. 249–78.

Kaufman, Carol. "Coupon Use in Ethnic Markets: Implications from a Retail Perspective." *Journal of Consumer Marketing*, Winter 1991, pp. 41–51.

Kelly, J. Patrick, Hugh Cannon, and H. Keith Hunt. "Customer Responses to Rainchecks." *Journal of Retailing*, Summer 1991, pp. 122–37.

Radder, Laetile. "The Marketing Practices of Independent Fashion Retailers: Evidence from South Africa." *Journal of Small Business Management* 34 (January 1996), pp. 78–84.

Redman, Russell. "Selling the Image." *Supermarket News*, March 18, 1996, pp. 1–2.

Srinivasan, Srini, Robert Leone, and Francis Mulhern. "The Advertising Exposure Effect of Free Standing Inserts." *Journal of Advertising*, March 22, 1995, pp. 29–38.

NOTES

1. "Cooking Up a Deep-Dish Database," *Business Week*, November 20, 1995, p. 160.

2. "Seven Pillars to Success," *Chain Store Age*, August 1, 1996, p. 11A.

3. "Department Store Frequency Marketing," *Colloquy* 4, no. 3 (1994), pp. 1–23.

4. *Financial and Operating Results of Department & Specialty Stores in 1996* (New York: National Retail Federation, 1993), p. 12.

5. "The Man Who Created Rudolph from an Idea That Almost Didn't Fly," *Chicago Tribune*, December 13, 1990, p. 1C.

6. See A. Coskun Samli, "Store Image Definition, Dimensions, Measurement, and Management," in *Retail Market Strategy*, ed. A. Samli (New York: Quorum, 1989).

7. See also "Sears Links to NCAA Women," *Advertising Age*, March 11, 1996, pp. 1, 35.

8. Chip Walker, "Word of Mouth," *American Demographics*, July 1995, pp. 38–43; Betsy Gelb and Madeline Johnson, "Word-of-Mouth Communications: Causes and Consequences," *Journal of Health Care Marketing*, Fall 1995, pp. 23–34; and Robin Higie, Lawrence Feick, and Linda Price, "Types and Amount of Word-of-Mouth Communications about Retailers," *Journal of Retailing* 63 (Fall 1987), pp. 260–78.

9. *Consumer Complaint Handling in America: An Update Study* (Washington, DC: White House Office of Consumer Affairs, 1986).

10. Steve Albrecht, *Crises Management for Corporate Self-Defense: How to Protect Your Organization in a Crisis* (New York: Random House, 1995).

11. "Top 100 Advertisers," *Advertising Age*, July 13, 1996, p. 16.

12. Janet Smith, "Integrated Marketing," *Marketing Tools*, November–December 1995, pp. 62–65.

13. David Aaker and J. Gary Shansby, "Positioning Your Product," *Business Horizons* 25 (May–June 1982), pp. 56–62; and Edward DiMingo, "The Fine Art of Positioning," *Journal of Business Strategy*, March–April 1989, pp. 34–38.

14. Anthony Cox and Dena Cox, "Competing on Price: The Role of Retail Price Advertisements in Shaping Store Price Image," *Journal of Retailing*, Winter 1990, pp. 428–45.

15. See Russell H. Colley, *Defining Advertising Goals for Measured Advertising Results* (New York: Association of National Advertisers, 1961); and R. Lavidge and G. A. Steiner, "A Model for Predictive Measurement of Advertising Effectiveness," *Journal of Marketing*, October 1961, pp. 59–62.

16. A number of different models and computer programs have been developed to help managers set promotion budgets. See Scott Neslin and John Quelch, "Developing Models for Planning Retailer Sales Promotions: An Application to Automobile Dealerships," *Journal of Retailing* 63 (Winter 1987), pp. 333–64; Paul Green, Vijay Manhajan, Stephen Goldberg, and Pradeep Kedia, "A Decision Support System for Developing Retail Promotion Strategy," *Journal of Retailing* 59 (Fall 1983), pp. 116–43; and Arthur Allaway, J. Barry Mason, and Gene Brown, "An Optimal Decision Support Model for Department-Level Promotion Mix Planning," *Journal of Retailing* 63 (Fall 1987), pp. 216–41.

17. Randall Chapman, "Assessing the Profitability of Retailer Couponing with a Low-Cost Field Experiment," *Journal of Retailing* 62 (Spring 1986), pp. 19–40; and Peter Doyle and B. Zeki Gidengil, "A Review of In-Store Experiments," *Journal of Retailing* 59 (Fall 1977), pp. 116–43.

18. Leonard Lodish, *Advertisers and Promotion Challenge: Vaguely Right or Precisely Wrong* (New York: Oxford University Press, 1986).

19. *Financial and Operating Results of Department & Specialty Stores in 1996*, p. 17.

20. Ronald Curhan and Robert Kopp, "Obtaining Retailer Support for Trade Deals: Key Success Factors," *Journal of Advertising Research* 27 (December 1987–January 1988), pp. 51–60.

21. Giles D'Souza and Arthur Allaway, "An Empirical Investigation of the Advertising Spending Decision of a Multiproduct Retailer," *Journal of Retailing* 71 (Fall 1995), pp. 279–96.

22. This example is adapted by William R. Swinyard, professor of business management, Brigham Young University, from "Overseas Airlines Service" case.

23. Gary Witkin, "Effective Use of Retail Data Base," *Direct Marketing*, December 1995, pp. 32–35.

24. Michael Rothschild, *Advertising* (Lexington, MA: D. C. Heath, 1987), pp. 663–64. See also John McCann, Ali Tadlaqui, and John Gallagher, "Knowledge Systems in Merchandising: Advertising Design," *Journal of Retailing*, Fall 1990, pp. 257–77; and Meryl Gardner and Michael Houston, "The Effects of Visual and Verbal Components of Retail Communications," *Journal of Retailing*, Summer 1986, pp. 65–78.

25. Rothschild, *Advertising*, p. 655.

26. "Top 100 Advertisers," p. 16.

27. Ibid., p. 31.

28. James Fredrick and Allene Symons, "Building an Image," *Drug Store News*, November 18, 1996, p. 9.

29. "Maximizing the Potential of Audio Advertising," *Chain Store Age*, March 1995, p. B13.

30. Fredrick and Symons, "Building an Image," pp. 9–10.

31. Tony Case, "A Rocky Road Predicted for Newspaper Advertising," *Editor & Publisher*, September 23, 1995, p. 27.

32. Cyndee Miller, "Outdoors Gets a Makeover," *Marketing News*, April, 10, 1995, pp. 1, 26; and Teresa Andreoli, "From Retailers to Consumers: Billboards Drive the Message Home," *Discount Store News*, September 19, 1994, p. 14.

33. "Free Papers Gain in Popularity as Ad Vehicles," *Chain Store Age Executive*, January 1988, p. 84.

34. Gabriella Stern, "With Sampling, There Is Too a Free Lunch," *The Wall Street Journal*, March 11, 1994, pp. B1, B5.

35. Ibid.

36. Kathleen Deveny and Richard Gibson, "Awash in Coupons? Some Firms Try to Stem the Tide," *The Wall Street Journal*, May 10, 1994, p. B1.

37. "The Future Is in the Cards," *Promo*, August 1995, p. S5.

38. "Dealing the Cards," *Promo*, August 1995, p. S5.

39. Robert R. Robichaud, "How to Milk a Store Opening for All It's Worth," *Marketing News*, March 16, 1984, p. 8; and Jules Abend, "Special Events," *Stores*, May 1984, pp. 39–42.

Store Management

SECTION IV FOCUSES ON IMPLEMENTATION ISSUES associated with store management, including managing store employees and controlling costs (Chapter 17), presenting merchandise (Chapter 18), providing service (Chapter 19), and selling merchandise (Chapter 20).

CHAPTER SEVENTEEN
Managing the Store

CHAPTER EIGHTEEN
Store Layout,
Design, and Visual
Merchandising

CHAPTER NINETEEN
Customer Service

CHAPTER TWENTY
Retail Selling

Traditionally, the issues concerning merchandise management were considered the most important retail implementation decisions, and buying was considered the best career path for achieving senior retail management positions. However, store management and operations are becoming more important. • Developing a strategic advantage through merchandise management is becoming more and more difficult. Competing stores often have similar assortments of branded merchandise. Since customers can find the same assortments in a number of conveniently located retail outlets, store management issues have become a critical basis for developing strategic advantage. Retailers are placing more emphasis on differentiating their offering from competitive offerings based on customer service, store design, and visual merchandising.

Anne Marie Johnson, District Manager, Home Depot

ALL OF HOME DEPOT'S RESOURCES are directed at supporting the associates working in the stores. Our company's success is based on selling merchandise to customers in our stores. Even though we are a $19.5 billion corporation, each store manager is an entrepreneur, running his or her own business, hiring, training, and motivating 150 employees. And each store takes on the personality of its manager. • We support this entrepreneurial philosophy by giving store managers the authority and responsibility for running their stores. I remember when I first became a store manager, I saw this product, a car wash kit, and thought it was going to be a big seller. I ordered 1,000 for my store, and after a few weeks we only sold 25. I had to call all of the stores in the area to ask them to take some of my inventory. My district manager encouraged the risk taking but explained the benefit of getting a partner. I learned the lesson at hand and continue to tell my associates that story so they too will feel comfortable taking a risk. • The real challenge in managing a store is getting employees to understand how important it is to take care of the customer. Some people don't like waiting on others, but our company was built on the principle that everyone needs to go the extra mile to make sure the customer is served. • The way to get promoted in our company is to develop the people who work for you. Sometimes it feels like I am counselor, priest, and the captain of the ship, all at the same time. But I love my job and have been successful. I am now 31 years old and am responsible for the 10 stores in my district. My income from salary and bonuses is more than eight times what it was when I started at Home Depot 13 years ago, and that doesn't include my stock options. But the most important rewards I get are dealing with the challenges of selling more merchandise and developing our future managers.

17

Managing the Store

THE WORLD OF RETAILING

↓

RETAILING STRATEGY

↓

MERCHANDISE MANAGEMENT
12. Planning Merchandise
    Assortments
13. Buying Systems
14. Buying Merchandise
15. Pricing
16. Retail Promotion Mix

STORE MANAGEMENT
17. Managing the Store
18. Store Layout, Design, and
    Visual Merchandising
19. Customer Service
20. Retail Selling

QUESTIONS

- What are the responsibilities of store managers?

- How should store managers recruit, select, motivate, train, and evaluate their employees?

- How should store managers compensate their salespeople?

- What legal and ethical issues must store managers consider in managing their employees?

- What can store managers do to increase productivity and reduce costs?

- How can store managers reduce inventory losses due to employee theft and shoplifting?

STORE MANAGERS ARE RESPONSIBLE for increasing the productivity of two of the retailer's most important assets: the firm's investments in its employees and real estate. Managers are on the firing line in retailing. Due to their daily contact with customers, they have the best knowledge of customer needs and competitive activity. From this unique vantage point, store managers play an important role in formulating and executing retail strategy. Buyers can develop exciting merchandise assortments and procure them at low cost, but the retailer only realizes the benefits of the buyer's effort when the merchandise is sold. Good merchandise doesn't sell itself. Store managers must present the merchandise effectively and offer services that stimulate and facilitate customer buying decisions.

Even in national chains, store managers are treated as relatively independent managers of a business within the corporation. Some department store managers are responsible for $150 million in annual sales and manage over 1,000 employees. For example, James Nordstrom (CEO of Nordstrom) tells store managers, "This is your business. Do your own thing. Don't listen to us in Seattle, listen to your customers. We give you permission to take care of your customers." And Michele Love, manager of the Nordstrom store in Skokie, Illinois, responded by building a mammography center in the store without asking anyone. The center has been booked solid since it opened.[1]

STORE MANAGEMENT RESPONSIBILITIES

The responsibilities of store managers are shown in Exhibit 17–1. These functions are divided into four major categories: managing employees, controlling costs, managing merchandise, and providing customer service. Issues concerning managing store employees and controlling costs are discussed in this chapter. The following chapters examine the store manager's responsibilities for presenting and managing merchandise and providing customer service.

An important function of store managers is increasing the productivity of the store's employees by recruiting and selecting effective people; improving their skills through training; and motivating, evaluating, and rewarding them to perform at higher levels. Retailing View 17.1 describes the special problems that German retailers have in increasing employee productivity.

In addition to increasing employee productivity, store managers also need to develop employees who can assume more responsibility and be promoted to higher-level management positions. By developing subordinates, managers help both their firm and themselves. The firm benefits from having more effective managers, and the manager benefits because the firm has a qualified replacement when the manager is promoted.[2]

The first portion of this chapter, focusing on the management of store employees, complements the strategic human resource management issues discussed in Chapter 10. Chapter 10 examines the organization of the tasks performed by the retailers and the general approaches for motivating retail employees and building their commitment to the firm. In this chapter, we discuss how store managers implement the retailer's human resource strategy.

REFACT In supermarkets, which are largely self-service, wages account for 65 percent of the store's controllable expenses.[3]

In addition to managing employees effectively, managers increase their stores' profits by reducing costs. The major costs are the compensation and benefits of employees. But store managers also need to control maintenance and energy costs and inventory loss due to shoplifting and employee theft. These cost control issues are discussed at the end of the chapter.

EXHIBIT 17–1

Responsibilities of Store Managers

MANAGING STORE EMPLOYEES (Chapter 17)

Recruiting and selecting
Socializing and training
Motivating
Evaluating and providing constructive feedback
Rewarding and compensating

CONTROLLING COSTS (Chapter 17)

Increasing labor and productivity
Reducing maintenance and energy costs
Reducing inventory losses

MANAGING MERCHANDISE

Displaying merchandise and maintaining visual standards (Chapter 18)
Working with buyers
   Suggesting new merchandise
   Buying merchandise
   Planning and managing special events
   Marking down merchandise

PROVIDING CUSTOMER SERVICE (Chapters 19 and 20)

17.1

German Retailers Think Americans Work Too Hard

MS. ANGIE CLARK and Mr. Andreas Drauschke have similar store management jobs with similar pay at two different department stores. However, Mr. Drauschke, in Germany, only works 37 hours a week (rarely at night or on weekends) and has six weeks of annual paid vacation. Ms. Clark, in the United States, works 44 hours a week (including evening and weekend shifts), frequently brings work home at night, and spends some off-time shopping the competitors. While Americans often marvel at German efficiency, Mr. Drauschke's workweek and benefits are typical in Germany where workers are guaranteed five weeks paid vacation by law and stores rarely are open more than one night a week and only a half-day on Saturday.

German retail sales associates serve an apprenticeship for two or three years. During this time, they learn the business and the merchandise inside out. In contrast, sales associates in U.S. department stores typically receive only two or three days of training before they start to work with customers.

Keeping work hours short is an obsession in Germany and a goal of the country's powerful labor unions. When Germany introduced Thursday-night shopping in 1989, retail workers went on strike. Mr. Drauschke still finds it difficult to staff the extra two hours on Thursday even though employees are given an hour less work overall. In contrast, many American retail employees work a second job to send their children through college or save money for a house.

However, the long, irregular hours for U.S. retail managers take their toll. Turnover among U.S. retail managers is as high as 40 percent while turnover among German retail managers is negligible.

Source: Daniel Benjamin and Tony Horwitz, "German View: 'You Americans Work Too Hard—and for What?'" *The Wall Street Journal*, July 14, 1994, pp. B1, B6.

Exhibit 17–2 outlines the steps in the employee management process that impact store employees' productivity. These steps are discussed in the following sections.

RECRUITING AND SELECTING STORE EMPLOYEES

The first step in the employee management process is recruiting and selecting employees. To effectively recruit employees, store managers need to undertake a job analysis, prepare a job description, find potential applicants with the desired capabilities, and screen the best candidates to interview.[4] (At the end of this book, Appendix A describes the recruiting and selection process from the perspective of people interested in pursuing retail careers and applying for management trainee positions.)

Job Analysis

The objective of the **job analysis** is to identify essential activities and to determine the qualifications employees need to perform them effectively. For example, retail salespeople's responsibilities vary from com-

EXHIBIT 17–2 Steps in the Employee Management Process

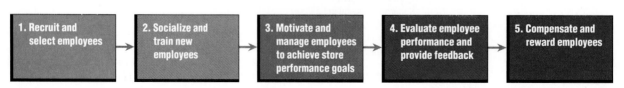

1. Recruit and select employees → 2. Socialize and train new employees → 3. Motivate and manage employees to achieve store performance goals → 4. Evaluate employee performance and provide feedback → 5. Compensate and reward employees

EXHIBIT **17–3**

Questions for
Undertaking a
Job Analysis

How many salespeople will be working in the department at the same time?
Do the salespeople have to work together in dealing with customers?
How many customers will the salesperson have to work with at one time?
Will the salesperson be selling on an open floor or working behind the counter?
How much and what type of product knowledge does the salesperson need?
Does the salesperson need to sell the merchandise or just ring up the orders and provide information?
Is the salesperson required to make appointments with customers and develop a loyal customer base?
Does the salesperson have the authority to negotiate price or terms of the sale?
Does the salesperson need to demonstrate the merchandise?
Will the salesperson be expected to make add-on sales?
Is the salesperson's appearance important? How should an effective salesperson look?
Will the salesperson be required to perform merchandising activities such as stocking shelves and setting up displays?
Who will the salesperson report to?
What compensation plan will the salesperson be working under?

pany to company and from department to department within a store. Clothing salespeople work on an open floor and need to approach customers. Cosmetic and jewelry salespeople work behind a counter, so their customers approach them. Due to these differences, effective open-floor selling requires more aggressive behavior than counter selling.

Managers can obtain the information needed for a job analysis by observing employees presently doing the job and by determining the characteristics of exceptional performers. Exhibit 17–3 lists some questions that managers should consider in a job analysis for sales associates. Information collected in the job analysis is used to prepare a job description.

The job analysis can also result in managers redefining the activities that need to be performed. For example, a job analysis resulted in waiters and waitresses in some Marriott restaurants never entering the kitchen. When the meals are ready, the kitchen beeps the server, a runner delivers the food, and the server puts it on the table. The manager of the Schaumberg, Illinois, Marriott says, "We've changed the job so the servers can do what they do best, provide services to customers."[5]

The job analysis can also lead to redefining the employee's authority as well as responsibilities. As discussed in Chapter 10, retailers are attempting to improve customer service by empowering sales associates to make more decisions. For example, sales clerks at Target's Greatland store can take the customer's word for items priced below $20 if the merchandise can't be scanned; give customers the sale price even if the sale's week has ended; and offer the customer comparable merchandise at the sale price rather than a rain check for out-of-stock items.[6]

Job Description

A **job description** includes (1) activities the employee needs to perform and (2) the performance expectations expressed in quantitative terms. The job description is a guideline for recruiting, selecting, training, and eventually evaluating employees. The description must be in writing so it can be communicated accurately and consistently to present and prospective employees.

Locating Prospective Employees

Staffing stores is a critical problem because the changing demographics is reducing the size of the labor pool. Sources of prospective salespeople include people who respond to newspaper ads; people who work for competitive retailers and other service-oriented businesses; unsolicited walk-in applicants; friends of employees; high school, junior college, and university students; and employment agencies.[7]

Frequently, firms involve their employees in the hunt for good recruits. For example, Professional Salon Concepts, a chain of beauty parlors, offers a referral bonus to its employees. Employees get $100 after a recommended recruit is on the job for 30 days, another $100 on the recruit's six-month anniversary, and $500 if the recruit works for the company for a year.[8]

Burger King aggressively pursues the growing number of immigrants as a source for new employees. Application forms are available in English and Spanish; prospective workers can bring a family member or friend to act as an interpreter during the interview. Training programs are developed for people who aren't familiar with U.S. business practices. For example, many foreign-born workers don't understand benefits like life insurance and are reluctant to report job-related injuries for fear of being fired.[9]

Other restaurants are focusing on hiring older people. These restaurants' managers have found that older employees have an excellent work ethic. They're rarely absent, use few sick days, and take their jobs seriously. However, some managers also report that elderly employees can be a source of friction when mixed with younger employees. Some older employees can't resist making comments like, "In my day we didn't take so many breaks."[10]

T. J. Maxx uses this ad to interest prospective employees in the entry-level position as assistant store manager.

Retail Management at T.J. Maxx . . .

For Corinne Fredericks, it's managing to make a difference.

Corinne Fredericks wanted a management career where she could make an impact on the bottom line. That's why she chose T.J. Maxx. Here, in addition to providing direction to her team of associates, she's ensuring customer satisfaction, overseeing the cash office, and managing the dozens of large and small details that make all the difference in a well-run multi-million dollar store operation.

Interested in learning more about a management style where "total store awareness" lets you make a real difference in bottom line profitability? If you have 3-5 years' retail management experience and are interested in an Assistant Store Manager position, send your resume to:

**Field Recruitment Coordinator
T.J. Maxx, Dept. ESS.
770 Cochituate Road
Framingham, MA 01701**

At T.J. Maxx, the $2.5 billion flagship division of The TJX Companies, Inc., our ongoing mission is to offer fashionable, quality, brand name merchandise at substantial savings for our customers at over 500 locations coast-to-coast. We're proud of our open corporate culture, which places great value on the contributions made by approximately 27,000 diverse and talented associates nationwide.

Maxximize Your Potential
We are an equal opportunity employer committed to workforce diversity.

Screening Applicants to Interview   The screening process matches applicants' qualifications with the job description. Sources of information about applicants include application forms, references, and test scores.[11]

Application Forms   **Job application forms** contain information about the applicant's employment history, previous compensation, reasons for leaving previous employment, education and training, personal health, and references. This information enables the manager to determine whether the applicant has the minimum qualifications and also provides information for interviewing the applicant.[12]

The applicant's job history is particularly important. Frequent job changes without good cause may indicate the applicant isn't committed to the work. Store managers need to give special attention to information not on the form. For example, there may be periods of time during which the applicant wasn't employed or in school. Managers should ask about these unexplained periods during a personal interview.

References   A good way to verify the application form's information is to contact the applicant's references. Contacting references is also helpful for collecting additional information from people who've worked with the applicant. Store managers should also check with former supervisors not listed as references. Due to potential legal problems, however, many companies have a policy of not commenting on past employees.[13]

Store managers generally expect to hear favorable comments from an applicant's references or even from previous supervisors who may not have thought highly of the applicant. The most useful information often comes when the manager asks probing questions in response to unusual comments, faint praise, hesitant responses, or inconsistent information provided by previous employers.

REFACT Seventy-two percent of retailers check references as part of the selection process; 34 percent do drug screening; and 33 percent use paper-and-pencil honesty tests.[15]

Test Scores   Intelligence, ability, personality, and interest tests can provide insights about potential employees. For example, intelligence tests yield data about the applicant's innate abilities and can be used to match applicants with job openings and to develop training programs. Due to potential losses from theft, many retailers such as Wal-Mart and Home Depot require applicants to take drug tests and use tests to assess applicants' honesty and ethics. Paper-and-pencil honesty tests include questions to find out if an applicant has ever thought about stealing and if he believes other people steal ("What percentage of people take more than $1 from their employer?").[14]

Some companies question the use of tests in the selection process because they may not be good predictors of performance. Candidates can fake responses to personality tests or can freeze up when taking aptitude tests. In addition, many tests discriminate against women and minorities who don't share the same values as middle-class white males.[16]

Realistic Job Preview   Turnover is reduced when the applicants understand both the attractive and unattractive aspects of the job. For example, PETsMART, a pet supply category specialist, has each applicant view a 10-minute video that begins with the advantages of being a company employee and then shows scenes of employees dealing with irate customers and cleaning up animal droppings. This type of job preview typically screens out 15 percent of the applicants who would most likely quit in three months if they were hired.[17]

Selecting Applicants   After screening applications, the selection process typically involves a personal interview. Since the interview is usually the critical factor in the hiring decision, the store manager needs to be well prepared and to have complete control over the interview.

Preparation for the Interview   The objective of the interview is to gather relevant information, not simply to ask a lot of questions. The questions should help the manager determine whether the candidate has the motivation and abilities to perform the required job activities.

To make sure that all the information needed to make a hiring decision is collected during the interview, the store manager should prepare a list of questions to ask the candidates. These questions are developed by reviewing the application form and the job description.

An effective approach to interviewing involves some planning by the managers but also allows some flexibility in selecting questions. Managers should develop objectives for what they want to learn about the candidate. Each topic area covered in the interview starts with a broad question, such as "Tell me about your last job," designed to elicit a lengthy response. The broad opening question is followed by a sequence of more specific questions, such as "What did you learn from that job?" or "How many subordinates did you have?"[18] Exhibit 17–4 shows questions the manager might ask.

Controlling the Interview   Some people feel that putting applicants under stress gives the best indication of their capabilities. However, the ability to cope with stress in an interview may not be a good indication of the applicant's performance on the job. Employees aren't typically under extreme stress when they're working.

Applicants are more likely to be open and forthright with the interviewer in a nonthreatening atmosphere. One approach for creating such an atmosphere is to describe the interview format to the applicant at the beginning of the interview. The techniques for asking questions and listening in an interview resemble salespeople's techniques to probe customers for information, which are described in Chapter 20.

Some managers interview candidates while giving a candidate a tour through the store. When the manager sees a display that's out of order, he might say, "While we're talking, would you help me straighten this out?" Some candidates will stand back; others will jump right in and help out. (Hint: You want to hire candidates from the second group.)

SOCIALIZING AND TRAINING NEW STORE EMPLOYEES   After hiring employees, the next step in developing effective employees (as Exhibit 17–2 shows) is introducing them to the firm and its policies. Retailers want the people they hire to become involved, committed contributors to the firm's successful performance. On the other hand, newly hired employees want to learn about their job responsibilities and the company they've decided to join. **Socialization** is the set of steps taken to transform new employees into effective, committed members of the firm. Socialization goes beyond simply orienting new employees to the firm. A principle objective of socialization is to develop a long-term relationship with new employees to reduce turnover costs.[19]

Orientation Program   Orientation programs are critical in overcoming entry shock and socializing new employees. Even the most knowledgeable and mature new employees encounter some surprises. College students who accept

EXHIBIT 17–4   Interviewing Questions

EDUCATION

What were your most favorite and least favorite subjects in college? Why?

What types of extracurricular activities did you participate in? Why did you select those activities?

If you had the opportunity to attend school all over again what, if anything, would you do differently? Why?

How did you spend the summers during college?

Did you have any part-time jobs? Which of your part-time jobs did you find most interesting? What did you find most difficult about working and attending college at the same time? What advice would you give to someone who wanted to work and attend college at the same time?

What accomplishment were you most proud of?

PREVIOUS EXPERIENCE

What's your description of the ideal manager? Subordinate? Coworker?

What did you like most/least about your last job?

What kind of people do you find it difficult/easy to work with? Why?

What has been your greatest accomplishment during your career to date?

Describe a situation at your last job involving pressure. How did you handle it?

What were some duties on your last job that you found difficult?

Of all the jobs you've had, which did you find the most/least rewarding?

What is the most frustrating situation you've encountered in your career?

Why do you want to leave your present job?

What would you do if . . . ?

How would you handle . . . ?

What would you like to avoid in future jobs?

What do you consider your greatest strength/weakness?

What are your responsibilities on your present job?

Tell me about the people you hired on your last job. How did they work out? What about the people you fired?

What risks did you take in your last job and what was the result of those risks?

Where do you see yourself in three years?

What kind of references will your previous employer give?

What do you do when you have trouble solving a problem?

QUESTIONS THAT SHOULD NOT BE ASKED PER EQUAL EMPLOYMENT OPPORTUNITY GUIDELINES

Do you have plans for having children/a family? What are your marriage plans? What does your husband/wife do? What happens if your husband/wife gets transferred or needs to relocate? Who will take care of your children while you're at work? (Asked of men) How would you feel about working for a woman?

How old are you? What is your date of birth? How would you feel working for a person younger than you? Where were you born? Where were your parents born?

Do you have any handicaps? As a handicapped person, what help are you going to need to do your work? How severe is your handicap?

What's your religion? What church do you attend? Do you hold religious beliefs that would prevent you from working on certain days of the week?

Do you feel that your race/color will be a problem in your performing the job? Are you of _____ heritage/race?

management trainee positions often are quite surprised by the differences between student and employee roles. Retailing View 17.2 describes some of these differences.[20]

Orientation programs can last from a few hours to several weeks. The orientation and training program for new salespeople might be limited to several hours during which the new salesperson learns the retailer's policies and procedures and how to use the POS terminal. On the other hand, the orientation program for a department or assistant store manager might take several weeks. For example, Burdines hires approximately 150 college students each year into its management training program. New trainees typically report to work at corporate headquarters in Miami. They're housed in a hotel for a four-week orientation during which they attend classes, meet company executives, and work on

17.2 The Transition from Student to Management Trainee

MANY STUDENTS HAVE some difficulty adjusting to the demands of their first full-time job, because student life and professional life are very different. Students typically "report" to three or four supervisors (professors). A student selects new "supervisors" every four months. On the other hand, management trainees have limited involvement, if any, in selecting the one supervisor they'll report to often for several years.

Student life has fixed time cycles—one-to-two–hour classes with a well-defined beginning and end. Retail managers are involved in a variety of activities with varied time horizons, ranging from a 5-minute interaction with a customer to developing and implementing a merchandise budget over a season.

The decision making students encounter differs dramatically from the decision making retail managers encounter. For example, business students might make several major decisions a day when they discuss cases in class. These decisions are made and implemented in one class period and then a new set of decisions is made and implemented in the next class. In a retail environment, strategic decisions evolve over a long time period. Most decisions, such as those regarding merchandise buying and pricing, are made with incomplete information. The buyers in real life often lack the extensive information provided in many business cases studied in class. Finally, there are long periods of time when retail managers undertake mundane tasks associated with implementing decisions and no major issues are being considered. Students typically don't have these mundane tasks to perform.

Source: Daniel Feldman, *Managing Careers in Organizations* (Reading, MA: Addison-Wesley, 1989), pp. 45–52.

projects. After completing the orientation program, they begin their initial assignment as a department manager in a store.

Effective orientation programs need to avoid information overload and one-way communication. When new hires are confronted with a stack of forms and company policies, they get the impression the company is very bureaucratic. Large quantities of information are hard to absorb in a short period of time. New employees learn information best when it's parceled out in small doses.

Store managers need to foster two-way communication when orienting new employees. Rather than just presenting information about their firm, managers need to give newly hired employees a chance to have their questions and concerns addressed.

Disney overhauled its orientation program to emphasize emotion rather than company policies and procedures. The new program begins with current employees, referred to as cast members, discussing their earliest memories of Disney, their visions of great service, and their understanding of teamwork. Then trainers relate "magic moments" they have witnessed to emphasize that insignificant actions can have a big impact on a guest. For example, a four-year-old trips and falls, spilling his box of popcorn. The boy cries, the mother is concerned, a costumed cast member, barely breaking stride, picks up the empty box, takes it to the popcorn stand for a refill, presents it to the child, and goes on his way.[21]

The orientation program is just one element in the overall training program. It needs to be accompanied by a systematic follow-up to ensure that any problems and concerns arising after the initial period are considered.

Training Store Employees

Effective training for new store employees includes both structured and on-the-job learning experiences.

17.3

Rib Tech, the College of Barbecue Knowledge

GATES BAR-B-Q, a seven-store restaurant chain and local institution in Kansas City, Missouri, devotes considerable time and effort training its employees. During a recent course for new employees, the instructor explains how a plate should look when it leaves the kitchen. "If it has barbecue sauce splattered on the sides of the plate, take it back."

Rib Tech is unusual because Gates only has 300 employees. But owner Ollie Gates says training really pays off. Seven two-hour courses are offered at Rib Tech with a test at the end of each class. All employees must attend the classes. In one class, employees learn how to cut a rib sandwich without leaving finger marks on the bread. Kiva Gates, Ollie's daughter and the course instructor, says, "The knife is the trick. It has to be very sharp."

The chain is a Kansas City landmark. Lines of tourists wait to get in; bottles of sauce are a favorite souvenir of the city. After President Clinton visited in 1994, Gates began selling a $48.95 "Presidential Platter" with ribs, ham, beef, turkey, chicken, and sausage.

Source: Kia Breauz, "In Ribs 101, Star Pupils Win Promotions," *The Wall Street Journal*, September 10, 1996, pp. B1–B2.

REFACT Annual spending by U.S. employers on training totals $200 billion—slightly more than annual public and private spending on elementary and secondary education.[22]

Structured Program During the structured program, new employees are taught the basic skills and knowledge they'll need to do their job. For example, salespeople learn what the company policies are, how to use the point-of-sale terminal, and how to perform basic selling skills; stockroom employees learn procedures for receiving merchandise. This initial training might include lectures, audiovisual presentations, manuals, and correspondence distributed to the new employees. In large firms, structured training may be done at a central location (such as the corporate headquarters or district office) under the human resources department's direction.

The initial structured program should be relatively short so new employees don't feel they are simply back in school. Effective training programs try to bring new recruits up to speed as quickly as possible and then get them involved in doing the job for which they've been hired.[23] Retailing View 17.3 describes how training built Gates Bar-B-Q into a Kansas City landmark.

On-the-Job Training The next training phase emphasizes on-the-job training. New employees are assigned a job, given responsibilities, and coached by their supervisor. The best way to learn is to practice what has been taught. New employees learn by doing activities, making mistakes, and then learning how not to make those mistakes again. Information learned through classroom lectures tends to be forgotten quickly unless it's used soon after the lecture.[24]

For example, students can learn about developing a merchandise budget plan by reading Chapter 13 of this text or by listening to a lecture. But they typically don't acquire all the necessary information or remember the information from these sources. The actual hands-on experience of making a plan and getting feedback provides more complete and lasting knowledge.

Store managers need to develop a plan to help new employees continually improve their skills and productivity. They should identify specific areas of improvement and spend time working with employees on those areas. Employees gain self-confidence in the job when they know their managers want to help them improve their skills.

The on-the-job training provided by this Hallmark manager gives the new employees an opportunity to make decisions and get constructive feedback.

Analyzing Successes and Failures   Every new employee makes mistakes. Unfortunately, some managers make new employees feel uncomfortable if they admit to making a mistake. When this happens, new employees have less opportunity to learn from their mistakes.[25]

Store managers should provide an atmosphere in which salespeople try out different approaches for providing customer service and selling merchandise. Store managers must recognize that some of these new approaches are going to fail, and when they do, managers shouldn't criticize the individual salesperson. Instead, they should talk about the situation, analyze why the approach didn't work, and discuss how the salesperson could avoid the problem in the future.

Similarly, managers should work with employees to help them understand and learn from their successes. For example, salespeople shouldn't just consider a large multiple-item sale to be simply due to luck. They should be encouraged to reflect on the sale, identify their key behaviors that facilitated the sale, and then remember these sales behaviors for future use.

It's important to help salespeople assign the right kinds of reasons for their performance. For example, some salespeople take credit for successes and blame the company, the buyers, or the merchandise for their failures. This tendency to avoid taking responsibility for failures doesn't encourage learning. When salespeople adopt this reasoning pattern, they aren't motivated to change their sales behavior because they don't take personal responsibility for losing a sale.[26]

Managers can help salespeople to constructively analyze their successes and failures by asking salespeople "why" questions that force them to analyze the reasons for effective and ineffective performance. To encourage learning, managers should get salespeople to recognize that they could have satisfied the customer if they had used a different approach or been more persistent. When salespeople accept such responsibility, they'll be motivated to search for ways to improve their sales skills.

MOTIVATING AND MANAGING STORE EMPLOYEES

After employees have received their initial training, managers must work with them to help them meet their performance goals. (Refer back to Exhibit 17–2.)

Leadership

Leadership is the process by which one person attempts to influence another to accomplish some goal or goals. Store managers are leaders of their group of employees. Managers use a variety of motivational techniques to increase productivity by helping employees achieve personal goals consistent with their firm's objectives.[27]

Leader Behaviors   Leaders engage in task performance and group maintenance behaviors. **Task performance behaviors** are the store manager's efforts to make sure that the store achieves its goals. Task performance behaviors are planning, organizing, motivating, evaluating, and coordinating store employees' activities.

Group maintenance behaviors are activities store managers undertake to make sure that employees are satisfied and work well together. These activities include considering employees' needs, showing concern for their well-being, and creating a pleasant work environment.[28]

Leader Decision Making   Store managers vary in how much they involve employees in making decisions. **Autocratic** store managers make all decisions on their own and then announce them to employees. They use the authority of their position to tell employees what to do. For example, an autocratic store manager determines who will work in each area of the store, when they'll take breaks, and what days they'll have off. On the other hand, a **democratic** store manager seeks information and opinions from employees and bases decisions on this information. Democratic store managers share their power and information with their employees. The democratic store manager asks employees where and when they want to work and makes a work schedule to accommodate employee desires.

Tom O'Donnell (right rear), manager of the Sandy City, Utah, Shopko store, is a democratic leader who holds meetings to keep employees informed about company and store activities and encourages suggestions for improving store performance.

Leadership Styles   Store managers tend to develop a specific leadership style. They emphasize either task performance or group maintenance behaviors. They're either autocratic or democratic in their decision-making style.

Which leadership style is best for store managers? After 60 years of research, psychologists have concluded there's no one best style. Effective managers use all styles, selecting the style most appropriate for each situation. For example, a store manager might be autocratic and relations-oriented with an insecure new trainee, but be democratic and task-oriented with an effective, experienced employee.

Effective store managers must consider both their firm's objectives and their employees' needs. They must recognize that employees aren't all the same. For some employees, promotions are crucial. Others want more compensation, and some simply want to be recognized for doing a good job. Some employees need to be motivated to work harder, while others need to be taught how to do their jobs effectively. Thus effective leaders use different approaches or styles for managing each employee.[29]

Transformational Leaders   The previous discussion and most of the chapter describe specific behaviors, activities, and programs store managers use to influence their employees. But the greatest leaders and store managers go beyond influencing employee behaviors to changing the beliefs, values, and needs of their employees. **Transformational leaders** get people to transcend their personal needs for the sake of the group or organization. They generate excitement and revitalize organizations.

Transformational store managers create this enthusiasm in their employees through their personal charisma. They're self-confident, have a clear vision that grabs employee attention, and communicate this vision through words and symbols. Finally, transformational leaders delegate challenging work to subordinates, have free and open communication with them, and provide personal mentoring to develop subordinates.[30]

Motivating Employees

Motivating employees to perform up to their potential may be store managers' most important and frustrating task.[31] The following hypothetical situation illustrates issues concerning employee motivation and evaluation.

After getting an associates degree at a local community college, Jim Taylor was hired for a sales position at the Foley's store in Denver's Cherry Creek Mall. The position offers first-hand knowledge of the firm's customers, managers, and policies. Taylor was told that if he did well in this assignment, he could become a management trainee.

His performance as a sales associate was average. After observing Taylor on the sales floor, his manager, Sally Rivera, felt he was effective only when working with customers like himself—young, career-oriented men and women. To encourage Taylor to sell to other types of customers, Rivera reduced his salary and increased his commission rate. She also reviewed Taylor's performance goals with him.

Taylor now feels a lot of pressure to increase his sales level. He's beginning to dread coming to work in the morning and is thinking about getting out of retailing and working for a bank.

In this hypothetical situation, Rivera focused on increasing Taylor's motivation by providing more incentive compensation. In discussing this illustration, we'll examine the appropriateness of this approach versus other approaches for improving Taylor's performance.

Setting Goals or Quotas   Employee performance improves when employees feel that (1) their efforts will enable them to achieve the goals set for them by their managers and (2) they'll receive rewards they value if they achieve their goals.

Thus managers can motivate employees by setting realistic goals and offering rewards employees want.[32]

For example, Sally Rivera set specific selling goals for Jim Taylor when he started to work in her department. Taylor, like all Foley's sales associates, had goals in five selling areas: sales per hour, average size of each sale, number of multiple-item (add-on) sales, number of preferred clients, and number of appointments made with preferred clients. (**Preferred clients** are customers who salespeople communicate with regularly, send notes to about new merchandise and sales in the department, and make appointments with for special presentations of merchandise.) Besides the selling goals, salespeople are evaluated on the overall department shrinkage due to stolen merchandise, the errors they make in using the point-of-sale terminal, and their contribution to maintaining the department's appearance.

Rivera also developed a program for Taylor's development as a sales associate. The activities she outlined over the next six months involved Taylor's attending classes to improve his selling skills. Rivera needs to be careful in setting goals for Taylor. If she sets goals too high, he might become discouraged, feel the goals are unattainable, and thus not be motivated to work harder. On the other hand, if she sets goals too low, Taylor can achieve them easily and won't be motivated to work to his full potential.

Rather than setting specific goals for each salesperson, Foley's uses the average performance for all salespeople as its goal. However, goals are most effective at motivating employees when they're based on the employee's experience and confidence. Experienced salespeople have confidence in their abilities and should have "stretch" goals—high goals that will make them work hard. New salespeople need lower goals that they have a good chance of achieving. The initial good experience in achieving and surpassing goals builds new salespeople's confidence and motivates them to improve their skills.[33] Later in the chapter we'll look at the use of rewards to motivate employees.

Maintaining Morale

Store morale is important in motivating employees. Typically morale goes up when things are going well and employees are highly motivated. But when sales aren't going well, morale tends to decrease and employee motivation declines. Here are some suggestions for building morale:

Sears builds morale and motivates its sales associates by holding "ready meetings" for each department before the store opens. At this meeting, the department manager discusses approaches for providing better customer service.

- Have storewide or department meetings prior to the store opening. Pass along information about new merchandise and programs and solicit opinions and suggestions from employees.
- Educate employees about the firm's finances, set achievable goals, and throw a pizza party when the goals are met.
- Divide the charity budget by the number of employees and invite the employees to suggest how their "share" should be used.
- Print stickers that tell customers that this sandwich was "wrapped by Roger" or this dress was "dry cleaned by Sarah."
- Give every employee a business card with the company mission printed on its back.[34]

Paula Hankins, a store manager for Pier 1 Imports, uses real-time sales data collected in her firm's information system (see Chapter 11) to build excitement among her employees. On the first day of the Christmas season, she wrote $3,159 on a blackboard in the store. That was the store's sales during the first day of the Christmas season last year. She tells her sales associates that beating that number is not enough. She wants a 36 percent increase, the same sales increase the store has achieved prior to the Christmas season.

By setting financial objectives and keeping sales associates informed of the up-to-the-minute results, an eight-hour shift of clock watchers is converted into an excited team of racers. All day, as customers come and go, sales associates take turns consulting the backroom computer recording sales from the stores' POS terminals. David Self, Hankins' regional manager, emphasizes, "The more information you give the associates, the more ownership they feel in the store's performance."[35]

EVALUATING STORE EMPLOYEES AND PROVIDING FEEDBACK

The fourth step in the management process (refer back to Exhibit 17–2) is evaluating and providing feedback to employees. The evaluation process's objective is to identify employees who are performing well and those who aren't. Based on the evaluation, high-performing employees should be rewarded. Plans need to be developed to increase the productivity of employees performing below expectations. Should poor performers be terminated? Do they need additional training? What kind of training do they need?[36]

Who Should Do the Evaluation?

In large retail firms, the evaluation system is usually designed by the human resources department. But the evaluation itself should be done by the employee's immediate supervisor—the manager who works most closely with the employee. For example, in a discount store, the department manager is in the best position to observe a salesperson in action and understand the reasons for the salesperson's performance. The department manager also oversees the recommendations that come out of the evaluation process. Inexperienced supervisors are often assisted by a senior manager in evaluating employees.

How Often Should Evaluations Be Made?

Most retailers evaluate employees annually or semiannually. Feedback from evaluations is the most effective method for improving employee skills. Thus, evaluation should be done more frequently when managers are developing inexperienced employees' skills. However, frequent formal evaluations are time-consuming for managers and may not give employees enough time to respond to suggestions. Managers should supplement these formal evaluations with frequent informal ones. For example, Sally Rivera should work with Jim Taylor informally and not wait for the formal six-month evaluation. The best time for Rivera to provide this informal feedback is immediately after she has obtained, through observations or reports, positive or negative information about Taylor's performance.

Format for Evaluation   Evaluations are only meaningful if employees know what they're required to do, what level of performance is expected, and how they'll be evaluated. Exhibit 17–5 shows The Gap's criteria for evaluating sales associates.

The Gap employee's overall evaluation is based on subjective evaluations made by the store manager and assistant managers. It places equal weight on individual sales/customer relations activities and activities associated with overall store performance. By emphasizing overall store operations and performance, The Gap's assessment criteria motivate sales associates to work together as a team.

The criteria used at Foley's to evaluate Jim Taylor are objective sales measures based on point-of-sale data rather than the subjective measures used by The Gap. Exhibit 17–6 summarizes Taylor's formal six-month evaluation. The evaluation form lists for various factors (1) what's considered average performance for company salespeople and (2) Taylor's actual performance. His department has done

EXHIBIT 17–5   Factors Used to Evaluate Sales Associates at The Gap

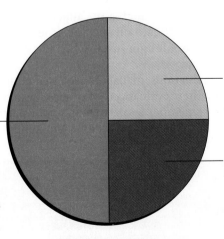

25%
OPERATIONS

1. Store appearance. Demonstrates an eye for detail (color and finesse) in the areas of display, coordination of merchandise on tables, floor fixtures, wall faceouts. Takes initiative in maintaining store presentation standards.

2. Loss prevention. Actively follows all loss prevention procedures.

3. Merchandise control and handling. Consistently achieves established requirements in price change activity, shipment processing, and inventory control.

4. Cash/wrap procedures. Accurately and efficiently follows all register policies and cash/wrap procedures.

50%
SALES/CUSTOMER RELATIONS

1. Greeting. Approaches customers within 1 to 2 minutes with a smile and friendly manner. Uses open-ended questions.

2. Product knowledge. Demonstrates knowledge of product information, fit, shrinkage, and price and can relay this information to the customer.

3. Suggests additional merchandise. Approaches customers at fitting room and cash/wrap areas.

4. Asks customers to buy and reinforces decisions. Lets the customer know they've made a wise choice and thanks them.

25%
COMPLIANCE

1. Dress code and appearance. Complies with dress code. Appears neat and well groomed. Projects current fashionable Gap image.

2. Flexibility. Able to switch from one assignment to another, open to schedule adjustments. Shows initiative, awareness of store priorities and needs.

3. Working relations. Cooperates with other employees, willingly accepts direction and guidance from management. Communicates to management.

EXHIBIT 17–6

Summary of Jim
Taylor's Six-Month
Evaluation

	AVERAGE PERFORMANCE FOR SALESPEOPLE IN THE COMPANY	JIM TAYLOR'S ACTUAL PERFORMANCE
Sales per hour	$75	$65
Average amount per transaction	$45	$35
Percent multiple transactions	55%	55%
Number of preferred customers	115	125
Number of preferred customer appointments	120	95
Departmental shrinkage	2.0%	1.8%
Systems errors	10	2
Merchandise presentation (10-point scale)	5	8

better than average on shrinkage control, and he has done well on system errors and merchandise presentation. However, his sales performance is below average even though he made more than the average number of presentations to preferred customers. These results suggest that Taylor's effort is good but his ability—his selling skills—may need improvement.

Evaluation Errors   Exhibit 17–7 shows some common errors that managers make when evaluating their employees. Managers must be realistic in evaluating salespeople and recognize that their employees are similar to employees in other stores or departments. Thus, they should avoid rating all their salespeople below average (strictness) or above average (leniency). Managers can make evaluation errors by first forming an overall opinion of the employee's performance and then allowing this opinion to influence the ratings of each performance factor (haloing). For example, a store manager might feel a salesperson's overall performance is below average and then rate the salesperson below average on selling skills, punctuality, appearance, and stocking. When an overall evaluation casts such a halo on specific aspects of a salesperson's performance, the evaluation is no longer useful for identifying specific areas that need improvement.

In making evaluations, managers are often unduly influenced by recent events (recency) and by their evaluations of other salespeople (contrast). For example, a manager might remember a salesperson's poor performance with a customer the day before and forget the salesperson's outstanding performance over the past

EXHIBIT 17–7

Common Evaluation
Errors

Strictness	Rating unduly negative
Leniency	Rating unduly positive
Haloing	Using the same rating on all aspects of the evaluation
Recency	Placing too much weight on recent events rather than evaluating performance over the entire period
Contrast	Having the evaluation of a salesperson unduly influenced by the evaluation of other salespeople
Attributions	Making errors in identifying causes of the salesperson's performance

The Gap store managers use a subjective approach to evaluating sales associates and providing feedback for improving their performance.

three months. Similarly, a manager might be unduly harsh in evaluating an average salesperson just after completing an evaluation of an outstanding salesperson.

Finally, managers have a natural tendency to attribute performance (particularly poor performance) to the salesperson and not to the environment the salesperson is working in (attributions). When making evaluations, managers tend to underemphasize effects of external factors such as merchandise in the department and competitors' actions.

The Foley's evaluation of sales associates (refer back to Exhibit 17–6's sample evaluation) avoids many of these potential biases because most ratings are based on objective data. In contrast, The Gap evaluation (Exhibit 17–5) considers a wider range of activities but uses more subjective measures of performance. Since subjective information about specific skills, attitudes about the store and customers, interactions with coworkers, enthusiasm, and appearance aren't used in the Foley's evaluation, performance on these factors may not be explicitly communicated to Jim Taylor. The subjective characteristics in The Gap evaluation are more prone to bias, but they also might be more helpful to salespeople as they try to improve their performance. To avoid bias when making subjective ratings, managers should observe performance regularly, record their observations, avoid evaluating many salespeople at one time, and remain conscious of the various potential biases.

COMPENSATING AND REWARDING EMPLOYEES

The fifth and final step in improving employee productivity in Exhibit 17–2 is compensating and rewarding employees. Store employees receive two types of rewards from their work: extrinsic and intrinsic. **Extrinsic rewards** are rewards provided by either the employee's manager or the firm such as compensation, promotion, and recognition. **Intrinsic rewards** are rewards employees get personally from doing their job well. For example, salespeople often like to sell because they think it's challenging and fun. Of course, they want to be paid, but they also find it rewarding to help customers and make sales.

Extrinsic Rewards

Managers can offer a variety of extrinsic rewards to motivate employees. However, store employees don't all seek the same rewards. For example, some salespeople want more compensation; others strive for a promotion in the company or public recognition of their performance. Jim Taylor wants a favorable evaluation from his manager so he can enter the management training program. Part-time salespeople often take a sales job to get out of the house and meet people. Their primary work objective isn't to make money.[37]

Because of these different needs, managers may not be able to use the same rewards to motivate all employees. Large retailers, however, find it hard to develop unique reward programs for each individual. One approach is to offer à la carte plans. For example, salespeople who achieve their goals could choose a cash bonus, extra days off, or a better discount on merchandise sold in the store. This type of compensation plan enables employees to select the rewards they want.

Recognition is an important nonmonetary extrinsic reward for many employees. (Compensation and financial rewards are discussed later.) Telling employees they've done a job well is appreciated. However, it's typically more rewarding when good performance is recognized publicly. In addition, public recognition can motivate all store employees, not just the star performers, because it demonstrates management's interest in rewarding employees.

Recognition can have a more lasting impact when it's recorded through a photograph or a plaque. Then the employee can show friends and relatives what she accomplished. The company also benefits because each time the picture or plaque is shown, the recipient's enthusiasm is reignited.

A note or a handshake from the department manager is appreciated, but recognition from a higher level of management, such as a district manager or company vice president, is even more rewarding. Finally, the more personal the recognition, the more effective it will be in motivating salespeople. An employee being recognized should be able to occupy center stage alone.

Intrinsic Rewards Most managers focus on extrinsic rewards to motivate employees. For example, a store manager might provide additional compensation if a salesperson achieves a sales goal. This emphasis on extrinsic rewards can make employees lose sight of their job's intrinsic rewards. They may feel that their only reason for working is to earn money and that the job isn't fun.[38]

Public recognition programs make employees feel they are appreciated and motivate them to improve their performance. For providing excellent customer service, the sales associates at the Mansfield, Ohio, Limited store were recognized with a "Hero Award."

Note that Sally Rivera tried to motivate Jim Taylor by using extrinsic rewards when she linked his compensation to how much he sold. This increased emphasis on financial rewards may be one reason Taylor now dreads to come to work in the morning. He might not think his job is fun anymore.

When employees find their jobs intrinsically rewarding, they're motivated to learn how to do them better. They act like a person playing a video game. The game itself is so interesting that the player gets rewards from trying to master it.

One approach to making work fun is to hold contests with relatively small prizes. Contests are most effective when everyone has a chance to win. Contests in which the best salespeople always win aren't exciting and may even be demoralizing. For example, consider a contest in which a playing card is given to a salesperson for each men's suit he sells during a two-week period. At the end of two weeks, the best poker hand wins. This contest motivates all salespeople during the entire period of the contest. A salesperson who sells only four suits can win with four aces. Contests should be used to create excitement and make selling challenging for everyone, not to pay the best salespeople more money.

Experienced employees often lose interest in their jobs. They no longer find them exciting and challenging. Extrinsic rewards, such as pay or promotion, might not be so attractive to them. They might be satisfied with their present income and job responsibilities.

More experienced employees can be motivated by providing intrinsic rewards through job enrichment. For example, they could be given responsibility for merchandising a particular area, training new salespeople, or planning and managing a special event.

Compensation Programs

The objectives of a compensation program are to attract and keep good employees, motivate them to undertake activities consistent with the retailer's objectives, and reward them for their effort. In developing a compensation program, the store manager must strike a balance between controlling labor costs and providing enough compensation to keep high-quality employees.

Compensation plans are most effective for motivating and retaining employees when the employees feel the plan is fair—when their compensation is related to their efforts. In general, simple plans are preferred to complex plans. Simple plans are easier to administer and employees have no trouble understanding them.

Types of Compensation Plans   Retail firms typically use one or more of the following compensation plans: straight salary, straight commission, salary plus commission, and quota-bonus.

Straight Salary Compensation   With **straight salary compensation,** salespeople or managers receive a fixed amount of compensation for each hour or week they work. For example, a salesperson might be paid $6 per hour, or a department manager $500 per week. This plan is easy for the employee to understand and for the store to administer.

Under a straight salary plan, the retailer has flexibility in assigning salespeople to different activities and sales areas. For example, salaried salespeople will undertake nonselling activities (such as stocking shelves) and won't be upset if they're transferred from a high–sales-volume department to a low–sales-volume department.

The major disadvantage of the straight salary plan is employees' lack of immediate incentives to improve their productivity. They know their compensation won't change, in the short run, whether they work hard or slack off. Another disadvantage for the retailer is that straight salary becomes a fixed cost the firm incurs even if sales decline.

Incentive Compensation Plan   **Incentive compensation plans** compensate employees based on their productivity. Many retailers now use incentives to motivate greater sales productivity. Under some incentive plans, a salesperson's income is based entirely on commission (straight commission). For example, a salesperson might be paid a commission based on a percentage of sales made minus merchandise returned. Normally, the percentage is the same for all merchandise sold (such as 7 percent). But some retailers use different percentages for different categories of merchandise (such as 4 percent for low-margin items and 10 percent for high-margin items). By using different percentages, the retailer provides additional incentives for its salespeople to sell specific items. Typically, compensation of salespeople selling high-priced items—such as men's suits, appliances, and consumer electronics—is based entirely on their commissions.

Incentive plans may include a fixed salary plus a smaller commission on total sales or a commission on sales over a quota. For example, a salesperson might receive a salary of $200 per week plus a commission of 2 percent on all sales over $50 per hour.

Incentive compensation plans are a powerful motivator for salespeople to sell merchandise, but they have a number of disadvantages. For example, it's hard to get salespeople who are compensated totally by commission to perform nonselling activities. Understandably, they're reluctant to spend time stocking shelves when they could be making money by selling. Also, salespeople will concentrate on the more expensive, fast-moving merchandise and neglect other merchandise. Incentives can also discourage salespeople from providing services to customers. Finally, salespeople compensated primarily by incentive don't develop loyalty to their employer. Since the employer doesn't guarantee them an income, they feel no obligation to the firm.[39]

Under a 100 percent straight commission plan, salespeople's income can fluctuate from week to week, depending on their sales. Since retail sales are seasonal, salespeople might earn most of their income during the Christmas season and much less during the summer months. To provide a more steady income for salespeople under high incentive plans, some retailers offer a drawing account. With a **drawing account,** salespeople receive a weekly check based on their estimated annual income. Then commissions earned are credited against the weekly payments. Periodically, the weekly draw is compared to the commission earned. If the draw exceeds earned commissions, the salespeople return the excess money they've been paid, and their weekly draw is reduced. If commissions earned exceed the draw, salespeople are paid the difference.

Quotas-Bonus Plans   **Quotas** are performance goals or objectives established to evaluate employee performance. Examples are sales per hour for salespeople and maintained margin and inventory turnover for buyers. For department store salespeople, selling quotas vary across departments due to differences in sales productivity. Quotas are often used with compensation plans. For example, in a quota-bonus plan, salespeople earn a bonus if their sales exceed their quota over a certain time period.

A quota-bonus plan's effectiveness depends on setting reasonable, fair quotas.[40] Setting effective quotas can be hard. Usually, quotas are set at the same level for everyone in a department. But salespeople in the same department may have

17.4

Incentive Plan Causes Problems for Sears

After a year-long investigation, the California Department of Consumer Affairs accused Sears of overcharging auto repair customers. Undercover agents reported they were overcharged for 90 percent of their repairs. The average overcharge was $223. Reacting to the report, Dr. Leonard Berry, director of the Retail Center at Texas A&M University, commented, "The confidence of customers is any company's most precious asset. Sears has suffered an incalculable loss from which full recovery is not possible."

Until February 1990, Sears paid its service advisors by the hour. Then in an effort to increase sales and decrease costs, Sears reduced service advisors' salaries, installed a commission compensation based on the auto services bought by customers, and set sales quotas. Sears acknowledged its compensation plan "created an environment where mistakes can occur."

Without an adequate control system, some service advisors systematically overcharged customers. After the overcharging was uncovered, Sears eliminated the incentive compensation plan and replaced it with a program rewarding service advisors for the quality, not the quantity, of their work.

Source: Julia Flynn, "Did Sears Take Other Customers for a Ride?" *Business Week,* August 3, 1992, pp. 24–25; Leonard Berry, Kenneth Galloway, Ike Lagnado, Sidney Doolittle, James Posner, Marvin Rothenberg, Susan O'Dell, R. Fulton MacDonald, Al Ries, and Peter Monash, "What Should Sears Do?" *Chain Store Age Executive,* August 1992, pp. 36–38; Tung Yin, "Sears Is Accused of Billing Fraud at Auto Centers," *The Wall Street Journal,* June 12, 1993, p. B1; and Gregory Patterson, "Sears's Brennan Accepts Blame for Auto Flap," *The Wall Street Journal,* June 23, 1993, p. B1.

different abilities and face different selling environments. For example, in the men's department, salespeople in the suit area have much greater sales potential than salespeople in the accessories area. Newly hired salespeople might have a harder time achieving a quota than more experienced salespeople. Thus, a quota based on average productivity may be too high to motivate the new salesperson and too low to effectively motivate the experienced salesperson. Quotas should be developed for each salesperson based on her experience and the nature of the store area where she works. Retailing View 17.4 outlines Sears' problems with its incentive compensation plan for auto repairs.

Group Incentives   To encourage employees in a department or store to work together, some retailers provide additional incentives based on the performance of the department or store as a whole. For example, salespeople might be paid a commission based on their individual sales and then receive additional compensation based on the amount of sales over plan or quota generated by all salespeople in the store. The group incentive encourages salespeople to work together on nonselling activities and handling customers so the department sales target will be achieved.[41]

Designing the Compensation Program   A compensation program's two elements are the amount of compensation and the percentage of compensation based on incentives. Typically, market conditions determine the amount of compensation. When economic conditions are good and labor is scarce, retailers pay higher wages. Retailers that hire inexperienced salespeople pay lower wages than those that recruit experienced salespeople with good skills and abilities. Incentives are most effective when a salesperson's performance can be measured easily and precisely. It's hard to measure individual performance when salespeople work in teams or when they must perform a lot of nonselling activities. Retailers can easily measure a salesperson's actual sales, but it's hard to measure their customer service or merchandising performance.[42]

When the saleperson's activities have a great impact on sales, incentives can provide additional motivation. For example, salespeople who are simply cashiers have little effect on sales and thus shouldn't be compensated with incentives. However, incentives are appropriate for salespeople who provide a lot of information and assistance about complex products such as designer dresses or stereo systems. Incentives are less effective with inexperienced salespeople because they inhibit learning. Inexperienced salespeople are less confident in their skills, and incentives can cause excessive stress.

Finally, compensation plans with too many incentives may not promote good customer service. Salespeople on commission become interested in selling anything they can to customers. They aren't willing to spend time helping customers buy the merchandise they need. They tend to stay close to the cash register or the dressing room exits so they can ring up a sale for a customer who's ready to buy.

Setting the Commission Percentage   Assume that a specialty store manager wants to hire experienced salespeople. To get the type of person she wants, she feels she must pay $12 per hour. Her selling costs are budgeted at 8 percent of sales. With compensation of $12 per hour, salespeople need to sell $150 worth of merchandise per hour ($12 divided by 8 percent) for the store to keep within its sales cost budget. The manager believes the best compensation would be one-third salary and two-thirds commission, so she decides to offer a compensation plan of $4 per hour salary (33 percent or $12) and a 5.33 percent commission on sales. If salespeople sell $150 worth of merchandise per hour, they'll earn $12 per hour ($4 per hour in salary plus $150 multiplied by 5.33 percent, which equals $8 per hour in commission).

LEGAL AND ETHICAL ISSUES IN MANAGING STORE EMPLOYEES

Store managers must conform to a number of federal, state, and local laws regulating employer–employee relationships. The primary store management activities covered by these laws are hiring and promotion selection, compensation, health and safety, sexual harassment, and labor relations.[43]

Hiring and Promotion

Heightened social awareness and government regulations emphasize the need to avoid discriminating against hiring the handicapped, women, minorities, and older workers. Title VII of the Civil Rights Act prohibits discrimination on the basis of race, national origin, sex, or religion in company personnel practices. Discrimination is specifically prohibited in the following human resource decisions: recruitment, hiring, discharge, layoff, discipline, promotion, compensation, and access to training. In 1974, the act was expanded to allow the **Equal Employment Opportunity Commission (EEOC)** to sue employers that violate the law. Several major retailers have been sued because they discriminated in hiring and promoting minorities and women.[44]

The **Age Discrimination and Employment Act** makes it illegal to discriminate in hiring and termination decisions concerning people between the ages of 40 and 70. Finally, the **Americans with Disabilities Act (ADA)** opens up job opportunities for the disabled by requiring employees to provide accommodating work environments.[45]

As discussed in Chapter 10, many retailers have taken proactive positions in terms of hiring these special groups. Special groups offer an attractive pool of potential employees at a time when the labor pool for retail workers is shrinking. In addition, retailers see advantages in having their work force mirror the diversity of their customers.[46]

REFACT A retailer incurs an additional $7,000 to 10,000 of expenses in medical costs, absences, turnover, and lost productivity when it hires a drug user.[47]

Selection

The use of lie detectors in testing employees is prohibited. Retailers and other employers have been discouraged from HIV testing for prospective employees. But testing for illegal drug use isn't prohibited because drug users are violating the law.

Compensation

The Fair Labor Standards Act of 1938 set minimum wages, maximum hours, child labor standards, and overtime pay provisions. Enforcement of this law is particularly important to retailers because they hire many low-wage employees and teenagers and have their employees work long hours.

The Equal Pay Act, now enforced by the EEOC, prohibits unequal pay for men and women who perform equal work or work of comparable worth. Equal work means that the jobs require the same skills, effort, and responsibility and are performed in the same working environment. Comparable worth implies that men and women who perform different jobs of equal worth should be compensated the same. Differences in compensation are legal when compensation is determined by a seniority system, an incentive compensation plan, or market demand.[48]

REFACT The grocery store industry ranked third in total recordable, job-related injuries and illnesses, with 250,000 cases.[49]

Health and Safety

The Occupational Safety and Health Act (OSHA) of 1970 requires employers to provide safe working conditions. Employers must keep records of workplace accidents and injuries and submit to on-site inspections.

Sexual Harassment

An important issue in managing employees is sexual harassment. **Sexual harassment** includes unwelcome sexual advances, requests for sexual favors, and other verbal and physical conduct. Harassment isn't confined to requests for sexual favors in exchange for job considerations such as a raise or promotion. Simply creating a hostile work environment can be considered sexual harassment.[50]

Actions that are considered sexual harassment include lewd comments, gestures, joking, and graffiti as well as showing obscene photographs, staring at a

Sexual harassment is an important issue confronting store managers. Managers must make sure that store employees avoid actions that are, or can be interpreted as, sexual harassment.

coworker in a sexual manner, alleging that an employee got rewards by engaging in sexual acts, and commenting on an employee's moral reputation.[51] Managers must prevent such behaviors because they're both unethical and illegal.

Sexual harassment is not restricted just to supervisors and fellow employees. It's even more of a problem when the offender is a customer. For example, female pharmacists find that some male customers demand lengthy discussions when they buy condoms. The pharmacists may have difficulty dealing with these situations because they want to keep the person as a customer and also protect themselves from abuse. Managers will need to respond to these situations as pharmacists shift their responsibility from simply dispensing to providing face-to-face information to customers.[52]

Labor Relations

The National Labor Relations Act legalized labor organizations (unions), prohibited employers from engaging in unfair labor practices, and established the National Labor Relations Board (NLRB) to conduct unionization elections and hearings about unfair practices.

REFACT Only 10 percent of retail employees are unionized. The largest union of retail workers, the United Food and Commercial Workers (UFCW), focuses on organizing supermarket employees.

The primary recent controversy between retailers and unions concerns incentive compensation based on performance. For example, the UFCW sued Nordstrom because sales associates weren't compensated for their overtime performing customer services encouraged by the company's culture. Nordstrom eventually signed an NLRB order settling the issue. One Nordstrom vendor says, "It's a trade-off. The best companies are not always the easiest employers." Nordstrom demands high performance from its employees but also compensates them better than competitors do.[53]

In the preceding sections, we have reviewed store managers' means to increase profit by increasing employee productivity. In the next section, we review some of the areas store managers address to reduce costs.

CONTROLLING COSTS

Labor scheduling, store maintenance, and energy management offer three opportunities for reducing store operating expenses.

Labor Scheduling

Using store employees efficiently is an important and challenging problem. Store employees provide customer service that can increase sales. On the other hand, employees are the largest store operating expense. **Labor scheduling** (determining the number of employees assigned to each area of the store) is difficult because of the multiple-shift and part-time workers needed to staff stores 12 hours a day, seven days a week. In addition, customer traffic varies greatly during the day and the week. Bad weather, holidays, and sales can dramatically alter normal shopping patterns and staffing needs.

REFACT Sixty percent of retailers use computer programs for merchandise planning, but only 37 percent use software for labor scheduling.[54]

Managers can spot obvious inefficiencies like long checkout lines and sales associates with nothing to do. But some inefficiencies are more subtle. For example, if 6 percent of a store's sales volume occurs between 2 and 3 P.M. and 9 percent of the total labor hours occur during this time period, the store might be overstaffed during this time period. Many stores use specially designed computer software to deal with the complexities of labor scheduling. Labor schedulers can reduce store payroll costs between 2 and 5 percent without affecting store sales.[55]

Efficient labor scheduling requires more than POS sales data by day and time of day. The manager also needs to know the traffic patterns and the impact of store employees on sales. For example, one store manager saw a downturn in sales during the hour before the store closed so she considered reducing the level of staffing. However, when traffic counters were installed, the manager discovered that the number of customers in the store did not decline during the last open hour. The manager then realized that employees were forsaking customer service and spending time preparing to close the store. Rather than reducing the staff, the manager extended the work hours so sales associates would realize the sales potential during the last hour.

Store Maintenance

Store maintenance is the activities involved with managing the exterior and interior physical facilities associated with the store. The exterior facilities include the parking lot, the entrances to the store, and signs on the outside of the store. The interior facilities include the walls, flooring, ceiling, and displays and signs.

Store maintenance affects both the sales generated in the store and the cost of running the store. A store's cleanliness and neatness affect consumer perceptions of the quality of its merchandise. Maintenance is costly. Floor maintenance for a 40,000–square-foot home center is about $10,000 a year. Poor maintenance shortens the useful life of air-conditioning units, floors, and fixtures.

Energy Management

Energy management is a major issue in store operations, especially in stores with special refrigeration needs such as supermarkets and restaurants. Wal-Mart has been very innovative in designing an energy-efficient store located in the City of Commerce, California. Rather than using individual energy-efficient systems for heating, air-conditioning, and lighting, the store uses a systems approach that results in an annual energy savings of $75,000. To use more daylight, the store has 180 skylights. Photo sensors continuously monitor the light levels so that as the amount of daylight increases, the artificial lighting in the store is reduced automatically, reducing the heat generated by the artificial lighting and the need for air-conditioning. Electronic sensors on faucets and toilets reduce water consumption in the store. Solar panels in the store's atrium provide 15 percent of the energy used in the store.[56]

REFACT Energy costs in a typical supermarket are between 1.0 and 1.4 percent of sales.[57]

REDUCING INVENTORY LOSSES

An important issue facing store management is reducing inventory losses due to employee theft, shoplifting, mistakes and inaccurate records, and vendor errors. Examples of employee mistakes are failing to ring up an item when it's sold and miscounting merchandise when it's received or when physical inventories are taken. Inventory shrinkage due to vendor mistakes arises when vendor shipments contain less than the amount indicated on the packing slip.

Although shoplifting receives most of the publicity, employee theft accounts for about the same amount of inventory loss. A recent survey attributes 39 percent of inventory shrinkage to employee theft, 36 percent to shoplifting, 19 percent to mistakes and inaccurate records, and 6 percent to vendor errors.[58]

In developing a loss prevention program, retailers confront a trade-off between providing shopping convenience and a pleasant work environment and, on the other hand, preventing losses due to shoplifting and employee theft. The key to an effective loss prevention program is determining the most effective

REFACT Computer and software retailers attribute 64 percent of their inventory shrinkage to employee theft, while music stores attribute 66 percent of their shrinkage to shoplifting.[59]

way to protect merchandise while preserving an open, attractive store atmosphere and a feeling among employees that they are trusted. Loss prevention requires coordination between store management, visual merchandising, and store design.

Calculating Shrinkage

Shrinkage is the difference between the recorded value of inventory (at retail prices) based on merchandise bought and received and the value of the actual inventory (at retail prices) in stores and distribution centers divided by retail sales during the period. For example, if accounting records indicate inventory should be $1,500,000, the actual count of the inventory reveals $1,236,000, and sales were $4,225,000, the shrinkage is 6.7 percent [($1,500,000 − $1,236,000) / $4,225,000]. Reducing shrinkage is an important store management issue. Retailers' annual loss from shrinkage is between 1 and 5 percent of sales. Every dollar of inventory shrinkage translates into a dollar of lost profit.

Detecting and Preventing Shoplifting

Losses due to shoplifting can be reduced by store design, employee training, and special security measures.

Store Design   Security issues need to be considered when placing merchandise near store entrances, delivery areas, and dressing rooms. For example, easily stolen merchandise such as jewelry and other small, expensive items should never be displayed near an entrance. Dressing room entrances should be visible to store employees so they can easily observe customers entering and exiting with merchandise.[60]

Employee Training   Store employees can be the retailer's most effective tools against shoplifting. They should be trained to be aware, visible, and alert to potential shoplifting situations. Exhibit 17–8 outlines rules for spotting shoplifters. Perhaps the best deterrent to shoplifting is an alert employee who is very visible.

EXHIBIT 17–8

Spotting Shoplifters

DON'T ASSUME THAT ALL SHOPLIFTERS ARE POORLY DRESSED

To avoid detection, professional shoplifters dress in the same manner as customers patronizing the store. Over 90 percent of all amateur shoplifters arrested have either the cash, checks, or credit to purchase the merchandise they stole.

SPOT LOITERERS

Amateur shoplifters frequently loiter in areas as they build up the nerve to steal something. Professionals also spend time waiting for the right opportunity, but less conspicuously than amateurs.

LOOK FOR GROUPS

Teenagers planning to shoplift often travel in groups. Some members of the group divert employees' attention while others take the merchandise. Professional shoplifters often work in pairs. One person takes the merchandise and passes it to a partner in the store's restroom, phone booths, or restaurant.

LOOK FOR PEOPLE WITH LOOSE CLOTHING

Shoplifters frequently hide stolen merchandise under loose-fitting clothing or in large shopping bags. People wearing a winter coat in the summer or a raincoat on a sunny day may be potential shoplifters.

WATCH THE EYES, HANDS, AND BODY

Professional shoplifters avoid looking at merchandise and concentrate on searching for store employees who might observe their activities. Shoplifters' movements might be unusual as they try to conceal merchandise.

Inventory shrinkage from employee theft and shoplifting is high for small, high-priced items such as CD ROMs and video discs. Music stores use a variety of techniques to reduce shrinkage, including video surveillance systems and EAS tags behind the merchandise labels.

Security Measures Exhibit 17–9 describes retailers' use of security measures. Department stores often chain expensive merchandise to fixtures. Another approach for deterring shoplifting is to embed dye capsules in the merchandise tags. If the tags aren't removed properly by a store employee, the capsules break and damage the merchandise.

By placing convex mirrors at key locations, employees can observe a wide area of the store. Closed-circuit TV cameras can be monitored from a central location, but purchasing the equipment and hiring people to monitor the system can be expensive. Some retailers install nonoperating equipment that looks like a TV camera to provide a psychological deterrent to shoplifters.

While these security measures reduce shoplifting, they can also make the shopping experience more unpleasant for honest customers. The atmosphere of a fashionable department store is diminished when guards, mirrors, and TV cameras are highly visible. Customers may find it hard to try on clothing secured with a lock-and-chain or an electronic tag. They can also be uncomfortable trying on clothing if they think they're secretly being watched via a surveillance monitor. Thus, when evaluating security measures, retailers need to balance the benefits of reducing shoplifting with the potential losses in sales.

REFACT Retailers lose more than $27 billion annually due to shrinkage.[61]

EXHIBIT 17–9

Uses of Security Measures by Retailers

LOSS PREVENTION MEASURE	% OF RETAILERS USING MEASURE
Live closed-circuit TV (CCTV)	64%
Observation mirrors	54
Mystery/Honest shoppers	49
Cables, locks, and chains	41
Secured displays	40
Plain-clothed detectives	35
Uniformed guards	34
Simulated CCTV	26
Radio frequency EAS tags	25
Magnetic EAS tags	22
Observation booths	17
Ink/dye tags	16
Microwave EAS tags	15
Fitting room attendants	11

Source: Richard Hollinger, *1996 National Retail Security Survey* (Gainesville, FL: Security Research Project, University of Florida, Department of Sociology, 1996), p. 24.

Electronic article surveillance is a promising approach for reducing shrinkage with little effect on shopping behavior. In **electronic article surveillance (EAS) systems,** special tags are placed on merchandise. When the merchandise is purchased, the tags are deactivated by the POS scanner. If a shoplifter tries to steal the merchandise, the active tags are sensed when the shoplifter passes a detection device at the store exit and an alarm is triggered.

EAS tags do not affect shopping behavior because customers do not realize they're on the merchandise. Due to the effectiveness of tags in reducing shoplifting, retailers can increase sales by displaying theft-prone, expensive merchandise openly rather than behind a counter or in a locked enclosure.

Some large national retailers insist that vendors install EAS tags during the manufacturing process because the vendors can install the tags at a lower cost than the retailers. In addition, retail installed tags can be removed more easily by shoplifters. Vendors are reluctant to get involved with installing EAS tags because industry standards have not been adopted. Without these standards, a vendor would have to develop unique tags and merchandise for each retailer.

Prosecution   Many retailers have a policy of prosecuting all shoplifters. They feel a strictly enforced prosecution policy deters shoplifters. Some retailers also sue shoplifters in civil proceedings for restitution of the stolen merchandise and the time spent in the prosecution.[62]

Reducing Employee Theft

The most effective approach for reducing employee theft and shoplifting is to create a trusting, supportive work environment. When employees feel they're respected members of a team, they identify their goals with the retailer's goals. Stealing from their employer becomes equivalent to stealing from themselves or their family and they go out of their way to prevent others from stealing from the "family." Thus retailers with a highly committed work force and low turnover typically have low inventory shrinkage. Additional approaches for reducing employee theft are carefully screening employees, creating an atmosphere that encourages honesty and integrity, using security personnel, and establishing security policies and control systems.

Redner's Warehouse Markets, a chain in Reading, Pennsylvania, has one of the industry's lowest inventory shrinkages, 0.16 percent of retail sales. Redner's achieves this low shrinkage by educating its employees about the causes and effects of shrinkage on the business. Then it backs this message with incentives. It annually budgets 0.50 percent for shrinkage—if a store improves on this budgeted level, the difference is paid back to its employees. Last year, employees earned $590,000 in bonuses for beating the budgeted shrinkage level.[63]

Screening Prospective Employees   Many retailers use paper-and-pencil honesty tests and make extensive reference checks to screen out potential employee theft problems. The major problem related to employee theft may be illegal drug use. Some retailers now require prospective employees to submit to drug tests as a condition of employment. Employees with documented performance problems, an unusual number of accidents, or erratic time and attendance records are also tested. Unless they're involved in selling drugs, employees who test positive are often offered an opportunity to complete a company-paid drug program, submit to random testing in the future, and remain with the firm.[64]

Using Security Personnel   In addition to uniformed guards, retailers use undercover shoppers to discourage and detect employee theft. These undercover security people pose as shoppers. They make sure salespeople ring up transactions accurately.

Establishing Security Policies and Control Systems   To control employee theft, some retailers adopt policies relating to certain activities that may facilitate theft (Exhibit 17–10). In addition, computer software is available to detect unusual activity at POS terminals. For example, a POS terminal where shortages are frequently reported or return activity is unusually high can be located and then employees using the terminal can be monitored. Transactions can also be analyzed to identify employees who ring up a lot of no-receipt returns or void other employees' returns.

SUMMARY   Effective store management can have a significant impact on a retail firm's financial performance. Store managers increase sales by increasing labor productivity, decrease costs through labor deployment decisions, and reduce inventory loss by developing a dedicated work force.

Increasing store employees' productivity is challenging because of the difficulties in recruiting, selecting, and motivating store employees. Employees typically have different skills and seek different rewards. Effective store managers need to motivate their employees to work hard and to develop skills so they improve their productivity. To motivate employees, store managers need to understand what rewards each employee is seeking and then provide an opportunity to realize those rewards. Store managers must establish realistic goals for employees that are consistent with the store's goals and must motivate each employee to achieve them.

Store managers also must control inventory losses due to employee theft, shoplifting, and clerical errors. Managers use a wide variety of methods in developing loss prevention programs, including security devices and employee screening during the selection process. However, the critical element of any loss prevention program is building employee loyalty to reduce employee interest in stealing and increase attention to shoplifting.

EXHIBIT 17–10

Policies for Reducing
Employee Theft

 Randomly search containers such as trash bins where stolen merchandise could be stored.

 Require store employees to enter and leave the store through designated locations.

 Assign salespeople to a specific POS terminal and require all transactions to be handled through that terminal.

 Restrict employee purchases to working hours.

 Provide customer receipts for all transactions.

 Have all refunds, returns, and discounts cosigned by a department or store manager.

 Change locks periodically and issue keys to authorized employees only.

 Have a locker room where all employee handbags, purses, packages, and coats must be checked.

KEY TERMS

ADA (Americans with Disabilities Act), *528*

Age Discrimination and Employment Act, *528*

autocratic leader, *517*

democratic leader, *517*

drawing account, *526*

EEOC (Equal Employment Opportunity Commission), *528*

electronic article surveillance (EAS) system, *534*

energy management, *531*

extrinsic reward, *523*

group maintenance behavior, *517*

incentive compensation plan, *526*

intrinsic reward, *523*

job analysis, *508*

job application form, *511*

job description, *509*

labor scheduling, *530*

leadership, *517*

preferred client, *519*

quota, *526*

sexual harassment, *529*

shrinkage, *532*

socialization, *512*

store maintenance, *531*

straight salary compensation, *525*

task performance behavior, *517*

transformational leader, *518*

DISCUSSION QUESTIONS & PROBLEMS

1. How do on-the-job training and classroom training differ? What are the benefits and limitations of each approach?

2. Give examples of a situation in which a manager of a McDonald's fast-food restaurant must utilize different leadership styles.

3. Job descriptions should be in writing so employees clearly understand what's expected of them. But what are the dangers of relying too heavily on written job descriptions?

4. Name some laws and regulations that affect the employee management process.

5. What's the difference between extrinsic rewards and intrinsic rewards?

6. Many large department stores—Penney, Sears, and Macy's—are changing their salespeople's reward system from a traditional salary or hourly reward system to a commission-based system. What problems can incentive compensation systems cause? How can department managers avoid these problems?

7. When evaluating retail employees, some stores use a quantitative approach that relies on checklists and numerical scores similar to the form in Exhibit 17–6. Other stores use a more qualitative approach whereby less time is spent checking and adding and more time is devoted to discussing strengths and weaknesses in written form. Which is the best evaluation approach?

8. What are the different methods for compensating employees? Discuss which methods you think would be best for compensating a sales associate, store manager, and buyer.

9. Is training more important for a small independent retailer or a large national chain? Why? How does training differ between these two types of retailers?

10. Discuss how retailers can reduce shrinkage from shoplifting and employee theft.

SUGGESTED READINGS

Allerton, Haidee. "Working Life: Rock Bottom." *Training & Development*, September 1993, pp. 87–88.

Caminiti, Susan. "What Team Leaders Need to Know." *Fortune*, February 20, 1995, pp. 93–100.

Clay, Joan, and Elvis Stephens. "Liability for Negligent Hiring: The Importance of Background Checks." *Cornell Hotel & Restaurant Administration Quarterly* 36 (October 1995), pp. 74–82.

Cox, Anthony, Dena Cox, Ronald Anderson, and George Moschis. "Social Influences on Adolescent Shoplifting: Theory, Evidence, and Implications for the Retail Industry." *Journal of Retailing* 69 (Summer 1993), pp. 234–46.

Fraedrich, John Paul. "The Ethical Behavior of Retail Managers." *Journal of Business Ethics* 12 (March 1993), pp. 207–18.

Golden, Marilyn. "The Americans with Disabilities Act—Its Impact on Retailers." *Retail Business Review*, January 1993, pp. 14–19.

Henkoff, Ronald. "Finding, Training, and Keeping the Best Service Workers." *Fortune*, October 3, 1994, pp. 120–25.

Jacobs, Bill. "Operating Stores." *Chain Store Age*, January 1994, pp. 22MH–25MH.

Lusch, Robert, and Bernard Jaworski. "Management Controls, Role Stress, and Retail Store Manager Performance." *Journal of Retailing* 67 (Winter 1991), pp. 397–419.

Reese, Susan. "Single-Employee Stores Raise Tough New Shrinkage Issues." *Stores*, September 1996, pp. 96–99.

"Staffing Shortfalls Plague Industry." *Hotel & Motel Management*, September 2, 1996, pp. 32–34.

Woodward, Ginger, Nancy Cassill, and David Herr. "The Relationship between Psychological Climate and Work Motivation in a Retail Environment." *The International Review of Retail, Distribution, and Consumer Research* 4 (July 1995), pp. 297–314.

Zuber, Amy. "Tapping a Human Resource: Restaurants Fight Labor Crunch with Training Programs." *Nation's Restaurant News*, July 8, 1996, pp. 33–36.

NOTES

1. Seth Lubovek, "Don't Listen to the Boss, Listen to the Customers," *Forbes*, December 4, 1995, pp. 45–46.

2. Joseph Carideo, "Developing Retail Talent," *Discount Merchandiser*, May 1993, pp. 117–18.

3. Steve Weinstein, "Motivating Forces," *Progressive Grocer*, September 1966, p. 32H.

4. R. D. Gatewood and H. S. Field, *Human Resource Selection* (Hinsdale, IL: Dryden, 1987); and Benjamin Schneider and Neil Schmit, *Staffing Organizations* (Glenview, IL: Scott, Foresman, 1986).

5. Ronald Henkoff, "Finding, Training, and Keeping the Best Service Workers," *Fortune*, October 3, 1994, p. 114.

6. "Delivering Customer Satisfaction," *Chain Store Age Executive*, January 1994, p. 25MH.

7. Frank Hammel, "The Coming Crunch: Dealing with the Growing Labor Shortage," *Supermarket Business*, June 1996, p. 93; Thomas Wotruba, Edwin Simpson, and Jennifer Reed, "The Recruiting Interview as Perceived by College Student Applicants for Sales Positions," *Journal of Personal Selling and Sales Management* 9 (Fall 1989), pp. 13–24; and T. Bergman and M. S. Taylor, "College Recruitment: What Attracts Students to Organizations?" *Personnel* 61 (1984), p. 34–46.

8. Michael Cronin, "Turning Employees into Headhunters," *Inc.*, June 1992, pp. 112–13.

9. Charlene Solomon, "Managing Today's Immigrants," *Personnel Journal*, July 1993, pp. 57–65.

10. Majorie Coeyman, "Two Takes on Seniors," *Restaurant Business*, March 1, 1996, p. 56.

11. George Kirk, Patrick Dunne, and James Wilson, "Pre-Employment Screening Devices: Are Retailers Using Them Correctly?" in Robert King, ed., *Retailing: Theories and Practices for Today and Tomorrow*, Proceedings of the Fourth Triennial National Retailing Conference, Richmond, VA, pp. 106–11.

12. Myron Gable, Charles Holland, and Frank Dangello, "Predicting Voluntary Management Trainee Turnover in a Large Retailing Organization from Information on an Employment Application Blank," *Journal of Retailing* 60 (Winter 1984), pp. 43–63.

13. Paul Barada, "Reference Checking Is More Important than Ever," *HRMagazine* 41 (November 1996), pp. 49–52; and Kirk Johnson, "Why References Aren't Available on Request," *New York Times*, June 9, 1985, pp. F8–F9.

14. John Bernardin and Donna Cooke, "Validity of an Honesty Test in Predicting Theft among Convenience Store Employees," *Academy of Management Journal* 36 (October 1993), pp. 1097–1109.

15. Richard Hollinger, *1996 National Retail Security Survey* (Gainesville, FL: Security Research Project, Department of Sociology, University of Florida, 1996), p. 17.

16. Neal Schmitt, Richard Gooding, Raymond Noe, and Michael Kirsch, "Meta-Analysis of Validity Studies Published between 1964 and 1982 and Investigation of Study Characteristics," *Personnel Psychology*, Autumn 1984, pp. 407–22; and J. E. Hunter, F. L. Schmidt, and R. Hunter, "Differential Validity of Employment Tests by Race," *Personnel Psychology*, July 1979, pp. 721–35.

17. Kal Lifson, "Turn Down Turnover to Turn Up Profits," *Chain Store Age*, November 1, 1996, pp. 64–66.

18. Peter Burgess, "How Those 'Innermost Thoughts' Are Revealed," *Grocer*, March 9, 1996, pp. 60–62; Laura Graves and Ronald Karren, "The Employee Selection Interview: A Fresh Look at an Old Problem," *Human Resource Management* 35 (Summer 1996), pp. 163–81; and Nancy Austin, "The New Job Interview: Beyond the Trick Question," *Working Woman*, March 1996, pp. 23–25.

19. Cheri Young and Craig Lundberg, "Creating a First Day on the Job," *Cornell Hotel and Restaurant Administration Journal*, December 1996, pp. 26–29.

20. Alice Starcke, "Building a Better Orientation Program," *HRMagazine*, November 1996, pp. 107–13.

21. Henkoff, "Finding, Training, and Keeping," p. 118.

22. "Education," *The Wall Street Journal*, February 9, 1991, p. R5.

23. Roy Canning, "Enhancing the Quality of Learning in Human Resource Development," *Journal of European Industrial Training* 20 (February 1996), pp. 3–11; Joy Riggs, "Faster, Shorter, Cheaper Drives Training Today," *Personnel Journal*, May 1996, pp. S1–S4; and Karen West, "Effective Training for a Revolving Door," *Training & Development*, September 1996, pp. 50–53.

24. Sarah Cohan, "Computer-Based Training Improves New Employee Customer Service at Color Tile," *Personnel Journal*, July 1993, p. 6; "Neiman-Marcus Sales Management in Training," *Stores*, November 1987, p. 100;

"Buyer Training," *Stores*, April 1981, pp. 47–48; "Computers as Classrooms," *Chain Store Executive*, January 1986, p. 128; and Arthur Bragg, "Are Good Salespeople Born or Made?" *Sales & Marketing Management*, September 1988, pp. 74–78.

25. Harish Sujan, Barton Weitz, and Mita Sujan, "Increasing Sales Productivity by Getting Salespeople to Work Smarter," *Journal of Personal Selling and Sales Management* 7 (August 1988), p. 919; and David Driscoll, "The Benefits of Failure," *Sales & Marketing Management*, April 1989, pp. 47–50.

26. Harish Sujan, "Smarter versus Harder: An Exploratory Attributional Analysis of Salespeople's Motivation," *Journal of Marketing Research* 23 (February 1986), pp. 41–49.

27. Warren Bennis, "Good Managers Are Good Leaders," *Across the Board*, October 1987, pp. 7–11; and A. Zaleznik, "The Leadership Gap," *The Executive*," February 1990, pp. 7–22.

28. J. P. Kotter, "What Leaders Really Do," *Harvard Business Review*, May–June 1990, pp. 103–11.

29. F. E. Fiedler and J. E. Garcia, *New Approaches for Effective Leadership* (New York: Wiley, 1986); V. H. Vroom and A. G. Jago, *The New Leadership* (Englewood Cliffs, NJ: Prentice-Hall, 1988); and Robert Tannenbaum and Warren Schmidt, "How to Choose a Leadership Style," *Harvard Business Review*, May–June 1973, pp. 162–80.

30. Bernard Bass, "Leadership: Good, Better, Best," *Organizational Dynamics*, Winter 1985, pp. 26–40; Noel Tichey and David Ulrich, "The Leadership Challenge—A Call for the Transformational Leader," *Sloan Management Review* 26 (Fall 1984), pp. 59–68; and B. Bass, B. Avolio, and L. Goodman, "Biography and the Assessment of Transformational Leadership at the World Class Level," *Journal of Management* 13 (1987), pp. 19–26.

31. Donald McNermey, "Creating a Motivated Workforce," *HR Focus*, August 1996, pp. 1–8.

32. G. P. Latham and E. A. Locke, "Goal Setting: A Motivational Technique That Works," *Organizational Dynamics*, Augumn 1979, pp. 68–80; R. D. Pritchard, P. L. Roth, S. D. Jones, P. J. Galgay, and M. Watson, "Designing a Goal Setting System to Enhance Performance: A Practical Guide," *Organizational Dynamics*, Summer 1988, pp. 69–78.

33. A. Bandura, "Self-Efficacy Mechanism in Human Agency," *American Psychologist* 37, no. 2 (1989), pp. 122–47; and M. E. Gist, "Self-Efficacy: Implications for Organizational Behavior and Human Resource Management," *Academy of Management Review* 12, no. 3 (1990), pp. 472–85.

34. Frank Hammel, "Becoming the Employer of Choice," *Supermarket Business*, June 1996, pp. 98–106.

35. Kevin Helliker, "Pressure at Pier 1: Beating the Sales Numbers of a Year Earlier Is a Storewide Obsession," *The Wall Street Journal*, December 7, 1995, pp. B1–B2.

36. Brian Smith, Jeffrey Hornsby, and Roslyn Shirmeyer, "Current Trends in Performance Appraisal: An Examination of Managerial Practice," *SAM Advanced*

Management Journal 61 (Summer 1996), pp. 10–16; Jane Pickard, "Assessment on the Sales Floor," *Personnel Management* 25 (March 1993), pp. 53–55; and Alan Dubinsky, Steven Skinner, and Thomas Whittler, "Evaluating Sales Personnel: An Attribution Theory Perspective," *Journal of Personal Selling and Sales Management* 9 (Spring 1989), pp. 9–22.

37. Daniel Feldman and Helen Doerpinghaus, "Missing Persons No Longer: Managing Part-Time Workers in the '90s," *Organizational Dynamics* 21 (Summer 1992), pp. 59–72; Daniel Feldman, "Reconceptualizing the Nature and Consequences of Part-Time Work," *Academy of Management Review* 15 (1990), pp. 103–12; and Roy Thiruk and Nico Van Der Wijst, "Part-Time Labor in Retailing," *Journal of Retailing* 60 (Fall 1984), pp. 62–80.

38. Lee Dyer and Donald Parker, "Classifying Outcomes in Work Motivation Research: An Examination of the Intrinsic–Extrinsic Dichotomy," *Journal of Applied Psychology* 60 (August 1975), pp. 455–58.

39. "Department Stores Debate Sales Commission System," *Stores*, November 1996, pp. 37–38.

40. Jhinuk Chowdhury, "Quota Setting and Salesperson Motivation: A Conceptual Framework," *Journal of Marketing Research*, February 1993, pp. 87–97.

41. James Terborg and Gerardo Ungson, "Group-Administered Bonus Pay and Retail Store Performance," *Journal of Retailing* 61 (Spring 1985), pp. 64–77.

42. George John and Barton Weitz, "Salesforce Compensation: An Empirical Investigation of Factors Related to Use of Salary versus Incentive Compensation," *Journal of Marketing Research* 26 (February 1989), p. 114; and K. M. Eisenhardt, "Agency- and Institutional-Theory Explanations: The Case of Retail Sales Compensation," *Academy of Management Journal*, 1988, pp. 591–602.

43. Steven Blackwell, Cheryl Szeinbach, Dewey Garner, and Mickey Smith, "Legal Issues in Personnel Management," *Drug Topics*, June 24, 1996, pp. 74–83; J. Ledvinka and V. Scarpello, *Federal Regulations of Personnel and Human Resource Management* (Boston: Kent, 1991); and M. D. Levin-Epstein, *Primer of Equal Employment Opportunity*, 6th ed. (Washington, DC: Bureau of National Affairs, 1996).

44. John McKinnon, "Retailers Beware!" *Florida Trend*, June 1996, pp. 20–21; and Shari Caudron, "Employees Use Diversity-Training Exercise against Lucky Stores in International Discrimination Suit," *Personnel Journal*, April 1993, p. 52.

45. Penny Gill, "American Spirit Award," *Stores*, June 1993, pp. 59–74; and Wayne Barlow and Edward Hane, "A Practical Guide to the Americans with Disabilities Act," *Personnel Journal*, June 1992, pp. 53–60.

46. Charlene Solomon, "Testing at Odds with Diversity Effort?" *Personnel Journal*, April 1996, pp. 131–40.

47. Julie Ross, "Hair Tests Gain Favor in Fight against Employee Drug Abuse," *Stores*, October 1996, pp. 75–76.

48. See Terry Leap, William Holley, and Hubert Field, "Equal Employment Opportunity and Its Implication for Personnel Practices," *Labor Law Journal* 11 (November 1980), pp. 669–82; and David Twomey, *A Concise Guide to Employment Law* (Cincinnati: South-Western, 1986).

49. Sarah Campany and Martin Personick, "Profiles in Safety and Health: Retail Grocery Stores," *Monthly Labor Review*, September 1992, pp. 9–16.

50. Carol Ukens, "Job Hazard," *Drug Topics*, May 20, 1996, p. 25; Kathryn Lewis and Pamela Johnson, "Preventing Sexual Harassment Complaints Based on Hostile Environments," *SAM Advanced Management Journal* 56 (Spring 1991), pp. 21–32; Sandra Galen, "Ending Sexual Harassment," *Business Week*, March 18, 1991, pp. 98–100; and Gretchen Morgenson, "Watch That Leer," *Forbes*, May 15, 1989, pp. 69–72.

51. Robert Ford and Frank McLaughlin, "Sexual Harassment at Work," *Business Horizons*, November–December 1988, pp. 14–19.

52. Carol Ukens, "Job Hazard," *Drug Topics*, May 29, 1996, p. 10.

53. Charlene Solomon, "Nightmare at Nordstrom," *Personnel Journal*, September 1990, pp. 76–83; Cyndee Miller, "Labor Strife Clouds Store's Service Policy," *Marketing News*, May 28, 1990, p. 1; and Francine Schwadel, "Irate Nordstrom Storming in Labor Fight," *The Wall Street Journal*, February 27, 1990, p. 26.

54. "Frugal Retailers Splurge on IS," *Chain Store Age*, January 1, 1997, p. 146.

55. "Retailers See Quick ROI in Automated Labor Scheduling," *Chain Store Age*, October 1996, pp. 78–82; and Bill Copeland, "The Latest and Greatest in People Planning," *Discount Merchandiser*, October 1995, pp. T66–T67.

56. Jennifer Pellet, "Wal-Mart's Rush for California Green," *Discount Merchandiser*, February 1996, pp. 62–63; and Marianne Wilson, "Cutting Costs with Energy-Efficient HVAC," *Discount Store News*, February 1996, p. 53.

57. "Budget-Minded Retailers Maximize Dollars," *Chain Store Age Executive*, July 1993, pp. 56–61.

58. Hollinger, *1996 National Retail Security Survey*, p. 13.

59. Ibid.

60. Tracy Dougherty, "Loss Prevention: Winning the War against Theft," *VM+SD*, October 1993, pp. 44–49; and Timothy Crowe, "The Secure Store: A Clean, Well-Lighted Place," *Security Management*, March 1992, pp. 22A–24A.

61. "Theft's Multibillion Dollar Impact on Retailers," *Chain Store Age*, January 1, 1997, p. 175.

62. Read Hayes, "The Civil Recovery Side of Shoplifting," *Security Management*, March 1992, pp. 30A–32A.

63. Denise Zimmerman, "Theft Deterrents at Work," *Supermarket Business*, January 15, 1996, p. 21.

64. J. Grant and T. Bateman, "An Experimental Test of the Impact of Drug-Testing Programs on Potential Job Applicants," *Journal of Applied Psychology* 75 (1990), pp. 127–31; David Evans, "A Dose of Drug Testing," *Security Management*, May 1992, pp. 48–53; and Jules Abend, "Drugs and Other Issues," *Stores*, June 1990, pp. 51–55.

Store Layout, Design, and Visual Merchandising

THE WORLD OF RETAILING

RETAILING STRATEGY

MERCHANDISE MANAGEMENT
12. Planning Merchandise
    Assortments
13. Buying Systems
14. Buying Merchandise
15. Pricing
16. Retail Promotion Mix

STORE MANAGEMENT
17. Managing the Store
**18. Store Layout, Design, and
    Visual Merchandising**
19. Customer Service
20. Retail Selling

QUESTIONS

● What are the critical issues in designing a store?

● What are the alternative methods of store layout?

● How is space assigned to merchandise and departments?

● What are the best techniques for merchandise presentation?

IN A TIME WHEN RETAILERS are finding it increasingly difficult to create a differential advantage on the basis of merchandise, price, promotion, and location, the store itself becomes a fertile opportunity for market differentiation. In fact, today's consumers have a multitude of shopping choices outside the store. They can shop via catalogs or on the Internet. (See Chapter 3.) The information highway of the future will facilitate shopping at home with video telephones and even **virtual reality**—an electronic three-dimensional experience in which all of the participant's senses become involved. Picture, for instance, being able to see, try on, and even feel a cashmere sweater electronically! Thus, even more than in the past, retailers must create an exciting store design with innovative merchandising techniques to make people want to get off their couches and go shopping.

Many retailers like to think of their store as a theater. The walls and floors represent the stage. The lighting, fixtures, and visual communications such as signs represent the sets. And the merchandise represents the show. Like the theater, the store design and all its components should work in harmony to support the merchandise, rather than competing with it. Most observers think of Border's Book Stores as expert implementers of the "store as theater" concept. Customers are encouraged to linger and explore the merchandise through comfortable sitting areas and an expresso coffeeshop. Consider the theatrical appeal of the Boomers! An Explosion of Fun! toy stores in Retailing View 18.1.

When designing or redesigning a store, managers must consider three objectives. First, the store's atmosphere must be consistent with the store's image and overall strategy. The second objective of a good store design is to help influence

18.1

Boomers! Puts Fun Back into Toy Stores

THINK OF IT AS A PLAYGROUND for adults or a toy store with attitude. Boomers! An Explosion of Fun! is dedicated to the child in everyone.

Boomers! is an adult toy and gift store, rated PG-13. It combines entertainment with retail for an experience that's pure fun. Boomers! An Explosion of Fun! has three stores in New Hope, Pennsylvania, Burlington, Vermont, and Littleton, New Hampshire.

Before opening the first store, Boomers! conducted an extensive, one-year survey of the nation's toy stores. The conclusion was that these toy stores had little entertainment value—a real anomaly for a toy store.

Boomers!, which sells an odd assortment of toys and novelties, occupies a unique niche in the marketplace. While young children will definitely be amused by the store, its primary target market is 13- to 40-year-olds.

What truly distinguishes Boomers! is its playful design and clever layout. With a heavy dollop of hip humor and a sure sense of the theatrical, Boomers! resembles a film set more than a traditional retail outlet. The friendly ambiance invites customers of all ages to touch and play with the merchandise.

Boomers! is divided into 10 moveable departments, or sets. Each is completely experiential and is delineated by backdrop, lighting, audio, video, and targeted merchandise. Merchandise is arranged by theme or subject rather than by product category. For instance, the "Survival of the Hippest" department offers hula hoops, Partridge Family hits, poodle skirts, and other treasures from the '50s, '60s and '70s, while familiar old TV shows play on an outdated console.

Source: Marianne Wilson, "Fun for All Ages at Boomers! Retailer Puts Fun Back into Toy Stores," *Chain Store Age Executive,* February 1995, pp. 36–37.

Boomers! An Explosion of Fun! is a toy store that brings theater to retailing. It's playful design and clever layout represents the set. The merchandise represents the show.

Stores must be designed to fit an image. Compare the San Francisco Eddie Bauer store (left) with the gondola in the discount store (right). Imagine switching store designs—bulk candy in the rich interior of the Eddie Bauer store, selling upscale outdoor clothing from a metal gondola. It just wouldn't work! Customers would find it hard to accurately judge value if the physical environment were inconsistent with the merchandise or prices.

customers' buying decisions. Finally, when making design decisions, managers must bear in mind the productivity of the retail space—how many sales can be generated out of each square foot of space.

To meet the first objective, retail managers must define the target customer and then design a store that complements customers' needs. Is the shop traditional or trendy, masculine or feminine? To illustrate, consider the San Francisco Eddie Bauer store in the accompanying picture. Its design appeals to its customers who are interested in the "great outdoors." The store has the rich feel of natural wood, metal, and leather. Stones are used for flooring. Customers view graphics of West Coast nature. In contrast, think of the long gondola fixtures and bare fluorescent lighting that complement discount and warehouse stores' no-frills, low-price image. (A *gondola* is an island-type of self-service counter with tiers of shelves, bins, or pegs.) Customers would find it hard to accurately judge value if the physical environment were inconsistent with the merchandise or prices. Throughout the chapter, keep in mind the relationships between the overall retail strategy and the store's image as it's portrayed by the store layout, merchandise display, and atmospheric design elements such as signs, graphics, lighting, color, music, and scent.

To meet the second design objective of influencing customer buying decisions, retailers concentrate on store layout and space-planning issues. Imagine a grocery store laid out like a women's specialty store, or an art gallery that looked like a tire store. Grocery stores are organized to facilitate an orderly shopping trip and to display as much merchandise as possible. Yet boutiques are laid out in a "free-form" design that allows customers to browse. Products are also located in certain areas to facilitate purchases. For instance, next time you visit a grocery or discount store, notice the merchandise displayed at the checkout area. **Impulse merchandise** (products purchased without prior planning such as candy, batteries, and *The National Enquirer*) are often located in these areas because people are often stuck in line with nothing else to do but buy.

Customers' purchasing behavior is also influenced by the store's atmosphere. Notice how your eye moves to an attractive, informative sign in a department store. On a more subtle level, have you ever been attracted to a Mrs. Fields Cookies store because of the chocolate chip cookie smell? Chances are the retailer planned this

This store is boring! It is cluttered. Everything is on one level. Customers cannot recognize distinct merchandise classifications because the store has failed to creatively use color, lighting, signage, and displays.

REFACT It costs over $20 million to build a new department store and $7 to $10 million for a redo.

and other sensory experiences to get your attention. This chapter explores such methods to positively influence consumers' purchase behavior.

Consistent with any retail decision, the third design objective is to consider the costs associated with each store design element versus the value received in terms of higher sales and profits. For instance, the free-form design found in many boutiques is much more costly than rows of gondolas in a discount store. Also, custom wood fixtures are more expensive than wire racks. Retailers must be aware of the financial ramifications of any store layout decision.

In Chapter 9 we examined the relative costs and space productivity associated with different store location decisions. Some issues examined there are relevant when determining where to locate certain departments and types of merchandise within a store. The best locations within a store are "worth" the most, so they're reserved for certain types of merchandise. For instance, many grocery stores place their produce near the store's entrance because it has a higher margin than other merchandise categories and it creates a nice atmosphere. Furniture and rugs are usually located off the beaten path in a department store because customers will seek out this merchandise. Retailers have developed maps called planograms that prescribe the location of merchandise based on profitability and other factors.

Finally, when considering atmospheric issues of store design, retailers must weigh the costs along with the strategy and customer attraction issues. For instance, certain types of lighting used to highlight expensive jewelry and crystal cost more than rows of bare fluorescent bulbs.

This chapter is part of the store management section. In it, we examine the store design objectives that we've been discussing. First, we start with the big picture—how should the overall store be laid out? Then, we look at how retailers plan and evaluate the location of departments, and merchandise within departments. Finally, we explore very specific methods of altering a store's atmosphere.

STORE LAYOUT

To design a good store layout, store designers must balance many objectives—objectives that often conflict. First, the store layout should entice customers to move around the store to purchase more merchandise than they may have originally planned. One method is to expose the customer to a layout that facilitates a specific traffic pattern. Customers should be enticed to follow what amounts to a "yellow brick road."[1] For instance, Toys "R" Us uses a layout that almost forces customers to move through sections of inexpensive impulse purchase products to get to larger, more expensive goods. It takes a very strong-willed parent to navigate through the balloons and party favors without making a purchase.

18.2

Using 3-D Animation to Design Stores

HOW DO RETAILERS like Blockbuster and B. Dalton Booksellers design their store layouts? Their aggressive schedule of new store openings demands the prototype be adapted quickly to a wide range of leases. Thus, the ability to quickly assess each new floor plan is essential. While the creative responsibility remains with a human designer, repetitive rendering of individual design elements is minimized through computerized three-dimensional store layouts.

Picture this: One by one, segments of a two-dimensional drawing begin to rise up from the computer screen's surface and assemble themselves into magical shapes. Wire-frame figures evolve into colorful three-dimensional forms.

This is where Alice would have ended up if she had followed a different rabbit. For retailers, 3-D animation is a powerful design, communication, and store-planning tool—one that will change the way stores are designed. Existing on the realism scale somewhere between conceptual drawing and actual construction, an animated rendering has the ability to convey spatial ideas more dramatically and realistically than an artist's rendering, and far less expensively than building a prototype.

Applied to a creative retail idea—prototype, fixture design, or floor plan configuration—a 3-D rendering doubles the dimensional firepower of a traditional conceptual drawing. To the two-dimensional drawing, CAD- (computer-aided–design-) driven modeling adds the Z axis, while the power of animation places the viewer in motion.

That means that a store designer can create a lifelike, three-dimensional, guided tour of any retail space using only her imagination and a desktop computer. Some of these systems run on mainstream Windows-based systems. You don't need to be a computer expert to run the program—just click the mouse and away you go.

Source: Sean O'Leary, "Revenge of the Sorcerer's Apprentice," *Visual Merchandising and Store Design*, December 1995, pp. 56–62.

Another method of helping customers move through the store is to provide variety. The store should be filled with little nooks and crannies that entice shoppers to wander around. If the "yellow brick road" comes to a dead end, customers will stop shopping. A store designer need not be satisfied with flat spaces filled with long rows of racks and shelves. Multilevels and ramps add variety. If the floor must be flat, at least display heights can be varied to avoid a monotonous presentation.

A second objective of a good layout is to provide a balance between giving customers adequate space in which to shop and productively using this expensive, often scarce resource for merchandise. A store with lots of people creates a sense of excitement and, hopefully, increases buying. But a store with too many racks and displays causes customers to get confused or even lost. Some department store chains have chopped their stores into so many small boutiques that customers don't know where to find even a simple silk blouse. Finally, when laying out stores, retailers must consider the special needs of the disabled.

To meet these objectives, store designers decide about (1) alternative design types, (2) allocating space to feature and bulk-of-stock selling areas, and (3) making efficient use of walls. At the same time, retailers must attempt to make their stores flexible so adjustments can be easy and inexpensive. Retailing View 18.2 describes how computers are currently being used to create store layouts.

Types of Design

Today's modern retailers use three general types of store layout design: grid, racetrack, and free-form.

EXHIBIT 18–1

Grid Store Layout

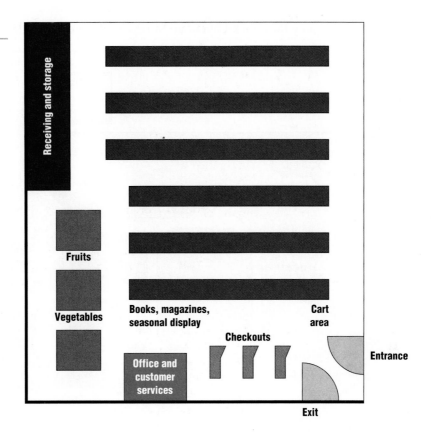

Grid   The **grid layout** is best illustrated by most grocery and drug store operations. It contains long gondolas of merchandise and aisles in a repetitive pattern (Exhibit 18–1). The grid isn't the most aesthetically pleasing arrangement, but it's very good for shopping trips in which the customer plans to move throughout the entire store. For instance, when customers do their weekly grocery shopping, they weave in and out of the aisles with great agility, picking up similar products every week. Since they know where everything is, they can minimize the time spent on a task that many don't especially enjoy. The grid layout is also cost-efficient. There's less wasted space with this design than with others because the aisles are all the same width and are designed to be just wide enough to accommodate shoppers and their carts. Since the grid design is used with long gondolas that have multiple shelf levels, the amount of merchandise on the floor can be significantly more than with other layouts. Thus, space productivity is enhanced. (Space productivity is discussed later in this chapter.) Finally, since the fixtures are generally standardized and repetitive, the fixturing cost is reduced.

REFACT In 1936, Sylvan Goldman, owner of two Oklahoma City supermarkets, noticed that customers quit shopping when their wicker baskets got too full or too heavy. So he designed the first grocery cart.[2]

Racetrack   One problem with the grid design is that customers aren't naturally drawn into the store. This isn't an issue in grocery stores, where most customers have a good notion of what they're going to purchase before they enter the store. But how can a store design pull customers through large shopping goods stores such as traditional department stores like Macy's or a discount store like Target?

The racetrack layout facilitates the goal of getting customers to visit multiple departments. The **racetrack layout** (also known as **loop**) is a type of store layout that provides a major aisle to facilitate customer traffic that has access to the

EXHIBIT 18–2   JCPenney Racetrack Layout at NorthPark Center in Dallas

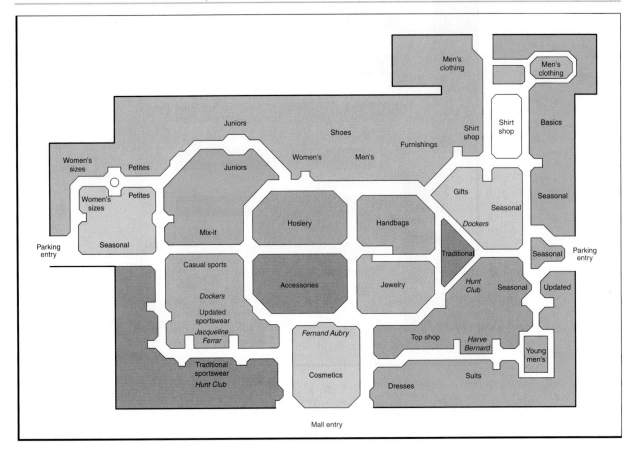

store's multiple entrances. This aisle "loops" through the store providing access to **boutiques** (departments designed to resemble smaller self-contained stores). The racetrack design encourages impulse purchasing. As customers go around the racetrack, their eyes are forced to take different viewing angles, rather than looking down one aisle as in the grid design.

Exhibit 18-2 shows the layout of JCPenney's store in the upscale NorthPark Center in Dallas, Texas. Since the store has multiple entrances, the loop design tends to place all departments on the "main aisle" by drawing customers through the store in a series of major and minor loops. To entice customers through the store, Penney's has placed some of the more important departments, like juniors, toward the rear of the store. The newest items are featured on the aisles to draw customers into departments and around the loop. To direct the customer through the store, the aisles must be defined by a change in surface or color. For instance, the aisle flooring is of marblelike tile, while the departments vary in material, texture, and color, depending on the desired ambiance.

Free-Form   A **free-form layout** (also known as **boutique layout**) arranges fixtures and aisles asymmetrically (Exhibit 18–3). It's successfully used primarily in smaller specialty stores or within the departments of larger stores. In this relaxed environment, customers feel like they're at someone's home, which facilitates shopping and browsing. A pleasant atmosphere isn't inexpensive, however. For

EXHIBIT **18–3**

Free-Form
Store Layout

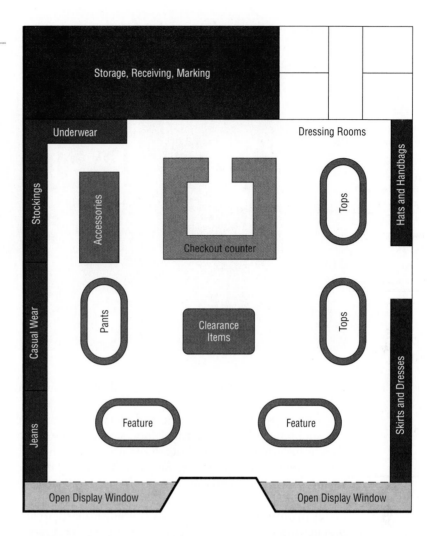

one thing, the fixtures are likely to be expensive custom units. Since the customers aren't naturally drawn around the store as they are in the grid and racetrack layouts, personal selling becomes more important. Also, since sales associates can't easily watch adjacent departments, theft is higher than with the grid design. Finally, the store sacrifices some storage and display space to create the more spacious environment. If the free-form layout is carefully designed, however, the increased costs can be easily offset by increased sales and profit margins because the customer feels at home.

To illustrate a free-form boutique within a racetrack layout, consider the Bloomingdale's I.C.B. boutique in the picture on the next page. The designers' objective was to create a simple, clear space that draws customers into the area. Fixtures with the latest garments are placed along the perimeter of the boutique. Yet the flooring and lighting clearly delineate the area from adjacent departments and the walkway.[3]

Types of Display Area

The three types of display area include feature areas, bulk of stock, and walls.

Feature Areas   **Feature areas** are designed to get the customer's attention. They include end caps, promotional aisles or areas, freestanding fixtures and

In this I.C.B. department at Bloomingdale's, fixtures with the latest garments are placed along the perimeter of the boutique to draw customers into the area. Flooring and lighting clearly delineate the area from adjacent departments and the walkway.

mannequins that introduce a soft goods department, windows, and point-of-sale areas.

End caps are located at the end of an aisle. The last time Howard Marmon was shopping at his local Kroger food store, a large end cap display of Coca-Cola caught his attention. The Coca-Cola was located near the rest of the soft drinks but was on sale. It's not always necessary to use end caps for sales, however. Due to their high visibility, end caps can also be used to feature special promotional items, like beer and potato chips before the Fourth of July.

A **promotional aisle** or **area** is used similarly to an end cap. Since Marmon was getting ready for the Christmas holidays, he stopped by a JCPenney store to stock up on ornaments. They were all in a special "trim-the-tree" department that seems to magically appear right after Halloween every year.

Freestanding fixtures and mannequins located on aisles are designed primarily to get customers' attention and bring them into a department. These fixtures often display and store the newest, most exciting merchandise in the department. (Reexamine the Bloomingdale's I.C.B. boutique in the picture on this page.)

Although windows are clearly external to the store, they can be an important component of the store layout. Properly used, window displays can help draw customers into the store. They provide a visual message about the type of merchandise for sale in the store and the type of image the store wishes to portray. Window displays should be tied to the merchandise and other displays in the store. For instance, say Howard Marmon notices a window display of bath towels, which draws him into a local boutique. The bath towels should then be prominently displayed inside. Otherwise, the drawing power of the window display is lost. Finally, windows can be used to set the shopping mood for a season or holiday like Christmas or Valentine's Day.

It is often impossible to resist purchasing something you really don't need at the point-of-sale. After all, you are almost held captive in that spot with nothing to do.

Point-of-sale areas (also known as **point-of-purchase** or **POP areas**) can be the most valuable piece of real estate in the store, because the customer is almost held captive in that spot. While waiting in a long checkout line at Kmart, Marmon picked up some batteries, candy, razors, and a copy of *People Magazine.* Did he need these items? Not really, but the wait bored him, so he spent the extra time shopping.

Bulk of Stock Area   The **bulk of stock area** contains the total assortment of merchandise. It is usually on gondolas in grocery and discount stores, and on free-standing fixtures for soft goods. This merchandise is usually introduced by a feature area. Presentation techniques for this merchandise are found later in this chapter.

Walls   Since retail space is often scarce and expensive, many retailers have successfully increased their ability to store extra stock, display merchandise, and creatively present a message by utilizing wall space. Merchandise can be stored on shelving and racks. The merchandise can be coordinated with displays, photographs, or

Since retail space is often scarce and expensive, many retailers have successfully increased their ability to store extra stock, display merchandise, and creatively present a message by utilizing wall space.

graphics featuring the merchandise. At Nike Town, for instance, a lot of merchandise is displayed relatively high on the wall. Not only does this allow the merchandise to "tell a story," but customers feel more comfortable because they aren't crowded by racks or other people, and they can get a perspective of the merchandise by viewing it from a distance.[4]

Flexibility of Store Design

As merchandise changes, so must a store's image. Thus, store planners attempt to design stores with maximum flexibility. Flexibility can take two forms: the ability to physically move store components and the ease with which components can be modified.

Most retailers have learned from the mistakes made by their predecessors following World War II. Stores during this period were often more like monuments, with inflexible wall-to-wall fixtures. The role of merchandise was almost an afterthought. Unfortunately, most of these architectural cathedrals quickly became outdated as tastes, attitudes, and the merchandise itself changed. Many of these landmark structures were made to last as long as the pyramids. Although they've long since closed for business, some still stand vacant as a sad tribute to what they once were, while others have been demolished. A few stores, like the Marshall Field's flagship store in Chicago, have been restored to their original splendor at a cost of millions of dollars.

Today, however, most stores are designed with flexibility in mind. For instance, IKEA, the Scandinavian furniture and home accessory retailer, has opened a small store in Manhattan called IKEA Marketing Outpost, that is completely reset every two to three months. Outpost was originally designed with displays of selected merchandise with a common theme so as to inspire New York shoppers to visit IKEA's full-size stores. But the Outpost has also become a successful retail location in its own right. The design is remarkably flexible. The walls, video displays, merchandise, and signage can easily be reconfigured. For instance, when the store opened, the theme "IKEA Cooks" focused on the chain's line of kitchen cabinetry, cookware, and accessories. After two months, the store closed for three days and reopened with an "IKEA plays" theme featuring juvenile furniture and toys.[5]

Recognizing the Needs of the Disabled

A critical consideration in any store design or redesign decision is the Americans with Disabilities Act (ADA).[6] This landmark federal civil rights law protects people with disabilities from discrimination in employment, transportation, public accommodations, telecommunications, and the activities of state and local government. Since both the owner of a shopping center and the retailer are responsible for compliance, the lease may delineate responsibilities, although the lease relieves neither party from its legal obligation not to discriminate.

The requirements for compliance with the ADA are different depending on whether it's an existing facility, a newly built facility, or a facility undergoing remodeling. It's easiest to comply in an existing facility. In essence, barriers must be removed if doing so doesn't involve much difficulty or expense. The ADA insists on higher standards for larger facilities. For most stores and shopping centers, the ADA requires building ramps, adding grab bars, rearranging restroom stall dividers, adding a handrail to stairs, providing Braille elevator buttons, and other measures.

Talk about flexibility, IKEA, the Scandinavian furniture store and home accessory retailer, has opened a small store in Manhattan called IKEA Marketing Outpost that is completely reset every two or three months.

Requirements for newly built facilities or those undergoing remodeling are more stringent. For instance, if a shopping center has five or more stores, it must have an elevator even if it's a small building under three stories or under 3,000 square feet per story.

SPACE PLANNING

Allocation of space to departments, categories, and finally items is one of store planners and category managers' most complicated and difficult decisions. They must answer four questions:

1. What items, vendors, categories, and departments should be carried?
2. How much of each item should be carried?
3. Where should the merchandise be located?
4. How much space should the merchandise take?

Chapter 12's discussion of assortment planning gave procedures for answering the first two questions. Now let's examine the last two questions.

Store planners in conjunction with category managers typically start by allocating space based on sales productivity. For instance, if knit shirts represent 15 percent of the total expected sales for the men's furnishings department, it will initially get 15 percent of the space. Store planners must then adjust the initial estimate based on the following five factors.

1. *How profitable is the merchandise?* The marginal analysis approach for allocating promotional expenditures to merchandise (as Chapter 16 related) also works for allocating space. In this situation, a retailer allocates space to SKUs to maximize

the merchandise category's profitability. Similar analyses can be performed for departments. Consider, for instance, allocating space for beer in a supermarket. At first glance, you might think that since Bud Light is the most profitable brand, it should get all the space. But if the store took this approach, it would lose sales on less profitable brands—and it might even lose customers who are loyal to other brands. Thus, the store should experiment with different shelf space allocations until it finds a combination that maximizes profits for the category.

2. *How will the planned inventory turnover and the resulting stock-to-sales ratio affect how many knit shirts will normally be carried in stock?* Recognize that (as in the merchandise budget plan) monthly inventory levels vary according to seasonal demands, holidays, and so on. Category managers and store planners must allocate space based on these seasonal needs rather than yearly averages. They must also estimate the proportion of merchandise kept on display versus backup stock. Merchandise kept as backup stock in a storage area takes much less room.

3. *How will the merchandise be displayed?* Merchandise and fixtures go hand in hand. Store planners design fixtures to go with the merchandise. But once the fixtures are in the store, category managers must consider the fixtures' physical limitations when assigning space to merchandise. Will the shirts be displayed on hangers or folded on tables? Customers can more easily examine merchandise on hangers, but this display method takes more space.

4. *What items does the retailer wish to emphasize?* The category managers have decided that this season will be particularly strong in knit shirts rather than woven shirts. They've bought accordingly, and planned additional advertising. As a result, knit shirts must also receive additional selling and display space.

5. *Will the location of certain merchandise draw the customer through the store, thus facilitating purchases?* Notice, for instance, the way the mannequins and fixtures are placed on the perimeter of the department in the Bloomingdale's I.C.B. boutique in the picture on page 548. Throughout this section, we examine how retailers locate departments and specific merchandise to facilitate purchases and encourage purchases of impulse and complementary products.

We've discussed in general terms how store planners and buyers plan the space requirements for a category like knit shirts or beer. Similar decisions are made for larger groups of merchandise like classifications, departments, and even merchandise groups. Now let's examine how retailers decide where to locate departments and where to locate merchandise within departments.

Location of Departments

Sandy Williams recently went to Nordstrom for a haircut. On the way in, she stopped at the cosmetics counter to buy makeup. Then on the escalator, she spotted a red dress to examine on her way out. Before leaving the store, she stopped by the lingerie department to browse.

Did she simply take a random walk through the store? Probably not. The departments she shopped—like all Nordstrom departments—are strategically located to maximize the entire store's profits. The profit-generating ability of various locations within a store aren't equal. (Remember the retail site selection techniques in Chapter 8.) The more traffic through a department, the better the location will be. Unfortunately, every department can't be situated in the best location. Retailers must consider additional demand-generating factors and the interrelations between departments when determining their locations.

Relative Location Advantages   The best locations within the store depend on the floor location, the position within a floor, and its location relative to traffic aisles, entrances, escalators, and so on. In general, in a multilevel store, a space's value decreases the further it is from the entry-level floor. As we've said, men aren't generally avid shoppers for clothing. Thus, many large stores locate the men's department on the entry-level floor to make shopping as easy as possible.

The position within a floor is also important when assigning locations to departments. The best locations are those closest to the store's entrances, main aisles, escalators, and elevators. Sandy Williams spotted the red dress because she could see it from the escalator. Multilevel stores often place escalators so customers must walk around the sales floor to get to the next level. Also, most customers turn right when entering a store or floor, so the right side will be especially desirable space. Finally, most customers won't get all the way to the center of the store, so many stores use the racetrack design to induce people to move into the store's interior.[7]

Impulse Products   **Impulse products**—like fragrances and cosmetics in department stores and magazines in supermarkets—are almost always located near the front of the store, where they're seen by everyone and may actually draw people into the store. Sandy Williams didn't plan her makeup purchase, for example, but decided she wanted some once she saw the displays.

Demand/Destination Areas   Children's, expensive specialty goods, and furniture departments as well as customer-service areas like beauty salons, credit offices, and photography studios are usually located off the beaten path—in corners and on upper floors. Due to the exclusive nature of Steuben Glass, for instance, the department is typically located in a low-traffic area of high-end stores like Neiman Marcus. A purchase of one of these unique, expensive pieces requires thought and concentration. Sandy Williams would probably become distracted if the department were adjacent to a high-traffic area. Besides, customers looking for these items will find them no matter where they're located in the store. These departments are known as **demand/destination areas** because *demand* for their products or services is created before customers get to their *destination*. Thus, they don't need prime locations.

Seasonal Needs   Some departments need to be more flexible than others. For instance, it's helpful to locate winter coats near sportswear. Extra space in the coat department can be absorbed by sportswear or swimwear in the spring when the bulk of the winter coats have been sold.

Physical Characteristics of Merchandise   Departments that require large amounts of floor space, like furniture, are often located in the less desirable locations. Some departments (like curtains) need significant wall space, while others (like shoes) require accessible storage.

Adjacent Departments   After trying on the red dress, Sandy found a complementary scarf and stockings nearby. Retailers often cluster complementary products together to facilitate multiple purchases.

Some stores are now combining traditionally separate departments or categories to facilitate multiple purchases using **market basket analysis.**[8] Stores are laid out based on the way customers purchase merchandise, rather than based on traditional categories or departments.

18.3

Why the Bread's in the Back of the Store

GROCERY SHOPPERS of the world, unite! Supermarkets know everything about you. It's time you learned something about them.

The barricade is the first thing you notice when you enter a Winn-Dixie supermarket. Everything, from checkout stands to grocery bins, pushes you to the right.

Meanwhile, the items almost everyone buys—milk, eggs, butter, and bread—are in the back left-hand corner. To get to them, a shopper tending right must travel half the store's perimeter and go past every aisle.

Most supermarkets steer shoppers immediately into the produce section. That's because they can see and feel and smell the food there, unlike the meat section, for instance, where items are hermetically sealed in plastic, or the snack section, where products are locked up in bags. The smell of fresh fruits and vegetables gets a shopper's mouth watering—and any supermarket manager can tell you that the best customer is a hungry customer.

The first produce item you see is apples, and that's no accident either. The apple is by far the most popular item in produce, almost twice as popular as oranges, bananas, lettuce, and potatoes, the runners-up.

Supermarkets prefer store brands because they carry higher profit margins than name brands. So, stock clerks place the former to the right of the latter. Why? Because most people are right-handed and to retrieve a name brand, will have to reach across the store brand to get it. Similarly, supermarkets display high-profit items on the right side of an aisle.

Source: Vince Staten, *Can You Trust a Tomato in January?* (New York: Simon & Schuster, 1993).

Using this technique, retailers analyze point-of-sale scanner data by individual customer to determine what predominant categories they're buying. For instance, if a market basket had more than 25 percent of the items made up of cosmetics or beauty care items, the basket would be categorized as belonging to a "Beauty Conscious" shopper. The market basket categories are based on the customers' personal needs, rather than traditional categories. The market basket for the "Beauty Conscious" customer might contain makeup, cotton balls, hair dye, and cologne—four different product categories in four different physical locations in the store.

Next, the buyer would analyze the profitability of each marketbasket category. Those with higher profits should receive more space. Items within a market basket should be merchandised together. For instance, if a large percentage of "Beauty Conscious" market baskets contained greeting cards, the retailer should try to locate them adjacent to the cosmetics.

Evaluating a Departmental Layout   Retailers have used traffic-counting systems for years to determine how many people travel to different parts of the store throughout a day. The more traffic, the more popular, and therefore, the more valuable the location.

In recent years, these systems have become quite sophisticated.[9] For instance, Marsh Supermarket in Indianapolis is using a system called The Tracker in which sensors are mounted on grocery carts, tracked with infrared sensors in the ceiling, and coordinated with point-of-sale terminals at the checkout. The system can collect the following data: actual path of the shopper, actual purchases, dollars spent, amount of time in the store by location, amount of time in the checkout line, and amount of time in front of specific products or displays. The system can be used to produce a thermal map of the store, thus revealing hot and cold selling spots.

A planogram prepared by Apollo Space Management System for the salad dressing section of a grocery store.

Next time you go grocery shopping, think about why things are located where they are. But first, read Retailing View 18.3.

Location of Merchandise within Departments: The Use of Planograms

To determine where merchandise should be located within a department, retailers of all types generate maps known as planograms. A **planogram** is a diagram created from photographs, computer output, or artists' renderings that illustrates exactly where every SKU should be placed. Technology for computer-generated planograms is readily available from commercial sources.[10]

Each planogram is accompanied by the following reports: a productivity report by SKU based on sales history; an ABC analysis by SKU (see Chapter 13); a space utilization report that describes the percentage of available space used in the planogram; and a comparison report that can describe productivity between any two retail spaces or between a current and a proposed space. (The comparison report is discussed in the next section.)

Electronic planogramming requires the user to input model numbers or UPC codes, product margins, turnover, sizes of product packaging or actual pictures of the packaging, and other pertinent information into the program. The computer plots the planogram based on the retailer's priorities. For instance, if the retailer wants prime shelf space given to products that produce the highest turns, the computer will locate those products in the best locations. If margins are more important, the computer will determine the shelf space priority and the optimal number of SKUs to stock in that space. Adjustments to the initial planogram can be made to see how additional space or different fixtures would affect the productivity measures.

Planograms are also useful for merchandise that doesn't fit nicely on gondolas in a grocery or discount store. The Gap and Banana Republic, for instance, provide their managers with photographs and diagrams of how merchandise should be displayed.

Recent advances in computer graphics and three-dimensional modeling allow planograms to be designed, tested with consumers, and changed, all in a "virtual" shopping environment.[11] A consumer can view merchandise on a computer screen that looks like a real store. The shopper can "pick up" a package by touching its image on the monitor. She can turn the package so it can be examined from all sides. If she wants, she can "purchase" the product. In the meantime, the computer tracks the time spent shopping and examining a particular product, and quantity purchased. Armed with this information, the retailer can "test" the effectiveness of different planograms.

In the next section, we describe how we use planograms to evaluate the productivity of space in a retail store.

Evaluating Space Productivity

Recall from Chapter 7 that a **productivity measure** (the ratio of an output to an input) determines how effectively a retailer uses a resource. Most retailers measure the productivity of space on a **sales-per-square-foot** basis, since rent and land purchases are assessed on a per-square-foot basis. But sometimes it's more efficient to measure profitability using **sales per linear foot.** For instance, in a grocery store, most merchandise is displayed on multiple shelves on long gondolas. Since the shelves have approximately the same width, only the length, or linear dimension, is relevant. Sales per cubic foot may be most appropriate for stores like wholesale clubs that use multiple layers of merchandise.

Exhibit 18–4 measures median and superior sales as well as gross margin per square foot for departments in department stores. Predictably, the cosmetics and drug departments have the highest net-sales and gross-margin-per-square-foot ratios ($425.50 and $455.90 for median and superior sales per square foot, and $160.40 and $177.00 for median and superior gross margin per square foot, respectively). These departments have relatively expensive merchandise that can be displayed in relatively small spaces.

When allocating space to merchandise or a department, a retail manager must consider the profit impact on all departments. Remember, the objective is to maximize the profitability of the store, not just a particular department. Since cosmetics and drugs has a relatively high gross margin per square foot, should management

EXHIBIT 18–4

Productivity of Space in Department Stores by Department, Measured in Dollars per Square Foot of Selling Space

DEPARTMENT	NET SALES		GROSS MARGIN	
	MEDIAN	SUPERIOR	MEDIAN	SUPERIOR
Female apparel	$153.20	$175.40	$56.90	$67.10
Adult female accessories	202.30	205.90	72.30	92.90
Men's and boys' apparel and accessories	185.40	223.80	58.00	67.70
Infants' and children's clothing and accessories	137.80	182.10	45.50	47.40
Cosmetics and drugs	425.50	455.90	160.40	177.00

Source: Alexandra Moran, ed., *MOR 1996 Edition: Merchandising and Operating Results of Retail Stores in 1995,* 71st ed. (New York: John Wiley & Sons, 1996), pp. 4–7.

EXHIBIT 18–5

Financial
Comparison Report
for Existing and
Proposed Salad
Dressing Planogram

BRAND	GROSS MARGIN PER WEEK	SALES PER WEEK	UNIT SALES PER WEEK	INVENTORY TURNOVER
Section: Salad Dressing current				
1. 7SEAS	$50.33	$273.68	222.00	35.52
2. HV RANCH	$26.01	$165.13	90.80	22.59
3. KENS STK	$46.76	$330.14	266.00	27.61
4. KRAFT	$59.83	$336.42	238.00	23.48
5. NWMN OW	$32.63	$186.06	114.00	34.87
6. PRS CHOI	$27.88	$122.18	82.00	59.22
7. WLD FRMS	$20.80	$109.85	65.00	45.07
8. WSHBN	$102.76	$590.03	431.00	25.73
Totals	$367.00	$2,113.49	1,508.80	28.53
Section: Salad Dressing revised				
1. 7SEAS	$50.33	$273.68	222.00	35.52
2. DUNNE	$6.97	$46.20	44.00	26.00
3. HV RANCH	$26.01	$165.13	90.80	22.59
4. KENS STK	$46.76	$330.14	266.00	27.61
5. KRAFT	$58.40	$326.97	229.00	27.13
6. NWMN OW	$32.63	$186.06	114.00	34.87
7. PRS CHOI	$27.88	$122.18	82.00	59.22
8. WLD FRMS	$20.80	$109.85	65.00	45.07
9. WSHBN	$102.76	$590.03	431.00	25.73
Totals	$372.54	$2,150.24	1,543.80	29.19
Net Change				
1. 7SEAS	$0.00	$0.00	0.00	0.00
2. DUNNE	$6.97	$46.20	44.00	26.00
3. HV RANCH	$0.00	$0.00	0.00	0.00
4. KENS STK	$0.00	$0.00	0.00	0.00
5. KRAFT	($1.43)	($9.45)	–9.00	3.64
6. NWMN OW	$0.00	$0.00	0.00	0.00
7. PRS CHOI	$0.00	$0.00	0.00	0.00
8. WLD FRMS	$0.00	$0.00	0.00	0.00
9. WSHBN	$0.00	$0.00	0.00	0.00
Totals	$5.54	$36.75	35.00	0.66

Source: Apollo Space Management System

give it more or less space? The answer depends on whether profitability of the entire store would increase if more space were alloted to this department. The department may be achieving its high productivity ratio because it's too small and has only a limited assortment. Conversely, a department may actually be too large—if so, almost as much profit could be generated with a smaller space. The buyer could buy smaller quantities more often, thereby making more productive use of a smaller space. If management decides to shrink cosmetics and the drugs department, more space would be available for, say, female apparel. If the departments' overall profitability would be increased by making this move, then the retailer should do it.[12]

Another way to evaluate the performance of retail space is to compare the productivity between any two retail spaces or between a current and a proposed space. Exhibit 18–5, on page 554, compares the performance of the salad dressing

Sales per cubic foot may be the most appropriate method for evaluating the productivity of space in stores like wholesale clubs that use multiple layers of merchandise.

planogram depicted earlier with one in which two Dunne dressings were added and two Kraft dressings were deleted. This report can be used to test different planograms and ask "what-if" questions. It provides information on gross margin per week, sales per week, unit sales per week, and inventory turnover for the current gondola and proposed gondola, and shows the net change between the two.

The revised gondola should improve gross margin by $5.54, sales by $36.75, unit sales by 35.00, and inventory turnover by .66. (See the last line of Exhibit 18–5.) The category manager or merchandiser planner for salad dressing should try several alternative configurations before settling on a new planogram for this gondola.

MERCHANDISE PRESENTATION TECHNIQUES

Many methods are available to retailers for effectively presenting merchandise to the customer. To decide which is best for a particular situation, store planners must consider the following four issues.

First, and probably most important, merchandise should be displayed in a manner consistent with the store's image. For instance, some stores display men's shirts by size so all size 15½–34 shirts are together. Thus the customer can easily determine what's available in his size. This is consistent with a no-nonsense image of the store. Other stores keep all color/style combinations together. This presentation evokes a more fashion-forward image and is more aesthetically pleasing, but it forces the customer to search in each stack for his size.

Second, store planners must consider the nature of the product. Basic jeans can easily be displayed in stacks, but skirts must be hung so the customer can more easily examine the design and style.

Third, packaging often dictates how the product is displayed. Discount stores sell small packages of nuts and bolts, for example, but hardware stores still sell these products by the unit. Although the per-unit price is significantly higher for the packages, self-service operations don't have adequate personnel to weigh and bag these small items.

Finally, products' profit potential influences display decisions. For example, low-profit/high-turnover items like back-to-school supplies don't require the same elaborate, expensive displays as Parker fountain pens.

In this section, we'll examine some specific presentation techniques. Then we'll describe the fixtures used in these merchandise presentations.

Idea-Oriented Presentation

Some retailers successfully use an **idea-oriented presentation**— a method of presenting merchandise based on a specific idea or the image of the store. Women's fashions, for instance, are often displayed to present an overall image or idea. Also, furniture is combined in room settings to give customers an idea of how it would look in their homes. Individual items are grouped to show customers how the items could be used and combined. This approach encourages the customer to make multiple complementary purchases.

Manufacturers with strong consumer demand are often merchandised together in the boutique layout described earlier in this chapter. This technique is similar to the idea-oriented presentation in that merchandise made by the same vendor will tend to be coordinated. Some apparel manufacturers like Liz Claiborne and Jaeger coordinate both style and color to influence multiple purchases within the line and enhance the line's overall image.

Style/Item Presentation

Probably the most common technique of organizing stock is by style or item. Discount stores, grocery stores, hardware stores, and drug stores employ this method for nearly every category of merchandise. Also, many apparel retailers use this technique. When customers look for a particular type of merchandise, such as a sweater, they expect to find all items in the same location.

Arranging items by size is a common method of organizing many types of merchandise, from nuts and bolts to apparel. Since the customer usually knows the desired size, it's easy to locate items organized in this manner.

Color Presentation

A bold merchandising technique is by color. For instance, in winter months women's apparel stores may display all white "cruise wear" together to let customers know that store is *the place* to purchase clothing for their winter vacation.

Price Lining

Organizing merchandise in price categories, or **price lining** (when retailers offer a limited number of predetermined price points within a classification), was discussed in Chapter 15. This strategy helps customers easily find merchandise at the price they wish to pay. For instance, men's dress shirts may be organized into three groups selling for $30, $45, and $60.

Vertical Merchandising

Another common way of organizing merchandise is **vertical merchandising.** Here merchandise is presented vertically using walls and high gondolas. Customers shop much as they read a newspaper— from left to right, going down each column, top to bottom. Stores can effectively organize merchandise to follow the eye's natural movement. Retailers take advantage of this tendency in several ways. Many grocery stores put national brands at eye level and store brands on lower shelves because customers scan from eye level down. Finally, retailers often display merchandise in bold vertical bands of an item. For instance, you'll see vertical columns of towels of the same color displayed in a department store or a vertical band of yellow-and-orange boxes of Tide detergent followed by a band of blue Cheer boxes in a supermarket.

Tonnage Merchandising

As the name implies, **tonnage merchandising** is a display technique in which large quantities of merchandise are displayed together. Customers have come to equate tonnage with low price, following the retail adage "stock it high and let it fly." Tonnage merchandising is therefore used to enhance and reinforce a store's price image. Using this display concept, the merchandise itself is the display. The retailer hopes customers will notice the merchandise and be drawn to it. For instance, before many holidays, grocery stores use an entire end of a gondola (i.e., an end cap) to display six-packs of Pepsi.

Frontal Presentation

Often, it's not possible to create effective displays and efficiently store items at the same time. But it's important to show as much of the merchandise as possible. One solution to this dilemma is the **frontal presentation** (a method of displaying merchandise in which the retailer exposes as much of the product as possible to catch the customer's eye). Book manufacturers, for instance, make great efforts to create eye-catching covers. But bookstores usually display books exposing only the spine. To create an effective display and break the monotony, book retailers often face the cover out like a billboard to catch the customer's attention. A similar frontal presentation is achieved on a rack of apparel by simply turning one item out to show the merchandise.

Fixtures

The primary purposes of fixtures are to efficiently hold and display merchandise. At the same time, they must help define areas of a store and encourage traffic flow. Fixtures must be in concert with the other physical aspects of the store, such as floor coverings and lighting, as well as the overall image of the store. For instance, in stores designed to convey a sense of tradition or history, customers automatically expect to see lots of wood rather than plastic or metal fixtures. Wood mixed with metal, acrylic, or stone changes the traditional orientation. The rule of thumb is that the more unexpected the combination of textures, the more contemporary the fixture.[13]

To create an effective display and break the monotony, book retailers often use a frontal presentation by facing some covers out like a billboard to catch the customer's attention.

Fixtures come in an infinite variety of styles, colors, sizes, and textures, but only a few basic types are commonly used. For apparel, retailers utilize the straight rack, rounder, and four-way. The mainstay fixture for most other merchandise is the gondola.

The **straight rack** consists of a long pipe suspended with supports going to the floor or attached to a wall (Exhibit 18–6A). Although the straight rack can hold a lot of apparel, it's hard to feature specific styles or colors. All the customer can see is a sleeve or a pant leg. As a result, straight racks are often found in discount and off-price apparel stores.

A **rounder** (also known as a **bulk** or **capacity fixture**) is a round fixture that sits on a pedestal (Exhibit 18–6B).

EXHIBIT 18-6

(a) Straight rack

(b) Rounder

(c) Four-way

(d) Gondola

Although smaller than the straight rack, it's designed to hold a maximum amount of merchandise. Since they're easy to move and efficiently store apparel, rounders are found in most types of apparel stores. But, as with the straight rack, customers can't get a frontal view of the merchandise.

A **four-way fixture** (also known as a **feature fixture**) has two crossbars that sit perpendicular to each other on a pedestal (Exhibit 18–6C). This fixture holds a large amount of merchandise and allows the customer to view the entire garment. The four-way is harder to properly maintain than the rounder or straight rack, however. All merchandise on an arm must be a similar style and color, or the customer may become confused. Due to their superior display properties, four-way fixtures are commonly utilized by fashion-oriented apparel retailers.

A **gondola** is an island type of self-service counter with tiers of shelves, bins, or pegs (Exhibit 18–6D). Gondolas are extremely versatile. They're used extensively, but not exclusively, in grocery and discount stores to display everything from canned foods to baseball gloves. Gondolas are also found displaying towels, sheets, and housewares in department stores. Folded apparel too can be efficiently displayed on gondolas, but, because the items are folded, it's even harder for customers to view apparel on gondolas than on straight racks.

An experimental method of selling merchandise without actually displaying it is with an interactive electronic kiosk. See Retailing View 18.4.

REFACT An Office Depot has over 1,700 linear feet of fixtures. A 100,000–square-foot Burdines Department Store has about 1,000 fixtures—half are for hanging apparel.

18.4

Interactive Electronic Kiosks

IMAGINE TRYING TO BUY a pair of shoes without the help of a salesperson or the ability to try them on. At some Reading, Pennsylvania, Boscov's stores, you can do just that at a Florsheim Express interactive kiosk. By pushing a button, customers tell the computer what type of shoe they want and how much they want to spend. The screen displays all available options.

Once the customer has made a selection, a printer in the kiosk generates an order form that the patron takes to the cash register. Orders are transmitted to the chain's master computer, which, in turn, sends the information to Florsheim. Florsheim then ships merchandise directly to patrons from its warehouses.

The stores benefit by reducing in-store inventory. They also expand their customer base by offering shoes in sizes and styles they wouldn't otherwise carry because of limited demand.

Some retailers haven't been so successful, however, because customers seem reluctant to use the kiosks. For instance, Hallmark has removed about 10,000 "Touch-Screen Greetings" personalized greeting card kiosks from a variety of different types of retailers.

Experts believe that for electronic interactive kiosks to succeed, retailers must consider the following issues:

To help facilitate the purchase of gifts for weddings and other special occasions, Crate & Barrel uses this electronic kiosk to help customers select gifts for those who have registered with their store.

- The industry must manufacture kiosks with a similar format so that consumers feel comfortable using them.
- Kiosks should be used only when they provide a significant improvement over current sales and merchandising techniques.
- Although the price of kiosks is falling, they're still expensive—up to $20,000 each. Their use must be cost-justified.

Source: Julie Ritzer Ross, "Standards Seek to Counter Kiosks' Customer Problem," *Stores*, January 1996, pp. 52–56.

ATMOSPHERICS

Atmospherics refers to the design of an environment via visual communications, lighting, colors, music, and scent to stimulate customers' perceptual and emotional responses and ultimately to affect their purchase behavior.[14] Many retailers have discovered the subtle benefits of developing atmospherics that complement other aspects of the store design and the merchandise. Now let's explore some basic principles of good atmospheric design and examine a few new, exciting, and somewhat controversial trends.

Visual Communications

Visual communications—comprising graphics, signs, and theatrical effects both in the store and in windows—help boost sales by providing information on products and suggesting items or special purchases. Signs and graphics also help customers find a department or merchandise. Graphics (such as photo panels) can add personality, beauty, and romance to the store's image.

Retailers should consider the following seven issues when designing visual communications strategies for their stores.

Coordinate Signs and Graphics with the Store's Image   Signs and graphics should act as a bridge between the merchandise and the target markets. The colors and tone of the signs and graphics should complement the merchandise. Colors that aren't pleasing to the overall presentation will visually destroy a good display and detract from the merchandise. For example, a pastel pink sign set in a bold red, white, and blue nautical display won't do a display justice. Also, a formally worded black-and-white rectangular sign doesn't relate to a children's display as well as a red-and-yellow circus tent design does. Color combinations should appeal to specific target customers or highlight specific merchandise—primary colors for kids, hot vivid colors for teens, pastels for lingerie, brights for sportswear, and so forth. Wall posters should depict merchandise used by the appropriate target market. Posters of teenagers in jeans should be used in the young men's department, for example.

Inform the Customer   Informative signs and graphics make merchandise more desirable. For instance, Crate & Barrel, the upscale home furnishings retailer, has a small white placard with black descriptive copy and price as an integral part of each display. The sign is foremost a sales tool designed to appeal to specific customer needs and wants. For example, one sign may explain how a food processor works; another may announce that a particular flatware pattern was an award winner.

Large photo panels depicting the merchandise in use or in an actual home help shoppers visualize how the merchandise will function in their lives. As retailers know, customers aren't just worried about buying the product per se. They're concerned with the solution to a problem or with the gratification the product offers.

Use Signs and Graphics as Props   Using signs or graphics that masquerade as props (or vice versa) is a great way to unify theme and merchandise for an appealing overall presentation. For instance, images of fruit slices of watermelons, oranges, lemons, limes, or kiwis make colorful signs that tie in with all kinds of summer sales and promotions. A retailer could plan a storewide sale incorporating fruit slices into signage, posters, shopping bags, window displays, banners, and so forth.

Keep Signs and Graphics Fresh   Signs and graphics should be relevant to the items displayed and shouldn't be left in the store or in windows after displays are removed. Forgotten, faded, and fraught with water spots, such signs do more to disparage a store's image than sell merchandise. Also, new signs imply new merchandise.

Limit the Copy of Signs   Since a sign's main purpose is to catch attention and inform customers, the copy is important to its overall success. As a general rule, signs with too much copy won't be read. Customers must be able to quickly grasp the information on the sign as they walk through the store.

Use Appropriate Typefaces on Signs   Using the appropriate typeface is critical to a sign's success. Different typefaces impart different messages and moods. For instance, carefully done calligraphy in an Old English script provides a very different message than a hastily written price reduction sign.

Create Theatrical Effects   Part of any theatrical set are special effects that transcend yet coordinate the other elements. To heighten store excitement and enhance store image, retailers have again borrowed from the theater. Theatrical effects may be simple extensions of more functional elements, like signs using colored fabric to identify a department. Or bold graphic posters or photographs can be hung from ceilings and walls to decorate, provide information, or camouflage less aesthetic areas, such as the ceiling structure.

Lighting   Good lighting in a store involves more than simply illuminating space. Lighting is used to highlight merchandise, sculpt space, and capture a mood or feeling that enhances the store's image. Lighting can also be used to downplay less attractive features that can't be changed.

REFACT A typical category killer store has about 150 lighting fixtures, whereas a 100,000–square-foot department store has over 1,000.

Highlight Merchandise   A good lighting system helps create a sense of excitement in the store. At the same time, lighting must provide an accurate color rendition of the merchandise. A green silk tie should look the same color in the store as at the office. Similarly, lighting should complement the customer. A department store's cosmetics area, for instance, requires more expensive lighting than the bare fluorescent lighting found in most grocery stores.

Another key use of lighting is called **popping the merchandise**—focusing spotlights on special feature areas and items. Using lighting to focus on strategic pockets of merchandise trains shoppers' eyes on the merchandise and draws customers strategically through the store.

Structure Space and Capture a Mood   When Greg Feffer was in The Broadway department store shopping for a suit, he noticed his mood changed as he moved from department to department and across aisles. Part of his mood change may have been due to the store planner's explicit lighting plan. Though there's no scientific proof, experience shows that a relaxed environment is reinforced by nonuniform lighting with warm, white light colors. Feffer noticed that the department store used this lighting strategy in the men's department, where he felt a sense of privacy, personalized service, and high quality. But when he moved to the more price-competitive sporting goods department, his mood changed. Here, higher light levels, cool tones of white, and peripheral wall brightness complemented the atmosphere of generic products, lower prices, and fewer sales associates.

Downplay Features   Lighting can hide errors and outmoded store designs. Cavanaugh's shoe store, for example, has outgrown its space. To increase its storage, it has created a false ceiling of wooden rafters with overstock above. Careful lighting deemphasizes this area, which could otherwise be an eyesore.

Color   The creative use of color can enhance a retailer's image and help create a mood. Research has shown that warm colors (red and yellow) produce opposite physiological and psychological effects from cool colors (blue and green), which are opposite on the color spectrum.[15] For example, red and warm colors have been found to increase blood pressure, respiratory rate, and other physiological responses. As we translate these findings to a retail store environment, warm colors are thought to attract customers and gain attention, yet they can be distracting and even unpleasant.

18.5

Sound Sells at Kinney's Colorado Stores

KINNEY'S COLORADO STORES, which sell high-end outdoor apparel, have a nature-themed environment. The New Age background music is interspersed with nature-related sound effects, such as babbling brooks and thunderstorms. They have one effect that brings to mind an eagle screeching as it flies through the sky. They integrate the effect at an angle, crossing the store space. The spatial effect is such that people actually look up as if expecting to see an eagle overhead.

Shoppers have reacted very positively to Colorado's sound backdrop. Customers want to buy the tape. More importantly, they stay in the store longer. The sound is so soothing that customers don't want to go back into the frenzy of the mall.

Sounds are even tied to specific merchandise. Motion sensors in the ceiling activate audio devices placed behind motorized boxes with rotating graphics on the wall. As a shopper approaches a display, a sensor kicks on the audio device and the appropriate sound is heard. If you're looking at a beach shoe, for example, you hear the sound of sea gulls and ocean surf.

Source: "The Sound of Retail," *Chain Store Age*, January 1996, pp. 3C–6C.

In contrast, research has shown that cool colors, like blue or green, are relaxing, peaceful, calm, and pleasant. Thus, cool colors may be most effective for retailers selling anxiety-causing products, such as expensive shopping goods. Alternatively, warm colors may be more appropriate in stores that want to generate excitement.

Music Like color and lighting, music can either add or detract from a retailer's total atmospheric package.[16] Unlike other atmospheric elements, however, music can be easily changed and adjusted with a mere change of tape or radio station. Seattle-based Muzak provides background music for many commercial enterprises, including retailing. It now offers a service that allows retailers to automatically change their music throughout the day to reflect different customers' tastes. For instance, a store might use adult contemporary in the morning and switch to Top 40 when teens start coming in after school.

Retailers can also use music to impact customers' behavior. Music can control the pace of store traffic, create an image, and attract or direct consumers' attention. For instance, The Limited's Express and Structure use French music to help create a chic international atmosphere that complements the merchandise. The Disney Stores pipe in soundtracks from famous Disney movies that are tied directly to the merchandise.

Music may also inhibit a customer's ability to evaluate merchandise because the brain can become overloaded with the music. Some customers may become so irritated that they leave the store, while others may actually purchase more because their resistance to sales presentations is lowered. Retailing View 18.5 explores how sound is used to sell high-end outdoor apparel.

Scent   Most buying decisions are based on emotions. Of all the human senses, smell has the greatest impact on our emotions.[18] "Smell, more than any other sense, is a straight line to feelings of happiness, hunger, disgust, and nostalgia—the same feelings marketers want to tap."[19] Although particular smells may put customers in a better mood or make them linger in a store longer, there's mixed evidence among researchers that better smells lead to better sales. Nonetheless, retailers from Federated Department Stores to The Limited are experimenting with scents in their stores. Most of the "proof" is anecdotal. Consider, for instance, that in the Aventura Shoe Store in Chicago's Watertower Place, sales tripled after it introduced an aroma that combined leather, citrus, and baby powder.

Retailers must carefully plan the scents that they use, depending on their target market. Gender of the target customer should be taken into account in deciding on the intensity of the fragrance in a store. Research has shown that women have a better ability to smell than men. Age and ethnic background are also factors. As people get older, their sense of smell decreases. Half of all people over 65 and three-quarters over 80 have almost no smell at all. Korean Americans have the best ability to smell; blacks, whites, and Hispanics are in the middle; and Japanese have the worst sense of smell.[20]

How are these scents introduced into the store? Retailers can use time-release atomizers available through janitorial supply vendors, or computerized heating and air conditioning systems. But polymer pellets soaked in fragrance and placed in ordinary light fixtures, where the lamp's heat activates the scent, are the most economical way to disperse fragrance.

SUMMARY   This chapter examined issues facing store designers, buyers, and merchandise planners. A good store layout helps customers find and purchase merchandise. Several types of layouts are commonly used by retailers. The grid design is best for stores in which customers are expected to explore the entire store, such as grocery stores and drugstores. Racetrack designs are more common in large upscale stores like department stores. Free-form designs are usually found in small specialty stores and within large stores' departments. Store planners also must carefully delineate different areas of the store. Feature areas, bulk of stock, and walls each have their own unique purpose but must also be coordinated to create a unifying theme.

There's more to assigning space to merchandise and departments than just determining where they'll fit. Departments' locations should be determined by the overall profitability and inventory turnover goals of the assortment, type of product, consumer buying behavior, the relationship with merchandise in other departments, and the physical characteristics of the merchandise. Planograms, both manual and computer-generated, are used to experiment with various space allocation configurations to determine the most productive use of space. When evaluating the productivity of retail space, retailers generally use sales per square foot.

Several tricks of the trade can help retailers present merchandise to facilitate sales. Retailers must attempt to empathize with the shopping experience and answer the following questions: How does the customer expect to find the merchandise? Is it easier to view, understand, and ultimately purchase merchandise when it's presented as a total concept or presented by manufacturer, style, size, color, or price? Ultimately, retailers must decide on the appropriate type of fixture to use for a particular purpose.

Retailers utilize various forms of atmospherics—graphics, signs, and theatrical effects—to facilitate the sale. Strategies involve lighting, colors, music, and scent.

KEY TERMS

atmospherics, *562*

boutique, *546*

bulk of stock area, *549*

demand/destination area, *553*

end cap, *548*

feature area, *547*

four-way fixture (feature fixture), *561*

free-form layout (boutique layout), *546*

freestanding fixture, *548*

frontal presentation, *560*

gondola, *561*

grid layout, *545*

idea-oriented presentation, *559*

impulse merchandise, *542*

impulse product, *553*

market basket analysis, *553*

planogram, *555*

point-of-sale area (point-of-purchase area, **POP** area), *549*

popping the merchandise, *564*

price lining, *559*

productivity measure, *556*

promotional aisle (promotional area), *548*

racetrack layout (loop), *545*

rounder (bulk fixture, capacity fixture), *560*

sales per linear foot, *556*

sales per square foot, *556*

straight rack, *560*

tonnage merchandising, *560*

vertical merchandising, *559*

virtual reality, *540*

DISCUSSION QUESTIONS & PROBLEMS

1. One of the fastest growing sectors of the population is the over-60 age group. But these customers may have limitations in their vision, hearing, and movement. How can retailers develop store designs with the older population's needs in mind?

2. Assume you have been hired as a consultant to assess a local discount store's space productivity. What analytical tools would you use to assess the situation? What would you suggest to improve space productivity?

3. Describe the different types of design that can be used in a store layout.

4. Generally speaking, departments located near entrances, on major aisles, and on the main level of multilevel stores have the best profit-generating potential. What additional factors help to determine the location of departments? Give examples of each factor.

5. A department store is building an addition. The merchandise manager for furniture is trying to convince the vice president to allot this new space to the furniture department. The merchandise manager for men's clothing is also trying to gain the space. What points should each manager use when presenting his or her rationale?

6. How would a retailer use information provided by a planogram?

7. How can a market basket analysis be used to allocate merchandise to space in a retail store?

8. Which retailers are particularly good at presenting their "store as theater"? Why?

9. Lighting in a store has been said to be similar to makeup on a model. Why?

10. Why do supermarkets put candy, gum, and magazines at the front of the store?

SUGGESTED READINGS

Areni, Charles S., and David Kim. "The Influence of Background Music on Shopping Behavior: Classical versus Top-Forty Music in a Wine Store." *Advances in Consumer Research* 20 (1993), pp. 336–40.

Baker, Julie, Michael Levy, and Dhruv Grewal. "An Experimental Approach to Making Retail Store Environmental Decisions." *Journal of Retailing* 68, no. 4 (Winter 1992), pp. 445–60.

Baker, Julie, Dhruv Grewal, and A. Parasuraman. "The Influence of Store Environment on Quality Inferences and Store Image." *Journal of the Academy of Marketing Sciences* 22 (Fall 1994), pp. 328–39.

Bellizzi, Joseph A., and Robert E. Hite. "Environmental Color, Consumer Feelings, and Purchase Likelihood." *Psychology and Marketing*, September–October 1992, pp. 347–63.

Bitner, Mary Jo. "Servicescapes: The Impact of Physical Surroundings on Customers and Employees." *Journal of Marketing* 56, no. 2 (Spring 1992) pp. 57–71.

Darden, William, and Barry Babin. "Exploring the Concept of Affective Quality: Expanding the Concept of Retail Personality." *Journal of Business Research*, February 29, 1994, pp. 101–9.

Donovan, Robert J., John R. Rossiter, Gilian Marcoolyn, and Andrew Nesdale. "Store Atmosphere and Purchasing Behavior." *Journal of Retailing* 70, no. 3 (Fall 1994), pp. 283–94.

Dreze, Xavier, Stephen Hoch, and Mary Park. "Shelf-Management and Space Elasticity." *Journal of Retailing* 70 (Winter 1994), pp. 301–26.

Dube, Laurette, Jean-Charles Chebat, and Sylvia Morin. "The Effects of Background Music on Consumers' Desire to Affliate in Buyer–Seller Interactions." *Psychology and Marketing* 12 (July 1995), pp. 305–20.

Herrington, J. Duncan, and Louis M. Capella. "Practical Applications of Music in Service Settings." *Journal of Services Marketing* 8, no. 3 (1994), pp. 50–65.

Spangenberg, Eric R., Ayn E. Crowley, and Pamela W. Henderson. "Improving the Store Environment: Do Olfactory Cues Affect Evaluations and Behaviors?" *Journal of Marketing* 60, no. 2 (Spring 1996), pp. 67–80.

Staten, Vince. *Can You Trust a Tomato in January?* New York: Simon & Schuster, 1993.

Ward, James C., Mary Jo Bitner, and John Barnes. "Measuring the Prototypicality and Meaning of Retail Environments." *Journal of Retailing* 68, no. 2 (Summer 1992), pp. 194–220.

Yalch, Richard F., and Eric Spangenberg. "Effects of Store Music on Shopping Behavior." *Journal of Services Marketing* 4, no. 1 (Winter 1990), pp. 31–39.

NOTES

1. "Enticing Shoppers to Follow the Yellow Brick Road," *Chain Store Age Executive*, August 1994, pp. 60–61.

2. Vince Staten, *Can You Trust a Tomato in January?* (New York: Simon & Schuster, 1993).

3. "International Interior Store Design Competition," *Visual Merchandising and Store Design*, February 1996, pp. 35–76.

4. "Enticing Shoppers to Follow the Yellow Brick Road."

5. "IKEA Holds Manhattan Outpost with Flexible Store Design," *Stores*, February 1996, pp. 65–66.

6. Marilyn Golden, "The Americans with Disabilities Act—Its Impact on Retailers," *Retail Business Review*, January 1993, pp. 14–19.

7. Adapted from Dale M. Lewison, *Retailing*, 4th ed. (New York: Macmillan, 1991), pp. 287–88.

8. Thomas J. Blischok, "Every Transaction Tells a Story," *Chain Store Age Executive*, March 1995, pp. 50–62. Market basket analysis is also useful for developing promotional strategies. See article for details.

9. Gary Robins, "Retailers Explore New Applications for Customer Counting Technology," *Stores*, September 1994, pp. 43–47.

10. Four of the most popular planogram programs are APOLLO (Information Resource Inc., Waltham, MA, 617-890-1100 or 671-290-0652), PEGMAN (MarketWare Inc., Norcross, GA, 404-246-1700, fax 404-246-1750), SPACEMAX (MarketMax Inc., Danvers, MA, 508-777-0057, fax 508-777-0195), and SPACEMAN III (Nielsen Marketing Research, Northbrook, IL, 708-498-6300).

11. Raymond R. Burke, "Virtual Shopping: Breakthrough in Marketing Research," *Harvard Business Review*, March–April 1996, pp. 120–34; and Lynn Fancher Canavan and Sean O'Leary, "Space Happens," *Visual Merchandising and Store Design*, October 1996, pp. 80–84.

12. See Heikki Rinne, Michael Geurts, and J. Patrick Kelly, "An Approach to Allocating Space to Departments in a Retail Store," *International Journal of Retailing* 2, no. 2 (1987), pp. 27–41; M. Corstjens and P. Doyle, "A Model for Optimizing Retail Space Allocations," *Management Science* 27, no. 7 (July 1981), pp. 822–33; and M. Corstjens and P. Doyle, "A Dynamic Model for Strategically Allocating Retail Space," *Journal of the Operational Research Society* 34, no. 10 (1983), pp. 943–52.

13. Bruce Fox, "Keeping the Customer Satisfied," *Chain Store Age Executive*, October 1989, p. 96.

14. The concept of atmospherics was introduced by Philip Kotler in "Atmosphere as a Marketing Tool," *Journal of Retailing* 49 (Winter 1973), pp. 48–64. The definition is adapted from Richard Yalch and Eric Spangenberg, "Effects of Store Music on Shopping Behavior," *The Journal of Services Marketing* 4, no. 1 (Winter 1990), pp. 31–39.

15. For a review of this research, see Joseph A. Bellizzi and Robert E. Hite, "Environmental Color, Consumer Feelings, and Purchase Likelihood," *Psychology and Marketing* 9, no. 5 (September–October 1992), pp. 347–63.

16. This section is adapted from Cyndee Miller, "The Right Song in the Air Can Boost Retail Sales," *Marketing News*, February 4, 1991, p. 2. Research attributed to Professor James Kellanis.

17. Susan Reda, "Dollars and Scents," *Stores*, August 1994, pp. 38–39.

18. Ibid.; and Cathleen McCarthy, "Aromatic Merchandising: Leading Customers by the Nose," *Visual Merchandising and Store Design*, April 1992, pp. 85–87.

19. Maxine Wilkie, "Scent of a Market," *American Demographics*, August 1995, pp. 40–49.

20. Cathleen McCarthy, "Aromatic Merchandising: Leading Customers by the Nose," *Visual Merchandising and Store Design*, April 1992, pp. 85–87.

19

Customer Service

THE WORLD OF RETAILING

RETAILING STRATEGY

MERCHANDISE MANAGEMENT
12. Planning Merchandise
    Assortments
13. Buying Systems
14. Buying Merchandise
15. Pricing
16. Retail Promotion Mix

STORE MANAGEMENT
17. Managing the Store
18. Store Layout, Design, and
    Visual Merchandising
19. Customer Service
20. Retail Selling

QUESTIONS

- What services do retailers offer customers?
- How can customer service build competitive advantage?
- How do customers evaluate a retailer's service?
- What obstacles hinder retailers in providing good service?
- How can retailers improve their customer service?

CUSTOMER SERVICE IS THE SET of activities and programs undertaken by retailers to make the shopping experience more rewarding for their customers. These activities increase the value customers receive from the merchandise and services they purchase. In a broad sense, all elements of the retailing mix provide services that increase the value of merchandise. For example, location, in-stock position, and assortments all increase customer convenience. However, this chapter focuses on services provided by the environment of the retail outlet and its employees.

Exhibit 19–1 lists some of the services provided by retailers. Most of these services furnish information about the retailer's offering and make it easier for customers to locate and buy products and services. However, some of the services (such as alterations and the assembly of merchandise) actually change merchandise to fit the needs of a specific customer. Some retailers are now exploring the ultimate example of tailoring merchandise to specific customers—mass customization.

Mass customization is the production of individually customized products at costs similar to mass-produced products. In Japan, for example, Paris Miki (the world's largest eyewear retailer) developed the Mikissimes Design System to customize rimless eyeglasses for its customers. Customers answer questions indicating the kind of look they want and then a digital picture is taken of their faces. Based on the customer's responses and the picture, the system recommends a lens size and shape and displays the lenses on an image of the consumer's face. Then opticians work with customers to adjust the shape and size of the lenses and help

EXHIBIT 19–1

Services Offered
by Retailers

	Department and specialty stores	Discount stores
Acceptance of credit cards	●	●
Alteration of merchandise	●	○
Assembling of merchandise	●	○
Bridal registry	●	○
Check cashing	●	◑
Child care facilities	○	○
Credit	●	◑
Delivery to home	○	○
Demonstrations of merchandise	●	◑
Displaying of merchandise	●	●
Dressing rooms	●	○
Extended store hours	○	●
Extensive signage to identify merchandise	○	●
Gift wrapping	●	●
Facilities for shoppers with special needs (physically handicapped, etc.)	○	○
Layaway plan	●	○
Parking	●	●
Personal assistance in selecting merchandise	●	◑
Personal shoppers	◑	○
Play areas for children	◑	◑
Presentations on how to use merchandise	◑	◑
Provisions for customers with special needs (wheelchairs, translators)	◑	○
Repair services	◑	○
Rest rooms	●	●
Return privileges	●	●
Rooms for checking coats and packages	○	○
Special orders	◑	◑
Warranties	●	●

● Frequently   ◑ Occasionally   ○ Rarely

customers select from a number of options for the nose bridge, hinges, and arms in order to complete the design. Finally, technicians grind the lenses and assemble the eyeglasses in the store in less than an hour.

Another example of mass customization is Custom Foot, a shoe store in Westport, Connecticut. Customers choose from among 150 styles of shoes. Their feet are measured and scanned by a computer to develop exact specifications. Data are sent via modem to factories in Italy, where the customized shoes are made. The final product is in the hands of the consumer in approximately two weeks with an average cost of $140 per pair, enabling customers to buy customized shoes at a mass-produced price.[2]

In the next section, we discuss retailers' opportunities to develop strategic advantage through customer service. Then we examine how retailers can take advantage of this opportunity by providing high-quality service.

STRATEGY ADVANTAGE THROUGH CUSTOMER SERVICE

Joan Tillman (general manager of Chicago's Saks Fifth Avenue department store) emphasizes that customer service is the key to retailing success in the 1990s:

You can buy the same merchandise at several places. If you're a Liz Claiborne customer, you can buy it at Bloomingdale's or buy it from Saks. Consumers are going to buy where they feel the most comfortable shopping. They will be most comfortable shopping when they feel attended to and where they find what they want in a reasonable amount of time.[3]

McDonald's, Nordstrom, L.L. Bean, Disney World, and Marriott differentiate their retail offering, build customer loyalty, and develop a sustainable competitive advantage by providing excellent customer service. Good service keeps customers returning to a retailer and generates positive word-of-mouth communication, which attracts new customers.

Nature of Customer Service

As discussed in Chapter 2, two important differences between the service and merchandise aspects of the retail offering are intangibility and inconsistency.[5] Most services are intangible—customers can't see or feel them. Clothing can be held and examined, but the assistance provided by a salesperson can't. Intangibility makes it hard for both retailers and customers to evaluate services. When evaluating merchandise, customers use tangible cues such as color, fit, style, weight, and size. Customers don't have these physical indicators to use when evaluating services. Intangibility also makes it hard to provide and maintain high-quality service. Retailers can't count, measure, or check service before it's delivered to customers.

REFACT Eighty-one percent of retailers indicate that improving customer service is their most important retailing issue.[4]

Automated manufacturing makes the quality of most merchandise consistent from item to item. For example, all Super Twist™ Skil electric screwdrivers look alike and typically perform alike. But the quality of retail service can vary dramatically from store to store and from customer to customer within a store. This is because most services are performed by people. It's hard for retailers to control the performance of employees who provide the service. Thus a salesperson may provide good service to one customer and poor service to the next customer.

The difficulty of providing consistent high-quality service provides an opportunity for a retailer to develop a sustainable competitive advantage. For example, Nordstrom devotes much time and effort to developing an organizational culture that stimulates and supports excellent customer service. Competing department stores would like to offer the same level of service, but find it hard to match Nordstrom's performance.

Small, independent retailers often attempt to develop a strategic advantage over large, national chains by providing customized customer service. Large chains can use their purchasing power to buy merchandise at lower prices than small local stores can. But small retailers can overcome this cost disadvantage by providing better customer service than a large, bureaucratic company. Retailing View 19.1 describes how providing excellent customer service enables a small independent auto tire outlet to maintain margins that are twice the industry average.

Customer Service Strategies

Customization and standardization are two approaches retailers use to develop a sustainable customer service advantage. Successful implementation of the customized approach relies on the performance of sales associates and service providers, while the standardization approach relies more on policy, procedures, and store design and layout.[6]

19.1

Customer Service Generates Profits for Direct Tire

AS CUSTOMERS APPROACH Direct Tire's 10,000–square-foot stores in Watertown and Norwood, Massachusetts, they see dozens of parked Ferraris, BMWs, and Porsches. Taking a closer look, however, they realize these high-performance cars are outnumbered by aging Honda Civics and Chevy Impalas. Outstanding service attracts a wide variety of customers to a store that sells tires for $10 to $20 more than the Goodyear outlet down the street.

The difference between Direct Tire and competing automotive outlets is apparent when customers walk through the door. Immaculate waiting rooms are stocked with current magazines (ranging from *Sports Illustrated* to *Vogue*) and freshly brewed coffee and donuts. The Norwood store even has an MCI Business Center outfitted with two phones and fax lines—free for customers' use.

Through windows in every wall, customers can watch Direct Tire's technicians work. Managers and salespeople wear ties and baseball-style jackets with the company logo. Everyone else wears dark blue pants and T-shirts with the company name and slogan. "I've never heard so many yes ma'ams and no ma'ams in my life," says a long-time customer.

If customers need to buy tires and have only an hour, they can schedule an appointment at their convenience. Customers who can't wait for service or to have new tires installed can take one of the company's seven loaner cars and then pick up their car later. Direct Tire also guarantees the tires they sell and the service work they do forever.

To keep its service promise to its customers, Direct Tire pays a 15 to 25 percent premium to hire the best mechanics and alignment specialists. Then it buys equipment to support these specialists. For example, the firm spent $25,000 for equipment that can diagnose alignment and hydraulic problems in 90 seconds. State-of-the-art equipment improves service and attracts the best technicians.

A $48,000 customized inventory control system reduces customer waiting time. Salespeople can immediately determine what tires are in stock and can print receipts to speed the checkout process. To satisfy the needs of its broad market, Direct Tire maintains an extensive tire inventory—for example, 140 sets of tires for a Porsche 928S.

Highly paid employees, lifetime guarantees, state-of-the-art equipment, and extensive inventory increase Direct Tire's costs. But customers are willing to pay more for good service, so Direct Tire's 3 percent profit on sales is twice the industry standard.

Source: Rosemary Herbert, "For Direct Tire, Business Is in Fast Lane," *The Boston Herald,* October 14, 1996, p. 46; Todd Hyten, "Steinberg Sells Service Direct," *Boston Business Journal,* April 28, 1995, p. 1; and Paul Brown, "The Real Cost of Customer Service," *Inc.,* September 1990, pp. 49–58.

Customization Approach   The **customization approach** encourages service providers to tailor the service to meet each customer's personal needs. For example, the opticians at Paris Miki design eyeglasses for customers, and salespeople at Custom Foot help customers order shoes that fit their feet.

Inspired by the Disney approach to customer service, Target launched its Guest Service program. Customers are treated as guests with store employees as their hosts. Stock clerks are taught that helping guests isn't an intrusion on their work. Several employees called guest ambassadors roam the store looking for customers who need assistance. Employees are also empowered to make sure that guests have a satisfying experience in the store. If the shelf price isn't on an item, checkout clerks can take the customer's word for prices up to $20. The guest doesn't have to wait for the clerk to check the price with someone on the floor.

When customers return merchandise without a receipt, employees at the Guest Service counter simply ask them how much they paid for the merchandise and give a refund.[7]

REFACT The word *service* is from the Latin *servus,* meaning slave.[8]

The customized approach typically results in customers' receiving superior service. But the service might be inconsistent because service delivery depends on the judgment and capabilities of the service providers. In addition, providing the customized service is costly since more well-trained service providers are required.

Standardization Approach   The **standardization approach** is based on service providers following a set of rules and procedures when providing service. By strict enforcement of these procedures, inconsistencies in the service are minimized. Through standardization, customers receive the same food and service at McDonald's restaurants across the globe. The food may not be exactly what customers want, but it's consistent and served in a timely manner at a low cost.

Store design and layout also play an important role in the standardization approach. In many situations, customers don't need the services store employees provide. They know what they want to buy, and their objective is to find it in the store and buy it quickly. In these situations, retailers offer good service by providing a store layout and signs that enable customers to locate merchandise easily, by having relevant information in displays, and by minimizing the time required to make a purchase.[9]

REFACT Shopping carts were first introduced in 1937 in a Humpty Dumpty store in Oklahoma City.[10]

To provide more assistance for their customers, self-service retailers are experimenting with placing computer terminals in kiosks throughout the store to help customers locate and select merchandise. For example, Best Buy stores have Answer Center kiosks which allow customers to view and print out customer information without the help of a sales associate. Data in the kiosks are updated regularly from a centralized database.[11]

Retailing View 19.2 shows how IKEA uses a standardized service approach—with some unique elements—to attract customers expecting the traditional customized approach employed in furniture retailing.

The layout and signage of this office supply center are an example of the standardized service approach that enables customers to locate merchandise quickly, without assistance from sales associates.

19.2

IKEA Offers a Different Type of Service than Traditional Furniture Stores

IKEA IS A GLOBAL furniture retailer based in Sweden. Its concept of service differs from the traditional furniture store. The typical furniture store has a showroom displaying some of the merchandise sold in the store. Complementing the inventory are books of fabric swatches, veneers, and alternative styles customers can order. Salespeople assist customers in going through the books. When the customer makes a selection, an order is placed with the factory, and the furniture is delivered to the customer's home in six to eight weeks. This system maximizes customization, but the costs are high.

In contrast, IKEA uses a self-service model based on extensive in-store displays. At information desks in the store, shoppers can pick up a map of the store plus a pencil, order form, clipboard, and tape measure. After studying the catalog and displays, customers proceed to a self-service warehouse and locate their selections using codes copied from the sales tags. Every product available is displayed in over 70 roomlike settings throughout the 150,000–square-foot warehouse store. Thus customers don't need a decorator to help them picture how the furniture will go together. Adjacent to the display room is a warehouse with ready-to-assemble furniture in boxes that customers can pick up when they leave the store.

Although IKEA uses a "customers do it themselves" approach, it does offer some services that traditional furniture stores do not, such as in-store child care centers and information on the quality of the furniture. Toddlers can be left in a supervised ballroom filled with 50,000 brightly colored plastic balls. There are changing rooms in each store complete with bottle warmers and disposable diaper dispensers. Displays cover quality of products in terms of design features and materials, with demonstration of testing procedures.

Source: Michael Porter, "What Is Strategy?" *Harvard Business Review,* November-December 1996, pp. 61–73; and "A+ Store: Self-Service = Better Service," *Stores,* February 1988, p. 37.

Cost of Customer Service

As indicated previously, providing high-quality service, particularly customized service, can be very costly. For example, due to its outstanding service, the Savoy Hotel in London maintains a special place in the hearts of the world's elite. The Savoy's special mattress—with "864 pocketed springs, two layers of pure cotton fleece, masses of the finest curled horse hair, and a generous layer of fleece wool"—makes sure that guests get a good night's sleep.

But the Savoy goes beyond providing a good night's sleep. Maids switch off vacuum cleaners and greet guests entering the hallway in the morning. Each floor has it own waiter on duty from 7 A.M. to 3 P.M. Guests can get cotton sheets instead of the standard Irish linen sheets if they wish. Preferred fruits are added to the complementary fruit bowl in each room. Rooms are personally furnished for customers who regularly have extended stays at the hotel. For example, Kerry Packer, the Australian media magnate, hardly leaves home when he comes to the Savoy during the Australian winter. The hotel staff moves his furniture—including personal pictures—into his room when he arrives in April.

However, this high level of personal attention is very costly to provide. The Savoy employs about three people for each of its 200 rooms, about double the average for a London hotel. The corporation that owns the Savoy is concerned that the lack of profits may indicate that the Savoy is providing too much service.[12]

However, from a long-term perspective, good customer service can actually reduce costs and increase profits. A study by Anderson Consulting estimates that it costs 5 to 15 times more to acquire a new customer than to generate repeat

KFC (left) provides good customer service by standardizing its policies and procedures, while Target (right) is using more of a customized service approach, encouraging its sales associates to tailor service to meet each customer's needs.

business from present customers, and a 5 percent increase in customer retention can increase profits by 25 to 40 percent.[13] Thus it costs much less to keep your existing customers satisfied and sell more merchandise to them than it costs to sell merchandise to people who aren't buying from you now.

Retailers need to consider the costs and benefits of service policies. For example, many retailers are reconsidering their "no questions asked" return policy. Wal-Mart now sets a 90-day limit for return to combat situations like a customer asking for a refund on a battered thermos that the supplier stopped manufacturing in the 50s. Best Buy won't take back merchandise unless the customer has a receipt. This policy prevents customers from taking merchandise off the shelf and taking it to the return counter for a reimbursement, claiming they lost the receipt. Best Buy customers are also charged a 15 percent restocking charge.[15]

In the next section, we examine how customers evaluate service quality.

REFACT Retailers that have satisfied customers can earn up to 9 percent more profits than retailers with poor customer satisfaction.[14]

CUSTOMER EVALUATION OF SERVICE QUALITY

When customers evaluate retail service, they compare their perceptions of the service they receive with their expectations.[16] Customers are satisfied when the perceived service meets or exceeds their expectations. They're dissatisfied when they feel the service falls below their expectations.

Role of Expectations

Customer expectations are based on a customer's knowledge and experiences with the retailer and its competitors.[17] For example, customers expect a supermarket to provide convenient parking, to be open from early morning to late evening, to have a wide variety of fresh and packaged food that can be located easily, to display products, and to offer fast checkout. They don't expect the supermarket to have store employees stationed in the aisle to offer information about groceries or how to prepare meals. On the other hand, when these same customers shop in a department store, they do expect the store to have knowledgeable salespeople who can provide information and assistance.

Since expectations aren't the same for all types of retailers, a customer may be satisfied with low levels of actual service in one store and dissatisfied with high service levels in another store. For example, customers have low service expectations for self-service retailers such as discount stores and supermarkets. Wal-Mart provides an unusual service for a discount store: An employee stands at the entrance to each store, greeting customers and answering questions. Because this service is unexpected in a discount store, customers evaluate Wal-Mart's service positively, even though the actual level of service is far below that provided by a typical department store.

Department stores have many more salespeople available to answer questions and provide information than Wal-Mart does. But customer service expectations are also higher for department stores. If department store customers can't locate a salesperson quickly when they have questions or want to make a purchase, they're dissatisfied.

Retailers can provide unexpected services to build customer satisfaction. These include:

- A restaurant that sends customers who have had too much to drink home in a taxi and then delivers their cars in the morning.
- A men's store that sews numbered tags on each garment so the customer will know what goes together.
- A gift store that keeps track of important customer dates and suggests appropriate gifts.[18]

Customer service expectations vary around the world. Although Germany's manufacturing capability is world renowned, its poor customer service is also well known. People wait years to have telephone service installed. Many restaurants do not accept credit cards, and customers who walk into stores near closing time often receive rude stares. Stores close at 1:30 P.M. on Saturday and don't open again until Monday morning. Because Germans are unaccustomed to good service, they don't demand it. But as retailing becomes global and new foreign competitors enter, German retailers are growing concerned.[19]

On the other hand, Japanese expect excellent customer service. In the United States, it's said that "the customer is always right." In Japan the equivalent expression is *okyakasuma wa kamisama desu*—the customer is God. When a customer comes back to a store to return merchandise, he's dealt with even more cordially than when the original purchase was made. Customer satisfaction isn't negotiable. The customer is never wrong. Even if the customer misused the product, retailers feel they were responsible for not telling the customer how to use it properly. The

This Wal-Mart employee greets customers when they enter the store and answers their questons. Since the service is unexpected in a discount store, it creates a favorable impression of Wal-Mart's customer service.

first person in the store who hears about the problem must take full responsibility for dealing with the customer even if the problem involved another department.[20]

Perceived Service   Customers base their evaluations of store service on their perceptions.[21] While these perceptions are affected by the actual service provided, service—due to its intangibility—is often hard to evaluate accurately. Exhibit 19–2 shows some cues customers use to evaluate services. Employees can play an important role in customer perceptions of service quality.[22] Customer evaluations of service quality are often based on the manner in which store employees provide the service, not just the outcome. Consider the following situation: A customer goes to a store to return an electric toothbrush that isn't working properly. In one case, company policy requires the employee to ask the customer for a receipt, check to see if the receipt shows the toothbrush was bought at the store, examine the toothbrush to see if it really doesn't work properly, ask a manager if a refund can be provided, complete some paperwork, and finally give the customer the amount paid for the toothbrush in cash.[23] In a second case, the store employee simply asks the customer how much he paid and gives him a cash refund. The two cases have the same outcome—the customer gets a cash refund. But the customer might be dissatisfied in the first case because the employee appeared not to trust the customer and took so much time providing the refund. In most situations, employees have a great effect on

EXHIBIT 19–2

Cues Customers Use to Evaluate Retail Service Quality

TANGIBLES	COURTESY
◆ Appearance of store	◆ Friendliness of employees
◆ Display of merchandise	◆ Respect shown to customers
◆ Appearance of salespeople	◆ Interest shown in customers
UNDERSTANDING AND KNOWING CUSTOMER	**ACCESS**
◆ Providing individual attention	◆ Short waiting time to complete sales transaction
◆ Recognizing regular customers	◆ Convenient operating hours
SECURITY	◆ Convenient location
◆ Feeling safe in parking lot	◆ Manager available to discuss problems
◆ Communications and transactions treated confidentially	**COMPETENCE**
CREDIBILITY	◆ Knowledgeable and skillful employees
◆ Reputation for honoring commitments	◆ Customer questions answered
◆ Trustworthiness of salespeople	**RESPONSIVENESS**
◆ Guarantees and warranties provided	◆ Returning a customer's call
◆ Return policy	◆ Giving prompt service
INFORMATION PROVIDED TO CUSTOMERS	**RELIABILITY**
◆ Explanation of service and its cost	◆ Accuracy in billing
◆ Notes sent to customers informing them of sales	◆ Performing service at designated time
◆ Assurances that a problem will be resolved	◆ Accuracy in completing sales transaction

Source: Adapted from Valarie Zeithaml, A. Parasuraman, and Leonard Berry, *Delivering Quality Service: Balancing Customer Perceptions and Expectations* (New York: Free Press, 1990), pp. 20–22; and A. Parasuraman, Valarie Zeithaml, and Leonard Berry, "A Conceptual Model of Service Quality and Its Implications for Future Research," *Journal of Marketing* 49 (Fall 1985), pp. 41–50.

the process of providing services and, thus, on the customer's eventual satisfaction with the services.

Situations That
Stimulate Satisfactory
and Unsatisfactory
Experiences

Most experiences customers have with retailers are quite ordinary. Customers visit a store, select an item, pay for it, and leave the store. These uneventful experiences may not stimulate customers to evaluate the service they received. But customers are motivated to evaluate service quality when an unexpected or unusual event occurs—when they have a problem locating merchandise, when they need or request special attention, or when a store employee undertakes an unprompted or unsolicited action. Exhibit 19–3 lists examples of situations that stimulate satisfactory or unsatisfactory service evaluations.

EXHIBIT 19–3

Situations
Stimulating
Customers to
Evaluate Service
Quality

SITUATION	MORE SATISFYING EXPERIENCE	LESS SATISFYING EXPERIENCE
Unavailable service Customer enters name in bridal registry but discovers desired merchandise was never listed.	Manager apologizes for losing merchandise listing and offers to call people invited to wedding.	No explanation, no apology, and no assistance.
Employee response to slow service Customer waits two weeks to have table delivered when a two-day delivery was promised.	Employee apologizes and finally says retailer will give customer a free tablecloth for the table.	Employee says table will be delivered in two days every two days.
Employee response to service failure Customer finds a frayed cord on a lamp and returns it, asking for a replacement.	Employee provides a replacement cord.	Employee suggests cord wasn't frayed when customer left store with it; suggests customer damaged it and is trying to rip store off.
Response to a special need Customer brings a baby into store and has trouble shopping and taking care of baby.	Salesperson holds baby while customer tries on clothing.	Salesperson suggests customer return to store when someone can watch baby.
Response to admitted error Customer leaves charge card in store after making purchase.	Salesperson notifies customer and then delivers card to customer's home.	Salesperson waits until customer discovers charge card is missing and returns to store to get it.
Response to customer need Customer wants a toaster oven in a size not in stock in the store.	Salesperson locates toaster oven in another store and has it delivered to customer's home.	Salesperson suggests customer check with other store to see if toaster oven is available.
Attention paid to customer Customer walks into store and asks for some assistance.	Salesperson treats customer like royalty, finding merchandise, putting clothing together to make outfits, and accessorizing outfits.	Salesperson acts as if customer is a bother, provides short answers, and turns attention to setting up a display.

Source: Adapted from Mary Jo Bitner, Bernard Booms, and Mary Stanfield Tetreault, "The Service Encounter: Diagnosing Favorable and Unfavorable Incidents," *Journal of Marketing* 54 (January 1990), pp. 71–84.

GAPS MODEL FOR IMPROVING RETAIL SERVICE QUALITY

The GAPS model (Exhibit 19–4) indicates what retailers need to do to provide high-quality customer service.[24] When customers' expectations are greater than their perceptions of the delivered service, customers are dissatisfied and feel the quality of the retailer's service is poor. Thus, retailers need to reduce the **service gap**—the difference between customers' expectations and perceptions of customer service—to improve customers' satisfaction with their service.

Four factors affect the service gap:

- **Knowledge gap:** The difference between customer expectations and the retailer's perception of customer expectations.
- **Standards gap:** The difference between the retailer's perceptions of customers' expectations and the customer service standards it sets.
- **Delivery gap:** The difference between the retailer's service standards and the actual service provided to customers.
- **Communication gap:** The difference between the actual service provided to customers and the service promised in the retailer's promotion program.

These four gaps add up to the service gap. The retailer's objective is to reduce the service gap by reducing each of the four gaps. Thus, the key to improving service quality is to (1) understand the level of service customers expect, (2) set standards

EXHIBIT 19–4

The GAPS Model for Improving Service Quality

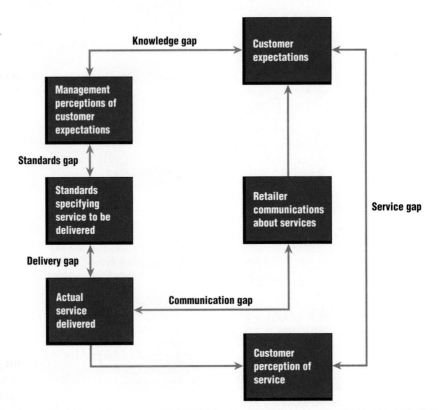

Source: Adapted from A. Parasuraman, Valarie Zeithaml, and Leonard Berry, "A Conceptual Model of Service Quality and Its Implications for Future Research," *Journal of Marketing* 49 (Fall 1985), pp. 41–50.

for providing customer service, (3) implement programs for delivering service that meets the standards, and (4) undertake communication programs to inform customers about the service offered by the retailer. The following sections describe these gaps and methods for reducing them.

KNOWING WHAT CUSTOMERS WANT: THE KNOWLEDGE GAP

The most critical step in providing good service is to know what the customer wants. Retailers often lack accurate information about what customers need and expect. This lack of information can result in poor decisions. For example, a supermarket might hire extra people to make sure the shelves are stocked so customers will always find what they want, but it may fail to realize that customers are most concerned about waiting at the checkout line. From the customer's perspective, the supermarket's service would improve if the extra employees were used to open more checkout lines rather than to stock shelves.

Retailers can reduce the knowledge gap and develop a better understanding of customer expectations by undertaking customer research, increasing interactions between retail managers and customers, and improving communication between managers and employees who provide customer service.

REFACT Consumers report that the greatest burden on their time is waiting in lines.[25]

Researching Customer Expectations and Perceptions

Market research can be used to better understand customers' expectations and the quality of service provided by a retailer. Methods for obtaining this information range from comprehensive surveys to simply asking some customers about the store's service.

Comprehensive Studies Some retailers have established programs for assessing customers' expectations and service perceptions. For example, every year JCPenney sales associates pass out questionnaires to shoppers in each store and its mall. Shoppers are asked about the service and merchandise offered by Penney and by competing department stores in the mall. Over 50,000 completed questionnaires are collected and analyzed. Since the same questionnaire is used each year, Penney can track service performance, determine whether it's improving or declining, and identify opportunities for improving service quality. The importance Penney places on customer service is revealed by its using the annual customer service profile to evaluate store manager performance.

The first step in providing quality customer service is understanding customer expectations. Customers expect limited hassle and waiting time when they are ready to buy merchandise.

Gauging Satisfaction with Individual Transactions   Another method for doing customer research is to survey customers immediately after a retail transaction has occurred. For example, Sears employees who deliver and assemble furniture in homes ask customers to complete a short survey describing how helpful, friendly, and professional the employees were. Airlines periodically ask passengers during a flight to evaluate the ticket-buying process, flight attendants, in-flight service, and gate agents.

Customer research on individual transactions provides up-to-date information about customers' expectations and perceptions. The research also indicates the retailer's interest in providing good service. Since the responses can be linked to a specific encounter, the research provides a method for rewarding employees who provide good service and correcting those who exhibit poor performance.

Customer Panels and Interviews   Rather than surveying many customers, retailers can use panels of 10 to 15 customers to gain insights into expectations and perceptions. For example, some store managers might meet once a month for an hour with a select group of customers who are asked to provide information about their experiences in the stores and to offer suggestions for improving service.

To reduce the knowledge gap, some supermarket managers go through the personal checks they receive each day and select customers who've made large and small purchases. They call these customers and ask them what they liked and didn't like about the store. With small purchasers, they probe to find out why the customers didn't buy more. Could they find everything they wanted? Did they get the assistance they expected from store employees?

Pier 1 Imports, a home furnishing chain, has a Customer Advisory Board (CAB) composed of 1,200 preferred customers representing a cross-section of the retailer's customer base. CAB members complete questionnaires three to four times a year on subjects like holiday shopping problems, in-store signage, and service quality. In exchange for their inputs, members receive a $5 gift certificate.[26]

Interacting with Customers   Owner-managers of small retail firms typically have daily contact with their customers and thus have accurate first-hand information about them. In large retail firms, managers often learn about customers through reports so they miss the rich information provided by direct contact with customers. Exhibit 19–5 lists common service complaints by customers.

Stanley Marcus, founder of Neiman Marcus, feels managers can become addicted to numbers and neglect the merchandise and customers. He uses suspenders as an example of how buyers can make poor decisions by only looking at the numbers. Originally, suspenders came in two sizes: short and long. By analyzing the numbers, buyers realized they could increase turnover by stocking one-size-only suspenders. The numbers looked good but the store had a lot of dissatisfied customers. With only one size, short men's pants fell down, while the fit was uncomfortable for tall men. "It comes back to the fact that the day is still only 24 hours long, and if you're a retailer, you've still got to spend some of those 24 hours with your customers and your products. You can't allow the computer to crowd them out as crucial sources of information."[27]

Many retailers require managers at all levels to spend time interacting with customers and observing service delivery. The entire headquarters staff at Weinstock's, a Sacramento department store chain, is required to work on the selling floor seven times a year. Headquarters staff thus found that credit authoriza-

REFACT Ninety-one percent of customers dissatisfied with a firm's offering never buy from the firm again. These dissatisfied customers will tell nine other people, on average, about their unsatisfactory experience.[28]

EXHIBIT 19–5

Common Service
Complaints

TRUE LIES
Blatant dishonesty or unfairness, such
as selling unneeded services.

AUTOMATIC PILOT
Impersonal, no-eye-contact, emotionless,
go through the motion interactions
with service providers.

RED ALERT
Retailers who think customers are
stupid and treat them disrespectfully.

SUFFERING IN SILENCE
Employees who don't bother to respond
to customers.

BROKEN PROMISES
Service providers who don't show up.

DON'T ASK
Sales associates who are put out by
requests for assistance.

I JUST WORK HERE
Powerless sales associates who lack
the authority, or desire, to solve
customer problems.

LIGHTS ON, NO ONE AT HOME
Clueless sales associates who don't
know the answers to commonly asked
questions.

THE BIG WAIT
Waiting in line because some of the
checkout aisles are closed.

MISPLACED PRIORITIES
Sales associates who visit with each
other or conduct personal business
while the customer waits.

tion took too long—something the sales associates had known for a long time. When company executives confronted this problem, they expedited the installation of dedicated phone lines to speed credit sales.[29]

Customer Complaints   Complaints allow retailers to interact with their customers and acquire detailed information about their service and merchandise. Handling complaints is an inexpensive means to isolate and correct service problems.[30]

REFACT Less than 5 percent of consumers with problems actually complain to companies.[31]

Catalog retailer L.L. Bean keeps track of all complaints and reasons for returned merchandise. These complaints and returns are summarized daily and given to customer service representatives so they can improve service. For example, a customer who returns a sweater might indicate the sweater was too large or the color tone differed from the picture in the catalog. With this information, customer service representatives can inform other customers who place an order for the sweater that it tends to be large and has a slightly different color than shown in the catalog. The information can also be used by buyers to improve vendor merchandise.

Miami's Baptist Hospital was very concerned when customer research found customer complaints among the city's growing Hispanic population were rising. "No one doubted the quality of the health care delivery," recalls Fred Messing, the hospital's CEO, "but there was a feeling we lacked sensitivity to cultural needs." Messing presented the problem to the hospital's Continuous Improvement Coordinating Committee, which developed Hispanic-friendly services like bilingual voice mail responses to outside calls, bilingual clinical brochures, additional translators in each department, and additional Hispanic dishes on patients' menus. "If you're truly committed to good customer service," says Messing, "you've got to know exactly where you are and be ready to move the instant you detect a problem."[32]

The buyer on the left is listening to the sales associate on the right explain why customers are not purchasing the sweaters that the buyer ordered.

Although customer complaints can provide useful information, retailers can't rely solely on this source of market information. Typically, dissatisfied customers don't complain. To provide better information on customer service, retailers need to encourage complaints and make it easy for customers to provide feedback about their problems. For example, some retailers set up a complaint desk in a convenient location where customers can get their problems heard and solved quickly.

Feedback from Store Employees Salespeople and other employees in regular contact with customers often have a good understanding of customer service expectations and problems. This information will improve service quality only if they're encouraged to communicate their experiences to high-level managers who can act on it.

Some retailers regularly survey their employees, asking questions like

- What is the biggest problem you face in delivering high-quality service to your customers?
- If you could make one change in the company to improve customer service, what would it be?

Using Customer Research

Collecting information about customer expectations and perceptions isn't enough. The service gap is reduced only when retailers use this information to improve service. For example, store managers should review the suggestions and comments made by customers daily, summarize the information, and distribute it to store employees and managers.

Feedback on service performance needs to be provided to employees in a timely manner. Reporting the July service performance in December makes it hard for employees to reflect on the reason for the reported performance.

Finally, feedback must be prominently presented so service providers are aware of their performance. For example, at Marriott, front desk personnel's performance feedback is displayed behind the front desk, while restaurant personnel's performance feedback is displayed behind the door to the kitchen.

SETTING SERVICE STANDARDS: THE STANDARDS GAP

After retailers gather information about customer service expectations and perceptions, the next step is to use this information to set standards and develop systems for delivering high-quality service. Service standards should be based on customers' perceptions rather than internal operations. For example, a supermarket chain might set an operations standard of a warehouse delivery every day to each store. But frequent warehouse deliveries may not result in more merchandise on the shelves or improve customers' impressions of shopping convenience.

To close the standards gap, retailers need to (1) commit their firms to providing high-quality service, (2) develop innovative solutions to service problems, (3) define the role of service providers, (4) set service goals, and (5) measure service performance.

Commitment to Service Quality

Service excellence occurs only when top management provides leadership and demonstrates commitment. Top management must be willing to accept the temporary difficulties and even the increased costs associated with improving service quality. This commitment needs to be demonstrated to the employees charged with providing the service. For example, a Lands' End poster prominently displays the following inscription for employees who process customer orders:

> What is a Customer? A Customer is the most important person in this office . . . in person or by mail. A Customer is not dependent on us . . . we are dependent on him. A customer is not an interruption in our work . . . he is the purpose of it. We are not doing him a favor by serving him . . . he is doing us a favor by giving us an opportunity to do so. A Customer is not someone to argue or match wits with.[33]

Top management's commitment sets service quality standards, but store managers are the key to achieving those standards. Managers must see that their efforts to provide service quality are noticed and rewarded. Providing incentives based on service quality makes service an important personal goal. Rather than basing bonuses only on store sales and profit, part of store managers' bonuses should be determined by the level of service provided. For example, some retailers use results of customer satisfaction studies to determine bonuses.

Exploring Solutions to Service Problems

Frequently, retailers don't set high service standards because they feel service improvements are either too costly or not achievable with available employees. This reflects an unwillingness to think creatively and to explore new approaches for improving service.

Innovative Approaches Finding ways to overcome service problems can improve customer satisfaction and, in some cases, reduce costs. For example, when customers complained about the long wait to check out, many hotels felt they couldn't do anything about the problem. Marriott, however, thought of a

Many pharmacists work in the back room filling prescriptions. At Rite Aid, pharmacists are available to answer customers' questions about their prescriptions or over-the-counter medications sold in the store.

creative approach to address this service problem. It invented Express Checkout—a system in which a bill is left under the customer's door the morning before checkout and, if the bill is accurate, the customer can check out by simply leaving the keys at the front desk and have the bill charged automatically to her credit card.

Parisian, a specialty department store chain headquartered in Birmingham, Alabama, holds a meeting before the Christmas season to identify and remove obstacles to improving customer service. At one meeting, store managers felt the policy of requiring a department manager's approval for personal checks over $250 was frustrating customers. During the hectic Christmas season, customers often had to wait 10 or 15 minutes while salespeople located their department managers. The vice president of stores suggested changing the policy and letting salespeople accept checks up to $5,000 without approval. The chief financial officer felt that changing the policy would increase the number of bad checks and reduce profits. But management decided that improving customer service was worth the risk. When the policy was implemented, the number of bad checks actually decreased because salespeople felt responsible and took time to verify the customers' identification. Previously, department managers had been so busy that they often just approved checks without looking closely at the identification.

Using Technology   Retailers can use technology to simplify and improve customer service. Routine, repetitious tasks can be handled by a system, freeing employees to deal with more demanding customer requests and problems. For example, Pizza Hut uses a computer system to centralize its home delivery business. Operators at a central location take all calls for home delivery. By training operators who specialize in order taking, Pizza Hut has reduced to 17 seconds the time required to take orders and verify directions to the caller's house. After calls are completed, orders are transmitted via computers to a printer in the restaurant closest to the caller's location. The system reduces delivery time and eliminates situations in which customers place calls at the "wrong" restaurant.[34]

Standardizing routine activities can actually improve service to important customers. For example, Marriott developed its Honored Guest program to provide extra service to its best customers. Customers who stay frequently at Marriott hotels or resorts automatically receive a special guest room, a gift, and a note from the hotel manager when they check in and show their Honored Guest card. Thus, these customers receive standardized special treatment.[35]

Pep Boys counter personnel go through extensive training so they can effectively use the company's information systems to help customers select the right part for automotive repairs.

Retailing View 19.3 describes how USAA, the most profitable insurance company in the United States, uses technology to provide outstanding customer service.

19.3

USAA Uses Technology to Service External and Internal Customers

BASED IN SAN ANTONIO, TEXAS, United Services Automobile Association (USAA) is the fastest growing and most profitable insurance company in the United States. Its strategy is providing insurance and other financial services to military officers and their dependents. The company, which is owned by its policy holders, provides coverage for 95 percent of the active-duty military officers. However, its market is shrinking. So USAA invested over $130 million in a paperless information system and database enabling its service providers to support the sales of a broader spectrum of financial services to its customers.

The system stores more than 65,000 documents a day electronically into a database containing over 150 million documents. The mail room in the auto and homeowners insurance area, scans 20,000 documents each day. The originals are held for two to three weeks for legal reasons or to be sure a document was accurately scanned. Then the paper is destroyed.

The company has also streamlined its claims process by equipping its adjusters with laptop computers. An adjuster inspects a dam-aged automobile, uploads the information over a cellular phone to USAA's computer system, prints an estimate, and usually issues a check on a portable printer right on the spot. Adjusters have even been given digital cameras to photograph damaged cars, and the digital information is fed back through remote access lines into USAA's system.

Using this system a USAA service representative can insure a member's new car, add a driver to the policy, shift investments from one mutual fund to another, and make a claim on a homeowner's policy. There are no callbacks or transfers needed. "In one five-minute phone call, you and our service representative have done all the work that used to take 55 steps, umpteen people, two weeks, and a lot of money," explains former CEO Robert McDermott.

Source: Steve Cocheo, "USAA: Stealth Bank or 'Bank' of the Future?" *ABA Banking Journal*, February 1996, pp. 43–48; Janet Purdy Levaux, "USAA's Robert McDermott," *Investor's Business Daily*, November 16, 1995, p. A1; and "USAA: Conquering a Paper Mountain," *Forbes*, October 9, 1995, p. 56.

Defining the Role of Service Providers

Managers can tell service providers that they need to provide excellent service, but not clearly indicate what excellent service means. Without a clear definition of the retailer's expectations, service providers are directionless.

The Ritz-Carlton Hotel Company, winner of the Baldrige National Quality Award, has its "Gold Standards" printed on a wallet-size card carried by all employees. The card contains the hotel's motto ("We Are Ladies and Gentlemen Serving Ladies and Gentlemen"), the three steps for high-quality service (warm and sincere greeting, anticipation and compliance with guests' needs, and fond farewell), and 20 basic rules for Ritz-Carlton employees including

- Any employee who receives a complaint "owns" the complaint.
- Instant guest gratification will be ensured by all. React quickly to correct problems immediately.
- "Smile—We are on stage." Always maintain positive eye contact.
- Escort guests rather than giving directions to another area of the hotel.[36]

Setting Service Goals

To deliver consistent high-quality service, retailers need to establish goals or standards to guide employees. Retailers often develop service goals based on their beliefs about the proper operation of the business

19.4

Domino's Abandons Its 30-Minute Delivery Standard

THE 30-MINUTE DELIVERY guarantee was the cornerstone on which Domino's became the largest pizza delivery retailer. If a phone order was delivered in more than 30 minutes, the customer got a $3 discount. After a woman who had been hit and injured by a Domino's delivery driver won a $78 million lawsuit, the company decided to drop the delivery guarantee.

Domino's screens the driving records of all delivery drivers and requires them to attend a defensive driving class. However, founder and CEO Thomas Monaghan comments, "No matter what we do in the areas of safety and training for our drivers, some of the public still have a negative perception about us because of the guarantee. So we are eliminating the element that creates that negative perception."

Domino's replaced the delivery time guarantee with a product satisfaction program. Unhappy customers will be given a free pizza. Thus Domino's is changing its service standards from delivery time to product quality.

Domino's changed its service standard when its 30-minute delivery guarantee resulted in a lawsuit.

Source: Krystal Miller and Richard Gibson, "Domino's Stops Promising Pizza in 30 Minutes," *The Wall Street Journal*, January 23, 1994, p. B1.

rather than the customers' needs and expectations. For example, a retailer might set a goal for all monthly bills to be mailed five days before the end of the month. This goal reduces the retailer's accounts receivable but offers no benefit to customers. Research undertaken by American Express showed customer evaluations of its service were based on perceptions of timeliness, accuracy, and responsiveness. Management then established goals (such as responding to all questions about bills within 24 hours) related to these customer-based criteria.[37]

Employees are motivated to achieve service goals when the goals are specific, measurable, and participatory in the sense that they participated in setting them. Vague goals, such as "Approach customers when they enter the selling area," don't fully specify what store employees should do, nor do such goals offer an opportunity to assess employee performance. A better goal would be "All customers should be approached by a salesperson within 30 seconds after entering a selling area." This goal is both specific and measurable.

Employee participation in setting service standards leads to better understanding and greater acceptance of the goals. Store employees resent and resist goals arbitrarily imposed on them by management. Chapter 17 says more on goal setting.

In setting service goals, retailers need to consider all consequences of these goals. Retailing View 19.4 describes Domino's Pizza's problems when it set a 30-minute delivery goal.

Measuring Service Performance

Retailers need to continuously assess service quality to ensure that goals will be achieved. Many retailers do periodic customer surveys to assess service quality. Many are using mystery shoppers to assess their service quality. **Mystery shoppers** are professional shoppers who "shop" a store to assess the service provided by store employees. Some retailers use their own employees as mystery shoppers but most contract with a firm to provide the assessment. Information typically reported by the mystery shoppers includes: (1) How long before a sales associate greeted you? (2) Did the sales associate act as if he wanted your business? (3) Was the sales associate knowledgeable about the merchandise?

Retailers typically inform salespeople that they have "been shopped" and provide feedback from the mystery shopper's report. Some retailers offer rewards to sales associates who receive high marks and request return visits to sales associates who get low evaluations.[38]

MEETING AND EXCEEDING SERVICE STANDARDS: THE DELIVERY GAP

To reduce the delivery gap and provide service that exceeds standards, retailers must give service providers the necessary knowledge and skills, provide instrumental and emotional support, improve internal communications and reduce conflicts, and empower employees to act in the customers' and firm's best interests.

Giving Information and Training

Store employees must know about the merchandise they offer as well as their customers' needs. With this information, employees can answer customers' questions and suggest products. This also instills confidence and a sense of competence, which are needed to overcome service problems.

In addition, store employees need training in interpersonal skills. Dealing with customers is hard—particularly when they're upset or angry. All store employees, even those who work for retailers that provide excellent service, will encounter dissatisfied customers. Through training, employees can learn to provide better service and to cope with the stress caused by disgruntled customers.[39]

Specific retail employees—salespeople and customer service representatives—are typically designated to interact with and provide service to customers. However, all retail employees should be prepared to deal with customers. For example, Walt Disney World provides four days of training for its maintenance workers, even though people can learn how to pick up trash and sweep streets in much less time. Disney has found that its customers are more likely to direct questions to maintenance people than to the clean-cut assistants wearing Ask me, I'm in Guest Relations buttons. Thus, Disney trains maintenance people to confidently handle the myriad of questions they'll be asked, rather than responding, "Gee, I dunno. Ask her."[40]

Toys "R" Us assesses customer satisfaction with checkout service by counting the number of abandoned shopping carts—carts with merchandise left in the store because customers became impatient with the time required to make a purchase. After the firm noticed an alarming increase in abandoned carts, it developed a unique program to reduce customers' time in line waiting to pay. Cashiers' motions while ringing up and bagging merchandise were studied. Based on this research, a training program was developed to show cashiers how to use their right hand to record purchases on the POS terminal and their left hand to push merchandise along the counter. Counters were redesigned to have a slot line with shopping bags in the middle of the counter. As the cashier pushes the merchandise along the counter, it drops into a bag. After the customer pays for the merchandise, the cashier simply lifts the bag from the slot and hands it to the customer, and a new bag pops into place.

To motivate cashiers to use the new system effectively, Toys "R" Us holds competitions in each store, district, and region to select the fastest cashiers. Regional winners receive a free vacation in New York City and participate in a competition at corporate headquarters to select a national champion.[41]

Providing Instrumental and Emotional Support

Service providers need to have the **instrumental support**—the appropriate systems and equipment—to deliver the service desired by customers. For example, a hotel chain installed a computer system to speed up the checkout process. A study of the new system's effectiveness revealed that checkout time was not reduced because clerks had to wait to use the one stapler available to staple the customer's credit card and hotel bill receipts.

In addition to instrumental support, service providers need **emotional support** from their coworkers and supervisors. Dealing with customer problems and maintaining a smile in difficult situations are psychologically demanding. For example, Ricky Anderson, a 20-year-old host at Disney's Tomorrowland, says, "Sometimes, you get hot in your costume, you get fed up dealing with angry guests who are tired of waiting in line. But then a kid asks you a question, you answer it, and she breaks into a smile. I realize that what I am doing is actually important and not to be taken for granted."[42] Service providers need to be in a supportive, understanding atmosphere to deal with these demands effectively.[43]

Improving Internal Communications and Reducing Conflict

When providing customer service, store employees must often manage the conflict between customers' needs and the retail firms' needs. For example, many retailers have a "no-questions-asked" return policy. Under this policy, the retailer will provide a refund at the customer's request even if the merchandise wasn't purchased at the store or was clearly used improperly. When JCPenney inaugurated this policy, some employees refused to provide refunds on merchandise that had been worn or damaged by the customer. They were loyal Penney employees and didn't want customers to take advantage of their firm.

Retailers can reduce such conflicts by having clear guidelines and policies concerning service and by explaining the rationale for these policies. Once Penney employees recognized that the goodwill created by the no-questions-asked policy generated more sales than the losses due to customers' abusing the policy, they implemented the policy enthusiastically.

Conflicts can also arise when retailers set goals inconsistent with the other behaviors expected from store employees. For example, if salespeople are expected to provide customer service, they should be evaluated on the service they provide, not just on the sales they make.

Finally, conflicts can also arise between different areas of the firm. Childress Buick/Kia, an auto dealer with an excellent customer service reputation, devotes considerable effort to reducing conflict by improving communication between its

19.5

Amy's Ice Cream Empowers Its Employees to Perform

AMY'S ICE CREAM (a seven-store chain of premium-ice-cream shops in Austin and Houston, Texas) sells terrific products and gives excellent service. But that's where the similarity to other scoop shops ends. Visit an Amy's store and you'll see employees performing in a manner you won't forget. They juggle with their serving spades, toss scoops of ice cream to one another behind the counter, and break-dance on the freezer top. If there's a line out the door, they might pass out samples—or offer free ice cream to any customer who'll sing or dance or recite a poem or mimic a barnyard animal, or who wins a 60-second cone-eating contest.

Amy Miller, the founder and CEO, obviously sells entertainment along with ice cream. To provide this atmosphere, she has to hire the right people and get them to be inventive. To identify employees who'll take the initiative, she uses the "white paper bag" test. Instead of an application form, prospective employees get a plain white paper bag along with the instructions to do anything they want with it and bring it back in a week. Those who just jot down a phone number will find that "Amy's isn't really for them," says Miller. But an applicant who produces "something unusual from a white paper bag tends to be an amusing person who would fit in with our environment."

One job seeker turned his into an elaborate pop-up jack-in-the box—and became a scooper at the Westbank Market store. That store's former manager painted an intricate green-and-blue sphere resembling the earth atop a waffle cone on his bag.

Source: John Case, "Corporate Culture," *Inc.,* November 1996, p. 42.

---

employees. The dealership holds a town hall in which employees feel free to bring up service problems. For example, Cheryl Pierson, a receptionist, discussed her frustration when she couldn't locate a sales rep for whom a customer had called. The customer finally said, "Well, I'll just take my business elsewhere." She used this example to emphasize that sales reps had to tell her when they slip out to run an errand. Now no one forgets that the front desk is the nerve center for the dealership.[44]

Empowering Store Employees

Empowerment means allowing employees at the firm's lowest level to make important decisions on how service is provided to customers. When the employees responsible for providing service are authorized to make important decisions, service quality improves. Service can be provided quickly without involving too many people. In our previous example, customer service improved when Parisian salespeople were given responsibility for authorizing customer checks without department managers' approval. Marshall Field's, a regional department store chain, empowered salespeople to make more decisions concerning returns when it trimmed its 36-page return policy to one page. Retailing View 19.5 shows how an ice cream parlor empowers employees to be creative.

Nordstrom provides an overall objective—satisfy customer needs—and then encourages employees to do whatever's necessary to carry out the objective. For example, a Nordstrom department manager bought 12 dozen pairs of hosiery from a competitor in the mall when her stock was depleted and the new shipment was delayed. Even though Nordstrom lost money on this hosiery, management applauded her actions to make sure customers found hosiery when they came to the store looking for it. Empowering service providers with only a rule like "Use your best judgment" can cause chaos. At Nordstrom, department managers avoid abuses by coaching and training salespeople. They help salespeople understand what "Use your best judgment" means.

However, empowering service providers can be difficult. Some employees prefer to have the appropriate behaviors clearly defined for them. They don't want to spend the time learning how to make decisions or assume the risks of making mistakes. For example, the First National Bank of Chicago found that when it empowered its tellers, the tellers were frightened to make decisions about large sums of money. The bank had to develop decision guideposts and rules until tellers felt more comfortable.[45]

In some cases, the benefits of empowering service providers may not justify the costs. For example, if a retailer uses a standardized service delivery approach like McDonald's, the cost of hiring, training, and supporting empowerment may not lead to consistent and superior service delivery.[46]

Providing Incentives

As we discussed in Chapter 17, many retailers use incentives, like paying commissions based on sales, to motive employees. But retailers have found that commissions on sales can decrease customer service and job satisfaction. Incentives can motivate high-pressure selling, which leads to customer dissatisfaction. However, incentives can be used effectively to improve customer service. For example, Kmart's "The Power to Please" program encourages sales associates to handle customer problems by providing hard-dollar rewards for successful customer service. Associates receive Knote bonuses from store and regional managers that convert into cash discounts. Kmart is also using nonmonetary forms of recognition such as the chairman's award and special certificates.[47]

COMMUNICATING THE SERVICE PROMISE: THE COMMUNICATIONS GAP

The fourth factor leading to a customer service gap is a difference between the service promised by the retailer and the service actually delivered. Overstating the service offered raises customer expectations. Then, if the retailer doesn't follow through, expectations exceed perceived service, and customers are dissatisfied. For example, if a store advertises that a customer will always be greeted by a friendly, smiling sales associate, customers may be disappointed if this doesn't occur. Raising expectations too high might bring in more customers initially, but it can also create dissatisfaction and reduce repeat business. The communication gap can be reduced by making realistic commitments and by managing customer expectations.

Realistic Commitments

Advertising programs are typically developed by the marketing department, while the store operations division delivers the service. Poor communication between these areas can result in a mismatch between an ad campaign's promises and the service the store can actually offer. This problem is illustrated by Holiday Inn's "No Surprises" ad campaign. Market research indicated hotel customers wanted greater reliability in lodging so Holiday Inn's agency developed a campaign promising no unpleasant surprises. Even though hotel managers didn't feel they could meet the claims promised in the ads, top management accepted the campaign. The campaign raised customer expectations to an unrealistic level and gave customers who did confront an unpleasant surprise an additional reason to be angry. The campaign was discontinued soon after it started.[48]

Managing Customer Expectations

How can a retailer communicate realistic service expectations without losing business to a competitor that makes inflated service claims? American Airlines' "Why Does It Seem Every Airline Flight Is Late?" ad campaign is an example of a communication program that addresses this issue. In print ads, American recognized its customers' frustration and explained some uncontrollable factors causing the problem: overcrowded airports, scheduling problems, and intense price competition. Then the ads described how American was improving the situation.

Sometimes service problems are caused by customers. Customers may use an invalid credit card to pay for merchandise, may not take time to try on a suit and have it altered properly, or may use a product incorrectly because they failed to read the instructions. Communication programs can also inform customers about their role and responsibility in getting good service, and can give tips on how to get better service (such as the best times of the day to shop and the retailer's policies and procedures for handling problems).

Now that we've discussed how retailers can improve customer service by reducing the knowledge, standards, delivery, and communications gaps, let's focus on an important issue retailers deal with daily—recovering from service problems.

SERVICE RECOVERY

As we said, delivery of customer service is inherently inconsistent so service failures are bound to arise. Rather than dwelling on negative aspects of customer problems, retailers should focus on the positive opportunities they generate. Service problems and complaints are an excellent source of information about the retailer's offering—its merchandise and service. Armed with this information, retailers can make changes to increase customer satisfaction. Marriott Corporation makes it easy for customers to complain by maintaining a 24-hour hotline in its hotels.[49]

Service problems also enable a retailer to demonstrate its commitment to providing high-quality customer service. By encouraging complaints and handling problems, a retailer has an opportunity to strengthen its relationship with its customers.

Most retailers have standard policies for handling problems. If a correctable problem is identified, such as defective merchandise, many retailers will make restitution on the spot and apologize for inconveniencing the customer. The retailer will either offer replacement merchandise, a credit toward future purchases, or a cash refund.

In many cases, the cause of the problem may be hard to identify (did the salesperson really insult the customer?), uncorrectable (the store had to close due to bad weather), or a result of the customer's unusual expectations (the customer didn't like his haircut). In this case, service recovery might be more difficult. The steps in effective service recovery are (1) listen to the customer, (2) provide a fair solution, and (3) resolve the problem quickly.

Listening to the Customer

Customers can become very emotional over their real or imaginary problems with a retailer. Often this emotional reaction can be reduced by simply giving customers a chance to get their complaints off their chests.

Store employees should allow customers to air their complaints without interruption. Interruptions can further irritate customers who may already be emotionally upset. It's very hard to reason with or satisfy an angry customer.

REFACT Less than two percent of the complaints made by customers are premeditated and fraudulent.[50]

Customers want a sympathetic response to their complaints. Thus, store employees need to make it clear they're happy that the problem has been brought to their attention. Satisfactory solutions rarely arise when store employees have an antagonistic attitude or assume that the customer is trying to cheat the store.

Employees also need to listen carefully to determine what the customer perceives to be a fair solution. For example, a hotel employee might assume that a customer irritated about a long wait to check in will be satisfied with an apology. But the customer might be expecting to receive a free drink as compensation for the wait. A supermarket employee may brusquely offer a refund for spoiled fruit, when the customer is also seeking an apology for the inconvenience of having to return to the store. Store employees shouldn't assume they know what the customer is complaining about or what solution the customer is seeking.

Providing a Fair Solution

When confronted with a complaint, store employees need to focus on how they can get the customer back, not simply how they can solve the problem.[51] Favorable impressions arise when customers feel they've been dealt with fairly. When evaluating the resolution of their problems, customers compare how they were treated in relation to others with similar problems. This comparison is based on observation of other customers with problems and/or on information about complaint handling learned from reading books and talking with others. Customers' evaluations of complaints' resolutions are based on distributive fairness and procedural fairness.

Distributive Fairness   **Distributive fairness** is customers' perceptions of the benefits received compared to their costs—their inconvenience or loss. Customers want to get what they paid for. The customer's need can affect the perceived correspondence between benefits and costs. For example, one customer might be satisfied with a raincheck for a food processor that was advertised at a discounted price but was sold out. This customer feels the low price for the food processor offsets the inconvenience of returning to the store. But another customer may need the food processor immediately. A rain check won't be adequate compensation for him. To satisfy this customer, the salesperson must locate a store that has the food processor and have it delivered to the customer's house.

Customers typically prefer tangible rather than intangible resolutions to their complaints. Customers may want to let off steam, but they also want to feel the retailer was responsive to their complaint. A low-cost reward—a free soft drink or a $1 discount—communicates more concern to the customer than a verbal apology. Store managers at Hechinger, a Maryland-based home-improvement center, offer tangible evidence of their concern by sending a dozen roses to particularly upset customers.[52]

If providing tangible restitution isn't possible, the next best alternative is to let customers see that their complaints will have an effect in the future. This can be done by making a note, in front of the customer, to a manager about the problem or writing to the customer about actions taken to prevent similar problems in the future.

Procedural Fairness   **Procedural fairness** is the perceived fairness of the process used to resolve complaints. Customers consider three questions when evaluating procedural fairness:

1. Did the employee collect information about the situation?
2. Was this information used to resolve the complaint?
3. Did the customer have some influence over the outcome?

Smith & Hawken resolves complaints quickly by talking with customers directly rather than communicating through the mail.

Discontent with the procedures used to handle a complaint can overshadow the benefits of a positive outcome. For example, customers might be less satisfied with their refund for a clerk's mistake in ringing up groceries if they get no chance to talk about their other problems with the clerk.

Customers typically feel they're dealt with fairly when store employees follow company guidelines. Guidelines reduce variability in handling complaints and lead customers to believe they're being treated like everyone else. But rigid adherence to guidelines can have negative effects. Store employees need some flexibility in resolving complaints, or customers may feel they had no influence in the resolution.

Resolving Problems Quickly

Customer satisfaction is affected by the time it takes to get an issue resolved. To respond to customers quickly, Smith & Hawken, a garden supply mail-order company, uses the telephone instead of the mail. The company feels that sending a letter is too time consuming and impersonal. Resolving complaints by phone can take minutes while sending letters can take weeks.

Retailers can minimize the time to resolve complaints by reducing the number of people the customer must contact, providing clear instructions, and speaking in the customer's language.[53]

Reducing the Number of Contacts   As a general rule, store employees who deal with customers should be made as self-sufficient as possible to handle problems. Customers are more satisfied when the first person they contact can resolve a problem. When customers are referred to several different employees, they waste a lot of time repeating their story. Also, the chance of conflicting responses by store employees increases.

Giving Clear Instructions   Customers should be told clearly and precisely what they need to do to resolve a problem. When American Express cardholders ask to have an unused airline ticket removed from their bill, they're told immediately that they must return the ticket to the airline or travel agency before a credit can be issued. Fast service often depends on providing clear instructions.

Speaking the Customer's Language   Customers can become annoyed when store employees use company jargon to describe a situation. To communicate clearly, store employees should use terms familiar to the customer. For example, a customer would be frustrated if a salesperson told her the slacks in her size were located on a rounder to the right of the four-way.[54]

Resolving customer complaints increases satisfaction. But when complaints are resolved too abruptly, customers might feel dissatisfied because they haven't received personal attention. Retailers must recognize the trade-off between resolving the problem quickly and taking time to listen to and show concern for the customer.

SUMMARY   Due to the inherent intangibility and inconsistency of service, providing high-quality customer service is challenging. However, customers also provide an opportunity for retailers to develop a strategic advantage. Retailers use two basic approaches for providing customer service—customization and standardization approaches. The customized approach relies primarily on sales associates. The standardized approach places more emphasis on developing appropriate rules and procedures and the store design.

Customers evaluate customer service by comparing their perceptions of the service delivered with their expectations. Thus, to improve service, retailers need to close the gaps between the service delivered and the customer's expectations. This gap is reduced by knowing what customers expect, setting standards to provide the expected service, providing support so store employees can meet the standards, and realistically communicating the service they offer to customers.

Due to inherent inconsistency, service failures are bound to arise. These lapses in service provide an opportunity for retailers to build even stronger relationships with their customers.

KEY TERMS

communication gap, *580*

customization approach, *573*

delivery gap, *580*

distributive fairness, *594*

emotional support, *590*

empowerment, *591*

instrumental support, *590*

knowledge gap, *580*

mass customization, *570*

mystery shopper, *589*

procedural fairness, *594*

service gap, *580*

standardization approach, *574*

standards gap, *580*

DISCUSSION QUESTIONS & PROBLEMS

1. Nordstrom and McDonald's are noted for their high-quality customer service. But their approaches to providing this quality service are different. Describe this difference and why the retailers elected to use these different approaches.

2. Providing customer service can be very expensive for retailers. When are the costs for providing high-quality services justified? What types of retailers find it financially advantageous to provide high-quality customer service? What retailers can't justify providing high-quality service?

3. Assume you're the department manager for menswear in a local department store that emphasizes empowering its managers. A customer returns a dress shirt that's no longer in the package it was sold in. The customer has no receipt, says that when he opened the package he found that the shirt was torn, and wants cash for the price the shirt is being sold at now. The shirt was on sale last week when the customer claims to have bought it. What would you do?

4. What unique aspects of customer service differentiate it from merchandise being sold?

5. How should store employees handle customer complaints?

6. Gaps analysis provides a systematic method of examining a customer service program's effectiveness. Kmart top management has told an information systems manager that customers are complaining about the long wait to pay for merchandise at the checkout station. How can the systems manager use Gaps analysis to analyze this problem and suggest approaches for reducing this time?

7. How could an effective customer service strategy cut a retailer's costs?

8. Employees play a critical role in customer perceptions of quality service. If you were hiring salespeople, what characteristics would you look for to assess their ability to provide good customer service?

9. Why is good communication between customer-contact employees and management important in providing high-quality customer service?

SUGGESTED READINGS

Anreoli, Teresa. "Hassle-Free Service Key to Repeat Biz." *Discount Store News*, May 6, 1996, pp. 62–66.

Baker, Julie, and Michaelle Cameron. "The Effects of the Service Environment on Affect and Consumer Perceptions of Waiting Time: An Integrative Review and Research Propositions." *Journal of the Academy of Marketing Science* 24 (Fall 1996), pp. 338–49.

Berry, Leonard. *On Great Customer Service: A Framework for Action.* New York: Free Press, 1995.

"Chains Soothe Nerves of the Time-Pressed." *Discount Store News*, May 6, 1996, pp. 90–94.

Dowling, Melissa. "Can We Afford Superior Service?" *Catalog Age*, July 1996, pp. 129–30.

Hartline, Michael, and O. C. Ferrell. "The Management of Customer-Contact Service Employees: An Empirical Investigation." *Journal of Marketing* 60 (October 1996), pp. 52–70.

Higgins, Kevin. "Room for Improvement: America's Innkeeper Polishes Its Image to Compete in the 90's." *Marketing Management*, Summer 1996, pp. 5–9.

Iacobucci, Dawn, Kent Grayson, and Amy Ostrom. "Customer Satisfaction Fables." *Sloan Management Review* 35 (Summer 1994), pp. 93–96.

Kelley, Scott, and Mark Davis. "Antecedents to Customer Expectations for Service Recovery." *Journal of the Academy of Marketing Science* 22 (Winter 1994), pp. 52–61.

Mittal, Banwari, and Walfried Lassar. "The Role of Personalization in Service Encounters." *Journal of Retailing* 72 (Spring 1996), pp. 95–109.

Reda, Susan. "Seven Keys to Better Service." *Stores*, January 1996, pp. 32–34.

"New Developments in Customer Service Training." *International Journal of Retail & Distribution Management* 24 (Summer 1996), pp. 12–15.

Schneider, Benjamin, and David Bowen. *Winning the Service Game.* Boston: Harvard Business School Press, 1995.

Spreng, Richard, Scott MacKenzie, and Richard Olshavsky. "A Reexamination of the Determinants of Consumer Satisfaction." *Journal of Marketing* 60 (July 1996), pp. 15–32.

Zeithaml, Valarie, Leonard Berry, and A. Parasuraman. "The Behavioral Consequences of Service Quality." *Journal of Marketing* 60 (April 1996), pp. 31–46.

NOTES

1. "Rating the Stores," *Consumer Reports*, November 1994, p. 714.

2. James Gilmore and B. Joseph Pine, "The Four Faces of Mass Customization," *Harvard Business Review*, January–February 1997, pp. 91–105; and Mark Kissling, "Survival of the Fittest," *Visual Merchandising and Store Design*, July 1996, pp. 30–34.

3. Sharon Stangenes, "Service with a Smile," *Chicago Tribune*, May 23, 1990, section 7, p. 1.

4. "Total Customer Service," *The KSAS Perspective* (New York: Kurt Salmon Associates, January 1991), p. 1.

5. Leonard Berry, "Services Marketing Is Different," *Business* 30 (May–June 1980), pp. 24–28; Duane Davis, Joseph Guiltinan, and Wesley Jones, "Service Characteristics, Consumer Search, and the Classification of Retail Services," *Journal of Retailing* 55 (Fall 1979), pp. 3–21; and G. Lynn Shostack, "Breaking Free from Product Marketing," *Journal of Marketing* 41 (April 1977), pp. 73–80.

6. Rikard Larsson and David Bowen, "Organization and Customer: Managing Design and Coordination of Services," *Academy of Management Review* 14 (1989), pp. 213–33.

7. Pete Hisey, "Customer Satisfaction Linked to Employee Training," *Discount Store News*, April 18, 1994, p. 41; and Richard Halverson, "Target Empowers Employees to Be Fast, Fun, and Friendly," *Discount Store News*, May 3, 1993, pp. 65–66.

8. Murray Raphael, "Tell Me What You Want and the Answer Is 'Yes,'" *Direct Marketing*, October 1996, p. 22.

9. Julie Baker and Michaelle Cameron, "The Effects of the Service Environment on Affect and Consumer Perceptions of Waiting Time: An Integrative Review and Research Propositions," *Journal of the Academy of Marketing Science* 24 (Fall 1996), pp. 338–49; Steve Weiner, "Many Stores Abandon Service with a Smile, Rely on Signs, Displays," *The Wall Street Journal*, March 16, 1991, pp. 1, 20.

10. "Retailers Join the War Effort," *Chain Store Age Executive*, June 1994, p. 15.

11. "RTIA: Electronic Stores Dominate," *Chain Store Age*, September 1995, pp. 74–75.

12. Janet Guyon, "Can the Savoy Cut Costs and Be the Savoy?" *The Wall Street Journal*, October 25, 1994, pp. B1, B5.

13. William Parsons, "Give the Lady What She Wants," *Chain Store Age*, November 1995, pp. 86–87.

14. Ibid., p. 87.

15. Louise Lee, "Without a Receipt, You May Get Charged for That Ugly Scarf," *The Wall Street Journal*, November 1996, pp. A1, A6. See also Melissa Dowling, "Can We Afford Superior Service?" *Catalog Age*, July 1996, pp. 129–30.

16. Valerie Taylor and Anthony Miyazaki, "Assessing Actual Service Performance: Incongruities between Expectations and Evaluative Criteria," in Frank Kardas and Mita Sujan, eds., *Advances in Consumer Research* 22 (Provo, UT: Association of Consumer Research, 1995), pp. 594–605; Pratibha Dabholkar, Dayle Thorpe, and Joseph Rentz, "A Measure of Service Quality for Retail Stores: Scale Development and Validation," *Journal of the Academy of Marketing Science* 24 (Winter 1996), pp. 3–16; A. Parasuraman, Valarie Zeithaml, and Leonard Berry, "A Conceptual Model of Service Quality and Its Implications for Future Research," *Journal of Marketing* 49 (Fall 1985), pp. 41–50; A. Parasuraman, Valarie Zeithaml, and Leonard Berry, "SERVQUAL: A Multiple-Item Scale for Measuring Consumer Perceptions of Service Quality," *Journal of Retailing* 64 (Spring 1988), pp. 12–21; and A. Parasuraman, Leonard Berry, and Valarie Zeithaml, "Understanding Customer Expectations of Service," *Sloan Management Review*, Spring 1991, pp. 39–48.

17. Ann Marie Thompson and Peter Kaminski, "Psychographic and Lifestyle Antecedents of Service Quality Expectations," *Journal of Services Marketing* 7 (1993), pp. 53–61.

18. Bill Pearson, "Customer Service . . . Expect the Unexpected," *Stores*, March 1994, p. 58.

19. Greg Steinmetz, "Customer-Service Era Is Reaching Germany Late, Hurting Business," *The Wall Street Journal*, June 1, 1995, pp. A1, A8. See also Peter Maass, "Service with a Snarl," *The Washington Post*, August 17, 1993, p. 42.

20. Alain Genestre, Paul Herbig, and Alan Shao, "What Does Marketing Really Mean in Japan?" *Marketing Intelligence & Planning* 13, no. 9 (1995), pp. 16–27.

21. Dayle Thorpe, "Meaning of Service Quality in the Retail Environment: The Customer's Perspective," in Robert King, ed., *Retailing: Theories and Practices for Today and Tomorrow*, Proceedings of the Fourth Triennial National Retailing Conference, Richmond, VA, pp. 61–63; and Kate Bertrand, "In Service, Perceptions Count," *Business Marketing*, April 1989, pp. 44–46.

22. Michael Hartline and O. C. Ferrell, "The Management of Customer-Contact Service Employees: An Empirical Investigation," *Journal of Marketing* 60 (October 1996), pp. 52–70; and Lois Mohr and Mary Jo Bittner, "The Role of Employee Effort in Satisfaction with Service Transactions," *Journal of Business Research* 32 (March 1995), pp. 239–52.

23. Chip Bell and Ron Zemke, "Do Service Procedures Tie Employees' Hands?" *Personnel Journal*, September 1988, pp. 77–83.

24. The following discussion of the Gaps Model and its implications is based on Valarie Zeithaml, A. Parasuraman, and Leonard Berry, *Delivering Quality Customer Service* (New York: Free Press, 1990); and Valarie Zeithaml, Leonard Berry, and A. Parasuraman, "Communication and Control Processes in the Delivery of Service Quality," *Journal of Marketing* 52 (April 1988), pp. 35–48.

25. Cynthia Crossen, "Americans Have It All, But It Is Not Enough," *The Wall Street Journal*, September 29, 1996, p. R4.

26. Leonard Berry, *On Great Customer Service: A Framework for Action* (New York: Free Press, 1996), p. 44.

27. "Merchant Prince: Stanley Marcus," *Inc.*, June 1987, pp. 41–44.

28. Thomas Peters and Nancy Austin, *A Passion for Excellence* (New York: Random House, 1985), p. 84.

29. "Weinstock's Tackles the Problem of Service," *Chain Store Age Executive*, January 1987, pp. 16–18.

30. Jagdip Singh and Robert Wilkes, "When Customers Complain: A Path Analysis of Key Antecedents of Customer Complaint Response Analysis," *Journal of the Academy of Marketing Science* 24 (Fall 1996), pp. 350–65. For an illustration of the importance of stimulating customer complaints, see Claus Fornell and B. Wernerfelt, "Defensive Marketing Strategy by Customer Complaint Management," *Journal of Marketing Research* 24 (November 1987), pp. 337–46.

31. Ron Zemke and Dick Schaaf, *The Service Edge: 101 Companies That Profit from Customer Care* (New York: Plume, 1990), pp. 319–21.

32. David Villano, "Secrets of Service," *Florida Trend,* September 1996, pp. 48–54.

33. Peters and Austin, *A Passion for Excellence,* p. 95.

34. "Mr. Winchester Orders a Pizza," *Fortune,* November 14, 1986, p. 134.

35. Malcolm Fleschner and Gerhard Gschwandtner, "The Marriott Miracle," *Selling Power,* September 1994, pp. 17–23.

36. Berry, *On Great Customer Service,* pp. 73–74.

37. "Boosting Productivity at American Express," *Business Week,* October 5, 1981, pp. 62, 66.

38. Kevin Helliker, "Smile: That Cranky Shopper May Be a Store Spy," *The Wall Street Journal,* November 10, 1994, pp. B1, B12.

39. "New Developments in Customer Service Training," *International Journal of Retail & Distribution Management* 24 (Summer 1996), pp. 12–18.

40. Bell and Zemke, "Service Procedures," p. 79.

41. See Michael Hui and David Tse, "What to Tell Consumers in Waits of Different Length: An Integrated Model of Service Evaluation," *Journal of Marketing* 60 (April 1996), pp. 81–90; and Gail Tom and Scott Lucey, "Waiting Time Delays and Customer Satisfaction in Supermarket," *Journal of Services Marketing* 9, no. 5 (1995), pp. 20–29.

42. Ronald Henkoff, "Finding, Training, and Keeping the Best Service Workers," *Fortune,* October 3, 1994, p. 120.

43. Mara Adelman and Aaron Ahuvia, "Social Support in the Service Sector: The Antecedents, Processes, and Consequences of Social Support in an Introductory Service," *Journal of Business Research* 32 (March 1995), pp. 273–82. Arlie Russell Hochschild, *The Managed Heart: Commercialization of Human Feelings* (Berkeley, CA: University of California Press, 1983), describes stress encountered by people who provide service to customers.

44. "The Informers," *Inc.,* March 1995, pp. 50–61.

45. Linda Cooper, "Polishing the Trophy—Enhancing the Service Commitment," *International Service Association Journal,* April 1991, pp. 25–28.

46. David Bowen and Edward Lawler, "The Empowerment of Service Workers: What, Why, How, and When?" *Sloan Management Review,* Spring 1992, pp. 32–44.

47. Alan Gilman, "Smart Compensation and Smart Selling," *Chain Store Age Executive,* September 1992, p. 134; and Pete Hisey, "Who Satisfies CE Shoppers Most: Commissioned or Noncommissioned Help?" *Discount Store News,* May 3, 1993, pp. 70–71.

48. William George and Leonard Berry, "Guidelines for the Advertising of Services," *Business Horizons,* May–June 1981, pp. 52–56.

49. Fredrick Reichheld, "Learning from Customer Defections," *Harvard Business Review,* March–April 1996, pp. 56–67.

50. "Improving Services Doesn't Always Require a Big Investment," *The Service Edge,* July–August, 1990, p. 3.

51. Linda Lash, "Complaints as a Marketing Strategy," *The Marketing Strategy Letter,* February 1993, p. 3; John F. Sherry, Jr., Mary Ann McGrath, and Sidney J. Levy, "The Disposition of the Gift and Many Unhappy Returns," *Journal of Retailing,* Spring 1992, pp. 40–65; and Doris Kincade, Ann Redwine, and Gregory Hancock, "Apparel Product Dissatisfaction and the Post-Complaint Process," *International Journal of Retail & Distribution Management,* September–October 1992, pp. 15–22.

52. Cathy Goodwin and Ivan Ross, "Customer Evaluations of Responses to Complaints: What's Fair and Why," *Journal of Consumer Marketing* 2 (Spring 1990), pp. 39–47.

53. Patricia Sellers, "Building Loyalty: Keeping the Buyers You Already Have," *Fortune,* November 22, 1993, pp. 56–58.

54. Richard Garfein, "Guiding Principles for Improving Customer Service," *Journal of Services Marketing* 2 (Spring 1988), pp. 37–41.

20 Retail Selling

THE WORLD OF RETAILING

RETAILING STRATEGY

MERCHANDISE MANAGEMENT
12. Planning Merchandise
    Assortments
13. Buying Systems
14. Buying Merchandise
15. Pricing
16. Retail Promotion Mix

STORE MANAGEMENT
17. Managing the Store
18. Store Layout, Design, and
    Visual Merchandising
19. Customer Service
20. Retail Selling

QUESTIONS

- What are retail salespeople's duties and responsibilities?

- Why are communication skills important for effective selling?

- What are the steps in selling merchandise to a customer?

- What knowledge and skills are required for effective retail selling?

- How can salespeople improve their listening skills?

A GOVERNMENT WORKER IN WASHINGTON, D.C., always tries to schedule a vacation day whenever she visits Dallas on business. She rents a car and drives 100 miles to Tyler to buy shoes from Cecile Satterwaite at Leon's Fashions, a privately owned women's clothing chain.

The attention Satterwaite gives her customers keeps them coming back. Satterwaite may bring out as many as 300 pairs of shoes from the stockroom for a single customer. She walks to the mirror with the customer each time the customer tries on a pair and then kneels down before the customer to slip the shoes on and off.

Satterwaite watches out for her customer's best interests. If a shoe doesn't fit, she won't let her buy it. She also discourages customers from buying a shoe that, she says, "doesn't look pretty on your foot." If the customer insists on buying it, she'll say, "If you buy that shoe, don't tell a soul I waited on you." Satterwaite sells over $600,000 of shoes and earns more than $100,000 each year.[1]

To many customers, salespeople like Ms. Satterwaite are the retailer. Typically, they're the only employees with whom customers come in contact. Salespeople help customers satisfy their needs by providing the retail services discussed in Chapter 19. Their actions can stimulate return visits to a store and build customer loyalty.

Salespeople help their store realize its goals by selling merchandise. Retailers make profits only when merchandise is sold. Thus, all of a retailer's employees are either providing customer service and selling merchandise, or supporting someone who does. Retailing View 20.1 describes the lessons a retailing entrepreneur learned about building her store's sales.

Effective Selling Leads to Retail Success

NANCY PRIDE LEARNED ABOUT the importance of personal selling when she opened Morgan Fitzgerald, a women's specialty store. Before she opened her store, Pride spent seven years teaching at Texas A&M.

"Selling is more than ringing up a cash register. Selling is determining the customers' needs and matching their needs to our products. That means our staff not only has to know our products and their features, but must listen to what our customers say. What looks good on the hanger may not look good on a particular customer. Nothing is as frustrating to a customer as trying on garment after garment and having nothing look good.

"As each customer enters the store, we evaluate her size, body shape, and color palette. We mentally scan the store for clothing that will fit. . . . A short, busty, slim-hipped lady needs a boxy, short jacket to balance the top to the bottom. A customer with a protruding stomach and slightly rounded shoulders needs . . . extra shoulder pad lifts. We have trained ourselves to look at these customers and determine the sizes before the customers have to tell us.

"We try not to pester a customer who wants to browse, but we recognize that unless we show the product, a customer may miss or fail to appreciate an appealing product feature. As a customer nears an item with a particular feature, we demonstrate the product and place it in the customer's hand.

"To make the garment seem complete, it needs accessories. Personal service means showing the customer how to accessorize the outfit. While she is trying on the clothes, we pull accessories to show her. Accessories should enhance the garment and be appropriate and functional for the customer. If the customer prefers clip earrings, we convert pierced earrings to clip."

By stressing selling and customer services, Nancy Pride's store increased sales 100 percent during its second year of operation and she forecasts a 50 percent increase during the third year.

Source: Nancy Pride, "Lessons of Retail Novice," *Arthur Andersen Retailing Issues Letter* (Center for Retail Studies, Texas A&M University), July 1995.

To be effective, store managers must understand the sales process. Many retailers require management trainees to spend considerable time selling during their first year in a management training program. Through this initial selling assignment, trainees develop understanding of the firm's customers—what they want and how they buy merchandise. They also gain appreciation for problems salespeople face.

ROLES OF SALESPEOPLE

Salespeople span the boundary between the retail firm and its customers. Even the most appealing merchandise doesn't sell itself. Retailers need to communicate with customers to stimulate needs, provide information to help customers evaluate merchandise, and encourage them to make a purchase decision. These communications are delivered by ads, sales promotions, publicity, signs and displays in the store, and salespeople.

As Chapter 16 said, these communication vehicles are used to affect different stages of the customer's decision-making process. Advertising, publicity, and sales promotions create awareness and build an image of the retailer. Messages delivered through these media presell the retailer's merchandise and services. Salespeople provide more detailed information and actually make the sale.

Salespeople have a unique capability as communication vehicles. They can develop and present a message tailored to each customer they encounter. Salespeople can also gauge the customer's reactions and alter the presentation during the interaction. This flexibility makes the salesperson the retailer's most effective communication vehicle—and the most expensive.

Many retailers call their salespeople **sales associates** or **sales consultants.** These terms recognize the important and professional nature of the sales function and avoid the negative image sometimes linked with the term *salesperson*. They also emphasize that salespeople's role is to use their knowledge about merchandise to help customers solve problems—just like a business consultant.

THE RETAIL SELLING PROCESS

To sell merchandise, salespeople must move customers through stages of the buying process discussed in Chapter 5. The **selling process** is a set of activities that salespeople undertake to facilitate the customer's buying decision. The stages in the selling process and the buying process are closely linked as Exhibit 20–1 shows.

In the first stage of the selling process, salespeople approach customers with unsatisfied needs and try to stimulate problem recognition. In the second stage, customers search for information to satisfy their needs, and salespeople collect information about customers so they can determine what merchandise might be appropriate. In the third stage, salespeople present and demonstrate merchandise to assist customers' evaluation of alternatives. Then the salespeople attempt to make a sale—to motivate customers to purchase merchandise. Finally, salespeople build future sales by influencing customers' postpurchase evaluations of the merchandise and offering follow-up service.

Not every sale goes through each step in the sales process, just as every purchase doesn't go through every step in the buying process. Sometimes steps occur in an order different from Exhibit 20–1's, but these steps do illustrate the set of activities retail salespeople perform as they sell merchandise.[2] In addition, customers also differ in the type of sales process they prefer. Retailing View 20.2 describes the sales process preferred by X-generation customers.

EXHIBIT 20–1

Steps in the Selling Process and Buying Process

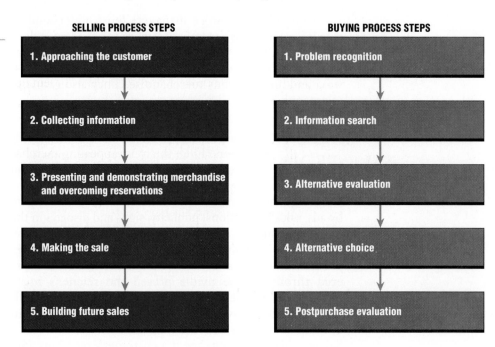

SELLING PROCESS STEPS	BUYING PROCESS STEPS
1. Approaching the customer	1. Problem recognition
2. Collecting information	2. Information search
3. Presenting and demonstrating merchandise and overcoming reservations	3. Alternative evaluation
4. Making the sale	4. Alternative choice
5. Building future sales	5. Postpurchase evaluation

20.2

Selling to Generation X

THE STAFF AT SEATTLE'S Speakeasy Cafe—a "cybercafe" that offers espresso and access to the Internet—is hands-off with customers. Mike Apgar, the cafe's 27-year-old president, says that salespeople approach only those customers who look lost. That may sound passive, but Apgar says that the approach works with his mostly 20-something customer base and complements managers' efforts to create a comfortable atmosphere for all patrons.

Many retailers across the United States are adopting similarly subtle approaches to attract Generation Xers. Generation Xers, more than other adult generations, are astute about slick sales tactics and can be turned off by sales clerks who try to push them. Here are some Xers complaints about retail salespeople selling sports equipment:

- Just assuming I'm going to buy something they show me, or trying to bully me into it. "Shall I wrap this up? Cash or charge?"

- Acting annoyed with my questions because they're too busy just trying to size me up as

to how much money they might make off of me. If I knew what I wanted and had all of the answers, I wouldn't ask the questions.

- Salespeople that are all over you when you first walk in the store and then you can't find them when you've had a chance to look around.

- Salespeople who try to make me spend more money than I can. I don't want to look cheap, but if I have a budget they should respect it.

- Trying to sell me stuff I don't need and know I don't need.

- No means no. If I say I'm not interested and not looking to buy, I don't want to be bugged.

Source: Laura Litvan, "X Marks the Spot for Low-Key Sales," *Nation's Business,* May 1996, pp. 32–35; and Patricia O'Connell, "The Secrets of Our Success," *The Times Mirror Magazine,* September 19, 1996, pp. 10–15.

Approaching Customers

The **approach** to a customer is a method for getting the customer's attention and building interest in the merchandise quickly. The approach is particularly important in retail selling. In many other sales situations, salespeople can obtain information about potential customers before they meet them. But in retail sales, salespeople are usually confronting customers for the first time and have only a few seconds to size them up.

Purpose of the Approach   While some customers visit a retailer when they have definite needs and seek a specific item, the majority of customers—even when they have a specific need—start their buying process by browsing. The purpose of the salesperson's approach is to narrow the customer's focus from a broad generalized interest to a consideration of specific items.

Elements in the Approach   The approach consists of greeting the customer with a genuine smile, introducing yourself by name, developing rapport, and getting the customer to consider specific merchandise. Many customers are anxious, particularly when considering a major purchase. Customers also may feel threatened, thinking a salesperson is going to be too aggressive. The customer's anxiety can be reduced by a smile, an introduction, and an opening comment about something other than the merchandise the customer is looking at. For example, an initial statement can be a flattering remark about something the customer is wearing or a comment about the weather.

This initial rapport building continues until the customer's verbal or non-verbal communications indicate she's ready to talk about the merchandise. Then the salesperson starts to direct the customer's attention by asking a question, mentioning a feature or benefit of the merchandise, discussing the good's manufacturer, or pointing out a special value. Here are examples of these techniques:

> "This shirt is 100 percent cotton. Cotton shirts are a lot more comfortable in hot weather than shirts made from synthetic fibers."
>
> "Try this remote control for the television. See how the channel and time are displayed when you change channels?"
>
> "It's real easy to change a kitchen faucet. This pamphlet shows you how to do it."
>
> "Club Med has resorts in some very exotic locations. What type of vacation are you looking for?"
>
> "Isn't that attaché case handsome? Bodega is probably the finest manufacturer of leather goods in the world."

Approaches that point out features or benefits help customers "see" the merchandise better. Many times customers don't recognize hidden features of the product, such as its multiple uses, the quality of its construction, or even the manufacturer's name.

The "Just-Looking" Customer   Salespeople should avoid using the simple approach "May I help you?" The response to this approach is often "I'm just looking." But most customers aren't just looking. They've come to buy something—and the salesperson is there to sell something.

Patience is the key to handling the "just-looking" customer. The effective salesperson shows an interest in helping the customer and then gives the customer a chance to look at the merchandise alone. Sandie Robbins, a furniture salesperson for JCPenney in Anchorage, Alaska, related a just-looking story:

> A couple told me they were not interested in anything in particular when I approached them. I kept an eye on them anyway. A little later, I noticed they seemed very interested in one piece. When they started checking the price, I approached them again. This time I cracked the shell. Since then I have been to their home three times to advise them, and they've bought almost $12,000 of furniture from me.[3]

Collecting Information

After the initial contact has been made, the next step in the retail sales process is to collect some information from the customer. The salesperson needs to determine the customer's needs and the type of merchandise the customer prefers. Basic information a salesperson should know about a customer includes

The type of service or merchandise the customer is looking for.

The price range the customer is considering.

How the customer plans to use the service or merchandise.

The customer's lifestyle.

What possessions the customer now has (such as wardrobe, appliances, or consumer electronics) might be used with the merchandise under consideration.

The customer's preferences for risk and returns in investments.

Salespeople collect this information by asking questions. For example, a salesperson might ask if a bank account that the customer is opening will be used for personal finances or business. The answer tells the salesperson whether to discuss services of interest to businesses like lock boxes. The customer should be encouraged to ask questions as the salesperson makes a presentation. These questions indicate how effectively the salesperson is communicating the bank account's features and benefits.

Through questioning, this Avon salesperson uncovers what the customer's needs are for cosmetics.

Customers often want to know the salesperson's opinion. Even when customers know the exact style of draperies they want, they might want to know the salesperson's opinion about the fabric's durability. Salespeople should have developed expertise about their merchandise—and they want to take advantage of this knowledge.

This conversation shows how a salesperson collects information from a customer.

Salesperson   Good morning. I'm Joe Turner. Have you shopped at Barney's before?

Customer   I've been in before to look at these sport coats, but I haven't bought anything.

Salesperson   If I could find out a little bit about what you're looking for, I can save you some time. Where will you be wearing the sport coat?

Customer   Well, as I said, I'm just looking. I want something sporty, something I can wear after work.

Salesperson   You look to be size 40 or 42. Is that right?

Customer   I usually wear a 42.

Salesperson   I think you'll be interested in the sports coats we have over here. Try this one on just to check the size.

Customer   OK. I'm not sure I like this one.

Salesperson   Why don't you like it?

Customer   The color, to begin with. I really don't like maroon.

Salesperson   What color do you like?

Customer   My wife says I look best in blue.

Salesperson   What kind of sports coats do you already have?

Customer   My two favorites are a navy blue blazer and a sports jacket that has a small pattern. Something like this one, only blue and gray. These are too dressy. I want something sportier.

Salesperson   Let's see. You want something that's not too severe in styling, something blue or that at least will coordinate with blue, and something with a casual look. I think you'd be interested in these jackets.

This interaction illustrates that effective selling requires a two-way flow of information between salesperson and customer. To satisfy customers' needs, salespeople must ask questions and then listen carefully to customers' replies and comments. Effective listening is the most important step in building rapport with customers.

Successful salespeople have a high degree of empathy for customers' feelings and attitudes. They recognize that the key to success over the long run is to have customers who are pleased with the merchandise they buy. Selling merchandise isn't enough. The salesperson must make sure that the merchandise will not be returned—but that the customers will. Later in this chapter, we'll detail the art of asking questions and listening.

Presenting the Merchandise

The third step in the retail sales process is presenting the merchandise or service and communicating its benefits to the customer.

Selling Benefits   Customers buy benefits, not features. A **benefit** is a specific need that's satisfied when a customer buys a product. In every buying situation, customers are asking themselves, What am I going to get out of buying this merchandise or service? Salespeople answer this question by explicitly indicating which needs expressed by the customer will be satisfied by the purchase.

EXHIBIT 20–2   Features and Benefits of Golf Clubs

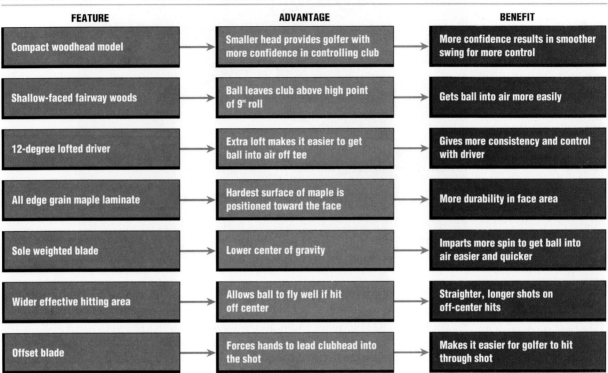

FEATURE	ADVANTAGE	BENEFIT
Compact woodhead model	Smaller head provides golfer with more confidence in controlling club	More confidence results in smoother swing for more control
Shallow-faced fairway woods	Ball leaves club above high point of 9" roll	Gets ball into air more easily
12-degree lofted driver	Extra loft makes it easier to get ball into air off tee	Gives more consistency and control with driver
All edge grain maple laminate	Hardest surface of maple is positioned toward the face	More durability in face area
Sole weighted blade	Lower center of gravity	Imparts more spin to get ball into air easier and quicker
Wider effective hitting area	Allows ball to fly well if hit off center	Straighter, longer shots on off-center hits
Offset blade	Forces hands to lead clubhead into the shot	Makes it easier for golfer to hit through shot

Features are a product's qualities or characteristics that provide benefits to customers. Exhibit 20–2 shows features and benefits of a certain brand of golf clubs.

An effective sales presentation must link the features to the benefits it provides the customer. A presentation that includes only features fails to answer the question, What's in it for me? A presentation that focuses only on benefits doesn't help the customer understand how and why the merchandise can deliver the benefits. Features are included in the presentation to assure customers that the benefits will be delivered. Exhibit 20–3 contrasts a presentation that emphasizes features with one that stresses benefits.

Demonstrating the Merchandise In-store shoppers, compared to catalog customers, can see the features and benefits of the product demonstrated. Demonstrations are most effective when they appeal to the senses of sound, touch, sight, taste, or smell.

EXHIBIT 20–3

Selling Benefits, Not Features

PRESENTATION EMPHASIZING FEATURES	PRESENTATION EMPHASIZING BENEFITS
This chinawear has a hard glaze that is applied after the pattern is on the cups and plates. The handles are molded into the cup before it is fired. All the china is fired at 2600°F.	This chinawear will last a long time. It is stronger than most chinawear because it is fired at 2600°F. To prevent the cup handles from breaking off, they are molded into the cup body before it is fired. The pattern will also last a long time. It won't fade because a hard leadless glaze is applied over the pattern.

Source: Barton Weitz, Stephen Castleberry, and John Tanner, *Selling: Building Parternships*, 3d ed. (Burr Ridge, IL: Irwin/McGraw-Hill, 1998).

This salesperson is demonstrating the benefits the customer will get from the unique features of the telescope.

A demonstration can generate excitement and enthusiasm by giving the customer hands-on experience with the product. Hands-on experience shows customers what the product will do for them. In cosmetics, customer involvement is usually the deciding factor in making a sale. When a customer isn't sure what color is best for her, the salesperson can help her try different colors to see how they look. By demonstrating a range of cosmetic products in a makeover, the salesperson can sell multiple items rather than a single product.

The most effective demonstrations occur when the customer gets actively involved: "Feel how soft this sweater is." "See how this suit makes you look thinner." "Hear the quality of these speakers."

Handling Reservations

Often customers have reservations about making a purchase. **Reservations** or **objections** are concerns raised by the customer. Salespeople must anticipate potential reservations and know how to respond to them.

Reservations can arise at each stage in the sales process. For example, a customer may not be willing to talk with a salesperson during the approach. Reservations can also arise when the salesperson is making a presentation.

Types of Reservations   Some common reservations (Exhibit 20–4) arise because the customer doesn't want to buy at the time or isn't satisfied with the price, merchandise, retailer, service, or salesperson.

Customers often resist making an immediate decision. They may say, "I haven't made up my mind," "I'll have to talk it over with my wife," or "I think I'll wait awhile." These reservations indicate the customer isn't convinced of the need for the offering or its benefits. The real reason for postponing the purchase may be the price or the offering itself. Also, some customers just don't like to make decisions. Reassurance works better than pressure with indecisive customers.

Price is probably the most common source of customers' reservations. Regardless of the price, someone will consider it too high, out of line, or higher than another retail outlet's price. Other common price reservations include "I can't afford it," "I was looking for a cheaper insurance policy," or "I'm going to wait for this to go on sale."

EXHIBIT 20-4

Types of Reservations

Objections involving the offering include "The quality of this screen door is poor," "The dress is the wrong size," "I don't like the entrees on your menu," or "I don't like the pediatrician in your HMO."

Customers might not like the retailer's place of business. For example, customers might visit a muffler repair shop to take advantage of special price. During the visit, they may feel uncomfortable because the waiting room is crowded. These customers might need special attention such as a pickup and delivery service.

Customers also can have reservations about a specific salesperson. The salesperson's personality, behavior, or dress might clash with the customer's expectations. The customer may be thinking, I don't like dealing with this person. The salesperson probably can't overcome this reservation so it's best for everyone involved to direct the customer to another salesperson. The store is more likely to make a sale, and the other salesperson may reciprocate.

Effective salespeople know the types of reservations likely to be raised. They may know that their service is more expensive than competitors', that their selection in a particular merchandise category is limited, or that the store doesn't accept a particular credit card. While not all reservations can be forestalled, effective salespeople can anticipate and handle some objections in their sales presentation. For example, a salesperson might say, "This vacation package is expensive, but let me tell you about the special activities included in the package."

Uncovering Reservations   Some salespeople make a mistake in treating an unfavorable comment as an objection. Here's an example:

Customer   Is this power drill expensive?

Salesperson   This drill really isn't that expensive. Are you concerned about whether it's worth it?

Customer   No, I just want to know the price.

The reservations customers state are often just excuses for not buying. Customers seldom say, "I don't have any reason—I just don't want to buy." Usually the customer gives a reason that appears to be the real reservation. Some customers agree to everything or make no comments. Then they decide not to buy the merchandise. The salesperson then must uncover the reason.

Salespeople can bring concealed reservations out into the open by observing how customers react to their sales presentation. When customers become less interested in a feature or the price, the salesperson should stop and begin a new approach or make a point clearer. Customers sometimes indicate the basis of their reservations by the way they handle the merchandise. For example, they may examine a shirt and then put it aside, implying "It doesn't look well-made to me" or "It's the wrong style [or color]." When these situations arise, the salesperson should ask a question such as "Did you see the double stitching around the collar?" Open-ended questions that encourage customers to talk more include "Would you like to tell me about it?" "Why is that?" and "Can we talk more about that?"

Methods for Handling Reservations   The best approach for handling reservations is to relax and listen. Allow customers to verbalize their feelings completely. Ask questions to clarify their reservations, but don't interrupt to provide an answer even though the answer might seem obvious.

Salespeople need to respond to reservations in a way that won't start an argument. One way is to turn the customer's statement into a question. If the customer says, "These bank accounts all require too high a minimum balance," the salesperson might reply, "Oh, what kind of minimum were you considering?" The answer will help the salesperson present an account that overcomes the customer's objection.

Answering a reservation with a question is usually more effective than trying to prove that the customer's reservation isn't valid. Asking a question sometimes leads customers to answer their own questions. A customer may say, "I can get this VCR much cheaper at Circuit City." A good reply is "Is price the only factor you're considering in buying a VCR?" The answer might be "No. I'm also interested in the service I'll get if it doesn't work. In fact, I came to your store because my friend said you have a great service department."

Responding to a reservation with a question is a good method for separating excuses from real objections. Inexperienced salespeople may be too quick to respond to a reservation, not realizing the initially expressed reservation isn't the real reason the customer isn't buying. Generalized reservations such as "I don't think I want to buy this mutual fund" are hard to handle. If a customer expresses a general reservation, the salesperson should ask questions to narrow the objection to specific points. For example, a customer might say, "I would like to look at the mutual funds you are selling, but I typically use a discount broker." A good response is "What don't you like about buying mutual funds from a bank?" The customer's answer to this question might reveal a misunderstanding or a point the salesperson can easily clarify. For example, the customer might say, "I don't like prices charged by banks when they sell mutual funds." Knowing this real reason for the customer's not purchasing, the salesperson can respond, "We have low prices on all mutual fund transactions if you bank with us."

Salespeople should aim to soften the reservation by getting on the customer's side. This can be done by agreeing with and then countering the reservation. Customers usually expect the salesperson to disagree with an objection. Instead, the salesperson should recognize that the objection is offered sincerely and respect the customer's view. A salesperson might say, "I know how you feel. Everything seems to cost so much today." After agreeing, the salesperson should proceed to provide information the customer might not be aware of. Skill is necessary in stating the counter. For example, a men's clothing salesperson might respond to the reservation "I don't like these new pleated pants" by saying, "You know, Mr. Smith, I felt the same way when I first saw these pants, but they're very comfortable and quite stylish. I bought a couple of pairs when they first came out a month ago, and now they're my favorite pants." With such a counter, the salesperson agrees that the customer's reaction isn't unusual but then proceeds to turn the objection into a benefit.

Price Concerns   Price reservations are the most common objections salespeople face. To avoid price reservations, salespeople need to establish the merchandise's benefits before they discuss price. If the customer feels the benefits don't justify the price, no sale will be made. On the other hand, when the customer feels the benefits exceed the price, there's a good chance of making a sale and having a satisfied customer.

Price reservations are best handled with a two-step approach. First, the salesperson should try to look at the reservations from the customer's viewpoint. Here are some questions to gain understanding of the customer's perspective:

> "We're usually quite competitive on this merchandise. What stores are selling this model at a lower price?"
>
> "You say you saw this at a lower price at Sears? I wonder if you were comparing apples with apples. What were the features on the Sears model?"

After learning more about the customer's perspective, the next step is to emphasize the item's benefits. All customers want to buy a less expensive product if they believe it has the same benefits as the more expensive one. But many customers will pay a higher price when additional benefits are pointed out to them. Many high-quality products look just like low-quality products so salespeople should emphasize features that justify the extra cost.

Some benefits are provided by intangible features—features customers can't see, such as durability of the merchandise, the quality of the health care provided, service provided by the store, the investment analysis done by specialists in the company, credit availability, the return policy, and the assortment that enables a customer to purchase an entire outfit in one store.

Finally, price reservations can be handled by suggesting merchandise with a lower price. But with this approach customers may not buy merchandise that best meets their needs.

Stalling   Another common reservation arises when a customer says, "I want to think it over." Here's an approach for handling this reservation:

Customer   I want to think this over. I can't make a decision now.

Salesperson   I understand how you feel. Many of our customers are uncertain before they buy a snowmobile. And you probably have several questions you still need to have answered before you make a decision, isn't that right?

Customer   Yes, that's right!

Salesperson   Let's make a list of some of your questions. Which of these questions is actually keeping you from making a decision now?

Making the Sale   The fourth step in the sales process involves getting the customer to make a purchase decision. Sales presentations are made to encourage purchase decisions. The salesperson must be ready to make a sale when the customer is ready to buy. The customer who says, "This table is scratched. Do

This customer is providing a buying signal when she takes the time to try on the jacket.

you have another one?" is giving the salesperson a chance to make a sale. Here it would be a mistake to present additional features and benefits. The customer is apparently ready to buy. The appropriate response to the customer's question is an answer and an attempt to make a sale such as "We have the same model in the warehouse. When would you like us to deliver it?"

Some salespeople make excellent presentations and then fail to ask the customer to purchase the product. This failure to close the sale often occurs because the salesperson is afraid the customer will say no. Many sales are lost due to this fear of asking to ring up the sale.

Timing   The right time to attempt to close a sale is when the customer appears ready to buy. There's no perfect psychological moment in a sales presentation to make the sale. Customers make up their minds to buy when they feel the benefits outweigh the price. For some customers, this point can occur when they first see the merchandise. For others, it might not occur until they've looked at a wide variety of options, contacted several retailers, and asked many questions.

Buying Signals   **Buying signals** are verbal or nonverbal communications from customers indicating they're ready to buy. Facial expressions often show when a customer isn't ready to buy. Customers who frown or seem to be puzzled may be indicating they aren't thoroughly sold on the merchandise. Customers' nonverbal signals indicating a salesperson should attempt to make a sale include

Resisting a salesperson's attempt to move merchandise out of the way.

Intently studying or reexamining the merchandise, handling it, and looking at it from different angles. For clothing, holding it against their body.

Smiling or appearing to be excited when looking at the item.

Handling or using a product for the second or third time.

Suggesting a move from the living room to a more work-oriented room such as the study (when the customer is talking to a salesperson at home).

Customers' comments are usually the best indicator that they're considering a purchase. The following statements may indicate they're about to make or have made a decision:

"I guess the blue paint goes better with my wallpaper than the gray paint."

"Can you alter the pants?"

"Do I understand you correctly that I can return this and get my money back?"

"Did you say that the return on the stock was 12.5 percent last year?"

"Do you have this desk in a darker wood?"

"I've always wanted to go to Cancun."

What If an Attempt to Make a Sale Fails? When an attempt fails, the salesperson needs to analyze the situation and determine why the customer declined to make a purchase. Sales attempts can fail for many reasons, including the salesperson's attempt to make a sale prematurely, misinterpreting the customer's interest in buying, making a poor presentation, emphasizing unimportant benefits to the customer, or not demonstrating the merchandise properly. Before salespeople can take corrective action, they must find out why the sales attempt failed.

When an attempt fails, the salesperson should continue to present the offering and look for another opportunity. The salesperson may have to collect additional information from the customer to determine the cause of failure.

An important lesson for inexperienced salespeople is that when a customer says no, the salesperson shouldn't presume that the sale is lost. A no might mean "Not now," or "I need more information," or "I don't understand."

Methods of Making a Sale No method or approach for making a sale works in all retail situations. Some approaches are to ask to ring up the sale, to assume the sale is made, to build a series of acceptances, and to emphasize an impending event. Often, a salesperson will use more than one approach during a presentation.

Asking for the order is the most straightforward and effective method for making a sale. But salespeople should be wary of appearing overly aggressive when using such a direct approach. The direct approach works best with decisive customers who want to get down to business.

In assuming the sale is made, the salesperson allows the customer to follow the path of least resistance. Again, be careful using this approach, because customers may feel that the salesperson is pushy. Here are some questions that can be used in an assumptive approach:

"Do you want to charge the lumber?"

"Why don't you try on the suit while I get the tailor to see if any alterations are necessary?"

Giving the customer a choice is another version of this approach. Remember, the choice is between two items or a set of items. It's never between buying the merchandise or not buying the merchandise. Examples that involve choices are

"Would you like the 30-piece or 48-piece set of this china?"

"Do you prefer to buy this on our monthly billing plan or pay for it now?"

Building a series of acceptances is actually a method for building up to a sale. Customers typically find it hard to refuse to buy merchandise when they agree that it satisfies their needs. By getting a customer to answer questions with a series of yeses, you help him make some easy decisions leading up to the buying decision. For example,

Salesperson   This tie goes well with your suit, don't you think?
Customer   Yes, it certainly does.
Salesperson   The 100 percent silk fabric certainly gives it a rich appearance, doesn't it?
Customer   Yes. Silk ties are very striking.
Salesperson   Is the tie in your price range?
Customer   It's a little high, but it's in the range.
Salesperson   Do you want to charge the tie or pay cash for it?

Emphasizing an impending event motivates a customer to buy immediately. The technique stresses that customers will lose something if they hesitate to purchase the merchandise. For example,

"The sale ends today. Tomorrow the price goes up $20."
"This is the only remote-control TV we have with stereo sound."
"The weather is beginning to turn cold, and these skis are going to sell fast."

Selling Multiple Items

Effective salespeople suggest additional items before the original sales transaction is completed. It's much easier to convince a customer to add on to a sale than to begin an entirely new sales process for additional items. Many retailers keep track of multiple-item sales and use this information to evaluate salesperson performance. (See Chapter 17.)

Customers appreciate new ideas and suggestions for items that will go with merchandise they've already decided to buy. Accessories, for example, can offer variety and excitement to a wardrobe. Effective salespeople can point out that adding the right look in scarves, wearing the right shoes, and/or pinning the right piece of jewelry to a scarf will create the special effect a customer is seeking.

When selling additional items, salespeople should avoid becoming too aggressive. The salesperson can mention available merchandise without offending a customer. But trying to sell a CD player to a customer who came in for a record might be annoying. When additional suggestions are appropriate, the salesperson should make them in a positive way. Asking "Anything else?" isn't as effective as saying "You'll need some film for your new camera."

Building Relationships and Future Sales

The relationship between a customer and a salesperson shouldn't end when a sale is made. It's becoming increasingly important for salespeople to build long-term relationships with customers so they'll return to the store and seek out the salesperson the next time they're buying.[4]

Goodwill is the value of customers' feeling or attitude toward the retailer and salesperson. The fundamental method for building goodwill is to make sure customers are satisfied with the merchandise they purchase. Customer satisfaction is achieved when salespeople are customer-oriented and not sales-oriented.[5] Customer-oriented salespeople focus their attention on the customer's needs, not just on making a sale.

For example, Edgar Hidalgo, Burdines' top salesperson, is 22 years old and sold over $500,000 in the Men's Guess Shop in the Dadeland Mall. He recalls how attention to the customers resulted in his largest sale:

> A lady approached me and asked me to help her find a gift. We ended up spending 40 minutes, but finally found one. The sale was $150. She apologized for taking so much of my time. I said it was a pleasure and I enjoyed helping her. Then she asked me if I was going to be in the next day and I said yes. The next day she came in and waited 40 minutes for me to finish with another customer. She decided to do her Christmas shopping and spent $3,500.[6]

Methods for building goodwill include reaffirming the customer's judgment, ensuring proper use of the merchandise, handling customer complaints, remembering the customer between visits, and providing "above-and-beyond" service.

Reaffirming the Customer's Judgment   Customers are often unsure about their decision after making a purchase, especially if the item is costly. Salespeople can increase the chances that customers will be satisfied with their purchases simply by reassuring them. A salesperson might say, "I'm sure you'll get a lot of good use out of your computer," or "Be sure to call me if you need any help. I'm eager to hear how your guests like your dress. Here's my card."

Many salespeople send handwritten notes to customers thanking them for making a purchase and ensuring them of good service in the future. Exhibit 20–5 shows an example.

EXHIBIT 20–5

Building Relationships with a Customer

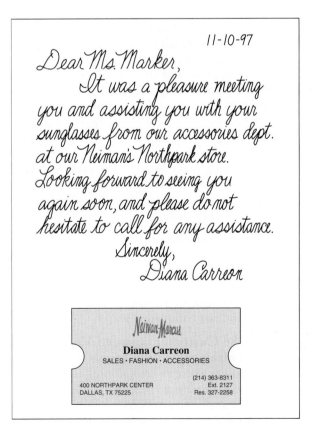

Liz Claiborne has repre-
sentatives that help train
store employees on the
benefits and features of
their merchandise.

Ensuring Proper Use of the Merchandise   If customers aren't familiar with the merchandise, they can become dissatisfied when they first use it. Computer salespeople can build goodwill by visiting a customer right after the computer is delivered to make sure the customer knows how to use it. A salesperson who has just sold several suits, ties, and shirts to a customer may make up a chart to show the different combinations that look good. This chart may help the customer realize the full potential benefits of the clothing he's purchased.

Customers may be satisfied with the merchandise they've purchased but may not get the maximum benefits from it if they're not aware of its capabilities. Salespeople should take the time after a sale to demonstrate how the merchandise is used. They should make sure customers receive instructions and special brochures provided by the manufacturer. When manufacturers provide new information, the salesperson has an excellent opportunity to develop goodwill by sending the information to customers who purchased the merchandise in the past.

Handling Customer Complaints   Responding to customer complaints gives the salesperson an excellent opportunity to build goodwill. Most customers don't go to the trouble of complaining to the store even if they're dissatisfied. When a customer takes the time to complain, salespeople should view it as an opportunity to demonstrate their concern for the customer's satisfaction. (Chapter 19 covered approaches for handling complaints.)

Remembering the Customer between Visits   Keeping in contact with customers between visits is an effective means to build goodwill. Some methods for maintaining customer contact are phoning a customer when new merchandise arrives, taking special orders to secure the merchandise sought by the customer, setting aside merchandise the customer might want, calling the customer to make an appointment for a private showing of new merchandise, and following up on merchandise sold to see if the customer is satisfied with it.

20.3

Selling at Nordstrom

AT NORDSTROM, SALESPEOPLE DON'T just tell customers how to solve their problems; they assume personal responsibility. Customers aren't told to go to a credit office to correct a mistake in a bill. They aren't passed along to different salespeople or directed to different departments. The salesperson they talk with is personally responsible for making the customer happy.

Tales of service above and beyond the call of duty abound. For example, a Nordstrom customer brought back a pair of shoes a year after buying them and asked if they could be repaired. The salesperson provided a new pair instead. In cold climates, salespeople have been known to warm up a customer's car while the customer pays for merchandise. If Nordstrom doesn't have a size or color that a customer wants, a salesperson will go to a competing store in the mall that carries the merchandise, buy it for the customer, and then sell it to the customer at the price charged at Nordstrom.

When merchandise is returned, the salesperson who made the original sale is debited, and commissions made on the sale are lost. This policy emphasizes to the salesperson that keeping customers satisfied is critical. The salesperson has a stake in making every sale the final sale.

New salespeople are given a "personal" book. The store manager explains that the personal book represents the salesperson's income. In the book, the salesperson keeps track of customers' names, telephone numbers, likes and dislikes, charge account numbers, and anything else that will help the salesperson become a personal shopper for the customer. New salespeople also receive personal and business cards and an open account to send thank-you notes or flowers to customers.

At Nordstrom, newly hired salespeople earn from $7 to $10 per hour, $2 per hour above the typical local retail wage. Compensation is based totally on sales generated. A top salesperson can gross between $50,000 and $80,000 per year.

Nordstrom pays salespeople well, but its expectations for them are high. Each salesperson's sales per hour are posted on bulletin boards near the employee entrances to the store. Nordstrom also stresses ethics and teamwork. A salesperson who knowingly takes sales from customers being serviced by another salesperson will be fired immediately.

Source: Penny Parker, "The Sole of Nordstrom," *The Denver Post,* August 11, 1996, p. H-01; Tibbett Speer, "How to Be a Friend to Your Customers," *American Demographics,* March 1995, pp. 14–15; and Michael Brogan, "Death of a Shoe Salesman," *Business Week,* February 20, 1995.

Providing Above-and-Beyond Service   Salespeople build long-term relationships with their customers by providing service above and beyond customer expectations. Here's an example of above-and-beyond service from a study of star salespeople:

> Cathy works in the jeans department, but you could not tell this from her sales records. She goes wherever her customers' needs take her. For example, one customer called and asked Cathy to pick out a birthday present for her granddaughter, who happens to like boyswear. Cathy went to the boys department, found some items she thought the little girl would like, charged them to the grandmother, had them gift wrapped, and sent them to the grandmother.[7]

Retailing View 20.3 describes sales practices at Nordstrom, a department store chain noted for its above-and-beyond service.

Building Special Relationships   Customers develop strong relationships with salespeople who offer functionality, friendship, and trust.[8] As Chapter 4 said, time is becoming a scarce resource for consumers. They have less time to shop and many consumers don't like to shop. Customers rely on salespeople who save them time and offer useful advice.

20.4

SteinMart's Boutique Ladies Sell through Personal Relationships

JAY STEIN, CHAIRMAN OF STEINMART (an off-price chain), says, "The boutique ladies are our secret weapon." Back in the 1980s, SteinMart began hiring wives of local business executives, doctors, and lawyers to sell merchandise in the store's designer boutique. The "boutique ladies" have limited work experience, but they have extensive networks of friends developed through volunteer charity work. They also have a flair for fashion and an enthusiasm that draws their friends to the store.

For example, when a shipment of $39 designer silk separates arrived, boutique lady Joy Abney (wife of the former managing partner of Coopers & Lybrand) "got right on the horn and told them to get over here." Her friends spent $2,000 in her department that day.

There's a waiting list to be a boutique lady at SteinMart. The 1,200 boutique ladies typically work one day a week and are excused from cash register duty and evening shifts. Many of the women are pleased to find out that an older woman without a resume is welcome in the workplace. "My husband thought the only thing I could do was carpool, but working here comes natural." It's a lot like volunteer work because "you are helping people. It's also fun to get a paycheck that's all mine."

Source: Teri Agins, "Clerking at SteinMart Is a Society Lady's Dream Come True," *The Wall Street Journal*, December 2, 1992, pp. A1, A5.

Sales associates often develop strong friendships with their customers, although these are business friendships and don't extend beyond the workplace. For example, a customer interviewed in a research project referred to a salesperson as being "like family" and brought baked goods to her to show her appreciation. Retailing View 20.4 describes how SteinMart, an off-price chain, hires society women to sell merchandise to their friends.

Trust is the critical element in building long-term relationships between salespeople and customers, and between vendors and retailers. Customers trust salespeople who are dependable, are honest, and take the customer's perspectives. A quote from the study of star salespeople reveals these traits.

> If I don't think it's going to look good on you, I will tell you. I find the key is being honest. If you can really speak truthfully from your heart, it works. Lots of salespeople just sell to make the sale, but I sell from the customer's point of view.[9]

In the next section, we look at knowledge and communication skills salespeople need to be effective during the sales process.

KNOWLEDGE AND SKILLS FOR EFFECTIVE SELLING

To be effective, retail salespeople must know the store's policies and merchandise. Skills they need to effectively manage the selling process include listening, questioning, interpreting and using nonverbal communications, and being flexible.

Knowledge

Policies When customers are about to make a buying decision, they often want information about the retailer's policies. For example, salespeople should be able to provide information about the firm's program for testing merchandise quality and safety or its unconditional guarantee to refund the purchase price in cash for all merchandise returned. Salespeople should know whom to contact in the company when questions arise they can't answer: whom to call to find out if an item is available in another store when it's sold out in their store, or a buyer to contact about a special order a customer wants to place.

Offering Knowledge of the merchandise or service is critical. Without it, the salesperson can't satisfy the customer's needs by matching the merchandise features to benefits sought by the customer. It's not enough for the salesperson to say, "This camera is a good buy. It's high-quality and has a low price." Customers expect specific information about merchandise: how to operate it, which features justify its price, or how one brand differs from another.

Patrick Conner (sales manager at The Strand in the Creste Butte ski resort) emphasizes the importance of product knowledge:

> We educate our customers, not just sell them. . . . And the key to educating customers is being educated yourself. Salespeople should go to every demo day and rep clinic they can, and read everything about a product you can get your hands on. Talk with your coworkers about products—whether it be a regularly scheduled meeting, or off the cuff.[10]

Some retailers seek out and hire people with considerable knowledge about their merchandise. For example, Home Depot salespeople usually have considerable do-it-yourself experience. With this knowledge, they can help customers select appropriate materials and tools and then advise them on how to use this information for home repair work. Similarly, Williams Sonoma prefers to hire salespeople with interest and experience in food preparation.

Most retailers provide training in selling skills. For example, at Parisian (a regional specialty department store chain) all newly hired salespeople get 45 hours of training before they interact with customers. During this training period, they spend at least one half-day shadowing a top salesperson in the department in which they'll be working. After 90 days on the job, they have an additional 12 hours of refresher training.

Salespeople at Lands' End get 75 hours of training before they're allowed to answer phones and take orders. During the training, they learn about and feel every product in the catalog. This product knowledge helps them answer questions like "What does the mesh knit shirt feel like?" or "Do the wool flannel trousers have buttons on both back pockets?"[11]

In addition, vendors provide information about their merchandise. Says Alfred Fuoco, chairman of Evan Picone (a manufacturer of high-quality women's clothing), "As store chains have grown larger, they've taken money out of their budget for sales help. That has hurt us." To address this problem, Evan Picone has 16 representatives who tour stores to train salespeople and to organize displays of its merchandise. Besides 15 consultants working with retail salespeople, Liz Claiborne has even hired architects to design selling areas for Liz clothing in department stores.[12]

Vendor sales representatives often meet with salespeople before the store opens to demonstrate new merchandise and answer questions. Vendor reps also spend time in the store working with salespeople and customers.

The Art of Listening
Inexperienced salespeople often believe effective selling is achieved by talking a lot. They go into each customer interaction thinking they have to out-talk the customer. Actually, listening is the most important part of effective communication. Salespeople who monopolize conversations will never learn what customers want or what they think of the merchandise being presented.

People can speak at a rate of 130 to 160 words per minute, but they can listen at a rate of 800 words per minute.[13] Because of this difference, salespeople are often lazy listeners. They don't pay attention, and they forget or miss a large part of what customers say.

Effective listening is an active endeavor. It's much more than just hearing what customers say. Good listeners project themselves into the customer's mind. If a customer says he wants a "fancy" computer, the salesperson needs to listen carefully to find out what *fancy* means to that customer. Through effective listening, the salesperson demonstrates concern for the customer's needs by selecting appropriate merchandise to present and demonstrate.

Effective listeners are actively thinking while they're listening. They're thinking about the conclusion the customer is leading up to, evaluating the information the customer is presenting, and sorting out important facts from unimportant facts. Active listening also means the salesperson attempts to draw as much information as possible from the customer.

Techniques for active listening include repeating or rephrasing information, summarizing conversations, and tolerating silences.[14]

Repeating or Rephrasing Information   During the sales process, salespeople need to verify information they collected from customers. Here's an example:

Customer   I'll take two high-quality blank videotapes and one standard-quality tape.

Salesperson   Sure, Mr. Johnson. That's two high-quality and one standard-quality.

Customer   Wait a minute. I got it backward. I want two standard-quality and one high-quality.

Salesperson   Fine. Two standard, one high-quality. Right?

Customer   Yes. That's right.

To verify a customer's intent, salespeople can restate the customer's comment in their own words.

Customer   The picture on that TV isn't what I expected.

Salesperson   I see. You're dissatisfied with the picture quality.

Customer   Oh, no. As a matter of fact, I think it's the clearest picture I've ever seen on a TV. I didn't expect it to be so clear.

Summarizing the Conversation   Active listening involves mentally summarizing points the customer makes. Somewhere in the presentation, the salesperson needs to check out these mental summaries.

Customer   . . . so I told him I wasn't interested.

Salesperson   Let me see if I got this straight. A salesperson at Discount Electronics told you he'd sell you this RCA console TV for $695. But then you found out that you had to buy a warranty because this was a special model made for Discount, and then you had to pay a shipping and handling charge. You thought that was a rip-off?

Customer   That's right.

Salesperson   Well, all of our TVs have a one-year warranty from the manufacturer, and we add on an additional one-year warranty at no cost to you. Plus we deliver the TV and install it with no charge.

Tolerating Silences   Perhaps this technique for better listening should be called "bite your tongue." Both salespeople and customers need time to think. Because people tend to exaggerate the amount of time passing during these silent periods, salespeople often feel they need to fill the gap by saying something. Tolerating silences, however, gives customers time to sell themselves.

Salesperson   Well, what do you think of our financial planning service?
Customer   [silence] Just a minute. . . . Let me think about it a little longer.
Salesperson   [silence]
Customer   It's certainly better than what I'm doing now.
Salesperson   Fine, Mr. Ruth. Would you be interested in going over the information we need now or should I set up an appointment in a few days?
Customer   Hmmmm . . .
Salesperson   [silence]
Customer   I think I'll work on it with you now.

The Art of Asking Questions

Salespeople should ask questions for several reasons. First, questions get the customer to participate in the sales process. By asking questions, salespeople encourage customers to actively engage in a conversation rather than passively listening to a presentation. Participating in a conversation makes them more likely to hear and remember what's said. Second, questions show customers the salesperson is interested in them. Finally, salespeople can collect valuable information using questions.

Types of Questions   Here are examples of questions that can be used to collect information:

> "What kind of wood paneling do you have now?"
> "How often do you play CDs on your stereo?"
> "What do you know about HMOs?"
> "*Consumer Reports* rated your brand as only average in torque. Is that your experience?"
> "Your stereo isn't compatible with your TV. I guess you can't put the soundtrack on the TV through your stereo system, can you?"

Here are some statements or questions that encourage customers to keep talking:

> "Uh-huh."
> "Can you give me an example of what you mean?"
> "Please tell me more about that."
> "That's interesting."
> "Is that so?"
> "You said you were dissatisfied with your present dishwasher?"
> "So you'd like to have more shelf space?"

Guidelines   Here are some guidelines for effective questioning:

1. *Encourage longer responses.* Don't ask questions that can be answered with a simple yes or no. For example, ask, "What do you know about our bank?" rather than "Have you heard of our bank?"

2. *Space out questions.* When a salesperson asks several questions one right after the other, customers may feel threatened. One method for spacing out questions is to encourage customers to elaborate on their responses.

3. *Ask short, simple questions.* Avoid questions with two or more parts. When faced with a complex question, customers might not know which part to answer, and the salesperson might not know which part of the question is being answered.

4. *Avoid leading questions.* Leading questions just put words into the customer's mouth and don't tell the salesperson what the customer is actually thinking. The question "Why do you think this is a good product?" gets at a customer's positive thoughts but doesn't reveal her reservations.

Interpreting and Using Nonverbal Communication

Nonverbal communications are nonspoken forms of expression—body language (body angle, face, arms, and hands), space, and appearance—that communicate thoughts and emotions. Salespeople need to (1) interpret customers' nonverbal signals and (2) use nonverbal communications to improve their selling effectiveness.

It's hard to interpret nonverbal signals by observing a single gesture or body position. Salespeople thus need to consider the pattern of signals a customer generates to interpret the person's feelings. Exhibit 20–6 shows some patterns of nonverbal communications.

To increase their effectiveness, salespeople can also use nonverbal signals as follows:

1. *Use cooperation signals* (see Exhibit 20–6) to indicate sincere interest in helping customers satisfy their needs. Avoid power signals. They intimidate customers and make them feel uncomfortable.

2. *Nothing creates rapport like a smile.* The smile should appear natural and comfortable—not a smirk or clownlike exaggerated grin. To get the smile right, practice in front of a mirror.

3. *Direct eye contact reflects sincerity.* Glancing from side to side or at a wall has the opposite effect. But staring can make a customer feel uncomfortable.

4. *Hand movements can have a dramatic effect.* Pointing a finger can be used to reinforce important points in the presentation. Too many hand gestures can distract attention from the verbal communication, however.

5. *Good voice and speech habits are critical.* To avoid monotony, salespeople should vary the rate and loudness of their speech. Simple messages may be delivered faster than more complex messages. Important points can be emphasized by increasing loudness. The clearest speech is made when the mouth is opened by the width of a finger. When the lips are too close together, enunciation is poor.[15]

Flexibility and Adaptive Selling

The chance to tailor the presentation to each customer is unique to personal selling communications. Thus, selling effectiveness is related to the salesperson's ability to exploit this opportunity. **Adaptive selling** is an approach to personal selling in which selling behaviors are altered based on information about the customer and the buying situation.[16]

Knowledge enables salespeople to be flexible and adapt their sales presentations. Salespeople need to know their customers—the different types of customers and the presentations that work best for each customer type. Retailing View 20.5 describes types of customers an undergraduate student encountered during her summer retailing internship.

EXHIBIT 20–6

Patterns of Nonverbal
Communications

INTERPRETATION	BODY ANGLE	FACE	ARMS	HANDS
Power, dominance, superiority	Exaggerated leaning over.	Piercing eye contact.	Hands on hips.	Hands behind neck or back. Steepling (fingertips touching).
Nervousness, submission, apprehension	Fidgeting or shifting from side to side.	Head down. Minimum eye contact. Constant blinking.	Hands to face, hair. Rubbing back of neck.	Wringing hands. Fingers clasped.
Disagreement, anger, skepticism	Turning body away.	Negative shake of head, frown. Lips pursing. Eyes squinting. Chin thrusting out.	Arms crossed. Finger under collar.	Fist. Finger pointing. Hands gripping edge of display.
Boredom, disinterest	Slouching against display.	Lack of eye contact. Looking at door, at watch, out window. Blank stare.		Playing with object on display case. Drumming on display case.
Suspicion, secretiveness, dishonesty	Moving body away. Sideways glance.	Avoid eye contact. Squinting eyes. Smirking.	Touching nose while speaking. Pulling ear while speaking.	Fingers crossed.
Uncertainty, indecision	Pacing back and forth.	Head down or tilted. Biting lip. Shifting eyes left and right.	Pinching bridge of nose. Tugging at clothes. Scratching head.	Pulling neck.
Evaluation	Head tilted slightly. Ear turned toward speaker.	Slight blinking of eyes, squinting. Eyebrows raised. Nodding.	Hand gripping chin. Putting glasses in mouth.	Putting index finger to lips.
Cooperation, confidence, honesty	Back and forth movement of body.	Good eye contact. Slight blinking. Smile.	Putting hands to chest. Free movement of arms and hands.	Open hands.

Source: Barton Weitz, Stephen Castleberry, and John Tanner, *Selling: Building Parternships,* 3d ed. (Burr Ridge, IL: Irwin/McGraw-Hill, 1998).

In theory, salespeople should treat each customer differently, but in practice, salespeople don't have time to develop unique strategies for each customer. Effective salespeople tend to categorize customers, as Cynthia Carter does in Retailing View 20.5. Each category contains a description of the customer and the most effective sales approach for that customer type. By developing a set of categories, salespeople reduce the complexity of retail selling and free up their mental capacity to think more creatively. Categorization also enables salespeople to use the knowledge gained through past experiences. When they encounter a customer with unusual needs—a customer who doesn't fit into an existing category—they add a new category to their repertoire.[17]

20.5

Retail Customers Come in 31 Flavors

CYNTHIA CARTER, A UNIVERSITY OF Florida undergraduate, spent 12 weeks during the summer as a paid intern at JCPenney's University Square Mall store in Tampa. Part of her internship was spent as a sales associate. Here she developed the following insights into how to effectively sell to different customer types.

"Experienced sales associates recognize that customers come in all shapes, sizes, and flavors. Some are more pleasant to deal with, but the true mark of a successful sales associate lies in the ability to assist every type of customer, all 31 flavors. Here are six of the customer flavors I encountered during my internship.

"The *vanilla customer* answers, 'I'm just looking,' to every question you ask or suggestion you offer. They're rather faceless and uninteresting, but they often actually need your assistance. It's most important that you don't threaten them by being overbearing. Simply let them know you're available when they realize they need your assistance.

"The *I'll take four cones*—chocolate, strawberry, bubble gum, and peanut butter and jelly—*customer* has three screaming children terrorizing the racks and dressing rooms. She doesn't have much time to shop. Ask her what she needs and she responds, 'Anything that doesn't need ironing.' She really needs your help. Give a 'hanger gun' to her kids, sit her in a dressing room, find out her size, and bring her clothes to try on. She'll be grateful for your help and will be back to spend money dressing her children.

"The *why-don't-you-have–banana-marshmallow-swirl customer* is very upset when she can't find what she wants. She freely criticizes the store for not having merchandise that everyone has. This customer needs to be handled with kid gloves. The key is to be very humble, very helpful, and very ready to point out similar items that the customer may find appealing. Use the JCPenney catalog as a backup since items in the catalog can be delivered in two days. Remember, never lose your cool and never tell the customer she's wrong.

"The *rum raisin customer* wants high quality and will pay high prices. Avoid polyester/cotton blends. Focus on the silks, suedes, and linens.

Salespeople use their past experiences to determine the most effective approaches for different types of customers. Cynthia Carter might characterize these customers as "four cone" types.

Give a lot of personal attention and fashion-conscious advice. Stress add-on sales. If you can win her fashion trust, you can make a big sale.

"The *tofu-granola-sorbet customer* needs sturdy fabrics with lots of big pockets for rock collecting in Montana. Durability and practicality are much more important than fashion. Forget the 24-inch triple-strand pearls and go for the durango khaki outfit. She'll pay the price for the right clothes.

"The *birthday-cake customer* is a frantic husband, boyfriend, or father who realizes over lunch that today's the big day, and he hasn't gotten anything yet. He usually doesn't know her size, let alone her weight or height. You can try to guess, but the best bet is suggesting a non-form-fitting sweater or coordinating earrings and necklace. You need to take control of the occasion and offer concrete advice. Tell him returns are handled most smoothly if he saves the receipt."

Source: Barton Weitz, Stephen Castleberry, and John Tanner, *Selling: Building Partnerships,* 3d ed. (Burr Ridge, IL: Irwin/McGraw-Hill, 1998).

Salespeople with more categories of customer types have more selling approaches to use and thus have a greater opportunity to adjust to a specific customer's needs. Salespeople can devise more categories by studying the customers they encounter and analyzing their successes and failures in selling to them.

SUMMARY   Salespeople are an important element in the retail mix. They're responsible for making sales and providing services that produce satisfied, loyal customers.

The sale begins when the salesperson approaches a customer, but the process doesn't end when the customer decides to buy something. The salesperson needs to encourage and assist the customer in buying complementary merchandise. These add-on sales are important aspects of a store's profitability, and they increase customers' satisfaction from their purchases. The sales process ends when a customer is satisfied with the merchandise and decides to return to the store. Making a sale is just one step in developing a loyal customer—the goal salespeople should have every time they interact with customers.

Effective communication skills—listening and questioning—enable salespeople to adapt their presentation to the needs of the customer. Through these skills, salespeople facilitate two-way communication. Adaptive selling also requires extensive knowledge of customer types and the most effective way to sell to each type.

Over two-thirds of all communication is nonverbal.

KEY TERMS

adaptive selling, *622*

approach, *603*

benefit, *606*

buying signals, *612*

feature, *607*

goodwill, *614*

nonverbal communication, *622*

reservation (objection), *608*

sales associate, *602*

sales consultant, *602*

selling process, *602*

DISCUSSION QUESTIONS & PROBLEMS

1. What do you think about the following statement? "Good salespeople need to be aggressive. They need to have a powerful voice and a winning smile."

2. Assume you're selling bedding—sheets and pillow cases. What questions might you ask a potential customer?

3. A customer raises the following reservations. How do you respond?
   a. "I really like all the things this copier does, but I don't think it's going to be very reliable. With all those features, something's got to go wrong."
   b. "Your price for this printer is higher than the price I saw advertised in a mail-order catalog."
   c. "These suits just never fit me right."

4. Some retail stores, such as Nordstrom, require salespeople to concentrate a significant amount of their effort on servicing customers. Speaking as a manager in charge of salespeople, discuss whether problems can arise when salespeople concentrate too much on providing service.

5. The sales profession has been accused of having more than its share of unethical people. Some people say the very nature of sales—convincing people to buy something—leaves it open to abuse. How can a salesperson be successful in sales and still maintain high ethical standards?

6. Because of increasing competition among retailers, price can differentiate one retailer from another. A retail salesperson often can't do much about an objection to price. What counterargument could you give a customer who objects to a price?

7. When handling a merchandise return, sometimes retail salespeople treat the customer with little interest and attention. In fact, some salespeople resent the customer's using up valuable selling time. How can the handling of merchandise returns build customer loyalty?

8. Distinguish between a product's benefits and features. Why must retail salespeople understand the difference?

9. "All methods for trying to get a customer to buy merchandise are devious and self-serving!" Comment.

10. Should a salesperson handle all complaints so that a customer is completely satisfied?

11. How can a salesperson oversell a customer?

SUGGESTED READINGS

Beatty, Sharon, Morris Mayer, James Coleman, and Kristy Reynolds. "Customer–Sales Associate Retail Relationships." *Journal of Retailing* 72 (Fall 1996), pp. 223–47.

Bloomquist, Randall. "Confessions of a Consumer Electronics Salesman." *The Washington Post*, August 28, 1996, pp. RO5–6.

"Blueprint for Retail Skills." *Stores*, February 1995, pp. 24–26.

Caldini, Robert. *Influence: Science and Practice*, 4th ed. New York: HarperCollins, 1997.

Castleberry, Stephen, and C. David Sheppard. "Effective Interpersonal Listening and Personal Selling." *Journal of Personal Selling and Sales Management* 1 (Winter 1993), pp. 35–50.

Gelman, Jan. "How to Make a Great First Impression." *Selling*, July–August 1995, pp. 58–65.

Goff, Brent, Danny Bellanger, and Carrie Stojack. "Cues to Consumer Susceptibility to Salesperson Influence: Implications for Adaptive Retail Selling." *Journal of Personal Selling and Sales Management* 14 (Spring 1994), pp. 25–40.

Peterson, Robert, Michael Cannito, and Steven Brown. "An Exploratory Investigation of Voice Characteristics and Selling Effectiveness." *Journal of Personal Selling and Sales Management* 15 (Winter 1995), pp. 1–16.

Pettijohn, Charles, Linda Pettijohn, and Albert Taylor. "The Relationship between Effective Selling and Effective Counseling." *Journal of Consumer Marketing* 12, no. 1 (1995), pp. 5–15.

Sharma, Arun, and Michael Levy. "Categorization of Customers by Retail Salespeople." *Journal of Retailing* 71 (Spring 1995), pp. 71–81.

Speer, Tibbett. "How to Be a Friend to Your Customers." *American Demographics*, March 1995, pp. 14–15.

Weitz, Barton, Stephen Castleberry, and John Tanner. *Selling: Building Partnerships*, 3d ed. Burr Ridge, IL: McGraw-Hill /Irwin, 1998.

NOTES

1. Monci Jo Williams, "America's Best Salesmen," *Fortune*, October 26, 1987, pp. 122–34.

2. For an in-depth treatment of the sales process, See Barton Weitz, Stephen Castleberry, and John Tanner, *Selling: Building Partnerships*, 3d ed. (Burr Ridge, IL: Irwin/McGraw-Hill, 1998).

3. "You and a Changing J.C. Penney," Holiday Issue 1986, p. 6. Company document.

4. Theodore Levitt, "After the Sale Is Over . . . ," *Harvard Business Review*, September–October 1983, pp. 87–93.

5. Lyndon Dawson, Barlow Soper, and Charles Pettijohn, "The Effects of Empathy on Salesperson Effectiveness," *Psychology & Marketing* 9 (July–August 1992), pp. 297–310; Robert Saxe and Barton Weitz, "The SOCO Scale: A Measure of the Customer Orientation of Salespeople," *Journal of Marketing Research* 17 (August 1982), pp. 343–51; and John Hawes, Kenneth Mast, and John Swan, "Trust Earning Perceptions of Sellers and Buyers," *Journal of Personal Selling and Sales Mangement* 9 (Spring 1989), pp. 30–41.

6. Lynn O'Rourke, "Edgar Hidalgo," *Daily News Record*, April 25, 1996, p. 12.

7. Sharon Beatty, "Relationship Selling in Retailing," *Retailing Issues Letter* (College Station: Center for Retailing Studies, Texas A&M University, November 1993), p. 2.

8. Ibid.

9. Ibid., p. 3.

10. Patricia O'Connell, "The Secrets of Our Success," *The Times Mirror Magazine*, September 19, 1996, pp. 10–15.

11. Ron Zemke and Dick Schaaf, *The Service Edge—101 Companies That Profit from Customer Care* (New York: Plume, 1990), p. 383.

12. Ann Hagendorn, "Apparel Makers Play Bigger Part on Sales Floor," *The Wall Street Journal*, March 2, 1988, p. 25.

13. Ruth Bennett and Rosemary Wood, "Effective Communications via Listening Styles," *Business* 39 (April–June 1989), p. 45.

14. Stephen Castleberry and C. David Sheppard, "Effective Interpersonal Listening and Personal Selling," *Journal of Personal Selling and Sales Management* 1 (Winter 1993), pp. 35–50; Om Kharbanda and Ernest Stallworthy, "A Vital Negotiating Skill," *Journal of Mangerial Psychology* 6

(1991), pp. 6–9, 49–52; Morey Stettner, "Salespeople Who Listen and What They Find Out," *Management Review*, June 1988, pp. 44–45; Kerry Johnson, "Salespeople: Are You Listening?" *Personal Selling Power*, May–June 1989, pp. 14–24; and Florence Wolff, *Perceptive Listening* (New York: Holt, Rinehart & Winston, 1983).

15. Mark Knapp and Judith Hall, *Non-Verbal Communications in Human Interactions*, 4th ed. (Fort Worth, TX: Holt, Rinehart and Winston, 1996); Robert Peterson, Michael Cannito, and Steven Brown, "An Exploratory Investigation of Voice Characteristics and Selling Effectiveness," *Journal of Personal Selling and Sales Management* 15 (Winter 1995), pp. 1–16; David Stewart, Sid Hecker, and John Graham, "It's More than What You Say: Assessing the Influence of Nonverbal Communication in Marketing," *Psychology and Marketing*, Winter 1987, pp. 302–22; and Gerhard Gschwandtner and Pat Garnett, *Non-Verbal Selling* (Englewood Cliffs, NJ: Prentice Hall, 1985).

16. Barton Weitz, Harish Sujan, and Mita Sujan, "Knowledge, Motivation and Adaptive Behavior: A Framework for Improving Selling Effectiveness," *Journal of Marketing* 50 (October 1986), pp. 174–91; and Morgan Miles, Danny Arnold, and Henry Nash, "Adaptive Communications: The Adaptation of the Seller's Interpersonal Style to the Stages of the Dyad's Relationship and the Buyer's Communication Style," *Journal of Personal Selling and Sales Management* 10 (February 1990), pp. 10–15.

17. Charles Gengler, "A Personal Construct Analysis of Adaptive Selling and Sales Experience," *Psychology & Marketing*, July 1995, pp. 287–304; Carolyn Predmore and Joseph Bonnice, "Sales Success as Predicted by a Process Measure of Adaptability," *Journal of Personal Selling and Sales Management* 14 (Fall 1994), pp. 56–65; Harish Sujan, Mita Sujan, and James Bettman, "Knowledge Structure Differences between Effective and Less Effective Salespeople," *Journal of Marketing Research*, February 1988, pp. 81–86; David Szymanski, "Determinants of Selling Effectiveness: The Importance of Declarative Knowledge to the Personal Selling Concept," *Journal of Marketing*, January 1988, pp. 64–77; and Leslie Fine, "Refining the Concept of Salesperson Adaptability," in Chris Allen et al., eds., *Marketing Theory and Applications* (Chicago, IL: American Marketing Association, 1992), pp. 42–49.

SECTION V

Cases

CASE	CHAPTER																			
	1	2	3	4	5	6	7	8	9	10	11	12	13	14	15	16	17	18	19	C
1. Cleveland Clinic	P	P				S														
2. Rainforest Cafe	P	P		S	S	S												S	S	S
3. Niketown	P	P		S	S	S												S		
4. Virtual Vineyards			P			S									S					
5. Home Shopping Network			P	S	S	S														S
6. Peapod			P	S	S	S														S
7. The Lab				P				S												
8. McGee's Buy Three Bicycles						P														
9. Bloomingdale's					P	P													S	
10. Toys "R" Us				S		P														S
11. Old Navy				S		P														
12. Sears						P				S										S
13. Lindy's Bridal Shoppe						P				S										S
14. Retailing in China				S		P														S
15. Winn-Dixie and Dillard						S	P													
16. Stephanie's Boutique						S		P												
17. Hutch									P											
18. Fuller's										P							S			
19. Marriott										P							S			
20. Lawson Sportswear											P									
21. Michaels						S						P								
22. Merchandising Planning Problems												P	S							
23. McFaddens												S	P							
24. Star Hardware												P	S							
25. Urban Outfitters												P					S			
26. Stan's Shirts													P							
27. Pricing Problems													P							
28. Advertising Plan																P				
29. Neiman Marcus																P			S	
30. Dexter Brown																	P			
31. Tardy Trainee																	P			
32. Borders																	P	S		
33. Best Display?																	S	P		
34. Olathe Lanes		S		S													P			
35. Levi Stores		S				S													P	
36. Delta Airlines		S		S															P	
37. Best Buy			S															S	P	

P Primary Use
S Secondary Use
C Comprehensive

Cleveland Clinic

FOR YEARS, Ohio's Cleveland Clinic has ranked with the top world-class providers of medical care. It pioneered coronary bypass surgery and developed the first kidney dialysis machine. King Hussein of Jordan uses the clinic, as does the royal family of Saudi Arabia.

Big-name health care institutions like the Cleveland Clinic are after new markets for their state-of-the-art medical care, and are posing a new threat to local physicians. The expansions are also disrupting traditional relationships between physicians and their patients, physicians and their hospitals, and physicians and their fellow physicians.

Like any business, the Cleveland Clinic keeps close tabs on its core market, and the outlook wasn't all that bright. Seven Midwestern states provided 90 percent of the clinic's business, though population growth in that region is expected to be flat through the year 2000. But not so southeastern Florida, where the population is still growing and, in many areas, is highly affluent.

Southeastern Florida appeared to be a dream market. Yachts lining the canals of the Intracoastal Waterway and a ubiquitous building boom reflect wealth and growth so palpable that clinic officials have come to call it immaculate consumption. Moreover, about 20 percent of the 3.7 million residents in Dade, Broward, and Palm Beach counties are over 65 years old. By the year 2000, about 50 percent of the population will be over 45—a potential mother lode of patients. "We felt there was room for us," Dr. Kiser, CEO of Cleveland Clinic, said. "We decided to go on our own rather than wait to be invited."

When the Cleveland Clinic opened an outpatient clinic in South Florida, a war broke out. In a full-page advertisement in the *Miami Herald*, Dr. Seropian, a local physician, pulled out the stops. He likened the clinic to dingoes (wild Australian dogs) that roam the bush, eating every kind of prey. The clinic filed suit in federal district court in Fort Lauderdale, charging, among other things, that some physicians had conspired to hamper its entry into Broward County.

Famous medical institutions like the Cleveland Clinic and Mayo are victims of their own success. Many of the once-exotic procedures that they invented are now routinely available across the country, reducing patients' need to travel to the medical meccas. For instance, the Cleveland Clinic might once have had a hold on coronary bypass surgery, but no more. In 1996, more than 250,000 patients had the operation at hospitals throughout the United States.

"These clinics used to be the court of last resort for complex medical cases," says Jeff Goldsmith, national health care advisor to Ernst & Young, the accounting firm. "Now, the flooding of the country with medical specialties and high-technology equipment has forced them to adopt a different strategy."

Their expertise and reputation mean formidable competition for the local medical community. "On one level," says Jay Wolfson, a health policy expert at the University of South Florida in Tampa, "it's like bringing in a McDonald's. If you're a mom-and-pop sandwich shop on the corner, you could get wiped out."

Discussion Questions

1. Compare the Cleveland Clinic to traditional retailers.
2. What was its retail mix?
3. What factors in its environment resulted in it changing its retail mix?

Rainforest Cafe: A Wild Place to Shop and Eat

STEVE SCHUSSLER opened the first Rainforest Cafe in the Mall of America, the largest enclosed mall in the world, in 1994. Before opening this unique retail store and theme restaurant, Schussler tested the concept for 12 years, eventually building a prototype in his Minneapolis home. It was not easy sharing a house with parrots, butterflies, tortoises, and tropical fish, but Schussler's creativity resulted in a highly profitable and fast-growing chain.

In 1996, the Rainforest Cafes (http://www.rainforest.com), located in Chicago, Washington, D.C., Fort Lauderdale, and Disney World in

Orlando, Florida, in addition to the Mall of Americas in Minneapolis, Minnesota, generated $48.7 million in sales and $5.9 million in profits. They offer a unique and exciting atmosphere, recreating a tropical rain forest in 20,000 to 30,000 square feet. The cafes are divided into a restaurant seating 300 to 600 people and a retail store stocking 3,000 SKUs of unique merchandise.

Retail merchandise accounts for 30 percent of the revenues generated by the cafes. Most theme restaurants stock fewer than 20 SKUs. The merchandise emphasizes eight proprietary jungle animals featured as animated characters in the restaurant. They include Bamba the gorilla, Cha Cha the tree frog, and Ozzie the orangutan. In addition to stuffed animals and toys, the characters are utilized on clothing and gifts and in animated films and children's books.

The cafes provide an environmentally conscious family adventure. The menu features dishes such as Rasta Pasta, Seafood Galapagos, Jamaica Me Crazy, and Eye of the Ocelot (meatloaf topped with sautéed mushrooms on a bed of caramelized onions). The restaurants have live tropical birds and fish plus animated crocodiles and monkeys, trumpeting elephants, gorillas beating their chests, cascading waterfalls surrounded by cool mist, simulated thunder and lightning, continuous tropical rain storms, and huge mushroom canapés. As Schussler said, "Our cafes feature the sophistication of a Warner Brothers store with the animation of Disney."

Rainforest Cafes contribute to the local community through an outreach program. Over 300,000 schoolchildren visit the cafes each year to hear curators talk about the vanishing rain forests and endangered species. All coins dropped into the Wishing Pond and Parking Meter in the cafes are donated to causes involving endangered species and tropical deforestation.

Technology is used in the Rainforest Cafes to increase efficiency and profits. When a party enters the restaurant, the host (called a tour guide) enters the party's name in a computer which prints a "passport" indicating the party's name, size, and estimated seating time. The party can then go shopping or sightseeing, knowing it will be ushered into the dining room within 5 to 10 minutes of the assigned seating time. When the party returns, the computer tells the "safari guide" the table at which the party will be seated. Tour and safari guides communicate with each other using headsets. This technology enables the Rainforest Cafes to turn tables five to six times a day compared to two to three turns in the typical restaurant.

Discussion Questions

1. What is Rainforest Cafe's retail offering and target market?

2. Why do you think the Rainforest Cafe is so profitable?

Source: This case was prepared by Barton Weitz, University of Florida.

CASE 3

NikeTown

SOME THINGS DON'T need much explanation. When you see the Golden Arches, you think of McDonald's. When you see a swirling red, white, and blue sphere, you think of Pepsi. And when you see the curvy little swoosh, "Just do it" comes to mind.

With so many nontraditional shopping alternatives competing for the customer's attention, a key to survival in the 90s is retailers' ability to maximize their in-store environments. Customers are bored with ordinary shopping experiences. Convenience and price aren't enough. They want to be entertained.

With this in mind, NikeTown was developed to create brand awareness about Nike as a company in an informative and fun way. It was established to promote a lifestyle as much as the product. "We wanted to engage the customer in both our products and the sport and fitness lifestyle that Nike represents," said Mary Burns, director of operations at Nike in Beavertown, Oregon.

There are six NikeTown stores in operation: in Portland, Oregon; Chicago; Atlanta; New York City; Costa Mesa, California; and San Francisco's Union Square. The stores are tourist attractions and it's easy to see why. If you were to visit the Portland store (the original NikeTown), this is what you would see: Flying superhumanly above the square is a life-sized statue of Michael Jordan. Nearby are other statues: Bo Jackson lifting weights and Andre Agassi running to smash a tennis ball.

NikeTown's background design is Disneylike characters and the city of the future, featuring the cartoon show "The Jetsons." Fourteen small, themed salesrooms, which Nike calls pavilions, feature an array of sports shoes and apparel for everything from tennis to hockey.

The majority of the pavilions feature the sounds associated with that sport. If you enter one basketball pavilion (The Flight Pavilion), you'll hear the distant sound of basketballs bouncing on hardwood floors. If you enter the tennis pavilion, you'll hear the sounds of the racket smashing against the little yellow ball.

In the Land of Barkley, named after basketball player Charles Barkley, basketball hoops hold up display shelves, and basketballs support benches. The sounds being played are shoes squeaking on hardwood. The actual floor is hardwood so "wannabe" Barkleys can pull on a pair of shoes and squeak them on the floors like the big guys. The tennis pavilion features a sunken, miniature tennis court; its most popular piece is John McEnroe's broken racket. There's even a kid's pavilion, with bootie-sized Air Jordan lookalikes and a measure on a wall that shows the height of Jordan's leap. At 40 inches, it's higher than some of his small fans' heads.

Even with all of this, one of the biggest attractions is the swim and volleyball area. The seats are surfboards. There's an aquarium with tropical fish and the floor features a center section designed to simulate a glass-bottomed boat, with videos of sea life playing.

Nike cares that customers carry away fond memories of the brand rather than only a new pair of sneakers. "NikeTowns provide Nike the opportunity to present the full scope of Nike's sports and fitness lines to our customers and to educate them on the value, quality, and benefits of Nike products," said Bruce Fabel, vice president of Nike's Retail Division. "Our research indicates customers who do not make a purchase at NikeTown will be more likely to buy Nike in the future from one of our retail accounts in the area."

Nike is not the only company pushing its own stores. A growing number of big-name manufacturers are turning into mainstream merchants, opening flashy stores called flagship stores all over the nation. Swimsuit maker Speedo, children's clothing company Oshkosh B'Gosh, and shoemaker Nine West are just a few that are opening stores similar to NikeTown, showcasing their brands and enhancing their image.

Discussion Questions

1. Why are manufacturers like Nike opening their own retail outlets?

2. How will consumers and retailers that sell Nike merchandise react to these new stores?

Source: This case was prepared by Laura Hooks, University of Florida.

C A S E 4

Virtual Vineyards: Wine On-Line

VIRTUAL VINEYARDS IS an electronic retailer providing Web shopping and information service. Its mission is to ensure that customers are offered the best possible products and to make shopping for these products pleasurable. Virtual Vineyards provides customers with information about wines and specialty foods produced by small, well-respected companies and limited production products from larger and widely recognized producers. Orders may also be placed through the Web site.

Robert Olson and Peter Granoff founded the business in 1994, and it went on-line in January 1995. Olson, nicknamed the Propeller Head, worked for over 21 years in system design, operating systems, software development, engineering management, and marketing.

Before Olson began his venture into Internet-based commerce in 1994, he needed to choose a product to market over the Internet. Olson believed that this product should be one whose purchase was influenced by information at the point of sale. Also, he searched for a product that was not readily available in all varieties. In May of that year, Olson chose California wines to be that product. Because of buyers' dependence on the recommendations at the time of purchase, wine seemed to be a perfect choice. Further, smaller wineries were unable to market as well as larger ones because of high costs. Olson believed that his business could improve the exposure of smaller wineries.

Granoff, the "Cork Dork," is a well-decorated veteran of the wine industry. He was admitted into the British Court of Master Sommeliers, which recognizes him as part of an elite group who are well educated in the elements of the wine industry. Granoff developed and trademarked "Peter's Tasting Court," which allows customers to view his perceptions of each wine. The primary characteristics that influence the taste and texture of wine are rated for each that he reviews. For each characteristic, he rates the wines on a continuum including delicate to powerful, bone dry to dessert, light body to very full body, and none to heavy tannin. All terms are described in detail, so that the average person can utilize Granoff's ratings in her selections.

Olson believed that another key to a successful Internet business was to provide invaluable information about the product from an expert. Granoff's expertise made him a perfect partner for Olson's business venture, and Virtual Vineyards was subsequently founded.

The "Wine List" and "Food Shop" are the two main paths found on Virtual Vineyards' home page World Wide Web Information (http://www.virtualvin.com). The wine list details the wines available by vineyard and their corresponding prices. A link is present for each wine, and a profile is called up when prompted. The profile includes a colorful, witty description of the wine, the date Granoff tasted it, his tasting chart ratings, and foods that would be good accompaniments. Also, the customer may choose to "remember" the selection by a click of the mouse. This creates a list of all of the wines the customer thought were interesting during his browsing of the site.

An order can easily be generated with a customer's selections. If a customer has asked to remember an item, it will appear on the order form, but does not commit him to order it. The person has the option of choosing the quantity, which can be zero or more. The order form was created to be simple to use. Shipping and handling charges are listed, along with a complete list of the products being ordered. Items can be removed or added and the total recalculated as many times as needed until the order is actually sent. Payment by major credit cards is accepted, and the card account numbers are sent over the Internet. Virtual Vineyards protects its customers by using encryption and security features for processing their on-line transactions.

A reoccurring issue with electronic retailing is the costs of the merchandise and shipping. Customers sometimes pay more for items over the Internet as a compromise for its convenience. A comparison shopping study conducted in Gainesville, Florida, investigated the cost difference of using Virtual Vineyards. The wine list from the Vineyards was taken to a local wine gallery known for its extensive assortment of wines and specialty foods.

Twenty-eight of the wines were available from both retailers, and the differences between the two were calculated. (See Exhibit 1.) The wines were separated by type (e.g., zinfandel, chardonnay) and the numbers of different wines within the category were listed. Overall, the 28 wines, based on cost per bottle, are shown to be more expensive when purchased through Virtual Vineyards.

If a case (12 bottles) of wine were sent to Atlanta, for example, the shipping cost would be $29.95, further elevating the price per bottle. Both retailers offer a 10 percent discount per case, but the shipping cost does not change. Depending on the wines ordered, the cost to order and receive wines from the Vineyard may be more.

While the cost may be slightly higher from Virtual Vineyards, many services are offered, such as a customer profile. Each time a customer comes to the site, he can sign in if he has created a personal account. The account allows a shopper to keep track of his past purchases and any personal comments about a wine purchased. Further, shipping and billing information is kept to speed the order process. Virtual Vineyards can personalize service through this customer profile.

EXHIBIT 1

Prices of Wines Available from Both Retailers

	VIRTUAL VINEYARDS	LOCAL GALLERY	DIFFERENCE (+/–OVER LOCAL GALLERY)
ALL 28 WINES	$554.23	$547.46	+$6.77
SAUVIGNON BLANC (3 BOTTLES)	25.50	22.98	+2.52
CHARDONNAY (6 BOTTLES)	112.50	106.96	+5.54
ZINFANDEL (2 BOTTLES)	30.00	29.98	+0.01
PINOT NOIR (3 BOTTLES)	62.00	60.86	+1.14
MERLOT (2 BOTTLES)	51.00	52.45	–1.45
CABERNET SAUVIGNON (2 BOTTLES)	42.99	43.99	–1.00

E-mail is an additional method for consumers to learn more about wines in general and, in particular, those available through the Vineyards. Granoff has a forum called "Ask the Cork Dork," which allows customers to E-mail questions to him. He will answer them either personally through an E-mail or on this forum. A list of the top 20 questions asked and a table of contents for subject areas of questions are presented on the Internet site.

Some questions in the forum regard the quality of the wines shipped. One person asked whether Granoff could guarantee their quality, and he responded with an emphatic yes. All wines may be returned if the customer is not satisfied. If taste is an issue, then the Vineyards staff will assist in finding a more pleasing wine and exchange the product.

Virtual Vineyards strives to provide customers with a wealth of information about wines. There are many avenues for browsers of this site to learn about its characteristics and how to describe their personal wine tastes. Granoff, a well-decorated wine professional, is at their disposal via E-mail to answer any questions. Wines may also be ordered from the comfort of a shopper's home or office.

Discussion Questions

1. Do you think that wine can be successfully sold over the Internet? Why?

2. What type of consumer would utilize a site such as Virtual Vineyards? How could the owners of the site market to these people?

Source: This case was prepared by Allison T. Knott, University of Florida.

C A S E **5**

The Home Shopping Network: Dealing with a Sales Slowdown

YOU'RE CHANNEL surfing on your television and you zoom by Ivana Trump. You pass the same station again and Olivia Newton-John and Suzanne Somers are talking about jewelry. You stop surfing to watch this star-studded talk show and discover you are watching the Home Shopping Club (HSC), a subsidiary of and primary revenue source for the Home Shopping Network, Inc. (HSN).

HSN began national operations in 1985 and is headquartered in St. Petersburg, Florida. The company has nearly 4,000 employees and operates one of the largest telemarketing centers in the world. HSN reaches approximately 69 million households through its different mediums; about 5 million of them are active Home Shopping households.

HSC, a leader in TV home shopping, is the best known division of HSN. HSC sells a variety of consumer goods and services on TV programs transmitted 24 hours a day, seven days per week via satellite to cable television systems, affiliated broadcast television stations, and satellite dish receivers.

The programming is divided into shows that include a host scheduled for certain time blocks. During each live show, she presents segments with different merchandise. The average segment begins with the host presenting a piece of merchandise and giving information about the product(s) shown, including price, quality, features, and benefits. Viewers are encouraged to call and discuss the product over the phone, as it is a live program. Some callers phone with their previous experience with an HSC item. Viewers, of course, may call and place an order via a toll-free phone number. In fact, HSN receives 155,000 to 200,000 calls and ships 62,000 packages daily. After a certain period of time, however, the item is no longer available, and the host moves to another item for sale.

HSC attempts to promote sales and customer loyalty through a combination of information, entertainment, and the creation of confidence in HSC and its products. HSC executives believe that satisfied customers will be loyal and purchase merchandise on a regular basis. HSC's customer service personnel and computerized voice response units (VRUs) staff the phones in order to assist customers seven days a week, 24 hours a day.

Who are HSC's customers, and are they, in fact, loyal? Fifty percent of customers make repeat purchases in a 12-month period; average purchases per customer total $367 a year. Company information reports that 85 percent are female and are from 35 to 54 years old with a median age of 45 years. The median Home Shopping household income is $45,000.

HSC's merchandise was always known to be competitively priced and unique in that it could not be found at department stores. In 1994, HSC changes its merchandise to be more upscale with higher prices and name brands of clothing and accessories. The company reported losses, and a change was made by President and CEO James Held and Chairman Barry Diller, who were both appointed in late 1995. They decided to return to emphasizing jewelry, housewares, and like items, while maintaining a modest level of clothing. This was apparently a more appropriate mix of merchandise for home shopping as profits rose again in 1996; however, annual sales have remained at about the same level over the past four years.

"It has to be value. It has to be unique," said Held in a 1996 interview about the merchandise change. "The predominant issue is variety with some entertainment value." The products that HSN sold were in four categories: jewelry (39 percent of sales), hardgoods (37 percent), softgoods (14 percent), and cosmetics (10 percent).

Discussion Questions

1. What benefits does TV home shopping offer to consumers?

2. How do these benefits compare to those offered by other retail formats such as stores and catalogs?

3. What can the Home Shopping Club do to increase its future sales and profits?

4. Annual sales for TV home shopping networks are about $5 billion, while annual catalog sales are 10 times greater. Do you think TV home shopping sales will grow relative to catalog sales? Why?

Source: This case was prepared by Allison T. Knott, University of Florida.

CASE 6

Peapod: Electronic Grocery Shopping

GONE ARE THE DAYS of searching for a can of potato soup on aisle 10 of the grocery store and waiting in a long checkout line. Electronic shopping is here. With decreasing amounts of spare time, customers can now dial Peapod from their personal computers or, in Columbus, Ohio, through an interactive television network to order groceries without ever leaving their homes. The concept is simple. Using special software and a modem, customers order groceries by computer, look to see what items are on special, and specify a time for delivery. Ordering groceries from the television network is just as easy. Dispatch Interactive TV and Kroger are joining together in this venture. They're making the service available in Columbus to start, but will eventually expand into Indianapolis.

Peapod (http://www.peapod.com) was established in 1989 and based in Evanston, Illinois. Currently the largest interactive, on-line grocery shopping and delivery service in the United States, it offers such services in Chicago through Jewel Food Stores, San Francisco through Safeway stores, and most recently Columbus through Kroger. When customers dial up Peapod, they can gain access to 25,000 to 30,000 grocery items stocked at their nearby supermarket. The system is set up so customers can browse by department (such as produce, dairy products, and cleaning supplies) or can search by item or brand.

Type "pasta" on your computer, for example, and Peapod lists everything in the store from fettucini to wheat lasagna noodles with brand name, price, and cost per ounce. By pushing a function key, all items are sorted by cost, so the customer can choose the most economical price. With another function key, customers are able to move federally mandated nutritional labels from the back of the can to their computer screen.

To speed up the ordering process, customers can start by selecting their "frequent shopping list" of items they buy on a regular basis—say, milk, eggs, bread, Butterball turkeys, and Oreo cookies. They can request substitutions in case an item is out of stock, or leave other instructions such as "pack bread carefully" or "pick overripe bananas for banana bread."

Peapod assembles orders by using its own employees, who are referred to as shoppers. At a typical store, 40 Peapod shoppers work alongside store staff. Besides hourly wages, these shoppers receive bonuses for accuracy. Deliveries are made

Tuesday through Sunday, between the hours of 9:30 A.M. and 9 P.M. on weekdays, and until 2 P.M. on weekends. Customers pick a 90-minute window for delivery and pay electronically by credit card or through a prearranged account with the service.

Peapod takes the unusual step of guaranteeing satisfaction on every order. "If we make a mistake, we'll make it right," promises a Peapod advertisement. Perishable products are carefully selected. Refrigerated items are delivered in temperature-controlled coolers.

Peapod has about 8,500 customers in Chicago and San Francisco. Right now less than 1 percent of groceries are bought from home and most of these are done by phone or fax orders. But when Bill Gates, chairman of Microsoft Corporation, predicts that one-third of food sales will be handled electronically by 2005, people tend to listen. Peapod has already experienced a 300 percent growth rate and has secured high-profile investors like Ameritech and the Tribune Company. Peapod is making money on a market-by-market basis, but the company overall is not yet profitable because it's reinvesting funds into expansion. But its net sales for 1995 were $16 million and sales are steadily increasing currently in 1996.

"Our customer is anyone with a limited amount of time who eats," says Derrick Milligan, marketing development manager for Peapod. One customer said the service is his salvation because it saves what little amount of free time he has. "Sure, we still go to the convenience store to pick up milk and soda when we run out and we would never abandon Kelly's Meats, but it's an incredible relief to download a mind-numbing task like grocery shopping."

Of course, this top-quality convenience of shopping via computer doesn't come cheap. Chicagoans pay $4.95 a month, plus $5 per delivery and 5 percent of the final bill—about $35 monthly for somebody with an average $100 grocery bill who shops three times per month. San Franciscans and Columbians pay a flat $29.95 monthly fee. In all three cities, there's a $29.95 software set-up fee.

Peapod is not the first to attempt an on-line supermarket service. Prodigy, the largest consumer-oriented on-line network, tested the field in 1988 with grocers in nine cities, but withdrew after three years because it didn't attract a substantial number of subscribers.

To Andrew Parkinson, the founder and CEO of Peapod, "Prodigy's problem was the same as virtually every other company that has gone into the supermarket home delivery business." They focus on the telemarketing aspect of the business, but fail to adequately get involved with the fulfillment aspects. Once they transmit an order to the retailer, they wash their hands of it, leaving it to the retailer to assemble the order and employ a third-party courier to deliver it.

Discussion Questions

1. Taking the customer's perspective, compare grocery shopping from Peapod and the other types of food retailers described in Chapter 2. What are the advantages and disadvantages of shopping from Peapod?

2. What types of customers will be attracted to Peapod? What types of customers will continue to shop at grocery stores?

Source: This case was prepared by Laura Hooks and Heather Zuilkoski, University of Florida.

CASE 7

The Lab: AKA the Antimall

IMAGINE SHOPPING AT a "mall" with broken walls scribbled with graffiti, weeds creeping up through the cracks in the cement floor, and ripped-up carpet—a mall without chrome, skylights, and food courts—one where you won't find the all too familiar Gap, Victoria's Secret, or Starbucks Coffee either.

This is The Lab, located in Costa Mesa, California. Its nickname is the Antimall. Its foundation consists of recycled oil barrels. And at the center of the mall is a "living room" sitting area that contains thrift shop furniture, all for sale. You won't hear Muzak piped into the mall, but you may hear live alternative rock.

It prides itself on being the first mall in the United States to be conceived for the X generation. This mall is aimed at the ultra-eccentric crowd who dare to be different. It's for those who are sick of the traditional mall with its cubicle stores that all seem similar to each other. The Lab is for the shopper who prefers a shopping experience scented with attitude, decay, and patchouli. Its appeal is to the 20-something crowd, although baby boomers, trying to relive their lost youth, can be found here too.

Shaheen Sadeghi, The Lab's creator, saw a trend of young adults opting to shop at Goodwill and Salvation Army instead of traditional stores. He found a niche that had not been served yet—hence the creation of the Antimall. Sadeghi took over a vacant military supply warehouse and transformed it into The Lab. "Malls are all marble and buffed out," Sadehi said. "This building is raw, soulful, and comfortable, a place where you can sip coffee, play chess, or read a book."

Although the luxurious South Coast Plaza is just down the road from The Lab, Sadeghi doesn't expect The Lab to compete with other malls in the area. He sees it as strong enough to support a smaller, alternative way to shopping. The age group targeted by The Lab represents a huge success opportunity because it is "the only group of people who actually want to spend more of their discretionary time shopping," said Watts Wacker, a futurist with Yankelovich and Partners in New York. Unfortunately for conventional retailers, these consumers are also "a group of people who feel unbelievably mistreated by the mainstream," according to Wacker.

The Lab has exposed wooden ceilings, massive iron roof beams, and cement floors. It is anchored by Urban Outfitters, which sells hip clothing and home decor, and Tower Records, which operates a large alternative music store. Urban Outfitters is the biggest store in The Lab. Here you can find such things as Q T-shirts meant to be worn a size too small, bowling bags cum evening bags, and black sunglasses. This cool, funky, freethinking apparel and home furnishings chain is excelling in the Generation X appeal. Its intention is to be a nonchain store. It is sure to win the hearts of those who hate pastels, orderly displays, and light wood interiors. Urban Outfitters stores are decorated in a style best described as a junk store. But behind the blown-apart dry walls, Salvation Army props, and haphazard fixtures is a carefully calculated, well–thought-out strategy that ropes in its audience.

Tower Alternative, a subsidiary of the Tower Records chain, was created specifically for The Lab, and stocks recordings of trendy bands such as The Cranberries, Green Day, and Garbage, as well as unsigned local bands from the area. It carries some mainstream pop, but little in the way of classical or country. Its stores rarely close before midnight.

The Lab houses more than a dozen shops, including a comic book shop called Collector's Library and a florist called Weeds. You can find ultracamp plastic Elvis busts and religious kitsch items at the Spanish Fly. Then you can drop by The Closet and pick up all your surfing, skating, and snow boarding equipment. And if you're tired from all the shopping, stop for a bite to eat at Havana, the Cuban restaurant, or for coffee at the Gypsy Den. But don't forget about your appointment at the interactive community garden where shoppers are encouraged to plant seeds so they have a stake in coming back to see how the plants do.

The retailer embraces the tastes, peculiarities, and interests of its customers. The background music in the stores is 100 percent alternative. Salespeople, who are often indistinguishable from the customers, are trained to be laid back. To be sure Urban Outfitters doesn't remind customers of their parents' favorite department store, it hires employees with tattoos and pierced body parts. The stores are filled with funky candles, affordable cotton throws, inexpensive T-shirts, and wool sweaters.

Apart from Urban Outfitters and Tower Alternatives, The Lab has no large chain stores because Sadeghi believes Generation X opposes the homogenization of American culture. Instead of having a food court, The Lab sells health foods and specialty coffees in an area furnished with lumpy sofas to lounge on.

The Lab also capitalizes on Generation X's desire for good causes. Instead of car expos and fashion shows, The Lab sponsors charity events. For example, it invited shoppers to buy broken tiles to decorate walls. Proceeds went to a charity for the homeless.

Discussion Questions

1. What characteristics of the X generation are reflected in The Lab?
2. Do you think antimalls like The Lab will be successful throughout the United States? Why?

Source: This case was prepared by Laura Hooks and Heather Zuilkoski, University of Florida.

The McGees Buy Three Bicycles

THE MCGEES LIVE in Riverside, California, west of Los Angeles. Terry is a physics professor at the University of California, Riverside. His wife Cheryl is a volunteer 10 hours a week at the Crisis Center. They have two children: Judy, age 10, and Mark, age 8.

In February, Cheryl's parents sent her $50 to buy a bicycle for Judy's birthday. They bought Judy her first bike when she was five. Now they wanted to buy her a full-size bike for her 11th birthday. Even though Cheryl's parents felt every child should have a bike, Cheryl didn't think Judy really wanted one. Judy and most of her friends didn't ride their bikes often and she was afraid to ride to school because of traffic. So Cheryl decided to buy her the cheapest full-size bicycle she could find.

Since most of Judy's friends didn't have full-size bikes, she didn't know much about them and had no preferences for a brand or type. To learn more about the types available and their prices, Cheryl and Judy checked the JCPenney catalog. After looking through the catalog, Judy said the only thing she cared about was the color. She wanted a blue bike, blue being her favorite color.

Using the Yellow Pages, Cheryl called several local retail outlets selling bikes. To her surprise, she found that a department store actually had the best price for a 26-inch bicycle, even lower than Toys "R" Us and Wal-Mart.

Cheryl drove to the department store, went straight to the toy department, and selected a blue bicycle before a salesperson approached her. She took the bike to the cash register and paid for it. Since making the purchase, the McGees found out that the bike was cheap in all senses. The chrome plating on the wheels was very thin and rusted away in six months. Both tires split and had to be replaced.

A year later, Cheryl's grandparents sent another $50 for a bike for Mark. Based on their experience with Judy's bike, the McGees by then realized that the lowest-priced bike might not be the least expensive option in the long run. Mark is very active and somewhat careless, so the McGee's wanted to buy a sturdy bike. Mark said he wanted a red, 10-speed, lightweight imported bike with lots of accessories: headlights, special foot pedals, and so forth. The McGees were concerned that Mark wouldn't maintain an expensive bike with all these accessories.

When they saw an ad for a bicycle sale at Montgomery Ward, Cheryl and Terry went to the store with Mark. A salesperson approached them at an outdoor display of bikes and directed them to the sporting goods department inside the store. There they found row after row of red three-speed bikes with minimal accessories—the type of bike Cheryl and Terry felt was ideal for Mark.

A salesperson approached them and tried to interest them in a more expensive bike. Terry dislikes salespeople trying to push something on him and interrupted her in mid-sentence. He said he wanted to look at the bikes on his own. With a little suggestion, Mark decided he wanted one of these bikes. His desire for accessories was satisfied when they bought a wire basket for the bike.

After buying a bike for Mark, Terry decided he'd like a bike for himself to ride on weekends. Terry had ridden bikes since he was five. In graduate school, before he was married, he'd owned a 10-speed. He frequently took 50-mile rides with friends. But he hadn't owned a bike since moving to Riverside 15 years ago.

Terry didn't know much about current types of touring bicycles. He bought a copy of *Touring* at the news stand to see what was available. He also went to the library to read *Consumer Reports'* evaluation of touring bikes. Based on this information, he decided he wanted a Serrato. It had all the features he wanted: light weight, durable construction, and flexible setup. When Terry called the discount stores and bicycle shops, he found they didn't carry Serrato. He then decided he might not really need a bike. After all, he'd done without one for 15 years.

One day, after lunch, he was walking back to his office and saw a small bicycle shop. The shop was run down with bicycle parts scattered across the floor. The owner, a young man in grease-covered shorts, was fixing a bike. As Terry was looking around, the owner approached him and asked him if he liked to bicycle. Terry said he used to but had given it up when he moved to Riverside. The owner said that was a shame because there were a lot of nice places to tour around Riverside.

As their conversation continued, Terry mentioned his interest in a Serrato and his disappointment in not finding a store in Riverside that sold them. The owner said that he could order a Serrato for Terry but that they weren't very reliable. He suggested a Ross and showed Terry one he had in stock. Terry thought the $400 price was too high, but the owner convinced him to try it next weekend. They would ride together in the country. The owner and some of his friends took a 60-mile tour with Terry. Terry really enjoyed the experience, recalling his college days. After the tour, Terry bought the Ross.

Discussion Questions

1. Outline the decision-making process for each of the McGees' bicycle purchases.

2. Compare the different purchase processes for the three bikes. What stimulated each of them? What factors were considered in making the store choice decisions and purchase decisions?

3. Construct a multiattribute model for each purchase decision. How do the attributes considered and importance weights vary for each decision?

Source: This case was prepared by Barton A. Weitz, University of Florida.

CASE 9

Bloomingdale's: Customer Service Reaches Abroad

IN **1872,** brothers Lyman and Joseph Bloomingdale opened their first retail outlet, the East Side Bazaar, in New York City. Bloomingdale's, now a division of Federated Department Stores, has grown into a national chain with 21 stores in Florida, Illinois, Maryland, Massachusetts, Minnesota, New York, New Jersey, Pennsylvania, and California.

With a reputation for quality, creativity, and uniqueness, Bloomingdale's has managed to stay at the forefront of retailing worldwide. The chain is known for its breadth of merchandise in all categories for women, men, children, and home as well as for its outstanding customer service. Bloomingdale's is more committed than ever to increasing and perfecting customer service. Personal shopping services available by appointment or by phone give customers access to all of Bloomingdale's unique merchandise collections. Bridal registry, delivery services, coat and package checks, restaurants, and gift wrapping are just some of the complimentary services available at Bloomingdale's. The retailer has mandated that every employee's goal is to make shopping an easy and enjoyable experience for each customer.

Due to Bloomie's unique merchandise and service it has become a tourist destination. Foreign customers are from almost every country with a strong representation from Japan, the United Kingdom, Brazil, Argentina, Germany, Australia, and Canada. These international patrons are affluent, educated, and typically from 35 to 55 years old.

Bloomingdale's has an extensive marketing department with professionals who specifically target international customers. Patti Freeman Evans, senior manager of international marketing for Bloomingdale's, says, "The mission of our department is to communicate with both current and potential customers who do not live near a Bloomingdale's location. We want to make it easy for everyone to shop at Bloomingdale's." To accomplish this mission, the department has developed a number of programs.

The international marketing division offers numerous services: shopping assistance in various languages; assistance with shipping; delivery to local hotels; news and information regarding what's happening at Bloomingdale's; and appointments with in-store services such as personal shoppers, alterations, spas, and beauty services. There is also a staff of visitors center consultants to assist traveling customers with any special needs. Special discounts, service coupons, and other benefits for tourist customers are available.

The International Club is a special program for foreign customers. Membership is available to any customer visiting from abroad who signs up in a Bloomingdale's store. It entitles them to exclusive benefits not offered to the general public: special in-store offers, gifts, services, and savings; Bloomingdale's catalogs mailed directly to their homes; semiannual editions of Bloomingdale's *International Club Newsletter;* notification of special events; private invitations; and more.

Most Bloomingdale's stores have International Service Desks/Visitors Centers. When a foreign customer comes to this area or customer service and asks for shopping assistance in her native language, the consultant will find an associate who speaks that language. If the associate is working elsewhere in the store that day, he will be released from his normal responsibilities to accompany the customer for as long as he is needed. A considerable number of international customers take advantage of this service.

Source: This case was prepared by Allison T. Knott, University of Florida.

Discussion Questions

1. What are the unique needs of international customers and what services can Bloomingdale's offer to satisfy those needs?

2. Are international customers an attractive market to pursue? Why?

3. Will their needs vary depending on their nationality?

4. How can Bloomingdale's market its international services to attract more international customers?

CASE **10**

Toys "R" Us: A New Beginning

"SANDY, WILL YOU and Johnny please stop fighting. We're leaving as soon as we find Glamour Barbie for the birthday party you're going to tonight. I just don't understand why we can't find them—they should be here with the other dolls. Now we just need someone to help us find it. Finally I think I see a guy who works here."

"Excuse me, could you tell me if you carry Glamour Barbie and, if so, where I can find it?"

"Ah, no. I just stock shelves, but I think maybe on aisle 10."

"Come on kids, we'll just go to Wal-Mart and we can get everything we need in one stop."

Has this type of situation ever happened to you? Have you ever felt like you are the only customer in the store, yet when you do find an employee, he hasn't got a clue? This type of situation was becoming synonymous with Toys "R" Us. It was a big powerhouse that didn't have to rely on customer service to create sales. Instead, its toys practically sold themselves because it was the only big-store toy discounter of its kind for 16 years, and consumers were willing to search, on their own, through piles of toys to find what they wanted. But with retail discounters and superstores, such as Wal-Mart, Kmart, and Target, becoming increasingly competitive in the toy industry, Toys "R" Us had to implement a major restructuring of its organization. And after having to shut down 25 of its 650 U.S. stores, including 12 Kids "R" Us stores,

Toys "R" Us realized it needed to revamp its business or prepare to surrender to the competitors.

Michael Goldstein, chief executive of Toys "R" Us, approved a $270 million restructuring plan for 1996 to get Toys "R" Us back on the right track. The main agenda was to expand and remodel its stores to better suit its customers' needs and wants and to take back its market share from competitors. First, Toys "R" Us introduced Babies "R" Us to compete directly with Baby Superstores and other baby-oriented stores. These stores offer parents a one-stop shopping trip for everything a baby needs—from diapers and clothing to nursery furniture and baby food and formula. Each store provides more than 30,000 items for babies with a floor plan featuring panoramic viewing, wide aisles, and skylights. The first store opened in May 1996 in Westbury, Long Island, and the chain plans to launch nine more before the year's end.

Along with these new stores, Toys "R" Us has developed "Concept 2000," which will be unveiled in approximately 14 locations, three of which will be retrofits of existing stores. These are Toys "R" Us/KidsWorld superstores which combine all of the "R" Us concepts under one roof. Superstores are an advantage to Toys "R" Us because these stores only require 90,000 square feet, whereas dividing products into different stores requires more space. It is also an advantage to consumers not only because of lower prices, but also because they can pick up all their children's needs and wants in one place.

Although superstores are an advantage, they can also discourage consumers because of their large size. Therefore, Toys "R" Us is not focusing all of its efforts on these stores only. In addition to the Concept 2000 format it's planning to open 35 new toy stores and 8 to 10 new Kids "R" Us stores in the United States this year. Internationally, it will add 55 new stores, including 20 franchise stores.

Many investors think that Toys "R" Us has gone about as far as it can in the United States, where it has captured about 23 percent of the $23 billion toy-and-video market. In their view, it will need strong international growth to earn more profits. "They can put up these new stores, but they are pretty saturated," said Greg Jackson, a portfolio manager at Yacktman Asset Management in Chicago, which has invested about $1.3 million in Toys "R" Us. Jackson feels there is tremendous growth potential internationally, particularly in Japan.

But despite the criticism, Toys "R" Us believes it is traveling down the right path by expanding domestically and abroad. It feels that there is going to be a larger demand in the near future because of several new product introductions, like new Star Wars figures, new Nintendo 64 videos, and toys that spin off films like *101 Dalmatians* and *Space Jam*. And when these toys fade out, there will always be new ones to take their place. Toys "R" Us feels the industry does have room to flourish—kids will always want toys, so it's just a matter of carrying the right ones.

Goldstein must keep in mind that he can't spend too much money revamping his stores because it could ruin his already shaky profit margins—but if he spends too little, his efforts may be for nothing.

The increased pressure from competition also forces Toys "R" Us to focus more on providing quality customer service and realizing that since the consumers now have control of the steering wheel, they have the power to decide the future of Toys "R" Us.

However, Toys "R" Us can help guide consumers by changing its no-frills, service-short shopping experience. Parents have grown intolerant of the lack of attention and the haphazard arrangements at Toys "R" Us, especially when they can go right down the street to a retail discounter and purchase products for the same price or sometimes even lower. Toys "R" Us must now find new ways to attract 1990s customers who have become accustomed to price wars and their spoils, and who are always searching for fresh concepts and new merchandise. The "supermarket style" Toys "R" Us has been noted for—which entails crowded aisles, toys stacked so high they cannot be reached, and plain decor—must be changed to a more desirable atmosphere for the consumer. Goldstein has recognized and begun rectifying this problem by reducing inventory carried in each store from 15,000 down to 11,000 and training the staff more carefully and requiring them to be more knowledgeable about toys.

As Goldstein sits in his office at company headquarters in Paramus, New Jersey, he does not seem too worried about the hard times. He points to a comic strip on the wall that celebrates his company and its world-renowned name. "This is one from the time we were really big. And we'll be there again."

Discussion Questions

1. Do you think that Toys "R" Us's expanding in the United States is an error in judgment? (Do you think this will overexpose Toys "R" Us?)

2. Do you think that Kids World superstores and Babies "R" Us will create a competitive edge for Toys "R" Us?

3. In what ways could Toys "R" Us improve its customer service?

Source: This case was prepared by Allison T. Knott, University of Florida.

CASE 11

The Gap Opens Old Navy

ARE DENIM JEANS, flannels, and T-shirts your favorite attire? If so, listen up. The Gap has started a new chain called Old Navy Clothing Stores. Analysts believe that the new division will eventually have as many stores as The Gap itself, which currently has over 1,426 stores worldwide. The Old Navy Clothing Stores will have the same kind of merchandise as The Gap, but will be able to keep its prices low by using lighter-weight, less expensive fabrics in addition to scaled-down store decor and lower-priced locations in strip shopping malls.

Old Navy is a part of The Gap's three-tiered retailing strategy. The Banana Republic chain is at the high end of the market. The Gap is in the middle, and Old Navy is at the low end.

The initial launch included three Old Navy stores in the Bay Area as well as one near Los Angeles. Others opened in Southern California,

Connecticut, and New York. The Gap first entered this niche market with the Gap Warehouse. The Gap Warehouse was a toned-down version of the familiar Gap shop featuring an assortment of basics—jeans, sweatshirts, and the like—at discount store prices.

According to the NDP Group (which tracks retail spending by direct queries of customers), consumers will spend nearly a third of their apparel dollars—$40 billion of them—at discount department stores, off-pricers, and factory outlets in 1997. There are several explanations for the strength of discount stores. The main attraction is the price. A cautious and financially unstable society has not wanted to invest a large percentage of its income on clothing, especially when there are house payments and doctor bills to be taken care of first.

It is not only price that drives consumers into discount stores for apparel. The industry has made great efforts in assortment, quality, and fashion. Discount stores have also come a long way in improving display, borrowing ideas from regular stores. Even the Old Navy discount Gap stores pride themselves on being clean, spacious places for customers to shop.

The Gap hopes Old Navy will serve as its next growth vehicle. Steven Kernkraut, an analyst at Bear Sterns, predicts Old Navy will steal a significant amount of business from Target and Sears. Kernkraut and other analysts predict that Old Navy will generate as much as $3 billion in revenues by the end of the decade, producing well over 20 percent annual growth in both revenues and earnings.

Discussion Questions

1. What types of growth strategy is The Gap pursuing with Old Navy?

2. Evaluate this growth strategy compared to The Gap's other growth strategies with Gap Kids and Baby Gap.

Source: This case prepared by Laura Hooks, University of Florida.

CASE **12**

Sears Rebounds from the Brink of Bankruptcy

SEARS, ROEBUCK and Company—an American institution—was on the verge of bankruptcy in 1992. Profits were only 0.7 percent on $31 billion in revenues. The company was experiencing significant cash flow problems. To avert disaster, then-CEO Ed Brennen decided to make a change.

Arthur Martinez was hired from Saks Fifth Avenue as the head of merchandising. In 1995, he was named CEO upon Brennen's retirement. He came to Sears with a mission to turn around the failing retailer. He took an aggressive position and began by cutting over 50,000 jobs, closing 113 stores, and eliminating the Sears Big Book, its 97-year-old catalog. Some thought these dramatic changes would be the demise of the 80-year-old retailer.

Sears has some of the most recognized brand names in hard goods: Kenmore appliances and Craftsman tools. Both brands ranked in the top 10 of 500 brands evaluated by consumers in a recent study. After touring stores, Martinez was struck by the store layout in which women purchasing lingerie would be next to men buying power tools. Martinez decided to place more emphasis on apparel, particularly women's apparel, in the mall-based department stores.

John Costello (executive vice president for marketing) developed and launched an advertising campaign, "The Softer Side of Sears," announcing this new direction in September 1993.

This shift to a more fashion-oriented department store was a result of extensive research showing that Sears management thought of their stores as men's stores. However, it was discovered that 70 percent of the purchases were by women.

Other changes brought on since the arrival of Martinez have included the addition of cosmetics departments to over 200 stores. Remodeling has also been part of Sears' overhaul. In mid-1996, over half of the renovation program was complete. About 6 million square feet of apparel selling space was added between 1994 and 1996; most of this space was converted from storage and office space.

Private-label merchandise has played an important role in Sears' new positioning. Circle of Beauty, an in-house brand of cosmetics, is expected to produce $500 million in revenues in 1996. Canyon River Blues, the new private-label brand of jeans and casual wear, reached $100 million in revenues only seven months after its introduction in 1995.

Before 1992, customers could only pay by cash or their Sears credit card. Martinez felt that this alienated customers and lowered the company's sales. Therefore, he changed this long-time policy, and the stores began to accept major credit cards.

By the end of 1996, Sears will once again be a retail-only company. Executives and board members agreed with prompting from Martinez to sell off Allstate Insurance Co., Homart, and Dean Witter. Sears also finalized the sale of its 50 percent ownership in the Prodigy on-line system.

Discussion Questions

1. If you were developing a new strategy for Sears, would you focus on apparel or hard goods in your mall-based department stores? Why?

2. Sears is planning to open one chain of home stores selling appliances, furniture, housewares, and bedding and another chain competing with Home Depot and Lowe's. How would you evaluate these new business opportunities for Sears?

Source: This case was prepared by Allison T. Knott, University of Florida.

CASE 13

Lindy's Bridal Shoppe

LOCATED IN RURAL Wilsonville (population 10,000), Lindy's Bridal Shoppe, a small bridal store, sells bridal gowns, prom gowns, accessories, and silk flowers. It also rents men's formal wear and performs various alteration services.

Lindy Armstrong, age 33, has owned the store since its founding in March 1997. She's married to a high school teacher and is the mother of three young children. A former nurse, she found the demands of hospital schedules left too little time for her young family. An energetic, active woman with many interests, she wanted to continue to work but also have time with her children.

The silk flowers market enabled Lindy to combine an in-home career with child rearing. She started Lindy's Silk Flowers with $75 of flower inventory in Vernon, a small town of about 1,000 people 10 miles from Wilsonville. Working out of her home, she depended on word-of-mouth communication among her customers (mainly brides) to bring in business. As Lindy's Silk Flowers prospered, a room was added onto the house to provide more space for the business. Lindy was still making all the flowers herself. Her flower-making schedule kept her extremely busy—long hours were the norm.

Lindy was approached by a young photographer named Dan Morgan, who proposed establishing a one-stop bridal shop. In this new business, Dan would provide photography, Lindy would provide silk flowers, and another partner, Karen Ross (who had expertise in the bridal market), would provide gowns and accessories. The new store would be located in Vernon in a rented structure. Shortly before the store was to open, Dan and Karen decided not to become partners and Lindy became the sole owner. She knew nothing about the bridal business. Having no merchandise or equipment, Lindy was drawn to an ad announcing that a bridal store in a major city was going out of business. She immediately called and arranged to meet the owner. Subsequently she bought all his stock (mannequins, racks, and carpet) for $4,000. The owner also gave her a crash course in the bridal business.

From March 1994 to December 1996, Lindy Armstrong owned and operated a bridal gown and silk flowers store named Lindy's Bridal Shoppe in Vernon. The location was chosen primarily because it was close to her home. While Vernon is a very small town, Lindy felt that location wasn't a critical factor in her store's success. She maintained that people would travel some distance to make a purchase as important as a bridal gown. Rent was $250 per month plus utilities. Parking was a problem.

During this period, Lindy's Bridal Shoppe grew. Bridal gowns and accessories as well as prom gowns sold well. As the time approached for Lindy to renew her lease, she wondered about the importance of location. A move to Wilsonville might be advisable.

A much larger town than Vernon, Wilsonville is the site of a state university. Lindy decided to move.

General Business Description

The majority of Lindy's Bridal Shoppe's current sales are made to individuals who order bridal gowns from the rack or from the catalogs of three major suppliers. At the time of the order, the customer pays a deposit (usually half of the purchase price). The balance is due in 30 days. Lindy would like payment in full at the time of ordering regardless of the delivery date. But payment is often delayed until delivery. Once ordered, a gown must be taken and the bill paid when delivered.

No tuxedos are carried in the store so customers must order from catalogs. Fitting jackets and shoes are provided to help patrons size their purchases. Lindy's Bridal Shoppe rents its men's formal wear from suppliers. Payment from the customer is due on delivery.

Certain times of the year see more formal events than others. Many school proms are held during late April and May, while June, July, and August are big months for weddings. Since traditional dates for weddings are followed less and less closely, Lindy believes that the business is becoming less seasonal, though January and February are quite slow.

Promotion Practices

Lindy's Bridal Shoppe engages in various promotional activities but is constrained by its limited financial ability. The firm has no operating budget, which prevents any formal appropriation for advertising expenses.

Newspaper ads constitute the primary promotional medium, though radio is occasionally used. Ads for prom gowns are run only during prom season. These ads usually feature a photograph of a local high school student in a Lindy's Bridal Shoppe gown plus a brief description of the student's activities.

Other promotional activities include bridal shows at a local mall. Lindy feels these have been very successful, though they're a lot of work. A recent prom show in a local high school used students as models. This proved to be an excellent way to stimulate sales. Lindy hopes to go into several other area high schools during the next prom season though this will demand much planning.

Personnel

Lindy Armstrong—the sole owner and also the manager of the firm—finds it hard to maintain a capable work force. A small company, Lindy's Bridal Shoppe can't offer premium salaries for its few positions. There's one full-time salesperson. The part-time staff includes a salesperson, alterations person, bookkeeper, and custodian.

Lindy handles all the paperwork. Her responsibilities include paying bills, ordering merchandise and supplies, hiring and firing personnel, fitting customers, and selling various items. She makes all the major decisions that directly affect the firm's operations. She also makes all the silk flowers herself. It's time consuming, but she isn't satisfied with how anyone else makes them.

Merchandise Offerings

Lindy's Bridal Shoppe's major product lines are new wedding, prom, and party gowns. No used gowns are sold. Discontinued styles or gowns that have been on the rack for a year are sold at reduced prices, primarily because discoloration is a major problem. Gowns tend to yellow after hanging on the racks for a year.

A wide variety of accessories are provided. Lindy believes it's important that her customers not have to go anywhere else for them. These accessories include shoes, veils, headpieces, jewelry, and foundations. Slips may be rented instead of purchased.

One room of Lindy's Bridal Shoppe is used only to prepare silk flowers.

Service Offerings

Lindy's Bridal Shoppe's major service offering is fitting and alteration. Most gowns must be altered, for which there's a nominal charge. Lindy Armstrong feels that personal attention and personal service set her apart from her competitors. Stressing customer satisfaction, she works hard to please each customer. This isn't always easy. Customers can be picky, and it takes time to deal with unhappy people.

Location

Lindy's Bridal Shoppe is located at the end of Wilsonville's main through street. Initially Lindy didn't think location was important to her bridal store's success, but she's changed her mind. Whereas business was good in Vernon, it's booming in Wilsonville. Vehicular traffic is high, and there's adequate, if not excess, parking.

Lindy's Bridal Shoppe has a $2\frac{1}{2}$ year lease. Rent ($1,800 per month) includes heat and water, but Lindy's Bridal Shoppe must pay for interior decoration. The physical facility is generally attractive, with open and inviting interior display areas. But some areas both inside and outside the store have an unfinished look.

Some storage areas require doors or screens to enhance the interior's appearance. The fitting room ceilings are unfinished, and the carpeting inside the front door may be unsafe. One other interior problem is insufficient space. There seems to be inadequate space for supporting activities such as flower preparation, customer fittings and merchandise storage, which gives the store a cluttered look.

Several external problems exist. The signs are ineffective, and there's a strong glare on the front windows. This detracts from the effectiveness of the overall appearance and interior window displays. The parking lot needs minor maintenance. Parking lines should be painted and curbs must be repaired. Much should be done to add color and atmosphere through basic landscaping.

Competition

Lindy's Bridal Shoppe is the only bridal shoppe in Wilsonville. Lindy believes she has four main competitors. Whitney's Bridal Shoppe is 20 miles from Wilsonville; Ender's Brides, a new shop with a good operation, is in Spartan City, 30 miles away; Carole's is a large, established bridal shop in Smithtown, 40 miles distant; and Gowns-n-Such is in Andersonville, 15 miles away. A new store in Yorktown (also 15 miles away) is selling used gowns and discontinued styles at very reduced prices. Lindy watches this new- and used-gown store closely.

Financial Considerations

Basic financial information includes

1. Markup: 50 percent.
2. 1997 sales: $200,000 (estimated).
3. Average inventory: $70,000.
4. Turnover: 3.0 (approximately).
5. Annual expenses are

   Rent: $19,200.
   Labor: $24,000.
   Utilities: $7,000.
   Supplies: $12,000.
   Equipment: $4,000.
   Miscellaneous: $4,000.

6. Estimated total costs ($200,000 sales): $170,200.
7. Implied profit including owner's salary: $29,800.
8. Capital invested (equipment, $8,000; inventory, $70,000): $78,000.
9. ROI: $5,800/$78,000 = 7.4 percent. (Assume owner salary of $24,000 per year.)

The Future

Lindy Armstrong is uncertain about the future. She enjoys the business but feels that she's working very hard and not making much money. During all the years of Lindy's Bridal Shoppe's operation, she hasn't taken a salary. She works 60 hours or more a week. Business is excellent and growing, but she's tired She has even discussed selling the business and returning to nursing.

Discussion Questions

1. Could Lindy change the emphasis of her merchandise mix to increase her sales?

2. Which products should have more emphasis? Which should have less?

3. What personnel decisions must Lindy face to improve her business?

4. How could someone like Lindy Armstrong balance the demands of her family and her business?

5. If one of Lindy's competitors were to offer her $150,000 for her business, should she sell?

Source: This case was prepared by Linda F. Felicetti and Joseph P. Grunewald, Clarion University of Pennsylvania.

CASE **14**

Retailing in China

SARAH HARRISON is president of Retail Expertise Associates (REA), a retail consulting firm based in Atlanta, Georgia. After 15 years in retailing culminating as a general merchandise manager for a major department chain, Sarah decided that she wanted to get out of the corporate retailing world and start her own business. She began REA as a consulting firm offering merchandising expertise to small and midsized department stores in the eastern United States.

Recently Sarah was contacted by one of her former professors after he returned from a three-month stay in the People's Republic of China, where he was teaching and doing research on Chinese marketing practices. Her professor had visited several department stores in the Shanghai area, all of which seemed to be in need of professional assistance. During his meetings with a department store general manager and his staff in Suzhou (a city of about 4 million people two hours west of Shanghai), the general manager of the store expressed an interest in working with Sarah or another retail consultant to help him identify the areas where improvements could be made.

Sarah agreed to go to China for a week of consulting with the First Department Store. As soon as she arrived in China, Sarah began a diary of her experiences. The following journal entries relate to her consulting work in China.

Day 1

Following a 16-hour flight from the United States, I was met at Shanghai airport by Professor Wong (a business professor from the university of Suzhou) and an interpreter hired by him to work with me during my stay. After two hours in transit from the Shanghai airport, we finally arrived at my hotel in Suzhou. It was late at night local time, and I was completely exhausted.

Day 2

When I got up it was overcast, which reminded me that I had forgotten to pack an umbrella. Buying an umbrella seemed like a good reason to take my first outing in China. I had plenty of time since Professor Wong was not scheduled to pick me up until late that afternoon. My hotel was on Suzhou's main shopping street, the Street of the People. I walked a few blocks and saw a multistory building with a large sign in English over its front door. The sign said WELCOME FOREIGN VISITORS—FIRST DEPARTMENT STORE. Since this was the store I had been invited to work with, it seemed like a good opportunity to take a quick look at the place as a customer, before employees in the store knew who I was.

As I approached the building, it became evident that the facade and entry were quite dirty and not very inviting. The outside of the building was simply bare concrete, badly discolored from the smog, which I had read was a hazard of city life in China. The entrance was a small door barely wide enough for one person to go through, and there was a small line of customers waiting to push their way in. The store was crammed with items for sale which were packed together with what seemed to me to be little organization. For instance, the first floor had sunglasses, umbrellas, cosmetics, appliances, bicycles, and motorcycles.

I was also struck by the number of employees in the store. Every merchandise area had several employees standing around. I was served by five different people as I tried to purchase an umbrella. As for buying the umbrella, what an experience! No one spoke English, despite the store's billboard welcoming foreign visitors. Through a combination of head nods and hand signals, I managed to select the umbrella I wanted. I took out some Chinese money to pay, but instead the sales clerk gave me what looked like a bill and pointed frantically toward another booth. It turned out that I had to take the invoice to another counter where my payment was computed on an abacus and change was made from a shoe box. Then I returned to the umbrella counter with the paid receipt to claim my purchase, which was neatly wrapped much like a present. I waited in line at the payment counter for almost 20 minutes and waited another 10 minutes back at the umbrella counter to pick up my purchase. The whole process took the better part of an hour. By the time I was done, I was frustrated and exhausted. By then it was midmorning and the store was getting crowded, so I decided to go back to my hotel to prepare for Professor Wong's arrival.

Professor Wong came by in the early afternoon to take me on a tour of Suzhou, an ancient city famous for its gardens and canals. We didn't go into any stores while we were on the tour, but I couldn't help noticing how many small retailers were in town. Most operate out of cramped stalls lining the side streets of the city. However, the main shopping street is wide and free of vendors. It resembles many shopping districts in the West. Stores on the street have conventional facades and fairly spacious interiors. People line the street throughout the day. It seems like this would be a retailer's paradise!

Day 3

Early this morning, Professor Wong met me at my hotel and brought me to my first meeting with the managers of the First Department Store. We were met at the front door by some of the store's managers and led to an elevator in the back of the store. The area near the elevator seemed untidy, and I thought we were taking a freight elevator to go up to the executive offices. However, Professor Wong informed me that this is the only elevator in the building and that it is used for both freight and customers, though most customers use the stairs. We entered a meeting room filled with overstuffed sofas and chairs. A table in the middle of the room held several teapots and cups. Inside were the general manager and his top assistants. Our introductions were brief. It turned out that the general manager is a close associate of Professor Wong. In fact, Professor Wong has done a lot of consulting for the store and has written a book on retailing based in part on his experiences at First. This was news to me, but will, no doubt, explain a lot about the job and the store's expectations from my work. In my research on

China, I had read about a system of relying on connections to do business (referred to as *Guanxi* in Chinese). It is an important part of getting things done. My readings explained how the Chinese accumulate favors like IOUs from each other and regularly trade them to do business. As I recalled that piece of information from my reading, I wondered who would be indebted to whom as a result of my work for First Department Store, and what obligations I'd be incurring during my meetings with the store's management.

My first exposure to a Chinese-style business meeting was an eye opener. I expected to begin with some questions to get a feel for the store's situation and where its main problems and challenges lie. Instead, the general manager pulled out a prepared speech, which he proceeded to read to me. The speech described the history of the store, how it operates as a state-owned entity, and how it is gearing itself up to eventually be sold to private investors and run as a for-profit venture. From the speech, I was able to glean that the store has annual sales of about Rmb 800 million (about $100 million), which is large by Chinese standards. The building is modern by Chinese standards, having been renovated in the early 1990s. It has over 8,000 square feet on six floors, with room to expand another 4,000 square feet. There are five floors of merchandise; administrative offices are on the sixth floor. The general manager stated the store's goal is to become the top department store in Suzhou and ultimately in all of China. To do that, he wants to upgrade the store's image. He also spoke of the store's need to export goods to the United States. This would earn the foreign currency needed to pay for more American, Japanese, and European goods, which he would like to sell in the store. Judging by the amount of time the general manager spent on the subject, it seemed that this was an important issue. This was not a complete surprise to me, but it is still unusual to think of retailers as exporters. The connection between retailing, exporting, importing, and foreign currency requirements will deserve some attention later on.

The general manager finished his speech by talking about China's 5,000-year-old history and culture, and how this is a tremendous source of pride for all Chinese people. The presentation took about 30 minutes. Afterwards, his two assistants gave brief speeches about their determination to make First Department Store the leading department store in the Suzhou area and about how proud they were of the progress the store has made to date.

Finally, it was my turn to say something. Professor Wong suggested that I should spend some time introducing myself and talking about my background rather than trying to elicit more information from the store managers. This took another half hour, at which point the general manager rose and told us that our meeting for today was over. He and Professor Wong arranged for me to come back tomorrow to take a full tour of the store and to ask any questions that I might have. I was somewhat frustrated by not being able to make some of the inquiries necessary for me to get going on my work. It became clear that doing my work in China will take a bit longer than what I was accustomed to in the United States.

Day 4

Professor Wong picked me up immediately after breakfast, and we walked over to the First Department Store. We were met at the door, as we had been yesterday. This time we were met by three of the store's managers and the general manager. From there we were taken on a floor-by-floor tour of the store. I was again struck by the number of staff in each area, most of whom seemed to have little to do. In both the men's and ladies' apparel departments, for example, sales clerks were posted at each rack and spent most of their time waiting for a customer to come around. I also noticed, again, that the store was dirty and cluttered. It was crammed with merchandise, and the excessively narrow walking areas were filled with customers, many of whom appeared to be window shopping. In addition, the aisles were crowded with customers who were waiting to pay at one of the designated "payment counters" or queuing a second time claim their purchases. I asked the general manager, through the interpreter, if this heavy store traffic was normal, and he told me that this was light compared to the store's peak periods!

Another thing that stood out as I toured the store was the displays. Along with being packed tightly, garments in the Apparel Department were hung on racks still in the protective plastic put on in the factory. Though this was explained to be a precaution to keep them from getting dirty as a result of customer handling and the environment, it was unattractive. Fitting rooms were nonexistent. Few mirrors were available in the apparel, shoes, or accessories areas. However, the store did have a few alcoves reserved for well-known international designer labels where the displays were more inviting, mannequins wore simple clothes, goods were hung up without the protective plastic, and there were fitting rooms with mirrors. In the nonapparel departments, such as toys and personal care products, goods were in glass counters, and customers asked sales staff for a closer look at the merchandise that they wanted to buy.

As we were walking through the bicycle department, I asked the general manager about the store's inventory management system. He replied that the store buyers place an order to replenish an item as the units on the display floor are sold. I asked him roughly how many times the store turned over its inventory. The interpreter had a hard time with this question—she and the general manager spent almost 10 minutes going back and forth. Finally, the general manager started talking about the quality of the bicycles. I suspected that neither he nor the interpreter understood what I meant by inventory turnover. We did see some computers in the administrative offices, and the general manager said they were used to prepare sales reports, not to track inventory or sales.

After the tour, we returned to the meeting room on the sixth floor. Here, I was introduced to another assistant manager, who spoke about the store's wholesale division. This manager noted that First Department Store acts as a wholesale outlet for several of the store's local suppliers, including manufacturers of mattresses, furniture, and clothing. After the assistant manager finished, the general manager invited me to ask questions and offer my ideas for improving the store's operations; but first he wanted to discuss how I could help First Department Store export goods to the United States. I said that I would have to do some research on that question as this was for me an uncommon feature of retailing. I did promise that I would get back to him with the names of possible buyers for the Chinese-made goods within a few weeks after I received from him a full descriptive list of the products First had to export. This seemed to satisfy him so we were able to move on to the questions and suggestions regarding store operations.

The first question I sought to ask the general manager was about the apparently excessive number of floor staff. Since I did not want to insult him, I asked him how he determined his staffing needs. As

soon as my question was translated for him, he broke into a broad grin. "Staffing," he said, "is a unique challenge in a government-owned entity like First." The store has almost 800 employees, a number he feels is excessive; however, the Chinese government sets an employee quota for the store. This government-imposed employment quota means that the store is saddled with many employees they may not need. As a result, motivating employees to do a good job is a real challenge. As the general manager put it, "It is difficult to motivate people who know they are not necessary and yet have a guaranteed job."

Next, I repeated the question I had asked earlier about inventory turnover. Again, the interpreter struggled with the question. One of the assistants tried to answer me; but instead of talking about inventory turnover, he proceeded to explain how the store carries 50,000 different items and how the store is organized into 10 departments—in descending order of sales, clothing, textiles, shoes and hats, furniture, jewelry and watches, televisions and video equipment, household appliances, sporting goods, educational materials, and toys. Though the assistant's answer was useful, it didn't get to the heart of my question and certainly didn't dispel my impression that no one at First understood the concept of inventory turnover. I was even less impressed when I asked about sales per square foot and sales per employee, only to get another indirect answer. Judging by the trouble Miss Tao and the managers had with both terms, it seemed that these were also unfamiliar terms to the store managers.

Since I wasn't getting far with questions related to hard data, I decided to ask my next question in an area that I felt confident the general manager would take great pride. I asked him to describe to me what had been done to date to advance his goal of improving the store's image. As I expected, he seemed proud of the store's efforts in this regard. They included plans to open an in-store art gallery, a new sales area for local specialty items such as silk handicrafts, a tea house on the fourth floor offering patrons a sweeping view of the city, and more floor areas set aside to feature international brand name goods. First Department Store also sponsors an employee chorus, which performs at local events and a local radio station. All these are positive steps, but it seemed to me that an image makeover would require more.

The general manager then looked at his watch and said that he would have to leave shortly as he was expected at another meeting. I still had a lot of unanswered questions for him. Patience is definitely a virtue when doing business in China! The general manager noted that the store had planned a welcome banquet for me this evening. Getting up to leave, he said that he looked forward to discussing my ideas and insights over dinner.

When evening came, Professor Wong and I took a taxi to an upscale restaurant where the First Department Store was hosting the banquet. I was still recovering from jet lag, and my body clock was a bit off, but I managed to fight off my tiredness by ingesting several cups of *Cha*, a strong Chinese tea. During dinner, I asked the general manager to identify the biggest challenges facing the store. He paused and then said that his main challenges are to improve the quality of the store's offerings and its customer service, to expand First's international activities, and to control costs so that the store can be more competitive with the city's many small retailers. In addition, he mentioned training for the store's employees as another top priority. I knew from my research that poor service by retail staff is one of Chinese consumers' main complaints and that much of this can be traced to poor employee training. The assistant general manager pointed out that many workers in China have poor attitudes because they think their jobs are guaranteed for life. The assistant manager also added that theft by employees had been a major problem at First, but the store has gotten this problem under control. Most of the rest of the evening was spent on social chitchat, and I decided not to force any more questions on the managers. All in all, the banquet was enjoyable, but I was beginning to see that there is a lot of work to be done at First Department Store.

Day 5

Over dinner last night, the general manager suggested that I tour one of the company's other outlets, which was in Kunshan, a city of 1 million people about halfway between Suzhou and Shanghai. The store provided a minivan and driver, and Professor Wong, Miss Tao, and I left Suzhou early in the morning. Upon our arrival we were met by the branch store's general manager and led to his office. He gave a brief speech on the outlet's history and objectives; then one of his assistants made a few remarks about the store's current performance. This store is smaller than the main store in Suzhou. It has 3,000 square feet organized in four floors (the administrative offices currently occupy part of the fourth floor). Annual sales are about Rmb. 200 million. All purchasing for the store is done by the main store in Suzhou. This gives First more bargaining power but, as the assistant general manager pointed out, it sometimes leads to the store being less sensitive to the demands of local consumers at their outlets. Most of the 270 employees at the store come from the main store in Suzhou. The Kunshan store even has apartments on the top floor for the senior managers who have been transferred from Suzhou. Before I had a chance to ask questions, the general manager suggested a store tour.

Walking through this branch of First, I saw many things I had observed at the main store. Again, it seems there are too many employees. Some were reading magazines or almost napping while standing around at counters or next to display racks. I also saw several instances of the kind of hastily prepared merchandise displays I had seen in Suzhou. However, the Kunshan store does have a different look and feel to it. Despite the basic nature of many of the displays, I also noticed several modern-looking display windows, especially near the store entrances. The store seemed to be better organized than the main store, with each of the four floors having a logical grouping of product categories. All of the employees in the Kunshan store wore a maroon tie and white shirt bearing the store's logo. As I recall, the staff of the main store wore a variety of smocks, some of which did not look very professional. Among the Kunshan store's plans for the future was the opening of an upscale restaurant on the top floor and refurbishing the building's dingy stairways, which were the principal means for customer movement between floors. This will include painting and decorating the stairways with more advertisements. I felt that a good cleaning would do wonders for the overall appearance of the stairwells!

The Kunshan store also had computers which were used primarily for inputting the daily sales and preparing reports. Near the computer room, there was a large room with an extensive security system, including television monitors and recording cameras. I was quite surprised, since my understanding was that crime in China was low. When I asked about the security system and the amount of shoplifting, the general manager explained that shoplifting was almost nonexistent but that the security and monitoring system had been installed to ensure that store employees were doing their jobs. This was not the answer I was expecting!

We returned to the meeting room where I got a chance to ask a few questions. The first thing I wanted to know was why there are so many differences between the operations of the main store in Suzhou and the branch here in Kunshan. The general manager replied that he has full autonomy to run the Kunshan outlet and that he may have more progressive ideas than the management team at headquarters. I wanted to know about inventory turnover and sales per square foot at the Kunshan outlet. I was beginning to think that there is no equivalent Chinese term for either figure, since it appeared that the interpreter and the general manager haggled for several minutes trying to get the question right. Finally, the general manager simply said that he did not have such "detailed statistics" but that the headquarters in Suzhou might.

I asked the managers to describe their competition to me. The assistant general manager gave me a thorough rundown, describing how the store is clearly beating its closest direct rival, another large multistory department store nearby, but that its main rivals are the thousands of small street vendors, who are often able to underprice First. One problem First Department Store faces in Kunshan and at all of its outlets, according to the assistant general manager, is that consumers window shop in the pleasant environment of their store but then do their buying wherever they can get the best price. According to the assistant general manager, the typical Chinese shopper operates according to the adage "Never make a purchase until you have compared three shops."

After about an hour in the meeting room, the general manager invited us to an elaborate lunch at a nearby restaurant. Once again, the food was fabulous; and once again, I got "the speech" about China's 5,000-year-old culture and how proud the Chinese are of it. I was tired and was starting to get a bit impatient with the slow pace of getting things done here and with the many rituals we had to go through to get to the point where I could get some hard information. After lunch, we drove back to Suzhou.

Day 6

Today, I decided to try another approach to gathering information so I went back to the main store to interview some store employees and department heads. From this I hoped to get a better feel for the day-to-day routine in the store. This turned out to be an exercise in futility. Many employees didn't seem to know much about how the store worked or about the merchandise they were supposed to be selling. Any time I asked a question that required the employees to express an opinion or that might lead to a criticism of the store, they became evasive and said that I had to speak to the general manager. I did get to meet 9 of the 10 department heads and sales staff from each department, but the information I got was hardly worth the time spent. By the end of the afternoon, both the interpreter and I were exhausted.

As I headed back to the hotel, Professor Wong told me that we would meet with the First Department Store's management team again for a second banquet the next evening, which would be my "good-bye banquet." Wong also told me that the First managers want to meet with me tomorrow afternoon before dinner and want me to offer suggestions to improve their store. Tomorrow, my last day in Suzhou, I must review my notes and prepare some preliminary recommendations for my Chinese hosts.

Discussion Questions

1. What are some of the unique aspects and challenges of doing business in China that Sarah Harrison has encountered?

2. What are the problems facing the store?

3. What recommendations should Sarah offer to the management of First Department Store? Why?

4. What other information should Sarah get to help her in making recommendations to the store's management?

Source: This case was prepared by Professors Robert Kenny, Robert Letovsky, and Debra Murphy, Saint Michael's College.

Winn-Dixie Stores, Inc., and Dillard Department Stores, Inc.: Comparing Strategic Profit Models

ELLIS JACKSON works in the Finance Department of Winn-Dixie Stores, Inc.—a major food retailer with 1,159 stores in 13 southeastern and southwestern states and the Bahama Islands. Winn-Dixie has divisions in Jacksonville, Greenville, Montgomery, Tampa, Atlanta, Raleigh, Louisville, New Orleans, Charlotte, Orlando, Miami, and Fort Worth. It also has 12 subsidiaries.

His new boss, Sam Frogg, was hired from Dillard Department Stores, Inc., to be the chief financial officer. Dillard operates stores in Arkansas, Tennessee, Texas, New Mexico, Oklahoma, Missouri, Nebraska, Kansas, Louisiana, Nevada, Arizona, Illinois, Alabama, Ohio, North Carolina, South Carolina, Mississippi, Iowa, Utah, Florida, and Kentucky.

Frogg is concerned and somewhat confused about why the key financial ratios for Winn-Dixie are so different from those of Dillard. Specifically, executives at Dillard always stressed the importance of net profit margin, and Dillard's net profit margin percentage is significantly higher than Winn-Dixie's.

You may do the strategic profit models by hand by using the form accompanying this case or you may prepare the plan using the *Integrated Interactive* module on the disk accompanying the text. After installing the disks, go through the *Strategic Profit Model Tutorial*. Then, open *Integrated Interactive*, and plug in the numbers from the case. On a separate sheet of paper, provide your explanation of why the ratios are different.

Discussion Questions

1. Construct strategic profit models using Exhibit 3 for Winn-Dixie and Dillard using data from the abbreviated income statements and balance sheets in Exhibits 1 and 2.

2. Explain, from a marketing perspective, why you would expect gross margin percentage, expense-to-sales ratio, net profit margin, inventory turnover, and asset turnover to be different for a grocery store chain versus a department store chain.

3. Assess which chain has better overall financial performance.

Source: This case was prepared by Evan Koenig, University of Miami.

EXHIBIT 1

Income Statements for Winn-Dixie Stores, Inc., and Dillard Department Stores, Inc.

	WINN-DIXIE (AS OF 6/29/94)	DILLARD (AS OF 1/28/95)
Net sales	$11,082,169	$5,728,588
Less: Cost of goods sold	$8,547,681	$3,614,628
Gross margin	$2,534,488	$2,113,960
Less: Operating expense	$2,171,718	$1,583,568
Less: Interest expense	$14,271	$124,282
Total expense	$2,185,989	$1,707,850
Net profit, pretax	$348,499	$406,110
Less: Taxes	$132,382	$154,320
Tax rate	37.99%	38.00%
Net profit after tax	$216,117	$251,790

Dollars are expressed in thousands.

EXHIBIT 2

Balance Sheet Information for Winn-Dixie Stores, Inc., and Dillard Department Stores, Inc.

	WINN-DIXIE (AS OF 6/29/94)	DILLARD (AS OF 1/28/95)
Assets		
Current assets		
Accounts receivable	$ 171,854	$ 1,102,104
Merchandise inventory	1,058,833	1,362,756
Cash	31,451	51,095
Other current assets	98,996	8,847
Total current assets	1,361,184	2,524,802
Fixed assets		
Building, equipment, and other fixed assets, less depreciation	785,390	2,052,955
Total assets	2,146,574	4,577,757

EXHIBIT 3   Strategic Profit Model

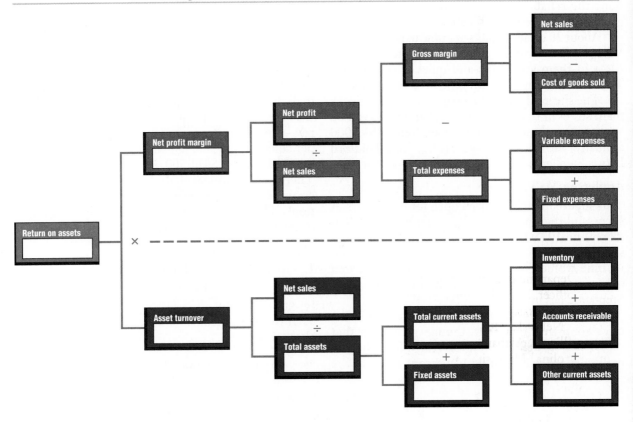

CASE 16

Stephanie's Boutique

STEPHANIE WILSON must decide where to open a ready-to-wear boutique she's been contemplating for several years. Now in her late 30s, she's been working in municipal government ever since leaving college, where she majored in fine arts. She's divorced with two children (aged five and eight) and wants her own business, at least partly to be able to spend more time with them.

She loves fashion, feels she has a flair for it, and has taken evening courses in fashion design and retail management. Recently she heard about a plan to rehabilitate an old arcade building in the downtown section of her midwestern city. This news crystallized her resolve to move now. She's considering three locations.

The Downtown Arcade

The city's central business district has been ailing for some time. The proposed arcade renovation is part of a master redevelopment plan, with a new department store and several office buildings already operating. Completion of the entire master plan is expected to take another six years.

Dating from 1912, the arcade building was once the center of downtown trade, but it's been vacant for the past 15 years. The proposed renovation includes a three-level shopping facility, low-rate garage with validated parking, and convention center complex. Forty shops are planned for the first (ground) floor, 28 more on the second, and a series of restaurants on the third.

The location Stephanie's considering is 30 feet square and situated near the main ground floor entrance. Rent is $20 per square foot, for an annual total of $18,000. If sales exceed $225,000, rent will be calculated at 8 percent of sales. She'll have to sign a three-year lease.

Tenderloin Village

The gentrified urban area of the city where Stephanie lives is nicknamed Tenderloin Village because of its lurid past. Today, however, the neat, well-kept brownstones and comfortable neighborhood make it feel like a yuppie enclave. Many residents have done the rehabilitation work themselves and take great pride in their neighborhood.

About 20 small retailers are now in an area of the Village adjacent to the convention center complex. Most of them are "ferns-and-quiche" restaurants. There are also three small women's clothing stores.

The site available to Stephanie is on the Village's main street in the ground floor of an old house. Its space is also about 900 square feet. Rent is $15,000 annually with no coverage clause. The landlord knows Stephanie and will require a two-year lease.

Appletree Mall

This suburban mall has been open for eight years. A successful regional center, it has three department stores and 100 smaller shops just off a major interstate highway about eight miles from downtown. Of its nine women's clothing retailers, three are in a price category considerably higher than what Stephanie has in mind.

Appletree has captured the retail business in the city's southwest quadrant, though growth in that sector has slowed in the past year. Nevertheless, mall sales are still running 12 percent ahead of the previous year. Stephanie learned of plans to develop a second shopping center east of town, which would be about the same size and character as Appletree Mall. But ground breaking is still 18 months away, and no renting agent has begun to enlist tenants.

The store available to Stephanie in Appletree is two doors from the local department store chain's mall outlet. At 1,200 square feet, it's slightly larger than the other two possibilities. But it's long and narrow—24 feet in front by 50 feet deep. Rent is $24 per square foot ($28,800 annually). In addition, on sales that exceed $411,500, rent is 7 percent of sales. There's an additional charge of 1 percent of sales to cover common-area maintenance and mall promotions. The mall's five-year lease includes an escape clause if sales don't reach $411,500 after two years.

Discussion Questions

1. Give the pluses and minuses of each location.

2. What type of store would be most appropriate for each location?

3. If you were Stephanie, which location would you choose? Why?

Source: This case was prepared by David Ehrlich, Marymount University.

CASE **17**

Hutch: Locating a New Store

IN JUNE, AFTER returning from a trip to the Bahamas, Dale Abell, vice president of new business development for the Hutch Corporation, began a search for a good location to open a new store. After a preliminary search, Abell narrowed the choice to two locations, both in Georgia. He now faces the difficult task of thoroughly analyzing each location and determining which will be the site of the next store.

Company Background

The Hutch store chain was founded in 1952 by John Henry Hutchison, a musician and an extremely successful insurance salesman. Hutchison established the headquarters in Richmond, Virginia, where both the executive offices and one of two warehouse-distribution centers are located. Hutch currently operates 350 popularly priced women's clothing stores throughout the Southeast and Midwest. Manufacturers ship all goods to these distribution centers. They are delivered "floor-ready" in that the vendor has attached price labels, UPC identifying codes, and source tags for security purposes, and has placed appropriate merchandise on hangers. Once at the distribution centers, the merchandise is consolidated for reshipment to the stores. Some staple merchandise, such as hosiery, is stored at these distribution centers. All Hutch stores are located within 400 miles of one of the distribution centers. This way, as Abell explains, "A truck driver can deliver to every location within a 400-mile radius in two days."

- **Hutch Fashions.** Hutch Fashions is considered one of the leading popular-priced women's fashion apparel chains in the Southeast. The stores carry trendy apparel selections in juniors', misses', and women's sizes, all at popular prices. The chain offers a complementary array of accessories in addition to its main features of dresses, coats, and sportswear. Located mainly in strip centers and malls, these shops typically require 4,000 to 5,000 square feet.
- **Hutch Extra.** Hutch Extra stores are primarily located in strip centers and malls. They bear a strong resemblance to Hutch Fashions. The difference is that Hutch Extra stores require less space—from 2,000 to 3,000 square feet—and cater to women

requiring large and half-size apparel. (Women who wear half-sizes require a larger size but are not tall enough to wear a standard large size. In other words, a size $18\frac{1}{2}$ is the same size 18 except that it is cut for a shorter woman.)

• **Hutch Fashions* Hutch Extra.** Although Hutch Fashions and Hutch Extra stores selectively appear as separate entries, the corporate goal is to position both as a single entity. The combination store emerged in 1986 and is now used for all new stores.

The Hutch Fashions* Hutch Extra combination occupies a combined space of 6,000 to 7,000 square feet with separate entrances for each entity. A partial wall separates the two frontal areas of the store but allows a combined checkout/customer service area in the rear. The new stores are primarily located in strip centers and can occasionally be found in malls. (Exhibit 1 shows a typical layout.)

Marketing Strategy

• **The Customers.** Hutch's target market is women between the ages of 18 and 40 who are in the lower-middle to middle-income range. Abel explains, "We don't cater to any specific ethnic group, only to women who like to wear the latest fashions."

• **Product/Price.** Hutch positions merchandise and price levels between the mass merchandisers and the department stores. You won't find any blue-light specials or designer boutiques in a Hutch store. By avoiding direct competition for customers with the large discounters (Kmart and Wal-Mart), and the high-fashion department stores and specialty shops, Hutch has secured a comfortable niche for itself. "Our products must be priced at a level where our customers perceive our products to be elegant and fashionable but not too expensive," notes Abell.

• **Location.** Hutch stores are located throughout the Southeast and Midwest and must be within a 400-mile radius of a Hutch distribution center. Within this geographic area, Hutch stores are located in communities with a population range from 10,000 to 50,000 and a trade area of 50,000 to 150,000. These locations are characterized by a large concentration of people in the low-to middle-income brackets who work in agriculture and industry.

EXHIBIT 1

Layout of a Hutch Fashions* Hutch Extra Store

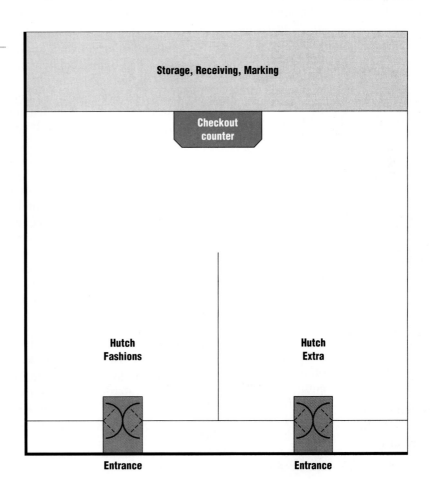

Hutch stores are primarily located in strip malls or strip centers—generally ones anchored by either a regional or national mass merchandiser (Wal-Mart or Kmart). In addition, these centers contain a mix of several nationally recognized and popular local tenants. Hutch stores are primarily located adjacent to the center's anchor. Mall locations must be on the main corridor as close to "Center Court" as economics (rent) will allow. Abell remarked, "We don't care if it's the only center in the country. If the only space available is at the end of the mall, we won't go in there. Our plan is to be a complement to the anchor and to feed off the traffic coming to it. We may have a reputation for being picky and having one of the toughest lease agreements in the business, but it's one of the main reasons for our continued success."

Data Sources

Abell is using several reports generated by Claritas/UDS Data Service to help him decide which location to choose for the next Hutch store. He has chosen reports that describe the 10-mile ring around each of the proposed locations.

Exhibits 2 and 3 summarize these reports. They contain detailed population, household, race, income, education, and employment data plus figures on retail sales and number of establishments. The reports also provide information about women's apparel sales and give a market index that estimates the annual per person spending potential for the trade area divided by the national average. (See Exhibit 3.) Dalton's 99 index means that the spending potential for women's clothing is slightly lower than the national average.

Finally, Abell is using Claritas/UDS's PRIZM™ lifestyle reports. These reports contain numeric figures and percentages of the population, households, families, sex, age, household size, and ownership of housing. An excerpt from the report is given in Exhibit 4. Some of the cluster group names and descriptions are described in Exhibit 5.

The Potential Locations

• **Dalton.** Dalton produces most of the carpeting in the United States. Consequently, the carpet mills are the major employers in Dalton. Stain Master carpeting has been putting a strain on the city's water supply. Stain Master is said to require seven times the amount of water as regular carpeting and is rapidly becoming the largest proportion of carpeting produced. Expressing concern over market validity, Abell said, "If the Dalton area were ever to experience a severe drought, the carpet mills would be forced to

drastically reduce production. The ensuing layoffs could put half the population on unemployment."

The proposed site for the new store is the Whitfield Square shopping center located off the main highway approximately two miles from the center of town. (See Exhibit 6.) After meeting with the developer, Abell was pleased with several aspects of the strip center. He learned that the center has good visibility from the highway, will be anchored by both Kmart and Kroger (a large grocery chain), and has ample parking. Abell is also reasonably pleased with the available location within the center, which is one spot away from Kmart. However, he was displeased with the presence of two large out-parcels in front of the center that would reduce the number of parking spaces and visibility directly of the center. (An out-parcel is a free-standing structure at the front of a mall—commonly a fast-food outlet, a bank, or a gas station.) Other tenants in the center include a nationally recognized shoe store, a beauty salon, two popular restaurants (Chinese and Mexican), and Little Caesar's Pizza at the end of the center, and a Century 21 real estate training school in the middle.

• **Hinesville.** Like Dalton, Hinesville has one major employer: the Fort Stuart army base. Abell recalls that popular-priced stores generally do very well in military towns. Additionally, Fort Stuart is a rapid-deployment–force base. Even though the United States currently enjoys stable relations with the rest of the world, Abell is concerned with a comment by a Hinesville native, "If these guys have to ship out, this place will be a ghost town."

The location under consideration is the Kmart Plaza at the junction of State Route 119 and US Highway 82. (See Exhibit 7.) The center is anchored by Kmart and a grocery store that is part of a popular eastern chain. The two anchors are located side by side in the middle of the center. The spot available in the center is a 6,800-square foot combination of three smaller units immediately adjacent to Kmart. Other tenants in the center include a bookstore, a waterbed store, a shoe store, an electronics retailer, a yogurt store, a video store, and a movie theater.

Discussion Questions

1. How do the people living in the trade areas compare with Hutch's target customer?

2. How do the proposed locations, including the cities, tenant mix, and the locations within the malls, fit with Hutch's locational requirements?

3. Which location would you select? Why?

Source: This case was prepared by Michael Levy, University of Miami.

EXHIBIT 2

Population and
Competitive Profile,
10-Mile Ring from
Center of Dalton and
Hinesville, Georgia

		DALTON	HINESVILLE
Population	2001 projection	93,182	64,195
	1996 estimate	87,293	57,945
	1990 Census	79,420	49,853
	1980 Census	71,373	34,125
	% change, 1990–96	9.9%	16.2%
	% change, 1980–90	11.3%	46.1%
	In group quarters (military base)		
	1996	.9%	11.2%
Household	2001 projection	35,570	20,010
	1996 estimate	33,140	17,541
	1990 Census	29,340	14,061
	1980 Census	24,302	8,557
	% change, 1990–96	12.9%	24.7%
	% change, 1980–90	20.7%	64.3%
Families	1996 estimate	24,347	14,277
Race, 1996	White	92.0%	54.1%
	Black	4.9%	38.3%
	American Indian	0.2%	0.5%
	Asian or Pacific Islander	0.6%	3.1%
	Other	2.3%	4.0%
Age, 1996	0–20	31.2%	40.2%
	21–44	37.1%	47.0%
	45–64	21.7%	9.2%
	65+	9.9%	3.4%
	Median Age, 1996	33.7	23.9
	Male	32.5	23.6
	Female	35.0	24.6
Household Size, 1996	1 person	21.0%	15.2%
	2 persons	32.3%	26.6%
	3–4 persons	38.1%	45.7%
	5+ persons	8.7%	12.6%
Income, 1996	Median household income	$30,516	$23, 686
	Average household income	$40,397	$28,677
Sex (% Male)		49.1%	55.8%
Education, 1990	Population age 25+	49,298	22,455
	No high school diploma	41.0%	15.5%
	High school only	28.6%	41.2%
	College, 1–3 years	19.1%	29.7%
	College, 4+ years	11.3%	13.5%
Industry	Manufacturing: nondurable goods	42.3%	7.2%
	Retail trade	12.6%	23.3%
	Professional and related services	13.3%	21.4%
	Public administration	2.2%	20.0%
Retail Sales, (000)	Total	$706,209	$172,802
	General merchandise stores		
	Apparel stores	$26,634	$9,339
Retail Establishments	General merchandise stores	12	3
	Women's apparel stores	21	8

EXHIBIT 3

Sales Potential Index for Women's Apparel

	AREA SALES ($ Mil.)	AREA SALES PER CAPITA	U.S. SALES PER CAPITA	INDEX (AREA SALES ÷ U.S. SALES)
Dalton	$18.01	$206.26	$207.65	99
Hinesville	$8.97	$154.74	$207.65	75

EXHIBIT 4

PRIZM Neighborhood Clusters

PRIZM CLUSTER	POPULATION, 1996	PERCENTAGE OF POPULATION
Dalton		
Big fish, small pond	4,727	5.4%
New homesteaders	6,030	6.9
Red, white & blues	31,123	35.7
Shotguns & pickups	8,881	10.2
Rural industrial	12,757	14.6
Mines & mills	7,694	8.8
Back country folks	4,293	4.9
Hinesville		
Military quarters	45,127	77.9
Scrub pine flats	3,476	6.0

EXHIBIT 5

PRIZM Lifestyle Clusters

BIG FISH, SMALL POND

Small-town executive families; upper-middle incomes; age groups 35–44, 45–54; predominantly white. This group is married, family-oriented, and conservative. Their neighborhoods are older. Best described as captains of local industry, they invest in their homes and clubs, and vacation by car in the U.S.

RURAL INDUSTRIAL

Low-income, blue-collar families; lower-middle incomes; age groups, <24, 25–34, predominantly white, high Hispanic. Once dependent on railroads and major markets, 18-wheelers freed light industry to go farther afield to seek the low-cost, nonunion labor found in this cluster, which is comprised of hundreds of blue-collar mill towns on American's rural backroads.

MINES & MILLS

Older families; mine and mill towns; poor; age groups 55–64, 65+; predominantly white. Down the Appalachians, across the Ozarks to Arizona, and up the Missouri, this cluster is exactly as its name implies. This older, mostly single population with a few children lives in the midst of scenic splendor.

SHOTGUNS & PICKUPS

Rural blue-collar workers and families; middle income; age groups 35–44, 45–54; predominantly white. This cluster is found in the Northeast, the Southeast, and in the Great Lakes and Piedmont industrial regions. They are in blue-collar jobs; most are married with school-age kids. They are churchgoers who also enjoy bowling, hunting, sewing, and attending car races.

BACK COUNTRY FOLKS

Older African-American farm families; lower-middle income; age groups 55–64, 65+; predominantly white. This cluster is centered in the Eastern uplands along a wide path from the Pennsylvania Poconos to the Arkansas Ozarks. Anyone who visits their playgrounds in Branson, Missouri, or Garlinburg, Tennessee, can attest that these are the most blue-collar neighborhoods in America. Centered in the Bible Belt, many back country folks are hooked on Christian and country music.

SCRUB PINE FLATS

Older African-American farm families; poor; age groups 55–64, 65+; predominantly black. This cluster is found mainly in the coastal flatlands of the Atlantic and Gulf states from the James to the Mississippi rivers. These humid, sleepy rural communities, with a mix of blacks and whites, live in a seemingly timeless, agrarian rhythm.

NEW HOMESTEADERS

Young middle-class families; middle income; age groups 35–44, 45–54; predominantly white. This cluster has above-average college education. Executives and professionals work in local service fields such as administration, communications, health, and retail. Most are married; the young have children, the elders do not. Life is homespun with a focus on crafts, camping, and sports.

RED, WHITE & BLUES

Small-town blue-collar families; middle income; age groups 35–54, 55–64; dominant white, with skilled workers primarily employed in mining, milling, manufacturing, and construction. Geocentered in the Appalachians, Great Lakes industrial region, and Western highlands, these folks love the outdoors.

MILITARY QUARTERS

GIs and surrounding off-base families; lower-middle income; age groups under 24, 25–34; ethnically diverse. Since this cluster depicts military life with personnel living in group quarters, its demographics are wholly atypical because they are located on or near military bases; this skews toward our principal harbors and defense perimeters. Racially integrated, and with the highest index for adults under 35, "Military Quarters" likes fast cars, bars, and action sports.

C-28

EXHIBIT 6

Whitfield Square
Shopping Center,
Dalton, Georgia

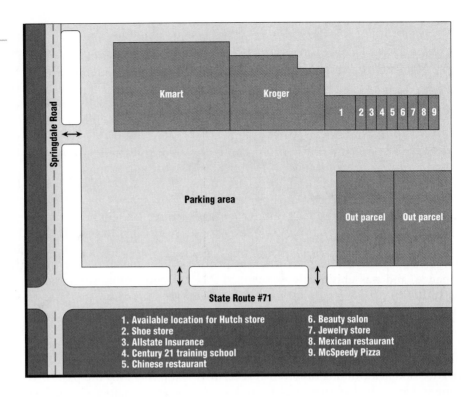

1. Available location for Hutch store
2. Shoe store
3. Allstate Insurance
4. Century 21 training school
5. Chinese restaurant
6. Beauty salon
7. Jewelry store
8. Mexican restaurant
9. McSpeedy Pizza

EXHIBIT 7

Kmart Plaza,
Hinesville, Georgia

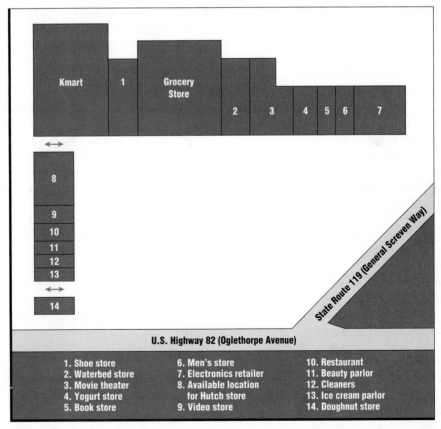

1. Shoe store
2. Waterbed store
3. Movie theater
4. Yogurt store
5. Book store
6. Men's store
7. Electronics retailer
8. Available location
   for Hutch store
9. Video store
10. Restaurant
11. Beauty parlor
12. Cleaners
13. Ice cream parlor
14. Doughnut store

Source: The Ben Tobin Companies.

Fuller's: Whom to Let Go?

RALPH JASON, president of Fuller's, was unhappy. He had just learned that Fuller's parent company, Consolidated Stores, had been acquired by a foreign financial group, and all Consolidated divisions had been ordered to reduce overhead expenses by at least 10 percent before the end of the fiscal year, four months away. Having gone through a similar exercise a few years earlier, he wasn't looking forward to doing it again. Fuller's was one of Consolidated's star divisions, with the best profit performance, and was universally recognized as a fashion leader in its California market. Jason had grown up with the store, starting as an assistant buyer 30 years earlier, and he knew almost everyone in his organization on a first-name basis. Furthermore, he'd been personally involved in virtually every financial decision made during his seven-year term as president and knew he had spent wisely. To have to reduce expenses as much as 10 percent seemed like killing the goose that laid the golden eggs, but he saw he had no choice.

So he reviewed the nonpersonnel areas of the business: have two fewer trucks and drivers, postpone the planned update of his computerized inventory systems, cut back the display department's budget, hold fewer fashion shows, reduce charitable contributions, and so on. But he was still short of the 10 percent goal, and he knew he had to face the hardest choice of all—to cut $240,000 in executive personnel expenses. Figuring that the fringe costs of employing executives was about 25 percent, he said, "I'll just have to find a combination of salaries that adds up to $180,000. I wish I didn't—these people have worked hard for me and shown great dedication."

Accordingly, Jason went through his executive personnel and came up with six possible candidates for termination, of whom he would have to settle on three. There were four men and two women: Louis Ingram, better coat buyer; Frank McCarthy, assistant warehouse manager; Charles Jordan, director of executive training; Marie Voltz, junior lingerie buyer; Lynne Cohen, a store manager; and Richard Morse, infants' buyer.

Ingram was 57 years old and had put in 15 years with the company. Having been in the coat business all his life, he knew everything about it and every-one in it. Prior to joining Fuller's, he had worked for a coat manufacturer in New York; before that, he had spent five years at the May Company. An experienced worker, he showed signs of slowing down as his children had finished college. But his sales increases were among the highest in Consolidated, and he was known throughout the trade as a pro.

McCarthy, age 52, had joined Fuller's out of high school as a stock boy, and had worked in the warehouse for 34 years. As his years in the job grew, so had his knowledge. He had uncovered several incidents of internal theft and had been rewarded each time. But over time, the warehouse jobs had become more sophisticated. Jason reflected that in years to come, he'd need people with state-of-the-art computer knowledge.

A graduate of a well-known business school, Jordan, age 54, had worked in personnel throughout his career—first with other divisions of Consolidated and then, for the past three years, with Fuller's. His wife (a skilled cosmetician) worked in the Estée Lauder counter in the company's best store, where her sales were outstanding. Charles Jordan had assumed control of a rather ineffectual internal training program and turned it around to the point where 30 top college graduates were now holding down positions of responsibility throughout the company. But Jordan had often said that when his job was completed, he would be happy to retire and tend his rose garden.

At age 61, Voltz had always bought the store's junior lingerie. She was a true old timer, and though she had long since agreed to forgo annual raises, she continued to produce well for the company. However, Consolidated had determined that junior lingerie was too hard to separate from the larger misses departments and had already phased it out in many of its divisions.

Cohen, age 34, was seen as a question mark. She had several assignments during her eight years with Fuller's, many of them difficult. She had handled most of them well but seemed to be having trouble in her current position. Her sales were lagging behind other stores', and Jason wondered whether she might not have run out of drive.

Morse, finally, was the 44-year-old father of six children. His family duties occasionally forced him to come in late to work, but he always made up the time. He was an extraordinarily willing worker.

Unfortunately, his business was plagued by a low birth rate in Fuller's market area and the fierce competition from local discount stores.

Jason thought over each of these six cases with a sigh. Every one of these people would normally be carried by the store for a variety of reasons. All had shown great devotion and at times had made huge contributions to the store's success. In selecting them as candidates for termination, Jason realized he had to make several other borderline decisions. But he felt in Ingram's case, he could combine better coats with budget coats, as the other coat buyer appeared restless and in need of more challenge. He felt that the warehouse organization could be revamped to take care of McCarthy's various duties, though he recognized that none of the "survivors" was over 32 years old. Executive training was a function that Jason had often thought he could and should handle personally, as he felt strongly that future leaders of the store should be developed internally. With respect to junior lingerie, he knew that he was fighting a losing battle with his superiors, though that department continued to produce significant profits. In Cohen's case, he realized he would simply have to take a chance on promoting another young hopeful, with no assurance that the job could be done any better. Finally, he said to himself that infants' and toddlers' could be bought by one person, with only a slight loss in volume, though he knew he was kidding himself.

The salaries of any three of these people would add up to the required dollar savings, so he was relieved that he would only have to dismiss three of them. But which three?

Discussion Questions

1. What criteria would you use to select people to terminate? Why?

2. What are the pros and cons of terminating each person?

3. As a neutral observer who knows none of the individuals involved, whom would you pick? Why?

Source: This case was prepared by David Ehrlich, Marymount University.

CASE 19

Marriott's Success Comes from Its Human Resources

IN OCTOBER 1993, the Marriott Corporation, known for its lodging services, divided into two separate companies: Marriott International and Host Marriott. Marriott International manages lodging service businesses and has operations in 28 countries with almost 200,000 employees and 1995 sales of more than $38 billion. The Host Marriott, formerly part of the Marriott Corporation, focuses on real estate ownership.

J. Willard ("Bill") Marriott and his wife Alice started the Marriott Corporation in 1927 by operating a root beer stand in Washington, D.C. Thirty years later, the couple opened the Twin Bridges Marriott Motor Hotel in Arlington, Virginia, near National Airport. The hotel boasted 300 rooms and a drive-in registration. It was the largest of its kind at that time.

In 1996, Marriott International grew to include over 1,000 hotels across six established hotel brands throughout the world. The brands include the four- and five-star Marriott Hotels, Resorts and Suites properties; moderately priced Courtyard by Marriott hotels; economy-minded Fairfield Inn Hotels; Residence Inn properties for extended-stay travelers; Marriott Conference Centers; and Marriott Vacation Club International (time share properties). In 1995, Marriott also purchased 49 percent interest in the Ritz-Carlton Hotel Company.

Although Marriott has become a major player in the lodging business, it maintains that relationships are an integral part of the company's mission. J. W. Marriott, Jr. (son of Bill Marriott), serves as the chairman and president of Marriott International. He is committed to enhancing the relations with the company's associates, guests, franchisees, owners, and others. To assist in this, a positive and open environment is established in each location. Associates are valued, treated with respect, appreciated for their cultural and intellectual diversity, given opportunities to learn and develop, and encouraged to be candid and innovative. The hope is that this environment will foster exceptional service for the guests so that the company may grow and prosper.

Mr. Marriott viewed his organization in the same way he viewed his own family. The principles of cooperation, support, and openness are applied to both "families." Marriott Jr. stated that his father felt that his employees should be looked after. "My father knew if he had happy employees, he would have happy customers and that would result in a good bottom line," said Marriott.

One way that Marriott is retaining its employees and increasing customer satisfaction is through "guest service associates" (also known as GSAs). This program empowers its associates to perform almost all tasks that would assist a guest upon her check-in to a hotel. The usual scenario begins with a GSA meeting guests at their vehicles, picking up keys to the assigned rooms, and escorting the guests immediately to their rooms. If there is a problem with the room assignment, the GSA can address it instead of having to solicit the help of a desk clerk. A GSA also performs the duties of a concierge; the associate can acquire tickets or reservations upon a guest's request.

The benefits of this service are apparent on many levels. The GSA becomes involved with the guests for the duration of their stay. This gives the GSA a sense of ownership of the business and a stake in each guest's happiness. GSAs also have the opportunity to earn higher tips from the guests.

The guests receive special attention from these GSAs, which is unique for today's consumers. Good, consistent customer service is increasingly hard to find. Customers seem to be grateful when they find extraordinary one-on-one treatment from any establishment.

Marriott executives believe that taking care of its associates is the key to its success. This is to be done by treating people fairly, ethically, honestly, and in a caring manner. Also, opportunity for an individual to grow professionally is important to the company. An environment that is positive and generates teamwork and instills pride is important as well.

Discussion Questions

1. What problems could arise from such open and supportive work environments? How could a manager combat them?

2. Marriott International is quite large and has diverse lodging divisions. How do you think the corporate headquarters keeps each division employee-oriented?

Source: This case was prepared by Allison T. Knott, University of Florida.

CASE 20

Lawson Sportswear

"WE NEED TO have vendors who can take this burden off of us," said Clifton Morris, Lawson Sportswear inventory manager. "We have had a sales increase of 20 percent over the last two years and my people can't keep up with it anymore."

Keith Lawson, general manager of Lawson Sportswear, reviewed the colorful chart showing the sales trend and replied, "I never thought I would have to complain about a sales increase, but it is obvious that the sales are well beyond our control. Something has to be done and that is why we are meeting today."

Lawson Sportswear was founded by George Lawson in 1963 in a major southwestern metropolitan area. For five years, Lawson Sportswear has been successful in the sportswear market. In 1995, George Lawson retired, and his son, Keith Lawson, was appointed general manager. From the beginning, Keith Lawson has been a real go-getter. Recently completing his MBA, he has wasted no time in locating new markets for Lawson Sportswear. He immediately contacted the two major universities and gained four-year exclusive contracts for apparel purchases made by the sports teams of their athletic departments. Soon after, Lawson's sportswear became popular among students. This growing demand for the company's products motivated Lawson to open two more retail stores. During the fall of 1997, the sales had increased beyond expectations. Although the company achieved a successful reputation in the marketplace, sales growth has generated major problems.

In the beginning, operations were fairly smooth and the company's inventory control department updated most of its procedures. Morris emphasized the crucial role of routinization in the overall inventory maintenance process to keep up with the increasing turnover. The sales increase was 20 percent, opposed to 12 percent that had been forecast for 1990. It was this increase that initiated a series of problems in the inventory control department. To temporarily alleviate the backlog, Lawson authorized Morris to lease an additional warehouse.

EXHIBIT 1

Sales for Lawson
Sportswear, 1996

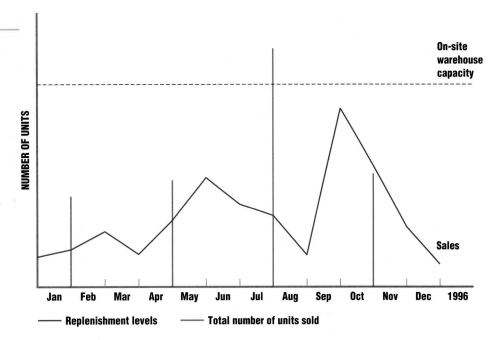

(See the replenishment level for July 1997 in Exhibit 1.) It was decided that the maximum 16 percent of the total inventory carrying costs were going to be dedicated to the off-premise inventory.

Worrying about not being able to meet demand on time, Clifton Morris met with suppliers and asked them to provide more timely delivery schedules to Lawson Sportswear. When he stated that the company was not going to tolerate any reasons for future delays, two major suppliers expressed their concerns about his lack of flexibility and requested price concessions. They simply indicated that Morris's demand had to be supported by providing cash and/or reducing quantity discounts. Morris ignored these comments and indicated how serious he really was by stating that Lawson Sportswear could always find new suppliers. By the end of a long discussion, arguments were beyond a manageable point and the two large suppliers decided to quit dealing with the company.

After the meeting, Morris received a memo from Lawson. Lawson was very concerned about the potential reactions of the rest of the vendors. He stated in his memo that since Lawson Sportswear was continuously growing, it was expected to present a more supportive attitude to its suppliers. He expressed his belief that the company needed a cohesive atmosphere with the rest of the channel members, especially with its vendors.

During the next six months, Morris had limited success in locating one or more large suppliers that would be able to deliver the products to Lawson Sportswear on a timely basis. Faced with growing demand from the surrounding high schools, he had to accumulate excess stock to avoid possible shortages. At the end of the six-month period, a memo from the accounting department of the company indicated the financial significance of the problem. In his memo, accounting manager Roger Noles simply addressed the high costs of inventory maintenance/security functions. (For details, see Exhibit 2.) He advised finding a substitute inventory policy to lower these cost figures. Specifically, he stated that the rental cost for the additional warehouse had leveled off at 16 percent, well beyond the maximum.

Keith Lawson immediately scheduled a meeting and asked the top managers to come up with the alternative plans to eliminate this problem.

"I should have never let those suppliers quit," said Morris. "It had a negative effect on our image, and now we all see the results."

"It's too late to worry about that," admonished Lawson. "Instead, we have to come up with a strategy to meet the demand effectively without increasing our costs to the detriment of profits. You realize that the university contracts will expire at the end of the year."

"That's the crucial fact," said Noles. "We simply cannot afford to stock up beyond the current level; it is just too expensive. It is well beyond the funds we have had even from the increased sales."

"In other words, the elimination of the excess inventory is necessary. Who are the vendors that we have at the moment?" asked Lawson.

"There are only three suppliers remaining after the last meeting," replied Morris. "They are fairly small businesses, but we've been dealing with them for quite some time. They have been successful in keeping up with us, and the details of their operations are summarized in their report."

"It seems like we have a good selection here," said Lawson, after looking at the report in front of him. "If they mostly work with us, we should be able to influence the future direction in their operations. In other words, it should not be difficult to convince them that they need to upgrade their deliveries in such a way that we can eliminate our excess inventory."

"That would cut down the rental costs that we incur from the additional warehouse," said Noles.

"Obviously!" Lawson replied impatiently. "We will probably need to provide those vendors with a comprehensive support program. If we can convert the floor space of the warehouse from storage to sales, we will have additional funds in retail operations. We can invest a portion of these funds in supporting our vendors and improve our image by forming a cohesive network with them. Of course, there will be a limit to this support. After all, it will be expensive for us to make the transition, too. Therefore, I would like you to come up with an analysis of converting the existing system to a more efficient one. I would like to know what we can do and how we can do it. To be very honest, gentlemen, I do not want to increase the sales if we do not know how to handle that increase."

Discussion Questions

1. How might the use of a Quick Response system affect the financial performance of Lawson?

2. What problems would Lawson have implementing a Quick Response system with vendors?

Source: This case was prepared by S. Alton Erdem, University of Minnesota–Duluth.

EXHIBIT 2

Comparative Statement of Profit and Loss for Years Ended December 31

	1997 (FORECAST)	1996	1995
Net sales	$165,000	$120,000	$100,000
Cost of sales			
Beginning inventory	7,000	6,000	4,000
Purchases (net)	140,000	92,000	62,000
	147,000	98,000	66,000
Ending inventory	9,000	7,000	6,000
	138,000	91,000	61,000
Gross profit	27,000	29,000	39,000
Expenses			
Stock maintenance	7,000	5,250	750
Rent	2,500	1,250	250
Insurance	4,500	3,500	1,500
Interest	4,500	2,500	1,000
Selling	3,500	2,500	2,000
Promotion	7,500	5,500	4,000
Supplies	2,750	1,500	250
Miscellaneous	2,250	1,500	250
	35,000	23,500	10,000
Net profit from operations	<8,000>	5,500	29,000
Other income			
Dividends	925	750	450
Interest	825	600	350
Miscellaneous	650	400	200
	2,400	1,750	1,000
Net profit before taxes	<5,600>	7,250	30,000
Provision for income taxes	1,008	1,305	8,100
Net profit after taxes	<4,592>	5,945	21,900

Michaels Decreases Its Merchandise Assortment

MICHAELS STORES, INC., is the world's largest specialty retailer of arts, crafts, and home decor. Its inventory includes silk and dried flowers, hobby and art supplies, creative crafts, and party, seasonal, and holiday merchandise. Picture framing materials and services are also mainstays in the stores. There are 448 Michaels locations in 45 states, Canada, and Puerto Rico. Aaron Brothers stores, also owned by Michaels, are 68 in number and are located primarily in California. Aaron Brothers stores offer approximately 6,500 items of picture framing and art supplies.

Michaels Stores, Inc., began with 11 Michaels locations, which were Ben Franklin licensees. They were Texas-based and purchased by Sam and Charles Wyly, owners of Peoples Restaurants, in 1983. The stock went public in 1984, which led the company into a strong 11-year stint of quick, enterprising growth. In fact, Michaels launched a rapid-growth program in 1991. The company acquired a large 28-store chain, bought three Helen's Arts and Crafts stores from Wal-Mart, and opened stores in Toronto, Ontario, Canada.

More aggressive growth came in 1994 when Michaels increased its store count more than 75 percent by year-end. Acquisitions included Treasure House Stores, Oregon Craft & Supply, and Leewards Creative Crafts. Aaron Brothers Holdings, Inc., a 71-store retailer, was purchased in 1995.

Michaels Stores offers a fun, exciting, and friendly atmosphere in each of its outlets, which is part of its success. Customer relationships are revered by the company and strengthened through special events. Customers are given the opportunity to attend approximately 20 weekly demonstrations and 30 seminars in each store. New products and craft techniques are demonstrated by the in-store crafting professionals. Free instruction is provided during workshops, which include faux finishing, candle making, fabric painting, and floral arranging. Each store also holds an annual Wedding Fair which highlights a wide range of wedding services available to customers. Wedding rentals and custom invitation programs are detailed, while floral, framing, cake decorating, and accessory merchandise are displayed. Throughout the year, class previews are held where customers find out about the classes, meet the instructors, and enjoy "work-in-progress" demonstrations.

The stores also involve children in the shopping experience. "Make-It-Take-It" projects let children complete their own fun and exciting crafts. Two annual children's events cosponsored with their vendors benefit the Ronald McDonald House Charities.

In 1995, Michaels Stores had over $1 billion in sales; however, the retailer reported losses of over $15 million in operating income and $20.4 in net income, leading to a loss of 95 cents per share. Michaels decided to take a new approach and focus more on higher profits and less on sales growth. This led to an analysis of company inventory.

Executives studied the merchandise assortment and the rate at which each piece was selling (its turn). They found that per-store inventories were up 20 percent from 1994's highest numbers. The company then began an "SKU Reduction" program. This included eliminating certain items and groups of items (lines) that were not selling quickly and thereby tying up inventory dollars. The overall goal was to reduce each store's inventory dollars by 5 percent by the end of fiscal 1995 as compared to the end of fiscal 1994.

SKU reduction led to the elimination of 7,500 items. These items were marked down and sold in clearance sales during June and July 1995. Michaels currently offers about 44,000 SKUs, as compared to the previous 50,000, in an average Michaels store during the course of a year. Approximately 33,000 of the items are considered standard and are stocked year-round.

The program cost Michaels over $64 million, but it made over $85 million in cash available during the fourth quarter of 1995, compared to $7 million in both 1993 and 1994. This allowed the company to pay down back debt and move the company toward becoming more profitable.

The company completed a new point-of-sale terminal rollout by the end of 1996. The company believes that a $30 million investment in technology during fiscal 1996 will benefit both customers and company. Customer service will be improved through accurate prices at the point of sale and quicker credit card authorizations. Reorders on merchandise will be generated automatically when certain items are sold. This is done when the computer system reads the item's bar code, determines the store's need for the item, and then produces an appropriate order with the vendor.

Store openings for both Michaels and Aaron Brothers resumed in late 1996. Although Michaels Stores, Inc., slowed its growth in 1995 for its Michaels stores, the company is on an upswing as sales continue to increase. In 1996, sales were 11 percent over what they were in 1995.

Discussion Questions

1. What positive and negative effects could the reduction in the SKUs have at the store level?

2. How should an employee in one of the Michaels stores explain the SKU reduction to a customer looking for one of the discontinued items?

Source: This case was prepared by Allison T. Knott, University of Florida.

CASE 22

Merchandise Planning Problems

1. SUSIE'S CASUALS has $10 million net sales. Average inventory at retail is $8.5 million. What is Susie's Casuals' inventory turnover?

2. What is inventory turnover of a pet shop chain with annual sales of $10 million, average inventory at cost of $3 million, and a gross margin of 40 percent?

3. What is the GMROI for each of the following merchandise categories in a bookstore?

	TEXTBOOKS	GENERAL READING	REFERENCE BOOKS	NEWSPAPERS, MAGAZINES
Annual sales	$800,000	$450,000	$600,000	$100,000
Average inventory (at cost)	$70,000	$110,000	$250,000	$10,000
Gross margin	10%	25%	40%	12%

Which of these categories is most profitable for the bookstore? Should the bookstore eliminate the least profitable category?

4. What is the annual inventory turnover for a retailer with the following monthly sales levels?

MONTH	SALES	BOM INVENTORY
January	$14,000	$40,000
February	13,800	38,000
March	13,000	39,000
April	17,500	41,000
May	16,000	40,500
June	14,800	38,500
July		40,000

5. What are the retail and cost inventory values of Hyde and Seek Records at the end of the month of October based on the following accounting information?

  a. BOM inventory worth $100,000 at cost and $150,000 at retail.

  b. Purchases made during the month worth $125,000 at cost and $175,000 at retail.

  c. $7,000 paid for freight charges.

  d. $130,000 net sales of retail, with a cost of goods sold at $90,000.

  e. $5,000 total markdowns.

  f. $150 in employee discounts.

  g. $2,400 allowance for shrinkage.

6. A specialty store had sales of $34,000 during June. Its end-of-month (EOM) stock was $100,000 and its BOM stock was $90,000. What was its additions to stock during June?

7. The annual sales of Harry's Hardware chain was $28,000,000. The average inventory at cost was $20,000,000 and the gross margin was 43 percent. What were the chain's GMROI, inventory turnover, and average stock-to-sales ratio?

8. A bicycle shop has developed the following merchandise plan:

Planned EOM stock	$45,000
Projected BOM stock	35,000
Actual on order (what is on order for the month)	25,000
Plan monthly sales	10,000
Plan reductions for the month	2,000

9. Crafts, Etc., a small gift-and-craft store, has the following plan for April:

Sales	$70,000
BOM stock	200,000
EOM stock	195,000
Planned reductions	2,500
Planned gross margin	40%

What are the planned purchases for the store at retail and at cost?

10. Based on the following information from the merchandise budget plan for a women's accessory department in a specialty store, what is the open-to-buy as of April 1?

Planned monthly sales	$62,000
BOM inventory	75,000
EOM inventory	80,000
April merchandise already received	45,000
April merchandise on order	18,000
Planned reductions	12,500

11. Forecast the sales for the next sales period for a retailer using exponential smoothing and the following information:

Old forecast	= 100 units
Actual demand	= 67 units
Alpha	= .08

12. What is the order point, and how many units should be ordered if a food retailer has an item with a 10-day lead-time, 3-day review time, and daily demand of 15 units? A total of 75 units are on hand and the retailer must take a safety stock of 50 units to maintain a 95 percent service level.

Source: These problems were prepared by Barton Weitz, University of Florida.

CASE 23

McFaddens Department Store: Preparation of a Merchandise Budget Plan

MCFADDENS DEPARTMENT Store has been a profitable family-owned business since its beginning in 1910. Last year's sales volume was $180 million.

More recently, however, many of its departments had been losing ground to national stores moving into the area. To complicate this problem the National Retail Federation (NRF) had predicted an upcoming recession. The NRF estimates a 6.5 percent drop in sales in the coming year for the Pacific Coast, where McFaddens operates.

Department 121 has one of the more profitable departments in the store maintaining a gross margin of 55 percent. Its basic merchandise is young men's clothing. Last year sales reached $2,780,750 for the July–December season. The highest sales period is the back-to-school period in August, when autumn fashions are supported by strong promotional advertising. Reductions, including markdowns, discounts to employees, and shrinkage, typically run 20 percent of sales. The percentage of reductions are spread throughout the season as follows:

JULY	AUG.	SEPT.	OCT.	NOV.	DEC.
10	20	15	10	10	35

By month the percentage of *annual* sales for Department 121 within this six-month period had been distributed as follows:

	JULY	AUG.	SEPT.	OCT.	NOV.	DEC.
1996	3.6	10.1	9.2	6.4	4.8	9.1
1997	3.5	10.3	9.6	6.8	5.3	8.6
1998	3.5	10.5	9.6	6.2	5.5	8.2
1999	3.0	10.3	9.8	6.6	5.5	8.0

A pre-Christmas sale has been planned in an attempt to counterbalance the slackened sales period following the first of the year. The buyer has decided to bring in some new merchandise for the sale to go along with the remaining fall fashion merchandise. The buyer expects that this will increase December's percentage of annual sales to 30 percent above what it would be without the sale. Top management has stressed that the department achieve a gross margin return on investment (GMROI) of 250 percent. Forecasted ending stock level in December is $758,000.

Additional information is available on the historical stock-to-sales ratio for this type of department. This information is taken from a similar department in another store which happens to have lower average stock-to-sales ratio.

JULY	AUG.	SEPT.	OCT.	NOV.	DEC.
3.0	1.9	2.1	2.4	2.5	2.2

In essence, this is the information that the manager of Department 121 has available for the preparation of his merchandise plan.

Assignment

Your task is to prepare a merchandise budget plan. You may do the plan by hand by using the form accompanying this case or you may prepare the plan using the Excel spreadsheet on the disk accompanying the text. You will have to prepare some intermediate calculations before inputting your answers onto the spreadsheet. After installing the disks, open the *Integrated Tutorial* and go through the merchandise budget plan segment., Then, open *Interactive Merchandise Budget*, and plug in the numbers from the case. On a separate sheet of paper, explain how you determined the sales forecast, percentage of sales per month, and the monthly stock-to-sales ratios.

Source: This case was prepared by Michael Levy, University of Miami, and Harold Koenig, Oregon State University.

McFaddens Merchandise Budget

Planning Data

SALES FORECAST $

$$\text{Planned GMROI} = \frac{\text{Gross Margin}}{\text{Net Sales}} \times \frac{\text{Net Sales}}{\text{Inventory Costs}}$$

$$= \frac{\$\ \square}{\square} \times \frac{\$\ \square}{\square}$$

	%	$
Markdowns		$
Discounts		$
Shortages		$
Total Reductions		$

$$\frac{\text{Sales}}{\text{Inventory Costs}} \times (100\% - GM\%) = \frac{\text{Inventory}}{\text{Turnover}}$$

$$\square \times \square \% = \square$$

$$12 \div \text{Inventory Turnover} = \text{B.O.M. Stock/Sales}$$

$$\square \div \square = \square$$

Forecasted Ending Inventory $ \square

The Plan

		Jan	Feb	Mar	Apr	May	Jun	Jul	Aug	Sept	Oct	Nov	Dec	Total (Average)	Remarks
% Distribution of Sales by Month	1													100.0%	History/Projection
Monthly Sales	2														Step (1) × Net Sales
% Distribution of Reductions/Mo	3													100.0%	History/Projection
Monthly Reductions	4														Step (3) × Reductions
B.O.M. Stock/Sales Ratios	5														Adjusted by mo. sales Fluctuations
B.O.M. Stock ($000)	6													(Forecasted End Inventory)	Step (2) × Step (5)
E.O.M. Stock ($000)	7														EOM Jan = BOM Feb
Monthly Additions to Stock ($000)	8														Steps 2 + 4 + 7−6 Sales + Reductions + EOM−BOM

C-38

Star Hardware

CYNTHIA TURK is an assistant buyer for Star Hardware, a chain of 10 hardware stores in a large Midwestern city. She works for Ramon Martinez, who is responsible for the hand tools merchandise categories. Mr. Martinez is concerned with the performance of the hand wrench category. He has assigned Ms. Turk to analyze the category and make recommendations to improve its performance.

Ms. Turk can use the following three reports in making her analysis:

1. The GMROI Summary Report ranking all of the SKUs in terms of their GMROI (Exhibit 1).
2. The Vendor Analysis Report listing the SKUs ordered from each vendor ranked by annual sales (Exhibit 2).
3. The Subcategory Report grouping the SKUs by subcategory (size) and ranking them by retail price (Exhibit 3).

EXHIBIT 1

GMROI Summary Report

SKU NUMBER	SIZE (INCHES)	VENDOR	RETAIL PRICE	ANNUAL SALES $	GROSS MARGIN $	GROSS MARGIN %	AVERAGE INVENTORY	INVENTORY TURNS	GMROI
E61	6	Eagle	$7.69	$21,165	$4,212	19.9%	1,895	8.9	178.0%
E101	10	Eagle	3.89	29,041	6,070	20.9%	2,894	7.9	165.9%
E151	15	Eagle	9.69	16,543	2,564	15.5%	1,391	10.0	155.8%
E121	12	Eagle	5.89	42,827	9,379	21.9%	4,738	7.1	154.6%
C101	10	Calder	3.29	6,667	1,693	25.4%	917	5.4	137.7%
L61	6	Locker	3.29	961	227	23.6%	134	5.5	129.4%
T101	10	Taylor	3.39	28,933	2,922	10.1%	2,050	12.7	128.1%
E41	4	Eagle	2.69	7,379	1,771	24.0%	1,112	5.0	121.0%
E82	8	Eagle	3.79	49,901	14,172	28.4%	8,601	4.2	118.0%
E181	18	Eagle	14.29	3,989	1,149	28.8%	742	3.8	110.2%
E122	12	Eagle	6.99	47,878	12,113	25.3%	8,250	4.3	109.7%
C61	6	Calder	2.99	4,317	1,083	25.1%	773	4.2	105.0%
E102	10	Eagle	4.89	49,392	11,805	23.9%	8,745	4.3	102.7%
E152	15	Eagle	10.79	17,696	4,778	27.0%	3,677	3.5	94.9%
E62	6	Eagle	3.39	33,900	7,899	23.3%	6,458	4.0	93.8%
C81	8	Calder	2.49	7,198	1,857	25.8%	1,524	3.5	90.4%
L121	12	Locker	5.79	384	120	31.3%	93	2.8	88.7%
E42	4	Eagle	3.29	11,300	2,859	25.3%	2,462	3.4	86.7%
C121	12	Calder	4.59	6,102	1,532	25.1%	1,349	3.4	85.1%
T121	12	Taylor	5.59	10,328	1,281	12.4%	1,329	6.8	84.4%
IM12	12	Import	3.89	4,328	1,108	25.6%	1,102	2.9	74.8%
L101	10	Locker	3.79	836	157	18.8%	175	3.9	72.9%
E81	8	Eagle	3.29	29,990	6,868	22.9%	7,437	3.1	71.2%
IM8	8	Import	2.19	4,565	1,109	24.3%	1,401	2.5	59.9%
E182	18	Eagle	18.19	8,950	2,300	25.7%	2,977	2.2	57.4%
T61	6	Taylor	2.49	4,396	316	7.2%	597	6.8	49.1%
IM10	10	Import	2.89	4,622	1,132	24.5%	1,967	1.8	43.5%
L81	8	Locker	3.19	1,141	247	21.6%	484	1.8	40.0%
IM6	6	Import	1.79	2,509	577	23.0%	1,215	1.6	36.6%
E242	24	Eagle	30.69	3,808	674	17.7%	1,906	1.6	29.1%
L181	18	Locker	13.59	3,322	246	7.4%	979	3.1	23.3%
T81	12	Taylor	2.99	5,356	407	7.6%	1,627	3.0	23.1%
		Total		469,724	104,627	22.3%	81,001	4.5	100.4%

Factors Mr. Martinez suggested that Ms. Turk consider in her analysis include (1) increasing the GMROI for the category, (2) maintaining the level of sales in the category, (3) providing a full line of wrenches, and (4) evaluating the performance of the vendors and private-label import program.

Discussion Questions

1. Should Ms. Turk recommend discontinuing some of the SKUs? If some SKUs should be discontinued, which ones should they be? Why?

2. Are the price points for the wrenches appropriate? Would you suggest any changes in the prices?

Source: This case was prepared by Barton Weitz, University of Florida.

EXHIBIT 2

Vendor Report

SKU NUMBER	SIZE (INCHES)	VENDOR	RETAIL PRICE	ANNUAL SALES $	GROSS MARGIN $	GROSS MARGIN %	AVERAGE INVENTORY	INVENTORY TURNS	GMROI
C81	8	Calder	$2.49	$7,198	$1,857	25.8%	1,524	3.5	90.4%
C101	10	Calder	3.29	6,667	1,693	25.4%	917	5.4	137.7%
C121	12	Calder	4.59	6,102	1,532	25.1%	1,349	3.4	85.1%
C61	6	Calder	2.99	4,317	1,083	25.1%	773	4.2	105.0%
				24,284	6,165	25.4%	4,563	4.0	100.8%
E82	8	Eagle	3.79	49,901	14,172	28.4%	8,601	4.2	118.0%
E102	10	Eagle	4.89	49,392	11,805	23.9%	8,745	4.3	102.7%
E122	12	Eagle	6.99	47,878	12,113	25.3%	8,250	4.3	109.7%
E121	12	Eagle	5.89	42,827	9,379	21.9%	4,738	7.1	154.6%
E62	6	Eagle	3.39	33,900	7,899	23.3%	6,458	4.0	93.8%
E81	8	Eagle	3.29	29,990	6,868	22.9%	7,437	3.1	71.2%
E101	10	Eagle	3.89	29,041	6,070	20.9%	2,894	7.9	165.9%
E61	6	Eagle	7.69	21,165	4,212	19.9%	1,895	8.9	178.0%
E152	15	Eagle	10.79	17,696	4,778	27.0%	3,677	3.5	94.9%
E151	15	Eagle	9.69	16,543	2,564	15.5%	1,391	10.0	155.8%
E42	4	Eagle	3.29	11,300	2,859	25.3%	2,462	3.4	86.7%
E182	18	Eagle	18.19	8,950	2,300	25.7%	2,977	2.2	57.4%
E41	4	Eagle	2.69	7,379	1,771	24.0%	1,112	5.0	121.0%
E181	18	Eagle	14.29	3,989	1,149	28.8%	742	3.8	110.2%
E242	24	Eagle	30.69	3,808	674	17.7%	1,906	1.6	29.1%
				373,759	88,613	23.7%	63,285	4.5	106.8%
IM10	10	Import	2.89	4,622	1,132	24.5%	1,967	1.8	43.5%
IM8	8	Import	2.19	4,565	1,109	24.3%	1,401	2.5	59.9%
IM12	12	Import	3.89	4,328	1,108	25.6%	1,102	2.9	74.8%
IM6	6	Import	1.79	2,509	577	23.0%	1,215	1.6	36.6%
				16,024	3,926	24.5%	5,685	2.1	52.1%
L181	18	Locker	13.59	3,322	246	7.4%	979	3.1	23.3%
L81	8	Locker	3.19	1,141	247	21.6%	484	1.8	40.0%
L61	6	Locker	3.29	961	227	23.6%	134	5.5	129.4%
L101	10	Locker	3.79	836	157	18.8%	175	3.9	72.9%
L121	12	Locker	5.79	384	120	31.3%	93	2.8	88.7%
				6,644	997	15.0%	1,865	3.0	45.4%
T101	10	Taylor	3.39	28,933	2,922	10.1%	2,050	12.7	128.1%
T121	12	Taylor	5.59	10,328	1,281	12.4%	1,329	6.8	84.4%
T81	12	Taylor	2.99	5,356	407	7.6%	1,627	3.0	23.1%
T61	6	Taylor	2.49	4,396	316	7.2%	597	6.8	49.1%
				49,013	4,926	10.1%	5,603	7.9	79.1%
			Grand total	469,724	104,627	22.3%	81,001	4.5	100.4%

EXHIBIT 3

Subcategory Report

SKU NUMBER	SIZE (INCH)	VENDOR	RETAIL PRICE	ANNUAL SALES $	GROSS MARGIN $	GROSS MARGIN %	AVERAGE INVENTORY	INVENTORY TURNS	GMROI
E41	4	Eagle	2.69	7,379	1,771	24.0%	1,112	5.0	121.0%
E42	4	Eagle	3.29	11,300	2,859	25.3%	2,462	3.4	86.7%
Sales $/SKU			9,340	18,679	4,630	24.8%	3,574	3.9	97.4%
IM6	6	Import	1.79	2,509	577	23.0%	1,215	1.6	36.6%
T61	6	Taylor	2.49	4,396	316	7.2%	597	6.8	49.1%
C61	6	Calder	2.99	4,317	1,083	25.1%	773	4.2	105.0%
L61	6	Locker	3.29	961	227	23.6%	134	5.5	129.4%
E62	6	Eagle	3.39	33,900	7,899	23.3%	6,458	4.0	93.8%
E61	6	Eagle	7.69	21,165	4,212	19.9%	1,895	8.9	178.0%
Sales $/SKU			11,208	67,248	14,315	21.3%	11,072	4.8	101.8%
IM8	8	Import	2.19	4,565	1,109	24.3%	1,401	2.5	59.9%
C81	8	Calder	2.49	7,198	1,857	25.8%	1,524	3.5	90.4%
L81	8	Locker	3.19	1,141	247	21.6%	484	1.8	40.0%
E81	8	Egle	3.29	29,990	6,868	22.9%	7,437	3.1	71.2%
E82	8	Eagle	3.79	49,901	14,172	28.4%	8,601	4.2	118.0%
Sales $/SKU			15,466	92,795	24,253	26.1%	19,447	3.5	92.1%
IM10	10	Import	2.89	4,622	1,132	24.5%	1,967	1.8	43.5%
C101	10	Calder	3.29	6,667	1,693	25.4%	917	5.4	137.7%
T101	10	Taylor	3.39	28,933	2,922	10.1%	2,050	12.7	128.1%
L101	10	Locker	3.79	836	157	18.8%	175	3.9	72.9%
E101	10	Eagle	3.89	29,041	6,070	20.9%	2894	7.9	165.9%
E102	10	Eagle	4.89	49,392	11,805	23.9%	8,745	4.3	102.7%
Sales $/SKU			19,915	119,491	23,779	19.9%	16,748	5.7	113.7%
T81	12	Taylor	2.99	5,356	407	7.6%	1,627	3.0	23.1%
IM12	12	Import	3.89	4,328	1,108	25.6%	1,102	2.9	74.8%
C121	12	Calder	4.59	6,102	1,532	25.1%	1,349	3.4	85.1%
T121	12	Taylor	5.59	10,328	1,281	12.4%	1,329	6.8	84.4%
L121	12	Locker	5.79	384	120	31.3%	93	2.8	88.7%
E121	12	Eagle	5.89	42,827	9,379	21.9%	4,738	7.1	154.6%
E122	12	Eagle	6.99	47,878	12,113	25.3%	8,250	4.3	109.7%
Sales $/SKU			16,743	117,203	25,940	22.1%	18,488	4.9	109.3%
E151	15	Eagle	9.69	16,543	2,564	15.5%	1,391	10.0	155.8%
E152	15	Eagle	10.79	17,696	4,778	27.0%	3,677	3.5	94.9%
Sales $/SKU			17,120	34,239	7,342	21.4%	5,068	5.3	113.8%
L181	18	Locker	13.59	3,322	246	7.4%	979	3.1	23.3%
E181	18	Eagle	14.29	3,989	1,149	28.8%	742	3.8	110.2%
E182	18	Eagle	18.19	8,950	2,300	25.7%	2,977	2.2	57.4%
Sales $/SKU			5,420	16,261	3,695	22.7%	4,698	2.7	60.8%
E242	24	Eagle	30.69	3,808	674	17.7%	1,906	1.6	29.1%
Sales $/SKU			3,808						
			Grand total	469,724	104,627	22.3%	81,001	4.5	100.4%

Urban Outfitters and the Coffee Crowd

URBAN OUTFITTERS (hereafter UO), the specialty store that poses as an ultra-cool department store for upscale 18-to-30–year-olds, has maintained a healthy balance sheet by carefully selecting its merchandise and store locations. The average merchandise buyer in this Philadelphia-based chain is in his or her mid-twenties, which keeps the selection current with its target market. The selection of men's and women's clothing, accessories, bath items, greeting cards, housewares, and tabletop decorations is quick to move with the times, having evolved through stages of preppy to punk to nostalgic to mod to 70s styles. There is always a note of irreverence in the merchandise and store design, which helps to maintain UO's cool image.

Mall locations would not be cool with UO's target customer, so UO seeks hip locations with vibrant urban street life. The stores are often surrounded by other cool retailers, cafes, and gourmet coffee shops that attract a large, well-educated, sophisticated, young crowd. Locations near large college populations indicate ripe opportunities with the target customer base, like Newbury Street in Boston and State Street in Madison, Wisconsin, or in hip urban areas, like Santa Monica, California, downtown Manhattan, Washington, D.C., and Georgetown. Because the cool areas can shift over time, UO leases its store locations. (UO is developing Anthropologie, a retail format aimed at a somewhat older, suburban customer with more money and a more established lifestyle than a typical UO customer has. These store are located in malls.)

A manager at one location noticed that many pedestrians could be seen walking by the store holding cups of gourmet coffee from one of the nearby upscale coffee shops. While UO has a policy against bringing food or beverages into the store, she considered the appeal of a small coffee bar within the store. She knew that some "lifestyle retailers" had installed coffee bars to encourage customers to spend more time in their stores, and that a gourmet coffee bar would further link the UO image with its clientele.

The manager called a few local gourmet coffee roasters/distributors to learn about the costs of various coffee bar options. The classy espresso machines that she so admired would probably not work. At more than $5,000 for a quality commercial machine and its related equipment, she doubted that the store could sell enough to cover the costs in the near future. In addition, operating an espresso machine takes much more skill than a traditional drip brewer. On the other hand, a commercial-grade coffee brewer could be purchased for $800, and an acceptable 2.2 liter (74-ounce) industrial-grade carafe could be purchased for $40. If the coffee bar was a success, she could consider upgrading these carafes to more attractive and durable $75 models. Given the local competition, and her desire to simplify the money-handling process, UO would charge $1 for a 10-ounce cup of coffee and still earn a 54 percent gross margin per pot after the cost of coffee, cream, sugar, add-ins (such as the obligatory cinnamon), cups, and napkins, and allowing for spillage and drips. This compared favorably to the average gross margins in the UO chain that have been steady at about 52 percent in recent years. Because brewing a carafe-size volume took longer than most customers wanted to wait, she would need a carafe and a spare if she wanted to offer one coffee type, but four if she wanted a "regular" coffee and a flavored brew. She assumed that cool people would not be interested in decaffeinated coffee.

One problem would be where to put the coffee bar. As with other stores in the chain, it was important to have adequate stock on the floor, but to maintain an uncluttered atmosphere to showcase the unique merchandise. (The lava lamps shouldn't be overlooked!) To set the ambiance and the potential for sales, the manager wanted customers to see the coffee station as soon as they entered the store. This meant that it could either be at the central checkout counter or occupy a 25-square-foot area on a wall in the front of the store. Locating the station close to a register would allow sales associates to monitor self-service coffee purchases. However, this would mean subsituting it for a jewelry case, which generates $600 per square foot at a gross margin of 72 percent.

A bar placed in the front of the store would have to compete with an average sales per square foot of $450, which is less than the average UO figure of $511, but still better than most specialty stores in the area. The gross profit on sales at this sale is similar to the recent corporate average: 52 percent. However, the manager wants to assign the responsibility for this area to a sales associate. He or she would pour coffee at this location to control "free sampling," monitor the fill level in each carafe, and clean the area as needed in addition to handling the regular floor duties.

Predicting the volume of coffee demanded is difficult, but the manager felt she could sell at least two carafes per day since she saw many people walking outside with coffee. Experience would help fine-tune the brewing amounts throughout each week.

Discussion Questions

1. Evaluate in financial terms the manager's plan to install a coffee bar in Urban Outfitters.

2. Evaluate the coffee station in terms of Urban Outfitters' retail strategy.

Source: This case was prepared by Jan Owens, University of Wisconsin, Madison.

CASE 26

Stan's Shirts

STAN SOPER has a 600-square-foot T-shirt store in a good mall location. He has all colors and sizes plus hundreds of designs for heat-embossing onto the shirts. Every shirt sells for $10. In his area, Stan estimates he has about a steady 12 percent share of a 100,000-units-per-year customized T-shirt market. Stan has found this to be a nonseasonal business. Sales hardly vary from one month to the next.

Stan's costs are

Store lease	$1,400 a month
T-shirts	$4 each
Embossing decals	$.50 each
Embossing equipment	$24,000
Store fixtures	$14,400
Telephone, postage, etc.	$125 per month

Stan's advertising budget is $200 per month. He pays one store assistant $240 per week ($1,040 a month) and draws a salary for himself of $300 per week ($1,300 a month). His waste (T-shirts spoiled by a poor or misapplied decal) runs around 2 percent of T-shirts sold.

Discussion Questions

1. What's the unit contribution for the T-shirts?

2. What's Stan's monthly break-even point?

3. What market share does he need to break even?

4. What's his monthly profit?

5. Because of some new fashion announcements he has just received, Stan expects T-shirt sales in his area to increase to about 144,000 next year. He's considering raising his advertising budget by $800 per month.

    a. If the advertising budget is raised, how many T-shirts must he sell to break even?

    b. How many T-shirts must he sell per month to get the same profit as this year?

    c. What must his market share be next year to get the same profit as this year?

    d. What must his market share be for him to have a monthly profit of $3,000?

Source: This case was prepared by William R. Swinyard, Brigham Young University.

CASE 27

Pricing Problems

SOME OF these problems can be solved using the computer disks accompanying the text. After installing the disks, open the *Integrated Tutorial* and go through the pricing and breakeven segments. Then, open *Integrated Interactive* and select either Cost/Retail Markup Page, Maintained Markup Page, or Breakeven page, and plug in the numbers from the case.

1. The cost of a new CD album is $8.75. The buyer plans to make an initial markup of 25 percent on the retail price. What should the retail price be?

2. The initial selling price for a blouse is $25. The cost was $14. What was the initial markup on retail?

3. A belt was originally priced at $17 and put on sale for $12. What was the markdown percentage on retail?

4. The cost of a bicycle is $200. The initial markup on retail is 40 percent. After offering the bicycle at the initial selling price, the bicycle was marked down by 20 percent and it sold at that price.

    a. What was the eventual selling price for the bicycle?

    b. What was the maintained markup?

5. A woman's dress suit was originally priced at $250. The first markdown was 20 percent on retail; the second markdown was an additional 30 percent. What is the selling price of the suit after the second markdown?

6. A buyer for men's ties wants to have a maintained markup of 40 percent. The buyer forecasts that the reduction as a percentage of sales will be 13 percent.
   a. What should the initial markup be?
   b. In the above example, if the cost of the ties is $12, what would be the initial selling price?

7. A buyer orders 500 cotton sweaters at a cost of $20 per sweater.
   a. What is the cost for all of the sweaters when they are sold?
   b. If the buyer wants to have a maintained markup of 50 percent, what total sales dollars must be generated by the sale of all 500 sweaters?
   c. The buyer sets the sweaters' initial selling price at $45. Two hundred sweaters are sold at that price. How many sales dollars were generated by the sales of the initial 200 sweaters?
   d. How many sales dollars must be generated by the remaining 300 sales to achieve a maintained markup of 50 percent?
   e. Sales of the sweaters are slowing so the buyer is going to mark them down. At what price does he need to sell each of the remaining 300 sweaters to realize 50 percent maintained markup?

f. How much of a markdown on retail can the buyer take to realize a 50 percent maintained markup on the sales of all 500 sweaters?

8. A buyer for women's hosiery is planning to buy merchandise to be sold during the summer season that will generate retail sales of $150,000. The buyer wants to have a maintained markup of 34 percent on retail for summer hosiery sales. Reductions will be very small and can be ignored. The buyer has already spent $53,250 for merchandise that will generate $75,450 at retail. What markup does the buyer need to have on the remainder of the planned purchases to realize the overall markup of 34 percent?

9. A buyer has purchased 100 handbags at $18 each. Some will be sold at $28 retail; others will be sold at $36 retail. How many handbags should be put at each price point to realize a maintained markup of 40 percent, assuming no reductions?

10. A retailer is considering the development of a collection of private-label men's ties. The ties, which will retail for $65 each, will incur an expense to the retailer that includes $15,000 in fixed costs and $19.50 per tie in variable costs. What is the retailer's break-even point expressed in both units and dollars?

Source: These case problems were prepared by Barton Weitz, University of Florida.

An Advertising Plan

A MAJOR department store in the Washington, D.C., area is planning a big rug sale in its suburban Virginia warehouse over the three-day Washington's Birthday weekend (Saturday through Monday). On sale will be nearly $2 million worth of rugs, assembled both from the company's inventory and from various market purchases. The average sale price of each rug is approximately $300. The company hopes to realize at least $900,000 in sales during the three days.

This is the first time the store has sold rugs from its warehouse, but previous experience with coats and furniture has been good. Two factors in particular were common to the previous events:

1. The first day's sales were 50 percent of the total. The second day's were 35 percent, and the last day's, 15 percent.
2. One of every two customers who came made a purchase.

It's known further that large numbers of people always flock to such sales—some driving as far as 50 miles. They come from all economic levels, but are all confirmed bargain hunters.

You're the assistant to the general merchandise manager, who has asked you to plan the event's campaign. The following information is at your disposal:

1. A full-page *Washington Post* ad costs $10,000; a half-page ad costs $6,000, and a quarter-page ad

costs $3,500. To get the maximum value from a newspaper campaign, it's company policy to always run two ads (not necessarily the same size) for such events.

2. The local Northern Virginia paper is printed weekly and distributed free to some 15,000 households. It costs $700 for a full page and $400 for a half page.

3. To get adequate TV coverage, at least three channels must be used, with a minimum of eight 30-second spots on each at $500 per spot, spread over three or more days. Producing a TV spot costs $3,000.

4. The store has contracts with three radio stations. One appeals to a broad general audience aged 25 to 34. One is popular with the 18-to-25 group. A classical music station has a small but wealthy audience. Minimum costs for a saturation radio campaign (incuding produc-

tion) on the three stations are $8,000, $5,000, and $3,000, respectively.

5. To produce and mail a full-color flyer to the store's 80,000 charge customers costs $10,000. When the company used such a mailing piece before, about 3 percent responded.

Discussion Questions

1. Knowing that the company wants a mixed-media ad campaign to support this event, prepare an ad plan for the general merchandise manager that costs no more than $40,000.
2. Work out the daily scheduling of all advertising.
3. Work out the dollars to be devoted to each medium.
4. Justify your plan.

Source: This case was prepared by David Ehrlich, Marymount University.

CASE **29**

Neiman Marcus's Preferred Customer Program

DALLAS-BASED department store retailer Neiman Marcus (NM) began the first preferred customer program, InCircle, in 1984. In such a program, purchases can only be completed with either the Neiman Marcus credit card, American Express Card, cash, or check. This retailer utilizes its own card to reward and provide incentives for its customers.

Customers must spend $3,000 on their Neiman Marcus charge in one calendar year to become eligible for the InCircle program. Once a part of this program, shoppers receive one InCircle point for each dollar charged to their Neiman Marcus card. These points must be redeemed at the end of the calendar year for prizes.

The rewards for InCircle membership include invitations to exclusive shopping events, a quarterly newsletter, free gift wrapping for purchases of $25 or more, double points on birthdays, and others. Prizes for points include Waterford crystal, engraved stationery, fine wines, and vacations.

In 1995, the customer programs division of Neiman Marcus developed different levels and programs within InCircle. Once an InCircle member has accumulated 1,500 points in a calendar year, she is extended an offer to become a Neiman Marcus Gold Card holder for a $50 annual fee. This status allows the member to earn double points for each dollar spent (up to $1,500). Other bonuses are given to the customer upon "earning" her Gold Card status, including a $50 American Airlines certificate for travel, a complimentary magazine subscription, free credit protection for charge cards, bonus InCircle points for certain events, and travel benefits.

The Platinum Card is offered to InCircle members who have accumulated 3,000 or more points. The $500 annual fee allows a customer to earn double points for the first $30,000 in purchases each year. Charter Platinum status is maintained by those who earn a minimum of 100,000 points yearly. Special gifts are available only to platinum members. They include restaurant gift certificates to exclusive establishments, such as Charlie Trotter's in Chicago. American Airlines travel certificates and unlimited Four Season's Hotel upgrades are also part of the platinum perks.

The goal of the InCircle programs is to appeal to each customer's distinctive buying habits and to foster further purchases. The rewards for each level of the program are distinctive and increasingly attractive.

"It's all about recognition and loyalty," said Billy Payton, vice president of marketing and customer programs. "It is important to make customers feel special by rewarding them for being good Neiman Marcus customers."

Other prizes include elaborate vacations available only to those with large numbers of points. In keeping with the high standards of Neiman Marcus's customer service, a full-time travel coordinator and assistant are on staff to personalize the trips earned by the InCircle customers.

All InCircle customers are invited to attend private shopping parties where they generally earn double points for their purchases. These dates, times, and locations are printed in the newsletter, *The InCircler*.

Special gifts and events are made available to members through the newsletter. Package trips/vacations, such as to the Olympics or Southern California, may be purchased. Distinctive items obtainable only by InCirclers are also featured.

InCircle not only benefits its members, it rewards sales professionals too. Loyalty will bring customers into Neiman Marcus to make more purchases, as the promise of the coveted points will also. This means more sales for a store's staff.

InCircle members are given the opportunity to present Exceptional Service Awards to deserving NM associates. These awards are in the form of a sticker and enclosed with each member's InCircle card. A sticker brings the member bonus points when it is presented to the associate, and the associate's name is entered into a quarterly prize drawing.

Other department stores have patterned preferred customer or valued customer programs after Neiman's InCircle. The company continues to add more prizes and privileges as its program develops. Currently, executives are planning for InCircle's thirteenth year.

"InCircle continues to be successful through gained market share and brand awareness," said Payton. "Our program perseveres because our customers enjoy and take advantage of their special perks and privileges."

Discussion Questions

1. How does InCircle build loyalty for Neiman Marcus versus other upscale retailers like Saks and Lord & Taylor?

2. How effective is the InCircle program in developing customer loyalty?

3. What obstacles might InCircle professionals face in further developing their program?

4. If all of Neiman Marcus's customers were ranked in terms of their annual purchases from the store, to which group should Neiman Marcus target their frequent shopper program? The top 10 percent? The second decile? The bottom 10 percent? Why?

Source: This case was prepared by Allison T. Knott, University of Florida.

CASE **30**

Dexter Brown, Star Salesperson

JANET GOULD (personnel administrator of Ian's, an elegant men's boutique in New York) had to decide what to do about her current problem child, salesman Dexter Brown.

Brown, a young man of 26 with movie-star good looks and a personality to go with them, had come to the store with wonderful references. He'd sold for two other men's stores (both somewhat less pricey than Ian's) and both his supervisors had said he was the best salesman they'd ever had. Indeed, he lived up to his advance billing. Ian's average salesman sold $1,000 a day on weekdays and $1,500 on Saturdays. In Brown's second week, he hit $2,000. Every day he was beating all the more experienced people hands down.

Salespeople at Ian's were paid a base salary plus a commission of 3 percent of sales of clothing (suits, sport jackets, and outerwear) and 1 percent of sales of furnishings (shirts, ties, sweaters, and accessories). Normally, a good commission salesperson would earn about $25,000 per year. The average longevity of the staff was five years. The average age of the selling staff was 35.

Dexter Brown was putting all the other employees to shame, and Gould wasn't sure whether this was the best or the worst thing that had ever happened to Ian's. His technique was quick and slick: He would stand near the front door and greet incoming shoppers with a cheery "Hi, I'm Dexter. When you're ready to make your purchase, please give me a call." He even had business cards with his name printed—at his own expense—and he handed them out liberally. Sometimes he'd give one to a shopper who was walking out and say, "Next time, be sure to ask for

Dexter." Naturally, other people in the department resented Dexter's methods, but they had to acknowledge that his sales technique was superb. He looked and dressed the part. Women in particular were drawn to him.

Overall, store sales were up since his joining the staff, but nowhere near 50 percent, which meant that he was in effect "stealing" some of the other men's business.

Gould had heard complaints from some of the others. Jim Green said, "I've got to admire that guy. I watch him all the time and learn something new each time. But he's eating into my commissions, and I don't like that. I've got a family to feed."

Art Ward was less complimentary. "That little rat, he's stealing my customers—my customers. He doesn't give them a chance to come in and say hello—he just grabs them. They've started listening to him."

And so it went. Brown had been with the store six months, and he was due for a review. Gould had to talk to him, but she wasn't sure whether to praise and raise him, or to let him go as a troublemaker.

Discussion Questions

1. What are the positive and negative aspects of Brown's behaviors?

2. Should the boutique fire Brown?

3. How can Gould emphasize the positive aspects of Brown's behavior and reduce the negative aspects?

4. What specifically would you say to Brown during the six-month review meeting?

Source: This case was prepared by David Ehrlich, Marymount University.

CASE **31**

The Tardy Trainee

THE METRO-DAY department store in downtown Seattle specializes in well-made clothing plus up-to-the-minute kitchen items and home furnishings. Of the six Metro-Day stores around the country, it's ranked number 1 in terms of sales volume and store standards. It's also the home of the company's Executive Training Program for future store managers.

A rising star with Metro-Day, Max Murphy had graduated from the training program himself only two years ago and had performed well with his first two assignments at other Metro locations. When an opening arose in the Seattle store, Max jumped at the chance. Not only would he be getting a promotion to sales manager of the Kitchen and Home Furnishings Department, he'd also get to teach that section of the training program. Max had done well in the training program and had gained the reputation of being a sharp, creative manager at both assignments prior to the Seattle promotion.

His first few months of managing the new department went smoothly. Max had gotten most of the usual personnel gripes under control and had familiarized and remerchandised the stock in his area to boost sales 20 percent over last year's figures. The first batch of two trainees came through the program with high marks, singing Max's praises. He was not only a smart merchant, but also a fair, honest, caring trainer.

Four people—twice the normal number—were going through the second training program. One of them, Sue Baker, presented Max with concerns. Sue would often show up late or work on written homework when she was supposed to be managing sections of the sales floor with the other trainees. Max knew he needed to sit down and talk with Sue after two weeks of working with her, but whenever he had a chance to talk with her, she was either absent—she was sick often—or somewhere other than the department. With three other trainees plus Christmas preparations, Max was very busy.

Max finally cornered Sue and spoke to her about her performance, highlighting his concerns. She seemed to take the conversation very personally. She said that Max didn't understand that she had car problems and allergies and that, not being a parent himself, wouldn't understand her responsibilities when her two children were sick. She claimed that when she was on the sales floor, he wasn't around. Max tried to be sympathetic to Sue's situation, but made it clear that she had responsibilities to the store. The conversation ended with both parties agreeing to try to do better.

Midway through the program, all trainees were to turn in progress sheets for Max to initial and rate. All did so but Sue. Max asked Sue for the report twice, but she never seemed to get it to him. By the end of the program, Max turned in a final report on all trainees. Now Sue came through with her midway review sheets as well. Both reports would need passing marks for the trainee to move on to the next section of the store. Sue's work on the second half was passable, but just barely. Looking over the review sheet for the first part of the program—with so much time passing between and the problems with Sue's attendance and work performance—made it almost impossible, in Max's mind, to evaluate Sue fairly.

Max was befuddled. He honestly didn't believe that Sue had successfully completed the program and couldn't fairly evaluate her on the first half. But he felt partly responsible for her failure since he hadn't pushed her harder to get her work turned in—though it's true that he had pushed her twice as hard as the other trainees. To further complicate matters, the program was a "self-motivated" one and the trainees knew from the start that Max wasn't there to baby-sit them.

Discussion Question
What should Max do?

Source: This case was prepared by Laura Bliss, Stephens College.

CASE 32

Borders Book Store

MICHAEL CHAIM, general manager of the Borders Bookstore in Madison, Wisconsin, was proud of his store. Located in a city that has one of the highest levels of book purchases per capita, Mr. Chaim felt Borders' selection, services, and location near the 40,000-student university served the community well. Even with competitive pressure from the newly opened Barnes and Noble on the west side of town, his bookstore-and-cafe was often a busy place.

Michael was taken aback when an article in a widely read "alternative" newspaper criticized the bookstore's merchandise arrangement as prejudiced. The store carries a large selection of literature and poetry, but separates some specialty categories, such as African American literature, gay and lesbian literature, and feminist literature, from the general literature and poetry sections. In part, this arrangement reflects Borders' college town roots in Ann Arbor, Michigan, where specialty collections were established to match course offerings.

The article described this arrangement as "ghetto-izing" authors who were not white males, although some female authors were in the general literature and poetry sections. The article and some follow-up letters to the newspaper's editor derided Borders for the few "nontraditional" authors who made it into the general literature collection. They felt that these African American, homosexual, Native American, and other nontraditional writers probably would have been separated from the general collection, had the management known the literature better.

While Madison is known as a very liberal community, Michael thought the accusation was very unfair. He strongly believed that he was doing his customers a service in highlighting authors and literary genres that may have been overlooked in a large, nondifferentiated collection. More immediately, he knew that he should respond to the article's accusations.

Discussion Questions
1. What should Michael Chaim do?
2. One option is to duplicate the titles that could be shelved in either the general literature section or in a specialty collection. What are the advantages and disadvantages of this tactic?

Source: This case was prepared by Jan Owens, University of Wisconsin.

CASE 33

The Best Display?

A MAJOR department store recognized that its first-floor selling fixtures had become outmoded so it set aside funds to renovate. The main floor had not been changed appreciably since the store was built in the 1920s. There were a number of handsome mahogany-paneled counter islands, which had always given the store an aura of tasteful elegance.

Jim Lewis, director of store fixturing, was debating the merits of several possible display systems. The selling departments that would be affected by the renovation were cosmetics; fine and costume jewelry; women's handbags, scarves, and belts; men's shirts, ties, and furnishings; women's sweaters; and gifts.

As Lewis saw it, the two major issues surrounding his decision were incompatible. On the one hand, the store wanted to make merchandise as accessible to customers as possible; on the other hand, experience had indicated that open-selling fixtures inevitably lead to more shoplifting.

As an experiment, the store had tried substituting self-service fixtures in its upstairs sweater department a year earlier. Sales jumped 30 percent, but inventory shrinkage in the department had gone from 2 to almost 5 percent.

A further consideration was that the size and quality of the staff on the selling floor had declined dramatically. In 1929, there were always two salespeople behind every counter, and customers could count on never having to wait for service. However, selling costs had since escalated, and the store's staff was less than half what it had been then. Furthermore, the store had instituted modern point-of-sale cash registers that enabled every salesperson to ring up a sale from any department in the store at any register. Most of the clerks were minimum-wage individuals who were only working there until something better turned up. Although some were able to provide useful selling information to the public, most could do little more than ring up sales.

The kind of open-selling fixtures Lewis was considering were contemporary and very attractive. They allowed the customer to pick up, unfold, or unpackage merchandise; try it on if appropriate; and then return it to the fixture. Such fixtures would unquestionably lead to more sales, especially since the customer could merely look for any salesperson or perhaps go to a central cashier to pay. However, it was equally unquestionable that such easy access to merchandise, especially to small goods, would encourage shoplifting and would increase the need for ongoing stock keeping.

Another disadvantage to the new type of fixturing was that in addition to being contemporary, it was somewhat trendy, which would lead to the need to replace it in a few years, thereby adding to capital costs.

An alternative system would be to retain the old counter islands, or a portion of them, but to put more goods on the countertops to encourage a measure of self-service. The disadvantage here, of course, would be the blocking of sight lines. Salespeople could not see customers, customers could not see salespeople, and the store security personnel could not see either. There would also need to be more policing by the store's display and merchandising staff to be sure the countertops looked inviting at all times. Manufacturers often contribute countertop displays to stores as part of the merchandise buying, and many of them might not be in harmony with the store's overall appearance.

Lewis recognized that he would have to make some compromises. Every affected department has its own peculiarities, and his job was to minimize those differences, rather than allow them to get out of hand. Some merchandise, such as fine jewelry, would obviously have to remain behind glass, but other departments would probably do much better by opening up their stocks to the public.

Discussion Questions

1. What display system would you recommend? Why?

2. Would you make the same recommendation for each of the affected departments? Why?

Source: This case was prepared by David Ehrlich, Marymount University.

CASE 34

Olathe Lanes East Bowling Center: Retail Space to Mirror Customers' Lifestyles

BJ'S LIFECODE Merchandising/Design is a company in Mission Hills, Kansas, that utilizes marketing techniques to redesign businesses' selling space. The executives examine customers' lifestyles rather than design trends to guide their layout and decorative decisions.

After the Olathe Lanes East bowling center burned in an electrical fire, the lanes' owner, Charlie Boyd, was eager to rebuild the lanes and reestablish his profitable business. Even though he had decided to keep the lanes as they were before the fire, he hired BJ's design firm to give him some ideas. However, the president of the design company, Barbara J. Eichhorn (the BJ in BJ's), had a vision for his business that came from her casual observations. It was as simple as the cars in Boyd's parking lot.

Since the fire, Boyd had been directing his Olathe Lanes East customers to Olathe Lanes West less than three miles away. When Eichhorn visited the West site on various days, she observed that there were different types of cars in the parking lot on certain nights of the week. Two nights had American-made cars and trucks, while two other evenings brought out owners of upper-end vehicles like Cadillacs and BMWs.

Boyd was impressed with Eichhorn's observations and agreed to allow BJ's to conduct research to define its clientele. A questionnaire was developed based on the VALS 2 psychographic scheme from SRI International. Some questions addressed customers' residences, attitudes, and buying styles.

The surveys revealed that the groups that frequented the separate facilities were, in fact, quite different. The Olathe West clients went to the bowling alley to gather with friends. While both women and men wanted to socialize, competition was still significant to their visits. There were a number of bowling leagues at this facility; most league members were employed in repetitive-task jobs.

The patrons of Olathe East used bowling as a means to relax. Sixty-five percent of the customers were women and children. The men reported their jobs as being mostly management positions. Therefore, the men bowled to release tension, not to compete. The Olathe East patrons did not need the bowling alley as a place to socialize; most indicated they had other outlets by which to interact with others.

Extensive profile research was performed from the data collected. BJ's staff used the PRIZM system from Claritas, which segments lifestyles. The Olathe East customers self-segmented themselves into three upper-class groups: young suburbia (38 percent), pools and patios (30 percent), and furs and station wagons (23 percent). The Olathe West patrons were in four predominantly blue-collar segments: blue collar nursery (17 percent), middle America (39 percent), blue chip blues (13 percent), and shotguns and pickups (9 percent). This information was used extensively in deciding on the interior changes to be made to the bowling alley.

Before BJ's decided on a design for the facility, executives asked Boyd which part of his business was most profitable. Interestingly enough, it was the refreshments. The design firm then changed the project's focus from the bowling component of the facility to food services.

Olathe Lanes East became one level, as opposed to its previous tier design. The new layout encouraged carrying food and drink into the bowling area. The centerpiece of the facility became the new concession area, consisting of a food court and bar. The tables behind the bowling area were purposely large—a well-known tactic. Customers have a tendency to fill their tables with food and drink, so the larger the better.

The design took a soft, art deco form. Since the Olathe East customers frequented the alley for relaxation, all edges of chair backs, walls, countertops, and signs were rounded.

To enhance the relaxing atmosphere, the issue of noise was addressed. To minimize the decibel level, decorative sound-refracting materials were used. New high-tech bowling equipment was also brought in to heighten the upscale look. Also, mahogany accents were used throughout the building. The restrooms were even upgraded with faux-marble–topped vanities and beveled mirrors.

Not leaving any detail to chance, BJ's examined the lighting of the facility. Concourse skylights and yuppie floor-to-ceiling windows were installed to increase the brightness of the alley. This created an open, active environment.

Well, did this overhaul help the financial status of the bowling alleys? Olathe Lanes East reported an outstanding increase of food and beverage sales. Over two and one-half times more refreshments were purchased for each line bowled than before the reconstruction. This obviously excited Boyd, and he asked the company to redesign his West location.

Since the Olathe West customers were competitive, squares and triangles were used as opposed to the soft edges of the East location; these were to demonstrate the customers' energy. The Southwestern style of the bowling alley utilized natural oak, peach stucco, and blue-green accents. The decor created a folksy, outdoors style.

Both locations provided a healthy and profitable business for Boyd. The customers were pleased with the new and unique locations.

BJ's Lifecode Merchandising/Design company made a dramatic change in the way it approached design. It began to rely on customers' lifestyles to direct decorative decisions, which has proved profitable for the businesses it has assisted. As BJ herself said, "Any retail environment—restaurant, appliance store, bank, or mall—can benefit by treating its exterior and interior as ready-made ads for the business."

1. What other changes in the business could Boyd have made to accompany the new look of his bowling alleys?

2. What could Boyd have done if he wasn't financially able to completely redo his Olathe West location?

Source: This case was prepared by Allison T. Knott, University of Florida.

CASE 35

Levi Stores: Mass Customization of Jeans

DO YOU EVER have problems finding the perfect pair of jeans? Are they too short? Too baggy? Too tight in the legs? Not big enough in the waist? If these problems seem familiar to you, Levi Strauss and Co. has a solution.

Their solution is "made-to-measure" jeans, called Personal Pair Jeans, a retail innovation that is the first of its type in the fashion industry. It's all done with a computer and tape measure. The process begins with a salesperson taking four measurements on the customer: waist, hips, inseam, and rise (the distance from the front waistband between the legs up to the back waistband). The measurements are then entered into a computer, which produces the number of the prototype pair of jeans with those measurements. The customer tries on the prototype, and the salesperson notes any modifications, which may be as minor as two inches in the fit. Once the modifications are determined, the new measurements are entered into a computer that produces another try-on prototype for the customer. "On average, it takes two or three prototypes before a customer is totally satisfied with the fit," a Levi spokesperson said.

The final fit numbers are electronically sent to a Levi's factory in Mountain City, Tennessee, where a bolt of denim is cut precisely to the customer's request. About three weeks later, they are sent for pickup at the Levi store, or they can be express-mailed directly to the customer for an additional $5. The cost of this service is about $58, which is about $10 higher than the conventional pair off the rack. Personal Pair is available at all Levi stores except the Manhattan one because of space constraints. Cassie Ederer, a Levi marketing specialist, comments, "The program is being watched carefully in the industry, because the ultimate promise of mass customization is no inventory, and therefore no markdowns." Annette Lim, a retail marketing services manager for Levi, adds, "You're not mass producing a product and hoping it sells. You've already got the sale."

Personal Pair is offered exclusively to purchasers of the women's Levi 512 jean, a fitted style. There are no plans to make this service available to men because market research indicates that women complain far more than men about difficulties in finding off-the-rack jeans.

The Personal Pair Jean is aimed at two types of women. "We see these jeans to be targeted to the woman who is discriminating about how her jeans fit or who is just a denim connoisseur in search of the 'ultimate,'" according to Lim.

What Levi is doing is part of an industrial trend called mass customization. The concept entails using computerized instructions to enable factories to tailor mass-market items to suit individual buyers. Other clothing retailers such as Tommy Hilfiger, Nautica, and Guess? have also begun to experiment with mass customization. Lee Apparel is also offering its customers a similar, but faster, service. Fit Finder is an interactive kiosk designed to provide women with a quick way of finding the size and style of Lee jeans that meet their personal preference by an in-store full-service computer. It is programmed with each store's individual inventory; the customer herself enters her measurements and the computer chooses the right Lee jean for her. Melissa Lewenstein, a spokesperson for Lee, believes her service is better than Levi's because "Customers don't have to find help, and don't have to pay a premium. And they don't have to wait for jeans to be made." Even with these advantages, Lee does not have the demand from consumers that Levi does; Levi sales have more than tripled over the past year. So, ladies, no more putting off that dreaded trip to the mall to find the perfect fit. It's now available right at your fingertips!

Discussion Questions

1. What are the advantages and the disadvantages of mass customization for the customer? For the retailer?

2. To what extent will mass customization affect the way in-store retailing is done? Will mass customization increase or decrease if electronic home shopping becomes more popular?

Source: This case was prepared by Laura Hooks and Heather Zuilkoski, University of Florida.

CASE **36**

Delta Airlines Finds Customer Service at a High Price

DURING THE 1980s, which was considered the airline's prime, Delta could boast about its tremendous customer service records. Readers of *Travel-Holiday* magazine rated it the number one U.S. air carrier. From 1984 to 1986, Delta averaged under one complaint per 100,000 passengers.

Delta was highly regarded not only by its passengers but also by its employees. The company allowed its workers to take ownership, which promoted a family atmosphere at Delta. The airline was nonunion by choice and determined to remain as such through excellent labor relations and low-key supervisory systems. There were few job rules. Employees were expected to guard their own performance and have pride in the services they provided. Cooperation was second nature to the workers, as flight crews were known to assist in ticketing passengers to cut customer delays.

One of the central, yet confidential, lines that Delta maintained was no layoffs or furloughs. This was validated in 1983, when the airline reported an operating income loss, the first in 39 years, and all jobs were spared. Previous to the loss, when all other airlines cut salaries in 1982, Delta rewarded its employees with an 8 percent raise. To show their appreciation to the company, employees banned together and purchased a $30 million Boeing 767 out of their own paychecks. There is no better example of the family spirit and loyalty felt within the company during that time.

The good will, however, deteriorated with the announcement on April 28, 1994, of Delta's Leadership 7.5 project. This program was developed to return the company to profitability by saving $2 billion over three years.

At that time, the average operating cost was 9.26 cents per available seat mile (ASM), the unit cost for carrying one seat one mile. The new project set a goal of 7.5 cents by June 1997. This reduction of ASM was to be achieved by improving efficiency and streamlining operations, which would eliminate 12,000 to 15,000 jobs, a 16 to 20 percent cutback.

Ron Allen, Delta chairman, president, and CEO, stated at the rollout of the program that the company wanted to reduce costs, not jobs, but that Delta would be changing the way it operated. He stated that the emergence of Leadership 7.5 was a direct result of fierce competition from low-frills airlines. Delta was forced to match rock-bottom fares but could not remain profitable at those prices.

Despite Allen's statement, many jobs were no longer needed because of the changes in Delta's operations. Employees were first offered options, such as leaves of absence and voluntary severance. The next phase was to offer early retirement to people age 52 and older. Finally, the layoffs began. Standard and Poor's Corporation said that Delta's program was the most ambitious cost-cutting initiative yet attempted in the U.S. airline industry.

This set of layoffs came not long after a previous job reduction plan that cut 7,400 jobs in a two-year period (June 1992 to April 1994). In February 1993, all workers, excluding the unionized pilots, took a 5 percent salary decrease to assist the company.

Part of Leadership 7.5's streamlining included 4,500 jobs cut from its customer service division. The duties from these jobs were diffused among remaining personnel, part-time workers, and outside contractors. The jobs included loading and unloading planes, cleaning and stocking planes, and working at gates and ticket counters.

Unfortunately, customer service became a casualty of the program. The U.S. Department of Transportation reported in early 1996 that the number of complaints about Delta were much greater than in the past year. Also, frequent fliers were upset about fewer meals, fewer flight attendants per flight, more mishandled baggage, more delayed flights, and longer check-in lines.

"Over the last six to nine months I have noticed it isn't the same," said Delta frequent flier Bob Fletcher in a 1996 interview. Fletcher added that he once felt privileged to fly Delta. As a result of the cutbacks, he complained that flying seemed like "riding a bus."

A journalist wrote that the attributes that the airline prided itself on—lifetime employment, high pay, lush in-flight services, and a blanket-the-territory route map—were plainly out of step in the deregulation era.

"They had to make decisions that ran contrary to a lot of their history, culture, and past practices," said Donald Carty, president of American Airlines in a 1996 interview.

Along with customer service, Delta's food budget fell below the industry average, whereas before it was higher than its competitors'. In December 1995, only 59 percent of its flights landed within 15 minutes of schedule, which was the worst among the major airlines and eight points below the average.

Delta executives announced in 1996 that their cutbacks may have been too extensive. Some problems with timeliness were attributed to less experienced workers completing tasks, such as cleaning and refueling, which delayed the take-off process. Complaints from employees that the maintenance

staff was too lean led to rehiring some mechanics whom Delta had previously released.

Many critics felt that one contributing factor to the customer service problem was a decline in morale within the company. Past research shows that the manner in which employees treat their customers is directly affected by the way they are treated by management. The once secure feeling that was rampant throughout Delta had been replaced with thoughts of betrayal and insecurity. In a survey of Delta flight attendants, 53 percent reported that they trusted "nobody" within the company. A feeling of needing to conform to save one's job was reported by many past and current workers.

Delta faced a problem that had no easy solution. The company was no longer profitable, so its executives had to make changes in order to save jobs and, potentially, the airline. While Delta was rapidly approaching its goal of $2 billion in savings, the company found itself in a black spin of low employee and customer satisfaction, a new combination for the once revered airline.

Discussion Questions

1. What could Delta have done differently to maintain high levels of customer service as staff numbers were decreasing?

2. How could Delta rebuild its employee morale and have it passed on to its passengers?

Source: This case was prepared by Allison T. Knott, University of Florida.

C A S E **37**

Best Buy Uses Kiosks to Improve Customer Service

BEST BUY COMPANY, Inc., a superstore electronics retailer, is a multibillion-dollar company based out of Eden-Prairie, Minnesota. It offers consumer electronics, home office products, entertainment software, and appliances to its customers. The firm decided that it was going to attract customers by making shopping fun and informative. It would provide unbiased information about the merchandise it sold and make it easy for customers to comparison shop with this information.

Best Buy was started by Richard M. Schulze, the present chairman and CEO, in 1966. The retailer began by selling audio component systems and called itself Sound of Music. In the early 1980s, Best Buy adopted its current name. Prompted by the development of the VCR, the retailer added video products and appliances to its inventory.

The store plans have evolved since its self-service approach in 1989. The first set of stores were about 28,000 square feet and based on a commission sales environment. These stores are now referred to as Concept I. By early 1992, Concept II stores were constructed with approximately 36,000 square feet. They were designed in a warehouse style where customers could browse and select merchandise on their own and then bring their choices to a central checkout. The sales force also incurred change as they became salaried employees. This was done to reduce pressure on customers.

Concept III are the most recent store plans, which have 45,000 to 58,000 square feet. A proportionate sales team of associates called "blue shirts," named for their work attire, is also part of the Concept III design.

The large stores were designed to be exciting, yet still low-pressure, for customers. The idea was to inform the customers and give honest, consistent answers to their electronics questions. Executives also wanted to develop an interactive store, where shoppers could examine and demonstrate the products. These stores included enhancements of their displays. The new prototype stores had demonstrations such as the virtual car, surround sound, and CD listening posts.

During the summer of 1994, Best Buy officers looked at designing and implementing a new point-of-sale system. Through their deliberations came the idea of Answer Centers, 10-foot-tall kiosks that stand alone in some Concept III stores. These kiosks should further their concept of interactive stores.

"As one of America's fastest growing retailers, Best Buy needed a flexible, fast, effective way to get unbiased product information to our customers and employees," said Clark Becker, vice president of MIS systems and programming for Best Buy, in a 1995 interview.

There are 12 Answer Centers in each Concept III-kiosk store. The centers quickly provide a wide range of information that includes text-based specifications, product descriptions, full-color graphics, and video clips. From the kiosk, the customer may learn about products' uses, features, and prices. The centers render accurate, consistent, and current data that do not instruct a customer to purchase a certain brand.

"Our customers need easy-to-understand product information that will enable them to make immediate buying decisions," said Becker.

Each center is strategically placed in the stores and provides a touch screen. Shoppers view and then select from photographs of the merchandise. Video tutorials on product features in stereo sound are provided by the kiosks. The customers may also print the information they find about the product(s). Therefore, they may comparison shop as informed consumers, carrying with them data supplied by Best Buy.

The kiosks allow customers to view items either by price, manufacturer, or groups, such as "CD players." Shoppers may learn more about equipment as a whole or by a certain component or feature.

"Lines of resolution on a TV screen—what does *lines of resolution* mean?" said Steve Anderson, Best Buy senior vice president of MIS and CIO, to give an example of the detail that the centers can provide. "If you go to the Answer Center and touch 'resolution,' it explains what that is and, based upon how you use your TV, how many lines of resolution you really need."

Best Buy teamed up with Microsoft and Digital to create the Answer Centers. The centers consist of a Pentium 590 PC and 17-inch monitor. These kiosks are fed information from the single Digital AlphaServer 2100 processor that is stored in a back room of each store. The system is on-line, meaning that both video and point-of-sale run from the same database. Therefore, there are no discrepancies between the kiosks and the checkout terminal. Also, price and information revisions are done in one location, which updates each kiosk across the country.

How does all of this affect the sales associates' jobs? Overall, it provides them with more information and more time to spend with customers. Not all Best Buy shoppers feel comfortable using the centers. The blue shirts are able, however, to give demonstrations and facts to the customers by using the kiosks. The information accessed is accurate and consistent. Inventory data of each store and warehouses are also available to the blue shirts via the centers, so that an item may be located for a shopper.

Another use of the centers is for training the over 35,500 employees. All employees may learn in their own store or travel to a nearby Concept III-kiosk store without having to trek to a central training site.

By the end of 1996, Best Buy will have over 270 total stores, including 157 Concept III stores, 24 with kiosks. Their popularity is growing as it is known as a fun place to shop. The environment encourages people to learn about products and make informed purchase decisions.

The Answer Centers project was expensive, but has paid off in sales over past years. Best Buy's sales for fiscal 1994 were $3 billion, $5 billion for 1995, and $7.2 billion for 1996; 1997 sales are projected at $8.5 billion.

According to Becker, kiosk-based technology is a key element of the retailer's future competitiveness. "The information that we provide with our kiosks is a major differentiator for us in the competitive electronic retail business."

Discussion Questions

1. What are potential weaknesses of the Concept III-kiosk stores?

2. What changes in management style would need to occur for a manager coming from a Concept I to a Concept III store?

Source: This case was prepared by Allison T. Knott, University of Florida.

Careers in Retailing

QUESTIONS

- What careers are available in retailing?
- Is retailing for me?
- What characteristics are necessary to be a successful retail executive?
- What are some commonly asked questions about a career in retailing?

RETAILING IS ONE OF THE MOST EXCITING, dynamic businesses in the world. Few other industries grant as many responsibilities to young managers. Where else can somebody be fully responsible for the profit-and-loss performance of a full business unit in just a few years? Also, few other industries provide as much opportunity to be entrepreneurial. Where else can an individual have an idea in the market, bring it back to the store, execute it in a few months—often at great financial risk—and at the same time have the indispensable support functions of colleagues at his or her call?

Retailing offers a variety of career paths such as buying, store management, sales promotion and advertising, personnel, operations/distribution, loss prevention, and finance in several different corporate forms such as department stores, specialty stores, food stores, and discount stores.

In addition, retailing offers almost immediate accountability for talented people to reach key management positions within a decade. Starting salaries are competitive, and the compensation of top management ranks among the highest in any industry.

CAREER OPPORTUNITIES

Did you know that the retailing industry is the nation's single largest employer? Within each type of retailing environment, career opportunities occur in the merchandising/buying, store management, and corporate functions. Corporate positions are found in such areas as accounting, finance, promotions and advertising, computer and distribution systems, and human resources.

The primary entry-level opportunities for a retailing career are in the areas of buying and store management. There are, however, more limited opportunities in the corporate staff. The corporate staff supports the organization's merchandising and operating efforts. A strong familiarity with merchandising is generally required to perform these corporate staff functions. Therefore, most executives in these support roles typically begin their careers in store management or buying.

Store Management

Successful store managers must have the ability to lead and motivate employees, as well as have an eye for detail—whether it be stock status reports or housekeeping and display. Store management involves all the disciplines necessary to run a successful business: sales planning and goal setting, overall store image and merchandise presentation, budgets and expense control, customer service and sales supervision, personnel administration and development, and community relations. The store manager works directly in the retail environment. Remote locations isolate him from the home office and create a sense of independence. His hours generally mirror his store's and can therefore include weekends and evenings. In addition, he spends much time during nonoperating hours tending to administrative responsibilities. His primary function is to manage the store's resources (merchandise, services, equipment, and personnel) with an end goal of satisfying the customer while maintaining a healthy retail operation. This requires good human management skills, general knowledge of several business disciplines (accounting, management, etc.), sales skills, creative decision-making skills, and common sense.

The typical career path in a department store usually begins as a department manager with responsibility for merchandise presentation, customer service, and inventory control. Next, you advance to a position known as area or group manager with responsibility for executing merchandising plans and achieving sales goals for several departments, as well as supervising training, and developing department managers. After these positions, you might become a general manager or store manager and eventually end up at corporate headquarters. Retailing View A.1 gives a glimpse into a successful career path at Wal-Mart.

Merchandising/Buying

Merchandise management attracts people with strong analytical capabilities, an ability to predict what merchandise will appeal to their target markets, and a skill to work with vendors as well as store management to get things done. Recently, many retailers have broken the merchandising/buying function into two different yet parallel career paths: buying and merchandise planning. Exhibit A–1 illustrates the career paths for buying and merchandise planning for a department store chain like Federated Department Stores, Inc.

Buyers are responsible for knowing customers' needs and wants, monitoring competition, and working with vendors to select and purchase merchandise. They must constantly stay in contact with their stores by visiting them, by talking to sales associates and managers, and by monitoring the sales data available on their merchandise management systems.

Planners have a more analytical role than buyers do. Their primary responsibility is to break down the merchandise budget into SKUs (i.e., determine how many styles, colors, sizes, and individual SKUs to purchase). Planners also control the open-to-buy and are responsible for allocating merchandise to stores. Once the merchandise is in the stores, planners closely monitor sales and work with buyers on decisions such as how much additional merchandise to purchase if the merchandise is doing well, or when to mark down merchandise if sales are below plan. Merchandise planners work very closely with distribution centers to make sure merchandise is in the stores when it is needed. Due to the analytical nature of these

A.1

From Intern to Store Manager

STEVE SCHULTHEIS is a Wal-Mart store manager in Lehighton, Pennsylvania. He began his retail career in 1988 through an internship with Wal-Mart. During his internship, Steve worked in one of the warehouses where he discovered a more efficient way to pack boxes. That year he saved Wal-Mart over $1 million in labor and supplies.

Steve graduated in 1989 with a bachelor of arts degree in marketing. His first position after graduation was with Wal-Mart as a management trainee. In June 1990, he was promoted to assistant manager. Soon after, Steve moved to Bentonville, Arkansas, where he worked as a training instructor. He returned to the stores as a co-manager in May 1991.

Steve's first store management position was offered to him in 1991. He managed stores in several locations: Venice, Bradenton, and Lake Worth, Florida.

As a store manager, Steve is responsible for the operations and merchandising of his store. He has four assistant managers and 220 associates at his location. He stated that the most challenging part of his job is "keeping these 224 people happy." Steve enjoys deciding what merchandise will be ordered for his location and predicting its sales.

When asked why he chose a retail career, Steve stated that his internship offered a close view of the opportunities in retail. Also, he felt that he could excel in a retail environment. Steve believes that retail is a very satisfying career; he is able to work with both the analytical and people aspects of a business.

Steve Schultheis

Steve advises students going into retail as their career, "When selecting an employer, choose a stable company that is projected to open more stores. When you've accepted an offer, remember to then pursue and accept various positions within your company. In these positions, you will meet many people and gain experience."

Source: *Career Opportunities in Retailing,* produced by the Center for Retailing Education and Research, University of Florida–Gainesville, p. 10.

positions, recruiters often look for students with quantitative backgrounds such as finance, accounting, management science, and computer information systems.

Buyers and planners are partners. They meld individual skills to work together for the success of the categories for which they are responsible.

Careers in Corporate (Support Areas)

Because these areas provide opportunities for individuals with specific skills and interests, related training programs tend to be tailored to an individual career plan. Although some companies recruit specifically for these careers, most require that college recruits begin their careers in either buying or store management to fully understand what the retail business is all about. This means that career opportunities in these areas are more difficult to break into.

EXHIBIT A–1

Buying and Merchandise Planning Career Paths at Department Store Chain

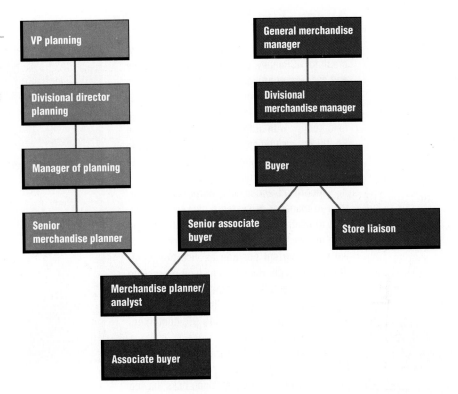

Computer Systems Experience with computer applications is an important plus when looking for a career in retailing. Such areas as data capture and application, Quick Response (QR) inventory systems to minimize inventory costs, expedient point-of-sale (POS) systems, and electronic data interchange (EDI) ensure retailers of an efficient merchandise flow.

Operations/Distribution People in this area oversee the movement of merchandise in an accurate, efficient, and timely manner. They are responsible for operating and maintaining the store's physical plant, for providing various customer services, for the receipt, ticketing, warehousing, and distribution of a store's inventory, and for buying and maintaining store supplies and operating equipment.

Many excellent opportunities exist in this area for people who are more interested in operating than in merchandising activities. These opportunities include store superintendent, warehouse manager, maintenance supervisor, customer service manager, receiving supervisor, and security.

Promotions/Advertising Sales promotion's many aspects include public relations, advertising, visual merchandising, and special events. The creative people in sales promotion departments try to presell the customer on the assumption that the best way to generate sales is to encourage people to want new merchandise. These departments offer stimulating career opportunities to creative men and women.

Loss Prevention Loss prevention people provide asset protection for associates, facilities, and merchandise. They are responsible for developing and maintaining loss prevention systems and controlling internal and external theft.

A.2

Twenty-Five Years and Counting

BILL ALCORN, vice president and director of credit for JCPenney, earned bachelor of science and bachelor of arts degrees in accounting from the University of Florida in 1971. His career began immediately following graduation as a field auditor with JCPenney. He traveled in the Southeast, visiting store locations, distribution centers, and credit service offices to evaluate their financial operations.

Alcorn advanced to a corporate auditor, then to manager of systems data processing, next to controller of the Penney's catalog, and then to assistant controller of JCPenney, which led to his current position as vice president/ director of credit. His duties include overseeing the credit operations, coordinating third-party charge operations, and outlining benefits of a JCPenney credit card for both the customers and the sales associates.

Mr. Alcorn suggests for those considering retail, "Before you choose retail as a career, make certain that you enjoy taking risks, having a lot of fun, and working in an exciting environment!" When asked what he enjoys about retail, he replies, "The dynamic environment! We are constantly evaluating our customers and what they are looking for. The customer is continually

Bill Alcorn

changing; therefore, the merchandise changes, too. Every day there is something new!"

Source: *Career Opportunities in Retailing,* produced by the Center for Retailing Education and Research, University of Florida–Gainesville, p. 8.

Finance/Control Sophisticated financial management and top financial officers are among the most highly paid people in retailing. Many retailers have been involved in complicated corporate restructuring leading to high levels of debt— and retail competition in general has become fierce. Most retailers also operate on a tight net profit margin. With such a fine line between success and failure, retailers continue to require top financial experts—and compensate them generously.

The finance/control division is responsible for the financial soundness of the company. This involves preparing the financial reports for all aspects of the business, including long-range forecasting and planning, economic trend analysis and budgeting, shortage control and internal audit, gross and net profit, accounts payable to vendors, and accounts receivable from charge customers.

Retailing View A.2 provides a view of a nonmerchandising/nonstore-management career path.

Store Design Retailers are finding that clearly defined, comfortable, and visually pleasing stores give them that extra edge over competition. Key elements of store design in the future include easy-to-shop, easy-to-maintain, and flexible store layouts. Talented, creative students in business, architecture, art, and other related fields will have innumerable opportunities for growth in the area of retail store design.

Human Resource Management   Human resource management is responsible for the effective selection, training, placement, advancement, and welfare of employees. Because there are seasonal peaks in retailing (such as Christmas when many extra people must be hired), human resource personnel must be flexible and highly efficient.

IS RETAILING FOR ME?

Possibly one of the most important decisions a student must make is whether to choose a career in retailing. A goal should be to pursue a career whose benefits are important to you and to avoid those whose disadvantages will impede your ability to succeed and be happy. Every career has its pros and cons. Finding the best fit, however, takes careful planning.

Compensation and Benefits

Retailing can be both financially and personally rewarding. Careers in retailing combine continuous personal development with almost immediate responsibility and new challenges. Each day is different, so sales associates and executives are rarely bored. Starting salaries are competitive, and the compensation of top management ranks with the highest in industry. For example, store managers with only a few years of experience can earn up to $100,000 or more, depending on bonuses. Top buyers, systems professionals, and other technical experts may earn just as much.

Compensation varies by category. Specialty store managers are generally paid less, but advancements are faster. Aggressive specialty store managers often run 8 to 15 units after a few years so they quickly move into higher pay brackets. Typical compensation for management trainees ranges from $22,000 to $28,000. A senior buyer for a department store earns from $50,000 to $90,000 or more. A department store manager can earn from $50,000 to $150,000; a discount store manager makes from $70,000 to $100,000 or more; and a specialty store manager earns from $35,000 to $60,000 or more.

Retailers have been strengthening the link between performance and compensation for top executives by supplementing base salaries with significant bonuses. A recent survey found, for example, that 95 percent of CEOs were eligible for incentives, which on average represented 61 percent of their salaries.[1] Similarly, about 83 percent of companies' top store and merchandising executives were eligible for incentives, although bonuses represented only a little less than 30 percent of their salaries. The survey also found evidence of the spread of incentive plans to other retail ranks. Even at the lower pay levels studied, roughly 82 percent of buyers and store managers, for example, were eligible for incentives.

Exhibit A–2 illustrates that, on average, top retail executives are well compensated. Because promotions in retailing tend to be based on individual performance (not on length of employment), advancement can be more rapid than in most industries. This means that how quickly people progress is largely up to them. A college graduate with a good performance record could become a buyer for a high–dollar-volume area in a large department store within two to three years, or manager of a specialty store in as little as one or two years.

A compensation package consists of more than salary alone. In retailing, the benefits package is often substantial. It may include a profit-sharing plan; savings plan; stock option plan; hospital, major medical, and dental insurance; life insurance; long-term disability protection and income protection plans; paid vacations and holidays; and bonus potential. Two additional benefits of retailing careers are that most retailers offer employees valuable discounts on the merchandise that they sell, and some buying positions include extensive foreign travel.

REFACT Joseph R. Hyde III (CEO of Auto Zone, a Memphis-based auto parts chain) received $1.1 million in salary and bonus in 1993, and earned $31.1 million by exercising his stock options.[2]

EXHIBIT A–2   Total Compensation for Retail Executives* (in thousands of dollars)

JOB TITLE	JOB DESCRIPTION	LOW (10TH PERCENTILE)	MEDIUM (50TH PERCENTILE)	HIGH (90TH PERCENTILE)
Chief Executive Officer	Has final responsibility to board of directors, parent company, or owners for current profits and long-range growth.	$253.0	$474.6	$927.0
Top Financial Executive	Heads all financial operations; supervises controller and treasury functions.	116.8	200.0	364.1
Top Merchandising Executive	Directs all buying-merchandising activities; supervises general merchandise managers or divisional merchandise managers.	105.8	197.5	381.2
Top Stores Executive	Is responsible for operation and profitability of retail stores; controls operating costs and implements merchandising programs.	84.0	152.3	259.9
Top Information Systems Executive	Is responsible for data processing activities.	89.6	138.6	225.8
General Merchandise Manager	Is responsible for development and implementation of merchandising activities for major groups of related merchandise.	84.8	136.1	201.4
Top Real Estate Executive	Is responsible for site selection, lease negotiation, and acquisition of real estate.	80.2	135.0	203.0
Top Marketing/Sales Promotion/Advertising Executive	Directs marketing/sales promotion/advertising programs.	76.6	125.8	222.4
Top Human Resources Executive	Develops and implements policies on recruitment, staffing, labor relations, compensation, and training.	77.5	120.0	206.5
Top Planning and Merchandise Distribution Executive	Is responsible for overall merchandise buying plans and merchandise allocation systems.	66.4	110.0	203.3
Treasurer	Directs most external financial activities, such as banking, investment, credit, and money management.	78.4	106.7	198.6
Controller	Is responsible for internal accounting policies and practices; maintains accounting records.	74.9	103.0	154.4
Divisional Merchandise Manager	Plans and executies merchandising activities for a related group of merchandise categories.	65.0	102.8	182.0
Top Distribution Center Executive	Ensures timely and cost-effective movement of merchandise to stores.	67.0	98.4	186.9
Top Loss Prevention Executive	Develops programs to protect company assets and safety of employees and customers.	54.3	80.5	119.8
Top Store Planning and Design Executive	Is responsible for architectural design of stores.	46.6	77.5	144.7
Top Store Planning/ Construction Executive	Is responsible for bidding, selection of contractors, and oversight of construction.	50.3	76.0	106.8
Senior Merchandise Planner/ Controller	Supports buying function and forecasts companywide sales plans.	40.0	62.0	82.3
Top Internal Auditor	Is responsible for internal audit program.	42.1	60.0	81.1

*Base salary plus reported bonus.

(continued)

EXHIBIT A–2   Total Compensation for Retail Executives* (in thousands of dollars) *(concluded)*

JOB TITLE	JOB DESCRIPTION	LOW (10TH PERCENTILE)	MEDIUM (50TH PERCENTILE)	HIGH (90TH PERCENTILE)
Buyer	Is responsible for purchasing, pricing, promotion, and sales of merchandise categories.	40.0	56.2	86.1
Merchandise Planner	Supports the buying function and develops distribution plans for specific merchandise categories and classes.	26.0	40.2	56.0
Store Manager	Is responsible for sales, expense control, display of merchandise, and customer service.	17.4	24.7	36.3

*Base salary plus reported bonus.

Source: Harrison Donnelly, "Are You Paid Enough?" *Stores*, December 1994, pp. 17, 19.

Working Conditions   Retailing has an often exaggerated reputation of offering long and odd hours. Superficially, this reputation is true. Store managers do work some evenings and weekends. But many progressive retailers have realized that if the odd hours aren't offset by time off at other periods in the week, many managers become inefficient, angry, and resentful—in a word, burned out. It's also important to put the concept of long hours into perspective. Most professional careers require more than 40 hours per week for the person to succeed. In a new job with new tasks and responsibilities, the time commitment is even greater.

People shouldn't go into retailing if they like a calm, orderly, peaceful work environment with no surprises. Retailing is for those who like having exciting days, making quick decisions, and dealing with a variety of assignments, tasks, and people—often all at once.

Responsibility   Retailing is also for people who like responsibility. Starting executives are given more responsibility more quickly than in other industries. Buyers are responsible for choosing, promoting, pricing, distributing, and selling millions of dollars worth of merchandise each season. The department manager, which is generally the first position after a training program, is often responsible for merchandising one or more departments as well as for managing 10 or more full- and part-time sales associates.

Employment Security   Retailing in general doesn't suffer from the severe shifts in the economy as badly as other industries such as the automotive industry. During recessions, people don't stop buying. They just buy less and shift their purchase patterns. Thus, sales and profits may suffer in retailing, but overall employment isn't impacted severely.

Retailing, on the other hand, is very results-oriented. Sales results are usually available immediately. Therefore, management knows who's successful and who isn't. Those who don't make the grade in the executive ranks move on rather quickly. Changes in ownership through mergers and acquisitions coupled with consolidations of systems and staffs have also made employment less secure in retailing. These changes, however, affect store management and human resources less than buyers and others in corporate staff positions.

Decentralized Job Opportunities

Depending on the type of retailer and the specific firm, retailing enables executives to change locations often or not at all. In general, a career path in store management has more opportunity for relocation than paths in buying/merchandising or corporate. Because buying and corporate offices are usually centrally located, these positions generally aren't subjected to frequent moves.

Career Advancement

Many opportunities for rapid advancement exist simply because of the sheer size of the retail industry. There are millions of retail establishments, and the larger ones have many different positions and multiple managerial levels. Yet in choosing a particular retailer, take care to choose a growth firm. Firms that have recently undergone corporate restructuring may have a glut of middle management positions. If store operations is an appealing career area, pursue chains with multiple outlets. But these stores don't present particularly good opportunities for people who seek a buying career, because they have relatively small buying staffs compared to the number of outlets. If buying is your primary career interest, choose a firm with a relatively large buying staff (e.g., a department store) or a firm with decentralized purchasing (e.g., JCPenney).

Women in Retailing

Many people consider retailing to be among the more gender-blind industries.[3] Women have made definite progress up the career ladder in the past decade or so. In 1978, *Stores* magazine conducted a survey that revealed few women held the title of general merchandise manager, controller, or senior or executive vice president. In 1990, a similar survey of 19 of the top specialty and department stores indicated that only five had no women in those positions, and most had more than one. Also, the 1978 survey indicated that there were only two self-made women among the ranks of department store presidents. Today, at least five hold the title of president, chairperson, chief executive officer, or chief operating officer. At least two women have achieved the position of chief financial officer. Retailing View A.3 tells how Carol Sanger made it to the top of her field.

CHARACTERISTICS NECESSARY TO BE A SUCCESSFUL RETAILER

Some of the many skills necessary to be a successful retail executive include:

1. *Analytical skills.* These skills include the ability to analyze data, develop plans, and alter these plans if set goals aren't realized. The ability to analyze past and present performance is critical to developing and modifying plans and producing profits.

2. *Decisiveness.* Retailers must be able to make decisions such as the price of thousands of items, which stores will receive certain items, and when and how much to mark down items. These decisions must typically be made quickly with only a limited amount of information.

3. *Creativity.* Successful retailers have the ability to develop novel, useful solutions to problems by blending imagination with analytical skills to beat the competition.

4. *Leadership.* Retailing is a very people-intensive business. Because retailers manage people, not machinery, successful retailers must be able to inspire their employees, delegate responsibility, and motivate people.

5. *Stress tolerance.* Because retailers have to make many important decisions in a rapidly changing, uncertain environment, a successful retailer must be able to perform under pressure.

A.3

Corporate Communications at the Top of Federated Department Stores, Inc.

UPON GRADUATION WITH A DEGREE in journalism and communications in 1970, Carol Sanger began her career as a newspaper reporter. Ms. Sanger's first position was with *The Cincinnati Post.* In 1975, she was the special assistant to the U.S. Secretary of Transportation in Washington, D.C. Next, she became the press secretary for a U.S. senator. Ms. Sanger then returned to print media as a business editor for *The Cincinnati Enquirer.*

In 1984, Federated Department Stores, Inc., offered her the position of vice president for public relations and public affairs. She accepted this opportunity for many reasons—most importantly because retailing is such a people-intensive, high-profile industry.

Ms. Sanger is currently vice president of corporate communications and external affairs for Federated Department Stores, Inc. She is responsible for all internal and external communications for Federated. Also, her position includes overseeing all government relations, community relations, and philanthropies.

Before considering a corporate communications career, a person should be well versed in journalism. In order for a person to be credible to the media, significant media exposure is necessary. According to Ms. Sanger, "Experience in the media also helps to have the skills you will need in a corporate public relations setting: the ability to absorb and synthesize facts, to deal with deadlines and a broad range of issues, to handle the crisis situations, and to be resourceful."

Ms. Sanger's advice to someone pursuing the corporate communications aspect of

Carol Sanger

retailing is simple: get experience in the media; work to perfect your oral and written communications skills; and develop the ability to take ambiguous, abstract ideas, disseminate facts, and then be creative enough to implement these facts into useful public relations techniques.

Source: *Career Opportunities in Retailing,* produced by the Center for Retailing Education and Research, University of Florida–Gainesville, p. 12.

---

6. *Organization.* To lessen the decision-making pressure, successful retailers must be good planners. By developing goals and lists of activities to accomplish, successful retailers can minimize the time spent on routine decisions, recognize important problems, and make adjustments.

7. *Communication.* The ability to present ideas and thoughts in a clear, concise manner is also important. In addition to expressing written ideas in an organized manner with proper grammar, successful retailers must be able to make oral presentations with persuasiveness and confidence.

The skills described above are important for someone interested in retailing. However, to be successful and enjoy a career in retailing, the following characteristics are also very helpful:

Interest in people.
Enjoyment of a challenge.
Desire for early recognition and rewards.
Pleasant personality.
Neat appearance.

COMMONLY ASKED QUESTIONS

Why Is a Job in Retailing Good for Starting Your Career?

There are three reasons for this:

1. It provides the best opportunity for getting experience in managing people and having profit-and-loss responsibility early in your career. These experiences are critical for promotion to upper-level management positions in all fields. You do not get this type of responsibility early in other careers.

2. Retail offers a wide diversity of activities. You don't do the same thing or make the same decisions day after day. It's a very challenging work environment. You don't have to sit behind a desk all the time. The fast-paced, diverse environment is a big benefit over other business careers like banking.

3. You have opportunities to get promoted and make a lot of money if you do a good job. Your company will know if you are doing a good job because it has the numbers. Objective performance measures can be traced down to the lowest-level job.

Will I Start Out as a Sales Associate?

No. After completing executive training, management trainees in department stores and discount stores usually start out as department sales managers (DSMs). The DSMs are responsible for the presentation of merchandise and the management of sales associates in an entire department. In specialty stores, you would enter as an assistant store manager responsible for all aspects of the store's operations.

How Quickly Can I Be Promoted and Receive Salary Increases?

Obviously, the different career paths within the various types of retail institutions will determine your rate and direction of advancement. How fast you advance really depends on your performance and the opportunities within your company. However, if you're above average in performance, you can expect to double your income within five years.

What Are the Training Programs Like?

Training programs are as different as the retailers that sponsor them. Some training programs emphasize on-the-job-training; others offer a very structured, classroom-type environment. Training periods can range from 12 weeks to two years. When you talk to various companies, ask what their specific training program entails.

If I Want to Become a Buyer, What Type of Retail Store Would Give Me That Opportunity?

It's harder to become a buyer in either a specialty store or a discount store than it is in a department store. Discount stores tend to have relatively few buyers and many store managers and operations people. Specialty stores also tend to be looking mainly for store managers because the same few buyers purchase for all of their stores. Department stores, on the other hand, are looking for both buyers and store managers. It is much easier to become a buyer for one of the many merchandise categories in a large department store than to become a buyer for one of the limited number of merchandise categories in a specialty store or for one of the large-volume categories in a discount store.

How Much Control Will I Have over Geographic Placement?

Although some companies will try to accommodate preferences, most companies are not able to consider personal preferences but instead emphasize the importance of flexibility. Most companies stress that the more willing you are to move, the faster you'll rise within the company since most moves are promotions. However, many companies won't require you to move if you're willing to accept a slower career path.

How Do I Decide Which Retail Store Is Best for Me?

In deciding which type of store environment is best for you, you must ask yourself several questions including

What corporate culture will I fit in with best?
Do I want to be in store management, buying, or a support function?
What kind of lifestyle do I want to lead?
Do I want the flexibility of switching career paths, say, from buying to store management?
Where do I want to be 5 or 10 years from now?

There are significant differences among the various types of retail institutions. These differences could have an effect on your choice of retailing as a career. Make it a point to discover the different career paths within the assorted types of retailers to determine how your interests and career needs may be better satisfied.

What Do You Need to Do to Get Promoted?

Do a good job in your present position, and don't worry about your next position until you get it. If you perform well and get good results, you'll be promoted when you're ready—often before you expect it.

GETTING READY FOR A RETAIL INTERVIEW

The following issues are worth considering prior to an interview:

• Visit prospective employers' stores before the interview. Actually seeing the store can give you insight for discussing the company intelligently throughout the interview process. Well-stocked and orderly departments (with the exception of deep-discount stores that sometimes purposely maintain a disorderly look) suggest (but don't prove) that the company is in good health. Signs of decay either could mean the store is planning a relocation or a massive renovation, or could indicate poor management or financial problems.[4]

- Read about the store. In conjunction with store visits, read the retailer's annual report to stockholders; examine reports from *Value Line* and other investment service firms; study trade publications such as *Discount Store News*, *Chain Store Age Executive*, and *Stores;* and visit their website on the Internet.
- Find out whether the retailer is hiring primarily for store or merchandise management positions. For example, if you're interested in fashion, a career in a department store or national off-price chain like T.J. Maxx or Marshalls may be the way to go. Be certain that its needs coincide with your goals.
- Determine whether there have been recent changes in ownership or top management. A change isn't necessarily bad, but it does add some uncertainty— and therefore risk—to the decision.
- Research the retailer's growth potential. Has it been expanding? Is it in strong markets? How strong and innovative are its competitors? Successful retailers in the 90s will increase their emphasis on marketing to satisfy customer needs by focusing heavily on service. Moreover, by employing creative organizational and management strategies, retailers will concentrate on giving buyers and store managers greater responsibility, while supporting them with logistics and systems specialists.
- Determine whether the retailer is known for innovation. An innovative retailer has a greater chance of long-term success than a stodgy one. To measure innovativeness, look at its stores and promotions. Are they modern? Do the stores and promotions reflect the times? Do they appeal to their target markets?
- Find out about the retailer's computers and distribution systems. Highly sophisticated retail technology symbolizes a view toward the future. Technology, if used properly, makes firms more efficient and therefore profitable. Finally, QR inventory management systems, EDI, and sophisticated POS terminals relieve managers from much of the tedious paperwork previously associated with careers in retailing.

Exhibit A–3 is an example of an interview guide that a retailer might use on a campus visit. To help prepare for an interview, study this exhibit carefully. Advance knowledge of some of the questions that may arise should boost your confidence, reduce your anxiety, and improve the interviewer's impression of you.

SUMMARY

Retailing isn't for everyone. This appendix has provided a framework for considering a career in retailing. A variety of careers available in the retail industry have been described. Advantages and disadvantages of a retailing career have been presented. The characteristics necessary to become a successful retail executive were examined. The appendix concluded with the answers to some commonly asked questions about a career in retailing and how to get ready for an interview.

NOTES

1. Harrison Donnelly, "Are you Paid Enough?" *Stores*, December 1994, pp. 16–19. The survey on executive compensation at specialty store chains was carried out by the National Retail Federation and William M. Mercer, Inc.

2. Ibid.

3. Penny Gill, "Women in Retailing: A Long Way?" *Stores*, September 1990, pp. 26–32.

4. "Careers in Retailing," A *Discount Store News* publication (New York: Lebhar-Friedman, 1991).

EXHIBIT A–3

The XYZ
Department Stores
Company Targeted
Selection Interview
Guide

Date: _____

Applicant's Name: _____   College/University: _____

Phone Number: _____   Best Time to Reach: _____

Interviewer: _____   Division _____

Overall GPA: _____   out of _____

Opening

- Greet Applicant: **Give name and position, and state that you represent XYZ Department Stores Company.**

- Explain Format: **Will be asked for specific behavioral examples. Will last approximately 30 minutes. Will be taking notes. Will provide applicant opportunity to ask questions.**

Dimensional Questions	Notes		
Background Review	Situation	Action	Result

Background Review
- **How did you become aware of XYZ?**
(Check as many as appropriate.)

_____ Open house/resume day		**Mentioned by:**
_____ Newspaper ad		_____ Faculty
_____ Personalized letter		_____ Placement office
_____ Pre-interview briefing		_____ Other students
_____ General reputation		_____ Alumni currently
_____ Class presentation		employed by
_____ Shop at your store		

- **Why did you choose your major? How does it relate to your career goals?**

Job motivation
- **Describe a situation that you found frustrating. What was the cause and how did you deal with it?**
- **Give me an example of when you worked the hardest and felt the greatest sense of achievement.**

Decision making
- **Describe a situation in which you received a procedure or set of instructions with which you disagreed. How did you handle it?**
- **In your last job, which decisions did you typically make? Which did you refer to a superior?**

Stress tolerance
- **Give an example of a task that you thought would go on forever. How did you deal with it? Result.**
- **When have you been under the most pressure?**
- **Describe a situation when someone has lost his/her temper or become irritated with you.**

Interview close
- **Review notes.**
- **Ask any additional questions to complete notes.**
- **Give applicant opportunity to ask questions.**
- **Explain that, at the conclusion of our first interviews, we will be in contact with some students for follow-up appointments. In any case, we will be getting back to everyone within two weeks.**
- **Thank applicant for a productive interview.**

(continued)

EXHIBIT A–3

The XYZ
Department Stores
Company Targeted
Selection Interview
Guide (*concluded*)

Interview recap	Applicant:	
Dimensions interviewed	**Comments**	**Rating**
1. Job motivation	_____	_____
2. Decision making	_____	_____
3. Stress tolerance	_____	_____
4. Oral communication skills	_____	_____
Remaining dimensional profile	**Comments**	**Rating**
1. Leadership	_____	_____
2. Initiative	_____	_____
3. Energy	_____	_____
4. Persuasiveness	_____	_____
5. Oral presentation skills	_____	_____
6. Planning and organizing	_____	_____

Future action

Overall comments _____

_____

_____

Ratings

5 Excessive

4 Superior   Reject   _____

3 Acceptable

- - - - - - - - -

2 Below standard

1 Unacceptable   Overall rating   _____

B Starting Your Own Retail Business

OWNING AND MANAGING A RETAIL BUSINESS is many people's dream. Are you interested in bringing this dream to reality? It sounds exciting, but starting your own business is very risky. Traditionally, 20 percent of all new businesses survive only five years.[1] Thus, many people who start new businesses suffer disappointment.

Ten major reasons why businesses fail are

1. Insufficient profits.
2. Poor growth.
3. Too much debt or too little equity.
4. Inexperience.
5. Heavy operating expenses.
6. Industry weakness.
7. Internal factors such as high interest rates, poor location, or competition.
8. Neglect.
9. Fraud.
10. Poor planning.[2]

Although there's little you can do to prevent a downturn in the economy, there's a lot you can do to avoid the other problems listed here. The essential prerequisite for making your dream come true is planning! Planning is defined as the anticipation and organization of what needs to be done to reach an objective. In this case, the objective is your business's long-term survival and profitability. Planning may sound simple, but it takes hard work and creativity to develop an effective business plan. Of course, there's no way to completely avoid the risks of starting your own retail business, but with proper planning you can significantly cut the chance of failure. You can begin the planning state by analyzing some basic questions about yourself, your marketing plan, your financial plan, and your external environment.

The following list of major questions is an outline for this appendix. These questions can also be your guide in preparing a comprehensive business plan and can help you identify the important issues you'll confront in converting your dream into reality.

1. Do you really have what it takes to run your own business? What are your decision-making capabilities?
    *   Are you emotionally and physically capable of handling the pressures of owning a business?
2. What should the business plan include?
    *   What should be included in marketing and financial plans?
    *   What aspects of the external environment must you consider?
    *   Where can you get help in formulating a business plan?
3. Where can you get the financing to start your business?
    *   Should you use equity or debt financing?
    *   Where can you borrow money?
    *   What must you do to get a loan?
4. What should you do if you're considering the purchase of an existing small business?
    *   Do you need a lawyer?
    *   What sort of investigation do you have to do?

DO YOU HAVE WHAT IT TAKES TO RUN YOUR OWN BUSINESS?

To answer this question, you must make an honest appraisal of your strengths and weaknesses. Exhibit B–1 is a checklist of personal characteristics required to own and manage a business. Use these questions to assess your capabilities for starting a retail business.

Demands in Owning a Business

Starting a retail business involves physical, emotional, and financial strain. The first few months—the most critical time for your business—will require tremendous personal dedication. Exhibit B–2's questions give you an idea of the demands that will be placed on you and your family.

Your business's success will depend on your skills and your level of self-confidence. Knowledge of retailing and the merchandise sold is vital to a new

EXHIBIT **B–1**

Personal Characteristics Needed to Own and Manage Your Own Retail Business

1. Are you a leader?
2. Do you like to make your own decisions?
3. Do others turn to you for help in making decisions?
4. Do you enjoy competition?
5. Do you have willpower and self-discipline?
6. Are you well organized? Do you plan ahead?
7. Do you like people?
8. Do you get along well with others?
9. Do you like being your own boss?
10. Are you physically fit?
11. Are you a hands-on manager?

If you answered yes to the majority of these questions, then you have many of the personal characteristics it takes to succeed in your business venture.

Source: Small Business Administration.

EXHIBIT B–2

Demands of Starting
Your Own Business

> 1. **Are you aware that planning your own business may require working 12 to 16 hours a day, six days a week, perhaps even Sundays and holidays?**
> 2. **Do you have the physical stamina to handle the work load and rigorous schedule?**
> 3. **Do you have the emotional strength to handle the strain?**
> 4. **Are you prepared to temporarily lower your standard of living until your business is firmly established?**
> 5. **Is your family prepared to go along with the strains they too must bear?**
> 6. **Are you prepared to lose your savings?**
> 7. **Do you have a strong belief in yourself and your capabilities?**
>
> **If you answered yes to all of these questions, then you have the personal dedication it takes to succeed in the first critical months of your own business venture.**

Source: Small Business Administration.

business's success. Of the owners who believed that their chances of success were at least 9 in 10, 82 percent survived the first three years. However, of those who indicated their odds were 6 in 10 or worse, only 67 percent survived.[3]

Your management style is also critical. Of the successful businesses surveyed, 91 percent of the owners spent more time working directly with the customers than on any other component of the business. This hands-on approach appears to have paid off.[4]

Opportunities and Potential Problems of Owning a Business

Another important predictor of success is whether the entrepreneur has a realistic picture of what to expect from his business and his environment. The following list of opportunities and problems will impart a practical understanding of small business ownership.

Opportunities

1. Significant personal profits.
2. Potential for innovation and flexibility in decision making.
3. Personal contacts with customers, suppliers, and employees.
4. Participation in community activities such as the local Chamber of Commerce.
5. High performance due to the owner-manager's active involvement.

Potential Problems

1. Difficulty in obtaining financing.
2. Inadequate management capabilities due to the wide variety of expertise required.
3. Poor competitive position due to lack of resources.
4. Limited knowledge of effective marketing techniques.
5. Difficulty in obtaining supplier credit.
6. Complexity of operations due to lack of systems for processing paperwork and record keeping.

Once you've realistically appraised yourself and your expectations from your business, you'll be prepared to advance to the next step of analysis: the business plan.

WHAT SHOULD THE BUSINESS PLAN INCLUDE?

The business plan includes the information needed to successfully begin and sustain a business. It also gives potential investors the documentation they need to understand and evaluate the business venture. The three primary components of a comprehensive business plan are the marketing plan, the financial plan, and legal considerations.

Marketing Plan

The marketing plan begins with an analysis of the business environment. This analysis supports the retail strategy that defines the specific target market you intend to focus on as well as your anticipated retail mix. Small retail businesses must find a niche or segment of the market that's either unfilled or undersupplied. But the target market must still be large enough to generate adequate profits. (Chapters 6 and 7 discuss evaluating opportunities from strategic and financial perspectives.)

The marketing plan should discuss the specific retail mix that will be used to attract the target market. Thus, the plan must describe in detail the following 10 elements:

1. *Merchandise offered.* Number and breadth of lines to be carried, styles of merchandise and accessories, names of suppliers, supplier credit terms, quality of merchandise, opening stock, inventory levels, and expected turnover rate. (See Chapters 12 through 14.)

2. *Customer services offered.* Customer service levels and contact provided, credit policies, exchange and return policies, alterations, and gift wrapping. (See Chapter 19.)

3. *Facilities.* Store appearance, any renovation required, interior decor, storefront, layout, lighting, window displays, wall displays, and overall atmosphere. (See Chapter 18.)

4. *Location.* Buy, lease, or rent; terms of contract; local ordinances; zoning regulations; parking; accessibility; local demographics; and conditions for remodeling. (See Chapters 8 and 9.)

5. *Pricing.* Price ranges to offer, competitive pricing, profitable pricing, margins, markdowns, and discount prices. (See Chapter 15.)

6. *Promotion.* One-year promotional plan, advertising budgets, selection of media, cost of local media options, promotional displays, cooperative advertising efforts, and public relations. (See Chapter 16.)

7. *Employees.* Compensation plan and wage scale to be offered; job specifications; employee training program; career and promotion schedule; employee benefits; social security taxes; sources and types of employees to hire (e.g., age, sex, appearance, education level); and policy on family employees. (See Chapter 17.)

8. *Security.* Security guards, fire and theft alarms, computer security system, windows, locks, merchandise protection devices, liability insurance, and other insurance. (See Chapter 17.)

9. *Equipment.* Cash register, sales desk, computer systems, display racks, office equipment, office supplies, and telephone systems. Computer system, management information system, software, cash register system, security systems, and personal computer requirements. (See Chapter 11.)

EXHIBIT **B-3**

Questions for Checking a Marketing Plan's Feasibility

1. Can you clearly identify and briefly discuss the business you plan to start?
2. Can you clearly define the retail format and mix you plan to offer?
3. Does your retail offering satisfy an unfilled need?
4. Will your retail offering serve an existing market where demand exceeds supply?
5. Will your retail offering be competitive based on its merchandise quality, assortment, price, and location?
6. Do you know who your customers will be?
7. Do you know where your customers live?
8. Will your promotional program be effective?
9. Do you understand how your business compares with those of your competitors?
10. Will your business be conveniently located for the people you plan to serve?

Answering yes to these questions means you're on the right track. A negative or incomplete answer indicates weakness in your plan.

Source: Small Business Administration.

10. *Controls.* Inventory and stock control method, register receipts, closing the register, record-keeping functions (separate from sales functions), accounting statements, and external audits.

Not only must these pieces in the retail mix have merit on their own, but they must also work together to form synergies for the entire business. Exhibit B–3 is a useful checklist to help you determine the feasibility of your business plan. The marketing plan should also include an extensive analysis of the competition's location, merchandise, target market, prices, promotions, and services.

Finally, the marketing plan should conclude with a statement of marketing objectives that can be expected due to the marketing strategy. Developing a well-constructed marketing plan may seem like a monumental task, but your business's success will hinge on the quality and depth of your analysis.

Financial Plan

A fully developed retail financial strategy includes a list of the financial requirements, an estimate of start-up expenses, a determination of the amount of financing needed, financial performance objectives, an estimate of sales and operating expenses, and an estimate of cash flows for the first year.

Financial Requirements   Exhibit B–4 gives a sample worksheet for determining the start-up costs associated with opening your business. Estimate both immediate and future costs to give you a realistic picture of the financial requirements for success.

An Estimate of Start-Up Expenses   Exhibit B–5 provides a sample worksheet to help estimate your expenses for one month. After estimating your monthly expenses, multiply that number by three. The new total will be the amount of cash required to cover your expenses for three months. This amount should be set aside to ensure the firm's survival through the critical first three months of operation.

From the initial opening of your business, you'll receive some cash from the sale of merchandise. However, the estimate of this income shouldn't be included to help defray your operating expenses in Exhibit B–5.

EXHIBIT B–4

Worksheet for
Estimating Start-Up
Costs

	IMMEDIATE COSTS	FUTURE COSTS
1. Fixtures and equipment	_____	_____
2. Decorating	_____	_____
3. Remodeling	_____	_____
4. Installation charges	_____	_____
5. Services required	_____	_____
6. Business supplies	_____	_____
7. Beginning inventory	_____	_____
8. Professional fees	_____	_____
9. License and permits	_____	_____
10. Telephone and utility deposits	_____	_____
11. Insurance coverage	_____	_____
12. Security costs	_____	_____
13. Initial advertising	_____	_____
14. Unanticipated expenses	_____	_____
15. Subtotal: Start-up costs	_____	_____
16. Total costs	_____	_____

Source: Small Business Administration.

Amount of Financing Required   A personal financial statement should be included in the financial plan. Exhibit B–6 provides an example. Such calculations will show your personal net worth.

    The total for the start-up costs worksheet (Exhibit B–4) should be added to the worksheet total for the three months of expenses (Exhibit B–5) to estimate the total financial requirements of operating your business for the first three months.

EXHIBIT B–5

Worksheet for
Estimating Monthly
Expenses

1. Your living costs	_____
2. Employee wages	_____
3. Rent	_____
4. Advertising	_____
5. Supplies	_____
6. Utilities	_____
7. Telephone	_____
8. Insurance	_____
9. Taxes	_____
10. Maintenance	_____
11. Delivery costs	_____
12. Professional fees	_____
13. Miscellaneous	_____
14. Total monthly costs	_____
Total monthly costs multiplied by three	_____

Source: Small Business Administration.

EXHIBIT **B–6**

Personal Financial
Statement

ASSETS		LIABILITIES	
Cash on hand	_____	Accounts payable	_____
Savings account	_____	Notes payable	_____
Stocks, bonds, securities	_____	Contracts payable	_____
Accounts/notes receivable	_____	Taxes	_____
Real estate	_____	Real estate loans	_____
Life insurance (cash value)	_____	Other liabilities	_____
Auto/other vehicles	_____		
Other liquid assets	_____		
Total assets	_____	Total liabilities	_____
		Net worth (assets minus liabilities)	_____

Subtract your calculated net worth (Exhibit B–6) from this total to determine the amount of financing needed.

Financial Performance Objectives   You must set expected return on investment, sales objectives with seasonal fluctuations, cost-of-goods-sold objectives, and other controllable expense objectives.

Estimated Sales and Operating Expenses for the First Year   These estimates should evolve from a combination of the marketing projections, the financial objectives, the competition's results, and a realistic appraisal of your current environment. The projected profit/loss worksheet in Exhibit B–7 will help you in this task.

Estimated Cash Flow for the Year   Businesses fail because they lack cash to pay their expenses. Thus, cash flow is more important than sales or profit. In determining how much funding will be required to start your business, you must calculate not only your starting costs, but also your projected losses in the early stages of your business.

You must determine if your monthly sales estimates will produce enough income to cover each month's bills. Exhibit B–8's worksheet will help you estimate your future monthly cash flows. Remember, this should start with the fourth month since you're going to set aside an adequate portion of the initial funds to cover the first three months' expenses.

This critical exercise will help determine whether there will be foreseeable problems with meeting expenses. If cash shortages become apparent, an alternate plan must be instituted, or additional financing will be required.

Important Considerations   In formulating the financial plan, consider the following factors, which frequently lead to new retail operations' downfall:

- Failure to recognize seasonal trends.
- Removal of excessive cash from the business for living expenses.
- Excessive investment in inventory.
- Overly aggressive expansion plans.
- Slow collection of accounts receivable from customers.

EXHIBIT **B–7**

Projected Profit and
Loss Statement

	%	J	F	M	A	M	J	J	A	S	O	N	D	Total
Total net sales														
Cost, goods sold														
Gross														
Controllable expense														
Salaries/wages														
Payroll taxes														
Legal/accounting														
Advertising														
Automobile														
Office supplies														
Dues/subscriptions														
Telephone														
Utilities														
Miscellaneous														
Total controllable expense														
Fixed expenses														
Rent														
Depreciation														
Insurance														
Licenses/permits														
Taxes														
Loan payments														
Total fixed expenses														
Total expenses														
Net profit/loss (before tax)														

Legal Requirements As the owner of a retail operation, you need a basic understanding of the laws and regulations affecting your venture. Most new entrepreneurs have a good idea of what to expect; however, the one area in which most new business owners aren't properly prepared is government regulation. Legal and regulatory constraints that will affect your business can be found through the following sources:

Your state's Department of Commerce.
Your state's Department of Economic Development.
U.S. Small Business Administration.
Your local Chamber of Commerce.

EXHIBIT **B–8**

Estimated Cash Flow Projection

	MONTH 4	MONTH 5	MONTH 6	MONTH 7
Cash in bank (first of month)				
Petty cash (first of month)				
Total cash (first of month)				
Anticipated cash sales				
Total receipts				
Total cash and receipts				
Disbursements for month (rent, loan payments, wages, utilities, etc.)				
Cash balance (end of month)				

A variety of critical legal considerations appear in Exhibit B–9. All permits, licenses, regulations, and so forth that pertain to your business venture should be analyzed thoroughly and included in your business plan. Hire an attorney who specializes in small business development. If you're planning to spend $50,000 on a business, you might as well spend $500 on legal fees to be certain of the business plan's thoroughness.

Business Plan Assistance   Most potential new business owners aren't experts in new business development or business plan preparation. Therefore, you should be prepared to look for expert assistance wherever possible. One of your best sources for guidance with your business plan is the U.S. Small Business Administration (SBA). The SBA can refer you to the Service Corps of Retired Executives (SCORE). SCORE is comprised of retired business executives who volunteer their time and knowledge to help new businesses get off the ground. Other sources of information are your local Chamber of Commerce, trade associations, local colleges, local banks, and library.

EXHIBIT **B–9**

Legal Considerations

		YES	NO
A.	Do I know which licenses and permits I need to operate my business?	___	___
B.	Do I know the business laws that I will have to obey?	___	___
C.	Do I have a lawyer who can advise me on legal matters?	___	___
D.	Am I aware of the following:	___	___
	◆ Occupational Safety and Health Administration (OSHA) requirements?	___	___
	◆ Regulations covering hazardous materials?	___	___
	◆ Local ordinances covering signs, parking, snow removal, and so forth?	___	___
	◆ Federal tax code provisions pertaining to a small business?	___	___
	◆ Federal regulations on withholding taxes and Social Security?	___	___
	◆ State workers' compensation laws?	___	___

Value of the Business Plan　Completing the business plan is a crucial step in starting a new operation. The business plan must contain all pertinent information regarding your business. The plan must be well written, factual, organized, professionally presented, and persuasive. A well-formed business plan will enable you to

Determine the feasibility of your business idea.

Present your business idea to potential investors.

Allocate resources effectively and efficiently.

Measure results of your actions.

Achieve a profit for your business.

WHERE CAN YOU GET THE FINANCING TO START YOUR BUSINESS?

Once your business plan is complete, you can approach sources of financial support. The size of your initial investment requirements will determine the type of financing you'll need. However, the commitment of your own funds is the first step in financing a new business. Your risking your own personal funds will improve potential investors' confidence dramatically. The following can be used as a rule of thumb:

FUNDS NEEDED	SOURCES
$0–$50,000	Personal and family savings
$50,000–$250,000	Private investors and banks
$250,000 and up	Venture capital and banks

The investors' objective is to maximize their profit potential by investing in the project or business that will provide the least risk and greatest return. Therefore, you must present potential investors with ample justification to place their money in your business. The following guidelines will help you persuade investors:

- Present a comprehensive, professional business plan.
- Explain how the investors' funds will be utilized.
- Show how and when profits will be generated.
- Provide a specific time frame telling when investors' initial investment will be repaid.
- Tailor your presentation to those groups from whom you're requesting funds.
- Present a realistic picture of the facts regardless of how positive or negative they are.

Numerous types of creative financing are available to an entrepreneur. However, all funding can be categorized as either equity financing or debt financing.

Equity Financing　Equity financing involves the division of business ownership among the investors who contribute capital to your new business venture. When considering equity financing, you should decide (1) what portion of the ownership you're willing to share with outside investors and (2) how much control of the operations you're willing to relinquish.

Partnership   The formation of a partnership is the traditional means of adding equity investments. A partnership may be general or limited. General partners contribute capital, management time, and personal liability, while limited partners contribute capital without management responsibilities or liabilities. This option overcomes the limitations of debt financing, which requires extensive documentation of income, credit, and collateral.

The venture capital investor becomes a partner in your business by relinquishing the demand for immediate repayment in return for an equity share of the business. Although this option may be attractive to small operators, the amount of venture capital available to new retail businesses is limited.

Sale of Stock   The formation of a corporation is an alternative to equity investment. Although corporations provide considerable advantages, such as limited liability, they also have significant disadvantages. Formation of a partnership or corporation should be thoroughly studied with a lawyer and accountant to determine the optimal structure for your unique situation.

Debt Financing
Debt financing is a popular alternative approach for obtaining money for your business. This option involves borrowing funds and then repaying the loan along with the interest. Sources of debt financing include nonprofessional loans, conventional loans (bank loans), and loans from the Small Business Administration.

Nonprofessional Loans   Nonprofessional loans normally come from a family member, friend, or other person looking for investment opportunities as a tax shelter. The lender knows the entrepreneur personally and is often more willing to support the new business venture than institutional investors are. Other incentives for nonprofessional investors are tax provisions that encourage investments in small businesses. But proceed with caution when using this type of financing. Nonprofessional investors may want to get involved with your daily operations. In addition, they're less likely to understand a delay in repaying the loan and are less able to sustain the loss of their investment.

Conventional Loans   Banks can also be a useful source of capital. Bankers often require extensive business plans from first-time borrowers. Most loans are granted on your ability to repay the loan, which is often determined from analysis of the projected profit/loss statements. However, depending on your credit history, you may be required to supply a cosigner and/or collateral before a bank will give you a loan.

Small Business Administration Loans   The SBA offers two types of loans. The first type, a guaranteed loan, is comprised of private lenders (usually banks) and is guaranteed up to 90 percent by the SBA. The maximum private-sector loan that the SBA will guarantee is $500,000. The loan process has three steps:

1. The applicant submits the loan application to the lender for initial review.
2. If the application is approved, the lender forwards it to the SBA.
3. If the SBA approves the application, the lender closes the loan and disburses the funds.

The second type of SBA loan, the direct loan, is available to an applicant who couldn't secure a guaranteed loan. The maximum loan available is $150,000. Before applying for a direct loan, the applicant must have sought financing from at least two other sources. These funds are extremely limited and at times are only available to certain types of borrowers, such as handicapped people or veterans.

WHAT SHOULD YOU DO IF YOU'RE CONSIDERING THE PURCHASE OF AN EXISTING SMALL BUSINESS?

Buying a business has proven to yield higher success rates than starting a business. While the long-term success rate of new businesses is only 20 to 30 percent, the survival rate of purchased businesses averages 70 percent. These statistics account for the high level of interest in existing businesses and for the large number of small businesses purchased each year.

But small business buyers can easily get burned. Be extremely cautious and thorough when investigating a small business. The following guidelines (adapted from advice prepared by Western States Business Consultants) will help you avoid the frequent pitfalls of buying a small business:

- Determine exactly why a company is for sale.
- Be sure that a seller hasn't made the business look more attractive than it really is.
- Hire an experienced lawyer to review all corporate records.
- Hire an accountant to analyze all financial statements.
- Tie financial statements to historical tax returns to spot deviations.
- Analyze major developments and trends within the company and the industry.
- Verify inventories and supplier relationships.
- Check personnel to determine if the sale will trigger benefits to employees or loss of key employees.
- Check records at the county assessor's office for information on the building and property.
- Verify that the sale won't trigger loss of vendors or customers.
- Confirm with the owner that she won't start another small business that could compete directly with the one she's trying to sell.

SUMMARY

As your first step in starting your own business, you must take a hard look at yourself. Carefully analyze your strengths and weaknesses to determine your entrepreneurial aptitude. The next crucial step is to develop the business plan. A well-organized, thorough, and persuasive business plan must then be presented to potential investors.

Remember, you need to obtain the financing required to sustain your business through the crucial start-up period. Only then are you ready to begin to implement your business plan and convert your dream into reality.

SUGGESTED READINGS

Apparel Shop Entrepreneurship. Stillwater: Center for Apparel Marketing and Merchandising (CAMM), Department of Design, Housing and Merchandising, Oklahoma State University, 1990.

Burstiner, Irving. *Run Your Own Store.* New York: Prentice-Hall, 1980.

Fisk, Irwin W. "Get the Facts before You Act." *Entrepreneur,* January 1991, pp. 94–99.

Ricklefs, Roger. "Road to Success Less Littered with Failures." *The Wall Street Journal,* October 10, 1989, pp. A1, A9.

Small Business Administration, Office of Business Development. *Checklist for Going into Your Own Business.* Washington, DC: U.S. Government Printing Office, 1987.

Small Business Administration, Office of Business Development. *Starting Your Own Business.* Washington, DC: U.S. Government Printing Office, 1987.

"The 1990 Guide to Small Business." *U.S. News & World Report,* October 1989, pp. 72–80.

NOTES

1. "Small-Business Buyers Find It's Easy to Get Burned," *The Wall Street Journal,* September 21, 1990.

2. "Checklist for Small Business," *U.S. News & World Report,* October 1989, pp. 72–80.

3. Ibid., p. 74.

4. Ibid., p. 77.

Starting a Franchise Business

LIKE BASEBALL AND APPLE PIE, franchising is an American institution. A proven means for realizing the entrepreneurial dream across the country, franchising is taking over a large part of the retail trade. Indeed, it's estimated that by the year 2000, half of all U.S. retail sales will take place in franchised outlets. But is it for you? This appendix explores the franchising option in terms of its merits, drawbacks, profitability potential, and application to your needs. With more than 2,300 franchises to choose from, finding the best one for you can be almost as hard as starting your own business. Though it's true that McDonald's franchises have proven extremely successful, most franchises aren't nearly so profitable.

Some franchisors will tell you that buying a franchise is a guarantee of success. You'll hear success rates of 95 to 99 percent espoused. But are all franchises secure investments? Chuck E Cheese Pizza Time Theater, Arthur Treacher's Fish and Chips, Mantle Men–Namath Girls, Jerry Lewis Theaters, Lums, Curry Copy Center, and Chicken Delight all have one thing in common: They failed. As a result, thousands of dreams were shattered and millions of dollars were lost. Buying a franchise can be a dream come true, or it can be a nightmare. The key is buying smart, and that means doing your planning and investigating before you sign the contract. Franchising can be a very satisfactory method of starting your own business. It can be extremely rewarding both personally and financially, and it can free you from having to work for someone else.

There are three ways to begin your own business: Start one, buy an already operating business, or buy a franchise. Although accurate statistics aren't available, an estimate of the success rates for each method shows the following:

- Starting a new business: A 20 percent chance for survival.
- Buying an existing business: A 70 percent chance for survival.
- Buying a franchise: A 90 percent chance for survival.

Thus, your chance of succeeding with your own business is 1.3 times better if you choose franchising over buying an existing business and 4.5 times better than if you start your own business.

WHY BUY A FRANCHISE?

When considering the franchise option, you should clearly understand the attractions and drawbacks to buying a franchise versus starting your own retail business.

Advantages of Buying a Franchise

Not every franchisor provides the following advantages, but most of the larger and better franchisors do.

- Franchises generally enjoy higher success rates.
- Risk is lower due to a proven method of doing business.
- Personal investment normally is lower.
- The franchisor may help with financing. The franchise's name alone could make financing more readily attainable.
- Operating manuals and employee training are available.
- A recognized name and image already exist.
- National advertising with advertising merchandise assistance is available.
- Centralized purchasing and economies-of-scale capabilities yield cost savings.
- Management consulting and assistance may be provided.
- New products and services are more readily available through the franchisor.
- You have a protected territory.
- Location analysis and counsel are obtainable.

Disadvantages of Buying a Franchise

Disadvantages of buying a franchise include

- Fees and royalties must be paid. The franchisee agrees to do practically all of the work in exchange for only a portion of the profit.
- Strict adherence to the franchisor's rules and guidelines is required. The decor is specific. Employees wear prescribed uniforms. Even the napkins must be a certain color and size.
- There are restrictions on canceling contracts and selling your business at a later time.
- Profits can be hurt by the franchisor's business errors.
- Assessing various franchisors' potentials and deciding on the right one is difficult.
- There is significant dependency on the franchisor.
- Franchisor–franchisee conflicts often occur.

ARE YOU READY?

Once you've completed this analysis, you must then take a hard look at yourself to determine whether you're the right type of person to buy a franchise. Are you ready to make the personal sacrifices of long hours, hard work, financial uncertainty, and potential family problems due to the strain of beginning your own business? Do you enjoy working with others? Are you a good leader? Are you an organized person? Are you buying a job? Do you have adequate financial resources to buy a franchise and keep it going for at least a year? These issues and all the points discussed in Appendix B on starting your own business also apply in buying a franchise. Think them through before actually considering specific franchise options.

You'll need a significant amount of money to buy a franchise. Generally, you must be able to afford

1. The franchise fee. The franchise fee is a one-time payment to acquire the franchise name and a license to use the franchisor's process. Franchise fees vary from a few thousand dollars to over $100,000.

2.   Supplies, equipment, and inventory that you may be required to buy from the franchisor or an approved source.

3.   Enough operating capital to sustain the business in its early months of operation.

4.   Purchase of any land or buildings.

In assessing your financial ability to buy a franchise, you must determine your net worth. (See Appendix B.) Franchisors ask for a personal background report on all potential franchisees. A typical background report or application includes the potential franchisee's personal financial statement, personal information, and business history.

The major difference in types of personalities needed to operate a franchise as opposed to owning your own business is the ability to conform with the franchisor's strict standards. To have a successful operation, a franchisor must have uniformity in appearance, quality of product, and service in the individual franchises. The franchisor's system must be followed because that's what makes it work. This system leaves little ground for your own creativity or your own business ideas, so you must be willing to adhere to standards set by others.

EVALUATING AND CHOOSING A FRANCHISE

Once you've determined your personal and financial ability to buy a franchise, you're ready to begin reviewing your franchise options before deciding on a franchise. The following seven-step evaluation process has been developed to simplify the franchise analysis.

Step 1: Initial Investigation

Once you decide what type of franchise you're interested in buying, pick 10 or 20 franchise options to review. For this initial review, you need to collect as much information as possible about these franchises. The following sources of information can give you a good overview of your candidates.

Uniform Franchise Offering Circular   One of your most important tools in reviewing various franchises is the franchisor disclosure document or Uniform Franchise Offering Circular (UFOC). This document is prepared by the franchisor and lists 23 categories of information about the franchisor and the franchise. The Federal Trade Commission (FTC) requires franchisors to give a UFOC to a prospective franchisee at least 10 days before a contract is signed. According to studies, nearly 70 percent of franchisees use the UFOC to make their selection. Buyers should be aware that there are no ironclad guarantees that the disclosure statement is accurate. However, 78 percent of the franchisees surveyed reported the UFOC reflected their own experience.

Ask yourself questions as you read through the document. Do you have the expertise to run it? Are there any lawsuits pending? Do the profitability projections seem reasonable? Do you have a thorough understanding of the fees and royalties? Can you handle the business financially? Are you required to purchase your supplies and services from a designated source?

Franchise Opportunities Handbook   An extremely useful source of information, the *Franchise Opportunities Handbook* lists over 1,000 franchisors and provides

- The name and address of the company.
- A brief description of the operation.

- The number of franchises.
- Year of inception.
- Equity capital needed.
- Any financial assistance available.
- Whether training is provided.
- Whether management assistance is provided.

Other Sources   Sources of government assistance include the U.S. Department of Commerce and the Small Business Administration. The Chamber of Commerce can provide local information. The public library can be used to research recent articles written about the franchise.

These sources of information should help you narrow your franchise alternatives to fewer than four. Now you're ready for a detailed investigation of the remaining candidates.

Step 2: Visiting Other Franchisees

As part of your overall investigation, visit or call existing franchises and ask a few key questions:

- When did you buy this franchise?
- Why did you pick this one?
- What was your background or business experience?
- What did you expect to gain from a franchise business? Are those expectations being fulfilled by this franchisor?
- What problems have you had?
- How big is your territory? Is it exclusive?
- What's your biggest complaint about your business?
- How are your dealings and relationship with the franchisor?
- Do you feel the franchise fee and royalties are fair?
- What's your personal work schedule? Does it vary? When are you busiest?
- What general advice can you give me?
- Would you buy this franchise again? Why or why not?

Compare what the franchisees tell you with the information provided in the disclosure documents and company booklets. Visit franchisees who failed and ask them the same questions. Then compare the two groups' answers. If the successful franchisees had certain backgrounds or experience the failures lacked, frankly evaluate your own attributes and deficiencies in these areas.

Step 3: Visiting the Franchisor's Headquarters

If you're still satisfied with franchise operations, plan to visit the company headquarters to get further details about the franchise. Exhibit C–1 lists 25 key questions a franchisor should be able to answer during your visit.

Step 4: Financial Analysis

There's no reason to invest in a franchise unless you can earn a profit from it. In predicting a venture's profitability, you'll need to estimate sales, your salary, net profits, total investment needed, return on investment, net present value, payback period, and break-even point. All these measures will help you determine the financial soundness of the franchise investment.

EXHIBIT C–1

Questions to Ask
the Franchisor

1. How much money can I make? Good franchisors will be cautious about this answer and the really good ones may even low-ball you (give you an extremely conservative estimate). It's certainly better to tell you to expect an annual salary of $25,000 and have you make $40,000 than the reverse. Some franchisors will give you a range that represents what other owners have experienced in their first year. Still others relate that figure to sales, in which case it's expressed as a percentage. For example, if you're told you can expect to take home 15 percent of sales as earnings, if you sell $100,000, you make $15,000; $200,000 in sales will net you $30,000, and so on.

2. When can I expect to begin making money? This is a vital question because you need to consider this factor in your financial planning. If you open a nationally known fast-food restaurant in virgin territory, you can expect to make money the first month or at least the second. If you open a service business or a retail business offering a new concept or product, it may take a year to build up sufficient clients or customers to turn a profit. For example, a franchise selling New England clam chowder may take less time to become established on Cape Cod than one selling California tacos. Franchised tutorial services may have to overcome parental reluctance to use them or provide proof of their merit before they can generate enough business to provide an income for their owners.

3. How much money must I personally invest? What does this include? How much is working capital?

4. Do you do any financing? If not, will you help me to secure it? NOTE: The majority of franchisors do neither, but you always ask because you might be dealing with the exception.

5. How many franchised locations do you have? How many are company-owned? How many of each have failed? Why did they fail?

6. What happens if I'm not successful due to my efforts? Suppose it's your fault—introducing products that don't sell, or picking the wrong location?

7. Is there any way you'll buy me back? Can either of us initiate this?

8. When do I pay you? This is important because some franchisors will allow you to stretch out the franchise fee. You also want to know how often you pay royalties.

9. How long is the process from contract signing to opening day?

10. Is the business seasonal? What affects business levels? One fast-food restaurant found its sales increased in recessionary periods. Some retail establishments experience their biggest rush during the Christmas season whereas those geared to tourist products and services may do the majority of their business in one particular season.

11. What is the nature of your training support? How long does it last? What will I learn? May I see the manuals?

12. What am I required to buy from you? Do I have to buy a minimum amount? What is your markup on what you sell to me?

13. What staff support can I count on? The larger, more established franchisors have internal consultants available. If this is the case here, must I pay for their services?

14. What advertising and promotion do you do? Am I expected to do a certain amount of local advertising? Are there advertising payments to you based on my sales?

15. Who will be my contact? What happens if that person leaves?

16. What are your plans for the next five years?

17. What makes you think this business will succeed in my area?

18. What are my hours of operation? Must I work full-time at the business? Can I start in my house?

19. What exactly is my territory?

20. Do I own the equipment?

21. Do you find the location for me? Who owns the real estate?

22. Do you have a newsletter?

23. What seminars and courses do you hold for present franchisees?

24. What exclusive rights do I have? Can I sell the business myself?

25. May I see a contract now? For how long is the contract good? Is it renewable? How can I terminate? How can you? What happens if I die?

Step 5: Professional Assistance   After you've examined the finances, have a qualified advisor (an attorney, accountant, banker, or other business professional) look them over too. The investment you make in professional assistance will be small compared to the dollar and time investments you'll be making in the franchise enterprise.

Step 6: Contract and Franchise Agreement   Carefully read and reread the actual franchise contract you'll be signing. Don't let yourself be rushed into signing this contract. Hire a lawyer to review the contract. To ensure that the franchise agreement contains all the necessary clauses, review the following points with your attorney:

1. Price and costs.
   - What's the total cost to you?
   - What are the initial fees?
   - What are the ongoing costs?
   - Are there hidden extras and costly tie-ins?
   - Are you restricted in your right to purchase goods?
2. Location and geography.
   - Where will you be located?
   - What's your territory?
   - What are your protections and limitations?
   - Who can compete with you?
   - Can the franchisor also become a retail competitor?
3. Control and support.
   - What controls are placed on you?
   - What policies or regulations govern you?
   - What support will you receive?
   - What training and ongoing supervision will you receive?
4. Advertising and assistance.
   - What national and local advertising will you receive?
   - For what advertising will you pay?
   - What marketing assistance will you receive?
5. Profits and losses.
   - If you're successful, what protection do you have for your earnings?
   - If you fail or are terminated, what obligations will remain for you to pay?
6. Transfer and death.
   - Will your franchise rights pass to your heirs upon your death?
   - Can you sell, transfer, or mortgage your franchise rights?
7. Duration and termination.
   - Who can cancel the contract and under what circumstances?
   - How long will your rights continue? Can they be renewed?

The most important determinant in avoiding future conflict in a franchise system is the contract. The contract shouldn't be one-sided in favor of the franchisor. The Better Business Bureau has developed several principles to guide franchise contract development:

- The contract should be frank, completely disclosing the relationship between the franchisor and the franchisee. The objective is to make explicit all mutual rights and obligations with performance standards to ensure that neither party may reasonably claim that it was deceived by the other.
- The provisions should be fair.
- The contract should be tailored to the specific situation.
- Criteria for new outlet penetration of given markets should be specified.
- Reasonable causes leading to termination by either party should be specified.
- How any potential conflict will be resolved should be delineated. If arbitration is necessary, who will arbitrate and who will bear the costs should be agreed to.

Step 7: Final Decision

Let's assume you still have three good franchise candidates. You've gotten sufficient information to remain interested, you've visited or called numerous franchisees within each franchise, you've been to the franchise headquarters, you've done extensive financial analysis, and you've investigated the contract and franchise agreement thoroughly. All three candidates have passed these tests. Now it's time to make a decision.

Before you analyze these options further, they must pass the following general criteria:

- The basic idea of the business appeals to you.
- You have the experience to run the business or believe the franchisor will train you.
- The franchisor has a proven track record.
- You like the franchisor's people.
- You can afford the franchise.
- The franchise can support you and your family.
- Running the business appears enjoyable.
- The financial analysis is sound.

Reflect on these qualities and be sure you aren't misleading yourself. Now imagine yourself as the owner of each of the three businesses. Does one feel better than the other? Rank them into first, second, and third choices. Exhibit C–2 depicts a franchise analysis form with extensive questions to consider for each franchise. Use your ranking, the franchise analysis, and the previous financial analysis to determine the optimal franchise operation. Don't make your decision solely on maximizing potential profits. This wouldn't be wise because you'll be spending a great deal of energy and time to make the venture succeed. If you don't enjoy the franchise concept or working with the franchisors, the franchise venture will be a miserable experience.

If you're willing to follow the seven steps outlined in this appendix, your chances of becoming the proud owner of a successful franchise will be greatly improved.

Good luck!

EXHIBIT **C–2**

Franchise Analysis
Form

Name of Franchisor:
Address:
City, State, Zip:

PART I

		Yes	No	Not Sure
A.	**THE FRANCHISOR**			
1.	Was I treated fairly and openly by the franchisor?	_____	_____	_____
2.	Do I believe the franchisor has met the spirit and intent of the FTC Rule?	_____	_____	_____
3.	Was I allowed to take my own time and not be hustled?	_____	_____	_____
4.	Were people professional and qualified?	_____	_____	_____
5.	Do I think the franchisor is honest?	_____	_____	_____
6.	Were all my questions answered to my satisfaction?	_____	_____	_____
7.	Does the franchisor have a good reputation?	_____	_____	_____
8.	Is the franchisor financially sound?	_____	_____	_____
9.	Are all the materials I've received clear and easy to understand?	_____	_____	_____
10.	Are the franchisor and its key people free from lawsuits?	_____	_____	_____
a.	FTC disclosure material?	_____	_____	_____
b.	A copy of the agreement?	_____	_____	_____
c.	Financial projections?	_____	_____	_____
d.	References?	_____	_____	_____
11.	Is the franchisor a member of the IFA?	_____	_____	_____
12.	Is the franchisor listed in *Franchise Opportunities Handbook?*	_____	_____	_____
13.	Does the franchisor have a newsletter?	_____	_____	_____
14.	Does the franchisor have a toll-free number?	_____	_____	_____
B.	**MARKETING/BUSINESS**			
1.	Has the product or service proven to be a success?	_____	_____	_____
2.	Does the product or service seem to have staying power?	_____	_____	_____
3.	Is the industry (fast food, business services) growing?	_____	_____	_____
4.	Is the franchisor growing?	_____	_____	_____
5.	Is the franchisor national in its operations?	_____	_____	_____
6.	Do I think this franchise will go in my area?	_____	_____	_____
7.	Does this franchise fulfill my personal goals?	_____	_____	_____
8.	Does the franchisor have a national advertising program?	_____	_____	_____
9.	Does the franchisor help me with local advertising— either financially or by providing ad copy?	_____	_____	_____
10.	Does the franchisor have a customer service department to answer my questions?	_____	_____	_____
11.	If applicable, does the franchisor provide sales leads?	_____	_____	_____
12.	Did the franchisor give me an idea of who or what my market is and who buys its product?	_____	_____	_____
13.	Do I know my competition well?	_____	_____	_____
14.	Does the franchisor have plans for new products and services?	_____	_____	_____

(continued)

EXHIBIT C–2

Franchise Analysis
Form *(continued)*

15. Do I have an exclusive territory? ___ ___ ___

16. Is the product or service protected by patents, trademarks, or copyrights? ___ ___ ___

C. OPERATIONS

1. Am I expected to work full-time at the business? ___ ___ ___

2. May I operate the business from my home? ___ ___ ___

3. If the answer to (2) above is no, may I lease the facility I need? ___ ___ ___

4. If the answer to (3) above is no, does the franchisor help in the design, construction, furnishing, or financing of the building? ___ ___ ___

5. Does the franchisor provide operations manuals? ___ ___ ___

6. May I buy equipment, supplies, and inventory from sources other than the franchisor? ___ ___ ___

7. Can I make a good living from this franchise? ___ ___ ___

8. Am I free to hire whom I want? ___ ___ ___

9. Do the financial ratios appear sound? ___ ___ ___

D. CONTRACT

Are the following items covered in the franchisor's contract?

1. The franchise fee. ___ ___ ___

2. Royalties and commissions. ___ ___ ___

3. Requirement to purchase from franchisor. ___ ___ ___

4. Advertising payments. ___ ___ ___

5. My duties and responsibilities. ___ ___ ___

6. Franchisor's duties and responsibilities. ___ ___ ___

7. Territory. ___ ___ ___

8. Training. ___ ___ ___

9. Causes for termination. ___ ___ ___

10. Ability to renew. ___ ___ ___

11. Financing. ___ ___ ___

12. Escape clauses. ___ ___ ___

E. TRAINING

1. Is the cost of initial training included in the franchise fee? ___ ___ ___

2. Is this initial training sufficient for me to be able to run this business? ___ ___ ___

3. Does the franchisor offer continuing education beyond the initial training? ___ ___ ___

(continued)

EXHIBIT **C–2**

Franchise Analysis
Form *(continued)*

PART II

1. If the franchisor is a division or subsidiary of a larger company, what is the name and address of that company?

2. Is the parent company, or the franchisor itself if there is no parent,

   a. A privately held company? _____

   b. A publicly traded company? _____

   c. If it's public, where is its stock traded? _____

      New York Stock Exchange. _____

      American Stock Exchange. _____

      Other stock exchange. _____

      Over the counter. _____

3. Concerning the franchise company,

   a. What year was it founded? _____

   b. In what year was the first franchise opened? _____

   c. What is the *total* number of franchise locations that have been opened? _____

   d. How many company-owned locations are there? _____

   e. How many *franchises* have failed? _____

   f. Compute the franchisor's failure rate: _____

      $$\frac{\text{No. of failures (from 3e)}}{\text{No. of total locations (from 3c)}} \times 100 = \underline{\hspace{3cm}}\%$$

      Note: If this figure is 20 percent or above, we suggest you be extremely cautious in considering this franchise.

   g. How many new franchises does the franchisor expect to sell in the next 12 months? _____

   h. Compute the growth rate for the next year:

      $$\frac{\text{No. of planned franchises (from 3g)}}{\text{No. of total locations (from 3c)}} \times 100 = \underline{\hspace{3cm}}\%$$

      Note: If this figure is 100 percent or greater, be cautious. Too rapid growth has buried many franchisors.

4. Briefly describe the business as you understand it now.

5. What is the biggest advantage of this business?

6. What are its greatest drawbacks?

7. Below, list any positive or negative facts about this franchisor you've discovered in your research.

   a. Discussion with Franchisee #1.   Name: _____

   b. Discussion with Franchisee #2.   Name: _____

(continued)

EXHIBIT **C–2**

Franchise Analysis
Form *(continued)*

   c.   **Discussion with Franchisee #3.**   **Name:** _____

   d.   **National Better Business Bureau reports.**

   e.   **FTC publications.**

   f.   **Local Better Business Bureau or Chamber of Commerce.**

   g.   **Research in newspaper and magazines.**

   h.   **Other.**

8.   **If you know the reasons for any failures, list them.**

9.   **Consider the community where you're thinking of locating. List your competition (which can be both franchised and nonfranchised businesses) and any appropriate comments—estimates of sales, strong and weak points, years in operation. Note: The Yellow Pages are your best place to start.**

           Name and Address of Competitor   **Comments**

   a.

   b.

   c.

   d.

   e.

   f.

   g.

10.   **What is the total franchise fee?**
     $_____

11.   **How much of the initial fee must I pay before I begin?**
     $_____

12.   **How much are my start-up costs (equipment, inventory, supplies)?**
     $_____

13.   **What do I need for working capital (money to run the business until it's profitable)?**
     $_____

14.   **If applicable, how much will it cost to buy land and build a building?**
     $_____

(continued)

EXHIBIT C–2

Franchise Analysis
Form (*continued*)

15. If other funds are required (special deposits, adance royalties, fees), how much are they?

    $_____

16. What is my total investment? (Add amounts in items 10, 12, 13, 14, and 15 above.)

    $_____

17. If the franchisor provides financing, how much of the total (from item 16 above) is covered?

    $_____

18. What interest rates does the franchisor charge?

    _____ percent

19. If the franchisor provides no financing, where can I go for it? (List banks, friends, relatives, and investors.)

    a.

    b.

    c.

    d.

20. How much, if any, of the initial fee will be refunded and under what circumstances? (For example, 100 percent refunded prior to training, 80 percent within five days after completing training.)

    $_____

21. Refer to your calculations in the previous chapter for the following four items:

    a. Cash required

       $_____

    b. Total investment

       $_____

    c. Sales

       $_____

    d. Earnings

       $_____

22. Next, record the five ratios:

    a. Cash/total investment

       _____ percent

    b. Sales/total investment

       _____ times

    c. Earnings/sales

       _____ percent

    d. Earnings/total investment

       _____ times

    e. Payback

       _____ years

23. What royalties do I pay and how are they computed? (Eight percent of net sales, for example.)

24. If there are any other fees, costs, assessments, or charges (for example, 1 percent of sales for national advertising, $1,000 annual auditing fee), list them below:

(*continued*)

EXHIBIT **C–2**

Franchise Analysis
Form *(concluded)*

25. According to the franchisor, how long will it be before the business breaks even and is self-sufficient? (If this figure is given in months or a combination of years and months, convert it to years expressed in decimals. For example, 18 months becomes 1.5 years.)

_____ years
(expressed in decimals)

Note: Compare this to the theoretical payback (item 22c). It should be longer because the payback was calculated based on the earnings of an *established* business. The time to achieve the break-even point is based on your starting from scratch.

26. How many people will I need to hire?

	Part-time	*Full-time*
a. To start with:		
b. After one year:		
c. After two years:		

27. Are there special skills or education my employees need?

Job Title	*Skills/Education Needed*
a.	a.
b.	b.
c.	c.
d.	d.

28. Who is my primary franchisor contact?

Name _____

Title _____

Address _____

City, state, zip _____

Phone _____

29. List any other franchisor contacts available to help:

a.

b.

c.

d.

30. Rate this business from 1 (a total dog, wouldn't take it if someone paid me) to 10 (absolutely perfect in every way) based on how you personally feel about it.

Rating: _____

Source: "Franchise Analysis Form," from *Buying a Franchise* by Brian R. Smith and Thomas L. West. Copyright © 1986 by Brian R. Smith and Thomas L. West. Used by permission of The Stephen Greene Press, an imprint of Penguin Books USA, Inc.

SUGGESTED READINGS

Answers to the Twenty-One Most Commonly Asked Questions about Franchising. Better Business Bureau, 1975.

Apparel Shop Entrepreneurship. Stillwater: Center for Apparel Marketing and Merchandising (CAMM), Department of Design, Housing and Merchandising, Oklahoma State University, 1990.

Facts on Selecting a Franchise. Better Business Bureau, 1975.

Fisk, Irwin W. "Get the Facts before You Act." *Entrepreneur,* January 1991, pp. 94–99.

Friedlander, Mark, and Gene Gurney. *Handbook of Successful Franchising.* Liberty Hall Press, 1990.

Kaufmann, David, and David Robbins. "Now Read This." *Entrepreneur,* January 1991, pp. 100–5.

Rosenberg, Kenneth. "Franchising American Style." *Entrepreneur,* January 1991, pp. 86–93.

Smith, Brian, and Thomas West. *Buying a Franchise.* Lexington, MA: Stephen Greene Press, 1986.

ABC analysis   an analysis that rank-orders SKUs by a profitability measure to determine which items should never be out of stock, should be allowed to be out of stock occasionally, or should be deleted from the stock selection.

abilities   the aptitude and skills of an employee.

accessibility   the degree to which customers can easily get into and out of a shopping center.

accessories   merchandise in apparel, department, and specialty stores used to complement apparel outfits. Examples include gloves, hosiery, handbags, jewelry, handkerchiefs, and scarves.

accordion theory   a cyclical theory of retailer evolution suggesting that changes in retail institutions are explained in terms of depth versus breadth of assortment. Retail institutions cycle from high-depth/low-breadth to low-depth/high-breadth stores and back again.

account opener   a premium or special promotion item offered to induce the opening of a new account, especially in financial institutions and stores operating on an installment credit basis.

accounts payable   the amount of money owed to vendors, primarily for merchandise inventory.

accounts receivable   the amount of money due to the retailer from selling merchandise on credit.

accrued liabilities   liabilities that accumulate daily but are paid only at the end of a period.

acquisition   a strategic growth activity in which one firm acquires another firm, usually resulting in a merger. See also **leveraged buyout.**

actionability   means that the definition of a market segment must clearly indicate what the retailer should do to satisfy its needs.

adaptive selling   an approach to personal selling in which selling behaviors are altered based on information about the customer and the buying situation.

additional markup   an increase in retail price after and in addition to original markup.

additional markup cancellation   the percentage by which the retail price is lowered after a markup is taken.

additional markup percentage   the addition of a further markup to the original markup as a percentage of net sales.

administered vertical marketing system   a form of vertical marketing system designed to control a line of classification of merchandise as opposed to an entire store's operation. Such systems involve the development of comprehensive programs for specified lines of merchandise. The vertically aligned companies, even though in a non-ownership position, may work together to reduce the total systems cost of such activities as advertising, transportation, and data processing. (See also **contractual vertical marketing system** and **corporate vertical marketing system.**)

advance order   an order placed well in advance of the desired time of shipment. By placing orders in advance of the actual buying season, a buyer is often able to get a lower price because the buyer gives the vendor business when the latter would normally be receiving little.

advertising   paid communications delivered to customers through nonpersonal mass media such as newspapers, television, radio, and direct mail.

advertising manager   a retail manager who manages advertising activities such as determining the advertising budget, allocating the budget, developing ads, selecting media, and monitoring advertising effectiveness.

advertising reach   the percentage of customers in the target market exposed to an ad at least once.

affinity marketing   marketing activities that enable consumers to express their identification with an organization. An example is offering credit cards tied to reference groups like the consumer's university or an NFL team.

affordable promotional budgeting   a budgeting method in which a retailer first sets a budget for every element of the retail mix except promotion and then allocates the leftover funds to a promotional budget.

agent   (1) a business unit that negotiates purchases, sales, or both but does not take title to the goods in which it deals. (2) a person who represents the principal (who, in the case of retailing, is the store or merchant) and who acts under authority, whether in buying or in bringing the principal into business relations with third parties.

aging   the length of time merchandise has been in stock.

all-purpose revolving account   a regular 30-day charge account that, if paid in full within 30 days from date of statement, has no service charge, but when installment payments are made, a service charge is made on the balance at the time of the next billing.

alteration costs   expenses incurred to change the appearance or fit, to assemble, or to repair merchandise.

Americans with Disabilities Act (ADA) a federal act that opens up job opportunities for the disabled by requiring employees to provide accommodating work environments.

analog approach a method of trade area analysis also known as the "similar store" or "mapping" approach. The analysis is divided into four steps: (1) describing the current trade areas through the technique of customer spotting, (2) plotting the customers on a map, (3) defining the primary, secondary, and tertiary area zones, and (4) matching the characteristics of stores in the trade areas with the potential new store to estimate its sales potential.

anchor store a large, well-known retail operation located in a shopping center and serving as an attracting force for consumers to the center.

ancillary services services such as layaway, gift wrap, credit, and any other service that is not directly related to the actual sale of a specific product within the store.

anticipation discount a discount offered by a vendor to a retailer in addition to the cash discount or dating, if the retailer pays the invoice before the end of the cash discount period.

anticompetitive leasing arrangement a lease that limits the type and amount of competition a particular retailer faces within a trading area.

antitrust legislation a set of laws directed at preventing unreasonable restraint of trade or unfair trade practices to foster a competitive environment. See also **restraint of trade.**

application form a form used for information on a job applicant's education, employment experience, hobbies, and references.

artificial barriers in site evaluations for accessibility, barriers such as railroad tracks, major highways, or parks.

assets economic resources of expected future economic benefit that are owned or controlled by an enterprise as a result of past transactions or events.

asset turnover net sales divided by total assets.

assortment the number of SKUs within a merchandise category.

assortment providing a function performed by retailers that enables customers to choose from a selection of brands, designs, sizes, and prices at one location.

atmospheric see **atmospherics.**

atmospherics the design of an environment via visual communications, lighting, colors, music, and scent to stimulate customers' perceptual and emotional responses and ultimately to affect their purchase behavior.

auction a market in which goods are sold to the highest bidder; usually well publicized in advance or held at specific times well-known in the trade.

autocratic method of store management when managers make all decisions on their own and then announce them to employees.

automatic reordering system a system for ordering staple merchandise using a predetermined minimum quantity of goods in stock. An automatic reorder can be generated by a computer on the basis of a perpetual inventory system and reorder point calculations.

average BOM stock-to-sales ratio the number of months in the period divided by planned inventory turnover for the period.

average inventory the sum of inventory on hand at several periods in time divided by the number of periods.

baby boomer the generational cohort of people born between 1946 and 1964.

back order a part of an order that the vendor has not filled on time and that the vendor intends to ship as soon as the goods in question are received, manufactured, or provided.

backward integration a form of vertical integration in which a retailer owns some or all of its suppliers.

bait-and-switch an unlawful deceptive practice that lures customers into a store by advertising a product at lower than usual prices (the bait) then inducing the customers to switch to a higher-price model (the switch).

balance sheet the summary of a retailer's financial resources and claims against the resources at a particular date; indicates the relationship between assets, liabilities, and owners' equity.

bank cards credit cards issued by banks, such as Visa and MasterCard.

bar code see **Universal Product Code (UPC).**

bargaining power of vendors the degree to which few vendors control the merchandise sold in a market.

barriers to entry conditions in a retail market that make it difficult for firms to enter the market.

basic merchandise see **staple merchandise.**

basic stock list the descriptive and record-keeping function of an inventory control system; includes the stock number, item description, number of units on hand and on order, and sales for the previous periods.

basic stock method an inventory management method used to determine the beginning-of-month (BOM) inventory by considering both the forecast sales for the month and the safety stock.

benchmarking   the practice of evaluating performance by comparing your performance with that of other retailers using a similar retail strategy.

benefits   the customer's specific needs that are satisfied when the customer buys a product.

benefit segmentation   a method of segmenting a retail market based on similar benefits sought in merchandise and/or services.

benefits/price effect   the condition that arises when customers' price sensitivity increases because they cannot perceive special benefits from a product.

black market   the availability of merchandise at a higher price when it is difficult or impossible to purchase under normal market circumstances; commonly involves illegal transactions.

blue laws   laws prohibiting retailers from being open two consecutive days of the weekend—ostensibly to allow employees a day of rest or religious observance. Most states no longer have blue laws.

bonus   additional compensation awarded periodically, based on a subjective evaluation of the employee's performance.

book inventory   see **retail inventory method.**

bottom-up planning   when goals are set at the bottom of the organization and filter up through the operating levels.

boutique layout   a store design that places all departments on the "main aisle" by drawing customers through the store in a series of major and minor loops; also known as a **loop layout.**

box store   see **limited-line warehouse store.**

brand   a distinctive grouping of products identified by corporate name, logo, design, symbol, or trademark.

brand loyal   customers who like and consistently buy a specific brand in a product category.

breadth of merchandise   see **variety.**

break-even analysis   a technique that evaluates the relationship between total revenue and total cost to determine profitability at various sales levels.

break-even point   the quantity at which total revenue equals total cost, and beyond which profit occurs.

breaking bulk   a function performed by retailers or wholesalers in which they receive large quantities of merchandise and sell them in smaller quantities.

breaking sizes   running out of stock on particular sizes.

broker   a middleman that serves as a go-between for the buyer or seller; assumes no title risks, does not usually have physical custody of products, and is not looked upon as a permanent representative of either the buyer or seller.

building codes   legal restrictions describing the size and type of building, signs, and type of parking lot, and so on that can be used at a particular location.

buffer stock   see **safety stock.**

bulk   see **rounder.**

bulk of stock   the store area in which the total assortment of merchandise is placed. Usually contains gondolas in grocery and discount stores and freestanding fixtures for soft goods in other types of stores.

buyer's market   market occurring in economic conditions that favor the position of the retail buyer (or merchandiser) rather than the vendor; in other words, economic conditions are such that the retailer can demand and usually get concessions from suppliers in terms of price, delivery, and other market advantages. Opposite of a seller's market.

buyer's report   information on the velocity of sales, availability of inventory, amount of order, inventory turnover, forecast sales, and, most important, the quantity that should be ordered for each SKU.

buying behavior   the activities customers undertake when purchasing a good or service.

buying calendar   a plan of a store buyer's market activities, generally covering a six-month merchandising season based on a selling calendar that indicates planned promotional events.

buying committee   a committee that has the authority for final judgment and decision making on such matters as adding or eliminating new products; especially common in supermarket companies and resident buying offices.

buying power   the customer's financial resources available for making purchases.

buying process   the stages customers go through to purchase merchandise or services.

buying situation segmentation   a method of segmenting a retail market based on customer needs in a specific buying situation such as a fill-in shopping trip versus a weekly shopping trip.

call system   a system of equalizing sales among salespersons—for example, some stores rotate salespeople, giving each an equal opportunity to meet customers.

capacity fixture   see **rounder.**

career path   the set of positions to which management employees are promoted within a particular organization, as their career progresses.

cart   a retail facility that offers the simplest presentation, is mobile, and is on wheels.

cash   money on hand.

cash discounts   reductions in the invoice cost that the vendor allows the retailer for paying the invoice prior to the end of the discount period.

catalog retailer   a nonstore retailer that communicates directly with customers using catalogs sent through the mail.

catalog showroom   a type of retailer that uses a showroom to display merchandise combined with an adjacent warehouse; typically specializes in hard goods such as housewares.

category   an assortment of items (SKUs) the customer sees as reasonable substitutes for each other.

category killer   discount retailer that offers a complete assortment in a category and thus dominates a category from the customer's perspective.

category life cycle   a merchandise category's sales pattern over time.

category specialist   see **category killer.**

caveat emptor   Latin term for "let the buyer beware."

census tracts   subdivisions of a standard metropolitan statistical area (SMSA), with an average population of 4,000.

central business district (CBD)   the traditional downtown business area of a city or town.

centralization   an organization structure in which the authority for making retail decisions is delegated to corporate managers rather than to geographically dispersed regional, district, and store management.

centralized buying   a situation in which a retailer makes all purchase decisions at one location, typically the firm's headquarters.

central market   see **market.**

central place   a center of retailing activity such as a town or city.

central place theory   Christaller's theory of retail location suggesting that retailers tend to locate in a central place. As more retailers locate together, more customers are attracted to the central place. See also **central place.**

chain   see **retail chain.**

chain discount   a number of different discounts taken sequentially from the suggested retail price.

channel of distribution   see **distribution channel.**

checking   the process of going through goods upon receipt to make sure that they arrived undamaged and that the merchandise received matches the merchandise ordered.

cherry-picking   customers visiting a store and buying only merchandise sold at big discounts.

classic   a fashion that has both a high level and a long duration of acceptance.

classification   a group of items or SKUs for the same type of merchandise, such as pants (as opposed to jackets or suits), supplied by different vendors.

classification dominance   an assortment so broad that customers should be able to satisfy all of their consumption needs for a particular category by visiting one retailer.

classification merchandising   divisions of departments into related types of merchandise for reporting and control purposes.

Clayton Act (1914)   an act passed as a response to the deficiencies of the Sherman Act; it specifically prohibits price discrimination, tying arrangements, and exclusive dealing contracts that have the effect of limiting free trade and provides for damage to parties injured as a result of violations of the act.

clearance sale   an end-of-season sale to make room for new goods; also pushing the sale of slow-moving, shopworn, and demonstration model goods.

close-out   an offer at a reduced price to clear slow-moving or incomplete stock; also, an incomplete assortment, the remainder of a line of merchandise that is to be discontinued, offered at a low price to ensure immediate sale.

close-out retailers   off-price retailers that sell a broad but inconsistent assortment of general merchandise as well as apparel and soft home goods, obtained through retail liquidations and bankruptcy proceedings.

cocooning   a term that describes a behavioral pattern of consumers who increasingly turn to the nice, safe, familiar environment of their homes to spend their limited leisure time.

COD (collect on delivery)   purchase terms in which payment for a product is collected at the time of delivery.

combination stores   food-based retailers between 30,000 and 100,000 square feet in size with over 25 percent of their sales from nonfood merchandise such as flowers, health and beauty aids, kitchen utensils, photo developing, prescription drugs, and videotape rentals.

commercial bribery   a vendor's offer of money or gifts to a buyer for the purpose of influencing purchasing decisions.

commission   compensation based on a fixed formula, such as percentage of sales.

committee buying   the situation whenever the buying decision is made by a group of people rather than by a single buyer. A multiunit operation is usually the type of firm that uses this procedure.

common stock   the type of stock most frequently issued by corporations. Owners of common stock usually have voting rights in the retail corporation.

communication objectives   specific goals for a communication program related to the effects of the communication program on the customer's decision-making process.

community center   shopping center that includes a discount store, specialty department store, super drug store, home-improvement center, and other convenience and shopping goods stores.

comparison shopping   a market research method in which retailers shop at competitive stores, comparing the merchandise, pricing, visual display, and service to their own offering.

compensation   monetary payments including salary, commission, and bonuses; also, paid vacations, health and insurance benefits, and a retirement plan.

competitive-oriented pricing   a pricing method in which a retailer uses competitor's prices (rather than demand or cost considerations) as guides.

competitive parity method   an approach for setting a promotion budget so that the retailer's share of promotion expenses is equal to its market share.

competitive rivalry   the frequency and intensity of reactions to competitors' actions.

competitor analysis   an examination of the strategic direction that competitors are likely to pursue and their ability to successfully implement their strategy.

composite segmentation   a method of segmenting a retail market using multiple variables including benefits sought, lifestyles, and demographics.

computerized checkout   see **point-of-sale (POS) terminal.**

conditional sales agreement   an agreement that passes title of goods to the consumer, conditional on full payment.

conditions of sale   see **terms of sale.**

conflict of interest   a situation in which a decision maker's personal interest influences or has the potential to influence his or her professional decision.

congestion   the amount of crowding of either cars or people.

consideration set   the set of alternatives the customer evaluates when making a merchandise selection.

consignment goods   items not paid for by the retailer until they are sold. The retailer can return unsold merchandise; however, the retailer does not take title until final sale is made.

consumer cooperatives   customers own and operate the retail establishment. Customers have ownership shares, hire full-time managers, and share in the store's profits through price reductions or dividends.

Consumer Goods Pricing Act (1975)   the statute that repealed all resale price maintenance laws and made it possible for retailers to sell products below suggested retail prices.

consumerism   the activities of government, business, and independent organizations designed to protect individuals from practices that infringe upon their rights as consumers.

contests   promotional activities in which customers compete for rewards. Contests can also be used to motivate retail employees.

contract distribution service companies   firms that perform all of the distribution functions for retailers or vendors, including transportation to the contract company's distribution center, merchandise processing, storage, and transportation to retailers.

contractual vertical marketing system   a form of vertical marketing system in which independent firms at different levels in the channel operate contractually to obtain the economies and market impacts that could not be obtained by unilateral action. Under this system, the identity of the individual firm and its autonomy of operations remain intact. See also **administered vertical marketing system** and **corporate vertical marketing system.**

contribution margin   gross margin less any expense that can be directly assigned to the merchandise.

convenience center   a shopping center that typically includes such stores as a convenience market, a dry cleaner, or a liquor store.

convenience products   products that the consumer buys from the most convenient location and that the consumer is not willing to spend the effort to evaluate prior to purchase.

convenience store   a store between 3,000 and 8,000 square feet in size providing a limited assortment of merchandise at a convenient location and time.

conventional supermarket   a self-service food store that offers groceries, meat, and produce with annual sales over $2 million and size under 20,000 square market.

cooperative   an establishment owned by an association of customers. In general, the distinguishing features of a cooperative are patronage dividends based on the volume of expenditures by the members and a limitation of one vote per member regardless of the amount of stock owned.

cooperative (co-op) advertising   a program undertaken by a vendor in which the vendor agrees to pay all or part of a promotion for its products.

cooperative buying   when a group of independent retailers work together to make large purchases from a single supplier.

copy   the text in an advertisement.

corporate vertical marketing system   a form of vertical marketing system in which all of the functions from production to distribution are at least partially owned and controlled by a single enterprise. Corporate systems typically operate manufacturing plants, warehouse facilities, and retail outlets. See also **administered vertical marketing system** and **contractual vertical marketing system.**

corporation   a firm that is formally incorporated under state law and that is a different legal entity from stockholders and employees.

cost code   the item cost information indicated on price tickets in code. A common method of coding is the use of letters from an easily remembered word or expression with nonrepeating letters corresponding to numerals. The following is illustrative:

y o u n g b l a d e
1 2 3 4 5 6 7 8 9 0

cost complement   the percentage of net sales represented by the cost of goods sold.

cost method of accounting   a method in which retailers record the cost of every item on an accounting sheet or include a cost code on the price tag or merchandise container. When a physical inventory is conducted, the cost of each item must be determined, the quantity in stock is counted, and the total inventory value at cost is calculated. See **retail inventory method.**

cost multiplier   the cumulative markup multiplied by 100 percent minus cumulative markup percentage.

cost-oriented method   a method for determining the retail price by adding a fixed percentage to the cost of the merchandise; also known as cost-plus pricing.

cost per thousand (CPM)   a measure that is often used to compare media. CPM is calculated by dividing an ad's cost by its reach.

counterfeit merchandise   goods that are made and sold without permission of the owner of a trademark.

coupon   printed material that offers a discount on the price of specific items when purchased at the store.

courtesy days   the days on which stores extend to credit customers the privilege of making purchases at sale prices in advance of public sale.

coverage   the theoretical number of potential customers in the retailer's target market that could be exposed to an ad in a given medium.

credible commitments   tangible investments in a relationship between retailer and vendor.

credit   money placed at a consumer's disposal by a retailer or financial or other institution. For purchases made on credit, payment is due in the future.

credit limit   the quantitative limit that indicates the maximum amount of credit that may be allowed to be outstanding on each individual customer account.

cross-docking   when merchandise is delivered to one side of a very narrow warehouse by vendors, is unloaded, and is immediately reloaded onto trucks that deliver merchandise to the stores. With cross-docking, merchandise spends very little time in the warehouse.

cross-selling   when sales associates in one department attempt to sell complementary merchandise from other departments to their customers.

cross-shopping   a pattern of buying both premium and low-priced merchandise or patronizing expensive status-oriented retailers and price-oriented retailers.

culture   the meaning and values shared by most members of a society.

cumulative attraction   the principle that a cluster of similar and complementary retailing activities will generally have greater drawing power than isolated stores that engage in the same retailing activities.

cumulative markup   the average percentage markup for the period; the total retail price minus cost divided by retail price.

cumulative quantity discounts   discounts earned by retailers when purchasing certain quantities over a specified period of time.

cumulative reach   the cumulative number of potential customers that would see an ad that runs several times.

current assets   cash or any assets that can normally be converted into cash within one year.

current liabilities   debts that are expected to be paid in less than one year.

current ratio   current assets divided by current liabilities; indicates the firm's ability to meet current debt with current assets.

customer allowance   an additional price reduction given to the customer.

customer buying process   the stages a customer goes through in purchasing a good or service. Stages include need recognition, information search, evaluation and choice of alternatives, purchase, and post-purchase evaluation.

customer loyalty   customers' commitment to shopping at a store.

customer returns   the amount of merchandise that customers return because it is damaged, doesn't fit, and so forth.

customer service   the set of retail activities that increase the value customers receive when they shop and purchase merchandise.

customer service department   the department in a retail organization that handles customer inquiries and complaints.

customer spotting   a technique used in trade area analysis that "spots" (locates) residences of customers for a store or shopping center.

customization service approach   an approach used by retailers to provide customer service that is tailored to meet each customer's personal needs.

cycle stock   inventory that results from the replenishment process and is required to meet demand when the retailer can predict demand and replenishment times (lead times) perfectly.

cyclical theories   theories of institutional change based on the premise that retail institutions change on the basis of cycles. See also **wheel of retailing** and **accordion theory.**

DAGMAR (defining advertising goals for measured advertising results)   a method for setting advertising goals based on communication objectives.

databased retailing   the development and implementation of retailing programs utilizing a computerized file **(data warehouse)** of customer profiles and purchase patterns.

data warehouse   a computerized file of customer profiles and purchase patterns.

dating   a process that determines when discounts can be taken and when the full invoice amount is due.

deal period   a limited time period allowed by manufacturers to purchase merchandise at a special price.

debit card   a card that resembles a credit card but allows the retailer to automatically subtract payments from a customer's checking account at the time of sale.

decentralization   an organization structure in which the authority for making retail decisions is delegated to geographically dispersed regional, district, and local managers.

deceptive advertising   any advertisement that contains a false statement or misrepresents a product or service.

deferred billing   an arrangement that enables customers to buy merchandise and not pay for it for several months, with no interest charge.

demand/destination areas   departments or areas in a store in which demand for the products or services offered is created before customers get to their destination.

demand-oriented method   a method of setting prices based on what the customers would expect or be willing to pay.

democratic method of store management   when a store manager seeks information and opinions from employees and bases decisions on this information.

demographics   factors such as age, sex, and income, commonly used to define market segments.

demographic segmentation   a method of segmenting a retail market using demographic characteristics of consumers.

department   a segment of a store with merchandise that represents a group of classifications the consumer views as being complementary.

departmentalization   an organizational design in which employees are grouped into departments that perform specific activities to achieve operating efficiencies through specialization.

department store   a retailer that carries a wide variety and deep assortment, offers considerable customer services, and is organized into separate departments for displaying merchandise.

depth interview   an unstructured personal interview in which the interviewer uses extensive probing to get individual respondents to talk in detail about a subject.

depth of merchandise   see **assortment.**

deseasonalized demand   the forecast demand without the influence of seasonality.

destination store   a retail store in which the merchandise, selection, presentation, pricing, or other unique feature acts as a magnet for customers.

dialectic theory   an evolutionary theory based on the premise that retail institutions evolve. The theory suggests that new retail formats emerge by adopting characteristics from other forms of retailers in much the same way that a child is the product of the pooled genes of two very different parents.

difficult comparison effect   the condition that arises when customers' price sensitivity increases because they find it difficult to compare existing brands.

direct mail catalog retailer   a retailer offering merchandise and/or services through catalogs mailed directly to customers.

direct mail retailer   a nonstore retailer that communicates directly with customers using letters and brochures sent through the mail.

direct marketing   a form of nonstore retailing in which customers are exposed to merchandise through print or electronic media and then purchase the merchandise by telephone or mail.

direct product profitability (DPP)   the profit associated with each category or unit of merchandise. DPP is equal to the per-unit gross margin less all variable costs associated with the merchandise such as procurement, distribution, sales, and the cost of carrying the assets. Also known as residual income.

direct response advertising   advertisements on TV and radio that describe products and provide an opportunity for customers to order them.

direct retailers   nonstore retailers that sell merchandise through salespeople who contact consumers directly or by telephone at home or place of work.

direct retailing   see **nonstore retailing.**

disclosure of confidential information   an unethical situation in which a retail employee discloses proprietary or confidential information about the firm's business to anyone outside the firm.

discount   a reduction in the original retail price granted to store employees as special benefits.

discount-anchored center   a shopping center that contains one or more discount stores and smaller retail tenants.

discount store   a general merchandise retailer that offers a wide variety of merchandise, limited service, and low prices.

disintermediation   when a manufacturer sells directly to consumers, thus bypassing retailers.

dispatcher   a person who coordinates deliveries to the distribution center.

display stock   merchandise placed on various display fixtures for customers to examine.

distribution   see **retail distribution.**

distribution center   a warehouse that receives merchandise from multiple vendors and distributes it to multiple stores.

distribution channel   a set of firms that facilitate the movement of products from the point of production to the point of sale to the ultimate consumer.

distribution intensity   the number of retailers carrying a particular category.

diversification   a strategic investment opportunity that involves an entirely new retail format directed toward a market segment not presently being served.

diversionary pricing   a practice sometimes used by retailers in which low price is stated for one or a few goods or services (emphasized in promotion) to give the illusion that the retailer's prices are all low.

diverter   a firm that buys unwanted merchandise from retailers and manufacturers and resells the merchandise to other retailers.

double coupon redemption   a retail promotion that allows the customer to double the face value of a coupon.

drawing account   a method of sales compensation in which salespeople receive a weekly check based on their estimated annual income.

drug store   specialty retail store that concentrates on pharmaceuticals and health and personal grooming merchandise.

dual distribution   when a manufacturer or wholesaler uses multiple channels of distribution to reach ultimate consumers.

economic order quantity (EOQ)   the order quantity that minimizes the total cost of processing orders and holding inventory.

electronic article surveillance (EAS)   special tags placed on merchandise in retail stores that are deactivated when the merchandise is purchased. The tags are used to discourage shoplifting.

electronic data interchange (EDI)   the computer-to-computer exchange of business documents from retailer to vendor, and back.

emotional support   supporting retail service providers with the understanding and positive regard to enable them to deal with the emotional stress created by disgruntled customers.

employee discount   a discount from retail price offered by most retailers to employees.

employee productivity   output generated by employee activities. One measure of employee productivity is sales per employee.

empowerment   the process of managers sharing power and decision-making authority with employees.

empty nesters   a segment of people whose children are no longer living with them.

end cap   display fixture located at the end of an aisle.

end-of-month dating (EOM)   a method of dating in which the discount period starts at the end of the month in which the invoice is dated (except when the invoice is dated the 25th or later).

environmental apparel   merchandise produced with few or no harmful effects on the environment.

escape clause a clause in a lease that allows the retailer to terminate its lease if sales don't reach a certain level after a specified number of years.

ethics a system or code of conduct based on universal moral duties and obligations that indicate how one should behave.

evaluation of alternatives the stage in the buying process in which the customer compares the benefits offered by various retailers.

everyday-low-price strategy a pricing strategy that attempts to have, on average, low prices on all items every day rather than periodically advertising price promotions on a few items.

evolutionary theories theories of institutional change based on the premise that retail institutions evolve. See **dialectic theory** and **natural selection.**

exclusive dealing agreement restriction a manufacturer or wholesaler places on a retailer to carry only its products and no competing vendors' products.

exclusive geographical territory a policy in which only one retailer in a certain territory is allowed to sell a particular brand.

exclusive use clause a clause in a lease that prohibits the landlord from leasing to retailers selling competing products.

executive training program (ETP) a training program for retail supervisors, managers, and executives.

expenses costs incurred in the normal course of doing business to generate revenues.

experiment a market research method in which a variable is manipulated under controlled conditions.

expert system computer program that incorporates knowledge of experts in a particular field. Expert systems are used to aid in decision making and problem solving.

exponential smoothing a sales forecasting technique in which sales in previous time periods are weighted to develop a forecast for future periods.

express warranty a guarantee supplied by either the retailer or the manufacturer that details the terms of the warranty in simple, easily understood language so customers know what is and what is not covered by the warranty.

extended problem solving a buying process in which customers spend considerable time at each stage of the decision-making process because the decision is important and they have limited knowledge of alternatives.

external source information provided by the media and other people.

extra dating a discount offered by a vendor in which the retailer receives extra time to pay the invoice and still take the cash discount.

extrinsic rewards rewards (such as money, promotion, and recognition) given to employees by their manager or the firm.

factoring a specialized financial function whereby manufacturers, wholesalers, or retailers sell accounts receivable to financial institutions, including factories, banks, and sales finance companies.

factory outlet store off-price retailer owned by a manufacturer.

fad a product with a very short life cycle.

fair trade laws see **vertical price fixing.**

fashion a category of merchandise that typically lasts several seasons, and sales can vary dramatically from one season to the next.

fashion-oriented shopping center shopping center usually containing a high-quality department store as well as small boutiques.

feature fixture see **four-way.**

features the qualities or characteristics of a product that provide benefits to customers.

Federal Trade Commission Act (1914) the congressional act that created the Federal Trade Commission (FTC) and gave it the power to enforce federal trade laws.

financial leverage a financial measure based on the relationship between the retailer's liabilities and owners' equity that indicates financial stability of the firm.

fixed assets assets that require more than a year to convert to cash.

fixed expenses expenses that remain constant for a given period of time regardless of the sales volume.

flattening the organization the reduction in the number of management levels.

flexible pricing a pricing strategy that allows consumers to bargain over selling prices.

flextime a job scheduling system that enables employees to choose the times they work.

floor-ready merchandise received at the store ready to be sold, without the need for any additional preparation by retail employees.

FOB (free on board) destination a term of sale designating that the shipper owns the merchandise until it is delivered to the retailer and is therefore responsible for transportation and any damage claims.

FOB (free on board) origin   a term of sale designating that the retailer takes ownership of the merchandise at the point of origin and is therefore responsible for transportation and any damage claims.

focus group   a marketing research technique in which a small group of respondents is interviewed by a moderator using a loosely structured format.

forward integration   a form of vertical integration in which a manufacturer owns wholesalers and/or retailers.

four-way   a fixture with two cross bars that sit perpendicular to each other on a pedestal.

franchising   a contractual agreement between a franchisor and a franchisee that allows the franchisee to operate a retail outlet using a name and format developed and supported by the franchisor.

free-form   a store design, used primarily in small specialty stores or within the boutiques of large stores, that arranges fixtures and aisles asymmetrically.

freestanding insert   an ad printed at the retailer's expense and distributed as a freestanding insert in the newspaper.

freestanding retailer   a location for a retailer that is not adjacent to other retailers.

freight collect   when the retailer pays the freight.

freight prepaid   when the freight is paid by the vendor.

frequency   how many times a potential customer is exposed to an ad.

frequent shopper program   a reward and communication program used by a retailer to encourage continued purchases from the retailer's best customers.

fringe trade area   see **tertiary trade zone.**

frontal presentation   a method of displaying merchandise in which the retailer exposes as much of the product as possible to catch the customer's eye.

full-line forcing   when a supplier requires a retailer to carry the supplier's full line of products if the retailer wants to carry any part of that line.

full warranty   a guarantee provided by either the retailer or manufacturer to repair or replace merchandise without charge and within a reasonable amount of time in the event of a defect.

functional discount   see **trade discount.**

functional needs   the needs satisfied by a product or service that are directly related to its performance.

functional product grouping   categorizing and displaying merchandise by common end uses.

functional relationships   a series of one-time market exchanges linked together over time.

future dating   a method of dating that allows the buyer additional time to take advantage of the cash discount or to pay the net amount of the invoice.

general merchandise discount store   a discount store that carries a broad variety of general merchandise.

general merchandise retailer   a retailer selling merchandise that is not refrigerated or perishable.

generational cohort   a group of people born during a specific time period who share common values because they have had similar life experiences.

Generation X   the generational cohort of people born between 1965 and 1976.

Generation Y   the generational cohort of people born between 1977 and 1998.

generic products   unbranded, unadvertised merchandise found mainly in drug, grocery, and discount stores.

gentrification   a process in which old buildings are torn down or are restored to create new offices, housing developments, and retailers.

geographic segmentation   segmentation of potential customers by where they live. A retail market can be segmented by countries, states, cities, and neighborhoods.

glass ceiling   an invisible barrier that makes it difficult for minorities and women to be promoted beyond a certain level.

gondola   an island type of self-service counter with tiers of shelves back-to-back.

graduated lease   a lease that includes precise rent increases over a specified period of time.

gray-market goods   merchandise that possesses a valid U.S. registered trademark and is made by a foreign manufacturer, but is imported into the United States without permission of the U.S. trademark owner.

green marketing   a strategic focus by retailers and their vendors to supply customers with environmentally friendly merchandise.

greeter   a retail employee who greets customers as they enter a store and who provides information and/or assistance.

grid layout   a store design, typically used by grocery stores, in which merchandise is displayed on long gondolas in aisles with a repetitive pattern.

gross margin   the difference between the price the customer pays for merchandise and the cost of the merchandise (the price the retailer paid the supplier of the merchandise). More specifically, gross margin = net sales – cost of goods sold (= maintained markup) – alteration cost + cash discounts.

gross margin return on investment (GMROI)   gross margin dollars divided by average (cost) inventory.

gross profit   see **gross margin.**

gross sales   the total dollar revenues received from the sales of merchandise and services.

group boycott   a concerted refusal by either retailers or vendors to deal with a particular business.

group maintenance behaviors   activities store managers undertake to make sure that employees are satisfied and work well together.

habitual decision making   a type of buying process in which customers routinize their purchase decisions and do not go through the stages of the buying process; also known as routine decision making.

historical center   a shopping center located in a place of historical interest.

home-improvement center   a category specialist combining the traditional hardware store and lumberyard.

horizontal price fixing   an agreement between retailers in direct competition with each other to charge the same prices.

Huff's model   a trade area analysis model used to determine the probability that a customer residing in a particular area will shop at a particular store or shopping center.

human resource management   management of a retailer's employees.

hypermarket   a very large retail store that offers low prices and combines a discount and a superstore food retailer in one warehouselike building.

idea-oriented presentation   a method of presenting merchandise based on a specific idea or the image of the store.

impact   an ad's effect on the audience.

implied warranty of merchantability   a guarantee that accompanies all merchandise sold by a retailer, assuring customers that the merchandise is up to standards for the ordinary purposes for which such goods are used.

impulse merchandise   products purchased without prior planning such as candy and batteries.

impulse purchase   an unplanned purchase by a customer.

incentive compensation plan   a compensation plan that rewards employees based on their productivity.

income statement   a summary of the financial performance of a firm for a certain period of time.

independent retailer   a retailer that owns only one retail store.

infomercial   a TV program, typically 30 minutes long, that mixes entertainment with product demonstrations and solicits orders placed by telephone from consumers.

information search   the stage in the buying process in which a customer seeks additional information to satisfy a need.

infringement   unauthorized use of a registered trademark.

ingress/egress   the ease of entering and exiting the parking lot of a retail site.

in-house credit system   see **proprietary store credit card system.**

initial markup   the difference between the cost of merchandise and the retail selling price originally placed on it.

input measures   performance measures used to assess the amount of resources or money used by the retailer to achieve outputs.

installment credit plan   a plan that enables consumers to pay their total purchase price (less down payment) in equal installment payments over a specified time period.

institutional advertisement   an advertisement that emphasizes the retailer's name and positioning rather than specific merchandise or prices.

instrumental support   support for retail service providers such as appropriate systems and equipment to deliver the service desired by customers.

integrated marketing communications   the strategic integration of multiple communication methods to form a comprehensive, consistent message.

intelligent agent   see **search engine.**

interactive electronic retailing   a system in which a retailer transmits data and graphics over cable or telephone lines to a consumer's TV or computer terminal.

interactive kiosk   a vending machine enabling consumers to interactively see the merchandise in use, have information about the merchandise, and use their credit cards to make a purchase.

interest   the amount charged by a financial institution to borrow money.

internal sources   information in a customer's memory such as the names, images, and past experiences with different stores.

Internet   a worldwide network of computers linked to facilitate communications between individuals, companies, and organizations.

intertype competition   competition between different types of retailers (e.g., Safeway versus Wal-Mart).

intratype competition   competition between the same type of retailers (e.g., Kroger versus Safeway).

intrinsic rewards   nonmonetary rewards employees get from doing their jobs.

inventory   goods or merchandise available for resale.

inventory management   the process of acquiring and maintaining a proper assortment of merchandise while keeping ordering, shipping, handling, and other related costs in check.

inventory shrinkage   see **shrinkage.**

inventory turnover   net sales divided by average retail inventory; used to evaluate how effectively managers utilize their investment in inventory.

invoice cost   the actual amount due for the merchandise after both trade and quantity discounts are taken.

item price removal   the practice of marking prices only on shelves or signs and not on individual items.

job analysis   identifying essential activities and determining the qualifications employees need to perform them effectively.

job description   a description of the activities the employee needs to perform and the firm's performance expectations.

job sharing   when two employees voluntarily are responsible for a job that was previously held by one person.

junk bond   bond that offers investors a higher-risk/higher-yield investment than conventional bonds.

key items   the items that are in greatest demand. Also referred to as best-sellers.

keystone method   a method of setting retail prices in which retailers simply double the cost of the merchandise to obtain the original retail selling price.

kickback   same as commercial bribery.

kiosk   a retail facility that is larger than a cart, is stationary, and has many conveniences of a store such as movable shelves, telephone, and electricity.

labor scheduling   the process of determining the number of employees assigned to each area of the store at each hour the store is open.

latchkey children   children in homes where both parents work outside the home.

layaway   a method of deferred payment in which merchandise is held by the store for the customer until it is completely paid for.

leader pricing   a pricing strategy in which certain items are priced lower than normal to increase the traffic flow of customers and/or to increase the sale of complementary products.

leadership   the process by which a person attempts to influence another to accomplish some goal or goals.

lead time   the amount of time between the recognition that an order needs to be placed and its arrival in the store, ready for sale.

leased department   a department in a retail store operated by an outside party. The outside party either pays fixed rent or a percentage of sales to the retailer for the space.

lessee   the party renting a property.

lessor   the party owning a property that is for rent.

less-than-carload-lot (LCL)   the rate that applies to less than full carload shipments.

level of support   see **service level.**

leveraged buyout (LBO)   a financial transaction in which a buyer (the firm's management or an outside individual or group) acquires a company by borrowing money from a financial institution or by issuing junk bonds using its assets as collateral. See also **merger** and **acquisition.**

liabilities   obligations of a retail enterprise to pay cash or other economic resources in return for past, present, or future benefits.

licensed brand   brand for which the licensor (owner of a well-known name) enters a contractual arrangement with a licensee (a retailer or a third party). The licensee either manufactures or contracts with a manufacturer to produce the licensed product and pays a royalty to the licensor.

lifestyle   the manner in which individual consumers or families (households) live and spend their time and money, what activities they pursue, and their attitudes and opinions about the world they live in.

lifestyle retailing   development of a retail format based on consumer living patterns.

lifestyle segmentation   a method of segmenting a retail market based on how consumers live, how they spend their time and money, what activities they pursue, and their attitudes and opinions about the world they live in.

limited-line warehouse store   discount food retailer that offers merchandise in a no-frills environment. They typically carry 1,500 items (one size and brand per item), with no refrigerated or perishable merchandise.

limited problem solving   a buying process that occurs when customers do not need to spend a great deal of time in each of the steps because of their knowledge and prior experience.

limited warranty   a type of guarantee in which any limitations must be stated conspicuously so that customers are not misled.

lines of authority and responsibility   the organizational principle that employees should be given the authority to accomplish the responsibilities assigned to them.

logistics   see **retail distribution.**

long-term liabilities   obligations the retailer commits to pay after at least one year (see **liabilities**). Long-term liabilities represent claims against assets.

loop layout   see **boutique layout.**

loss leader   an item priced near or below cost to attract customer traffic into the store.

mail-order retailer   see **direct mail catalog retailer.**

maintained markup   the amount of markup the retailer wishes to maintain on a particular category of merchandise; net sales minus cost of goods sold.

maintenance-increase-recoupment lease   a provision of a lease that can be used with either a percentage or straight lease. This type of lease allows the landlord to increase the rent if insurance, property taxes, or utility bills increase beyond a certain point.

management by objectives   a popular method for linking the goals of a firm to goals for each employee and providing information to employees about their role.

managing diversity   a set of human resource management programs designed to realize the benefits of a diverse work force.

manufacturer brand   a brand that is produced and controlled by and that carries the name of a manufacturer; also known as national brand.

manufacturer's agent   an agent who generally operates on an extended contractual basis; often sells within an exclusive territory; handles noncompeting but related lines of goods; and possesses limited authority with regard to prices and terms of sale.

manufacturer's outlet store   a discount retail store owned and operated by a manufacturer.

mapping   see **analog approach.**

marginal analysis   a method of analysis used in setting a promotional budget or allocating retail space, based on the economic principle that firms should increase expenditures as long as each additional dollar spent generates more than a dollar of additional contribution.

markdown   the percentage reduction in the initial retail price.

markdown cancellation   the percentage increase in the retail price after a markdown is taken.

markdown money   funds provided by a vendor to a retailer to cover decreased gross margin from markdowns and other merchandising issues.

market   a group of vendors in a concentrated geographic location or even under one roof; also known as a central market.

market attractiveness–competitive position matrix   a method for analyzing opportunities that explicitly considers the capabilities of the retailer and the attractiveness of retail markets.

market development   see **market penetration opportunity.**

market exchange   a short-term transaction between a buyer and vendor who do not expect to be involved in future transactions with each other.

market expansion opportunity   a strategic investment opportunity that employs the same retailing format in new market segments.

marketing segmentation   the process of dividing a retail market into homogeneous groups. See **retail market segment.**

market penetration opportunity   an investment opportunity strategy that focuses on increasing sales to present customers using the same retailing format.

market positioning   see **positioning.**

market research   the systematic collection and analysis of information about a retail market.

market share   a retailer's sales divided by the sales of all competitors within the same market.

market week   see **trade show.**

markup   the increase in the retail price of an item after the initial markup percentage has been applied but before the item is placed on the selling floor.

marquee   a sign used to display a store's name and/or logo.

mass customization   the production of individually customized products at costs similar to mass-produced products.

Mazur plan   a method of retail organization in which all retail activities fall into four functional areas: merchandising, publicity, store management, and accounting and control.

media coverage   the theoretical number of potential customers in a retailer's market who could be exposed to an ad.

memorandum purchases   items not paid for by a retailer until they are sold. The retailer can return unsold merchandise; however, the retailer takes title on delivery and is responsible for damages. See **consignment goods.**

mentoring program   the assigning of higher-level managers to help lower-level managers learn the firm's values and meet other senior executives.

merchandise budget plan a plan used by buyers to determine how much money to spend in each month on a particular merchandise category, given the firm's sales forecast, inventory turnover, and profit goals.

merchandise category see **category.**

merchandise classification see **classification.**

merchandise management the analysis, planning, acquisition, promotion, and control of merchandise sold by a retailer.

merchandise show see **trade show.**

merchandising see **merchandise management.**

merger a financial strategy in which one larger firm acquires a smaller firm. This term is used interchangeably with **acquisition.** See also **leveraged buyout.**

metropolitan statistical area (MSA) a city with 50,000 or more inhabitants or an urbanized area of at least 50,000 inhabitants and a total MSA population of at least 100,000 (75,000 in New England).

mission statement a broad description of the scope of activities a retailer plans to undertake.

mixed-use development (MXDs) shopping centers that have office towers, hotels, residential complexes, civic centers, and convention complexes on top of or attached to the shopping areas.

model stock list a list of fashion merchandise that indicates in very general terms (product lines, colors, and size distributions) what should be carried in a particular merchandise category; also known as model stock plan.

monthly additions to stock the amount to be ordered for delivery in each month, given the firm's turnover and sales objectives.

motivation the drive within people to expend effort to achieve goals.

multiattribute attitude model a model of customer decision making based on the notion that customers see a retailer or a product as a collection of attributes or characteristics.

multiattribute method see **multiple-attribute method.**

multilevel direct selling a form of direct selling in which people sell directly to customers and serve as master distributors and recruit other people to become distributors in their network. The master distributors either buy merchandise from the firm and resell it to their distributors or receive a commission on all merchandise purchased by the distributors in their network.

multiple-attribute method a method for evaluating vendors that uses a weighted average score based on various issues and the vendor's performance on those issues.

multiple-unit pricing practice of offering two or more similar products or services for sale at one price.

national brand see **manufacturer brand.**

natural barriers barriers, such as rivers or mountains, that limit the size of a trade area.

natural selection those institutions best able to adapt to changes in customers, technology, competition, and legal environments have the greatest chance for success.

needs the basic psychological forces that motivate customers to act.

negligence a product liability suit that occurs if a retailer or a retail employee fails to exercise the care that a prudent person usually would.

negotiation an interaction between two or more parties to reach an agreement.

neighborhood business district (NBD) a group of stores directed toward convenience shopping needs of customers in a neighborhood; typically includes a supermarket and is located on the major street(s) of a residential area.

neighborhood center a shopping center that includes a supermarket, drugstore, home-improvement center, or variety store. Neighborhood centers often include small stores, such as apparel, shoe, camera, and other shopping goods stores.

net invoice price the net value of the invoice or the total invoice minus all other discounts.

net lease a lease that requires all maintenance expenses such as heat, insurance, and interior repairs to be paid by the retailer.

net profit a measure of the overall performance of a firm; revenues (sales) minus expenses and losses for the period.

net sales the total amount of dollars received by a retailer after all funds have been paid to customers for returned merchandise.

network direct selling see **multilevel direct selling.**

net worth see **owners' equity.**

never-out list a list of key items or best-sellers that are separately planned and controlled. These items account for large sales volume and are stocked in a manner so they are always available. These are A items in an **ABC analysis.**

noncumulative quality discount discount offered to retailers as an incentive to purchase more merchandise on a single order.

nondurable perishable product consumed in one or a few uses.

nonstore retailing a form of retailing to ultimate consumers that is not store-based. Nonstore retailing is conducted through vending machines, direct selling, and direct marketing.

notes payable current liabilities representing principal and interest the retailer owes to financial institutions (banks) that are due and payable in less than a year.

objective-and-task method a method for setting a promotion budget in which the retailer first establishes a set of communication objectives and then determines the necessary tasks and their costs.

observation a type of market research in which customer behavior is observed and recorded.

odd price a price ending with an odd number (such as 57 cents or 63 cents) or just under a round number (such as $98 instead of $100).

off-price retailer a retailer that offers an inconsistent assortment of brand-name, fashion-oriented soft goods at low prices.

off-price shopping centers centers that specialize in off-price retail tenants such as T.J. Maxx or Burlington Coat Factory.

off-the-job training training conducted in centralized classrooms away from the employee's work environment.

one hundred percent location the retail site in a major business district that has the greatest exposure to a retail store's target market customers.

one-price policy a policy that, at a given time, all customers pay the same price for any given item of merchandise.

one-price retailer a store that offers all merchandise at a single fixed price.

on-the-job training a decentralized approach in which job training occurs in the work environment where employees perform their jobs.

open-to-buy the plan that keeps track of how much is spent in each month (and how much is left to spend).

opinion leaders persons whose attitudes, opinions, preferences, and actions influence those of others.

opportunity cost of capital the rate available on the next-best use of the capital invested in the project at hand. The opportunity cost should be no larger than the rate at which a firm borrows funds, since one alternative is to pay back borrowed money. It can be higher, however, depending on the range of other opportunities available. Typically, the opportunity cost rises with investment risk.

optical character recognition (OCR) an industry-wide classification system for coding information onto merchandise; enables retailers to record information on each SKU when it is sold and to transmit the information to a computer.

option credit account a revolving account that allows partial payments without interest charges if a bill is paid in full when due.

option-term revolving credit a credit arrangement that offers customers two payment options: (1) pay full amount within a specified number of days and avoid any finance charges or (2) make a minimum payment and be assessed finance charges on the unpaid balance.

order form a legally binding contract when signed by both parties, specifying the terms and conditions under which a purchase transaction is to be conducted.

order point the amount of inventory below which the quantity available shouldn't go or the item will be out of stock before the next order arrives.

organizational culture a firm's set of values and customs that guide employee behavior.

organization chart a graphic that displays the reporting relationships within a firm.

organization structure the plan according to which a retailer assigns authority and responsibility for performing retail functions and activities to employees.

outlet center typically features stores owned by retail chains or manufacturers that sell excess and out-of-season merchandise at reduced prices.

outlet store off-price retailer owned by a manufacturer or a department or specialty store chain.

output measures measures that assess the results of retailers' investment decisions.

outshopping customers shopping in other areas because their needs are not being met locally.

overstored a description of an area that has too many stores to profitability satisfy demand.

owners' equity the amount of assets belonging to the owners of the retail firm after all obligations (liabilities) have been met; also known as net worth.

pallet a platform, usually made of wood, that provides stable support for several cartons. Pallets are used to help move and store merchandise.

partnership an ongoing, mutually beneficial relationship with each party having concern for the other party's well-being.

party plan system salespeople encourage people to act as hosts and invite friends or coworkers to a "party" at which the merchandise is demonstrated. The host or hostess receives a gift or commission for arranging the meeting.

perceived risk the level of risk a consumer believes to exist regarding the purchase of a specific good or service.

percentage lease   a lease that relates the amount of rent to a retailer's sales or profits.

percentage lease with specified maximum   a lease that pays the lessor, or landlord, a percentage of sales up to a maximum amount.

percentage lease with specified minimum   the retailer must pay a minimum rent no matter how low sales are.

percentage-of-sales method   a method for setting a promotion budget based on a fixed percentage of forecast sales.

percentage variation method   an inventory planning method wherein the actual stock on hand during any month varies from average planned monthly stock by only half of the month's variation from average estimated monthly sales.

periodic reordering system   an inventory management system in which the review time is a fixed period (e.g., two weeks), but the order quantity can vary.

perpetual book inventory   see **retail inventory method.**

perpetual ordering system   the stock level is monitored perpetually and a fixed quantity, known as **EOQ (economic order quantity),** is purchased when the inventory available reaches a prescribed level.

personal selling   a communication process in which salespeople assist customers in satisfying their needs through face-to-face exchange of information.

physical inventory   a method of gathering stock information by using an actual physical count and inspection of the merchandise items.

pick ticket   a document that tells the order filler how much of each item to get from the storage area.

pilferage   the stealing of a store's merchandise. See also **shoplifting.**

planogram   a diagram created from photographs, computer output, or artists' renderings that illustrates exactly where every SKU should be placed.

PM   see **push money.**

point-of-purchase display   an interior display that provides customers with information and promotes the merchandise.

point-of-sale (POS) terminal   a cash register that has the capability to electronically scan a UPC code with a laser and electronically record a sale; also known as computerized checkout.

polygons   trade areas whose boundaries conform to streets and other physical characteristics rather than being concentric circles.

popping the merchandise   focusing spot lights on special feature areas and items.

population density   the number of people per unit area (usually square mile) who live within a geographic area.

positioning   the design and implementation of a retail promotion program to create an image in the customer's mind of the retailer relative to its competitors.

postpurchase behavior   a customer's further purchases and/or reevaluation based on a purchase.

postpurchase evaluation   the evaluation of merchandise or services after the customer has purchased and consumed them.

poverty of time   a condition in which greater affluence results in less, rather than more, free time because the alternatives competing for customers' time increase.

power retailer   see **category killer** or **category specialist.**

power shopping center   an open-air-shopping center with the majority of space preleased to several well-known anchor retail tenants—**category killers**—with high credit ratings.

predatory pricing   a method for establishing merchandise prices for the purpose of driving competition from the marketplace.

preferred client   customers salespeople communicate with regularly, send notes to about new merchandise and sales in the department, and make appointments for, for special presentations or merchandise.

premarking   the price is marked by manufacturer or other supplier before goods are shipped to a retail store. Also called **prepricing.**

premium   merchandise offered at a reduced price, or free, as an additional incentive for a customer to make a purchase.

prepricing   see **premarking.**

preprint   an advertisement printed at the retailer's expense and distributed as a freestanding insert in a newspaper.

press conference   a meeting with representatives of the news media that is called by a retailer.

press release   a statement of facts or opinions that the retailer would like to see published by the news media.

prestige pricing   a system of pricing based on the assumption that consumers will not buy goods and services at prices they feel are two low.

price bundling   the practice of offering two or more different products or services for sale at one price.

price comparison   a comparison of the price of merchandise offered for sale with a higher "regular" price or a manufacturer's list price.

price discrimination   an illegal practice in which a vendor sells the same product to two or more retailers at different prices.

price elasticity of demand   a measure of the effect a price change has on consumer demand; percentage change in demand divided by percentage change in price.

price fixing   an illegal pricing activity in which several marketing channel members establish a fixed retail selling price for a product line within a market area. See **vertical price fixing** and **horizontal price fixing.**

price guarantee   a term of purchase that protects retailers against price declines. In the event that a retailer cannot sell merchandise at a given price, the manufacturer pays the retailer the difference between the planned retail and the actual retail selling price.

price lining   a pricing policy in which a retailer offers a limited number of predetermined price points within a classification.

pricing experiment   an experiment in which a retailer actually changes the price of an item in a systematic manner to observe changes in customers' purchases or purchase intentions.

primary data   marketing research information collected through surveys, observations, and experiments to address a problem confronting a retailer.

primary trade zone   the geographical area from which the store or shopping center derives 60 to 65 percent of its customers.

private-label brand   a brand of products designed, produced, controlled by, and carrying the name of the store or a name owned by the store; also known as a store brand or dealer brand.

private-label store credit-card system   a system in which credit cards have the store's name on them, but the accounts receivable are sold to a financial institution.

PRIZM (potential rating index for ZIP markets)   a database combining census data, nationwide consumer surveys, and interviews with hundreds of people across the country into a geodemographic segmentation system.

product attributes   characteristics of a product that affect customer evaluations.

productivity measure   the ratio of an output to an input determining how effectively a retailer uses a resource.

product liability   a tort (or wrong) that occurs when an injury results from the use of a product.

product line   a group of related products.

profitability   a company's ability to generate revenues in excess of the costs incurred in producing those revenues.

profit margin   net profit after taxes divided by net sales.

prohibited use clause   a clause in a lease that limits the landlord from leasing to certain kinds of tenants.

promotion   activities undertaken by a retailer to provide consumers with information about the retailer's store and its retail mix.

promotional advertising   advertising intended to inform prospective customers of special sales; it announces the arrival of new and seasonal goods; and it features, creates, and promotes a market for the merchandise items in regular stock.

promotional allowance   an allowance given by vendors to retailers to compensate the latter for money spent in advertising a particular item.

promotional department store   a department store that concentrates on apparel and sells a substantial portion of its merchandise on weekly promotion.

promotional or discount-oriented center   a type of specialty shopping center that contains one or more discount stores plus smaller retail tenants.

promotional stock   a retailer's stock of goods offered at an unusually attractive price in order to obtain sales volume; it often represents special purchases from vendors.

promotion from within   a staffing policy emphasizing that employees are only hired for low-level positions, while promotions to higher levels are given to employees of the firm rather than outsiders.

proprietary store credit card system   a system in which credit cards have the store's name on them and the accounts receivable are administered by the retailer; also known as in-house credit system.

psychographics   see **lifestyle.**

psychographic segmentation   see **lifestyle segmentation.**

psychological needs   needs associated with the personal gratification that customers get from shopping or from purchasing and owning a product.

publicity   communications through significant unpaid presentations about the retailer (usually a news story) in impersonal media.

puffing   an advertising or personal selling practice in which a retailer simply exaggerates the benefits or quality of a product in very broad terms.

pull logistics strategy   orders for merchandise are generated at the store level on the basis of demand data captured by point-of-sale terminals.

purchase visibility curve   a display technique in which the retailer tilts lower shelves so more merchandise is in direct view.

push logistics strategy   merchandise is allocated to stores based on historical demand, the inventory position at the distribution center, as well as the stores' needs.

push money (PM)   an incentive for retail salespeople provided by a vendor to promote, or push, a particular product; also known as spiff.

quantity discount   the practice of granting lower prices to retailers who buy in higher quantities.

quick-response (QR) delivery system   system designed to reduce the lead time for receiving merchandise, thereby lowering inventory investment, improving customer service levels, and reducing distribution expenses; also known as just-in-time inventory management system.

quota   performance goal or objective established to evaluate employee performance, such as sales per hour for salespeople and maintained margin and turnover for buyers.

racetrack layout   a type of store layout that provides a major aisle to facilitate customer traffic that has access to the store's multiple entrances.

raincheck   when sale merchandise is out of stock, a promise to customers to sell them that merchandise at the sale price when it arrives.

reach   the actual number of customers in the target market exposed to an advertising medium. See **advertising reach**.

rebate   money returned to the buyer in the form of cash based on a portion of the purchase price.

receipt of goods (ROG) dating   a dating policy in which the cash discount period starts on the day the merchandise is received.

receiving   the process of filling out paperwork to record the receipt of merchandise that arrives at a store or distribution center.

recruitment   activity performed by a retailer to generate job applicants.

reductions   markdowns; discounts to employees and customers; and inventory shrinkage due to shoplifting, breakage, or loss.

reference group   one or more people whom a person uses as a basis of comparison for his beliefs, feelings, and behaviors.

refusal to deal   a legal issue in which either a vendor or a retailer reserves the right to deal or refuse to deal with anyone they choose.

region   in retail location analysis refers to the part of the country, a particular city, or Metropolitan Statistical Area (MSA).

regional center   a shopping center that includes up to three department stores plus shopping or specialty stores rather than convenience stores. Super-regionals are similar but have at least four department stores.

Reilly's law   a model used in trade area analysis to define the relative ability of two cities to attract customers from the area between them.

related diversification   a diversification opportunity strategy in which the retailer's present offering and market share something in common with the market and format being considered.

relational partnerships   long-term business relationships in which the buyer and vendor have a close, trusting interpersonal relationship.

remarking   the practice of remarking merchandise due to price changes, lost or mutilated tickets, or customer returns.

reorder point   the stock level at which a new order is placed.

resale price maintenance   see **vertical price fixing**.

resident buying office   an office owned and operated by a retailer that is located in an important market area (source of supply) and provides valuable information and contacts.

restraint of trade   any contract that tends to eliminate or stifle competition, create a monopoly, artificially maintain prices, or otherwise hamper or obstruct the course of trade and commerce as it would be carried on if left to the control of natural forces; also known as unfair trade practices.

retail accordion theory   see **accordion theory**.

retail audit   see **situation audit**.

retail chain   a firm that consists of multiple retail units under common ownership and usually has some centralization of decision making in defining and implementing its strategy.

retail distribution   the organization process of managing the flow of merchandise from the source of supply—the vendor, wholesaler, or distributor—through the internal processing functions—warehouse and transportation—until the merchandise is sold and delivered to the customer; also known as logistics.

retailer   a business that sells products and services to ultimate consumers.

retail format   a type of retail mix that is used by a number of retailers.

retail format development opportunity   an investment opportunity strategy in which a retailer offers a new retail format to present customers.

retail information system   system that provides the information needed by retail managers by collecting, organizing, and storing relevant data continuously and directing the information to the appropriate managers.

retailing   the set of business activities involved in selling products and services to ultimate consumers.

retailing concept   a management orientation that holds that the key task of a retailer is to determine the needs and wants of its target markets and to direct the firm toward satisfying those needs and wants more effectively and efficiently than competitors do.

retail institution   a group of retailers that provide a similar retail mix.

retail inventory method (RIM)   an accounting procedure whose objectives are to maintain a perpetual or book inventory in retail dollar amounts and to maintain records that make it possible to determine the cost value of the inventory at any time without taking a physical inventory; also known as book inventory system or perpetual book inventory.

retail market   a group of consumers with similar needs (a segment) and a group of retailers using similar retail mixes (types of merchandise, prices, promotions, and services) to satisfy those consumer needs.

retail market segment   a group of customers whose needs will be satisfied by the same retail offering because they have similar needs and go through similar buying processes.

retail merchandising units (RMU)   a relatively new and sophisticated location alternative that offers the compactness and mobility of a cart, but the more sophisticated features of a kiosk. They can also be locked or enclosed, so they can serve as a display when closed for business.

retail mix   the factors used by a retailer to satisfy customer needs and influence their purchase decisions; includes merchandise and services offered, pricing, advertising and promotions, store design and location, and visual merchandising.

retail-sponsored cooperative   an organization owned and operated by small, independent retailers to improve operating efficiency and buying power. Typically, the retail-sponsored cooperative operates a wholesale buying and distribution system and requires its members to concentrate their purchases from the cooperative wholesale operation.

retail strategy   a statement that indicates (1) the target market toward which a retailer plans to commit its resources, (2) the nature of the retail offering that the retailer plans to use to satisfy the needs of the target market, and (3) the bases upon which the retailer will attempt to build a sustainable competitive advantage over competitors.

retained earnings   the portion of owners' equity that has accumulated over time through profits but has not been paid out in dividends to owners.

return on assets   net profit after taxes divided by total assets.

return on owners' equity   net profit after taxes divided by owners' equity; also known as return on net worth.

review time   the period of time between reviews of a line for purchase decisions.

revolving credit   a consumer credit plan that combines the convenience of a continuous charge account and the privileges of installment payment.

ribbon center   see **strip center.**

road condition   includes the age, number of lanes, number of stoplights, congestion, and general state of repair of roads in a trade area.

road pattern   a consideration used in measuring the accessibility of a retail location via major arteries, freeways, or roads.

Robinson-Patman Act (1946)   the Congressional act that revised Section 2 of the Clayton Act and specifically prohibits price discrimination.

role clarity   the degree to which employees know what their duties and responsibilities are.

role conflict   the degree to which employees receive mixed messages about the scope of their activities.

rounder   a round fixture that sits on a pedestal, smaller than the straight rack. It is designed to hold a maximum amount of merchandise.

routine decision making   see **habitual decision making.**

SKU   see **stock keeping unit.**

safety stock   merchandise inventory used as a safety cushion for cycle stock so the retailer won't run out of stock if demand exceeds the sales forecast.

sale-leaseback   the practice in which retailers build new stores and sell them to real-estate investors who then lease the buildings back to the retailers on a long-term basis.

sales associate   the same as a salesperson, but is used to recognize the importance and professional nature of the sales function and avoids the negative image sometimes linked with the term *salesperson.*

sales consultant   see **sales associate.**

sales per cubic foot   a measure of space productivity appropriate for stores like wholesale clubs that use multiple layers of merchandise.

sales per linear foot   a measure of space productivity used when most merchandise is displayed on multiple shelves of long gondolas, such as in grocery stores.

sales per square foot   a measure of space productivity used by most retailers since rent and land purchases are assessed on a per-square-foot basis.

sales productivity   the efficiency of salespeople, typically measured by sales per hour.

sales promotions   paid impersonal communication activities that offer extra value and incentives to customers to visit a store and/or purchase merchandise during a specific period of time.

satisfaction   a postconsumption evaluation of the degree to which a store or product meets or exceeds customer expectations.

scale economies   cost advantages due to the size of a retailer.

scanning   the process in point-of-sales (service) systems wherein the input into the terminal is accomplished by passing a coded ticket over a reader or having a hand-held wand pass over the ticket.

scrambled merchandising   a merchandising practice in which a retailer offers unrelated merchandise categories.

search engine   a computer program that locates and selects alternatives based on some predetermined characteristics.

seasonal discount   an additional discount offered as an incentive to retailers to place orders for merchandise in advance of the normal buying season.

seasonal merchandise   inventory whose sales fluctuate dramatically according to the time of the year.

secondary data   market research information previously gathered for purposes other than solving the current problem under investigation.

secondary shopping district   outside the central business district, a cluster of stores that serves a large population within a section or part of a large city; it is similar in character to the main shopping district of a smaller city.

secondary trade zone   the geographic area of secondary importance in terms of customer sales, generating about 20 percent of a store's sales.

security   an operating unit within a retail organization that is responsible for protecting merchandise and other assets from pilferage (internal or external). Those working in security may be employees or outside agency people.

self-analysis   an internally focused examination of a business's strengths and weaknesses.

self-service retailer   a retailer that offers minimal customer service.

selling agent   an agent who operates on an extended contractual basis; the agent sells all of a specified line of merchandise or the entire output of the principal, and usually has full authority with regard to prices, terms, and other conditions of sale. The agent occasionally renders financial aid to the principal.

selling process   a set of activities that salespeople undertake to facilitate the customer's buying decision.

selling space   the area set aside for displays of merchandise, interactions between sales personnel and customers, demonstrations, and so on.

sell-through analysis   a comparison between actual and planned sales to determine whether early markdowns are required or whether more merchandise is needed to satisfy demand.

service level   a measure used in inventory management to define the level of support or level of product availability; the number of items sold divided by the number of items demanded. Service level should not be confused with customer service. See **customer service.**

services   retailing organizations that offer services to consumers—such as banks, hospitals, health spas, doctors, legal clinics, entertainment firms, and universities.

services retailer   a retailer that primarily sells services rather than merchandise to end users.

sexual harassment   unwelcome sexual advances, requests for sexual favors, or other verbal and physical conduct with sexual elements.

Sherman Antitrust Act (1890)   the act protecting small businesses and consumers from large corporations by outlawing any person, corporation, or association from engaging in activities that restrain trade or commerce.

shoplifting   the act of stealing merchandise from a store by customers or people posing as customers.

shopping goods product   product for which consumers will spend time comparing alternatives.

shopping guide   free paper delivered to all residents in a specific area.

shopping malls   generally more planned than strip centers and with more pedestrian activity, they can be either open-air or enclosed.

shortage   see **shrinkage.**

shrinkage   the difference between the recorded value of inventory (at retail) based on merchandise bought and received and the value of actual inventory in stores and distribution centers divided by retail sales during a time period. Shrinkage is caused by employee theft, by customer shoplifting, and by merchandise being misplaced, damaged, or mispriced.

silver streakers   the generational cohort of people born before 1946.

single-price retailer   see **one-price retailer.**

situation audit   an analysis containing three elements: (1) the assessment of the attractiveness of different retail markets in which the business is competing or might compete, (2) the assessment of the objectives and capabilities of competitors, and (3) the assessment of the strengths and weaknesses of the business relative to its competition.

sliding scale   a part of some leases that stipulates how much the percentage of sales paid as rent decreases as sales go up.

slotting allowance   fee paid by a vendor for space in a retail store.

socialization   the steps taken to transform new employees into effective, committed members of the firm.

sole proprietorship   an arrangement in which an unincorporated retail firm is owned by one person.

span of control   the number of subordinates reporting to a manager.

specialization   a form of organization in which employees are assigned a limited set of tasks to perform.

specialty center   see **promotional or discount-oriented center** and **fashion-oriented shopping center.**

specialty department store   a store with a department store format that focuses primarily on apparel and soft home goods (such as Neiman Marcus or Parisian).

specialty product   product for which the customer will expend considerable effort to buy.

specialty store   concentrates on a limited number of complementary merchandise categories and provides a high level of service.

spiff   see **push money.**

split shipment   a vendor ships part of a shipment to a retailer and back orders the remainder because the entire shipment could not be shipped at the same time.

spot   a local television commercial.

spot check   used particularly in receiving operations when goods come in for reshipping to branch stores in packing cartons. Certain cartons are opened in the receiving area of the central distribution point and spot-checked for quality and quantity.

spotting techniques   see **analog approach.**

staging area   area in which merchandise is accumulated from different parts of the distribution center and prepared for shipment to stores.

standardization   involves requiring service providers to follow a set of rules and procedures when providing service.

standardization service approach   an approach used by retailers to provide customer service by using a set of rules and procedures so that all customers consistently receive the same service.

staple merchandise   inventory that has continuous demand by customers (also known as basic merchandise).

stock balance   trade-offs associated with determining variety, assortment, and service levels.

stockholders' equity   see **owners' equity.**

stock keeping unit (SKU)   the smallest unit available for keeping inventory control. In soft goods merchandise, an SKU usually means size, color, and style.

stock overage   the amount by which a retail book inventory figure exceeds a physical ending inventory.

stock-to-sales ratio   the beginning-of-month (BOM) inventory divided by sales for the month. The average stock-to-sales ratio is 12 divided by planned inventory turnover. This ratio is an integral component of the merchandise budget plan.

store atmosphere   see **atmospherics.**

store brand   see **private-label brand.**

store image   the way a store is defined in a shopper's mind. The store image is based on the store's physical characteristics, its retail mix, and a set of psychological attributes.

store loyalty   a condition in which a customer regularly patronizes a specific retailer.

store visibility   see **visibility.**

straight lease   a type of lease in which the retailer pays a fixed amount per month over the life of the lease.

straight rack   a type of fixture that consists of a long pipe suspended with supports going to the floor or attached to a wall.

straight salary   a compensation plan in which salespeople or managers receive a fixed amount of compensation for each hour or week they work.

strategic partnership   long-term relationship in which partners make significant investments to improve both parties' profitability.

strategic profit model (SPM)   a tool used for planning a retailer's financial strategy based on both margin management (net profit margin), asset management (asset turnover), and financial leverage management (financial leverage ratio). Using the SPM, a retailer's objective is to achieve a target return on owners' equity.

strategic retail plan a grand design or blueprint indicating the retail strategy and the steps for implementing the plan.

strengths-and-weaknesses analysis a critical aspect of the situation audit in which a retailer determines its unique capabilities—its strengths and weaknesses relative to its competition.

strict product liability a product liability suit in which the injury to the customer may not have been intentional or under the retailer's control.

strip center a small shopping center that comprises several adjacent stores located along a major street or highway; also known as a ribbon center.

style the characteristic or distinctive form, outline, or shape of a product.

subculture a distinctive group of people within a culture. Members of a subculture share some customs and norms with the overall society but also have some unique perspectives.

subjective employee evaluation assessment of employee performance based on a supervisor's ratings rather than on objective measures such as sales per hour.

substitute awareness effect a condition in which customers become more price-sensitive because they can find a lot of substitutes for a product or for a retailer.

supercenter a retail format combining a superstore (a large supermarket) and a general merchandise discount store in stores ranging from 150,000 to 200,000 square feet.

supermarket see **conventional supermarket.**

superstore a large supermarket between 20,000 and 50,000 square feet in size.

superwarehouse a warehouse food retail format with stores ranging in size from 50,000 to 70,000 square feet and generating from $30 to $50 million in sales per store.

survey a method of data collection, using telephone, personal interview, mail, or any combination thereof.

sustainable competitive advantage a distinct competency of a retailer relative to its competitors that can be maintained over a considerable time period.

sweepstake a promotion in which customers win prizes based on chance.

tall wall unit retail facility that is a six-to-seven–foot selling space placed against a wall in a mall instead of in the middle of an aisle as a cart or kiosk would be.

target market the customer group to which a retailer targets its retail mix.

target segment see **target market.**

task performance behaviors planning, organizing, motivating, evaluating, and coordinating store employees' activities.

terms of purchase conditions in a purchase agreement with a vendor that include the type(s) of discounts available and responsibility for transportation costs.

terms of sale conditions in a sales contract with customers including such issues as charges for alterations, delivery, or gift wrapping, or the store's exchange policies.

tertiary trade zone the outermost ring of a trade area; includes customers who occasionally shop at the store or shopping center. Also known as fringe trade area.

theme center a shopping center that tries to replicate a historical place and typically contains tenants similar to those in specialty centers, except there usually is no large specialty store or department store as an anchor. See **historical center.**

thrift store a retail format offering used merchandise.

ticketing and marking procedures for making price labels and placing them on the merchandise.

tie-in an approach used to attract attention to a store's offering by associating the offering with an event.

tonnage merchandising a technique in which a large quantity of merchandise is displayed together.

top-down planning one side of the process of developing an overall retail strategy where goals are set at the top of the organization and filter down through the operating levels.

total expenditure effect a condition in which customer price sensitivity increases when the total expenditure is large.

trade area a geographic sector that contains potential customers for a particular retailer or shopping center.

trade discount reduction in a retailer's suggested retail price granted to wholesalers and retailers; also known as functional discount.

trade show a temporary concentration of vendors that provides retailers opportunities to place orders and view what is available in the marketplace; also known as a merchandise show.

trademark any mark, work, picture, or design associated with a particular line of merchandise or product.

traffic appliance small portable appliance.

transformational leader a leader who gets people to transcend their personal needs for the sake of realizing the group goal.

transportation cost   the expense a retailer incurs if it pays the cost of shipping merchandise from the vendor to the stores.

travel time contours   used in trade area analysis to define the rings around a particular site based on travel time instead of distances.

triple coupon promotion   a retail promotion that allows the customer triple the face value of the coupon.

turnover   the percentage of employees at the beginning of a time period (usually a year) who aren't employed by the firm at the end of the time period.

tying contract   an agreement between a vendor and a retailer requiring the retailer to take a product it does not necessarily desire (the "tied product") to ensure that it can buy a product it does desire (the "tying product").

ultimate consumers   individuals who purchase goods and services for their own personal use or for use by members of their household.

undercover shopper   person hired by or working for a retailer who poses as a customer to observe the activities and performance of employees.

unit pricing   the practice of expressing price in terms of both the total price of an item and the price per unit of measure.

unity of command   the appropriate relationship between managers and their subordinates.

Universal Product Code (UPC)   the black-and-white bar codes found on most merchandise used to collect sales information at the point of sale using computer terminals that read them. This information is transmitted computer-to-computer to buyers, distribution centers, and then to vendors, who in turn quickly ship replenishment merchandise.

unrelated diversification   diversification in which there is no commonality between the present business and the new business.

URL (Uniform Resource Locator)   the standard for a page on the World Wide Web (e.g., http://www.nrf.orf).

utility   the consumer's perception of the benefits of the product and services offered by the retailer.

value pricing   setting prices based on fair value for both the service provider and the consumer.

variable direct costs   costs that vary with the level of sales and can be applied directly to the decision in question.

variety   the number of different merchandise categories within a store or department.

vending machine retailing   a form of nonstore retailing in which customers purchase and receive merchandise from a machine.

vendor   any firm from which a retailer obtains merchandise.

vertical integration   a firm that performs more than one function in the channel.

vertical merchandising   a method whereby merchandise is organized to follow the eye's natural up-and-down movement.

vertical price fixing   agreements to fix prices between parties at different levels of the same marketing channel (for example, retailers and their vendors). Also known as resale price maintenance or fair trade laws.

video kiosk   see **interactive kiosk.**

videotex retailing   an interactive electronic system in which a retailer transmits data and graphics over cable or telephone lines to a consumer's TV or computer terminal.

visibility   the customers' ability to see the store and enter the parking lot safely.

visual communications   the act of providing information to customers through graphics, signs, and theatrical effects both in the store and in windows to help boost sales by providing information on products and by suggesting items or special purchases.

want book   information collected by retail salespeople to record out-of-stock or requested merchandise. Similar to want slip.

warehouse club   a general merchandise retailer that offers limited merchandise assortment with little service at low prices to ultimate consumers and small businesses.

warehouse store   a discount food retailer that offers merchandise in a no-frills environment.

Web site   a page or series of pages on the Internet, identified by a unique address (URL) that can provide information and/or facilitate electronic commerce.

week's supply method   an inventory management method most similar to the stock-to-sales method. The difference is that everything is expressed in weeks rather than months.

wheel of retailing   a cyclical theory of retail evolution whose premise is that retailing institutions evolve from low–price/service to higher–price/service operations.

wholesale club   a general merchandise retailer that offers a limited merchandise assortment with little service at low prices and sells to ultimate consumers and member trade people.

wholesaler a merchant establishment operated by a concern that is primarily engaged in buying, taking title to, usually storing, and physically handling goods in large quantities, and reselling the goods (usually in smaller quantities) to retailers or to industrial or business users.

wholesale-sponsored voluntary cooperative group an organization operated by a wholesaler offering a merchandising program to small, independent retailers on a voluntary basis.

word of mouth communications about a retailer delivered to the customer by other people.

WWW (World Wide Web) the user-friendly area of the Internet that consists of linked pages containing graphics, text, sound, and video.

yuppies young urban professionals.

zoning the regulation of the construction and use of buildings in certain areas of a municipality.

CREDITS

Chapter 13

374 © Vic Bider/PhotoEdit **376** Courtesy Pelco **382** Courtesy of Mothers Work, Inc. **383** Courtesy Target Stores **385** © Hiroyuki Watsumoto/Tony Stone Images **389** © Elena Rooraid/PhotoEdit **391** © Michael Newman/PhotoEdit **391** © Michael Newman/PhotoEdit

Chapter 14

403 © David Young-Wolff/PhotoEdit **408** Courtesy of Sears, Roebuck and Co. **411** © Jeff Greenberg/PhotoEdit **414** SuperStock International **416** © Rudi Von Briel/PhotoEdit **417** © Robert Brenner/PhotoEdit **418** © Tony Freeman/PhotoEdit

Chapter 15

441 © Jose Carrillo/PhotoEdit **443** © Michael Newman/PhotoEdit **443** © Michael Newman/PhotoEdit **445** © Robert Brenner/PhotoEdit **446** © Tony Freeman/PhotoEdit **447** © David Young-Wolff/PhotoEdit **447** © David Young-Wolff/PhotoEdit **448** © Michael Newman/PhotoEdit **449** © Tony Freeman/PhotoEdit **454** © Michael Newman/PhotoEdit

Chapter 16

475 Larry Fleming **478** © Myrleen Ferguson/PhotoEdit **479** Courtesy of Fashion Bug **479** Courtesy Payless ShoeSource, Inc. **490** Courtesy Kmart Properties, Inc. **496** © Tony Freeman/PhotoEdit **496** © David Young-Wolff/PhotoEdit **497** Courtesy Advanced Promotion Technologies **500** © Jeff Greenberg/PhotoEdit

Chapter 17

510 Courtesy The TJX Companies, Inc. **516** © Michael Newman/PhotoEdit **517** Courtesy Shopko Stores, Inc. **519** Courtesy Sears, Roebuck & Company/Photography by Mark Joseph **523** Chicago Tribune Photo by Walter Kale **524** Courtesy The Limited, Inc. **529** © Frank Garner/The Stock Market **533** © David Young-Wolff/PhotoEdit **534** © Amy C. Etra/PhotoEdit **534** Courtesy Sensormatic

Chapter 18

541 Courtesy of Boomers **542** Paul Bielenberg/Bielenberg Associates **542** © Tony Freeman/PhotoEdit **543** © Mitch Kezar/Tony Stone Images **548** © Paul Warchol/Warchol Photography **549** © Mark Richards/ PhotoEdit **549** © Tony Freeman/PhotoEdit **551** Courtesy of Jericho Promotions **555** Courtesy of Information Resources **558** © Mark Richards/PhotoEdit **560** © David Young-Wolff/PhotoEdit **561** Sharon Hoogstraten **562** © Myrleen Ferguson/PhotoEdit

Chapter 19

574 Courtesy Miller/Zell **576** Courtesy Kentucky Fried Chicken (KFC) Corporation, Louisville, KY **576** Discount Store News **577** Courtesy Will & Deni McIntyre **581** © Mark Richards/PhotoEdit **584** Courtesy Mercantile Stores Company, Inc. **585** © David Young-Wolff/PhotoEdit **586** Courtesy The Pep Boys–Manny, Moe & Jack **588** Courtesy Domino's Pizza **595** © Michael Newman/PhotoEdit

Chapter 20

604 © Myrleen Ferguson/PhotoEdit **605** © Tom McCarthy/PhotoEdit **608** © Rhoda Sidney/PhotoEdit **612** © Amy C. Etra/PhotoEdit **616** Courtesy Liz Claiborne, Inc. **624** © Amy C. Etra/PhotoEdit

NAME INDEX

Aaker, David, 189, 193n, 195n, 478, 502n
Abend, Jules, 312n, 503n, 539n
Achabal, Dale D., 283n, 368, 369, 502
Adelman, Mara, 599n
Agins, Teri, 119n, 438n, 471n, 618
Ahuvia, Aaron, 599n
Ailawadi, Karim, 25
Ailawadi, Kusum L., 223, 427
Alba, Joseph, 95n
Albaum, Gerald, 91, 94n
Alberts, William, 229n
Albrecht, Steve, 502n
Alcorn, Bill, A4
Allaway, Arthur, 503n
Allerton, Haidee, 537
Anderson, Duncan, 50
Anderson, Erin, 193n, 438n
Anderson, John, 94n
Anderson, Monroe, 156n
Anderson, Phillip, 311
Anderson, Ricky, 590
Anderson, Ronald, 537
Andreoli, Teresa, 503n, 597
Andrews, J. Craig, 281, 283n
Ansoff, H. Igor, 193n
Antonni, Joseph, 27n
Apfel, Ira, 254n
Apgar, Mike, 603
Appel, David, 64n
Applebaum, William, 268
Areni, Charles S., 568
Arnold, Danny, 627n
Arnold, Helen, 179
Assuncao, Joao, 27n
Austin, Nancy, 538n, 598n, 599n
Avolio, B., 538n

Babin, Barry, 155n, 568
Baczko, Joseph R., 193n
Baker, Julie, 568, 597, 598n
Ballen, Kate, 94n
Bamerji, Shumet, 427
Bandura, A., 538n
Barada, Paul, 538n
Barlow, Wayne, 539n
Barmmash, Isadore, 25
Barnes, John, 568
Barrett, Patrick, 478
Barrett, Paul M., 471n
Bartlett, Richard, 91
Baskin, Carlisle W., 282n
Bass, Bernard, 538n
Bateman, T., 539n
Bauer, Connie, 94n

Baum, Richard N., 192n, 194n
Bawa, Kapil, 470n
Bearden, William O., 470n
Beatty, Sharon E., 155n, 157n, 626, 626n
Beaumont, J.R., 283n
Behr, Mary, 95n
Belch, George, 502
Belch, Michael, 502
Bell, Alice T., 223, 229n
Bell, Chip, 598n, 599n
Bellanger, Danny, 626
Bellizzi, Joseph A., 568, 569n
Benjamin, Daniel, 508
Bennett, P.D., 155n
Bennett, Ruth, 626
Bennis, Warren, 538n
Berens, John S., 401n
Berger, Michelle, 598n
Bergman, T., 537n
Bergmann, Joan, 194n
Bernardin, John, 538n
Berner, Robert, 318
Berry, Jon, 154n
Berry, Leonard L., 58, 64n, 193n, 469, 527, 578, 580, 597, 597n, 598n, 599n
Bertrand, Kate, 598n
Bessen, Jim, 334, 335n
Bettman, James R., 155n, 156n, 627n
Bezos, Jeffrey, 88
Bienstock, Carol C., 334
Bier, Michael, 193n
Bird, Laura, 382, 470n
Bird, Monroe Murphy, 334
Birou, Laura M., 438n
Bitner, Mary Jo, 58, 59, 193n, 568, 579, 598n
Bivens, Jacquelyn, 27n, 155n
Black, William C., 155n
Blackwell, Steven, 539n
Blake, S., 312n
Blank, Arthur, 284, 290–291
Blattberg, Robert C., 27n, 334n, 335n, 368, 369n, 470n
Blischok, Thomas J., 568n
Bliss, Laura, C48
Block, Peter, 155n
Bloomquist, Randall, 626
Boardman, Anthony, 192n
Boje, David, 312n
Bonnice, Joseph, 627n
Booms, Bernard, 579
Bordat, Alain, 415–416
Borin, Norm, 25, 223, 427

Boucicaut, Aristide, 61
Boughton, Paul, 194n
Bounds, Wendy, 37
Boutlier, Robert, 156n
Bowen, David, 597, 598n, 599n
Bragg, Arthur, 538n
Braus, Patricia, 117, 118n
Breauz, Kia, 515
Britney, Robert, 439n
Britt, Steward Henderson, 470n
Broderick, Amanda, 150
Brogan, Michael, 617
Brookman, Faye, 332, 369n, 439n
Brossi, Mario, 95n
Browder, Seanna, 308
Brown, Caryne, 94n
Brown, Gene, 503n
Brown, James, 27n
Brown, Paul, 573
Brown, Stephen, 58, 65n, 281
Brown, Steven, 156n, 626, 627n
Browning, E.S., 179, 438n
Bruner, Gordon, 155n
Bucklin, Louis P., 439n
Burdett, John, 312n
Burdine, William M., 23
Burgess, Peter, 538n
Burke, Raymond R., 568n
Burns, David J., 254
Burstiner, Irving, A27
Burt, Steve, 150
Buzek, Tereska, 64n
Buzzell, Robert D., 195n, 334, 427

Caldini, Robert, 626
Callahan, Thomas, 303
Cameron, Michaelle, 597
Caminiti, Susan, 27n, 155n, 537
Cammaratus, Bernard, 485
Campany, Sarah, 539n
Campbell, James Quick, 305
Campeau, Robert, 54
Canning, Roy, 538n
Cannito, Michael, 626, 627n
Cannon, Hugh M., 368, 502
Capella, Louis M., 568
Cappelli, Peter, 311
Carideo, Joseph, 537n
Caroll. C., 27n
Carr, Karen A., 193n
Carsky, Mary, 150
Carter, Cynthia, 623, 624
Cartwright, Donna, 194n
Casati, Mary Ann, 194n
Case, John, 312n, 591

I

Case, Tony, 503n
Cash, R. Patrick, 396
Cassill, Nancy, 537
Castleberry, Stephen, 607, 623, 624, 626, 626n
Castellano, Joseph F., 229n
Caudron, Shari, 539n
Chakravarthy, B.S., 228n
Chandler, Susan, 27n, 438n
Chanil, Debra, 27n, 193n, 199
Chao, Paul, 438n
Chapman, Randall, 503n
Chase, Marilyn, 369n
Chatterjee, Patrali, 95n
Chebat, Jean Charles, 568
Chen, Yung-Fang, 194n
Chouinard, Tvon, 16
Chow, James, 223
Chowdhury, Jhinuk, 539n
Christ, Paul F., 334, 335n
Christaller, Walter, 275, 276, 282n
Christiansen, Tim, 155n
Clark, Angie, 508
Clark, Terry, 194n
Claxton, Reid, 95n
Clay, Joan, 537
Cocheo, Steve, 587
Cochrane, J.L., 401n
Coeyman, Marjorie, 537n
Cohan, Sarah, 538n
Cohen, Eric, 254
Coleman, James, 626
Colley, Russell H., 502n
Collins, David, 189, 193n
Comer, Gary, 15, 16
Compeau, Larry D., 469, 471n
Compton, Ted R., 223, 229n
Conder, J., 312n
Conner, Patrick, 619
Conry, Edward J., 439n
Converse, P.D., 275, 276, 282n
Cooke, Donna, 538n
Cooke, John, 193n
Cooper, L.G., 283n
Cooper, Linda, 599n
Cooper, Martha, 335n
Cooper, Peter, 470n
Cooper, Robin, 223, 229n
Copeland, Bill, 539n
Corley, Robert N., 471n
Corstjens, M., 568n
Cortez, John, 27n
Coughlin, Ann, 64n
Cox, Anthony, 502n, 537
Cox, Dena, 502n, 537
Cox, T., 312n
Craig, C. Samuel, 281, 283n
Crail, Frank, 39
Crissy, W.J.E., 229n
Critchfield, Melissa A., 229n

CrockerHefler, Anne, 311
Cron, William, 439n
Cronin, Michael, 537n
Crossen, Cynthia, 94n, 598n
Crowe, Timothy, 539n
Crowley, Ayn E., 568
Cuneo, Alice, 502
Curhan, Ronald, 503n
Curry, Bruce, 281
Czinkota, Michael R., 326, 335n, 438n

Dabholkar, Pratibha, 598n
Dangello, Frank, 538n
Darden, William R., 155n, 312n, 401n, 568
Darwin, Charles, 63
Dauber, Daniel M., 199
Daugherty, Patricia J., 335
D'Aveni, R.A., 228n
Davidson, William R., 27n, 369n
Davies, R.L., 254, 269, 281, 282n, 283n
Davis, Duane, 597n
Davis, Fred R., 194n
Davis, Mark, 597
Dawson, Lyndon, 626n
Dawson, Peter, 155n
Dawson, Scott, 155n
Day, George, 27n, 194n
De Santa, Richard, 497
Deighton, John, 91, 334, 335n
Della Bitta, Albert J., 439n
Delusia, Ann, 379
DeMoss, Michelle, 155n
Deogun, Nikhil, 95n
DeSarbo, Wayne, 156n
DesMarteau, Kathleen, 335n
Deutscher, Terry, 155n
Deveny, Kathleen, 503n
Dick, Alan S., 427
Dickinson, Rachel J., 357
Dickinson, Roger, 150, 369
Dickson, Peter R., 95n, 154n, 155n, 469, 470n
DiMingo, Edward, 502n
Dingus, Anne, 499
Dodds, William B., 471n
Doerpinghaus, Helen, 539n
Dolan, Carrie, 194n
Dolan, Kerry, 311, 312n
Donnelly, Harrison, 335n, A7, A12n
Donovan, Robert J., 568
Donthu, Naveen, 282
Doocey, Paul, 194n, 239
Doolittle, Sidney, 527
Dortch, Shannon, 117, 118n
Dougherty, Tracy, 539n
Douthitt, Robin, 156n
Dowling, Melissa, 69, 597, 598n
Doyle, Peter, 503n, 568n

Drauschke, Andreas, 508
Dreesmann, A.C.R., 65n
Dreves, Robert, 155n
Drexler, Mickey, 15
Dreze, Xavier, 469, 568
Drezner, Tammy, 254, 281, 283n
Driscoll, David, 538n
Droge, Cornelia, 335
Drucker, Stephen, 193n
Drummey, G.L., 269, 282n
D'Souza, Giles, 503n
Dube, Laurette, 568
Dubinsky, Alan, 539n
Dudley, Joe, 76
Duff, Christina, 153, 254n, 361
Dunn, Steven C., 335
Dunne, Patrick, 282n, 401n, 538n
Durand, Richard, 155n
Durvasula, Srinivas, 281, 283n
Dwyer, Robert, 438n
Dyer, Lee, 539n
Dziedzic, Anita, 198

Edelson, Sharon, 64n, 94n, 238, 369n
Ehrlich, David, C24, C31, C45, C47, C49
Eiselt, H.A., 281, 283n
Eisenhardt, K.M., 539n
El-Ansary, Adel, 27n, 64n
Ellis, Joseph H., 118n, 194n, 444
Emmelhainz, Larry W., 368
Emmelhainz, Margaret A., 368
Emondson, Brad, 117, 118n
Epen, Gary, 27n
Erdem, S. Alton, C34
Erickson, Gary M., 438n
Eroglu, Sevgin, 255n
Etgar, Michael, 439n
Ettenson, Richard, 401n
Evans, David, 539n
Evans, Kenneth, 155n
Evans, Martin, 282
Evered, Roger, 192n
Everett, Peter, 155n

Faber, Ronald, 155n
Fabricant, Florence, 156n
Faiola, Anthony, 422
Falk, Edgar, 502
Fancher Canavan, Lynn, 568n
Farnsworth Riche, Martha, 118n, 146, 157n
Farris, Laura, 337
Farris, Paul W., 25, 223, 427
Fawcett, Stanley E., 438n
Fedyk, Jaoanne, 156n
Feffer, Greg, 564
Feick, Lawrence, 155n, 502n
Feinberg, Samuel, 235
Feldman, Daniel, 514, 539n

Felicetti, Linda F., C16
Ferrell, O.C., 597, 598n
Ferrera, Gerald R., 439n
Fiedler, F.E., 538n
Field, H.S., 537n
Field, Hubert, 539n
Fields, William, 50
Filipczak, Bob, 308
Fine, Leslie, 627n
Finkelstein, Sydney, 311
Finn, Adam, 155n, 194n, 254
Fiorito, Susan S., 311, 334
Fischer, Paul M., 229n
Fisher, Christy, 117, 118n, 141, 156n
Fisher, Donald, 15
Fisher, Roger, 427, 439n
Fisk, Irwin W., A27, A41
Fleischman, John, 254n
Fleschner, Malcolm, 599n
Flynn, Julia, 527
Ford, Henry, 329
Ford, Robert, 539n
Forester, Murray, 65n
Fornell, Claus, 598n
Foster, Irene, 156n
Foust, Dean, 64n
Fox, Bruce, 95n, 369n, 569n
Fox, Edward J., 368, 369n
Fox, Karla H., 439n
Fox, Neil J., 109
Fox, Richard J., 357
Fraedrich, John Paul, 537
Fram, Eugene, 118n, 155n
Frank, Bertrand, 27n
Frank, Robert, 369n
Franklin, Benjamin, 70
Frederick, James, 503n
Frederick, Joanne, 27n, 64n
Freedman, Alix M., 471n
Friedlander, Mark, A41
Friedman, Arthur, 369n, 438n
Fruhan, William, 229n
Fuoco, Alfred, 619
Fyock, C., 313n

Gabbott, Mark, 150
Gable, Myron, 194n, 311, 538n
Gade, Michael, 27n
Galbraith, J.R., 311
Galceran, Ignacio, 154n
Gale, Bradley, 195n
Galen, Sandra, 539n
Galgay, P.J., 538n
Gallagher, John, 503n
Galloway, Kenneth, 527
Ganesan, Shankar, 312n, 427
Garcia, J.E., 538n
Gardiner, Stanley C., 223
Gardner, Meryl, 503n
Garfein, Richard, 599n

Garner, Dewey, 539n
Garnett, Pat, 627n
Garry, Michael, 64n
Gates, Ollie, 515
Gatewood, R.D., 537n
Gault, Jack, 334, 335n
Gebhardt, Randall, 282n
Gehrt, Kenneth, 91
Gelb, Betsy, 502n
Gelfand, Michael, 64n
Gelman, Jan, 626
Genestre, Alain, 598n
Gengler, Charles, 627n
Gentry, James, 312n
George, William, 599n
Gerlich, R. Nicholas, 189
Germain, Richard, 335
Geurts, Michael, 568n
Ghemawat, Pankaj, 316
Ghosh, Avijit, 254, 281, 283n
Giblen, Gary, 470n
Gibson, Richard, 254n, 503n, 588
Gibson, Stan, 95n
Gidengil, B. Zeki, 503n
Gill, James, 155n
Gill, Lynn E., 401n
Gill, Penny, 27n, 539n, A12n
Gilliam, Margaret, 193n
Gilman, Alan, 599n
Gilmore, James, 597n
Ginzberg, Eli, 470n
Gist, M.E., 538n
Gladwell, Malcolm, 150
Glazer, Rashi, 193n
Goff, Brent, 626
Goldberg, Bruce, 39
Goldberg, Stephen, 503n
Golden, Linda L., 193n
Golden, Marilyn, 537, 568n
Goldman, Arieh, 64n, 65n
Goldman, Sylvan, 545
Goldsmith, Harold, 218
Goldsmith, Ronald, 156n
Good, Linda, 312n
Gooding, Richard, 538n
Goodman, L., 538n
Goodwin, Cathy, 599n
Goodwin, David R., 396
Gordon, Jay, 326
Gordon, Mary Ellen, 91, 94n
Gorr, W.L., 283n
Graham, Ellen, 94n
Graham, John, 627n
Graham, Thomas R., 438n
Gralla, Heidi, 254n
Grant, Hugh, 109
Grant, J., 539n
Grant, Linda, 54
Gratiot, Preston, 499
Graves, Laura, 538n

Grayson, Kent, 597
Grazin, Kent L., 427
Greco, Alan, 58
Greco, Susan, 193n
Green, Paul, 503n
Greenberg, Barnett, 65n
Greenberg, Larry, 64n
Gresham, Larry, 193n
Grewal, Dhruv, 469, 471n, 568
Grewal, Diana S., 469, 471n
Griffin, Mitch, 155n
Grossman, Laurie M., 118n
Grunewald, Joseph P., C16
Gschwandtner, Gerhard, 599n, 627n
Gubernick, Lisa, 155n
Guiltinan, Joseph P., 470n, 597n
Gundlach, Gregory T., 427
Gurney, Gene, A41
Guy, William, 303
Guyon, Janet, 598n

Hagan, Patti, 170
Hagendorn, Ann, 626n
Haggin, Jeff, 27n
Haley, George T., 335
Hall, Judith, 627n
Hallowell, Roger, 300
Halstead, Diane, 193n
Halverson, Richard, 598n
Hambrick, D.C., 228n
Hamel, Gary, 193n, 194n
Hammel, Frank, 312n, 537n, 538n
Hammonds, Keith, 311, 312n
Hampton, Ronald, 312n
Hancock, Gregory, 599n
Hane, Edward, 539n
Hankins, Paula, 520
Hansen, Robert, 155n
Harper, Rosanne, 37
Harrell, Gilbert D., 255n
Harris, L., 25
Harrison, David, 218
Hartline, Michael, 597, 598n
Hartnet, Michael, 6
Hatch, David, 12
Hathcote, Jan, 502
Hauser, John, 155n, 156n
Hawes, John, 626n
Hax, A., 229n
Hayes, Read, 438n, 539n
Hazel, Debra, 239, 254n, 282n
Hecker, Sid, 627n
Helliker, Kevin, 156n, 453, 538n, 599n
Henderson, Pamela W., 568
Henkoff, Ronald, 537, 537n, 538n, 599n
Henkoff, Susan, 311
Herbert, Rosemary, 573
Herbig, Paul, 598n
Hernandez, Del, 14

Herr, David, 537
Herrington, J. Duncan, 568
Hessen, Wendy, 357
Hidalgo, Edgar, 615
Higby, Mary A., 117
Higgins, Kevin, 597
Higie, Robin, 155n, 502n
Hirschman, Elizabeth C., 401n
Hisey, Pete, 344, 466, 598n, 599n
Hite, Robert E., 568, 569n
Hoch, Stephen, 427, 469, 568
Hodges, James S., 281
Hoeffel, John, 117, 118n
Hof, Robert, 95n
Hoffman, Donna, 95n
Holland, Charles, 538n
Hollander, Stanley, 25, 65n
Holley, William, 539n
Hollinger, Richard, 533, 538n, 539n
Holton, Lisa, 255n
Homer, Pamela, 157n
Hong, Sung-Tai, 438n
Honzik, Nicole, 198
Hooks, Laura, C3, C7–C8, C13, C52
Hornsby, Jeffrey, 538n
Horwitz, Tony, 508
House, Robert G., 391, 396, 401n
Houston, Michael, 503n
Howard, Daniel J., 229n, 470n
Howard, J.D., 439n
Howell, Roy D., 312n, 439n
Hoyer, Wayne, 156n
Hudson, Jason, 73, 94n
Huff, David L., 283n
Hui, Michael, 599n
Huizenga, Wayne, 50
Hunt, H. Keith, 368, 502
Hunt, Shelby, 189, 427
Hunter, George, 198
Hunter, J.E., 538n
Hunter, R., 538n
Husling, David, 427
Hutchins, Vickie, 72
Hwang, Suein, 132
Hyde, Joseph R., A5
Hyten, Todd, 573

Iacobucci, Dawn, 597
Ingene, Charles A., 229n
Ingram, Bob, 142
Irons, Jeremy, 109

Jacobs, Bill, 537
Jacobson, Robert, 195n
Jaffee, Thomas, 27n
Jago, A.G., 538n
Jain, Arun K., 283n, 427
James, Don, 155n
Janiszewski, Chris, 95n
Jap, Sandy, 438n

Jaworski, Bernard, 312n, 537
Jeuland, Abel P., 439n
Joachimsthaler, Erich, 478
Johansson, Johny K., 438n
John, George, 539n
Johnson, Anne Marie, 505
Johnson, Eric, 156n
Johnson, Jay, 193n, 194n
Johnson, Jonathan, 10
Johnson, Kerry, 627n
Johnson, Kirk, 538n
Johnson, Madeline, 502n
Johnson, Pamela, 539n
Johnson, William, 312n
Jones, Ken, 281, 282
Jones, S.D., 538n
Jones, Wesley, 597n
Jun, Sung Youl, 469

Kahle, Lynne, 157n
Kalapurakai, Rosemary, 155n
Kalyanam, Kirthi, 281
Kaminski, Peter, 598n
Kang, Yong-Soon, 155n
Kanungo, R., 312n
Kaplan, Robert S., 223, 229n
Karan, Donna, 75
Karande, Kiram, 502
Karande, Kiran W., 469
Karch, Nancy, 192n
Kardas, Frank, 598n
Karren, Ronald, 538n
Kartomkin, Bjorn, 27n
Kasuhs, Jack, 118n
Katz, D.R., 25
Katzen, Lawrence R., 194n
Kaufman, Carol, 502
Kaufmann, David, A41
Kaufmann, Patrick J., 469
Kaye, G. Roland, 194n
Kedia, Pradeep, 503n
Kelleher, Herbert, 304, 305
Kelley, Scott, 312n, 597
Kelly, J. Patrick, 368, 502, 568n
Kelly, Mary Ellen, 118n, 194n
Kenny, Robert, C21
Kerin, Roger, 193n, 194n, 229n
Kerr, Jeffrey, 193n
Kerrigan, Phillip, 233
Kharbanda, Om, 626n
Kibarian, Thomas, 470n
Kim, David, 568
Kincade, Doris, 599n
Kindal, Sharen, 156n
King, Robert, 598n
King, Thomas R., 242
Kingdom, Mark, 254n, 369n
Kiotabe, Masaaki, 156n
Kirk, George, 538n
Kirsch, Michael, 538n

Kissling, Mark, 597n
Klein, Calvin, 75
Klein, Ellen, 439n
Klein, Lisa, 95n
Kline, Barbara, 368
Knapp, Mark, 627n
Knecht, G. Bruce, 88, 156n
Knott, Allison T., C5, C11–C12, C14, C32, C36, C46, C51, C53, C55
Koenig, Evan, C22
Koenig, Harold, C38
Koh, Anthony, 223
Kohler, Keith, 194n
Kohsaka, Hiroyuki, 282
Konarski III, John, 254n
Kopp, Robert, 503n
Kotler, Philip, 569n
Kotter, J.P., 538n
Kramer, Louise, 27n
Kranzin, Kent, 150
Krapel, Robert, 427, 438n
Kreitzman, Howard, 439n
Krishnan, R., 335
Krishnan, Trichy V., 469
Krueger, Richard, 369n
Kullen, King, 33
Kumar, V., 469, 502
Kuzdrall, Paul, 439n

Lachman, Conway, 156n
Laczniak, Gene R., 438n
Lagnado, Ike, 527
Laker, Jane, 193n
Lal, Rajiv, 439n
LaLonde, Bernard J., 229n, 335n
Lambert, Douglas M., 223, 229n, 335, 335n, 369n, 396, 401n, 470n
Lanasa, John, 156n
Langrehr, Fred, 27n
Laporte, G., 281, 283n
Larke, Roy, 58
Larsson, Rikard, 598n
Lash, Linda, 599n
Lassar, Walfried, 597
Latham, G.P., 538n
Lavidge, R., 502n
Lavin, Marilyn, 156n
Lawler, Edward, 599n
Lawson, Diana, 91
Lazarus, Jr., Fred, 19
Leap, Terry, 539n
LeBlanc, Ronald, 156n
Ledvinka, J., 539n
Lee, Georgia, 335n
Lee, Julian, 478
Lee, Louise, 95n, 598n
Lee, Tom, 306
Lehmann, Donald, 189, 194n
Lenahan, Margaret, 470n
Leone, Robert, 470n, 502

Letovsky, Robert, C21
Levin-Epstein, M.D., 539n
Levinson, Barry, 218
Levitt, Theodore, 626n
Levy, Michael, 229n, 439n, 470n, 568, 626, C26–C29, C38
Levy, Sidney J., 599n
Lewis, Kathryn, 539n
Lewis, Robin, 438n
Lewison, Dale M., 62, 63, 65n, 568n
Liebeck, Laura, 118n, 194n
Lieberman, Joshua, 27n
Lifson, Kal, 538n
Lisanti, Tony, 194n
Litvan, Laura, 603
Locke, E.A., 538n
Lodish, Leonard, 503n
Loeb, Walter, 312n
Longfellow, Timothy, 312n
Lord, J. Dennis, 282n
Louviere, Jordan, 155n, 254
Love, Michele, 506
Lubinger, Bill, 198
Lubovek, Seth, 537n
Lucas, George, 193n
Lucey, Scott, 599n
Lumpkin, James, 154n
Lundberg, Craig, 538n
Lusch, Robert F., 282n, 401n, 537
Lutz, Richard J., 95n, 155n, 156n
Lynch, John, 95n
Lynds, Charles D., 282n

Maass, Peter, 598n
Macarenhus, Oswald A.J., 117
McCann, John, 503n
McCarthy, Cathleen, 569n
McCarthy, Patrick, 311
McClenahen, John, 312n
McCloud, John, 254n
MacCrimmon, Kenneth R., 401n
McDermott, Robert, 587
Macdonald, R. Fulton, 527
McDowell, Edwin, 27n
McGrath, Mary Ann, 599n
McIntyre, Shelby H., 368, 369, 502
MacKenzie, Scott, 597
MacKenzie-Child, Richard, 499
MacKenzie-Child, Victoria, 499
McKinnon, John, 539n
McLafferty, Sara L., 254, 281, 283n
McLaughlin, Frank, 539n
McMurray, Scott, 167
McNeal, James, 150
McNermey, Donald, 538n
McNulty, Eric, 79
McQuaid, Sara, 312n
McTaggart, James, 229n
Maes, Patricia, 95n

Mahajan, Vijay, 193n, 194n, 228n, 283n, 469, 503n
Mahoney, Marianne, 94n
Mahoney, Tom, 65n
Majluf, N., 229n
Malehorn, Jack, 312n
Mamis, Robert, 94n
Mammarella, James, 193n
Manning, Kenneth H., 229n
Manoff, Mark, 119n
Marcoolyn, Gilian, 568
Marcus, Bernard, 284, 290, 291
Marcus, Joshua, 193n
Marcus, Stanley, 193n, 194n, 582
Mardon, Lawson, 312n
Maremont, Mark, 27n
Marino, Joseph, 95n
Markin, Rom J., 401n
Markowitz, Arthur, 194n
Marmon, Howard, 548–549
Maronick, Thomas J., 65n
Marsh, Barbara, 255n
Martin, Joann, 72
Martin, John, 300
Martin, Justin, 179, 218
Martin, Michael, 95n
Martin, Scott, 118n
Martinez, Arthur, 167, 318
Maslow, Abraham, 155n
Mason, J. Barry, 503n
Massey, William F., 401n
Mast, Kenneth, 626n
Matus, Alina, 183
Matzer, Marla, 72
May, Eleanor G., 334
Mayer, Morris, 626
Mazumdar, Tridib, 469
Mazur, Paul M., 290, 312n
Mazursky, David, 401n
Mead, Gary, 472
Meadus, Amanda, 357
Mecimore, Charles D., 223, 229n
Mentzer, John T., 334, 335n
Messing, Fred, 583
Meyer, Robert, 27n, 156n
Michman, Ronald, 58
Mick, David, 155n
Miglautsch, John, 94n
Milbank, Dana, 233
Miles, Morgan, 627n
Miller, Amy, 591
Miller, Christopher M., 368
Miller, Cyndee, 64n, 73, 79, 118n, 123, 156n, 167, 503n, 539n, 569n
Miller, Krystal, 588
Miller, Leslie, 95n
Miller, Stephen, 194n
Mills, D. Quinn, 312n
Milne, George, 91, 94n
Mintzberg, Henry, 195n

Mish, David, 193n
Mitchell, Susan, 99, 117, 282n
Mittal, Banwari, 597
Miyazaki, Anthony, 598n
Mogelonsky, Marcia, 438n
Mohr, Jakki, 427
Mohr, Lois, 598n
Moin, David, 369
Monaghan, Thomas, 15, 16, 17, 588
Monahan, James, 439n
Monash, Peter, 527
Monroe, Kent B., 439n, 469, 470n, 471n
Montgomery, Cynthia, 189, 193n
Moore, William, 27n
Moran, Alexandra, 223, 228n, 348, 556
Morgan, John, 109
Morgan, Robert, 189, 427
Morgenson, Gretchen, 539n
Morin, Sylvia, 568
Morris, Betsy, 155n
Morris, Eugene, 117, 118n
Morris, Tim, 189
Morwitz, Vicki G., 369
Moschis, George P., 117, 150, 537
Mossman, Frank H., 229n
Moutinho, Luiz, 281
Mubndt, Kevin, 308
Mudambi, Susan, 193n
Mueller, Rene, 150
Mulhern, Francis J., 469, 470n, 502
Mullin, Tracy, 27n, 194n
Mulvihill, Nari-Aylssa, 50
Mundt, Kevin, 192n
Murphy, Debra, C21
Murphy, Patrick E., 154n, 427, 438n
Murra, Matt, 64n
Myers, Gerry, 468

Nagle, Thomas T., 469, 470n, 471n
Nakanishi, M., 283n
Nanadan, Shiva, 369
Nash, Henry, 627n
Neiman, Al, 166
Nesdale, Andrew, 568
Neslin, Scott, 503n
Nevin, John R., 427
Niemira, Michael P., 118n
Noe, Raymond, 538n
Nolan, Johannah, 438n
Nordstrom, James, 506
Norrdewier, Thomas, 335n
Nourse, Hugh O., 282
Novack, Janet, 25, 27n
Novack, Robert, 439n
Novak, Thomas, 95n
Nowak, Glen, 94n
Nowatakhtar, Susan, 59
Nystrom, Paul, 194n

Ochtenstein, Donald R., 470n
O'Connell, Patricia, 603, 626n
O'Dell, Susan, 527
O'Donnell, Tom, 517
Oh, Sejo, 438n
Okoruwa, Ason A., 282
O'Leary, Sean, 544, 568n
Oliver, Richard L., 156n
Olsen, Janeen E., 427
Olshavsky, Richard, 156n, 597
Olson, Jerry C., 118n, 128, 143, 150, 154n
Olson, Paul, 335n
O'Malley, Lisa, 282
Omura, Glenn, 25
Ono, Yumiko, 156n
O'Reilly, Charles, 312n
O'Rourke, Lynn, 626n
Ortega, Bob, 176, 312n, 466
Ortmeyer, Gwen, 334, 427, 469, 470n
Ostrom, Amy, 597
Oswades, Ruth, 170
Ouchi, William, 312n
Owens, Jan, C43, C48
Oxenfeldt, Alfred, 27n
Ozzard, Janet, 439n

Pacelle, Mitchell, 238
Pacino, Al, 109
Packer, Arnold, 312n
Packer, Kerry, 575
Padgett, Daniel T., 469
Pagonis, William G., 318
Parasuraman, A., 64n, 568, 578, 580, 597, 598n
Park, Mary, 568
Parker, Donald, 539n
Parker, Penny, 617
Parker-Pope, Tara, 95n
Parrish, Jean, 401n
Parsons, William, 598n
Patterson, Gregory, 527
Patterson, Maurice, 282
Pearson, Bill, 372, 598n
Pellet, Jennifer, 95n, 539n
Pelter, James, 94n
Penney, James Cash, 303
Peppers, Don, 25, 189
Peracchio, Laura A., 117
Pereira, Joseph, 485
Perry, N., 313n
Personiek, Martin, 539n
Pessimier, Edgar D., 155n
Peter, J. Paul, 118n, 128, 143, 150, 154n
Peters, Thomas, 598n, 599n
Peterson, Robert A., 91, 94n, 117, 626, 627n
Pettijohn, Charles, 626n
Pettijohn, Linda, 626
Pfeffer, Jeffrey, 311
Phillips, Joanne, 179–180, 182–186, 196, 209–210, 213–214, 217, 221

Phillips, Joseph, 94n
Phillips, Lisa, 335
Pickard, Jane, 539n
Pierson, Cheryl, 591
Pinches, G.E., 229n
Pine, B. Joseph, 597n
Pirto, Rebecca, 157n
Piton, Francis, 154n
Pogoda, Dianne, 156n
Pol, Louis, 254, 282
Polegate, Rosemary, 132
Pomazal, Richard, 155n
Pope, Kyle, 27n
Porter, Jennifer, 64n
Porter, Michael E., 27n, 189, 194n, 282n, 575
Posner, James, 527
Powers, James T., 396, 401n
Prahalad, C.K., 193n, 194n
Predmore, Carolyn, 627n
Price, Linda, 502n
Price, Sol, 197
Pride, Nancy, 601
Pride, William, 194n
Prie, Linda, 155n
Pritchard, R.D., 538n
Pritchett, Lou, 418
Punj, Girish, 155n
Purdy Levaux, Janet, 587
Purk, Mary E., 469
Putler, Daniel S., 281

Quelch, John A., 95n, 427, 470n, 503n
Questrom, Alan, 54
Quinn, James Brian, 195n, 311

Radder, Laetile, 502
Rajendram, K.N., 469
Ramey, Joanna, 438n
Ramirez, A., 313n
Rankin, Ken, 471n
Rao, Akshay R., 471n
Rao, Ram C., 469
Raphael, Murray, 498, 598n
Rappaport, Alfred, 194n, 223, 229n
Rappoport, Carla, 179
Raucher, A., 27n
Rayport, Jeffrey, 91
Reda, Susan, 118n, 167, 192n, 193n, 312n, 335n, 408, 438n, 569n, 597
Redman, Mel, 193n
Redman, Russell, 502
Redwell, Sara, 306
Redwine, Ann, 599n
Reed, Dan, 305
Reed, Jennifer, 537n
Reed, O. Lee, 471n
Reese, Jennifer, 27n
Reese, Susan, 537
Reichheld, Fredrick, 599n

Reilly, W.J., 275, 282n
Rennie, W.R., 95n
Rentz, Joseph, 598n
Retiman, Valarie, 94n
Reynolds, Kristy, 626
Rice, Faye, 98, 439n
Richardson, Paul S., 427
Ricklefs, Roger, 369n, A27
Ridgeway, Nancy, 155n
Ries, Al, 527
Rigdon, Joan, 95n
Riggs, Joy, 538n
Rink, David, 438n
Rinne, Heikki J., 470n, 568n
Ritzer Ross, Julie, 562
Robbins, David, A41
Robbins, Gary, 313n, 335n, 357, 568n
Robbins, Sandie, 605
Roberts, Bob, 305
Roberts, Jenney, 438n
Robeson, James F., 391, 396, 401n
Robichaud, Robert R., 503n
Robinson, John, 117, 118n
Roca, Ruben A., 282
Rock, Dennis, 154n
Roddick, Anita, 478
Roebuck, Alvah, 73
Roehm, Harper A., 229n
Rogers, Dale S., 254, 269, 281, 282n, 283n, 335
Rogers, Martha, 25, 189
Rohwedder, Cacilie, 233
Rolfson, Chuck, 495
Ronkainen, Ilkka A., 326, 335n, 438n
Rose, Herman, 150
Rosenberg, Kenneth, A41
Rosenbloom, Bert, 192n
Ross, Ivan, 599n
Ross, John, 335n
Ross, Julie, 539n
Rossiter, John R., 568
Roth, P.L., 538n
Rothenberg, Marvin, 527
Rothschild, Michael, 494, 503n
Rothschild, R.L., 192n
Rothschild, William, 194n
Rudnitsky, Howard, 192n
Rushton, G., 283n
Russell, Cheryl, 117, 118n
Russell, George, 155n
Rust, Roland T., 228n, 282

St. James, Lynn, 476
Salmon, Walter J., 193n, 470n
Salmond, Deborah, 427, 438n
Samiee, Saeed, 189, 194n
Samli, A. Coskun, 502n
Sanders, Colonel, 15
Sanger, Carol, A8–A9
Saporito, Bill, 12, 312n
Satterwaite, Cecile, 600

Savvas, Jim D., 401n
Sawyer, Alan, 155n, 470n
Saxe, Robert, 626n
Scammon, Debra L., 95n
Scarpello, V., 539n
Schaaf, Dick, 599n, 626n
Schiller, Zachary, 470n
Schindler, Robert M., 470n
Schiro, Thomas J., 177, 194n
Schlesinger, Leonard, 300
Schmidt, F.L., 538n
Schmidt, Warren, 538n
Schmitt, Bernd, 193n
Schmitt, Neal, 537n, 538n
Schmittlein, David, 228n, 369
Schneider, Benjamin, 537n, 597
Schribowsky, John, 94n
Schultheis, Steve, A2
Schultz, David, 59, 195n
Schultz, Howard, 308
Schurr, Paul, 438n
Schwadel, Francine, 539n
Schwartz, Joe, 156n
Sears, Richard, 73
Seiders, Kathleen, 58
Selbert, Roger, 118n
Sele, Michael, 183
Self, David, 520
Sellers, Patricia, 12, 27n, 50, 312n, 599n
Sethuraman, Raj, 438n
Sewall, Murphy, 156n
Shamdasani, Prem, 369n
Shansby, J. Gary, 502n
Shao, Alan, 598n
Sharav, Itzhak, 439n
Sharma, Arun, 626
Sharma, Subhash, 228n, 281, 283n
Shaw, Deborah, 118n
Sheffet, Mary Jane, 95n
Sheppard, C. David, 626, 626n
Shermach, Kelly, 94n
Sherman, Elaine, 91
Shern, Stephanie S., 118n
Sherry, John F., 599n
Sheth, Jagdish, 154n, 155n
Shields, Grainne, 91
Shim, Soyean, 94n
Shirmeyer, Roslyn, 538n
Shoemaker, Robert W., 470n
Shore, Andrew, 470n
Shostack, G. Lynn, 597n
Shugan, Steven M., 439n
Simmons, Jim, 281, 282
Simone, John, 94n
Simonson, Alex, 193n
Simonson, Itamar, 470n
Simpson, Edwin, 537n
Simpson, Eithel, 193n
Sims, J., 65n

Singh, Jagdip, 156n, 598n
Sisler, Grovalynn, 312n
Sjkrova, Sandra, 64n
Skelly, Gerald, 154n
Skinner, Steven, 539n
Skolnik, Amy M., 177, 194n
Slesin, Suzanne, 153
Sloane, Leonard, 65n
Slocum, John, 312n
Slywatsky, Adrian, 192n, 308
Smart, Denise, 189, 193n
Smith, Brian, 538n
Smith, Brian R., A32, A40–A41
Smith, David, 415–416
Smith, Gerald, 193n, 311, 469
Smith, Janet, 502n
Smith, Kenard E., 255n, 282n
Smith, Mary, 150
Smith, Mickey, 539n
Smith, N. Craig, 469
Smith, Scott M., 27n, 155n
Smith, Stephen A., 369n, 502
Sneath, Julie, 150
Soderquist, Don, 312n
Solano-Mendez, Robert, 189, 193n
Solomon, Barbara, 54, 389
Solomon, Charlene, 537n, 539n
Solomon, Michael R., 150, 438n
Solomons, David, 223, 229n
Soper, Barlow, 626n
Spangenberg, Eric R., 568, 569n
Spector, Robert, 311
Speer, Tibbett, 617, 626
Spekman, Robert, 427, 438n
Spiggle, Susan, 156n
Spreng, Richard, 597
Spriggs, Mark T., 427
Srinivasan, Srini, 502
Staelin, Richard, 439n
Stalk, G., 194n
Stallworthy, Ernest, 626n
Stampfl, Ronald W., 27n, 369n
Stanfield Tetreault, Mary, 579
Stangenes, Sharon, 597n
Stank, Theodore P., 335
Starcke, Alice, 538n
Staten, Vince, 555, 568, 568n
Steidmann, Carl, 118n, 119n
Stein, Jay, 618
Steiner, G.A., 502n
Steinhauer, Jennifer, 218
Steinmetz, Greg, 598n
Stephens, Elvis, 537
Stern, Gabriella, 503n
Stern, Louis, 27n, 64n
Sternberg, Lawrence, 312n
Sternquist, Barbara, 194n
Stettner, Morey, 627n
Stewart, David, 369n, 627n
Stisser, Peter, 117, 119n

Stock, James R., 223, 229n, 335n, 368, 369n, 396, 401n, 470n
Stojack, Carrie, 626
Stone, Kenneth, 183
Strachan, George C., 199
Straughn, Katherine, 334
Sujan, Harish, 538n, 627n
Sujan, Mita, 538n, 598n, 627n
Sultan, Ralph, 195n
Sviokla, John, 91
Swamidass, Paul M., 427
Swan, John, 438n, 626n
Sweeney, Daniel J., 27n, 369n
Swinyard, William R., 27n, 503n, C43
Switzer, Gerald J., 396
Sykes, Debra, 119n
Symons, Allene, 297, 503n
Szeinbach, Cheryl, 539n
Szymanski, David, 627n

Tadlaqui, Ali, 503n
Tannenbaum, Robert, 538n
Tanner, Jeffery, 626n
Tanner, John, 607, 623, 624, 626
Tauber, Edward, 155n
Taylor, Albert, 626
Taylor, Alex, 6
Taylor, Bernard, 470n
Taylor, Charles G., 396
Taylor, M.S., 537n
Taylor, Valerie, 598n
Tayman, Jeff, 254, 282
Tedeschi, Mark, 57
Tedlow, Richard, 25
Teel, Jesse E., 470n
Tellis, Gerald J., 469, 471n
Terborg, James, 539n
Terza, Joseph V., 282
Thaler, Richard, 471n
Thiruk, Roy, 539n
Thisse, J.F., 281, 283n
Thomas, David, 15
Thomas, Melinda Lou, 15
Thomas, R. Roosevelt, 312n
Thompson, Ann Marie, 598n
Thompson, John S., 254, 273, 282, 282n
Thompson, Roger, 64n
Thorpe, Dayle, 193n, 598n
Thorton, Emily, 8
Tichey, Noel, 538n
Tillman, Joan, 571
Titus, Philip, 155n
Tom, Gail, 599n
Topol, Martin, 91, 194n, 311
Tordjman, Andre, 25
Tosh, Mark, 369n, 438n
Trachtenberg, Jeffrey A., 54, 438n
Trawick, I. Fred, 438n
Treadgold, Alan, 194n

Tse, David, 599n
Turcsik, Richard, 142
Turf, Barbara, 153, 361
Turley, L.W., 156n
Twomey, David, 539n

Ukens, Carol, 539n
Ulrich, David, 538n
Underhill, Paco, 117, 118n
Ungson, Gerardo, 539n
Urban, Glen, 155n
Urbany, Joel E., 154n, 155n, 469
Ury, William, 427, 439n

Valentin, Erhard, 150
van Breda, Michael, 229n, 439n
Van Der Wijst, Nico, 539n
Varadarajan, P. Rajan, 193n, 194n
Varaiya, Nikhil, 229n
Venkatesh, R., 469
Venkatraman, Meera, 193n
Verdi, Ellis, 470n
Verdisco, Robert, 193n
Verity, John, 95n
Villano, David, 599n
Vining, Aidan, 192n
Vollmers, Stacy, 156n
Vroom, V.H., 538n

Wagner, Janet, 368, 401n
Wahl, Michael, 155n
Walker, Bruce J., 65n
Walker, Chip, 150, 502n
Walkup, Carolyn, 27n
Walsh, Matt, 497
Walters, Rockney G., 470n
Walton, Sam, 12, 304
Wanamaker, John, 465, 571
Ward, Cheryl, 193n
Ward, James C., 568
Warshaw, Michael, 50
Watson, M., 538n
Wayne, Beverly, 64n
Wayne, Curtis, 64n
Weber, Thomas, 95n
Webster, Cynthia, 312n
Weeks, David, 229n

Weinberg, Bruce, 155n
Weiner, Steve, 598n
Weinglass, Leonard "Boogie," 218
Weinstein, Steve, 194n, 313n, 537n
Weishar, Joseph, 255n
Weiss, Michael J., 282
Weitz, Barton, 95n, 192n, 193n, 312n, 438n, 538n, 539n, 607, 623, 624, 626, 626n, 627n, C2, C10, C37, C40, C44,
Wells, Ken, 156n
Wensley, Robin, 27n, 192n, 194n, 195n
Werner, Manuel, 312n
Wernerfeldt, Birger, 156n
Wernerfelt, B., 598n
Werther, William, 193n
West, Diane, 481–483
West, Karen, 538n
West, Thomas L., A32, A40–A41
Westbrook, Robert A., 155n
Westegren, Jeffrey, 64n
Wexner, Leslie, 15
Whalen, Bruce, 154n
Whitefield, Mimi, 107
Whittelsey, Frances Cerra, 468
Whittler, Thomas, 539n
Widdows, Richard, 59
Wiesendanger, Betsy, 156n
Wilcox, James B., 439n
Wilkenson, I., 65n
Wilkes, Robert, 598n
Wilkie, Maxine, 569n
Wilkie, William L., 95n, 154n, 155n
Williams, Monci Jo, 626n
Williams, Robert H., 470n
Williams, Sandy, 552–553
Williams, Tina, 496–497
Wills, Gordon, 470n
Wilson, B.L., 282n
Wilson, James, 538n
Wilson, Marianne, 118n, 313n, 539n, 541
Wiman, Alan R., 470n
Winer, Russell, 189, 194n
Wines, Leslie, 189, 193n
Wirebach, John, 192n
Wisniewski, Kenneth, 470n
Witkin, Gary, 492, 503n

Witkowski, Terrence, 156n
Wolff, Florence, 627n
Wood, Rosemary, 626n
Wood, Stacy, 95n
Woods, Michael D., 229n
Woods, Robert, 189
Woodside, A.G., 65n, 155n
Woodward, Ginger, 537
Woolf, Brian, 498
Wortzel, Lawrence, 193n
Wotruba, Thomas, 537n
Writing, Julie, 57
Wu, Haw-Jan, 335
Wyer, Robert S., 438n
Wylie, David, 170

Xu, Xian Zhong, 194n

Yadav, Manjit S., 469
Yalch, Richard F., 568, 569n
Yale, Laura, 91
Yamaguchi, Mari, 69
Yamamoto, Yoshito, 156n
Yang, Catherine, 311, 312n
Yasai-Ardekani, Masoud, 194n
Yeh, Chyon-Hwa, 150
Yin, Tung, 527
Yoshihashi, Pauline, 199
Young, Cheri, 538n
Yovovich, B.G., 438n

Zaichowsky, Judith, 132
Zaleznik, A., 538n
Zeithaml, Valerie A., 59, 64n, 471n, 578, 580, 597, 598n
Zeleny, M., 401n
Zellner, Wendy, 193n
Zemke, Ron, 598n, 599n, 626n
Zhang, Janet, 194n
Zill, Nicholas, 117, 118n
Zimmer, Mary R., 193n
Zimmerman, Denise, 539n
Zinn, Laura, 27n
Zornitsky, Jeffery, 300
Zuber, Amy, 537
Zuilkoski, Heather, C7–C8, C52
Zusman, Pinhas, 439n

AAMCO, 48
AARP/Prudential, 71
Abercrombie & Fitch, 15, 53
Abraham & Strauss, 54
Ace Hardware, 53
Aetna Life & Casualty, 13
Ahold, 179
Air Canada, 326
Alamo, 48
Alberton, 475
Albertson's, 13
Aldus Manutius, 70
Alfred Dunhill, 249
Allied, 6, 54
Allstate, 13, 48
Amazon.com, 88, 89, 127
AMC, 48
America Online, 48
America West, 85
American Airlines, 48, 85, 324, 593
American Drug Stores, 38, 296
American Express, 48, 179, 588, 595
American Stores, 13, 34
Americo Group Inc., 331
Ames, 6
AMR (American Airlines), 13
Amy's Ice Cream, 591
Anderson Consulting, 224, 575
Ann Taylor, 38, 54, 111, 249, 260, 445
A&P, 4, 34, 92, 113, 179, 403, 407
Apollo Space Management System, 554
Arbor Drugs, 93
Arthur Treacher's Fish and Chips, A28
Associated Merchandising Corporation
    (AMC), 416
AT&T, 48, 71
AUCHAN, 92
Automobile Association, 71
AutoZone, 38, 93, 161, 162, A5
Aventura Shoe Store, 566
Avis, 48
Avon, 9, 75, 201, 605

B. Dalton Booksellers, 544
Baby Superstores, 44
Bally's, 48
Banana Republic, 111, 144, 361–363,
    403, 410, 413, 556
Bank of America, 48
Bargain Finder, 81–82
Barnes & Noble, 44, 88, 127, 161, 183
Barney's New York, 115
Bath & Body Works, 15
Bed, Bath & Beyond, 44, 330
Ben Franklin, 12

Benetton, 424
Bergstroms, 144
Best Buy, 4, 44, 93, 167, 214, 371, 574,
    576, C53–C55
Best Products, 6, 46
Bi-Lo, 179
Black & Decker, 325, 403, 417, 434
Blockbuster Video, 18, 19, 48, 49, 50, 93,
    96, 130, 176, 234, 544
Bloomingdale's, 19, 24, 54, 71, 86, 92,
    163, 165–166, 239, 243, 295, 301,
    342, 407, 547–548, 552, 572,
    C10–C11
Bob's Western Wear Store, 424
Body & Bath Works, 53
The Body Shop, 93, 103, 114, 477–478,
    604
Bolen's Hallmark Shop, 249
Bombay Co., 38
Bon Marche, 19, 61, 235, 295
Bon-Ton Stores, 92
Bonwit Teller, 54
Boomers!, 540–541
Borden, 464
Borders Book Store, C48
Borders Books and Music, 44, 53, 93,
    113, 127, 540
Boscov's Department Stores, 92, 562
Boucheron, 423
British Airways, 48
The Broadway, 54, 564
Brooks Brothers, 45, 54, 410
Budget, 48, 55
Bud's Warehouse Outlets, 45
Builder's Square, 43, 53, 165, 173
Bullock's, 14, 54
Burdines, 23, 24, 54, 163, 295, 513, 615
Burger King, 55, 261, 510
Burlington Coat Factory, 43, 93, 240,
    428
Burpee, 70

Cacique, 15, 53
Calvin Klein, 99, 101, 410
Calyx & Corolla, 170
Camelot Music, 105
Campbell Soup, 420
Campbell's, 8
Campeau Corporation, 54
CarMax, 6
Carnival, 141, 142
Carrefour, 92, 179
Carson Pirie Scott, 92, 371
Carson Wagonlit, 55
Carter Hawley-Hale, 6
Cartier, 422

Casual Man/Big & Tall, 93
Catalina Marketing, 497
Century 21, 48, 55
Chanel, 422, 461
Charming Shop, 38, 163
Chemlawn, 48, 205
Chess King, 218
Chicken Delight, A28
Chisolm Larsson Gallery, 66
Chuck E Cheese's Pizza, A28
Cigna, 13
Circle K, 29, 34
Circuit City, 4, 6, 41, 44, 83, 93, 130,
    167, 191, 214, 236, 289, 295, 478,
    610
Citibank, 48
Cityvision PLC, 176
Claritas Corporation, 266
Classic Creations, 183
Cleveland Clinic, C1
Coca-Cola, 405
Coldwell Banker, 48, 55, 172
Comcast Cable, 71
Community Pride Food Stores, 10
Comp-U-Card, 71
CompUSA, 44, 93, 238
CompuServe, 48
Computer City, 44
Computer Renaissance, 56
Comshare Retail, 371–373
Consolidated Stores, 109
Consumer Electronics, 44
Container Store, 93
Continental Cablevision, 71
Costco Warehouse; see Price/Costco
Costco Wholesale Corporation, 199
County Seat, 361–365
Cox Communication, 71
Craftsman, 403
Crate & Barrel, 112, 153, 240, 360, 361,
    410, 562–563
Cullum, 46
Curry Copy Center, A28
Custom Foot, 571
CVS, 38, 53, 93
Cybersmith, 78, 79

Daffy's, 445
Daiei, 8
Dairy Queen, 55
Days Inn, 48, 167, 308
Dayton Co., 235
Dayton Hudson, 13, 38, 40, 41, 53, 295,
    332, 414, 440, 444
De Beers, 423

Dean Witter, 48, 172
Dell Computer, 6, 7, 71
Deloitte & Touche, 224
Delta, 13, 48, C52–C53
Denny's, 55
Dillard's Department Store, 13, 92, 214, 249, 440, 444, 453, 485, C22
Direct Tire's, 573
Disc Go Round, 56
Disney; *see* Walt Disney
Disney World, 589
Dollar General, 109
Dollar Tree, 45
Domain, 98
Domino's Pizza, 15, 17, 140, 472, 588
Donegar Group, 415–416
Drug Emporium, 93
Dudley Products, 76
Dunkin' Donuts, 55

Eastern Airlines, 305
Eaton's, 92
Eatzi's, 5, 36, 113
Eckerd Drug, 13, 38, 53, 93, 493
Eddie Bauer, 69, 93, 306, 373, 414, 542
Edwards, 179
Electric Avenue, 28
Electric Boutique, 93
Electronic Boutique, 478
Elizabeth Arden, 182
Estee Lauder, 182, 344, 496
Evan Picone, 45, 619
Expedia, 86
Express, 93, 121, 565

Fabri-Centers of America, 44
Family Dollar, 168
Famous Footwear, 38
FAO Schwarz, 93, 240
Fashion Bug, 479
Father/Son Shoes, 60
Federal Express, 48, 170, 353
Federated Department Stores, 6, 13, 24, 38, 53, 54, 71, 92, 214, 243, 290, 293–296, 321, 406, 416, 566, A1, A9
Federated Merchandising, 416
Federated Specialty Store, 295
Federated Stores, Inc., 342
Ferguson's Lobster Pound, Ltd, 326
Ferrari Automobile Company, 423
Filene's, 54, 182, 456
Filene's Basement, 54
Fingerhut, 71, 329
First National Bank of Chicago, 592
Fisher-Price, 99
The Florida Store, 23, 24
Foley's, 243, 460, 518–519, 521, 523
Food Lion, 4, 13, 33, 34, 92, 179, 214
Foot Locker, 63, 93, 105, 249, 373
Ford Motor, 115

F&R Lazarus, 54
Fred Meyers, 47, 92
Frederick Atkins Inc., 416
Fresh Farm, 496
Fuller Brush, 76
Fuller's, C30–C31

Galeries Lafayette, 179
The Gap, 6, 8, 10, 15, 38, 93, 109, 121, 144, 151, 163–164, 166, 171–172, 214, 218, 230, 238, 244–245, 290, 292, 295–296, 342, 358–359, 371, 403, 408, 410, 414, 458–459, 461, 491, 521, 523, 556, C12–C13
GapKids, 15, 171, 191
Gateway 2000, 71
GEICO, 71
Geldof Chocolatier, 69
General Foods, 420
General Motors, 7, 327
General Nutrition Alive, 4, 5, 144
Genuardi's Family Market, 100
Georgio Armani, 410
Giant Foods, 179, 310
Gifts To Go, 179–185, 196, 201, 209, 214–217
Givenchy, 422, 423
GNC, 55
Godiva Chocolates, 86
Gold Circle, 54
Gold's Gym, 48, 362
Goldsmith's, 54, 290, 293, 295
Goodwill, 56
Gooseberry Patch, 17, 72
Gottschalks, 92
Gourmet To Go, 113
Goya Foods, 106
Grand Union, 6
Gray Goods, Inc., 422
Great American & Pacific Tea Company, 13
The Great Atlantic & Pacific Tea Company (A&P), 330
Grow Biz International, 56, 109
Guess? Inc., 405, 410
Gymboree, 48, 161, 162

Haagen-Dazs, 176
Hagger, 123
Hanes, 319–324
Hannaford, 92
Harley-Davidson, 410
Harrod's, 80, 86
Harry and David, 70
Harry Rosen, 168
Harry's Video, 18
Hartz Mountain, 424
Harwyns, 60
Haverty Furniture, 38
HCA, 48
H.E. Butt, 92

HealthSouth, 213
Hechinger, 43, 594
Heileg-Meyers, 38
Helzberg Diamonds, 38
Henri Bendel, 15, 53
Hermanos, 135
Hertz, 48
Holiday Inn, 55, 167, 592
Home Depot, 6, 8–9, 13, 43, 94, 110, 138, 165, 167, 182–183, 236, 245–246, 284–285, 290–291, 302, 305, 308, 441, 443, 460, 505, 511, 619
Home Shopping Network, 9, 74, 75, 206, C5–C6
Horne's, 54
H&R Block, 48
Hudson's, 240
Hudson's Bay Company, 41, 67
Humana, 48
Humpty Dumpty, 574
Hutch Corporation, C24–C26
Hyatt, 48, 138
Hypermart*USA, 46

Ian's, C46–C47
IBM, 115, 123, 383, 405
IKEA, 38, 44, 138, 140, 178, 550–551, 574, 575
Independent Groceries Alliance (IGA), 53, 92
InfoScan, 359, 462
Intimate Brands, 38, 53

James River, 417
Japan Airlines, 326
Jazzercise, 48, 55
JCPenney, 5, 10, 12–13, 21–22, 28, 38, 41, 53, 60–61, 69–71, 78, 87, 92, 105–106, 109, 114–115, 136–137, 141–142, 144, 147–148, 163–164, 166, 172, 176, 182, 184, 249, 298–299, 302–303, 305, 310, 318, 361, 374, 407–408, 411, 414, 417–418, 444, 460, 476, 488, 491, 546, 581, 590, 605, 624, A4, A8
Jenny Craig, 48
Jerry Lewis Theaters, A28
Jiffy Lube, 47, 48, 124, 164
Johnson & Johnson (J&J), 419
Jordan Marsh, 54
Joske's, 54
J. Sainsbury, 92

Kalame Jewelry Store, 197–199
Kay-Bee Toy Stores, 53, 371
Kellogg, 8, 354, 403
KFC, 15, 55, 576
Kids "R" Us, 191, 407
Kimberly-Clark, 444
Kindercare, 48
King Soopers, 407
Kinney Shoe Store, 93, 249

Kinney's, 565
K&K True Value Hardware, 183
Kmart, 9, 13, 19, 28, 34–35, 41, 47, 53–54, 61, 63, 92, 103, 105, 109, 113, 125, 128, 142, 163, 165–166, 168, 173, 176, 214, 224, 247, 251, 389, 407–408, 419, 421, 433, 440, 444–445, 474, 490, 549, 592
Kou, 8
Kraft, 8
Kraft General Foods, 417
Kroger Company, 13, 34, 214, 268, 295, 406, 484, 485, 548

La Madeline Bakery, 197, 199
The Lab, C7–C8
Land's End, 5, 15, 16, 69, 71, 72, 78, 81, 94, 163, 202, 214, 585, 619
Lane Bryant, 15, 53, 142, 477
Langleys, 233
LaQuinta, 167
Lawson Sportswear, C32–C34
Lazarus Department Stores, 19, 144, 290, 293, 295, 342
Lechmere, 100
LensCrafter, 38, 48, 93
Leon's Fashions, 600
Lerner Shops, 15, 53
Lever Brothers, 423
Levi Strauss, 4, 15, 84, 88, 98, 101, 114, 116, 341, 344, 350–351, 355–366, 403, 405, 408, 410, 417–418, 421, 422, 424, 460, C51–C52
Levitz, 38
Liberty House, 92
The Limited, 6, 10, 13, 15, 38, 53, 142, 163, 165–166, 172, 186, 214, 244–245, 249, 295, 325, 406–407, 410, 465, 524, 565–566
Limited Express, 15, 142, 407
Limited Two, 15
Lindy's Bridal Shoppe, C14–C16
Linen's N Things, 44
Little Caesar's, 234, 472
Liz Claiborne, 46, 121, 127, 344, 405, 414, 453, 616, 619
L.L. Bean, 9, 66, 69, 72, 78, 94, 113, 126, 130, 139, 373, 572, 583
Loehmann's, 62, 163, 166, 428, 440
Loews/Sony, 48
Long John Silver's, 55
Longs Drug Store, 297
Lord & Taylor, 249, 422, 427–432, 460, 491
Lowe's 9, 13, 43, 94, 309
Lufthansa, 85
Lums, A28

McCormick, 8
McDonald's, 4, 12, 13, 50, 55, 100, 169, 176, 179, 251, 261, 272, 476, 572, 574, 592, A28

McFaddens Department Store, C37–C38
MacFrugal's, 45
McGraw-Hill, 134
McKinsey & Co, 233
Macy's, 6, 9–10, 14, 18–19, 24, 28, 53–54, 92, 115, 121–122, 127, 129, 163, 182, 239, 295, 360, 407, 460, 475, 545
Mail Boxes Etc., 55
Makro, 179
Manco, 344
Mantle Men-Namath Girls, A28
Marks & Spencer, 92
Marriott, 13, 48, 141, 143, 205, 306, 509, 572, 584, 585, 586, 593, C31–C32
Mars, 341
Marsh Supermarkets, 554
Marshall Field's, 53, 92, 460, 550, 591
Marshall's, 43, 53, 123, 163, 166, 236, 428, 440, 456, 485
Martin Bayer Associates, 416
Mary Kay Corporation, 6, 69, 111
Mast Industries, 172
MasterCard, 48
Mattel, 99
May Company, 54, 92
May Department Store, 13, 38, 104, 214, 243, 416, 422, 463
May Merchandising, 416
MCA, 242
MCI, 48, 71
Media Play, 93
Medicine Shoppe, 55
Meijer, 47, 94
Mel's Jewelry Store, 422
Melville, 13, 53, 54
Men's Warehouse, 115
Mercantile Stores, 92
Merrill Lynch, 48, 146
Merry Maids, 55
Merry-Go-Round, 218
Mervyn's, 40, 53, 109, 163, 359, 440
Metro-Day, C47–C48
Metropolitan Life Insurance, 13
Mi Amore Pizza & Pasta, 472–473
Michaels, 9, 44, 93, C35–C36
Micro Warehouse, 71
Microsoft, 260
Midas, 48, 55
Miller's, 54
Mini Maid, 9, 48
Minyard, 142
Mobil, 425
Montgomery Ward, 112, 474
Morgan Fitzgerald, 601
Mothers Work Inc., 382
Motorola, 352
Mr. CB's Bait & Tackle, 183
Mr. I's Optical Boutique, 246–247, 259–260, 264–271

Mrs. Fields Cookies, 542
Music Go Round, 56
Musicland, 38
Muzak, 565

Nationwide Life, 13
The Nature Company, 93, 145, 478
NCNB, 48, 86
Neiman Marcus, 18, 40, 86, 92, 108, 112–113, 151, 163, 165–167, 176, 184, 224, 240, 244, 249, 322, 371, 407, 416, 442, 453, 456, 460, 478, 491, 498–499, 553, 582, C45–C46
New Balance Athletic Shoe Co., 464
New York Life, 13
Nike, 410
NikeTown, 5, 79, 550, C2–C3
Noah's Bagels, 47
Nordstrom, 19, 41, 46, 88, 92, 112, 138, 141, 161, 165–166, 169, 184, 197–198, 200–211, 213–214, 216, 222, 239–240, 244, 298–299, 304, 360, 407, 440, 478, 506, 552, 572, 591–592, 617
Northwest Airlines, 13
Northwest Mutual Life, 13
N.W. Ayer, 488

Odd Lots/Big Lots, 45
Office Depot, 13, 42, 44, 53, 83, 182, 236, 441, 561
OfficeMax, 44, 53, 93, 111, 113, 180, 182
Olathe Lanes East, C49–C51
Old Navy Clothing Company, 15, 109, 238, C12–C13
Olive Garden, 52
Once Upon A Child, 56
Orvis, 70
Osco, 93
Otto Versand, 71

Pace Warehouse, 173
Palm Beach, 45
Pan Am, 305
Paris Miki, 570, 573
Parisian, 40, 301, 586, 591, 619
Patagonia, 9, 16, 17, 69, 72, 94, 113
Patek Philippe, 422
Payless, 479
Payless Cashways, 43, 94
Payless Shoe Source, 38, 234, 238
Peapod, C6–C7
Pearle Vision, 38, 48
Pegman, 556
Peoples Jewelry, 272
Pep Boys, 38, 93, 164, 167, 586
PepsiCo, 13, 410
Pet Food Giant, 53
Petco, 238
PETsMART, 44, 53, 70, 71, 93, 236, 511

Petstuff, 53
Pier 1 Imports, 38, 93, 371, 486, 520, 582
Pizza Hut, 48, 55, 100, 176, 472, 586
Play It Again Sports, 9, 56
Pockets Men's Store, 415
Potomac Mills, 5
Price Breakers, 416
Price/Costco, 13, 34, 43, 62, 94, 197, 199–211, 213, 216, 222, 236, 246, 289, 440
Primrose Fashions, 449
Proctor & Gamble, 13, 403, 417, 418, 444, 484, 487
Professional Salon Concepts, 510
Prudential Insurance of America, 13
Publix Supermarkets, 13, 106, 107, 113, 295, 496

QVC, 74, 75

RaceTrac, 92
Rackes Direct, 167
Radio Shack, 93, 238
Rainforest Cafe, C1–C2
Ralph Lauren, 45, 126, 127, 240, 344, 410
Ralph's, 54, 92
Rampage, 37
Rand McNally, 240
Reader's Digest, 71
Recreational Equipment Inc. (REI), 57, 373
Redner's Warehouse Markets, 535
Reebok, 45
REI, 57, 373
Revco, 6, 38, 93
Rib Tech, 515
Rich's, 54, 163, 290–296, 298, 300
Rike's, 54
Rite Aid, 38, 93, 585
Ritz-Carlton, 51, 587
RJR Nabisco, 13
R.L. Polk and Company, 269
Rocky Mountain Chocolate Factory, 39
Rolex, 422
Roots, 93
Ross Stores, 43, 93, 163
Roto-Rooter, 48
Royal Cashmere, 66
Rubbermaid, 384–385, 490
Ryder, 48

Safeway, 9, 13, 34, 53, 96, 214, 224, 341, 407, 479–480
Sainsbury, 179
Saks Fifth Avenue, 45, 75, 112, 114–115, 128, 163, 166, 231, 240, 324, 332, 407–408, 456, 460, 571–572
Salvation Army, 56
Sam's Warehouse Club, 8, 34, 43, 62, 94, 440

Sam's Wholesale Club, 246
Save-on Drugs, 93
Savoy Hotel, 575
Sears, 13, 22, 29, 38, 41, 61, 72–73, 88, 92, 115, 141, 165–167, 173, 184, 239, 295, 306, 317–319, 321–323, 403, 407–408, 460, 476, 519, 527, 582, 611, C13–C14
Service Merchandise, 28, 46, 214, 328, 411, 492
7-Eleven, 4, 13, 29, 34, 55, 92, 135, 136, 231, 259, 478
Sharper Image, 102, 145
Shaw's, 4, 179
Sheraton, 48
Sherwin-Williams, 371
Shillito's, 54
Shop Rite, 113
Shopko, 517
Showscan Corp., 242
Singapore Airways, 48
Six Flags, 48
Smith & Hawken, 70, 595
Sony, 410, 420
South Gate West, 486
Southland, 13
Southwest Airlines, 304–305
Spalding Sports Worldwide, 406
Speakeasy Cafe, 603
Spiegel, 71, 105, 163, 214
The Spoke, 412
Sporting Dog Specialty, 70, 71
Sports and Recreation, 44
Sports Authority, 44, 53, 63, 93, 173, 236, 245
The Sportsman's Wife, 243
Sprint, 48
SRI International, 145, 146
Stan's Shirts, C43
Staples, 13, 44, 53, 93, 182
Star Hardware, C39–C41
Starbucks, 47, 161, 169, 170, 307, 308, 410
State Farm, 13, 48
Stein Mart, 163, 416, 618
Stephanie's Boutique, C23–C24
Sterling Jewelers, 38
Stern's, 54, 295
Stop & Shop, 4, 179
The Strand, 619
Strategic Weather Services, 357
Structures, 15, 53, 565
Subway, 55
Sulka, 109
Sunglass Hut, 38
Super Kmart centers, 47
Susie's Casuals, C36–C37

Taco Bell, 47, 55, 257, 300
Talbots, 111, 161–163, 171, 173, 330, 407

Target, 41, 53, 61, 92, 109, 113, 115, 144, 163, 166, 236, 298, 389, 408, 440, 509, 545, 573, 576
Tele-Communications, 71
Tengelmann, 179
Tesco, 92
Texaco, 425
Texas Instruments, 83
TGI Friday's, 48, 176
This End Up, 53
Thrifty, 38
Thrifty Gifts, 214–217
TIAA, 13
Tiffany & Co, 38, 201, 214
Tiffany's, 410, 449
Time Warner, 13, 71, 420
T.J. Maxx, 43, 165, 166, 240, 290, 428, 440, 456, 485, 510
TJX, 54, 485
Tommy Hilfiger, 427–432
Tops, 179
Toshiba, 83
Tower Records, 38
Toys "R" Us, 6, 12–13, 20, 30–32, 42, 44, 63, 93, 100, 105, 171–172, 174, 176, 183, 230, 233, 236, 242, 245–246, 259–260, 302, 309, 325, 342, 362, 441, 446, 448, 543, 589–590, C11–C12
Trader Joe's, 92, 477
Travelosity, 85
Tuesday Morning, 93

UAL (United Airlines), 13, 161
U-Haul, 48
United Parcel Services of America, Inc. (UPS), 48, 353
United Services, 71
Universal, 48
Universal Studios, 48
UPS, 48, 353
Uptons, 40
Urban Decision Systems, 261, 264, 359
Urban Outfitters, C42–C43
U.S. Postal Service, 48
USAA, 13, 70, 586–587
USAirways, 13, 85

Van Heusen, 45
Viacom, 13, 50
Victoria's Secret, 15, 53, 371
Virgin Sound, 406
Virtual Vineyards, C3–C5
VISA, 48
Vision, 406
Von Maur, 258
Vons Companies Inc., 214

Walgreens, 13, 38, 47, 93, 96–97, 234, 491

Wal-Mart, 4–6, 9, 12–13, 18–20, 28, 30–32, 34–35, 41–43, 45–47, 50, 53, 61, 63, 68, 78, 86–87, 92, 109, 112–114, 130, 163, 166, 168, 172, 175–176, 179, 183–184, 211, 214, 233, 238, 242, 251, 257–258, 261, 286, 298, 302–305, 315–316, 320, 331–333, 337, 342, 406–408, 414, 417, 433, 440–441, 443–445, 455, 463–466, 478, 511, 531, 576–577, A1–A2
Wal-Mart Supercenters, 47
Walt Disney, 13, 48, 93, 354, 514, 565, 572–573, 590

Warnaco, 45
Warner Brothers, 5, 93, 565
Warner Brothers Consumer Products, 406
Warner Brothers Interactive Entertainment, 406
WBCP, 406
Wegman's Food Market, 37, 92, 113
Weight Watchers, 48
Weinstock's, 582
Wendy's International, 15, 48
Western Auto, 38, 93
Western States Business Consultants, A26

Westin, 176
Whole Foods Market, 92
Wickes Lumber, 94
Williams Sonoma, 108, 619
Wilson's, 53
Winn-Dixie, 13, 34, 407, 555, C22–C23
Woodward and Lothrop, 166
Woolworth, 13, 20
W.S. Babcock, 38

Young & Rubicam, 15

Zales, 6, 38, 172, 371, 461

ABC analysis, 390–391
Accessibility
    market segmentation and, 143
    site evaluation and, 247–248
Accordion theory, 62–63
Accountability, 220
Accounts payable, 210
Accounts receivable, 204–205, 215
Accrued liabilities, 210
Actionability, market segmentation and, 142
Activity-based costing, 224–228
Adaptive selling, 622–625
Adjacent departments, 553–554
Administrative management, 286–288, 293–294
Advanced shipping notice (AWN), 328
Advertising; see also Promotion programs
    agencies, use of, 489
    allowances, 44, 429
    budget for, C43
    comparative price, 465–466
    cooperative, 429, 487–490
    defined, 474
    direct mail, 491–492, C45
    direct-response, 74
    frequency of, 495
    image, 487–488
    local markets, 489
    magazines, 491
    media selection factors, 493–495
    newspapers, 490–491, C44–C45
    outdoor, 493
    radio, 492, C45
    shopping guides, 493
    television, 493, C45
    timing, 495
    yellow pages, 493
Advertising plans, C44–C45
Affinity marketing, 139
Affordable method, 483–484
African-Americans, 105, 140–141
Age Discrimination and Employment Act, 528
Age distribution demographics, 97–104
Allocation
    merchandise, 387–389
    promotion budget, 485–486
    space, 227–228, 551–558
Altruism, 305
Americans with Disabilities Act (ADA), 528, 550–551
Analog approach, to measure sales potential, 268–271
Anticipation discounts, 436–437

Arthur, merchandise management system, 371–373, 379–380
Artificial barriers to location selection, 247
Asia, 178
Asian-Americans, 106–108
Assets
    current, 204–208
    defined, 203
    fixed, 208, 216
    turnover of, 197–199, 203–204, 209–210, 216–217, 350
Assortment plan, 339, 365–367, 389
Assortment planning, 8–9, 338–369
    backup stock, 339, 364–365, 385
    category management, 339–344
    classification system, 341–344
    corporate philosophy and, 363
    improvement of, 315–316, C39–C41
    product availability, 315, 332, 361–365, 385
    reduction of, C35–C36
    sales forecasting; see Sales forecasting
    service retailers, 362
    space and, 363
    variety and assortment, 30–32, 361–363, C42–C43
Atmospherics, 562–566
Attitude models, multiattribute, 130–134, C9–C10
Attractiveness factors, used to choose location, 260–261
Authority, assigned to employees, 288–289, 300–301
Autocratic management style, 517
Automated selling, 113
Availability, of products, 315, 332, 361–365, 385

Baby boomers, 97–103
Backup stock, 339, 364–365, 385
Backward integration, 172
Bait-and-switch tactics, 466–467
Balance sheets, 203–211, 215–216, C22
Balancing careers and families, 306–307, C14–C16
Bar coding, 319, 321, 323
Bargaining power, of vendors, 182–183
Barriers, site evaluation and, 247
Barriers to entry into the retail market, 182
Base stock, 364
Basic merchandise, 355
Basic stock list, 384–385
Basic stock method, 400
Benefit, of purchase, 606–607
Benefit segmentation, 147

Benefits/price effect, 461
Big box food retailers, 34–35
Billboard advertising, 493
Bonuses, 302, 526–527
Bottom-up planning, 219
Boutique layout, 546–547
Boutiques, 546
Box stores, 34
Brands
    choice of, 402–403
    generic, 409
    licensed, 405–406
    loyalty to, 123
    manufacturer, 403–405
    national, 403–405
    private label, 22, 41, 186, 224, 404, 406–409, 460
    store, 406–409
Breadth of merchandise, 30–32, 361–363
Break-even analysis, 458–460, C43
Breaking bulk shipments, 9
Breaking sizes, 363
Bribery, commercial, 420–421
Budgeting
    advertising, C43
    affordable method, 483–484
    allocation of, 485–486
    competitive parity method, 484
    marginal analysis method, 481–482, 551–552
    merchandise budget plan, 370–379, C37–C38
    objective-and-task method, 482–483
    percentage-of-sales method, 483–484
    rule-of-thumb methods, 483–484
Buffer stock, 364–365, 385
Building codes, store locations and, 252
Bulk fixtures, 560–561
Bulk of stock area, 549
Bulk shipments, breaking, 9
Business climate, as a location factor, 260–261
Business failure, reasons for, A15
Business plan, for new businesses, A18–A24
Buyer(s)
    career as a, A1–A3, A11
    category managers, 340–341
    coordination with store management, 297–299
    responsibilities of, 291–292, 337
Buying behavior; see Customer buying behavior
Buying decisions; see Customer buying behavior

Buying merchandise; *see* Merchandise, purchase of
Buying Power Index (BPI), 261, 264, 280, 359
Buying process, 124–137
  defined, 124
  evaluation of alternatives, 130–136, C9–C10
  information search, 129–130
  need recognition, 125–128
  postpurchase evaluation, 137, 581–582
  purchase of goods/services, 136–137
  stages of the, 125
Buying signals, 612–613
Buying situation market segmentation, 146–147
Buying system(s), 370–401; *see also* Inventory management
  allocation of merchandise, 387–389
  fashion merchandise, 371–382
  merchandise budget plan, 370–379, C37–C38
  open-to-buy, 379–382, C37
  reordering system, 386–387
  staple merchandise, 383–387
Bylined articles, as a publicity tool, 499

Capacity fixtures, 560–561
Careers, retail, A0–A14
  advancement, A8
  common questions, A10–A11
  compensation and benefits, A5–A7
  interview preparation, A11–A14
  job security, A7
  opportunities, A0–A5, 14–15, 310
  responsibility, A7
  skills needed, A8–A10
  women and, A8–A9, C14–C16
  working conditions, A7
Carrying costs, of inventory, 9, 43, 225, 412
Carts, 242–243
Cash, as an asset, 207
Cash discounts, 434–436
Catalog retailing/sales, 69–73, 113, 499
Catalog showroom, 46
Categories, of merchandise, 343–344
Category, defined, 339, 343
Category captain, 341
Category killers, 42, 63, 173–176
Category life cycles, 351–355
Category management, 339–344
Category managers, 340–341
Category specialist
  advantages of, 42, 46, 48, 259
  location strategies of, 245–246
  types of, 42–44
CBDs, 231–232, 243–244
CD ROM catalogs, 73
Census Bureau data, as an information source, 261–263, 265

Census of Retail Trade, 29, 267
Central business districts (CBDs), 231–232, 243–244
Central place theory, 276–277
Centralization, of buying activities, 21–22, 295–299
Chain discounts, 433
Chain stores, allocation of merchandise, 387–389
Child care assistance, 306
China, retail opportunities, 178–179, C16–C21
Christaller Central Place Theory, 276–277
Classification of merchandise, 341–344
Classification of retailers, 29–30
Closeout retailers, 45
Cocooning, 115
Color, store atmosphere and, 564–565
Color presentation, 559
Combination stores, 34
Commercial bribery, 420–421
Commission, on sales, 302, 526, 592, C46–C47
Common goals, shared with vendors, 419
Common stock, 211
Communication; *see also* Advertising; Promotion programs
  comparison of methods, 475–476
  improving, 297–298
  integrated marketing, 476–477
  nonverbal, 622–623
  objectives, 479–480
  paid impersonal, 474, 476
  paid personal, 475–476
  unpaid impersonal, 475–476
  unpaid personal, 475–476
  with vendors, importance of good, 419
  visual, 562–564
  word of mouth, 475–476
Communications gap, 580, 592–593
Community centers, 236
Community service, 97, 100, 113–114
Comparative price advertising, 465–466
Comparison shopping, 59–60, 83
Compatibility, of fashion, 153
Compensation, 523–528
  bonuses, 302, 526–527
  commissions, 302, 526, 592, C46–C47
  design of plans, 527–528
  drawing accounts, 526
  of executives, A5–A7
  incentives plan, 302–303, 526–527, 592
  legal issues, 529
  quotas, 526–527
  stock ownership, 285, 302–303
  straight salary, 525–526
Competition, 17–19
  competitive factors, 182–183
  in food retailing, 35–36

Competition—*Cont.*
  intertype, 18
  intratype, 17
  measuring, 267–268
  rivalry, 183
  scale economics, 182
  shopping the, 360
Competitive advantage
  customer service and, 166, 570–573
  gaining, 164–170, 316
  multiple sources of, 169–170
  store location and, 18, 167, 230, 261
  strategic opportunities and, 173
Competitive parity method, 484
Competitive position matrix, 186–187, 190–192
Complaints, 583–584, 593–596, 616
Complexity, of fashion, 153
Complimentary merchandise, 363
Composite approach, to market segmentation, 147
Computerized systems; *see also* Interactive home shopping; Internet
  Arthur merchandise management system, 371–373, 379–380
  automated selling, 113
  customer service and, 586–587
  databased retailing, 166, 168, 314, 329–331, 472, 491–492
  for distribution/transportation, 5, 322
  electronic data interchange, 168, 316, 328, 331, 333
  electronic kiosks, 113, 561–562, 574, C53–C55
  online services as a source of information, 263
  quick response systems, 314, 322, 331–333, 349, 413, C32–C34
  virtual reality, 540, 556
  voice recognition technology, 320
Conflicting customer needs, 127
Conflicts, 590–591
Consideration set, 135
Consignment, of goods, 178
Consistency, of retail mix, 167
Consumer cooperatives, 56–57
Consumer Goods Pricing Act, 464
Consumer panel data, 463
Consumer trends, 19, 113–116
Contests, 496, 525, 590
Contracts
  franchise, A33–A34
  leasing, 251
  terms and conditions of, 403, 432–437, 465
  tying, 424
Contribution margin, 390
Convenience stores, 29, 35–36
Conventional supermarkets, 33–34; *see also* Supermarkets

Converse's Breaking Point Model, 276
Cooperative advertising, 429, 487–490
Cooperative buying groups
  consumer, 56–57
  retail, 52–53
Cooperative/associated office, 416
Corporate culture, 303–305
Corporate retail chains, 53–54
Cost(s)
  capital, 225, 412
  controlling, 530–531
  cost per thousand measure (CPM), 494
  customer service, 575–576
  distribution, 315–316
  fixed, 458
  holding/carrying inventory, 9, 43, 225, 412
  international sourcing, 409–413
  labor, 40, 285, 530
  logistics, 332–333
  merchandise, 83–84
  operating costs, 169, 201–202, 350–351
  publicity, 476
  transportation, 9, 351, 413, 428
  variable, 458
  variety and assortment, 31–32
Cost oriented pricing method, 449–459
Cost per thousand (CPM) measure, 494
Council of Logistics Management, 328
Counterfeit merchandise, 421–422
Country risk assessment, 175
Country-of-origin, 410–411
Coupons, 329, 445–446, 496–497
Coverage, of advertising, 493
Credible commitments, 419
Credit cards, 139, C45–C46
Cross-docking, 316, 321, 331
Cross-selling, 171
Cross-shopping, 127–128
Culture, customer buying behavior and, 140–141
Culture, organizational, 303–305
Cumulative attraction, principle of, 249
Cumulative reach, 494
Currency fluctuations, 411
Current assets, 204–208
Current liabilities, 210
Customer allowances, 201
Customer buying behavior, 120–157
  attitude model, 130–134, C9–C10
  buying process; see Buying process
  buying signals, 612–613
  cocooning, 115
  culture and, 140–141
  decision making process, 120–124, C9–C10
    factors affecting, 137–141
  toward fashion, 150–154
  implications for retailers, 134–136
  market segmentation, 141–148

Customer buying behavior—Cont.
  performance and, 131–133, 135–136
  price sensitivity factors, 460–461
  reservations and, 608–611
  risks and, 121–122
Customer information, obtaining, 359–360, 581–584, 605–606
Customer interviews, 582
Customer loyalty, 123–124, 165–167, 405, C45–C46
Customer returns, 201, 576, 583, 590
Customer service, 570–599
  above-and-beyond, 617
  competitive advantage and, 166, 570–573
  complaints, 583–584, 593–596, 616
  conflict reduction, 590–591
  costs of, 575–576
  customization, 570–574, C51–C52
  empowerment, 112, 301–302, 573–574, 591–592, C31–C32
  evaluation of quality, 576–579
  examples of good, 198, C31–C32
  expectations, 576–578, 593
  Gaps model; see Gaps customer service model
  goal setting, 587–588
  goodwill, building, 614–615
  improvement of, 112, 585–587
  intangibility, 572
  international customers and, C10–C11
  layoffs, impact on, C52–C53
  market research and, 581–584
  measuring service performance, 589
  perceptions, 578–579
  personalized, 112, 127, C10, C31–C32
  preferred customers, 519, C45–C46
  quality commitment, 585
  self-service, 41–42, 574–575
  service recovery, 593–596
  services provided as a, 570–571, 577
  standardization, 572, 574
  technology, use of, 586–587
Customer spotting, 268–270
Customization, of service, 570–574, C51–C52
Cycle stock, 364–365
Cyclical theories, of retail evolution, 61–63

Data warehouse, 166, 168, 328
Databased retailing, 166, 168, 314, 329–331, 472, 491–492
Dating (cash discounts), 435–436
Deal periods, 442
Dealing agreements, exclusive, 424
Debt financing, A25–A26
Decennial Census of the United States, 261–265, 280
Decentralization of buying activities, 22, 296–299

Decision-making process, 17–24, 120–124
Decline in acceptance and obsolescence, in fashion, 154
Delivery gap, 580, 589–592
Delivery terms, negotiation of, 429
Demalling, 238
Demand
  deseasonalized, 386
  forecasting of, 264
  measurement of, 261–265
Demand/destination areas, 553
Demand-oriented pricing method, 449, 460–463
Democratic management style, 517
Demographic data vendors, 264–267
Demographic market segmentation, 144–145
Demographics, 96–113
  age distribution, 97–104
  baby boomers, 97–103
  changes in values, 113–116
  defined, 97
  ethnic diversity and, 104–107, 285, 307–310
  Generation X, 97, 100–101, 603, C7–C8
  Generation Y, 98–100
  generational cohorts, 97–104
  household managers, 110–111
  income distribution and, 107–110
  market segmentation by, 144–145
  older population, 96, 103–104
  store location and, 260, 264–267
  time-poor society, 111–113
  Women's market, 110–111
Department stores
  location strategies, 243–244
  organizational structure, 290–295
  promotional, 40
  types of, 38–41
Departments
  adjacent, 553–554
  demand/destination areas, 553
  leased, 39
  location of, 552–555
Depreciation, 208
Depth interview, 359
Depth of merchandise, 30–32, 361–363
Deseasonalized demand, 386
Destination areas, 553
Destination stores, 246, 259–260
Dialectic process, 63
Difficult comparison effect, 460
Direct mail
  advertising, 491–492, C45
  retailing, 69–73
Direct product profitability (DPP), 224
Direct selling/retailing, 67–68, 75–76
Direct-response advertising, 74
Disabled, designing stores for, 550–551

Disabled workers, use of, 309
Discount stores, 35, 41–42
Discounts
    anticipation, 436–437
    cash, 434–436
    chain, 433
    employee, 375
    functional, 432–433, 463
    quantity, 433–434, 463
    seasonal, 434
    trade, 432–433, 463
Discrimination, 528–529
Disintermediation, 89–90
Dispatchers, 320
Display areas, 547–550, 560–561, C48–C49
Distribution centers, 319–322, 325–327
Distribution system(s), 314–335; see also Logistics system(s)
    channel, 7–10
    cost of, 315–316
    cross-docking, 316, 321, 331
    distribution centers, 319–322, 325–327
    dual, 424–425
    efficiency of, 89
    flow of information, 328
    intensity, 352–353
    Japanese system, 8, 178
    point-of-sale data, 21, 322, 331, 349
    strategic advantages from, 168–170
    U.S. system, 8
Distributive fairness, 594
Diversification, as a growth strategy, 172–173
Diversity, 104–107, 285, 307–310
Diverted merchandise, 421–423
Drawing accounts, 526
Dress-down fashion, 115
Drug stores, 38
Drug testing, 511, 529, 535
Dual distribution, 424–425
Duty, 411

EDI, 168, 316, 328, 331, 333
EDLP, 33–34, 441–445
EEOC, 528
Efficient consumer response (ECR), 331
80–20 principle, 390–391
Electronic agents, 129
Electronic article surveillance (EAS) systems, 534
Electronic data interchange (EDI), 168, 316, 328, 331, 333
Electronic kiosks, 113, 561–562, 574, C53–C55
Electronic retailing, 4, 74, 129, C3–C7; see also Interactive home shopping; Internet
Emotional needs, 126
Emotional support, during conflict, 590

Employee discounts, 375
Employee stock ownership plans, 285, 302–303
Employee theft, 531–536
Employee turnover, 304–307
Employees; see Human resource management
Employment trends, 260–261
Empowerment, 112, 301–302, 573–574, 591–592, C31–C32
Empty nest syndrome, 102, 110
End caps, 548
End-of-month (EOM) dating, 435–436
End-of-season sales, 442–443
Energy management, 531
Entertainment, used to draw shoppers, 79, 238, 242, 541, C2–C3
Entrepreneurship, A15–A27
    business failure factors, A15
    buying existing businesses, A26
    characteristics needed, A16
    demands of, A16–A17
    financial plan, A19–A23
    financing, sources for, A24–A26
    franchises; see Franchise businesses
    legal requirements, A22–A23
    marketing plan, A18–A19
    opportunities, 15–17, A17
    potential problems, A17
Environment
    green marketing, 101, 114
    recycling, 177
    store location, 252
Environmental factors, affecting market attractiveness, 184
Environmental Protection Agency (EPA), 252
EOM dating, 435–436
Equal Employment Opportunity Commission (EEOC), 528
Equal Pay Act, 529
Equity financing, A24–A25
Errors, in employee evaluations, 522–523
Escape clause, in a lease, 251
Estimate regression equation, 272–274
Ethics, 419–425; see also Legal issues
    commercial bribery, 420–421
    dual distribution, 424–425
    exclusive dealing agreements, 424
    exclusive territories, 423
    gifts and, 421
    gray-market goods and, 421–423
    management of employees and, 528–530
    standards, 19–20
    tying contracts, 424
Ethnic diversity, 104–107, 285, 307–310
Europe, retail opportunities in, 176–178
European Community (EC), 176–177
Evaluation of alternative products/stores, 130–136

Evaluation of employee performance, 520–523
Everyday low pricing (EDLP), 33–34, 441–445
Exclusive dealing agreements, 424
Exclusive geographic territories, 423
Exclusive use clause, in a lease, 251
Expectations, of customers, 576–578, 593
Expenses, 201–202
Experiments with pricing, 462
Exponential smoothing, 385–386, C36
Extended problem solving, 121–122
External information sources, 129–130
Extra dating, 436
Extrinsic rewards, 523–524

Factory outlets, 45, 240–241
Fads, 354–355
Fair Labor Standards Act, 529
Fair trade laws, 88, 464
Family life cycle, 138–139
Family members, influence on buying decisions, 137–139
Fashion, 115–116, 123, 150–154, 355
Fashion consultants, 112
Fashion merchandise, buying system for, 371–382
Fashion/specialty centers, 239–240
Feature display areas, 547–550
Feature fixtures, 561
Features, of products, 607
Federal Trade Commission, A40, 464
Filling orders, 322
Financial analysis, 214–217, A29–A31
Financial management, as a career, A4
Financial strategy, 196–229; see also Budgeting; Price/pricing
    activity-based costing, 224–228
    balance sheets, 203–211, 215–216, C22
    break-even analysis, 458–460, C43
    direct product profitability (DPP), 224
    income statements, 200–202, C22
    integrated with marketing strategy, 214–217
    merchandise management, 344–360
        GMROI, 338, 345–348, C36, C39–C41
        inventory turnover analysis, 205–207, 215–216, 346, 348–351, 376–377, 385, C36
    new businesses and, A19–A23, C14–C16
    return on investment (ROI), 316–317
    strategic profit model, 197–199, 211–214, 217, 345, C22–C23
    value-based planning, 228
Financing, sources for, A24–A26
Fitness and youth, as a selling strategy, 103
Fixed assets, 208, 216
Fixed costs, 458

Fixed-rate lease, 250
Fixtures, 548, 560–561, C48–C49
Flextime, 306
Floor-ready merchandise, 322–324
FOB terms, 437
Focus groups, 360
Food Marketing Institute, 47, 92
Food retailers, 33–36, 246, C6–C7
Forecast demand, 386
Forecasting of demand, 264
Forecasting sales; *see* Sales forecasting
Foreign trade zones, 412
Formats, retail, 78–79, 161–164, 171
Four-way fixtures, 561
Fragrance, store atmosphere and, 566
Franchise businesses, 55–56, A28–A41
    advantages/disadvantages of buying,
        A28–A29
    analysis form, A35–A40
    financial analysis, A29–A31
    investigation of options, A30–A32
    legal issues, A33–A34
    success rates of, A28
Franchise Opportunities Handbook,
    A30–A31
Free-form layout, 546–547
Freestanding fixtures, 548
Free-standing insert (FSI), 491
Freestanding sites, 242
Freight charges, 437
Freight forwarders, 325
Frequency, of advertising, 495
Frequent shopper programs, 100,
    473–474, 496–498
Frontal presentations, 560
Functional discounts, 432–433, 463
Functional needs, buying process and,
    125–126

Games, as a promotional tool, 496
Gaps customer service model, 580–593
    communications gap, 580, 592–593
    delivery gap, 580, 589–592
    knowledge gap, 580–584
    standards gap, 580, 584–589
Garment District, 415–416
GATT, 411
Gender differences, in shopping behav-
    ior, 132
General Agreement on Tariffs and Trade
    (GATT), 411
General merchandise discount stores,
    41–42
General merchandise manager (GMM),
    responsibilities of, 291, 342
General merchandise retailers, 36–42
Generation X, 97, 100–101, 603, C7–C8
Generation Y, 98–100
Generational cohorts, 97–104
Generic brands, 409
Gentrification, 231–232

Geographic Information Systems (GIS),
    263
Geographic market segmentation, 144
Geographic territories, exclusive, 423
Gifts, from vendors, 421
Glass ceiling, 310
GMROI, 338, 345–348, C36, C39–C41
Gondola, 542, 561
Goodwill, 614–615
Graduated lease, 250
Gravity models, used to measure trade
    potential, 274–279
Gray-market goods, 421–423
Green marketing, 101, 114
Greeter, for customers, 112, 576–577
Grid store layout, 545
Grocery Manufacturers Association, 92
Grocery stores, 246; *see also* Food retailers
Gross margin, 201, 214–215, 450–451
Gross margin return on inventory
    investment (GMROI), 338,
    345–348, C36, C39–C41
Gross profit, 201, 450
Group maintenance behaviors, 517
Growth, strategies for, 170–173,
    C12–C13

Habitual decision making, 123–124
Haloing effect, 522
Hard goods, 46
Hazardous materials, 252
Health and safety issues, 529
High assay principle, 486
High-low pricing strategy, 33–34,
    441–445
Hiring and promotion, legal and ethical
    issues, 528–530
Hispanic-Americans, 105–106, 140–141
HIV testing, 529
Home shopping; *see* Interactive home
    shopping (IHS)
Home-improvement centers, 42–43
Horizontal price-fixing, 464–465
Household managers, 110–111
Huff's Gravity Model, 277–279
Human resource management, 284–313;
    see also Careers, retail
    balancing careers and families,
        306–307; C14–C16
    career development and promotions,
        305–306, 310
    compensation; *see* Compensation
    corporate culture, 303–305
    diversity, 104–107, 285, 307–310
    drug testing, 511, 529, 535
    employee motivation, 349, 517–520
        contests, 525, 590
        effective leadership and, 517–518
        goal setting, 518–519, 587–588
    employee theft, 531–536
    empowerment, 112, 301–302,
        573–574, 591–592, C31–C32

Human resource management—*Cont.*
    evaluating employee performance,
        520–523, C47–C48
    hiring and promotion, 528–530
    labor relations, 530
    legal and ethical issues, 528–530
    morale, 519–520, C52–C53
    objectives of, 286
    organizational structure; *see*
        Organizational structure
    orientation program, 512–514
    productivity, of employees, 286
    promotion from within, as a policy,
        305–306, 310
    recruitment/hiring, 508–513
        interviewing, 512–513, A11–A14
        job analysis, 508–509
        job descriptions, 509–510
        locating prospective employees, 510
        screening/testing of applicants, 511,
            535
    responsibility and authority, 288–289,
        300–301, A7
    rewarding employees, 523–528; *see also*
        Compensation
    sexual harassment, 529–530
    skills needed, A8–A10
    socialization, of employees, 512–516
    specialization, 287–289
    task assignment, 286–288
    teaming, 300
    termination of employees, C30–C31,
        C52
    training of employees, 285, 306, 308,
        510, 512–516, 532, 589–590,
        619, A10
    turnover of employees, 304–307
Hypermarkets, 46–47

Idea-oriented presentation, 559
Identifiability, market segmentation and,
    142
IHS; *see* Interactive home shopping
Image advertising, 487–488
Impact of advertising, 494–495
Importance weights, used to evaluate
    stores, 131–133, 136
Impulse buying/merchandise, 122–123,
    542, 553
Inbound transportation, management
    of, 320
Incentives, used to motivate employees,
    302–303, 526–527, 592
Income distribution, and demographics,
    107–110
Income statements, 200–202, C22
Independent, single–store establish-
    ments, 52–53
Independent agents, 75
Influencing customers, approaches to,
    134–136
Infomercials, 74
INFOREM, 383

Information search
  buying process and, 129–130
  selling process and, 605–606
Informing customers, by promotion, 473
Initial markup, 451–452
Input measure, used to measure performance, 220–221
In-store demonstrations, 495, 607–608
Instrumental support, 590
Intangibility, of service, 572
Integrated marketing communication, 476–477
Intelligent agent, 81–82
Interactive home shopping (IHS), 77–90, C5–C6; *see also* Internet
  benefits of, 79–84, 87
  growth potential, 79
  impact on retail industry, 86–90
  types of merchandise sold, 84–86
Interest expense, 201
Internal information sources, 129
International Council of Shopping Centers, 233–234
International retailing, 173–179, C10–C11, C16–C21
International sourcing, 409–414
  cost issues, 409–413
  country of origin, 410–411
  currency fluctuations, 411
  foreign trade zones, 412
  inventory carrying costs, 412
  Made in America, 413–414
  NAFTA, 176, 411–413
  quality issues, 413
  tariffs, 411
Internet; *see also* Interactive home shopping (IHS)
  purchasing from, 6, 66, 78–84, 88, C3–C5
  search engines/intelligent agents, 81–82
  selling services through, 85–86
Internet exercises, 5, 29, 47, 78, 81, 97, 116, 134, 145, 162, 167, 211, 234, 238, 266, 315, 328, 359, 372, 383, 414, 444, 447, 492, 496, 531
Intertype competition, 18
Interviewing, of job applicants, 512–513, A11–A14
Interviews, customer, 582
Intratype competition, 17
Intrinsic rewards, 523–525
Inventory management; *see also* Merchandise management
  ABC analysis, 390–391
  allocation of merchandise, 387–389
  backup/safety stock, 339, 364–365, 385, 442
  bar coding, 319, 321, 323
  basic stock list, 384–385
  basic stock method, 400
  databased retailing, 166, 168, 314, 329–331, 472, 491–492

Inventory management—*Cont.*
  fads/fashion, affect on, 355–356
  GMROI, 338, 345–348, C36, C39–C41
  holding/carrying, cost of, 9, 43, 225, 412
  INFOREM, 383
  lead time, 331–332, 365, 387, 412
  loss prevention, 531–535
  percentage variation method, 400–401
  physical count, 349
  quick response system, 314, 322, 331–333, 349, 413, C32–C34
  reduction of inventory, 318, 332, C32–C36
  reordering system, 386–387
  reports, 384–387
  retail inventory method (RIM), 396–399
  staple merchandise, 355, 383–387
  turnover, 205–207, 215–216, 346, 348–351, 376–377, 385, C36
  week's supply method, 400

Japan, retail opportunities, 178
Job analysis, 508–509
Job application forms, 511
Job descriptions, 509–510
Job preview, 511
Job security, A7
Job sharing, 306

Keystone method, 449
Kickbacks, 420–421
Kiosks, 113, 242–243, 561–562, 574, C53–C55
Knowledge gap, 580–584

Labor costs, 40, 285, 530
Labor relations, 530
Labor scheduling, 530
Labor shortage, 286
Latchkey children, 101
Latin America, retail opportunities, 175–176
Layaway, 112
Lead time, 331–332, 365, 387, 412
Leader pricing, 446, 448
Leadership styles, 517–518
Leased departments, 39
Leasing, 230, 249–251
Legal issues, 19–20
  commercial bribery, 420–421
  counterfeit merchandise, 421–422
  disabled, access for, 528, 550–551
  discrimination, 528–529
  exclusive dealing agreements, 424
  exclusive territories, 423
  fair trade laws, 88, 464
  franchises, A33–A34
  gray-market and diverted merchandise, 421–423

Legal issues—*Cont.*
  management of store employees and, 528–530
  new businesses, A22–A23
  pricing, 463–467
  Robinson–Patman Act, 428–429, 433, 455
  store location and, 251–252
  tying contracts, 424
Lessee, defined, 251
Lessor defined, 251
Level of support (product availability), 361–365
Liabilities, 203, 210–211
Licensed brands, 405–406
Licensing requirements, 252
Lie detectors, used in the hiring process, 529
Life cycles, of products, 351–355
Lifestyle market segmentation, 145–146, C49–C50
Lifestyling retailing, 37
Lighting, store atmosphere and, 564
Limited problem solving, 122–123
Limited-line warehouse stores, 34
Liquidating markdown merchandise, 456
Listening skills, 619–621
Loans, as a source of financing, A25–A26
Location; *see* Store location(s)
Location allocation models, 279
Logistics system(s), 314–335; *see also* Distribution system(s)
  competitive advantage and, 315–317
  costs, 332–333, 351
  defined, 317
  distribution centers, 319–322, 325–327
  electronic data interchange, 168, 316, 328, 331, 333
  examples of effective, 316, 318
  information flow, 317, 319, 328
  outsourcing, 323–325
  pull/push strategy, 327, 388–389
  quick response systems, 314, 322, 331–333, 349, 413, C32–C34
  return on investment and, 316–317
  third–party services, 324–326
Long-term liabilities, 210–211
Loop store layout, 545–546
Loss leaders, 446, 448
Lower income markets, 108–110
Loyalty, customer, 123–124, 165–167, 405, C45–C46

Made in America, 413–414
Magazines, advertising in, 491
Mail-order sales; *see* Catalog retailing/sales
Maintained markup, 450–452
Maintenance, of stores, 531
Maintenance-increase-recoupment lease, 250
Malls, shopping, 232, 237–242, C7–C8

Management
  career opportunities, 14–15, A1
  customer interaction, 582–583
  decision-making process, 17–24
  human resources; *see* Human resource
    management
  labor scheduling, 530
  organizational structure; *see*
    Organizational structure
Management by walking around, 298
Management information systems,
  168–169, 299, 315–317; *see also*
  Computerized systems
Manufacturer brands, 403–405
Maquiladores, 411–412
Marginal analysis method, 481–482,
  551–552
Markdown cancellation, 457
Markdown money, 455
Markdowns, 44, 349, 375, 453–458,
  C43–C44
Market, as a place to find vendors,
  414–415
Market, target, 17, 20, 161–164, C2
Market analysis, 181
Market attractiveness analysis, 186–187,
  190–192
Market basket analysis, 553–554
Market expansion opportunity, 171, 173,
  C11–C12
Market factors, 181–182
Market penetration opportunity,
  170–171
Market research, information to collect,
  134, 581–584
Market segmentation, 141–148
  benefit, 147
  buying situation, 146–147
  composite approach, 147
  criteria for, 142–144
  demographic, 144–145
  geographic, 144
  lifestyle, 145–146, C49–C50
  women's apparel, 147–148
Market weeks, 415
Marketing; *see also* Promotion programs
  affinity, 139
  green, 101, 114
  plan for new business, A18–A19
  target, 17, 20, 161–164
Markups, 450–452, 458, C43–C44
Mass customization, 570–571, C51–C52
Mass middle income customers, 108–110
Mass-market theory, of fashion development, 152
Mentoring programs, 309–310
Merchandise; *see also* Merchandise management; Store layout/design
  ABC analysis, 390–391
  analyzing performance, 389–394
  availability, 315, 332, 361–365, 385
  basic, 355

Merchandise—*Cont.*
  brands/branding; *see* Brands
  classification of, 341–344
  competitive advantage and, 167
  complimentary, 363
  counterfeit, 421–422
  customer loyalty and, 123–124,
    165–167, 405, C45–C46
  demonstration of, 495, 607–608
  depth/breadth of, 30–32, 361–363
  display areas, 547–550, 560–561,
    C48–C49
  distribution; *see* Distribution system(s)
  diverted, 421–423
  fixtures, 560–561, C48–C49
  floor-ready, 322–324
  generic products, 409
  gray-market, 421–423
  impulse, 122–123, 542, 553
  inventory; *see* Inventory management
  life cycles, 351–355
  location within department, 555–558
  logistics; *see* Logistics system(s)
  markdowns, 44, 349, 375, 453–458,
    C43–C44
  mix, 22–24, 29, 167, 187, 362–363,
    C1, C14–C16
  presentation of, 59, 558–562,
    606–607, C48
  purchase of, 402–439
    branding strategies; *see* Brands
    ethical and legal issues, 419–425
    international sources, 409–414
    negotiation, 6, 403, 427–432
    terms and conditions, 403, 432–437,
      465
    vendors; *see* Vendor(s)
  receiving and checking, 320
  scrambled, 17–18
  seasonal, 355, 374
  shrinkage, 375, 532–533
  staple, 355, 383–387
  ticketing and marking, 321–322
  tonnage, 560
  traffic appliances, 454
  types of, 29–32
  variety and assortment of, 30–32,
    361–363, C42–C43
  vertical, 559
Merchandise budget plans, 370–379,
  C37–C38
Merchandise group, 342
Merchandise management; *see also*
  Inventory management; Merchandise
  allocation of merchandise, 387–389
  Arthur system, 371–373, 379–380
  assortment planning; *see* Assortment
    planning
  buying system; *see* Buying system(s)
  career opportunities in; *see* Careers,
    retail
  category management, 339–344

Merchandise management—*Cont.*
  defined, 338
  distribution centers, 319–322,
    325–327
  financial plans; *see* Financial strategy
  organization for; *see* Organizational
    structure
  performance measures
    ABC analysis, 390–391
    GMROI, 338, 345–348, C36,
      C39–C41
    sell-through analysis, 392, 455
  pricing; *see* Price/pricing
  sales forecasting; *see* Sales forecasting
Merchandise planners, 340, A1–A3
Merchandise retailers vs services retailers,
  49–52
Merchandise shows, 415
Metropolitan Statistical Area (MSA),
  256, 263
Mexico, retail opportunities, 176
Minorities; *see* Diversity
Minority owned businesses, 105
Mission statement, 180
Mixed-use developments (MXDs), 243
Mom-and-pop stores, 233
Monthly Retail Trade Report, 359
Morale, of employees, 519–520, C52–C53
Motivation, of employees; *see* Human
  resource management
MSA, 256, 263
Multiattribute attitude model, 130–134,
  C9–C10
Multiattribute method of evaluating
  vendors, 392–394
Multilevel sales network, 76
Multiple regression analysis, 271–274
Multiple-attribute method of evaluating
  vendors, 392–394
Multiple-unit pricing, 447
Music, store atmosphere and, 565
Mutual trust, in a partnership, 418–419
MXDs, 243
Mystery shoppers, 589

NAFTA, 176, 411–413
National Association of Convenience
  Stores, 92
National brands, 403–405
National Grocer Association, 92
National Labor Relations Act, 530
National Labor Relations Board, 530
National Retail Federation, 47, 92, 330,
  341–342
National Retail Hardware Association, 92
National-America Wholesale Grocers
  Association, 92
Natural barriers, 247
Natural selection theory of retailing, 63
Need recognition, buying process and,
  125–128
Negotiation, 6, 403, 427–432

Neighborhood CBD, 232
Neighborhood centers, 235
Net lease, 250
Net profit, 202
Net profit margins, 215
Net sales, 201
Net sales ratio, 215
Newspapers, advertising in, 490–491, C44–C45
NLRB, 530
Nonstore retailing; *see also* Interactive home shopping (IHS)
    benefits of, 68–69
    catalog and direct mail, 69–73, 113, 491–492, 499
    defined, 67
    direct selling, 67–68, 75–76
    electronic, 4, 74, 129, C3–C7
    versus store–based, 67–69
    television, 9, 11, 74–75, C5–C6
    types of, 9, 67–68
    vending machine, 73–74
Nonverbal communication, 622–623
North American Free Trade Agreement (NAFTA), 176, 411–413
Notes payable, 210

Objective-and-task method, 482–483
Objectives setting, planning process and, 187, 218–219
Observability, of fashion, 154
Obsolescence and markdowns, elimination of, 349
Occupancy terms, 249–252
Occupational Safety and Health Act, 529
Odd price strategy, 448–449
Off-price retailers, 43–45
Older population
    selling to, 103–104
    workers from, 96, 510
One-stop shopping, 96, 113
Online services, as a source of information, 263
Open-to-buy system, 379–382, C37
Operating expenses/costs, 169, 201–202, 350–351
Operations, as a career, A3
Opportunity cost of capital, 225, 412
Order point, 386–387, C36
Order quantity, 387
Orders, filling of, 322
Organizational culture, 303–305
Organizational structure, 286–302; *see also* Human resource management
    administrative division, 286–288, 293–294
    centralization, 21–22, 295–299
    coordination between buyer and store owner, 297–299
    decentralization, 22, 296–299
    department stores, 290–295
    flattening of the, 300

Organizational structure—*Cont.*
    merchandise division, 291–292
    reporting relationships, 289
    small store, 289–290
    stores division, 293
Orientation programs for new employees, 512–514
OSHA, 529
Outbound transportation, 322
Outdoor advertising, 493
Outlet stores/centers, 45–46, 240–241
Outparcel, 251
Output measure, used to measure performance, 220–221
Outsourcing, 301, 323–325
Overstored trade area, 261, 460
Owners' equity, 203, 210–211
Ownership, types of, 52–56

Paid impersonal communication, 474, 476
Paid personal communication, 475–476
Parasite store, 260
Parking facilities, 247
Partnership, as a source of financing, A25
Party plan system, 76
Penetration pricing strategy, 353
Percentage leases, 249
Percentage variation method, 400–401
Percentage-of-sales method, 483–484
Perceptions, of customers, 578–579
Perceptual maps, 165–166
Performance measures
    ABC analysis, 390–391
    customer buying behavior and, 131–133, 135–136
    employee; *see* Human resource management
    GMROI, 338, 345–348, C36, C39–C41
    multiple-attribute method, 392–394
    sell-through analysis, 392, 455
    setting objectives, 218–219
    of strategic plans, 187
    types of, 220–221
    used to predict sales, 272
    vendors, 392–394
Periodic reordering system, 387
Perishability, 51
Perpetual ordering system, 386
Personal selling, 475–476, C10
Personalized service, for customers, 112, 127, C10, C31–C32
Persuading customers, 473
Physical flow of materials; *see* Logistics system(s)
Pick ticket, 322
Planograms, 341, 555–558
Point-of-purchase display areas, 549
Point-of-sale display area, 549
Point-of-sale (POS) system, 21, 314, 322, 331, 349

Policies and procedures, 302
Polygons, 258
Popping the merchandise, 564
POS, 21, 314, 322, 331, 349
Positioning, 165–167, 477–479
Postpurchase evaluation, 137, 581–582
Potential Rating Index for Zip Markets, 266–267, C26, C28, C50
Power, customer need for, 127
Power centers, 236–237
Power retailers; *see* Category specialist
Predatory pricing, 465–466
Preferred customers, 519, C45–C46
Premiums, 496
Preprints, in advertising, 491
Press conferences, 498
Press releases, 498
Price/pricing, 440–471; *see also* Discounts
    adjustments to initial, 453–458
    bundling, 446–447
    comparative, 465–466
    competition, 87–89
    consumer panel data, 463
    cost oriented method, 449–459
        break-even analysis, 458–460, C43
        markdowns, 453–458; C43–C44
        markups, 450–452, 458, C43–C44
    coupons, 329, 445–446, 496–497
    customer reservations about, 611
    customer sensitivity and, 460–461
    demand oriented method, 449, 460–463
    discrimination, 463–464
    everyday low price (EDLP), 33–34, 441–445
    experiments, 462
    fixing, 464–465
    high-low, 33–34, 441–445
    keystone method, 449
    leader pricing, 446, 448
    legal issues, 463–467
    lining, 448, 559
    multiple-unit, 447
    odd, 448–449
    penetration, 353
    price wars, 183, 442
    rebates, 446
    Robinson-Patman Act, 428–429, 433, 455
    skimming, 353
Primary zones, 258
Principle of cumulative attraction, 249
Private label brands, 22, 41, 186, 224, 404, 406–409, 460
Private office, 416
PRIZM, 266–267, C26, C28, C50
Procedural fairness, 594–595
Product availability, 315, 332, 361–365, 385
Product life cycle, 351–355
Productivity measures, 221, 286, 556–558

Profit
  gross, 201, 450
  net, 202, 215
Profit margin, increased by EDLP, 442
Profit margin models, 200
Profit path, as a strategy, 197, 199–200, 214
Profitability of merchandise mix, 362–363
Profit-sharing, 302–303
Prohibited use clause, 251
Promotion from within, as a corporate policy, 305–306, 310
Promotion programs, 472–503; *see also* Communication
  advertising; *see* Advertising
  budgeting, 481–487; *see also* Budgeting
  career opportunities and, A3
  choosing a medium, 490–495
  communication methods, 474–477
  evaluation of opportunities, 484–487
  positioning, 165–167, 477–479
  preferred customers, 519, C45–C46
  publicity, 475–476, 497–500
  sales, 474, 495–497
  setting objectives, 477–480
  tasks of, 473–474
  types of media, 490–493
Promotional aisle/area, 548
Promotional stores, 33, 40
Psychological needs, buying process and, 125–127
Public warehouses, 325
Publicity programs, 475–476, 497–500; *see also* Promotion programs
Pull logistics strategy, 327, 388–389
Purchase decision process; *see* Customer buying behavior
Purchasing cooperative, 52–53
Purchasing of merchandise; *see* Merchandise, purchase of
Push logistics strategy, 327, 388–389
Pyramid schemes, 76

Quality control, in international sourcing, 413
Quantity discounts, 433–434, 463
Quantity to order, 387
Questioning skills, 621–622
Quick response delivery/inventory systems, 314, 322, 331–333, 349, 413, C32–C34
Quotas/bonus plans, 526–527

Racetrack store layout, 545–546
Radio advertising, 492, C45
Rain checks, 442
Reach, of advertising, 494
Rebates, 446
Receipt of goods (ROG) dating, 435
Receiving, 320

Recruiting and selecting store employees, 508–513
Recycling, 177
Reductions, 451
Reengineering, 300
Reference groups, affect on buying decisions, 139
Reference price, 465–466
References, job, 511
Refusals to deal, 424
Regional centers, 237
Region/market area, 256, 258–261
Regression analysis, 271–274
Reilly's Law of Retail Gravitation, 275–276
Related diversification, 172–173
Relative location advantages, 553
Reminding customers, 473–474
Reordering system, 386–387
Resale price maintenance laws, 464
Reservations, overcoming customer, 608–611
Resident buying offices, 360, 402, 415–416
Resource allocation, 187
Responsibility and authority, 288–289, 300–301, A7
Restriction of competition, legal issues, 423–424
Retail chains, 53–54
Retail gravitation, 274–279
Retail institutions, 29–52
  catalog and direct mail, 69–73, 113, 491–492, 499
  category specialist, 42–44, 46, 48, 245–246, 259
  department stores, 38–41, 112, 243–244, 290–295
  discount stores, 35, 41–42
  food stores, 33–36, 246, C6–C7
  general merchandise, 36–42
  home-improvement centers, 42–43
  mom-and-pop stores, 233
  nonstore; *see* Nonstore retailing
  off-price, 43–45
  specialty apparel, 244–245
  warehouse clubs, 6, 8, 43, 48–49
Retail inventory method (RIM), 396–399
Retail markets, 141, 162–164
Retail merchandising units (RMU), 242–243
Retail mix, 22–24, 29, 167, 187, C1, C14–C16
Retail strategy; *see* Strategy, retail
Retailer sponsored cooperatives, 52–53
Retailers/retailing; *see also* Retail institutions
  accordion theory of, 62–63
  classification, 29–30
  closeout, 45
  concept of, 17
  decision making process, 17–24

Retailers/retailing—*Cont.*
  defined, 7–9
  distribution channels, 7–10
  economic significance of, 11
  entrepreneurial opportunities, 15–17
  environmental factors, 17–20
  evolution of, 61–63
  format, 78–79, 161–164, 171
  functions, 8–9
  largest, 12–13
  ownerships, types of, 52–56
  sales statistics, 11–13, 31, 41
  services, 47–52, 85–86, 213, 231, 353
  trade publications for, 25–27
  types of, 29–32
  value-added services, 9–10, 17
  wheel of retailing, 61–62
Retained earnings, 211
Return on assets, 211–213, 217, 316, 345–346
Return on investment (ROI), 316–317; *see also* GMROI
Return privileges, 44
Returns, customer, 201, 576, 583, 590
RIM, 396–399
Rivalry, competitive, 183
RMU, 242–243
Roads, site evaluation and, 247–248
Robinson–Patman Act, 428–429, 433, 455
ROI, 316–317
Rounder (fixture), 560–561
Rule-of-thumb methods, 483–484

Safety stock, 364–365, 385, 442
Salaried/fee office, 416
Salaries; *see* Compensation
Sales & Marketing Management's Buying Power Index, 261, 264, 280, 359
Sales data; *see* Point-of-sale (POS) system
Sales forecasting
  analog approach, 268–271
  category life cycles, used in, 351–355
  deseasonalized demand, 386
  development of, 355–360
  exponential smoothing, 385–386, C36
  gravity models, 274–279
  obtaining customer information, 359–360
  previous sales volume, 355–358
  published information sources, 358–359
  regression analysis and, 271–274
  by season, 358
  service retailers and, 353
  weather, used in, 356–357
Sales goals, 479
Sales growth, 226
Sales promotion programs, 474, 495–497; *see also* Promotion programs

Salespeople; *see also* Selling process
  adaptive selling, 622–625
  compensation; *see* Compensation
  effective questioning, 621–622
  ethics and, C46–C47
  knowledgeable, 618–619
  listening skills, 619–621
  nonverbal communication, 622–623
  role of, 601–602
Sales-per-linear-foot, 556
Sales-per-square-foot, 556
Sales-to-stock ratio, 346, 376–378
Sampling, of merchandise, 495
Satisfaction, with purchase, 137
Saturated trade area, 261
Saturation, of the fashion market, 154
Scale economics, 182
Scent, store atmosphere and, 566
Scrambled merchandise, 17–18
Screening process, of job applicants, 511, 535
Search engines, 81–82
Seasonal discounts, 434
Seasonal merchandise, 355, 374
Seasonal needs, 553
Secondary zones, 259
Security measures, to prevent shoplifting, 533–535
Segmentation of markets; *see* Market segmentation
Self-analysis, strategic planning process and, 184–185
Self-reward, customer need for, 127
Self-service approach, 41–42, 574–575
Selling, direct, 67–68, 75–76
Selling process, 600–627; *see also* Salespeople
  approaching customers, 602–605
  buying signals, 612–613
  cross selling, 171
  demonstrating merchandise, 495, 607–608
  future sales, 614–618
  information gathering, 605–606
  making the sale, 611–614
  multiple item sales, 614
  presenting merchandise, 606–607
  reservations/objectives, overcoming, 608–611
  steps in, 602
Sell-through analysis, 392, 455
Service levels (product availability), 361–365
Services retailing, 213
  assortment planning, 362
  difference between merchandise retailers, 49–52
  location and, 231
  sales forecasting, 353
  types of retailers, 47–48
  via the Internet, 85–86

Sexual harassment, 529–530
Shipping terms and conditions, 437
Shop the competition, 360
Shoplifting, 531–534
Shopping, comparison, 59–60, 83
Shopping centers, 232–236, 244
Shopping goods, 245
Shopping guides, 493
Shopping malls, 232, 237–242, C7–C8
Shrinkage, of inventory, 375, 532–533
Signs
  restriction of use, 252
  store atmosphere and, 562–564
Silver-streakers, 103–104
Similar store approach, 268–271
Single-price retailers, 45
Site evaluation, 247–252
Situation audit/analysis, conducting, 181–185
Situation effect, 461
Size, market segmentation and, 144
Skimming, as a pricing strategy, 353
SKUs, 30, 315–316, 344
Sliding scale, in a lease, 249–250
Slotting allowances/fees, 420
Small Business Administration, A23, A25–A26, A31
Small store, organizational structure of, 289–290
Social consciousness, 97, 100, 113–114, 478, C8
Social experience, customer need for, 127
Socialization, of new employees, 512–516
Source tagging, 323–324
Space allocation, retail, 227–228, 551–558
Space planning; *see* Store layout/design
Spatial analysis, 256–257
Specialization, of employees, 287–289
Specialty apparel stores, 244–245
Specialty stores, 36–38, 40
Speeches, as a publicity tool, 499
Spots, television, 493
Stability, market segmentation and, 144
Standard Industrial Classification (SIC), 29–30
Standardization, 572, 574
Standards gap, 580, 584–589
Staple merchandise, 355, 383–387
Start-up costs, of a new business, A19–A20
Status, customer need for, 127
Stimulation, customer need for, 126
Stock keeping units, 30, 315–316, 344
Stock ownership, for employees, 285, 302–303
Stockholders' equity, 203, 210–211
Stock-to-sales ratio, 377–378, 399–401
Store atmosphere, 474, 562–566
Store brands, 406–409; *see also* Private label brands

Store layout/design, 540–569, C49–C50
  assortment planning, 363, C48
  atmospherics, 474, 562–566
  careers and, A4
  disabled, designed for, 550–551
  display areas, 547–550, 560–561, C48–C49
  evaluation of, 554
  fixtures, 560–561, C48–C49
  flexibility of, 550–551
  free-form layout, 546–547
  grid layout, 545
  merchandise presentation techniques, 59, 558–562, 606–607, C48
  objectives of design and layout, 540–544
  racetrack, 545–546
  signage, 252, 562–564
  space planning, 227–228
    location of departments, 552–555
    planograms, 341, 555–558
    productivity measures, 556–558
Store location(s), 230–283, C24–C29
  accessibility and, 247–248
  attractiveness factors, 260–261, C42–C43
  as competitive advantage, 18, 167, 230, 261
  decision-making process, 256–257, C23–C24
  demographics and, 260, 264–267
  environmental issues and, 252
  legal considerations, 251–252
  licensing requirements, 252
  measuring trade area potential, 268–279, C24–C29
    analog approach, 268–271
    gravity models, 274–279
    multiple regression analysis, 271–274
  occupancy terms, 249–251
  region/market area, 256, 258
  signs and, 252
  site evaluation methods, 247–252
  strategies, 21, 243–247
  trade areas, 230, 257–260
  types of, 231–243
    central business districts, 231–232, 243–244
    freestanding sites, 242
    malls, 232, 237–242, C7–C8
    mixed–use developments, 243
    shopping centers, 232–236, 244
    strip shopping centers, 232, 234–237
  zoning and building codes, 252
Store loyalty, 123–124, 165–167, 405
Store maintenance, 531
Store management, 286–288, 293
  career opportunities and, A1
  controlling costs, 530–531
  coordination between buyers and, 297–299

Store management—*Cont.*
  energy management, 531
  extended hours, 111
  human resource issues; *see* Human
    resource management
  maintenance, 531
  responsibilities of manager, 506–507
Store opening, publicity and, 499–500
Store visits, 298
Straight racks, 560–561
Straight salary compensation plan,
  525–526
Strategic alliance/partnerships, 168, 315,
  341, 403, 413, 416–419, C32–C34
Strategic planning; *see* Strategy, retail
Strategic profit model, 197–199,
  211–214, 217, 345, C22–C23
Strategy, financial; *see* financial strategy
Strategy, retail, 160–195
  changes in, C13–C14
  children's needs and, 100
  competitive advantage, 164–170, 316
  customer loyalty, 123–124, 165–167,
    405, C45–C46
  defined, 160–162
  development of, 20–22
  distribution and, 168–170, 315–317
  diversification opportunities, 172–173
  financial strategy; *see* Financial strategy
  green marketing, 101, 114
  growth, 170–173, C12–C13
  implementation of, 22–24
  international, 173–179, C10–C11,
    C16–C21
  market attractiveness, 186–187, 190–192
  market expansion, 171, 173, C11–C12
  organizational structure and, 289
  planning process, 179–188
    bottom-up, 219
    define mission, 180–181
    develop retail mix, 187
    establish objectives, 187
    evaluate opportunities, 186–187
    evaluate performance, 187
    identify opportunities, 185–186
    situation audit, 181–185
    top–down, 219
  positioning as a, 165–167, 444–479
  pricing; *see* Price/pricing
  promotional; *see* Promotion programs
  saving time for consumers, 111–113
  selling natural, 103
  selling technology, 103
  selling youth and fitness, 103
  store location and; *see* Store location(s)
  target markets, 17, 20, 161–164, C2
Strength and weakness analysis, 184–185
Strip shopping centers, 232, 234–237
Style/item presentation, 559
Subculture theory, of fashion development, 152

Subcultures, 140–141
Substitute awareness effect, 460
Supercenters, 35, 46–47
Supermarkets, 33–36, 48
Superregional centers, 238–239
Superstores, 6, 34, C11–C12
Super-warehouse, 35
Supply and demand, 51
Surveys, used to gather information
  about customers, 269–270
Sweepstakes, 496
SWOT analysis, 184–185
Syndicated office, 416

Tall wall units, 242–243
Target markets, 17, 20, 161–164, C2
Tariffs, 411
Task performance behaviors, 517
Teams, concept of, 300
Teen boards, used by department stores,
  139
Television advertising, 493, C45
Television home shopping, 9, 11, 74–75,
  C5–C6
Termination of employees, C30–C31, C52
Terms and conditions, in a contract, 403,
  432–437, 465
Tertiary zone, 259
Test scores, of job applicants, 511
Testing new merchandise, 429
Theft, 531–536
Theme/festival centers, 241–242
Third-party logistics services, 324–326
Ticketing and marking of new merchan-
  dise, 321–322
TIGER, 263
Time-poor society, demographic
  changes and, 111–113
Timing, of advertising, 495
Timing, of a sale, 612
Tonnage merchandising, 560
Top-down planning, 219
Topologically Integrated Geographic
  Encoding and Reference System
  (TIGER), 263
Total expenditure effect, 460
Touch-and-feel information, 84
Trade areas, 230, 257–260
Trade discounts, 432–433, 463
Trade publications, 25–27
Trade shows, used to locate vendors, 415
Trademark Counterfeiting Act of 1984, 421
Trademarks, 421
Training, 285, 306, 308, 510, 512–516,
  532, 589–590, 619, A10
Transformational leaders, 518
Transportation; *see also* Distribution sys-
  tem(s); Logistics system(s)
  costs, 9, 351, 413, 428
  inbound, 320
  outbound, 322
  outsourcing, 323–325

Transportation—*Cont.*
  terms and conditions of contract, 437
  third-party services, 324–326
Travel-time contours, 264
Treasury bill, 212
Triability, of fashion, 153–154
Trickle-down theory, of fashion develop-
  ment, 152
Turnover
  of assets, 197–199, 203–204, 209–210,
    216–217, 350
  of employees, 304–307
  of inventory, 205–207, 215–216, 346,
    348–351, 376–377, 385, C36
Turnover path; *see* Strategic profit model
TV home shopping, 9, 11, 74–75
Tying contracts, 424

Understored trade area, 261
Uniform Franchise Offering Circular, A30
Unions, 530
Universal Product Codes (UPC), 21,
  319, 321, 323
Unpaid impersonal communication,
  475–476
Unpaid personal communication,
  475–476
Unrelated diversification, 172
UPCs, 21, 319, 321, 323
Upscale customers, 107–109
Used merchandise, 109

Vacant space problems, 238
VALS2 lifestyle segmentation, 145–146,
  C50
Value-added networks (VANs), 324, 333
Value-added services, 9–10, 17
Value-based planning, 228
Values, changes in consumer, 113–116
VANs, 324, 333
Variable costs, 458
Variety and assortment, of merchandise,
  30–32, 361–363, C42–C43
Vending machine retailing, 73–74
Vendor(s)
  bargaining power, 182–183
  category captain, 341
  cooperative advertising and, 429,
    487–490
  ethical issues; *see* Ethics
  international; *see* International sourcing
  lead time, 331–332, 365, 387, 412
  legal issues; *see* Legal issues
  measuring performance, 392–394
  negotiations, 6, 403, 427–432
  promotion programs and, 484–485
  sources for locating, 414–416
  strategic alliances/partnerships, 168,
    315, 341, 403, 413, 416–419,
    C32–C34
  terms and conditions, 403,
    432–437, 465

Vertical integration, 9–10, 172
Vertical merchandising, 559
Vertical pricing-fixing, 464
Village clusters, 240
Virtual reality, 540, 556
Visibility, site evaluation and, 247–248
Visual communication, 562–564
Visual merchandise department, 24
Visual merchandising, 127–128
Voice recognition technology, 320

Wall display areas, 549–550
Want books, used to plan merchandise, 359

Warehouse clubs, 6, 8, 43, 48–49
    financial strategy, 197–213
Warehouse stores, 34–35
Warehousing, 325
Weather, used to forecast sales, 356–357
Week's supply method, 400
Wheel of retailing, 61–62
Wholesale market centers, 415
Wholesalers, 7–8
Wholesale-sponsored voluntary
    group/cooperative, 52–53
Window displays, 128, 548

Women's market
    changes in, 110–111
    segmentation of apparel for, 147–148
    working women, 308–310, A8–A9
Word of mouth advertising, 475–476
Working conditions, A7
World wide web; see Internet

Yellow pages, advertising in, 493
Yuppies, 102

Zoning, store location and, 252